CONTINENTAL LITERATURE: AN ANTHOLOGY

THE LIPPINCOTT COLLEGE ENGLISH SERIES

Under the Editorship of
Albert J. Guerard, Stanford University

VOLUME *2* SINCE THE RENAISSANCE

Continental Literature

AN ANTHOLOGY

EDITED BY
DOROTHY VAN GHENT

AND

JOSEPH S. BROWN

with the assistance of Willard Maas, Assistant
Professor of English, University of Puerto Rico

J. B. Lippincott Company
PHILADELPHIA AND NEW YORK

Preface

It is a commonplace that any anthology must be, in some way, inadequate. Philosopher and poet, scholar and dilletante, teacher and student — everyone takes exception to a particular selection, or omission; but an anthology of *Continental Literature* — of literature in translation — which presumes to be both comprehensive and distinctive, representative and surprising, risks offending more than the usual number of passionate readers. The classicist will look for the pre-Socratic philosophers; Dante without his Paradise will dismay the medievalist; a Renaissance man would eagerly sacrifice Ibsen to more of *Gargantua;* the philosopher looks for Kant, unless he is a logical positivist; and college freshmen demand more Camus, less St. Augustine. Nevertheless, the anthologist begins with the assumption (and ends with the hope) that what he forms out of the existing literature will demonstrate critical judgment and imaginative taste; he tries to forestall the obvious objections, sometimes at the risk of taking them more seriously than they deserve, and then he writes a preface ostensibly outlining his rationale, but in fact justifying the limitations of that rationale. The editors of *Continental Literature* do not pretend to be different.

The teachers who use *Continental Literature* are more likely to be students of literature or literary scholars than philosophers or historians. Therefore, at certain critical moments, intellectual prose had to yield to fiction, drama, and poetry. The needs of students are sometimes more difficult to fix. Horace declared almost two thousand years ago that "The poet's aim is teaching or delight," and that tiny "or" has generated two thousand years of argument, and confusion. For the student the issue is uncomplicated: what he ought to read is not always what he wants to read. For the teacher attempting to blur the distinction between pleasure and pain the difficulties multiply. For the anthologist looking in two directions the conflict seems insoluble. The standards we chose — although teachers may object and students doubt — were delightful accessibility and hard, instructive relevance. Thus we have tried to substitute "and" for Horace's "or," serving bread that tastes like cake. Sometimes, of course, the sweetness is barely detectable, but once discerned, it lingers, and the aftertaste never surfeits. Kierkegaard meditating on Abraham, Freud redefining the tragedy of Oedipus, Thucydides and Boccaccio describing the plagues which destroyed their cities — we believe that the selections we have chosen cast long shadows. Their significance is not only self-contained but is reinforced by the intellectual apprehension of continuity, and change.

We also believe that *Continental Literature* has two special distinctions. Except in the rare case where permission was not granted, the translations reflect the best work being done in a difficult, if not impossible, discipline: Nabokov's *Eugene Onegin*, Wilbur's *Tartuffe*, Lowell's *Phaedra*, Marianne Moore's *Fables*, among many others, suggest the renewed artistic vitality of a neglected form. And we decided to include examples of the kind of essay which is produced when a creative, disciplined mind confronts a masterpiece: Mann on Goethe's *Faust*, Santayana on *The Divine Comedy*, Jaeger on the *Symposium* — all demonstrate what criticism is capable of achieving. Such essays become themselves works of art.

The sudden death, during the preparation of this anthology, of Dorothy Van Ghent stopped, *in medias res*, a collaboration to which she brought the same qualities that distinguished her literary criticism: the passionate brilliance of her mind and the discrimination of her incomparable taste. Her students and friends know — and the readers of this book will discover — what they have lost.

JOSEPH S. BROWN

Department of Humanities
Massachusetts Institute of Technology
Cambridge, Massachusetts
February, 1968

Contents

THE NEOCLASSICAL WORLD

THE MODERN WORLD: BEGINNINGS

THE MODERN WORLD: TWENTIETH CENTURY

The Neoclassical World

Erasmus believed that there need be no conflict between the new learning, which affirmed the value of the intellect and reason, and Christianity, which exalted faith. Montaigne, even as he exploited the classical past in support of his meditations on the nature of man, rejected the view that man can control himself and his environment merely by an exercise of reason; but he did not accept the certainty with which religion presumed to establish man's place in a world ordered according to some mysterious principle. It was in answer to Montaigne that Pascal began to accumulate "his pensées, his thoughts." Almost a century separates the two men, and during that time the unhampered, self-indulgent exuberance of Renaissance humanism began to be tempered by a stricter adherence to classical form, which exemplified the virtues of restraint and moderation. That reason Erasmus valued so highly sharpened the distinction between what the intellect said was true and what religion affirmed as truth. The satisfactions of science as a way of understanding nature became greater than those of religion; the quarrel between reason and faith was exacerbated. An emphasis on form in literature and art reflected both a desire for the securities of the past and a determination to conform to rules which demonstrated the ability of reason to order all human activity.

Pascal began his creative life as a scientist; he is said to have lived extravagantly in Paris as a young man; and his submission to the discipline of Jansenism suggests that the Neoclassical World he introduces was, in part, a reaction against the excesses of Rabelais and the Epicureanism of Montaigne. The Jansenists, named after Cornelius Jansen, bishop of Ypres, founded a school at the Abbey of Port-Royal and there taught the strict doctrine of predestined salvation for the few. Their moral code was an ascetic one, full of rigid self-discipline and conformity to severe rules of behavior. Pascal's *Pensées*, his apology of Christianity, reflects the hard, unyielding submission of self which Jansenism demanded. Yet for all the sweet clarity and strength with which Pascal accepts the truth of revelation and religious intuition, there is that which sets him apart from the age in which he is placed. Neoclassicism has been judged as a movement demanding those restraints which the writer who prizes freedom sees as stifling originality and ignoring the qualities in human nature that give to the experience of life its depth and value. Such a view does an injustice to the spirit which animates the best products of the age, but critics of the judgment have not been completely successful in dislodging it. As a result, the Pascal to whom the modern reader is likely to respond is the man capable of expressing, not his certainty about the soul's triumphant salvation, but the terror of being merely and inescapably human:

The eternal silence of these infinite spaces frightens me.

And although his "thoughts" move him to the conclusion that Christianity is ultimately the force which gives man his freedom, he communicates a sense of despair about the human predicament which can still elicit sympathetic apprehension:

Let us imagine a number of men in chairs, and all condemned to death, where some are killed each day in the sight of others, and those who remain see their own fate in that of their fellows, and wait their turn, looking at each other sorrowfully and without hope. It is an image of the condition of men.

The passion with which men argue their theological differences is reflected in the blood spilled when Luther's revolution initiated the Counter-Reformation. France emerged, after the violent suppression of the Huguenots, a unified Catholic state; the only challenge to orthodoxy would come from movements like Jansenism, which was itself suppressed in 1709, or from free thinking *philosophes* who presumably liberated their world by enlightening it. The fear of orthodoxy that the new spirit was anti-religious justified attacks on the most perceptive critics of human weakness when they seemed to be probing the institutions of organized religion. The history of Molière's *Tartuffe* is a perfect example of the defensiveness with which men responded to a work that suggested the dangers of an empty piety. After an initial performance before Louis XIV, the play was kept off the stage until Molière had revised it to the satisfaction of those who saw in it an attempt to undermine religious faith. We do not know the precise nature of the revisions, although it is probable that, for example, Cléante's attempt to distinguish between true and false piety represents Molière's willingness to make his intention clearer. In spite of his concessions to orthodoxy, however, Molière reveals enough of his attitude toward pretensions of goodness to suggest that the enlightenment he is concerned with does not touch on divine truth. The vice being dramatically exposed is, of course, hypocrisy; but although the particular form it takes is that of a man who only professes to be pious, the implications of that vice for an age which valued social forms and decorum are more critical than the inferences the church chose to draw from Molière's ironic exposure of the vice. The perfect hypocrite is the personification of appearance — an actor of such convincing distinction that his audience accepts the mask as reality, the form as substance. Against such deception, reason finds defense difficult, since the actor observes all the rules, never departing from accepted principles of behavior. Common sense, which is the counterpart, in nature, of reason, demands that we examine critically, not skeptically, protestations of uncompromising righteousness; but common sense is the first victim of hypocrisy when man is only concerned with appearances. Nor is faith of any value when it is called in to argue against the decorum of a consistent illusion. The worst threat, however, that hypocrisy offers to civilized behavior lies in the ease with which it stimulates excess. The play begins with the assumption of Orgon's credulity. Tartuffe has already overthrown common sense in the house he is usurping; but Molière proceeds to dramatize the descent into madness of a man who has been freed of the restraints of reasonable understanding:

> The more you loathe the man, and dread him,
> The more ennobling it will be to wed him.
> Marry Tartuffe, and mortify your flesh!

Such a speech would, in a slightly different context, foreshadow a more tragic conclusion to the Iago-like manipulations of Tartuffe as he sets out to destroy a family. But Orgon is only absurd, not tragic; unlike Othello, he learns to recognize in time his flaw, which is an excess that need not be fatal:

> Ah, there you go — extravagant as ever!
> Why can you not be rational? You never
> Manage to take the middle course, it seems,
> But jump, instead, between absurd extremes.

To be unreasonable is to be absurd, like lovers who agree to a marriage neither wants in order to be polite. The ultimate absurdity which hypocrisy can wrest from guillibility occurs when Tartuffe tells the truth to Orgon in order not to be believed — possibly the greatest achievement of a life dedicated to the reality of illusions. When a man can so master the art of appearances, only a more accomplished actor will defeat him, and so the play ends happily with the entrance of a messenger from Louis XIV, unmasking Tartuffe and re-establishing that harmony which comes from an observance of etiquette, in this case the flattery of sovereigns. In an enlightened time, the Sun King must inevitably triumph.

French Neoclassical tragedy also reflects the preoccupations and values of the age. In its logical, analytic dissection of the dangers of excess, Racine's *Phaedra* achieves a level of concentrated inevitability that the Elizabethan dramatist (and audience) would probably not have found satisfying. Using the *Hippolytus* of Euripides, a study of *hubris* in a young man who dares to deny the power of love, Racine creates a tragedy in which human nature is seen as an uneasy balance between those forces that would plunge us into irrational passion and the spirit of self-control. In the original Greek version, Phaedra was almost a minor character, never confronting Hippolytus on stage; she acknowledges the shame of her love but is concerned mainly with her reputation after her death, which occurs off stage. Racine's heroine, on the other hand, dominates the play as she exposes the exorbitant range of her emotions within the bounds of Racine's tense couplets. Always aware of what is happening to her — of the extent to which she has yielded to her passionate nature — and therefore wracked by her sense of guilt, she moves inexorably toward the fate of all those who have given in to the power of the dark instincts. In the famous scene in Act II, in which she confesses the passion to her stepson with the self-loathing precision of one of Dante's damned souls, Racine has managed the impossibly difficult task of realizing, by a concentrated objectivity of means, the emotional intensity of a tragic heroine confronted by a situation that will produce equally disastrous effects no matter what choice she makes. At such a moment the French tragedian demonstrates the vitality of the rules which the Neoclassical World believed necessary in the creation of art.

In drama, the classical rules to be observed were the unities of time, place, and action, although only the last had actually been formulated by Aristotle in his *Poetics*. Such rules, difficult as they were to obey, gave, or so it was thought, a clarity and coherence to the drama which would allow writers to come closer to the perfections of classical literature. The same assumption about the value of form may be seen operating in the work of writers like La Rochefoucauld (1613–80) and La Bruyère (1645–96). The former spent his creative life distilling experience into a series of concise maxims that depended for their effect on the pleasures to be received from the ironic wit with which conventional truths are projected. La Bruyère worked in the genre of the "portrait," in which social types are satirically exposed, usually within the limits of a short, descriptive paragraph of acutely observed analysis. His source was the *Characters* of Theophrastus (fourth century B.C.), but his subjects were his contemporaries as they conformed to the appearances demanded by an empty decorum. La Fontaine also exploited an old form, and as in the maxims of La Rochefoucauld, the pleasures of his translations stem from the witty precision with which he transforms Aesop's prose into a verse of delicate, balanced harmonies. Nor do the "morals" which adorn the fables intrude on their simplicity. Rather, they give to the values implicit in the miniature dramas a formal completeness that makes the fables a significant vehicle for the expression of La Fontaine's cynical appreciation of the absurdities of experience. In their elegant control they justify Neoclassical formalism.

During the Regency period following the death of Louis XIV in

1715, Montesquieu published *The Persian Letters*. The narrative device of the book is still being imitated: visitors from a strange land observe and comment on the customs and people of the host country. It is a strategy perfectly suited to the satiric exposure of empty or absurd values. Montesquieu, however, is also concerned with the institutions which men create to govern themselves; his criticism of the French monarchy and the legal alternatives he proposed were used, in part, by revolutionists later in the eighteenth century. In *The Persian Letters* he deals with a France that could no longer be certain of the stability imposed on it by a strong monarch; and that transitional insecurity is ironically dramatized in the deterioration of social order in Usbek's seraglio while he is traveling in Europe to "become educated in Western Sciences." The comparative study of institutions — the beginning of the discipline of social science — became Montesquieu's passion. The evidence he accumulated at last suggested to him that absolutes like "the divine right of kings" are neither predestined nor unchanging. Experience tells us that nothing lasts forever, that reason cannot dictate order, that institutions do not survive the decay of the forces which produced them. In the history of the Troglodytes, Montesquieu allegorizes many of the beliefs that he spent his life attempting to corroborate: it is at once the ideological core of the book and a foreshadowing both of his mature judgments on social organizations and of the philosophical assumptions of the revolutionary spirit which destroyed the old forms. The history of governments is cyclical: man moves from tyranny to monarchy to democracy — a process often repeated. Many of the details of the Troglodyte experience come, for example, from Thucydides' *History of the Peloponnesian War*. No institution is fixed forever in time; and although Montesquieu suggests in these letters that virtue is natural to man, he came to believe that all values are artificial, and therefore transient.

The satirist is, by nature, a reformer: the passage in Letter XII which describes the edemic state of the early Troglodytes as yet uncorrupted by their social environment became a commonplace in revolutionary theory. In *Candide* Voltaire, whose philosophical tales reflect Montesquieu's influence on eighteenth-century French literature, also uses the device of a journey to foreign lands to present his radical reevaluation of human nature and institutions. Like Montesquieu, he offers, in the midst of all the carnage of Candide's experience, a glimpse of the utopian possibilities of life on earth, although Candide betrays his greed and ambition by refusing to submit to a paradise where all men are equally blessed. Yet for all the bitterness with which Voltaire views man's vicious irrationality, Candide's hellish journey arouses a quiet pity for, in Jacques' words, the "featherless, two-legged creature with a soul" who tries so desperately to make sense of a world gone mad. Men, the honest Anabaptist asserts, "were not born wolves." Candide discovers the extent to which men have *become* wolves; but in spite of all the meaningless attempts to justify the evils which both man and nature (in the form of earthquakes) commit, it is still possible to survive — not believing that "all is for the best," but affirming the right to make of existence what one wishes. The enlightenment Voltaire tries to bring to his world demands that the individual reject all those forms and institutions which give neither coherence nor value to his life. Once stripped of the burden of belief in an artificial, unchanging order, man — no longer a wolf — can begin again to create an order which reflects his true nature.

Blaise Pascal (1623–1662) *

LIFE: French mathematician, physicist, and religious philosopher. Before he was sixteen, Pascal had written a paper on conic sections that attracted the attention of leading mathematicians; at nineteen he invented a calculating machine; he is credited with founding the modern theory of probability; he created what is known in mathematics as "Pascal's triangle," and contributed to the development of differential calculus; his experiments in physics increased knowledge of atmospheric pressure through barometric measurements, and established what is known as "Pascal's law" on the equilibrium of fluids. But this astonishingly gifted genius is known best through his notes and memoranda in a personal journal called *Pensées* (Thoughts), where his chief concern is with the inadequacy of pure reason to solve human difficulties or to realize human hopes, and the consequent necessity of religious faith.

WORKS: In addition to his various mathematical and scientific papers, Pascal also wrote *The Provincial Letters* (1656–1657).

PENSÉES †

Section I: Thoughts on Mind and on Style

3

Those who are accustomed to judge by feeling do not understand the process of reasoning, for they would understand at first sight, and are not used to seek for principles. And others, on the contrary, who are

* From *The Essential Prose* by Dorothy Van Ghent and Willard Maas, copyright © 1965, by the Bobbs-Merrill Company, Inc., reprinted by permission of the publishers.
From *Pensées* by Blaise Pascal. Translated by W. F. Trotter. Everyman's Library Edition. Reprinted by permission of E. P. Dutton & Co., Inc.

† The fragments of what Pascal conceived as a book on the "evidences of religion" were published by his friends in 1670.

accustomed to reason from principles, do not at all understand matters of feeling, seeking principles, and being unable to see at a glance.

9

When we wish to correct with advantage, and to show another that he errs, we must notice from what side he views the matter, for on that side it is usually true, and admit that truth to him, but reveal to him the side on which it is false. He is satisfied with that, for he sees that he was not mistaken, and that he only failed to see all sides. Now, no one is offended at not seeing everything; but one does not like to be mistaken, and that perhaps arises from the fact that man naturally cannot see everything, and that naturally he cannot err in the side he looks at, since the perceptions of our senses are always true.

19

The last thing one settles in writing a book is what one should put in first.

44

Do you wish people to believe good of you? Don't speak.

143

Diversion. — Men are entrusted from infancy with the care of their honour, their property, their friends, and even with the property and the honour of their friends. They are overwhelmed with business, with the study of languages, and with physical exercise; and they are made to understand that they cannot be happy unless their health, their honour, their fortune and that of their friends be in good condition, and that a single thing wanting will make them unhappy. Thus they are given cares and business which make them bustle about from break of day. — It is, you will exclaim, a strange way to make them happy! What more could be done to make them miserable? — Indeed! what could be done? We should only have to relieve them from all these cares; for then they would see themselves: they would reflect on what they are, whence they came, whither they go, and thus we cannot employ and divert them too much. And this is why, after having given them so much business, we advise them, if they have some time for relaxation, to employ it in amusement, in play, and to be always fully occupied.

How hollow and full of ribaldry is the heart of man!

172

We do not rest satisfied with the present. We anticipate the future as too slow in coming, as if in order to hasten its course; or we recall the past, to stop its too rapid flight. So imprudent are we that we wander in the times which are not ours, and do not think of the only one which belongs to us; and so idle are we that we dream of those times which are no more, and thoughtlessly overlook that which alone exists. For the present is generally painful to us. We conceal it from our sight, because it troubles us; and if it be delightful to us, we regret to see it pass away. We try to sustain it by the future, and think of arranging matters which are not in our power, for a time which we have no certainty of reaching.

Let each one examine his thoughts, and he will find them all occupied with the past and the future. We scarcely ever think of the present; and if we think of it, it is only to take light from it to arrange the future. The present is never our end. The past and the present are our means; the future alone is our end. So we never live, but we hope to live; and, as we are always preparing to be happy, it is inevitable we should never be so.

183

We run carelessly to the precipice, after we have put something before us to prevent us seeing it.

Section III: Of the Necessity of the Wager

194

. . . Let them at least learn what is the religion they attack, before attacking it. If this religion boasted of having a clear view of God, and of possessing it open and unveiled, it would be attacking it to say that we see nothing in the world which shows it with this clearness. But since, on the contrary, it says that men are in darkness and estranged from God, that He has hidden Himself from their knowledge, that this is in fact the name which He gives Himself in the Scriptures, *Deus absconditus;* [1] and finally, if it endeavours equally to establish these two things: that God has set up in the Church visible signs to make Himself known to those who should seek Him sincerely, and that He has nevertheless so disguised them that He will only be perceived by those who seek Him with all their heart; what advantage can they obtain, when, in the negligence with which they make profession of being in search of the truth, they cry out that nothing reveals it to them; and since that darkness in which they are, and with which they upbraid the Church, establishes only one of the things which she affirms, without touching the other, and, very far from destroying, proves her doctrine?

In order to attack it, they should have protested that they had made every effort to seek Him everywhere, and even in that which the Church proposes for their instruction, but without satisfaction. If they talked in this manner, they would in truth be attacking one of her pretensions. But I hope here to show that no reasonable person can speak thus, and

1. God who stands apart.

I venture even to say that no one has ever done so. We know well enough how those who are of this mind behave. They believe they have made great efforts for their instruction, when they have spent a few hours in reading some book of Scripture, and have questioned some priest on the truths of the faith. After that, they boast of having made vain search in books and among men. But, verily, I will tell them what I have often said, that this negligence is insufferable. We are not here concerned with the trifling interests of some stranger, that we should treat it in this fashion; the matter concerns ourselves and our all.

The immortality of the soul is a matter which is of so great consequence to us, and which touches us so profoundly, that we must have lost all feeling to be indifferent as to knowing what it is. All our actions and thoughts must take such different courses, according as there are or are not eternal joys to hope for, that it is impossible to take one step with sense and judgment, unless we regulate our course by our view of this point which ought to be our ultimate end.

Thus our first interest and our first duty is to enlighten ourselves on this subject, whereon depends all our conduct. Therefore among those who do not believe, I make a vast difference between those who strive with all their power to inform themselves, and those who live without troubling or thinking about it.

I can have only compassion for those who sincerely bewail their doubt, who regard it as the greatest of misfortunes, and who, sparing no effort to escape it, make of this inquiry their principal and most serious occupation.

But as for those who pass their life without thinking of this ultimate end of life, and who, for this sole reason that they do not find within themselves the lights which convince them of it, neglect to seek them elsewhere, and to examine thoroughly whether this opinion is one of those which people receive with credulous simplicity, or one of those which, although obscure in themselves, have nevertheless a solid and immovable foundation, I look upon them in a manner quite different.

This carelessness in a matter which concerns themselves, their eternity, their all, moves me more to anger than pity; it astonishes and shocks me; it is to me monstrous. I do not say this out of the pious zeal of a spiritual devotion. I expect, on the contrary, that we ought to have this feeling from principles of human interest and self-love; for this we need only see what the least enlightened persons see.

We do not require great education of the mind to understand that here is no real and lasting satisfaction; that our pleasures are only vanity; that our evils are infinite; and, lastly, that death, which threatens us every moment, must infallibly place us within a few years under the dreadful necessity of being for ever either annihilated or unhappy.

There is nothing more real than this, nothing more terrible. Be we as heroic as we like, that is the end which awaits the noblest life in the world. Let us reflect on this, and then say whether it is not beyond doubt that there is no good in this life but in the hope of another; that we are happy only in proportion as we draw near it; and that, as there are no more woes for those who have complete assurance of eternity, so there is no more happiness for those who have no insight into it.

Surely then it is a great evil thus to be in doubt, but it is at least an indispensable duty to seek when we are in such doubt; and thus the doubter who does not seek is altogether completely unhappy and completely wrong. And if besides this he is easy and content, professes to be so, and indeed boasts of it; if it is this state itself which is the subject of his joy and vanity, I have no words to describe so silly a creature.

How can people hold these opinions? What joy can we find in the expectation of nothing but hopeless misery? What reason for boasting that we are in impenetrable darkness? And how can it happen that the following argument occurs to a reasonable man?

"I know not who put me into the world, nor what the world is, nor what I myself am. I am in terrible ignorance of everything. I know not what my body is, nor my senses, nor my soul, not even that part of me which thinks what I say, which reflects on all and on itself, and knows itself no more than the rest. I see those frightful spaces of the universe which surround me, and I find myself tied to one corner of this vast expanse, without knowing why I am put in this place rather than in another, nor why the short time which is given me to live is assigned to me at this point rather than at another of the whole eternity which was before me or which shall come after me. I see nothing but infinites on all sides, which surround me as an atom, and as a shadow which endures only for an instant and returns no more. All I know is that I must soon die, but what I know least is this very death which I cannot escape.

"As I know not whence I come, so I know not whither I go. I know only that, in leaving this world, I fall for ever either into annihilation or into the hands of an angry God, without knowing to which of these two states I shall be for ever assigned. Such is my state, full of weakness and uncertainty. And from all this I conclude that I ought to spend all the days of my life without caring to inquire into what must happen to me. Perhaps I might find some solution to my doubts, but I will not take the trouble, nor take a step to seek it; and after treating with scorn those who are concerned with this care, I will go without foresight and without fear to try the great event, and let myself be led carelessly to death, uncertain of the eternity of my future state."

Who would desire to have for a friend a man who talks in this fashion? Who would choose him out from others to tell him of his affairs? Who would have recourse to him in affliction? And indeed to what use in life could one put him?

In truth, it is the glory of religion to have for enemies men so unreasonable; and their opposition to it is so little dangerous that it serves on the contrary to establish its truths. For the Christian faith goes mainly to establish these two facts: the corruption of nature, and redemption by Jesus Christ. Now I contend that if these men do not serve to prove the truth of the redemption by the holiness of their behaviour, they at least serve admirably to show the corruption of nature by sentiments so unnatural.

Nothing is so important to man as his own state, nothing is so formidable to him as eternity; and thus it is not natural that there should be men indifferent to the loss of their existence, and to the perils of everlasting suffering. They are quite different with regard to all other things. They are afraid of mere trifles; they foresee them; they feel them. And this same man who spends so many days and nights in rage and despair for the loss of office, or for some imaginary insult to his honour, is the very one who knows without anxiety and without emotion that he will lose all by death. It is a monstrous thing to see in the same heart and at the same time this sensibility to trifles and this strange insensibility to the greatest objects. It is an incomprehensible enchantment, and a supernatural slumber, which indicates as its cause an allpowerful force.

There must be a strange confusion in the nature of man, that he should boast of being in that state in which it seems incredible that a single individual should be. However, experience has shown me so great a number of such persons that the fact would be surprising, if we did not know that the greater part of those who trouble themselves about the matter are disingenuous, and not in fact what they say. They are people who have heard it said that it is the fashion to be thus daring. It is what they call shaking off the yoke, and they try to imitate this. But it would not be difficult to make them understand how greatly they deceive themselves in thus seeking esteem. This is not the way to gain it, even I say among those men of the world who take a healthy view of things, and who know that the only way to succeed in this life is to make ourselves appear honourable, faithful, judicious, and capable of useful service to a friend; because naturally men love only what may be useful to them. Now, what do we gain by hearing it said of a man that he has now thrown off the yoke, that he does not believe there is a God who watches our actions, that he considers himself the sole master of his conduct, and that he thinks he is accountable for it only to himself? Does he think that he has thus brought us to have henceforth complete confidence in him, and to look to him for consolation, advice, and help in every need of life? Do they profess to have delighted us by telling us that they hold our soul to be only a little wind and smoke, especially by telling us this in a haughty and self-satisfied tone of voice? Is this a thing to say gaily? Is it not, on the contrary, a thing to say sadly, as the saddest thing in the world?

If they thought of it seriously, they would see that this is so bad a mistake, so contrary to good sense, so opposed to decency, and so removed in every respect from that good breeding which they seek, that they would be more likely to correct than to pervert those who had an inclination to follow them. And indeed, make them give an account of their opinions, and of the reasons which they have for doubting religion, and they will say to you things so feeble and so petty, that they will persuade you of the contrary. The following is what a person one day said to such a one very appositely: "If you continue to talk in this manner, you will really make me religious." And he was right, for who would not have a horror of holding opinions in which he would have such contemptible persons as companions!

Thus those who only feign these opinions would be very unhappy, if they restrained their natural feelings in order to make themselves the most conceited of men. If, at the bottom of their heart, they are troubled at not having more light, let them not disguise the fact; this avowal will not be shameful. The only shame is to have none. Nothing reveals more an extreme weakness of mind than not to know the misery of a godless man. Nothing is more indicative of a bad disposition of heart than not to desire the truth of eternal promises. Nothing is more dastardly than to act with bravado before God. Let them then leave these impieties to those who are sufficiently ill-bred to be really capable of them. Let them at least be honest men, if they cannot be Christians. Finally, let them recognise that there are two kinds of people one can call reasonable; those who serve God with all their heart because they know Him, and those who seek Him with all their heart because they do not know Him.

But as for those who live without knowing Him and without seeking Him, they judge themselves so little worthy of their own care, that they are not worthy of the care of others; and it needs all the charity of the religion which they despise, not to despise them even to the point of leaving them to their folly. But because this religion obliges us always to regard them, so long as they are in this life, as capable of the grace which can enlighten them, and to believe that they may, in a little time, be more replenished with faith than we are, and that, on the other hand, we may fall into the blindness wherein they are, we must do for them what we would they should do for us if we were in their place, and call upon them to have pity upon themselves, and to take at least some steps in the endeavour to find light. Let them give to reading this some of the hours which they otherwise employ so uselessly; whatever aversion they may bring to the task, they will perhaps gain something, and at least will not lose much. But as for those who bring to the task perfect sincerity and a real desire to meet with truth, those I hope will be satisfied and convinced of the proofs of a religion so divine, which I have here collected, and in which I have followed somewhat after this order . . .

195

Before entering into the proofs of the Christian religion, I find it necessary to point out the sinfulness of those men who live in indifference to the search for truth in a matter which is so important to them, and which touches them so nearly.

Of all their errors, this doubtless is the one which most convicts them of foolishness and blindness, and in which it is easiest to confound them by the first glimmerings of common sense, and by natural feelings.

For it is not to be doubted that the duration of this life is but a moment; that the state of death is eternal, whatever may be its nature; and that thus all our actions and thoughts must take such different directions according to the state of that eternity, that it is impossible to take one step with sense and judgment, unless we regulate our course by the truth of that point which ought to be our ultimate end.

There is nothing clearer than this; and thus, according to the principles of reason, the conduct of men is wholly unreasonable, if they do not take another course.

On this point, therefore, we condemn those who live without thought of the ultimate end of life, who let themselves be guided by their own inclinations and their own pleasures without reflection and without concern, and, as if they could annihilate eternity by turning away their thought from it, think only of making themselves happy for the moment.

Yet this eternity exists, and death, which must open into it, and threatens them every hour, must in a little time infallibly put them under the dreadful necessity of being either annihilated or unhappy for ever, without knowing which of these eternities is for ever prepared for them.

This is a doubt of terrible consequence. They are in peril of eternal woe and thereupon, as if the matter were not worth the trouble, they neglect to inquire whether this is one of those opinions which people receive with too credulous a facility, or one of those which, obscure in themselves, have a very firm, though hidden, foundation. Thus they know not whether there be truth or falsity in the matter, nor whether there be strength or weakness in the proofs. They have them before their eyes; they refuse to look at them; and in that ignorance they choose all that is necessary to fall into this misfortune if it exists, to await death to make trial of it, yet to be very content in this state, to make profession of it, and indeed to boast of it. Can we think seriously on the importance of this subject without being horrified at conduct so extravagant?

This resting in ignorance is a monstrous thing, and they who pass their life in it must be made to feel its extravagance and stupidity, by having it shown to them, so that they may be confounded by the sight of their folly. For this is how men reason, when they choose to live in such ignorance of what they are, and without seeking enlightenment. "I know not," they say . . .

199

Let us imagine a number of men in chains, and all condemned to death, where some are killed each day in the sight of the others, and those who remain see their own fate in that of their fellows, and wait their turn, looking at each other sorrowfully and without hope. It is an image of the condition of men.

205

When I consider the short duration of my life, swallowed up in the eternity before and after, the little space which I fill, and even can see, engulfed in the infinite immensity of spaces of which I am ignorant, and which know me not, I am frightened, and am astonished at being here rather than there; for there is no reason why here rather than there, why now rather than then. Who has put me here? By whose order and direction have this place and time been allotted to me?

206

The eternal silence of these infinite spaces frightens me.

210

The last act is tragic, however happy all the rest of the play is; at the last a little earth is thrown upon our head, and that is the end for ever.

221

Atheists ought to say what is perfectly evident; now it is not perfectly evident that the soul is material.

222

Atheists. — What reason have they for saying that we cannot rise from the dead? What is more difficult, to be born or to rise again; that what has never been should be, or that what has been should be again? Is it more difficult to come into existence than to return to it? Habit makes the one appear easy to us; want of habit makes the other impossible. A popular way of thinking!

Why cannot a virgin bear a child? Does a hen not lay eggs without a cock? What distinguishes these outwardly from others? And who has told us that the hen may not form the germ as well as the cock?

230

It is incomprehensible that God should exist, and it is incomprehensible that He should not exist; that the soul should be joined to the body, and that we should have no soul; that the world should be created, and that it should not be created, etc.; that original sin should be, and that it should not be.

231

Do you believe it to be impossible that God is infinite, without parts? — Yes. I wish therefore to show you an infinite and indivisible thing.

It is a point moving everywhere with an infinite velocity; for it is one in all places, and is all totality in every place.

Let this effect of nature, which previously seemed to you impossible, make you know that there may be others of which you are still ignorant. Do not draw this conclusion from your experiment, that there remains nothing for you to know; but rather that there remains an infinity for you to know.

232

Infinite movement, the point which fills everything, the moment of rest; infinite without quantity, indivisible and infinite.

233

Infinite — nothing. — Our soul is cast into a body, where it finds number, time, dimension. Thereupon it reasons, and calls this nature necessity, and can believe nothing else.

Unity joined to infinity adds nothing to it, no more than one foot to an infinite measure. The finite is annihilated in the presence of the infinite, and becomes a pure nothing. So our spirit before God, so our justice before divine justice. There is not so great a disproportion between our justice and that of God, as between unity and infinity.

The justice of God must be vast like His compassion. Now justice to the outcast is less vast, and ought less to offend our feelings than mercy towards the elect.

We know that there is an infinite, and are ignorant of its nature. As we know it to be false that numbers are finite, it is therefore true that there is an infinity in number. But we do not know what it is. It is false that it is even, it is false that it is odd; for the addition of a unit can make no change in its nature. Yet it is a number, and every number is odd or even (this is certainly true of every finite number). So we may well know that there is a God without knowing what He is. Is there not one substantial truth, seeing there are so many things which are not the truth itself?

We know then the existence and nature of the finite, because we also are finite and have extension. We know the existence of the infinite, and are ignorant of its nature, because it has extension like us, but not limits like us. But we know neither the existence nor the nature of God, because He has neither extension nor limits.

But by faith we know His existence; in glory we shall know His nature. Now, I have already shown that we may well know the existence of a thing, without knowing its nature.

Let us now speak according to natural lights.

If there is a God, He is infinitely incomprehensible, since, having neither parts nor limits, He has no affinity to us. We are then incapable of knowing either what He is or if He is. This being so, who will dare to undertake the decision of the question? Not we, who have no affinity to Him.

Who then will blame Christians for not being able to give a reason for their belief, since they profess a religion for which they cannot give a reason? They declare, in expounding it to the world, that it is a foolishness, *stultitiam;* and then you complain that they do not prove it! If they proved it, they would not keep their word; it is in lacking proofs that they are not lacking in sense. "Yes, but although this excuses those who offer it as such, and takes away from them the blame of putting it forward without reason, it does not excuse those who receive it." Let us then examine this point, and say, "God is, or He is not." But to which side shall we incline? Reason can decide nothing here. There is an infinite chaos which separated us. A game is being played at the extremity of this infinite distance where heads or tails will turn up. What will you wager? According to reason, you can do neither the one thing nor the other; according to reason, you can defend neither of the propositions.

Do not then reprove for error those who have made a choice; for you know nothing about it. "No, but I blame them for having made, not this choice, but a choice; for again both he who chooses heads and he who chooses tails are equally at fault, they are both in the wrong. The true course is not to wager at all."

Yes; but you must wager. It is not optional. You are embarked. Which will you choose then? Let us see. Since you must choose, let us see which interests you least. You have two things to lose, the true and the good; and two things to stake, your reason and your will, your knowledge and your happiness; and your nature has two things to shun, error and misery. Your reason is no more shocked in choosing one rather than the other, since you must of necessity choose. This is one point settled. But your happiness? Let us weigh the gain and the loss in wagering that God is. Let us estimate these two chances. If you gain, you gain all; if you lose, you lose nothing. Wager, then, without hesitation that He is. — "That is very fine. Yes, I must wager; but I may perhaps wager too much." — Let us see. Since there is an equal risk of gain and of loss, if you had only to gain two lives, instead of one, you might still wager. But if there were three lives to gain, you would have to play (since you are under the necessity of playing), and you would be imprudent, when you are forced to play, not to chance your life to gain three at a game where there is an equal risk of loss and gain. But there is an eternity of life and happiness. And this being so, if there were an infinity of chances, of which one only would be for you, you would still be right in wagering one to win two, and you would act stupidly, being obliged to play, by refusing to stake one life against three at a game in which out of an infinity of chances there is one for you, if there were an infinity of an infinitely happy life to gain. But there is here an infinity of an infinitely happy life to gain, a chance of gain against a finite number of chances of loss, and what you stake is finite. It is all divided; wherever the infinite is and there is not an infinity of chances of loss against that of gain, there is no time to hesitate, you must give all. And thus, when one is forced to play, he must renounce reason to preserve his life, rather than risk it for infinite gain, as likely to happen as the loss of nothingness.

For it is no use to say it is uncertain if we will gain, and it is certain that we risk, and that the infinite distance between the *certainty* of what is staked and the *uncertainty* of what will be gained, equals the finite good which is certainly staked against the uncertain infinite. It is not so, as every player stakes a certainty to gain an uncertainty, and yet he stakes a finite certainty to gain a finite uncertainty, without transgressing against reason. There is not an infinite distance between the certainty staked and the uncertainty of the gain; that is untrue. In truth, there is an infinity between the certainty of gain and the certainty of loss. But the uncertainty of the gain is proportioned to the certainty of the stake according to the proportion of the chances of gain and loss. Hence it comes that, if there are as many risks on one side as on the other, the course is to play even; and then the certainty of the stake is equal to the uncertainty of the gain, so far is it from fact that there is an infinite distance between them. And so our proposition is of infinite force, when there is the finite to stake in a game where there are equal risks of gain and of loss, and the infinite to gain. This is demonstrable; and if men are capable of any truths, this is one.

"I confess it, I admit it. But, still, is there no means of seeing the faces of the cards?" — Yes, Scripture and the rest, etc. "Yes, but I have my hands tied and my mouth closed; I am forced to wager, and am not free. I am not released, and am so made that I cannot believe. What, then, would you have me do?"

True. But at least learn your inability to believe, since reason brings you to this, and yet you cannot believe. Endeavour then to convince yourself, not by increase of proofs of God, but by the abatement of your passions. You would like to attain faith, and do not know the way; you would like to cure yourself of unbelief, and ask the remedy for it. Learn of those who have been bound like you, and who now stake all their possessions. These are people who know the way which you would follow, and who are cured of an ill of which you would be cured. Follow the way by which they began; by acting as if they believed, taking the holy water, having masses said, etc. Even this will naturally make you believe, and deaden your acuteness. — "But this is what I am afraid of." — And why? What have you to lose?

But to show you that this leads you there, it is this which will lessen the passions, which are your stumbling-blocks.

The end of this discourse. — Now, what harm will befall you in taking this side? You will be faithful, honest, humble, grateful, generous, a sincere friend, truthful. Certainly you will not have those poisonous pleasures, glory and luxury; but will you not have others? I will tell you that you will thereby gain in this life, and that, at each step you take on this road, you will see so great certainty of gain, so much nothingness in what you risk, that you will at last recognise that you have wagered for something certain and infinite, for which you have given nothing.

"Ah! This discourse transports me, charms me," etc.

If this discourse pleases you and seems impressive, know that it is made by a man who has knelt, both before and after it, in prayer to that Being, infinite and without parts, before whom he lays all he has, for you also to lay before Him all you have for your own good and for His glory, that so strength may be given to lowliness.

234

If we must not act save on a certainty, we ought not to act on religion, for it is not certain. But how many things we do on an uncertainty, sea voyages, battles! I say then we must do nothing at all, for nothing is certain, and that there is more certainty in religion than there is as to whether we may see to-morrow; for it is not certain that we may see to-morrow, and it is certainly possible that we may not see it. We cannot say as much about religion. It is not certain that it is; but who will venture to say that it is certainly possible that it is not? Now when we work for to-morrow, and so on an uncertainty, we act reasonably; for we ought to work for an uncertainty according to the doctrine of chance which was demonstrated above.

Saint Augustine has seen that we work for an uncertainty, on sea, in battle, etc. But he has not seen the doctrine of chance which proves that we should do so. Montaigne has seen that we are shocked at a fool, and that habit is all-powerful; but he has not seen the reason of this effect.

All these persons have seen the effects, but they have not seen the causes. They are, in comparison with those who have discovered the causes, as those who have only eyes are in comparison with those who have intellect. For the effects are perceptible by sense, and the causes are visible only to the intellect. And although these effects are seen by the mind, this mind is, in comparison with the mind which sees the causes, as the bodily senses are in comparison with the intellect.

Section IV: Of the Means of Belief

267

The last proceeding of reason is to recognise that there is an infinity of things which are beyond it. It is but feeble if it does not see so far as to know this. But if natural things are beyond it, what will be said of supernatural?

277

The heart has its reasons, which reason does not know. We feel it in a thousand things. I say that the heart naturally loves the Universal Being, and also itself naturally, according as it gives itself to them; and it hardens itself against one or the other at its will. You have rejected the one, and kept the other. Is it by reason that you love yourself?

280

The knowledge of God is very far from the love of Him.

282

We know truth, not only by the reason, but also by the heart, and it is in this last way that we know first principles; and reason, which has no part in it, tries in vain to impugn them. The sceptics, who have only this for their object, labour to no purpose. We know that we do not dream, and however impossible it is for us to prove it by reason, this inability demonstrates only the weakness of our reason, but not, as they affirm, the uncertainty of all our knowledge. For the knowledge of first principles, as space, time, motion, number, is as sure as any of those which we get from reasoning. And reason must trust these intuitions of the heart, and must base them on every argument. (We have intuitive knowledge of the tri-dimensional nature of space, and of the infinity of number, and reason then shows that there are no two square numbers one of which is double of the other. Principles are intuited, propositions are inferred, all with certainty, though in different ways.) And it is as useless and absurd for reason to demand from the heart proofs of her first principles, before admitting them, as it would be for the heart to demand from reason an intuition of all demonstrated propositions before accepting them.

This inability ought, then, to serve only to humble reason, which would judge all, but not to impugn our certainty, as if only reason were capable of instructing us. Would to God, on the contrary, that we had never need of it, and that we knew everything by instinct and intuition! But nature has refused us this boon. On the contrary, she has given us but very little knowledge of this kind; and all the rest can be acquired only by reasoning.

Therefore, those to whom God has imparted religion by intuition are very fortunate, and justly convinced. But to those who do not have it, we can give it only by reasoning, waiting for God to give them spiritual insight, without which faith is only human, and useless for salvation.

Section VI: The Philosophers

347

Man is but a reed, the most feeble thing in nature; but he is a thinking reed. The entire universe need not arm itself to crush him. A vapour, a drop of water suffices to kill him. But, if the universe were to crush him, man would still be more noble than that which killed him, because he knows that he dies and the advantage which the universe has over him; the universe knows nothing of this.

All our dignity consists, then, in thought. By it we must elevate ourselves, and not by space and time which we cannot fill. Let us endeavour, then, to think well; this is the principle of morality.

378

Scepticism. — Excess, like defect of intellect, is accused of madness. Nothing is good but mediocrity. The majority has settled that, and finds fault with him who escapes it at whichever end. I will not oppose it. I quite consent to put myself there, and refuse to be at the lower end, not because it is low, but because it is an end; for I would likewise refuse to be placed at the top. To leave the mean is to abandon humanity. The greatness of the human soul consists in knowing how to preserve the mean. So far from greatness consisting in leaving it, it consists in not leaving it.

396

Two things instruct man about his whole nature; instinct and experience.

397

The greatness of man is great in that he knows himself to be miserable. A tree does not know itself to be miserable. It is then being miserable to know oneself to be miserable; but it is also being great to know that one is miserable.

Jean-Baptiste Poquelin Molière (1622–1673)

LIFE: Born Jean-Baptiste Poquelin. Like Shakespeare, he began his dramatic career as an actor, shared in the profits of the company which performed his plays, had royal patronage, and made an unfortunate marriage. But while the attacks on Shakespeare's work were, on the whole, merely part of the general war on all popular drama, the controversies which Molière inspired were more personal: only the intervention of Louis XIV prevented *Tartuffe* from being permanently silenced. His comedies — in which language is purged of excess and character of triviality — are an accurate reflection of the man who wrote them: sane, moderate, objective, disciplined, natural. He was himself sick when he wrote his last play, *Le Malade imaginaire*, about a man who only imagines he is sick; and not wanting to disappoint his audience he acted the main role a few hours before he died.

WORKS: Molière wrote farces, social comedies, and *comedie-ballets* (for the court of Louis XIV), but his major plays usually possess characteristics of all three forms. Among them are: *Les Précieuses ridicules* (1659), *L'École des maris* (1662), *Le Misanthrope, Le Médecin malgré lui* (1666), *Tartuffe* (1667), *L'Avare* (1668), *Le Bourgeois gentilhomme* (1671), *Le Malade imaginaire* (1673).

TARTUFFE *

Characters

MME. PERNELLE, *Orgon's mother*
ORGON, *Elmire's husband*
ELMIRE, *Orgon's wife*
DAMIS, *Orgon's son, Elmire's stepson*
MARIANE, *Orgon's daughter, Elmire's stepdaughter, in love with Valère*
VALÈRE, *in love with Mariane*
CLÉANTE, *Orgon's brother-in-law*
TARTUFFE, *a hypocrite*
DORINE, *Mariane's lady's-maid*
M. LOYAL, *a bailiff*
A POLICE OFFICER
FLIPOTE, *Mme. Pernelle's maid*

The scene throughout: Orgon's house in Paris

ACT I

SCENE I

MADAME PERNELLE *and* FLIPOTE, *her maid,* ELMIRE,
MARIANE, DORINE, DAMIS, CLÉANTE

MME. PERNELLE: Come, come, Flipote; it's time I left this place.
ELMIRE: I can't keep up, you walk at such a pace.
MME. PERNELLE: Don't trouble, child; no need to show me out.
It's not your manners I'm concerned about.
ELMIRE: We merely pay you the respect we owe.   5
But, Mother, why this hurry? Must you go?

Molière's *Tartuffe* translated by Richard Wilbur, © 1961, 1962, 1963, by Richard Wilbur. Reprinted by permission of Harcourt, Brace & World, Inc.

* The first three acts were first performed in 1664 at Versailles. The complete play was given its first public performance in 1667.

MME. PERNELLE: I must. This house appals me. No one in it
Will pay attention for a single minute.
Children, I take my leave much vexed in spirit.
I offer good advice, but you won't hear it.   10
You all break in and chatter on and on.
It's like a madhouse with the keeper gone.
DORINE: If . . .
MME. PERNELLE: Girl, you talk too much, and I'm afraid
You're far too saucy for a lady's-maid.
You push in everywhere and have your say.   15
DAMIS: But . . .
MME. PERNELLE: You, boy, grow more foolish every day.
To think my grandson should be such a dunce!
I've said a hundred times, if I've said it once,
That if you keep the course on which you've started,
You'll leave your worthy father broken-hearted.   20
MARIANE: I think . . .
MME. PERNELLE: And you, his sister, seem so pure,
So shy, so innocent, and so demure.
But you know what they say about still waters.
I pity parents with secretive daughters.
ELMIRE: Now, Mother . . .
MME. PERNELLE: And as for you, child, let me add   25
That your behavior is extremely bad,
And a poor example for these children, too.
Their dear, dead mother did far better than you.
You're much too free with money, and I'm distressed
To see you so elaborately dressed.   30
When it's one's husband that one aims to please,
One has no need of costly fripperies.
CLÉANTE: Oh, Madam, really . . .
MME. PERNELLE: You are her brother, Sir,
And I respect and love you; yet if I were
My son, this lady's good and pious spouse,   35
I wouldn't make you welcome in my house.
You're full of worldly counsels which, I fear,
Aren't suitable for decent folk to hear.
I've spoken bluntly, Sir; but it behooves us
Not to mince words when righteous fervor moves us.   40
DAMIS: Your man Tartuffe is full of holy speeches . . .
MME. PERNELLE: And practises precisely what he preaches.
He's a fine man, and should be listened to.
I will not hear him mocked by fools like you.
DAMIS: Good God! Do you expect me to submit   45
To the tyranny of that carping hypocrite?
Must we forgo all joys and satisfactions
Because that bigot censures all our actions?

DORINE: To hear him talk — and he talks all the time —
There's nothing one can do that's not a crime.   50
He rails at everything, your dear Tartuffe.
MME. PERNELLE: Whatever he reproves deserves reproof.
He's out to save your souls, and all of you
Must love him, as my son would have you do.
DAMIS: Ah no, Grandmother, I could never take   55
To such a rascal, even for my father's sake.
That's how I feel, and I shall not dissemble,
His every action makes me seethe and tremble
With helpless anger, and I have no doubt
That he and I will shortly have it out.   60
DORINE: Surely it is a shame and a disgrace
To see this man usurp the master's place —
To see this beggar who, when first he came,
Had not a shoe or shoestring to his name
So far forget himself that he behaves   65
As if the house were his, and we his slaves.
MME. PERNELLE: Well, mark my words, your souls would fare far better
If you obeyed his precepts to the letter.
DORINE: You see him as a saint. I'm far less awed;
In fact, I see right through him. He's a fraud.   70
MME. PERNELLE: Nonsense!
DORINE: His man Laurent's the same, or worse;
I'd not trust either with a penny purse.
MME. PERNELLE: I can't say what his servant's morals may be;
His own great goodness I can guarantee.
You all regard him with distaste and fear   75
Because he tells you what you're loath to hear,
Condemns your sins, points out your moral flaws,
And humbly strives to further Heaven's cause.
DORINE: If sin is all that bothers him, why is it
He's so upset when folk drop in to visit?   80
Is Heaven so outraged by a social call
That he must prophesy against us all?
I'll tell you what I think: if you ask me,
He's jealous of my mistress' company.
MME. PERNELLE: Rubbish! (*To Elmire:*) He's not alone, child, in com-
        plaining   85
Of all your promiscuous entertaining.
Why, the whole neighborhood's upset, I know,
By all these carriages that come and go,
With crowds of guests parading in and out
And noisy servants loitering about.   90
In all of this, I'm sure there's nothing vicious;
But why give people cause to be suspicious?
CLÉANTE: They need no cause; they'll talk in any case.

Madam, this world would be a joyless place
If, fearing what malicious tongues might say,   95
We locked our doors and turned our friends away.
And even if one did so dreary a thing,
D'you think those tongues would cease their chattering?
One can't fight slander; it's a losing battle;
Let us instead ignore their tittle-tattle.   100
Let's strive to live by conscience' clear decrees,
And let the gossips gossip as they please.
DORINE: If there is talk against us, I know the source:
It's Daphne and her little husband, of course.
Those who have greatest cause for guilt and shame   105
Are quickest to besmirch a neighbor's name.
When there's a chance for libel, they never miss it;
When something can be made to seem illicit
They're off at once to spread the joyous news,
Adding to fact what fantasies they choose.   110
By talking up their neighbor's indiscretions
They seek to camouflage their own transgressions,
Hoping that others' innocent affairs
Will lend a hue of innocence to theirs,
Or that their own black guilt will come to seem   115
Part of a general shady color-scheme.
MME. PERNELLE: All that is quite irrelevant. I doubt
That anyone's more virtuous and devout
Than dear Orante; and I'm informed that she
Condemns your mode of life most vehemently.   120
DORINE: Oh, yes, she's strict, devout, and has no taint
Of worldliness; in short, she seems a saint.
But it was time which taught her that disguise;
She's thus because she can't be otherwise.
So long as her attractions could enthrall,   125
She flounced and flirted and enjoyed it all,
But now that they're no longer what they were
She quits a world which fast is quitting her,
And wears a veil of virtue to conceal
Her bankrupt beauty and her lost appeal.   130
That's what becomes of old coquettes today:
Distressed when all their lovers fall away,
They see no recourse but to play the prude,
And so confer a style on solitude.
Thereafter, they're severe with everyone,   135
Condemning all our actions, pardoning none,
And claiming to be pure, austere, and zealous
When, if the truth were known, they're merely jealous,
And cannot bear to see another know
The pleasures time has forced them to forgo.   140

MME. PERNELLE (*Initially to Elmire:*) That sort of talk is what you
    like to hear;
Therefore you'd have us all keep still, my dear,
While Madam rattles on the livelong day.
Nevertheless, I mean to have my say.
I tell you that you're blest to have Tartuffe   145
Dwelling, as my son's guest, beneath this roof;
That Heaven has sent him to forestall its wrath
By leading you, once more, to the true path;
That all he reprehends is reprehensible,
And that you'd better heed him, and be sensible.   150
These visits, balls, and parties in which you revel
Are nothing but inventions of the Devil.
One never hears a word that's edifying:
Nothing but chaff and foolishness and lying,
As well as vicious gossip in which one's neighbor   155
Is cut to bits with epee, foil, and saber.
People of sense are driven half-insane
At such affairs, where noise and folly reign
And reputations perish thick and fast.
As a wise preacher said on Sunday last,   160
Parties are Towers of Babylon, because
The guests all babble on with never a pause;
And then he told a story which, I think . . .
(*To Cléante:*) I heard that laugh, Sir, and I saw that wink!
Go find your silly friends and laugh some more!   165
Enough; I'm going; don't show me to the door.
I leave this household much dismayed and vexed;
I cannot say when I shall see you next.
(*Slapping Flipote:*) Wake up, don't stand there gaping into space!
I'll slap some sense into that stupid face.   170
Move, move, you slut.

SCENE II

CLÉANTE, DORINE

CLÉANTE: I think I'll stay behind;
I want no further pieces of her mind.
How that old lady . . .
DORINE: Oh, what wouldn't she say
If she could hear you speak of her that way!
She'd thank you for the *lady*, but I'm sure   175
She'd find the *old* a little premature.
CLÉANTE: My, what a scene she made, and what a din!
And how this man Tartuffe has taken her in!
DORINE: Yes, but her son is even worse deceived;

161. *Towers of Babylon:* she means, of course, the Tower of Babel.

His folly must be seen to be believed. 180
In the late troubles, he played an able part
And served his king with wise and loyal heart,
But he's quite lost his senses since he fell
Beneath Tartuffe's infatuating spell.
He calls him brother, and loves him as his life, 185
Preferring him to mother, child, or wife.
In him and him alone will he confide;
He's made him his confessor and his guide;
He pets and pampers him with love more tender
Than any pretty mistress could engender, 190
Gives him the place of honor when they dine,
Delights to see him gorging like a swine,
Stuffs him with dainties till his guts distend,
And when he belches, cries "God bless you, friend!"
In short, he's mad; he worships him; he dotes; 195
His deeds he marvels at, his words he quotes,
Thinking each act a miracle, each word
Oracular as those that Moses heard.
Tartuffe, much pleased to find so easy a victim,
Has in a hundred ways beguiled and tricked him, 200
Milked him of money, and with his permission
Established here a sort of Inquisition.
Even Laurent, his lackey, dares to give
Us arrogant advice on how to live;
He sermonizes us in thundering tones 205
And confiscates our ribbons and colognes.
Last week he tore a kerchief into pieces
Because he found it pressed in a *Life of Jesus:*
He said it was a sin to juxtapose
Unholy vanities and holy prose. 210

Scene III

ELMIRE, MARIANE, DAMIS, CLÉANTE, DORINE

ELMIRE (*To Cléante:*) You did well not to follow; she stood in the door
And said *verbatim* all she'd said before.
I saw my husband coming. I think I'd best
Go upstairs now, and take a little rest.
CLÉANTE: I'll wait and greet him here; then I must go. 215
I've really only time to say hello.
DAMIS: Sound him about my sister's wedding, please.
I think Tartuffe's against it, and that he's
Been urging Father to withdraw his blessing.
As you well know, I'd find that most distressing. 220

181. *late troubles:* The Fronde, or civil war, in which the nobles, the church, the people, and the *parlement* of Paris fought for power while Louis XIV was too young to assume his sovereignty.

Unless my sister and Valère can marry,
My hopes to wed *his* sister will miscarry,
And I'm determined . . .
DORINE: He's coming.

SCENE IV

ORGON, CLÉANTE, DORINE

ORGON: Ah, Brother, good-day.
CLÉANTE: Well, welcome back. I'm sorry I can't stay.
How was the country? Blooming, I trust, and green? 225
ORGON: Excuse me, Brother; just one moment.
(*To Dorine:*) Dorine . . .
(*To Cléante:*) To put my mind at rest, I always learn
The household news the moment I return.
(*To Dorine:*) Has all been well, these two days I've been gone?
How are the family? What's been going on? 230
DORINE: Your wife, two days ago, had a bad fever,
And a fierce headache which refused to leave her.
ORGON: Ah. And Tartuffe?
DORINE: Tartuffe? Why, he's round and red,
Bursting with health, and excellently fed.
ORGON: Poor fellow!
DORINE: That night, the mistress was unable 235
To take a single bite at the dinner-table.
Her headache-pains, she said, were simply hellish.
ORGON: Ah. And Tartuffe?
DORINE: He ate his meal with relish,
And zealously devoured in her presence
A leg of mutton and a brace of pheasants. 240
ORGON: Poor fellow!
DORINE: Well, the pains continued strong,
And so she tossed and tossed the whole night long,
Now icy-cold, now burning like a flame.
We sat beside her bed till morning came.
ORGON: Ah. And Tartuffe?
DORINE: Why, having eaten, he rose 245
And sought his room, already in a doze,
Got into his warm bed, and snored away
In perfect peace until the break of day.
ORGON: Poor fellow!
DORINE: After much ado, we talked her
Into dispatching someone for the doctor. 250
He bled her, and the fever quickly fell.
ORGON: Ah. And Tartuffe?
DORINE: He bore it very well.
To keep his cheerfulness at any cost,

And make up for the blood *Madame* had lost,
He drank, at lunch, four beakers full of port.   255
ORGON: Poor fellow!
DORINE: Both are doing well, in short.
I'll go and tell *Madame* that you've expressed
Keen sympathy and anxious interest.

SCENE V

ORGON, CLÉANTE

CLÉANTE: That girl was laughing in your face, and though
I've no wish to offend you, even so   260
I'm bound to say that she had some excuse.
How can you possibly be such a goose?
Are you so dazed by this man's hocus-pocus
That all the world, save him, is out of focus?
You've given him clothing, shelter, food, and care;   265
Why must you also . . .
ORGON: Brother, stop right there.
You do not know the man of whom you speak.
CLÉANTE: I grant you that. But my judgment's not so weak
That I can't tell, by his effect on others . . .
ORGON: Ah, when you meet him, you two will be like brothers!   270
There's been no loftier soul since time began.
He is a man who . . . a man who . . . an excellent man.
To keep his precepts is to be reborn,
And view this dunghill of a world with scorn.
Yes, thanks to him I'm a changed man indeed.   275
Under his tutelage my soul's been freed
From earthly loves, and every human tie:
My mother, children, brother, and wife could die,
And I'd not feel a single moment's pain.
CLÉANTE: That's a fine sentiment, Brother; most humane.   280
ORGON: Oh, had you seen Tartuffe as I first knew him,
Your heart, like mine, would have surrendered to him.
He used to come into our church each day
And humbly kneel nearby, and start to pray.
He'd draw the eyes of everybody there   285
By the deep fervor of his heartfelt prayer;
He'd sigh and weep, and sometimes with a sound
Of rapture he would bend and kiss the ground;
And when I rose to go, he'd run before
To offer me holy-water at the door.   290
His serving-man, no less devout than he,
Informed me of his master's poverty;
I gave him gifts, but in his humbleness
He'd beg me every time to give him less.

"Oh, that's too much," he'd cry, "too much by twice!   295
I don't deserve it. The half, Sir, would suffice."
And when I wouldn't take it back, he'd share
Half of it with the poor, right then and there.
At length, Heaven prompted me to take him in
To dwell with us, and free our souls from sin.   300
He guides our lives, and to protect my honor
Stays by my wife, and keeps an eye upon her;
He tells me whom she sees, and all she does,
And seems more jealous than I ever was!
And how austere he is! Why, he can detect   305
A mortal sin where you would least suspect;
In smallest trifles, he's extremely strict.
Last week, his conscience was severely pricked
Because, while praying, he had caught a flea
And killed it, so he felt, too wrathfully.   310
CLÉANTE: Good God, man! Have you lost your common sense —
Or is this all some joke at my expense?
How can you stand there and in all sobriety . . .
ORGON: Brother, your language savors of impiety.
Too much free-thinking's made your faith unsteady,   315
And as I've warned you many times already,
'Twill get you into trouble before you're through.
CLÉANTE: So I've been told before by dupes like you:
Being blind, you'd have all others blind as well;
The clear-eyed man you call an infidel,   320
And he who sees through humbug and pretense
Is charged, by you, with want of reverence.
Spare me your warnings, Brother; I have no fear
Of speaking out, for you and Heaven to hear,
Against affected zeal and pious knavery.   325
There's true and false in piety, as in bravery,
And just as those whose courage shines the most
In battle, are the least inclined to boast,
So those whose hearts are truly pure and lowly
Don't make a flashy show of being holy.   330
There's a vast difference, so it seems to me,
Between true piety and hypocrisy:
How do you fail to see it, may I ask?
Is not a face quite different from a mask?
Cannot sincerity and cunning art,   335
Reality and semblance, be told apart?
Are scarecrows just like men, and do you hold
That a false coin is just as good as gold?
Ah, Brother, man's a strangely fashioned creature
Who seldom is content to follow Nature,   340
But recklessly pursues his inclination

Beyond the narrow bounds of moderation,
And often, by transgressing Reason's laws,
Perverts a lofty aim or noble cause.
A passing observation, but it applies.   345
ORGON: I see, dear Brother, that you're profoundly wise;
You harbor all the insight of the age.
You are our one clear mind, our only sage,
The era's oracle, its Cato too,
And all mankind are fools compared to you.   350
CLÉANTE: Brother, I don't pretend to be a sage,
Nor have I all the wisdom of the age.
There's just one insight I would dare to claim:
I know that true and false are not the same;
And just as there is nothing I more revere   355
Than a soul whose faith is steadfast and sincere,
Nothing that I more cherish and admire
Than honest zeal and true religious fire,
So there is nothing that I find more base
Than specious piety's dishonest face —   360
Than these bold mountebanks, these histrios
Whose impious mummeries and hollow shows
Exploit our love of Heaven, and make a jest
Of all that men think holiest and best;
These calculating souls who offer prayers   365
Not to their Maker, but as public wares,
And seek to buy respect and reputation
With lifted eyes and sighs of exaltation;
These charlatans, I say, whose pilgrim souls
Proceed, by way of Heaven, toward earthly goals,   370
Who weep and pray and swindle and extort,
Who preach the monkish life, but haunt the court,
Who make their zeal the partner of their vice —
Such men are vengeful, sly, and cold as ice,
And when there is an enemy to defame   375
They cloak their spite in fair religion's name,
Their private spleen and malice being made
To seem a high and virtuous crusade,
Until, to mankind's reverent applause,
They crucify their foe in Heaven's cause.   380
Such knaves are all too common; yet, for the wise,
True piety isn't hard to recognize,
And, happily, these present times provide us
With bright examples to instruct and guide us.
Consider Ariston and Périandre;   385
Look at Oronte, Alcidamas, Clitandre;
Their virtue is acknowledged; who could doubt it?
But you won't hear them beat the drum about it.

They're never ostentatious, never vain,
And their religion's moderate and humane;   390
It's not their way to criticize and chide:
They think censoriousness a mark of pride,
And therefore, letting others preach and rave,
They show, by deeds, how Christians should behave.
They think no evil of their fellow man,   395
But judge of him as kindly as they can.
They don't intrigue and wangle and conspire;
To lead a good life is their one desire;
The sinner wakes no rancorous hate in them;
It is the sin alone which they condemn;   400
Nor do they try to show a fiercer zeal
For Heaven's cause than Heaven itself could feel.
These men I honor, these men I advocate
As models for us all to emulate.
Your man is not their sort at all, I fear: 405
And, while your praise of him is quite sincere,
I think that you've been dreadfully deluded.
ORGON: Now then, dear Brother, is your speech concluded?
CLÉANTE: Why, yes.
ORGON: Your servant, Sir. (*He turns to go.*)
CLÉANTE: No, Brother; wait.
There's one more matter. You agreed of late   410
That young Valère might have your daughter's hand.
ORGON: I did.
CLÉANTE: And set the date, I understand.
ORGON: Quite so.
CLÉANTE: You've now postponed it; is that true?
ORGON: No doubt.
CLÉANTE: The match no longer pleases you?
ORGON: Who knows?
CLÉANTE: D'you mean to go back on your word?   415
ORGON: I won't say that.
CLÉANTE: Has anything occurred
Which might entitle you to break your pledge?
ORGON: Perhaps.
CLÉANTE: Why must you hem, and haw, and hedge?
The boy asked me to sound you in this affair . . .
ORGON: It's been a pleasure.
CLÉANTE: But what shall I tell Valère?   420
ORGON: Whatever you like.
CLÉANTE: But what have you decided?
What are your plans?
ORGON: I plan, Sir, to be guided
By Heaven's will.
CLÉANTE: Come, Brother, don't talk rot.

He lost his fortune, as he says himself,
Because he cared for Heaven alone, and so
Was careless of his interests here below.
I mean to get him out of his present straits   65
And help him to recover his estates —
Which, in his part of the world, have no small fame.
Poor though he is, he's a gentleman just the same.
DORINE: Yes, so he tells us; and, Sir, it seems to me
Such pride goes very ill with piety.   70
A man whose spirit spurns this dungy earth
Ought not to brag of lands and noble birth;
Such worldly arrogance will hardly square
With meek devotion and the life of prayer.
. . . But this approach, I see, has drawn a blank;   75
Let's speak, then, of his person, not his rank.
Doesn't it seem to you a trifle grim
To give a girl like her to a man like him?
When two are so ill-suited, can't you see
What the sad consequence is bound to be?   80
A young girl's virtue is imperilled, Sir,
When such a marriage is imposed on her;
For if one's bridegroom isn't to one's taste,
It's hardly an inducement to be chaste,
And many a man with horns upon his brow   85
Has made his wife the thing that she is now.
It's hard to be a faithful wife, in short,
To certain husbands of a certain sort,
And he who gives his daughter to a man she hates
Must answer for her sins at Heaven's gates.   90
Think, Sir, before you play so risky a role.
ORGON: This servant-girl presumes to save my soul!
DORINE: You would do well to ponder what I've said.
ORGON: Daughter, we'll disregard this dunderhead.
Just trust your father's judgment. Oh, I'm aware   95
That I once promised you to young Valère;
But now I hear he gambles, which greatly shocks me;
What's more, I've doubts about his orthodoxy.
His visits to church, I note, are very few.
DORINE: Would you have him go at the same hours as you,   100
And kneel nearby, to be sure of being seen?
ORGON: I can dispense with such remarks, Dorine.
(*To Mariane:*) Tartuffe, however, is sure of Heaven's blessing,
And that's the only treasure worth possessing.
This match will bring you joys beyond all measure;   105
Your cup will overflow with every pleasure;
You two will interchange your faithful loves
Like two sweet cherubs, or two turtle-doves.

No harsh word shall be heard, no frown be seen,
And he shall make you happy as a queen.   110
DORINE: And she'll make him a cuckold, just wait and see.
ORGON: What language!
DORINE: Oh, he's a man of destiny;
He's *made* for horns, and what the stars demand
Your daughter's virtue surely can't withstand.
ORGON: Don't interrupt me further. Why can't you learn   115
That certain things are none of your concern?
DORINE: It's for your own sake that I interfere.
> (*She repeatedly interrupts Orgon just as he is turning to speak
> to his daughter:*)
ORGON: Most kind of you. Now, hold your tongue, d'you hear?
DORINE: If I didn't love you . . .
ORGON: Spare me your affection.
DORINE: I'll love you, Sir, in spite of your objection.   120
ORGON: Blast!
DORINE: I can't bear, Sir, for your honor's sake,
To let you make this ludicrous mistake.
ORGON: You mean to go on talking?
DORINE: If I didn't protest
This sinful marriage, my conscience couldn't rest.
ORGON: If you don't hold your tongue, you little shrew . . .   125
DORINE: What, lost your temper? A pious man like you?
ORGON: Yes! Yes! You talk and talk. I'm maddened by it.
Once and for all, I tell you to be quiet.
DORINE: Well, I'll be quiet. But I'll be thinking hard.
ORGON: Think all you like, but you had better guard   130
That saucy tongue of yours, or I'll . . .
(*Turning back to Mariane:*) Now, child,
I've weighed this matter fully.
DORINE (*Aside:*) It drives me wild
That I can't speak.
> (*Orgon turns his head, and she is silent.*)
ORGON: Tartuffe is no young dandy,
But, still, his person . . .
DORINE (*Aside:*) Is as sweet as candy.
ORGON: Is such that, even if you shouldn't care   135
For his other merits . . .
> (*He turns and stands facing Dorine, arms crossed.*)
DORINE (*Aside:*) They'll make a lovely pair.
If I were she, no man would marry me
Against my inclination, and go scot-free.
He'd learn, before the wedding-day was over,
How readily a wife can find a lover.   140
ORGON (*To Dorine:*) It seems you treat my orders as a joke.

DORINE: Why, what's the matter? 'Twas not to you I spoke.

ORGON: What *were* you doing?

DORINE: Talking to myself, that's all.

ORGON: Ah! (*Aside:*) One more bit of impudence and gall,
And I shall give her a good slap in the face.   145
    (*He puts himself in position to slap her; Dorine, whenever he
    glances at her, stands immobile and silent:*)
Daughter, you shall accept, and with good grace,
The husband I've selected . . . Your wedding-day . . .
(*To Dorine:*) Why don't you talk to yourself?

DORINE: I've nothing to say.

ORGON: Come, just one word.

DORINE: No thank you, Sir. I pass.

ORGON: Come, speak; I'm waiting.

DORINE: I'd not be such an ass.   150

ORGON (*Turning to Mariane:*) In short, dear Daughter, I mean to be
    obeyed,
And you must bow to the sound choice I've made.

DORINE (*Moving away:*) I'd not wed such a monster, even in jest.
                  (*Orgon attempts to slap her, but misses.*)

ORGON: Daughter, that maid of yours is a thorough pest;
She makes me sinfully annoyed and nettled.   155
I can't speak further; my nerves are too unsettled.
She's so upset me by her insolent talk,
I'll calm myself by going for a walk.

Scene III

DORINE, MARIANE

DORINE (*Returning:*) Well, have you lost your tongue, girl? Must I play
Your part, and say the lines you ought to say?   160
Faced with a fate so hideous and absurd,
Can you not utter one dissenting word?

MARIANE: What good would it do? A father's power is great.

DORINE: Resist him now, or it will be too late.

MARIANE: But . . .

DORINE: Tell him one cannot love at a father's whim;   165
That you shall marry for yourself, not him;
That since it's you who are to be the bride,
It's you, not he, who must be satisfied;
And that if his Tartuffe is so sublime,
He's free to marry him at any time.   170

MARIANE: I've bowed so long to Father's strict control,
I couldn't oppose him now, to save my soul.

DORINE: Come, come, Mariane. Do listen to reason, won't you?
Valère has asked your hand. Do you love him, or don't you?

MARIANE: Oh, how unjust of you! What can you mean   175
By asking such a question, dear Dorine?
You know the depth of my affection for him;
I've told you a hundred times how I adore him.
DORINE: I don't believe in everything I hear;
Who knows if your professions were sincere?   180
MARIANE: They were, Dorine, and you do me wrong to doubt it;
Heaven knows that I've been all too frank about it.
DORINE: You love him, then?
MARIANE: Oh, more than I can express.
DORINE: And he, I take it, cares for you no less?
MARIANE: I think so.
DORINE: And you both, with equal fire,   185
Burn to be married?
MARIANE: That is our one desire.
DORINE: What of Tartuffe, then? What of your father's plan?
MARIANE: I'll kill myself, if I'm forced to wed that man.
DORINE: I hadn't thought of that recourse. How splendid!
Just die, and all your troubles will be ended!   190
A fine solution. Oh, it maddens me
To hear you talk in that self-pitying key.
MARIANE: Dorine, how harsh you are! It's most unfair.
You have no sympathy for my despair.
DORINE: I've none at all for people who talk drivel   195
And, faced with difficulties, whine and snivel.
MARIANE: No doubt I'm timid, but it would be wrong . . .
DORINE: True love requires a heart that's firm and strong.
MARIANE: I'm strong in my affection for Valère,
But coping with my father is his affair.   200
DORINE: But if your father's brain has grown so cracked
Over his dear Tartuffe that he can retract
His blessing, though your wedding-day was named,
It's surely not Valère who's to be blamed.
MARIANE: If I defied my father, as you suggest,   205
Would it not seem unmaidenly, at best?
Shall I defend my love at the expense
Of brazenness and disobedience?
Shall I parade my heart's desires, and flaunt . . .
DORINE: No, I ask nothing of you. Clearly you want   210
To be Madame Tartuffe, and I feel bound
Not to oppose a wish so very sound.
What right have I to criticize the match?
Indeed, my dear, the man's a brilliant catch.
Monsieur Tartuffe! Now, there's a man of weight!   215
Yes, yes, Monsieur Tartuffe, I'm bound to state,
Is quite a person; that's not to be denied;
'Twill be no little thing to be his bride.

The world already rings with his renown;
He's a great noble — in his native town;   220
His ears are red, he has a pink complexion,
And all in all, he'll suit you to perfection.
MARIANE: Dear God!
DORINE: Oh, how triumphant you will feel
At having caught a husband so ideal!
MARIANE: Oh, do stop teasing, and use your cleverness   225
To get me out of this appalling mess.
Advise me, and I'll do whatever you say.
DORINE: Ah no, a dutiful daughter must obey
Her father, even if he weds her to an ape.
You've a bright future; why struggle to escape?   230
Tartuffe will take you back where his family lives,
To a small town aswarm with relatives —
Uncles and cousins whom you'll be charmed to meet.
You'll be received at once by the elite,
Calling upon the bailiff's wife, no less   235
Even, perhaps, upon the mayoress,
Who'll sit you down in the *best* kitchen chair.
Then, once a year, you'll dance at the village fair
To the drone of bagpipes — two of them, in fact —
And see a puppet-show, or an animal act.   240
Your husband . . .
MARIANE: Oh, you turn my blood to ice!
Stop torturing me, and give me your advice.
DORINE (*Threatening to go:*) Your servant, Madam.
MARIANE: Dorine, I beg of you . . .
DORINE: No, you deserve it; this marriage must go through.
MARIANE: Dorine!
DORINE: No.
MARIANE: Not Tartuffe! You know I think him . . .   245
DORINE: Tartuffe's your cup of tea, and you shall drink him.
MARIANE: I've always told you everything, and relied . . .
DORINE: No. You deserve to be tartuffified.
MARIANE: Well, since you mock me and refuse to care,
I'll henceforth seek my solace in despair: 250
Despair shall be my counsellor and friend,
And help me bring my sorrows to an end.
                                                        (*She starts to leave.*)
DORINE: There now, come back; my anger has subsided.
You do deserve some pity, I've decided.
MARIANE: Dorine, if Father makes me undergo   255
This dreadful martyrdom, I'll die, I know.
DORINE: Don't fret; it won't be difficult to discover
Some plan of action . . . But here's Valère, your lover.

Scene IV

VALÈRE, MARIANE, DORINE

VALÈRE: Madam, I've just received some wondrous news
Regarding which I'd like to hear your views.   260
MARIANE: What news?
VALÈRE: You're marrying Tartuffe.
MARIANE: I find
That Father does have such a match in mind.
VALÈRE: Your father, Madam . . .
MARIANE: . . . has just this minute said
That it's Tartuffe he wishes me to wed.
VALÈRE: Can he be serious?
MARIANE: Oh, indeed he can;   265
He's clearly set his heart upon the plan.
VALÈRE: And what position do you propose to take,
Madam?
MARIANE: Why — I don't know.
VALÈRE: For heaven's sake —
You don't know?
MARIANE: No.
VALÈRE: Well, well!
MARIANE: Advise me, do.
VALÈRE: Marry the man. That's my advice to you.   270
MARIANE: That's your advice?
VALÈRE: Yes.
MARIANE: Truly?
VALÈRE: Oh, absolutely.
You couldn't choose more wisely, more astutely.
MARIANE: Thanks for this counsel; I'll follow it, of course.
VALÈRE: Do, do; I'm sure 'twill cost you no remorse.
MARIANE: To give it didn't cause your heart to break.   275
VALÈRE: I gave it, Madam, only for your sake.
MARIANE: And it's for your sake that I take it, Sir.
DORINE (*Withdrawing to the rear of the stage:*) Let's see which fool
    will prove the stubborner.
VALÈRE: So! I am nothing to you, and it was flat
Deception when you . . .
MARIANE: Please, enough of that.   280
You've told me plainly that I should agree
To wed the man my father's chosen for me,
And since you've deigned to counsel me so wisely,
I promise, Sir, to do as you advise me.
VALÈRE: Ah, no, 'twas not by me that you were swayed.   285
No, your decision was already made;
Though now, to save appearances, you protest
That you're betraying me at my behest.

VALÈRE (*To Mariane:*) On such a question, why ask advice of *me?*
DORINE: Oh, you're impossible. Give me your hands, you two. 355
(*To Valère:*) Yours first.
VALÈRE (*Giving Dorine his hand:*) But why?
DORINE (*To Mariane:*) And now a hand from you.
MARIANE (*Also giving Dorine her hand:*) What are you doing?
DORINE: There: a perfect fit.
You suit each other better than you'll admit.
 (*Valère and Mariane hold hands for some time without looking
 at each other.*)
VALÈRE (*Turning toward Mariane:*) Ah, come, don't be so haughty.
 Give a man
A look of kindness, won't you, Mariane? 360
     (*Mariane turns toward Valère and smiles.*)
DORINE: I tell you, lovers are completely mad!
VALÈRE (*To Mariane:*) Now come, confess that you were very bad
To hurt my feelings as you did just now.
I have a just complaint, you must allow.
MARIANE: *You* must allow that you were most unpleasant . . . 365
DORINE: Let's table that discussion for the present;
Your father has a plan which must be stopped.
MARIANE: Advise us, then; what means must we adopt?
DORINE: We'll use all manner of means, and all at once.
(*To Mariane:*) Your father's addled; he's acting like a dunce. 370
Therefore you'd better humor the old fossil.
Pretend to yield to him, be sweet and docile,
And then postpone, as often as necessary,
The day on which you have agreed to marry.
You'll thus gain time, and time will turn the trick. 375
Sometimes, for instance, you'll be taken sick,
And that will seem good reason for delay;
Or some bad omen will make you change the day —
You'll dream of muddy water, or you'll pass
A dead man's hearse, or break a looking-glass. 380
If all else fails, no man can marry you
Unless you take his ring and say "I do."
But now, let's separate. If they should find
Us talking here, our plot might be divined.
(*To Valère:*) Go to your friends, and tell them what's occurred, 385
And have them urge her father to keep his word.
Meanwhile, we'll stir her brother into action,
And get Elmire, as well, to join our faction.
Good-bye.
VALÈRE (*To Mariane:*) Though each of us will do his best,
It's your true heart on which my hopes shall rest. 390
MARIANE (*To Valère:*) Regardless of what Father may decide,
None but Valère shall claim me as his bride.

VALÈRE: Oh, how those words content me! Come what will . . .
DORINE: Oh, lovers, lovers! Their tongues are never still.
Be off, now.
VALÈRE (*Turning to go, then turning back:*) One last word . . .
DORINE: No time to chat: 395
You leave by this door; and *you* leave by that.
        (*Dorine pushes them, by the shoulders, toward opposing doors.*)

ACT III

SCENE I

DAMIS, DORINE

DAMIS: May lightning strike me even as I speak,
May all men call me cowardly and weak,
If any fear or scruple holds me back
From settling things, at once, with that great quack!
DORINE: Now, don't give way to violent emotion.   5
Your father's merely talked about this notion,
And words and deeds are far from being one.
Much that is talked about is left undone.
DAMIS: No, I must stop that scoundrel's machinations;
I'll go and tell him off; I'm out of patience.   10
DORINE: Do calm down and be practical. I had rather
My mistress dealt with him — and with your father.
She has some influence with Tartuffe, I've noted.
He hangs upon her words, seems most devoted,
And may, indeed, be smitten by her charm.   15
Pray Heaven it's true! 'Twould do our cause no harm.
She sent for him, just now, to sound him out
On this affair you're so incensed about;
She'll find out where he stands, and tell him, too,
What dreadful strife and trouble will ensue   20
If he lends countenance to your father's plan.
I couldn't get in to see him, but his man
Says that he's almost finished with his prayers.
Go, now. I'll catch him when he comes downstairs.
DAMIS: I want to hear this conference, and I will.   25
DORINE: No, they must be alone.
DAMIS: Oh, I'll keep still.
DORINE: Not you. I know your temper. You'd start a brawl,
And shout and stamp your foot and spoil it all.
Go on.
DAMIS: I won't; I have a perfect right . . .
DORINE: Lord, you're a nuisance! He's coming; get out of sight.   30
        (*Damis conceals himself in a closet at the rear of the stage.*)

Scene II

TARTUFFE, DORINE

TARTUFFE (*Observing Dorine, and calling to his manservant offstage:*)
Hang up my hair-shirt, put my scourge in place,
And pray, Laurent, for Heaven's perpetual grace.
I'm going to the prison now, to share
My last few coins with the poor wretches there.
DORINE (*Aside:*) Dear God, what affectation! What a fake!   35
TARTUFFE: You wished to see me?
DORINE: Yes . . .
TARTUFFE (*Taking a handkerchief from his pocket:*)
For mercy's sake,
Please take this handkerchief, before you speak.
DORINE: What?
TARTUFFE: Cover that bosom, girl. The flesh is weak,
And unclean thoughts are difficult to control.
Such sights as that can undermine the soul.   40
DORINE: Your soul, it seems, has very poor defenses,
And flesh makes quite an impact on your senses.
It's strange that you're so easily excited;
My own desires are not so soon ignited,
And if I saw you naked as a beast,   45
Not all your hide would tempt me in the least.
TARTUFFE: Girl, speak more modestly; unless you do,
I shall be forced to take my leave of you.
DORINE: Oh, no, it's I who must be on my way;
I've just one little message to convey.   50
Madame is coming down, and begs you, Sir,
To wait and have a word or two with her.
TARTUFFE: Gladly.
DORINE (*Aside:*) *That* had a softening effect!
I think my guess about him was correct.
TARTUFFE: Will she be long?
DORINE: No: that's her step I hear.   55
Ah, here she is, and I shall disappear.

Scene III

ELMIRE, TARTUFFE

TARTUFFE: May Heaven, whose infinite goodness we adore,
Preserve your body and soul forevermore,
And bless your days, and answer thus the plea
Of one who is its humblest votary.   60
ELMIRE: I thank you for that pious wish. But please,
Do take a chair and let's be more at ease.

(They sit down.)

TARTUFFE: I trust that you are once more well and strong?
ELMIRE: Oh, yes: the fever didn't last for long.
TARTUFFE: My prayers are too unworthy, I am sure, 65
To have gained from Heaven this most gracious cure;
But lately, Madam, my every supplication
Has had for object your recuperation.
ELMIRE: You shouldn't have troubled so. I don't deserve it.
TARTUFFE: Your health is priceless, Madam, and to preserve it 70
I'd gladly give my own, in all sincerity.
ELMIRE: Sir, you outdo us all in Christian charity.
You've been most kind. I count myself your debtor.
TARTUFFE: 'Twas nothing, Madam. I long to serve you better.
ELMIRE: There's a private matter I'm anxious to discuss. 75
I'm glad there's no one here to hinder us.
TARTUFFE: I too am glad; it floods my heart with bliss
To find myself alone with you like this.
For just this chance I've prayed with all my power —
But prayed in vain, until this happy hour. 80
ELMIRE: This won't take long, Sir, and I hope you'll be
Entirely frank and unconstrained with me.
TARTUFFE: Indeed, there's nothing I had rather do
Than bare my inmost heart and soul to you.
First, let me say that what remarks I've made 85
About the constant visits you are paid
Were prompted not by any mean emotion,
But rather by a pure and deep devotion,
A fervent zeal . . .
ELMIRE: No need for explanation.
Your sole concern, I'm sure, was my salvation. 90
TARTUFFE (*Taking Elmire's hand and pressing her fingertips:*)
Quite so; and such great fervor do I feel . . .
ELMIRE: Ooh! Please! You're pinching!
TARTUFFE: 'Twas from excess of zeal.
I never meant to cause you pain, I swear.
I'd rather . . .
(He places his hand on Elmire's knee.)
ELMIRE: What can your hand be doing there?
TARTUFFE: Feeling your gown; what soft, fine-woven stuff! 95
ELMIRE: Please, I'm extremely ticklish. That's enough.
(She draws her chair away; Tartuffe pulls his after her.)
TARTUFFE (*Fondling the lace collar of her gown:*)
My, my, what lovely lacework on your dress!
The workmanship's miraculous, no less.
I've not seen anything to equal it.
ELMIRE: Yes, quite. But let's talk business for a bit. 100
They say my husband means to break his word

And give his daughter to you, Sir. Had you heard?
TARTUFFE: He did once mention it. But I confess
I dream of quite a different happiness.
It's elsewhere, Madam, that my eyes discern   105
The promise of that bliss for which I yearn.
ELMIRE: I see: you care for nothing here below.
TARTUFFE: Ah, well — my heart's not made of stone, you know.
ELMIRE: All your desires mount heavenward, I'm sure,
In scorn of all that's earthly and impure.   110
TARTUFFE: A love of heavenly beauty does not preclude
A proper love for earthly pulchritude;
Our senses are quite rightly captivated
By perfect works our Maker has created.
Some glory clings to all that Heaven has made;   115
In you, all Heaven's marvels are displayed.
On that fair face, such beauties have been lavished,
The eyes are dazzled and the heart is ravished;
How could I look on you, O flawless creature,
And not adore the Author of all Nature,   120
Feeling a love both passionate and pure
For you, his triumph of self-portraiture?
At first, I trembled lest that love should be
A subtle snare that Hell had laid for me;
I vowed to flee the sight of you, eschewing   125
A rapture that might prove my soul's undoing;
But soon, fair being, I became aware
That my deep passion could be made to square
With rectitude, and with my bounden duty.
I thereupon surrendered to your beauty.   130
It is, I know, presumptuous on my part
To bring you this poor offering of my heart,
And it is not my merit, Heaven knows,
But your compassion on which my hopes repose.
You are my peace, my solace, my salvation;   135
On you depends my bliss — or desolation;
I bide your judgment and, as you think best,
I shall be either miserable or blest.
ELMIRE: Your declaration is most gallant, Sir,
But don't you think it's out of character?   140
You'd have done better to restrain your passion
And think before you spoke in such a fashion.
It ill becomes a pious man like you . . .
TARTUFFE: I may be pious, but I'm human too:
With your celestial charms before his eyes,   145
A man has not the power to be wise.
I know such words sound strangely, coming from me,
But I'm no angel, nor was meant to be,

And if you blame my passion, you must needs
Reproach as well the charms on which it feeds.   150
Your loveliness I had no sooner seen
Than you became my soul's unrivalled queen;
Before your seraph glance, divinely sweet,
My heart's defenses crumbled in defeat,
And nothing fasting, prayer, or tears might do   155
Could stay my spirit from adoring you.
My eyes, my sighs have told you in the past
What now my lips make bold to say at last,
And if, in your great goodness, you will deign
To look upon your slave, and ease his pain, —   160
If, in compassion for my soul's distress,
You'll stoop to comfort my unworthiness,
I'll raise to you, in thanks for that sweet manna,
An endless hymn, an infinite hosanna.
With me, of course, there need be no anxiety,   165
No fear of scandal or of notoriety.
These young court gallants, whom all the ladies fancy,
Are vain in speech, in action rash and chancy;
When they succeed in love, the world soon knows it;
No favor's granted them but they disclose it   170
And by the looseness of their tongues profane
The very altar where their hearts have lain.
Men of my sort, however, love discreetly,
And one may trust our reticence completely.
My keen concern for my good name insures   175
The absolute security of yours;
In short, I offer you, my dear Elmire,
Love without scandal, pleasure without fear.
ELMIRE: I've heard your well-turned speeches to the end,
And what you urge I clearly apprehend.   180
Aren't you afraid that I may take a notion
To tell my husband of your warm devotion,
And that, supposing he were duly told,
His feelings toward you might grow rather cold?
TARTUFFE: I know, dear lady, that your exceeding charity   185
Will lead your heart to pardon my temerity;
That you'll excuse my violent affection
As human weakness, human imperfection;
And that — O fairest! — you will bear in mind
That I'm but flesh and blood, and am not blind.   190
ELMIRE: Some women might do otherwise, perhaps,
But I shall be discreet about your lapse;
I'll tell my husband nothing of what's occurred
If, in return, you'll give your solemn word
To advocate as forcefully as you can   195
The marriage of Valère and Mariane,

Renouncing all desire to dispossess
Another of his rightful happiness,
And . . .

Scene IV

DAMIS, ELMIRE, TARTUFFE

DAMIS (*Emerging from the closet where he has been hiding:*)
  No! We'll not hush up this vile affair;
I heard it all inside that closet there,   200
Where Heaven, in order to confound the pride
Of this great rascal, prompted me to hide.
Ah, now I have my long-awaited chance
To punish his deceit and arrogance,
And give my father clear and shocking proof   205
Of the black character of his dear Tartuffe.
ELMIRE: Ah no, Damis; I'll be content if he
Will study to deserve my leniency.
I've promised silence — don't make me break my word;
To make a scandal would be too absurd.   210
Good wives laugh off such trifles, and forget them;
Why should they tell their husbands, and upset them?
DAMIS: You have your reasons for taking such a course,
And I have reasons, too, of equal force.
To spare him now would be insanely wrong.   215
I've swallowed my just wrath for far too long
And watched this insolent bigot bringing strife
And bitterness into our family life.
Too long he's meddled in my father's affairs,
Thwarting my marriage-hopes, and poor Valère's.   220
It's high time that my father was undeceived,
And now I've proof that can't be disbelieved —
Proof that was furnished me by Heaven above.
It's too good not to take advantage of.
This is my chance, and I deserve to lose it   225
If, for one moment, I hesitate to use it.
ELMIRE: Damis . . .
DAMIS: No, I must do what I think right.
Madam, my heart is bursting with delight,
And, say whatever you will, I'll not consent
To lose the sweet revenge on which I'm bent.   230
I'll settle matters without more ado;
And here, most opportunely, is my cue.

Scene V

ORGON, DAMIS, TARTUFFE, ELMIRE

DAMIS: Father, I'm glad you've joined us. Let us advise you
Of some fresh news which doubtless will surprise you.

You've just now been repaid with interest 235
For all your loving-kindness to our guest.
He's proved his warm and grateful feelings toward you;
It's with a pair of horns he would reward you.
Yes, I surprised him with your wife, and heard
His whole adulterous offer, every word. 240
She, with her all too gentle disposition,
Would not have told you of his proposition;
But I shall not make terms with brazen lechery,
And feel that not to tell you would be treachery.
ELMIRE: And I hold that one's husband's peace of mind 245
Should not be spoilt by tattle of this kind.
One's honor doesn't require it: to be proficient
In keeping men at bay is quite sufficient.
These are my sentiments, and I wish, Damis,
That you had heeded me and held your peace. 250

Scene VI

ORGON, DAMIS, TARTUFFE

ORGON: Can it be true, this dreadful thing I hear?
TARTUFFE: Yes, Brother, I'm a wicked man, I fear:
A wretched sinner, all depraved and twisted,
The greatest villain that has ever existed.
My life's one heap of crimes, which grows each minute; 255
There's naught but foulness and corruption in it;
And I perceive that Heaven, outraged by me,
Has chosen this occasion to mortify me.
Charge me with any deed you wish to name;
I'll not defend myself, but take the blame. 260
Believe what you are told, and drive Tartuffe
Like some base criminal from beneath your roof;
Yes, drive me hence, and with a parting curse:
I shan't protest, for I deserve far worse.
ORGON (To Damis:) Ah, you deceitful boy, how dare you try 265
To stain his purity with so foul a lie?
DAMIS: What! Are you taken in by such a bluff?
Did you not hear . . . ?
ORGON: Enough, you rogue, enough!
TARTUFFE: Ah, Brother, let him speak: you're being unjust.
Believe his story; the boy deserves your trust. 270
Why, after all, should you have faith in me?
How can you know what I might do, or be?
Is it on my good actions that you base
Your favor? Do you trust my pious face?
Ah, no, don't be deceived by hollow shows; 275
I'm far, alas, from being what men suppose;

Though the world takes me for a man of worth,
I'm truly the most worthless man on earth.
(*To Damis:*) Yes, my dear son, speak out now: call me the chief
Of sinners, a wretch, a murderer, a thief;   280
Load me with all the names men most abhor;
I'll not complain; I've earned them all, and more;
I'll kneel here while you pour them on my head
As a just punishment for the life I've led.
ORGON (*To Tartuffe:*) This is too much, dear Brother.
(*To Damis:*) Have you no heart?   285
DAMIS: Are you so hoodwinked by this rascal's art . . . ?
ORGON: Be still, you monster.
(*To Tartuffe:*) Brother, I pray you, rise.
(*To Damis:*) Villain!
DAMIS: But . . .
ORGON: Silence!
DAMIS: Can't you realize . . . ?
ORGON: Just one word more, and I'll tear you limb from limb.
TARTUFFE: In God's name, Brother, don't be harsh with him.   290
I'd rather far be tortured at the stake
Than see him bear one scratch for my poor sake.
ORGON (*To Damis:*) Ingrate!
TARTUFFE: If I must beg you, on bended knee,
To pardon him . . .
ORGON (*Falling to his knees, addressing Tartuffe:*) Such goodness can-
not be!
(*To Damis:*) Now, *there's* true charity!
DAMIS: What, you . . . ?
ORGON: Villain, be still!   295
I know your motives; I know you wish him ill:
Yes, all of you — wife, children, servants, all —
Conspire against him and desire his fall,
Employing every shameful trick you can
To alienate me from this saintly man.   300
Ah, but the more you seek to drive him away,
The more I'll do to keep him. Without delay,
I'll spite this household and confound its pride
By giving him my daughter as his bride.
DAMIS: You're going to force her to accept his hand?   305
ORGON: Yes, and this very night, d'you understand?
I shall defy you all, and make it clear
That I'm the one who gives the orders here.
Come, wretch, kneel down and clasp his blessed feet,
And ask his pardon for your black deceit.   310
DAMIS: I ask that swindler's pardon? Why, I'd rather . . .
ORGON: So! You insult him, and defy your father!
A stick! A stick! (*To Tartuffe:*) No, no — release me, do.

(*To Damis:*) Out of my house this minute! Be off with you,
And never dare set foot in it again.   315
DAMIS: Well, I shall go, but . . .
ORGON: Well, go quickly, then.
I disinherit you; an empty purse
Is all you'll get from me — except my curse!

Scene VII

ORGON, TARTUFFE

ORGON: How he blasphemed your goodness! What a son!
TARTUFFE: Forgive him, Lord, as I've already done.   320
(*To Orgon:*) You can't know how it hurts when someone tries
To blacken me in my dear Brother's eyes.
ORGON: Ahh!
TARTUFFE: The mere thought of such ingratitude
Plunges my soul into so dark a mood . . .
Such horror grips my heart . . . I gasp for breath,   325
And cannot speak, and feel myself near death.
ORGON: (*He runs, in tears, to the door through which he has just driven
    his son.*)
You blackguard! Why did I spare you? Why did I not
Break you in little pieces on the spot?
Compose yourself, and don't be hurt, dear friend.
TARTUFFE: These scenes, these dreadful quarrels, have got to end.   330
I've much upset your household, and I perceive
That the best thing will be for me to leave.
ORGON: What are you saying!
TARTUFFE: They're all against me here;
They'd have you think me false and insincere.
ORGON: Ah, what of that? Have I ceased believing in you?   335
TARTUFFE: Their adverse talk will certainly continue,
And charges which you now repudiate
You may find credible at a later date.
ORGON: No, Brother, never.
TARTUFFE: Brother, a wife can sway
Her husband's mind in many a subtle way.   340
ORGON: No, no.
TARTUFFE: To leave at once is the solution;
Thus only can I end their persecution.
ORGON: No, no, I'll not allow it; you shall remain.
TARTUFFE: Ah, well; 'twill mean much martyrdom and pain,
But if you wish it . . .
ORGON: Ah!
TARTUFFE: Enough; so be it.   345
But one thing must be settled, as I see it.
For your dear honor, and for our friendship's sake,

There's one precaution I feel bound to take.
I shall avoid your wife, and keep away . . .
ORGON: No, you shall not, whatever they may say.   350
It pleases me to vex them, and for spite
I'd have them see you with her day and night.
What's more, I'm going to drive them to despair
By making you my only son and heir;
This very day, I'll give to you alone   355
Clear deed and title to everything I own.
A dear, good friend and son-in-law-to-be
Is more than wife, or child, or kin to me.
Will you accept my offer, dearest son?
TARTUFFE: In all things, let the will of Heaven be done.   360
ORGON: Poor fellow! Come, we'll go draw up the deed.
Then let them burst with disappointed greed!

ACT IV

Scene I

CLÉANTE, TARTUFFE

CLÉANTE: Yes, all the town's discussing it, and truly,
Their comments do not flatter you unduly.
I'm glad we've met, Sir, and I'll give my view
Of this sad matter in a word or two.
As for who's guilty, that I shan't discuss;   5
Let's say it was Damis who caused the fuss;
Assuming, then, that you have been ill-used
By young Damis, and groundlessly accused,
Ought not a Christian to forgive, and ought
He not to stifle every vengeful thought?   10
Should you stand by and watch a father make
His only son an exile for your sake?
Again I tell you frankly, be advised:
The whole town, high and low, is scandalized;
This quarrel must be mended, and my advice is   15
Not to push matters to a further crisis.
No, sacrifice your wrath to God above,
And help Damis regain his father's love.
TARTUFFE: Alas, for my part I should take great joy
In doing so. I've nothing against the boy.   20
I pardon all, I harbor no resentment;
To serve him would afford me much contentment.
But Heaven's interest will not have it so:
If he comes back, then I shall have to go.
After his conduct — so extreme, so vicious —   25
Our further intercourse would look suspicious.

God knows what people would think! Why, they'd describe
My goodness to him as a sort of bribe;
They'd say that out of guilt I made pretense
Of loving-kindness and benevolence —   30
That, fearing my accuser's tongue, I strove
To buy his silence with a show of love.
CLÉANTE: Your reasoning is badly warped and stretched,
And these excuses, Sir, are most far-fetched.
Why put yourself in charge of Heaven's cause?   35
Does Heaven need our help to enforce its laws?
Leave vengeance to the Lord, Sir; while we live,
Our duty's not to punish, but forgive;
And what the Lord commands, we should obey
Without regard to what the world may say.   40
What! Shall the fear of being misunderstood
Prevent our doing what is right and good?
No, no; let's simply do what Heaven ordains,
And let no other thoughts perplex our brains.
TARTUFFE: Again, Sir, let me say that I've forgiven   45
Damis, and thus obeyed the laws of Heaven;
But I am not commanded by the Bible
To live with one who smears my name with libel.
CLÉANTE: Were you commanded, Sir, to indulge the whim
Of poor Orgon, and to encourage him   50
In suddenly transferring to your name
A large estate to which you have no claim?
TARTUFFE: 'Twould never occur to those who know me best
To think I acted from self-interest.
The treasures of this world I quite despise;   55
Their specious glitter does not charm my eyes;
And if I have resigned myself to taking
The gift which my dear Brother insists on making,
I do so only, as he well understands,
Lest so much wealth fall into wicked hands,   60
Lest those to whom it might descend in time
Turn it to purposes of sin and crime,
And not, as I shall do, make use of it
For Heaven's glory and mankind's benefit.
CLÉANTE: Forget these trumped-up fears. Your argument   65
Is one the rightful heir might well resent;
It *is* a moral burden to inherit
Such wealth, but give Damis a chance to bear it.
And would it not be worse to be accused
Of swindling, than to see that wealth misused?   70
I'm shocked that you allowed Orgon to broach
This matter, and that you feel no self-reproach;
Does true religion teach that lawful heirs

May freely be deprived of what is theirs?
And if the Lord has told you in your heart   75
That you and young Damis must dwell apart,
Would it not be the decent thing to beat
A generous and honorable retreat,
Rather than let the son of the house be sent,
For your convenience, into banishment?   80
Sir, if you wish to prove the honesty
Of your intentions . . .
TARTUFFE: Sir, it is half-past three.
I've certain pious duties to attend to,
And hope my prompt departure won't offend you.
CLÉANTE (*Alone:*) Damn.

SCENE II

ELMIRE, MARIANE, CLÉANTE, DORINE

DORINE: Stay, Sir, and help Mariane, for Heaven's sake!   85
She's suffering so, I fear her heart will break.
Her father's plan to marry her off tonight
Has put the poor child in a desperate plight.
I hear him coming. Let's stand together, now,
And see if we can't change his mind, somehow,   90
About this match we all deplore and fear.

SCENE III

ORGON, ELMIRE, MARIANE, CLÉANTE, DORINE

ORGON: Hah! Glad to find you all assembled here.
(*To Mariane:*) This contract, child, contains your happiness,
And what it says I think your heart can guess.
MARIANE (*Falling to her knees:*) Sir, by that Heaven which sees me
        here distressed,   95
And by whatever else can move your breast,
Do not employ a father's power, I pray you,
To crush my heart and force it to obey you,
Nor by your harsh commands oppress me so
That I'll begrudge the duty which I owe —   100
And do not so embitter and enslave me
That I shall hate the very life you gave me.
If my sweet hopes must perish, if you refuse
To give me to the one I've dared to choose,
Spare me at least — I beg you, I implore —   105
The pain of wedding one whom I abhor;
And do not, by a heartless use of force,
Drive me to contemplate some desperate course.
ORGON (*Feeling himself touched by her:*) Be firm, my soul. No human
        weakness, now.

MARIANE: I don't resent your love for him. Allow   110
Your heart free rein, Sir; give him your property,
And if that's not enough, take mine from me;
He's welcome to my money; take it, do,
But don't, I pray, include my person too.
Spare me, I beg you; and let me end the tale   115
Of my sad days behind a convent veil.
ORGON: A convent! Hah! When crossed in their amours,
All lovesick girls have the same thought as yours.
Get up! The more you loathe the man, and dread him,
The more ennobling it will be to wed him.   120
Marry Tartuffe, and mortify your flesh!
Enough; don't start that whimpering afresh.
DORINE: But why . . . ?
ORGON: Be still, there. Speak when you're spoken to.
Not one more bit of impudence out of you.
CLÉANTE: If I may offer a word of counsel here . . .   125
ORGON: Brother, in counseling you have no peer;
All your advice is forceful, sound, and clever;
I don't propose to follow it, however.
ELMIRE (*To Orgon:*) I am amazed, and don't know what to say;
Your blindness simply takes my breath away.   130
You are indeed bewitched, to take no warning
From our account of what occurred this morning.
ORGON: Madam, I know a few plain facts, and one
Is that you're partial to my rascal son;
Hence, when he sought to make Tartuffe the victim   135
Of a base lie, you dared not contradict him.
Ah, but you underplayed your part, my pet;
You should have looked more angry, more upset.
ELMIRE: When men make overtures, must we reply
With righteous anger and a battle-cry?   140
Must we turn back their amorous advances
With sharp reproaches and with fiery glances?
Myself, I find such offers merely amusing,
And make no scenes and fusses in refusing;
My taste is for good-natured rectitude,   145
And I dislike the savage sort of prude
Who guards her virtue with her teeth and claws,
And tears men's eyes out for the slightest cause:
The Lord preserve me from such honor as that,
Which bites and scratches like an alley-cat!   150
I've found that a polite and cool rebuff
Discourages a lover quite enough.
ORGON: I know the facts, and I shall not be shaken.
ELMIRE: I marvel at your power to be mistaken.
Would it, I wonder, carry weight with you   155

If I could *show* you that our tale was true?
ORGON: Show me?
ELMIRE: Yes.
ORGON: Rot.
ELMIRE: Come, what if I found a way
To make you see the facts as plain as day?
ORGON: Nonsense.
ELMIRE: Do answer me; don't be absurd.
I'm not now asking you to trust our word.   160
Suppose that from some hiding-place in here
You learned the whole sad truth by eye and ear —
What would you say of your good friend, after that?
ORGON: Why, I'd say . . . nothing, by Jehoshaphat!
It can't be true.
ELMIRE: You've been too long deceived,   165
And I'm quite tired of being disbelieved.
Come now: let's put my statements to the test,
And you shall see the truth made manifest.
ORGON: I'll take that challenge. Now do your uttermost.
We'll see how you make good your empty boast.   170
ELMIRE (*To Dorine:*) Send him to me.
DORINE: He's crafty; it may be hard
To catch the cunning scoundrel off his guard.
ELMIRE: No, amorous men are gullible. Their conceit
So blinds them that they're never hard to cheat.
Have him come down (*To Cléante & Mariane:*) Please leave us, for
     a bit.   175

Scene IV

ELMIRE, ORGON

ELMIRE: Pull up this table, and get under it.
ORGON: What?
ELMIRE: It's essential that you be well-hidden.
ORGON: Why there?
ELMIRE: Oh, Heavens! Just do as you are bidden.
I have my plans; we'll soon see how they fare.
Under the table, now; and once you're there,   180
Take care that you are neither seen nor heard.
ORGON: Well, I'll indulge you, since I gave my word
To see you through this infantile charade.
ELMIRE: Once it is over, you'll be glad we played.
                    (*To her husband, who is now under the table:*)
I'm going to act quite strangely, now, and you   185
Must not be shocked at anything I do.
Whatever I may say, you must excuse
As part of that deceit I'm forced to use.

I shall employ sweet speeches in the task
Of making that imposter drop his mask;   190
I'll give encouragement to his bold desires,
And furnish fuel to his amorous fires.
Since it's for your sake, and for his destruction,
That I shall seem to yield to his seduction,
I'll gladly stop whenever you decide   195
That all your doubts are fully satisfied.
I'll count on you, as soon as you have seen
What sort of man he is, to intervene,
And not expose me to his odious lust
One moment longer than you feel you must.   200
Remember: you're to save me from my plight
Whenever . . . He's coming! Hush! Keep out of sight!

Scene V

TARTUFFE, ELMIRE, ORGON

TARTUFFE: You wish to have a word with me, I'm told.
ELMIRE: Yes. I've a little secret to unfold.
Before I speak, however, it would be wise   205
To close that door, and look about for spies.
             (*Tartuffe goes to the door, closes it, and returns.*)
The very last thing that must happen now
Is a repetition of this morning's row.
I've never been so badly caught off guard.
Oh, how I feared for you! You saw how hard   210
I tried to make that troublesome Damis
Control his dreadful temper, and hold his peace.
In my confusion, I didn't have the sense
Simply to contradict his evidence;
But as it happened, that was for the best,   215
And all has worked out in our interest.
This storm has only bettered your position;
My husband doesn't have the least suspicion,
And now, in mockery of those who do,
He bids me be continually with you.   220
And that is why, quite fearless of reproof,
I now can be alone with my Tartuffe,
And why my heart — perhaps too quick to yield —
Feels free to let its passion be revealed.
TARTUFFE: Madam, your words confuse me. Not long ago,   225
You spoke in quite a different style, you know.
ELMIRE: Ah, Sir, if that refusal made you smart,
It's little that you know of woman's heart,
Or what that heart is trying to convey
When it resists in such a feeble way!   230

Always, at first, our modesty prevents
The frank avowal of tender sentiments;
However high the passion which inflames us,
Still, to confess its power somehow shames us.
Thus we reluct, at first, yet in a tone   235
Which tells you that our heart is overthrown,
That what our lips deny, our pulse confesses,
And that, in time, all noes will turn to yesses.
I fear my words are all too frank and free,
And a poor proof of woman's modesty;   240
But since I'm started, tell me, if you will —
Would I have tried to make Damis be still,
Would I have listened, calm and unoffended,
Until your lengthy offer of love was ended,
And been so very mild in my reaction,   245
Had your sweet words not given me satisfaction?
And when I tried to force you to undo
The marriage-plans my husband has in view,
What did my urgent pleading signify
If not that I admired you, and that I   250
Deplored the thought that someone else might own
Part of a heart I wished for mine alone?
TARTUFFE: Madam, no happiness is so complete
As when, from lips we love, come words so sweet;
Their nectar floods my every sense, and drains   255
In honeyed rivulets through all my veins.
To please you is my joy, my only goal;
Your love is the restorer of my soul;
And yet I must beg leave, now, to confess
Some lingering doubts as to my happiness.   260
Might this not be a trick? Might not the catch
Be that you wish me to break off the match
With Mariane, and so have feigned to love me?
I shan't quite trust your fond opinion of me
Until the feelings you've expressed so sweetly   265
Are demonstrated somewhat more concretely,
And you have shown, by certain kind concessions,
That I may put my faith in your professions.
ELMIRE (*She coughs, to warn her husband.*)
Why be in such a hurry? Must my heart
Exhaust its bounty at the very start?   270
To make that sweet admission cost me dear,
But you'll not be content, it would appear,
Unless my store of favors is disbursed
To the last farthing, and at the very first.
TARTUFFE: The less we merit, the less we dare to hope,   275
And with our doubts, mere words can never cope.

We trust no promised bliss till we receive it;
Not till a joy is ours can we believe it.
I, who so little merit your esteem,
Can't credit this fulfillment of my dream,   280
And shan't believe it, Madam, until I savor
Some palpable assurance of your favor.
ELMIRE: My, how tyrannical your love can be,
And how it flusters and perplexes me!
How furiously you take one's heart in hand,   285
And make your every wish a fierce command!
Come, must you hound and harry me to death?
Will you not give me time to catch my breath?
Can it be right to press me with such force,
Give me no quarter, show me no remorse,   290
And take advantage, by your stern insistence,
Of the fond feelings which weaken my resistance?
TARTUFFE: Well, if you look with favor upon my love,
Why, then, begrudge me some clear proof thereof?
ELMIRE: But how can I consent without offense   295
To Heaven, toward which you feel such reverence?
TARTUFFE: If Heaven is all that holds you back, don't worry.
I can remove that hindrance in a hurry.
Nothing of that sort need obstruct our path.
ELMIRE: Must one not be afraid of Heaven's wrath?   300
TARTUFFE: Madam, forget such fears, and be my pupil,
And I shall teach you how to conquer scruple.
Some joys, it's true, are wrong in Heaven's eyes;
Yet Heaven is not averse to compromise;
There is a science, lately formulated,   305
Whereby one's conscience may be liberated,
And any wrongful act you care to mention
May be redeemed by purity of intention.
I'll teach you, Madam, the secrets of that science;
Meanwhile, just place on me your full reliance.   310
Assuage my keen desires, and feel no dread:
The sin, if any, shall be on my head.
        (*Elmire coughs, this time more loudly.*)
You've a bad cough.
ELMIRE: Yes, yes. It's bad indeed.
TARTUFFE (*Producing a little paper bag:*) A bit of licorice may be
    what you need.
ELMIRE: No, I've a stubborn cold, it seems. I'm sure it   315
Will take much more than licorice to cure it.
TARTUFFE: How aggravating.
ELMIRE: Oh, more than I can say.
TARTUFFE: If you're still troubled, think of things this way:
No one shall know our joys, save us alone,
And there's no evil till the act is known;   320

It's scandal, Madam, which makes it an offense,
And it's no sin to sin in confidence.
ELMIRE (*Having coughed once more:*) Well, clearly I must do as you
    require,
And yield to your importunate desire.
It is apparent, now, that nothing less   325
Will satisfy you, and so I acquiesce.
To go so far is much against my will;
I'm vexed that it should come to this; but still,
Since you are so determined on it, since you
Will not allow mere language to convince you,   330
And since you ask for concrete evidence, I
See nothing for it, now, but to comply.
If this is sinful, if I'm wrong to do it,
So much the worse for him who drove me to it.
The fault can surely not be charged to me.   335
TARTUFFE: Madam, the fault is mine, if fault there be,
And . . .
ELMIRE: Open the door a little, and peek out;
I wouldn't want my husband poking about.
TARTUFFE: Why worry about the man? Each day he grows
More gullible; one can lead him by the nose.   340
To find us here would fill him with delight,
And if he saw the worst, he'd doubt his sight.
ELMIRE: Nevertheless, do step out for a minute
Into the hall, and see that no one's in it.

Scene VI

ORGON, ELMIRE

ORGON (*Coming out from under the table:*) That man's a perfect mon-
    ster, I must admit!   345
I'm simply stunned. I can't get over it.
ELMIRE: What, coming out so soon? How premature!
Get back in hiding, and wait until you're sure.
Stay till the end, and be convinced completely;
We mustn't stop till things are proved concretely.   350
ORGON: Hell never harbored anything so vicious!
ELMIRE: Tut, don't be hasty. Try to be judicious.
Wait, and be certain that there's no mistake.
No jumping to conclusions, for Heaven's sake!
          (*She places Orgon behind her, as Tartuffe re-enters.*)

Scene VII

TARTUFFE, ELMIRE, ORGON

TARTUFFE (*Not seeing Orgon:*) Madam, all things have worked out to
    perfection;   355
I've given the neighboring rooms a full inspection;

No one's about; and now I may at last . . .
ORGON (*Intercepting him:*) Hold on, my passionate fellow, not so fast!
I should advise a little more restraint.
Well, so you thought you'd fool me, my dear saint!   360
How soon you wearied of the saintly life —
Wedding my daughter, and coveting my wife!
I've long suspected you, and had a feeling
That soon I'd catch you at your double-dealing.
Just now, you've given me evidence galore;   365
It's quite enough; I have no wish for more.
ELMIRE (*To Tartuffe:*) I'm sorry to have treated you so slyly,
But circumstances forced me to be wily.
TARTUFFE: Brother, you can't think . . .
ORGON: No more talk from you;
Just leave this household, without more ado.   370
TARTUFFE: What I intended . . .
ORGON: That seems fairly clear.
Spare me your falsehoods and get out of here.
TARTUFFE: No, I'm the master, and you're the one to go!
This house belongs to me, I'll have you know,
And I shall show you that you can't hurt *me*   375
By this contemptible conspiracy,
That those who cross me know not what they do,
And that I've means to expose and punish you,
Avenge offended Heaven, and make you grieve
That ever you dared order me to leave.   380

Scene VIII

ELMIRE, ORGON

ELMIRE: What was the point of all that angry chatter?
ORGON: Dear God, I'm worried. This is no laughing matter.
ELMIRE: How so?
ORGON: I fear I understood his drift.
I'm much disturbed about that deed of gift.
ELMIRE: You gave him . . . ?
ORGON: Yes, it's all been drawn and signed.   385
But one thing more is weighing on my mind.
ELMIRE: What's that?
ORGON: I'll tell you; but first let's see if there's
A certain strong-box in his room upstairs.

ACT V

Scene I

ORGON, CLÉANTE

CLÉANTE: Where are you going so fast?
ORGON: God knows!

CLÉANTE: Then wait;
Let's have a conference, and deliberate
On how this situation's to be met.
ORGON: That strong-box has me utterly upset; 5
This is the worst of many, many shocks.
CLÉANTE: Is there some fearful mystery in that box?
ORGON: My poor friend Argas brought that box to me
With his own hands, in utmost secrecy;
'Twas on the very morning of his flight.
It's full of papers which, if they came to light, 10
Would ruin him — or such is my impression.
CLÉANTE: Then why did you let it out of your possession?
ORGON: Those papers vexed my conscience, and it seemed best
To ask the counsel of my pious guest.
The cunning scoundrel got me to agree 15
To leave the strong-box in his custody,
So that, in case of an investigation,
I could employ a slight equivocation
And swear I didn't have it, and thereby,
At no expense to conscience, tell a lie. 20
CLÉANTE: It looks to me as if you're out on a limb.
Trusting him with that box, and offering him
That deed of gift, were actions of a kind
Which scarcely indicate a prudent mind.
With two such weapons, he has the upper hand, 25
And since you're vulnerable, as matters stand,
You erred once more in bringing him to bay.
You should have acted in some subtler way.
ORGON: Just think of it: behind that fervent face,
A heart so wicked, and a soul so base! 30
I took him in, a hungry beggar, and then . . .
Enough, by God! I'm through with pious men:
Henceforth I'll hate the whole false brotherhood,
And persecute them worse than Satan could.
CLÉANTE: Ah, there you go — extravagant as ever! 35
Why can you not be rational? You never
Manage to take the middle course, it seems,
But jump, instead, between absurd extremes.
You've recognized your recent grave mistake
In falling victim to a pious fake; 40
Now, to correct that error, must you embrace
An even greater error in its place,
And judge our worthy neighbors as a whole
By what you've learned of one corrupted soul?
Come, just because one rascal made you swallow 45
A show of zeal which turned out to be hollow,
Shall you conclude that all men are deceivers,
And that, today, there are no true believers?

Let atheists make that foolish inference;
Learn to distinguish virtue from pretense, 50
Be cautious in bestowing admiration,
And cultivate a sober moderation.
Don't humor fraud, but also don't asperse
True piety; the latter fault is worse,
And it is best to err, if err one must, 55
As you have done, upon the side of trust.

Scene II

DAMIS, ORGON, CLÉANTE

DAMIS: Father, I hear that scoundrel's uttered threats
Against you; that he pridefully forgets
How, in his need, he was befriended by you,
And means to use your gifts to crucify you. 60
ORGON: It's true, my boy. I'm too distressed for tears.
DAMIS: Leave it to me, Sir; let me trim his ears.
Faced with such insolence, we must not waver.
I shall rejoice in doing you the favor
Of cutting short his life, and your distress. 65
CLÉANTE: What a display of young hotheadedness!
Do learn to moderate your fits of rage.
In this just kingdom, this enlightened age,
One does not settle things by violence.

Scene III

MADAME PERNELLE, MARIANE, ELMIRE, DORINE, DAMIS, ORGON, CLÉANTE

MME. PERNELLE: I hear strange tales of very strange events. 70
ORGON: Yes, strange events which these two eyes beheld.
The man's ingratitude is unparalleled.
I save a wretched pauper from starvation,
House him, and treat him like a blood relation,
Shower him every day with my largesse, 75
Give him my daughter, and all that I possess;
And meanwhile the unconscionable knave
Tries to induce my wife to misbehave;
And not content with such extreme rascality,
Now threatens me with my own liberality, 80
And aims, by taking base advantage of
The gifts I gave him out of Christian love,
To drive me from my house, a ruined man,
And make me end a pauper, as he began.
DORINE: Poor fellow!
MME. PERNELLE: No, my son, I'll never bring 85
Myself to think him guilty of such a thing.

ORGON: How's that?

MME. PERNELLE: The righteous always were maligned.

ORGON: Speak clearly, Mother. Say what's on your mind.

MME. PERNELLE: I mean that I can smell a rat, my dear.
You know how everybody hates him, here. 90

ORGON: That has no bearing on the case at all.

MME. PERNELLE: I told you a hundred times, when you were small,
That virtue in this world is hated ever;
Malicious men may die, but malice never.

ORGON: No doubt that's true, but how does it apply? 95

MME. PERNELLE: They've turned you against him by a clever lie.

ORGON: I've told you, I was there and saw it done.

MME. PERNELLE: Ah, slanderers will stop at nothing, Son.

ORGON: Mother, I'll lose my temper . . . For the last time,
I tell you I was witness to the crime. 100

MME. PERNELLE: The tongues of spite are busy night and noon,
And to their venom no man is immune.

ORGON: You're talking nonsense. Can't you realize
I saw it; saw it; saw it with my eyes?
Saw, do you understand me? Must I shout it 105
Into your ears before you'll cease to doubt it?

MME. PERNELLE: Appearances can deceive, my son. Dear me,
We cannot always judge by what we see.

ORGON: Drat! Drat!

MME. PERNELLE: One often interprets things awry;
Good can seem evil to a suspicious eye. 110

ORGON: Was I to see his pawing at Elmire
As an act of charity?

MME. PERNELLE: Till his guilt is clear,
A man deserves the benefit of the doubt.
You should have waited, to see how things turned out.

ORGON: Great God in Heaven, what more proof did I need? 115
Was I to sit there, watching, until he'd . . .
You drive me to the brink of impropriety.

MME. PERNELLE: No, no, a man of such surpassing piety
Could not do such a thing. You cannot shake me.
I don't believe it, and you shall not make me. 120

ORGON: You vex me so that, if you weren't my mother,
I'd say to you . . . some dreadful thing or other.

DORINE: It's your turn now, Sir, not to be listened to;
You'd not trust us, and now she won't trust you.

CLÉANTE: My friends, we're wasting time which should be spent 125
In facing up to our predicament.
I fear that scoundrel's threats weren't made in sport.

DAMIS: Do you think he'd have the nerve to go to court?

ELMIRE: I'm sure he won't: they'd find it all too crude
A case of swindling and ingratitude. 130

CLÉANTE: Don't be too sure. He won't be at a loss
To give his claims a high and righteous gloss;
And clever rogues with far less valid cause
Have trapped their victims in a web of laws.
I say again that to antagonize   135
A man so strongly armed was most unwise.
ORGON: I know it; but the man's appalling cheek
Outraged me so, I couldn't control my pique.
CLÉANTE: I wish to Heaven that we could devise
Some truce between you, or some compromise.   140
ELMIRE: If I had known what cards he held, I'd not
Have roused his anger by my little plot.
ORGON (*To Dorine, as M. Loyal enters:*) What is that fellow looking
        for? Who is he?
Go talk to him — and tell him that I'm busy.

Scene IV

MONSIEUR LOYAL, MADAME PERNELLE, ORGON, DAMIS, MARIANE, DORINE, ELMIRE, CLÉANTE

MONSIEUR LOYAL: Good day, dear sister. Kindly let me see   145
Your master.
DORINE: He's involved with company,
And cannot be disturbed just now, I fear.
MONSIEUR LOYAL: I hate to intrude; but what has brought me here
Will not disturb your master, in any event.
Indeed, my news will make him most content.   150
DORINE: Your name?
MONSIEUR LOYAL: Just say that I bring greetings from
Monsieur Tartuffe, on whose behalf I've come.
DORINE (*To Orgon:*) Sir, he's a very gracious man, and bears
A message from Tartuffe, which, he declares,
Will make you most content.
CLÉANTE: Upon my word,   155
I think this man had best be seen, and heard.
ORGON: Perhaps he has some settlement to suggest.
How shall I treat him? What manner would be best?
CLÉANTE: Control your anger, and if he should mention
Some fair adjustment, give him your full attention.   160
MONSIEUR LOYAL: Good health to you, good Sir. May Heaven confound
Your enemies, and may your joys abound.
ORGON (*Aside, to Cléante:*) A gentle salutation: it confirms
My guess that he is here to offer terms.
MONSIEUR LOYAL: I've always held your family most dear;   165
I served your father, Sir, for many a year.
ORGON: Sir, I must ask your pardon; to my shame,
I cannot now recall your face or name.

MONSIEUR LOYAL: Loyal's my name; I come from Normandy,
And I'm a bailiff, in all modesty.   170
For forty years, praise God, it's been my boast
To serve with honor in that vital post,
And I am here, Sir, if you will permit
The liberty, to serve you with this writ . . .
ORGON: To — *what?*
MONSIEUR LOYAL: Now, please, Sir, let us have no friction: 175
It's nothing but an order of eviction.
You are to move your goods and family out
And make way for new occupants, without
Deferment or delay, and give the keys . . .
ORGON: I? Leave this house?
MONSIEUR LOYAL: Why yes, Sir, if you please.   180
This house, Sir, from the cellar to the roof,
Belongs now to the good Monsieur Tartuffe,
And he is lord and master of your estate
By virtue of a deed of present date,
Drawn in due form, with clearest legal phrasing . . .   185
DAMIS: Your insolence is utterly amazing!
MONSIEUR LOYAL: Young man, my business here is not with you,
But with your wise and temperate father, who,
Like every worthy citizen, stands in awe
Of justice, and would never obstruct the law.   190
ORGON: But . . .
MONSIEUR LOYAL: Not for a million, Sir, would you rebel
Against authority; I know that well.
You'll not make trouble, Sir, or interfere
With the execution of my duties here.
DAMIS: Someone may execute a smart tattoo   195
On that black jacket of yours, before you're through.
MONSIEUR LOYAL: Sir, bid your son be silent. I'd much regret
Having to mention such a nasty threat
Of violence, in writing my report.
DORINE (*Aside:*) This man Loyal's a most disloyal sort!   200
MONSIEUR LOYAL: I love all men of upright character,
And when I agreed to serve these papers, Sir,
It was your feelings that I had in mind.
I couldn't bear to see the case assigned
To someone else, who might esteem you less   205
And so subject you to unpleasantness.
ORGON: What's more unpleasant than telling a man to leave
His house and home?
MONSIEUR LOYAL: You'd like a short reprieve?
If you desire it, Sir, I shall not press you,
But wait until tomorrow to dispossess you.   210
Splendid. I'll come and spend the night here, then,

Most quietly, with half a score of men.
For form's sake, you might bring me, just before
You go to bed, the keys to the front door.
My men, I promise, will be on their best   215
Behavior, and will not disturb your rest.
But bright and early, Sir, you must be quick
And move out all your furniture, every stick:
The men I've chosen are both young and strong,
And with their help it shouldn't take you long.   220
In short, I'll make things pleasant and convenient,
And since I'm being so extremely lenient,
Please show me, Sir, a like consideration,
And give me your entire cooperation.
ORGON (*Aside:*) I may be all but bankrupt, but I vow   225
I'd give a hundred louis, here and now,
Just for the pleasure of landing one good clout
Right on the end of that complacent snout.
CLÉANTE: Careful; don't make things worse.
DAMIS: My bootsole itches
To give that beggar a good kick in the breeches.   230
DORINE: Monsieur Loyal, I'd love to hear the whack
Of a stout stick across your fine broad back.
MONSIEUR LOYAL: Take care: a woman too may go to jail if
She uses threatening language to a bailiff.
CLÉANTE: Enough, enough, Sir. This must not go on.   235
Give me that paper, please, and then begone.
MONSIEUR LOYAL: Well, *au revoir*. God give you all good cheer!
ORGON: May God confound you, and him who sent you here!

Scene V

ORGON, CLÉANTE, MARIANE, ELMIRE, MADAME PERNELLE,
DORINE, DAMIS

ORGON: Now, Mother, was I right or not? This writ
Should change your notion of Tartuffe a bit.   240
Do you perceive his villainy at last?
MME. PERNELLE: I'm thunderstruck. I'm utterly aghast.
DORINE: Oh, come, be fair. You mustn't take offense
At this new proof of his benevolence.
He's acting out of selfless love, I know.   245
Material things enslave the soul, and so
He kindly has arranged your liberation
From all that might endanger your salvation.
ORGON: Will you not ever hold your tongue, you dunce?
CLÉANTE: Come, you must take some action, and at once.   250
ELMIRE: Go tell the world of the low trick he's tried.
The deed of gift is surely nullified,

By such behavior, and public rage will not
Permit the wretch to carry out his plot.

Scene VI

VALÈRE, ORGON, CLÉANTE, ELMIRE, MARIANE,
MADAME PERNELLE, DAMIS, DORINE

VALÈRE: Sir, though I hate to bring you more bad news,   255
Such is the danger that I cannot choose.
A friend who is extremely close to me
And knows my interest in your family
Has, for my sake, presumed to violate
The secrecy that's due to things of state,   260
And sends me word that you are in a plight
From which your one salvation lies in flight.
That scoundrel who's imposed upon you so
Denounced you to the King an hour ago
And, as supporting evidence, displayed   265
The strong-box of a certain renegade
Whose secret papers, so he testified,
You had disloyally agreed to hide.
I don't know just what charges may be pressed,
But there's a warrant out for your arrest;   270
Tartuffe has been instructed, furthermore,
To guide the arresting officer to your door.
CLÉANTE: He's clearly done this to facilitate
His seizure of your house and your estate.
ORGON: That man, I must say, is a vicious beast!   275
VALÈRE: Quick, Sir; you mustn't tarry in the least.
My carriage is outside, to take you hence;
This thousand louis should cover all expense.
Let's lose no time, or you shall be undone;
The sole defense, in this case, is to run.   280
I shall go with you all the way, and place you
In a safe refuge to which they'll never trace you.
ORGON: Alas, dear boy, I wish that I could show you
My gratitude for everything I owe you.
But now is not the time; I pray the Lord   285
That I may live to give you your reward.
Farewell, my dears; be careful . . .
CLÉANTE: Brother, hurry.
We shall take care of things; you needn't worry.

Scene VII

THE OFFICER, TARTUFFE, VALÈRE, ORGON, ELMIRE,
MARIANE, MADAME PERNELLE, DORINE, CLÉANTE, DAMIS

TARTUFFE: Gently, Sir, gently; stay right where you are.
No need for haste; your lodging isn't far.   290

You're off to prison, by order of the Prince.
ORGON: This is the crowning blow, you wretch; and since
It means my total ruin and defeat,
Your villainy is now at last complete.
TARTUFFE: You needn't try to provoke me; it's no use.   295
Those who serve Heaven must expect abuse.
CLÉANTE: You are indeed most patient, sweet, and blameless.
DORINE: How he exploits the name of Heaven! It's shameless.
TARTUFFE: Your taunts and mockeries are all for naught;
To do my duty is my only thought.   300
MARIANE: Your love of duty is most meritorious,
And what you've done is little short of glorious.
TARTUFFE: All deeds are glorious, Madam, which obey
The sovereign prince who sent me here today.
ORGON: I rescued you when you were destitute;   305
Have you forgotten that, you thankless brute?
TARTUFFE: No, no, I well remember everything;
But my first duty is to serve my King.
That obligation is so paramount
That other claims, beside it, do not count;   310
And for it I would sacrifice my wife,
My family, my friend, or my own life.
ELMIRE: Hypocrite!
DORINE: All that we most revere, he uses
To cloak his plots and camouflage his ruses.
CLÉANTE: If it is true that you are animated   315
By pure and loyal zeal, as you have stated,
Why was this zeal not roused until you'd sought
To make Orgon a cuckold, and been caught?
Why weren't you moved to give your evidence
Until your outraged host had driven you hence?   320
I shan't say that the gift of all his treasure
Ought to have damped your zeal in any measure;
But if he is a traitor, as you declare,
How could you condescend to be his heir?
TARTUFFE (*To the Officer:*) Sir, spare me all this clamor; it's growing shrill.
    325
Please carry out your orders, if you will.
OFFICER: Yes, I've delayed too long, Sir. Thank you kindly.
You're just the proper person to remind me.
Come, you are off to join the other boarders
In the King's prison, according to his orders.   330
TARTUFFE: Who? I, Sir?
OFFICER: Yes.
TARTUFFE: To prison? This can't be true!
OFFICER: I owe an explanation, but not to you.

(*To Orgon:*) Sir, all is well; rest easy, and be grateful.
We serve a Prince to whom all sham is hateful,
A Prince who sees into our inmost hearts, 335
And can't be fooled by any trickster's arts.
His royal soul, though generous and human,
Views all things with discernment and acumen;
His sovereign reason is not lightly swayed,
And all his judgments are discreetly weighed. 340
He honors righteous men of every kind,
And yet his zeal for virtue is not blind,
Nor does his love of piety numb his wits
And make him tolerant of hypocrites.
'Twas hardly likely that this man could cozen 345
A King who's foiled such liars by the dozen.
With one keen glance, the King perceived the whole
Perverseness and corruption of his soul,
And thus high Heaven's justice was displayed:
Betraying you, the rogue stood self-betrayed. 350
The King soon recognized Tartuffe as one
Notorious by another name, who'd done
So many vicious crimes that one could fill
Ten volumes with them, and be writing still.
But to be brief: our sovereign was appalled 355
By this man's treachery toward you, which he called
The last, worst villainy of a vile career,
And bade me follow the impostor here
To see how gross his impudence could be,
And force him to restore your property. 360
Your private papers, by the King's command,
I hereby seize and give into your hand.
The King, by royal order, invalidates
The deed which gave this rascal your estates,
And pardons, furthermore, your grave offense 365
In harboring an exile's documents.
By these decrees, our Prince rewards you for
Your loyal deeds in the late civil war,
And shows how heartfelt is his satisfaction
In recompensing any worthy action, 370
How much he prizes merit, and how he makes
More of men's virtues than of their mistakes.
DORINE: Heaven be praised!
MME. PERNELLE: I breathe again, at last.
ELMIRE: We're safe.
MARIANE: I can't believe the danger's past.
ORGON (*To Tartuffe:*) Well, traitor, now you see . . .
CLÉANTE: Ah, Brother, please, 375

Let's not descend to such indignities.
Leave the poor wretch to his unhappy fate,
And don't say anything to aggravate
His present woes; but rather hope that he
Will soon embrace an honest piety,   380
And mend his ways, and by a true repentance
Move our just King to moderate his sentence.
Meanwhile, go kneel before your sovereign's throne
And thank him for the mercies he has shown.
ORGON: Well said: let's go at once and, gladly kneeling,   385
Express the gratitude which all are feeling.
Then, when that first great duty has been done,
We'll turn with pleasure to a second one,
And give Valère, whose love has proven so true,
The wedded happiness which is his due.   390

Jean Racine (1639–1699)

LIFE: Racine's education, after the death of his parents, at Port-Royal, which was the center of Jansenism, no doubt predetermined his later religious conversion; but for 14 years of his maturity he worked in the theater, producing ten plays and forming with Boileau, La Fontaine, and Molière the "society of the four," which added French literature to that of the world. Racine offers yet another example of a man who was both unencumbered artist and court flatterer (he began his career with odes to Louis XIV), ascetic and libertine, secularist and devout believer. When *Phaedra* was driven off the stage by an opposition company, the strength of his moral convictions turned him from the theater; he tried to enter a Carthusian monastery, settled instead for a prudent Christian marriage which produced seven children and a retirement which produced *Esther* and *Athalia,* written for the edification of schoolgirls. But in spite of any qualifications about the sincerity of his conversion, the plays remain as testimony to the fitness of his artistic judgment and taste.

WORKS: Racine wrote ten plays before his retirement: *The Thebaid* (1664), *Alexander the Great* (1665), *Andromache* (1667), *The Suitors* (1668), *Britannicus* (1669), *Berenice* (1670), *Bajazet* (1672), *Mithridates* (1673), *Iphegenia* (1674), and *Phaedra* (1677); after his retirement he wrote the two biblical dramas (*Esther* and *Athalia*) and a history of Port-Royal.

PHAEDRA *

Characters

THESEUS, *son of Aegeus and King of Athens*
PHAEDRA, *wife of Theseus and daughter of Minos and Pasiphaë*
HIPPOLYTUS, *son of Theseus and Antiope, Queen of the Amazons*
ARICIA, *princess of the royal blood of Athens*
OENONE, *nurse of Phaedra*
THERAMENES, *tutor of Hippolytus*
ISMENE, *friend of Aricia*
PANOPE, *waiting-woman of Phaedra*
Guards

Pronunciation:

   Phaedra = Pheédra   Aricia = Arísha
   Oenone = Eenónee   Theramenes = Therámeneés
   Ismene = Ismeénee   Panope = Pánopeé
          Pasiphaë = Pásiphá-ee

ACT I

SCENE I

Hippolytus, Theramenes

HIPPOLYTUS: No, no, my friend, we're off! Six months have passed
since Father heard the ocean howl and cast
his galley on the Aegean's skull-white froth.
Listen! The blank sea calls us — off, off, off!
I'll follow Father to the fountainhead   5
and marsh of hell. We're off. Alive or dead,
I'll find him.

THERAMENES: Where, my lord? I've sent a host
of veteran seamen up and down the coast;
each village, creek and cove from here to Crete
has been ransacked and questioned by my fleet;   10
my flagship skirted Hades' rapids, furled
sail there a day, and scoured the underworld.
Have you fresh news? New hopes? One even doubts
if noble Theseus wants his whereabouts
discovered. Does he need helpers to share   15
the plunder of his latest love affair;
a shipload of spectators and his son

Reprinted with permission of Farrar, Straus & Giroux, Inc. from *Phaedra and Figaro* by Robert Lowell.
Copyright © 1960, 1961 by Robert Lowell.

  * First performed on New Year's day, 1677.

to watch him ruin his last Amazon —
some creature, taller than a man, whose tanned
and single bosom slithers from his hand,   20
when he leaps to crush her like a waterfall
of honeysuckle?
HIPPOLYTUS: You are cynical,
my friend. Your insinuations wrong a king,
sick as myself of his philandering.
His heart is Phaedra's and no rivals dare   25
to challenge Phaedra's sole possession there.
I sail to find my father. The command
of duty calls me from this stifling land.
THERAMENES: This stifling land? Is that how you deride
this gentle province where you used to ride   30
the bridle-paths, pursuing happiness?
You cured your orphaned childhood's loneliness
and found a peace here you preferred to all
the blaze of Athens' brawling protocol.
A rage for exploits blinds you. Your disease   35
is boredom.
HIPPOLYTUS: Friend, this kingdom lost its peace,
when Father left my mother for defiled
bull-serviced Pasiphaë's child. The child
of homicidal Minos is our queen!
THERAMENES: Yes, Phaedra reigns and rules here. I have seen   40
you crouch before her outbursts like a cur.
When she first met you, she refused to stir
until your father drove you out of court.
The news is better now; our friends report
the queen is dying. Will you cross the seas,   45
desert your party and abandon Greece?
Why flee from Phaedra? Phaedra fears the night
less than she fears the day that strives to light
the universal ennui of her eye —
this dying woman, who desires to die!   50
HIPPOLYTUS: No, I despise her Cretan vanity,
hysteria and idle cruelty.
I fear Aricia; she alone survives
the blood-feud that destroyed her brothers' lives.
THERAMENES: Prince, Prince, forgive my laughter. Must you fly   55
beyond the limits of the world and die,
floating in flotsam, friendless, far from help,

18. *Amazon:* it was during his expedition against the Amazons that Theseus won Hippolytus'
mother, Antiope.
28. *this stifling land:* Troezen, the setting of the play.
38. *Pasiphaë's child:* Phaedra was the daughter of Minos, king of Crete, and Pasiphaë, whose
union with a bull produced the Minotaur, the half-bull and half-man killed by Theseus in the
Cretan labyrinth.

and clubbed to death by Tartars in the kelp?
Why arm the shrinking violet with a knife?
Do you hate Aricia, and fear for your life,   60
Prince?
HIPPOLYTUS: If I hated her, I'd trust myself
and stay.
THERAMENES: Shall I explain you to yourself?
Prince, you have ceased to be that hard-mouthed, proud
and pure Hippolytus, who scorned the crowd
of common lovers once and rose above   65
your wayward father by despising love.
Now you justify your father, and you feel
love's poison running through you, now you kneel
and breathe the heavy incense, and a god
possesses you and revels in your blood!   70
Are you in love?
HIPPOLYTUS: Theramenes, when I call
and cry for help, you push me to the wall.
Why do you plague me, and try to make me fear
the qualities you taught me to revere?
I sucked in prudence with my mother's milk.   75
Antiope, no harlot draped in silk,
first hardened me. I was my mother's son
and not my father's. When the Amazon,
my mother, was dethroned, my mind approved
her lessons more than ever. I still loved   80
her bristling chastity. Later, you told
stories about my father's deeds that made me hold
back judgment — how he stood for Hercules,
a second Hercules who cleared the Cretan seas
of pirates, throttled Scirron, Cercyon,   85
Procrustes, Sinnis, and the giant man
of Epidaurus writhing in his gore.
He pierced the maze and killed the Minotaur.
Other things turned my stomach: that long list
of women, all refusing to resist.   90
Helen, caught up with all her honeyed flesh
from Sparta; Periboea, young and fresh,
already tired of Salinis. A hundred more,
their names forgotten by my father — whore
and virgin, child and mother, all deceived,   95
if their protestations can be believed!

84. *a second Hercules:* like Hercules, Theseus was a legendary Greek hero who might have been
a real person; his accomplishments are indeed herculean.
91. *Helen:* this legendary beauty seems to have been abduction-prone, although she was only a
child when Theseus caught her up.
92. *Periboea:* she was to be one of the maidens sacrificed to the Minotaur the year Theseus
slew it; later she became the mother of Ajax.
93. *Salinis:* the island of Salamis, in the Saronic Gulf.

Ariadne declaiming to the rocks,
her sister, Phaedra, kidnapped. Phaedra locks
the gate at last! You know how often I
would weary, fall to nodding and deny   100
the possibility of hearing the whole
ignoble, dull, insipid boast unroll.
And now I too must fall. The gods have made me creep.
How can I be in love? I have no specious heap
of honors, friend. No mastered monsters drape   105
my shoulders — Theseus' excuse to rape
at will. Suppose I chose a woman. Why
choose an orphan? Aricia is eternally
cut off from marriage, lest she breed
successors to her fierce brothers, and seed   110
the land with treason. Father only grants
her life on one condition. This — he wants
no bridal torch to burn for her. Unwooed
and childless, she must answer for the blood
her brothers shed. How can I marry her,   115
gaily subvert our kingdom's character,
and sail on the high seas of love?
THERAMENES: You'll prove
nothing by reason, for you are in love.
Theseus' injustice to Aricia throws
her in the light; your eyes he wished to close   120
are open. She dazzles you. Her pitiful
seclusion makes her doubly terrible.
Does this innocent passion freeze your blood?
There's sweetness in it. Is your only good
the dismal famine of your chastity?   125
You shun your father's path? Where would you be,
Prince, if Antiope had never burned
chastely for Theseus? Love, my lord, has turned
the head of Hercules, and thousands — fired
the forge of Vulcan! All your uninspired,   130
cold moralizing is nothing, Prince. You have changed!
Now no one sees you riding, half-deranged
along the sand-bars, where you drove your horse
and foaming chariot with all your force,
tilting and staggering upright through the surf —   135
far from their usual course across the turf.
The woods are quiet . . . How your eyes hang down!
You often murmur and forget to frown.
All's out, Prince. You're in love; you burn. Flames, flames,
Prince! A dissimulated sickness maims   140

97. *Ariadne:* although she showed Theseus how to escape from the labyrinth, he left her on the
island of Dia.

the youthful quickness of your daring. Does
lovely Aricia haunt you?
HIPPOLYTUS: Friend, spare us.
I sail to find my father.
THERAMENES: Will you see
Phaedra before you go?
HIPPOLYTUS: I mean to be
here when she comes. Go, tell her. I will do   145
my duty. Wait, I see her nurse. What new
troubles torment her?

SCENE II

Hippolytus, Theramenes, Oenone

OENONE: Who has griefs like mine,
my lord? I cannot help the queen in her decline.
Although I sit beside her day and night,
she shuts her eyes and withers in my sight.   150
An eternal tumult roisters through her head,
panics her sleep, and drags her from her bed.
Just now she fled me at the prime
of day to see the sun for the last time.
She's coming.
HIPPOLYTUS: So! I'll steal away. My flight   155
removes a hateful object from her sight.

SCENE III

Phaedra, Oenone

PHAEDRA: Dearest, we'll go no further. I must rest.
I'll sit here. My emotions shake my breast,
the sunlight throws black bars across my eyes.
My knees give. If I fall, why should I rise,   160
Nurse?
OENONE: Heaven help us! Let me comfort you.
PHAEDRA: Tear off these gross, official rings, undo
these royal veils. They drag me to the ground.
Why have you frilled me, laced me, crowned me, and wound
my hair in turrets? All your skill torments   165
and chokes me. I am crushed by ornaments.
Everything hurts me, and drags me to my knees!
OENONE: Now this, now that, Madam. You never cease
commanding us then cancelling your commands.
You feel your strength return, summon all hands   170
to dress you like a bride, then say you choke!
We open all the windows, fetch a cloak,
rush you outdoors. It's no use, you decide

that sunlight kills you, and only want to hide.
PHAEDRA: I feel the heavens' royal radiance cool   175
and fail, as if it feared my terrible
shame has destroyed its right to shine on men.
I'll never look upon the sun again.
OENONE: Renunciation or renunciation!
Now you slander the source of your creation.   180
Why do you run to death and tear your hair?
PHAEDRA: Oh God, take me to some sunless forest lair . . .
There hoof-beats raise a dust-cloud, and my eye
follows a horseman outlined on the sky!
OENONE: What's this, my lady?
PHAEDRA: I have lost my mind.   185
Where am I? Oh forget my words! I find
I've lost the habit now of talking sense.
My face is red and guilty — evidence
of treason! I've betrayed my darkest fears,
Nurse, and my eyes, despite me, fill with tears.   190
OENONE: Lady, if you must weep, weep for your silence
that filled your days and mine with violence.
Ah deaf to argument and numb to care,
you have no mercy. Spare me, spare
yourself. Your blood is like polluted water,   195
fouling a mind desiring its own slaughter.
The sun has died and shadows filled the skies
thrice now, since you have closed your eyes;
the day has broken through the night's content
thrice now, since you have tasted nourishment.   200
Is your salvation from your terrified
conscience this passive, servile suicide?
Lady, your madness harms the gods who gave
you life, betrays your husband. Who will save
your children? Your downfall will orphan them,   205
deprive them of their kingdom, and condemn
their lives and future to the discipline
of one who abhors you and all your kin,
a tyrant suckled by an amazon,
Hippolytus . . .
PHAEDRA: Oh God!
OENONE: You still hate someone;   210
thank heaven for that, Madam!
PHAEDRA: You spoke his name!
OENONE: Hippolytus, Hippolytus! There's hope
in hatred, Lady. Give your anger rope.
I love your anger. If the winds of love
and fury stir you, you will live. Above   215

your children towers this foreigner, this child
of Scythian cannibals, now wild
to ruin the kingdom, master Greece, and choke
the children of the gods beneath his yoke.
Why dawdle? Why deliberate at length?   220
Oh, gather up your dissipated strength.
PHAEDRA: I've lived too long.
OENONE: Always, always agonized!
Is your conscience still stunned and paralyzed?
Do you think you have washed your hands in blood?
PHAEDRA: Thank God, my hands are clean still. Would to God   225
my heart were innocent!
OENONE: Your heart, your heart!
What have you done that tears your soul apart?
PHAEDRA: I've said too much. Oenone, let me die;
by dying I shall escape blasphemy.
OENONE: Search for another hand to close your eyes.   230
Oh cruel Queen, I see that you despise
my sorrow and devotion. I'll die first,
and end the anguish of this service cursed
by your perversity. A thousand roads
always lie open to the killing gods.   235
I'll choose the nearest. Lady, tell me how
Oenone's love has failed you. Will you allow
your nurse to die, your nurse, who gave up all —
nation, parents, children, to serve in thrall.
I saved you from your mother, King Minos' wife!   240
Will your death pay me for giving up my life?
PHAEDRA: What I could tell you, I have told you. Nurse,
only my silence saves me from the curse
of heaven.
OENONE: How could you tell me anything
worse than watching you dying?
PHAEDRA: I would bring   245
my life and rank dishonor. What can I say
to save myself, or put off death a day.
OENONE: Ah Lady, I implore you by my tears,
and by your suffering body. Heaven hears,
and knows the truth already. Let me see.   250
PHAEDRA: Stand up.
OENONE: Your hesitation's killing me!
PHAEDRA: What can I tell you? How the gods reprove me!
OENONE: Speak!
PHAEDRA: Oh Venus, murdering Venus! love

217. *Scythian cannibals:* the Greeks named Scythia the country between the Carpathians and the
River Don.

gored Pasiphaë with the bull.
OENONE: Forget
your mother! When she died, she paid her debt.   255
PHAEDRA: Oh Ariadne, oh my Sister, lost
for love of Theseus on that rocky coast.
OENONE: Lady, what nervous languor makes you rave
against your family; they are in the grave.
PHAEDRA: Remorseless Aphrodite drives me. I,   260
my race's last and worst love-victim, die.
OENONE: Are you in love?
PHAEDRA: I am insane with love!
OENONE: Who is he?
PHAEDRA: I'll tell you. Nothing love can do
could equal . . . Nurse, I am in love. The shame
kills me. I love the . . . Do not ask his name.   265
OENONE: Who?
PHAEDRA: Nurse, you know my old loathing for the son
of Theseus and the barbarous amazon?
OENONE: Hippolytus! My God, oh my God!
PHAEDRA: You,
not I, have named him.
OENONE: What can you do,
but die? Your words have turned my blood to ice.   270
Oh righteous heavens, must the blasphemies
of Pasiphaë fall upon her daughter?
Her Furies strike us down across the water.
Why did we come here?
PHAEDRA: My evil comes from farther off. In May,   275
in brilliant Athens, on my marriage day,
I turned aside for shelter from the smile
of Theseus. Death was frowning in an aisle —
Hippolytus! I saw his face, turned white!
My lost and dazzled eyes saw only night,   280
capricious burnings flickered through my bleak
abandoned flesh. I could not breathe or speak.
I faced my flaming executioner,
Aphrodite, my mother's murderer!
I tried to calm her wrath by flowers and praise,   285
I built her a temple, fretted months and days
on decoration. I even hoped to find
symbols and stays for my distracted mind,
searching the guts of sacrificial steers.
Yet when my erring passions, mutineers   290
to virtue, offered incense at the shrine

273. *Furies:* the spirits of punishment.

of love, I failed to silence the malign
Goddess. Alas, my hungry open mouth,
thirsting with adoration, tasted drouth —
Venus resigned her altar to my new lord —   295
and even while I was praying, I adored
Hippolytus above the sacred flame,
now offered to his name I could not name.
I fled him, yet he stormed me in disguise,
and seemed to watch me from his father's eyes.   300
I even turned against myself, screwed up
my slack courage to fury, and would not stop
shrieking and raging, till half-dead with love
and the hatred of a stepmother, I drove
Hippolytus in exile from the rest   305
and strenuous wardship of his father's breast.
Then I could breathe, Oenone; he was gone;
my lazy, nerveless days meandered on
through dreams and daydreams, like a stately carriage
touring the level landscape of my marriage.   310
Yet nothing worked. My husband sent me here
to Troezen, far from Athens; once again the dear
face shattered me; I saw Hippolytus
each day, and felt my ancient, venomous
passion tear my body limb from limb;   315
naked Venus was clawing down her victim.
What could I do? Each moment, terrified
by loose diseased emotions, now I cried
for death to save my glory and expel
my gloomy frenzy from this world, my hell.   320
And yet your tears and words bewildered me,
and so endangered my tranquillity,
at last I spoke. Nurse, I shall not repent,
if you will leave me the passive content
of dry silence and solitude.   325

Scene IV

Phaedra, Oenone, Panope

PANOPE: My heart breaks. Would to God, I could refuse
to tell your majesty my evil news.
The King is dead! Listen, the heavens ring
with shouts and lamentations for the King.
PHAEDRA: The King is dead? What's this?
PANOPE: In vain   330
you beg the gods to send him back again.
Hippolytus has heard the true report,

he is already heading for the port.
PHAEDRA: Oh God!
PANOPE: They've heard in Athens. Everyone
is joining factions — some salute your son,   335
others are calling for Hippolytus;
they want him to reform and harden us —
even Aricia claims the loyalty
of a fanatical minority.
The Prince's captains have recalled their men.   340
His flag is up and now he sails again
for Athens. Queen, if he appear there now,
he'll drag the people with him!
OENONE: Stop, allow
the Queen a little respite for her grief.
She hears you, and will act for our relief.   345

SCENE V

Phaedra, Oenone

OENONE: I'd given up persuading you to live;
death was your refuge, only death could give
you peace and save your troubled glory. I
myself desired to follow you, and die.
But this catastrophe prescribes new laws: 350
the king is dead, and for the king who was,
fate offers you his kingdom. You have a son;
he should be king! If you abandon
him, he'll be a slave. The gods, his ancestors,
will curse and drive you on your fatal course.   355
Live! Who'll condemn you if you love and woo
the Prince? Your stepson is no kin to you,
now that your royal husband's death has cut
and freed you from the throttling marriage-knot.
Do not torment the Prince with persecution,   360
and give a leader to the revolution;
no, win his friendship, bind him to your side.
Give him this city and its countryside.
He will renounce the walls of Athens, piled
stone on stone by Minerva for your child.   365
Stand with Hippolytus, annihilate
Aricia's faction, and possess the state!
PHAEDRA: So be it! Your superior force has won.
I will live if compassion for my son,
devotion to the Prince, and love of power   370
can give me courage in this fearful hour.

---

365. *Minerva:* identified with Athena (the patron goddess of Athens); she was also the Italian
goddess of handcrafts.

ACT II

Scene I

Aricia, Ismene

ARICIA: What's this? The Prince has sent a messenger?
The Prince begs me to wait and meet him here?
The Prince begs! Goose, you've lost your feeble wits!
ISMENE: Lady, be calm. These are the benefits
of Theseus' death: first Prince Hippolytus   5
comes courting favors; soon the populous
cities of Greece will follow — they will eat
out of your hand, Princess, and kiss your feet.
ARICIA: This felon's hand, this slave's! My dear, your news
is only frivolous gossip, I refuse   10
to hope.
ISMENE: Ah Princess, the just powers of hell
have struck. Theseus has joined your brothers!
ARICIA: Tell
me how he died.
ISMENE: Princess, fearful tales
are circulating. Sailors saw his sails,
his infamous black sails, spin round and round   15
in Charybdis' whirlpool; all hands were drowned.
Yet others say on better evidence
that Theseus and Pirithoüs passed the dense
darkness of hell to rape Persephone.
Pirithoüs was murdered by the hound;   20
Theseus, still living, was buried in the ground.
ARICIA: This is an old wives' tale. Only the dead
enter the underworld, and see the bed
of Queen Persephone. What brought him there?
ISMENE: Princess, the King is dead — dead! Everywhere   25
men know and mourn. Already our worshipping
townsmen acclaim Hippolytus for their king;
in her great palace, Phaedra, the self-styled
regent, rages and trembles for her child.
ARICIA: What makes you think the puritanical   30
son of Theseus is human. Will he recall
my sentence and relent?
ISMENE: I know he will.

16. *Charybdis:* the monster (daughter of Poseidon and Mother Earth) who inhabited one of the cliffs at the Straits of Messina, she created a whirlpool by sucking in and spewing out water; on the other side of the Straits lived Scylla, her fellow-monster, daughter of Hecate, who ate sailors (see Book XII of Homer's *Odyssey*).
18. *Pirithoüs:* king of the Lapiths, he was the instigator and sharer of many of Theseus' wild adventures, including the abduction of Helen, but their most famous exploit was the attempted rape of Persephone, wife of Hades, lord of the underworld. In the next speech Aricia dismisses the legend and in Act III, Scene V, Theseus gives his own version of what happened.

ARICIA: You know nothing about him. He would kill
a woman, rather than be kind to one.
That wolf-cub of a fighting amazon   35
hates me above all women. He would walk
from here to hell, rather than hear me talk.
ISMENE: Do you know Hippolytus? Listen to me.
His famous, blasphemous frigidity,
what is it, when you've seen him close at hand?   40
I've watched him like a hawk, and seen him stand
shaking beside you — all his reputation
for hating womenkind bears no relation
to what I saw. He couldn't take his eyes
off you! His eyes speak what his tongue denies.   45
ARICIA: I can't believe you. Your story's absurd!
How greedily I listen to each word!
Ismene, you know me, you know how my heart
was reared on death, and always set apart
from what it cherished — can this plaything of   50
the gods and furies feel the peace of love?
What sights I've seen, Ismene! "Heads will roll,"
my brothers told me, "we will rule." I, the sole
survivor of those fabulous kings, who tilled
the soil of Greece, have seen my brothers killed,   55
six brothers murdered! In a single hour,
the tyrant, Theseus, lopped them in their flower.
The monster spared my life, and yet decreed
the torments of this childless life I lead
in exile, where no Greek can look on me;   60
my forced, perpetual virginity
preserves his crown; no son shall bear my name
or blow my brothers' ashes into flame.
Ismene, you know how well his tyranny
favors my temperament and strengthens me   65
to guard the honor of my reputation;
his rigor fortified my inclination.
How could I test his son's civilities?
I'd never even seen him with my eyes!
I'd never seen him. I'd restrained my eye,   70
that giddy nerve, from dwelling thoughtlessly
upon his outward grace and beauty — on mere
embellishments of nature, a veneer
the Prince himself despises and ignores.
My heart loves nobler virtues, and adores   75
in him his father's hard intelligence.
He has his father's daring and a sense

55. *my brothers:* called the Pallantids, they were the sons of Pallas, who was the brother of
Aegeus, Theseus' father. Theseus murdered them to ensure his control of Athens.

of honor his father lacks. Let me confess,
I love him for his lofty haughtiness
never submitted to a woman's yoke.   80
How could Phaedra's splendid marriage provoke
my jealousy? Have I so little pride,
I'd snatch at a rake's heart, a heart denied
to none — all riddled, opened up to let
thousands pass in like water through a net?   85
To carry sorrows to a heart, alone
untouched by passion, inflexible as stone,
to fasten my dominion on a force
as nervous as a never-harnessed horse —
this stirs me, this enflames me. Devilish Zeus   90
is easier mastered than Hippolytus;
heaven's love-infatuated emperor
confers less glory on his conqueror!
Ismene, I'm afraid. Why should I boast?
His very virtues I admire most   95
threaten to rise and throw me from the brink
of hope. What girlish folly made me think
Hippolytus could love Aricia?
ISMENE: Here
he is. He loves you, Princess. Have no fear.

SCENE II

Aricia, Ismene, Hippolytus

HIPPOLYTUS: Princess, before   100
I leave here, I must tell you what's in store
for you in Greece. Alas, my father's dead.
The fierce forebodings that disquieted
my peace are true. Death, only death, could hide
his valor from this world he pacified.   105
The homicidal Fates will not release
the comrade, friend and peer of Hercules.
Princess, I trust your hate will not resent
honors whose justice is self-evident.
A single hope alleviates my grief,   110
Princess, I hope to offer you relief.
I now revoke a law whose cruelty
has pained my conscience. Princess, you are free
to marry. Oh enjoy this province, whose
honest, unhesitating subjects choose   115
Hippolytus for king. Live free as air,
here, free as I am, much more free!
ARICIA: I dare
not hope. You are too gracious. Can you free

Aricia from your father's stern decree?
HIPPOLYTUS: Princess, the Athenian people, torn in two   120
between myself and Phaedra's son, want you.
ARICIA: Want me, my Lord!
HIPPOLYTUS: I've no illusions. Lame
Athenian precedents condemn my claim,
because my mother was a foreigner.
But what is that? If my only rival were   125
my younger brother, his minority
would clear my legal disability.
However, a better claim than his or mine
now favors you, ennobled by the line
of great Erectheus. Your direct descent   130
sets you before my father; he was only lent
this kingdom by adoption. Once the common
Athenian, dazed by Theseus' superhuman
energies, had no longing to exhume
the rights that rushed your brothers to their doom.   135
Now Athens calls you home; the ancient feud
too long has stained the sacred olive wood;
blood festers in the furrows of our soil
to blight its fruits and scorch the farmer's toil.
This province suits me; let the vines of Crete   140
offer my brother a secure retreat.
The rest is yours. All Attica is yours;
I go to win you what your right assures.
ARICIA: Am I awake, my lord? Your sayings seem
like weird phantasmagoria in a dream.   145
How can your sparkling promises be true?
Some god, my lord, some god, has entered you!
How justly you are worshiped in this town;
oh how the truth surpasses your renown!
You wish to endow me with your heritage!   150
I only hoped you would not hate me. This rage
your father felt, how can you put it by
and treat me kindly?
HIPPOLYTUS: Princess, is my eye
blind to beauty? Am I a bear, a bull, a boar,
some abortion fathered by the Minotaur?   155
Some one-eyed Cyclops, able to resist
Aricia's loveliness and still exist?
How can a man stand up against your grace?
ARICIA: My lord, my lord!

130. *Erectheus:* a legendary king of Athens, he was the son of Earth and raised by Athena.
132. *adoption:* Theseus was the son of Poseidon and Aethra, but the god allowed Aegeus, King of Athens, to claim him.
156. *Cyclops:* the most famous of these legendary giants was Polyphemus, son of Poseidon (see Book IX of Homer's *Odyssey*).

HIPPOLYTUS: I cannot hide my face,
Princess! I'm driven. Why does my violence   160
so silence reason and intelligence?
Must I be still, and let my adoration
simmer away in silent resignation?
Princess, I've lost all power to restrain
myself. You see a madman, whose insane   165
pride hated love, and hoped to sit ashore,
watching the galleys founder in the war;
I was Diana's liegeman, dressed in steel.
I hoped to trample love beneath my heel —
alas, the flaming Venus burns me down,   170
I am the last dependent on her crown.
What left me charred and writhing in her clutch?
A single moment and a single touch.
Six months now, bounding like a wounded stag,
I've tried to shake this poisoned dart, and drag   175
myself to safety from your eyes that blind
when present, and when absent leave behind
volleys of burning arrows in my mind.
Ah, Princess, shall I dive into the sea,
or steal the wings of Icarus to flee   180
love's Midas' touch that turns my world to gold?
Your image drives me stumbling through the cold,
floods my deserted forest caves with light,
darkens the day and dazzles through my night.
I'm grafted to your side by all I see;   185
all things unite us and imprison me.
I have no courage for the Spartan exercise
that trained my hand and steeled my energies.
Where are my horses? I forget their names.
My triumphs with my chariot at the games   190
no longer give me strength to mount a horse.
The ocean drives me shuddering from its shores.
Does such a savage conquest make you blush?
My boorish gestures, headlong cries that rush
at you like formless monsters from the sea?   195
Ah, Princess, hear me! Your serenity
must pardon the distortions of a weak
and new-born lover, forced by you to speak
love's foreign language, words that snarl and yelp . . .
I never could have spoken without your help.   200

168. *Diana's liegeman:* Diana (the Greek Artemis) was goddess of the hunt and fertility; Venus will take her revenge on Diana's liegeman.
180. *Icarus:* his father Daedalus fashioned wings to flee Minos of Crete, but Icarus, in the ecstasy of flight, moved too close to the sun and fell to the sea when the wax which bound the feathers of his wings melted.
181. *Midas:* the legendary Phrygian king whom Dionysus granted the golden touch, which he prayed to lose when he discovered it also metamorphosed his food.

Scene III

Aricia, Ismene, Hippolytus, Theramenes

THERAMENES: I announce the Queen. She comes hurriedly,
looking for you.
HIPPOLYTUS: For me!
THERAMENES: Don't ask me why;
she insisted. I promised I'd prevail
on you to speak with her before you sail.
HIPPOLYTUS: What can she want to hear? What can I say?   205
ARICIA: Wait for her, here! You cannot turn away.
Forget her malice. Hating her will serve
no purpose. Wait for her! Her tears deserve
your pity.
HIPPOLYTUS: You're going, Princess? And I must go
to Athens, far from you. How shall I know   210
if you accept my love.
ARICIA: My lord, pursue
your gracious promise. Do what you must do,
make Athens tributary to my rule.
Nothing you offer is unacceptable;
yet this empire, so great, so glorious,   215
is the least precious of your gifts to us.

Scene IV

Hippolytus, Theramenes

HIPPOLYTUS: We're ready. Wait, the Queen's here. I need you.
You must interrupt this tedious interview.
Hurry down to the ship, then rush back, pale
and breathless. Say the wind's up and we must sail.   220

Scene V

Hippolytus, Oenone, Phaedra

PHAEDRA: He's here! Why does he scowl and look away
from me? What shall I do? What shall I say?
OENONE: Speak for your son, he has no other patron.
PHAEDRA: Why are you so impatient to be gone
from us, my lord? Stay! we will weep together.   225
Pity my son; he too has lost his father.
My own death's near. Rebellion, sick with wrongs,
now like a sea-beast, lifts its slimy prongs,
its muck, its jelly. You alone now stand
to save the state. Who else can understand   230
a mother? I forget. You will not hear
me! An enemy deserves no pity. I fear
your anger. Must my son, your brother, Prince,

be punished for his cruel mother's sins?
HIPPOLYTUS: I've no such thoughts.
PHAEDRA: I persecuted you   235
blindly, and now you have good reason to
return my impudence. How could you find
the motivation of this heart and mind
that scourged and tortured you, till you began
to lose the calm composure of a man,   240
and dwindle to a harsh and sullen boy,
a thing of ice, unable to enjoy
the charms of any civilized resource
except the heavy friendship of your horse,
that whirled you far from women, court and throne,   245
to course the savage woods for wolves alone?
You have good reason, yet if pain's a measure,
no one has less deserved your stern displeasure.
My lord, no one has more deserved compassion.
HIPPOLYTUS: Lady, I understand a mother's passion,   250
a mother jealous for her children's rights.
How can she spare a first wife's son? Long nights
of plotting, devious ways of quarrelling —
a madhouse! What else can remarriage bring?
Another would have shown equal hostility,   255
pushed her advantage more outrageously.
PHAEDRA: My lord, if you had known how far my love
and yearning have exalted me above
this usual weakness . . . Our afflicting kinship
is ending . . .
HIPPOLYTUS: Madam, the precious minutes slip   260
by. I fatigue you. Fight against your fears.
Perhaps Poseidon has listened to our tears,
perhaps your husband's still alive. He hears
us, he is surging home — only a short
day's cruise conceals him, as he scuds for port.   265
PHAEDRA: That's folly, my lord. Who has twice visited
black Hades and the river of the dead
and returned? No, the poisonous Acheron
never lets go. Theseus drifts on and on,
a gutted galley on that clotted waste —   270
he woos, he wins Persephone, the chaste . . .
What am I saying? Theseus is not dead.
He lives in you. He speaks, he's taller by a head,
I see him, touch him, and my heart — a reef . . .
Ah Prince, I wander. Love betrays my grief . . .   275
HIPPOLYTUS: No, no, my father lives. Lady, the blind

---

262. *Poseidon:* god of the sea and putative father of Theseus.
268. *Acheron:* a river leading to Hades.

furies release him; in your loyal mind,
love's fullness holds him, and he cannot die.
PHAEDRA: I hunger for Theseus. Always in my eye
he wanders, not as he appeared in hell,   280
lascivious eulogist of any belle
he found there, from the lowest to the Queen;
no, faithful, airy, just a little mean
through virtue, charming all, yet young and new,
as we would paint a god — as I now see you!   285
Your valiant shyness would have graced his speech,
he would have had your stature, eyes, and reach,
Prince, when he flashed across our Cretan waters,
the loved enslaver of King Minos' daughters.
Where were you? How could he conscript the flower   290
of Athens' youth against my father's power,
and ignore you? You were too young, they say;
you should have voyaged as a stowaway.
No dawdling bypath would have saved our bull,
when your just vengeance thundered through its skull.   295
there, light of foot, and certain of your goal,
you would have struck my brother's monstrous soul,
and pierced our maze's slow meanders, led
by Ariadne and her subtle thread.
By Ariadne? Prince, *I* would have fought   300
for precedence; my every flaming thought,
love-quickened, would have shot you through the dark,
straight as an arrow to your quaking mark.
Could I have waited, panting, perishing,
entrusting your survival to a string,   305
like Ariadne, when she skulked behind,
there at the portal, to bemuse her mind
among the solemn cloisters of the porch?
No, Phaedra would have snatched your burning torch,
and lunged before you, reeling like a priest   310
of Dionysus to distract the beast.
I would have reached the final corridor
a lap before you, and killed the Minotaur!
Lost in the labyrinth, and at your side,
would it have mattered, if I lived or died?   315
HIPPOLYTUS: What are you saying, Madam? You forget
my father is your husband!
PHAEDRA: I have let
you see my grief for Theseus! How could I

299. *her subtle thread:* given to her by Daedalus, it allowed Theseus to penetrate the labyrinth,
kill the Minotaur, and find his way out alive.
311. *Dionysus:* the god inspired an ecstatic religious frenzy in his followers, who were mostly
women.

forget my honor and my majesty,
Prince?

HIPPOLYTUS: Madam, forgive me! My foolish youth 320
conjectured hideous untruths from your truth.
I cannot face my insolence. Farewell . . .

PHAEDRA: You monster! You understood me too well!
Why do you hang there, speechless, petrified,
polite! My mind whirls. What have I to hide? 325
Phaedra in all her madness stands before you.
I love you! Fool, I love you, I adore you!
Do not imagine that my mind approved
my first defection, Prince, or that I loved
your youth light-heartedly, and fed my treason 330
with cowardly compliance, till I lost my reason.
I wished to hate you, but the gods corrupt
us; though I never suffered their abrupt
seductions, shattering advances, I
too bear their sensual lightnings in my thigh. 335
I too am dying. I have felt the heat
that drove my mother through the fields of Crete,
the bride of Minos, dying for the full
magnetic April thunders of the bull.
I struggled with my sickness, but I found 340
no grace or magic to preserve my sound
intelligence and honor from this lust,
plowing my body with its horny thrust.
At first I fled you, and when this fell short
of safety, Prince, I exiled you from court. 345
Alas, my violence to resist you made
my face inhuman, hateful. I was afraid
to kiss my husband lest I love his son.
I made you fear me (this was easily done);
you loathed me more, I ached for you no less. 350
Misfortune magnified your loveliness.
I grew so wrung and wasted, men mistook
me for the Sibyl. If you could bear to look
your eyes would tell you. Do you believe my passion
is voluntary? That my obscene confession 355
is some dark trick, some oily artifice?
I came to beg you not to sacrifice
my son, already uncertain of his life.
Ridiculous, mad embassy, for a wife
who loves her stepson! Prince, I only spoke 360
about myself! Avenge yourself, invoke
your father; a worse monster threatens you

353. *Sibyl:* a prophetess. The one at Cumae had longevity but not youthful beauty.

than any Theseus ever fought and slew.
The wife of Theseus loves Hippolytus!
See, Prince! Look, this monster, ravenous   365
for her execution, will not flinch.
I want your sword's spasmodic final inch.
OENONE: Madam, put down this weapon. Your distress
attracts the people. Fly these witnesses.
Hurry! Stop kneeling! What a time to pray!   370

SCENE VI

Theramenes, Hippolytus

THERAMENES: Is this Phaedra, fleeing, or rather dragged away
sobbing? Where is your sword? Who tore
this empty scabbard from your belt?
HIPPOLYTUS: No more!
Oh let me get away! I face disaster.
Horrors unnerve me. Help! I cannot master   375
my terror. Phaedra . . . No, I won't expose
her. No! Something I do not dare disclose . . .
THERAMENES: Our ship is ready, but before you leave,
listen! Prince, what we never would believe
has happened: Athens has voted for your brother.   380
The citizens have made him king. His mother
is regent.
HIPPOLYTUS: Phaedra is in power!
THERAMENES: An envoy sent from Athens came this hour
to place the scepter in her hands. Her son
is king.
HIPPOLYTUS: Almighty gods, you know this woman!   385
Is it her spotless virtue you reward?
THERAMENES: I've heard a rumor. Someone swam aboard
a ship off Epirus. He claims the King
is still alive. I've searched. I know the thing
is nonsense.
HIPPOLYTUS: Search! Nothing must be neglected.   390
If the king's dead, I'll rouse the disaffected
people, crown Aricia, and place our lands,
our people, and our lives in worthy hands.

ACT III

SCENE I

Phaedra, Oenone

PHAEDRA: Why do my people rush to crown me queen?
Who can even want to see me? They have seen

---

388. *Epirus:* in western Greece.

my downfall. Will their praise deliver me?
Oh bury me at the bottom of the sea!
Nurse, I have said too much! Led on by you,   5
I've said what no one should have listened to.
He listened. How could he pretend my drift
was hidden? Something held him, and made him shift
his ground . . . He only wanted to depart
and hide, while I was pouring out my heart.   10
Oh how his blushing multiplied my shame!
Why did you hold me back! You are to blame,
Oenone. But for you, I would have killed
myself. Would he have stood there, iron-willed
and merciless, while I fell upon his sword?   15
He would have snatched it, held me, and restored
my life. No! No!
OENONE: Control yourself! No peace
comes from surrendering to your disease,
Madam. Oh daughter of the kings of Crete,
why are you weeping and fawning at the feet   20
of this barbarian, less afraid of fate
than of a woman? You must rule the state.
PHAEDRA: Can I, who have no courage to restrain
the insurrection of my passions, reign?
Will the Athenians trust their sovereignty   25
to me? Love's despotism is crushing me,
I am ruined.
OENONE: Fly!
PHAEDRA: How can I leave him?
OENONE: Lady, you have already banished him.
Can't you take flight?
PHAEDRA: The time for flight has passed.
He knows me now. I rushed beyond the last   30
limits of modesty, when I confessed.
Hope was no longer blasting through my breast;
I was resigned to hopelessness and death,
and gasping out my last innocent breath,
Oenone, when you forced me back to life.   35
You thought I was no longer Theseus' wife,
and let me feel that I was free to love.
OENONE: I would have done anything to remove
your danger. Whether I'm guilty or innocent
is all the same to me. Your punishment   40
should fall on one who tried to kill you, not
on poor Oenone. Lady, you must plot
and sacrifice this monster, whose unjust
abhorrence left you dying in the dust.
Oh humble him, undo him, oh despise   45
him! Lady, you must see him with my eyes.

PHAEDRA: Oenone, he was nourished in the woods;
he is all shyness and ungracious moods
because the forests left him half-inhuman.
He's never heard love spoken by a woman! 50
We've gone too far. Oenone, we're unwise;
perhaps the young man's silence was surprise.
OENONE: His mother, the amazon, was never moved
by men.
PHAEDRA: The boy exists. She must have loved!
OENONE: He has a sullen hatred for our sex. 55
PHAEDRA: Oh, all the better; rivals will not vex
my chances. Your advice is out of season;
now you must serve my frenzy, not my reason!
You tell me love has never touched his heart;
we'll look, we'll find an undefended part. 60
He's turned his bronze prows seaward; look, the wind
already blows like a trumpeter behind
his bulging canvas! The Acropolis
of Athens and its empire shall be his!
Hurry, Oenone, hunt the young man down, 65
blind him with dazzling visions of the crown.
Go tell him I relinquish my command,
I only want the guidance of his hand.
Let him assume these powers that weary me,
he will instruct my son in sovereignty. 70
Perhaps he will adopt my son, and be
the son and mother's one divinity!
Oenone, rush to him, use every means
to bend and win him; if he fears the Queen's
too proud, he'll listen to her slave. Plead, groan, 75
insist, say I am giving him my throne . . .
No, say I'm dying!

SCENE II

Phaedra

PHAEDRA: Implacable Aphrodite, now you see
the depths to which your tireless cruelty
has driven Phaedra — here is my bosom;
every thrust and arrow his struck home! 80
Oh Goddess, if you hunger for renown,
rise now, and shoot a worthier victim down!
Conquer the barbarous Hippolytus,
who mocks the graces and the power of Venus,
and gazes on your godhead with disgust. 85
Avenge me, Venus! See, my cause is just,
my cause is yours. Oh bend him to my will! . . .
You're back, Oenone? Does he hate me still?

Scene III

Phaedra, Oenone

OENONE: Your love is folly, dash it from your soul,
gather your scattered pride and self-control,   90
Madam! I've seen the royal ship arrive.
Theseus is back, Theseus is still alive!
Thousands of voices thunder from the docks.
People are waving flags and climbing rocks.
While I was looking for Hippolytus . . .   95
PHAEDRA: My husband's living! Must you trouble us
by talking? What am I living for?
He lives, Oenone, let me hear no more
about it.
OENONE: Why?
PHAEDRA: I told you, but my fears
were stilled, alas, and smothered by your tears.   100
Had I died this morning, I might have faced
the gods. I heeded you and die disgraced!
OENONE: You are disgraced!
PHAEDRA: Oh Gods of wrath,
how far I've travelled on my dangerous path!
I go to meet my husband; at his side   105
will stand Hippolytus. How shall I hide
my thick adulterous passion for this youth,
who has rejected me, and knows the truth?
Will the stern Prince stand smiling and approve
the labored histrionics of my love   110
for Theseus, see my lips, still languishing
for his, betray his father and his King?
Will he not draw his sword and strike me dead?
Suppose he spares me? What if nothing's said?
Am I a gorgon, or Circe, or the infidel   115
Medea, stifled by the flames of hell,
yet rising like Aphrodite from the sea,
refreshed and radiant with indecency?
Can I kiss Theseus with dissembled poise?
I think each stone and pillar has a voice.   120
The very dust rises to disabuse
my husband — to defame me and accuse!
Oenone, I want to die. Death will give
me freedom; oh it's nothing not to live;
death to the unhappy's no catastrophe!   125
I fear the name that must live after me,
and crush my son until the end of time.

115–116. *gorgon . . . Circe . . . Medea:* these legendary women personify female viciousness: the most famous of the Gorgons was Medusa, with snakes for hair and eyes that turned men to stone; Circe could change men into swine (see Book X of Homer's *Odyssey*); Medea, the "cunning one," had a full-blooded life of carnage and plays a part in Phaedra's tragedy.

Is his inheritance his mother's crime,
his right to curse me, when my pollution stains
the blood of heaven bubbling in his veins?   130
The day will come, alas, the day will come,
when nothing will be left to save him from
the voices of despair. If he should live
he'll flee his subjects like a fugitive.
OENONE: He has my pity. Who has ever built   135
firmer foundations to expose her guilt?
But why expose your son? Is your contribution
for his defense to serve the prosecution?
Suppose you kill yourself? The world will say
you fled your outraged husband in dismay.   140
Could there be stronger evidence and proof
than Phaedra crushed beneath the horse's hoof
of blasphemous self-destruction to convince
the crowds who'll dance attendance on the Prince?
The crowds will mob your children when they hear   145
their defamation by a foreigner!
Wouldn't you rather see earth bury us?
Tell me, do you still love Hippolytus?
PHAEDRA: I see him as a beast, who'd murder us.
OENONE: Madam, let the positions be reversed!   150
You fear the Prince; you must accuse him first.
Who'll dare assert your story is untrue,
if all the evidence shall speak for you:
your present grief, your past despair of mind,
the Prince's sword so luckily left behind?   155
Do you think Theseus will oppose his son's
second exile? He has consented once!
PHAEDRA: How dare I take this murderous, plunging course?
OENONE: I tremble, Lady, I too feel remorse.
If death could rescue you from infamy,   160
Madam, I too would follow you and die.
Help me by being silent. I will speak
in such a way the King will only seek
a bloodless exile to assert his rights.
A father is still a father when he smites,   165
You shudder at this evil sacrifice,
but nothing's evil or too high a price
to save your menaced honor from defeat.
Ah Minos, Minos, you defended Crete
by killing young men? Help us! If the cost   170
for saving Phaedra is a holocaust
of virtue, Minos, you must sanctify
our undertaking, or watch your daughter die.

I see the King.
PHAEDRA: I see Hippolytus!

Scene IV

Phaedra, Theseus, Hippolytus, Oenone

THESEUS: Fate's heard me, Phaedra, and removed the bar   175
that kept me from your arms.
PHAEDRA: Theseus, stop where you are!
Your raptures and endearments are profane.
Your arm must never comfort me again.
You have been wronged, the gods who spared your life
have used your absence to disgrace your wife,   180
unworthy now to please you or come near.
My only refuge is to disappear.

Scene V

Theseus, Hippolytus

THESEUS: What a strange welcome! This bewilders me.
My son, what's happened?
HIPPOLYTUS: Phaedra holds the key.
Ask Phaedra. If you love me, let me leave   185
this kingdom. I'm determined to achieve
some action that will show my strength. I fear
Phaedra. I am afraid of living here,
THESEUS: My son, you want to leave me?
HIPPOLYTUS: I never sought
her grace or favor. Your decision brought   190
her here from Athens. Your desires prevailed
against my judgment, Father, when you sailed
leaving Phaedra and Aricia in my care.
I've done my duty, now I must prepare
for sterner actions, I must test my skill   195
on monsters far more dangerous to kill
than any wolf or eagle in this wood.
Release me, I too must prove my manhood.
Oh Father, you were hardly half my age,
when herds of giants writhed before your rage —   200
you were already famous as the scourge
of insolence. Our people saw you purge
the pirates from the shores of Greece and Thrace,
the harmless merchantman was free to race
the winds, and weary Hercules could pause   205
from slaughter, knowing you upheld his cause.
The world revered you. I am still unknown;
even my mother's deeds surpass my own.

Some tyrants have escaped you; let me meet
with them and throw their bodies at your feet.   210
I'll drag them from their wolf-holes; if I die,
my death will show I struggled worthily.
Oh, Father, raise me from oblivion;
my deeds shall tell the universe I am your son.
THESEUS: What do I see? Oh gods, what horror drives   215
my queen and children fleeing for their lives
before me? If so little warmth remains,
oh why did you release me from my chains?
Why am I hated, and so little loved?
I had a friend, just one. His folly moved   220
me till I aided his conspiracy
to ravish Queen Persephone.
The gods, tormented by our blasphemous
designs, befogged our minds and blinded us —
we invaded Epirus instead of hell.   225
There a diseased and subtle tyrant fell
upon us as we slept, and while I stood
by, helpless, monsters crazed for human blood
consumed Pirithoüs. I myself was chained
fast in a death-deep dungeon. I remained   230
six months there, then the gods had pity,
and put me in possession of the city.
I killed the tyrant; now his body feasts
the famished, pampered bellies of his beasts.
At last, I voyaged home, cast anchor, furled   235
my sails. When I was rushing to my world —
what am I saying? When my heart and soul
were mine again, unable to control
themselves for longing — who receives me? All run
and shun me, as if I were a skeleton.   240
Now I myself begin to feel the fear
I inspire. I wish I were a prisoner
again or dead. Speak! Phaedra says my home
was outraged. Who betrayed me? Someone come
and tell me. I have fought for Greece. Will Greece, 245
sustained by Theseus, give my enemies
asylum in my household? Tell me why
I've no avenger? Is my son a spy?
You will not answer. I must know my fate.
Suspicion chokes me, while I hesitate   250
and stand here pleading. Wait, let no one stir.
Phaedra shall tell me what has troubled her.

226. *tyrant:* Aidoneus. Theseus rejects his legendary harrowing of Hades for a more realistic version of the exploit.

Scene VI

Hippolytus

HIPPOLYTUS : What now? His anger turns my blood to ice.
Will Phaedra, always uncertain, sacrifice
herself? What will she tell the King? How hot   255
the air's becoming here! I feel the rot
of love seeping like poison through this house.
I feel the pollution. I cannot rouse
my former loyalties. When I try to gather
the necessary strength to face my father,   260
my mind spins with some dark presentiment . . .
How can such terror touch the innocent?
I LOVE ARICIA! Father, I confess
my treason to you is my happiness!
I LOVE ARICIA! Will this bring you joy,   265
our love you have no power to destroy?

ACT IV

Scene I

Theseus, Oenone

THESEUS : What's this, you tell me he dishonors me,
and has assaulted Phaedra's chastity?
Oh heavy fortune, I no longer know
who loves me, who I am, or where I go.
Who has ever seen such disloyalty   5
after such love? Such sly audacity!
His youth made no impression on her soul,
so he fell back on force to reach his goal!
I recognize this perjured sword; I gave
him this myself to teach him to be brave!   10
Oh Zeus, are blood-ties no impediment?
Phaedra tried to save him from punishment!
Why did her silence spare this parricide?
OENONE : She hoped to spare a trusting father's pride.
She felt so sickened by your son's attempt,   15
his hot eyes leering at her with contempt,
she had no wish to live. She read out her will
to me, then lifted up her arm to kill
herself. I struck the sword out of her hand.
Fainting, she babbled the secret she had planned   20
to bury with her in the grave. My ears
unwillingly interpreted her tears.
THESEUS : Oh traitor! I know why he seemed to blanch
and toss with terror like an aspen branch

when Phaedra saw him. Now I know why he stood   25
back, then embraced me so coldly he froze my blood.
Was Athens the first stage for his obscene
attentions? Did he dare attack the Queen
before our marriage?
OENONE: Remember her disgust
and hate then? She already feared his lust.   30
THESEUS: And when I sailed, this started up again?
OENONE: I've hidden nothing. Do you want your pain
redoubled? Phaedra calls me. Let me go,
and save her. I have told you what I know.

Scene II

Theseus, Hippolytus

THESEUS: My son returns! Oh God, reserved and cool,   35
dressed in a casual freedom that could fool
the sharpest. Is it right his brows should blaze
and dazzle me with virtue's sacred rays?
Are there not signs? Should not ADULTERER
in looping scarlet script be branded there?   40
HIPPOLYTUS: What cares becloud your kingly countenance,
Father! What is this irritated glance?
Tell me! Are you afraid to trust your son?
THESEUS: How dare you stand here? May the great Zeus stone
me, if I let my fondness and your birth   45
protect you! Is my strength which rid the earth
of brigands paralysed? Am I so sick
and senile, any coward with a stick
can strike me? Am I a schoolboy's target? Oh God,
am I food for vultures? Some carrion you must prod   50
and poke to see if it's alive or dead?
Your hands are moist and itching for my bed,
Coward! Wasn't begetting you enough
dishonor to destroy me? Must I snuff
your perjured life, my own son's life, and stain   55
a thousand glories? Let the gods restrain
my fury! Fly! live hated and alone —
there are places where my name may be unknown.
Go, find them, follow your disastrous star
through filth; if I discover where you are,   60
I'll add another body to the hill
of vermin I've extinguished by my skill.
Fly from me, let the grieving storm-winds bear
your contagion from me. You corrupt the air.
I call upon Poseidon. Help me, Lord   65
of Ocean, help your servant! Once my sword

heaped crucified assassins on your shore
and let them burn like beacons. God, you swore
my first request would be fulfilled. My first!
I never made it. Even through the worst   70
torments of Epirus I held my peace;
no threat or torture brought me to my knees
beseeching favors; even then I knew
some greater project was reserved for you!
Poseidon, now I kneel. Avenge me, dash   75
my incestuous son against your rocks, and wash
his dishonor from my household; wave on wave
of roaring nothingness shall be his grave.
HIPPOLYTUS: Phaedra accuses me of lawless love!
Phaedra! My heart stops, I can hardly move   80
my lips and answer. I have no defense,
if you condemn me without evidence.
THESEUS: Oh coward, you were counting on the Queen
to hide your brutal insolence and screen
your outrage with her weakness! You forgot   85
something. You dropped your sword and spoiled your plot.
You should have kept it. Surely you had time
to kill the only witness to your crime!
HIPPOLYTUS: Why do I stand this, and forbear to clear
away these lies, and let the truth appear?   90
I could so easily. Where would you be,
if I spoke out? Respect my loyalty,
Father, respect your own intelligence.
Examine me. What am I? My defense
is my whole life. When have I wavered, when   95
have I pursued the vices of young men?
Father, you have no scaffolding to rig
your charges on. Small crimes precede the big.
Phaedra accused me of attempting rape!
Am I some Proteus, who can change his shape?   100
Nature despises such disparities.
Vice, like virtue, advances by degrees.
Bred by Antiope to manly arms,
I hate the fever of this lust that warms
the loins and rots the spirit. I was taught   105
uprightness by Theramenes. I fought
with wolves, tamed horses, gave my soul to sport,
and shunned the joys of women and the court.
I dislike praise, but those who know me best
grant me one virtue — it's that I detest   110
the very crimes of which I am accused.

100. *Proteus:* a minor god of the sea whose power to assume any shape could be subdued if he were held tight until he took on his true identity.

How often you yourself have been amused
and puzzled by my love of purity,
pushed to the point of crudeness. By the sea
and in the forests, I have filled my heart   115
with freedom, far from women.
THESEUS: When this part
was dropped, could only Phaedra violate
the cold abyss of your immaculate
reptilian soul. How could this funeral urn
contain a heart, a living heart, or burn   120
for any woman but my wife?
HIPPOLYTUS: Ah no!
Father, I too have seen my passions blow
into a tempest. Why should I conceal
my true offense? I feel, Father, I feel
what other young men feel. I love, I love   125
Aricia. Father, I love the sister of
your worst enemies. I worship her!
I only feel and breathe and live for her!
THESEUS: You love Aricia? God! No, this is meant
to blind my eyes and throw me off the scent.   130
HIPPOLYTUS: Father, for six months I have done my worst
to kill this passion. You shall be the first
to know . . . You frown still. Nothing can remove
your dark obsession. Father, what will prove
my innocence? I swear by earth and sky,   135
and nature's solemn, shining majesty. . . .
THESEUS: Oaths and religion are the common cant
of all betrayers. If you wish to taunt
me, find a better prop than blasphemy.
HIPPOLYTUS: All's blasphemy to eyes that cannot see.   140
Could even Phaedra bear me such ill will?
THESEUS: Phaedra, Phaedra! Name her again, I'll kill
you! My hand's already on my sword.
HIPPOLYTUS: Explain
my terms of exile. What do you ordain?
THESEUS: Sail out across the ocean. Everywhere   145
on earth and under heaven is too near.
HIPPOLYTUS: Who'll take me in? Oh who will pity me,
and give me bread, if you abandon me?
THESEUS: You'll find fitting companions. Look for friends
who honor everything that most offends.   150
Pimps and jackals who praise adultery
and incest will protect your purity!
HIPPOLYTUS: Adultery! Is it your privilege
to fling this word in my teeth? I've reached the edge
of madness . . . No, I'll say no more. Compare   155

my breeding with Phaedra's. Think and beware . . .
She had a mother . . . No, I must not speak.
THESEUS: You devil, you'll attack the queen still weak
from your assault. How can you stand and face
your father? Must I drive you from this place   160
with my own hand. Run off, or I will flog
you with the flat of my sword like a dog!

SCENE III

Theseus

THESEUS: You go to your inevitable fate,
Child — by the river immortals venerate.
Poseidon gave his word. You cannot fly: 165
death and the gods march on invisibly.
I loved you once; despite your perfidy,
my bowels writhe inside me. Must you die?
Yes; I am in too deep now to draw back.
What son has placed his father on such a rack?   170
What father groans for such a monstrous birth?
Oh gods, your thunder throws me to the earth.

SCENE IV

Theseus, Phaedra

PHAEDRA: Theseus, I heard the deluge of your voice,
and stand here trembling. If there's time for choice,
hold back your hand, still bloodless; spare your race!   175
I supplicate you, I kneel here for grace.
Oh, Theseus, Theseus, will you drench the earth
with your own blood? His virtue, youth and birth
cry out for him. Is he already slain
by you for me — spare me this incestuous pain!   180
THESEUS: Phaedra, my son's blood has not touched my hand;
and yet I'll be avenged. On sea and land,
spirits, the swift of foot, shall track him down.
Poseidon owes me this. Why do you frown?
PHAEDRA: Poseidon owes you this? What have you done   185
in anger?
THESEUS: What! You wish to help my son?
No, stir my anger, back me to the hilt,
call for blacker colors to paint his guilt.
Lash, strike and drive me on! You cannot guess
the nerve and fury of his wickedness.   190
Phaedra, he slandered your sincerity,
he told me your accusation was a lie.
He swore he loved Aricia, he wants to wed
Aricia. . . .

PHAEDRA: What, my lord!
THESEUS: That's what he said.
Of course, I scorn his shallow artifice. 195
Help me, Poseidon, hear me, sacrifice
my son. I seek the altar. Come! Let us both
kneel down and beg the gods to keep their oath.

Scene V

Phaedra

PHAEDRA: My husband's gone, still rumbling his own name
and fame. He has no inkling of the flame 200
his words have started. If he hadn't spoken,
I might have . . . I was on my feet, I'd broken
loose from Oenone, and had just begun
to say I know not what to save his son.
Who knows how far I would have gone? Remorse, 205
longing and anguish shook me with such force,
I might have told the truth and suffered death,
before this revelation stopped my breath:
Hippolytus is not insensible,
only insensible to me! His dull 210
heart chases shadows. He is glad to rest
upon Aricia's adolescent breast!
Oh thin abstraction! When I saw his firm
repugnance spurn my passion like a worm,
I thought he had some magic to withstand 215
the lure of any woman in the land,
and now I see a schoolgirl leads the boy,
as simply as her puppy or a toy.
Was I about to perish for this sham,
this panting hypocrite? Perhaps I am 220
the only woman that he could refuse!

Scene VI

Phaedra, Oenone

PHAEDRA: Oenone, dearest, have you heard the news?
OENONE: No, I know nothing, but I am afraid.
How can I follow you? You have betrayed
your life and children. What have you revealed, 225
Madam?
PHAEDRA: I have a rival in the field,
Oenone.
OENONE: What?
PHAEDRA: Oenone, he's in love —
this howling monster, able to disprove
my beauty, mock my passion, scorn each prayer,

230
and face me like a tiger in its lair —
he's tamed, the beast is harnessed to a cart;
Aricia's found an entrance to his heart.
OENONE: Aricia?
PHAEDRA: Nurse, my last calamity
has come. This is the bottom of the sea.
235
All that preceded this had little force —
the flames of lust, the horrors of remorse,
the prim refusal by my grim young master,
were only feeble hints of this disaster.
They love each other! Passion blinded me.
240
I let them blind me, let them meet and see
each other freely! Was such bounty wrong?
Oenone, you have known this all along,
you must have seen their meetings, watch them sneak
off to their forest, playing hide-and-seek!
245
Alas, such rendezvous are no offence:
innocent nature smiles of innocence,
for them each natural impulse was allowed,
each day was summer and without a cloud.
Oenone, nature hated me. I fled
250
its light, as if a price were on my head.
I shut my eyes and hungered for my end.
Death was the only God my vows could bend.
And even while my desolation served
me gall and tears, I knew I was observed;
255
I never had security or leisure
for honest weeping, but must steal this pleasure.
Oh hideous pomp; a monarch only wears
the robes of majesty to hide her tears!
OENONE: How can their folly help them? They will never
enjoy its fruit.
260
PHAEDRA: Ugh, they will love forever —
even while I am talking, they embrace,
they scorn me, they are laughing in my face!
In the teeth of exile, I hear them swear
they will be true forever, everywhere.
265
Oenone, have pity on my jealous rage;
I'll kill this happiness that jeers at age.
I'll summon Theseus; hate shall answer hate!
I'll drive my husband to annihilate
Aricia — let no trivial punishment,
270
her instant death, or bloodless banishment . . .
What am I saying? Have I lost my mind?
I am jealous, and call my husband! Bind
me, gag me; I am frothing with desire.
My husband is alive, and I'm on fire!

For whom? Hippolytus. When I have said   275
his name, blood fills my eyes, my heart stops dead.
Imposture, incest, murder! I have passed
the limits of damnation; now at last,
my lover's lifeblood is my single good.
Nothing else cools my murderous thirst for blood.   280
Yet I live on! I live, looked down upon
by my progenitor, the sacred sun,
by Zeus, by Europa, by the universe
of gods and stars, my ancestors. They curse
their daughter. Let me die. In the great night   285
of Hades, I'll find shelter from their sight.
What am I saying? I've no place to turn:
Minos, my father, holds the judge's urn.
The gods have placed damnation in his hands,
the shades in Hades follow his commands.   290
Will he not shake and curse his fatal star
that brings his daughter trembling to his bar?
His child by Pasiphaë forced to tell
a thousand sins unclassified in hell?
Father, when you interpret what I speak,   295
I fear your fortitude will be too weak
to hold the urn. I see you fumbling for
new punishments for crimes unknown before.
You'll be your own child's executioner!
You cannot kill me; look, my murderer   300
is Venus, who destroyed our family;
Father, she has already murdered me.
I killed myself — and what is worse I wasted
my life for pleasures I have never tasted.
My lover flees me still, and my last gasp   305
is for the fleeting flesh I failed to clasp.
OENONE: Madam, Madam, cast off this groundless terror!
Is love now an unprecedented error?
You love! What then? You love! Accept your fate.
You're not the first to sail into this strait.   310
Will chaos overturn the earth and Jove,
because a mortal woman is in love?
Such accidents are easy, all too common.
A woman must submit to being woman.
You curse a failure in the source of things.   315
Venus has feasted on the hearts of kings;
even the gods, man's judges, feel desire,
Zeus learned to live with his adulterous fire.

283. *Europa:* the mother of Minos, who was the product of a union between Europa and Zeus in the shape of a bull.
288. *judge's urn:* Zeus made Minos a judge of the dead in the underworld.
318. *his adulterous fire:* Zeus's love affairs are famous for their number and ingenuity.

PHAEDRA: Must I still listen and drink your poisoned breath?
My death's redoubled on the edge of death.   320
I'd fled Hippolytus and I was free
till your entreaties stabbed and blinded me,
and dragged me howling to the pit of lust.
Oenone, I was learning to be just.
You fed my malice. Attacking the young Prince   325
was not enough; you clothed him with my sins.
You wished to kill him; he is dying now,
because of you, and Theseus' brutal vow.
You watch my torture; I'm the last ungorged
scrap rotting in this trap your plots have forged.   330
What binds you to me? Leave me, go, and die,
may your punishment be to terrify
all those who ruin princes by their lies,
hints, acquiescence, filth, and blasphemies —
panders who grease the grooves of inclination,   335
and lure our willing bodies from salvation.
Go die, go frighten false flatterers, the worst
friends the gods can give to kings they've cursed!
OENONE: I have given all and left all for her service,
almighty gods! I have been paid my price!   340

ACT V

SCENE I

Hippolytus, Aricia

ARICIA: Take a stand, speak the truth, if you respect
your father's glory and your life. Protect
yourself! I'm nothing to you. You consent
without a struggle to your banishment.
If you are weary of Aricia, go;   5
at least do something to prevent the blow
that dooms your honor and existence — both
at a stroke! Your father must recall his oath;
there is time still, but if the truth's concealed,
you offer your accuser a free field.   10
Speak to your father!
HIPPOLYTUS: I've already said
what's lawful. Shall I point to his soiled bed,
tell Athens how his marriage was foresworn,
make Theseus curse the day that he was born?
My aching heart recoils. I only want   15
God and Aricia for my confidants.
See how I love you; love makes me confide
in you this horror I have tried to hide

from my own heart. My faith must not be broken;
forget, if possible, what I have spoken. 20
Ah Princess, if even a whisper slips
past you, it will perjure your pure lips.
God's justice is committed to the cause
of those who love him, and uphold his laws;
sooner or later, heaven itself will rise 25
in wrath and punish Phaedra's blasphemies.
I must not. If I rip away her mask,
I'll kill my father. Give me what I ask.
Do this! Then throw away your chains; it's right
for you to follow me, and share my flight. 30
Fly from this prison; here the vices seethe
and simmer, virtue has no air to breathe.
In the confusion of my exile, none
will even notice that Aricia's gone.
Banished and broken, Princess, I am still 35
a force in Greece. Your guards obey my will,
powerful intercessors wish us well:
our neighbors, Argos' citadel
is armed, and in Mycenae our allies
will shelter us, if lying Phaedra tries 40
to hurry us from our paternal throne,
and steal our sacred titles for her son.
The gods are ours, they urge us to attack.
Why do you tremble, falter and hold back?
Your interests drive me to this sacrifice. 45
While I'm on fire, your blood has changed to ice.
Princess, is exile more than you can face?
ARICIA: Exile with you, my lord? What sweeter place
is under heaven? Standing at your side,
I'd let the universe and heaven slide. 50
You're my one love, my king, but can I hope
for peace and honor, Prince, if I elope
unmarried? This . . . I wasn't questioning
the decency of flying from the King.
Is he my father? Only an abject 55
spirit honors tyrants with respect.
You say you love me. Prince, I am afraid.
HIPPOLYTUS: Aricia, you shall never be betrayed;
accept me! Let our love be sanctified,
then flee from your oppressor as my bride. 60
Bear witness, oh you gods, our love released
by danger, needs no temple or a priest.
It's faith, not ceremonial, that saves.

38. *Argos:* a city in Peloponnesus.
39. *Mycenae:* six miles from Argos.

Here at the city gates, among these graves
the resting places of my ancient line,   65
there stands a sacred temple and a shrine.
Here, where no mortal ever swore in vain,
here in these shadows, where eternal pain
is ready to engulf the perjurer;
here heaven's scepter quivers to confer   70
its final sanction; here, my Love, we'll kneel,
and pray the gods to consecrate and seal
our love. Zeus, the father of the world will stand
here as your father and bestow your hand.
Only the pure shall be our witnesses: 75
Hera, the guarantor of marriages,
Demeter and the virgin Artemis.
ARICIA: The King is coming. Fly. I'll stay and meet
his anger here and cover your retreat.
Hurry. Be off, send me some friend to guide   80
my timid footsteps, husband, to your side.

SCENE II

Theseus, Ismene, Aricia

THESEUS: Oh God, illuminate my troubled mind.
Show me the answer I have failed to find.
ARICIA: Go, Ismene, be ready to escape.

SCENE III

Theseus, Aricia

THESEUS: Princess, you are disturbed. You twist your cape   85
and blush. The Prince was talking to you. Why
is he running?
ARICIA: We've said our last goodbye,
my lord.
THESEUS: I see the beauty of your eyes
moves even my son, and you have gained a prize
no woman hoped for.
ARICIA: He hasn't taken on   90
your hatred for me, though he is your son.
THESEUS: I follow. I can hear the oaths he swore.
He knelt, he wept. He has done this before
and worse. You are deceived.
ARICIA: Deceived, my lord?
THESEUS: Princess, are you so rich? Can you afford   95
to hunger for this lover that my queen
rejected? Your betrayer loves my wife.

76. *Hera:* the wife of Zeus.
77. *Demeter:* the Greek corn-goddess, mother of Persephone and bringer of fertility.

ARICIA: How can you bear to blacken his pure life?
Is kingship only for the blind and strong,
unable to distinguish right from wrong? 100
What insolent prerogative obscures
a light that shines in every eye but yours?
You have betrayed him to his enemies.
What more, my lord? Repent your blasphemies.
Are you not fearful lest the gods so loathe 105
and hate you they will gratify your oath?
Fear God, my lord, fear God. How many times
he grants men's wishes to expose their crimes.
THESEUS: Love blinds you, Princess, and beclouds your reason.
Your outburst cannot cover up his treason. 110
My trust's in witnesses that cannot lie.
I have seen Phaedra's tears. She tried to die.
ARICIA: Take care, your Highness. What your killing hand
drove all the thieves and reptiles from the land,
you missed one monster, one was left alive, 115
one . . . No, I must not name her, Sire, or strive
to save your helpless son; he wants to spare
your reputation. Let me go. I dare
not stay here. If I stayed I'd be too weak
to keep my promise. I'd be forced to speak. 120

SCENE IV

Theseus

THESEUS: What was she saying? I must try to reach
the meaning of her interrupted speech.
Is it a pitfall? A conspiracy?
Are they plotting together to torture me?
Why did I let the rash, wild girl depart? 125
What is this whisper crying in my heart?
A secret pity fills my soul with pain.
I must question Oenone once again.
My guards, summon Oenone to the throne.
Quick, bring her. I must talk with her alone. 130

SCENE V

Theseus, Panope

PANOPE: The Queen's deranged, your Highness. Some accursed
madness is driving her; some fury stalks
behind her back, possesses her, and talks
its evil through her, and blasphemes the world.
She cursed Oenone. Now Oenone's hurled 135
herself into the ocean, Sire, and drowned.

Why did she do it? No reason can be found.
THESEUS: Oenone's drowned?
PANOPE: Her death has brought no peace.
The cries of Phaedra's troubled soul increase.
Now driven by some sinister unrest,   140
she snatches up her children to her breast,
pets them and weeps, till something makes her scoff
at her affection, and she drives them off.
Her glance is drunken and irregular,
she looks through us and wonders who we are;   145
thrice she has started letters to you, Sire,
thrice tossed the shredded fragments in the fire.
Oh call her to you. Help her!
THESEUS: The nurse is drowned? Phaedra wishes to die?
Oh gods! Summon my son. Let him defend   150
himself, tell him I'm ready to attend.
I want him!
Exit Panope
Neptune, hear me, spare my son!
My vengeance was too hastily begun.
Oh why was I so eager to believe
Oenone's accusation? The gods deceive   155
the victims they are ready to destroy!

Scene VI

Theseus, Theramenes

THESEUS: Here is Theramenes. Where is my boy,
my first-born? He was yours to guard and keep.
Where is he? Answer me. What's this? You weep?
THERAMENES: Oh, tardy, futile grief, his blood is shed.   160
My lord, your son, Hippolytus, is dead.
THESEUS: Oh gods, have mercy!
THERAMENES: I saw him die. The most
lovely and innocent of men is lost.
THESEUS: He's dead? The gods have hurried him away
and killed him? . . . just as I began to pray . . .   165
What sudden thunderbolt has struck him down?
THERAMENES: We'd started out, and hardly left the town.
He held the reins; a few feet to his rear,
a single, silent guard held up a spear.
He followed the Mycenae highroad, deep   170
in thought, reins dangling, as if half asleep;
his famous horses, only he could hold,
trudged on with lowered heads, and sometimes rolled
their dull eyes slowly — they seemed to have caught
their master's melancholy, and aped his thought.   175

Then all at once winds struck us like a fist,
we heard a sudden roaring through the mist;
from underground a voice in agony
answered the prolonged groaning of the sea.
We shook, the horses' manes rose on their heads, 180
and now against a sky of blacks and reds,
we saw the flat waves hump into a mountain
of green-white water rising like a fountain,
as it reached land and crashed with a last roar
to shatter like a galley on the shore. 185
Out of its fragments rose a monster, half
dragon, half bull; a mouth that seemed to laugh
drooled venom on its dirty yellow scales
and python belly, forking to three tails.
The shore was shaken like a tuning fork, 190
ships bounced on the stung sea like bits of cork,
the earth moved, and the sun spun round and round,
a sulphur-colored venom swept the ground.
We fled; each felt his useless courage falter,
and sought asylum at a nearby altar. 195
Only the Prince remained; he wheeled about,
and hurled a javelin through the monster's snout.
Each kept advancing. Flung from the Prince's arm,
dart after dart struck where the blood was warm.
The monster in its death-throes felt defeat, 200
and bounded howling to the horses' feet.
There its stretched gullet and its armor broke,
and drenched the chariot with blood and smoke,
and then the horses, terror-struck, stampeded.
Their master's whip and shouting went unheeded, 205
they dragged his breathless body to the spray.
Their red mouths bit the bloody surf, men say
Poseidon stood beside them, that the god
was stabbing at their bellies with a goad.
Their terror drove them crashing on a cliff, 210
the chariot crashed in two, they ran as if
the Furies screamed and crackled in their manes,
their fallen hero tangled in the reins,
jounced on the rocks behind them. The sweet light
of heaven never will expunge this sight: 215
the horses that Hippolytus had tamed,
now dragged him headlong, and their mad hooves maimed
his face past recognition. When he tried
to call them, calling only terrified;
faster and ever faster moved their feet, 220
his body was a piece of bloody meat.
The cliffs and ocean trembled to our shout,
at last their panic failed, they turned about,

and stopped not far from where those hallowed graves,
the Prince's fathers, overlook the waves.   225
I ran on breathless, guards were at my back,
my master's blood had left a generous track.
The stones were red, each thistle in the mud
was stuck with bits of hair and skin and blood.
I came upon him, called; he stretched his right   230
hand to me, blinked his eyes, then closed them tight.
"I die," he whispered, "it's the gods' desire.
Friend, stand between Aricia and my sire —
some day enlightened, softened, disabused,
he will lament his son, falsely accused;   235
then when at last he wishes to appease
my soul, he'll treat my lover well, release
and honor Aricia. . . ." On this word, he died.
Only a broken body testified
he'd lived and loved once. On the sand now lies   240
something his father will not recognize.
THESEUS: My son, my son! Alas, I stand alone
before the gods. I never can atone.
THERAMENES: Meanwhile Aricia, rushing down the path,
approached us. She was fleeing from your wrath,   245
my lord, and wished to make Hippolytus
her husband in God's eyes. Then nearing us,
she saw the signs of struggle in the waste,
she saw (oh what a sight) her love defaced,
her young love lying lifeless on the sand.   250
At first she hardly seemed to understand;
while staring at the body in the grass,
she kept on asking where her lover was.
At last the black and fearful truth broke through
her desolation! She seemed to curse the blue   255
and murdering ocean, as she caught his head
up in her lap; then fainting lay half dead,
until Ismene somehow summoned back her breath,
restored the child to life — or rather death.
I come, great King, to urge my final task,   260
your dying son's last outcry was to ask
mercy for poor Aricia, for his bride.
Now Phaedra comes. She killed him. She has lied.

Scene VII

Theseus, Phaedra, Panope

THESEUS: Ah Phaedra, you have won. He's dead. A man
was killed. Were you watching? His horses ran   265
him down, and tore his body limb from limb.
Poseidon struck him, Theseus murdered him.

I served you! Tell me why Oenone died?
Was it to save you? Is her suicide
A proof of your truth? No, since he's dead, I must   270
accept your evidence, just or unjust.
I must believe my faith has been abused;
you have accused him; he shall stand accused.
He's friendless even in the world below.
There the shades fear him! Am I forced to know   275
the truth? Truth cannot bring my son to life.
If fathers murder, shall I kill my wife
too? Leave me, Phaedra. Far from you, exiled
from Greece, I will lament my murdered child.
I am a murdered gladiator, whirled   280
in black circles. I want to leave the world;
my whole life rises to increase my guilt —
all those dazzled, dazzling eyes, my glory built
on killing killers. Less known, less magnified,
I might escape, and find a place to hide.   285
Stand back, Poseidon. I know the gods are hard
to please. I pleased you. This is my reward:
I killed my son. I killed him! Only a god
spares enemies, and wants his servants' blood!
PHAEDRA: No, Theseus, I must disobey your prayer.   290
Listen to me. I'm dying. I declare
Hippolytus was innocent.
THESEUS: Ah Phaedra, on your evidence, I sent
him to his death. Do you ask me to forgive
my son's assassin? Can I let you live?   295
PHAEDRA: My time's too short, your highness. It was I,
who lusted for your son with my hot eye.
The flames of Aphrodite maddened me;
I loathed myself, and yearned outrageously
like a starved wolf to fall upon the sheep.   300
I wished to hold him to me in my sleep
and dreamt I had him. Then Oenone's tears,
troubled my mind; she played upon my fears,
until her pleading forced me to declare
I loved your son. He scorned me. In despair,   305
I plotted with my nurse, and our conspiracy
made you believe your son assaulted me.
Oenone's punished; fleeing from my wrath,
she drowned herself, and found a too easy path
to death and hell. Perhaps you wonder why   310
I still survive her, and refuse to die?
Theseus, I stand before you to absolve
your noble son. Sire, only this resolve
upheld me, and made me throw down my knife.

I've chosen a slower way to end my life — 315
Medea's poison; chills already dart
along my boiling veins and squeeze my heart.
A cold composure I have never known
gives me a moment's poise. I stand alone
and seem to see my outraged husband fade 320
and waver into death's dissolving shade.
My eyes at last give up their light, and see
the day they've soiled resume its purity.
PANOPE: She's dead, my lord.
THESEUS: Would God, all memory
of her and me had died with her! Now I 325
must live. This knowledge that has come too late
must give me strength and help me expiate
my sacrilegious vow. Let's go, I'll pay
my son the honors he has earned today.
His father's tears shall mingle with his blood. 330
My love that did my son so little good
asks mercy from his spirit. I declare
Aricia is my daughter and my heir.

Jean de la Fontaine (1621–1695)

LIFE: Son of the superintendent of the royal preserves at Château-Thierry, he left his wife, after two years of marriage, and settled eventually in Paris, where his personal charm and indisputable gifts as a writer ensured him continuing success, whatever the changing fortunes of his various patrons. He lived at the home of the elegant Mme. de la Sablière for nearly twenty years, in the midst of the luxury his talents earned him, and was elected to the French Academy in 1684. He died repenting slightly the hedonism of his life.

WORKS: He is best known for his *Fables*, published in twelve volumes between 1668 and 1694, and the *Contes* (1664).

FABLES *

The Grasshopper and the Ant [1]

Until fall, a grasshopper
    Chose to chirr;

* The first six books were published in 1668; the next five in 1678–79; the twelfth book in 1694.
1. Book I, No. 1.

With starvation as foe
When northeasters would blow,
And not even a gnat's residue   5
Or caterpillar's to chew,
She chirred a recurrent chant
Of want beside an ant,
Begging it to rescue her
With some seeds it could spare   10
Till the following year's fell.
"By August you shall have them all,
Interest and principal."
Share one's seeds? Now what is worse
For any ant to do?   15
Ours asked, "When fair, what brought you through?"
— "I sang for those who might pass by chance —
Night and day. Please do not be repelled.
— "Sang? A delight when someone has excelled.
A singer! Excellent. Now dance."   20

The Town Rat and the Country Rat [2]

In this ancient parable,
Town rat proffered country rat
A fashionable meal
As a change from this and that,

Where on a rug from Turkey,   5
A feast for two was ready.
Fond fancy alone could see
The pair's joint ecstasy.

Fine food made each's plate replete —
More dainties there than greed could paint,   10
But as they were about to eat,
Noises were heard; the pair felt faint.

At the door, sniff and smell.
What was scratching steadily?
Both frightened ill, half fell,   15
Then fled confusedly.

When they had dared to reappear,
In seclusion with relief,
The city rat resumed, "My dear,
Come now, divide the beef."   20

2. Book I, No. 9.

— "I have dined," the field rat said;
"Be my guest, pray, a day hence,
Though you'll not find, I am afraid,
Similar magnificence.

Yet I'm never in danger: I've supped,   25
Carefree from year to year;
And so farewell. What is good cheer
Which death threats can disrupt?"

The Fox and the Stork [3]

Shrewd Master Fox had been such a courtier
That stately Miss Stork had said she'd dine with him;
But his preparations involved no great flutter,
      It being the rascal's whim
To provide consommé; thrift seemed important.   5
The broth was offered the stork upon a dinner plate:
Her long beak caught so little, the creature scarcely ate,
Yet the rogue lapped all of his up in an instant.
      Later, to requite his perfidy,
The stork offered him hospitality.   10
"I'm charmed," he said, "and to those I know intimately
      Come enthusiastically."
     On the hour he was punctually
      At his hostess's address,
      Blessing her for her thoughtfulness;   15
      That the meal was not quite done
Gave him an appetite; foxes are famed for one.
Oh, the scent of meat; it made his whole being expand!
Cut fine, he inferred, and turned by a careful hand.
      Yet what had he not to endure,   20
Since it was served in a tall, very small-mouthed ewer.
The stork's bill was so long, the vase was scarcely taller,
But what fox-nose can probe a mere aperture!
The embarrassed guest was soon trotting home hungry,
Looking as if caught robbing a hennery —   25
      Ears and tail limp, not caring how they were.

      My words here are particularly
      Addressed to foxes without fur.

The Child and the Schoolmaster [4]

That fools' preaching is devoid of power
Is what I am trying to explain.

3. Book I, No. 18.
4. Book I, No. 19.

A child all but drowned in an idle hour
When frolicking on a bank of the Seine.
Yet fairly near the little fellow 5
Providence had placed an enormous willow.
Well, as the child clutched some branches that trailed,
A teacher approached and his ears were assailed
By cries of, "Help! I'm drowning. Rescue me."
The schoolmaster, pausing impersonally 10
As though reproving iniquities,
Said, "The little blockhead has fallen in!
See? Punishment for stupidities!
Think of undertaking the rogues. Imagine.
Unlucky parents who must keep a watchful eye 15
On the renegades, alert for tricks they may try.
Pitiful. I am pained for them to the core!"
He ranted, and then drew the child ashore.
Many more types are implied than I include —
The loose-tongued, carpers, prigs who cannot unbend; 20
Self-evident, those to whom I allude;
A whole tribe represented by a single trend.
The Creator blessed the seed of each brood.
They find, whatever their occupation,
    A pretext for talking all day. 25
Ah, friend, first effect my salvation,
    Then tell me what you have to say.

The Lion and the Gnat [5]

"Begone, objectionable gnat; you pollute the air!"
        The lion affected this tone
        In addressing the little one,
        Who himself shrilled a challenge to war.
"Do you think the name king," he said to the great cat, 5
        "Has sovereign power to terrify?
        An ox though harder to combat,
        Behaves as fancy dictates to me."
        He had scarcely expressed the thought
        That he'd taken charge of the campaign, 10
        When his gnat note rang out.
        He circled the enemy's mane,
        Took his time and bit the great cat
        On the neck. Almost crazed by the gnat,
The quadruped foamed. Lightning shot from his eyeball. 15
He roared. The neighbors trembled and rushed underground,
        Cowering from what had disorganized all.

5. Book II, No. 9.

      A mere gnat held them terrorbound.
The minute pest was intolerable;
A hundred times stung the spine, forced the mouth to close,   20
      Then ventured up into the nose.
Whereupon the victim really lost his head.
The invisible foe laughed at the great beast's despair,
Whose own teeth and claws were drawing blood —
Defeat costing the cause of it not a care.   25
The miserable cat tore grooves in his own frame,
His whirling tail lashed his flanks with a smiting sound.
He beat the blameless air, self-tormented till tame —
And with muscles slack, sank exhausted upon the ground.
Mars' insect withdrew in a halo of fire.   30
As he'd bugled the charge, he announced he'd retire —
His last taunt to the tamed; then encountered a skein
      He'd not seen, of a web which some spider had spread.
      He would never tame lions again.

And what is the moral that has been conveyed?   35
A double one: don't underrate an enemy;
The direst enemy may be too small to see;
The other: we may surmount what few could bear;
      Then something minute end our earthly career.

The Fox and the Grapes [6]

A fox of Gascon, though some say of Norman descent,
When starved till faint gazed up at a trellis to which grapes were tied —
      Matured till they glowed with a purplish tint
      As though there were gems inside.
Now grapes were what our adventurer on strained haunches chanced to
                                  crave, 5
      But because he could not reach the vine
He said, "These grapes are sour; I'll leave them for some knave."

Better, I think, than an embittered whine.

The Hare and the Tortoise [7]

If you don't start on time, you might as well not try:
As proved by the tortoise when a boaster finished last.
"Wager who'll be winner?" the tortoise said. "It's I.
You'll see which is the plodder and which is really fast."
      The fleeter asked, "Are you sober?   5
      Take herbs as a purge, good mother.

6. Book III, No. 11.
7. Book VI, No. 10.

Say four grains of hellebore;
Sane or not, you have a competitor."
The two set forth and wickets were placed
To show them the goal toward which they raced: 10
As for me, I did not see the pair
Or the judging that was done.
Master Hare had no more than four leaps to take before he would win
    the dare;
I mean the sort of bounds he makes when dogs nearly run him down —
When he draws so fast he would take till Greek Kalends to find,   15
    With pack nosing the ground he has left behind;
So he could afford to do some browsing,
    Furthermore spare time for dozing;
    Snuffing the wind while the tortoise came
    Festina lente like a senator   20
    Perseveringly toward phantom fame,
    Following him who had sped before.
Now the hare did not fancy a sinecure;
    To defeat a tortoise is scarcely a lure,
    So thought he'd allow her to think she could score,   25
And started late. He browsed and then would doze,
    Amusing himself as a rabbit does,
    And the race was deferred. But seeing presently
That the tortoise might win and there was no time to spare,
He was off like a dart. Belated energy!   30
The tortoise, alas, was ahead of Master Hare.
"Well!" she cried. "Was I right to say I could do what I've done?
    Did your speed achieve success?
    I've brought it off! And what of your tardiness
    If you'd carried a tortoiseshell as you ran?"   35

20. *Festina lente:* making haste slowly.

The Cobbler and the Financier [8]

He'd sing from break of day till the sun would disappear,
    Like a seraph; any there
Stood still to hear the arpeggios sink
    Deeper than seven sages think.
Nearby a man with a fortune of which to take care,   5
    Seldom sang and with careworn eyes ajar,
    Was a slave to fear of expense.
Before the sky could clear or one ought to start the day,
He would wake with a jerk, aroused by the cobbler's lay,
    And, "Oh, that Providence," he would say,   10
    "Could grant us the convenience
Of buying sleep as we buy provender —

8. Book VIII, No. 2.

Food and drink that we require."
Requesting the cobbler to come and confer,
Our complainer said, "Master Gregory, I would ask, if I may
                                                    inquire,   15
How much do you earn in a year?" — "Do I earn, sir, in a year?"
    The dear man smiled at the financier
With a gentle air and said, "I don't know, am not quite sure;
I can't say what I earn; never count what's so poor,
    Just work for hire; but in the end it is plain   20
      As the seasons roll away,
      That I've earned our bread again."
— "Well then, how much might you earn, say, in a day?"
— "Sometimes more, sometimes less. A thing I deplore
(If it were not for this, what a round sum I'd make)   25
Is that every other day I lock the door
    And can't work, though the holidays we take
Seem alike, I swear; the priest, dear sir, should be blamed,
Since each new saint's day he has a discourse to drone."
The financier smiled as he said, "I'm ashamed.   30
Permit me to say that henceforth all your hours are your own:
Here are a hundred crowns — patrimony, I mean:
    To which to turn when times are lean."
The cobbler thought it the whole round earth's amassed dower —
    Say, the assets of each generation   35
    That were meant to advantage everyone.
Whereupon he went home and that very same hour
    Buried his gold and his joy at a stroke,
    Sang no more; in fact he could scarcely croak.
Then since he must guard the wealth which he had found,   40
    Slept by fits and starts, with uneasy
    Imagination busy.
    His suspicions were stirred by each sound.
    Both ears and eyes were alert all day, and at night,
    If so much as a cat trod light,   45
He thought it would thieve his fund. In the end the poor man
Sped to him whose night's rest was really rest,
To say, "Take your hundred crowns; I crave to have back
    The songs and sleep thieves don't molest."

The Rat and the Elephant [9]

I fear that appearances are worshiped throughout France:
    Whereas pre-eminence perchance
    Merely means a pushing person.
    An extremely French folly —

9. Book VIII, No. 15.

A weakness of which we have more than our share — 5
Whereas false pride, I'd say, has been the Spaniard's snare.
      To be epigrammatical,
      They're foolish folk; we're comical.
      Well, I've put us in this tale
      Which came to mind as usable. 10

A mite of a rat was mocking an elephant
As it moved slowly by, majestically aslant,
      Valued from antiquity,
      Towering in draped solemnity
      While bearing along in majesty 15
      A queen of the Levant —
      With her dog, her cat, and sycophant,
Her parakeet, monkey, anything she might want —
      On their way to relics they wished to see.
      But the rat was not one whom weight could daunt 20
And asked why observers should praise mere size.
"Who cares what space an object occupies?"
He said. "Size does not make a thing significant!
All crowding near an elephant? Why must I worship him?
Servile to brute force at which mere tots might faint? 25
Should persons such as I admire his heavy limb?
      I pander to an elephant!"
      About to prolong his soliloquy
      When the cat broke from captivity
      And instantly proved what her victim would grant: 30
      That a rat is not an elephant.

Charles de Montesquieu (1689–1755)

LIFE: Born at the Château La Brède near Bordeaux, Charles de Secondat, Baron de la Brède et de Montesquieu, served that city's government as counselor of the parlement and then its president until his deteriorating eyesight turned him to the researches into politics, law, and philosophy which were his passion. He spent two years in England, studying its institutions, enjoying its society, and finally concluding that its constitution was worthy of Europe's praise. At the time of his death he was completely blind.

WORKS: His most ambitious work, *The Spirit of the Laws,* was published anonymously in 1748 and went through twenty-two editions in two years.

THE PERSIAN LETTERS *

Letter VIII

Usbek to his friend Rustan in Ispahan

Your letter was delivered to me at Erzerum, where I now am. I was quite sure that my departure would cause talk. I am not at all upset by it. Which would you have me follow: the good judgment of my enemies, or my own?

I came to court at a very early age. I can say that my heart was in no way corrupted there. I even formed a noble resolution: I dared to be virtuous in those surroundings. So soon as I recognized vice, I withdrew from it, but I came back to it again to unmask it. I carried truth to the very steps of the throne. I spoke there a hitherto unknown language; I brought flattery to confusion, and astonished at once both the worshippers and their idol.

But when I realized that my sincerity had made enemies for me, that I had drawn on myself the jealousy of ministers without having won the favor of the Prince, and that in a corrupt court I managed to buoy myself up only by an already enfeebled virtue, then I decided to leave. I pretended to possess a great devotion to learning, and by dint of pretense, such devotion actually came to me. I became involved in no more intrigues and withdrew to my country house. But this solution had its own disadvantages. I still remained exposed to the malice of my enemies, but I had almost completely removed the means of protecting myself from them. Some confidential advice made me think seriously about my future. I decided to exile myself from my country, and my withdrawal from the court provided me with a plausible pretext. I went to the King. I pointed out to him my great desire to become educated in Western sciences. I hinted that he might draw some profit from my travels. I found understanding in his eyes. I left and thereby robbed my enemies of a victim.

There, Rustan, is the true motive for my trip. Let them talk in Ispahan. Come to my defense only with my friends. Leave to my enemies their evil interpretations. I am only too happy that this should be the only harm they can do me.

At the present moment there is talk of me. Perhaps I shall be only too easily forgotten hereafter and my friends . . . No, Rustan, I shall not give myself over to such a sad thought. I shall always be dear to them. I count on their fidelity as I do on your own.

From Erzerum, the 20th of the
Moon of Gemmadi II, 1711.

Reprinted from *The Persian Letters* by Charles de Montesquieu, edited and translated by J. Robert Loy. By permission of The World Publishing Company. Copyright © 1961 by Meridian Books, Inc.

* First published anonymously in 1721.

Letter IX

The first eunuch to Ibbi in Erzerum

You are following your former master in his voyages; you are passing through provinces and kingdoms. Vexations could not possibly make any impression on you. Every moment brings you new things to see. All that you are seeing diverts you and makes you pass the time without feeling it.

Such is not the case with me, closed up as I am in a fearful prison, ever surrounded by the same objects and consumed by the same griefs. I sigh, overwhelmed as I am by the weight of fifty years of cares and anxieties. In the course of a long life I can say that I have had not one peaceful day nor any tranquil moment.

When my first master had settled on the cruel plan of entrusting his women to me and had obliged me by seductions doubled with a thousand threats to separate me forever from myself, I planned, weary of the most laborious tasks, to sacrifice my passions to tranquillity and fortune. Unhappy man that I was! My preoccupation of mind made me see the recompense but not the loss. I hope to be delivered from the seizure of love by my impotence to satisfy it. Alas for me! The effect of passion was snuffed out in me without extinguishing the cause, and far from being comforted, I found myself surrounded by objects that provoked my passion without cease. I entered into the harem, where everything aroused the regret of what I had lost. I found myself excited every moment; a thousand natural charms seemed to be displayed to my eyes only to torment me. As the crowning stroke to my misery, I had ever before my eyes a happy man. During these troubled times, I never led a woman to my master's bed, I never undressed her without returning to my room with rage in my heart and horrible desolation in my soul.

That is how I spent my miserable youth. I had only myself for intimate friend. The cares and vexations with which I was laden, I was forced to consume within myself. The same women whom I was tempted to behold with such tender eyes, I could look at only with severity. I would have been lost if they had understood. What advantage they would have taken of me!

I remember that one day I was putting a woman in her bath and I felt so carried away that I lost my reason completely and dared to move my hand to a dread spot. At first I thought that day would be my last. I was, however, fortunate enough to escape a thousand deaths. But the beauty who became thus party to my weakness sold her silence dearly. I lost my authority over her completely, and she has since that time forced me into complaisances that have exposed me a thousand times to losing my life.

Finally, the flames of youth have passed. I am old, and as concerns all that, I am at peace. I behold women with indifference, and I return to them all the scorn and torture they have made me suffer. I remember always that I was born to command them, and it seems to me that I become a man again when I can still do so. I have detested them ever since the moment I was able to consider them objectively, since my reason has allowed me to see all their weaknesses. Although I watch over them for another, the pleasure of making myself obeyed gives me a secret joy. When I deprive them of everything, I feel I do so for my own benefit, and indirectly, I always receive great satisfaction from it. In the seraglio it is as if I were in a small empire, and my ambition, the sole passion left to me, is satisfied a little. I can see with pleasure that everything turns on me and that I am needed every moment. I accept willingly the hate of all those women, and this strengthens me in my position. Still, they are not dealing with an ungrateful wretch: they always find me co-operative in their most innocent pleasures. I represent to them an unshakable barrier: they dream up plans, and I put an immediate stop to them. I fortify myself with refusal; I bristle with scruples. There are never any other words in my mouth save duty, virtue, decency, and modesty. I bring them to despair by talking continually about the weakness of their sex and the authority of the master. I thereupon complain of having to be so severe, and I pretend to want them to understand that I act from no other motive than their own well-being and my great affection for them.

This does not mean that I do not suffer, in my turn, an infinite amount of unpleasantness, or that these vindictive women do not each day try to return to me, twofold, the unpleasantness I cause them. They are capable of terrible revenge. There exists between us something like an ebb and flow of dominion and submission. They always arrange to have the most humiliating tasks fall on me. They make a show of unexampled scorn, and with no regard for my advanced age, they cause me to get up at night for the most inconsequential whim. I am forever weighed down under orders, commands, chores, and fancies. They seem to spell each other at harassing me; they seem to arrange their whims. Often they take pleasure in making me redouble my attentions. They arrange to involve me in false intrigue: now one of them comes to tell me that a young man has appeared around the walls; another time, that they have heard a noise or that a letter is to be delivered. All this unnerves me, and they laugh at my confusion. They are delighted to see me torment myself in this way. On other occasions they keep me behind their door and chain me there day and night; they know very well how to feign sickness, fainting, and fright; they do not lack pretexts for leading me to the point where they want me. On such occasions one must show blind obedience and limitless compliance. A refusal coming from the mouth of a man like me would be unheard of, and were I to hesitate in obeying them, they would have the right to punish me. I should rather lose my life completely, dear Ibbi, than descend to such humiliation.

Nor is that the whole story. I am never for one moment sure of being in my master's favor. I have all these enemies in his heart, intent only upon destroying me. The women pass through moments when I am not obeyed at all, moments when they give in to my every bidding, moments when I am always in the wrong. I take angered women to my master's bed. Do you think they work in my behalf there, or that my side is the stronger? I have everything to fear from their tears, from their sighs, from their embraces, from their very pleasures. They are in their glory there. Their charms can become terrible for me. Present services rendered wipe out in one moment all my services of the past, and there is no being sure of a master who is no longer himself.

How many times has it happened to me to retire in favor and arise in disgrace! That day when I was so scandalously whipped all over the seraglio, what had I done? I left a woman in my master's arms. As soon as she saw that he was excited, she poured forth a torrent of tears. She complained and arranged her bewailing so well that this added to the measure of love she was arousing. How could I possibly have justified myself at such a time? I was lost when I expected it least. I was the victim of amorous negotiation, of a treaty made with sighs. That, dear Ibbi, is the cruel situation in which I have ever lived.

How fortunate you are! Your cares are limited only to Usbek's person. It is easy for you to please him and to keep yourself in his favor until the end of your days.

> From the seraglio at Ispahan, the last
> of the Moon of Saphar, 1711.

Letter X

Mirza to his friend Usbek in Erzerum

You are the only person who could make up for the absence of Rica, and there was only Rica who could console me for yours. We miss you, Usbek; you were the soul of our circle. What violence does it take to break the ties formed by heart and mind!

We discuss many things here. Our discussions usually turn about the subject of ethics. Yesterday we argued the question whether men were happy through the pleasures and satisfactions of the senses or through the practice of virtue. I have often heard you say that men were born to be virtuous and that justice is a quality as proper to man as existence. Explain to me, I beg of you, what you mean.

I have spoken to some mullahs [1] who drive me to desperation with their passages of the Koran, for I do not speak to them as true believer but rather as man, citizen, and father.

Farewell.

> From Ispahan, the last of the
> Moon of Saphar, 1711.

1. Roughly, a doctor of religion.

Letter XI

Usbek to Mirza in Ispahan

You renounce your own reason and fall back on mine. You condescend to consult me; you judge me capable of instructing you. My dear Mirza, there is one thing that flatters me still more than the good opinion you have had of me: your friendship, which procures that opinion for me.

To carry out what you have required of me, I did not think it proper to use much abstract reasoning. There are certain truths that it is not enough to impress by rational conviction, that must be felt. Such are the verities of ethics. Perhaps this bit of history will touch you more than some subtle philosophy.

There once lived in Arabia a small tribe called Troglodytes, descended from those ancient Troglodytes who, if one is to believe the historians, resembled beasts more closely than men. These people were not at all deformed, nor were they hairy like wolves, nor did they hiss. They had two eyes, but they were so wicked and so ferocious that there existed among them no principle of equity and justice.

They had a king, of foreign origin, who, wishing to correct the wickedness of their natural dispositions, treated them with great severity. But they conspired against him, killed him, and exterminated the whole royal family.

This action completed, they assembled to choose a new government, and after much dissension, they created magistrates. But scarcely had they elected the magistrates when they found the new men unbearable and massacred them.

This race, freed of the new yoke, turned for guidance solely to their innate savage character. All the individuals agreed that they would no longer obey anyone and that each would look out strictly for his own interests without regard to the interests of others.

This unanimous resolution pleased all the individuals extremely well. They would say: "Why should I kill myself working for people I don't care a thing about? I shall think only of myself and I shall live happily. What matter to me whether others can do so or not? I shall provide for all my needs and so long as I have managed that, it matters nothing to me that all the other Troglodytes should be miserable."

It was the season for planting the fields. Each man said: "I shall cultivate my land only enough to furnish what grain I need to eat. A larger amount would be useless to me; I shall not go to such trouble for nothing."

The soils of this little realm were not of equal quality. There were dry, mountainous terrains, and then others that, lying lower, were watered by several streams. That year the drought was great, so that the elevated terrain lacked all sustenance, whereas the ground that could be watered was very fertile. Thus practically all the mountain people perished of hunger because of the hard hearts of the others, who refused to share their harvest.

The following year was very rainy. The elevated lands were extraordinarily fertile, and the low-lying lands were submerged. Half of the people again cried famine, but these miserable people came up against men as hard as they had been themselves.

One of the leading inhabitants had an extremely beautiful wife; his neighbor fell in love with her and abducted her. There arose a great quarrel and after many insults and many blows, they agreed to refer the matter to the decision of a certain Troglodyte, a man who during the Republic, had enjoyed a good reputation. They went before him and tried to give their sides of the affair. "What does it matter to me," said this man, "whether the woman is yours, or yours? I have my field to cultivate, and it's just possible I am not going to use up my time settling your differences and working at your affairs while I neglect my own. I pray you to leave me in peace and distract me no more with your quarrels." Thereupon he left them and went off to work his land. The wife-stealer, who was stronger than the other fellow, swore that he would die rather than give back the woman, and the other fellow, grieved by his neighbor's injustice and by the judge's harshness, was returning home in despair, when on his road he found a young and beautiful woman coming back from the fountain. He had no wife now; this one pleased him. And she pleased him even more when he learned that she was the wife of the man he had wanted to judge the case, the man who had been so insensitive to his misfortune. He abducted her and took her home.

There was a man who owned a rather fertile field, which he cultivated with great care. Two of his neighbors joined together, chased him from his house, and took over his field. They made between themselves an agreement of mutual protection against all those who might wish to rob them, and in effect, they managed to uphold each other thereby for several months. But then one of them, tired of sharing what he could have alone, killed the other and became sole owner of the field. His dominion did not last long. Two other Troglodytes came and attacked him. He was too weak to defend himself, and he was killed.

A Troglodyte, very close to being naked, saw some wool for sale. He asked the price. The merchant said to himself: "Naturally, I ought not expect from my wool more than the wherewithal to buy two measures of grain. But I am going to sell it for four times more money and thus get eight measures." The buyer had to give in and pay the price asked. "I am quite happy with this transaction," said the merchant, "and now I need some grain."

"What's that you say?" replied the buyer. "You need some grain? I happen to have some for sale. It's just that the price might surprise you, for you must know that grain is extremely dear and that famine is the rule almost everywhere. But give me back my money and I shall give you one measure of wheat. For I should not choose to dispose of it on any other terms were you to die of hunger."

Meanwhile, a cruel sickness was ravaging the countryside. A clever physician came from a neighboring country and gave such fitting remedies that he cured all those who put themselves under his care. When the sickness had stopped, he went to all he had treated and asked for his payment. But he met everywhere with nothing but refusals to pay. He returned to his own country and arrived there broken by the vigors of such a long journey. Soon after he learned that the same disease was making itself felt once again and was more than ever afflicting that ungrateful country. This time they came to him and did not wait for him to come to them. "Be off," he said to them, "be off, evil men. You have in your souls a poison more fatal than the disease you seek to cure. You do not deserve to occupy a place on the earth, for you have no humanity and the rules of justice are unknown to you. I should feel I was offending the gods as they punish you, were I to oppose the justice of their wrath."

From Erzerum, the 3rd of the
Moon of Gemmadi II, 1711.

Letter XII

Usbek to the same in Ispahan

You have seen, my dear Mirza, how the Troglodytes perished by reason of their very wickedness and how they were victims of their own injustice. Out of all these families there remained only two to escape the misfortunes of the nation. There were in that country two extraordinary men: they possessed humanity; they were acquainted with justice; they loved virtue. As bound together by their uprightness of heart as were the others by their corruption, they could see the general desolation and reacted to it only with pity. This was the motive for a new union. They worked with common solicitude for the common welfare. Their only differences were those that a sweet and tender friendship can give rise to, and in the most remote region of the country, separated from compatriots unworthy of their company, they were leading a peaceful and happy life. The earth, cultivated by these virtuous hands, seemed to produce of her own accord.

They loved their wives and were, in turn, tenderly cherished by them. The whole of their efforts was turned to bringing up their children in the paths of virtue. They continually pointed out to them the misfortunes of their compatriots, continually held up before their eyes this sad example. Above all, they made them feel that the welfare of the individual is always to be found in the common good, and that to want to stray from it is to seek destruction; they taught them that virtue is not something that should cost us effort, that it is not to be considered a painful exercise; and that justice to others is like charity to ourselves.

They soon had the reward of virtuous fathers, which is to have children like themselves. The young people growing up under their eyes increased in number through happy marriages. Their numbers continued to grow; their union remained the same, and virtue, far from weakening amid this multitude, was, on the contrary, fortified by a greater number of examples.

Who could describe here the happiness of the Troglodytes? Such a just people must have been cherished by the gods. As soon as the Troglodytes opened their eyes and knew them, they learned to fear them, and religion came to smooth off any excess of roughness left in their customs by nature.

They instituted celebrations in honor of the gods. Young boys and flower-bedecked young ladies celebrated these festivals with dancing and the sweet accords of country music. Afterward, there were banquets in which joy took no lesser role than frugality. It was in such congregation that simple Nature made herself heard: it was here they learned to give and take hearts; it was here that virginal chastity made, amid blushes, its surprised confession, a confession soon confirmed by the father's consent; it was here that mothers took joy in foreseeing from afar a tender and faithful union.

They would go to the temple to seek the favors of the gods. The prayers were not for riches or for burdensome abundance — such were unworthy of our happy Troglodytes. They could envisage favors only for their compatriots. They came to the foot of the altar only to ask for the health of their fathers, the marriage of their brothers, the tender love of their wives, the affection and obedience of their children. Girls came only to lay down the tender sacrifice of their hearts and sought no other blessing than that of making a Troglodyte happy.

In the evening, when the flocks had left the plains and the weary oxen had brought the plow home, they would congregate, and over a frugal meal, sing of the injustice and misfortunes of the first Troglodytes, of the rebirth of virtue in a new people, and of its felicity. They would celebrate the grandeur of the gods and their ever-present favors to men who turn to them, as well as their inevitable wrath visited upon those who fear them not. Then they would describe the delights of country living and the happiness that accompanies a way of life continually crowned with innocence. Soon they would yield to a slumber never interrupted by cares and worries.

Nature ministered no less to their desires than to their needs. In this happy country, cupidity was completely foreign. They would exchange presents in such a way that the giver always felt he had the advantage. The Troglodyte people thought of themselves as a single family. Their flocks were almost always intermixed; the only trouble they ordinarily spared themselves was trying to separate them.

From Erzerum, the 6th of the
Moon of Gemmadi II, 1711.

Letter XIII

Usbek to the same

I could not possibly say enough to you about the virtue of the Troglodytes. One day, one of them said: "Tomorrow my father must plow his field. I shall get up two hours before he does, and when he goes to his field, he will find it already plowed."

Another would say to himself: "I think my sister feels an inclination for one of our Troglodyte relatives. I must speak to my father about this young man and persuade him to arrange a marriage."

They came to another to say that thieves had taken his herd. "I am quite angry about that," he said, "for there was a pure white heifer I wanted to offer to the gods."

You might hear another of them say: "I must go to the temple with thanks for the gods because my brother, whom my father loves so much and whom I cherish dearly, has recovered his health."

Or perhaps: "There is a field that borders on a field of my father, and the workers there are always exposed to the intense heat of the sun. I must plant a couple of trees so that those poor people can from time to time rest in the shade."

One day when several Troglodytes were gathered together, an old man spoke of a young man whom he suspected of an evil action and reproached him for it. "We cannot believe that he has committed this crime," said the young Troglodytes. "But if he has done it, then may he be the last of his family to die!"

It was announced to a Troglodyte that strangers had put his house to pillage and had carried off everything. "If they were not unjust men," he replied, "I should wish that the gods might give them longer benefit from it than I had."

So much prosperity was not observed without envy. Neighboring peoples came together, and on some empty pretext, resolved to seize the Troglodyte flocks. As soon as they learned of such a resolve, the Troglodytes sent ambassadors to them and addressed them thus:

"What have the Troglodytes done to you? Have they carried off your wives? Stolen your cattle? Ravaged your fields? No, for we are just and fear the gods. What then do you ask of us? Would you like wool to make clothes for yourselves? Would you like milk for your animals, or the fruits of our soil? Put down your arms; come among us, and we shall give you all of that. But we swear by all that is most sacred that if you come into our lands as enemies, we shall consider you an unjust people and we shall treat you as we should treat wild beasts."

These words were turned down with scorn. The savage tribes came armed into the lands of the Troglodytes, for they thought they were defended only by their innocence.

But the Troglodytes were well prepared for their own defense. They

had placed their wives and children in their midst. They were astonished not by the numbers of the enemy but by their injustice. A renewed enthusiasm took hold of their hearts: one man wanted to die
for his father; another, for his wife and children; one chose to die
for his brothers; another, for his friends; and every man, for the
Troglodyte people. The position of a man dying in battle was immediately taken by another who in addition to the common cause, now
had a particular death to avenge.

Such was the battle of Injustice and Virtue. Those cowardly peoples
who sought only booty were not ashamed to flee; they yielded to the
virtue of the Troglodytes, without even being touched.

From Erzerum, the 9th of the
Moon of Gemmadi II, 1711.

Letter XIV

Usbek to the same

As their tribe was growing every day, the Troglodytes thought it a
proper time to choose a king. They agreed that they should tender the
crown to the man who was the most upright among them, and they
all cast their eyes on an old man, venerated for his years and for a
long record of virtue. He had not wanted to take part in their assembly.
He had withdrawn to his house, his heart sore with sadness.

When they sent the deputies to inform him that their choice had
fallen on him, he said: "God forbid that I should commit this wrong
against the Troglodytes and that anyone could think that there is no
one among you more just than myself! You are offering me the crown,
and if you absolutely insist on it, I shall naturally have to take it.
But realize that I shall die of grief to have seen Troglodytes born free
and now see them subjects." On these words, he began to pour forth
a torrent of tears. "Oh, unhappy day!" he said, "why did I have to
live so long?" Then he cried out in a stern voice: "I can see what is
happening, O Troglodytes! Your virtue is beginning to weigh upon
you. In the present state of affairs, with no chief, you must be virtuous
in spite of yourselves. Otherwise you couldn't subsist and would fall
into the misfortunes of your forefathers. But this yoke seems too hard
to you. You prefer to be subjects of a prince and obey his laws, for
they are less restrictive than your customs. You know that from now
on, you can satisfy your ambition, acquire riches, and languish in soft
luxury, and that so long as you avoid falling into great crimes, you
will have no need of virtue." He stopped a moment as his tears flowed
more profusely than before. "Well then, what would you have me do?
How could I give orders to a Troglodyte? Do you hope that he will
commit a virtuous deed because I command him to do so, a man who
would do it anyhow, without me and by the sole inclination of nature?
O Troglodytes, I am coming to the end of my days. My blood stands

frozen in my veins. I shall soon see your sacred forebears. Why would you have me afflict them and oblige me to tell them that I have left you here under any yoke other than that of Virtue?"

It was a grand spectacle to see all the Troglodytes joyous, while the Prince dissolved in tears. The next day he appeared before the Troglodytes with a face that betrayed neither sadness nor joy. He seemed now intent only on taking charge of the government. But the secret care that devoured him soon put him in his tomb. And thus died the greatest king who ever governed men.

He was mourned for forty days; every man thought to have lost his father. Everyone said: "What has happened to the hope of the Troglodytes? We lose you, dear Prince! You believed you were not worthy to rule us. Heaven has made clear that we were not worthy to obey you. But we swear by your sacred shade, that since you did not want to govern us by your laws, we shall conduct ourselves by your example."

Another prince had to be elected, and there was one remarkable thing about it — of all the relatives of the late monarch, not a one sought the crown. From that family, the wisest and most just of all was chosen.

Toward the end of his reign, some people believed it necessary to establish commerce and the arts among the Troglodytes. The Nation was convoked, and that move was decided.

The King spoke thus: "You wished me to take the crown and believed me sufficiently virtuous to govern you. Heaven is my witness that since that time, the happiness of the Troglodytes has been the sole object of my solicitude. I have the great honor of knowing that my reign has not been sullied by the cowardice of a single Troglodyte. Would you now prefer riches to your virtue?"

"My lord," said one of them to him, "we are happy. We work on excellent soil. May I dare say it? It is you alone who will decide whether riches will be dangerous for your people or not. If they see that you prefer them to virtue, they will quickly accustom themselves to do the same, and in this, your taste will determine their own. If you elevate a man into high government function, or share your intimate confidence with him, solely because of his wealth, be sure that this will be a mortal blow delivered by you to his virtue, and that bit by bit you will make as many dishonest men as there were men who took note of that cruel discrimination. You know, my lord, the foundation on which your people's virtue is built — it is education. Change that education, and the man who was not daring enough to be criminal will soon blush at being virtuous.

"We have two things to do: to deflate and bring to naught avarice, and equally, prodigality. Every man must be accountable to the state for the administration of his possessions. And may the coward who will lower himself to the point of robbing himself of an honest subsistence be punished no less severely than the man who runs through the patrimony of his children. Each citizen must be a fair dispenser of his own wealth, just as he would be of the wealth of another."

"Troglodytes," said the King, "riches will come into your land. But I declare before you that if you are not virtuous, you will be one of the most unfortunate peoples on earth. In your present condition, I have only to be more just than you — this is the mark of my royal authority, and I couldn't possibly find any more august mark. If you seek to distinguish yourselves only by your wealth (which is nothing in itself) I shall have to distinguish myself by the same methods in order not to remain in a poverty you would scorn. Thus I should have to overwhelm you with taxes, and you would use a great part of your subsistence in keeping up the pomp and glitter that would serve to make me respectable. At present I find all my wealth within myself, but then, you would have to wear yourselves out to make me rich, and these riches, of which you make so much, would give you no pleasure for they would all flow into my treasury. O Troglodytes! we can be united by a lovely tie: if you are virtuous, I shall be; if I am virtuous, you will be."

> From Erzerum, the 10th of the
> Moon of Gemmadi II, 1711.

Letter XV

The first eunuch to Jaron, black eunuch, in Erzerum

I pray that heaven bring you back into these precincts and shield you from all dangers.

Although I have scarcely ever known that tie called friendship, although I have consciously been wrapped up entirely in myself, you have yet made me feel that I still possess a heart; and while for all the slaves living under my orders, I was as hard as bronze, I saw your childhood advance with pleasure.

The time came when my master cast his eyes on you. Nature was far from having her word when the blade separated you forever from nature. I shall not say whether I pitied you or whether I felt pleasure in seeing you raised to my level. I quieted your tears and your outcries. I thought of you as having a second birth and taking leave of a servitude in which you always had to obey, to enter another kind of servitude, where you were to command. I took care of your education. My severity, ever joined to my precepts, made you unaware for a long time that you were dear to me. And yet you were dear to me, and I should tell you that I loved you as a father loves his son, if these terms father and son could apply to our destiny.

You will travel through countries inhabited by Christians who have never been believers. It is not possible for you to do so without being subjected to many defilements. How could the Prophet keep an eye on you in the midst of so many millions of his enemies? When he returns,

I should like my master to make the pilgrimage to Mecca. You could all purify yourselves in the land of the angels.

Farewell.

> From the seraglio of Ispahan, the 10th
> of the Moon of Gemmadi II, 1711.

François-Marie Arouet de Voltaire (1694–1778)

LIFE: Only Rabelais may be said to have lived a life as hectic and varied as Voltaire's. Continually exiled from Paris for his irreligious or seditious opinions, he lived at different times in England, Prussia, Switzerland, the low countries; his three years with Frederick the Great were comedy after the manner of an impure French classicism; his liaisons with married women were French farce at its most incredible, and human. But with all the diversions at his wish and command his productivity was gargantuan: between 50 and 60 plays; an almost uncountable number of poems; a great mass of history; the correspondence, unbelievably vast; general criticism and miscellaneous works; the prose tales by which he is chiefly known outside France. His triumphant return to Paris in 1778, at the age of 84, after 28 years of exile, was the only kind of final act with which a man of such prodigious passion and talent might have been satisfied.

WORKS: *The Henriad* (an epic poem, first published in 1723); *History of Charles XII, King of Sweden* (1731); *Zaïre* (a play, 1732); *Letters on the English* (1733–34); *Zadig* (a philosophical tale, 1748); *Philosophical Dictionary* (1764).

CANDIDE *

CHAPTER I

How Candide Was Brought Up in a Noble Castle and How He Was Expelled from the Same

In the castle of Baron Thunder-ten-tronckh in Westphalia [1] there lived a youth, endowed by Nature with the most gentle character. His face was the expression of his soul. His judgment was quite honest and he was extremely simple-minded; and this was the reason, I think, that he was named Candide. Old servants in the house suspected that he was the son of the Baron's sister and a decent honest gentleman of the neighborhood, whom this young lady would never marry because he

---

* 1759. Translator unknown.
1. A poor agricultural province of Germany.

could only prove seventy-one quarterings,[2] and the rest of his genea-
logical tree was lost, owing to the injuries of time.

The Baron was one of the most powerful lords in Westphalia, for his
castle possessed a door and windows. His Great Hall was even decorated
with a piece of tapestry. The dogs in his stable-yards formed a pack
of hounds when necessary; his grooms were his huntsmen; the village
curate was his Grand Almoner. They all called him "My Lord," and
laughed heartily at his stories.

The Baroness weighed about three hundred and fifty pounds, was
therefore greatly respected, and did the honors of the house with a dignity which rendered her still more respectable. Her daughter Cunegonde,
aged seventeen, was rosy-cheeked, fresh, plump and tempting. The
Baron's son appeared in every respect worthy of his father. The tutor
Pangloss was the oracle of the house, and little Candide followed his
lessons with all the candor of his age and character.

Pangloss[3] taught metaphysico-theologo-cosmolonigology.[4] He proved
admirably that there is no effect without a cause and that in this best
of all possible worlds, My Lord the Baron's castle was the best of castles
and his wife the best of all possible Baronesses.

" 'Tis demonstrated," said he, "that things cannot be otherwise; for,
since everything is made for an end, everything is necessarily for the
best end. Observe that noses were made to wear spectacles; and so we
have spectacles. Legs were visibly instituted to be breeched, and we
have breeches. Stones were formed to be quarried and to build castles;
and My Lord has a very noble castle; the greatest Baron in the province
should have the best house; and as pigs were made to be eaten, we eat
pork all the year round; consequently, those who have asserted that all
is well[5] talk nonsense; they ought to have said that all is for the best."

Candide listened attentively and believed innocently; for he thought
Mademoiselle Cunegonde extremely beautiful, although he was never
bold enough to tell her so. He decided that after the happiness of being
born Baron of Thunder-ten-tronckh, the second degree of happiness was
to be Mademoiselle Cunegonde; the third, to see her every day; and the
fourth to listen to Doctor Pangloss, the greatest philosopher of the
province and therefore of the whole world.

One day when Cunegonde was walking near the castle, in a little wood
which was called The Park, she observed Doctor Pangloss in the bushes,
giving a lesson in experimental physics to her mother's waiting maid,
a very pretty and docile brunette. Mademoiselle Cunegonde had a great
inclination for science and watched breathlessly the reiterated experiments she witnessed; she observed clearly the Doctor's sufficient reason,
the effects and the causes, and returned home very much excited, pensive, filled with the desire of learning, reflecting that she might be the
sufficient reason of young Candide and that he might be hers.

2. Divisions on coats of arms.
3. That is, "all-tongue."
4. Or meaningless philosophy.
5. The moral position of Alexander Pope in his *Essay on Man.*

On her way back to the castle she met Candide and blushed; Candide also blushed. She bade him good-morning in a hesitating voice; Candide replied without knowing what he was saying. Next day, when they left the table after dinner, Cunegonde and Candide found themselves behind a screen; Cunegonde dropped her handkerchief, Candide picked it up; she innocently held his hand; the young man innocently kissed the young lady's hand with remarkable vivacity, tenderness and grace; their lips met, their eyes sparkled, their knees trembled, their hands wandered. Baron Thunder-ten-tronckh passed near the screen, and, observing this cause and effect, expelled Candide from the castle by kicking him in the backside frequently and hard. Cunegonde swooned; when she recovered her senses, the Baroness slapped her in the face; and all was in consternation in the noblest and most agreeable of all possible castles.

CHAPTER II

What Happened to Candide among the Bulgarians

Candide, expelled from the earthly paradise, wandered for a long time without knowing where he was going, weeping, turning up his eyes to Heaven, gazing back frequently at the noblest of castles which held the most beautiful of young Baronesses; he lay down to sleep supperless between two furrows in the open fields; it snowed heavily in large flakes. The next morning the shivering Candide, penniless, dying of cold and exhaustion, dragged himself towards the neighboring town, which was called Waldberghoff-trarbkdikdorff. He halted sadly at the door of an inn. Two men dressed in blue noticed him.

"Comrade," said one, "there's a well-built young man of the right height." They went up to Candide and very civilly invited him to dinner.

"Gentlemen," said Candide with charming modesty, "you do me a great honor, but I have no money to pay my share."

"Ah, sir," said one of the men in blue, "persons of your figure and merit never pay anything; are you not five feet five tall?"

"Yes, gentlemen," said he, bowing, "that is my height."

"Ah, sir, come to table; we will not only pay your expenses, we will never allow a man like you to be short of money; men were only made to help each other."

"You are in the right," said Candide, "that is what Doctor Pangloss was always telling me, and I see that everything is for the best."

They begged him to accept a few crowns, he took them and wished to give them an I O U; they refused to take it and all sat down to table. "Do you not love tenderly . . ."

"Oh, yes," said he. "I love Mademoiselle Cunegonde tenderly."

"No," said one of the gentlemen. "We were asking if you do not tenderly love the King of the Bulgarians." [6]

"Not a bit," said he, "for I have never seen him."

6. A reference to Frederick the Great of Prussia.

"What! He is the most charming of Kings, and you must drink his health."

"Oh, gladly, gentlemen." And he drank.

"That is sufficient," he was told. "You are now the support, the aid, the defender, the hero of the Bulgarians; your fortune is made and your glory assured."

They immediately put irons on his legs and took him to a regiment. He was made to turn to the right and left, to raise the ramrod and return the ramrod, to take aim, to fire, to double up,[7] and he was given thirty strokes with a stick; the next day he drilled not quite so badly, and received only twenty strokes; the day after, he only had ten, and was looked on as a prodigy by his comrades.

Candide was completely mystified and could not make out how he was a hero. One fine spring day he thought he would take a walk, going straight ahead, in the belief that to use his legs as he pleased was a privilege of the human species as well as of animals. He had not gone two leagues when four other heroes, each six feet tall, fell upon him, bound him and dragged him back to a cell. He was asked by his judges whether he would rather be thrashed thirty-six times by the whole regiment or receive a dozen lead bullets at once in his brain. Although he protested that men's wills are free and that he wanted neither one nor the other, he had to make a choice; by virtue of that gift of God which is called *liberty,* he determined to run the gauntlet thirty-six times and actually did so twice. There were two thousand men in the regiment. That made four thousand strokes which laid bare the muscles and nerves from his neck to his backside. As they were about to proceed to a third turn, Candide, utterly exhausted, begged as a favor that they would be so kind as to smash his head; he obtained this favor; they bound his eyes and he was made to kneel down. At that moment the King of the Bulgarians came by and inquired the victim's crime; and as this King was possessed of a vast genius, he perceived from what he learned about Candide that he was a young metaphysician very ignorant in worldly matters, and therefore pardoned him with a clemency which will be praised in all newspapers and all ages. An honest surgeon healed Candide in three weeks with the ointments recommended by Dioscorides.[8] He had already regained a little skin and could walk when the King of the Bulgarians went to war with the King of the Abares.[9]

CHAPTER III

How Candide Escaped from the Bulgarians and What Became of Him

Nothing could be smarter, more splendid, more brilliant, better drawn up than the two armies. Trumpets, fifes, hautboys, drums, cannons,

7. That is, double-time.
8. An army physician of the first century A.D., he wrote a book of pharmacology.
9. A reference to the French-Austrian alliance against Frederick the Great in the Seven Years' War.

formed a harmony such as has never been heard even in hell. The cannons first of all laid flat about six thousand men on each side; then the musketry removed from the best of worlds some nine or ten thousand blackguards who infested its surface. The bayonet also was the sufficient reason for the death of some thousands of men. The whole might amount to thirty thousand souls. Candide, who trembled like a philosopher, hid himself as well as he could during this heroic butchery.

At last, while the two Kings each commanded a *Te Deum* [10] in his camp, Candide decided to go elsewhere to reason about effects and causes. He clambered over heaps of dead and dying men and reached a neighboring village, which was in ashes; it was an Abare village which the Bulgarians had burned in accordance with international law. Here, old men dazed with blows watched the dying agonies of their murdered wives who clutched their children to their bleeding breasts; there, disembowelled girls who had been made to satisfy the natural appetites of heroes gasped their last sighs; others, half-burned, begged to be put to death. Brains were scattered on the ground among dismembered arms and legs.

Candide fled to another village as fast as he could; it belonged to the Bulgarians, and Abarian heroes had treated it in the same way. Candide, stumbling over quivering limbs or across ruins, at last escaped from the theatre of war, carrying a little food in his knapsack, and never forgetting Mademoiselle Cunegonde. His provisions were all gone when he reached Holland; but, having heard that everyone in that country was rich and a Christian, he had no doubt at all but that he would be as well treated as he had been in the Baron's castle before he had been expelled on account of Mademoiselle Cunegonde's pretty eyes.

He asked an alms of several grave persons, who all replied that if he continued in that way he would be shut up in a house of correction to teach him how to live. He then addressed himself to a man who had been discoursing on charity in a large assembly for an hour on end. This orator, glancing at him askance, said: "What are you doing here? Are you for the good cause?"

"There is no effect without a cause," said Candide modestly. "Everything is necessarily linked up and arranged for the best. It was necessary that I should be expelled from the company of Mademoiselle Cunegonde, that I ran the gauntlet, and that I beg my bread until I can earn it; all this could not have happened differently."

"My friend," said the orator, "do you believe that the Pope is Anti-Christ?"

"I had never heard so before," said Candide, "but whether he is or isn't, I am starving."

"You don't deserve to eat," said the other. "Hence, rascal; hence, you wretch; and never come near me again."

The orator's wife thrust her head out of the window and seeing a man who did not believe that the Pope was Anti-Christ, she poured on

10. A hymn of thanks to God for victory.

his head a full . . . O Heavens! To what excess religious zeal is carried by ladies!

A man who had not been baptized, an honest Anabaptist [11] named Jacques, saw the cruel and ignominious treatment of one of his brothers, a featherless two-legged creature with a soul; he took him home, cleaned him up, gave him bread and beer, presented him with two florins, and even offered to teach him to work at the manufacture of Persian stuffs which are made in Holland. Candide threw himself at the man's feet, exclaiming: "Doctor Pangloss was right in telling me that all is for the best in this world, for I am vastly more touched by your extreme generosity than by the harshness of the gentleman in the black cloak and his good lady."

The next day when he walked out he met a beggar covered with sores, dull-eyed, with the end of his nose fallen away, his mouth awry, his teeth black, who talked huskily, was tormented with a violent cough and spat out a tooth at every cough.

CHAPTER IV

How Candide Met His Old Master in Philosophy, Doctor Pangloss, and What Happened

Candide, moved even more by compassion than by horror, gave this horrible beggar the two florins he had received from the honest Anabaptist, Jacques. The phantom gazed fixedly at him, shed tears and threw its arms round his neck. Candide recoiled in terror.

"Alas!" said the wretch to the other wretch, "don't you recognise your dear Pangloss?"

"What do I hear? You, my dear master! You, in this horrible state! What misfortune has happened to you? Why are you no longer in the noblest of castles? What has become of Mademoiselle Cunegonde, the pearl of young ladies, the masterpiece of Nature?"

"I am exhausted," said Pangloss. Candide immediately took him to the Anabaptist's stable where he gave him a little bread to eat; and when Pangloss had recovered: "Well!" said he, "Cunegonde?"

"Dead," replied the other.

At this word Candide swooned; his friend restored him to his senses with a little bad vinegar which happened to be in the stable. Candide opened his eyes. "Cunegonde dead! Ah! best of worlds, where are you? But what illness did she die of? Was it because she saw me kicked out of her father's noble castle?"

"No," said Pangloss. "She was disembowelled by Bulgarian soldiers, after having been raped to the limit of possibility; they broke the Baron's head when he tried to defend her; the Baroness was cut to pieces; my poor pupil was treated exactly like his sister; and as to the castle, there is not one stone standing on another, not a barn, not a

11. A Protestant sect opposing infant baptism.

sheep, not a duck, not a tree; but we were well avenged, for the Abares did exactly the same to a neighboring barony which belonged to a Bulgarian Lord." At this, Candide swooned again; but, having recovered and having said all that he ought to say, he inquired the cause and effect, the sufficient reason which had reduced Pangloss to so piteous a state.

"Alas!" said Pangloss, " 'tis love; love, the consoler of the human race, the preserver of the universe, the soul of all tender creatures, gentle love."

"Alas!" said Candide, "I am acquainted with this love, this sovereign of hearts, this soul of our soul; it has never brought me anything but one kiss and twenty kicks in the backside. How could this beautiful cause produce in you so abominable an effect?"

Pangloss replied as follows: "My dear Candide! You remember Paquette, the maidservant of our august Baroness; in her arms I enjoyed the delights of Paradise which have produced the tortures of Hell by which you see I am devoured; she was infected and perhaps is dead. Paquette received this present from a most learned monk, who had it from the source; for he received it from an old countess, who had it from a cavalry captain, who owed it to a marchioness, who derived it from a page, who had received it from a Jesuit, who, when a novice, had it in a direct line from one of the companions of Christopher Columbus. For my part, I shall not give it to anyone, for I am dying."

"O Pangloss!" exclaimed Candide, "this is a strange genealogy! Wasn't the devil at the root of it?"

"Not at all," replied that great man. "It was something indispensable in this best of worlds, a necessary ingredient; for, if Columbus in an island of America had not caught this disease, which poisons the source of generation, and often indeed prevents generation, we should not have chocolate and cochineal; it must also be noticed that hitherto in our continent this disease is peculiar to us, like theological disputes. The Turks, the Indians, the Persians, the Chinese, the Siamese and the Japanese are not yet familiar with it; but there is a sufficient reason why they in their turn should become familiar with it in a few centuries. Meanwhile, it has made marvellous progress among us, and especially in those large armies composed of honest, well-bred stipendiaries who decide the destiny of States; it may be asserted that when thirty thousand men fight a pitched battle against an equal number of troops, there are about twenty thousand with the pox on either side."

"Admirable!" said Candide. "But you must get cured."

"How can I?" said Pangloss. "I haven't a sou, my friend, and in the whole extent of this globe, you cannot be bled or receive an enema without paying or without someone paying for you."

This last speech determined Candide; he went and threw himself at the feet of his charitable Anabaptist, Jacques, and drew so touching a picture of the state to which his friend was reduced that the good easy man did not hesitate to succor Pangloss; he had him cured at his own expense. In this cure Pangloss only lost one eye and one ear. He could write well and knew arithmetic perfectly. The Anabaptist made him his bookkeeper. At the end of two months he was compelled to go to Lisbon on business and took his two philosophers on the boat with him. Pangloss explained to him how everything was for the best. Jacques was not of this opinion.

"Men," said he, "must have corrupted nature a little, for they were not born wolves, and they have become wolves. God did not give them twenty-four-pounder cannons or bayonets, and they have made bayonets and cannons to destroy each other. I might bring bankruptcies into the account and Justice which seizes the goods of bankrupts in order to deprive the creditors of them."

"It was all indispensable," replied the one-eyed doctor, "and private misfortunes make the public good, so that the more private misfortunes there are, the more everything is well."

While he was reasoning, the air grew dark, the winds blew from the four quarters of the globe and the ship was attacked by the most horrible tempest in sight of the port of Lisbon.

CHAPTER V

Storm, Shipwreck, Earthquake, and What Happened to Dr. Pangloss, to Candide and the Anabaptist Jacques

Half the enfeebled passengers, suffering from that inconceivable anguish which the rolling of a ship causes in the nerves and in all the humors of bodies shaken in contrary directions, did not retain strength enough even to trouble about the danger. The other half screamed and prayed; the sails were torn, the masts broken, the vessel leaking. Those worked who could, no one cooperated, no one commanded. The Anabaptist tried to help the crew a little; he was on the main deck; a furious sailor struck him violently and stretched him on the deck; but the blow he delivered gave him so violent a shock that he fell head-first out of the ship. He remained hanging and clinging to part of the broken mast. The good Jacques ran to his aid, helped him to climb back, and from the effort he made was flung into the sea in full view of the sailor, who allowed him to drown without condescending even to look at him. Candide came up, saw his benefactor reappear for a moment and then be engulfed for ever. He tried to throw himself after him into the sea; he was prevented by the philosopher Pangloss, who proved to him that the Lisbon roads had been expressly created for the Anabaptist to be drowned in them. While he was proving this *a priori*,[12] the vessel sank, and every one perished except Pangloss, Candide and the brutal sailor who had drowned the virtuous Anabaptist; the blackguard swam successfully to the shore and Pangloss and Candide were carried there on a plank.

12. That is, by deductive reasoning, which argues from a premise that is assumed to be true.

When they had recovered a little, they walked toward Lisbon; they had a little money by the help of which they hoped to be saved from hunger after having escaped the storm. Weeping the death of their benefactor, they had scarcely set foot in the town when they felt the earth tremble under their feet; the sea rose in foaming masses in the port and smashed the ships which rode at anchor. Whirlwinds of flame and ashes covered the streets and squares; the houses collapsed, the roofs were thrown upon the foundations, and the foundations were scattered; thirty thousand inhabitants of every age and both sexes were crushed under the ruins. Whistling and swearing, the sailor said: "There'll be something to pick up here."

"What can be the sufficient reason for this phenomenon?" said Pangloss.

"It is the last day!" cried Candide.

The sailor immediately ran among the debris, dared death to find money, found it, seized it, got drunk, and having slept off his wine, purchased the favors of the first woman of good will he met on the ruins of the houses and among the dead and dying. Pangloss, however, pulled him by the sleeve. "My friend," said he, "this is not well, you are disregarding universal reason, you choose the wrong time."

"Blood and 'ounds!" he retorted, "I am a sailor and I was born in Batavia; four times have I stamped on the crucifix during four voyages to Japan; [13] you have found the right man for your universal reason!"

Candide had been hurt by some falling stones; he lay in the street covered with debris. He said to Pangloss: "Alas! Get me a little wine and oil; I am dying."

"This earthquake is not a new thing," replied Pangloss. "The town of Lima felt the same shocks in America last year; similar causes produce similar effects; there must certainly be a train of sulphur underground from Lima to Lisbon."

"Nothing is more probable," replied Candide; "but, for God's sake, a little oil and wine."

"What do you mean, probable?" replied the philosopher; "I maintain that it is proved."

Candide lost consciousness, and Pangloss brought him a little water from a neighboring fountain.

Next day they found a little food as they wandered among the ruins and regained a little strength. Afterwards they worked like others to help the inhabitants who had escaped death. Some citizens they had assisted gave them as good a dinner as could be expected in such a disaster; true, it was a dreary meal; the hosts watered their bread with their tears, but Pangloss consoled them by assuring them that things could not be otherwise. "For," said he, "all this is for the best; for, if there is a volcano at Lisbon, it cannot be anywhere else; for it is impossible that things should not be where they are; for all is well."

13. An act merchants had to perform to prove they weren't Catholics.

A little, dark man, a familiar of the Inquisition,[14] who sat beside him, politely took up the conversation, and said: "Apparently, you do not believe in original sin; for, if everything is for the best, there was neither fall nor punishment."

"I most humbly beg your excellency's pardon," replied Pangloss still more politely, "for the fall of man and the curse necessarily entered into the best of all possible worlds."

"Then you do not believe in free will?" said the familiar.

"Your excellency will pardon me," said Pangloss; "free will can exist with absolute necessity; for it was necessary that we should be free; for in short, limited will . . ."

Pangloss was in the middle of his phrase when the familiar nodded to his armed attendant who was pouring out port or Oporto wine for him.

CHAPTER VI

How a Splendid Auto-da-fé Was Held to Prevent Earthquakes, and How Candide Was Flogged

After the earthquake which destroyed three-quarters of Lisbon, the wise men of that country could discover no more efficacious way of preventing a total ruin than by giving the people a splendid *auto-da-fé*.[15] It was decided by the university of Coimbre [16] that the sight of several persons being slowly burned in great ceremony is an infallible secret for preventing earthquakes. Consequently they had arrested a Biscayan convicted of having married his fellow-godmother, and two Portuguese who, when eating a chicken, had thrown away the bacon; [17] after dinner they came and bound Dr. Pangloss and his disciple Candide, one because he had spoken and the other because he had listened with an air of approbation; they were both carried separately to extremely cool apartments, where there was never any discomfort from the sun; a week afterwards each was dressed in a sanbenito [18] and their heads were ornamented with paper mitres; Candide's mitre and sanbenito were painted with flames upside down and with devils who had neither tails nor claws; but Pangloss's devils had claws and tails, and his flames were upright.

Dressed in this manner they marched in procession and listened to a most pathetic sermon, followed by lovely plain song music. Candide was flogged in time to the music, while the singing went on; the Biscayan and the two men who had not wanted to eat the bacon were burned, and Pangloss was hanged, although this is not the custom. The very same day, the earth shook again with a terrible clamor.

Candide, terrified, dumbfounded, bewildered, covered with blood, quiv-

14. An officer of the Inquisition, which was instituted to eradicate heresy.
15. That is, an act of faith — or the burning of heretics at the stake.
16. A city north of Lisbon.
17. They were thus probably Jewish.   18. The frock worn by a condemned heretic.

ering from head to foot, said to himself: "If this is the best of all possible worlds, what are the others? Let it pass that I was flogged, for I was flogged by the Bulgarians, but, O my dear Pangloss! The greatest of philosophers! Must I see you hanged without knowing why! O my dear Anabaptist! The best of men! Was it necessary that you should be drowned in port! O Mademoiselle Cunegonde! The pearl of women! Was it necessary that your belly should be slit!"

He was returning, scarcely able to support himself, preached at, flogged, absolved and blessed, when an old woman accosted him and said: "Courage, my son, follow me."

CHAPTER VII

How an Old Woman Took Care of Candide and How He Regained That Which He Loved

Candide did not take courage, but he followed the old woman to a hovel; she gave him a pot of ointment to rub on, and left him food and drink; she pointed out a fairly clean bed; near the bed there was a suit of clothes. "Eat, drink, sleep," said she, "and may our Lady of Atocha, my Lord Saint Anthony of Padua and my Lord Saint James of Compostella take care of you; I shall come back tomorrow."

Candide, still amazed by all he had seen, by all he had suffered, and still more by the old woman's charity, tried to kiss her hand. " 'Tis not my hand you should kiss," said the old woman, "I shall come back tomorrow. Rub on the ointment, eat and sleep."

In spite of all his misfortune, Candide ate and went to sleep. Next day the old woman brought him breakfast, examined his back and smeared him with another ointment; later she brought him dinner, and returned in the evening with supper. The next day she went through the same ceremony.

"Who are you?" Candide kept asking her. "Who has inspired you with so much kindness? How can I thank you?"

The good woman never made any reply; she returned in the evening without any supper. "Come with me," said she, "and do not speak a word."

She took him by the arm and walked into the country with him for about a quarter of a mile; they came to an isolated house, surrounded with gardens and canals. The old woman knocked at a little door. It was opened; she led Candide up a back stairway into a gilded apartment, left him on a brocaded sofa, shut the door and went away. Candide thought he was dreaming, and felt that his whole life was a bad dream and the present moment an agreeable dream. The old woman soon reappeared; she was supporting with some difficulty a trembling woman of majestic stature, glittering with precious stones and covered with a veil.

"Remove the veil," said the old woman to Candide. The young man advanced and lifted the veil with a timid hand. What a moment! What a surprise! He thought he saw Mademoiselle Cunegonde, in fact he was looking at her, it was she herself. His strength failed him, he could not utter a word and fell at her feet. Cunegonde fell on the sofa. The old woman dosed them with distilled waters; they recovered their senses and began to speak: at first they uttered only broken words, questions and answers at cross purposes, sighs, tears, exclamations. The old woman advised them to make less noise and left them alone.

"What! Is it you?" said Candide. "You are alive, and I find you here in Portugal! Then you were not raped? Your belly was not slit, as the philosopher Pangloss assured me?"

"Yes, indeed," said the fair Cunegonde; "but those two accidents are not always fatal."

"But your father and mother were killed?"

" 'Tis only too true," said Cunegonde, weeping.

"And your brother?"

"My brother was killed too."

"And why are you in Portugal? And how did you know I was here? And by what strange adventure have you brought me to this house?"

"I will tell you everything," replied the lady, "but first of all you must tell me everything that has happened to you since the innocent kiss you gave me and the kicks you received."

Candide obeyed with profound respect; and, although he was bewildered, although his voice was weak and trembling, although his back was still a little painful, he related in the most natural manner all he had endured since the moment of their separation. Cunegonde raised her eyes to heaven; she shed tears at the death of the good Anabaptist and Pangloss, after which she spoke as follows to Candide, who did not miss a word and devoured her with his eyes.

[*Cunegonde escaped death at the hands of the Bulgarians, only to be sold to Don Issachar, who is in turn forced to share her services with the Grand Inquisitor. Candide kills both her masters; they escape to Cadiz, where Candide becomes captain of a company sailing to Paraguay to "Bring to reason the Reverend Jesuit Fathers"; but when they land at Buenos Ayres, the Governor there proposes marriage to Cunegonde and she accepts on the advice of the old woman, who also tells Candide that knowledge of his murder of the Grand Inquisitor has reached the New World. With his valet Cacambo he flees, reaches Paraguay, and discovers the Reverend Provincial Father of the Jesuits to be Cunegonde's brother: But their reunion is short-lived: Candide thrusts his sword into his belly when the Jesuit Father, for various reasons, resists the idea of Candide's marriage to his sister, and with his valet Candide is forced once again to become a fugitive.*]

CHAPTER XVII

ARRIVAL OF CANDIDE AND HIS VALET IN THE COUNTRY OF ELDORADO [19]
AND WHAT THEY SAW THERE

When they reached the frontiers of the Oreillons,[20] Cacambo said to Candide: "You see this hemisphere is no better than the other; take my advice, let us go back to Europe by the shortest road."

"How can we go back," said Candide, "and where can we go? If I go to my own country, the Bulgarians and the Abares are murdering everybody; if I return to Portugal I shall be burned; if we stay here, we run the risk of being spitted at any moment. But how can I make up my mind to leave that part of the world where Mademoiselle Cunegonde is living?"

"Let us go to Cayenne," [21] said Cacambo, "we shall find Frenchmen there, for they go all over the world; they might help us. Perhaps God will have pity on us."

It was not easy to go to Cayenne. They knew roughly the direction to take, but mountains, rivers, precipices, brigands and savages were everywhere terrible obstacles. Their horses died of fatigue; their provisions were exhausted; for a whole month they lived on wild fruits and at last found themselves near a little river fringed with cocoanut-trees which supported their lives and their hopes.

Cacambo, who always gave advice as prudent as the old woman's, said to Candide: "We can go no farther, we have walked far enough; I can see an empty canoe in the bank, let us fill it with cocoanuts, get into the little boat and drift with the current; a river always leads to some inhabited place. If we do not find anything pleasant, we shall at least find something new."

"Come on then," said Candide, "and let us trust to Providence."

They drifted for some leagues between banks which were sometimes flowery, sometimes bare, sometimes flat, sometimes steep. The river continually became wider; finally it disappeared under an arch of frightful rocks which towered up to the very sky. The two travellers were bold enough to trust themselves to the current under this arch. The stream, narrowed between walls, carried them with horrible rapidity and noise. After twenty-four hours they saw daylight again; but their canoe was wrecked on reefs; they had to crawl from rock to rock for a whole league and at last they discovered an immense horizon, bordered by inaccessible mountains. The country was cultivated for pleasure as well as for necessity; everywhere the useful was agreeable. The roads were covered or rather ornamented with carriages of brilliant material and shape, carrying men and women of singular beauty, who were rapidly drawn along by large red sheep whose swiftness surpassed that of the finest horses of Andalusia, Tetuan, and Mequinez.[22]

19. The legendary land of gold.
20. A tribe of Indians; Candide had just managed to escape being eaten by them.
21. Capital of French Guiana.
22. Tetuan and Mequinez are Moroccan towns.

"This country," said Candide, "is better than Westphalia."

He landed with Cacambo near the first village he came to. Several children of the village, dressed in torn gold brocade, were playing quoits outside the village. Our two men from the other world amused themselves by looking on; their quoits were large round pieces, yellow, red and green which shone with peculiar lustre. The travellers were curious enough to pick up some of them; they were of gold, emeralds and rubies, the least of which would have been the greatest ornament in the Mogul's throne.

"No doubt," said Cacambo, "these children are the sons of the King of this country playing at quoits."

At that moment the village schoolmaster appeared to call them into school.

"This," said Candide, "is the tutor of the Royal Family."

The little beggars immediately left their game, abandoning their quoits and everything with which they had been playing. Candide picked them up, ran to the tutor, and presented them to him humbly, giving him to understand by signs that their Royal Highnesses had forgotten their gold and their precious stones. The village schoolmaster smiled, threw them on the ground, gazed for a moment at Candide's face with much surprise and continued on his way. The travellers did not fail to pick up the gold, the rubies and the emeralds.

"Where are we?" cried Candide. "The children of the King must be well brought up, since they are taught to despise gold and precious stones."

Cacambo was as much surprised as Candide. At last they reached the first house in the village, which was built like a European palace. There were crowds of people round the door and still more inside; very pleasant music could be heard and there was a delicious smell of cooking. Cacambo went up to the door and heard them speaking Peruvian; it was his maternal tongue, for everyone knows that Cacambo was born in a village of Tucuman where nothing else is spoken.

"I will act as your interpreter," he said to Candide, "this is an inn, let us enter."

Immediately two boys and two girls of the inn, dressed in cloth of gold, whose hair was bound up with ribbons, invited them to sit down to the table d'hôte. They served four soups each garnished with two parrots, a boiled condor which weighed two hundred pounds, two roast monkeys of excellent flavor, three hundred colibris in one dish and six hundred hummingbirds in another, exquisite ragouts and delicious pastries, all in dishes of a sort of rock crystal. The boys and girls brought several sorts of drinks made of sugarcane. Most of the guests were merchants and coachmen, all extremely polite, who asked Cacambo a few questions with the most delicate discretion and answered his in a satisfactory manner.

When the meal was over, Cacambo, like Candide, thought he could pay the reckoning by throwing on the table two of the large pieces of gold he had picked up; the host and hostess laughed until they had to hold their sides. At last they recovered themselves.

"Gentlemen," said the host, "we perceive you are strangers; we are not accustomed to seeing them. Forgive us if we began to laugh when you offered us in payment the stones from our highways. No doubt you have none of the money of this country, but you do not need any to dine here. All the hotels established for the utility of commerce are paid for by the government. You have been ill entertained here because this is a poor village; but everywhere else you will be received as you deserve to be."

Cacambo explained to Candide all that the host had said, and Candide listened in the same admiration and disorder with which his friend Cacambo interpreted. "What can this country be," they said to each other, "which is unknown to the rest of the world and where all nature is so different from ours? Probably it is the country where everything is for the best; for there must be one country of that sort. And, in spite of what Dr. Pangloss said, I often noticed that everything went very ill in Westphalia."

CHAPTER XVIII

WHAT THEY SAW IN THE LAND OF ELDORADO

Cacambo informed the host of his curiosity, and the host said: "I am a very ignorant man and am all the better for it; but we have here an old man who has retired from the court and who is the most learned and most communicative man in the kingdom." And he at once took Cacambo to the old man. Candide now played only the second part and accompanied his valet. They entered a very simple house, for the door was only of silver and the panelling of the apartments in gold, but so tastefully carved that the richest decorations did not surpass it. The antechamber indeed was only encrusted with rubies and emeralds; but the order with which everything was arranged atoned for this extreme simplicity.

The old man received the two strangers on a sofa padded with colibri feathers, and presented them with drinks in diamond cups; after which he satisfied their curiosity in these words: "I am a hundred and seventy-two years old and I heard from my late father, the King's equerry, the astonishing revolutions of Peru of which he had been an eye-witness. The kingdom where we now are is the ancient country of the Incas, who most imprudently left it to conquer part of the world and were at last destroyed by the Spaniards. The princes of their family who remained in their native country had more wisdom; with the consent of the nation, they ordered that no inhabitants should ever leave our little kingdom, and this it is that has preserved our innocence and our felicity. The Spaniards had some vague knowledge of this country, which they called Eldorado, and about a hundred years ago an English-

man named Raleigh [23] came very near to it; but, since we are surrounded by inaccessible rocks and precipices, we have hitherto been
exempt from the rapacity of the nations of Europe who have an inconceivable lust for the pebbles and mud of our land and would kill us to
the last man to get possession of them."

The conversation was long; it touched upon the form of the government, manners, women, public spectacles and the arts. Finally Candide,
who was always interested in metaphysics, asked through Cacambo
whether the country had a religion.

The old man blushed a little. "How can you doubt it?" said he. "Do
you think we are ingrates?"

Cacambo humbly asked what was the religion of Eldorado.

The old man blushed again. "Can there be two religions?" said he.
"We have, I think, the religion of every one else; we adore God from
evening until morning."

"Do you adore only one God?" said Cacambo, who continued to act
as the interpreter of Candide's doubts.

"Manifestly," said the old man, "there are not two or three or four.
I must confess that the people of your world ask very extraordinary
questions."

Candide continued to press the old man with questions; he wished
to know how they prayed to God in Eldorado.

"We do not pray," said the good and respectable sage, "we have
nothing to ask from him; he has given us everything necessary and we
continually give him thanks."

Candide was curious to see the priests; and asked where they were.

The good old man smiled. "My friends," said he, "we are all priests;
the King and all the heads of families solemnly sing praises every
morning, accompanied by five or six thousand musicians."

"What! Have you no monks to teach, to dispute, to govern, to intrigue and to burn people who do not agree with them?"

"For that, we should have to become fools," said the old man; "here
we are all of the same opinion and do not understand what you mean
with your monks."

At all this Candide was in an ecstasy and said to himself: "This is
very different from Westphalia and the castle of His Lordship the
Baron; if our friend Pangloss had seen Eldorado, he would not have
said that the castle of Thunder-ten-tronckh was the best of all that
exists on the earth; certainly, a man should travel."

After this long conversation the good old man ordered a carriage to
be harnessed with six sheep and gave the two travellers twelve of his
servants to take them to court. "You will excuse me," he said, "if my
age deprives me of the honor of accompanying you. The King will receive you in a manner which will not displease you and doubtless you
will pardon the customs of the country if any of them disconcert you."

23. That is, Sir Walter Raleigh, who believed that Eldorado existed.

Candide and Cacambo entered the carriage; the six sheep galloped off and in less than four hours they reached the King's palace, which was situated at one end of the capital. The portal was two hundred and twenty feet high and a hundred feet wide; it is impossible to describe its material. Anyone can see the prodigious superiority it must have over the pebbles and sand we call *gold* and *gems*.

Twenty beautiful maidens of the guard received Candide and Cacambo as they alighted from the carriage, conducted them to the baths and dressed them in robes woven from the down of colibris; after which the principal male and female officers of the Crown led them to his Majesty's apartment through two files of a thousand musicians each, according to the usual custom. As they approached the throneroom, Cacambo asked one of the chief officers how they should behave in his Majesty's presence; whether they should fall on their knees or flat on their faces, whether they should put their hands on their heads or on their backsides; whether they should lick the dust of the throneroom; in a word, what was the ceremony?

"The custom," said the chief officer, "is to embrace the King and to kiss him on either cheek."

Candide and Cacambo threw their arms round his Majesty's neck; he received them with all imaginable favor and politely asked them to supper. Meanwhile they were carried to see the town, the public buildings rising to the very skies, the market-places ornamented with thousands of columns, the fountains of rose-water and of liquors distilled from sugarcane, which played continually in the public squares paved with precious stones which emitted a perfume like that of cloves and cinnamon.

Candide asked to see the law courts; he was told there were none, and that nobody ever went to law. He asked if there were prisons and was told there were none. He was still more surprised and pleased by the palace of sciences, where he saw a gallery two thousand feet long, filled with instruments of mathematics and physics.

After they had explored all the afternoon about a thousandth part of the town, they were taken back to the King. Candide sat down to table with his Majesty, his valet Cacambo and several ladies. Never was better cheer, and never was anyone wittier at supper than his Majesty. Cacambo explained the King's witty remarks to Candide and even when translated they still appeared witty. Among all the things which amazed Candide, this did not amaze him the least.

They enjoyed this hospitality for a month. Candide repeatedly said to Cacambo: "Once again, my friend, it is quite true that the castle where I was born cannot be compared with this country; but then Mademoiselle Cunegonde is not here and you probably have a mistress in Europe. If we remain here, we shall only be like everyone else; but if we return to our own world with only twelve sheep laden with Eldorado pebbles, we shall be richer than all the kings put together;

we shall have no more Inquisitors to fear and we can easily regain Mademoiselle Cunegonde."

Cacambo agreed with this; it is so pleasant to be on the move, to show off before friends, to make a parade of the things seen on one's travels, that these two happy men resolved to be so no longer and to ask his Majesty's permission to depart.

"You are doing a very silly thing," said the King. "I know my country is small; but when we are comfortable anywhere we should stay there; I certainly have not the right to detain foreigners, that is a tyranny which does not exist either in our manners or our laws; all men are free, leave when you please, but the way out is very difficult. It is impossible to ascend the rapid river by which you miraculously came here and which flows under arches of rock. The mountains which surround the whole of my kingdom are ten thousand feet high and are perpendicular like walls; they are more than ten leagues broad, and you can only get down from them by way of precipices. However, since you must go, I will give orders to the directors of machinery to make a machine which will carry you comfortably. When you have been taken to the other side of the mountains, nobody can proceed any farther with you; for my subjects have sworn never to pass this boundary and they are too wise to break their oath. Ask anything else of me you wish."

"We ask nothing of your Majesty," said Cacambo, "except a few sheep laden with provisions, pebbles and the mud of this country."

The King laughed. "I cannot understand," said he, "the taste you people of Europe have for our yellow mud; but take as much as you wish, and much good may it do you."

He immediately ordered his engineers to make a machine to hoist these two extraordinary men out of his kingdom. Three thousand learned scientists worked at it; it was ready in a fortnight and only cost about twenty million pounds sterling in the money of that country. Candide and Cacambo were placed on the machine; there were two large red sheep saddled and bridled for them to ride on when they had passed the mountains, twenty sumpter sheep [24] laden with provisions, thirty carrying presents of the most curious productions of the country and fifty laden with gold, precious stones and diamonds. The King embraced the two vagabonds tenderly. Their departure was a splendid sight and so was the ingenious manner in which they and their sheep were hoisted on to the top of the mountains. The scientists took leave of them after having landed them safely, and Candide's only desire and object was to go and present Mademoiselle Cunegonde with his sheep.

"We have sufficient to pay the governor of Buenos Ayres," said he, "if Mademoiselle Cunegonde can be bought. Let us go to Cayenne, and take ship, and then we will see what kingdom we will buy."

24. Pack-sheep.

CHAPTER XIX

What Happened to Them at Surinam and How Candide Made the Acquaintance of Martin

Our two travellers' first day was quite pleasant. They were encouraged by the idea of possessing more treasures than all Asia, Europe and Africa could collect. Candide in transport carved the name of Cunegonde on the trees. On the second day two of the sheep stuck in a marsh and were swallowed up with their loads; two other sheep died of fatigue a few days later; then seven or eight died of hunger in a desert; several days afterwards others fell off precipices. Finally, after they had travelled for a hundred days, they had only two sheep left.

Candide said to Cacambo: "My friend, you see how perishable are the riches of this world; nothing is steadfast but virtue and the happiness of seeing Mademoiselle Cunegonde again."

"I admit it," said Cacambo, "but we still have two sheep with more treasures than ever the King of Spain will have, and in the distance I see a town I suspect is Surinam,[25] which belongs to the Dutch. We are at the end of our troubles and the beginning of our happiness."

As they drew near the town they came upon a negro lying on the ground wearing only half his clothes, that is to say, a pair of blue cotton drawers; this poor man had no left leg and no right hand. "Good heavens!" said Candide to him in Dutch, "what are you doing there, my friend, in that horrible state?"

"I am waiting for my master, the famous merchant Monsieur Vanderdendur."

"Was it Monsieur Vanderdendur," said Candide, "who treated you in that way?"

"Yes, sir," said the negro, "it is the custom. We are given a pair of cotton drawers twice a year as clothing. When we work in the sugar mills and the grindstone catches our fingers, they cut off the hand; when we try to run away, they cut off a leg. Both these things happened to me. This is the price paid for the sugar you eat in Europe. But when my mother sold me for ten patagons on the coast of Guinea, she said to me: 'My dear child, give thanks to our fetishes, always worship them, and they will make you happy; you have the honor to be a slave of our lords the white men and thereby you have made the fortune of your father and mother.' Alas! I do not know whether I made their fortune, but they certainly did not make mine. Dogs, monkeys and parrots are a thousand times less miserable than we are; the Dutch fetishes who converted me tell me that we are all of us, whites and blacks, the children of Adam. I am not a genealogist, but if these preachers tell the truth, we are all second cousins. Now, you will admit that no one could treat his relatives in a more horrible way."

"O Pangloss!" cried Candide. "This is an abomination you had not

25. In Dutch Guiana.

guessed; this is too much, in the end I shall have to renounce optimism."

"What is optimism?" said Cacambo.

"Alas!" said Candide, "it is the mania of maintaining that everything is well when we are wretched." And he shed tears as he looked at his negro; and he entered Surinam weeping.

The first thing they inquired was whether there was any ship in the port which could be sent to Buenos Ayres. The person they addressed happened to be a Spanish captain, who offered to strike an honest bargain with them. He arranged to meet them at an inn. Candide and the faithful Cacambo went and waited for him with their two sheep. Candide, who blurted everything out, told the Spaniard all his adventures and confessed that he wanted to elope with Mademoiselle Cunegonde.

"I shall certainly not take you to Buenos Ayres," said the captain. "I should be hanged and you would, too. The fair Cunegonde is his Lordship's favorite mistress."

Candide was thunderstruck; he sobbed for a long time; then he took Cacambo aside. "My dear friend," said he, "this is what you must do. We have each of us in our pockets five or six millions worth of diamonds; you are more skilful than I am; go to Buenos Ayres and get Mademoiselle Cunegonde. If the governor makes any difficulties give him a million; if he is still obstinate give him two; you have not killed an Inquisitor so they will not suspect you. I will fit out another ship, I will go and wait for you at Venice; it is a free country where there is nothing to fear from Bulgarians, Abares, Jews or Inquisitors."

Cacambo applauded this wise resolution; he was in despair at leaving a good master who had become his intimate friend; but the pleasure of being useful to him overcame the grief of leaving him. They embraced with tears. Candide urged him not to forget the good old woman. Cacambo set off that very same day; he was a very good man, this Cacambo.

Candide remained some time longer at Surinam waiting for another captain to take him to Italy with the two sheep he had left. He engaged servants and bought everything necessary for a long voyage. At last Monsieur Vanderdendur, the owner of a large ship, came to see him.

"How much do you want," he asked this man, "to take me straight to Venice with my servants, my baggage and these two sheep?"

The captain asked for ten thousand piastres. Candide did not hesitate. "Oh! Ho!" said the prudent Vanderdendur to himself, "this foreigner gives ten thousand piastres immediately! He must be very rich." He returned a moment afterwards and said he could not sail for less than twenty thousand.

"Very well, you shall have them," said Candide.

"Whew!" said the merchant to himself, "this man gives twenty thousand piastres as easily as ten thousand." He came back again, and said he could not take him to Venice for less than thirty thousand piastres.

"Then you shall have thirty thousand," replied Candide.

"Oho!" said the Dutch merchant to himself again, "thirty thousand piastres is nothing to this man; obviously the two sheep are laden with immense treasures; I will not insist any further; first let me make him pay the thirty thousand piastres, and then we will see."

Candide sold two little diamonds, the smaller of which was worth more than all the money the captain asked. He paid him in advance. The two sheep were taken on board. Candide followed in a little boat to join the ship which rode at anchor; the captain watched his time, set his sails and weighed anchor; the wind was favorable. Candide, bewildered and stupefied, soon lost sight of him. "Alas!" he cried, "this is a trick worthy of the old world."

He returned to shore, in grief; for he had lost enough to make the fortunes of twenty kings. He went to the Dutch judge; and, as he was rather disturbed, he knocked loudly at the door; he went in, related what had happened and talked a little louder than he ought to have done. The judge began by fining him ten thousand piastres for the noise he had made; he then listened patiently to him, promised to look into his affair as soon as the merchant returned, and charged him another ten thousand piastres for the expenses of the audience.

This behavior reduced Candide to despair; he had indeed endured misfortunes a thousand times more painful; but the calmness of the judge and of the captain who had robbed him, stirred up his bile and plunged him into a black melancholy. The malevolence of men revealed itself to his mind in all its ugliness; he entertained only gloomy ideas.

At last a French ship was about to leave for Bordeaux and, since he no longer had any sheep laden with diamonds to put on board, he hired a cabin at a reasonable price and announced throughout the town that he would give the passage, food and two thousand piastres to an honest man who would make the journey with him, on condition that this man was the most unfortunate and the most disgusted with his condition in the whole province. Such a crowd of applicants arrived that a fleet would not have contained them. Candide, wishing to choose among the most likely, picked out twenty persons who seemed reasonably sociable and who all claimed to deserve his preference. He collected them in a tavern and gave them supper, on condition that each took an oath to relate truthfully the story of his life, promising that he would choose the man who seemed to him the most deserving of pity and to have the most cause for being discontented with his condition, and that he would give the others a little money. The sitting lasted until four o'clock in the morning. As Candide listened to their adventures he remembered what the old woman had said on the voyage to Buenos Ayres and how she had wagered that there was nobody on the boat who had not experienced very great misfortunes. At each story which was told him, he thought of Pangloss.

"This Pangloss," said he, "would have some difficulty in supporting his system. I wish he were here. Certainly, if everything is well, it is only in Eldorado and not in the rest of the world."

He finally determined in favor of a poor man of letters who had worked ten years for the booksellers at Amsterdam. He judged that there was no occupation in the world which could more disgust a man.[26] This man of letters, who was also a good man, had been robbed by his wife, beaten by his son, and abandoned by his daughter, who had eloped with a Portuguese. He had just been deprived of a small post on which he depended and the preachers of Surinam were persecuting him because they thought he was a Socinian.[27] It must be admitted that the others were at least as unfortunate as he was; but Candide hoped that this learned man would help to pass the time during the voyage. All his other rivals considered that Candide was doing them a great injustice; but he soothed them down by giving each of them a hundred piastres.

CHAPTER XX

What Happened to Candide and Martin at Sea

So the old man, who was called Martin, embarked with Candide for Bordeaux. Both had seen and suffered much; and if the ship had been sailing from Surinam to Japan by way of the Cape of Good Hope they would have been able to discuss moral and physical evil during the whole voyage. However, Candide had one great advantage over Martin, because he still hoped to see Mademoiselle Cunegonde again, and Martin had nothing to hope for; moreover, he possessed gold and diamonds; and, although he had lost a hundred large red sheep laden with the greatest treasures on earth, although he was still enraged at being robbed by the Dutch captain, yet when he thought of what he still had left in his pockets and when he talked of Cunegonde, especially at the end of a meal, he still inclined towards the system of Pangloss.

"But what do you think of all this, Martin?" said he to the man of letters. "What is your view of moral and physical evil?"

"Sir," replied Martin, "my priests accused me of being a Socinian; but the truth is I am a Manichean." [28]

"You are poking fun at me," said Candide, "there are no Manicheans left in the world."

"I am one," said Martin. "I don't know what to do about it, but I am unable to think in any other fashion."

"You must be possessed by the devil," said Candide.

"He takes so great a share in the affairs of this world," said Martin, "that he might well be in me, as he is everywhere else; but I confess that when I consider this globe, or rather this globule, I think that God has abandoned it to some evil creature — always excepting Eldo-

26. Voltaire speaks from personal experience with publishers.
27. Similar to a Unitarian.
28. The schismatic Manicheans threatened Christianity and reached the peak of their influence at the time of St. Augustine.

rado. I have never seen a town which did not desire the ruin of the next town, never a family which did not wish to exterminate some other family. Everywhere the weak loathe the powerful before whom they cower and the powerful treat them like flocks of sheep whose wool and flesh are to be sold. A million drilled assassins go from one end of Europe to the other murdering and robbing with discipline in order to earn their bread, because there is no honester occupation; and in the towns which seem to enjoy peace and where the arts flourish, men are devoured by more envy, troubles and worries than the afflictions of a besieged town. Secret griefs are even more cruel than public miseries. In a word, I have seen so much and endured so much that I have become a Manichean."

"Yet there is some good," replied Candide.

"There may be," said Martin, "but I do not know it."

In the midst of this dispute they heard the sound of cannon. The noise increased every moment. Every one took his telescope. About three miles away they saw two ships engaged in battle; and the wind brought them so near the French ship that they had the pleasure of seeing the fight at their ease. At last one of the two ships fired a broadside so accurately and so low down that the other ship began to sink. Candide and Martin distinctly saw a hundred men on the main deck of the sinking ship; they raised their hands to Heaven and uttered frightful shrieks; in a moment all were engulfed.

"Well!" said Martin, "that is how men treat each other."

"It is certainly true," said Candide, "that there is something diabolical in this affair."

As he was speaking, he saw something of a brilliant red swimming near the ship. They launched a boat to see what it could be; it was one of his sheep. Candide felt more joy at recovering this sheep than grief at losing a hundred all laden with large diamonds from Eldorado.

The French captain soon perceived that the captain of the remaining ship was a Spaniard and that the sunken ship was a Dutch pirate; the captain was the very same who had robbed Candide. The immense wealth this scoundrel had stolen was swallowed up with him in the sea and only a sheep was saved.

"You see," said Candide to Martin, "that crime is sometimes punished; this scoundrel of a Dutch captain has met the fate he deserved."

"Yes," said Martin, "but was it necessary that the other passengers on his ship should perish too? God punished the thief, and the devil punished the others."

Meanwhile the French and Spanish ships continued on their way and Candide continued his conversation with Martin. They argued for a fortnight and at the end of the fortnight they had got no further than at the beginning. But after all, they talked, they exchanged ideas, they consoled each other. Candide stroked his sheep. "Since I have found you again," said he, "I may very likely find Cunegonde."

[*After various adventures Candide and Martin reach Venice, where Cacambo was supposed to bring Cunegonde.*]

CHAPTER XXVI

How Candide and Martin Supped with Six Strangers and Who They Were

One evening when Candide and Martin were going to sit down to table with the strangers who lodged in the same hotel, a man with a face the color of soot came up to him from behind and, taking him by the arm, said: "Get ready to come with us, and do not fail."

He turned round and saw Cacambo. Only the sight of Cunegonde could have surprised and pleased him more. He was almost wild with joy. He embraced his dear friend.

"Cunegonde is here, of course? Where is she? Take me to her, let me die of joy with her."

"Cunegonde is not here," said Cacambo. "She is in Constantinople."

"Heavens! In Constantinople! But, were she in China, I would fly to her; let us start at once."

"We will start after supper," replied Cacambo. "I cannot tell you any more; I am a slave, and my master is waiting for me; I must go and serve him at table! Do not say anything; eat your supper, and be in readiness."

Candide, torn between joy and grief, charmed to see his faithful agent again, amazed to see him a slave, filled with the idea of seeing his mistress again, with turmoil in his heart, agitation in his mind, sat down to table with Martin (who met every strange occurrence with the same calmness), and with six strangers, who had come to spend the Carnival at Venice.

Cacambo, who acted as butler to one of the strangers, bent down to his master's head towards the end of the meal and said: "Sire, your Majesty can leave when you wish, the ship is ready." After saying this, Cacambo withdrew.

The guests looked at each other with surprise without saying a word, when another servant came up to his master and said: "Sire, your Majesty's post chaise is at Padua, and the boat is ready." The master made a sign and the servant departed.

Once more all the guests looked at each other, and the general surprise was increased twofold. A third servant went up to the third stranger and said: "Sire, believe me, your Majesty cannot remain here any longer; I will prepare everything." And he immediately disappeared.

Candide and Martin had no doubt that this was a Carnival masquerade. A fourth servant said to the fourth master: "Your Majesty can leave when you wish." And he went out like the others. The fifth servant spoke similarly to the fifth master. But the sixth servant spoke differently to the sixth stranger who was next to Candide, and said: "Faith, sire, they will not give your Majesty any more credit nor me either, and we may very likely be jailed tonight, both of us; I am going to look to my own affairs, good bye."

When the servants had all gone, the six strangers, Candide and Martin remained in profound silence. At last it was broken by Candide.

"Gentlemen," said he, "this is a curious jest. How is it you are all kings? I confess that neither Martin nor I are kings."

Cacambo's master then gravely spoke and said in Italian: "I am not jesting, my name is Achmet III. For several years I was Sultan; I dethroned my brother; my nephew dethroned me; they cut off the heads of my viziers; I am ending my days in the old seraglio; my nephew, Sultan Mahmoud, sometimes allows me to travel for my health, and I have come to spend the Carnival at Venice."

A young man who sat next to Achmet spoke after him and said: "My name is Ivan; I was Emperor of all the Russias; I was dethroned in my cradle; [29] my father and mother were imprisoned and I was brought up in prison; I sometimes have permission to travel, accompanied by those who guard me, and I have come to spend the Carnival at Venice."

The third said: "I am Charles Edward, King of England; [30] my father gave up his rights to the throne to me and I fought a war to assert them; the hearts of eight hundred of my adherents were torn out and dashed in their faces. I have been in prison; I am going to Rome to visit the King, my father, who is dethroned like my grandfather and me; and I have come to spend the Carnival at Venice."

The fourth then spoke and said: "I am the King of Poland; [31] the chance of war deprived me of my hereditary states; my father [32] endured the same reverse of fortune; I am resigned to Providence like the Sultan Achmet, the Emperor Ivan and King Charles Edward, to whom God grant long life; and I have come to spend the Carnival at Venice."

The fifth said: "I also am the King of Poland, [33] I have lost my kingdom twice; but Providence has given me another state in which I have been able to do more good than all the kings of the Sarmatians together have been ever able to do on the banks of the Vistula; I also am resigned to Providence and I have come to spend the Carnival at Venice."

It was now for the sixth monarch to speak. "Gentlemen," said he, "I am not so eminent as you; but I have been a king like anyone else. I am Theodore; [34] I was elected King of Corsica; I have been called Your Majesty and now I am barely called Sir. I have coined money and do not own a farthing; I have had two Secretaries of State and now have scarcely a valet; I have occupied a throne and for a long time

29. Ivan VI was indeed dethroned, when he was a year old. All the kings mentioned are historical.
30. The "Young Pretender," son of James Stuart.
31. Augustus III (1696–1763).
32. Augustus II (1670–1733).
33. Stanislas Leczinski, who was the father-in-law of Louis XV, the French king. He was a friend of Voltaire's.
34. Born Baron von Neuhoff, an eighteenth century German adventurer who was King of Corsica for a few months in 1736.

lay on straw in a London prison. I am much afraid I shall be treated in the same way here, although I have come, like your Majesties, to spend the Carnival at Venice."

The five other kings listened to this speech with a noble compassion. Each of them gave King Theodore twenty sequins [35] to buy clothes and shirts; Candide presented him with a diamond worth two thousand sequins.

"Who is this man," said the five kings, "who is able to give a hundred times as much as any of us, and who gives it?"

As they were leaving the table, there came to the same hotel four serene highnesses who had also lost their states in the chance of war, and who had come to spend the rest of the Carnival at Venice; but Candide did not even notice these newcomers, he could think of nothing but of going to Constantinople to find his dear Cunegonde.

CHAPTER XXVII

CANDIDE'S VOYAGE TO CONSTANTINOPLE

The faithful Cacambo had already spoken to the Turkish captain who was to take Sultan Achmet back to Constantinople and had obtained permission for Candide and Martin to come on board. They both entered this ship after having prostrated themselves before his miserable Highness.

On the way, Candide said to Martin: "So we have just supped with six dethroned kings! And among those six kings there was one to whom I gave charity. Perhaps there are many other princes still more unfortunate. Now, I have only lost a hundred sheep and I am hastening to Cunegonde's arms. My dear Martin, once more, Pangloss was right, all is well."

"I hope so," said Martin.

"But," said Candide, "this is a very singular experience we have just had at Venice. Nobody has ever seen or heard of six dethroned kings supping together in a tavern."

"'Tis no more extraordinary," said Martin, "than most of the things which have happened to us. It is very common for kings to be dethroned; and as to the honor we have had of supping with them, 'tis a trifle not deserving our attention."

Scarcely had Candide entered the ship when he threw his arms round the neck of his old valet, of his friend Cacambo.

"Well!" said he, "what is Cunegonde doing? Is she still a marvel of beauty? Does she still love me? How is she? Of course you have bought her a palace in Constantinople?"

"My dear master," replied Cacambo, "Cunegonde is washing dishes on the banks of Propontis [36] for a prince who possesses very few dishes; she is a slave in the house of a former sovereign named

35. A Venetian gold coin.
36. Now the Sea of Marmora.

Ragotsky,[37] who receives in his refuge three crowns a day from the Grand Turk; but what is even more sad is that she has lost her beauty and has become horribly ugly."

"Ah! beautiful or ugly," said Candide, "I am a man of honor and my duty is to love her always. But how can she be reduced to so abject a condition with the five or six millions you carried off?"

"Ah!" said Cacambo, "did I not have to give two millions to Señor Don Fernando d'Ibaraa y Figueora y Mascarenes y Lampourdos y Souza, Governor of Buenos Ayres, for permission to bring away Mademoiselle Cunegonde? And did not a pirate bravely strip us of all the rest? And did not this pirate take us to Cape Matapan, to Milo, to Nicaria, to Samos, to Petra, to the Dardanelles, to Marmora, to Scutari? Cunegonde and the old woman are servants to the prince I mentioned, and I am slave to the dethroned Sultan."

"What a chain of terrible calamities!" said Candide. "But after all, I still have a few diamonds; I shall easily deliver Cunegonde. What a pity she has become so ugly."

Then, turning to Martin, he said: "Who do you think is the most to be pitied, the Sultan Achmet, the Emperor Ivan, King Charles Edward, or me?"

"I do not know at all," said Martin. "I should have to be in your hearts to know."

"Ah!" said Candide, "if Pangloss were here he would know and would tell us."

"I do not know," said Martin, "what scales your Pangloss would use to weigh the misfortunes of men and to estimate their sufferings. All I presume is that there are millions of men on the earth a hundred times more to be pitied than King Charles Edward, the Emperor Ivan and the Sultan Achmet."

"That may very well be," said Candide.

In a few days they reached the Black Sea channel. Candide began by paying a high ransom for Cacambo and, without wasting time, he went on board a galley with his companions bound for the shores of Propontis, in order to find Cunegonde however ugly she might be. Among the galley slaves were two convicts who rowed very badly and from time to time the Levantine captain applied several strokes of a bull's pizzle to their naked shoulders. From a natural feeling of pity Candide watched them more attentively than the other galley slaves and went up to them. Some features of their disfigured faces appeared to him to have some resemblance to Pangloss and the wretched Jesuit, the Baron, Mademoiselle Cunegonde's brother. This idea disturbed and saddened him. He looked at them still more carefully. "Truly," said he to Cacambo, "if I had not seen Dr. Pangloss hanged, and if I had not been so unfortunate as to kill the Baron, I should think they were rowing in this galley."

37. Once King of Transylvania.

At the words Baron and Pangloss, the two convicts gave a loud cry, stopped on their seats and dropped their oars. The Levantine captain ran up to them and the lashes with the bull's pizzle were redoubled.

"Stop! Stop, sir!" cried Candide. "I will give you as much money as you want."

"What! Is it Candide?" said one of the convicts.

"What! Is it Candide?" said the other.

"Is it a dream?" said Candide. "Am I awake? Am I in this galley? Is that my Lord the Baron whom I killed? Is that Dr. Pangloss whom I saw hanged?"

"It is, it is," they replied.

"What! Is that the great philosopher?" said Martin.

"Ah! sir," said Candide to the Levantine captain, "how much money do you want for My Lord Thunder-ten-tronckh, one of the first Barons of the empire, and for Dr. Pangloss, the most profound metaphysician of Germany?"

"Dog of a Christian," replied the Levantine captain, "since these two dogs of Christian convicts are Barons and metaphysicians, which no doubt is a high rank in their country, you shall pay me fifty thousand sequins."

"You shall have them, sir. Row back to Constantinople like lightning and you shall be paid at once. But, no, take me to Mademoiselle Cunegonde."

The captain, at Candide's first offer had already turned the bow towards the town, and rowed there more swiftly than a bird cleaves the air.

Candide embraced the Baron and Pangloss a hundred times. "How was it I did not kill you, my dear Baron? And, my dear Pangloss, how do you happen to be alive after having been hanged? And why are you both in a Turkish galley?"

"Is it really true that my dear sister is in this country?" said the Baron.

"Yes," replied Cacambo.

"So once more I see my dear Candide!" cried Pangloss.

Candide introduced Martin and Cacambo. They all embraced and all talked at the same time. The galley flew; already they were in the harbor. They sent for a Jew, and Candide sold him for fifty thousand sequins a diamond worth a hundred thousand, for which he swore by Abraham he could not give any more. The ransom of the Baron and Pangloss was immediately paid. Pangloss threw himself at the feet of his liberator and bathed them with tears; the other thanked him with a nod and promised to repay the money at the first opportunity. "But is it possible that my sister is in Turkey?" said he.

"Nothing is so possible," replied Cacambo, "since she washes up the dishes of a prince of Transylvania."

They immediately sent for two Jews; Candide sold some more diamonds; and they all set out in another galley to rescue Cunegonde.

CHAPTER XXVIII

WHAT HAPPENED TO CANDIDE, TO CUNEGONDE, TO PANGLOSS, TO MARTIN, ETC.

"Pardon once more," said Candide to the Baron, "pardon me, reverend father, for having thrust my sword through your body."

"Let us say no more about it," said the Baron. "I admit I was a little too sharp; but since you wish to know how it was you saw me in a galley, I must tell you that after my wound was healed by the brother apothecary of the college, I was attacked and carried off by a Spanish raiding party; I was imprisoned in Buenos Ayres at the time when my sister had just left. I asked to return to the Vicar-General in Rome. I was ordered to Constantinople to act as almoner to the Ambassador of France. A week after I had taken up my office I met towards evening a very handsome young page of the Sultan. It was very hot; the young man wished to bathe; I took the opportunity to bathe also. I did not know that it was a most serious crime for a Christian to be found naked with a young Mahometan. A cadi [38] sentenced me to a hundred strokes on the soles of my feet and condemned me to the galley. I do not think a more horrible injustice has ever been committed. But I should very much like to know why my sister is in the kitchen of a Transylvanian sovereign living in exile among the Turks."

"But, my dear Pangloss," said Candide, "how does it happen that I see you once more?"

"It is true," said Pangloss, "that you saw me hanged; and in the natural course of events I should have been burned. But you remember, it poured with rain when they were going to roast me; the storm was so violent that they despaired of lighting the fire; I was hanged because they could do nothing better; a surgeon bought my body, carried me home and dissected me. He first made a crucial incision in me from the navel to the collarbone. Nobody could have been worse hanged than I was. The executioner of the holy Inquisition, who was a sub-deacon, was marvellously skilful in burning people, but he was not accustomed to hang them; the rope was wet and did not slide easily and it was knotted; in short, I still breathed. The crucial incision caused me to utter so loud a scream that the surgeon fell over backwards and, thinking he was dissecting the devil, fled away in terror and fell down the staircase in his flight. His wife ran in from another room at the noise; she saw me stretched out on the table with my crucial incision; she was still more frightened than her husband, fled, and fell on top of him. When they had recovered themselves a little, I heard the surgeon's wife say to the surgeon: 'My dear, what were you thinking of, to dissect a heretic? Don't you know the devil always possesses them? I will go and get a priest at once to exorcise him.'

"At this I shuddered and collected the little strength I had left to shout: 'Have pity on me!' At last the Portuguese barber grew bolder;

38. Judge.

he sewed up my skin; his wife even took care of me, and at the end of a fortnight I was able to walk again. The barber found me a situation and made me lackey to a Knight of Malta who was going to Venice; but, as my master had no money to pay me wages, I entered the service of a Venetian merchant and followed him to Constantinople.

"One day I took it into my head to enter a mosque; there was nobody there except an old Imam and a very pretty young devotee who was reciting her prayers; her breasts were entirely uncovered; between them she wore a bunch of tulips, roses, anemones, ranunculus, hyacinths and auriculas; she dropped her bunch of flowers; I picked it up and returned it to her with a most respectful alacrity. I was so long putting them back that the Imam grew angry and, seeing I was a Christian, called for help. I was taken to the cadi, who sentenced me to receive a hundred strokes on the soles of my feet and sent me to the galleys. I was chained on the same seat and in the same galley as My Lord the Baron. In this galley there were four young men from Marseilles, five Neapolitan priests and two monks from Corfu, who assured us that similar accidents occurred every day. His Lordship the Baron claimed that he had suffered a greater injustice than I; and I claimed that it was much more permissible to replace a bunch of flowers between a woman's breasts than to be naked with one of the Sultan's pages. We argued continually, and every day received twenty strokes of the bull's pizzle, when the chain of events of this universe led you to our galley and you ransomed us."

"Well! my dear Pangloss," said Candide, "when you were hanged, dissected, stunned with blows and made to row in the galleys, did you always think that everything was for the best in this world?"

"I am still of my first opinion," replied Pangloss, "for after all I am a philosopher; and it would be unbecoming for me to recant, since Leibnitz [39] could not be in the wrong and pre-established harmony is the finest thing imaginable like the plenum and subtle matter."

CHAPTER XXIX

How Candide Found Cunegonde and the Old woman Again

While Candide, the Baron, Pangloss, Martin and Cacambo were relating their adventures, reasoning upon contingent or non-contingent events of the universe, arguing about effects and causes, moral and physical evil, free will and necessity, and the consolation to be found in the Turkish galleys, they came to the house of the Transylvanian prince on the shores of Propontis.

The first objects which met their sight were Cunegonde and the old woman hanging out towels to dry on the line. At this sight the Baron grew pale. Candide, that tender lover, seeing his fair Cunegonde sunburned, blear-eyed, flat-breasted, with wrinkles round her eyes and red,

39. Gottfried Wilhelm Leibnitz (1646–1716), the famous German philosopher and mathematician whose "optimism" Voltaire has been satirizing.

chapped arms, recoiled three paces in horror, and then advanced from mere politeness. She embraced Candide and her brother. They embraced the old woman; Candide bought them both.

In the neighborhood was a little farm; the old woman suggested that Candide should buy it, until some better fate befell the group. Cunegonde did not know that she had become ugly, for nobody had told her so; she reminded Candide of his promises in so peremptory a tone that the good Candide dared not refuse her. He therefore informed the Baron that he was about to marry his sister.

"Never," said the Baron, "will I endure such baseness on her part and such insolence on yours; nobody shall ever reproach me with this infamy; my sister's children could never enter the chapters [40] of Germany. No, my sister shall never marry anyone but a Baron of the Empire."

Cunegonde threw herself at his feet and bathed them in tears; but he was inflexible.

"Madman," said Candide, "I rescued you from the galleys, I paid your ransom and your sister's; she was washing dishes here, she is ugly, I am so kind as to make her my wife, and you pretend to oppose me! I should re-kill you if I listened to my anger."

"You may kill me again," said the Baron, "but you shall never marry my sister while I am alive."

CHAPTER XXX

Conclusion

At the bottom of his heart Candide had not the least wish to marry Cunegonde. But the Baron's extreme impertinence determined him to complete the marriage, and Cunegonde urged it so warmly that he could not retract. He consulted Pangloss, Martin and the faithful Cacambo. Pangloss wrote an excellent memorandum by which he proved that the Baron had no rights over his sister and that by all the laws of the empire she could make a left-handed marriage [41] with Candide. Martin advised that the Baron should be thrown into the sea; Cacambo decided that he should be returned to the Levantine captain and sent back to the galleys, after which he would be returned by the first ship to the Vicar-General at Rome. This was thought to be very good advice; the old woman approved it; they said nothing to the sister; the plan was carried out with the aid of a little money and they had the pleasure of duping a Jesuit and punishing the pride of a German Baron.

It would be natural to suppose that when, after so many disasters, Candide was married to his mistress, and living with the philosopher Pangloss, the philosopher Martin, the prudent Cacambo and the old woman, having brought back so many diamonds from the country of the

40. Knightly assemblies.
41. A so-called morganatic marriage, which would not admit Candide to the noble rank of his wife.

ancient Incas, he would lead the most pleasant life imaginable. But he was so cheated by the Jews [42] that he had nothing left but his little farm; his wife, growing uglier every day, became shrewish and unendurable; the old woman was ailing and even more bad tempered than Cunegonde. Cacambo, who worked in the garden and then went to Constantinople to sell vegetables, was overworked and cursed his fate. Pangloss was in despair because he did not shine in some German university.

As for Martin, he was firmly convinced that people are equally uncomfortable everywhere; he accepted things patiently. Candide, Martin and Pangloss sometimes argued about metaphysics and morals. From the windows of the farm they often watched the ships going by, filled with effendis, pashas, and cadis, who were being exiled to Lemnos, to Mitylene and Erzerum. They saw other cadis, other pashas and other effendis coming back to take the place of the exiles and to be exiled in their turn. They saw the neatly impaled heads which were taken to the Sublime Porte.[43] These sights redoubled their discussions; and when they were not arguing, the boredom was so excessive that one day the old woman dared to say to them: "I should like to know which is worse, to be raped a hundred times by negro pirates, to have a buttock cut off, to run the gauntlet among the Bulgarians, to be whipped and flogged in an *auto-da-fé*, to be dissected, to row in a galley, in short, to endure all the miseries through which we have passed, or to remain here doing nothing?"

" 'Tis a great question," said Candide.

These remarks led to new reflections, and Martin especially concluded that man was born to live in the convulsions of distress or in the lethargy of boredom. Candide did not agree, but he asserted nothing. Pangloss confessed that he had always suffered horribly; but, having once maintained that everything was for the best, he had continued to maintain it without believing it.

One thing confirmed Martin in his detestable principles, made Candide hesitate more than ever, and embarrassed Pangloss. And it was this. One day there came to their farm Paquette [44] and Friar Giroflée, who were in the most extreme misery; they had soon wasted their three thousand piastres,[45] had left each other, made it up, quarrelled again, been put in prison, escaped, and finally Friar Giroflée had turned Turk. Paquette continued her occupation everywhere and now earned nothing by it.

"I foresaw," said Martin to Candide, "that your gifts would soon be wasted and would only make them the more miserable. You and Cacambo were once bloated with millions of piastres and you are no happier than Friar Giroflée and Paquette."

42. Voltaire's bias stems in part from the losses he suffered when his Jewish bankers went bankrupt.
43. The Gate of the Turkish Sultan's palace, which was also the Palace of Justice.
44. Pangloss' former mistress.
45. Candide had given them money when he saw them in Venice.

"Ah! Ha!" said Pangloss to Paquette, "so Heaven brings you back to us, my dear child? Do you know that you cost me the end of my nose, an eye and an ear! What a plight you are in! Ah! What a world this is!"

This new occurrence caused them to philosophise more than ever. In the neighborhood there lived a very famous Dervish, who was supposed to be the best philosopher in Turkey; they went to consult him; Pangloss was the spokesman and said: "Master, we have come to beg you to tell us why so strange an animal as man was ever created."

"What has it to do with you?" said the Dervish. "Is it your business?"

"But, reverend father," said Candide, "there is a horrible amount of evil in the world."

"What does it matter," said the Dervish, "whether there is evil or good? When his highness sends a ship to Egypt, does he worry about the comfort or discomfort of the rats in the ship?"

"Then what should we do?" said Pangloss.

"Hold your tongue," said the Dervish.

"I flattered myself," said Pangloss, "that I should discuss with you effects and causes, this best of all possible worlds, the origin of evil, the nature of the soul and pre-established harmony."

At these words the Dervish slammed the door in their faces.

During this conversation the news went round that at Constantinople two viziers and the mufti had been strangled and several of their friends impaled. This catastrophe made a prodigious noise everywhere for several hours. As Pangloss, Candide and Martin were returning to their little farm, they came upon an old man who was taking the air under a bower of orange trees at his door. Pangloss, who was as curious as he was argumentative, asked him what was the name of the mufti who had just been strangled.

"I do not know," replied the old man. "I have never known the name of any mufti or of any vizier. I am entirely ignorant of the occurrence you mention; I presume that in general those who meddle with public affairs sometimes perish miserably and that they deserve it; but I never inquire what is going on in Constantinople; I content myself with sending there for sale the produce of the garden I cultivate."

Having spoken thus, he took the strangers into his house. His two daughters and his two sons presented them with several kinds of sherbert which they made themselves, caymac flavored with candied citron peel, oranges, lemons, limes, pineapples, dates, pistachios and Moccha coffee which had not been mixed with the bad coffee of Batavia and the Isles. After which this good Mussulman's two daughters perfumed the beards of Candide, Pangloss and Martin.

"You must have a vast and magnificent estate?" said Candide to the Turk.

"I have only twenty acres," replied the Turk. "I cultivate them with my children; and work keeps at bay three great evils: boredom, vice and need."

As Candide returned to his farm he reflected deeply on the Turk's remarks. He said to Pangloss and Martin: "That good old man seems to me to have chosen an existence preferable by far to that of the six kings with whom we had the honor to sup."

"Exalted rank," said Pangloss, "is very dangerous, according to the testimony of all philosophers; for Eglon, King of the Moabites, was murdered by Ehud; Absalom was hanged by the hair and pierced by three darts; King Nadab, son of Jeroboam, was killed by Baasha; King Elah by Zimri; Ahaziah by Jehu; Athaliah by Jehoiada; the Kings Jehoiakim, Jeconiah and Zedekiah were made slaves. You know in what manner died Crœsus, Astyages, Darius, Denys of Syracuse, Pyrrhus, Perseus, Hannibal, Jugurtha, Ariovistus, Cæsar, Pompey, Nero, Otho, Vitellius, Domitian, Richard II of England, Edward II, Henry VI, Richard III, Mary Stuart, Charles I, the three Henrys of France, the Emperor Henry IV.[46] You know . . ."

"I also know," said Candide, "that we should cultivate our gardens."

"You are right," said Pangloss, "for, when man was placed in the Garden of Eden, he was placed there *ut operaretur eum,* to dress it and to keep it; which proves that man was not born for idleness."

"Let us work without theorizing," said Martin; " 'tis the only way to make life endurable."

The whole small fraternity entered into this praiseworthy plan, and each started to make use of his talents. The little farm yielded well. Cunegonde was indeed very ugly, but she became an excellent pastry cook; Paquette embroidered; the old woman took care of the linen. Even Friar Giroflée performed some service; he was a very good carpenter and even became a man of honor; and Pangloss sometimes said to Candide: "All events are linked up in this best of all possible worlds; for, if you had not been expelled from the noble castle, by hard kicks in your backside for love of Mademoiselle Cunegonde, if you had not been clapped into the Inquisition, if you had not wandered about America on foot, if you had not stuck your sword in the Baron, if you had not lost all your sheep from the land of Eldorado, you would not be eating candied citrons and pistachios here."

" 'Tis well said," replied Candide, "but we must cultivate our gardens."

46. Voltaire is satirizing (from the grave) those editors who would footnote all these references.

The Modern World: Beginnings

The need to confess may reflect the certainty of salvation, as in St. Augustine. A man sins and repents, acknowledging his guilt, feeling cleansed. He may be ruthlessly honest in his confession as he details the extent to which he has fallen, making clear the nature of his sinful life, which becomes a Christian exemplum, illuminating the way for all sinners. The confession, then, is not intrinsically significant: it looks continually beyond itself toward some idea of absolute order in which a divine principle is at work redeeming the life of the lowliest sinner. The particular case yields to a universal good. But there is a confession which is not teleological: it satisfies, ostensibly, only the need to know oneself, without the inevitability of redemption. Such a confession does not necessarily assume that the life exemplifies a sinful nature; nor does it imply an acute sense of guilt. The confessor's only salvation is his commitment to the truth:

> I am commencing an undertaking, hitherto without precedent, and which will never find an imitator. I desire to set before my fellows the likeness of a man in all the truth of nature, and that man myself.

Thus Rousseau begins his *Confessions*. His is the autobiographical impulse which, in part at least, motivated Cellini to put his life on paper; but Cellini's confession usually suggests that he suppresses those details which might blur the image he wishes to project of a man in control of his environment — triumphing over all his enemies. It is, in its own way, as tendentious as the *Confessions* of St. Augustine. Rousseau, on the other hand, does not consciously wish to justify himself or to score points against foes both imaginary and real.

> I have taken the first and most difficult step in the dark and dirty labyrinth of my confessions. . . . Henceforth I am sure of myself; after having ventured to say so much, I can shrink from nothing.

1319

The strategy, then, is one of convincing the reader that everything is being revealed, that the most sordid and the least flattering details of the life are not being hidden for reasons of taste or pride or deception. Rousseau moves into the labyrinth without the certainty that he will find his way out; he believes in the necessity, the rightness, of an absolute fidelity to himself as he is, not as he wishes to be — a self full of unresolved contradictions, of dark ambiguities, of irrational desires and degrading needs. He is stepping into the only past he believes worth discovering — his own personal history — and his single purpose is the recovery of a knowledge about himself that might illuminate, however tentatively, the forces which conjoin to form a man. Yet for all the strategic sincerity with which Rousseau projects his soul, he is finally no less tendentious than St. Augustine or Cellini: The willful commitment to the truth, no matter how ugly, becomes a matter of pride. Even at his most disgusting and least rational, man assumes the shape of a hero, both in his own eyes and those of the world.

The phenomenon which is called "Romanticism" — a term critics have found even more inadequate than the Renaissance as a description of a particular time in the history of Western civilization — has as one of its major characteristics the determination to redefine the nature of heroic activity, to believe that triumph can issue from those qualities which were formerly considered vicious. Man's moral nature, which it was once optimistically assumed would lead him to act as one ultimately redeemable, was no longer taken for granted. Man as rebel became the new ideal; not only was he actively engaged in denying the values of a fixed social order and working to destroy that order, but he was also determined to assert his individual identity by consciously commiting himself to what the world assumed to be his evil nature, triumphing as devil rather than god, heroic in his damnation. As Don Juan, as Faust, as Eugene Onegin, as Rousseau, man plunged into the various circles of Dante's hell, daring God or man to condemn him. Reason, too, as the only human way to achieve order in a world no longer ruled by God was exposed as an inadequate force for evolutionary progress. Man is not a reasonable creature. He does not naturally do what his reason tells him is to his best advantage. The Romantic temperament celebrates the individual ego in all its passionate contradictions — transforming it into an object no less formal than the most decorous impositions of the Neoclassical World. The difference is that the Romantics posited an irrevocable conflict between the expressive needs of the individual and the world against which he rebelled. The grounds of the Romantic imagination were not external to it: the only world worth exploring was the world within, a world in which the objects of love and hate exist as an extension of self, of the eye perceiving and transforming those objects. The nature one holds a mirror up to is one's own.

Something of that morbid fascination with the self — and the curiously passive detachment which may result — can be seen in both Balzac's story "The Elixir of Life" and Pushkin's narrative poem *Eugene Onegin*. Balzac is famous as a writer of realistic fiction, a genre which exalts the details of external reality, of men interacting within a social context. The reader does not sense the presence of a subjective artist between him and the world being created; the artist seems to disappear, like the God of the Deists, as he projects imaginatively an objective· reality. Yet Balzac's version of the legend of Don Juan indicates how even the most determined of the realists could be drawn to a subject that fascinated the Romantic writers of the early nineteenth century. Part of that fascination was for a past to which the Romantics fled in their rebellion against the present: in England and Germany, the Medieval World was idealized as a time when the human passions had been uncorrupted by the enticements of reason. The legend also furnishes Balzac with an opportunity to deal ironically with the men who corrupted the institutions of the Church. He moves from an apparently detached, realistic presentation of the sordid life of a sinful man to the sensational melodrama of the Don's canonization. "Don Juan," the story by E. T. A. Hoffman to which Balzac refers in his introduction ("To The Reader"), is an excellent example of the romantic tale, full of improbable happenings, ghosts, and damned souls — all filtered through the excited imagination of the artist· Balzac, of course, claims for his version of the legend a realism that is to be less than sensational:

> When you have read the account of Don Juan's decorous parricide, try to picture to yourself the part which would be played under very similar circumstances by honest folk who, in this nineteenth century, will take a man's money and undertake to pay him a life annuity on the faith of a chill, or let a house to an ancient lady for the term of her natural life.

He is arguing that the events of his story ought to be familiar, that the world he is creating is no different from that of his readers; but the elixir is right out of medieval alchemy, and the Don himself, for whom nothing is sacred and everything possible, is merely the romantic rebel racing through a world he scornfully exposes. His only punishment is the boredom which results from living a life dedicated to the pursuit of pleasures that never satisfy the need driving him to hunt them. And that boredom merely reinforces his detachment from the world he scorns, gradually attenuating his rebellion until he begins curiously to resemble, up to the melodramatic climax, the alienated man who was to become the new hero in the twentieth century.

The two strains — the corruptions of society and the boredom which can deteriorate into melancholy — are beautifully exposed in Pushkin's great poem. The irony with which Pushkin presents Onegin's life as a fop does not, however, quite manage to submerge the sympathetic understanding of his hero that the poet feels and communicates. Eugene is indifferent to the world, and yet he knows that there is nothing which can compensate him for its emptiness. This double sense of both his superiority and his limitations paralyzes him: he can neither cry defiance nor commit himself to what he knows to be worthless, and in that state of suspension he only succeeds in destroying the people for whom he can feel nothing. Such a condition arouses compassion, and becomes tragic in its implications when Eugene, after his aimless wanderings, returns to society to discover that perhaps he *had* lost something of value. Just as he had condescended to teach Tatiana the only lesson he felt life could offer, she instructs him; but for all the irony with which Pushkin exposes Onegin's love for her, Tatiana's moral triumph does not destroy the sympathetic intensity of his despair, the sense of loss that results from his new consciousness of what he had thrown away. The conflict in the soul of Onegin, like the conflict between Pushkin's sympathy for and judgment of his hero, reflects the Romantic impulses of the period in which it was written; but the poem also foreshadows the psychological ambiguities of the age which followed, as well as the peculiarly Russian products of that age.

The critical problems raised by *Madame Bovary* stem in part, as in the work of Balzac, from the conventional view that Flaubert brought to perfection the aims and methods of realism. The picture of Flaubert has been fixed by the letters he wrote during the creation of his novel — that of a man struggling for years to discover the precise words to represent a reality untainted by the subjective distortions of a creator. Flaubert took as his object a world for which he felt complete contempt, the world of provincial, bourgeois France, and attempted to present it as it was, in all its stifling, degrading ugliness. It was a world that believed it was evolving to the point where the advances of science and the application of reason were producing the best possible life for those shrewd enough to take advantage of them. "The Agricultural Show" dramatizes the reality of that world, presumably without authorial comment, and the mere act of observing it as it is allows the reader to make the inevitable and necessary judgment. But the irony of Flaubert's presentation — the juxtaposition of romantic love and manure — is, of course, no less a subjective rendering of experience than Pushkin's most explicit intrusions into the world of Eugene Onegin. Even more significant, however, is the rendering of Emma Bovary, for whom Flaubert was also presumed to have felt nothing but contempt. There is, first of all, the strategic challenge: how to portray a character one detests, how to dramatize her emotional life without appearing to force the reader to make the judgment which can so easily be dictated by direct authorial comment. But Emma becomes more than an artistic challenge. One does not need to know Flaubert's famous comment — "Madame Bovary, c'est moi!" — to discover the extent to which Flaubert as passionate creator comes between his reader and his heroine, or to realize the intense ambiguity of his feelings for her. His hatred of the meaningless, empty progress that is affirmed at the Agricultural Show is matched by his equally sharp scorn for the man

Emma believes capable of satisfying her. Madame Bovary is a "romantic." She longs for an intense experience as rewarding as the past she idealizes:

> Emma's eyes kept turning in spite of themselves towards that old man with the drooping lips, as though to some august curiosity. He had lived at Court, had lain in the Queen's bed!

Flaubert is mocking Emma, but he shares her disgust for the life she was born into. The past becomes an escape for her as she sentimentalizes its beauties. Through her Flaubert exposes both the emptiness of contemporary life, with its stupid belief in the value of evolutionary progress, and the follies of sentimentality, which was one of the excesses of Romanticism. Emma luxuriates lovingly in self-pity:

> At last she sighed. 'What can be more distressing than to drag out a futile existence like mine? If only our sorrows could be of use to someone, we might find some consolation in the thought of our sacrifice.'

Flaubert's irony deepens as he takes Emma and Léon through the Rouen Cathedral, a monument to the past she idealizes, and then on the famous carriage ride through the city streets — one of scenes that shocked the bourgeois sensibilities Flaubert scorned and resulted in his prosecution for obscenity. The technique, then, is one of objective, detailed representation of the external world; but that technique, no less than Rousseau's subjective confessions, is a function of the most personal vision of life. The tension between Flaubert's rigorous control of his authorial presence and the intensity of emotional involvement which is implicit in his irony reaches its climax with Emma's death, an experience about which the reader cannot easily make a moral judgment. Flaubert's passionate determination to make the reality speak for itself is rewarded by the reader's willingness to feel that Emma does not, after all her foolish dreams and actions, really deserve the kind of death which the society both she and Flaubert detested has forced on her.

The ambiguities of judgment and identification which distinguish the conception of Emma Bovary are even more involved, and radical, in Dostoevsky's short novel *Notes from Underground*, which may be read as a uniquely Russian thematic variation on what Flaubert saw as the profound inadequacies of the values of his age. The narrator of *Notes* rejects that nineteenth-century optimism which asserts that progress is inevitable, that the scientific and industrial revolutions must lead to a richer, better life for the individual and for society. His scorn for the prophets of evolution becomes psychopathic in its intensity as he explores the depths of his own rage and impotence. Like Rousseau, he is confessing — revealing "The likeness of a man in all the truth of nature" — but he rejects Rousseau's "truth," which he sees as no less an evasion, and evil, than the most scientific and rational view of the world. For all the honesty of his confessions about the sordid psychological drives which have formed his character, Rousseau has an optimistically moral conception of the human soul, an idea that man, corrupted by his environment, can become better if that environment is transformed. Dostoevsky, however, is much more despairing about the possibilities of human redemption, and his rejection of reason, of the power to control oneself and one's world, is much more radical:

> One may choose what is contrary to one's own interests, and sometimes one *positively ought* . . .

Part I, "Underground," is a monologue in which the narrator addresses an imaginary audience of gentlemen — the world from which he has withdrawn — and reveals what he has learned about himself. The symbolic confrontation dramatizes the schizoid division of his mind: he longs to become part of the world he scorns, but he knows he cannot; he believes intensely in the freedom of the will, but the only way he can demonstrate that freedom is by imprisoning himself inside the pain of his withdrawal; he seeks love, but he masochistically plunges into experiences which can only produce hate. The idea of a man so acutely conscious of what it means to be human that he is paralyzed, unable to act, has become an archetype of the modern soul. He is "sick," "spiteful," "unattractive" — a mouse — and yet he has got hold of a truth the discovery of which makes him nothing less than heroic. He is mad, but he sees more clearly and profoundly into the human condition than any ordinary heroic man of action. His vision is a tragic one: he comes to believe that the only way left for him to demonstrate his freedom is to destroy himself, a terrible fate but ultimately a triumph:

> . . . if he does not find means he will contrive destruction and chaos, will contrive sufferings of all sorts, only to gain his point! He will launch a curse upon the world, and as only man can curse (it is his privilege, the primary distinction between him and other animals), maybe by his curse alone he will attain his object — that is, convince himself that he is a man and not a piano-key!

In Part II, "À propos of the Wet Snow," the man who has gone underground reveals the experience which drove him there, as well as dramatizing the validity of the theory he has offered in Part I. He shows himself again and again acting against his own best interests; he continually places himself in situations which are bound to humiliate and degrade him, out of a willful drive to assert his independence of all conventional or predetermined ideas of human behavior. Yet his confrontation with Liza suggests, in spite of his rejection of her love, the possibilities for redemption which were implicit in Part I; for in his refusal to accept the power of immutable laws independent of man's will lies the hope of salvation. Man can change even as he suffers:

paralysis (or madness) is not the only effect of acute self-consciousness, not the only product of tragic understanding. Dostoevsky's belief in the power of Christ does not, however, save the man who has gone underground.

Like Dostoevsky, Tolstoy is concerned with the redemptive possibilities of human experience as well as the moral emptiness of the conventional world; but unlike the Dostoevsky who created *Notes from Underground,* he is at the center of the great nineteenth-century tradition of omniscient writers who see their task as one of capturing as fully as possible, with words, the illusion of life and who do not hesitate to impose explicitly their own judgments and values on the characters and the world they are creating.

> In reality [Ivan's house] was just what is usually seen in the houses of people of moderate means who want to appear rich, and therefore succeed only in resembling others like themselves . . .

There is no uncertainty, no ambiguity, in the drama of Ivan's life; there is no psychotic division in his soul; there is no attempt, as in Dostoevsky, to mask the vision in madness, thus obscuring the presence of the author. We see Ivan as Tolstoy wishes us to see him, in all the clear horror of his life and death. But the meaning of that experience touches so profoundly on all the fears and needs of the human being that the story becomes an allegory of man, whatever his time or environment, as he confronts the finality of a death which calls into question the purpose of his life. If death is the ultimate reality, it demands of us a response that acknowledges its power. Against it, all the defenses which society has built to deny that power, are useless. Ivan must fight his way through the darkness that inevitably results when man discovers he is alone in the bloody confrontation to a rage which weakens the power and then to a certainty which destroys it. The light Ivan falls to is, of course, faith, the intense belief in a personal God which became Tolstoy's strength after his conversion. But the artist in Tolstoy — that part of him he so violently rejected that he condemned the books he wrote before his conversion — triumphs over the preacher. There is only one specific reference to God after Ivan's transformation:

> He tried to add, 'forgive me,' but said 'forego' and waved his hand, knowing that He whose understanding mattered would understand.

Otherwise, Ivan's redemption is represented only as a personal defeat of death, which has been the great antagonist in his life. Tolstoy's artistic control of his moral obsessions has helped to render dramatically every moment in that conflict and has made Ivan's triumph an individual one, even as it becomes a parable of the life of everyman.

The Romantic movement did not produce drama that was actable: Goethe's *Faust* is not often performed on the stage. The subjective, ideosyncratic vision of the poet usually collides with the communal demands of the theater, where emotions are public and must be immediately shared. But as the nineteenth century moved towards the new "naturalism," the vitality of the drama began to reassert itself. The techniques of naturalism — the meticulous, almost scientific attention to the details of the real world — could be more easily applied to the conventions of the stage, which began to take up the same criticism of life that had been the concern of novelists. In *Hedda Gabler,* Ibsen attacks a world in which moral judgments are expressed by social disapproval. Like Flaubert he uses irony to expose the inadequacy of such responses to the irrationality and ugliness of human nature:

> But, good God! People don't do such things!

In this way does Judge Brack reveal the limitations of his understanding when confronted by the final action of a woman he presumed to understand. But Ibsen, like Dostoevsky, is concerned with more than ironic self-exposure. The conception of Hedda Gabler suggests the interest in psychological ambiguity and neurotic behavior which was to become a central preoccupation of post-Freudian writers. Although Ibsen emphasizes boredom as the dominant emotion in Hedda's life, he also adduces enough evidence to suggest that there are more troublesome, and complicated, reasons for her suicide. Her refusal to acknowledge her pregnancy, her obsessive care of her father's guns, her indifference to her husband, her destruction of the manuscript which demonstrated the return of Loevborg's creative powers — much of what Hedda does reflects her tortured refusal to affirm her sexual identity. And her need to exercise power over others — in particular men — becomes more than merely an expression of the desire for independence which Ibsen saw as characterizing modern women. Whatever the limitations of an analysis that places Hedda at the beginning of a long line of sexually insecure heroines, it does not distort her character to make her a witness to the disintegration of the personality as a theme peculiar to the Modern World.

The influence that writers like Dostoevsky and Ibsen had in preparing the ground for the techniques and attitudes of the twentieth century has its counterpart in the poetry of Baudelaire, Rimbaud, and Mallarmé. The image of the poet as satanic outlaw — a romantic extension of the experience of Villon — was uniquely suited to the demands of lyric poetry, which does not, in its celebration of the individual soul, assume that human activity must conform to predetermined standards, or rules. The lyric poet begins with the world defined, and contained, by that self which perceives, suffers, or triumphs; but he does not reject the natural world. Baudelaire, like Rimbaud, wrote lyrics which used journeys as the central metaphor, to suggest that one of the ways the self achieves its unrestricted identity is by a willing submission to the whole universe in all its chaotic completeness:

One morning we set sail, with brains on fire,
And hearts swelled up with rancorous emotion,
Balancing, to the rhythm of its lyre,
Our infinite upon the finite ocean.
                    (Baudelaire, "The Voyage")

And since then I've been bathing in the Poem
Of star-infused and milky Sea,
Devouring the azure greens, where, flotsam pale,
A brooding corpse at times drifts by . . .
                    (Rimbaud, *The Drunken Boat*)

This plunge into sensuous experience becomes the vehicle for an expression of the power of the poet to convey, and then order, in a way
that the exercise of mere reason could never match, the infinite range
and vitality of that world which the poet seeks to apprehend. Mallarmé
simply extended the implications of the journey by subordinating the
natural world so irrevocably to the perceiving eye that the words on
the page — and their contextual, grammatical relationships — assumed
a symbolic reality which no longer demanded reference to any object
outside the verbal world. The symbolist movement in France affirmed
the primacy of the created poem, and challenged the existence of anything beyond it. The power of art to rival all creation became a received
truth in the twentieth century — and the resulting interest in the psychological processes by which the artist creates, an obsessive preoccupation.

Jean-Jacques Rousseau (1712–1778)

LIFE: Born in Geneva, raised by an indifferent father, he ran away at sixteen to begin a life of wandering, controversy, fame, and disillusionment. It was during his stay in England at the invitation of the philosopher David Hume that he wrote down the *Confessions,* which ruthlessly exposed the motivating forces, facts, and movements of that life — including the succession of women, some beautiful, some powerful, with whom he formed his passionate, egocentric, disturbed liaisons. And it was in his final years that the psychological complexities he revealed in the *Confessions* bore deadly fruit: he died insane, the fine strands of his nature having at last been broken.

WORKS: *Social Contract* (1762); *Émile* (1762); *The New Heloise* (1761); *Musings of a Solitary Stroller* (1782); *Confessions* (published 1781–1788).

CONFESSIONS *

Part the First

BOOK I

[1712–1719]

I am commencing an undertaking, hitherto without precedent, and which will never find an imitator. I desire to set before my fellows the likeness of a man in all the truth of nature, and that man myself.

Myself alone! I know the feelings of my heart, and I know men. I am not made like any of those I have seen; I venture to believe that I am not made like any of those who are in existence. If I am not better, at least I am different. Whether Nature has acted rightly or wrongly in destroying the mould in which she cast me, can only be decided after I have been read.

Let the trumpet of the Day of Judgment sound when it will, I will present myself before the Sovereign Judge with this book in my hand. I will say boldly: "This is what I have done, what I have thought,

---

* Published 1781–1788. Translator unknown.

what I was. I have told the good and the bad with equal frankness. I have neither omitted anything bad, nor interpolated anything good. If I have occasionally made use of some immaterial embellishments, this has only been in order to fill a gap caused by lack of memory. I may have assumed the truth of that which I knew might have been true, never of that which I knew to be false. I have shown myself as I was: mean and contemptible, good, high-minded and sublime, according as I was one or the other. I have unveiled my inmost self even as Thou hast seen it, O Eternal Being. Gather round me the countless host of my fellow-men; let them hear my confessions, lament for my unworthiness, and blush for my imperfections. Then let each of them in turn reveal, with the same frankness, the secrets of his heart at the foot of the Throne, and say, if he dare, '*I was better than that man!*' "

I was born at Geneva, in the year 1712, and was the son of Isaac Rousseau and Susanne Bernard, citizens. The distribution of a very moderate inheritance amongst fifteen children had reduced my father's portion almost to nothing; and his only means of livelihood was his trade of watchmaker, in which he was really very clever. My mother, a daughter of the Protestant minister Bernard, was better off. She was clever and beautiful, and my father had found difficulty in obtaining her hand. . . .

My father, after the birth of my only brother, set out for Constantinople, whither he was summoned to undertake the post of watchmaker to the Sultan. During his absence, my mother's beauty, intellect and talents gained for her the devotion of numerous admirers. M. de la Closure, the French Resident, was one of the most eager to offer his. His passion must have been great, for, thirty years later, I saw him greatly affected when speaking to me of her. To enable her to resist such advances, my mother had more than her virtue: she loved her husband tenderly. She pressed him to return; he left all, and returned. I was the unhappy fruit of this return. Ten months later I was born, a weak and ailing child; I cost my mother her life, and my birth was the first of my misfortunes. . . .

Such were the authors of my existence. Of all the gifts which Heaven had bestowed upon them, a sensitive heart is the only one they bequeathed to me; it had been the source of their happiness, but for me it proved the source of all the misfortunes of my life. . . .

I felt before I thought: this is the common lot of humanity. I experienced it more than others. I do not know what I did until I was five or six years old. I do not know how I learned to read; I only remember my earliest reading, and the effect it had upon me; from that time I date my uninterrupted self-consciousness. My mother had left some romances behind her, which my father and I began to read after supper. At first it was only a question of practising me in reading by the aid of amusing books; but soon the interest became so lively, that we used to read in turns without stopping, and spent whole nights in this occupation. We were unable to leave off until the volume was finished. Sometimes, my father, hearing the swallows begin to twitter in the early morning, would say, quite ashamed, "Let us go to bed; I am more of a child than yourself."

In a short time I acquired, by this dangerous method, not only extreme facility in reading and understanding what I read, but a knowledge of the passions that was unique in a child of my age. I had no idea of things in themselves, although all the feelings of actual life were already known to me. I had conceived nothing, but felt everything. These confused emotions which I felt one after the other, certainly did not warp the reasoning powers which I did not as yet possess; but they shaped them in me of a peculiar stamp, and gave me odd and romantic notions of human life, of which experience and reflection have never been able wholly to cure me. . . .

The children of kings could not be more carefully looked after than I was during my early years — worshipped by all around me, and, which is far less common, treated as a beloved, never as a spoiled child. Till I left my father's house, I was never once allowed to run about the streets by myself with the other children; in my case no one ever had to satisfy or check any of those fantastic whims which are attributed to Nature, but are all in reality the result of education. I had the faults of my age: I was a chatterbox, a glutton, and, sometimes, a liar. I would have stolen fruits, bonbons, or eatables; but I have never found pleasure in doing harm or damage, in accusing others, or in tormenting poor dumb animals. I remember, however, that I once made water in a saucepan belonging to one of our neighbours, Madame Clot, while she was at church. I declare that, even now, the recollection of this makes me laugh, because Madame Clot, a good woman in other respects, was the most confirmed old grumbler I have ever known. Such is the brief and true story of all my childish offences.

How could I become wicked, when I had nothing but examples of gentleness before my eyes, and none around me but the best people in the world? My father, my aunt, my nurse, my relations, our friends, our neighbours, all who surrounded me, did not, it is true, obey me, but they loved me; and I loved them in return. My wishes were so little excited and so little opposed, that it did not occur to me to have any. I can swear that, until I served under a master, I never knew what a fancy was. Except during the time I spent in reading or writing in my father's company, or when my nurse took me for a walk, I was always with my aunt, sitting or standing by her side, watching her at her embroidery or listening to her singing; and I was content. Her cheerfulness, her gentleness and her pleasant face have stamped so deep and lively an impression on my mind that I can still see her manner, look, and attitude; I remember her affectionate language: I could describe what clothes she wore and how her head was dressed, not forgetting the two little curls of black hair on her temples, which she wore in accordance with the fashion of the time.

I am convinced that it is to her I owe the taste, or rather passion, for music, which only became fully developed in me a long time after-wards. She knew a prodigious number of tunes and songs which she used to sing in a very thin, gentle voice. This excellent woman's cheer-fulness of soul banished dreaminess and melancholy from herself and all around her. The attraction which her singing possessed for me was so great, that not only have several of her songs always remained in my memory, but even now, when I have lost her, and as I grew older, many of them, totally forgotten since the days of my childhood, return to my mind with inexpressible charm. Would anyone believe that I, an old dotard, eaten up by cares and troubles, sometime find myself weep-ing like a child, when I mumble one of those little airs in a voice already broken and trembling? . . .

Such were my earliest emotions on my entry into life; thus began to form or display itself in me that heart at once so proud and tender, that character so effeminate but yet indomitable, which, ever wavering between timidity and courage, weakness and self-control, has throughout my life made me inconsistent, and has caused abstinence and enjoyment, pleasure and prudence equally to elude my grasp.

This course of education was interrupted by an accident, the conse-quences of which have exercised an influence upon the remainder of my life. My father had a quarrel with a captain in the French army, named Gautier, who was connected with some of the members of the Common Council. This Gautier, a cowardly and insolent fellow (whose nose happened to bleed during the affray), in order to avenge himself, ac-cused my father of having drawn his sword within the city walls. My father, whom they wanted to send to prison, persisted that, in accord-ance with the law, the accuser ought to be imprisoned as well as him-self. Being unable to have his way in this, he preferred to quit Geneva and expatriate himself for the rest of his life, than to give way on a point in which honour and liberty appeared to him to be compromised.

I remained under the care of my uncle Bernard, who was at the time employed upon the fortifications of Geneva. His eldest daughter was dead, but he had a son of the same age as myself. We were sent together to Bossey, to board with the Protestant minister Lambercier, in order to learn, together with Latin, all the sorry trash which is included under the name of education.

Two years spent in the village in some degree softened my Roman roughness and made me a child again. At Geneva, where no tasks were imposed upon me, I loved reading and study, which were almost my only amusements; at Bossey, my tasks made me love the games which formed a break in them. The country was so new to me, that my enjoy-ment of it never palled. I conceived so lively an affection for it, that it has never since died out. The remembrance of the happy days I have spent there filled me with regretful longing for its pleasures, at all periods of my life, until the day which has brought me back to it. M. Lambercier was a very intelligent person, who, without neglecting our education, never imposed excessive tasks upon us. The fact that, in spite of my dislike of restraint, I have never recalled my hours of study with any feeling of disgust — and also that, even if I did not learn much from him, I learnt without difficulty what I did learn and never forgot it — is sufficient proof that his system of instruction was a good one. . . .

The life which I led at Bossey suited me so well that, had it only lasted longer, it would have completely decided my character. Tender, affectionate and gentle feelings formed its foundation. I believe that no individual of our species was naturally more free from vanity than myself. I raised myself by fits and starts to lofty flights, but immediately fell down again into my natural languor. My liveliest desire was to be loved by all who came near me. I was of a gentle disposition; my cousin and our guardians were the same. During two whole years I was neither the witness nor the victim of any violent feeling. Everything nourished in my heart those tendencies which it received from Nature. I knew no higher happiness than to see all the world satisfied with me and with everything. I shall never forget how, if I happen to hesitate when saying my catechism in church, nothing troubled me more than to observe signs of restlessness and dissatisfaction on Mademoiselle Lambercier's face. That alone troubled me more than the disgrace of failing in public, which, nevertheless, affected me greatly: for, although little susceptible to praise, I felt shame keenly; and I may say here that the thought of Mademoiselle's reproaches caused me less uneasiness than the fear of offending her.

When it was necessary, however, neither she nor her brother were wanting in severity; but, since this severity was nearly always just, and never passionate, it pained me without making me insubordinate. Failure to please grieved me more than punishment, and signs of dissatisfaction hurt me more than corporal chastisement. It is somewhat embarrassing to explain myself more clearly, but, nevertheless, I must do so. How differently would one deal with youth, if one could more clearly see the remote effects of the usual method of treatment, which is employed always without discrimination, frequently without discretion! The important lesson which may be drawn from an example as common as it is fatal makes me decide to mention it.

As Mademoiselle Lambercier had the affection of a mother for us, she also exercised the authority of one, and sometimes carried it so far as to inflict upon us the punishment of children when we had deserved it. For some time she was content with threats, and this threat of a punishment that was quite new to me appeared very terrible; but, after it had been carried out, I found the reality less terrible than the expectation; and, what was still more strange, this chastisement made me still more devoted to her who had inflicted it. It needed all the strength of this devotion and all my natural docility to keep myself from doing something which would have deservedly brought upon me a repetition of it; for I had found in the pain, even in the disgrace, a mixture of sensuality which had left me less afraid than desirous of experiencing it again from the same hand. No doubt some precocious sexual instinct was mingled with this feeling, for the same chastisement inflicted by her brother would not have seemed to me at all pleasant. But, considering his disposition, there was little cause to fear the substitution; and if I kept myself from deserving punishment, it was solely for fear of displeasing Mademoiselle Lambercier; for, so great is the power exercised over me by kindness, even by that which is due to the senses, that it has always controlled the latter in my heart.

The repetition of the offence, which I avoided without being afraid of it, occurred without any fault of mine, that is to say, of my will, and I may say that I profited by it without any qualm of conscience. But this second time was also the last; for Mademoiselle Lambercier, who had no doubt noticed something which convinced her that the punishment did not have the desired effect, declared that it tired her too much, and that she would abandon it. Until then we had slept in her room, sometimes even in her bed during the winter. Two days afterwards we were put to sleep in another room, and from that time I had the honour, which I would gladly have dispensed with, of being treated by her as a big boy.

Who would believe that this childish punishment, inflicted upon me when only eight years old by a young woman of thirty, disposed of my tastes, my desires, my passions, and my own self for the remainder of my life, and that in a manner exactly contrary to that which should have been the natural result? When my feelings were once inflamed, my desires so went astray that, limited to what I had already felt, they did not trouble themselves to look for anything else. In spite of my hot blood, which has been inflamed with sensuality almost from my birth, I kept myself free from every taint until the age when the coldest and most sluggish temperaments begin to develop. In torments for a long time, without knowing why, I devoured with burning glances all the pretty women I met; my imagination unceasingly recalled them to me, only to make use of them in my own fashion, and to make of them so many Mlles. Lambercier.

Even after I had reached years of maturity, this curious taste, always abiding with me and carried to depravity and even frenzy, preserved my morality, which it might naturally have been expected to destroy. If ever a bringing-up was chaste and modest, assuredly mine was. My three aunts were not only models of propriety, but reserved to a degree which has long since been unknown amongst women. My father, a man of pleasure, but a gallant of the old school, never said a word, even in the presence of women whom he loved more than others, which would have brought a blush to a maiden's cheek; and the respect due to children has never been so much insisted upon as in my family and in my presence. In this respect I found M. Lambercier equally careful; and an excellent servant was dismissed for having used a somewhat too free expression in our presence. Until I was a young man, I not only had no distinct idea of the union of the sexes, but the confused notion which I had regarding it never presented itself to me except in a hateful and disgusting form. For common prostitutes I felt a loathing which has never been effaced: the sight of a profligate always filled me with contempt, even with affright. My horror of debauchery became thus pronounced ever since the day when, walking to Little Sacconex by a hollow way, I saw on both sides holes in the ground, where I was told that these creatures carried on their intercourse. The thought of the one always brought back to my mind the copulation of dogs, and the bare recollection was sufficient to disgust me.

This tendency of my bringing-up, in itself adapted to delay the first outbreaks of an inflammable temperament, was assisted, as I have already said, by the direction which the first indications of sensuality took in my case. Only busying my imagination with what I had actually felt, in spite of most uncomfortable effervescence of blood, I only knew how to turn my desires in the direction of that kind of pleasure with which I was acquainted, without ever going as far as that which had been made hateful to me, and which, without my having the least suspicion of it, was so closely related to the other. In my foolish fancies, in my erotic frenzies, in the extravagant acts to which they sometimes led me, I had recourse in my imagination to the assistance of the other sex, without ever thinking that it was serviceable for any purpose than that for which I was burning to make use of it.

In this manner, then, in spite of an ardent, lascivious and precocious temperament, I passed the age of puberty without desiring, even without knowing of any other sensual pleasures than those of which Mademoiselle Lambercier had most innocently given me the idea; and when, in course of time, I became a man, that which should have destroyed me again preserved me. My old childish taste, instead of disappearing, became so associated with the other, that I could never banish it from the desires kindled by my senses; and this madness, joined to my natural shyness, has always made me very unenterprising with women, for want of courage to say all or power to do all. The kind of enjoyment, of which the other was only for me the final consummation could neither be appropriated by him who longed for it, nor guessed by her who was able to bestow it. Thus I have spent my life in idle longing, without saying a word, in the presence of those whom I loved most. Too bashful to declare my taste, I at least satisfied it in situations which had reference to it and kept up the idea of it. To lie at the feet of an imperious mistress, to obey her commands, to ask her forgiveness — this was for me a sweet enjoyment; and, the more my lively imagination heated my blood, the more I presented the appearance of a bashful lover. It may be easily imagined that this manner of making love does not lead to very speedy results, and is not very dangerous to the virtue of those who are its object. For this reason I have rarely possessed, but have none the less enjoyed myself in my own way — that is to say, in imagination. Thus it has happened that my senses, in harmony with my timid disposition and my romantic spirit, have kept my sentiments pure and my morals blameless, owing to the very tastes which, combined with a little more impudence, might have plunged me into the most brutal sensuality.

I have taken the first and most difficult step in the dark and dirty labyrinth of my confessions. It is easier to admit that which is criminal than that which is ridiculous and makes a man feel ashamed. Henceforth I am sure of myself; after having ventured to say so much, I can shrink from nothing. One may judge what such confessions have cost me, from the fact that, during the whole course of my life, I have never dared to declare my folly to those whom I loved with the frenzy of a passion which deprived me of sight and hearing, which robbed me of my senses and caused me to tremble all over with a convulsive movement. I have never brought myself, even when on most intimate terms, to ask women to grant me the only favour of all which was wanting. This never happened to me but once — in my childhood, with a girl of my own age; even then, it was she who first proposed it.

While thus going back to the first traces of my inner life, I find elements which sometimes appear incompatible, and yet have united in order to produce with vigour a simple and uniform effect; and I find others which, although apparently the same, have formed combinations so different, owing to the co-operation of certain circumstances, that one would never imagine that these elements were in any way connected. Who, for instance, would believe that one of the most powerful movements of my soul was tempered in the same spring from which a stream of sensuality and effeminacy has entered my blood? Without leaving the subject of which I have just spoken, I shall produce by means of it a very different impression.

One day I was learning my lesson by myself in the room next to the kitchen. The servant had put Mademoiselle Lambercier's combs in front of the fire-place to dry. When she came back to fetch them, she found one with a whole row of teeth broken. Who was to blame for the damage? No one except myself had entered the room. On being questioned, I denied that I had touched the comb. M. and Mademoiselle Lambercier both began to admonish, to press, and to threaten me; I obstinately persisted in my denial; but the evidence was too strong, and outweighed all my protestations, although it was the first time that I had been found to lie so boldly. The matter was regarded as serious, as in fact it deserved to be. The mischievousness, the falsehood, the obstinacy appeared equally deserving of punishment; but this time it was not by Mademoiselle Lambercier that chastisement was inflicted. My uncle Bernard was written to, and he came. My poor cousin was accused of another equally grave offence; we were involved in the same punishment. It was terrible. Had they wished to look for the remedy in the evil itself and to deaden for ever my depraved senses, they could not have set to work better, and for a long time my senses left me undisturbed.

They could not draw from me the desired confession. Although I was several times brought up before them and reduced to a pitiable condition, I remained unshaken. I would have endured death, and made up my mind to do so. Force was obliged to yield to the diabolical obstinacy of a child — as they called my firmness. At last I emerged from this cruel trial, utterly broken, but triumphant.

It is now nearly fifty years since this incident took place, and I have no fear of being punished again for the same thing. Well, then, I declare in the sight of heaven that I was innocent of the offence, that I neither broke nor touched the comb, that I never went near the fireplace, and had never even thought of doing so. It would be useless to ask me how the damage was done: I do not know, and I cannot understand; all that I know for certain is, that I had nothing to do with it.

Imagine a child, shy and obedient in ordinary life, but fiery, proud, and unruly in his passions: a child who had always been led by the voice of reason and always treated with gentleness, justice, and consideration, who had not even a notion of injustice, and who for the first time becomes acquainted with so terrible an example of it on the part of the very people whom he most loves and respects! What an upset of ideas! what a disturbance of feelings! what revolution in his heart, in his brain, in the whole of his little intellectual and moral being! Imagine all this, I say, if possible. As for myself, I feel incapable of disentangling and following up the least trace of what then took place within me.

I had not yet sense enough to feel how much appearances were against me, and to put myself in the place of the others. I kept to my own place, and all that I felt was the harshness of a frightful punishment for an offence which I had not committed. The bodily pain, although severe, I felt but little: all I felt was indignation, rage, despair. My cousin, whose case was almost the same, and who had been punished for an involuntary mistake as if it had been a premeditated act, following my example, flew into a rage, and worked himself up to the same pitch of excitement as myself. Both in the same bed, we embraced each other with convulsive transports: we felt suffocated; and when at length our young hearts, somewhat relieved, were able to vent their wrath, we sat upright in bed and began to shout, times without number, with all our might: *Carnifex! carnifex! carnifex!* [1] . . .

With the above incident the tranquillity of my childish life was over. From that moment I ceased to enjoy a pure happiness, and even at the present day I feel that the recollection of the charms of my childhood ceases there. We remained a few months longer at Bossey. We were there, as the first man is represented to us — still in the earthly paradise, but we no longer enjoyed it; in appearance our condition was the same, in reality it was quite a different manner of existence. Attachment, respect, intimacy, and confidence no longer united pupils and guides: we no longer regarded them as gods, who were able to read in our hearts; we became less ashamed of doing wrong and more afraid of being accused; we began to dissemble, to be insubordinate, to lie. All

1. Executioner, torturer.

the vices of our age corrupted our innocence and threw a veil of ugliness over our amusements. Even the country lost in our eyes that charm of gentleness and simplicity which goes to the heart. It appeared to us lonely and sombre: it seemed as it were covered with a veil which concealed its beauties from our eyes. We ceased to cultivate our little gardens, our plants, our flowers. We no longer scratched up the ground gently, or cried with joy when we saw the seed which we had sown beginning to sprout. We were disgusted with the life, and others were disgusted with us; my uncle took us away, and we separated from M. and Mademoiselle Lambercier, having had enough of each other, and feeling but little regret at the separation. . . .

After long deliberation as to the bent of my natural inclination, a profession was determined upon for which I had the least taste; I was put with M. Masseron, the town clerk, in order to learn, under his tuition, the useful trade of a *fee-grabber*.[2] This nickname was extremely distasteful to me; the hope of gaining a number of crowns in a somewhat sordid business by no means flattered my pride; the occupation itself appeared to me wearisome and unendurable; the constant application, the feeling of servitude completed my dislike, and I never entered the office without a feeling of horror, which daily increased in intensity. M. Masseron, on his part, was ill-satisfied with me, and treated me with contempt; he continually reproached me with my dulness and stupidity, dinning into my ears every day that my uncle had told him that I knew something, whereas, in reality, I knew nothing; that he had promised him a sharp lad, and had given him a jackass. At last I was dismissed from the office in disgrace as being utterly incapable, and M. Masseron's clerks declared that I was good for nothing except to handle a file.

My calling being thus settled, I was apprenticed, not, however, to a watchmaker, but to an engraver. The contempt with which I had been treated by M. Masseron had made me very humble, and I obeyed without a murmur. My new master, M. Ducommun, was a rough and violent young man, who in a short time succeeded in tarnishing all the brightness of my childhood, stupefying my loving and lively nature, and reducing me, in mind as well as in position, to a real state of apprenticeship. My Latin, my antiquities, my history, were all for a long time forgotten; I did not even remember that there had ever been any Romans in the world. My father, when I went to see him, no longer found in me his idol; for the ladies I was no longer the gallant Jean Jacques; and I felt so certain myself that the Lamberciers would not have recognised their pupil in me, that I was ashamed to pay them a visit, and have never seen them since. The vilest tastes, the lowest street-blackguardism took the place of my simple amusements and effaced even the remembrance of them. I must, in spite of a most upright training, have had a great propensity to degenerate; for the change took place with great rapidity, without the least trouble . . .

My master's tyranny at length made the work, of which I should have

2. *Grapignan:* a slang term for a lawyer.

been very fond, altogether unbearable, and filled me with vices which I should otherwise have hated, such as lying, idleness and thieving. The recollection of the alteration produced in me by that period of my life has taught me, better than anything else, the difference between filial dependence and abject servitude. Naturally shy and timid, no fault was more foreign to my disposition than impudence; but I had enjoyed an honourable liberty, which hitherto had only been gradually restrained, and at length disappeared altogether. I was bold with my father, unrestrained with M. Lambercier, and modest with my uncle; I became timid with my master, and from that moment I was a lost child. Accustomed to perfect equality in my intercourse with my superiors, knowing no pleasure which was not within my reach, seeing no dish of which I could not have a share, having no desire which I could not have openly expressed, and carrying my heart upon my lips — it is easy to judge what I was bound to become, in a house in which I did not venture to open my mouth, where I was obliged to leave the table before the meal was half over, and the room as soon as I had nothing more to do there; where, incessantly fettered to my work, I saw only objects of enjoyment for others and of privation for myself; where the sight of the liberty enjoyed by my master and companions increased the weight of my servitude; where, in disputes about matters as to which I was best informed, I did not venture to open my mouth; where, in short, everything that I saw became for my heart an object of longing, simply because I was deprived of all. . . .

In this manner I learnt to covet in silence, to dissemble, to lie, and, lastly, to steal — an idea which, up to that time, had never even entered my mind, and of which since then I have never been able to cure myself completely. Covetousness and weakness always lead in that direction. This explains why all servants are rogues, and why all apprentices ought to be; but the latter, in a peaceful state of equality, where all that they see is within their reach, lose, as they grow up, this disgraceful propensity. Not having had the same advantages, I have not been able to reap the same benefits.

It is nearly always good, but badly-directed principles, that make a child take the first step towards evil. In spite of continual privations and temptations, I had been more than a year with my master without being able to make up my mind to take anything, even eatables. My first theft was a matter of obliging some one else, but it opened the door to others, the motive of which was not so praiseworthy.

My master had a journeyman, named M. Verrat, whose house was in the neighbourhood, and had a garden some way off which produced very fine asparagus. M. Verrat, who was not too well supplied with money, conceived the idea of stealing some of his mother's young asparagus and selling it in order to provide himself with two or three good breakfasts. As he was unwilling to run the risk himself, and was not very active, he selected me for the expedition. After some preliminary cajoleries, which the more easily succeeded with me as I did not see their aim, he proposed it to me as an idea that had struck him on the spur of the moment. I strongly opposed it; he persisted. I have never been able to resist flattery: I gave in. I went every morning to gather a crop of the finest asparagus, and carried it to the Molard, where some good woman, who saw that I had just stolen it, told me so to my face in order to get it cheaper. In my fright I took whatever she chose to offer me, and took it to Verrat. The amount was immediately converted into a breakfast, of which I was the purveyor, and which he shared with another companion; I myself was quite satisfied with a few scraps, and never even touched their wine.

This little arrangement continued several days, without its even occurring to me to rob the robber, and to levy my tithe of the proceeds of M. Verrat's asparagus. I performed my part in the transaction with the greatest loyalty; my only motive was to please him who prompted me to carry it out. And yet, if I had been caught, what blows, abuse, and cruel treatment should I have had to endure, while the wretch, who would have been sure to give me the lie, would have been believed on his word, and I should have suffered double punishment for having had the impudence to accuse him, seeing that he was a journeyman, while I was only an apprentice! So true it is that, in every condition of life, the strong man who is guilty saves himself at the expense of the innocent who is weak.

In this manner I learned that stealing was not so terrible a thing as I had imagined, and I soon knew how to make such good use of my discovery, that nothing I desired, if it was within my reach, was safe from me. I was not absolutely ill-fed, and abstinence was only rendered difficult to me from seeing that my master observed it so ill himself. The custom of sending young people from the table when the most appetising dishes are brought on appears to me admirably adapted to make them gluttons as well as thieves. In a short time I became both the one and the other; and, as a rule, I came off very well; occasionally, when I was caught, very badly.

I shudder, and at the same time laugh, when I remember an apple-hunt which cost me dear. These apples were at the bottom of a store-room, which was lighted from the kitchen by means of a high grating. One day, when I was alone in the house, I climbed upon the kneading-trough, in order to look at the precious fruit in the garden of the Hesperides, which was out of my reach. I went to fetch the spit to see if I could touch the apples; it was too short. To make it longer, I tied on to it another little spit which was used for small game, for my master was very fond of sport. I thrust several times without success; at last, to my great delight, I felt that I had secured an apple. I pulled very gently; the apple was close to the grating; I was ready to catch hold of it. But who can describe my grief, when I found that it was too large to pass through the bars? How many expedients I tried, to get it through! I had to find supports to keep the spit in its place, a knife long enough to divide the apple, a lath to hold it up. At last I managed to divide it, and hoped to be able to pull the pieces towards me one after the other; but no sooner were they separated than they both fell into the store-room. Compassionate reader, share my affliction!

I by no means lost courage; but I had lost considerable time. I was afraid of being surprised. I put off a more lucky attempt till the following day, and returned to my work as quietly as if I had done nothing, without thinking of the two tell-tale witnesses in the store-room.

The next day, finding the opportunity favourable, I made a fresh attempt. I climbed upon my stool, lengthened the spit, adjusted it, and was ready to make a lunge . . . but, unfortunately, the dragon was not asleep; all at once the door of the store-room opened, my master came out, folded his arms, looked at me, and said, "Courage!" . . . the pen falls from my hand.

In consequence of continuous ill-treatment I soon became less sensitive to it, and regarded it as a kind of compensation for theft, which gave me the right to continue the latter. Instead of looking back and considering the punishment, I looked forward and thought of revenge. I considered that, if I were beaten as a rogue, I was entitled to behave like one. I found that stealing and a flogging went together, and constituted a sort of bargain, and that, if I performed my part, I could safely leave my master to carry out his own. With this idea, I began to steal more quietly than before. I said to myself: "What will be the result? I shall be flogged. Never mind; I am made to be flogged." . . .

This being understood, it will be easy to comprehend one of my apparent inconsistencies — the union of an almost sordid avarice with the greatest contempt for money. It is a piece of furniture in which I find so little convenience, that it never enters my mind to long for it when I have not got it, and that, when I have got it, I keep it for a long time without spending it, for want of knowing how to make use of it in a way to please myself; but if a convenient and agreeable opportunity presents itself, I make such good use of it that my purse is empty before I know it. Besides this, one need not expect to find in me that curious characteristic of misers — that of spending for the sake of ostentation; on the contrary, I spend in secret for the sake of enjoyment; far from glorying in my expenditure, I conceal it. I feel so strongly that money is of no use to me, that I am almost ashamed to have any, still more to make use of it. If I had ever had an income sufficient to live comfortably upon, I am certain that I should never have been tempted to be a miser. I should have spent it all, without attempting to increase it; but my precarious circumstances make me careful. I worship freedom; I abhor restraint, trouble, dependence. As long as the money in my purse lasts, it assures my independence; it relieves me of the trouble of finding expedients to replenish it, a necessity which always inspired me with dread; but the fear of seeing it exhausted makes me hoard it carefully. The money which a man possesses is the instrument of freedom; that which we eagerly pursue is the instrument of slavery. Therefore I hold fast to that which I have, and desire nothing.

My disinterestedness is, therefore, nothing but idleness; the pleasure of possession is not worth the trouble of acquisition. In like manner, my extravagance is nothing but idleness; when the opportunity of spending agreeably presents itself, it cannot be too profitably employed. Money tempts me less than things, because between money and the possession of the desired object there is always an intermediary, whereas between the thing itself and the enjoyment of it there is none. If I see the thing, it tempts me; if I only see the means of gaining possession of it, it does not. For this reason I have committed thefts, and even now I sometimes pilfer trifles which tempt me, and which I prefer to take rather than to ask for; but neither when a child nor a grown-up man do I ever remember to have robbed anyone of a farthing, except on one occasion, fifteen years ago, when I stole seven *livres* ten *sous*. The incident is worth recording, for it contains a most extraordinary mixture of folly and impudence, which I should have found difficulty in believing if it concerned anyone but myself.

It took place at Paris. I was walking with M. de Franceuil in the Palais-Royal about five o'clock. He pulled out his watch, looked at it, and said: "Let us go to the Opera." I agreed; we went. He took two tickets for the amphitheatre, gave me one, and went on in front with the other. I followed him; he went in. Entering after him, I found the door blocked. I looked, and seeing everybody standing up, thought it would be easy to lose myself in the crowd, or at any rate to make M. de Franceuil believe that I had lost myself. I went out, took back my check, then my money, and went off, without thinking that as soon as I had reached the door everybody had taken their seats, and that M. de Franceuil clearly saw that I was no longer there.

As nothing was ever more foreign to my disposition than such behaviour, I mention it in order to show that there are moments of semi-delirium during which men must not be judged by their actions. I did not exactly want to steal the money, I wanted to steal the employment of it; the less of a theft it was, the greater its disgracefulness.

I should never finish these details if I were to follow all the paths along which, during my apprenticeship, I descended from the sublimity of heroism to the depths of worthlessness. And yet, although I adopted the vices of my position, I could not altogether acquire a taste for them. I wearied of the amusements of my companions; and when excessive restraint had rendered work unendurable to me, I grew tired of everything. This renewed my taste for reading, which I had for some time lost. This reading, for which I stole time from my work, became a new offence which brought new punishment upon me. The taste for it, provoked by constraint, became a passion, and soon a regular madness. La Tribu, a well-known lender of books, provided me with all kinds of literature. Good or bad, all were alike to me; I had no choice, and read everything with equal avidity. I read at the work-table, I read on my errands, I read in the wardrobe, and forgot myself for hours together; my head became giddy with reading; I could do nothing else. My master watched me, surprised me, beat me, took away my books. How many volumes were torn, burnt, and thrown out of the window! how many works were left in odd volumes in La Tribu's stock! When I had no more money to pay her, I gave her my shirts, neckties and clothes; my three sous of pocket-money were regularly taken to her every Sunday.

Well, then, I shall be told, money had become necessary to me. That is true; but it was not until my passion for reading had deprived me of all activity. Completely devoted to my new hobby, I did nothing but read, and no longer stole. Here again is one of my characteristic peculiarities. In the midst of a certain attachment to any manner of life, a mere trifle distracts me, alters me, rivets my attention, and finally becomes a passion. Then everything is forgotten; I no longer think of anything except the new object which engrosses my attention. My heart beat with impatience to turn over the leaves of the new book which I had in my pocket; I pulled it out as soon as I was alone, and thought no more of rummaging my master's work-room. I can hardly believe that I should have stolen even if I had had more expensive tastes. Limited to the present, it was not in my way to make preparations in this manner for the future. La Tribu gave me credit, the payments on account were small, and, as soon as I had my book in my pocket, I forgot everything else. The money which came to me honestly passed in the same manner into the hands of this woman; and, when she pressed me, nothing was easier to dispose of than my own property. It required too much foresight to steal in advance, and I was not even tempted to steal in order to pay.

In consequence of quarrels, blows, and secret and ill-chosen reading, my disposition became savage and taciturn; my mind became altogether perverted, and I lived like a misanthrope. However, if my good taste did not keep me from silly and insipid books, my good fortune preserved me from such as were filthy and licentious; not that La Tribu, a woman in all respects most accommodating, would have made any scruple about lending them to me; but, in order to increase their importance, she always mentioned them to me with an air of mystery which had just the effect of making me refuse them, as much from disgust as from shame; and chance aided my modest disposition so well, that I was more than thirty years old before I set eyes upon any of those dangerous books which a fine lady finds inconvenient because they can only be read with one hand.

In less than a year I exhausted La Tribu's little stock, and want of occupation, during my spare time, became painful to me. I had been cured of my childish and knavish propensities by my passion for reading, and even by the books I read, which, although ill-chosen and frequently bad, filled my heart with nobler sentiments than those with which my sphere of life had inspired me. Disgusted with everything that was within my reach, and feeling that everything which might have tempted me was too far removed from me, I saw nothing possible which might have flattered my heart. My excited senses had long clamoured for an enjoyment, the object of which I could not even imagine. I was as far removed from actual enjoyment as if I had been sexless; and, already fully developed and sensitive, I sometimes thought of my crazes, but saw nothing beyond them. In this strange situation, my restless imagination entered upon an occupation which saved me from myself and calmed my growing sensuality. This consisted in feeding myself upon the situations which had interested me in the course of my reading, in recalling them, in varying them, in combining them, in making them so truly my own that I became one of the persons who filled my imagination, and always saw myself in the situations most agreeable to my taste; and that, finally, the fictitious state in which I succeeded in putting myself made me forget my actual state with which I was so dissatisfied. This love of imaginary objects, and the readiness with which I occupied myself with them, ended by disgusting me with everything around me, and decided that liking for solitude which has never left me. In the sequel we shall see more than once the curious effects of this disposition, apparently so gloomy and misanthropic, but which is really due to a too affectionate, too loving and too tender heart, which, being unable to find any in existence resembling it, is obliged to nourish itself with fancies. For the present, it is sufficient for me to have defined the origin and first cause of a propensity which has modified all my passions, and which, restraining them by means of themselves, has always made me slow to act, owing to my excessive impetuosity in desire.

In this manner I reached my sixteenth year, restless, dissatisfied with myself and everything, without any of the tastes of my condition of life, without any of the pleasures of my age, consumed by desires of the object of which I was ignorant, weeping without any cause for tears, sighing without knowing why — in short, tenderly caressing my chimeras, since I saw nothing around me which counterbalanced them. On Sundays, my fellow-apprentices came to fetch me after service to go and amuse myself with them. I would gladly have escaped from them if I had been able; but, once engaged in their amusements, I became more excited and went further than any of them; it was as difficult to set me going as to stop me. Such was always my disposition. During our walks outside the city I always went further than any of them without thinking about my return, unless others thought of it for me. Twice I was caught: the gates were shut before I could get back. The next day I was treated as may be imagined; the second time I was promised such a reception if it ever happened again, that I resolved not to run the risk of it; yet this third time, so dreaded, came to pass. My watchfulness was rendered useless by a confounded Captain Minutoli, who always shut the gate at which he was on guard half-an-hour before the others. I was returning with two companions. About half a league from the city I heard the retreat sounded: I doubled my pace: I heard the tattoo beat, and ran with all my might. I arrived out of breath and bathed in perspiration; my heart beat; from a distance I saw the soldiers at their posts; I rushed up and cried out with a voice half-choked. It was too late! Twenty paces from the outposts, I saw the first bridge raised. I shuddered when I saw those terrible horns rising in the air — a sinister and fatal omen of the destiny which that moment was opening for me.

In the first violence of my grief I threw myself on the *glacis* and bit the ground. My companions, laughing at their misfortune, immediately made up their minds what to do. I did the same, but my resolution was different from theirs. On the spot I swore never to return to my master; and the next morning, when they entered the city after the gates were opened, I said good-bye to them for ever, only begging them secretly to inform my cousin Bernard of the resolution I had taken, and of the place where he might be able to see me once more. . . .

BOOK V

[1732–1736]

. . . I do not know how to describe my condition; it was a kind of fright mingled with impatience, during which I was so afraid of what I longed for, that I sometimes seriously endeavoured to think of some decent way of avoiding the promised happiness. Consider my ardent and lascivious temperament, my heated blood, my heart intoxicated with love, my vigorous health, my age. Remember that, in this condition, thirsting after women, I had never yet touched one; that imagination, need, vanity, and curiosity, all combined to devour me with the burning desire of being a man and showing myself one. Add to this, above all — for it must never be forgotten — that my tender and lively attachment to her,[3] far from diminishing, had only become warmer every day, that I was never happy except with her; that I never left her except to think of her; that my heart was full, not only of her goodness and amiability, but of her sex, her form, her person; in a word, of her, under every aspect in which she could be dear to me. Do not imagine, that, because she was ten or twelve years older than myself, she had either grown old, or appeared so to me. During the five or six years since the first sight of her had so enchanted me, she had really altered very little, and, in my eyes, not at all. She had always appeared charming to me, and, at that time, everyone still considered her so. Her figure alone had become a little stouter. In other respects, it was the same eye, the same complexion, the same bosom, the same features, the same beautiful fair hair, the same cheerfulness, even the voice was the same, the silvery voice of youth, which always made so deep an impression upon me, that, even now, I cannot hear without emotion the tones of a pretty girlish voice.

What I had to fear in the expectation of possessing one who was so dear to me, was naturally the anticipation of it, and the inability to

3. Mme. de Warens.

control my desires and imagination sufficiently to remain master of myself. It will be seen that, at an advanced age, the mere idea of certain trifling favours which awaited me in the company of the person I loved, heated my blood to such a degree that it was impossible for me to make with impunity the short journey which separated me from her. How then was it that, in the flower of my youth, I felt so little eagerness for the first enjoyment? How was it that I could see the hour approach with more pain than pleasure? How was it that, instead of the rapture which should have intoxicated me, I almost felt repugnance and fear? There is no doubt that, if I had been able to escape my happiness with decency, I should have done so with all my heart. I have promised singularities in the history of my attachment to her; this is surely one which would never have been expected.

The reader, already disgusted, is doubtless of opinion that, being already possessed by another man, she degraded herself in my eyes by distributing her favours, and that a feeling of dis-esteem cooled those with which she had inspired me. He is mistaken. This distribution was certainly very painful to me, as much in consequence of a very natural feeling of delicacy as because I really considered it unworthy of her and myself; but it never altered my feelings towards her, and I can swear that I never loved her more tenderly than when I had so little desire to possess her. I know too well her modest heart and her cold temperament to think for a moment that sensual pleasure had anything to do with this abandonment of herself; I was perfectly convinced that nothing but anxiety to save me from dangers that were otherwise almost inevitable and to preserve me entirely for myself and my duties, caused her to violate a duty which she did not regard in the same light as other women, as will be shown later. I pitied her and pitied myself. I should have liked to say to her: "No, mamma, it is not necessary; I will answer for myself without that." But I did not dare to do so — first, because it was not a thing to say, and, in the second place, because in the main I felt that it was not true, and that, in reality, there was only *one* woman who could protect me against other women and secure me against temptations. Without desiring to possess her, I was very glad that she prevented me from desiring the possession of other women, to such an extent did I look upon everything as a misfortune which would draw me away from her. Our long-continued and innocent intercourse, far from weakening my feelings for her, had strengthened them, but, at the same time, had given them a different turn, which made them more affectionate, more tender perhaps, but also less sensual. Having so long called her mamma, having enjoyed with her the intimacy of a son, I had become accustomed to look upon myself as one. I believe that this was really the cause of the little eagerness I felt to possess her, although she was so dear to me. I well remember that my early feelings, without being livelier, were more sensual. At Annecy,[4] I was intoxicated; at Chambéri, I was no longer so. I still

4. Where Rousseau first met Mme. de Warens.

loved her as passionately as possible; but I loved her more for her own sake than for my own, or, at least, I sought happiness with her, rather than enjoyment; she was for me more than a sister, more than a mother, more than a friend, even more than a mistress; and for that very reason she was not a mistress for me. In short, I loved her too well to desire to possess her; that is most clearly prominent in my ideas.

The day, more dreaded than wished for, at length arrived. I promised everything, and kept my word. My heart sealed all my vows, without desiring their reward. However, I obtained it. For the first time I found himself in the arms of a woman, a woman whom I adored. Was I happy? No; I tasted pleasure. A certain unconquerable feeling of melancholy poisoned its charm; I felt as if I had been guilty of incest. Two or three times, while pressing her in ecstasy to my arms, I wetted her bosom with my tears. She, on the other hand, was neither sad nor excited; she was tender and calm. As she was by no means sensual and had not looked for enjoyment, she felt no gratification, and never experienced remorse.

I repeat it: all her faults were due to her errors, none to her passions. She was well born, her heart was pure, she loved propriety; her inclinations were upright and virtuous, her taste was refined; she was formed for an elegance of manners which she always loved but never followed, because, instead of listening to her heart, which always guided her aright, she listened to her reason, which guided her wrongly; for when the latter is led astray by false principles, these are always belied by its real feelings; but, unfortunately, she rather prided herself on her philosophy, and the morals which she drew from it corrupted those which her heart dictated.

M. de Tavel, her first lover, was her instructor in philosophy, and the principles which he taught her were those which he found necessary, in order to seduce her. Finding her attached to her husband, devoted to her duties, always cold, calculating, and inaccessible to sensual feelings, he endeavoured to reach her by sophistries, and succeeded in convincing her that the duties, to which she was so attached, were so much catechism-nonsense, intended solely for the amusement of children; that the union of the sexes was in itself a matter of the greatest indifference; that conjugal fidelity was merely an apparent obligation, the inner morality of which only had reference to public opinion; that the husband's repose was the only rule of duty which the wife need respect, so that secret acts of unfaithfulness, being nothing to him against whom they were committed, were equally nothing to the conscience; in short, he persuaded her that the thing was nothing in itself, that only scandal called it into existence, and that every woman who appeared virtuous owed it to that alone. In this manner the wretch attained his object, by corrupting the mind of a child whose heart he had been unable to corrupt. He was punished for it by an all-devouring jealousy, being convinced that she treated him as he had persuaded her to treat her husband. I do not know whether he was mistaken in this.

The minister Perret was supposed to have been his successor. All I know is, that the cold temperament of this young woman, which ought to have protected her against this system, was just what subsequently prevented her from abandoning it. She could not conceive that anyone should attach such importance to that which possessed no importance for her. She never honoured by the name of virtue an abstinence which cost her so little.

She hardly ever misused these false principles for her own sake; but she misused them for the sake of others, and that in consequence of another maxim almost equally false, but more in harmony with the goodness of her heart. She always believed that nothing attached a man so strongly to a woman as possession; and, although her love for her friends was only friendship, it was a friendship so tender, that she employed all possible means at her disposal to attach them more strongly to her. The remarkable thing is, that she nearly always succeeded. She was so truly amiable, that, the greater the intimacy in which one lived with her, the more one found fresh reasons for loving her. Another thing worthy of notice is that, after her first weakness, she rarely bestowed her favours except upon the unfortunate; persons of distinction spent their labour upon her in vain; but, if she once began to feel sympathy for a man, he must have been little deserving of love if she did not end by loving him. If she sometimes chose those who were unworthy of her, the blame rested, not on any low inclinations, which were far removed from her noble heart, but only on her too generous, too kindly, too compassionate, and too feeling disposition, which she did not always control with sufficient judgment.

If some false principles led her astray, how many admirable ones did she possess, to which she always remained constant! By how many virtues did she make up for her weaknesses, if those errors can be so called, with which the senses had so little to do! The same man, who deceived her in one point, instructed her admirably in a thousand others; and, as her passions were not so unruly as to prevent her from following her reason, she took the right path when her sophisms did not mislead her. Her motives, even in her errors, were praiseworthy; owing to her mistaken ideas, she might do wrong, but she was incapable of doing so wilfully. She abhorred duplicity and lying; she was just, fair, humane, disinterested, faithful to her word, her friends, and the duties which she regarded as such, incapable of revenge or hatred, without the least idea that there was any merit in forgiveness. Finally, to return to those qualities which less admit of excuse, without knowing how to estimate the value of her favours, she never made a common trade of them; she was lavish of them, but she never sold them, although she was always at her wit's end how to live; and I venture to assert, that if Socrates could esteem Aspasia,[5] he would have respected Madame de Warens.

5. The famous Milesian courtesan who became the mistress of Pericles; she was also known for her intellectual distinction.

I know beforehand, that, when I ascribe to her a sensitive disposition and a cold temperament, I shall, as usual, be accused of contradiction, and with as much reason. It may be that Nature was wrong, and that this combination ought not to have existed; I only know that it did exist. All who have known Madame de Warens, many of whom are still alive, know well that this was the case. I will even venture to add, that she never knew but *one* real pleasure in life — to procure enjoyment for those whom she loved. Anyone is at liberty to judge of that as he pleases, and learnedly prove that it is not true. My duty is to state the truth, not to make people believe it.

By degrees I became acquainted with all I have just said in the course of the conversations which succeeded our union, and which alone rendered it delightful. She had been right in hoping that her complaisance would be useful to me; I derived great advantages from it as regards my instruction. Hitherto, she had only spoken to me of myself alone as if she had been talking to a child. She now began to treat me as a man, and spoke to me of herself. All that she said to me was so interesting, and I felt so touched by it, that, when I reflected, I derived greater advantage from these confidences than from her instructions. When we truly feel that the heart speaks, our own opens to receive its confidences, and all the morality of a pedagogue will never be worth the tender and loving chatter of a clever woman, who has gained our affection. . . .

It is sometimes said that the sword wears out the scabbard. That is my history. My passions have made me live, and my passions have killed me. What passions? will be asked. Trifles, the most childish things in the world, which, however, excited me as much as if the possession of Helen or the throne of the universe had been at stake. In the first place — women. When I possessed one, my senses were calm; my heart, never. The needs of love devoured me in the midst of enjoyment; I had a tender mother, a dear friend; but I needed a mistress. I imagined one in her place; I represented her to myself in a thousand forms, in order to deceive myself. If I had thought that I held mamma in my arms when I embraced her, these embraces would have been no less lively, but all my desires would have been extinguished; I should have sobbed from affection, but I should never have felt any enjoyment. Enjoyment! Does this ever fall to the lot of man? If I had ever, a single time in my life, tasted all the delights of love in their fulness, I do not believe that my frail existence could have endured it; I should have died on the spot.

Thus I was burning with love, without an object; and it is this state, perhaps, that is most exhausting. I was restless, tormented by the hopeless condition of poor mamma's affairs, and her imprudent conduct, which were bound to ruin her completely at no distant date. My cruel imagination, which always anticipates misfortunes, exhibited this particular one to me continually, in all its extent and in all its results. I already saw myself compelled by want to separate from her to whom

I had devoted my life, and without whom I could not enjoy it. Thus my soul was ever in a state of agitation; I was devoured alternately by desires and fears. . . .

The decline in my health affected my temper and moderated the ardour of my imagination. Feeling myself weaker, I became quieter, and lost, in some degree, my mania for travelling. I remained more at home, and was attacked, not by ennui, but by melancholy; my passions were succeeded by hysteria; my languor changed to sadness; I wept and I sighed about nothing; I felt life slipping away from me before I had enjoyed it. I sighed over the state in which I was leaving my poor mamma; over the state into which I saw her ready to fall. I can assert that my only regret was at leaving her, and leaving her in so lamentable a condition. At length, I became really ill. She nursed me more tenderly than any mother ever nursed her child; and this was beneficial to herself, since it diverted her from schemes, and kept away the promoters of them. How sweet would death have been if it had come then! If I had not enjoyed many of the good things of life, I had felt but few of its sorrows. My peaceful soul would have departed without that cruel feeling of the injustice of mankind, which poisons both life and death. I should have had the consolation that I was surviving myself in the better half of me; it could hardly have been called death. Had it not been for the uneasiness I felt concerning her lot, I could have died as easily as I could have fallen asleep; and my very uneasiness was connected with an affectionate and tender object, which softened its bitterness. I said to her: "My whole being is in your hands; make it happy." Two or three times, when I was worse than usual, I got up during the night and dragged myself to her room, to give her advice upon her conduct, which I may say was thoroughly correct and sensible, but in which my sympathy for her was more marked than anything else. As if tears had been food and medicine, those which I shed by her side, sitting on her bed, holding her hands in mine, seemed to give me strength. The hours slipped away in these nightly conversations, and I left her, feeling better than when I entered; calm and content with the promises which she had made me, with the hopes with which she had inspired me, I went to sleep, peace in my heart, and resigned to Providence.

After I have had so many reasons to hate life, after all the storms which have shaken my existence, and only make it a burden to me, may God grant that the death which is to end it may not be more cruel than it would have been to me at that moment!

By her unremitting attention and watchfulness, and incredible exertions she saved me; and it is certain that she alone could have done so. I have little faith in the medicine of physicians, but a great deal in that of true friends; those things on which our happiness depends are always more salutary than anything else. If there is such a thing as a delightful sensation in life, it is that which we felt when we were restored to each other. Our mutual attachment was not increased, that was impossible; but it assumed a more intimate form which I cannot explain, more touching in its great simplicity. I became entirely her work, entirely her child, more so than if she had been really my mother. We began, without thinking of it, to be inseparable, to share, as it were, our existence in common; and feeling that we were not only necessary, but sufficient, for each other, we accustomed ourselves to think of nothing that was foreign to us, to limit our happiness and all our desires to that possession of each other, which was, perhaps, unique of its kind amongst human beings, which, as I have said, was not love, but a more real possession, which, without being dependent upon the senses, sex, age or personal appearance, was concerned with all that which makes one what one is, and which one can only lose by ceasing to exist. . . .

Johann Wolfgang Von Goethe (1749–1832)

LIFE: He was educated for the law, but his genius would not be confined, so it is as poet, dramatist, and scientist that he made early nineteenth century Germany the intellectual capital of Europe. His private life was characterized by passionate and rather disorderly attachments, until he married Christiane Vulpe, who had born him a son years before; his public life included meetings with Beethoven and Napoleon; and his life as a poet produced one of the authentic masterpieces of western literature.

WORKS: *Faust* (Part I, 1808, Part II, 1832); *The Sorrows of Young Werther* (1774); *Wilhelm Meister's Apprenticeship* (1796); *Wilhelm Meister's Travels* (1821); *Truth and Poetry* (1811–1832).

FAUST: PART I *

Prologue in Heaven †

(*The Lord, the Heavenly Host, and later Mephistopheles. The three Archangels come forward and speak.*)

RAPHAEL: The sun sings in the ancient major,
in song-match with its brother-spheres,
and finishes its ordained journey

* Part I, published in 1808. Goethe's Dedication, The Prologue at the Theater, and The Walpurgis Night's Dream are omitted.
† See the first two chapters of Job for the source of this scene.

with thunder-crash about their ears.
Its face gives strength to all the angels   5
though none of them can fathom why;
the inconceivably great work shines,
new as on the founding day.
GABRIEL: And swift, past understanding swift,
the splendor of the earth whirls past,   10
changing the paradisial brightness
for the night's deepness, shuddering, vast.
Broadly the ocean currents, foaming
out of the depths, are tossed and swirled,
and rocks and water hurtle onward   15
forever with the racing worlds.
MICHAEL: And tempests bluster in a wager,
from sea to land, from land to sea,
raging, forging an encoiling
chain of deepest energy.   20
A dazzling desolation is flaming
with thundering strokes along the way.
But, Lord, your messengers must honor
the gentle power of your day.
ALL THREE: This vision gives the angels power   25
though none of them can fathom you;
and all your wonderful creations
are splendid as on their first day.
MEPHISTOPHELES: Since you, O Lord, once more approach and ask
how we are getting on, and since you used   30
to see me gladly, I have taken the risk
and come among your servants; but I can't
make pretty speeches, though the crowd here scoff
and scorn me, lest my pathos make you laugh —
if long ago you'd not dispensed with laughter.   35
I don't know how the suns and worlds are turned,
I only see how men will plague themselves.
The little earth-god's stamped in the old way
and is as odd as on creation day.
He'd be much better, Lord, if you'd not let   40
him have the merest glimpse of heavenly light
which he calls reason, using it at best
only to grow more bestial than the beasts.
He seems to me — I hope I'm not improper —
exactly like a spindly-legg'd grasshopper   45
that flits and flies and jumps,
then landing in the grass, will always sing
the same old worn-out song.
I wish that he were lost forever in the grass!
He digs his nose in every sort of trash.   50

THE LORD: And is there nothing else you want to say?
Do you come here only to lodge complaints?
Is there nothing at all upon the earth that suits you?
MEPHISTOPHELES: No, Lord! I find things there, as always, pretty bad.
Men grieve me so with the days of their lamenting,   55
I even hate to plague them with my torments.
THE LORD: Do you know Faust?
MEPHISTOPHELES: The Doctor?
THE LORD: He's my servant!
MEPHISTOPHELES: He serves you very strangely then, indeed.   60
For nothing earthly will he eat or drink, the fool.
A yeasty yearning has driven him so far,
he's only half-aware that he is mad.
He wants from the sky the fairest star,
and from earth the highest joy that's to be had;   65
yet everything near and everything far
can never satisfy his deeply stirred desire.
THE LORD: Since, though confused, he serves me still,
I'll lead him soon toward a clearer view.
The gardener knows that when the branches green,   70
soon fruit and flowers will show what time can do.
MEPHISTOPHELES: What will you bet? You'd lose him yet
if you let me lead him gently down my street!
THE LORD: As long as he lives on earth,
I'll not forbid your trying.   75
Man is doomed to err as long as he is striving.
MEPHISTOPHELES: Thank you. Because I always hate
to get involved with the dead and dying.
I'd rather have the fresh and rounded cheeks.
I'm never at home to a corpse.   80
I prefer, like a cat, to play with a mouse that squeaks.
THE LORD: Very well then. It shall be as you wish.
Pervert this soul from its first source,
lead him — if you can get hold of him —
along your downward path; but when you lose   85
stand up and admit defeat.
A good man, struggling in his darkness,
will always be aware of the true course.
MEPHISTOPHELES: Good, Lord, and it won't take me long!
I'll not be worried about this wager!   90
But when I win, please let me take
my triumph fully. He must gorge on dust,
and love it, like my aunt, the celebrated snake.
THE LORD: Do as you will. I give you a free hand.
I have no hatred for the like of you.   95
Among destroyers, you must understand,
the rogue's the least offensive of the lot.

Man's active spirit easily falls asleep;
he's much too readily seduced by sloth.
Therefore, I gladly give him a companion   100
who prods and twists and must act as a devil.

(*turning to the good angels*)

But you, who are the real sons of The Lord,
rejoice in beauty's live dominions.
May the Becoming, which eternally moves and lives,
surround you with the friendly walls of love!   105
To all that wavers you must minister,
basing it firmly in enduring thoughts.

(*The heavens close and the angels go out.*)

MEPHISTOPHELES (*alone*): I like to see the Old Boy now and then,
and I take care not to cross him by a word.
It's very decent of so great a lord   110
to gossip with the Devil like a man.

The Tragedy: First Part

NIGHT

(*Faust sits restlessly at his desk in a high-vaulted, narrow, Gothic
room.*)

FAUST: Now I have studied philosophy,
medicine and the law,
and unfortunately, theology,
wearily sweating, yet I stand now,
poor fool, no wiser than I was before;   5
I am called Master, even Doctor,
and for these last ten years have led
my students by the nose — up, down,
crosswise and crooked. Now I see
that we know nothing finally.   10

This burns my heart, but I know, at least,
that I'm cleverer than all the conceited pedagogues,

the doctors, masters, clerks, and priests;
I am not troubled by doubts or scruples,
I'm not afraid of Hell or the Devil —   15
but, in return, all joy has been torn from me.

I don't presume to know anything now,
nor imagine I can teach anyone

how he can grow better. I have no
property, I haven't any money,   20
no decorations, or glories of this earth —
not even a dog would want to live like me.

Therefore I've turned to magic,
hoping a spirit will give me power
to fathom some of the secrets   25
so that I need no longer say, with sour sweat,
things that I don't know anything about;
so I may learn the fabric of the world,
see all the seeds, watch the wheels run,
and stop this rummaging around with words.   30

O radiant full moon, if only for the last time
you were looking down on my misery!
So many midnights when I've watched
beside my desk, over the books and papers,
you have appeared, my melancholy friend!   35
If I could only go along the mountain tops
under your friendly light,
ride round the mountain caverns with the spirits,
float over the meadows in your glimmering,
purged of the smoke of knowledge,   40
and bathe myself back to health in your dew!

Alas, am I still stuck in this prison?
This damned damp hole in the wall
where the sweet light of heaven
breaks gloomily through the painted panes!   45

Shut in by this heap of worm-gnawed
dust-covered books, that reach to the high arches
where smoke-stained paper clings;
cluttered with glassware and boxes,
with instruments stacked on all sides,   50
and crammed with inherited rubbish —
this is your world! Or what is called a world!
And do you still wonder why your heart
is cramped with fear?
Why this inexplicable hurt   55
represses all your lust for life?
Instead of living nature
in which God created man,
you're surrounded by smoke and rot,
animals' skeletons and dead men's bones.   60

Escape from this! Bestir yourself!
Move into the wider realm.
Is not this mysterious book by Nostradamus
sufficient company for you?
You'll understand the stars' procession,   65
and when Nature has instructed you,
the strength of your own soul will be revealed
as spirit speaks to spirit.
All this dry plodding never can explain
the holy symbols to you. Hover about me,   70
spirits, and answer if you hear me!

(*He opens the book and sees the sign of the Macrocosm.**)

Oh, what delight thrills through me
from this sudden sight!
I feel a young and holy zest for life flow,
newly glowing, through my veins and nerves.   75
Was it a god who drew these signs
which still my inner ravings,
fill my wretched heart with joy,
and with mysterious impulses unveil
the powers of nature around me?   80
Am I a god? All becomes clearer to me!
I see in these pure lines
creative nature lying open before my soul.
Now I begin to understand what the sage means:
"The world of spirits is not closed;   85
but your senses are shut, your heart is dead!
Up, neophyte, and undismayed
bathe your mortality in the morning light!"

(*He gazes at the sign.*)

How everything moves toward the whole;
each in the other works and lives,
like seraphs climbing up and down,   90
passing to one another golden buckets!
On blessed fragrant wings
pressing from heaven through earth,
all sounding through the All with harmony!   95

What a great spectacle! But, yet, it's nothing more!
Eternal nature, where shall I grasp you?
Where are you, breasts, you springs of life

63. *Nostradamus:* the French astrologer Michel de Notredame (1503–1566), whose rhymed prophecies were first published in 1555.
* The great world or universe. The neoplantonists believed in a mystical correspondence between macrocosm and microcosm. For a description of the latter see the selection from Castiglione's *The Book of the Courtier* in this anthology.

on which hang heaven and earth,
toward which the parched heart presses?   100
You flow, you suckle — must I do without you?

(*He leafs through the book impatiently and finds the sign of the Earth-Spirit.*)

How differently this symbol works on me!
Spirit of the Earth, you are nearer to me;
already I feel my powers increasing,
already I glow as if I'd drunk new wine.   105
I have the courage to venture into the world,

to bear the woe and joy of earth,
to tussle with storms,
and not to fear the crash of shipwreck.
Clouds gather above me —   110
the moon now hides her light —
the lamp goes out!
Mists rise! — red gleams dart
round my head — cold horror
is dropping from the arches to seize me!   115
Spirit whom I implored, I feel you near me.
Unveil yourself!
You're tearing at my heart!
My senses burst
with strange new feelings!   120
My heart is utterly yielded to you!
Come! You must come! Although it costs my life!

(*He seizes the book and mysteriously speaks the spell. The Spirit appears in a red flame.*)

SPIRIT: Who calls me?
FAUST (*turning away*): Terrible apparition!
SPIRIT: Powerfully you have summoned me;   125
long have you sucked for nourishment from my sphere,
and now —
FAUST: I can't endure you!
SPIRIT: Breathlessly, you prayed to behold me,
to hear my voice, to see my face;   130
the strong petitions of your soul have touched me —
and here I am! What pitiful terror
now overwhelms this superman! Where is the soul's cry?
Where is this mind that conceived a world within,
bore it and cherished it, joyously trembling,   135
and puffed itself up to rival us spirits?

103. *Spirit of the Earth:* symbolizing the force of the powerful elementary world.

Where are you, Faust, whose voice I heard,
who drove yourself toward me with all your strength?
Is this you, encompassed by my breath,
who tremble in your inmost being,   140
a worm that wriggles away in fear?
FAUST: O flame-form, must I yield to you?
I am Faust! I am your equal!
SPIRIT: Like the swirling of life, the storm of action,
I rise and fall,   145
moving here and there!
I am the womb and the tomb,
an eternal ocean,
a changing, glowing
life in ferment: 150
thus working on the roaring loom of time,
I weave God's living garment.
FAUST: O active spirit, how near I feel to you!
You who swirl round the whole wide world.
SPIRIT: You resemble the spirit which you comprehend,   155
not me!

(*The Spirit vanishes.*)

FAUST (*overpowered*): Not you?
Whom then?
I, the image of godhead,
yet not so much as you?   160

(*There is a knock.*)

O death! I know it — that's my assistant!
My greatest chance will come to nothing!
This boring plodder will destroy
the abundance of these revelations!

(*Wagner, ready for bed, in a nightcap and dressing gown, comes in with a lamp. Faust turns round impatiently.*)

WAGNER: Excuse me! I heard you declaiming;   165
You're reading a part from some Greek tragedy?
That is an art from which I'd like to profit,
for nowadays everyone should know about it.
I've often heard it said that people
skilled in acting can instruct a parson.   170
FAUST: Yes, if the preacher is an actor,
as happens very often in these times.
WAGNER: When one's so cooped up in his little study
and scarcely sees the world on a holiday,
and as though through a telescope, it's so far away —   175

how can he ever persuade or lead anybody?
FAUST: Unless you feel it, you will never achieve it.
If it doesn't flow from your soul
with natural easy power,
your listeners will not believe it.   180
You can sit down and paste phrases together by the hour,
cook up a little stew from others' feasts;
you can blow up miserable flames
from your heap of ashes
that will amaze children and monkeys —   185
if such little triumphs please your taste —
but you'll never move others, heart to heart,
unless your speech comes from your own heart.
WAGNER: But orators depend for success
on elocution, and there I'm far behind.   190
FAUST: Seek only honest gain.
Don't be a jingling jester!
Common sense and understanding
can go far with little art.
If you've something serious to say,   195
the words will come to you.
Glib tongues frill up their hash of knowledge
for mankind in polished speeches
that are no more than vaporous winds
rustling the fallen leaves in autumn.   200
WAGNER: O God, art is so long!
And life so short.
Often during my philological studies
I lose heart and courage.
How hard it is to earn the means   205
to reach the sources!
And before a man can get half-way,
generally he dies, poor devil!
FAUST: Is parchment then the blessed spring
whose water quenches your thirst forever?   210
What does not burst from your own soul
will never refresh you.
WAGNER: Excuse me! It is the greatest pleasure
to put oneself in the spirit of the ages,
for by comparison with wise men before us   215
we see how far our own time has advanced.
FAUST: Oh yes, up to the stars! My friend,
the past is a book of seven seals, and what
you call the spirit of the times, in the end,
is merely the spirit of those gentlemen   220

201–202. *art . . . short:* "ars longa, vita brevis," a famous aphorism attributed to Hippocrates.

in whom the times are mirrored.
And often as not they're a pretty sad lot!
At the first glance one runs away.
The garbage cans, the attics, the high-flown political dramas
have been raked for the proper didactic maxims   225
for the marionettes to mouth.
WAGNER: But the world, the mind and heart of men!
Everyone yearns to learn about them.
FAUST: To learn about them, yes, after a fashion.
But who dares call the child by its right name?   230
The few who know anything about it
are foolish not to guard it in their hearts;
those who have shown the rabble their feelings and thoughts
have been finally crucified or burned at the stake.
But it's late, my friend, and we'd better   235
break off for tonight.
WAGNER: I'd have liked to go right on, wide-awake
and talking here so learnedly with you.
But tomorrow's the first day of Easter vacation,
and maybe you'll answer another question or two.   240
I've been so eager and busy and patient;
I know a lot already, but I'd like to be omniscient.

(*He goes out.*)

FAUST (*alone*): How can anyone clinging to such trash
keep any hope in his head?
With greedy hands he digs for treasure,   245
and is happy when he finds earthworms!
How could the voice of such a man dare sound
here where a host of spirits hovered round me?
But I must thank you, this once,
poorest son of earth, for what you've done.   250
You tore me loose from the despair
that had almost driven me to frenzy.
The apparition was so huge a giant,
that I felt like a dwarf.

I, the image of godhead, who thought myself   255
near to the mirror of eternal truth,
enjoying myself in heaven's clear radiance
and stripping off all mortality;
I, more than a cherub, I, whose free strength
already dreamed it flowed through the veins of nature   260
and dared presume to enjoy
the creative life of gods — I must do penance for that.
A word of thunder swept me far away.

I dare not liken myself to you!
If I had the power to draw you,   265
I would have no strength to hold you.
In that happy instant you were near me
I felt myself so small, and yet so great . . .
ruthlessly you thrust me back
into humanity's ambiguous fate.   270
Who will teach me? What must I avoid?
Shall I yield to impulse and ask the spirits' help?
Alas, our acts, as well as our sufferings,
cramp the course of our lives.

Things — alien and ever more foreign   275
intrude on the mind's most noble conceptions.
When we achieve some good here in our world,
we call the better merely deceit and illusion.
The glorious aspirations that made us alive
turn torpid in the earthly turmoil.   280
Though fancy once with daring hopeful flight
expanded toward infinity, now a speck
of space contents her when joy after joy
founders in the great maelstrom of time.
Anxiety nests deeply in the heart,   285
working her sorrow in secret;
restlessly she cradles herself, disturbing
joy and peace, with new masks veiling
her face, or else appearing
as house and property, as wife and child,   290
as fire, water, poison and dagger.
You worry about so many things which may not happen
and weep for things you may never lose.

I am not like the gods! I feel that so deeply;
I am the worm that crawls in dust,   295
lives there and must feed on dust, and dies,
crushed and buried under the wanderer's heel.

Is it not dust that cramps this lofty wall
with a hundred shelves around me?
This rubbish with a thousand trifles   300
that stifle me in this world of moths?
Shall I find here what I lack?
Shall I, perhaps, read in a thousand books
that everywhere men plague themselves,
with only here and there one happy man?   305

What are you grinning at me hollow skull, except
that in your brain, confused like mine, once lived
something that sought bright day, desiring truth,
yet in the heavy dusk went miserably astray?
Surely this apparatus mocks me with its wheels,   310
rollers, cogs, and tackle. I stood at the gateway;
these should have been the key. The wards
are intricately made, but move no bolts.
Mysterious even in the light of day,
nature will never let her veil be stolen,   315
and what she will not show your mind
you'll not get out of her with screws and levers.
These ancient tools that I have never used
are here because my father needed them.
This scroll of parchment has been stained with smoke   320
since first the lamp was lighted on this desk.
Better if I had squandered my slight possessions,
than to be sweating here now with this worthless burden.
What you inherit from your father
must first be earned before it's yours.   325
What you don't use becomes a heavy load;
the moment creates the tool to serve its need.

But why is now my gaze drawn to that spot?
Can that flask be a magnet to my eyes?
What is this sudden gentle radiance   330
like moonlight drifting through the woods at night?

Hail, precious phial! With awe
I take you down and honor man's cunning art.
Essence of kindly opiates,
extract of subtle and deadly agents,   335
now give your favor to your master!
I see you and my pain is soothed;
I grasp you, and at once my struggles are calmed;
the flood-tide of the spirit ebbs away.
I am shown the path above the ocean   340
where mirror-waters glisten at my feet;
a new day lures me to new shores.

On light wings a fiery chariot hovers,
gliding toward me. I feel ready
to pierce new pathways in the ether,   345
into new spheres of action without limits.
Exalted existence, godlike delight!
Can I, no better than a worm, deserve them?
Firmly resolved, I turn my back

to the bright sun of earth. Be bold to burst open   350
the gates past which others would gladly go slinking!
Now it is time to show that man's dignity
vies with the high gods, and will not tremble
before that dark cavern where phantasy, self-damned,
lives among torments; then on to the passage   355
whose narrow mouth flames with all Hell's seething.
Serenely determine to take this final step
though you risk the danger of plunging to nothingness.

Come down, pure crystal goblet, from your case.
For many years I have not thought of you.   360
You shone at gay ancestral feasts
and used to cheer the solemn guests
when one touched you to another for a toast.
The elaborate images carved and wrought on you —
it was the drinker's task to rhyme on them   365
and drain your bowl with one long drink.
Now they recall those nights of youth.

Now I shall never pass you gaily to my neighbor,
or show my wit off on your art.
Here is a juice that quickly makes men drunk.   370
I pour the brown stream in the cup.
I have prepared it, now I choose it
and take the final drink with all my will,
a solemn festal pledge to Easter morning!

(*He raises the goblet to his lips. But, as he does so, there comes the sound of chimes and a chorus of voices.*)

CHORUS OF ANGELS: Christ is arisen!   375
Joy to the mortal
whom baneful, insidious,
inherited failings
of earth had entwined.
FAUST: With that deep resonance, what bright sound   380
now forcibly pulls the goblet from my lips?
Those booming bells, do they announce the first glad hour
of Easter? Is the choir already singing
the hymn of consolation
which through the night of the tomb   385
rang from the angels' lips, pledging a new covenant?
CHORUS OF WOMEN: With myrrh and spices
we tenderly tended him.
We, his most faithful ones,

---

375. *Christ is arisen:* Goethe's source is a German Easter hymn of the Middle Ages.

laid him away; 390
in swathings and grave clothes
we cleanly wrapped him.
Alas! for we find now
Christ is not here.
CHORUS OF ANGELS: Christ is arisen! 395
Blest is the loving one
who has transcended
the wholesome and chastening
trials that beset him!
FAUST: Gentle and mighty music of heaven, 400
why do you seek me here in the dust?
Ring rather to soft-hearted men.
I hear your message, but I lack belief.
Miracle is the darling child of faith.
I dare not struggle up to those high spheres 405
where the glad tidings ring;
and yet from childhood I was used
to these same sounds, and now they call me back to life.
In other times the kiss of heavenly love
fell on me in the solemn Sabbath stillness; 410
the full chimes rang prophetically;
a prayer was ardent pleasure; a longing,
sweet, unfathomable, drove me through woods and fields,
and while I shed a thousand burning tears,
I felt a new world rise within me. 415
This song announced the happy sports of youth,
the free and joyous festival of spring;
now memory with childlike feelings keeps me
from this last decisive step.
Oh, ring, sweet heavenly songs! Ring out! 420
My tears flow and earth has me back again!
CHORUS OF DISCIPLES: He who was buried
is risen already,
alive and sublimely
exalted on high. 425
To the joy of becoming,
to the gladness of creation,
now he is near.
But here down on earth
we stand in affliction. 430
He has left us, who loved us,
we pine for him here.
Master, we weep for you,
weep for your happiness!
CHORUS OF ANGELS: Christ is arisen 435
from the womb of corruption.

Joyfully loosen
yourselves from your bonds!
If you live, praising him,
showing all love to him, 440
with brotherly feasting,
journeying and preaching,
promising joy,
the master will be near you,
the master is here! 445

OUTSIDE THE TOWN * GATE

(*Various classes of people are promenading.*)

APPRENTICES: Why do you go that way?
OTHERS: We're off to the Hunters' Lodge.
THE FIRST: We're going down to the mill.
ANOTHER: I'd rather go to the inn by the water.
THE SECOND: The road there is not very pretty. 5
OTHERS: What will you do?
THE THIRD: I'll just go along with the rest.
THE FOURTH: Come up to Burgdorf. You'll find there
the prettiest girls and the strongest beer,
and there's always something doing. 10
THE FIFTH: Well, you're too much for me!
Does your hide itch for a third beating?
I'm afraid of the place.
I'll not go there.
A SERVANT GIRL: No, no! I'm going back to town. 15
A SECOND: We'll surely find him there by the poplars.
THE FIRST: Well isn't that a piece of luck for me!
He'll walk with you, he'll dance
with no one else but you.
What good will all your fun do me? 20
THE SECOND: Today he's not alone.
He said that Curly would come with him.
A STUDENT: Wow! look at that pair just going by!
Come on, brother, let's try to pick them up.
Beer with a head, tobacco that bites, 25
and a girl like that will suit my appetite.
A BURGHER'S DAUGHTER: Just watch those good looking boys!
Now aren't they awful?
When they could have the best society,
they'd rather chase after those housemaids! 30
THE SECOND STUDENT: Don't go so fast! Here come
a couple of really nice looking girls.

* Probably Frankfurt.

That one there lives next door to me
and I like her a lot. They look shy,
but they'll let us go along with them. 35
THE FIRST STUDENT: No, brother, thanks, but I don't like them tame.
Quick! or we'll lose the ones we want to get.
The arm that wields a broom on Saturday
on Sunday always snuggles you the best!
A BURGHER: I don't like our new mayor. Since the election 40
he acts like a dictator. And what has he done
for the city? Every day it's getting worse.
We're regimented and taxed as never before.
A BEGGAR (*singing*): Sweet ladies and kind gentlemen,
red-cheeked, in such fine clothes, 45
be gracious and remember me,
take pity on my woes.
Don't let me grind my organ in vain!
Only the generous are gay.
A time when people celebrate 50
should be my harvest-day.
A SECOND BURGHER: It's fine on a Sunday or holiday
to sit snugly and talk of war and the noise of battles;
how they're fighting down in Turkey, far away.
You stand by the tavern window and empty your bottle 55
and look at the river where gay boats glide past;
then go home at evening, happy, and praising peace.
A THIRD: That's right, neighbor, no foreign intervention!
Let them crack each others' heads open.
However things go there, we'd better 60
stay at home and stick to the old customs.
A BAWDY OLD WOMAN (*to the Burghers' daughters*):
So smartly dressed! Oh, the gay young blood!
Who could resist falling in love with you?
Now I know exactly — don't act so shocked — 65
just how to manage the thing that you'd like.
THE GIRL: Hurry up, Agatha! We must be careful
not to be seen in public with a witch.
But just last Hallowe'en she showed me
my future lover, real as flesh and blood. 70
THE OTHER GIRL: She called up mine, too, in a crystal:
he was a soldier, marching with his troop.
Since then I've looked around for him everywhere,
But so far I haven't been able to find him.
CHORUS OF SOLDIERS MARCHING PAST: Castles with mighty walls, 75
towers, and battlements,
girls who are haughty

69. *Hallowe'en:* in the original German, St. Andrew's Night (November 29), when young girls
pray that their future husbands will appear to them in a dream.

and scornful and hard—
we'd like to win all of them!
Daring's the doing, 80
and great the reward.

Hear how the trumpets
woo us to pleasure,
and coax us to peril.
Oh what a life it is! 85
Oh what a storm!
Castles and girls as well
yield in the end.
Daring's the doing,
great the reward! 90
And the soldiers go marching
away down the road.

(*Faust and Wagner enter.*)

FAUST: Now spring's reviving glance has freed
the ice from stream and river.
The valley turns green with the joy of hope. 95
Old winter, growing impotent, crawls back
to the rough mountains; as he flees, he hurls
fitful gusts of icy-kerneled sleet
in streaks on the green meadows.
But the sun allows no whiteness; 100
growth and creation stir and strive
to cover everything with color.
And since the landscape still lacks flowers, the sun
must use the color of peoples' clothes instead.
Turn round and from this hill-top 105
look at the town. Now from the towered
gloomy gateway streams a motley swarm
eager to sun themselves today.
They celebrate the resurrection
of the Lord; for they themselves 110
are newly risen from the tenements,
from the damp rooms and the press
of mills and factories, from the weight
of roofs and gables and the stifling
crush of alleys, from the solemn 115
venerable gloom of churches —
now they come out into the sunlight.
See how lively now the crowd
scatters through the fields and gardens,
while, up and down, there on the river 120
bob the merry little row-boats,

and the last skiff, over-laden
and almost sinking, pushes off.

Even from the mountain pathways
bright-colored dresses are shining.   125
Already I hear the bustle of the village.
Here's the heaven of the people;
rich and poor are happy and shouting.
Here I feel, and dare feel, like a man.
WAGNER: It's an honor to go walking with you, Doctor,   130
and also profitable; but I wouldn't care
to lose myself alone here, since I'm opposed
to everything that's vulgar. Fiddling, shouting,
and nine-pins are noises that I hate.
The people riot, driven by the Devil,   135
and call it joy and think it's music.

(*There are peasants under a linden tree, dancing and singing.*)

THE PEASANTS: The shepherd was all dressed up for the dance,
with wreath and ribbons and leather pants,
and he was making a show.
Already under the linden tree   140
the crowd was dancing crazily.
Jukey! Jukey!
Jubilo!
So went the fiddle-bow.

As he pushed swiftly through the swirl,   145
he bumped a pretty peasant girl
sharply with his elbow.
The jolly maiden turned around
and said, "Well, you're a clumsy clown!"
Jukey! Jukey!   150
Jubilo!
"And your behavior's low."

Then in a circle, twirling swift,
they danced to the right, they danced to the left —
and the skirts whirled out and rose.   155
They got red and they got warm,
and rested, puffing, arm in arm.
Jukey! Jukey!
Jubilo!
Hip against elbow.   160

"Don't be familiar! How many men
wheedle and lie to their sweethearts, then

off and away they go!"
But he coaxed her aside with flattery
while the music rang round the linden tree: 165
Jukey! Jukey!
Jubilo!
Oh, the shouts and that fiddle-bow!
AN OLD PEASANT: Doctor, it is good of you
not to disdain today   170
to come among us farmers,
though you're a great scholar.
Pray take the finest tankard,
brimming with our freshest draught.
May it quench your thirst, and each drop   175
be a day added to your life.
FAUST: I take it gladly, this refreshing drink;
here's to your health and many thanks!

(*The people gather round him.*)

OLD PEASANT: You have kindly come to share
our happy day, as long ago   180
in evil times you helped us here.
There's many a man stands here alive
saved by your father from the rage
of the hot fever when he stopped
the pestilence. A young man then,   185
you went in every stricken house;
many a corpse was carried out,
but you kept well and bore hard trials.
The Helper yonder helped the helper here.
ALL: Long life to this well-proven man,   190
long may he live and help us!
FAUST: Bow down to Him above
Who teaches and sends help!

(*He goes on with Wagner.*)

WAGNER: O great man, what a feeling
all this honor from the crowd must give you!   195
Happy is he who from his skill
can gain such benefits! Each father calls
his boy to look at you. The people rush up
and stand around you, asking questions.
The dancers stop, the fiddle's still.   200
They stand in rows to watch you pass;
throw their caps in the air. And almost

186–187. *you went . . . out:* Goethe is recalling an episode from the life of Nostradamus, who helped to relieve a plague in Provence.

get on their knees, as if you were the sacred Host.
FAUST: A few steps farther, to that stone.
We'll rest after our walk. How many times   205
I've brooded here, tortured myself with prayers
and fastings, rich in hope and firm in faith;
with sighs and tears, wringing my hands, I thought
to force the Lord in heaven to end the plague.
The crowd's applause now sounds like scorn.   210
If they could read my mind, they'd see
how little both father and son deserve their praise.

My father was an obscure gentleman
who loved, quite honestly, in his odd way
to ponder on nature and her sacred workings,   215
with a crank's unsystematic zeal.
He shut himself in the black kitchen
with a group of expert alchemists,
seeking by many a recipe
to make the incompatibles agree.   220

There the red Lion, a brisk chaser,
married the Lily in a lukewarm bath,
and both above the open flame
were tortured from one bride-chamber to another.
Then, if the young queen appeared   225
with varied colors in the glass retort,
that was the medicine! The patients died;
and no one asked: "Who recovered?"
Thus, with Hell's electuaries,
we brought more destruction than the plague   230
among these mountains and valleys.
I have poisoned many thousands;
they pined away from our drugs, yet I must live
to hear the reckless murderers praised.
WAGNER: Why let it worry you? Does not the good man   235
fulfill his duty when he practices
skilfully and scrupulously the art
transmitted to him? If in your youth you honor
your father, you will gladly learn from him.
If in your manhood you carry this knowledge farther,   240
maybe your son will reach a higher goal.
FAUST: Oh, happy the man with any hope
of rising out of error's ocean!
You need just what you do not know,
and what you really know is worthless.   245
But let us not embitter this blessed hour

221–227. *red Lion . . . medicine:* Goethe is using the language of medieval alchemy.

with melancholy thoughts.
See how the green-encircled huts
shine in the glow of the evening sun.
The day is over; the sun yields and hastens   250
onward to quicken new life. Oh, that wings
could lift me from the earth to follow,
struggling in the sun-wake! I would see
beneath my feet the silent world
glowing in the eternal evening;   255
each peak on fire, each valley calm,
the silver brooks flowing to golden rivers.
And the wild mountain with its gorges
could not check my godlike flight.
Already the ocean with its sun-warmed bays   260
broadens beneath my astonished eye.
Yet finally the sun appears to sink;
and a new instinct awakens.
I hurry onward to drink his eternal light,
the day before me, and the night behind,   265
the sky above, the waves below —
a splendid dream until the sun fades out.

Ah, if only the wings that raise the spirit
might be brothered by strong earthly wings!
Man is born with a desire   270
that drives his feeling upward, onward,
when overhead, lost in blue space,
the skylark sings his quavering song;
when over craggy fir-topped heights
he sees the out-spread eagle soaring,   275
or the crane struggling homeward
over lakes and swampy moors.
WAGNER: I've often had strange whims myself,
but never such an urge as that.
You soon get bored with fields and forests;   280
I'll never envy any bird his flight.
How differently the spirit's pleasures bear us,
from page to page, through volume after volume.
Then winter nights are cheerful and friendly,
warm delight steals through the bones,   285
and ah, when you unroll some precious parchment,
Heaven itself comes down to you!
FAUST: You know the one impulse only.
It's better if you never learn the other.
Alas, there are two souls that live in me   290
and one would like to leave its brother;
one with gripping organs clings to earth

with a rough and hearty lust;
the other rises powerfully from the dirt
up toward the region of the great forefathers.   295
If there are lordly spirits in the air
roaming between the earth and sky,
let them come down from the golden atmosphere
and lead me to a new, more vivid life!
Yes, if I had a magic cloak to carry me   300
to foreign lands, I would not trade it
for the richest robes, or for the mantle of a king.
WAGNER: Do not invoke the much-feared throng of demons
that rush about the murky air,
preparing evils, thousands of them, for mankind   305
from every quarter of the sky.
Out of the North the sharp-toothed ghosts
sweep down on you with tongues like arrows;
out of the East they come to quench
their thirst and feed upon your lungs;   310
if the Southwind swirls them up from the desert,
pouring heat-waves on your skull,
then the West will send its swarm, reviving you first with rain,
then drowning you and the fields and meadows.
Being full of mischief, they love to listen;   315
they gladly obey, for they like to betray you,
pretending to be sent from Heaven,
and lisping like angels, while they lie.
But let us go. The world turns gray,
the air grows cool, the fog blows in.   320
Only at evening can you really value home —
But why do you stand like that and look amazed?
What is it fascinates you in the twilight?
FAUST: Do you see that black dog sneaking
through the stubble and the grain?   325
WAGNER: I saw him long ago. It seemed unimportant.
FAUST: Look at him closely. What kind of animal is it?
WAGNER: It's a poodle, sniffing after
the footsteps of his master, as they all do.
FAUST: But see in what wide spirals   330
he stalks us, always coming closer.
And unless my eyes deceive me,
a fiery whirlpool is following his path.
WAGNER: I don't see anything except a plain black poodle.
It must be just an optical illusion.   335
FAUST: It seems to me he's drawing magic nooses
around our feet to make a snare.
WAGNER: All that I notice is that he jumps uncertainly about
because he sees two strangers, not his master.

FAUST: The circle narrows. Now he's getting near.　340
WAGNER: You see! It's nothing but a dog. No spectre there.
He snarls and hesitates, crawls on his belly
and wags his tail — all common canine habits.
FAUST: Here, boy! here! Come here!
WAGNER: It's only a stupid poodle. You stand still,　345
and he'll sit up and beg; you speak and he jumps up on you.
Lose something, and he'll hunt for it
or jump into the water for your stick.
FAUST: You're right. I don't find any traces
of the supernatural. It is just his training.　350
WAGNER: A well-trained dog can win a learned man.
He's worth your favor, for it's clear
that he's a scholar of the students,
who have taught him tricks.

(*They enter the city gates.*)

FAUST'S STUDY

(*Faust comes in with the poodle.*)

FAUST: I have left the fields and meadows
hidden deeply in the veil of night
that wakens the true soul with holy
and prophetic shudderings. Now violent actions
and the wild impulses are asleep;　5
love for mankind revives,
and the love of God is stirring in the heart.

Be quiet, poodle, don't run back and forth!
What are you sniffing at there by the threshold?
Lie down behind the stove, I'll give you　10
my best cushion. Up there on the hillside
your games amused me; now I'll keep you here
if you can act like a quiet and welcome guest.

Ah, when the lamp again burns friendly
in our little study,　15
then all glows bright within us,
in the heart that understands itself.
Reason begins to speak again, hope blooms;
we yearn then for the springs of life,
and long to attain its very source.　20

Stop growling, poodle!
That brutish noise is not in tune
with the holy tones that fill my soul.

We are used to men who jeer at what
they do not understand, who grumble
at the beautiful and good which often are difficult.   25
Must dogs snarl at them, too?

But now, although I want it, I no longer feel
that inner peacefulness.
Why must the stream run dry so soon and leave us   30
thirsting once again? I have gone through it all so often.
And yet, this want can be relieved. We learn
to prize the supernatural; we yearn for revelation
which never burned more beautifully, more nobly,
than here in the New Testament. Now I must open   35
the original text, with this my honest purpose,
once and for all, to turn the holy scripture
into my own beloved German.

(*He opens the book and begins.*)

It is written: "In the beginning was the *Word!*"
I'm stopped already. Who will help me further?   40
I cannot possibly rate the *Word* so highly.
I must translate it otherwise,
if I am rightly enlightened by the spirit.
It is written: "In the beginning was the *Thought!*"
Consider the first line well,   45
lest the pen write too hastily.
Is it the *Thought* that works and creates all?
Should it not be: "In the beginning was the *Power!*"
Yet, even as I write it down.
I feel I can not let that stand.   50
The spirit helps me! Suddenly I have it,
and confidently write: "In the beginning was the *Deed!*"

Poodle, if I must share this room with you,
then stop that growling,
and that howling!   55
I can't stand a companion who's a nuisance.
One of us must leave
I hate to withdraw
my hospitality, but the door is open.
The way is free.   60
But what is this I see?
Can such things happen naturally?
Is it shadow or reality?
How my poodle grows long and broad!

39. *It is written:* see John 1:1.

He swells with power.   65
That's no dog's form!
What phantom have I brought into the house?
Now he looks like a hippopotamus
with fiery eyes and a terrible jaw of teeth.
Ah, now I'm sure of you!   70
Solomon's Key is good
for creatures of such Hellish blood!
SPIRITS (*in the corridor*): Someone is caught in there!
Don't follow. Stay safe here!
Like a fox in a gin,   75
Hell's lynx quakes within.
But take care!
Hover here, hover there,
up and down.
Soon he'll be free.   80
If you can serve him,
help now to save him;
for he has done
good turns for everyone.
FAUST: I cannot meet this beast until   85
I quell him with the Spell of Four:

Let salamander glow
and undine coil,
sylph disappear
and goblin toil!   90

Who is ignorant
of the four elements,
their potencies
and properties,
shall never master   95
the spirits.

Vanish in flames, salamander!
Undines,
flow gurgling together.
Sylphs,   100
be bright as meteors.
Incubus, to all in-doors
be helpful; incubus,
come forth and put an end to this!

71. *Solomon's Key:* a book called *Clavicula Salomonis*, it was associated with Solomon because of his reputation as a magician and was used in magical rites of conjuration and exorcism.
86. *Four:* that is, the elementary spirits of fire (salamander), water (undine), air (sylph), and earth (goblin or gnome).

None of the four   105
is in the beast.
He lies at rest
and grins at me.
I haven't hurt him yet;
now he shall hear me conjure   110
with a mightier sorcery.

(*He shows the beast a crucifix.*)

Are you a fugitive from Hell?
Behold this sign!
To this the black hosts
of Hell bow down.   115

He swells up now, with bristling hair.

Rejected creature,
can you read this symbol?
Sign of the uncreated,
the unnamable.   120
Him through all realms diffused,
Who was wantonly spear-pierced?

Forced by my spells behind the stove,
he's swelling like an elephant.
Now he fills the room completely,   125
he's about to dissolve in vapor.
Don't rise to the ceiling!
Lie down at your master's feet!
You see I don't threaten vainly.
I'll scorch you with holy fire!   130
Do not wait
for the triple-glowing light!
Do not wait
for the full strength of my arts!

(*Mephistopheles* * *comes from behind the stove while the mist vanishes.
He is dressed like a traveling scholar.*)

MEPHISTOPHELES: Why all the noise?   135
How may I serve you, Sir?
FAUST: So that was the poodle's kernel!
A vagabond scholar! It makes me laugh.
MEPHISTOPHELES: I salute you, learned Sir.
You certainly made me sweat.   140
FAUST: What is your name?

* It is generally agreed that the name means "not loving the light."

MEPHISTOPHELES: Now that seems to me rather petty
in one so scornful of the Word,
one who is sceptical of appearances,
and looks only for the depths of being.   145
FAUST: We can usually recognize the identity
of such gentlemen as you by the name,
which shows itself all too plainly
when they call you the God of Flies, the Destroyer,
the Liar. So then, who are you?   150
MEPHISTOPHELES: A part of that power
which always wills evil and always works good.
FAUST: What does that riddle mean?
MEPHISTOPHELES: I am the spirit that always denies! A good thing, too,
for all that exists deserves to be destroyed.   155
It would be much better if nothing were ever created.
So I'm everything that you call sin and destruction,
in short, evil — these are my proper element.
FAUST: You call yourself a part, yet stand there whole.
MEPHISTOPHELES: I speak the modest truth. Though man,   160
that silly little microcosm,
commonly thinks himself an entity.
I am part of the part that at first was all,
part of the darkness that gave birth to light,
that supercilious light which now disputes   165
with Mother Night her ancient rank and realm,
and yet can not succeed; however much it struggles,
it sticks to matter and can't get free.
Light flows from substance, makes it beautiful;
solids can check its path, so I hope it won't be long   170
till light and the world-stuff are destroyed together.
FAUST: Now I understand your important duties!
You can't destroy things quite wholesale,
So you've started on a smaller scale.
MEPHISTOPHELES: And really I haven't got far with it.   175
In spite of all I've undertaken
I can't get under the skin of this fat world,
this something that opposes the nothing.
Earth-quakes, tidal-waves, hurricanes, fires — no use,
the land and sea remain as calm as ever.   180
And that damned trash, the race of beasts and men — ?
I can't get at them either, as I'd like.
How many of them I've buried!
Yet always there's fresh new blood
to go on circulating, on and on,   185
until I'm almost crazy! For out of the waters,
and out of the earth and the air,

149–150. *God of Flies, the Destroyer, the Liar:* Beelzebub, Abaddon, Satan.

thousands of seeds are unfolding everywhere,
in drouth and moisture, in heat and cold.
If I hadn't reserved fire for myself 190
I'd certainly have very little.
FAUST: You dare to raise your cold devil's fist,
clenched vainly in malice,
against the ever-working, healing, creative power?
Try something else, you wayward son of Chaos! 195
MEPHISTOPHELES: We'll take the matter under advisement
and consider it at our next meeting.
And now, may I go?
FAUST: I don't see why you ask.
I've just now made your acquaintance. 200
Visit me when you wish.
Here is the door, there is the window,
and there's the old reliable chimney.
MEPHISTOPHELES: To tell the truth, I can't leave,
there's a little obstacle: the swan-foot-print 205
of the incubus on your threshold.
FAUST: So the pentagram's giving you trouble?
But tell me, you son of Hell,
if that stops you, how did you get in?
What was it tricked a devil like you? 210
MEPHISTOPHELES: Just look closely! It's not well-drawn;
the angle pointing out is not connected.
FAUST: A lucky accident! I've got you prisoner?
A splendid opportunity for me!
MEPHISTOPHELES: The poodle didn't see it when he jumped in; 215
but things look different now.
In fact, the Devil can't get out.
FAUST: But why not through the window?
MEPHISTOPHELES: Oh, that's just one of those things: a law for spirits
and demons — wherever they steal in they must go out. 220
We can choose the first but are bound by the second.
FAUST: Then even Hell itself has laws?
I think that's fine, because some binding pact
might be arranged between us.
MEPHISTOPHELES: What's promised you'll enjoy in full. 225
Nothing shall be pinched from it.
But the matter's not so easily settled.
We'll talk it over next time. For the present,
with your permission, I'll withdraw.
FAUST: But stay a moment and tell me some good news. 230
MEPHISTOPHELES: Let me go now! I'll come back soon;
then you can question me to your heart's content.
FAUST: I set no trap for you. You walked into the meshes.

205. *Swan-foot-print:* or pentagram, a five-pointed star which warded off evil spirits.

Let him who's caught the Devil hold him!
He won't be caught so soon a second time.   235
MEPHISTOPHELES: If it will please you, I'm prepared
to stay — on one condition:
to pass the time I'll demonstrate
my art as a magician.
FAUST: I'd like that. Anything you wish,   240
but make it something pleasant.
MEPHISTOPHELES: My friend, you'll get more from this hour
to delight your senses than you could get
in a year of academic monotony.
All that the dainty spirits sing,   245
and all their pretty pictures,
are not mere empty sorcery.
They'll tickle your nose, refresh your palate,
and finally ravish your feelings.
It doesn't require rehearsal,   250
and so, since we're all ready, then let's go!
SPIRITS: Vanish, O gloomy
arches above us!
Let the blue ether gaze
tenderly down on us.   255
Let the black cumulus
clouds scud away from us!
Little stars glitter,
and milder suns shine.
Ethereal beauty   260
of bright sons of heaven,
wavering, lean to us,
hovering over us;
and wistful yearning
comes following after.   265
Fluttering ribbons
of the bright garments
cover the countryside,
cover the arbors
where dreaming lovers   270
swear love forever.
Leaves, what a wealth of leaves!
Tendrils still budding!
Heavily grape-clusters
fall in the must-vats.   275
How the juice gushes now,
crushed out by presses,
falling in torrents
of red-foaming wine,
purling round purest gems,   280

leaving the hills behind,
spreading in lakes and ponds,
bathing in pleasure
the flanks of green hillocks.
Now all the birds come   285
and drink it with joy,
then fly toward the sunlight,
fly to bright islands
that dance on the waves.
We hear in a chorus   290
voices rejoicing,
and over the meadows
see dancers amusing
themselves in the open.
People are climbing   295
over the mountains;
and some are sailing
over the water;
others are flying:
all move toward living,   300
all toward the distant
earth loving stars
blessed and kind.
MEPHISTOPHELES: He sleeps! Well done, my delicate airy rascals!
Your lullaby has really made him sleep.   305
I am indebted to you for this concert.
You're not the man yet who can hold the Devil!
Weave sweet phantom-forms around him;
plunge him in the ocean of delusion.
And now I need some sharp rat-teeth   310
to splinter this magic threshold.
But I shan't have to conjure long.
Already one comes scampering to obey me.

The lord of mice and rats,
bed-bugs, flies, frogs and lice,   315
orders you to come. Be bold
and gnaw this threshold for him
as soon as he's smeared a spot with oil —
here you come hopping. Start your work.
The point at the edge there has me caught.   320
Another nibble, and the trick is done.
Now, Faust, dream on until we meet again.
FAUST (*awakening*): Have I been deceived again and led astray?
Can such a throng of spirits disappear?
Was it a lying dream that the Devil was here,   325
and *was* it a poodle that ran away?

FAUST'S STUDY

(Faust and Mephistopheles.)

FAUST: Who knocks? Come in! Who's bothering me again?
MEPHISTOPHELES: Just me.
FAUST: Come in!
MEPHISTOPHELES: You must ask three times.
FAUST: Come in, then!   5
MEPHISTOPHELES: I like you this way.
I hope we'll hit it off together!
Here I am, come to chase away your wild moods,
gotten up as a nobleman in a red doublet trimmed with gold,
with a stiff silk cloak, a cock's feather   10
in my hat, and a long pointed sword.
I advise you to dress the same way.
Then we may travel easily,
while you discover what life can be.   15
FAUST: Whatever the clothes, I still would feel the pain
of this earth's narrow life. I am too old
for play, too young to live without desire.
What more can the world allow me? Renounce!
You must renounce! That's the eternal song   20
every man hears ringing in his ear,
singing hoarsely every hour,
his whole life long.
I wake at dawn with horror; I could weep
bitterly, to see another day   25
which in its course will not fulfill one wish, not one:
a day that lessens with capricious disappointments
all my anticipated pleasures.
A day that checks my creative power
with a thousand grinning goblins of life.   30
Then when night sinks down, I must stretch out
on a bed of desperation that gives me no rest;
for even there wild dreams will frighten me.
The god who lives within can stir me deeply,
can sit like a king. throned on my own strength,   35
but has no power over external things;
and so, existence is a burden,
death wished-for, and life hated.
MEPHISTOPHELES: And yet death's never a wholly welcome guest.
FAUST: Happy that man whose brow death winds
with bloody laurels in the splendor of victory;   40
or he who is taken in a girl's arms
after the nimble maddening dance.
Oh, would that I had fallen dead,

overcome by the might of the great spirit!
MEPHISTOPHELES: Yet, wasn't there someone on a certain night   45
who didn't drink the brown juice from the jug?
FAUST: It seems, you like to spy.
MEPHISTOPHELES: I'm not omniscient, but I do know many things.
FAUST: Although a sweet familiar tone drew me
from dreadful frenzy and deceived the remnant   50
of childhood's feelings with echoes of happy times,
now I curse all that holds the soul with lures
and hocus-pocus, all that confines it with blinding flattery
to this cave of gloom. I curse above all
that false self-exaltation with which the mind   55
befuddles itself. Cursed be the blinding
of illusion that wraps our senses.
A curse on cheating dreams,
obsessions of glory and desire for an immortal name.
Cursed be all flattering possessions, like wife and child,   60
servant and plough. Damned be Mammon
when he incites us to rash acts
with hopes of wealth, or when he softens our beds
for futile pleasures. Cursed be the balsam-juice
of the grape, and the delights of love.   65
Accursed be hope and faith and, above all, patience!
CHORUS OF SPIRITS (off-stage): Woe, woe!
You have destroyed
the splendid world
with a mighty fist.
It is shattered, and falls!   70
A demi-god broke it!
We carry the fragments
back to the nothingness.
We make lamentation   75
over lost beauty.
O mighty one
among earth's sons,
build it again, build it greater,
build it within yourself!
Begin the new way of life   80
brightly, more cheerfully,
and new songs will praise it!
MEPHISTOPHELES: These little fellows
belong to my faction.
Hear how they shrewdly   85
advise you to·act
and enjoy yourself.
Try the wide world;
abandon this solitude,   90

which dries up the brain
and stagnates the blood.

Stop playing with your grief
which, like a vulture, eats your life.
The worst society will let you feel 95
that you're a man among men.
And yet I don't mean that you should
be thrust among the stupid masses.
I'm not a high ranking devil, but if you'd like
to try your luck with me in a new life, 100
I'll gladly put myself at your disposal —
go where you will, do what you'd like to do,
be your companion — and if I suit you,
I'll be your servant and your slave.
FAUST: What must I do for you in return? 105
MEPHISTOPHELES: The debt can be handled on quite a long term.
FAUST: No, no! The Devil is an egoist
and certainly not inclined to help
anyone for god's charity. State your conditions clearly;
a servant like you must be expensive. 110
MEPHISTOPHELES: I'll bind myself to your service *here*
and do everything you ask of me;
Then when we meet over *yonder,* you shall do
as much for me as I've done for you.
FAUST: What lies beyond doesn't worry me. 115
Suppose you break this world to bits, another may arise.
My joy springs from this earth,
this sun shines on my sorrows.
When I leave here, let come what must.
What do I care about it now, if hereafter 120
men hate or love, or if in those other spheres
there be an Above or a Below?
MEPHISTOPHELES: In this mood you'll go far.
Commit yourself, and in the days to come
I'll use my arts for your pleasure. 125
I'll give you things that no man ever saw.
FAUST: Poor devil, what have you to give?
Was ever the ambitious spirit of man
understood by one of your kind?
If you have food — it never satisfies; 130
you have red gold — that's fickle as mercury
and runs from the hands; a game — nobody wins;
a girl — right in my arms
she would make eyes at someone else;
suppose you give the godlike joy of honor — 135
it vanishes like a meteor!

Show me the fruit that rots before it's picked,
and trees that grow green again each day!
MEPHISTOPHELES: I'm not afraid of such demands.
I can bring you such treasures without trouble.   140
But, my friend, the time will come
when we shall want to feast in peace.
FAUST: If I ever rest on a lazy bed of ease,
then let me die at once. If you can beguile me
with blandishments, satisfy me with what I am,   145
or deceive me with pleasure,
let that be my last day. I'll bet on that!
MEPHISTOPHELES: Taken!
FAUST: Yes, taken and taken again!
If ever I say to any moment: 150
"Linger — you are so wonderful!"
Then you may throw me in chains.
I'll be ready for the earth.
Then let the death-bells toll, you'll be released.
The clock may stand still, the hands drop down,   155
and time come to an end, for all of me!
MEPHISTOPHELES: Consider this carefully. We'll not forget it.
FAUST: Stand on your legal rights.
My action is not rash. I'll not regret it.
As soon as I stagnate, I become a slave.   160
So what does it matter whose I am?
MEPHISTOPHELES: I'll begin my service at once. Tonight
at the faculty dinner. But one thing more:
to provide for contingencies,
give me a couple of lines.   165
FAUST: O you pedant, to want a written statement!
Did you never know a man who kept his word?
Isn't it enough that my spoken word
rules all my days until eternity?
Doesn't the world go raging in all its currents,   170
and would a promise bind me?

Yet, man has a fixation on this illusion;
and who would like to rid himself of it?
Happy is he who has the pure truth in him.
He will regret no sacrifice that keeps it.   175
But a parchment, signed and sealed, is a ghost
that everybody fears. The word dies on the pen,
and wax and leather remain our masters. Spirit of evil,
what do you want of me: bronze, marble, vellum, paper?
Shall I write with chisel, engraving tool, or goose-quill?   180
I let you have your choice.
MEPHISTOPHELES: Come now! Don't get excited,

and oratorical!
A scrap of paper is enough for me,
and a little drop of blood to sign it.   185
FAUST: If this will satisfy you fully,
then let's carry out the farce.
MEPHISTOPHELES: Blood is a very special kind of juice.
FAUST: Don't worry. I'll not break the bargain.
The goal of all my struggling's been just this   190
that I now promise. I aspired too high.
I'm merely on the level of the Devil.
The mighty spirit has scorned me;
nature has closed herself to me.
The thread of thought is broken;   195
and long ago all knowledge made me sick.
Let me put out my burning passion
in sloughs of lechery!
Let every wonder be made ready
that hides behind magic veils.   200
Let us throw ourselves into the rush of time,
into the swirls of chance, where pain and pleasure,
success and disappointment,
change and shift as luck goes:
restless activity's the only thing for man.   205
MEPHISTOPHELES: Neither moderation nor goal is set for you.
You can sample and nibble at everything;
and snatch at things as you fly past.
And may you prosper in your pleasures,
but start at once and don't be timid!   210
FAUST: Listen! It's not a question of joy.
I vow myself to excitement, intoxication,
the bitterest pleasures, amorous hatred,
and stirring remorse. My heart, now free
of the longing for learning, shall close itself   215
to no future pain. I mean to enjoy
in my innermost being all that is offered to mankind,
to seize the highest and the lowest,
to mix all kinds of good and evil,
and thus expand my Self till it includes   220
the spirit of all men — and, with them,
I shall be ruined and perish in the end.
MEPHISTOPHELES: Listen to me, for I have chewed
this same tough food for many thousand years:
from cradle to coffin there's no man   225
who can digest this ancient sour dough.
You can believe me that this world was made
to suit a god who dwells in eternal light.
He has cast us devils into darkness;

for you it's enough to have only night and day. 230
FAUST: But I will!
MEPHISTOPHELES: A proper answer!
But I'm still troubled by one thing:
time is short and art is long.
I'd think you'd let yourself be instructed. 235
Associate yourself with a poet
and let him gallop through the fields of thought
and heap all noble qualities on your honored head:
the lion's courage, the stag's speed,
the fiery Italian blood, 240
the Northman's fortitude;
let him solve for you the secret that binds
cunning with magnanimity, and teaches you
how, with the instincts of youth's hot desires,
to fall in love according to a plan. 245
I'd like myself to meet with such man,
and I'd name him Sir Microcosm.
FAUST: But what am I if I should fail to gain
the crown of mankind for which I struggle
with all my senses? 250
MEPHISTOPHELES: In the end, you are exactly — what you are.
Put on a wig with a million curls,
put the highest heeled boots on your feet,
yet you remain in the end just what you are.
FAUST: I feel how every effort has been in vain 255
to encompass human wisdom in my head,
and when I sit down finally
no new strength comes to me,
and I'm not taller by a hair or any nearer to infinity.
MEPHISTOPHELES: My dear man, these things seem to you 260
just as they do to others.
We must manage more cleverly
before the joys of life escape us.
Damn it all! You must use hands and feet,
and head and sex to gain your ends! 265
And because I enjoy all these in play,
are they in any way less mine?
If I can hire six stallions,
is not all their power mine?
I dash away and act as big 270
as if I had two dozen legs.
Quick now, give up this idle pondering!
And let's be off into the great wide world!
I tell you: the fool who speculates on things
is like some animal on a dry heath, 275

234. *time . . . long:* see the note to ll. 201–202 in the first scene of the tragedy.

led by an evil fiend in endless circles,
while fine green pastures lie on every side.
FAUST: When do we start?
MEPHISTOPHELES: As soon as we can.
This place is a torment. 280
What sort of life is it where a man
bores both himself and his students?
Leave that to your neighbor, Doctor Paunch!
Why should you slave to thresh out that old straw?
The best you know you can't show to the boys. 285
Right now I hear one at the door.
FAUST: It's quite impossible for me to see him.
MEPHISTOPHELES: The poor boy's waited so long already,
he mustn't go away uncomforted.
Come, give me your doctor's gown and hood. 290
This mask will suit me wonderfully.

(*He changes his clothes.*)

Go now and leave it to my wits!
A quarter-hour is all I'll need,
in which time go get ready for our trip!

(*Faust goes out.*)

MEPHISTOPHELES (*in the doctor's gown*)
Scoff at all knowledge and despise 295
reason and science, those flowers of mankind.
Let the father of all lies
with dazzling necromancy make you blind,
then I'll have you unconditionally —
fate gave him a spirit that's ever pressing forward, 300
uncurbed; his rash impulses overleap
the joys of earth. I'll drag him through the wild life,
through the flat wasteland. I'll let him flounder,
stiffen, stick fast, and food and drink
shall bait his insatiate sense, 305
hovering before his greedy lips.
Vainly he'll beg me for refreshment,
and even if he hadn't given himself to the Devil,
he'd still be ruined in the end.

(*A Student enters.*)

STUDENT: I've been here just a little while 310
and come, full of devotion,
to meet and know a man of whom
the world speaks with such reverence.
MEPHISTOPHELES: I'm flattered by your courtesy.

You see a man like any other. 315
Have you already been around elsewhere?
STUDENT: Please, sir, assist me. I have come
with the best intentions, good health, and a little money.
My mother didn't like to have me leave her;
I want to learn something here that's practical. 320
MEPHISTOPHELES: That's fine. You've come to the right place.
STUDENT: But honestly I don't like it here at all
and would love to get away from these walls and halls
and these narrow gloomy lecture-rooms.
I feel so cramped: no grass, no trees — 325
and on a bench in the auditorium
I cannot think and I am deaf and dumb.
MEPHISTOPHELES: That comes with practice; as a child at first
unwillingly receives the mother's breast,
but soon takes to the feeding eagerly; 330
so you, nursed on the breasts of wisdom,
will satisfy your thirst more gladly every day.
STUDENT: I'll hang with joy about her neck!
But only tell me the best means to use.
MEPHISTOPHELES: Before proceeding, you must tell me: 335
what subject will you choose?
STUDENT: I want to be very learned and understand
the secrets of the earth and of the firmament —
the natural sciences, that is to say!
MEPHISTOPHELES: You're starting out on the right paths, 340
but you mustn't let any distraction lead you astray.
STUDENT: I'm set upon it, body and soul;
but I'd like some time to play
in freedom and not have to study
during the summer holidays! 345
MEPHISTOPHELES: Use your time well. It glides away so swiftly,
but system will teach you how to conserve it.
My friend, take logic. There your spirit's deftly
laced in the tight Spanish boot.
Thereafter you'll proceed more circumspectly, 350
crawling down the road of reason, but never veer,
like a will o' the wisp, and criss-cross here and there.
Each day you'll learn that what required no thought
for its performance, as when you eat and drink,
must now be done in order — one, two, three! 355
And really in these thinking-mills
it's like a masterpiece worked on a weaver's loom:
one treadle moves like a thousand threads on spools;
the humming shuttles dart from side to side;
threads flow invisibly; one stroke 360

349. *Spanish boot:* a torture device.

will tie a thousand knots — then the philosopher steps in
and shows you that it must be so:
the first was thus and the second so;
therefore the third and fourth are likewise so;
but if it weren't for the first and second,   365
the third and fourth just never could have been.
Everywhere the scholars praise
this sort of thing, but never become weavers.
The man who wants to know   370
organic truth and describe it well
seeks first to drive the living spirit out;
he's got the parts in hand there,
it's merely the breath of life that's lacking.
The chemists call it *encheiresin naturae*   375
and mock themselves and don't know how or why.
STUDENT: I don't quite understand you.
MEPHISTOPHELES: You'll get the hang of it by and by.
Everything will be simplified
after it's properly classified.   380
STUDENT: I'm all confused from what you've said,
as if a mill-wheel were turning in my brain.
MEPHISTOPHELES: Then, before studying any further,
you must try metaphysics; but take care
to grasp the deepest meanings and explore   385
what isn't suitable for human brains.
There's always a pompous word to serve
for what we may or may not understand.
See that throughout the first semester
you follow the routine most carefully.   390
When the chimes ring in the tower,
be at class punctually — don't miss a day.
Be well prepared for five long lectures;
study each paragraph so well
that you can check up on the teacher;   395
don't let him put in a syllable
that isn't in the book.
And busily write down his every word
as though the Holy Ghost were dictating to you!
STUDENT: That you won't have to tell me more than once!   400
I think that's very good advice.
What one gets down in black and white in notes
he can carry home to comfort him at night.
MEPHISTOPHELES: Now you must choose your major subject.
STUDENT: The study of law does not seem too attractive.
MEPHISTOPHELES: I can't hold that against you, I admit,   405
for I know well just how that matter stands.

374. *encheiresin naturae:* the force of nature.

The statutes and the laws are handed on
like some disease that never ends,
stealthily creeping from race to race.
Reason turns nonsense; beneficence becomes a plague.   410
It's too bad that you're a grandchild, my lad.
But of natural rights, unfortunately,
there's never any question.
STUDENT: You have increased my own aversion for the law.
The students you teach are lucky indeed.   415
Maybe I'd like to study theology.
MEPHISTOPHELES: I wouldn't want to be leading you astray,
but in the subject matter of this field
it's difficult to keep on the right track;
there's so much poison hidden here   420
it's hard to tell it from the medicine.
You'll find it's best to have just one professor
and swear by the master's words. In general,
stick fast to words, and through that trusty gateway
you'll get into the temple of assurance.   425
STUDENT: But there ought to be some idea behind a word.
MEPHISTOPHELES: Of course! But don't torment yourself too much.
Just where the idea's lacking a word pops up.
Words are splendid weapons for fighting;
with words you can prepare a system;   430
words are grand to put your faith in —
and you can't take anything from one.
STUDENT: Excuse me if I ask too many questions;
but won't you please make some suggestions for the study
of medicine? Three years go by so quickly   435
and, God, the field's so wide!
If only I could get a pointer
then I could grope my way ahead.
MEPHISTOPHELES (aside): I'm bored with this dry tone
and now I'll really play the Devil again.   440

(aloud)

The spirit of medicine is easily comprehended;
you study through the macrocosm and microcosm,
but in the end let it all go, as pleases God.
In vain you rummage learnedly far and wide;
each one learns only what he can;   445
but he who seizes the instant boldly,
he is the clever one!
Now you, you're pretty well built
and will not be lacking in daring.
As long as you thoroughly trust yourself,   450
all the simple souls will have confidence in you.

Above all, learn how to manage the women:
all their eternal Ah's and Oh's
of a thousand sorts
can be cured at a single point.   455
And if you act discreetly,
you'll keep them all under your thumb.
First, your M. D. will give them confidence
that your skill and learning are immense.
Right at the start you can fumble them here and there,   460
when another man would have to coax for years.
Learn how to press the pulse in the little wrist
and with fiery furtive glances slip
your arm around her slender hips
to see how tightly she is laced.   465
STUDENT: Already it seems better!
Now I begin to see the where and how.
MEPHISTOPHELES: My friend, all theory is gray,
and the golden tree of life is green.
STUDENT: I swear to you it's like a dream.   470
May I return another time and trouble you
to expound your system to the bottom?
MEPHISTOPHELES: I'll do all that I can for you and more.
STUDENT: I cannot possibly leave
until I get your autograph.   475
I wonder if you'd be so kind.
MEPHISTOPHELES: With pleasure.

(*He writes in the book and returns it.*)

STUDENT (*reading*): *Eritis sicut Deus, scientes bonum et malum.*
(*He closes the book reverently and goes out.*)

MEPHISTOPHELES: Just follow the old proverb and my cousin the snake;
and in spite of your likeness to God,   480
your soul will soon be quaking!

(*Faust comes in.*)

FAUST: Where do we go from here?
MEPHISTOPHELES: Wherever you please. First we can see
the world of little people, then the great.   485
With pleasure and profit
you can crib through the course.
FAUST: But admit that it's pretty hard to be
a man of the world, with a beard as long as mine.
I lack the *savoir vivre*. I won't succeed.   490
I never did know how to get around;
indeed, I feel so small before most other men,

478. *Eritis . . . malum*: "You shall be as God, knowing good and evil" [translator's note].

that often I could sink into the dirt.
MEPHISTOPHELES: Time will take care of that, my friend.
Gain some self-confidence and you'll know how to live.
FAUST: But how shall we get away from here?
Where have you a coach, driver and horses? 495
MEPHISTOPHELES: We only need to spread this cloak
and it will carry us through the sky.
Of course, upon this daring journey
your baggage must be very light.
A puff of hydrogen which I'll prepare 500
will hoist us quickly to the upper regions.
Congratulations on your new career!

AUERBACH'S CELLAR IN LEIPSIC

(*A lively drinking party is in progress.*)

FROSCH: Will no one drink? Nobody laugh?
I'll teach you how to make faces!
Today you're all like soggy straw,
but usually you're all ablaze.
BRANDER: And you're to blame; you've given us
neither nonsense or bawdiness. 5
FROSCH (*pouring a glass of wine over his head*): There now! You've
both.
BRANDER: You double-swine!
FROSCH: You asked for it! And there it is!
SIEBEL: Throw all brawlers out of doors!
Swill and shout and sing the chorus! 10
Hurray, hurrah, and heidy ho!
ALTMAYER: Damn you, shut up! Bring me some cotton.
He's broken my ear-drum.
SIEBEL: When the ceiling echoes back the song,
then you can feel that rolling bass. 15
FROSCH: That's right! Put out the man who doesn't like it!
Oh! tara lara lay!
ALTMAYER: Oh! tara lara lay!
FROSCH: That's the right tune. Let's go.
20

(*He sings.*)

The darling Roman Empire, oh,
what holds the thing together?
BRANDER: That's a nasty song! To hell with politics!
No more of that. And thank God every day
that you weren't born to rule
the Roman Empire. You can bet I'm glad 25
I'm not the Kaiser or his chancellor!

But we must have a chief, so let's elect a Pope.
You know the one essential quality
that turns the scale and raises up a man.   30
FROSCH (*singing*): Soar to the sky, O nightingale,
and greet my love ten thousand times!
SIEBEL: No songs to girls! I can't stand that.
FROSCH: Just try to stop me! Greetings and kisses to my girl!

(*He sings.*)
                                                                             35
Unbolt the door in the quiet night.
Unbolt the door. My love sleeps light.
But now it's dawn so bolt it tight!
SIEBEL: Yes, sing! Go on and brag of her!
I'll have my turn for laughter soon.   40
She led me on — I followed, but
she'll do the same to you. She needs a goblin
to play with her at a dark cross-road.
An old he-goat galloping from the Brocken
may bleat Good Night to her! A flesh and blood   45
lover is far too good for that little bitch.
The only greeting she'll get from me
is when I bash in her window.
BRANDER (*pounding on the table*): Quiet, all you, and listen to me.
Admit I know what's what. We've got   50
some lovesick fellows sitting here.
And I must give them something cheerful
to make them feel a little better.
So here's a brand new song. Now open up
and bear down on the choruses.

(*He sings.*)
                                                                             55
In a nest in the cellar lived a rat
that fed on butter, grease, and lard
till she achieved a paunch as fat
as Doctor Luther's, round and hard.
The cook smeared poison out one night —   60
and the rat's world soon grew small and tight,
as though she had love in her belly.
CHORUS (*shouting*): As though she had love in her belly!
BRANDER: The rat raced here, the rat raced there,
she lapped up puddle-water,   65
tore up the whole house, everywhere,
but nothing made her better.
She hopped and leaped in agony
as though she had love in her belly!
CHORUS: As though she had love in her belly!

BRANDER: Driven by torment to the light,   70
she ran about the kitchen,
fell on the hearth and gasped and lay,
most piteously twitching.
Then laughed the poisoner: Bless my soul!
she's whistling now on the final hole —   75
as though she had love in her belly!
CHORUS: As though she had love in her belly!
SIEBEL: How these dull birds amuse themselves!
It strikes me it's a mighty art
to sprinkle poison for the poor old rats!   80
BRANDER: So you like them, do you?
ALTMAYER: Misfortune has turned tame and mild
this old pot-gut with the shiny skull.
He looks at the bloated rat and sees
his portrait, lifelike as could be.   85

(*Faust and Mephistopheles come in.*)

MEPHISTOPHELES: First now I must introduce you
to some lively fellows who'll amuse you.
Here you can see how pleasant life can be
when every day's a holiday.
With slender wit and plenty of leisure
each man dances his little round,   90
like kittens chasing their tails for pleasure.
And while no hang-overs spoil their fun,
and the host lets the little bills run on,
they are happy and free from worry.
BRANDER: These gentlemen are traveling.   95
You can see that from their foreign air;
they've not been here in town an hour.
FROSCH: You're right. But my Leipsic's the place for me!
It's a little Paris and gives its people refinement.
SIEBEL: Who do you guess these strangers are?   100
FROSCH: Just let me at them! Over a full glass
I'll pull the worms of fact
from the fellow's nose like a baby's tooth.
They appear to me to be noblemen,
they look so proud and discontented.   105
BRANDER: They're phonies, I'll bet you.
ALTMAYER: Maybe so.
FROSCH: Watch me. I'll screw their secret out.
MEPHISTOPHELES (*to Faust*): These little sods here wouldn't suspect
the Devil if he had them by the neck!
FAUST: Good evening, gentlemen!   111
SIEBEL: And we return the compliment with thanks.

99–100. *But my Leipsic's . . . refinement:* These lines are ironic.

(Softly, as he looks at Mephistopheles from the side.)

Why does the rascal limp with his left foot?
MEPHISTOPHELES: May we sit here? Instead of a decent drink, 115
which can't be had, we'll have good company.
ALTMAYER: You're spoiled, or used to the best, I guess.
FROSCH: Have you just come from Rippach?
Did you dine with Master Hans tonight?
MEPHISTOPHELES: Today we went by without stopping, 120
but the last time we spoke to him
he talked a lot about his relatives
and gave us many greetings to bring you!

(He bows to Frosch.)

ALTMAYER *(softly)*: There now! He understands what you're up to!
SIEBEL: A clever customer! 125
FROSCH: Just wait a minute. I'll get him soon.
MEPHISTOPHELES: Unless I'm wrong, I heard just now
some well-trained voices singing a chorus.
The arches here must make fine echoes.
FROSCH: Perhaps you're a virtuoso. 130
MEPHISTOPHELES: I'd like to sing but I haven't the voice.
ALTMAYER: Give us a song.
MEPHISTOPHELES: All you want of them.
SIEBEL: But let it be new as a nail!
MEPHISTOPHELES: We've recently returned from Spain, 135
that lovely country of song and wine.

(He sings)

Once on a time a monarch
had a flea, a giant one . . .
FROSCH: Hear that! You understand? A flea!
A neat little customer, not for me! 140
MEPHISTOPHELES *(singing)*: Once on a time a monarch
had a flea, a giant one,
which he loved no less fondly
than if it were his son.
He called the royal tailor, 145
the tailor to him came.
"Measure Milord for a coat
and breeches to match the same!"
BRANDER: Don't forget to tell the tailor
he must really measure carefully; 150
if he wants to keep his head

---

119. *Hans:* "Hans Arsch, the fictitious hero of a student's joke, which is not too delicate" [translator's note]. He was also called Hans von Rippach; Rippach is on the road to Leipsic.
141ff. *Once on a time . . . :* Goethe is satirizing the Court of Weimar.

those trousers will have to be a good fit!
MEPHISTOPHELES (*singing*): Soon in silk and velvet
the flea was grandly dressed;
he had ribbons on his clothing
and a cross upon his chest. 155
He became a high official
and wore a gorgeous star.
He found jobs for his relations
at court, and they went far. 160
Of course, the lords and ladies
were exceedingly provoked.
The queen and her maid-in-waiting
were pinched and plagued and poked;
but didn't dare to crack them 165
or scratch them off at night.
But we can smother and crunch them
as soon as they start to bite.
CHORUS (*shouting*): We can smother and crunch them
as soon as they start to bite! 170
FROSCH: Bravo! bravo! That was fine.
SIEBEL: The same to every flea!
BRANDER: Squash them with your finger-tips.
ALTMAYER: Hurray for wine and liberty!
MEPHISTOPHELES: I'd like to drink to freedom myself, 175
if your wine were only a little bit better.
SIEBEL: You'd better not let us hear that again!
MEPHISTOPHELES: If the landlord wouldn't be offended,
I'd like to stand you, as my guests,
a round of the best drinks from *our* cellar. 180
SIEBEL: Just bring them on. I'll take the blame.
FROSCH: Give us a good drink, and we'll praise you.
But see that it's not too small.
For if you want my judgment,
I must have a real mouthful. 185
ALTMAYER (*aside*): I've smelled it out. They're from the Rhine.
MEPHISTOPHELES: Bring me an auger.
BRANDER: What will you do with that?
Have you got some kegs outside the door?
ALTMAYER (*aside*): The landlord's tool-box is back there. 190
MEPHISTOPHELES (*taking the auger, to Frosch*): Tell me, what's your
favorite wine?
FROSCH: What do you mean? Have you several kinds?
MEPHISTOPHELES: I'll give each of you what he likes best.
ALTMAYER (*to Frosch*): Ah ha! already you're smacking your lips.
FROSCH: Good. If I can choose, I'll take Rhine wine, 195
the best gift of our fatherland.

MEPHISTOPHELES (*as he bores a hole in the table's edge at Frosch's place*): Get wax and make some stoppers at once.
ALTMAYER: Ridiculous! This is some sleight of hand.
MEPHISTOPHELES (*to Brander*): And you?
BRANDER: I'd like champagne, and with plenty of sparkle!   200

(*Mephistopheles bores. Meanwhile stoppers are made and the holes plugged.*)

BRANDER: You can't steer clear of everything that's foreign.
Often the best things come from far away.
A German hates the French with all his heart
and yet he gladly drinks their wine.
SIEBEL (*as Mephistopheles approaches his place*): I must admit, I don't like sour.   205
Give me a glass of something really sweet.
MEPHISTOPHELES (*as he bores*): Just wait a minute, and Tokay will pour.
ALTMAYER: No, gentlemen! Look me in the eye!
You're pulling our legs.
MEPHISTOPHELES: No, no, with noble guests like you   210
that would be going too far.
But speak up quickly!
What kind of wine do you want?
ALTMAYER: Anything. Only, hurry with it.
MEPHISTOPHELES (*after the holes have been bored and plugged, with strange gestures*): Clustered grapes the vine has borne,   215
and the billy goat wears horns.
The stalks are food, the sap is new,
the wooden table can give wine too.
Gaze deeply in nature and believe!
Here is a miracle achieved!   220
Pull corks and fill your glasses to the top!

(*As each draws a stopper, the wine asked for flows into his glass.*)

ALL: Beautiful fountain, may it never stop flowing!
MEPHISTOPHELES: Be careful not to spill a drop!

(*They drink freely.*)

ALL (*singing*): We're all as gay as cannibals,   225
or as five hundred sows!
MEPHISTOPHELES: See how they lap it and like it! They're doing fine.
FAUST: I'd like to go now.
MEPHISTOPHELES: First you must see
their splendid bestiality.

(*Siebel, drinking carelessly, spills some wine on the floor. It bursts into flames.*)

SIEBEL: Help! Fire! Help! Hell's burning! 230
MEPHISTOPHELES (*as he charms the flame*): Be quiet, friendly element!

(*to Siebel*)

This time it was just a drop of purgatorial fire.
SIEBEL: What's this? Just wait! We'll pay you back!
It seems you don't know who we are.
FROSCH: Just think again before you try it a second time! 235
ALTMAYER: We'd better pack him off on the quiet!
SIEBEL: What, sir? Do you dare insult us
with this outrageous hocus-pocus?
MEPHISTOPHELES: Shut up, you old wine-keg!
SIEBEL: You broom-stick, you!
You dare insult us! 240
BRANDER: Just wait! Blows will fall here, black and blue!

(*Altmayer draws a cork from the table and flames leap forth.*)

ALTMAYER: I'm burning! I'm burning!
SIEBEL: It's sorcery!
Hit him! He's anybody's game! 245

(*They draw knives and attack Mephistopheles.*)

MEPHISTOPHELES (*with solemn gestures*): False images and words,
ensnare their senses and change the scene.
Be here . . . be there!

(*They stand amazed and look at one another.*)

ALTMAYER: Where am I? What a lovely land!
FROSCH: Vineyards! Am I seeing things?
SIEBEL: And these beautiful bunches of grapes! 250
BRANDER: Look at these vine branches
under the spreading leaves!

(*He seizes Siebel by the nose. The others, with raised knives, do the same.*)

MEPHISTOPHELES (*with more gestures*): Illusion take the veils from their eyes!
And you, see how the Devil plays a trick! 255

(*He vanishes with Faust. The drinkers come to their senses, startled.*)

SIEBEL: What happened?
ALTMAYER: How did we get this way?
FROSCH: Was that your nose?
BRANDER (*to Siebel*): And I have hold of yours!
ALTMAYER: Somebody knocked me out.
Get me a chair. I'm going to faint. 260

FROSCH: Can anybody tell me just what happened?
SIEBEL: Where has he gone? When I find him,
he'll not get off alive.
ALTMAYER: I saw him riding a cask through the tavern door, 265
but my feet stuck to the floor, heavy as lead.

(*turning to the table*)

I wonder if the wine still flows.
SIEBEL: It was all fake and deception.
FROSCH: I thought I was drinking wine.
BRANDER: And weren't those real grapes either? 270
ALTMAYER: Can you believe in miracles? Who knows?

THE WITCH'S KITCHEN

(*A big cauldron hangs over a fire on a low hearth. In the rising vapor various forms appear. A She-ape is skimming the broth. The He-ape and their young ones are sitting nearby. The walls and ceiling are covered with fantastic witches' apparatus. Faust and Mephistopheles come in.*)

FAUST: This crazy sorcery disgusts me. Promise me
I'll recover in this chaos of madness.
Must I ask help from this old hag?
And can this messy cookery take thirty years
from my body? Too bad you know nothing better! 5
I've neither heart nor hope for this.
Have nature and some noble mind
been able to find no other formula?
MEPHISTOPHELES: My friend, you're talking sense again.
There is a natural method for recapturing youth; 10
but that's in another book, in a curious chapter.
FAUST: I want to know it.
MEPHISTOPHELES: Good! The remedy requires no money,
physician nor magic. Just go out in the field
and begin to dig and plough.
Keep your whole life within a little circle, 15
eat simple food, live with the beasts as a beast,
don't be too proud to dung the field you reap.
That's the best method, believe me,
to keep yourself young at eighty.
FAUST: But I'm not used to that sort of thing. 20
I can't even dig with a spade.
The narrow life doesn't suit me.
MEPHISTOPHELES: Then you must try the witch.
FAUST: Will no one do but this old hag?
Can't you yourself work up a brew? 25

MEPHISTOPHELES: Now, wouldn't that be a pretty pastime!
In the same time I could build a thousand bridges.
It isn't science or art alone;
it takes lots of patience to do this work.
A quiet spirit keeps busy with it for years;⁣   30
for only time produces the fermentation.
And everything about it is a wonderful business!
The Devil taught her how to brew it,
yet the devil alone isn't able to make it.

(*He sees the animals.*)

Look! What an ornamental pair!   35
That's the slavey. And there's the house-boy.

(*to the apes*)

The old lady isn't at home, it seems?
THE APES: She's at a party!
She flew up the chimney!
Out of the house.   40
MEPHISTOPHELES: How long is she usually off on a revel?
THE APES: As long as it takes us to warm our paws.
MEPHISTOPHELES (*to Faust*): What do you think of these dainty crea-
        tures?
FAUST: I never saw anything so absurd!
MEPHISTOPHELES: No — a little discourse with such beasts   45
can prove amusing indeed.

(*to the apes*)

Now tell me, you damned puppets,
what are you stirring there in the porridge pot?
THE APES: We're cooking some waterish beggars' soup.
MEPHISTOPHELES: You'll have plenty of customers for that.   50
HE-APE (*making up to Mephistopheles*): Oh, roll the dice
that can make me rich,
and let me win!
My luck's so bad,
but if I had money   55
then I'd have brains.
MEPHISTOPHELES: This monkey here would love to bet
in any kind of lottery.

(*The young apes have been playing with a big globe, which they now
roll forward.*)

HE-APE: This is the world.
It rises and falls   60
and continually whirls.

It rings like glass —
how soon it breaks!
It's hollow inside. 65
Here it shines bright,
and here even more.
Now me, I'm lively!
But, my dear son,
you keep away — 70
you too must die!
It's made of clay
and will crumble to bits.

MEPHISTOPHELES: What good's that sieve?

HE-APE (*taking it down*): If you were a thief, 75
I could tell it at once.

(*He runs to the She-ape and lets her look through it.*)

Look through the sieve.
Do you recognize The Thief
but dare not name him?

MEPHISTOPHELES (*going toward the fire*): And what's this pot? 80

THE APES: The silly idiot
doesn't know the pot!
He doesn't know the kettle!

MEPHISTOPHELES: You ill-bred brute!

HE-APE: Take the whisk-broom to it 85
and settle down on the settle!

(*He makes Mephistopheles sit down.*)

FAUST (*who has been looking in a mirror, now approaching, then drawing back from it*): What do I see? What a heavenly picture
shows itself in this magic mirror!
O love, lend me your swiftest wings
and lead me straight to her. 90
But alas, when I move forward from this spot
and try to approach, she fades away in mist,
this lovely image of a woman.
Is it possible that she can be so beautiful?
Do I not see in this reclining body 95
the very essence of heaven?
"Earth has not anything more fair."

MEPHISTOPHELES: Why, naturally, if God worked six whole days
and shouted Bravo! at the finish,
he must have done something pretty impressive. 100
For the present gaze your fill. I know
exactly where to spy out just such a treasure.
And happy the man whose luck it is
to lead her home as his bride.

(*Faust continues to look at the mirror. Mephistopheles is stretched on the bench and plays with the broom.*)

I sit here like a king on his throne.
Here is my sceptre, but where's the crown?   105

(*The apes, who have been playing pranks, bring him a crown, and shriek.*)

THE APES: Just be so good,
as with sweat and blood
to glue this crown together!

(*They fight for the crown. It breaks and they dance with the pieces.*)

Now it's done for and broke,
we talk and we look,   110
we listen and make verses.
FAUST (*before the mirror*): God, I'm almost crazy!
MEPHISTOPHELES (*pointing to the apes*): It makes even me a little bit
        dizzy.
THE APES: If the rhyme goes well
and fits, who can tell   115
but there may be some thought in it?
FAUST: My heart begins to burn.
Quick! Let's get away from here.
MEPHISTOPHELES: Well, at least it's good to learn
some poets are sincere.   120

(*The kettle, neglected by the She-ape, boils over. A great flame leaps up, and the Witch comes down the chimney, shrieking.*)

THE WITCH: Aouw! Aouw!
You damned beast! You sow!
You've forgotten the kettle and burned me!
Damned beast!

(*She sees the visitors.*)

What is this here?   125
Who are you?
What do you want?
How did you sneak in?
Let the torture of fire
burn your bones!   130

(*She dips the ladle in the pot and throws flames at everyone. The apes whimper.*)

MEPHISTOPHELES (*turning the brush end for end and smashing the glass-
        ware and pots*): Be broken in two!
I'll spatter your stew!

The glass is broken,
but it's all a joke.
You carcass, it's only the time   135
and beat of your rhyme!

(*as the Witch steps back in anger and horror*)

Don't you know me, skeleton, scarecrow?
Don't you recognize your lord and master?
Why don't I give you a beating,
and crush you and your ape-spirits?   140
Have you no longer any respect for the scarlet jacket?
Did you never see the cock's feather before?
Is this face disguised? Must I tell you my name?
THE WITCH: Master, pardon my raw greeting!
But I don't see the horse's hoof.   145
And where are your two ravens?
MEPHISTOPHELES: This time you can get away with it.
It's been a long while, I'll admit,
since we have seen each other.
And then, since culture has taken a lick at the world,   150
the Devil's also been touched up a bit.
The phantom of the North is seen no longer.
Can you detect any horns or tail or claws?
And as for the hoof, which I can't quite spare,
it would prejudice people against me;   155
therefore, I do as many a buck has done
and have worn false calves for many years.
THE WITCH (*dancing*): I almost go out of my head
when I see Squire Satan here again!
MEPHISTOPHELES: I forbid you, woman, to call me by that name!   160
THE WITCH: Why so? Has it done you any harm?
MEPHISTOPHELES: It's long been buried in the book of fables,
but men have grown no better:
They're free of the Evil One, but the evil ones remain.
Just call me Baron; that's all right.   165
I'm merely a cavalier like any other.
If you've any doubt about my noble blood,
just look at the splendid coat-of-arms I bear!

(*He makes an indecent gesture.*)

THE WITCH (*laughing immoderately*): Ha! ha! That's your old self:
the same old rascal you always were!   170
MEPHISTOPHELES (*to Faust*): My friend, learn this:
the way to handle witches.
THE WITCH: Now tell me, gentlemen, how can I oblige you?
MEPHISTOPHELES: A good glass of your famous liquor.

The very oldest, if you please! 175
For age puts double strength in it.
THE WITCH: Gladly! I've got here a bottle
from which I sometimes tipple myself.
It's lost at last all trace of stink.
I'll give you a little glass of it with pleasure. 180

(*softly, to Mephistopheles*)

But if this man drinks it unprepared,
he will not live an hour, as you know.
MEPHISTOPHELES: He's a good friend and will thrive on it.
I don't begrudge him your kitchen's best.
Draw your circle and speak your spells, 185
and let him have a good full cup.

(*With fantastic gestures the Witch makes a circle and puts curious
things in it. Meanwhile the glasses ring and the kettle makes music.
Finally she brings a large book and arranges the apes to serve as a
lectern and hold torches. She beckons Faust to approach.*)

FAUST (*to Mephistopheles*): What's all this crazy apparatus?
I've seen this frantic nonsense and trickery before
and have always despised them.
MEPHISTOPHELES: It's a sort of mummery. She's only joking. 190
Don't be so particular.
She's like a doctor with her hocus-pocus
that makes the potion work the miracle.

(*He gets Faust into the circle.*)

THE WITCH (*with great emphasis, declaiming from the book*): Watch
    me and then
from one get ten,
drop two, then three, 195
make it even, see!
Now you are rich.
Then drop the four.
From five and six,
so says the witch, 200
make seven and eight.
Then all's complete.
And nine is one,
and ten is none.
That is the witch's multiplication-table! 205
FAUST: The old girl is raving in a delirium.
MEPHISTOPHELES: There's a lot more yet where that came from.
I know it well; the whole book sounds the same.
And I have lost much time on it, because 210
the perfect contradiction remains

as much a mystery to the wise as to the fools.
My friend, the art is old and new.
It's been the custom in all ages   215
through three and one, and one and three,
to hide the truth and propagandize error.
Untroubled, they chatter and teach it in the schools —
and why concern yourself with idiots?
When he hears words man's likely to believe   220
that they convey ideas and have meaning.
THE WITCH (*continuing*): The exalted skill
of science still
from the world is well-concealed.
Who doesn't think   225
gets in a wink
the whole affair revealed.
FAUST: What craziness is that she is drooling?
My head is almost splitting.
I seem to hear a hundred thousand fools   230
speaking in one vast chorus.
MEPHISTOPHELES: Enough, O excellent sibyl!
Give us the panacea
and fill the cup to the rim.
This little drink won't hurt my friend: 235
he's taken many honorary degrees
and plenty of good gulps with them.

(*With much ceremony, the Witch pours the elixir. As Faust raises the cup to his lips, a little flame rises.*)

MEPHISTOPHELES: Bottoms up! Quickly! It will do
your heart a lot of good. For shame!
You're the Devil's intimate friend,   240
yet you're afraid of a little fire?

(*The Witch breaks the ring. Faust comes out.*)

MEPHISTOPHELES: Now, hurry! You should not rest.
THE WITCH: May this little swallow do you good!
MEPHISTOPHELES (*to the Witch*): If I can do a favor for you,
you need only mention it on Walpurgis Night.
THE WITCH: Here's a song! Whenever you sing it,   245
you'll get a remarkable reaction.
MEPHISTOPHELES (*to Faust*): Hurry! And let me guide you. You must
        sweat
to make its power work through your whole body.
And then I'll teach you how to pass
your time in noble idleness.   250
Soon you'll feel, with pleasant surprise
how Cupid stirs in you and sets things going.
FAUST: Just one more glimpse in that looking-glass!

That woman's image was magnificent!
MEPHISTOPHELES: No, no! Soon you'll see the very model   255
of beauty in solid human flesh.

(*aside*)

With that drink in your belly,
you'll think you're seeing Helen of Troy
in every woman you meet.

A STREET

(*Faust sees Margaret* * *going by.*)

FAUST: Beautiful lady, I wonder if I may
offer my arm to escort you anywhere?
MARGARET: I'm neither a lady, nor am I pretty,
and I know my own way home.

(*She goes out.*)

FAUST: By heaven! that's a lovely child!   5
I've never seen one like that before.
Modest and virtuous, unspoiled,
and yet with some snap in her too.
Her lips were red, her cheeks were bright —
Will I ever forget   10
how my heart jumped, how she dropped her eyes?
Even her curtness filled me with ecstasy.

(*Mephistopheles enters.*)

FAUST: Listen! You must get that girl for me!
MEPHISTOPHELES: Which one?
FAUST: The one that just went by.   15
MEPHISTOPHELES: Oh, that one! She was just coming from the priest,
and he absolved her of every sin.
I sneaked up close behind the box;
she's the most innocent little thing,
with less than nothing to confess.
I have no power over her.   20
FAUST: Yet she must be fourteen or more.
MEPHISTOPHELES: You talk like any libertine
Who wants each tender flower, and imagines
she has nothing that can't be picked;
but it doesn't always turn out like that.   25
FAUST: Come off your perch. Don't preach again
to me of morals. I tell you, short and plain:
unless that girl with her fresh young blood

* "Goethe also calls her Gretchen in some of the later scenes" [translator's note].

sleeps in my arms tonight, our contract's void. 30
MEPHISTOPHELES: Hold on now. Think what may and might happen.
Allow me at least a fortnight
to feel around for an opportunity.
FAUST: If I had seven hours, I'd have no need
for the Devil's help. I could seduce 35
the little creature by myself.
MEPHISTOPHELES: You talk like any French roué.
Buck up. Don't be downhearted.
Why do you want to enjoy her right away?
The pleasure isn't half so great 40
as if, with various softening tricks,
you slowly mold her and get her ready,
just as they do in Italian stories.
FAUST: I've appetite enough without all that.
MEPHISTOPHELES: Yet, without jesting or joking 45
I tell you that this young beauty
can't be had so easily.
It depends less on passion than on cunning.
FAUST: Get me something that belongs to that angel.
Lead me to her room, or bring me the kerchief 50
from her breast, or her garter for my love's delight!
MEPHISTOPHELES: So that you'll see how willingly
I work to remedy your pain and gloom,
I'll take you, without losing an instant,
right into her bedroom itself. 55
FAUST: And I'll see her? I'll have her?
MEPHISTOPHELES: No! She'll be visiting a neighbor.
But you can pasture your hope on the perfume
and dream of future joys, alone in her room.
FAUST: Can't we go now? 60
MEPHISTOPHELES: It's still too early.
FAUST: Get me a little present for her.

(*Faust goes out.*)

MEPHISTOPHELES: What! Gifts so soon? That's gallant.
Oh, you'll surely get her.
I know of several caches of ancient treasure. 65
But I'll have to reconnoitre them a bit.

(*He goes out.*)

EVENING. A NEAT LITTLE ROOM

(*Margaret is braiding and putting up her hair.*)

MARGARET: I'd give a penny if I knew
who that was I saw today.

He looked so gallant, like a nobleman.
That was plain from his manner,
and explains his being so forward.   5

(*She goes out. Faust and Mephistopheles enter.*)

MEPHISTOPHELES: Come in! But quietly. Come in!
FAUST (*after a silence*): Leave me here alone, I beg you.
MEPHISTOPHELES (*snooping around*): Not every girl keeps things so
    tidy.

(*He goes out.*)

FAUST (*looking around*): Welcome, sweet twilight glow
that permeates this blessed place.   10
Seize my heart, sweet pains of love that live
in yearning on the dews of hope.
Around me breathes the feeling
of calmness, order and contentment.
In this poverty what plenty;   15
in this narrow cell what happiness!

(*He sits down in the arm chair by the bed.*)

In times long past this chair with open arms
received all joy and sorrow!
How often children must have played
around this father-throne!   20
Perhaps here my darling,
grateful for some Christmas gift,
piously kissed grandfather's wrinkled hand
with her full childish lips.
I feel the spirit of order and fulness   25
instructing her daily, like a mother,
to lay the table cloth and spread it smoothly,
to strew the sand in patterns on the floor.
Her darling hands have turned this cottage
into a paradise. And here —   30

(*He raises the bed-curtain.*)

What makes me tremble so?
Here I could linger many an hour.
Here nature lightly created in dreams
this little native angel.
Here lay the child, with warm life   35
filling her tender body,
and here by pure and holy molding
the image of a goddess was created.

And you! What brings you here?
How deeply I am stirred.   40
What do you want? Why is your heart so heavy?
Unhappy Faust, I no longer understand you.

Is this enchantment's fragrance that surrounds me?
I was driven by lust for immediate pleasure,
yet now I am softly dissolved in a dream of love!   45
Are we playthings for every gust of wind?

And if she came in right now,
how you'd do penance for this sacrilege!
How the bragging Jack would grow small
and lie melting, at her feet!   50
MEPHISTOPHELES (*entering*): Quickly! I see her coming below.
FAUST: Away from this! I'll never return.
MEPHISTOPHELES: Here's a fairly heavy box of jewels
that I got in a certain place.
Just put it in the chest at once.   55
I swear to you, she'll lose her mind over it.
I put enough little trinkets in it for you
to win any woman. And certainly
a girl's a girl and fun is always fun!
FAUST: I don't know. Should I?   60
MEPHISTOPHELES: Why do you hesitate?
Or maybe you'd like to keep the things yourself.
Then I advise your lustfulness to waste
no more of this sweet daylight and my trouble.
I hope you're not a miser.   65
I scratch my head, I rub my hands —

(*He puts the box in the chest and locks it.*)

Come on. Hurry! All this to turn
the sweet young ninny's fancy to you —
yet you look as though you had to go
to the lecture room where, gray and incarnate,   70
Physics and Metaphysics had come to life before you.
Come on!

(*They go out. Margaret enters with a lamp.*)

MARGARET: It's so close and stuffy here,

(*She opens a window.*)

yet outside it's not so warm.
I feel so — I don't know how —   75
but I wish mother would come home.

Now I'm trembling all over —
I'm just a fearful silly woman.

(*While she undresses she sings.*)

There was a king in Thule,
faithful to the grave,
to whom his dying sweetheart
a golden goblet gave.   80

There was nothing he liked better,
he drained it at every feast;
he wept while he was drinking,
but he held the goblet fast.   85

When he felt death nearing,
he tallied his towns and lands,
consigned them to his successor,
but he kept the cup in his hands.   90

He sat at the royal banquet,
and his knights sat, knee to knee,
in the tall ancestral chamber
in the castle there by the sea.

Drinking his life's passion,   95
the aged drunkard stood,
and he hurled the holy goblet
down into the flood.

He watched it plunging and drinking
till the water brimmed the top.   100
His eyelids closed and he never
drank another drop.

(*She opens the chest and sees the jewel box.*)

How did this pretty box get here?
I certainly locked the chest.
It's very strange. What can be in it?
Maybe someone left it as a pledge   105
and mother made a loan on it.
Here's a little key on a ribbon.
I think I'll open it.
What's this! O God in heaven! Look!
I've never seen such things in all my life: 110
jewels a noble lady might wear on a high feast day.

79ff. *There was a king* . . . : this ballad, first written in 1774, was published in 1782.

I wonder how this chain would look on me?
And whose can they be?

(*She puts on the chain and looks in the glass.*)

If only these ear-rings were mine!   115
I look entirely different with them on.
What good are beauty and young blood?
It's fine if you can have them, but just the same
people let you alone or praise you in half-pity.
Everyone strives for gold,   120
everyone clings to gold.
Alas, we poor folk!

A STREET

(*Faust is walking back and forth in meditation.*)

MEPHISTOPHELES (*entering*): By all rejected love! By the fires of hell!
I wish I knew something worse to swear by!
FAUST: What's the matter? What's pinching you?
I never saw such a face in all my life.
MEPHISTOPHELES: I'd like to give myself to the Devil,   5
if I weren't the Devil myself!
FAUST: Have you gone crazy?
It certainly suits you to rave like a maniac!
MEPHISTOPHELES: Imagine this! A priest has carried off
the jewels I brought to Margaret. Listen!   10
The mother saw them and got scared at once.
The woman has a nose!
She's always sniffling her prayer-book,
whiffing at everything till she's sure
whether its pure or naughty;   15
and she knew very well when she smelled the gems
that very little holiness clung to them.
"My child," says she, "ill-gotten goods
snare the soul and suck out the blood.
We'll give them to God's mother,   20
and she'll shower down manna on us."
Little Maggie made a wry face
and thought: "A gift horse is all right;
there can be no great impiety
in whoever it was who brought these things."   25
But mother called a priest. He came,
saw how things lay, and circumspectly said:
"You've reasoned as you should.
He wins the most who learns to tame his greed.
The Church has a strong stomach,   30

she has gobbled many lands and realms,
yet never suffered surfeit from it,
or greasy qualms. My daughters, for illegal goods
I recommend the Church's sound digestion."
FAUST: That's the way they always do,   35
and a Jew or a king can do it as well.
MEPHISTOPHELES: With that, he swept rings, chain, and brooch,
like so many mushrooms, into his pouch,
hardly thanking them any more
than if it had been a basketful of nuts.   40
He promised them both a heavenly reward
and left them feeling very righteous.
FAUST: And Margaret?
MEPHISTOPHELES: Has the fidgets now,
doesn't know what she wants to do.   45
She thinks of the jewels night and day,
but more about him who brought them.
FAUST: The little darling's trouble hurts me.
Get her some new trinkets at once.
The others weren't much, anyway.   50
MEPHISTOPHELES: You think getting them is child's play?
FAUST: Do what I tell you.
And stick close to her neighbor.
Don't get soft! Be a real devil,
and bring another box of jewels.   55
MEPHISTOPHELES: Yes, gracious sir, with all my heart.

(*Faust goes out.*)

Such a love-sick fool would puff out the sun,
moon and stars, in thin air, to make sport
for his lady-love.

(*He leaves.*)

THE NEIGHBOR'S HOUSE

(*Martha is alone.*)

MARTHA: God pardon my poor husband!
He did not behave too well by me.
Off into the world he's gone,
leaving me alone in the straw.
I never crossed or bothered him;   5
God knows how well I petted him!

(*She weeps.*)

Maybe he's dead — How terrible! —
If I only had his death-certificate!

(Margaret comes in.)

MARGARET: Martha!
MARTHA: Margaret, what's the trouble?   10
MARGARET: My knees are almost giving away!
Just now I found another little box
in my dresser, made of ebony,
and the things in it are more expensive
and wonderful than the others were.   15
MARTHA: You mustn't say anything to your mother;
she'd take them to the confessional like the others.
MARGARET: But look now! Just look!
MARTHA *(putting the things on Margaret)*: You lucky creature!
MARGARET: But I wouldn't dare be seen with them   20
at church or on the street, or anywhere.
MARTHA: Whenever you want to you can bring
your treasures here and try them on;
parade before the mirror for an hour,
and in that way we'll have our fun.   25
Then on some big occasion, like a feast,
you can show off one piece, to start with:
a chain at first, then a pearl at your ear —
your mother won't notice, or we'll make up a story.
MARGARET: But who could have brought them both?   30
Things that are right don't happen this way.

(Someone knocks.)

O God, that must be mother!
MARTHA *(peeking through the curtains)*: It's a strange man. Come in!

(Mephistopheles comes in.)

MEPHISTOPHELES: If I have been a little free in walking in,
I pray you ladies to pardon me.   35

(He steps back respectfully from Margaret.)

Is this where Mrs. Martha Schwerdtlein lives?
MARTHA: That's me. What is it that you want?
MEPHISTOPHELES *(softly to her)*: I know you now and that's enough.
You've such distinguished company.
So please excuse the liberty I've taken;   40
I'll call again this afternoon.
MARTHA *(aloud)*: Think, child — of all things in the world —
This gentleman takes you for a well-born lady!
MARGARET: I am poor and of humble blood.
Heavens, the gentleman is too kind: 45
The jewels are not mine.
MEPHISTOPHELES: It isn't merely all this finery;

you've a distinguished look and a certain air.
I'm glad that you will let me stay.
MARTHA: What is your business? I want very much —   50
MEPHISTOPHELES: I wish I had more cheerful news for you.
I hope you won't make me repent it.
Your husband's dead, and sent you a last greeting.
MARTHA: He's dead? That faithful heart! Oh! Oh!
My husband's dead! Let me die too!   55
MARGARET: Dear Martha, don't be so upset!
MEPHISTOPHELES: You must hear the mournful story.
MARGARET: I never want to fall in love at all.
A loss like this would kill me.
MEPHISTOPHELES: Joy must have sorrow and sorrow, joy.   60
MARTHA: Tell me about his last days.
MEPHISTOPHELES: He lies buried in Padua,
near the Church of St. Anthony
in holy ground that has been consecrated
for cool and eternal rest.   65
MARTHA: Did you bring nothing else but this news?
MEPHISTOPHELES: Oh yes, one last request that's very serious:
you should have three hundred masses sung for him.
Aside from this, my pocket's empty.
MARTHA: What! Not a souvenir or a medal   70
such as every journeyman keeps in his bag?
A token he will not part with,
even though he's hungry or has to beg?
MEPHISTOPHELES: Madam, I'm very sorry from my heart;
he really didn't squander all his money.   75
He felt sincere repentance for his faults
and lamented his misfortunes even more.
MARGARET: Oh, why must men be so unfortunate?
I shall say many a prayer for him.
MEPHISTOPHELES: You're ready to be married now yourself.   80
You are a child who's worthy of being loved.
MARGARET: Oh no, not for a long time still.
MEPHISTOPHELES: If not a husband, then a handsome beau.
For it is one of heaven's greatest gifts
to hold a loved one in one's arms.   85
MARGARET: That's not the custom in this town.
MEPHISTOPHELES: Custom or not, it's often done!
MARTHA: Oh, tell me more!
MEPHISTOPHELES: I stood by his death-bed —
it was a little better than manure,
being half-rotten straw. He died a Christian,   90
and felt that he had left too much unsettled.
"Oh, how I hate myself!" he cried. "I left my wife

and my business. Ah, the memory strikes me dead.
If only she'd forgive me in this life! — " 95
MARTHA (*weeping*): The good man! I forgave him long ago.
MEPHISTOPHELES: " — Though she, God knows, was more to blame
than I!"
MARTHA: A lie! And right on the brink of the grave!
MEPHISTOPHELES: In his last agonies his senses wandered,
if I'm anything of a connoisseur. 100
"There was no time in life for play," he cried.
"First the children, then to get them bread,
and bread in the broadest sense,
and never time to eat my share in peace."
MARTHA: Did he forget my love's fidelity, 105
my drudgery for him, day and night?
MEPHISTOPHELES: Oh, no! He mentioned all that tenderly.
"When I left Malta how I prayed
for my wife and the little tots!" he said.
"And heaven blessed us. We were lucky. 110
Our vessel captured a Turkish merchantman
which carried a treasure of the mighty Sultan.
For my bravery I got a share of it."
MARTHA: How much? Where is it? Do you think he buried it?
MEPHISTOPHELES: Who knows where the four winds carried it? 115
When he was a stranger in Naples
a pretty tart adopted him as her friend
and gave him such loving devotion that he didn't
get rid of her little gift till his blessed end.
MARTHA: The villain! stealing from his children, 120
and all our misery and need
couldn't restrain him from his evil living!
MEPHISTOPHELES: But think: because of it he's dead.
If I were in your place, I'd mourn
a decent year for him and then 125
look around for another love.
MARTHA: O God! A man like my first man
I'll never find on earth again!
And so good-hearted, though he never stayed home,
but liked strange women and foreign liquor 130
and never could let the wicked dice alone.
MEPHISTOPHELES: There, there, all could have gone on well
if he had overlooked some little slips
of yours. On such a basis, isn't it possible
that you and I might trade lovers' rings? 135
MARTHA: It amuses the gentleman to joke.
MEPHISTOPHELES (*aside*): I'd better get away in time.
She'd hold the Devil himself to his word.

(*to Margaret*)

How are things going with your heart, my dear?
MARGARET: What do you mean, Sir?
MEPHISTOPHELES (*aside*): You innocent sweet thing! 140

(*aloud*)

Farewell, ladies!
MARGARET: Good-by.
MARTHA: Tell me quickly before you go:
I wish I had a witness to where and how 145
my dear man died and was buried.
I've always liked things to be right
and want to read about it in the weekly paper.
MEPHISTOPHELES: Well, my good woman, what two witnesses will swear
is everywhere considered valid evidence. 150
And I've a good friend who, I know,
will go right with us to the judge and testify.
I'll bring him here.
MARTHA: Oh yes, please do!
MEPHISTOPHELES: And this young lady will she still be here? 155
He's a fine lad who's traveled widely
and knows how to pay the ladies his respect.
MARGARET: I'm afraid he'd make me blush for shame.
MEPHISTOPHELES: You wouldn't need to blush before a king.
MARTHA: We'll expect you gentlemen this evening 160
in the garden back of the house.

A STREET

(*Faust is with Mephistopheles.*)

FAUST: How is it going? Have you made some progress?
MEPHISTOPHELES: Fine! So you're all on fire for her.
Gretchen will soon be yours.
Tonight you'll see her at Neighbor Martha's.
Now there's a woman, if ever there was one, 5
made to play the gypsy and procuress.
FAUST: That's good!
MEPHISTOPHELES: But she'll want something for her trouble.
FAUST: Well, one good turn deserves another.
MEPHISTOPHELES: We'll have to witness a certificate 10
that her husband's remains
lie in holy ground in Padua.
FAUST: Clever! But first we'll have to go there!
MEPHISTOPHELES: *Sancta Simplicitas!* There's no need to do that;
just sign the deposition as though you knew it. 15
FAUST: If that's the way it is, you must give up the plan.

MEPHISTOPHELES: Oh, you righteous and holy man!
Is this the first time in your life
you've told a lie? Haven't you defined,
with pompous words and brash effrontery,   20
God, the world, and living things, and man —
what stirs in his heart and runs through his mind?
And if you want to take it up, confess
you know just as much of Mr. Schwerdtlein's death
as you really do of things like those.   25
FAUST: Once and for all, you're a sophist and a liar.
MEPHISTOPHELES: Yes, if you don't look any deeper.
But tomorrow, will you not yourself
deceive poor little Margaret, in all honor,
swearing your whole soul's love to her?   30
FAUST: Yes, and with all my heart.
MEPHISTOPHELES: That's perfectly splendid!
Then you pledge her eternal love and faith,
whispering about one all-absorbing passion —
will that too come from your heart?   35
FAUST: Stop this! It will! When I feel this great emotion,
this tumult, and try to name it, but cannot;
when my mind searches the world for words
to call this flame that burns me,
this thing that must be eternal — is that nothing   40
but a devilish playing with lies?
MEPHISTOPHELES: And still I'm right!
FAUST: Just hear me out, I pray, and spare my lungs.
A man determined to be right who has a tongue
will always have the final word. But come,   45
I'm sick of talking. And besides, what makes you right
is that I cannot act in any other way.

A GARDEN

(*Margaret on Faust's arm, with Martha and Mephistopheles, walking back and forth.*)

MARGARET: I feel you're only sparing me
and stooping to make me feel ashamed.
A traveler gets used to accommodating
himself good-naturedly. I know very well
my poor words can't amuse a man of the world.   5
FAUST: A glance, a word from you are worth
more than all the wisdom of this world.

(*He kisses her hand.*)

MARGARET: Don't put yourself out! Why should you want to kiss
a hand as rough and coarse as mine?

I've so much work to do at home,
and mother is so exacting, too.   10

(*They walk on.*)

MARTHA: And are you always on the go?
MEPHISTOPHELES: Alas, my duties and business drive me on!
With what regret we leave so many places,
and yet we can't stay always in one spot!   15
MARTHA: It's all very fine in your active years
to galavant around the world,
but it's not so good when the evil days draw near
and the bachelor slips toward the brink
of the grave alone: that's not so pleasant.   20
MEPHISTOPHELES: It makes me shudder merely to think of it.
MARTHA: Then, worthy sir, consider it in time.

(*They go on.*)

MARGARET: Yes, out of sight is out of mind.
It's easy enough for you to flatter.
You can find so many friends more sensible than I.   25
FAUST: Believe me, my dear, what men call sense
is often just pretence and narrow-mindedness.
MARGARET: What do you mean?
FAUST: Oh, I mean that innocence and simplicity
so seldom know their worth.   30
That meekness and lowliness, the highest gifts
of loving bountiful nature —
MARGARET: If only you'll remember me a little;
I shall have time enough to think of you.
FAUST: You're often alone, then?   35
MARGARET: Yes, our household is very small
but still it must be looked after. We've no servant:
I have to cook, sweep, knit, and do the sewing,
run all the errands, early and late, and mother
is so particular about everything!   40
Not that she has to skimp herself —
we could make more show than many others;
for father left us a nice little property:
a little house and garden outside the town.
But now my life is quiet.   45
My brother is a soldier;
my little sister is dead.
I had my blessed trials with the child!
Yet I would gladly go through it all again,
because I loved her so.   50
FAUST: She was an angel if she was like you.

MARGARET: I brought her up and she was fond of me.
My father died before she came.
Mother lay sick to death. We gave her up.   55
But slowly she recovered, little by little.
But she couldn't dream of nursing the poor little worm,
and so I raised her myself,
on milk and water. So she really was mine!
She nestled in my arms, played in my lap,   60
she was friendly and kicked and grew.
FAUST: You've certainly felt the purest happiness.
MARGARET: But many a heavy hour too.
The little one's cradle stood at night
beside my bed, and if she stirred, I wakened;   65
sometimes I had to give her a drink, sometimes
take her in bed with me; then, if she wouldn't hush,
get out of bed and dance her up and down
around the room; early each morning
I was up, doing the washing in the tubs,   70
going to market, doing the cooking.
And so it went, each day was like the last.
I'm not always too cheerful;
but it makes me like my supper and my bed.

(*They walk on.*)

MARTHA: We women are badly off. It's hard   75
to bring a bachelor to his senses.
MEPHISTOPHELES: Till I met you I hadn't heard
anyone so convincing.
MARTHA: But tell me: have you never found anyone
to whom your heart felt bound?   80
MEPHISTOPHELES: The proverb is so true:
a man's own hearth and a good wife
are better than gold and pearls.
MARTHA: I mean, have you never been stirred by a passion?
MEPHISTOPHELES: I've been entertained everywhere most cordially.
MARTHA: I wanted to say: were you ever serious, ever?   85
MEPHISTOPHELES: One shouldn't ever trifle with the ladies.
MARTHA: Ah, you don't understand me!
MEPHISTOPHELES: I'm so sorry! But I do understand
that you're very kindly disposed to me.

(*They go on.*)

FAUST: You knew me again, you little angel,   90
as soon as I came in the garden?
MARGARET: Didn't you see it? I lowered my eyes.
FAUST: And do you forgive the freedom —

my boldness when I tried to talk to you
as you came out of church?
MARGARET: I was upset. It never happened before,   95
and no one could say one bad thing about me.
I thought: has he seen something in my manner
that is immodest or unbecoming?
It seemed to strike him all at once: that girl
is easy to flirt with. But I must admit,   100
I don't know what but something in me began at once
to take your part, and I was very angry
with myself because I couldn't be angrier with you.
FAUST: You darling!
MARGARET: Just a minute!   105

(*She picks a star-flower and strips off the petals slowly.*)

FAUST: What's that? A posy?
MARGARET: No, it's only a game.
FAUST: What game?
MARGARET: Go away. You'd laugh at me.   110

(*She pulls off the petals.*)

FAUST: What are you murmuring?
MARGARET (*under her breath*): He loves me . . . he loves me not.
FAUST: Heaven is in your face!
MARGARET (*pulling off the last petals joyfully*): He loves me . . . not
  . . . loves me . . . not . . . he loves me!   115
FAUST: Yes, child! Let this flower's decision
be the gods' oracle to you. He loves you!
You understand what that means? He loves you!

(*He takes her hands.*)

MARGARET: It makes me tremble.
FAUST: Don't shudder! Look at me.
Let our hands say what can't be said.   120
To give yourself up wholly and feel joy
that must last forever! Forever! . . . Its end
would be desperation. No, no end! No end!

(*Margaret presses his hands, frees herself and runs off. He stands
thoughtfully a moment and then follows.*)

MARTHA (*entering*): It's almost night.
MEPHISTOPHELES: Yes, and we must leave.   125
MARTHA: I'd ask you to stay longer, but this is a wicked place.
Nobody is ever too busy to stare at his neighbor's
comings and goings. A woman gets talked about,
no matter how she acts. But where are our love-birds?   130

MEPHISTOPHELES: They fluttered up the path there.
Like summer butterflies!
MARTHA: He seems to like her.
MEPHISTOPHELES: And she him. It's the way of the world.

A GARDEN HOUSE

(Margaret runs in and hides behind the door, with her finger at her lips, and looking through the crack.)

MARGARET: He's coming!

(Faust enters.)

FAUST: Ah, you rascal, you're teasing me!
I've got you now.

(He kisses her.)

MARGARET *(returning his kiss)*: Dearest, I love you with all my heart!

(Mephistopheles knocks.)

FAUST *(provoked)*: Who's there?   5
MEPHISTOPHELES: A friend!
FAUST: You're a beast!
MEPHISTOPHELES: It's time to go.
MARTHA *(coming)*: It's really getting late, Sir.
FAUST: Can't I take you home?   10
MARGARET: Mother wouldn't . . . no, good-by!
FAUST: Must I leave you? Good-by!
MARTHA: Adieu!
MARGARET: Till we meet soon!

(Faust and Mephistopheles go out.)

MARGARET: Dear God, was there ever such a man?   15
What things he thinks about!
I stand before him, all ashamed,
and just say "yes" to everything.
I'm a poor ignorant girl
and I don't know what he sees in me.   20

(She goes out.)

FOREST AND CAVERN

(Faust is alone.)

FAUST: Spirit sublime, you gave me, gave me all
I asked for. Not for nothing did you turn
your face to me out of the fire. And for my kingdom

you gave me glorious nature, the power to feel
and enjoy her, not merely in cold astonished visits;   5
but you allowed me to look deep within her,
as one looks into the heart of a friend.
You lead the procession of living creatures before me,
and teach me to know my brothers
in the silent thickets, in the air and water.   10
And when the storm in the forest roars and creaks,
when the giant fir tree crashes down,
crushing the neighboring branches and trunks;
when the hills rumble with hollow thunder;
then you lead me to the sheltered cavern   15
and show me myself, and in my mind
deep and secret wonders are revealed.
Before my eyes the pure moon rises, softening everything,
and from rock-walls, out of damp bushes,
the silver phantoms of a bygone world drift before me,   20
to temper the stern delight of contemplation.
Oh, I know now that for man there is no perfection.
With this joy leading me nearer and nearer to the gods,
you gave me a companion whom I can no longer spare,
though scornfully and coldly, he degrades me before myself   25
and with a word-breath changes your gifts to nothing.
Busily he fans a raging fire in my heart
for that beautiful image.
So from desire I stagger toward enjoyment,
and in getting that I languish again for desire.   30

(*Mephistopheles enters.*)

MEPHISTOPHELES: Won't you have had enough of this life soon?
In the long run how can it please you?
It was all right to try it once, but soon now
we ought to be getting along to something new.
FAUST: I wish you had other things to do   35
than plague me on a happy day.
MEPHISTOPHELES: All right, all right, I'll gladly let you be;
you wouldn't dare say that in earnest.
A companion so crazy, cross and ungracious
certainly wouldn't be much of a loss.   40
All day you're a handful! And never from your looks
can I get any idea what you like or don't.
FAUST: Now isn't that just the tone!
He wants to be thanked for having bored me.
MEPHISTOPHELES: You miserable earthling, before I came   45
how well did you manage your life?
For a time I saved you
from all this rubbish of the imagination;

if it were not for me then long ago
you'd have walked off this earth-ball. 50
Why do you sit in these caves and fissures like an owl,
sucking your food from dripping stones
and wet moss like a toad?
A fine and pleasant pastime!
The Doctor still sticks in your bones. 55
FAUST: Can you not understand the new life-energy
this roaming in the wasteland has given me?
If you could guess what it means to me,
you'd be devil enough, I suppose, to begrudge me it.
MEPHISTOPHELES: A super-natural pleasure! 60
To lie in the night dew on a mountain side,
to embrace heaven and earth in ecstasy,
to puff yourself up to godhead size
and wallow through earth's marrow with prescient force,
to feel the six days' creation within yourself, 65
to enjoy in your haughty power I don't know what,
now to flood everything with a surge of love,
your earthly nature completely transcended,
and then the ultimate intuition . . .

(*with a flippant gesture*)

I mustn't say how you will achieve it! 70
FAUST: You're rotten!
MEPHISTOPHELES: So, you don't like it!
Well, you have the right to say so.
I mustn't mention to the modest ear
the very thing the chaste heart can't forbear. 75
But, to be brief, I can't deny you the pleasure
of deluding yourself with occasional evasions;
but you can't hold out much longer.
You're already exhausted, and if it goes on like this
you'll be driven to madness, or anguish and horror. 80
So enough! Your little darling's waiting,
shut up by herself and feeling sad.
She's thinking about you constantly;
she's overpoweringly in love with you.
At first your passion overflowed, 85
like a torrent swollen with melting snow;
you poured it into her heart — but now
your little brook has run quite dry again.
Instead of sitting enthroned in the woods,
shouldn't your lordship reward 90
the little monkey for her devotion?
Now time is dragging pitifully for her;
she stands by the window and watches the clouds

drifting over the old town-walls.
"If only I were a little bird!" so runs her song　　95
the whole day long and half the night.
Sometimes she is lively, but more often troubled,
sometimes she's quite wept-out,
then calm again, or so she seems,
and always love-sick for you.　　100
FAUST: You serpent! You snake!
MEPHISTOPHELES (*aside*): That's right! But I'll catch you yet!
FAUST: Get out, you reprobate!
Don't mention that lovely creature!
Don't stir up desire for her sweet body　　105
in my half-mad senses again!
MEPHISTOPHELES: What *do* you want, then? She thinks you've left her,
and more or less, that's what you've done.
FAUST: No, I am near her even now,
and if I were ever so far away,　　110
I could never forget or lose her.
I even envy the Holy Sacrament
when her lips touch it.
MEPHISTOPHELES: Very good, my friend! I've often envied you
those little twins that feed among the roses.　　115
FAUST: You pimp, get out!
MEPHISTOPHELES: All right! Swear at me, I have to laugh.
When God fashioned boy and girl,
he knew the duty of this noblest profession
was to arrange the opportunity for meeting.　　120
Let's get along now. It's agony!
You're going to your sweetheart's room,
not to your death!
FAUST: What is the heavenly joy that's in her arms?
Let me be warm upon her breast!　　125
Am I not always feeling her distress?
Am I not homeless and a fugitive?
A monster without aim or peace,
roaring like a cataract from crag to crag,
with greedy rage toward the abyss?　　130
While she, with vague and childish feelings,
in a tiny hut on a little Alpine meadow by the stream,
with all her homely problems
is locked in her little world.
And I, with God's hate on me, was still not satisfied　　135
to grip the rocks and break them into pieces!
No, I must undermine her, and destroy her peace!
O Hell, do you demand this sacrifice?
Now help me, demon, to shorten the time of anguish!
May that which is doomed to happen happen soon!　　140

Let her fate crash down on me
and hurl us both together to one ruin!
MEPHISTOPHELES: What's all this seething and fireworks about?
You fool, go in and comfort her!
Whenever a pin-head sees no way out,   145
he imagines at once it's the end of everything.
Live dangerously and you live right!
You've played the devil already with quite a flair,
and there's nothing in this world that's more absurd
than a devil who can't make up his mind.   150

GRETCHEN'S ROOM

GRETCHEN (*alone, at her spinning wheel*): My peace is gone —
my heart is sore —
I shall find it never,
no, never more.

Where I don't have him   5
it's a grave for me.
And all the world
becomes gall to me.

Oh my poor head
is dazed and numb;   10
and my poor brains
are dull and dumb.

My peace is gone —
My heart is sore —
I shall find it never,   15
no, never more.

From my window
I watch for him;
I only go walking
to look for him.   20

His manly walk,
his noble ways,
the smile of his mouth,
the power of his eyes,

and the way he talks,   25
his magic speech,
the touch of his hand,
the kiss of his lips!

My peace is gone —
my heart is sore —
I shall find it never,
no, never more.   30

My heart would follow
wherever he goes.
If I could embrace him
and hold him close,   35

and kiss and kiss him
as much as I wish
and finally die
beneath his kiss.   40

MARTHA'S GARDEN

(*Margaret and Faust are together.*)

MARGARET: Promise me, Henry!
FAUST: If I can.
MARGARET: Tell me: what do you think about religion?
You're a loving, wonderful man,
but it seems to me you don't think much about it.   5
FAUST: Let's leave that, child. You know I'm fond of you;
I'd give my flesh and blood for those I love,
and I'd never rob anyone of his feelings and faith.
MARGARET: That's not enough. You must believe!
FAUST: Must I?   10
MARGARET: Oh, if I had the power to change you!
You don't even honor the Holy Sacrament.
FAUST: I do honor it.
MARGARET: Yes, but you don't partake of it.
How long since you have been to mass or confession?   15
Do you believe in God?
FAUST: My dear, who dares to say:
I believe in God?
Question any priest or philosopher,
and his answer will seem to mock you.   20
MARGARET: So you don't believe?
FAUST: Don't misunderstand me, my love.
Who dares name him?
Who can declare:
I believe in him?
Who can feel   25
and be bold enough to say:
I don't believe in him?

Does not the all-encompassing,
the all-supporting, 30
embrace and uphold us,
you, me, and Himself?
Does not the sky arch over us?
Does not the earth stand firmly below us?
Do not the eternal stars arise, 35
looking down kindly upon us?
When we gaze in each other's eyes,
is there not a surging in your heart and head,
formed by the eternal mystery,
invisibly and visibly about you! 40
Fill your great heart with that,
and when you're wholly overcome by the feeling,
then call it what you will:
call it joy, or heart, or love, or God!
I have no name for it! 45
Feeling is everything;
the name is sound and smoke
beclouding the glow of heaven.
MARGARET: All that is fine and true.
The preacher talks very much the same, 50
only with slightly different words.
FAUST: All hearts beneath the light of day
say it everywhere, each in his own tongue;
then why not I in mine?
MARGARET: That sounds all right, and yet 55
there's something warped about it.
Like that, you're not a Christian.
FAUST: Dear child!
MARGARET: It's worried me so long
to see you in such company. 60
FAUST: How so?
MARGARET: That man who comes with you,
deep in my soul, I hate him.
Nothing in all my life has stabbed me to the heart
like his repulsive face. 65
FAUST: My darling, don't be afraid of him.
MARGARET: His presence chills my blood.
Toward everyone else I feel good will;
but, though I long to see you,
he fills me with a secret horror — 70
and I think he's a scoundrel too,
though God forgive me, if I do him an injustice!
FAUST: But there must be a few such odd fish in the world.
MARGARET: I wouldn't want to live with a man like him!
When he comes to the door 75

he always looks mocking and half-way angry.
You can see he has sympathy for nothing.
It's written on his forehead
that he can love no one.
I feel so happy in your arms, 80
so happy and yielding and warm,
but when he comes, my heart is suddenly shut.
FAUST: You're a foreboding little angel!
MARGARET: It overcomes me so
that when we meet him, I even feel 85
as if I didn't love you any more.
And when he's near me, I can never pray.
And that eats into my heart.
Henry, you must feel it too.
FAUST: It's just a prejudice! 90
MARGARET: I must go now.
FAUST: Can we never spend a little hour of peace
close to each other, body and soul?
MARGARET: If only I slept by myself!
I'd gladly leave the door unbolted for you tonight; 95
but mother's a light sleeper,
and if she found us out,
it would kill me.
FAUST: You angel, don't worry about that.
Here is a little bottle. Three drops of this 100
mixed in her drink and she will sleep
the deep sleep that pleases nature.
MARGARET: There's nothing I wouldn't do for you.
But will it hurt her?
FAUST: Darling, would I give it to you if it would? 105
MARGARET: O best of men, when I look at you,
something makes me do what you want.
I've done so much for you already:
there's almost nothing left that I can do.

(*She leaves. Mephistopheles enters.*)

MEPHISTOPHELES: Well, has the little monkey gone? 110
FAUST: Spying again?
MEPHISTOPHELES: I heard it all in great detail.
The Doctor has been catechized!
I hope it will do him a lot of good.
Girls nowadays are keen on knowing 115
if a man is pious and simple in the old way.
They think: if he gives in there, he'll yield to us too.
FAUST: Monster, you cannot understand
how this true-loving soul,
filled with her faith, which quite alone 120
assures her of salvation,

can suffer awful anguish
if she thinks her lover is damned.
MEPHISTOPHELES: You transcendental sensualist,
a little minx is leading you by the nose.   125
FAUST: You vile abortion of dung and fire!
MEPHISTOPHELES: And how she knows her physiognomies!
When she's near me, she feels — she doesn't know what.
She finds a hidden meaning behind my mask.
She feels I'm surely a spirit,   130
perhaps the Devil himself!
Now, about tonight — ?
FAUST: What's that to you?
MEPHISTOPHELES: Never mind. I get my pleasure from it too!

AT THE WELL

(*Gretchen and Lilybeth have come to fill pitchers.*)

LILYBETH: You heard about Barbara?
GRETCHEN: Not a word. I don't go out very much.
LILYBETH: But it's true, for Sibyl told me today!
She's finally made a fool of herself,
with all her affectations.   5
GRETCHEN: How do you mean?
LILYBETH: It smells!
She's feeding two when she eats and drinks.
GRETCHEN: Ah!
LILYBETH: At last she's got what was coming to her.   10
How long she's been hanging on to that fellow!
All that parading about with him,
in the dance halls and around the town,
always trying to show herself off,
while he was treating her with wine   15
and little pastries. She was so vain
about her looks. And all her shameless behavior
in taking the presents he gave her.
With all her kissing and petting,
finally she's lost that little virgin flower.   20
GRETCHEN: Poor thing!
LILYBETH: So you still pity her?
When girls like us were at the spinning-wheel
and our mothers wouldn't let us go out at night,
she was with her lover in the dark hall,   25
and the hours weren't too long on the bench by the door.
She's got to humble herself now
and do penance at church in the sinner's shirt!
GRETCHEN: But he'll marry her, surely.
LILYBETH: He'd be a fool! A slick fellow   30

like him can get along anywhere.
He's gone already.
GRETCHEN : That isn't right!
LILYBETH : If she should get him, you can be sure
the boys would tear off her bridal-wreath   35
and strew chopped straw for shame at her door!

(*She goes out.*)

GRETCHEN (*starting homeward*) : Once, how boldly I'd have run down
any girl that got herself in trouble!
My tongue would have found hard words
for her sins, to smear them black and blacker   40
and still not black enough.
And I'd have blessed myself
and been so good and smug —
but now we're tarred with the same brush!
Yet — all that led to it, O God,   45
it was so good! It was so sweet!

BY THE TOWN WALL

(*Gretchen is putting flowers in vases before the image of the Mater
Dolorosa* * which stands in a niche.*)

GRETCHEN : O rich-in-sorrow,
turn your face
graciously to my distress!

With the sword in your heart
and a thousand hurts,   5
you are gazing up where your son lies dead.

You look to the father
and sigh to him
the pain in you and the pain in him.

Who feels   10
the grief
in my body and bones?
How my heart is afraid
and trembles and yearns
you only know, and you alone!   15

Wherever I go,
what woe, what woe, what woe
I carry with me!

* The Virgin Mary.

And when I'm alone
I weep, I weep, I weep   20
till my heart is broken.

My tears fell and wet
the pots by my window
when this morning early
I broke you these blossoms.   25

When the sun shone early,
so bright in my bedroom,
I sat on my bed,
awake with my misery.

Help me! And save me   30
from death and disgrace!
Turn your eyes toward me,
O my sister in sorrow!

NIGHT IN THE STREET IN FRONT OF GRETCHEN'S HOUSE

(*Valentine, a soldier, Gretchen's brother, is standing in the street.*)

VALENTINE: Often at some drinking-party
when my companions would boast
about their sweethearts,
praising them drunkenly
and washing the words down with full cups,   5
I'd sit there, head propped on my elbows,
complacently listening to their bragging,
and smile at ease and stroke my beard,
then take a full glass in my hand
and say: Each man to his own taste!   10
But is there one in all the land
like my faithful Gretchen,
one worthy to stand by my sister?
"None! That's right!" Clink, clink!
"She's the best of all the girls in town!"   15
And all the braggarts would sit there, dumb.
But now! — I could tear out my hair
and knock my head against the walls!
With nasty names, they thumb their noses,
and any bastard dares insult me!   20
Like a bankrupt debtor, I must sit,
and be the butt of every joke,
sweating to smash them into bits —
yet I can't call them liars.

Who comes there? Who is sneaking near?   25
Unless I'm wrong, there are two. If it's he,
he'll never leave here alive.

(*Faust and Mephistopheles come along.*)

FAUST: As from the window of the chancel there
the glow of the eternal lamp flames upward,
glimmering weaker and weaker at the sides,   30
while darkness presses round; so gloom
makes night in my thoughts.
MEPHISTOPHELES: And I'm a yearning tom-cat
sneaking up fire-escapes and creeping stealthily
along the tops of walls.   35
I feel virtuous but thievish,
and a bit like a ram,
for premonitions of Walpurgis Night
are spooking through my body.
It's just two days away, and then   40
you'll see what keeps a man awake.
FAUST: Isn't that some buried treasure that I see
glinting and rising in the air?
MEPHISTOPHELES: Soon you can have the pleasure
of lifting the kettle out.   45
Not long ago I peeked in
and it's full of lion-dollars.
FAUST: And no jewelry, or perhaps a ring,
as a present for the girl?
MEPHISTOPHELES: I think I did see some such thing,   50
a sort of rope of pearls.
FAUST: That's good! I don't like going there
without some little gift for her.
MEPHISTOPHELES: Really, it ought not to annoy you
to get some pleasures free.   55
Now the sky is glowing, full of stars,
you'll hear a musical masterpiece;
I'll sing a moral song to her
and make a fool of her through the ear.

(*He sings, playing on a zither.*)

What do you there   60
by your true-love's door,
Ophelia dear,
at break of day?

60–75. *What do you . . . a ring:* the source of this song is Ophelia's song in Shakespeare's *Hamlet,* Act IV, Scene 5.

Ah, let it alone,
you'll go as a maid,   65
but when you come out
you'll not be one.

Take care of yourself!
If the deed is done,
why, then Good-night,   70
poor little thing!
For your own sake
don't steal or take
any love unless
you've got a ring.   75
VALENTINE (*coming forward*): What are you after? By the body and
    blood!
You damned rat-catcher!
To the devil with your zither!
Then I'll send the singer after it!
MEPHISTOPHELES: He's broken my zither! It's no good now.   80
VALENTINE: And next I'll smash your skull!
MEPHISTOPHELES (*to Faust*): Stand fast, Doctor! Keep cool!
Stick tight to me. I'll help you.
Out with your feather-duster!
You thrust! I'll parry!   85
VALENTINE: Parry that!
MEPHISTOPHELES: And why not!
VALENTINE: And that!
MEPHISTOPHELES: Yes indeed!
VALENTINE: I think it's the Devil who's fighting me!   90
What's that? He's got my hand.
MEPHISTOPHELES (*to Faust*): Let him have it.
VALENTINE (*falling*): Aaah!
MEPHISTOPHELES: Now the fool's tamed!
But quick! We've got to vanish.   95
Already someone's yelling Murder!
I get along splendidly with the police,
but in penal court the blood-ban's hard to manage.
MARTHA (*at her window*): Help! Help!
GRETCHEN (*at hers*): Bring a light!   100
MARTHA: They're cursing and scuffling, shouting and fighting!

(*A crowd gathers.*)

PEOPLE: Someone's been killed already!
MARTHA (*coming out*): Where did the murderers go?
GRETCHEN (*coming out*): Who lies there?

PEOPLE: Your mother's son. 105
GRETCHEN: Almighty God! How horrible!
VALENTINE: I'm dying. That is quickly said
and quicker for me to do.
Why do you women stand there and howl?
Come here and listen to me. 110

(*They gather round him.*)

Listen, Gretchen. You're still young;
but you've not been smart enough.
You've managed your business badly.
Confidentially, I've got
a sister who's become a whore! 115
Well, be a real one then.
GRETCHEN: My brother! God! Such words to me?
VALENTINE: Just leave God out of this!
What's done, unfortunately, is done,
and what's to come will surely come. 120
You started with one, on the sly;
but others will follow soon enough
and when you've had a dozen,
then the whole town can have you.
When shame is born, how secretly 125
she is brought into the world;
over her head and ears
the veils of night are drawn.
Oh yes, you'd like to murder her,
but she gets so bold when she starts to grow 130
that she goes out naked in daytime,
and though she's gotten no lovelier,
the more loathsome that she looks,
the more she seeks the light of day.
Already I foresee the time 135
when every decent person in the town
will turn away from you, you slut,
as though you were a rotting carcass.
And then your heart will despair
when they look you in the eyes. 140
You'll never wear a golden chain!
You'll never stand near the altar in church!
Or enjoy yourself on the dancing floor,
dressed in a pretty lace collar.
In some dark corner of misery 145
you'll hide among beggars and cripples,
and even though God may pardon you,
on earth you shall be damned!
MARTHA: Commend your soul to the grace of God.

Must you add slander to your burden? 150
VALENTINE: If I could reach your withered body,
you shameless, coupling pimp,
then I might get full pardon
for all the sins of my life!
GRETCHEN: My brother! what agony! 155
VALENTINE: I tell you: no more tears!
When you first lost your honor
you gave my heart its death-blow.
Now I go, like an honest soldier,
through the sleep of death to God. 160

IN THE CATHEDRAL
SERVICE, ORGAN, AND CHOIR

(*Gretchen stands among many people. An evil spirit is behind her.*)

THE EVIL SPIRIT: How different, Gretchen, it was once
when you, still innocent,
came here to the altar
and prattled your prayer
from the well-worn little book, 5
half in childish play,
half with God in your heart!
Gretchen, what are you thinking?
What crime is brooding
in your heart? 10
Are you praying for your mother's soul,
who slept, because of you,
into the long, long torment?
Whose blood is that on your threshold?
— And underneath your heart 15
what stirs, quickening already,
torturing you and itself
with its ominous presence?
GRETCHEN: O God!
If I could be free of these thoughts
that go through me, back and forth, 20
accusing me!
CHORUS: *Dies irae, dies illa*
solvet saeclum in favilla.

(*There is organ music.*)

THE EVIL SPIRIT: Wrath seizes you!
The trumpet sounds! 25
The graves quake!

22–23. *Dies . . . favilla:* "Day of wrath, day that shall scatter the world to ashes" [translator's note]. The choir's chant was written by Thomas of Celano in the thirteenth century.

And your heart,
recreated,
trembles forth
from the peace of ashes   30
toward fiery torment!
GRETCHEN: I wish I were outside!
I feel as if the organ
throttled my breath,
and the anthem had loosened   35
the depths of my heart.
CHORUS: *Judex ergo cum sedebit,*
quidquid latet adparebit,
nil inultum remanebit.
GRETCHEN: It is so close here!   40
The walls and pillars
oppress me! The ceiling
crushes me! . . . I must have air!
THE EVIL SPIRIT: Hide yourself!
Sin and shame cannot be hidden.   45
Air? Light?
Woe unto you!
CHORUS: *Quid sum miser tunc dicturus?*
Quem patronum rogaturus?
Cum vix justus sit securus.   50
THE EVIL SPIRIT: The transfigured spirits
turn away from you.
The pure ones shudder
to reach you their hands.
Woe!   55
CHORUS: *Quid sum miser tunc dicturus?*
GRETCHEN: Neighbor! Your smelling salts!

(*She faints.*)

WALPURGIS NIGHT * — THE HARZ MOUNTAINS
IN THE NEIGHBORHOOD OF SCHIERKE AND ELEND

(*Faust and Mephistopheles.*)

MEPHISTOPHELES: Wouldn't you love to have a broomstick?
I wish I were straddling a good stout ram.
Our goal is still a long way off.
FAUST: As long as I still feel fresh on my legs,
this knotty staff's enough.   5

37–39. *Judex . . . remanebit:* "When the judge shall take his seat, what is hidden shall appear, nothing shall be unavenged" [translator's note].
48–50. *Quid sum . . . securus:* "What shall I, the wretched, say then? Whom appeal to for protection? The just man barely shall be safe" [translator's note].
* The Witches' Sabbath occurred on the night between April 30 and May 1, on the summit of Mount Brocken.

Why should you want to shorten the way? —
To wander through this labyrinth of valleys,
to climb these rocks where springs gush,
spitting spray forever: these are the pleasures
that make the path spicy! 10
Spring stirs the birches,
even the fir trees feel it already;
ought not the season to work in our bodies?
MEPHISTOPHELES: Really, I don't feel a thing. It's winter
in my bones, and I would rather 15
snow and frost lay on my pathway.
How drearily the lop-sided disk
of the red moon rises with its belated glow!
And it's bad illumination too! At every step
you crack your shins against a stone or stump! 20
Let me call a Jack o' Lantern.
There's one blazing away so cheerfully.
Ho, there friend! Won't you help us?
You're burning yourself out for no reason.
Be so kind as to light our way upward! 25
JACK O' LANTERN: Out of respect, I hope I shall succeed
in restraining my vacillating disposition.
It's our nature to go zigzag.
MEPHISTOPHELES: Ah, well, he's trying to imitate mankind.
But go, ahead now, in the Devil's name! 30
Or I'll blow your flicker-flame life out.
JACK O' LANTERN: I plainly see you're the master of the place
and shall readjust myself to suit the situation.
But remember: the mountain is bewitched tonight;
and if a will o' the wisp is to guide you correctly, 35
you mustn't take his directions too exactly.

(*All three, singing in turn, as they climb.*)

MEPHISTOPHELES: In the dream-and-magic-spheres
we have entered, it appears.
Lead us well and get our praises
when we soon succeed in climbing 40
to the wide and desert places.
JACK O' LANTERN: Through the trees that grow here thickly
see us rush and pass them quickly.
All the cliffs bow down before us,
and the long rock-snouts snore for us. 45
How they puff and blow!
FAUST: Through the stones and through the grasses
streams and little brooklets pass us.
Do I hear singing on the air
and the charming lover's prayer, 50

voices of our heavenly days?
What we love and long to seize!
And the echo chimes and rhymes
like a saga of old times.
MEPHISTOPHELES: Uhu! Shuhu! Can you hear? 55
Lapwing, owl, and jay are near.
It is late for them to waken!
Are those newts there in the bracken? —
their bodies are fat but their legs are long!
How the tangled tree-roots throng 60
like serpents through the stones and soil
twined in marvelous coil on coil,
stretching out to catch and grip
like the tentacles of a polyp,
reaching from a rocky lair 65
for an unsuspecting wanderer.
Mice of every color and shade
scamper through the heathery glade.
And glowworms crowd in swarms to fly
a bewildering escort in the sky. 70
FAUST: Tell me if we stay or go,
everything is whirling so!
Rocks and trees are making faces
and the firefly darts and chases,
seems to multiply and grow. 75
MEPHISTOPHELES: Hold my coat-tail tightly!
Here's a midway ridge. From here
people can see with astonishment
how Evil burns inside the mountain.
FAUST: How strangely a troubled dawn-like red 80
glimmers through the gorges!
In the chasms of the abyss it darts its gleams.
Reek is rising, vapor is drifting,
and a glow burns through the fog-veil,
creeping like a slender thread 85
till it bursts out like a spring.
Its hundred veins, twisting a long way,
are knotted through the valley,
here, compressed in a sharp elbow,
then suddenly spread far and wide. 90
Now sparks are sputtering
like scattered golden sand!
Look how the rocky walls are kindled
and blazing to their highest peaks.
MEPHISTOPHELES: Didn't Mammon light his palace 95
marvelously for the revel?
You're lucky that you got to see it.

Already I hear the rowdy guests approaching.
FAUST: How the whirlwind is raging!
It's almost breaking my neck! 100
MEPHISTOPHELES: Cling tightly to these rocky ribs,
or you'll be hurled into the chasm.
Mist thickens the night.
Hear how the forest crashes!
The owls are flying away in terror. 105
Listen! the pillars of the eternal
green palace are splintering.
Branches moan and are broken!
Tree trunks groan mightily,
creeping roots gaping. 110
Then in fearful confusion
they're hurtled together,
crashing over each other.
Through the wreck-cluttered chasms
the air howls and hisses. 115
You hear those voices in the sky?
Near and far, down the mountain ridges
flows a furious incantation!
THE WITCHES (*in a chorus*): Up to the Brocken the witches speed,
the stubble is yellow, green is the seed. 120
A thronging crowd will gather there,
with Old Nick sitting high in the air.
So over stock and stone we go;
the witch breaks wind and the goat lets go.
A VOICE: Old lecherous Baubo is coming now, 125
riding along on a mother-sow.
THE CHORUS: Honor her now who is worthy of honor!
Forward, Dame Baubo, to lead the rout!
A tough old sow with her mother upon her,
and the witches dancing a roundabout. 130
A VOICE: Which road did you come by?
ANOTHER VOICE: I came by Ilsenstein.
There I peeked in an owl's eyes,
and she stared in mine.
ANOTHER VOICE: Oh, go to Hell! 135
Why do you ride so fast?
ANOTHER VOICE: She has gored me.
Look at the wound!
THE WITCHES' CHORUS: The road is long, the road is broad.
Did you ever see such a crazy crowd? 140
The broom it scratches, the pitch-fork pokes,
the mother pops open, but baby chokes.

122. *Old Nick:* that is, the devil.
125. *Baubo:* the old nurse of the Greek goddess Demeter, she symbolizes gross sensuality.

A HALF-CHORUS OF SORCERERS: We creep along like a snail in her house;
the women are in the lead.
For, when we're hell-bent on a carouse,   145
the female is always ahead.
THE OTHER HALF: That's not the way it goes, exactly.
With a thousand steps a woman must creep;
no matter how she hurries quickly,
the man can make it with a leap!   150
A VOICE (*from above*): Come along, come along, from Rocky Lake!
VOICES (*from below*): We'd love to fly with you up there.
We scour ourselves, all white and bare;
but we're barren still, as we always were.
BOTH CHORUSES: The stars have fled, the wind is still,   155
the dreary moon is glad to retire.
The magic chorus, whizzing wildly,
sputters a thousand sparks of fire.
A VOICE (*from below*): Stop! Stop!
A VOICE (*from above*): Who calls down there from the stone-abyss?
A VOICE (*from below*): Take me with you, oh, take me too!   161
Three long centuries I've been climbing,
and still I can't get to the top.
I want to be with my own kind.
BOTH CHORUSES: We ride the broom and the walking-stick,   165
we ride the pitch-fork and the buck;
whoever can't find a steed today
is lost and will never get away.
HALF-WITCH (*below*): I've been tottering on for such a long time;
but the others are all so far ahead.   170
At home I've neither rest nor peace,
and even here I still can't find them.
WITCHES' CHORUS: There's a magic salve puts pluck in a hag.
You can make a sail from any old rag.
A trough can be a wonderful boat.   175
But who doesn't now, will never float.
BOTH CHORUSES: And when we finally get up there,
We'll cover the ground and fill the air;
The mountain heather's farthest reaches
will be swarming with us spooks and witches   180

(*They alight.*)

MEPHISTOPHELES: They shove and jostle, push and clatter,
They hiss and swirl, and rattle and rush!
They glow, spray sparks and stink and flare!
Truly a world of the witches.
Keep close or we'll be separated.   185
Where are you?
FAUST (*in the distance*): Here!

MEPHISTOPHELES: Already torn away?
I'll have to claim my house-rights here.
Attention! Squire Voland the Seducer is here. 190
Make room, good people, if you please, make room!
Here, Doctor, hold me tightly.
In one leap we'll leave this mob,
that's even too mad for me.
Something shines there, gleaming weirdly, 195
luring me to this thicket. Let's slip in.
FAUST: Spirit of contradiction! Yes, I'll follow you.
I still think that you've done it cleverly;
we're on the Brocken for Walpurgis Night,
yet we arrange to draw apart 200
and watch things from the side.
MEPHISTOPHELES: Look! what many-colored flames!
That's a jolly little club there.
In a little circle you're never alone.
FAUST: I'd rather be up there. Already I see 205
the glow and the swirling smoke.
There the crowd streams toward the Evil One;
and many a riddle will be untied.
MEPHISTOPHELES: And many will be knotted, too.
Let the great world riot and rave; 210
we'll hide a while here, on the quiet.
It's an old saw that from large worlds
we make the little ones. But look —
the younger witches go naked and bare,
while the old ones cover up cleverly. 215
Be friendly to them, for my sake;
it isn't much bother, and it can be fun.
I hear the sound of their instruments!
What a damned noise! But we've got to get used to it.
Come on! Come on! We'd better start. 220
I'll go ahead and make the introductions —
and, incidentally, this ratifies our bond.
What do you say, my friend? Up here
there's lots of space. You can't see the end.
A hundred fires are burning, rows of them; 225
they dance and chatter, cook and drink, make love;
where will you find it better, tell me that.
FAUST: Now when you introduce us at this revel,
will you present yourself as devil or magician?
MEPHISTOPHELES: Really, I'm used to going incognito, 230
but on a gala day we sport our orders.
I haven't got the Garter to set me up,
but here the horse's hoof is held in high esteem.

190. *Voland:* another name for the devil, it means "the evil one" or "seducer."

You see the snail there, crawling toward us,
she's smelled me out with searching feelers.   235
I can't disguise myself here as I would like to.
But come, let's go from fire to fire.
I am the pander and you be the wooer.

(*to a group by a dying fire*)

Venerable gentlemen, why are you in the rear?
If I found you in the middle of the party,   240
with riot and revelry around you,
I'd praise you; but you're enough alone at home.
A GENERAL: Who now can trust the nations?
No matter what we've done for them,
the fickle people, like women,   245
give the prize to younger men.
A MINISTER: Man stands so far from justice now;
I praise the good old times;
when we had all the power,
those were the golden days.   250
A PARVENU: Really, we aren't exactly dumb,
though often we did things we shouldn't;
but now the world whirls round and round,
just when we want to hold it.
AN AUTHOR: Who is there now will read a book,   255
that's written with real intelligence?
And the younger generation
is getting cockier than ever.
MEPHISTOPHELES (*who suddenly looks very old*): I feel mankind is ripe
        for Judgment Day,
and never again will I climb up the Brocken.   260
My little keg is dripping less,
and the world, like me, is on the wane.
A HUCKSTER-WITCH: Gentlemen, stop! Don't pass me by.
This is your opportunity!
Inspect my little stock with care.   265
You'll find here vast variety;
in all the world there's no such shop.
There's nothing here that hasn't done
malicious evil to somebody.
There is no dagger here that's not drawn blood;   270
no goblet that's not poured destructive poison
into some healthy body. And each jewel
has bought some lovely female's person.
There's not a sword here that's not cut a pact
or stabbed an enemy in the back.   275
MEPHISTOPHELES: Now, aunty, you don't understand the times.
What's done is gone! What's gone is done!

Stock up your booth with something new,
for only novelties can please our taste.
FAUST: I'll lose my wits if I don't watch out.   280
Now this is what I really call a fair!
MEPHISTOPHELES: The whole swirl struggles to get to the top;
you think you're pushing but you're being shoved.
FAUST: Who is that there?
MEPHISTOPHELES: Look at her closely!   285
That's Lilith.
FAUST: Who?
MEPHISTOPHELES: "Of Adam's first wife Lilith it is said . . ."
beware of her beautiful hair —
she's famous for it!   290
When a young fellow falls for it,
he doesn't soon get loose — she has him.
FAUST: Look at that couple, the hag and the girl!
They've done some pretty good whirls and leaps.
MEPHISTOPHELES: No one can rest a minute tonight.   295
Here's another dance starting. Let's get in it!
FAUST (*dancing with the girl*): Once I had a lovely dream:
I dreamt that on an apple tree,
I saw two pretty apples gleam —
I climbed for them most eagerly.   300
THE PRETTY WITCH: These little apples have seduced
man since the days of Eden.
I want to treat you as you're used,
and am I glad you need them!
MEPHISTOPHELES (*with the Old Witch*): Once I had a bawdy dream
of an old tree that was split.   306
It had a —— —— ——
that pleased me quite a bit.
THE OLD WITCH: It gives me pleasure to salute
the knight who bears the horse's foot.   310
Let him get ready a proper cork
if a large —— doesn't cramp his work.
THE PROCTOPHANTASMIST *: Damned rabble! How dare you!
Haven't I proved conclusively
that ghosts don't have ordinary feet — ?   315
But here you're dancing like mortals!
THE PRETTY WITCH (*dancing*): Then what is he doing at our ball?
FAUST: Oh, that fellow gets around everywhere.
While others dance, he judges all their steps.
If he doesn't find them sound,   320
they're as good as never taken.

286. *Lilith:* the legendary first wife of Adam became a witch who seduced men.
* "Friedrich Nicolai, who published in 1799 a paper on ghosts and the curative power of leeches. He also wrote several travel books and professed himself the leader of the 'Age of Enlightenment' " [translator's note].

What riles him most is when we go ahead;
but if we just keep going in a circle —
like him with his old windmill —
he's sure to think it quite all right,   325
especially if you consult him with respect!
THE PROCTOPHANTASMIST: Are you still here? This is unheard-of!
Vanish at one! This nonsense has been cleared up!
This devil-pack just won't observe the law.
We are so wise, yet ghosts can still haunt Tegel.   330
How long I've tried to clean away this folly!
But everything's still dirty. It's impossible!
THE PRETTY WITCH: Oh, stop boring us!
THE PROCTOPHANTASMIST: I tell you spirits to your face,
I'll not put up with this spectral despotism;   335
my spirit can't endure it.

(*The dancing continues.*)

I see that I will not succeed today,
but I always carry a copy of my *Travels*,
and hope before I make my final tour,
I'll overcome the devils and the poets.   340
MEPHISTOPHELES: Now he'll sit down in the nearest puddle,
for he knows his trouble and how to cure it:
the leeches at his bum will phlebotomize his muddle,
and he'll recover from these spirits and from spirit.

(*to Faust, who has stopped dancing*)

But why did you let that pretty piece go   345
who sang so sweetly while she was dancing?
FAUST: Because right in the middle of her song
out of her mouth sprang a little red mouse!
MEPHISTOPHELES: That was all right. Don't be alarmed!
It doesn't matter as long it wasn't gray.   350
And when you're on this kind of a date, why worry?
FAUST: And I saw too —
MEPHISTOPHELES: What?
FAUST: Mephistopheles, can't you see
that beautiful girl there, standing alone
and far away? Slowly she drags herself along,   355
as if her feet were chained. It seems to me,
she's very like my Gretchen.
MEPHISTOPHELES: Now let that one alone! She's no good!
In fact, it's a magic image, lifeless, a phantom.   360
It's bad luck to meet her.
That rigid stare would "thick men's blood with cold"

---

338. *Travels:* Nicolai's twelve volume description of a journey through Germany and Switzerland;
it represented all that Goethe detested in the German character and literature.

and almost turn you into stone.
Haven't you ever heard about Medusa?
FAUST: Truly, they are the eyes of a dead girl,   **365**
unclosed by any loving hand.
That is the breast that Gretchen gave me.
That is the sweet body I enjoyed.
MEPHISTOPHELES: It's sorcery, deluded simpleton!
Every man sees in her his own beloved!   **370**
FAUST: What joy and what torture!
I cannot leave this vision.
How strangely that one scarlet thread,
no thicker than the blade of a knife,
adorns her lovely neck!   **375**
MEPHISTOPHELES: That's right! I see it too.
She can carry her own head away, under her arm,
for Perseus sliced it off.
You've always this hankering for illusion!
But come, let's climb this little hill.   **380**
It's as lively as the Prater Park in Vienna.
And unless someone's put a spell on me,
I really see a theater. What's going on?
A STAGE-HAND: The play will soon begin: a brand-new piece,
the last of a series of seven,   **385**
for here it's the custom
to put them on in batches.
A dilettante wrote it,
and dilettanti act in it.
Excuse me, gentlemen, I've got to go,   **390**
with dilettantish joy, to hoist the curtain.
MEPHISTOPHELES: I'm glad to find you on the Brocken,
for you belong here, that's certain.*

A GLOOMY DAY IN A FIELD

(Faust and Mephistopheles.)

FAUST: In misery! Desperate! Pitifully wandering all this long time on earth, and now imprisoned! That lovely ill-fated being, shut in a dungeon like a criminal, and exposed to horrible tortures! It has come to this! To this! — Perfidious, contemptible demon, to have concealed this from me! — Stop! Stand there, and roll your hellish eyes in their sockets with rage! Stand and defy me with your unendurable presence! In prison! In irreparable extremity! Given up to evil spirits and to mankind which damns without mercy! And you, you cradled me all this

364. *Medusa:* the Gorgon of Greek mythology.
381. *Prater Park:* a famous public park.
* The Walpurgis Night's Dream which follows is always cut from performances of *Faust* and is here omitted.

while in insipid dissipations, and hid from me her growing anguish and let her perish without help!

MEPHISTOPHELES: She's not the first one.

FAUST: You dog! Detestable brute! — O Infinite Spirit, turn this vermin back into that dog-shape in which he liked to trot before me, the unsuspecting wanderer, rolling at my feet, or leaping on my shoulders when I fell down. Turn him back again to his favorite form, so that he can crawl on his belly in the sand while I kick him — the depraved creature! — Not the first one! — God's wounds! Can the human spirit conceive that more than one being has sunk into these depths of wretchedness, and that the first one, writhing in the agony of death, was not enough to expiate the guilt of all others in the eyes of the eternal pardoner! Her misery cuts clean to the marrow of my life; yet you grin coolly at the doom of thousands!

MEPHISTOPHELES: Here we are again at our wits' end, where human reason snaps. Why do you try to join up with us, if you can't go through with it? You want to fly, but you get dizzy! Did we intrude on you, or you on us?

FAUST: Don't gnash your hungry fangs at me! You make me sick! — Glorious and Mighty Spirit who condescended to manifest yourself to me, you who know my heart and my soul, why did you chain me to this miscreant who feeds on suffering and gluts himself on destruction?

MEPHISTOPHELES: Is that all now?

FAUST: Save her, or you'll be sorry! May you suffer an awful curse for thousands of years!

MEPHISTOPHELES: I cannot loosen the avenger's chains, nor shoot back his bolts. — Save her! — Who was it ruined her, you or I?

(*Faust looks wildly about.*)

Do you want to seize the thunder? It's a good thing, you miserable mortals can't do it! It's the tyrant's nature to smash the innocent bystander into bits; it helps him out of the mess.

FAUST: Take me to her! She must be freed!

MEPHISTOPHELES: And what of the dangers you lay yourself open to? Did it ever occur to you that you're guilty of murder in that town? Avenging furies hover over the place where a man has been slain, and they lurk in waiting for the return of the killer.

FAUST: That, too, from you? All the murder and death of a world be upon you, monster! Lead me there, I tell you, and set her free!

MEPHISTOPHELES: I'll take you there, and I'll tell you what I *can* do! Am I all-powerful in heaven or on earth? I'll muddle the jailer's brains while you get the keys and lead her out. A human hand must do it. I'll stand on guard. The magic horses are ready. I'll carry you off. That much I can do.

FAUST: Then hurry!

NIGHT. IN THE OPEN COUNTRY

(*Faust and Mephistopheles are galloping on black horses.*)

FAUST: What are they doing there at the Ravenstone gibbet?
MEPHISTOPHELES: I wouldn't know what their cookery's concocting.
FAUST: They're soaring and swooping, bowing and scraping.
MEPHISTOPHELES: It's the witches' union holding a meeting.
FAUST: They're making a magic spell.   5
MEPHISTOPHELES: Come on! Come along!

1. *Ravenstone:* a place of execution.

A DUNGEON

(*Faust, with a bunch of keys and a lamp, is standing before an iron door.*)

FAUST: A feeling of awe runs through me —
such as I have not felt for a long time;
all the misery of mankind grips me.
Here she lives behind these damp walls,
yet her crime was only a dear illusion.   5
You hesitate to go to her?
You fear to see her again?
On now! Your irresolution draws death nearer.

(*He takes hold of the lock. There is singing within.*)

My mother, the whore,
she murdered me!   10
My father, the villain,
has eaten me.
My wee little sister
gathered my bones
and hid them away   15
beneath cool stones;
then I turned into a pretty bird.
Fly away! fly away!
FAUST (*unlocking the door*): She does not dream that her lover is listening,
that he hears the chains rattling and the straw rustling.   20

(*He goes in.*)

MARGARET (*hiding in the bed*): They're coming for me! Oh bitter death!
FAUST (*softly*): Hush, hush! I've come to free you.
MARGARET (*throwing herself before him*): If you're a man, take pity on my misery!
FAUST: Your cries will waken the guard!

(*He starts to unlock the fetters.*)

MARGARET (*on her knees*): Executioner, who gave you this power?   25
It's only midnight, yet you come for me.
Have pity on me and let me live!
Is not tomorrow morning soon enough?

(*She stands up.*)

I'm still so young, so young!
Yet soon to die!   30
And I was beautiful — that was my ruin.
My lover was near, but now he's far away.
The wreath is torn and the blossoms are scattered.
Don't clutch me so roughly!
Spare me! What have I done to you?   35
Don't let me beg you in vain.
I've never seen you before in all my life!
FAUST: Can I endure this agony?
MARGARET: Now I'm completely in your power.
Only first, let me suckle my baby again.   40
I cuddled it to me all night long;
but they took it away to hurt me,
and now they say I've murdered it.
And I'll never be happy again.
They sing songs about me! It's wicked of the people!   45
There's an old tale that ends so . . .
but why do they mix me up in it?
FAUST (*throwing himself at her feet*): Your lover lies at your feet,
come to free you from this misery and anguish.
MARGARET (*throwing herself beside him*): Oh, let us kneel and call to
        the saints!   51
See, under these steps,
under the threshold
Hell is seething!
The Evil One
in a fearful rage   55
is making a hub-bub!
FAUST (*aloud*): Margaret! Margaret!
MARGARET (*listening*): That was my lover's voice!

(*She jumps up. The chains fall off.*)

Where is he? I heard him call me.
I am free! No one can stop me!
I will go to him and lie close to him!   60
He called "Margaret!" He stood on the threshold,
and through the shrieking and the clatter of Hell,
through the angry scoffings of the devils,

I recognized that sweet and tender voice. 65
FAUST: It is I!
MARGARET: You! Oh, say it again!

(*She embraces him.*)

It is he! It is he! Where now is all my misery?
The suffering in this dungeon? The chains?
It is you come to save me! 70
I am saved! —
I see the street again where I first met you,
and the garden
where I waited for you with Martha.
FAUST (*urging her to leave*): Come now! Come! 75
MARGARET: Oh, wait!
I want to stay here, just with you!

(*She caresses him.*)

FAUST: Hurry!
If you don't hurry,
we shall have to pay for it dearly. 80
MARGARET: What? Can't you kiss any more?
My love, we were only parted a little while,
and yet you have forgotten how to kiss?
Why am I so afraid in your arms?
Just a word or look from you 85
made heaven come down to me,
and you used to kiss me
as though you wanted to smother me.
Kiss me! Or I'll kiss you!

(*She embraces him.*)

Oh, your lips are cold and silent. 90
Where has your love hidden?
Who has stolen it from me?

(*She turns away from him.*)

FAUST: Come, follow me! Darling, be brave!
I love you more than ever before;
but follow me, I beg you. 95
MARGARET (*turning to him*): And is it you? And is it really you?
FAUST: Of course. But come!
MARGARET: You undo the chains,
and you hold me close to you again.
How is it that you aren't afraid of me? — 100
And do you really know whom you're setting free?
FAUST: Come! It's almost daylight.

MARGARET: I have killed my mother,
I have drowned my child.
Wasn't it given to you and me? 105
To you too — It *is* you! I can hardly believe it.
Give me your hand! It isn't a dream!
Your dear hand! — But, oh, it's wet!
Wipe it off! It seems to me
that there's blood on it. 110
O God, what have you done?
Put up your sword, I beg you!
FAUST: Forget what is past.
You're torturing me!
MARGARET: No, you must go on living! 115
I'll tell you about their graves.
You must see to them
the first thing in the morning.
Give the best place to mother;
put my brother close by. 120
Put me a little to one side —
only not too far away!
And the baby on my right breast.
No one else will ever lie beside me!
It was a dear sweet joy 125
to be close beside you.
But it isn't like that any more.
Now it's as if I must force myself toward you,
and you were thrusting me away.
And yet it's you, and you seem so good and kind 130
FAUST: If you feel this, then come!
MARGARET: Out there?
FAUST: To freedom.
MARGARET: If the grave is there
and death lurks for me, then I'll come! 135
From here to the eternal bed of rest
but farther not one step —
Are you going?
O Henry, if I could only go with you!
FAUST: You can if you will. The door is open. 140
MARGARET: I dare not go out. There is nothing for me to hope.
What would it help if I fled? They're waiting to catch me.
It's miserable to have to beg,
and worse with an evil conscience!
It is miserable having to wander in a strange land. 145
And finally I'd be caught!
FAUST: I'll stay with you.
MARGARET: Quickly! Quickly!
Save your poor child.

Run! Straight up the path 150
along the brook,
over the foot-bridge,
into the woods,
to the left where the plank
is in the pond. 155
Seize it quickly!
It's trying to keep afloat,
it is still struggling.
Save it! Save it!
FAUST: Think! Please think! 160
One step and you're free!
MARGARET: If we were only beyond the hill!
My mother sits there on a stone —
it's as if a cold hand had me by the hair!
My mother sits there on a stone 165
and wags her head.
She doesn't beckon, she doesn't nod. Her head is so heavy.
She has slept so long, and will never waken.
She slept so that we could enjoy ourselves,
and those were happy times! 170
FAUST: My begging and my words are no help.
I must carry you away.
MARGARET: Let me go! I'll not be forced!
Don't take hold of me so murderously!
Didn't I once do everything you wanted? 175
FAUST: Dearest, it will soon be dawn!
MARGARET: Dawn! Soon daylight! My last day is breaking;
it was to have been my wedding-day!
Don't tell a soul you've been with Margaret already.
Alas my virgin's wreath 180
is a thing of the past now!
We'll see each other again,
but not at the dance.
The crowd presses nearer. No one speaks.
The square and the streets 185
can't hold them all.
The bell tolls, the judge's staff is broken.
They seize me and bind me!
I'm taken to the bloody block.
Each one imagines above his own neck 190
the sharp sword trembling over mine.
The world lies hushed as a grave.
FAUST: I wish I had never been born!
MEPHISTOPHELES (*appearing outside*): Come! Or you're lost.
This futile hesitation! This wavering and babbling! 195

My horses are shuddering
because the day is breaking.
MARGARET: What rises there from the ground?
It is he! He! Oh, send him away!
What does he want in this holy place?   200
He wants me!
FAUST: You shall live!
MARGARET: I give myself up to the judgment of God!
MEPHISTOPHELES (to Faust): Come along! Or I'll leave you in the
lurch with her!
MARGARET: Father, I am yours! Save me!   205
Angels and hosts of heaven,
gather your forces around me! Protect me!
Henry — I am afraid for you!
MEPHISTOPHELES: She is judged and doomed!
A VOICE (from above): She is saved!   210
MEPHISTOPHELES (to Faust): Come with me!

(They vanish.)

MARGARET'S VOICE (from within, dying away): Henry! Henry!

Thomas Mann

GOETHE'S "FAUST" *

. . . In the sixteenth century, after the coming of the printing-press,
there was a great need for matter to feed the presses and exploit the
popular possibilities of the new invention. Almost any sort of material
would do; and the printer, in order to be able to keep on turning it
out, often became his own author. Thus the oldest Faust-book, of the
year 1587, was probably compiled in Frankfurt by the printer, Spies.
It was a collection of popular legends of the black art, up to then
circulated by word of mouth; they grouped themselves round the figure
of a Dr. Johannes Faustus, a charlatan who had lived some fifty years
before and now embodied in the popular fancy the conception of the
invoker of evil spirits. His name, it seems, was Georg Helmstätter, but
he assumed the highsounding cognomen of Sabellicus, and later, for a
definite reason, the name of Faustus. On the Easter Sunday walk,
Goethe makes Faust discourse to Wagner in brilliant verse, disclosing
various characteristic and probable-sounding things about his ante-

From *Essays*, by Thomas Mann and translated by H. T. Lowe-Porter. Copyright 1938 by Alfred A.
Knopf, Inc. Reprinted by permission.

* [Delivered in English as a public lecture at Princeton University in 1938.]

cedents and origins and about his father, the alchemist and quack physician, that *"dunkler Ehrenmann."*

I mention this old book because it has a chapter, copied down by the printer from some source or other, in which Helena appears. Dr. Faustus summons up the most beautiful woman in the world before the eyes of his fortunate students; but then he falls in love with her himself and demands her as bedfellow from the devil who serves him, whose name is already Mephistopheles. The description of Helena's famous or infamous person is amorous, though somewhat conventional. It has elements from the Trojan tales of various literatures; and all the epithets used by Byzantine, mediæval and troubadour poets to characterize the European ideal of female beauty are lavished with somewhat mechanical enthusiasm upon it.

The idea of a love-affair between the sixteenth-century charlatan and the regal hetæra of classical antiquity is in itself rather striking. But the combination was not new, its roots strike deep down in time. The Faust-Helena combination is one of those pregnant inventions which can make a period of two thousand years seem like a single span of human life. The end of the classic age, the period of struggle between the classic and the Christian world, must have had elements of similarity with the age of the Reformation. Both were times of fanaticism and mental confusion, and in the earlier as in the later there flourished a host of charlatans, religious impostors, illusionists and self-delusionists. One of these, called Simon, came from Samaria and figures in apostolic history as having scandalously offered money to Peter to buy himself the gift of the Holy Ghost. This Simon was in fact altogether a scandal: he was held in abhorrence by the Fathers of the church because he founded a heretical sect, the Simonians, and shamelessly gave himself out as divine. Also because he took about with him a female, a former prostitute, now acclaimed by her master and his accomplices as the second highest godhead in the universe, the female deity for whom the world had been waiting. He called her Helena.

All that was true mythological hocus-pocus. The adventurer Simon confused the name of Helena with that of Selene, the moon- and mother-goddess and paramour, Astarte. It was an intentional conflation of the erotic and the idea of redemption — today, when we are entering upon another epoch of legend-building quackery, we can gauge its popular appeal better than could some of our ancestors who lived in intervening centuries more firmly anchored to the rational. Well, then, Simon and his Helena were one of those pairs of impostors such as early Christianity knew all too well. We learn from Suetonius that Simon gave an exhibition of flying before the Emperor Nero — the first in history — and crashed. Here, in the flight motif, we have a theme beloved of all the legends of necromancy and witchcraft. Flying is one of man's earliest wish-dreams; and since its fulfilment in actuality lay in the dim future, he transferred it to the realm of magic. The magnificent passage from the Easter Sunday walk, where Faust talks to Wagner about the joys of flying, bears witness to the inward marriage of the poet with his supernatural material.

> *Ach, zu des Geistes Flügel wird so leicht*
> *Kein körperlicher Flügel sich gesellen.*
> *Doch ist es jedem eingeboren,*
> *Dass sein Gefühl hinauf und vorwärts drängt,*
> *Wenn über uns, im blauen Raum verloren,*
> *Ihr schmetternd Lied die Lerche singt;*
> *Wenn über schroffen Fichtenhöhen*
> *Der Adler ausgebreitet schwebt,*
> *Und über Flächen, über Seen*
> *Der Kranich nach der Heimat strebt.*

> Alas, our bodies have no wings to vie
> With the swift pinions of the lofty spirit!
> And yet 'tis nature to aspire
> Upward to heights of our desire,
> Whenas above, in the blue ether soaring,
> We hear the lark her warbling song outpouring,
> Above the rugged fir-clad steep
> The outspread eagle floats and sways,
> And high above o'er plains and lakes
> The crane his swift way homeward takes.

The dream has been fulfilled. As the dreams of men usually are. The whirring plane has made it a disillusioning reality. Flying is a neutral, mechanical experience; you read the paper as you soar godlike in the air. And when the incendiary bombs fall from immense heights upon cities and towns, then we sympathize with Wagner, the timid pedant, who disclaims any sympathy with Faust's ideas, saying:

> *Wie anders tragen uns die Geistesfreuden*
> *Von Buch zu Buch, von Blatt zu Blatt!*

> 'Tis otherwise when intellectual pleasures
> Bear us from book to book, from page to page!

To return to Simon, the Samaritan: he survived in a novel of the early Christian age. It was called *Recognitiones* (*Recognitions*), and in it, under the name of Magus, he and his disreputable companion play a thrilling role, performing all the conjuring tricks (including flying) which have become the permanent stock-in-trade in the literature of magic and diabolism. However, it says in this novel that Simon, when he and Helena made their flight, took the name of Faust.

Fifty generations later it was Georg Helmstätter's turn to practise humbuggery upon this earth. He came to Basel, and left his quack visiting-cards upon humanists and theologians. It was the year 1526, and the old *Recognitiones* was in a new edition. The taste of the time is sufficiently revealed by the fact that the antiquated trash became the fashion and went through many impressions. Helmstätter read it and straightway gave himself out as the successor to Magus, calling himself Magus II and Faustus Junior on his visiting-cards. Also, he conformed with the pattern by getting himself a travelling-companion named Helena. Obviously it was an age of great sympathetic understanding of the myth, even though the myth had long since become a species of charlatanry. Helmstätter was not merely the successor of Faustus; there was something else in play, and that was the principle of identification, the abrogation of the individual in the type. Helmstätter-Faustus continued for eleven years to practise his sense-deluding mystery. Then he died; and fifty years later, in Frankfurt, the popular Faust-book was compiled in memory of him.

Thus it came about that the name of Helena, the legendary queen of antiquity, remained bound up with that of the sixteenth-century witch-doctor. Nor had Goethe, in the beginning, any other intention than to bring his Helena at once on the stage with his Faustus. But the autobiographical triumphed temporarily over the legend. In Frankfurt there had been an early-loved Gretchen, in Alsace there was a Friederike, basely left; and these two flesh-and-blood memories put the classic shade so far in the background that the sweet and sorrowful Gretchen dominates the whole first part of *Faust*. Gretchen put Helena in the shade — yet not quite, and not even altogether in the *Faust Erster Teil*. Thanks to the folk-character of Goethe's genius, Faust and Gretchen rank among the famous lovers of literature. They are as secure a possession of our imagination as are Romeo and Juliet, Hero and Leander, Petrarch and Laura, Paolo and Francesca, Abélard and Héloïse — or Goethe's own Werther and Lotte. But in Goethe's masterpiece the pair of lovers has an interchangeable female half. Faust-Gretchen, Faust-Helena — there is an extraordinary combination indeed! Not alone because the magnificent Helena episode in the second part is, in its highly developed, highly literary way, as full of genius as are the priceless Gretchen scenes in the first part. No; I mean that in the first part itself there are dreamlike transferences. In the scene in the witches' kitchen, written in Rome, Faust, before he drinks the magic draught, beholds in the magic mirror Woman in all the splendour of her supreme loveliness, and enraptured sees in that recumbent form the summary and brief abstract of heaven itself. Whom does he there see? Obviously no individual woman, rather a wish-picture of sensual loveliness — the pattern of the female kind, as Mephistopheles says, while promising Faust that he shall soon see that pattern before him in the flesh. But she whom he will actually see — that is not Helena, it is sweet Gretchen, for whom "the pattern of the female kind" is certainly rather a high-flown description. If Faust finds her that, then the only explanation is that given in Mephisto's words:

Du siehst mit diesem Trank im Leibe
Bald Helenen in jedem Weibe

With this drink inside you, presently
Helen in every female you will see.

There, for the first time in the play, the name of Helena appears; in anticipation, and as a symbol of all that feminine beauty and delight which the sweet, simple German burgher-maid is shortly to embody. Yet it is strange to see that Goethe, in that rapturous outburst of Faust after the first meeting with Gretchen, remains faithful to the description of Helena in the old Faust-book:

Beim Himmel, dieses Kind ist schön!
So etwas hab ich nie gesehn!

Heavens, but that child was fair!
Her like I've not seen anywhere!

cries the Faust of the poem.

Der Lippe rot, der Wange Licht,
Die Tage der Welt vergesse ich's nicht!

So red her lips, her cheek so bright,
Ne'er shall I forget the sight!

And in the Faust-book it says of Helena: *"Ihre Leffzen rot wie Kirschen, rote Bäcklein wie ein Rösslin"* ("Her lips as cherries red, her cheeks like rosebuds"). And her face is described as *"überaus schön gleissend"* ("so shining fair"), of which there is a clear reminiscence in the striking phrase of Goethe: *"der Wange Licht."* And *"etwas schnippisch doch zugleich"* ("rather tart withal") is the demure Gretchen:

Wie sie kurz angebunden war
Das ist nun zum Entzücken gar!

Her pretty, shrewish speech —
It was enchanting!

That, I would wager, is a memory, in a more charmingly turned phrase, of the "pert and roguish face" given to Helena in the Faust-book.

In short, Gretchen betrays traits, half-obliterated, of Helena. She was originally Helena, and Helena, in some small degree, she is still. Yet what an infinitely more lifelike figure the young poet created when he turned the luxurious beauty of the legend into the sweet and hapless little daughter of the pawnbroker! Infinitely more lifelike than if he had followed the old legend, instead of drawing on his own. *"Bewundert viel und viel gescholten,"* "much admired and censured much," Helena will duly appear in the second part. But her phantasmagorical figure is far from having the vivid emotional appeal of Gretchen's. She remains an episode. When Faust has dreamed to the end his enchanted dream with her — laden as that is with all the weight of Goethe's mind and art — when that is over she disappears, she vanishes from Faust's sight and memory. Gretchen it is, *una pœnitentium,* who in the fullness of time becomes the instrument by which the end of Faust's story and of his life are linked to their beginning: ˙

> *Neige, neige,*
> *Du Ohnegleiche,*
> *Du Strahlenreiche,*
> *Dein Antlitz gnädig meinem Glück!*
> *Der Frühgeliebte,*
> *Nicht mehr getrübte,*
> *Er kommt zurück.*

> Bend down, bend down,
> Incomp'rable one,
> Thy radiant face
> Upon my bliss, in grace!
> My early lover,
> No more in sorrow,
> Comes back to me.

The lines, with their parallelism to those of his early years:

> *Neige, neige,*
> *Du Schmerzensreiche,*

> Bend down, bend down,
> Thou suffering one,

round out the great circle of the poet's life. A life so abundant and manifold that there was ever present danger of its being squandered, here asserts, by the power of memory, its essential unity. *Faust* is the representative achievement, the symbol of Goethe's whole life. He himself said of it:

> *Des Menschen Leben ist ein ähnliches Gedicht;*
> *Es hat wohl einen Anfang, hat ein Ende,*
> *Allein ein Ganzes ist es nicht.*

> Man's life's a poem similar to this;
> It has, of course, beginning, has an end too —
> But yet a whole it does not come to.

It is touching to see how his mind, in the later, elder time, reaches back to give to the fragmentary and illimitable work the unity that in his deepest heart he craved. "He is," he said, "the most fortunate man who can bring the end of his life round to its beginning again."

It is always a pleasure to speak to the young, to beginning students of Goethe's great poem. For it belongs to their age, it is the conception of one like-minded to them. Originally it was nothing more than the work of a highly gifted student, wherein the author calls faculties and professors over the coals and amuses himself enormously with playing the clever mentor, in diabolic disguise, to the timid freshman newly come up. A contemporary critic — the man's name was Pustkuchen, as one might say Popover — remarked peevishly: "Faust's attack on all human knowledge is not precisely that of an Alexander standing at the known limits of the world and sighing for more to conquer. It is more like that of a student making fun of his professor — however, it was enough for the needs of the majority of his readers." And the hard-pushed critic continues: "But as it goes on, it follows the course of all the Goethian poetry. The great sinner, the titanic figure who outbids the powers of the Devil himself . . . he becomes in the writer's hands a hero like all his other heroes. A love-story unfolds, like a thousand others . . . there is a good-hearted, limited middle-class girl, like Clärchen in *Egmont*. . . ."

Yes, really, the man, in his good-hearted, limited way, is quite right in inveighing against a poetic realism which must have seemed to him like a derogation into intimate personalities of material in itself very lofty. The critic is always on the side of the material, against the poet who irreverently deals with it as an instrument, a pretext for his own personal ends. But what such critics fail to see is the remarkable phenomenon displayed in *Faust*: the genius of student youth here usurps the role of humanity itself, and the whole Western world has accepted this valuation and recognized in the symbolism of the Faust-figure its own deepest essence. Much honour is done to youth by this poem and the greatness it achieved. Its uncompromisingness, its spirit of untamed revolt, its scorn of limitations, of peace and quiet, its yearning and heaven-storming soul, are precisely the expression of what age likes to call "youthful immaturity." But, thanks to the power of genius, this immaturity becomes the representative of humanity; youth stands for the human being at large; what was youthful storm and stress becomes ageless and typical.

Of course, in the play it is not a youth but a reverend and learned doctor whom we see at his desk in the dark vault. The filthy brewage of the witches' kitchen is to take thirty years from his age, and he must be a man some thirty years old when he first addresses Gretchen; so at the beginning of the play he would be not less than sixty years old, and as such he is represented on the stage. Yet of this sixty-year-old man Mephistopheles says to God:

> *Fürwahr, er dient euch auf besonderer Weise.*
> *Nicht irdisch ist des Thoren Trank und Speise.*
> *Ihn treibt die Gährung in die Ferne,*
> *Er ist sich seiner Tollheit halb bewusst;*
> *Von Himmel fordert er die schönsten Sterne*
> *Und von der Erde jede höchste Lust,*
> *Und alle Näh und alle Fern*
> *Befriedigt nicht die tiefbewegte Brust.*

> Indeed, he serves you in the strangest fashion!
> Not earthly food or drink do feed his passion.
> His inner ferment drives him far,
> Of his own frenzy he is half aware;
> From heaven he demands the fairest star,
> From earth all bliss supremely rare —
> And yet not near nor far
> Can he find easement for his anguished breast.

Those are not words that fit a man on the threshold of old age. The poet transplants his youthful urgency into the breast of a man at the same time of life as Goethe's own when he wrote the *Elective Affinities*. His Faust is humanity itself, object at once of the divine solicitude and of the lust for conquest of the powers of darkness. But the young poet who so facilely sketched this cosmic figure gave it his own traits, his own nature; and thus the youth became a man, the man a youth.

But this particular youth strives for, and achieves, critical detachment even from his own youngness, from his unbounded urge for freedom and the Absolute. Detachment implies irony; and his need of irony just as strongly demands poetic expression as do his other cravings. Irony is his "second soul"; and Goethe makes Faust speak with a sigh of the two souls within his breast: the one the lusty hunger for love, the clinging sensuality; the other his longing for the pure and spiritual. The sigh he breathes is half-hypocritical: as well might he lament the duality of irony and enthusiasm, for well he knows that dualism is the soil and the mystery of creative fruitfulness. Enthusiasm — that is fullness with God; and what then is irony? The author of *Faust* is youth enough to see in that urge for the Absolute the divine in man; and in irony the diabolic. But this diabolism of his does not stand on such a bad footing with the divine. The Lord God says of it:

> *Ich habe deinesgleichen nie gehasst.*
> *Von allen Geistern die verneinen*
> *Ist mir der Schalk am wenigsten zur Last.*

> Hatred for your sort I have never felt.
> Of all the spirits that deny
> I find the thorough rascal least offensive.

The diabolism is of an amusing, witty kind, and God has tolerant understanding of it. It is acidulous, unprejudiced worldly sense, unapt for the emotions of the angels but not without sympathy for ordinary human need: "I feel a pity for the pains of men," says Mephisto. It makes superior mock of youthful enthusiasm; it is creative inventiveness and conscious anticipation of maturity and experience, fanaticism and worldly good sense; these are the contradiction, the "two souls" that Goethe likes to project into the dramatic form. Later he will divide himself into Tasso and Antonio; here, on a grander scale, he divides himself into Faust and Mephistopheles. Mephistopheles is the ironic self-corrective to Goethe's youthful titanism.

Mephistopheles is the most vital figure of a devil in all literature; the clearest-cut, the most animated by creative genius. He has not the emotional appeal of Klopstock's and Milton's devils; yet the characterization is so fresh and amusing, so sharply outlined and yet so various, that despite its spirit of ironic self-abrogation it made a permanent conquest of the human imagination for all time. The name Mephistopheles comes from the old Faust-book and the literature of demonology. Has it to do with mephitic? Does it signify sulphurous, pestilential? At any rate, it has the right sound, for the fellow is foul, foul in the grand style, with a sense of humour about his own foulness. He is the presiding genius of all vermin — rats, mice, frogs, bugs, lice and so on. But his protection of the more repulsive manifestations of creation is really an expression of his nihilism, his denial of creation and of life altogether.

He says so straight out, and his words have become proverbial:

> *Ich bin der Geist der stets verneint!*
> *Und das mit Recht; denn alles was entsteht*
> *Ist wert, dass es zu Grunde geht;*
> *Drum besser wär's, dass nichts entstünde.*

> I am the spirit that ever denies!
> And rightly so; for all that's born on earth
> Merits destruction from its birth
> And better 'twere it had not seen the light.

And much later on, in the second part of the tragedy, when Faust dies, he shrugs his shoulders at the angel's word: "Over!" and mocks at life's lament over its own transitoriness:

> *Vorbei! Ein dummes Wort.*
> *Warum vorbei?*
> *Vorbei und reines Nichts, vollkommenes Einerlei!*

Was soll uns denn das ew'ge Schaffen?
Geschaffenes zu Nichts hinwegzuraffen!
Da ist's vorbei! Was ist daran zu lesen?
Es ist so gut, als wär' es nicht gewesen,
Und treibt sich doch im Kreis, als wenn es wäre.
Ich liebte mir dafür das Ewig-leere.

Over! A silly word.
Why over?
Over, and sheerest nothing, quite the same!
Then what's the use, eternally to strive,
When all that's made at nothing does arrive?
Over it is! What shall we learn from that?
It is as good as though it never were,
Runs round and round, the same old end to see —
The eternal void is good enough for me.

The grey-haired poet makes his devil speak just as the audacious youth had made him do, in the selfsame accents. And we must not think that the devil's nihilism, his critique of life as it is and just because it is, was remote from the poet and foreign to his soul. Through the mouth of Faust he stands up for life, "the healing, creative force," to which Mephisto opposes the "cold devil's fist." But what Mephisto says springs just as much from Goethe's own nature and feelings as does his apologia for life. Goethe, like Mephisto, is no angelic flatterer of creation; and he invents a devil in order to have a mouthpiece for all the rebellion, denial, and critical bitterness he feels in himself.

But Mephistopheles is not only the presiding genius of all the vermin. Above all he is the genius of *fire,* he has reserved to himself that destructive, sterilizing, annihilating element. The red waistcoat and the cock's feather are the outward signs of his infernal nature. It is true that the witch misses in him the other classic attributes, the cloven hoof, the two ravens, which the Christian Devil inherited from the pagan Wotan. But in Mephisto the devil of the myth is tamed down in accordance with the cosmopolitan pose which he humorously finds more appropriate to the times. The cloven hoof is replaced by a slight limp. Wotan's ravens do indeed appear in the second part ("I see my raven pair, what message do they bear?"); but they are as a rule invisible. Mephisto regards himself as a cultural product, and seeks to dissociate himself from the legendary "northern phantom." He lays aside horns, claws, and tail; as for the cloven hoof, that, he feels, would do him harm in society. He refuses to be addressed as Squire Satan, and prefers the title of Herr Baron, as a gentleman among other gentlemen. Satan, he feels, has become a fable; he accepts the man-of-the-world version of him; though at the same time he asserts that mankind has not gained very much by doing away with the Devil. "They are rid of the Evil One, the evils remain." He completely departs from the role, turns his scepticism upon himself, and quite in the spirit of the Enlightenment regards his own existence as a superstition, or at most as so moderated by enlightenment as to fit the new age. The drollest implications arise, as for instance that scene, in only four verses, wherein Faust and Mephistopheles pass by a crucifix. "Mephisto, why so fast?" says Faust. "And why cast down your eyes before the Cross?" His companion replies:

> *Ich weiss es wohl, es ist ein Vorurteil,*
> *Allein genug, mir ist's einmal zuwider.*

> I realize it is a prejudice —
> Anyhow, there it is: I do not like it.

The fear of the crucifix was a mark of the mediæval Devil. But when Mephisto speaks of prejudice, that is good eighteenth-century, and a proper modernized Satan to match. His enlightenment is not religious, it is not the crucifix that he speaks of as a prejudice, it is his own mediæval, traditional fear to which he refers, and he excuses it as a weakness and caprice which, despite all his modern culture, he has been unable to overcome.

We see how the poet plays with his conception of the Evil One, limiting at moments its reality, making it display at times a satiric abrogation of its own identity. But after all it is actually there, actually a devil, who comes when called, and is subject to the laws of demonology. "I make my homage to the learned man: you certainly have made me sweat quite soundly," he acknowledges to Faust. Sometimes one might suspect that he is only playing his part in the game; in the witches' kitchen he behaves with good-humoured, sceptical condescension towards the magic claptrap and objectionable humbug which so offend Faust's humanistic feeling.

> *Ei Possen, das ist nur zum Lachen.*
> *Seid nur nicht ein so strenger Mann!*
> *Sie muss als Arzt ein Hokuspokus machen.*

> Oh, suchlike little games — one laughs
> At them! My good sir, don't be such an ass!
> She is the doctor, she must do her stuff.

He defends the nonsensical *Einmaleins* (one times one) incantation by an attack on the pious absurdity of the Holy Trinity, in a sarcastic line or so. Yet Mephisto seems to be caught by the pentagram and subject to it; also the signature in blood, to Faust a meaningless gesture, he appears actually to need in order to execute the pact in good mediæval demonological style.

Thus we see the artist playing with the traditional figure; making it hover in changeful light or even avaunt and void the sight of its own identity. It is even uncertain, for instance, and is deliberately left uncertain, whether this is actually *the* Devil or only *a* devil; only a representative of the infernal powers (*ein Teil von jener Kraft*) or the Evil One himself in person. In the Prologue in Heaven he is plainly the Satan of the Book of Job; for why should a lesser one than he ask permission of God to try a human soul? And at the very end, when Faust's immortal soul is in question, he cannot well be other than Satan himself, the thwarted Devil of legend. But in between he functions, so to speak, as a limited liability company; refers to "us" and "folk like us"; says: "Bethink thee well, for we shall not forget," and "Did we force ourselves on you, or you on us?" Goethe even wrote for the Walpurgisnacht a scene in which Satanas himself, Herr Urian, sits on the peak of the Brocken and holds his horrid court. But this was to introduce confusion: to include the scene would have condemned Mephisto to second place in the hierarchy, and Goethe left it out, so that the Prince of Hell, the Whole, might not derogate from the importance of the part.

Mephisto's language is sharply contrasted with the earnest, emotional, passionate key in which Faust speaks. The devil's line is brisk and worldly; it has a careless wit; is eminently critical and contemptuous, spiced with foreign words, altogether diverting. He speaks as it were *en passant;* the result is happy, casual, and most effective:

> *Mein guter Herr, ihr seht die Sachen*
> *Wie man die Sachen eben sieht;*
> *Wir müssen das gescheiter machen —*

> Yes, my good sir, you look at things
> Precisely as in fact one does;
> From now on we must manage better —

and so on. That is the tone. It is the superiority of the man of the world (and Mephisto is at bottom nothing but a worldling) who shrugs his shoulders over the man with the deep and troubled emotional nature. Faust, in worldly matters, is Mephisto's pupil; he lets himself be led; and in despair over his own striving for the highest things, even strikes a bargain with the devil. Mephisto's relation to Faust is that of the experienced travelling-companion and tutor who knows his way about; he is courier, *maître des plaisirs;* again he is simply the resourceful servant who Lothario-like makes opportunities for his master. He is all these things by turns, with versatility and wit. In the Paralipomenon, one of the numerous rejected drafts, the devil pictures himself as the corrupt tutor of a young eighteenth-century nobleman:

> *Der junge Herr ist freilich schwer zu führen,*
> *Doch als erfahrener Gouverneur*
> *Weiss ich den Wildfang zu regieren,*

Und afficiert mich auch nichts mehr.
Und lass ihn so in seinen Lüsten wandeln,
Mag ich doch auch nach meinen Lüsten handeln,
Ich rede viel und lass ihn immer gehn;
Ist ja ein allzudummer Streich geschehen
Dann muss ich meine Weisheit zeigen,
Dann wird er bei den Haarn herausgeführt,
Doch gibt man gleich, indem man's repariert,
Gelegenheit zu neuen dummen Streichen.

True, my young master is a trifle wilful,
But birds like that aren't hard to tame.
A tutor's job has made me skilful,
Naught he can do puts me to shame.
Go where he will, I follow with due meekness,
Since for my own ways I still have a weakness,
I preach a lot — and let him have his way.
And when some extra-stupid prank he'll play,
Then my good sense it is my turn to show,
And drag him out of harm's way by the hair:
Leaving him, while the damage we repair,
Always an opening for some new folly.

Goethe continually rhymes *zeigen* and *streichen, neigen* and *reichen,* as though his Frankfurt pronunciation *zeichen* and *neichen* were the universal one. It is certainly a hard pill to swallow, from the greatest lyric poet of Germany. It shows a naïve persistence in local tradition — we have simply to put up with it, and console ourselves with the thought that it is nice to hear how Goethe spoke. The rejected verses just quoted are a good illustration of the wit and variety in Goethe's portrayal of the devil: how it makes itself large and then small, expanding from the satirical human being into the magnificently diabolic and back again at will.

But in the end Mephistopheles is the personification of the hatred of light and life; he is primal night and Chaos' son, the emissary of the void — after his own kind he is on a very grand scale. "Thou vile abortion, born of filth and fire!" — thus Faust once rails at him, and it is a splendid description. Something about it, we realize, corresponds to the human intellectual elements which both impress and offend us. The filth, that is the cynicism, the obscene wit, launched by the fires of his infernal will to destruction. The essence of his nature is the profoundest lovelessness. Hatred fairly scintillates in the creature's slanting yellow tiger-eyes. "The bottomless rage that leads thee to destroy," Faust says to him: "thy tig'rish glare, thy all-compelling face. . . ." Here the humorous side fades out, and the devil emerges in all his specific majesty; not without a certain admiration the poet sees and feels it.

Goethe's own attitude towards evil is not uniform; it hovers between recognition and contempt. He says, in one of the Proverbs:

> *Ich kann mich nicht bereden lassen:*
> *Macht mir den Teufel nur nicht klein!*
> *Ein Kerl, den alle Menschen hassen,*
> *Der muss was sein.*

> I still remain quite unconvinced
> That it's good sense to paint the devil small:
> There must be something in a chap
> Who's hated so by all.

But in portraying Mephistopheles as the embodiment of evil, Goethe sometimes injects into the character a trace of self-contempt, a hang-dog note: Mephistopheles will sometimes betray his suspicion that the devil is no great shakes when all is said and done:

> *Mich darf niemand aufs Gewissen fragen,*
> *Ich schäme mich oft meines Geschlechts;*
> *Sie meinen, wenn Sie Teufel sagen,*
> *So sagen Sie was Rechts.*

> Let nobody ask me on my oath
> Whether I shame me for my kind;
> But you, when you speak the words "the devil" —
> You've something big in mind.

When you say "the devil," you really are not saying much; in other words, evil is a poor thing after all. The poet could scarcely make the idea more impressive than by putting it in the Evil One's own mouth! And in the Prologue, Mephisto feels flattered by the fact that God condescends to converse with him, the old nihilist:

> *Es ist gar hübsch von einem grossen Herrn*
> *So menschlich mit dem Teufel selbst zu sprechen!*

> It's very handsome of so great a lord
> To talk with the devil as man to man!

Not for nothing have these two light-hearted lines become so famous. Their humour is complex and subtle. Here is the Divine Absolute, in the role of the Grand Seigneur who is human enough to discuss with the Opposition; and here is the Opposition, flattered by the complaisance and recognizing its own inferiority — truly a cosmic jest, a regular poet's joke, and very characteristic of this particular poet; for when in the presence of opposition and negation, Goethe always thought of himself as the grand seigneur and representative of the government.

"If I had had the *misfortune* to be in the Opposition," he once said in conversation. And yet it was precisely Goethe who created, and invested with lyric meaning, the figure of the arch-nihilist, Mephistopheles.

And further: what character in this play — racked, it is true, by disillusionment, bitterness, yearning, and despair — utters the most crushing, nihilistic words in the whole poem: the great malediction upon life, its joys and its seduction; the great curse upon spirit and sense, fame and possessions, love, hope, faith, endurance — so that the chorus of spirits must lament:

> *Weh! Weh!*
> *Du hast sie zerstört,*
> *Die schöne Welt,*
> *Mit mächtiger Faust;*
> *Sie stürzt, sie zerfällt!*
> *Ein Halbgott hat sie zerschlagen!*
> *Wir tragen*
> *Die Trümmer ins Nichts hinüber*
> *Und klagen*
> *Über die verlorne Schöne!*

> Woe! Woe!
> Thou hast laid low
> With violent blow
> The beautiful world —
> It totters, it falls,
> A demigod hath struck it.
> We have borne
> Its ruins into the void
> And we mourn
> For the beauty destroyed!

Which character is it? Mephisto? He could never have summoned the pity or pain for such an anathema against life and joy. No, it is the anguished human being, it is Goethe-Faust who utters the frightful words. Here the roles are reversed, and the nihilistic devil becomes the practical and worldly advocate for life against the desperate and rebellious human spirit.

> *Hör auf, mit deinem Gram zu spielen,*
> *Der, wie ein Geier, Dir im Leben frisst,*
> *Die schlechteste Gesellschaft lässt Dich fühlen,*
> *Dass Du ein Mensch mit Menschen bist.*

> Do stop playing with your sorrows,
> That like vultures feed upon your breast!
> Even from the lowest company one borrows
> A sense that one's a man like all the rest.

The character of Faust in the poem is no simpler, no more uniform, than that of his diabolic mentor. It varies in the same way. Or rather the whole poem in which they play their parts possesses this variability of the Time-Spirit; since the scene, ostensibly, is laid in the sixteenth century, but continually plays over into the eighteenth, the poet's own. Wagner, the famulus, speaks the language of the age of Enlightenment, praises the periods of Gottsched, and feels that science and mankind have made glorious progress. Faust-Goethe, on the contrary, stands for Herder's ideas about the "age of genius." The nature-mysticism of his soliloquies, and the religious feeling he shows to Gretchen — all that is inspired by Swedenborg, Ossian, and Lavater, in particular by the northern mystic, who died in 1772, and whose name Goethe replaced by that of Nostradamus in order to preserve the historical perspective. I spoke of Faust's humanism, the intellectual attitude that makes him fundamentally despise magic as despicable rigmarole, although he surrenders to it, that "through the spirit's mouth and might, mysteries might see the light." As a matter of fact, he remained, as Mephisto's patron, addicted to it up to his old age and made use of it in all his adventures, first with Gretchen, and then in the world, at the Kaiser's court, in battle, in the affair with Helena, whom he wins only by enchantment and illusion. Not till very late does there stir in him the desire "magic from out his path to put away." Yet even so, his attitude towards it from the beginning is highly fastidious — or at least towards its practicants and technicians and their obscene trafficking. He inveighs against the witches' kitchen as a *"Wust von Raserei"* (crazy rubbish). "Why just that old hag?" he asks in disgust. He finds the whole thing as unappetizing as anything he ever saw. Bad taste, offensive — that is his humanistic judgment on the whole of magic art: "frantic stuff, wild goings-on, disgusting humbug" — he knows and despises it already. The blood-pact — vital to Mephisto because after all, in God's name, he really *is* the devil — Faust knows about that too, it is as familiar as repulsive to him; he refers to the pact with contempt, as a piece of tomfoolery. Why must they have such a superstitious flourish as the signature in blood, when after all, in the eternal flux of things, there can be no such thing as a binding promise, however much a high-minded man would wish to cling to the delusion of truth? Mephisto duly utters his mediæval patter, just as it stands in the legend:

> *Ich will mich hier zu deinem Dienst verbinden*
> *Auf deinen Wink nicht rasten und nicht ruhn:*
> *Wenn wir uns drüben wiederfinden,*
> *Dann sollst Du mir das Gleiche tun.*

> Here I bind myself unto your service,
> Ever at your beck and call to be;
> When we find ourselves in the hereafter,
> Then you shall do the same for me.

He speaks of the hereafter as an actuality in the popular mind and his own — in the Prologue, indeed, he stands before God among the heavenly host. But Faust answers him as a humanist and earth-bound human spirit, who does not believe in a hereafter, or at least is not interested in one:

> *Aus dieser Erde quillen meine Freuden,*
> *Und diese Sonne scheinet meinen Leiden;*
> *Kann ich mich erst von ihnen scheiden,*
> *Dann mag was will und kann geschehn.*
> *Davon will ich nichts weiter hören. . . .*

> My joys all spring from earthly sources,
> My griefs are shined on by this very sun;
> When I can sever me from earthly courses,
> Let come what can and will; my race is run.
> I'll hear no more of it.

Neither understands the other — either temporally or morally. The bargain is struck on the basis of two different conceptions: one primitive and diabolic, the other more evolved and with some knowledge of human dignity. *"Was willst du, armer Teufel, geben?"* asks Faust. ("And what, poor devil, can you give, at best?")

> *Ward eines Menschen Geist, in seinem hohen Streben*
> *Von deinesgleichen je gefasst?*

> When was the human spirit's striving
> E'er understanded of a thing like thee?

He makes his pact with the devil out of the same high and human aspiration that mind, science, knowledge had been unable to satisfy; with the same absolute and insatiable passion that made him despair of thought he gives himself to pleasure. And all the while he knows but too well that it will be as impotent as knowledge to still his craving for infinity.

> *Werd ich beruhigt je mich auf ein Faulbett legen,*
> *So sei es gleich um mich getan!*
> *Kannst du mich schmeichelnd je belügen,*
> *Dass ich mir selbst gefallen mag,*
> *Kannst du mich mit Genuss betrügen,*
> *Das sei für mich der letzte Tag!*

> If ever on bed of idleness I lay me,
> May I that moment die!
> When thou by flattery canst wile me

In self-complacency to rest,
Or e'er with pleasant lusts beguile me —
Then may that moment be my last!

"Beguile with pleasant lusts." Thus no voluptuary speaks. Rather he who takes up with pleasure as earlier he did with things of the mind, and recognizes but one kind of slavery: inertia and ease.

> *Des Denkens Faden ist zerrissen,*
> *Mir ekelt lange vor allem Wissen.*
> *Lass in den Tiefen der Sinnlichkeit*
> *Uns glühende Leidenschaften stillen. . . .*
> *Stürzen wir uns in das Rauschen der Zeit,*
> *Ins Rollen der Begebenheit!*
> *Da mag denn Schmerz und Genuss,*
> *Gelingen und Verdruss,*
> *Miteinander wechseln wie es kann;*
> *Nur rastlos betätigt sich der Mann.*

> All threads of thought I sever.
> Knowledge abjure forever,
> And in the senses deep
> My glowing passions steep. . . .
> Plunged in time's whirling surge,
> Rolled round in life's unending urge,
> Let success or failure come,
> Alternates of joy and woe
> Mingle together how they can;
> But let man only striving know.

Thus no voluptuary speaks. Thus speaks an activist, who seeks not pleasure but life, and binds himself to the devil only so far as a man of intellect does who gives himself to life. The formal bond he despises as pedantic and futile, there being no reason to doubt his complete surrender.

> *Nur keine Furcht, dass ich dies Bündnis breche!*
> *Das Streben meiner ganzen Kraft*
> *Ist gerade das was ich verspreche.*

> There needs no fear this promise shall be broken:
> The uttermost of all my powers
> Is bent to keep what I have spoken.

One asks oneself, indeed, what does actually come of that plumbing of the depths of sense, of the intoxications of life and time, of that furious masculine activity of Faust during his companionship with Mephistopheles. I will not extend the question to the second part of the poem. There it is only after a multitude of involved adventures in magic that Faust engages in any kind of activity that could be called unresting or masculine. As for the first part, we must admit that Goethe has not gone very far towards poetic realization of the depths of sensuality or the life of action, fluctuating between success and failure, to which his hero would devote himself. What does Mephisto do for his hopeful pupil? He takes him to Auerbach's cellar, where the two perform conjuring tricks before bawling philistines just as in the chapbook. Well, at least that is by way of illustration to the lines:

> *Die schlechteste Gesellschaft lässt dich fühlen*
> *Dass du ein Mensch mit Menschen bist —*

> Even from the lowest company one borrows
> A sense that one's a man like all the rest —

though it is hardly even that, for Faust does not succeed in being hail fellow well met with his brother topers in the cellar. He and the devil behave more like high-born travelling foreigners, very spoilt and capricious at that, and with a snack of the charlatan that would make them suspect to middle-class minds. We hear that they have just got back from Spain; if that is true, what have they been doing there? We do not learn. We are equally puzzled by Faust's remark at the beginning of the Gretchen episode, when he demands that Mephisto deliver the little one straight into his arms:

> *Hätt ich nur sieben Stunden Ruh,*
> *Brauchte den Teufel nicht dazu*
> *So ein Geschöpfchen zu verführen.*

> If I had only seven hours free,
> I should not need to call the Devil in
> To teach that little creature how to sin.

If that is only said in order to excuse him for not being able to seduce the poor child by his own efforts, but needing the powers of hell to help him to do it, then we must deduce that he is occupied indeed — and with what, and how? We remain in the dark. None of the deceased charlatan's famous deeds or misdeeds come into the first part; the Gretchen story stands alone, for nothing stronger had the young poet to give! He magnified it into his own tragedy, he reduced all the rest of the Faustian program to this one exploration of the life of passion. And who would regret the fact? For the result was the loveliest, sincerest, saddest love-story in the German language, perhaps in any language, told in the simplest, most natural, convincing, and moving accents in the world.

We must repeat what has so often been said already: this little Gretchen, the pawnbroker's daughter, as we see her move before our mind's eye, in her grief, her humanness and femininity, her childlike purity, her love and devotion, her vicarious, pitiful fate, is a figure of immortal beauty. We see her in the little German imperial city, a small, idyllic setting, with spinning-wheel and fountain, christening feast and gossiping neighbours. But how the young creature, so simple, yet so warm with life, is lifted out of her lowliness and transfigured by the masculine guilt and remorse! At the end she is nothing less than the spirit of love itself, watching from above over the struggles of the erring one and preparing his welcome and redemption. Like Mignon in Goethe's great novel, she has two of her creator's most marvellous lyrics put in her mouth: *"Meine Ruh ist hin,"* and *"Es war ein König in Thule."* But she is herself a *"Lied,"* a folk-song refined by the most personal art. At the end, in desolation and madness, in her prison cell, her soul and her song slip away into the most wondrous, awesome sphere of all folk-poesy:

> *Meine Mutter die Hur,*
> *Die mich ungebracht hat!*
> *Mein Vater der Schelm,*
> *Der mich gessen hat!*
> *Mein Schwesterlein klein*
> *Hub auf die Bein,*
> *An einem kühlen Ort;*
> *Da ward ich ein schönes Waldvögelein,*
> *Fliege fort, fliege fort!*

> My mother the whore,
> She did me to death!
> My father the knave,
> My flesh eaten hath!
> My sister so small
> My bones gathered all
> And laid them to cool.
> And then I was turned to a sweet wood bird —
> Fly away, fly away!

Such simple, native accents of uncanny fantasy are unknown to Clärchen in *Egmont*. Yet the two are sisters, Clärchen and Gretchen, unmistakably visualized and created by their author to like though varying tragic destinies. One becomes the heroine, the other the martyr of her sex. And just as they are sisters, so their lovers, Faust and Egmont, are brothers, true sons of Goethe both, representing the characteristic Goethian eroticism, a little narcissistic; which finds its peculiar ecstasy in the beguilement of simple innocence, of the little maid of the people by a lordly masculinity stooping down from loftier spheres, and in her utter surrender to her blissful fate. Egmont shows himself to the virtuous Clärchen in Spanish court dress; nothing could be more characteristic of Goethe's own wish-dream world than this scene. In *Faust*, the court dress and the golden fleece are of a metaphysical kind. An elegant, fastidious traveller, from an intellectual sphere unknown to Gretchen's bourgeois simplicity and most impressive; half nobleman, half scholar, Faust appears as from another world, and dreaming of him she says:

> *Ich gäb was drum, wenn ich nur wüsst'*
> *Wer heut der Herr gewesen ist!*
> *Eh sah gewiss recht wacker aus*
> *Und ist aus einem edlen Haus:*
> *Das konnt' ich ihm an der Stirne lesen —*
> *Er wär' auch sonst nicht so keck gewesen.*

> How much I'd give if I could say
> Who that gallant was today!
> He looked so very fine and proud,
> And I could tell, from some high family:
> A nobleman, 'twas plain to see,
> So forward else he had not been with me.

Delightful lines. Gretchen betrays in them her profound curiosity and emotion after the first meeting. She is flattered that he approached her, yet feels her modesty offended and, having given no occasion for his boldness, explains it by his high rank. The childlike words betray the specific charm which lay for the poet in such a situation — as does also the later dialogue:

> MARGARETE:
> *Ich fühl es wohl, dass mich der Herr nur schont,*
> *Herab sich lässt, mich zu beschämen;*
> *Ein Reisender ist so gewohnt*
> *Aus Gütigkeit fürlieb zu nehmen;*
> *Ich weiss zu gut, dass solch erfahrnen Mann*
> *Mein arm Gespräch nicht unterhalten kann.*

> FAUST:
> *Ein Blick von dir, ein Wort mehr unterhält*
> *Als alle Weisheit dieser Welt.*

> MARGARETE:
> I realize, the gentleman is kind,
> And lowers himself, it puts me quite to shame;
> For travellers are not to blame
> For simply taking up with what they find.
> I know too well, my simple chatter,
> To such a man as you are, could not matter.

FAUST:
One look from thee, one word is more to me
Than all the wisdom of this world can be.

In this everyday fragment of talk there lies great richness of feeling. It is so typical of student life; it is so typically the love-story of the university man, the academic, the Herr Doctor, and the little girl of the people, who cannot think what the clever gentleman sees in her. *In abstracto*, it is beauty, poor in spirit, blushing before the wooing of the intellect. Beauty, and "wisdom"; and the sensual abrogation of the one before the other, with all the dangers of seduction and ruin which lie for innocence and beauty in this appeal of intellect and sensuality combined. Thus intellect becomes guilty before beauty, and thus Faust became guilty before Gretchen. Certainly the Gretchen story is the tragedy of intellect becoming mortally guilty to beauty, with the cynical connivance of the devil. And here, more than anywhere else, does Goethe betray himself a revolutionary, in that he would stir our emotions against the cruelty of human society, which punishes the beauty that falls victim to the beguilement of the superior mind. This once, and never again, Goethe, owing to his own tragic sense of guilt, becomes an accuser and rebel against society. In the prose scene: "Grey day, a field," taken bodily out of the *Urfaust* and put unchanged into the fragment as well as the finished poem, Faust, after the repulsive distractions of the Blocksburg and the Walpurgisnacht dream, learns that Gretchen is in prison and has been handed over to the justice of cruel, unthinking men. Mephistopheles flings at him his cynical "She is not the first."

"Not the first! Oh, horror, horror! How can any human being understand that the writhing death-agony of the first was not enough to atone for the guilt of the rest, in the eyes of the All-Merciful! The agony of this single one pierces me to the heart — and you can stand there and grin at the fate of thousands!"

The scene is written in rough, savage, almost clumsy prose, devoid of irony; it scarcely seems to belong to a poem that otherwise, in all its inward significance, its profound human symbolism, moves with such light-footed creative objectivity. Shall we call it uncharacteristic? Certainly Goethe seems to have found it so. When the *Faust* was performed at Weimar, he left this scene out. And it is said that as a member of the government he gave society its due by signing the death-sentence upon a young girl accused of child-murder, although the Duke himself would have shown her mercy.

If this story be true, it bears witness to a stern self-disciplining of his own kindliness and pity, and their suppression in favour of established order. For order the mature Goethe held in such honour that he openly declared it to be better to commit injustice than to tolerate disorder. That too has its fine side; but more youthfully beautiful, certainly, is the rebellion against order, grounded on the remorseful feelings of Friederike Brion's unfaithful lover, and mounting in the Faust

poem almost to destructive heights. Gretchen's destruction is almost
the ruin of Faust as well. Nowhere else does he, the human being, fall
so foul of his companion as here; nowhere does he fling the scorn of
his anguished heart so furiously in the grinning face of the demon
who mocks at man's double nature: *"Hund! Abscheuliches Untier!"*
("Dog! Detestable monster!")

"Hab' ich doch meine Freude dran!" ("I get my fun out of it too.")

Goethe, in *Faust,* has depicted love as a regular devil's holiday: the
"high intuition" whose conclusion and consummation Mephisto indicates with an obscene gesture. It begins so tenderly, with such extravagant soulfulness, and reaches its end in guilty despair. *"Doch, alles was
mich dazu trieb, Gott! war so gut, ach! war so lieb!"* ("And all that
drove me thereunto, God! was so dear, ah! was so true!") So poor
Gretchen sighs; and her seducer will not have it at any price that he
is betraying her when he whispers her eternal loyalty and love. Faust
replies to the mockery of his companion:

> . . . *wenn ich empfinde,*
> *Für das Gefühl, fur das Gewühl*
> *Nach Namen suche, keinen finde,*
> *Dann durch die Welt mit allen Sinnen schweife,*
> *Nach allen höchsten Worten greife,*
> *Und diese Glut, von der ich brenne,*
> *Unendlich, ewig, ewig nenne,*
> *Ist das ein teuflisch Lügenspiel?*

> . . . when for my feeling,
> When for the tumult in my breast,
> I seek a name, and find no healing,
> When through the world I range and try
> With all my senses to express
> This ecstasy with which I burn,
> And call eternal, infinite —
> Is that a devilish lie?

And the Evil One replies: "And yet I'm right!" For youthful love, the
most human thing in the world, wherein the spirit and the body, the
natural and the divine, mingle in a way so symbolic and so exemplary
for all humanity, is truly the devil's playground, the theatre of his
most prized triumphs. There he most easily performs his traditional
task of betraying the highest in man to the basest. There truly is his
immemorial striving: to seize on that higher part of man, so mingled
with his baser self, and in the baser swallow up the higher. And he
would triumph, were it not that the Eternal Goodness, with whom in
the Prologue the devil is so cringingly conversable, and who sees the
highest in the lowest, not, as the devil does, the lowest in the highest,
opposes his will to destruction.

The whole Faust-poem is based on the Prologue in Heaven. Or rather the Prologue was afterwards shoved underneath the youthful, light-heartedly conceived composition, to prop it up. For it is in the Prologue that the figure of Faust becomes the protagonist and symbol of man, in whom the Eternal Goodness had a share, as he in it. Faust's human trait, which makes him strive after the universally human, is his noble side, the goodness which is at the same time godliness in him. So it comes about that he and the devil, who has no understanding of the painstaking spirit of man, misunderstand each other when they make their pact. When Faust says: "Let us still our glowing passions in the depth of sense," he means something quite different from what the devil thinks; he means even the sensuality with a difference: as something nobler, deeper, more serious and fervent. Despairing of thought, he turns to the world and to life. But of joy, he says, there can be no thought.

Dem Taumel weih' ich mich, dem schmerzlichen Genuss. . . .
Mein Busen, der von Wissensdrang geheilt ist,
Soll keinen Schmerzen künftig sich verschliessen,
Und was der ganzen Menschheit zugeteilt ist,
Will ich mit meinem inneren Selbst geniessen,
Mit meinem Geist das Höchst und Tiefste greifen,
Ihr Wohl und Weh auf meinen Busen häufen,
Und so mein eigen Selbst zu ihrem Selbst erweitern. . . .

To tumult I am vowed, and ecstasy of pain. . . .
My bosom, now of wisdom's craving healed,
Shall to no sorrows from this day be sealed,
But all the pangs that human lot befall,
In my own heart henceforth I'll know them all,
And with my spirit grasp their depth and height.
Their weal and woe my breast shall know,
And so my own self to their self shall grow.

The Mephistophelian "world" (the devil is only a worldling) becomes for Faust life, with its tortures and desires; but surrender to it takes on at once a human character; he wishes to live, in the fullest, most human sense, he would be a son of man, would take upon himself and exhaust, as representative and sacrifice, all the joys and sorrows of mankind. And we recall those words, spoken as in a dream, which Goethe murmured to himself on a moonlight night in his youth, mounting out of the Ilm:

Alles geben die Götter, die Unendlichen,
Ihren Lieblingen ganz:
Alle Freuden, die Unendlichen,
Alle Schmerzen, die Unendlichen,
Ganz.

> All do the gods give, the eternal,
> To their favourites, wholly:
> All the joys, the eternal,
> All the pangs, the eternal,
> Wholly.

To take the joys and sufferings of mankind upon himself, in giving himself to life — nothing else is it that Faust promises the devil. But this "striving to attain man's utmost height," infinite as it always is, and sinful in the sense that it is presumptuous titanism, is after all more allied to God than to the devil; it is generous, upright, and good, and despite all the perils it entails, it never from the first holds out any great hopes to the devil.

In a poem written at the time of his betrothal to Lili Schönemann, we hear Goethe call himself *"ein guter Junge"* ("a good lad"). "Why," he asks:

> *Warum ziehst du mich unwiderstehlich,*
> *Ach, in jene Pracht?*
> *War ich* guter Junge, *nicht so selig*
> *In der öden Nacht?*

> Ah, why dost thou so resistless draw me
> To thy splendour bright?
> Was I not, *good lad,* so happy,
> In the lonely night?

"Ich guter Junge." It is touching to hear Goethe so address himself; and whatever the intellectual heights he reached, however reverend he became to himself, it remained to the end a good description. We know how mild he was, how tolerant, what universal benevolence he possessed. We know his lifelong wish, "to do good to men," "to teach them to live"; we know his confession, that after every flight into solitude he needed but to see a human face "to love again." And the man of the Faustian strivings and efforts, he too is "a good boy." Just as he means well by himself, and feels that he can be saved, so also he means well by humanity: he wants its good, would have it assisted, positively, lovingly, reasonably; would not have it bewildered, would have it satisfied. In a Paralipomenon Faust says to Mephistopheles:

> *So höre denn, wenn du es niemals hörtest:*
> *Die Menschheit hat einfein Gehör,*
> *Ein reines Wort erreget schöne Taten.*
> *Der Mensch fühlt sein Bedürfnis nur zu sehr*
> *Und lässt sich gern im Ernste ratem.*

So hearken now, if thou hast never heard:
The human hearing's very keen,
And glorious deeds can follow one clear word.
Man knows only too sore his human need,
And gladly counsel he will heed.

And again:

> *Von allem ist dir nichts gewährt.*
> *Was weisst du, was der Mensch begehrt?*
> *Dein widrig Wesen, bitter, scharf,*
> *Was weiss es was der Mensch bedarf?*

> Nothing of all is granted thee.
> Then how canst thou men's longing read?
> Thy warped nature, bitter, curst,
> What can it know of human need?

Nothing could be more Goethian, nothing more Faustian. Its conception of man, its attitude towards the human being, are a part of the Everlasting Goodness; and no differently speaks the Eternal Goodness itself, God the Lord, in the Prologue, whose characterization of man is young Goethe's characterization of himself; in it self-love grows till it embraces humanity:

> *Wenn er mir jetzt auch nur verworren dient,*
> *So werd ich ihn bald in die Klarheit führen.*
> *Weiss doch der Gärtner, wenn das Bäumchen grünt,*
> *Dass Blüt' und Frucht die künftigen Jahre zieren.*

> Though still he serve me with a darkened mind,
> Soon to the light of truth I'll lead his feet.
> Knows not the gardener when the tree is green
> That flower and fruit the coming year shall greet?

And then that primal word of the Eternal Goodness:

> *Es irrt der Mensch so lang er strebt.*

> For man must err, so long as man must strive.

And that final pronouncement of God, which in its lofty and trusting mildness has become proverbial for all mankind:

> *Und steh' beschämt, wenn du erkennen musst,*
> *Ein guter Mensch, in seinem dunklen Drange,*
> *Ist sich des rechten Weges wohl bewusst.*

> And stand abashed, when you at last must say,
> The good man, howsoever dark his striving,
> Is ever mindful of the better way.

A good man, a good boy. For our time, which seems to have fallen a
helpless prey to evil and cynicism, how welcome were some kindly
greatness, which should know what man needs and instead of offering
him mocking sophisms, could give him serious advice in his necessities!
A "clear word" and a benevolent, pointing out the better course, seems
powerless today; world events pass all such over with brutal disregard.
But let us hold fast to the anti-diabolic faith, that mankind has after
all a "keen hearing," and that words born of one's own striving may
do it good and not perish from its heart.

Honoré de Balzac (1799–1850)

LIFE: Like one of the characters of his fiction, he lived out his life
beyond the ordinary limits of human energy and capacity: rejecting
the law he had studied, he became a Parisian hack, bankrupt business
speculator, and finally the creator of the *Human Comedy,* a projected
fictional history of contemporary civilization — and lived to produce 85
books in twenty years. Three months before he died he married Madame
Hanska, a wealthy Polish widow with whom he had been corresponding
for many years.

WORKS: Among his novels are: *The Wild Ass's Skin* (1831); *Eugénie
Grandet* (1833); *Old Goriot* (1834); *Lost Illusions* (1837–43); *Cousin
Betty* (1846).

THE ELIXIR OF LIFE *

To the Reader

At the very outset of the writer's literary career, a friend, long since
dead, gave him the subject of this Study. Later on he found the same
story in a collection published about the beginning of the present century. To the best of his belief, it is some stray fancy of the brain of
Hoffmann of Berlin; probably it appeared in some German almanack,
and was omitted in the published editions of his collected works. The
Comédie Humaine is sufficiently rich in original creations for the author
to own to this innocent piece of plagiarism; when, like the worthy La
Fontaine, he has told unwittingly, and after his own fashion, a tale
already related by another. This is not one of the hoaxes in vogue in the
year 1830, when every author wrote his "tale of horror" for the amuse-

* 1830. Translated by Ellen Marriage.

ment of young ladies. When you have read the account of Don Juan's decorous parricide, try to picture to yourself the part which would be played under very similar circumstances by honest folk who, in this nineteenth century, will take a man's money and undertake to pay him a life annuity on the faith of a chill, or let a house to an ancient lady for the term of her natural life. Would they be for resuscitating their clients? I should dearly like a connoisseur in consciences to consider how far there is a resemblance between a Don Juan and fathers who marry their children to great expectations. Does humanity, which, according to certain philosophers, is making progress, look on the art of waiting for dead men's shoes as a step in the right direction? To this art we owe several honourable professions, which open up ways of living on death. There are people who rely entirely on an expected demise; who brood over it, crouching each morning upon a corpse, that serves again for their pillow at night. To this class belong bishops' coadjutors, cardinals' supernumeraries, *tontiniers,* and the like. Add to the list many delicately scrupulous persons eager to buy landed property beyond their means, who calculate with dry logic and in cold blood the probable duration of the life of a father or of a stepmother, some old man or woman of eighty or ninety, saying to themselves, "I shall be sure to come in for it in three years' time, and then —— " A murderer is less loathsome to us than a spy. The murderer may have acted on a sudden mad impulse; he may be penitent and amend; but a spy is always a spy, night and day, in bed, at table, as he walks abroad; his vileness pervades every moment of his life. Then what must it be to live when every moment of your life is tainted with murder? And have we not just admitted that a host of human creatures in our midst are led by our laws, customs, and usages to dwell without ceasing on a fellow-creature's death. There are men who put the weight of a coffin into their deliberations as they bargain for Cashmere shawls for their wives, as they go up the staircase of a theatre, or think of going to the Bouffons, or of setting up a carriage; who are murderers in thought when dear ones, with the irresistible charm of innocence, hold up childish foreheads to be kissed with a "Good-night, father!" Hourly they meet the gaze of eyes that they would fain close for ever, eyes that still open each morning to the light, like Belvidero's in this Study. God alone knows the number of those who are parricides in thought. Picture to yourself the state of mind of a man who must pay a life annuity to some old woman whom he scarcely knows; both live in the country with a brook between them, both sides are free to hate cordially, without offending against the social conventions that require two brothers to wear a mask if the older will succeed to the entail, and the other to the fortune of a younger son. The whole civilisation of Europe turns upon the principle of hereditary succession as upon a pivot; it would be madness to subvert the principle; but could we not, in an age that prides itself upon its mechanical inventions, perfect this essential portion of the social machinery?

If the author has preserved the old-fashioned style of address *To the Reader* before a work wherein he endeavours to represent all literary forms, it is for the purpose of making a remark that applies to several of the Studies, and very specially to this. Every one of his compositions has been based upon ideas more or less novel, which, as it seemed to him, needed literary expression; he can claim priority for certain forms and for certain ideas which have since passed into the domain of literature, and have there, in some instances, become common property; so that the date of the first publication of each Study cannot be a matter of indifference to those of his readers who would fain do him justice.

Reading brings us unknown friends, and what friend is like a reader! We have friends in our own circle who read nothing of ours. The author hopes to pay his debt, by dedicating this work *Diis ignotis*.

One winter evening, in a princely palace at Ferrara, Don Juan Belvidero was giving a banquet to a prince of the house of Este. A banquet in those times was a marvellous spectacle which only royal wealth or the power of a mighty lord could furnish forth. Seated about a table lit up with perfumed tapers, seven laughter-loving women were interchanging sweet talk. The white marble of the noble works of art about them stood out against the red stucco walls, and made strong contrasts with the rich Turkey carpets. Clad in satin, glittering with gold, and covered with gems less brilliant than their eyes, each told a tale of energetic passions as diverse as their styles of beauty. They differed neither in their ideas nor in their language; but the expression of their eyes, their glances, occasional gestures, or the tones of their voices supplied a commentary, dissolute, wanton, melancholy, or satirical, to their words.

One seemed to be saying — "The frozen heart of age might kindle at my beauty."

Another — "I love to lounge upon cushions, and think with rapture of my adorers."

A third, a neophyte at these banquets, was inclined to blush. "I feel remorse in the depths of my heart! I am a Catholic, and afraid of hell. But I love you, I love you so that I can sacrifice my hereafter to you."

The fourth drained a cup of Chian wine. "Give me a joyous life!" she cried; "I begin life afresh each day with the dawn. Forgetful of the past, with the intoxication of yesterday's rapture still upon me, I drink deep of life — a whole lifetime of pleasure and of love!"

The woman who sat next to Juan Belvidero looked at him with a feverish glitter in her eyes. She was silent. Then — "I should need no hired bravo to kill my lover if he forsook me!" she cried at last, and laughed, but the marvellously wrought gold comfit box in her fingers was crushed by her convulsive clutch.

"When are you to be Grand Duke?" asked the sixth. There was the frenzy of a Bacchante in her eyes, and her teeth gleamed between the lips parted with a smile of cruel glee.

"Yes, when is that father of yours going to die?" asked the seventh, throwing her bouquet at Don Juan with bewitching playfulness. It was a childish girl who spoke, and the speaker was wont to make sport of sacred things.

"Oh! don't talk about it," cried Don Juan, the young and handsome giver of the banquet. "There is but one eternal father, and, as ill luck will have it, he is mine."

The seven Ferrarese, Don Juan's friends, the Prince himself, gave a cry of horror. Two hundred years later, in the days of Louis XV., people of taste would have laughed at this witticism. Or was it, perhaps, that at the outset of an orgy there is a certain unwonted lucidity of mind? Despite the taper light, the clamour of the senses, the gleam of gold and silver, the fumes of wine, and the exquisite beauty of the women, there may perhaps have been in the depths of the revellers' hearts some struggling glimmer of reverence for things divine and human, until it was drowned in glowing floods of wine! Yet even then the flowers had been crushed, eyes were growing dull, and drunkenness, in Rabelais' phrase, had "taken possession of them down to their sandals."

During that brief pause a door opened; and as once the Divine presence was revealed at Belshazzar's feast, so now it seemed to be manifest in the apparition of an old white-haired servant, who tottered in, and looked sadly from under knitted brows at the revellers. He gave a withering glance at the garlands, the golden cups, the pyramids of fruit, the dazzling lights of the banquet, the flushed scared faces, the hues of the cushions pressed by the white arms of the women.

"My Lord, your father is dying!" he said; and at those solemn words, uttered in hollow tones, a veil of crape seemed to be drawn over the wild mirth.

Don Juan rose to his feet with a gesture to his guests that might be rendered by, "Excuse me; this kind of thing does not happen every day."

Does it so seldom happen that a father's death surprises youth in the full-blown splendour of life, in the midst of the mad riot of an orgy? Death is as unexpected in his caprice as a courtesan in her disdain; but Death is truer — Death has never forsaken any man.

Don Juan closed the door of the banqueting-hall; and as he went down the long gallery, through the cold and darkness, he strove to assume an expression in keeping with the part he had to play; he had thrown off his mirthful mood, as he had thrown down his table napkin, at the first thought of this *rôle*. The night was dark. The mute servitor, his guide to the chamber where the dying man lay, lighted the way so dimly, that Death, aided by cold, silence, and darkness, and it may be by a reaction of drunkenness, could send some sober thoughts through the spendthrift's soul. He examined his life, and became thoughtful, like a man involved in a lawsuit on his way to the Court.

Bartolommeo Belvidero, Don Juan's father, was an old man of ninety, who had devoted the greatest part of his life to business pursuits. He had acquired vast wealth in many a journey in magical Eastern lands, and knowledge, so it was said, more valuable than the gold and diamonds, which had almost ceased to have any value for him.

"I would give more to have a tooth in my head than for a ruby," he would say at times with a smile. The indulgent father loved to hear Don Juan's story of this and that wild freak of youth. "So long as these follies amuse you, dear boy — " he would say laughingly, as he lavished money on his son. Age never took such pleasure in the sight of youth; the fond father did not remember his own decaying powers while he looked on that brilliant young life.

Bartolommeo Belvidero, at the age of sixty, had fallen in love with an angel of peace and beauty. Don Juan had been the sole fruit of this late and short-lived love. For fifteen years the widower had mourned the loss of his beloved Juana; and to this sorrow of age, his son and his numerous household had attributed the strange habits that he had contracted. He had shut himself up in the least comfortable wing of his palace, and very seldom left his apartments; even Don Juan himself must first ask permission before seeing his father. If this hermit, unbound by vows, came or went in his palace or in the streets of Ferrara, he walked as if he were in a dream, wholly engrossed, like a man at strife with a memory, or a wrestler with some thought.

The young Don Juan might give princely banquets, the palace might echo with clamorous mirth, horses pawed the ground in the courtyards, pages quarrelled and flung dice upon the stairs, but Bartolommeo ate his seven ounces of bread daily and drank water. A fowl was occasionally dressed for him, simply that the black poodle, his faithful companion, might have the bones. Bartolommeo never complained of the noise. If huntsmen's horns and baying dogs disturbed his sleep during his illness, he only said, "Ah! Don Juan has come back again." Never on earth has there been a father so little exacting and so indulgent; and, in consequence, young Belvidero, accustomed to treat his father unceremoniously, had all the faults of a spoiled child. He treated old Bartolommeo as a wilful courtesan treats an elderly adorer; buying indemnity for insolence with a smile, selling good-humour, submitting to be loved.

Don Juan, beholding scene after scene of his younger years, saw that it would be a difficult task to find his father's indulgence at fault. Some new-born remorse stirred the depths of his heart; he felt almost ready to forgive this father now about to die for having lived so long. He had an accession of filial piety, like a thief's return in thought to honesty at the prospect of a million adroitly stolen.

Before long Don Juan had crossed the lofty chilly suite of rooms in which his father lived; the penetrating influences of the damp close air, the mustiness diffused by old tapestries and presses thickly covered with dust had passed into him, and now he stood in the old man's antiquated room, in the repulsive presence of the death-bed, beside a dying fire.

A flickering lamp on a Gothic table sent broad uncertain shafts of light, fainter or brighter, across the bed, so that the dying man's face seemed to wear a different look at every moment. The bitter wind whistled through the crannies of the ill-fitting casements; there was a smothered sound of snow lashing the windows. The harsh contrast of these sights and sounds with the scenes which Don Juan had just quitted was so sudden, that he could not help shuddering. He turned cold as he came towards the bed; the lamp flared in a sudden vehement gust of wind and lighted up his father's face; the features were wasted and distorted; the skin that cleaved to their bony outlines had taken wan livid hues, all the more ghastly by force of contrast with the white pillows on which he lay. The muscles about the toothless mouth had contracted with pain and drawn apart the lips; the moans that issued between them with appalling energy found an accompaniment in the howling of the storm without.

In spite of every sign of coming dissolution, the most striking thing about the dying face was its incredible power. It was no ordinary spirit that wrestled there with Death. The eyes glared with strange fixity of gaze from the cavernous sockets hollowed by disease. It seemed as if Bartolommeo sought to kill some enemy sitting at the foot of his bed by the intent gaze of dying eyes. That steady remorseless look was the more appalling because the head that lay upon the pillow was passive and motionless as a skull upon a doctor's table. The outlines of the body, revealed by the coverlet, were no less rigid and stiff; he lay there as one dead, save for those eyes. There was something automatic about the moaning sounds that came from the mouth. Don Juan felt something like shame that he must be brought thus to his father's bedside, wearing a courtesan's bouquet, redolent of the fragrance of the banqueting-chamber and the fumes of wine.

"You were enjoying yourself!" the old man cried as he saw his son.

Even as he spoke the pure high notes of a woman's voice, sustained by the sound of the viol on which she accompanied her song, rose above the rattle of the storm against the casements, and floated up to the chamber of death. Don Juan stopped his ears against the barbarous answer to his father's speech.

"I bear you no grudge, my child," Bartolommeo went on.

The words were full of kindness, but they hurt Don Juan; he could not pardon this heart-searching goodness on his father's part.

"What a remorseful memory for me!" he cried, hypocritically.

"Poor Juanino," the dying man went on, in a smothered voice, "I have always been so kind to you, that you could not surely desire my death?"

"Oh, if it were only possible to keep you here by giving up a part of my own life!" cried Don Juan.

("We can always *say* this sort of thing," the spendthrift thought; "it is as if I laid the whole world at my mistress's feet.")

The thought had scarcely crossed his mind when the old poodle barked.

Don Juan shivered; the response was so intelligent that he fancied the dog must have understood him.

"I was sure that I could count upon you, my son!" cried the dying man. "I shall live. So be it; you shall be satisfied. I shall live, but without depriving you of a single day of your life."

"He is raving," thought Don Juan. Aloud he added, "Yes, dearest father, yes; you shall live, of course, as long as I live, for your image will be for ever in my heart."

"It is not that kind of life that I mean," said the old noble, summoning all his strength to sit up in bed; for a thrill of doubt ran through him, one of those suspicions that come into being under a dying man's pillow. "Listen, my son," he went on, in a voice grown weak with that last effort, "I have no more wish to give up life than you to give up wine and mistresses, horses and hounds, and hawks and gold —— "

"I can well believe it," thought the son; and he knelt down by the bed and kissed Bartolommeo's cold hands. "But, father, my dear father," he added aloud, "we must submit to the will of God."

"I am God!" muttered the dying man.

"Do not blaspheme!" cried the other, as he saw the menacing expression on his father's face. "Beware what you say; you have received extreme unction, and I should be inconsolable if you were to die before my eyes in mortal sin."

"Will you listen to me?" cried Bartolommeo, and his mouth twitched.

Don Juan held his peace; an ugly silence prevailed. Yet above the muffled sound of the beating of the snow against the windows rose the sounds of the beautiful voice and the viol in unison, far off and faint as the dawn. The dying man smiled.

"Thank you," he said, "for bringing those singing voices and the music, a banquet, young and lovely women with fair faces and dark tresses, all the pleasures of life! Bid them wait for me; for I am about to begin life anew."

"The delirium is at its height," said Don Juan to himself.

"I have found out a way of coming to life again," the speaker went on. "There, just look in that table drawer, press the spring hidden by the griffin, and it will fly open."

"I have found it, father."

"Well, then, now take out a little phial of rock crystal."

"I have it."

"I have spent twenty years in —— " but even as he spoke the old man felt how very near the end had come, and summoned all his dying strength to say, "As soon as the breath is out of me, rub me all over with that liquid, and I shall come to life again."

"There is very little of it," his son remarked.

Though Bartolommeo could no longer speak, he could still hear and see. When those words dropped from Don Juan, his head turned with appalling quickness, his neck was twisted like the throat of some marble statue which the sculptor has condemned to remain stretched out for ever, the wide eyes had come to have a ghastly fixity.

He was dead, and in death he lost his last and sole illusion.

He had sought a shelter in his son's heart, and it had proved to be a sepulchre, a pit deeper than men dig for their dead. The hair on his head had risen and stiffened with horror, his agonised glance still spoke. He was a father rising in just anger from his tomb, to demand vengeance at the throne of God.

"There! it is all over with the old man!" cried Don Juan.

He had been so interested in holding the mysterious phial to the lamp, as a drinker holds up the wine-bottle at the end of a meal, that he had not seen his father's eyes fade. The cowering poodle looked from his master to the elixir, just as Don Juan himself glanced again and again from his father to the flask. The lamplight flickered. There was a deep silence; the viol was mute. Juan Belvidero thought that he saw his father stir, and trembled. The changeless gaze of those accusing eyes frightened him; he closed them hastily, as he would have closed a loose shutter swayed by the wind of an autumn night. He stood there motionless, lost in a world of thought.

Suddenly the silence was broken by a shrill sound like the creaking of a rusty spring. It startled Don Juan; he all but dropped the phial. A sweat, colder than the blade of a dagger, issued through every pore. It was only a piece of clockwork, a wooden cock that sprang out and crowed three times, an ingenious contrivance by which the learned of that epoch were wont to be awakened at the appointed hour to begin the labours of the day. Through the windows there came already a flush of dawn. The thing, composed of wood, and cords, and wheels, and pulleys, was more faithful in its service than he in his duty to Bartolommeo — he, a man with that peculiar piece of human mechanism within him that we call a heart.

Don Juan the sceptic shut the flask again in the secret drawer in the Gothic table — he meant to run no more risks of losing the mysterious liquid.

Even at that solemn moment he heard the murmur of a crowd in the gallery, a confused sound of voices, of stifled laughter and light footfalls, and the rustling of silks — the sounds of a band of revellers struggling for gravity. The door opened, and in came the Prince and Don Juan's friends, the seven courtesans, and the singers, dishevelled and wild like dancers surprised by the dawn, when the tapers that have burned through the night struggle with the sunlight.

They had come to offer the customary condolence to the young heir.

"Oho! is poor Don Juan really taking this seriously?" said the Prince in Brambilla's ear.

"Well, his father was very good," she returned.

But Don Juan's night-thoughts had left such unmistakable traces on his features, that the crew was awed into silence. The men stood motionless. The women, with wine-parched lips and cheeks marbled with kisses, knelt down and began a prayer. Don Juan could scarce help trembling when he saw splendour and mirth and laughter and song and youth and beauty and power bowed in reverence before Death. But in those times, in that adorable Italy of the sixteenth century, religion and revelry went hand in hand; and religious excess became a sort of debauch, and a debauch a religious rite!

The Prince grasped Don Juan's hand affectionately, then when all faces had simultaneously put on the same grimace — half-gloomy, half-indifferent — the whole masque disappeared, and left the chamber of death empty. It was like an allegory of life.

As they went down the staircase, the Prince spoke to Rivabarella: "Now, who would have taken Don Juan's impiety for a boast? He loves his father."

"Did you see that black dog?" asked La Brambilla.

"He is enormously rich now," sighed Bianca Cavatolino.

"What is that to me?" cried the proud Veronese (she who had crushed the comfit-box).

"What does it matter to you, forsooth?" cried the Duke. "With his money he is as much a prince as I am."

At first Don Juan was swayed hither and thither by countless thoughts, and wavered between two decisions. He took counsel with the gold heaped up by his father, and returned in the evening to the chamber of death, his whole soul brimming over with hideous selfishness. He found all his household busy there. "His lordship" was to lie in state to-morrow; all Ferrara would flock to behold the wonderful spectacle; and the servants were busy decking the room and the couch on which the dead man lay. At a sign from Don Juan all his people stopped, dumbfounded and trembling.

"Leave me alone here," he said, and his voice was changed, "and do not return until I leave the room."

When the footsteps of the old servitor, who was the last to go, echoed but faintly along the paved gallery, Don Juan hastily locked the door, and, sure that he was quite alone, "Let us try," he said to himself.

Bartolommeo's body was stretched on a long table. The embalmers had laid a sheet over it, to hide from all eyes the dreadful spectacle of a corpse so wasted and shrunken that it seemed like a skeleton, and only the face was uncovered. This mummy-like form lay in the middle of the room. The limp clinging linen lent itself to the outlines it shrouded — so sharp, bony, and thin. Large violet patches had already begun to spread over the face; the embalmer's work had not been finished too soon.

Don Juan, strong as he was in his scepticism, felt a tremor as he opened the magic crystal flask. When he stood over that face, he was trembling so violently, that he was actually obliged to wait for a moment. But Don Juan had acquired an early familiarity with evil; his morals had been corrupted by a licentious court, a reflection worthy of the Duke of Urbino crossed his mind, and it was a keen sense of curiosity that goaded him into boldness. The devil himself might have whispered the words that were echoing through his brain, *Moisten one of the eyes with the liquid!* He took up a linen cloth, moistened it sparingly with the precious fluid, and passed it lightly over the right eyelid of the corpse. The eye unclosed. . . .

"Aha!" said Don Juan. He gripped the flask tightly, as we clutch in dreams the branch from which we hang suspended over a precipice.

For the eye was full of life. It was a young child's eye set in a death's head; the light quivered in the depths of its youthful liquid brightness. Shaded by the long dark lashes, it sparkled like the strange lights that travellers see in lonely places in winter nights. That eye seemed as if it would fain dart fire at Don Juan; he saw it thinking, upbraiding, condemning, uttering accusations, threatening doom; it cried aloud, and gnashed upon him. All anguish that shakes human souls was gathered there; supplications the most tender, the wrath of kings, the love in a girl's heart pleading with the headsman; then, after all these, the deeply searching glance a man turns on his fellows as he mounts the last step of the scaffold. Life so dilated in this fragment of life that Don Juan shrank back; he walked up and down the room, he dared not meet that gaze, but he saw nothing else. The ceiling and the hangings, the whole room was sown with living points of fire and intelligence. Everywhere those gleaming eyes haunted him.

"He might very likely have lived another hundred years!" he cried involuntarily. Some diabolical influence had drawn him to his father, and again he gazed at that luminous spark. The eyelid closed and opened again abruptly; it was like a woman's sign of assent. It was an intelligent movement. If a voice had cried "Yes!" Don Juan could not have been more startled.

"What is to be done?" he thought.

He nerved himself to try to close the white eyelid. In vain.

"Kill it? That would perhaps be parricide," he debated with himself.

"Yes," the eye said, with a strange sardonic quiver of the lid.

"Aha!" said Don Juan to himself, "here is witchcraft at work!" And he went closer to crush the thing. A great tear trickled over the hollow cheeks, and fell on Don Juan's hand.

"It is scalding!" he cried. He sat down. This struggle exhausted him; it was as if, like Jacob of old, he was wrestling with an angel.

At last he rose. "So long as there is no blood —— " he muttered.

Then, summoning all the courage needed for a coward's crime, he extinguished the eye, pressing it with the linen cloth, turning his head away. A terrible groan startled him. It was the poor poodle, who died with a long-drawn howl.

"Could the brute have been in the secret?" thought Don Juan, looking down at the faithful creature.

Don Juan Belvidero was looked upon as a dutiful son. He reared a white marble monument on his father's tomb, and employed the greatest sculptors of the time upon it. He did not recover perfect ease of mind till the day when his father knelt in marble before Religion, and the heavy weight of the stone had sealed the mouth of the grave in which he had laid the one feeling of remorse that sometimes flitted through his soul in moments of physical weariness.

He had drawn up a list of the wealth heaped up by the old merchant in the East, and he became a miser: had he not to provide for a second lifetime? His views of life were the more profound and penetrating; he grasped its significance, as a whole, the better, because he saw it across a grave. All men, all things, he analysed once and for all; he summed up the Past, represented by its records; the Present in the law, its crystallised form; the Future, revealed by religion. He took spirit and matter, and flung them into his crucible, and found — Nothing. Thenceforward he became Don Juan.

At the outset of his life, in the prime of youth and the beauty of youth, he knew the illusions of life for what they were; he despised the world, and made the utmost of the world. His felicity could not have been of the bourgeois kind, rejoicing in periodically recurrent *bouilli*, in the comforts of a warming-pan, a lamp of a night, and a new pair of slippers once a quarter. Nay, rather he seized upon existence as a monkey snatches a nut, and after no long toying with it, proceeds deftly to strip off the mere husks to reach the savoury kernel within.

Poetry and the sublime transports of passion scarcely reached ankle-depth with him now. He in nowise fell into the error of strong natures who flatter themselves now and again that little souls will believe in a great soul, and are willing to barter their own lofty thoughts of the future for the small change of our life-annuity ideas. He, even as they, had he chosen, might well have walked with his feet on the earth and his head in the skies; but he liked better to sit on earth, to wither the soft, fresh, fragrant lips of a woman with kisses, for, like Death, he devoured everything without scruple as he passed; he would have full fruition; he was an Oriental lover, seeking prolonged pleasures easily obtained. He sought nothing but a woman in women, and cultivated cynicism, until it became with him a habit of mind. When his mistress, from the couch on which she lay, soared and was lost in regions of ecstatic bliss, Don Juan followed suit, earnest, expansive, serious as any German student. But he said I, while she, in the transports of intoxication, said We. He understood to admiration the art of abandoning himself to the influence of a woman; he was always clever enough to make her believe that he trembled like some boy fresh from college before his first partner at a dance, when he asks her, "Do you like dancing?" But, no less, he could be terrible at need, could unsheath a formidable sword and make short work of Commandants. Banter lurked beneath his simplicity, mocking laughter behind his tears — for he had tears at need, like any woman nowadays who says to her husband, "Give me a carriage, or I shall go into a consumption."

For a merchant the world is a bale of goods or a mass of circulating bills; for most young men it is a woman, and for a woman here and there it is a man; for a certain order of mind it is a salon, a coterie, a quarter of the town, or some single city; but Don Juan found his world in himself.

This model of grace and dignity, this captivating wit, moored his bark by every shore; but wherever he was led he was never carried away, and was only steered in a course of his own choosing. The more he saw, the more he doubted. He watched men narrowly, and saw how, beneath the surface, courage was often rashness; and prudence, cowardice; generosity, a clever piece of calculation; justice, a wrong; delicacy, pusillanimity; honesty, a *modus vivendi;* and by some strange dispensation of fate, he must see that those who at heart were really honest, scrupulous, just, generous, prudent, or brave were held cheaply by their fellow-men.

"What a cold-blooded jest!" said he to himself. "It was not devised by a God."

From that time forth he renounced a better world, and never uncovered himself when a Name was pronounced, and for him the carven saints in the churches became works of art. He understood the mechanism of society too well to clash wantonly with its prejudices; for, after all, he was not as powerful as the executioner, but he evaded social laws with the wit and grace so well rendered in the scene with M. Dimanche. He was, in fact, Molière's Don Juan, Goethe's Faust, Byron's Manfred, Mathurin's Melmoth — great allegorical figures drawn by the greatest men of genius in Europe, to which Mozart's harmonies, perhaps, do no more justice than Rossini's lyre. Terrible allegorical figures that shall endure as long as the principle of evil existing in the heart of man shall produce a few copies from century to century. Sometimes the type becomes half-human when incarnate as a Mirabeau, sometimes it is an inarticulate force in a Bonaparte, sometimes it overwhelms the universe with irony as a Rabelais; or, yet again, it appears when a Maréchal de Richelieu elects to laugh at human beings instead of scoffing at things, or when one of the most famous of our ambassadors goes a step further and scoffs at both men and things. But the profound genius of Juan Belvidero anticipated and resumed all these. All things were a jest to him. His was the life of a mocking spirit. All men, all institutions, all realities, all ideas were within its scope. As for eternity, after half an hour of familiar conversation with Pope Julius II. he had said, laughing —

"If it is absolutely necessary to make a choice, I would rather believe in God than in the Devil; power combined with goodness always offers more resources than the spirit of Evil can boast."

"Yes; still God requires repentance in this present world —— "

"So you always think of your indulgences," returned Don Juan Belvidero. "Well, well, I have another life in reserve in which to repent of the sins of my previous existence."

"Oh, if you regard old age in that light," cried the Pope, "you are in danger of canonisation —— "

"After your elevation to the Papacy nothing is incredible." And they went to watch the workmen who were building the huge basilica dedicated to Saint Peter.

"Saint Peter, as the man of genius who laid the foundation of our double power," the Pope said to Don Juan, "deserves this monument. Sometimes, though, at night, I think that a deluge will wipe all this out as with a sponge, and it will be all to begin over again."

Don Juan and the Pope began to laugh; they understood each other. A fool would have gone on the morrow to amuse himself with Julius II. in Raphael's studio or at the delicious Villa Madama; not so Belvidero. He went to see the Pope as pontiff, to be convinced of any doubts that he (Don Juan) entertained. Over his cups the Rovere would have been capable of denying his own infallibility and of commenting on the Apocalypse.

Nevertheless, this legend has not been undertaken to furnish materials for future biographies of Don Juan; it is intended to prove to honest folk that Belvidero did not die in a duel with stone, as some lithographers would have us believe.

When Don Juan Belvidero reached the age of sixty he settled in Spain, and there in his old age he married a young and charming Andalusian wife. But of set purpose he was neither a good husband nor a good father. He had observed that we are never so tenderly loved as by women to whom we scarcely give a thought. Doña Elvira had been devoutly brought up by an old aunt in a castle a few leagues from San Lucar in a remote part of Andalusia. She was a model of devotion and grace. Don Juan foresaw that this would be a woman who would struggle long against a passion before yielding, and therefore hoped to keep her virtuous until his death. It was a jest undertaken in earnest, a game of chess which he meant to reserve till his old age. Don Juan had learned wisdom from the mistakes made by his father Bartolommeo; he determined that the least details of his life in old age should be subordinated to one object — the success of the drama which was to be played out upon his deathbed.

For the same reason the largest part of his wealth was buried in the cellars of his palace at Ferrara, whither he seldom went. As for the rest of his fortune, it was invested in a life annuity, with a view to give his wife and children an interest in keeping him alive; but this Machiavellian piece of foresight was scarcely necessary. His son, young Felipe Belvidero, grew up as a Spaniard as religiously conscientious as his father was irreligious, in virtue, perhaps, of the old rule, "A miser has a spendthrift son." The Abbot of San-Lucar was chosen by Don Juan to be the director of the consciences of the Duchess of Belvidero and her son Felipe. The ecclesiastic was a holy man, well shaped, and admirably well proportioned. He had fine dark eyes, a head like that of Tiberius, worn with fasting, bleached by an ascetic life, and, like all dwellers in the wilderness, was daily tempted. The noble lord had hopes, it may be, of despatching yet another monk before his term of life was out.

But whether because the Abbot was every whit as clever as Don Juan himself, or Doña Elvira possessed more discretion or more virtue than Spanish wives are usually credited with, Don Juan was compelled to spend his declining years beneath his own roof, with no more scandal under it than if he had been an ancient country parson. Occasionally he would take wife and son to task for negligence in the duties of religion, peremptorily insisting that they should carry out to the letter the obligations imposed upon the flock by the Court of Rome. Indeed, he was never so well pleased as when he had set the courtly Abbot discussing some case of conscience with Doña Elvira and Felipe.

At length, however, despite the prodigious care that the great magnifico, Don Juan Belvidero, took of himself, the days of decrepitude came upon him, and with those days the constant importunity of physical feebleness, an importunity all the more distressing by contrast with the wealth of memories of his impetuous youth and the sensual pleasures of middle age. The unbeliever who in the height of his cynical humour had been wont to persuade others to believe in laws and principles at which he scoffed, must repose nightly upon a *perhaps*. The great Duke, the pattern of good breeding, the champion of many a carouse, the proud ornament of Courts, the man of genius, the graceful winner of hearts that he had wrung as carelessly as a peasant twists an osier withe, was now the victim of a cough, of a ruthless sciatica, of an unmannerly gout. His teeth gradually deserted him, as at the end of an evening the fairest and best-dressed women take their leave one by one till the room is left empty and desolate. The active hands became palsy-stricken, the shapely legs tottered as he walked. At last, one night, a stroke of apoplexy caught him by the throat in its icy clutch. After that fatal day he grew morose and stern.

He would reproach his wife and son with their devotion, casting it in their teeth that the affecting and thoughtful care that they lavished so tenderly upon him was bestowed because they knew that his money was invested in a life annuity. Then Elvira and Felipe would shed bitter tears and redouble their caresses, and the wicked old man's insinuating voice would take an affectionate tone — "Ah, you will forgive me, will you not, dear friends, dear wife? I am rather a nuisance. Alas, Lord in heaven, how canst Thou use me as the instrument by which Thou provest these two angelic creatures? I who should be the joy of their lives am become their scourge . . ."

In this manner he kept them tethered to his pillow, blotting out the memory of whole months of fretfulness and unkindness in one short hour when he chose to display for them the ever-new treasures of his pinchbeck tenderness and charm of manner — a system of paternity that yielded him an infinitely better return than his own father's indulgence had formerly gained. At length his bodily infirmities reached a point when the task of laying him in bed became as difficult as the navigation of a felucca in the perils of an intricate channel. Then came the day of his death; and this brilliant sceptic, whose mental faculties alone had survived the most dreadful of all destructions, found himself between his two special antipathies — the doctor and the confessor. But he was jovial with them. Did he not see a light gleaming in the future beyond the veil? The pall that is like lead for other men was thin and translucent for him; the light-footed, irresistible delights of youth danced beyond it like shadows.

It was on a beautiful summer evening that Don Juan felt the near approach of death. The sky of Spain was serene and cloudless; the air was full of the scent of orange-blossom; the stars shed clear, pure gleams of light; nature without seemed to give the dying man assurance of resurrection; a dutiful and obedient son sat there watching him with loving and respectful eyes. Towards eleven o'clock he desired to be left alone with this single-hearted being.

"Felipe," said the father, in tones so soft and affectionate that the young man trembled, and tears of gladness came to his eyes; never had that stern father spoken his name in such a tone. "Listen, my son," the dying man went on. "I am a great sinner. All my life long, however, I have thought of my death. I was once the friend of the great Pope Julius II; and that illustrious Pontiff, fearing lest the excessive excitability of my senses should entangle me in mortal sin between the moment of my death and the time of my anointing with the holy oil, gave me a flask that contains a little of the holy water that once issued from the rock in the wilderness. I have kept the secret of this squandering of a treasure belonging to Holy Church, but I am permitted to reveal the mystery *in articulo mortis* to my son. You will find the flask in a drawer in that Gothic table that always stands by the head of the bed. . . . The precious little crystal flask may be of use yet again for you, dearest Felipe. Will you swear to me, by your salvation, to carry out my instructions faithfully?"

Felipe looked at his father, and Don Juan was too deeply learned in the lore of the human countenance not to die in peace with that look as his warrant, as his own father had died in despair at meeting the expression in his son's eyes.

"You deserved to have a better father," Don Juan went on. "I dare to confess, my child, that while the reverend Abbot of San-Lucar was administering the Viaticum I was thinking of the incompatibility of the co-existence of two powers so infinite as God and the Devil —— "

"Oh, father!"

"And I said to myself, when Satan makes his peace he ought surely to stipulate for the pardon of his followers, or he will be the veriest scoundrel. The thought haunted me; so I shall go to hell, my son, unless you carry out my wishes."

"Oh, quick; tell me quickly, father."

"As soon as I have closed my eyes," Don Juan went on, "and that may be in a few minutes, you must take my body before it grows cold and lay it on a table in this room. Then put out the lamp; the light of the stars should be sufficient. Take off my clothes, reciting *Aves* and *Paters* the while, raising your soul to God in prayer, and carefully anoint my lips and eyes with this holy water; begin with the face, and proceed successively to my limbs and the rest of my body; my dear son, the power of God is so great that you must be astonished at nothing."

Don Juan felt death so near, that he added in a terrible voice, "Be careful not to drop the flask."

Then he breathed his last gently in the arms of his son, and his son's tears fell fast over his sardonic, haggard features.

It was almost midnight when Don Felipe Belvidero laid his father's body upon the table. He kissed the sinister brow and the grey hair; then he put out the lamp.

By the soft moonlight that lit strange gleams across the country without, Felipe could dimly see his father's body, a vague white thing among the shadows. The dutiful son moistened a linen cloth with the liquid, and, absorbed in prayer, he anointed the revered face. A deep silence reigned. Felipe heard faint, indescribable rustlings; it was the breeze in the tree-tops, he thought. But when he had moistened the right arm, he felt himself caught by the throat, a young strong hand held him in a tight grip — it was his father's hand! He shrieked aloud; the flask dropped from his hand and broke in pieces. The liquid evaporated; the whole household hurried into the room, holding torches aloft. That shriek had startled them, and filled them with as much terror as if the Trumpet of the Angel sounding on the Last Day had rung through earth and sky. The room was full of people, and a horror-stricken crowd beheld the fainting Felipe upheld by the strong arm of his father, who clutched him by the throat. They saw another thing, an unearthly spectacle — Don Juan's face grown young and beautiful as Antinoüs, with its dark hair and brilliant eyes and red lips, a head that made horrible efforts, but could not move the dead, wasted body.

An old servitor cried, "A miracle! a miracle!" and all the Spaniards echoed, "A miracle! a miracle!"

Doña Elvira, too pious to attribute this to magic, sent for the Abbot of San-Lucar; and the Prior beholding the miracle with his own eyes, being a clever man, and withal an Abbot desirous of augmenting his revenues, determined to turn the occasion to profit. He immediately gave out that Don Juan would certainly be canonised; he appointed a day for the celebration of the apotheosis in his convent, which thenceforward, he said, should be called the convent of San Juan of Lucar. At these words a sufficiently facetious grimace passed over the features of the late Duke.

The taste of the Spanish people for ecclesiastical solemnities is so

well known, that it should not be difficult to imagine the religious pantomime by which the Convent of San-Lucar celebrated the translation
of the *blessed Don Juan Belvidero* to the abbey-church. The tale of
the partial resurrection had spread so quickly from village to village,
that a day or two after the death of the illustrious nobleman the report
had reached every place within fifty miles of San-Lucar, and it was as
good as a play to see the roads covered already with crowds flocking
in on all sides, their curiosity whetted still further by the prospect of a
Te Deum sung by torchlight. The old abbey-church of San-Lucar,
a marvellous building erected by the Moors, a mosque of Allah, which
for three centuries had heard the name of Christ, could not hold the
throng that poured in to see the ceremony. Hidalgos in their velvet
mantles, with their good swords at their sides, swarmed like ants, and
were so tightly packed in among the pillars that they had not room to
bend the knees, which never bent save to God. Charming peasant girls,
in the basquina that defines the luxuriant outlines of their figures, lent
an arm to white-haired old men. Young men, with eyes of fire, walked
beside aged crones in holiday array. Then came couples tremulous with
joy, young lovers led thither by curiosity, newly wedded folk; children
timidly clasping each other by the hand. This throng, so rich in colour-
ing, in vivid contrasts, laden with flowers, enamelled like a meadow,
sent up a soft murmur through the quiet night. Then the great doors
of the church opened.

Late comers who remained without saw afar, through the three great
open doorways, a scene of which the theatrical illusions of modern
opera can give but a faint idea. The vast church was lighted up by
thousands of candles, offered by saints and sinners alike eager to win
the favour of this new candidate for canonisation, and these self-
commending illuminations turned the great building into an enchanted
fairyland. The black archways, the shafts and capitals, the recessed
chapels with gold and silver gleaming in their depths, the galleries, the
Arab traceries, all the most delicate outlines of that delicate sculpture,
burned in the excess of light like the fantastic figures in the red heart
of a brazier. At the further end of the church, above that blazing sea,
rose the high altar like a splendid dawn. All the glories of the golden
lamps and silver candlesticks, of banners and tassels, of the shrines of
the saints and votive offerings, paled before the gorgeous brightness
of the reliquary in which Don Juan lay. The blasphemer's body sparkled
with gems, and flowers, and crystal, with diamonds and gold, and
plumes white as the wings of seraphim; they had set it up on the altar,
where the picture of Christ had stood. All about him blazed a host of
tall candles; the air quivered in the radiant light. The worthy Abbot
of San-Lucar, in pontifical robes, with his mitre set with precious
stones, his rochet and golden crosier, sat enthroned in imperial state
among his clergy in the choir. Rows of impassive aged faces, silver-
haired old men clad in fine linen albs, were grouped about him, as the

saints who confessed Christ on earth are set by painters, each in his place, about the throne of God in heaven. The precentor and the dignitaries of the chapter, adorned with the gorgeous insignia of ecclesiastical vanity, came and went through the clouds of incense, like stars upon their courses in the firmament.

When the hour of triumph arrived, the bells awoke the echoes far and wide, and the whole vast crowd raised to God the first cry of praise that begins the *Te Deum*. A sublime cry! High, pure notes, the voices of women in ecstasy, mingled in it with the sterner and deeper voices of men; thousands of voices sent up a volume of sound so mighty, that the straining, groaning organ-pipes could not dominate that harmony. But the shrill sound of children's singing among the choristers, the reverberation of deep bass notes, awakened gracious associations, visions of childhood, and of man in his strength, and rose above that entrancing harmony of human voices blended in one sentiment of love.

Te Deum laudamus!

The chant went up from the black masses of men and women kneeling in the cathedral, like a sudden breaking out of light in darkness, and the silence was shattered as by a peal of thunder. The voices floated up with the clouds of incense that had begun to cast thin bluish veils over the fanciful marvels of the architecture, and the aisles were filled with splendour and perfume and light and melody. Even at the moment when that music of love and thanksgiving soared up to the altar, Don Juan, too well bred not to express his acknowledgments, too witty not to understand how to take a jest, bridled up in his reliquary, and responded with an appalling burst of laughter. Then the Devil having put him in mind of the risk he was running of being taken for an ordinary man, a saint, a Boniface, a Pantaleone, he interrupted the melody of love by a yell; the thousand voices of hell joined in it. Earth blessed, Heaven banned. The church was shaken to its ancient foundations.

Te Deum laudamus! cried the many voices.

"Go to the devil, brute beasts that you are! *Dios! Dios! Carajos demonios!* Idiots! What fools you are with your dotard-God!" and a torrent of imprecations poured forth like a stream of red-hot lava from the mouth of Vesuvius.

"Deus Sabaoth! . . . Sabaoth!" cried the believers.

"You are insulting the majesty of Hell," shouted Don Juan, gnashing his teeth. In another moment the living arm struggled out of the reliquary, and was brandished over the assembly in mockery and despair.

"The saint is blessing us," cried the old women, children, lovers, and the credulous among the crowd.

And note how often we are deceived in the homage we pay; the great man scoffs at those who praise him, and pays compliments now and again to those whom he laughs at in the depths of his heart.

Just as the Abbot, prostrate before the altar, was chanting *"Sancte Johanneš, ora pro nobis!"* he heard a voice exclaim sufficiently distinctly: *"O coglione!"*

"What can be going on up there?" cried the Sub-prior, as he saw the reliquary move.

"The saint is playing the devil," replied the Abbot.

Even as he spoke, the living head tore itself away from the lifeless body, and dropped upon the sallow cranium of the officiating priest.

"Remember Doña Elvira!" cried the thing, with its teeth set fast in the Abbot's head.

The Abbot's horror-stricken shriek disturbed the ceremony; all the ecclesiastics hurried up and crowded about their chief.

"Idiot, tell us now if there is a God!" the voice cried, as the Abbot, bitten through the brain, drew his last breath.

Alexander Pushkin (1799–1837)

LIFE: He was descended from an Abyssinian brought as a slave to the court of Peter I of Russia in the early years of the eighteenth century, entered the service of his government in 1817, was exiled to Southern Russia in 1820 for his liberal politics, and did not return to Moscow, his birthplace, until 1825, the year Nicholas I became Tsar. In 1831 he married Natalia Goncharov and six years later was killed in a duel with Baron Georges Charles d'Anthès, whom he had called out in an affair of honor involving his wife.

WORKS: *Boris Godunov* (1831); *Ruslan and Lyudmila* (1820); *Prisoner of the Caucusus* (1822); *Eugene Onegin* (1825–1832).

EUGENE ONEGIN *

To live it hurries and to feel it hastes.

Prince Vyazemski †

CHAPTER ONE

I

"My uncle has most honest principles:
when he was taken gravely ill,

Eugene Onegin by Aleksandr Pushkin, translated from the Russian, with a Commentary, by Vladimir Nabokov. Bollingen Series LXXII. Copyright 1964 by Bollingen Foundation, New York. Distributed by Princeton University Press. Reprinted by permission of Bollingen Foundation.

* First published in one volume in 1833.
† A minor poet, Pushkin's friend.

he forced one to respect him
and nothing better could invent.
To others his example is a lesson;   5
but, good God, what a bore to sit
by a sick person day and night, not stirring
a step away!
What base perfidiousness
to entertain one half-alive,   10
adjust for him his pillows,
sadly serve him his medicine,
sigh — and think inwardly
when *will* the devil take you?"

II

    15
Thus a young scapegrace thought
as with post horses in the dust he flew,
by the most lofty will of Zeus
the heir of all his kin.
Friends of Lyudmila and Ruslan!   20
The hero of my novel,
without preambles, forthwith,
I'd like to have you meet:
Onegin, a good pal of mine,
was born upon the Neva's banks,   25
where maybe you were born,
or used to shine, my reader!
There formerly I too promenaded —
but harmful is the North to me.

III

Having served excellently, nobly,
his father lived by means of debts;   30
gave three balls yearly
and squandered everything at last.
Fate guarded Eugene:
at first, Madame looked after him;
later, Monsieur replaced her.   35
The child was boisterous but charming.
Monsieur l'Abbé, a poor wretch of a Frenchman,
not to wear out the infant,
taught him all things in play,
bothered him not with stern moralization,   40
scolded him slightly for his pranks,
and to the Letniy Sad took him for walks.

19. *Lyudmila and Ruslan:* a reference to Pushkin's poetic epic published in 1820.
24. *Neva:* in St. Petersburg.
42. *Letniy Sad:* Le Jardin d'Eté (Summer Garden), a public park along the Neva.

IV

Then, when the season of tumultuous youth
for Eugene came,
season of hopes and tender melancholy,   45
Monsieur was ousted from the place.
Now my Onegin is at large:
hair cut after the latest fashion,
dressed like a London Dandy —
and finally he saw the World.
In French impeccably   50
he could express himself and write,
danced the mazurka lightly, and
bowed unconstrainedly —
what would you more? The World decided   55
that he was clever and most charming.

V

All of us had a bit of schooling
in something and somehow:
hence in our midst it is not hard,
thank God, to flaunt one's education.
Onegin was, in the opinion   60
of many (judges resolute and stern),
a learned fellow but a pedant.
He had the happy talent,
without constraint, in conversation
slightly to touch on everything,   65
keep silent, with an expert's learned air,
during a grave discussion, and provoke
the smiles of ladies with the fire
of unexpected epigrams.   70

VI

Latin has gone at present out of fashion;
still, to tell you the truth,
he had enough knowledge of Latin
to make out epigraphs,
expatiate on Juvenal,
put at the bottom of a letter *vale*,   75
and he remembered, though not without fault,
two lines from the *Aeneid*.
He had no inclination
to rummage in the chronological
dust of the earth's historiography,   80
but anecdotes of days gone by,

75. *Juvenal:* the Roman satirist (c. A.D. 60–c. 140).
76. *vale:* farewell.

from Romulus to our days,
he did keep in his memory.

VII

85

Lacking the lofty passion not to spare
life for the sake of sounds,
an iamb from a trochee —
no matter how we strove — he could not tell apart.
Theocritus and Homer he disparaged,
but read, in compensation, Adam Smith,   90
and was a deep economist:
that is, he could assess the way
a state grows rich,
what it subsists upon, and why
it needs not gold   95
when it has got the simple product.
His father could not understand him,
and mortgaged his lands.

VIII

All Eugene knew besides
I have no leisure to recount;   100
but where he was a veritable genius,
what he more firmly knew than all the arts,
what since his prime had been to him
toil, torment, and delight,
what occupied the livelong day   105
his fretting indolence —
was the art of soft passion
which Naso sang,
wherefore a sufferer
his brilliant and unruly span   110
he ended, in Moldavia,
deep in the steppes, far from his Italy.

IX *

[The ardor of the heart torments us early.
Witching deceit —
Chateaubriand or Staël, not nature —   115
teaches us love.
We yearn to learn life in advance —

83. *Romulus:* the legendary founder of Rome.
89. *Theocritus:* Greek poet of the third century B.C., best known for his pastoral poetry.
90. *Adam Smith:* the major work of this eighteenth century Scottish economist is *Wealth of Nations*.
108. *Naso:* Ovid, who ended his life in exile from Rome.
* In the 1837 edition of the poem (published just before Pushkin's death) this stanza was missing.
115. *Chateaubriand:* François René de Chateaubriand (1768–1848), author of the romantic French
novel *René. Staël:* Madame de Staël (1766–1817), the French writer who knew all the political and
literary figures of her time.

and learn it from a novel.
We have learned everything; meantime
nothing have we enjoyed.
Anticipating nature's voice,   120
we only injure happiness,
and then too late, too late
young ardency flies after it.
Onegin had experienced this — but then how well
women he'd come to know!]   125

X

How early he was able to dissemble,
conceal a hope, show jealousy,
shake one's belief, make one believe,
seem gloomy, pine away,
appear proud and obedient,   130
attentive or indifferent!
How languorously he was silent,
how fierily eloquent,
in letters of the heart, how casual!   135
With one thing breathing, one thing loving,
how self-oblivious he could be!
How quick and tender was his gaze,
bashful and daring, while at times
it shone with an obedient tear!   140

XI

How he was able to seem new,
in jest astonish innocence,
alarm with ready desperation,
amuse with pleasant flattery,
capture the minute of softheartedness;   145
the prejudices of innocent years
conquer by means of wits and passion,
wait for involuntary favors,
beg or demand avowals,
eavesdrop upon a heart's first sound,   150
pursue love — and all of a sudden
obtain a secret assignation,
and afterward, alone with her,
amid the stillness give her lessons!

XII

How early he already could disturb   155
the hearts of the professed coquettes!
Or when he wanted to annihilate

his rivals,
how bitingly he'd tattle!
What snares prepare for them! 160
But you, blest husbands,
you remained friends with him:
him petted the sly spouse,
Faublas' disciple of long standing, 165
and the distrustful oldster,
and the majestical cornuto,
always pleased with himself,
his dinner, and his wife.

XIII *

[How well he knew how to attract
the pious gaze of a meek widow 170
and with her, modest and confused,
start, blushing, a conspiracy,
to captivate her with a tender inexperience,
a stanch devotion,
which are no longer in the world, 175
and with the fervor of innocent years!
How well he could with any lady
discuss Platonic love,
and with an unexpected epigram
confuse her — and at last 180
snatch the triumphal crown!]

XIV

[Thus the maidservant's frisky pet,
guard of the garner, whiskered tom,
leaves the stove ledge to stalk a mouse,
stretches, walks on, walks on, 185
his eyes half closed, approaches,
curls up, lumplike, plays with his tail,
prepares the claws of cunning paws —
and, all at once, he scrabs the poor thing up.
Thus, the rapacious wolf, anguished with hunger, 190
comes out of the dense depth of woods
and prowls near the unwatchful dogs,
around the inexperienced flock.
All sleeps. And suddenly the fierce thief whisks
a lamb away into the thick fir forest.] 195

164. *Faublas:* the hero of a picaresque novel by Jean Baptiste Louvet de Couvrai (1760–97).
166. *cornuto:* cuckold.
* "These two stanzas [XIII and XIV] were omitted. After stanza XII in the 1837 edition, the
Roman numerals are followed by three lines of dots" [translator's note]. The translator's indication
that line 174 is incomplete and that there is a line missing in stanza XIII is not reproduced here.

XV

It happened, he'd be still in bed
when little billets would be brought him.
What? Invitations? Yes, indeed,
to a soiree three houses bid him:
here, there will be a ball; elsewhere, a children's fete.   200
So whither is my scamp to scurry?
Whom will he start with? Never mind:
'tis simple to get everywhere in time.
Meanwhile, in morning dress,
having donned a broad bolivar,   205
Onegin drives to the boulevard
and there goes strolling unconfined
till vigilant Bréguet
to him chimes dinner.

XVI

'Tis dark by now. He gets into a sleigh.
The cry "Way, way!" resounds.   210
With frostdust silvers
his beaver collar.
To Talon's he has dashed off: he is certain
that there already waits for him [Kavérin];
has entered — and the cork goes ceilingward,   215
the flow of comet wine spurts forth,
a bloody roast beef is before him,
and truffles, luxury of youthful years,
the best flower of French cookery,
and a decayless Strasbourg pie   220
between a living Limburg cheese
and a golden ananas.

XVII

Thirst is still clamoring for beakers
to drown the hot fat of the cutlets;
but Bréguet's chime reports to them   225
that a new ballet has begun.
The theater's unkind
lawgiver; the inconstant
adorer of enchanting actresses;
an honorary citizen of the coulisses,   230

205. *bolivar:* "hat à la Bolivar" (Pushkin's note in the 1837 edition). "This was a silk hat, slightly funnelform, with a wide, upturned brim, especially fashionable in Paris and Petersburg in 1819" [translator's note].

208. *Bréguet:* "An elegant repeater made by the celebrated French watchmaker, Abraham Louis Bréguet (1747–1823)" [translator's note].

214. *Talon:* "well-known restaurateur" [Pushkin's note].

215. *Kavérin:* a friend of Pushkin's, he was known for his gay but dissipated life.

223. *ananas:* pineapple.

Onegin has flown to the theater,
where, breathing criticism,
each is prepared to clap an *entrechat*,
hiss Phaedra, Cleopatra,   235
call out Moëna — for the purpose
merely of being heard.

XVIII

A magic region! There in olden years
the sovereign of courageous satire,
sparkled Fonvízin, freedom's friend,   240
and imitational Knyazhnín;
there Ózerov involuntary tributes
of public tears, of plaudits
shared with the young Semyónova;
there our Katénin resurrected   245
Corneille's majestic genius;
there caustic Shahovskóy brought forth the noisy
swarm of his comedies;
there, too, Didelot did crown himself with glory;
there, there, beneath the shelter of coulisses,   250
my young days sped.

XIX

My goddesses! What has become of you?
Where are you? Hearken to my woeful voice:
Are all of you the same? Have other maidens
taken your place without replacing you?   255
Am I to hear again your choruses?
Am I to see Russian Terpsichore's
soulful volation?
Or will the mournful gaze not find
familiar faces on the dreary stage,   260
and at an alien world having directed
a disenchanted lorgnette,
shall I, indifferent spectator
of merriment, yawn wordlessly
and bygones recollect?   265

235. *Phaedra:* According to the translator, this is probably a reference to an opera by J. B. Lemoyne, *Phèdre,* which was based on Racine's tragedy. *Cleopatra:* which Cleopatra Pushkin had in mind is uncertain.

236. *Moëna:* the heroine of Ózerov's *Fingal,* which was derived from the *Fingal* of James Macpherson (1736–96), who claimed that it was a translation of a Gaelic epic poem.

240. *Fonvízin:* eighteenth-century comic dramatist.

241. *Knyazhnín:* second-rate dramatist (1741–91).

242. *Ózerov:* another minor dramatist.

244. *Semyónova:* a famous actress.

245. *Katénin:* He translated Corneille's *Cid* into Russian (1822). Pierre Corneille (1606–84) was France's first great dramatist.

247. *Shahovskóy:* another second-rate dramatist.

249. *Didelot:* French dancer and choreographer, ballet-master in St. Petersburg.

XX

By now the house is full; the boxes blaze;
parterre and stalls — all seethes;
in the top gallery impatiently they clap,
and, soaring up, the curtain swishes.
Resplendent, half ethereal,   270
obedient to the magic bow,
surrounded by a throng of nymphs,
Istómina stands: she,
while touching with one foot the floor,
gyrates the other slowly,   275
and lo! a leap, and lo! she flies,
she flies like fluff from Eol's lips,
now twines and now untwines her waist
and beats one swift small foot against the other.

XXI

All clap as one. Onegin enters: 280
he walks — on people's toes — between the stalls;
askance, his double lorgnette trains
upon the loges of strange ladies;
he has scanned all the tiers;
he has seen everything; with faces, garb,   285
he's dreadfully displeased;
with men on every side
he has exchanged salutes; then at the stage
in great abstraction he has glanced,
has turned away, and yawned,   290
and uttered: "Time all were replaced;
ballets I long have suffered,
but even of Didelot I've had enough."

XXII

Amors, diaboli, and dragons
still on the stage jump and make noise;   295
still at the carriage porch the weary footmen
on the pelisses are asleep;
still people have not ceased to stamp,
blow noses, cough, hiss, clap;
still, outside and inside,   300
lamps glitter everywhere;
still, chilled, the horses fidget,
bored with their harness,
and round the fires the coachmen curse their masters

273. *Istómina:* a ballerina.
277. *Eol:* Aeolus, god of the winds.

and beat their palms together;
and yet Onegin has already left;
he's driving home to dress.

XXIII

Shall I present a faithful picture
of the secluded cabinet,
where fashions' model pupil
is dressed, undressed, and dressed again?
Whatever, for the lavish whim,
London the trinkleter deals in
and o'er the Baltic waves to us
ships in exchange for timber and for tallow;
whatever hungry taste in Paris,
choosing a useful trade,
invents for pastimes,
for luxury, for modish mollitude;
all this adorned the cabinet
of a philosopher at eighteen years of age.

XXIV

Amber on Tsargrad's pipes,
porcelain and bronzes on a table,
and — joyance of the pampered senses —
perfumes in crystal cut with facets;
combs, little files of steel,
straight scissors, curvate ones, and brushes
of thirty kinds —
these for the nails, those for the teeth.
Rousseau (I shall observe in passing) was unable
to understand how the dignified Grimm
dared clean his nails in front of *him,*
the eloquent crackbrain.
The advocate of liberty and rights
was in the present case not right at all.

XXV

One can be an efficient man —
and mind the beauty of one's nails:
why vainly argue with the age?
Custom is despot among men.
My Eugene, a second [Chadáev],
being afraid of jealous censures,

305

310

315

320

325

330

335

340

---

322. *Tsargrad:* Constantinople.
331. *Grimm:* Frédéric Melchior Grimm (1723–1807), French encyclopedist.
340. *Chadáev:* "Colonel Pyotr Chaadaev (1793–1856) was in Onegin's day a strange and brilliant personality, fop and philosopher, a man of mercy and wit, and an influential freethinker — to be later engulfed in organized mysticism" [translator's note].

was in his dress a pedant
and what we've called a fop.
Three hours, at least,
he spent in front of glasses, 345
and from his dressing room came forth
akin to giddy Venus
when, having donned a masculine attire,
the goddess drives to a masqued ball.

XXVI

With toilette in the latest taste 350
having engaged your curious glance,
I might before the learned world
describe here his attire;
this would, no doubt, be daring;
however, 'tis my business to describe; 355
but "dress coat," "waistcoat," "pantaloons" —
in Russian all these words are not;
in fact, I see (my guilt I lay before you)
that my poor idiom as it is
might be diversified much less 360
with words of foreign stock,
though I did erstwhile dip
into the Academic Dictionary.

XXVII

Not this is our concern at present:
we'd better hurry to the ball 365
whither headlong in a hack coach
already my Onegin has sped off.
In front of darkened houses,
alongst the sleeping street in rows
the twin lamps of coupés 370
pour forth a cheerful light
and project rainbows on the snow.
Studded around with lampions,
glitters a splendid house;
across its whole-glassed windows shadows move: 375
there come and go the profiled heads
of ladies and of modish quizzes.

XXVIII

Up to the porch our hero now has driven;
past the hall porter, like a dart,
he has flown up the marble steps, 380

363. *Dictionary:* The famous dictionary began to be assembled by the French Academy in the seven-
teenth century and is still being assembled.

has run his fingers through his hair,
has entered. The ballroom is full of people;
the music has already tired of dinning;
the crowd is occupied with the mazurka;
there's all around both noise and squeeze; 385
there clink the cavalier guard's spurs;
the little feet of winsome ladies flit;
upon their captivating tracks
flit flaming glances,
and by the roar of violins is drowned 390
the jealous whispering of fashionable women.

XXIX

In days of gaieties and desires
I was mad about balls:
there is no safer spot for declarations
and for the handing of a letter. 395
O you, respected husbands!
I'll offer you my services;
pray, mark my speech:
I wish to warn you.
You too, mammas: most strictly 400
follow your daughters with your eyes;
hold up your lorgnettes straight!
Or else . . . else — God forbid!
If this I write it is because
I have long ceased to sin. 405

XXX

Alas, on various pastimes I have wasted
a lot of life!
But to this day, if morals did not suffer,
I'd still like balls.
I like riotous youth, 410
the crush, the glitter, and the gladness,
and the considered dresses of the ladies;
I like their little feet; but then 'tis doubtful
that in all Russia you will find
three pairs of shapely feminine feet. 415
Ah me, I long could not forget
two little feet! . . . Despondent, fervorless,
I still remember them, and in sleep they
disturb my heart.

XXXI

So when and where, in what desert, will you 420
forget them, madman? Little feet,

ah, little feet! Where are you now?
Where do you trample vernant blooms?
Brought up in Oriental mollitude,
on the Northern sad snow
you left no prints: 425
you liked the sumptuous contact
of yielding rugs.
Is it long since I would forget for you
the thirst for fame and praises,
the country of my fathers, and confinement?   430
The happiness of youthful years has vanished
as on the meadows your light trace.

XXXII

Diana's bosom, Flora's cheeks, are charming,
dear friends! Nevertheless, for me   435
something about it makes more charming
the small foot of Terpsichore.
By prophesying to the gaze
an unpriced recompense,
with token beauty it attracts the willful   440
swarm of desires.
I like it, dear Elvina,
beneath the long napery of tables,
in springtime on the turf of meads,
in winter on the hearth's cast iron,   445
on mirrory parquet of halls,
by the sea on granite of rocks.

XXXIII

I recollect the sea before a tempest:
how I envied the waves
running in turbulent succession   450
with love to lie down at her feet!
How much I wished then with the waves
to touch the dear feet with my lips!
No, never midst the fiery days
of my ebullient youth   455
did I long with such anguish
to kiss the lips of young Armidas,
or the roses of flaming cheeks,
or bosoms full of languor —
no, never did the surge of passions   460
thus rive my soul!

442. *Elvina:* a fictitious name for a supposedly real lady, whose identity cannot be established with certainty.
457. *Armidas:* Armida is the beautiful sorceress in Tasso's *Jerusalem Delivered* (1581).

XXXIV

I have remembrance of another time:
in chary fancies now and then
I hold the happy stirrup
and feel a small foot in my hand.   465
Again imagination seethes,
again that touch has kindled
the blood within my withered heart,
again the ache, again the love!
But 'tis enough extolling haughty ones   470
with my loquacious lyre:
they are not worth either the passions
or songs by them inspired;
the words and gaze of the said charmers
are as deceptive as their little feet.   475

XXXV

And my Onegin? Half asleep,
he drives from ball to bed,
while indefatigable Petersburg
is roused already by the drum.
The merchant's up, the hawker's out,   480
the cabby to the hack stand drags,
the Okhta girl hastes with her jug,
the morning snow creaks under her.
Morn's pleasant hubbub has awoken,
unclosed are shutters, chimney smoke   485
ascends in a blue column, and the baker,
a punctual German in a cotton cap,
has more than once already
opened his *vasisdas*.

XXXVI
                                                     490
But by the tumult of the ball fatigued,
and turning morning into midnight,
sleeps peacefully in blissful shade
the child of pastimes and of luxury.
He will awake past midday, and again   495
till morn his life will be prepared,
monotonous and motley, and tomorrow
'twill be the same as yesterday.
But was my Eugene happy —
free, in the bloom of the best years,   500
amidst resplendent conquests,
amidst delights of every day?

482. *Okhta:* east of St. Petersburg.
489. *vasisdas:* a small transom.

Was it to him of no avail
midst banquets to be rash and hale?

XXXVII

No, feelings early cooled in him.
Tedious to him became the social hum.   505
The fairs remained not long
the object of his customary thoughts.
Betrayals had time to fatigue him. Friends
and friendship palled,
since plainly not always could he   510
beefsteaks and Strasbourg pie
sluice with a champagne bottle
and scatter piquant sayings when
he had the headache;
and though he was a fiery scapegrace,   515
he lost at last his liking
for strife, saber and lead.

XXXVIII

A malady, the cause of which
'tis high time were discovered,
similar to the English "spleen" —   520
in short, the Russian "chondria" —
possessed him by degrees.
To shoot himself, thank God,
he did not care to try,
but toward life became quite cold.   525
He like Childe Harold, gloomy, languid,
appeared in drawing rooms;
neither the gossip of the *monde* nor boston,
neither a winsome glance nor an immodest sigh,
nothing touched him;   530
he noticed nothing.

XLII *

Capricious belles of the *grand monde!*
Before all others you he left;
and it is true that in our years
the upper *ton* is rather tedious.   535
Although, perhaps, this or that dame

520. *spleen:* generally, melancholy.
526. *Childe Harold:* the hero of Byron's romantic poem.
528. *boston:* a card game.
* "Nothing in Pushkin's manuscripts has been found that might lend itself to an insertion under these stanza headings [XXXIX, XL, XLI]. In the fair copy, XLII immediately follows XXXVIII. It is not unthinkable that this gap is a fictitious one, with some musical value — the artifice of a wistful pause, the imitation of a missed heartbeat, the mirage of an emotional horizon, false asterisks of false suspense" [translator's note].

interprets Say and Bentham,
in general their conversation
is insupportable, though harmless tosh.
On top of that they are so pure,   540
so stately, so intelligent,
so full of piety,
so circumspect, so scrupulous,
so inaccessible to men,
that the mere sight of them begets the spleen.   545

XLIII

And you, young beauties, whom
at a late hour daredevil droshkies
carry away over the pavement
of Petersburg,
you also were abandoned by my Eugene.   550
Apostate from the turbulent delights,
Onegin locked himself indoors;
yawning, took up a pen;
wanted to write; but persevering toil
to him was loathsome: nothing   555
from his pen issued, and he did not get
into the cocky guild of people
on whom I pass no judgment — for the reason
that I belong to them.

XLIV
    560
And once again to idleness consigned,
oppressed by emptiness of soul,
he settled down with the laudable aim
to make his own another's mind;
he crammed a shelf with an array of books,   565
and read, and read — and all for nothing:
here there was dullness; there, deceit and raving;
this one lacked conscience; that one, sense;
on all of them were different fetters;
and outworn was the old, and the new raved   570
about the old.
As he'd left women, he left books
and, with its dusty tribe, the shelf
with funerary taffeta he curtained.

XLV

Having cast off the burden of the *monde*'s conventions,
    575
having, as he, from vain pursuits desisted,

537. *Say:* Jean Baptiste Say (1767–1832), French political economist and disciple of Adam Smith.
Bentham: Jeremy Bentham (1748–1832), the English writer who popularized Utilitarian ethics.

with him I made friends at that time.
I liked his traits,
to dreams the involuntary addiction,
nonimitative oddity,
and sharp, chilled mind; 580
I was embittered, he was gloomy;
the play of passions we knew both;
on both, life weighed;
in both, the heart's glow had gone out;
for both, there was in store the rancor 585
of blind Fortuna and of men
at the very morn of our days.

XLVI

He who has lived and thought
cannot help in his soul despising men;
him who has felt disturbs 590
the ghost of irrecoverable days;
for him there are no more enchantments;
him does the snake of memories,
him does repentance gnaw.
All this often imparts 595
great charm to conversation.
At first, Onegin's language
would disconcert me; but I grew
accustomed to his biting argument
and banter blent halfwise with bile 600
and virulence of somber epigrams.

XLVII

How oft in summertide, when limpid
and luminous is the nocturnal sky
above the Neva, and the gay
glass of the waters 605
does not reflect Diana's visage —
rememorating intrigues of past years,
rememorating a past love,
impressible, carefree again,
the breath of the benignant night 610
we mutely quaffed!
As to the greenwood from a prison
a slumbering clogged convict is transferred,
so we'd be carried off in fancy
to the beginning of young life. 615

XLVIII

With soul full of regrets,
and leaning on the granite,

Eugene stood pensive — as himself
the Poet has described.
'Twas stillness all; only night sentries   620
to one another called,
and the far clip-clop of some droshky
resounded suddenly from Million Street;
only a boat, oar swinging,
swam on the dozing river,   625
and, in the distance, captivated us
a horn and a brave song.
But, 'mid the night's diversions, sweeter
is the strain of Torquato's octaves.

XLIX

Adrian waves,   630
O Brenta! Nay, I'll see you
and, filled anew with inspiration,
I'll hear your magic voice!
'Tis sacred to Apollo's nephews;
through the proud lyre of Albion   635
to me 'tis known, to me 'tis kindred.
In the voluptuousness of golden
Italy's nights at liberty I'll revel,
with a youthful Venetian,
now talkative, now mute,   640
swimming in a mysterious gondola;
with her my lips will find
the tongue of Petrarch and of love.

L

Will the hour of my freedom come?
'Tis time, 'tis time! To it I call;   645
I roam above the sea, I wait for the right weather,
I beckon to the sails of ships.
Under the cope of storms, with waves disputing,
on the free crossway of the sea
when shall I start on my free course?   650
'Tis time to leave the dull shore of an element
inimical to me,
and sigh, 'mid the meridian swell, beneath the
sky of my Africa,

619. *Poet:* Mihail Muravyov (1757–1807).
629. *Torquato's octaves:* the poetic stanzas of the Italian writer Torquato Tasso.
630. *Adrian:* Adriatic.
631. *Brenta:* river near Venice.
634. *Apollo's nephews:* poets.
635. *proud lyre of Albion:* the poetry of Byron, whose influence on Pushkin, through French prose
translations, was enormous.
643. *tongue:* Italian. For examples of Petrarch's love poetry see the selections in this anthology.
654. *Africa:* "The author, on his mother's side, is of African descent" [Pushkin's note].

for somber Russia, where
I suffered, where I loved,
where I buried my heart.

655

LI

Onegin was prepared with me
to see strange lands;
but soon we were to be by fate
sundered for a long time.
'Twas then his father died.
Before Onegin there assembled
a greedy host of creditors.
Each has a mind and notion of his own.
Eugene, detesting litigations,
contented with his lot,
abandoned the inheritance to them,
perceiving no great loss therein,
or precognizing from afar
the demise of his aged uncle.

660

665

670

LII

All of a sudden he indeed
got from the steward
a report that his uncle was nigh death in bed
and would be glad to bid farewell to him.
Eugene, the sad epistle having read,
incontinently to the rendezvous
drove headlong, traveling post,
and yawned already in anticipation,
preparing, for the sake of money,
for sighs, boredom, and guile
(and 'tis with this that I began my novel);
but when he reached apace his uncle's manor,
he found him laid already on the table
as a prepared tribute to earth.

675

680

685

LIII

He found the grounds full of attendants;
to the dead man from every side
came driving foes and friends,
enthusiasts for funerals.
The dead man was interred,
the priests and guests ate, drank,
and solemnly dispersed thereafter,
as though they had been sensibly engaged.
Now our Onegin is a rural dweller,
of workshops, waters, forests, lands,

690

695

absolute lord (while up to then he'd been
an enemy of order and a wastrel),
and very glad to have exchanged
his former course for something.

LIV

For two days new to him   700
seemed the secluded fields,
the coolness of the somber park,
the bubbling of the quiet brook;
by the third day, grove, hill, and field   705
did not engage him any more;
then somnolence already they induced;
then plainly he perceived
that in the country, too, the boredom was the same,
although there were no streets, no palaces,
no cards, no balls, no verses.   710
The hyp was waiting for him on the watch,
and it kept running after him
like a shadow or faithful wife.

LV

I was born for the peaceful life,
for country quiet: 715
the lyre's voice in the wild is more resounding,
creative dreams are more alive.
To harmless leisures consecrated,
I wander by a wasteful lake
and *far niente* is my rule.   720
By every morn I am awakened
unto sweet mollitude and freedom;
little I read, a lot I sleep,
volatile fame do not pursue.
Was it not thus in former years,   725
that in inaction, in the [shade],
I spent my happiest days?

LVI

Flowers, love, the country, idleness,
ye fields! my soul is vowed to you.
I'm always glad to mark the difference   730
between Onegin and myself,
lest a sarcastic reader
or else some publisher
of complicated calumny,

711. *hyp:* that is, "spleen."
720. *far niente:* the Italian phrase meaning "doing nothing" is so written in the original poem.

collating here my traits,   735
repeat thereafter shamelessly
that I have scrawled my portrait
like Byron, the poet of pride
— as if we were no longer able
to write long poems   740
on any other subject than ourselves!

LVII

In this connection I'll observe: all poets
are friends of fancifying love.
It used to happen that dear objects
I'd dream of, and my soul   745
preserved their secret image;
the Muse revived them later:
thus I, carefree, would sing
a maiden of the mountains, my ideal,
as well as captives of the Salgir's banks.   750
From you, my friends, at present
not seldom do I hear the question:
"For whom does your lyre sigh?
To whom did you, among the throng
of jealous maidens, dedicate its strain?   755

LVIII

"Whose gaze, while stirring inspiration,
with a dewy caress rewarded
your pensive singing? Whom did your
verse idolize?"
Faith, nobody, my friends, I swear!   760
Love's mad anxiety
I cheerlessly went through.
Happy who blent with it the fever
of rhymes: thereby the sacred frenzy
of poetry he doubled,   765
striding in Petrarch's tracks;
as to the heart's pangs, he allayed them
and meanwhile fame he captured too —
but I, when loving, was stupid and mute.

LIX

Love passed, the Muse appeared,   770
and the dark mind cleared up.
Once free, I seek again the concord
of magic sounds, feelings, and thoughts;
I write, and the heart does not pine;

749. *maiden:* in Pushkin's *The Caucasian Captive* (1822).
750. *captives:* in Pushkin's *The Fountain of Bahchisaray* (1824). *Salgir:* in the Crimea.

the pen draws not, lost in a trance,   775
next to unfinished lines,
feminine feet or heads;
extinguished ashes will not flare again;
I still feel sad; but there are no more tears,
and soon, soon the storm's trace   780
will hush completely in my soul:
then I shall start to write a poem
in twenty-five cantos or so.

LX

I've thought already of a form of plan
and how my hero I shall call.   785
Meantime, my novel's
first chapter I have finished;
all this I have looked over closely;
the inconsistencies are very many,
but to correct them I don't wish.   790
I shall pay censorship its due
and give away my labors' fruits
to the reviewers for devourment.
Be off, then, to the Neva's banks,
newborn work! And deserve for me   795
fame's tribute: false interpretations,
noise, and abuse!

Onegin strikes up a friendship with Lenski, a neighboring land-owner who has just returned from a German university and who introduces him to the Larin family, in particular the two daughters, Olga and Tatania. Lenski loves Olga and Tatania falls in love with Onegin, who remains bored. She writes him a romantic love letter which he doesn't answer, and when they meet he lectures her condescendingly on the need for self-control. Lenski's courtship of Olga continues through the autumn and winter; they are to be married in January; but at a party two weeks before the wedding Onegin flirts with Olga, is challenged to a duel by Lenski, and kills him. He has been traveling for three years when, in Chapter Eight, he returns to St. Petersburg.

CHAPTER EIGHT

I

In those days when in the Lyceum's gardens
I bloomed serenely,

1. *Lyceum:* "The reference is to the Aleksandrovskiy Litsey, Lycée de l'Empereur Alexandre I, founded by that tsar Aug. 12, 1810, at Tsarskoe Selo (now Pushkin), twenty-two versts from St. Petersburg. Pushkin passed the entrance examinations in August, 1911. . . . In modern terms, the Lyceum might be defined as a boarding school for young gentlemen, which offered three years of preparatory school and three years of junior college . . . [translator's note].

would eagerly read Apuleius,
did *not* read Cicero;
in those days, in mysterious valleys,   5
in springtime, to the calls of swans,
near waters shining in the stillness,
the Muse began to visit me.
My student cell was all at once
radiant with light: in it the Muse   10
opened a banquet of young fancies,
sang childish gaieties,
and glory of our ancientry,
and the heart's tremulous dreams.

II

And with a smile the world received her;   15
the first success provided us with wings;
the aged Derzhavin noticed us — and blessed us
as he descended to the grave.
And Dmitrev was not our detractor;
and the custodian of Russian lore,   20
leaving his scrolls, would heed us and caress
[our] timid Muse.
And you, deeply inspired
bard of all that is beautiful,
you, idol of virginal hearts: 25
was it not you who, by partisanship
carried away, would stretch a hand to me
and summon to pure fame?

III

And I, setting myself for law
only the arbitrary will of passions,   30
sharing emotions with the crowd,
I led my frisky Muse into the hubbub
of feasts and turbulent discussions —
the terror of midnight patrols;
and to them, in mad feasts,   35
she brought her gifts,
and like a little bacchante frisked,

3. *Apuleius:* Lucius Apuleius, Roman philosopher and novelist of the second century A.D. His most famous book is *The Metamorphoses,* or *The Golden Ass,* a slightly bawdy novel.
17. *Derzhavin:* Gavrila Derzhavin (1743–1816), Russian poet.
19. *Dmitrev:* "a poetical elision of Dmitriev" (translator's note); Ivan Dmitriev (1760–1837) was a minor Russian poet.
20. *custodian:* "The reference is to Nikolay Karamzin (1766–1826). Pushkin had been well acquainted with him in 1818–20, and appreciated him chiefly as a reformer of language and as the historian of Russia" [translator's note].
23. *you:* "The reference is to Vasiliy Zhukovski (1783–1852), Pushkin's lifelong friend, a prudent mediator in our poet's clashes with the government, and his amiable teacher in matters of prosody and poetical idiom" [translator's note].

over the bowl sang for the guests;
and the young people of past days
would turbulently dangle after her;
and I was proud 'mong friends
of my volatile mistress.

IV

But I dropped out of their alliance —
and fled afar . . . she followed me.
How often the caressive Muse
for me would sweeten the mute way
with the bewitchment of a secret tale!
How often on Caucasia's crags,
Lenorelike, by the moon,
with me she'd gallop on a steed!
How often on the shores of Tauris
she in the gloom of night
led me to listen the sound of the sea,
Nereid's unceasing murmur,
the deep eternal chorus of the billows,
the praiseful hymn to the sire of the worlds.

V

And the far capital's glitter and noisy feasts
having forgotten in the wilds
of sad Moldavia,
she visited the humble tents
of wandering tribes;
and among them grew savage, and forgot
the language of the gods
for scant, strange tongues,
for songs of the steppe dear to her.
Suddenly everything around
changed, and lo! in my garden she appeared
as a provincial miss,
with a sad thought in her eyes, with a French
book in her hands.

VI

And now my Muse for the first time
I'm taking to a high-life rout;
at her steppe charms
with jealous apprehensiveness I look.
Through a dense series of aristocrats,

40

45

50

55

60

65

70

75

49. *Lenorelike:* "*Lenore* is the celebrated ballad written at Gelliehausen, near Gottingen, in the summer of 1773, by Gottfried August Bürger" [translator's note].
72. *rout:* "an evening assembly without dances; means properly crowd" [Pushkin's note].

of military fops, of diplomats
and haughty dames, she glides; now quietly
she has sat down and looks, admiring
the noisy crush,
the flickering of dress and speech,   80
the apparition of slow guests
in front of the young hostess,
and the dark frame of men
around ladies, as about pictures.

VII

She likes the stately order   85
of oligarchic colloquies,
and the chill of calm pride,
and this mixture of ranks and years.
But who's that standing in the chosen throng,
silent and nebulous?   90
To everyone he seems a stranger.
Before him faces come and go
like a series of tedious specters.
What is it — spleen or smarting morgue
upon his face? Why is he here?   95
Who is he? Is it really — Eugene?
He, really? So, 'tis he, indeed.
— Since when has he been blown our way?

VIII

Is he the same, or grown more peaceful?
Or does he still play the eccentric?   100
Say, in what guise has he returned?
What will he stage for us meanwhile?
As what will he appear now? As a Melmoth?
a cosmopolitan? a patriot?
a Harold? a Quaker? a bigot?   105
Or will he sport some other mask?
Or else be simply a good fellow
like you and me, like the whole world?
At least here's my advice:
to drop an antiquated fashion.   110
Sufficiently he's gulled the world . . .
— You know him? — Yes and no.

103. *Melmoth:* a reference to *Melmoth the Wanderer* (1820), a gothic novel by the Irish writer
Charles Robert Maturin (1782–1824).
105. *Harold:* "Byron's *Childe Harold*, friend of the mountains, companion of the caverns, familiar of
the ocean, but in man's dwelling a restless stranger who looks at the painted world with a smile of
despair and crushes his enemies with the curse of forgiveness" [translator's note].

IX

— Why so unfavorably then
do you report on him?
Because we indefatigably   115
fuss, judge of everything?
Because of fiery souls the rashness
to smug nonentity is either
insulting or absurd?
Because, by liking room, wit cramps?   120
Because too often conversations
we're glad to take for deeds,
because stupidity is volatile and wicked?
Because to grave men grave are trifles,
and mediocrity alone   125
is to our measure and not odd?

X

Blest who was youthful in his youth;
blest who matured at the right time;
who, with the years, the chill of life
was gradually able to withstand;   130
who never was addicted to strange dreams;
who did not shun the fashionable rabble;
who was at twenty fop or dasher,
and then at thirty, profitably married;
who rid himself at fifty   135
of private and of other debts;
who gained repute, money, and rank
calmly in turn;
about whom lifelong one kept saying:
N. N. is an excellent man.   140

XI

But it is sad to think that youth
was given us in vain,
that we betrayed it every hour,
that it duped us;
that our best aspirations,   145
that our fresh dreamings,
in quick succession have decayed
like leaves in putrid autumn.
It is unbearable to see before one
only of dinners a long series,   150
to look on life as on a rite,
and in the wake of the decorous crowd

to go, not sharing with it either
the general opinions or the passions.

XII

When one becomes the subject   155
of noisy comments, it's unbearable
(you will agree) to pass among
sensible people for a feigned eccentric
or a sad crackbrain,
or a satanic monster,   160
or even for my Demon.
Onegin (let me take him up again),
having in single combat killed his friend,
having without a goal, without exertions,
lived to the age of twenty-six,   165
irked by the inactivity of leisure,
without employment, wife, or occupation,
could think of nothing to take up.

XIII

A restlessness took hold of him,
the inclination to a change of places   170
(a most excruciating property,
a cross that few deliberately bear).
He left his countryseat,
the solitude of woods and fields,
where an ensanguined shade   175
daily appeared to him,
and started upon travels without aim,
accessible to one sensation;
and to him journeys,
like everything on earth,   180
grew boring. He returned and found himself,
like Chatski, come from boat to ball.

XIV

But lo! the throng has undulated,
a murmur through the hall has run. . . .
Toward the hostess there advanced a lady,   185
followed by an imposing general.
She was unhurried,
not cold, not talkative,
without a flouting gaze for everyone,
without pretensions to success,   190
without those little mannerisms,

161. *Demon:* an allusion to Pushkin's poem *The Demon* (1823).
182. *Chatski:* a reference to a character in the satiric comedy *Woe from Wit* by A. S. Griboedov (1795–1829).

without mimetic artifices. . . .
All about her was quiet, simple.
She seemed a faithful reproduction
du comme il faut. . . . ([Shishkov,] forgive me: 195
I do not know how to translate.)

XV

Closer to her the ladies moved;
old women smiled to her;
the men bowed lower, sought
to catch her gaze;   200
maidens before her passed more quietly
across the room; and higher
than anyone lifted his nose and shoulders
the general who had come in with her.
None could have called her   205
a beauty; but from head to foot
none could have found in her
what is by autocratic fashion
in the high London circle
called "vulgar." (I'm unable —   210

XVI

— of that word I am very fond,
but am unable to translate it; in our midst
for the time being it is new
and hardly bound to be in favor;
it might do nicely in an epigram. . . .   215
But to our lady let me turn.)
Winsome with carefree charm,
she at a table sat
with brilliant Nina Voronskóy,
that Cleopatra of the Neva;   220
and, surely, you would have agreed
that Nina with her marble beauty
could not — though dazzling —
eclipse her neighbor.

XVII
                                                                     225
"Can it be possible?" thinks Eugene.
"Can it be she? . . . But really . . . No . . .
What! From outback steppe villages . . ."
and a tenacious quizzing glass
he keeps directing every minute

195. *du comme il faut:* "vulgar" (see line 210). [*Shishkov*]: "The reference is to the leader of the Archaic group of writers, Admiral Aleksandr Shishkov (1754–1841), publicist, statesman, president of the Academy of Sciences, and a cousin of my great-grandmother" [translator's note].

at her whose aspect vaguely has   230
recalled to him forgotten features.
"Tell me, Prince, you don't know
who is it there in the *framboise* beret
talking with the Spanish ambassador?"
The prince looks at Onegin: 235
"Aha! Indeed, long have you not been in the *monde*.
Wait, I'll present you."
"But *who* is she?" "My wife."

XVIII

"So you are married! Didn't know before.
How long?" "About two years."
"To whom?" "The Larin girl." "Tatiana!"   240
"She knows you?" "I'm their neighbor."
"Oh, then, come on." The prince goes up
to his wife and leads up to her
his kin and friend.
The princess looks at him . . . and whatsoever   245
troubled her soul,
however greatly
she was surprised, astounded,
nothing betrayed her,
her *ton* remained the same,   250
her bow was just as quiet.

XIX

Forsooth! It was not merely that she didn't
flinch, or blanch suddenly, or flush —
she simply never moved an eyebrow,
did not even compress her lips.   255
Though he looked with the utmost care,
not even traces of the old Tatiana could
Onegin find.
With her he wished to start a conversation —
and . . . and could not. She asked: How long   260
had he been there? And whence came he —
from their own parts, maybe?
Then on her spouse she turned a look
of lassitude; glided away. . . .
And moveless he remained.   265

XX

Could it be that the same Tatiana
to whom, alone with her,
at the beginning of our novel

233. *framboise:* raspberry.

back in a stagnant, distant region,   270
in the fine fervor of moralization
precepts he once had preached;
the one from whom a letter he preserves
where the heart speaks,
where all it out, all unrestrained;   275
that little girl — or is he dreaming? —
that little girl whom in her humble state
he had passed over — could it be that now
she had been so indifferent,
so bold with him?   280

XXI

He leaves the close-packed rout,
he drives home, pensive; by a fancy
now sad, now charming,
his first sleep is disturbed.
He wakes; is brought   285
a letter: Prince N. begs the honor of his presence
at a soiree. Good God — to her?
I will, I will! And rapidly a courteous
reply he scrawls. What is the matter
with him? In what strange daze is he?   290
What has stirred at the bottom of that cold
and sluggish soul?
Vexation? Vanity? Or once again
youth's worry — love?

XXII

Once more Onegin counts the hours,   295
once more he can't wait for the day to end.
But ten strikes: he drives off,
he has flown forth, he's at the porch;
with tremor he goes in to the princess:
he finds Tatiana   300
alone, and for some minutes
they sit together. From Onegin's lips
the words come not. Ill-humored,
awkward, he barely, barely
replies to her. His head   305
is full of a persistent thought.
Persistently he looks: she sits
easy and free.

XXIII

The husband comes. He interrupts
this painful tête-à-tête;   310
he with Onegin recollects

the pranks, the jests of former years.
They laugh. Guests enter.
Now with the large-grained salt of high-life malice
the conversation starts to be enlivened.
Before the lady of the house, light nonsense   315
flashed without stupid affectation,
and meantime interrupted it
sensible talk, without trite topics,
eternal truths, or pedantry,
nor did its free vivacity   320
shock anybody's ears.

XXIV

Yet here was the flower of the capital,
both high nobility and paragons of fashion;
the faces one meets everywhere,
the fools one cannot go without;   325
here were, in mobcaps and in roses,
elderly ladies, wicked-looking;
here were several maidens —
unsmiling faces;
here was an envoy, speaking   330
of state affairs;
here was, with fragrant hoary hair,
an old man in the old way joking —
with eminent subtility and wit,
which is somewhat absurd today!   335

XXV

Here was, to epigrams addicted
a gentleman cross with everything:
with the too-sweet tea of the hostess,
the ladies' platitudes, the *ton* of men,
the comments on a foggy novel,   340
the badge two sisters had been granted,
the falsehoods in reviews, the war,
the snow, and his own wife.

XXVI

Here was [. . .], who had gained   345
distinction by the baseness of his soul
and blunted in all albums,
Saint-P[riest], your pencils;
in the doorway another ball dictator

348. *Saint-P[riest]*: "The reference is to Count Emmanuil Sen-Pri (1806–28), said to have been a gifted cartoonist. . . . This young artist shot himself, according to some, on Easter Day in Italy, in church, or, according to others, in the presence of an eccentric Englishman who had promised to pay his gambling debts if granted the spectacle of self-murder" [translator's note].

stood like a fashion plate,   350
as rosy as a Palm Week cherub,
tight-coated, mute and motionless;
and a far-flung traveler,
an overstarched jackanapes,
provoked a smile among the guests   355
by his studied deportment,
and an exchange of silent glances was
his universal condemnation.

XXVII

But my Onegin the whole evening heeds
only Tatiana: 360
not the shy little maiden,
enamored, poor and simple —
but the indifferent princess,
the inaccessible
goddess of the luxurious, queenly Neva.   365
O humans! All of you resemble
ancestress Eve:
what's given to you does not lure,
incessantly the serpent calls you
to him, to the mysterious tree: 370
you *must* have the forbidden fruit supplied to you,
for paradise without that is no paradise to you.

XXVIII

How changed Tatiana is!
Into her role how firmly she has entered!
The ways of a constricting rank   375
how fast she has adopted!
Who'd dare to seek the tender little lass
in this majestic,
this careless legislatrix of salons?
And he had stirred her heart!   380
About him in the dark of night,
as long as Morpheus had not come flying,
time was, she virginally brooded,
raised to the moon a dying eye,
dreaming that someday she might make   385
with him life's humble journey!

XXIX

All ages are to love submissive;
but to young virgin hearts
its impulses are beneficial
as are spring storms to fields.   390

They freshen in the rain of passions,
and renovate themselves, and ripen,
and vigorous life gives
both rich bloom and sweet fruit.
But at a late and barren age, 395
at the turn of our years,
sad is the trace of a dead passion. . . .
Thus storms of the cold autumn
into a marsh transform the meadow
and strip the woods around. 400

XXX

There is no doubt: alas! Eugene
in love is with Tatiana like a child.
In throes of amorous designs
he spends both day and night.
Not harking to the mind's stern protests, 405
up to her porch, glass vestibule,
daily he drives.
He chases like a shadow after her;
he's happy if he casts
the fluffy boa on her shoulders, 410
or touches torridly
her hand, or if he parts in front of her
the motley host of liveries, or picks up
her handkerchief.

XXXI

She does not notice him, 415
no matter how he strives — even to death;
receives him freely at her house; at those
of others says two or three words to him;
sometimes welcomes with a mere bow,
sometimes does not take any notice: 420
there's not a drop of coquetry in her,
the high world does not tolerate it.
Onegin is beginning to grow pale;
she does not see or does not care;
Onegin wastes away: 425
he's practically phthisical.
All send Onegin to physicians;
in chorus these send him to spas.

XXXII

Yet he's not going. He beforehand
is ready to his forefathers to write 430

of an impending meeting; yet Tatiana
cares not one bit (such is their sex).
But he is stubborn, won't desist,
still hopes, bestirs himself;
a sick man bolder than one hale,   435
he with a weak hand to the princess
writes an impassioned missive.
Though generally little sense in letters
he saw, not without reason;
but evidently torment of the heart   440
had now passed his endurance.
Here you have his letter word for word.

ONEGIN'S LETTER TO TATIANA

I foresee everything: the explanation
of a sad secret will offend you.
What bitter scorn   445
your proud glance will express!
What do I want? What is my object
in opening my soul to you?
What wicked merriment
perhaps I give occasion to!   450

Chancing to meet you once,
noting in you a spark of tenderness,
I did not venture to believe in it:
did not give way to a sweet habit;
my tedious freedom   455
I did not wish to lose. Another thing
yet separated us:
a hapless victim Lenski fell. . . .
From all that to the heart is dear
then did I tear my heart away;   460
alien to everybody, tied by nothing,
I thought: liberty and peace are
a substitute for happiness. Good God!
How wrong I was, how I am punished!

No — every minute to see you; to follow   465
you everywhere;
the smile of your lips, movement of your eyes,
to try to capture with enamored eyes;
to listen long to you, to comprehend
all your perfection with one's soul;   470
to melt in agonies before you,
grow pale and waste away . . . that's rapture!

And I'm deprived of that; for you
I drag myself at random everywhere;
to me each day is dear, each hour is dear,   475
while I in futile dullness squander
the days told off by fate — they are
sufficiently oppressive anyway.
I know: my span is well-nigh measured;   480
but that my life may be prolonged
I must be certain in the morning
of seeing you during the day.
I fear: in my meek plea
your severe gaze will see   485
the schemes of despicable cunning —
and I can hear your wrathful censure.
If you but knew how terrible it is
to languish with the thirst of love,
burn — and by means of reason hourly   490
subdue the tumult in one's blood;
wish to embrace your knees
and, in a burst of sobbing, at your feet
pour out appeals, avowals, plaints,
all, all I could express,   495
and in the meantime with feigned coldness
arm speech and gaze,
maintain a placid conversation,
glance at you with a cheerful glance! . . .

But let it be: against myself
I've not the force to struggle any more;   500
all is decided: I am in your power,
and I surrender to my fate.

XXXIII

There is no answer. He sends a new missive.
To the second, to the third letter —
there is no answer. He drives out to some   505
reception. Hardly has he entered — there she is
coming in his direction. How severe!
He is not seen, to him no word is said.
Ugh! How surrounded she is now   510
with Twelfthtide cold!
How anxious are to hold back indignation
her stubborn lips!
Onegin peers with a keen eye:
where, where are discomposure, sympathy,   515
where the tearstains? None, none!
There's on that face but the imprint of wrath . . .

XXXIV

plus, possibly, a secret fear
lest husband or *monde* guess
the escapade, the casual foible,   520
all my Onegin knows. . . .
There is no hope! He drives away,
curses his folly —
and, deeply plunged in it,
the *monde* he once again renounces   525
and in his silent study comes to him
the recollection of the time
when cruel chondria
pursued him in the noisy *monde,*
captured him, took him by the collar,   530
and shut him up in a dark hole.

XXXV

Again, without discrimination,
he started reading. He read Gibbon,
Rousseau, Manzoni, Herder,
Chamfort, Mme de Staël, Bichat, Tissot.   535
He read the skeptic Bayle,
he read the works of Fontenelle,
he read some [authors] of our own,
without rejecting anything —
the "almanacs" and the reviews   540
where sermons into us are drummed,
where I'm today abused so much
but where *such* madrigals addressed to me
I used to meet with now and then:
e sempre bene, gentlemen.   545

XXXVI

And lo — his eyes were reading, but his thoughts
were far away;
chimeras, desires, sorrows
kept crowding deep into his soul.
Between the printed lines   550
he with spiritual eyes
read other lines. It was in *them*

533–37. *Gibbon . . . Fontenelle:* Edward Gibbon (1737–94), the English historian, author of
Decline and Fall of the Roman Empire; Rousseau — see the selection in this anthology; Alessandro
Manzoni (1785–1873), Italian writer whose most famous book is the novel *The Betrothed* (1827);
Johann Gottfried Herder (1744–1803), German critic and poet; Nicolas Sébastian Roch Chamfort
(1741–94), French writer famous for his maxims; Mme de Staël (1766–1817), as famous for her
personality as for her writing; Marie François Xavier Bichat (1771–1802), famous physician and
physiologist; Simon André Tissot (1728–97), Swiss doctor and author; Pierre Bayle (1647–1706),
French critic and philosopher; Bernard le Bovier de Fontenelle (1657–1757), who during his hundred
years worked in almost every literary form.

that he was utterly absorbed.
These were the secret legends of the heart's
dark ancientry;   555
dreams unconnected
with anything; threats, rumors, presages;
or the live tosh of a long tale,
or a young maiden's letters.

XXXVII

And by degrees into a lethargy   560
of feelings and of thoughts he falls,
while before him Imagination
deals out her motley faro deck.
Now he sees: on the melted snow,
as at a night's encampment sleeping,   565
stirless, a youth lies; and he hears
a voice: "Well, what — he's dead!"
Now he sees foes forgotten,
calumniators, and malicious cowards,
and a swarm of young traitresses,   570
and a circle of despicable comrades;
and now a country house, and by the window
sits *she* . . . and ever she!

XXXVIII

He grew so used to lose himself in this
that he almost went off his head   575
or else became a poet. (Frankly,
that would have been a boon, indeed!)
And true: by dint of magnetism,
the mechanism of Russian verses
my addleheaded pupil   580
at that time nearly grasped.
How much a poet he resembled
when in a corner he would sit alone,
and the hearth blazed in front of him,
and he hummed "Benedetta"   585
or "Idol mio," and into the fire
dropped now a slipper, now his magazine!

XXXIX

Days rushed. In warmth-pervaded air
winter already was resolving;
and he did not become a poet,   590

585. *"Benedetta"*: " 'Benedetta sia la madre,' 'Let the mother be blessed,' a Venetian barcarolle" [translator's note].

586. *"Idol mio"*: " 'Idol mio, piu pace non ho,' 'My idol, I have no peace any longer': the refrain in a duettino . . . by Vincenzo Gabussi (1800–46)" [translator's note].

he did not die, did not go mad.
Spring quickens him: for the first time
his close-shut chambers, where he had
been hibernating like a marmot,
his double windows, inglenook —   595
he leaves on a bright morning,
he fleets in sleigh along the Neva's bank.
Upon blue blocks of hewn-out ice
the sun plays. In the streets
the furrowed snow thaws muddily: 600
whither, upon it, his fast course

XL

directs Onegin? You beforehand
have guessed already. Yes, exactly:
apace to her, to his Tatiana,
my unreformed eccentric comes.   605
He walks in, looking like a corpse.
There's not a soul in the front hall.
He enters the reception room. On! No one.
A door he opens. . . . What is it
that strikes him with such force?   610
The princess before him, alone,
sits, unadorned, pale, reading
some kind of letter,
and softly sheds a flood of tears,
her cheek propped on her hand.   615

XLI

Ah! Her mute sufferings —
in this swift instant who would not have read!
Who would not have the former Tanya,
poor Tanya, recognized now in the princess?
In throes of mad regrets,   620
Eugene falls at her feet;
she gives a start,
and is silent, and looks,
without surprise, without wrath, at Onegin. . . .
His sick, extinguished gaze,   625
imploring aspect, mute reproof,
she takes in everything. The simple maid,
with the dreams, with the heart of former days
again in her has resurrected now.

XLII

She does not bid him rise   630
and, not taking her eyes off him,

does not withdraw
her limp hand from his avid lips. . . .
What is her dreaming now about?
A lengthy silence passes, 635
and finally she, softly:
"Enough; get up. I must
frankly explain myself to you.
Onegin, do you recollect that hour
when in the garden, in the avenue, fate brought us 640
together and so meekly
your lesson I heard out.
Today it is my turn.

XLIII

"Onegin, I was younger then,
I was, I daresay, better-looking, 645
and I loved you; and what then, what
did I find in your heart?
What answer? Mere severity.
There wasn't — was there? — novelty for you
in a meek little maiden's love? 650
Even today — good heavens! — my blood freezes
as soon as I remember
your cold glance and that sermon. . . . But I do not
accuse you; at that awful hour
you acted nobly, 655
you in regard to me were right,
to you with all my soul I'm grateful. . . .

XLIV

"*Then* — is it not so? — in the wilderness,
far from vain Hearsay,
I was not to your liking. . . . Why, then, *now* 660
do you pursue me?
Why have you marked me out?
Might it not be because I must
now move in the *grand monde;*
because I have both wealth and rank; 665
because my husband has been maimed in battles;
because for that the Court is kind to us?
Might it not be because my disrepute
would be remarked by everybody now
and in society might bring you 670
scandalous honor?

639–642. *do you recollect . . . out:* Tatiana refers to the scene in Chapter Four in which Onegin lectured her about the letter she had sent him.

XLV

"I'm crying. . . . If your Tanya
you've not forgotten yet,
then know: the sharpness of your blame,
cold, stern discourse,   675
if it were only in my power
I'd have preferred to an offensive passion,
and to these letters and tears.
For my infantine dreams
you had at least some pity then,   680
at least consideration for my age.
But *now!* . . . What to my feet
has brought you? What a trifle!
How, with your heart and mind,
be the slave of a trivial feeling?   685

XLVI

"But as to me, Onegin, this magnificence,
a wearisome life's tinsel, my successes
in the world's vortex,
my fashionable house and evenings,
what do I care for them? . . . At once I'd gladly   690
give all the frippery of this masquerade,
all this glitter, and noise, and fumes,
for a shelfful of books, for a wild garden,
for our poor dwelling,
for those haunts where for the first time,   695
Onegin, I saw you,
and for the humble churchyard where
there is a cross now and the shade
of branches over my poor nurse.

XLVII

"Yet happiness had been so possible,   700
so near! . . . But my fate is already
settled. Imprudently,
perhaps, I acted.
My mother with tears of conjurement
beseeched me. For poor Tanya   705
all lots were equal.
I married. You must,
I pray you, leave me;
I know: in your heart are
both pride and genuine honor.   710
I love you (why dissimulate?);

but to another I belong:
to him I shall be faithful all my life."

XLVIII

She has gone. Eugene stands
as if by thunder struck.   715
In what a tempest of sensations
his heart is now immersed!
But there resounds a sudden clink of spurs,
and there appears Tatiana's husband,
and here my hero,   720
at an unfortunate minute for him,
reader, we now shall leave
for long . . . forever. . . . After him
sufficiently along one path
we've roamed the world. Let us congratulate   725
each other on attaining land. Hurrah!
It long (is it not true?) was time.

XLIX

Whoever, O my reader,
you be — friend, foe — I wish to part
with you at present as a pal.   730
Farewell. Whatever in these careless strophes
you might have looked for as you followed me —
tumultuous recollections,
relief from labors,
live images or witticisms,   735
or faults of grammar —
God grant that in this book, for recreation,
for dreaming, for the heart,
for justs in journals,
you find at least a crumb.   740
Upon which, let us part, farewell!

L

You, too, farewell, my strange traveling companion,
and you, my true ideal,
and you, my live and constant,
though small, work. I have known with you   745
all that a poet covets:
obliviousness of life in the world's tempests,
the sweet discourse of friends.
Rushed by have many, many days
since young Tatiana, and with her   750
Onegin, in a blurry dream
appeared to me for the first time —

and the far stretch of a free novel
I through a magic crystal
still did not make out clearly.   755

LI

But those to whom at amicable meetings
its first strophes I read —
"Some are no more, others are distant,"
as erstwhiles Sadi said.
Without them was Onegin's picture finished.   760
And she from whom was fashioned
the dear ideal of "Tatiana" . . .
Ah, much, much has fate snatched away!
Blest who left life's feast early,
not having to the bottom drained   765
the goblet full of wine;
who never read life's novel to the end
and all at once could part with it
as I with my Onegin.

759. *Sadi:* Persian poet of the thirteenth century.

Søren Kierkegaard (1813–1855)

LIFE: Born and educated in Copenhagen, he traveled in Germany and then returned to his native city, where he spent his last years. The critical act of his life was the purposeful rejection of the woman to whom he was engaged to be married; out of that period came his first great work, *Either/Or,* the source book of contemporary existentialism, and *Fear and Trembling.*

WORKS: *Either/Or* (1843); *Fear and Trembling* (1843); *The Sickness Unto Death* (1849).

FEAR AND TREMBLING *

Prelude

Once upon a time there was a man who as a child had heard the beautiful story about how God tempted Abraham, and how he endured temptation, kept the faith, and a second time received again a son con-

Fear and Trembling, by Søren Kierkegaard. Translated by Walter Lowrie (1941). Reprinted by permission of Princeton University Press. Copyright 1954 Princeton University Press.

* 1843.

trary to expectation.[1] When the child became older he read the same story with even greater admiration, for life had separated what was united in the pious simplicity of the child. The older he became, the more frequently his mind reverted to that story, his enthusiasm became greater and greater, and yet he was less and less able to understand the story. At last in his interest for that he forgot everything else; his soul had only one wish, to see Abraham, one longing, to have been witness to that event. His desire was not to behold the beautiful countries of the Orient, or the earthly glory of the Promised Land, or that godfearing couple whose old age God had blessed, or the venerable figure of the aged patriarch, or the vigorous young manhood of Isaac whom God had bestowed upon Abraham — he saw no reason why the same thing might not have taken place on a barren heath in Denmark. His yearning was to accompany them on the three days' journey when Abraham rode with sorrow before him and with Isaac by his side. His only wish was to be present at the time when Abraham lifted up his eyes and saw Mount Moriah afar off, at the time when he left the asses behind and went alone with Isaac up unto the mountain; for what his mind was intent upon was not the ingenious web of imagination but the shudder of thought.

That man was not a thinker, he felt no need of getting beyond faith; he deemed it the most glorious thing to be remembered as the father of it, an enviable lot to possess it, even though no one else were to know it.

That man was not a learned exegete, he didn't know Hebrew, if he had known Hebrew, he perhaps would easily have understood the story and Abraham. . . .

A Panegyric Upon Abraham

If there were no eternal consciousness in a man, if at the foundation of all there lay only a wildly seething power which writhing with obscure passions produced everything that is great and everything that is insignificant, if a bottomless void never satiated lay hidden beneath all — what then would life be but despair? If such were the case, if there were no sacred bond which united mankind, if one generation arose after another like the leafage in the forest, if the one generation replaced the other like the song of birds in the forest, if the human race passed through the world as the ship goes through the sea, like the wind through the desert, a thoughtless and fruitless activity, if an eternal oblivion were always lurking hungrily for its prey and there was no power strong enough to wrest it from its maw — how empty then and comfortless life would be! But therefore it is not thus, but as God created man and woman, so too He fashioned the hero and the poet or orator. The poet cannot do what that other does, he can only admire, love and rejoice in the hero. Yet he too is happy, and not less so, for

1. See Genesis 22.

the hero is as it were his better nature, with which he is in love, rejoicing in the fact that this after all is not himself, that his love can be admiration. He is the genius of recollection, can do nothing except call to mind what has been done, do nothing but admire what has been done; he contributes nothing of his own, but is jealous of the intrusted treasure. He follows the option of his heart, but when he has found what he sought, he wanders before every man's door with his song and with his oration, that all may admire the hero as he does, be proud of the hero as he is. This is his achievement, his humble work, this is his faithful service in the house of the hero. If he thus remains true to his love, he strives day and night against the cunning of oblivion which would trick him out of his hero, then he has completed his work, then he is gathered to the hero, who has loved him just as faithfully, for the poet is as it were the hero's better nature, powerless it may be as a memory is, but also transfigured as a memory is. Hence no one shall be forgotten who was great, and though time tarries long, though a cloud of misunderstanding takes the hero away, his lover comes nevertheless, and the longer the time that has passed, the more faithfully will he cling to him.

No, not one shall be forgotten who was great in the world. But each was great in his own way, and each in proportion to the greatness of that which he *loved*. For he who loved himself became great by himself, and he who loved other men became great by his selfless devotion, but he who loved God became greater than all. Everyone shall be remembered, but each became great in proportion to his *expectation*. One became great by expecting the possible, another by expecting the eternal, but he who expected the impossible became greater than all. Everyone shall be remembered, but each was great in proportion to the greatness of that with which he *strove*. For he who strove with the world became great by overcoming the world, and he who strove with himself became great by overcoming himself, but he who strove with God became greater than all. So there was strife in the world, man against man, one against a thousand, but he who strove with God was greater than all. So there was strife upon earth: there was one who overcame all by his power, and there was one who overcame God by his impotence. There was one who relied upon himself and gained all, there was one who secure in his strength sacrificed all, but he who believed God was greater than all. There was one who was great by reason of his power, and one who was great by reason of his wisdom, and one who was great by reason of his hope, and one who was great by reason of his love; but Abraham was greater than all, great by reason of his power whose strength is impotence, great by reason of his wisdom whose secret is foolishness, great by reason of his hope whose form is madness, great by reason of the love which is hatred of oneself.

By faith Abraham went out from the land of his fathers and became a sojourner in the land of promise. He left one thing behind, took one thing with him: he left his earthly understanding behind and took faith with him — otherwise he would not have wandered forth but would have thought this unreasonable. By faith he was a stranger in the land of promise, and there was nothing to recall what was dear to him, but by its novelty everything tempted his soul to melancholy yearning — and yet he was God's elect, in whom the Lord was well pleased! Yea, if he had been disowned, cast off from God's grace, he could have comprehended it better; but now it was like a mockery of him and of his faith. There was in the world one too who lived in banishment [2] from the fatherland he loved. He is not forgotten, nor his Lamentations when he sorrowfully sought and found what he had lost. There is no song of Lamentations by Abraham. It is human to lament, human to weep with them that weep, but it is greater to believe, more blessed to contemplate the believer.

By faith Abraham received the promise that in his seed all races of the world would be blessed. Time passed, the possibility was there, Abraham believed; time passed, it became unreasonable, Abraham believed. There was in the world one who had an expectation, time passed, the evening drew nigh, he was not paltry enough to have forgotten his expectation, therefore he too shall not be forgotten. Then he sorrowed, and sorrow did not deceive him as life had done, it did for him all it could, in the sweetness of sorrow he possessed his delusive expectation. It is human to sorrow, human to sorrow with them that sorrow, but it is greater to believe, more blessed to contemplate the believer. There is no song of Lamentations by Abraham. He did not mournfully count the days while time passed, he did not look at Sarah with a suspicious glance, wondering whether she were growing old, he did not arrest the course of the sun, that Sarah might not grow old, and his expectation with her. He did not sing lullingly before Sarah his mournful lay. Abraham became old, Sarah became a laughing-stock in the land, and yet he was God's elect and inheritor of the promise that in his seed all the races of the world would be blessed. So were it not better if he had not been God's elect? What is it to be God's elect? It is to be denied in youth the wishes of youth, so as with great pains to get them fulfilled in old age. But Abraham believed and held fast the expectation. If Abraham had wavered, he would have given it up. If he had said to God, "Then perhaps it is not after all Thy will that it should come to pass, so I will give up the wish. It was my only wish, it was my bliss. My soul is sincere, I hide no secret malice because Thou didst deny it to me" — he would not have been forgotten, he would have saved many by his example, yet he would not be the father of faith. For it is great to give up one's wish, but it is greater to hold it fast after having given it up, it is great to grasp the eternal, but it is greater to hold fast to the temporal after having given it up.

Then came the fulness of time. If Abraham had not believed, Sarah surely would have been dead of sorrow, and Abraham, dulled by grief, would not have understood the fulfilment but would have smiled at it

2. See Jeremiah.

as at a dream of youth. But Abraham believed, therefore he was young; for he who always hopes for the best becomes old, and he who is always prepared for the worst grows old early, but he who believes preserves an eternal youth. Praise therefore to that story! For Sarah, though stricken in years, was young enough to desire the pleasure of motherhood, and Abraham, though gray-haired, was young enough to wish to be a father. In an outward respect the marvel consists in the fact that it came to pass according to their expectation, in a deeper sense the miracle of faith consists in the fact that Abraham and Sarah were young enough to wish, and that faith had preserved their wish and therewith their youth. He accepted the fulfilment of the promise, he accepted it by faith, and it came to pass according to the promise and according to his faith — for Moses smote the rock with his rod, but he did not believe.

Then there was joy in Abraham's house, when Sarah became a bride on the day of their golden wedding.

But it was not to remain thus. Still once more Abraham was to be tried. He had fought with that cunning power which invents everything, with that alert enemy which never slumbers, with that old man who outlives all things — he had fought with Time and preserved his faith. Now all the terror of the strife was concentrated in one instant. "And God tempted Abraham and said unto him, Take Isaac, thine only son, whom thou lovest, and get thee into the land of Moriah, and offer him there for a burnt offering upon the mountain which I will show thee."

So all was lost — more dreadfully than if it had never come to pass! So the Lord was only making sport of Abraham! He made miraculously the preposterous actual, and now in turn He would annihilate it. It was indeed foolishness, but Abraham did not laugh at it like Sarah when the promise was announced. All was lost! Seventy years of faithful expectation, the brief joy at the fulfilment of faith. Who then is he that plucks away the old man's staff, who is it that requires that he himself shall break it? Who is he that would make a man's gray hairs comfortless, who is it that requires that he himself shall do it? Is there no compassion for the venerable oldling, none for the innocent child? And yet Abraham was God's elect, and it was the Lord who imposed the trial. All would now be lost. The glorious memory to be preserved by the human race, the promise in Abraham's seed — this was only a whim, a fleeting thought which the Lord had had, which Abraham should now obliterate. That glorious treasure which was just as old as faith in Abraham's heart, many, many years older than Isaac, the fruit of Abraham's life, sanctified by prayers, matured in conflict — the blessing upon Abraham's lips, this fruit was now to be plucked prematurely and remain without significance. For what significance had it when Isaac was to be sacrificed? That sad and yet blissful hour when Abraham was to take leave of all that was dear to him, when yet once more he was to lift up his head, when his countenance would shine like that of the Lord, when he would concentrate his whole soul in a blessing which was potent to make Isaac blessed all his days — this time would not come! For he would indeed take leave of Isaac, but in such a way that he himself would remain behind; death would separate them, but in such a way that Isaac remained its prey. The old man would not be joyful in death as he laid his hands in blessing upon Isaac, but he would be weary of life as he laid violent hands upon Isaac. And it was God who tried him. Yea, woe, woe unto the messenger who had come before Abraham with such tidings! Who would have ventured to be the emissary of this sorrow? But it was God who tried Abraham.

Yet Abraham believed, and believed for this life. Yea, if his faith had been only for a future life, he surely would have cast everything away in order to hasten out of this world to which he did not belong. But Abraham's faith was not of this sort, if there be such a faith; for really this is not faith but the furthest possibility of faith which has a presentiment of its object at the extremest limit of the horizon, yet is separated from it by a yawning abyss within which despair carries on its game. But Abraham believed precisely for this life, that he was to grow old in the land, honored by the people, blessed in his generation, remembered forever in Isaac, his dearest thing in life, whom he embraced with a love for which it would be a poor expression to say that he loyally fulfilled the father's duty of loving the son, as indeed is evinced in the words of the summons, "the son whom thou lovest." Jacob had twelve sons, and one of them he loved; Abraham had only one, the son whom he loved.

Yet Abraham believed and did not doubt, he believed the preposterous. If Abraham had doubted — then he would have done something else, something glorious; for how could Abraham do anything but what is great and glorious! He would have marched up to Mount Moriah, he would have cleft the fire-wood, lit the pyre, drawn the knife — he would have cried out to God, "Despise not this sacrifice, it is not the best thing I possess, that I know well, for what is an old man is comparison with the child of promise; but it is the best I am able to give Thee. Let Isaac never come to know this, that he may console himself with his youth." He would have plunged the knife into his own breast. He would have been admired in the world, and his name would not have been forgotten; but it is one thing to be admired, and another to be the guiding star which saves the anguished.

But Abraham believed. He did not pray for himself, with the hope of moving the Lord — it was only when the righteous punishment was decreed upon Sodom and Gomorrha that Abraham came forward with his prayers.

We read in those holy books: "And God tempted Abraham, and said unto him, Abraham, Abraham, where art thou? And he said, Here am I." Thou to whom my speech is addressed, was such the case with thee? When afar off thou didst see the heavy dispensation of providence approaching thee, didst thou not say to the mountains, Fall on me, and to the hills, Cover me? Or if thou wast stronger, did not thy foot move slowly along the way, longing as it were for the old path? When a call was issued to thee, didst thou answer, or didst thou not answer perhaps in a low voice, whisperingly? Not so Abraham: joyfully, buoyantly, confidently, with a loud voice, he answered, "Here am I." We read further: "And Abraham rose early in the morning" — as though it were to a festival, so he hastened, and early in the morning he had come to the place spoken of, to Mount Moriah. He said nothing to Sarah, nothing to Eleazar. Indeed who could understand him? Had not the temptation by its very nature exacted of him an oath of silence? He cleft the wood, he bound Isaac, he lit the pyre, he drew the knife. My hearer, there was many a father who believed that with his son he lost everything that was dearest to him in the world, that he was deprived of every hope for the future, but yet there was none that was the child of promise in the sense that Isaac was for Abraham. There was many a father who lost his child; but then it was God, it was the unalterable, the unsearchable will of the Almighty, it was His hand took the child. Not so with Abraham. For him was reserved a harder trial, and Isaac's fate was laid along with the knife in Abraham's hand. And there he stood, the old man, with his only hope! But he did not doubt, he did not look anxiously to the right or to the left, he did not challenge heaven with his prayers. He knew that it was God the Almighty who was trying him, he knew that it was the hardest sacrifice that could be required of him; but he knew also that no sacrifice was too hard when God required it — and he drew the knife.

Who gave strength to Abraham's arm? Who held his right hand up so that it did not fall limp at his side? He who gazes at this becomes paralyzed. Who gave strength to Abraham's soul, so that his eyes did not grow dim, so that he saw neither Isaac nor the ram? He who gazes at this becomes blind. — And yet rare enough perhaps is the man who becomes paralyzed and blind, still more rare one who worthily recounts what happened. We all know it — it was only a trial.

If Abraham when he stood upon Mount Moriah had doubted, if he had gazed about him irresolutely, if before he drew the knife he had by chance discovered the ram, if God had permitted him to offer it instead of Isaac — then he would have betaken himself home, everything would have been the same, he has Sarah, he retained Isaac, and yet how changed! For his retreat would have been a flight, his salvation an accident, his reward dishonor, his future perhaps perdition. Then he would have borne witness neither to his faith nor to God's grace, but would have testified only how dreadful it is to march out to Mount Moriah. Then Abraham would not have been forgotten, nor would Mount Moriah, this mountain would then be mentioned, not like Ararat where the Ark landed, but would be spoken of as a consternation, because it was here that Abraham doubted.

Venerable Father Abraham! In marching home from Mount Moriah thou hadst no need of a panegyric which might console thee for thy loss; for thou didst gain all and didst retain Isaac. Was it not so? Never again did the Lord take him from thee, but thou didst sit at table joyfully with him in thy tent, as thou dost in the beyond to all eternity. Venerable Father Abraham! Thousands of years have run their course since those days, but thou hast need of no tardy lover to snatch the memorial of thee from the power of oblivion, for every language calls thee to remembrance — and yet thou dost reward thy lover more gloriously than does any other; hereafter thou dost make him blessed in thy bosom; here thou dost enthral his eyes and his heart by the marvel of thy deed. Venerable Father Abraham! Second Father of the human race! Thou who first wast sensible of and didst first bear witness to that prodigious passion which disdains the dreadful conflict with the rage of the elements and with the powers of creation in order to strive with God; thou who first didst know that highest passion, the holy, pure and humble expression of the divine madness which the pagans admired — forgive him who would speak in praise of thee, if he does not do it fittingly. He spoke humbly, as if it were the desire of his own heart, he spoke briefly, as it becomes him to do, but he will never forget that thou hadst need of a hundred years to obtain a son of old age against expectation, that thou didst have to draw the knife before retaining Isaac; he will never forget that in a hundred and thirty years thou didst not get further than to faith. . . .

Problemata: Preliminary Expectoration

I am not unacquainted with what has been admired as great and noble in the world, my soul feels affinity with it, being convinced in all humility that it was in my cause the hero contended, and the instant I contemplate his deed I cry out to myself, *jam tua res agitur*.[3] I *think* myself into the hero, but into Abraham I cannot think myself; when I reach the height I fall down, for what I encounter there is the paradox. I do not however mean in any sense to say that faith is something lowly, but on the contrary that it is the highest thing, and that it is dishonest of philosophy to give something else instead of it and to make light of faith. Philosophy cannot and should not give faith, but it should understand itself and know what it has to offer and take nothing away, and least of all should fool people out of something as if it were nothing. I am not unacquainted with the perplexities and dangers of life, I do not fear them, and I encounter them buoyantly. I am not unacquainted with the dreadful, my memory is a faithful wife, and my imagination is (as I myself am not) a diligent little maiden who all day sits quietly at her work, and in the evening knows how to chat to me about it so prettily that I must look at it, though not always, I must say, is it landscapes, or flowers, or pastoral idyls she paints. I have seen the dreadful before my own eyes, I do not flee from it timorously, but

3. "Quoted from Horace's *Letters*, I, 18, 84: 'It's your affair when the neighbor's house is afire' " [translator's note].

I know very well that, although I advance to meet it, my courage is not the courage of faith, nor anything comparable to it. I am unable to make the movements of faith, I cannot shut my eyes and plunge confidently into the absurd, for me that is an impossibility . . . but I do not boast of it. I am convinced that God is love, this thought has for me a primitive lyrical validity. When it is present to me, I am unspeakably blissful, when it is absent, I long for it more vehemently than does the lover for his object; but I do not believe, this courage I lack. For me the love of God is, both in a direct and in an inverse sense, incommensurable with the whole of reality. I am not cowardly enough to whimper and complain, but neither am I deceitful enough to deny that faith is something much higher. I can well endure living in my way, I am joyful and content, but my joy is not that of faith, and in comparison with that it is unhappy. I do not trouble God with my petty sorrows, the particular does not trouble me, I gaze only at my love, and I keep its virginal flame pure and clear. Faith is convinced that God is concerned about the least things. I am content in this life with being married to the left hand, faith is humble enough to demand the right hand — for that this is humility I do not deny and shall never deny.

But really is everyone in my generation capable of making the movements of faith, I wonder? Unless I am very much mistaken, this generation is rather inclined to be proud of making what they do not even believe I am capable of making, viz. incomplete movements. It is repugnant to me to do as so often is done, namely, to speak inhumanly about a great deed, as though some thousands of years were an immense distance; I would rather speak humanly about it, as though it had occurred yesterday, letting only the greatness be the distance, which either exalts or condemns. So if (*in the quality of a tragic hero,* for I can get no higher) I had been summoned to undertake such a royal progress to Mount Moriah, I know well what I would have done. I would not have been cowardly enough to stay at home, neither would I have laid down or sauntered along the way, nor have forgotten the knife, so that there might be a little delay — I am pretty well convinced that I would have been there on the stroke of the clock and would have had everything in order, perhaps I would have arrived too early in order to get through with it sooner. But I also know what else I would have done. The very instant I mounted the horse I would have said to myself, "Now all is lost. God requires Isaac, I sacrifice him, and with him my joy — yet God is love and continues to be that for me; for in the temporal world God and I cannot talk together, we have no language in common." Perhaps one or another in our age will be foolish enough, or envious enough of the great, to want to make himself and me believe that if I really had done this, I would have done even a greater deed than Abraham; for my prodigious resignation was far more ideal and poetic than Abraham's narrow-mindedness. And yet this is the greatest falsehood, for my prodigious resignation was the surrogate for faith, nor could I do more than make the infinite movement, in order to find myself and again repose in myself. In that case I would not have loved Isaac as Abraham loved. That I was resolute in making the movement might prove my courage, humanly speaking; that I loved him with all my soul is the presumption apart from which the whole thing becomes a crime, but yet I did not love like Abraham, for in that case I would have held back even at the last minute, though not for this would I have arrived too late at Mount Moriah. Besides, by my behavior I would have spoiled the whole story; for if I had got Isaac back again, I would have been in embarrassment. What Abraham found easiest, I would have found hard, namely to be joyful again with Isaac; for he who with all the infinity of his soul, *propio motu et propiis auspiciis* [by his own power and on his own responsibility], has performed the infinite movement [of resignation] and cannot do more, only retains Isaac with pain.

But what did Abraham do? He arrived neither too *soon* nor too late. He mounted the ass, he rode slowly along the way. All that time he believed — he believed that God would not require Isaac of him, whereas he was willing nevertheless to sacrifice him if it was required. He believed by virtue of the absurd; for there could be no question of human calculation, and it was indeed the absurd that God who required it of him should the next instant recall the requirement. He climbed the mountain, even at the instant when the knife glittered he believed . . . that God would not require Isaac. He was indeed astonished at the outcome, but by a double-movement he had reached his first position, and therefore he received Isaac more gladly than the first time. Let us go further. We let Isaac be really sacrificed. Abraham believed. He did not believe that some day he would be blessed in the beyond, but that he would be happy here in the world. God could give him a new Isaac, could recall to life him who had been sacrificed. He believed by virtue of the absurd; for all human reckoning had long since ceased to function. That sorrow can derange a man's mind, that we see, and it is sad enough. That there is such a thing as strength of will which is able to haul up so exceedingly close to the wind that it saves a man's reason, even though he remains a little queer, that too one sees. I have no intention of disparaging this; but to be able to lose one's reason, and therefore the whole of finiteness of which reason is the broker, and then by virtue of the absurd to gain precisely the same finiteness — that appalls my soul, but I do not for this cause say that it is something lowly, since on the contrary it is the only prodigy. Generally people are of the opinion that what faith produces is not a work of art, that it is coarse and common work, only for the more clumsy natures; but in fact this is far from the truth. The dialectic of faith is the finest and most remarkable of all; it possesses an elevation, of which indeed I can form a conception, but nothing more. I am able to make from the springboard the great leap whereby I pass into infinity, my back is like that of a tight-rope dancer, having been twisted in my childhood, hence

I find this easy; with a one-two-three! I can walk about existence on my head; but the next thing I cannot do, for I cannot perform the miraculous, but can only be astonished by it. Yes, if Abraham the instant he swung his leg over the ass's back had said to himself, "Now, since Isaac is lost, I might just as well sacrifice him here at home, rather than ride the long way to Moriah" — then I should have no need of Abraham, whereas now I bow seven times before his name and seventy times before his deed. For this indeed he did not do, as I can prove by the fact that he was glad at receiving Isaac, heartily glad, that he needed no preparation, no time to concentrate upon the finite and its joy. If this had not been the case with Abraham, then perhaps he might have loved God but not believed; for he who loves God without faith reflects upon himself, he who loves God believingly reflects upon God.

Upon this pinnacle stands Abraham. The last stage he loses sight of is the infinite resignation. He really goes further, and reaches faith; for all these caricatures of faith, the miserable lukewarm indolence which thinks, "There surely is no instant need, it is not worth while sorrowing before the time," the pitiful hope which says, "One cannot know what is going to happen . . . it might possibly be after all" — these caricatures of faith are part and parcel of life's wretchedness, and the infinite resignation has already consigned them to infinite contempt.

Abraham I cannot understand, in a certain sense there is nothing I can learn from him but astonishment. If people fancy that by considering the outcome of this story they might let themselves be moved to believe, they deceive themselves and want to swindle God out of the first movement of faith, the infinite resignation. They would suck worldly wisdom out of the paradox. Perhaps one or another may succeed in that, for our age is not willing to stop with faith, with its miracle of turning water into wine, it goes further, it turns wine into water. . . .

Gustave Flaubert (1821–1880)

LIFE: Except for a brief period reluctantly spent studying law in Paris, he lived as a writer, dedicating himself with a nervous and intense passion to the construction of a few books that might succeed in realizing his imaginative vision; neither the affair with Louise Colet, the poetess who encouraged him to recreate a bourgeois world he detested, nor the attacks of that world on his masterpiece, *Madame Bovary*, which was condemned as immoral, could disturb the monastic life he chose in fulfillment of his esthetic passion.

WORKS: *Madame Bovary* (first published serially in 1856, in book form in 1857); *Sentimental Education* (1869); *The Temptation of St. Anthony* (1874); *Three Tales* (1877); *Bouvard and Pécuchet* (1881).

MADAME BOVARY *

The Ball at La Vaubyessard †

The château, a modern building in the Italian style with two project-ing wings and three flights of steps in front of it, sprawled at the bot-tom end of a wide stretch of parkland, where cows grazed between ordered clumps of tall trees, and an assortment of green shrubs, rhodo-dendron, syringa and guelder-rose, bulged out unevenly over the wind-ing gravel drive. A stream ran under a bridge, and through the mist you could detect thatched buildings dotted about over the grassland, which was bounded on either side by a gently rising wooded slope, while among the groves behind the house, in two parallel lines, stood the coach-houses and stables, all that remained of the old château that had been pulled down.

Charles drove up to the middle flight of steps. Servants appeared. The Marquis came forward, offered his arm to the doctor's wife, and led her inside.

The hall was lofty, paved with marble, and it echoed footsteps and voices like a church. Facing the entrance was a straight staircase; on the left, overlooking the garden, a balcony led to the billiard-room, where the click of ivory balls met you as you opened the door. As she went through to the drawing-room, Emma saw round the table a group of dignified-looking gentlemen with cravats high up round their chins, all wearing decorations, and smiling silently as they made their stroke. On the dark wood panelling hung large gilt frames with names in black lettering on their lower borders. She read: "Jean Antoine d'Andervilliers d'Yverbonville, Comte de la Vaubyessard and Baron de la Fresnaye, killed at the Battle of Coutras, 20th October 1587." On another: "Jean Antoine Henry Guy d'Andervilliers de la Vaubyessard, Admiral of France and Knight of the Order of St Michael, wounded in the battle at La Hougue St Waast, 29th May 1692, died at La Vaubyessard 23rd January 1693." The ones that followed were barely discernible, for the lamplight was directed on to the green baize of the billiard-table, and cast round the rest of the room a flickering radiance that mellowed the hanging canvases and broke into delicate streaks where it fell on the cracks in the varnish. On all those great dark gold-framed rectangles were patches of paint that stood out brighter — a pale forehead, a pair of eyes that looked straight at you, red coats with perukes flowing down over powdery shoulders, the buckle of a garter above a plump calf.

The Marquis opened the door into the drawing-room. One of the

From *Madame Bovary*, translated by Alan Russell. Reprinted by permission of Penguin Books, Ltd.

* First published serially in 1856, and then as a book in 1857.
† From Part One, chapter 8. Emma Rouault has recently married Charles Bovary, a country doctor who does not satisfy her romantic passions, and is already yielding to self-pity when the Marquis d'Andervilliers, whom her husband had successfully treated for an abscess in the mouth, invites them to his home.

ladies rose; it was the Marchioness. She came forward to greet Emma, took her to sit beside her on an ottoman, and began talking as freely as if they were old friends. She was a woman of forty or so, with fine shoulders, a hooked nose and a drawling voice. Over her auburn hair she was wearing tonight a simple lace neckerchief that came down in a point at the back. A fair-haired young woman sat on a high-backed chair nearby, and round the fireplace gentlemen with little flowers in their button-holes stood talking to the ladies.

Dinner was at seven. The men, who were in the majority, sat down at the first table in the hall, the ladies at the second, in the dining-room, with their host and hostess.

As she went in, Emma felt herself plunged into a warm atmosphere compounded of the scent of flowers and of fine linen, of the savour of meat and the smell of truffles. The candles in the chandeliers glowed on the silver dish-covers with elongated flames. The pieces of cut glass had steamed over, and reflected a dull glimmer from one to the other. Bunches of flowers were set in a row down the whole length of the table, and on the wide-rimmed plates stood serviettes folded in the form of a bishop's mitre, each with an oval-shaped roll inside the fold. The red claws of the lobsters lay over the edge of the dishes. Luscious fruits were piled on moss in open baskets. The quails still had their feathers on them. The fumes rose. Solemn as a judge in his silk stockings and knee-breeches, his white cravat and frilled shirt, the major-domo handed the dishes, ready carved, between the guests' shoulders, and flicked the piece you chose on to your plate with his spoon. On the big porcelain stove with its copper rod, a statue of a woman draped to the chin stared fixedly at the roomful of people.

Madame Bovary noticed that several of the ladies had not put their gloves in their glasses.

At the top end of the table, alone among all these women, sat one aged man, crouched over his plate, with his serviette tied round his neck like a bib, dribbling gravy as he ate. His eyes were bloodshot, and he wore a little pigtail wound round with black ribbon. This was the Marquis' father-in-law, the old Duc de Laverdière, once favourite of the Comte d'Artois, in the days of the Marquis de Conflans' hunting-parties at La Vaudreuil; he was said to have been the lover of Marie Antoinette, between Messieurs de Coigny and de Lauzun. He had filled his life with riot and debauch, with duels, wagers and abductions; had squandered his wealth and been the terror of his family. He pointed to the dishes, mumbling, and a footman stationed behind him named them aloud in his ear. Emma's eyes kept turning in spite of themselves towards that old man with the drooping lips, as though to some august curiosity. He had lived at Court, had lain in the Queen's bed!

Iced champagne was served. Emma shivered all over at the cold taste of it in her mouth. She had never seen pomegranates before, or tasted a pineapple. Even the castor sugar looked finer and whiter than elsewhere.

After dinner the ladies went upstairs to get ready for the ball.

Emma dressed with the meticulous care of an actress making her début. She did her hair in the style her hairdresser had recommended, and put on her muslin dress, which had been laid out on the bed. Charles' trousers were too tight for him round his stomach.

"And these straps will be awkward for dancing," he said.

"Dancing?" said Emma.

"Yes!"

"Why, you must be off your head! They'd laugh at you! You stay in your seat! It's not quite the thing for a doctor to dance, anyhow," she added.

Charles relapsed into silence, then started pacing up and down, waiting for Emma to finish dressing.

He watched her from behind, in the mirror, between the two candles. Her black eyes looked blacker than ever. The braids of her hair, gently curving over her ears, had a rich blue lustre upon them, and in her chignon was a rose, trembling on its fragile stem, with artificial dewdrops at the tips of the leaves. Her dress was a pale saffron set off by three bunches of pompon roses and a spray of green. Charles came to kiss her on the shoulder.

"Let me alone!" she said. "You'll rumple me."

They heard a flourish from a violin, then the note of a horn. She descended the stairs, resisting an impulse to run.

The dancing had started. Guests were arriving, and the hall was crowded. She sat down on a little settee just inside the door.

When the quadrille was over, the floor was left to the men, who stood talking in groups, and the liveried servants bringing round large trays. Along the row of seated women went a fluttering of painted fans. Smiling faces were half hidden behind bouquets, gold-stoppered scent-bottles twirled in cupped hands whose white gloves showed the outline of finger-nails, and pinched the flesh at the wrist. Lace frills, diamond brooches, medallion bracelets, trembled on their bodices, gleamed on their breasts, jingled on their bare arms. On their hair, which was stuck down firmly on their foreheads and coiled up at the nape of the neck, were forget-me-nots, jasmine, pomegranate-blossom, wheatears or corn-flowers, in garlands, bunches or sprays. Red turbans crowned the wry-faced matrons who sat immovably in their seats.

Emma's heart beat a little faster when, her partner holding her by the tips of her fingers, she took her place in line and waited for the sweep of the fiddler's bow to start them off. Her nervousness soon vanished, and away she went, swaying to the rhythm of the orchestra, gently nodding her head as she glided forward. A smile rose to her lips at certain subtleties from the violin, playing solo. When the rest of the instruments were silent, you could hear the gold coins clinking on the baize tables in the next room. Then they all joined in again, the cornet blew a rousing blast, the dancers picked up the time, skirts swelled out and brushed together, hands were caught and released, eyes that lowered before you came back again to fix themselves on yours.

Scattered among the dancers, or talking in the doorways, were some dozen or more men, of twenty-five to forty, who were distinguishable from the rest of the crowd by a family likeness, which cut across all differences of age, dress or appearance. Their coats looked better cut, from finer cloth, and their hair, brought forward over the forehead in ringlets, seemed to glisten with more delicate pomades. They had the complexion of wealth, that clear white skin which is accentuated by the pallor of porcelain, the shimmer of satin, the "finish" on handsome furniture, and is maintained at its best by a modest diet of the most exquisite foods. Their necks moved freely in low cravats, their long side-whiskers rested upon turn-down collars, the handkerchiefs with which they wiped their lips were embroidered with large monograms and emitted a delicious scent. The older among them retained a youthful air, while the young ones revealed a certain maturity. Their nonchalant glances reflected the quietude of passions daily gratified; behind their gentleness of manner one could detect that peculiar brutality inculcated by dominance in not over-exacting activities such as exercise strength and flatter vanity — the handling of thoroughbreds and the pursuit of wantons.

A few paces from Emma, a gentleman in a blue coat was talking about Italy to a pale young woman with an ornament of pearls. They extolled the size of the pillars in St Peter's; then Tivoli and Vesuvius, Castellamare and the Cascine, the roses of Genoa and the Coliseum by moonlight. With her other ear, Emma was listening to a conversation full of words she didn't understand. In the centre of a group was a youth who the week before had beaten Miss Arabella and Romulus and won two thousand pounds jumping a ditch in England. One man complained about his racers getting fat, another of the way the printers had garbled his horse's name.

It was stuffy in the ballroom. The lamps were dimming. There was a general movement into the billiard-room. A servant climbing up on a chair broke a couple of window-panes; at the sound of the glass smashing, Madame Bovary turned, and caught sight of some peasants outside, with their faces pressed to the window. It reminded her of Les Bertaux: she saw the farmhouse and the muddy pond, her father in his smock beneath the apple-trees, and herself back in the dairy again, skimming cream off the milk with her fingers. But her past life, till now so clear in her mind, had begun to slip right away from her amid the splendours of the present moment; she could not be quite sure it had ever happened. Here she was, at the ball. Outside, over everything else, hung a dark veil. She was eating a maraschino ice, holding the silver-gilt shell in her hand, half-closing her eyes as she put the spoon to her lips.

A lady sitting near her dropped her fan as a gentleman passed.

"Would you be so kind, sir," said she, "as to pick up my fan from behind this sofa?"

The gentleman bowed, and as he reached for the fan Emma saw the young lady's hand drop a little white triangular object into his hat. He retrieved the fan and presented it to her respectfully. She inclined her head in thanks and buried her nose in her bouquet.

After supper — at which Spanish wines and Rhine wines flowed freely, accompanied by shell-fish soup and milk-of-almond soup, Trafalgar puddings, and every variety of cold meat, in trembling aspic — the carriages began to move off in ones and twos. If you drew aside the edge of the muslin curtain you could see the lamps gliding away into the darkness. The settees emptied; but some of the card-players still sat on. The musicians moistened the tips of their fingers on their tongues. Charles leaned against a door, half-asleep.

At three in the morning the cotillion began. Emma didn't know how to waltz. Everyone was waltzing, Mademoiselle d'Andervilliers herself, and the Marchioness. There remained now only the dozen guests who were staying the night at the château.

One of the men, who was familiarly addressed as "Viscount" and wore a very low-cut waistcoat that looked as if it had been moulded upon him, came up and repeated his request to Madame Bovary, promising to guide her, and insisting that she would manage it successfully.

They started slowly, then got faster. They turned, and everything turned round them — the lamps and chairs, the panelling, the parquet floor — like a disc on a pivot. As they swept past a door, Emma's skirt swirled out against her partner's trousers. Their legs intertwined. He looked down at her and she looked up at him; a numb feeling came over her, she stopped still. Then they were off again, and the Viscount whirled her away still faster, till they were out of sight at the end of the gallery. She was panting for breath, she nearly fell, for an instant she leaned her head on his chest. Still turning, but more gently, he brought her back to her seat. She sank back against the wall and covered her eyes with her hands.

When she opened them again, there was a lady sitting on a footstool in the centre of the floor, with three gentlemen kneeling at her feet; she chose the Viscount, and the violin struck up again.

All eyes were upon them. Round and round they went, she holding her body quite stiff, with her head lowered, he all the while in the same pose, shoulders square, elbow rounded, chin well forward. And how that woman could waltz! They went on and on, and tired out everyone else.

After a few more minutes' conversation, the house-party said goodnight, or rather good-morning, and went to bed.

Charles dragged himself upstairs clinging to the bannisters; his legs were ready to drop off. He had been standing upright by the whisttables for five hours on end, watching the play without knowing what it was all about; and it was with a deep sigh of relief that he pulled off his boots.

Emma slipped a shawl over her shoulders, opened the window and leaned out.

It was a dark night. A few drops of rain were falling. She breathed the moist wind, and felt it cool on her eyelids. The dance music was still strumming in her ears. She strained to keep awake and so prolong the spell of this luxurious life she must so soon abandon.

Day began to break. She looked long at the windows of the château, trying to guess whereabouts all the people were whom she had noticed during the evening. She would have liked to know all about them, to enter into their lives, become involved in them.

But she was shivering with cold. She undressed and huddled up against Charles, who was already asleep.

There was a large party at breakfast, which lasted only ten minutes, and at which no liqueurs were served, to the doctor's surprise. Afterwards Mademoiselle d'Andervilliers gathered up the remains of the rolls in a basket and took them to the swans in the lake, while the guests strolled round the greenhouses, where fantastic bristly plants rose up in pyramids beneath hanging vases which, with their long green intertwining tendrils falling over the edge, looked like overcrowded snakes'-nests. From the orangery at the far end a covered way led to the outhouses. To amuse the young woman, the Marquis took her to look at the stables. Above the basket-shaped racks porcelain slabs gave the names of the horses in black lettering. Each of the animals stirred in its stall as you went past and clicked your tongue. The boards of the saddle-room glittered to the eye like a parquet floor. The coach harness stood in the middle on two revolving posts, and bits and whips and stirrups and curbs were arrayed along the wall.

Meanwhile Charles went to ask one of the grooms to put his horse to. The trap was brought round to the front, and when all the luggage had been stowed in, the Bovarys took leave of their host and hostess, and set off for home.

Emma sat silent, watching the wheels go round. Charles, perched right on the edge of the seat, drove with the reins held wide apart, and the little horse ambled gently along in the shafts, which were too wide for it. The slack reins jogging against its rump grew wet with foam, and the box roped on behind kept up a steady bumping against the body of the trap.

They had reached the high ground at Thibourville when suddenly a number of horsemen appeared in front of them and passed by, laughing, with cigars in their mouths. Emma thought she recognised the Viscount. She turned and looked back, but all she saw against the sky was a group of heads bobbing up and down in the varying tempo of trot or gallop.

A mile further on the breech-band snapped, and they had to stop and tie it together.

As he was giving the harness a final glance, Charles noticed something lying on the ground between the horse's feet. He picked up a cigar-case, with a green silk border all round it and a coat of arms in the centre, like a carriage-door.

"A couple of cigars inside, too," he said. "They'll do for after dinner tonight."

"You smoke, then?" she asked.

"Sometimes. When I get the chance."

He pocketed his find and whipped up the nag.

When they reached home, dinner was not ready. Madame flew into a rage. Nastasie answered back.

"Leave the room!" said Emma. "The impertinence! You're dismissed!"

For dinner there was onion soup and a piece of veal cooked with sorrel. Charles, seated opposite Emma, rubbed his hands together gleefully.

"It's good to be home again!" he said.

They could hear Nastasie crying. The poor old girl had kept him company many a long evening after his first wife died, and he was fond of her. She was his first patient and oldest acquaintance in the place.

"Have you really given her notice?" he said at last.

"Yes. Why shouldn't I?"

They warmed themselves in the kitchen while the bedroom was being got ready. Charles lit one of the cigars; he smoked with his lips rounded, spitting at each instant, recoiling at every puff.

"You'll make yourself ill," she said scornfully.

Suddenly he put the cigar down and ran out to swallow a glass of cold water at the pump. Emma snatched up the cigar-case and hurled it to the back of the cupboard.

The next day went, oh, so slowly! She walked round the garden, up and down the same few paths, stopping in front of the flower-beds or the fruit-wall or the plaster *curé*, staring in bewilderment at all these old familiar things. How far away the ball seemed already! Why should there be such a gulf between Wednesday morning and Friday evening? The visit to La Vaubyessard had made a gap in her life, like those great chasms that a mountain-storm will sometimes scoop out in a single night. But she resigned herself to the inevitable. Reverently she put away in the chest of drawers her lovely dress and her satin slippers, the soles of which were yellowed with the wax from the dance floor. Her heart was like that. Contact with riches had left upon it a coating that would never wear off.

And so it gave Emma something to do, to think about the ball. Each time Wednesday came round she woke saying to herself, "A week ago . . . Two weeks ago . . . Three weeks ago, I was there!" Gradually faces blurred in her memory, she forgot the dance tunes, no longer saw the liveried servants and the big rooms so clearly: some of the details vanished, but her yearning for it all remained.

The Agricultural Show *

The famous Show did indeed arrive. From early morning on the great day the village folk had been standing at their doors discussing the preparations. The façade of the Town Hall was festooned with ivy, a marquee had been erected in one of the meadows, and in the middle of the market-place, opposite the church, stood a kind of cannon that was to announce the arrival of the Prefect and salute the successful competitors. The militia from Buchy — there was none at Yonville — had come to augment the fire-brigade, captained by Binet.[1] He wore an even higher collar than usual to-day; and, buttoned tight into his uniform, the upper part of his body was so stiff and motionless that it seemed as if all the life in him had descended to his legs, which rose and fell with wooden exactitude as he marked time. A certain rivalry existed between the tax-collector and the colonel of the militia, and to display their talents they drilled their men separately. Red epaulettes and black breastplates crossed and recrossed alternately, starting off again and again, never ending. Never had there been such a parade! A number of citizens had washed their houses overnight; tricolours hung from open windows; all the inns were full. In the fine weather, starched bonnets, gold crosses and coloured neckerchiefs stood out dazzling as snow, glittering in the bright sunshine, relieving with their scattered motley the sombre monotony of the frock-coats and blue smocks. The farmers' wives from the surrounding district had tucked their dresses up, to avoid getting them splashed, with thick pins which they removed on dismounting. Their menfolk were concerned rather with their hats, covering them with their pocket-handkerchiefs, one corner of which they held between their teeth.

The crowds were flocking into the main street from both ends of the village, pouring out of lanes and byways and houses. Now and then a door-knocker banged back behind a lady in cotton gloves who was stepping out to see the sights. The principal attraction was a pair of long stands covered with fairy lights, flanking the platform on which the authorities were to sit. And against each of the four pillars of the Town Hall stood a pole bearing a little dark-green pennant emblazoned with an inscription in gold lettering. One said "Trade," another "Agriculture," the third "Industry" and the fourth "The Arts."

However, the jubilation that beamed on every face seemed to cast a cloud upon Madame Lefrançois at the "Lion." She stood on her kitchen steps muttering under her breath.

"Tomfoolery! A lot of tomfoolery, with their tent thing! I suppose they imagine the Prefect'll enjoy having his dinner down there under canvas, like a circus clown? And all that nonsense is — 'for the good of the district.' . . . Then why go and get that bottle-washer of theirs

---

* From Part Two, chapter 8. Emma and Charles have moved to Yonville-L'Abbaye, a small town twenty-four miles from Rouen, and there her self-indulgent boredom leads her into a flirtation (and eventually an affair) with Rodolphe Boulanger, "thirty-four years old, hard of heart and shrewd of head, with much experience and understanding of women."
1. The tax-collector.

all the way from Neufchâtel? And who's it for, anyway — a lot of cowherds and ragamuffins. . . ."

The chemist [2] came in sight. He was wearing a dress-coat and nankeen trousers, beaver shoes and, unusually for him, a hat — a hat with a low crown.

"How d'ye do!" he called. "You'll excuse me, I'm in a hurry."

The stout widow asked where he was going.

"Aha, surprised to see me out? A man who's for ever poked away in his laboratory, like the rat in the old chap's cheese!"

"What cheese?" said the landlady.

"Oh, nothing, nothing," answered Homais, "I was merely trying to convey to you, Madame Lefrançois, that in the ordinary course of things I am quite a recluse. Today being a special occasion, however, I have to . . ."

"Ah, that's where you're going!" she said with an air of scorn.

"Why, yes!" replied the chemist in astonishment. "Am I not a member of the committee?"

Widow Lefrançois stared at him a moment and then replied with a smile:

"Oh, I see! But how do you come to be mixed up with farming? Do you know anything about it?"

"Certainly I do. I am a chemist. And chemistry being, Madame Lefrançois, the study of the reciprocal molecular action of all natural bodies, it follows that agriculture falls within its sphere! After all — composition of manures, fermentation of liquids, analysis of gases, effect of miasmas — what is all that, I ask you, but chemistry pure and simple?"

The landlady made no answer.

"Do you think," Homais continued, "that you need actually till the soil or fatten fowls yourself to be an agriculturist? No: it's the chemical composition of the relevant substances that you must know about, the geological deposits, atmospheric effects, soil properties, properties of minerals and rain-water, the varying densities of bodies, their capillary attraction and so on and so forth. Then you must have your principles of hygiene off thoroughly, in order to supervise and criticise the construction of buildings, the feeding of your livestock, the provisioning of your men! Furthermore, Madame Lefrançois, you must master botany! Be able to tell one plant from another, you follow me? Know which ones are beneficial and which deleterious, which unproductive and which nutritive, whether you'd do well to pull them up here and reset them there, to propagate some and destroy others. In short, you've got to keep abreast of science in the pamphlets and published papers, and always be on the alert, to point out improvements. . . ."

The landlady was gazing steadfastly at the door of the Café Français.

2. Homais.

"Would to heaven our farmers were trained chemists," Homais proceeded, "or at least paid more attention to scientific teaching! You know, I myself recently wrote a striking little work, a treatise of over seventy-two pages, entitled 'Cider: its Manufacture and Operation; with some original observations thereon,' and I sent it up to the Agricultural Society of Rouen. It earned me the distinction of being admitted to membership of that body, in the Agricultural Section, Pomology Sub-section. Well, now, if my work had only been given to the general public . . ."

The chemist paused, noting the landlady's air of preoccupation.

"Look at 'em!" she said. "It's beyond everything! A cookshop like that!"

And with a shrugging of her shoulders, that pulled her jumper up over her bosom, she pointed with both hands to her rival's establishment, whence issued the sound of singing.

"Well, it won't be for long now," she added. "Another week'll see the end of it!"

Homais stepped back in amazement. She came down the three steps and spoke in his ear:

"D'you mean to say you've not heard? The bailiffs are going in this week. Lheureux's selling him up. He's been the death of 'em with his bills."

"What a shocking tragedy!" exclaimed the chemist, who always had the right form of words for every conceivable occasion.

The landlady proceeded to tell him what had happened. She had heard it from Théodore, the man at Monsieur Guillaumin's. Much as she abominated Tellier, she censured Lheureux; he was a wheedling, grovelling creature.

"Hullo, there he is!" she said. "Going through the market! He's bowing to Madame Bovary. She's got a green hat on: and look, she's on Monsieur Boulanger's arm!"

"Madame Bovary!" exclaimed Homais. "I must run and pay her my respects. She might like to have a seat in the enclosure, under the peristyle."

And turning a deaf ear to the rest of the Widow Lefrançois' story, the chemist hurried off, with a smile on his lips, a jaunty stride, and any number of bowings in all directions, taking up a great deal of space with the long tails of his dress-coat flapping in the breeze behind him.

Rodolphe had noticed him from a distance and quickened his pace, but as Madame Bovary got out of breath, he slowed up again, smiling at her as he explained brusquely:

"That was to escape from the heavy fellow — you know, the chemist."

She gave him a nudge.

"What's the meaning of that?" he asked himself, and as he walked along he surveyed her out of the corner of his eye.

Her calm profile gave no hint. It showed clear in the light, framed in the oval of her bonnet, which was tied with pale reed-like ribbons. She was looking straight in front of her, beneath her long curving lashes, and though her eyes were fully open they appeared slightly narrowed because of the blood that pulsated gently beneath the fine skin that covered her cheek-bones. Where her nostrils met was a pale pink glow. Her head leaned a little to one side, and between her parted lips you saw the pearly tips of her white teeth.

"Is she laughing at me?" Rodolphe wondered.

Emma's nudge had been simply a warning, however. Monsieur Lheureux was walking along beside them. Every now and then he made some conversational remark, such as "What a glorious day!" "Everybody's out of doors!" "The wind's in the east!"

Madame Bovary took as little notice of his advances as did Rodolphe, though the draper came sidling up to them at their least movement, touching his hat and saying, "Beg pardon?"

Outside the blacksmith's, instead of keeping on up to the gate along the roadway, Rodolphe turned abruptly down a side-path, drawing Madame Bovary with him.

"Farewell, Monsieur Lheureux!" he called out. "Till we meet again!"

"How you got rid of him!" she said with a laugh.

"Why let people hang on to one?" he answered. "And to-day, when I'm fortunate enough to be with you . . ."

Emma blushed. He left the sentence unfinished, and started talking about the lovely weather, and the delight of walking on the grass.

Some daisies were growing there.

"What pretty daisies!" he said. "Oracles in plenty for all the local girls in love! . . . Suppose I pick one," he added. "What do you say?"

"Are *you* in love?" she asked, with a little cough.

"Eh! eh! who knows?" answered Rodolphe.

The show-ground was beginning to fill up, and the women helpers kept bumping into you with their big umbrellas, their baskets and their babies. You had frequently to be getting out of the way of a long row of peasant-girls, maidservants in blue stockings and flat shoes, with silver rings on their fingers, who smelt of milk when you came close to them. They spread out hand in hand all across the field, from the row of aspens up to the marquee. By now the judging was due to start, and one after another the farmers were filing into a kind of arena marked off by a long rope hung on stakes.

Inside were the animals, their muzzles towards the rope, their rumps jostling together in a rough line. Somnolent pigs sank their snouts in the ground, calves lowed, sheep bleated, cows sprawled their bellies out on the grass, with one leg bent beneath them, and chewed with deliberation, blinking their heavy eyelids as the midges buzzed round them. Shirt-sleeved wagoners were holding the restive stallions, which kept neighing vociferously in the direction of the mares. These stood quite quiet, stretching out their necks, their manes drooping, while their foals rested in their shadows, or came up from time to time to suck. Above the undulating line of massed beasts, you saw a white mane ruffling up like a wave in the breeze, a pair of sharp horns jutting out, or the heads of some men running. Outside the arena, a hundred yards farther on, a big black bull stood apart, muzzled, with an iron ring through its nostrils, moving no more than an animal of bronze. A ragged child held it by a rope.

Sundry gentlemen were now advancing with heavy tread between the two rows of animals, examining each in turn and then conferring together in low tones. One, who looked more important than the rest, made jottings in a notebook as he went. This was the chairman of the judges, Monsieur Derozerays de la Panville. The minute he recognised Rodolphe he stepped briskly towards him.

"What's this, Monsieur Boulanger?" he said, with a pleasant smile. "Are you deserting us?"

Rodolphe assured him he was coming directly. But when the chairman was once more out of earshot he said, "I think not! When I can be with you!"

While ridiculing the Show, Rodolphe nevertheless produced his blue ticket, so that they could move about wherever they pleased, and he even halted occasionally in front of one of the fine "exhibits." Noticing, however, that Madame Bovary was unimpressed by these, he started making fun of the Yonville ladies and the way they were turned out. He apologised for being so carelessly dressed himself. His clothes were an incongruous mixture of the workaday and the elegant, such as is taken by the vulgar to denote an eccentric way of life, an emotional disturbance, or a subservience to aesthetics, combined always with a certain contempt for convention, by which they are either fascinated or exasperated. Frilly at the cuffs, his cambric shirt fluttered out in front between the revers of his grey drill waistcoat wherever the breeze took it. His broad-striped trousers terminated at the ankle above a pair of nankeen boots vamped with patent leather. These were so highly polished that you could see the grass in them; and in them he went trampling over the horse-dung, with one hand in his jacket pocket, his straw hat tilted to the side of his head.

"But then, when you live in the country . . ." he added.

". . . There's no point in bothering," said Emma.

"Exactly!" Rodolphe replied. "Just fancy, there's not one of all these good people who's capable of understanding so much as the cut of a coat."

They spoke of the dullness of the country, the lives that were smothered by it, the illusions that perished there.

"That's why," said Rodolphe, "I'm sinking into such a state of gloom. . . ."

"You!" she exclaimed in surprise. "Why, I thought you were a very cheerful person."

"Oh, on the surface, yes. I wear my jester's mask in public. But how often I've looked at a graveyard in the moonlight and wondered whether I wouldn't be better off lying there asleep with the rest of them!"

"Oh! But what about your friends?" she said. "Don't you think of them?"

"My friends? What friends? Have I got any? Is there anyone who cares about me?" — and he accompanied these last words with a little hissing sound.

However, they had to step aside for a man coming up behind them with an immense scaffolding of chairs. He was so loaded that you could see nothing of him but the toes of his sabots and the tips of his outstretched arms. It was Lestiboudois the sexton, carting round the church chairs among the crowd. Full of ideas where his own interests were concerned, he had hit upon this method of turning the Show to account; and his enterprise was rewarded, for he had more customers than he could cope with. The villagers, feeling the warmth, had actually started squabbling over those straw seats that reeked of incense; and against their stout backs, covered with blobs of candle-grease, they were leaning with a certain awe.

Madame Bovary took Rodolphe's arm again.

"Yes," he went on as though to himself, "I've missed a lot, always being alone. If only I'd had some aim in life. If I'd met with affection. If I'd found someone . . . Oh, I'd have used all the energy I possessed — conquered everything, smashed down every obstacle."

"It doesn't seem to me you've got much to grumble about," said Emma.

"You think not?"

"After all, you're free" — she hesitated — "and rich."

"You're laughing at me!" he exclaimed.

She assured him she was not. As she spoke, they heard the boom of a cannon. Everybody at once started rushing back to the village.

It was a false alarm; there was no sign of the Prefect. The judges were in a quandary: should they wait, or open the proceedings?

At last, from the far end of the square, appeared a large hired landau drawn by a pair of skinny horses, which were being roundly lashed by a coachman in a white hat. Binet just had time to shout "Fall in!" and the Colonel to follow suit. There was a dive for the piled rifles. In the commotion, some of the men forgot to fasten their collars. The official equipage seemed to divine their discomfiture, however, for the pair of hacks slowed up, tugging at their chain, and ambled to a halt outside the Town Hall, just as the militia and the fire-brigade were deploying to the beat of the drums.

"Mark time!" shouted Binet.

"Halt!" shouted the Colonel. "Into line — left — turn!"

After a "Present arms," in which the smacking of the bands came rattling out like a copper kettle rolling downstairs, all the rifles were lowered again.

Thereupon a gentleman in a short silver-trimmed jacket was seen to step out of the carriage. He was bald in front and tufted behind, sallow-complexioned, and with an appearance of the utmost benignity. He narrowed his large heavy-lidded eyes to scan the crowd, lifted his pointed nose in the air and set a smile on his sunken mouth. Recognising the Mayor by his sash, he explained that the Prefect had been prevented from coming. He himself was an official on the Prefect's staff. He added a few words of apology. Tuvache responded in complimentary terms. The visitor declared himself overwhelmed. So they stood there face to face, their foreheads almost touching, surrounded by the judges, the councillors, the important personages, the militia, and the crowd at large. Holding his little black three-cornered hat against his chest, the great man reiterated his greetings, while Tuvache, bent like a bow, smiled back at him, stuttering and stammering and making protestation of his loyalty to the throne and his appreciation of the honour that was being done to Yonville.

Hippolyte, the groom from the inn, came limping up on his club-foot to take the reins from the coachman, and led the horses off beneath the archway of the Golden Lion, where a crowd of peasants gathered round to inspect the carriage. There was a tattoo on the drums, the howitzer thundered, and the gentlemen filed up and took their places on the platform, in the easy-chairs of red Utrecht velvet lent by Madame Tuvache.

A homogeneous group they were, with their soft, fair, slightly tanned faces, the colour of new cider, and their bushy whiskers sticking out above tall stiff collars supported by white cravats tied in a floppy bow. Every one of the waistcoats had velvet revers, every watch carried an oval cornelian seal at the end of a long band. Hands all rested on thighs, carefully lifting the creases of their trousers, which were of unsponged cloth and shone more brilliantly than their stout leather boots.

The ladies of the party kept at the back, between the pillars in the vestibule, while the body of the crowd faced them, standing up, or seated on Lestiboudois' chairs. For he had brought a load along with him from the meadow, and was all the while running off to get more from the church, causing such congestion with his trade that one had great difficulty in reaching the platform steps.

"I think myself," said Monsieur Lheureux to the chemist, as the latter passed along to take his seat, "that they ought to have put up a couple of Venetian masts, with something rich and a bit severe in the way of draping. It would have made a fine sight."

"Certainly it would," answered Homais. "But there, what can you expect? The Mayor *would* do the whole thing on his own. Poor old Tuvache, he hasn't got much taste; in fact, he's completely lacking in any sort of artistic sense."

Meanwhile Rodolphe and Madame Bovary had gone up to the Council Chamber on the first floor of the Town Hall. It was empty, and so he declared that they would be able to enjoy the spectacle in comfort up there. Fetching three stools from the oval table under the bust of the King, he placed them by one of the windows, and they sat down side by side.

There was a great commotion on the platform, much whispering and parleying, and at last the Prefect's deputy rose. His name, now known to be Lieuvain, was being passed round among the crowd. After collecting his papers together and holding them close up to his eyes to see them better, he began:

"Gentlemen,

"Let me first be permitted, before addressing you on the object of our gathering here to-day — and this sentiment will, I am sure, be shared by all of you — let me be permitted, I say, to pay fitting tribute to the Authorities, to the Government and, gentlemen, to our beloved Monarch and Sovereign Lord the King, to whom no branch of public or private prosperity is indifferent, and who steers the chariot of state with a hand at once so firm and so wise, amid the ceaseless perils of a stormy sea — who knows, moreover, how to gain respect for peace no less than for war — for Trade and for Industry, for Agriculture and for the Arts."

"I ought to get a bit farther back," said Rodolphe.

"Why?" said Emma.

But at that moment the official's voice rose to a remarkable pitch as he declaimed:

"Those days are past, gentlemen, when civil discord stained our public places with blood, when landowner, merchant, and working-man alike, as they courted peaceful slumbers, would tremble lest they be awakened by the clang of the tocsin; when the most subversive slogans were aimed in all audacity at the very foundations — "

"They might see me from down there," Rodolphe explained, "and then I'd have to spend a fortnight apologising. And with my bad reputation . . ."

"What a thing to say about yourself!"

"No, no, it's abominable, I assure you."

"However, gentlemen," the speaker proceeded, "if, driving those sombre pictures from my mind, I turn my gaze now to the present state of our fair land, what do I see? Everywhere, trade and the arts flourish. Everywhere new paths of communication, new arteries within the body politic, are opening up new contacts. Our great manufacturing centres thrive once more. Religion finds new strength and smiles in every heart. Our ports are full. Confidence returns. At last France breathes again!"

"Though I dare say I deserve it by ordinary standards," Rodolphe added.

"How is that?" she asked.

"Why, do you not know that there are souls for ever in turmoil? Souls that must have dream and action turn and turn about — a passion of utter purity, and an orgy of self-indulgence? It leads one into all kinds of adventures and escapades."

She gazed at him then as one might gaze at a traveller who has journeyed through strange lands.

"We poor women haven't even that diversion," she remarked.

"Sorry diversion, for it never brings happiness."

"Does anything?"

"Yes," he answered, "it comes along one day."

"And this," the distinguished visitor was saying, "this you have realised, you who cultivate the land and labour in the fields, peaceable pioneers in a true task of civilisation! Progressive and high-minded men! You have realised, I say, that the storms of political strife are, in very truth, more devastating than the riot of the elements!"

"It comes along one day," Rodolphe repeated, "all of a sudden, just when you are despairing of it. Then, new vistas open. It's as if a voice cried out 'Behold!' You feel you must reveal yourself, give everything, sacrifice everything, to that person. Nothing need be said. You know! You have seen each other in your dreams" — and his eyes rested on hers. "There before you, shining, sparkling, is the treasure you have sought so long. Still you doubt. You dare not believe. You stand dazed as if you had stepped out of darkness into light."

Here Rodolphe helped out his words with motions, passing his hand over his face like a man in a trance. Then he let it fall on Emma's. She withdrew hers. The official read on:

"And who can wonder at it, gentlemen? Only he who remains so blind, so immersed, so deeply immersed, I do not fear to say, in the prejudices of a past age, as still to misconceive the spirit of our agricultural communities. Where, indeed, can one find more patriotism than in the country, more devotion to the common weal, in a word, more intelligence? I do not mean, gentlemen, a superficial intelligence — that vain embellishment of idle minds — but a profound and balanced intelligence that applies itself first and foremost to the pursuit of useful ends, contributing thus to the good of each, to the general advancement, and to the upholding of the State — the fruit of respect for law and fulfilment of duty!"

"Duty again!" said Rodolphe. "Always on about duty. I'm sick to death of the word. What a lot of flannel-waistcoated old fogeys they are, pious old women with beads and bedsocks, for ever twittering in our ears about 'Duty, duty!' To feel nobly and to love what is beautiful — that's our duty. Not to accept all the conventions of society and the humiliations society imposes on us."

"Still . . . all the same . . ." Madame Bovary demurred.

"No! Why inveigh against the passions? Are they not the one beautiful thing there is on earth; the source of all heroism and enthusiasm, poetry, music, art, everything?"

"All the same," said Emma, "we must take some notice of what the world thinks, and conform to its morality."

"But you see, there are two moralities," he replied. "One is the petty, conventional morality of men, clamorous, ever-changing, that flounders about on the ground, of the earth earthy, like that mob of nincompoops down there. The other, the eternal morality, is all about and above us, like the countryside that surrounds us and the blue heavens that give us light."

Monsieur Lieuvain had just wiped his mouth with his handkerchief. He resumed:

"Now what should I be doing here, gentlemen, demonstrating the usefulness of farming to *you*? Who supplies our wants, who provides us with the means of life, but the farmer? The farmer, gentlemen, who, sowing with laborious hand the fertile furrows of our countryside, brings forth the corn which, crushed and ground by ingenious machinery, issues thence in the guise of flour, to be conveyed to our cities and speedily delivered to the baker, who makes it into a food for rich and poor alike. Is it not the farmer, again, who fattens his rich flocks to give us clothes? How should we clothe, or feed, ourselves were it not for the farmer? Nay, gentlemen, need we go even so far afield for our examples? Who has not frequently pondered on the great importance to us of that homely animal, the adornment of our poultry-yards, that provides us with soft pillows to sleep on, succulent flesh for our tables, and eggs? — But I could go on for ever enumerating, one by one, the various products that the well-tended earth lavishes like a bountiful mother upon her children. Here the vine, there the cider apple, elsewhere colza, cheese, or flax — gentlemen, let us not forget flax! — which has made such strides in recent years, and to which I would more especially draw your attention."

He had no need to draw it, for the multitude sat open-mouthed to drink in his words. Tuvache, next to him, listened with staring eyes. Monsieur Derozerays gently closed his now and then. Farther along, the chemist, with his son Napoléon between his knees, had his hand cupped behind his ear so as not to lose a single syllable. The rest of the judges nodded their chins slowly up and down in their waistcoats to signify assent. The fire-brigade leaned on their bayonet-scabbards at the foot of the platform, and Binet stood motionless, his elbow stuck out, the point of his sabre in the air. He may have heard, but he could not have seen anything for the visor of his helmet, which came right down over his nose. His lieutenant, Monsieur Tuvache's youngest son, had his visor at a still more exaggerated angle. He was wearing an enormous helmet that wobbled on top of his head and allowed one end of his calico handkerchief to slip down behind. He smiled beneath it with a perfectly child-like sweetness, and his little white face, running with sweat, wore an expression of enjoyment, exhaustion and somnolence.

The crowd stretched right across to the houses on the far side of the square. There were people leaning out of every window, standing in every doorway. Justin, outside the chemist's shop, seemed quite transfixed by the sight that met his eyes. In spite of the silence, Monsieur Lieuvain's voice failed to carry in the air, and reached you only in fragmentary phrases, drowned here and there by the scraping of

chairs among the crowd. Then all of a sudden you heard the long low-
ing of a bullock behind you, or lambs bleating to each other at the
corners of the streets. They had been driven down by the shepherds
and cowherds, and gave voice from time to time as their tongues
snatched at a morsel of foliage hanging above their muzzles.

Rodolphe had drawn closer to Emma and was talking rapidly in a
low voice.

"Doesn't this conspiracy of society revolt you? Is there a single
feeling it does not condemn? The noblest instincts, the purest sympathies, are reviled and persecuted, and if ever two poor souls do meet,
then everything is organised to prevent their union. They'll attempt it
all the same, they'll flap their wings and call to one another. And no
matter what happens, sooner or later, in six months or ten years, they'll
meet again and love — because Fate ordains it, because they were born
for one another."

He sat with his arms folded on his knees. Raising his eyes to Emma's,
he gazed at her closely, fixedly. She saw little gleams of gold playing
about his dark pupils. She was near enough to him to smell the cream
on his glossy hair. She felt limp, she remembered the Viscount who
had waltzed with her at La Vaubyessard: his beard had exhaled that
same perfume of lemon and vanilla. Mechanically her eyelids narrowed
as she breathed in the scent. She straightened up in her chair, and as
she did so she caught a glimpse, right away on the farthest horizon,
of the ancient *Hirondelle* slowly descending Leux Hill, trailing a long
plume of dust behind it. It was in that yellow coach that Léon [3] had so
often come back to her; and along that road that he had gone from
her for ever. She had a vision of him at his window across the way.
Then everything blurred, the sky clouded over, and it seemed to her
that she was still circling in the waltz, in the glare of the chandeliers,
on the Viscount's arm, and Léon was not far away, he was just coming. . . . But all the while she was conscious of Rodolphe's face beside
her. Her old desires became imbued with the sweetness of the present
sensation, and, on this subtle breath of perfume that was being shed
upon her soul, they were tossed about like grains of sand in a gust of
wind. Her nostrils dilated rapidly, vigorously, breathing in the freshness of the ivy round the tops of the columns. She took off her gloves,
wiped her hands, fanned her face with her handkerchief, while through
the throbbing at her temples she could hear the hum of the crowd
below and the speaker still droning out his singsong.

"Keep steadily ahead!" he was saying. "Listen neither to the voice
of hidebound habit nor to the impulsive counsels of rash experiment!
Work above all at the improvement of the soil, at producing rich fer-
tilisers, at breeding fine horses and cattle, fine sheep and pigs! Let this
Agricultural Show be a peaceful arena where victor extends the hand
of brotherhood to vanquished and wishes him success next time! . . .

3. Léon Depuis is a young clerk who was too timid and unsure of himself to take advantage of
Emma's boredom when she first arrived at Yonville. He has left for Paris.

And now, to all those venerable retainers, lowly servants whose laborious toils have never before been recognised by any Government, I say: Come forward and receive the meed of your silent virtues! Rest assured that from this day forth the State will never lose sight of you, that it will encourage and protect you, will satisfy your just demands, and lighten, so far as in it lies, the painful burden of your sacrifice!"

And Monsieur Lieuvain sat down.

Monsieur Derozerays rose and began his speech. This was far less ornate than the official's, and recommended itself by a more positive flavour — a matter of more specialised knowledge and more exalted reflections. Eulogistic reference to the Government had less place in it, farming and religion had more. The bond that existed between the two was made clear — they had always worked together for civilisation . . . While Rodolphe was talking to Madame Bovary about dreams, presentiments and magnetic attraction, the speaker went back to the infancy of society, to those savage times when men lived on acorns in the heart of great forests; from which he passed on to the period at which they had given up animals' skins for a covering of cloth, had ploughed the land and planted the vine. Now was this an improvement? Were there not perhaps more disadvantages than advantages in these discoveries? Monsieur Derozerays asked himself the question. Rodolphe had led on gradually from magnetism to affinities; and while the Chairman alluded to Cincinnatus [4] at his plough, to Diocletian [5] among his cabbages, to the Chinese emperors ushering in the new year with the sowing of seed, the young man was explaining to the young woman that the cause of these irresistible attractions lay in some previous existence.

"We, now, why did we meet? What turn of fate decreed it? Was it not that, like two rivers gradually converging across the intervening distance, our own natures propelled us towards one another?"

He took her hand, and she did not withdraw it.

"General Prize!" cried the Chairman.

"Just now, for instance, when I came to call on you . . ."

"Monsieur Bizet of Quincampoix."

". . . how could I know that I should escort you here?"

"Seventy francs!"

"And I've stayed with you, because I couldn't tear myself away, though I've tried a hundred times."

"Manure!"

"And so I'd stay tonight and tomorrow and every day for all the rest of my life."

"To Monsieur Caron of Argueil, a Gold Medal!"

"For I have never been so utterly charmed with anyone before."

---

4. An historical figure who, according to tradition, left his farm, was made dictator, saved his country from an enemy invasion, and then returned to his farm — all within the space of two or three weeks.

5. This Roman Emperor (died A.D. 313) is unfortunately more famous for his persecution of the Christians.

"To Monsieur Bain of Givry St Martin."

"And so I shall cherish the memory of you."

"For a merino ram . . ."

"But you'll forget me. I shall have passed like a shadow . . ."

"To Monsieur Belot of Notre-Dame . . ."

"No, say I shan't! Tell me I shall count for something in your thoughts, in your life?"

"Pigs: Prize divided! Monsieur Lehérissé and Monsieur Cullembourg, sixty francs each!"

Rodolphe squeezed her hand. He felt it warm and vibrant in his, like a captive turtle-dove trying to take wing. Whether she was trying to withdraw it, or responding to his pressure, her fingers made a movement.

"Oh, thank you, you do not repulse me!" he cried. "How sweet you are! You know that I am yours! Only let me look at you, let me gaze upon you!"

A breeze from the window ruffled the cloth on the table, and down in the square the peasant women's big bonnets lifted up, fluttering like white butterflies' wings.

"Oil-cake," the Chairman continued. He began to go faster: "Flemish fertiliser — Flax — Drainage — Long Leases — Domestic Service."

Rodolphe had stopped speaking. They looked at one another, and their dry lips quivered in a supreme desire. Gently, effortlessly, their fingers intertwined.

"Catherine Nicaise Elisabeth Leroux of Sassetot la Guerrière: For fifty-four years' service at the same farm: Silver Medal, value twenty-five francs!"

"Where is she? Catherine Leroux!" the official repeated.

There was no sign of her. Voices could be heard whispering:

"Go on!"

"No."

"Over there on the left!"

"Don't be afraid!"

"Stupid creature!"

"Well, is she there or not?" cried Tuvache.

"Yes, here she is!"

"Then let her come up!"

Thereupon a timorous-looking little old woman was seen to step up on to the platform, wizened and shrunken in her tattered garments. She wore heavy clogs on her feet and a big blue apron round her waist. Her thin face, framed in a borderless cap, was wrinkled as a withered russet, and from the sleeves of her red bodice appeared two drooping hands, gnarled at the joints, and so caked and chapped and hardened by barn-dust, wool-grease and washing-soda that they looked dirty though they had been rinsed in fresh water. Years of service had left them hanging open as if to bear their own humble witness to the many hardships they had endured. A touch of cloistral austerity lent some expression to her face, but her pale stare was softened by no shade of sadness or of feeling. Living among animals, she had grown placid and mute as they. This was the first time she had ever found herself the centre of such a crowd of people. Inwardly terrified by the flags and drums, the frock-coated gentlemen and the official's Legion of Honour, she stood stock-still, not knowing whether to advance or to run, or why they kept pushing her forward or why the judges smiled at her. There she stood, before those beaming bourgeois, an embodied half-century of servitude.

"Come, venerable Catherine Nicaise Elisabeth Leroux!" said the official, who had taken the list of prizewinners from the Chairman. "Come along, come along!" he coaxed her in fatherly fashion, looking alternately at the sheet of paper in his hand and at the aged crone in front of him.

"Is she deaf?" said Tuvache, bouncing up in his armchair. He started shouting in her ear:

"Fifty-four years' service! Silver Medal! Twenty-five francs! For you!"

Having got her medal, she gazed at it, and a blissful smile overspread her features. As she trotted off, she could be heard muttering: "I'll give it to our *curé*, to say mass for me."

"Fanatical!" exclaimed the chemist, leaning across to the lawyer.

The proceedings were over. The crowds dispersed. The speeches had been delivered, and now everybody resumed his station and things reverted to normal. Masters bullied servants. Servants belaboured the animals — those indolent conquerors returning to their sheds, their horns garlanded with green.

Meanwhile the militia had gone up to the first floor of the Town Hall, with cakes spitted on their bayonets, and the regimental drummer carrying a basketful of bottles. Madame Bovary took Rodolphe's arm and he saw her home. They parted at her door, and then he went off for a stroll in the meadow until it was time for the feast to begin.

The feast was long and noisy and badly served. The guests were wedged in so tight they could hardly move, and the narrow planks that were doing duty as benches very nearly gave way beneath the weight of the assembled company. They ate hugely. Everyone set to and did his share. Sweat poured down every forehead, and a pallid steam hovered between the lamps above the table, like a river-mist on an autumn morning. Rodolphe leant back against the side of the marquee, too deep in his thoughts of Emma to hear a thing. On the grass behind him, servants were piling up the dirty plates. His neighbours spoke to him and received no answer. They refilled his glass, but though the hubbub grew around him, all was quiet within his mind. He was thinking of the things she had said, and of the shape of her lips. Her face appeared to him in the cap badges of the militia, shining as in a magic mirror. The pleats of her dress hung down the walls; and days of love unfolded endlessly before him in the long vistas of the future.

In the evening he saw her again, at the fireworks, but she was with her husband and Monsieur and Madame Homais. The chemist, much perturbed about the danger of stray squibs, kept breaking away from the party every other minute to go and offer Binet his advice.

The fireworks had been delivered to Monsieur Tuvache, who, with excessive caution, had stored them in his cellar. The powder was consequently damp and wouldn't light, and the principal feature, which was to have been a dragon biting its tail, completely miscarried. Occasionally a paltry little Roman candle went off and drew from the gaping crowd a great roar of applause, with which there mingled the shrieks of women who were being tickled under cover of the darkness. Emma nestled silently against Charles, then raised her chin as she followed the flash of the rockets across the black sky. Rodolphe watched her in the glimmer of the lanterns.

The lanterns burned down one by one. The stars shone out.

A few drops of rain began to fall, and Emma tied her scarf over her hair.

At that moment the official's cab drove out of the inn yard. The coachman was drunk and immediately dropped into a doze, and from some way off you could see, above the hood, between the two lamps, his unwieldy body swinging to and fro with the rocking of the vehicle.

"Drunkenness really ought to be dealt with severely!" said the chemist. "I'd like to see a special list put up every seven days on the door of the Town Hall, with the names of all those who have been under the influence of alcohol during the week. From the statistical point of view, you'd have a kind of public record, which might come in . . . Excuse me!" — and once more he ran off to speak to the Captain.

That gentleman was just going home — home to his lathe.

"It wouldn't be a bad idea," said Homais to him, "if you sent one of your men, or went round yourself . . ."

"Don't come bothering me. There's nothing to make a fuss about," answered the tax-collector.

"Nothing to worry about!" said the chemist as he rejoined his friends. "Monsieur Binet assures me that everything has been attended to. There won't be any sparks, and the pumps are full. We can go home to bed."

"My word, I can do with it, too!" observed Madame Homais, who was yawning tremendously. "But who cares? We've had a lovely day for our Show."

"A very lovely day!" agreed Rodolphe under his breath, his eyes tender.

They said good-night and went their ways.

Two days later, a big report of the Show appeared in the *Rouen Beacon*. Homais had composed it in style the following morning.

"Whence these festoons, these flowers, these garlands? Whither bound these throngs like the billows of a raging ocean, beneath a tropical sun that pours upon our leas its warmth torrential?"

He went on to speak of the condition of the peasants: the Government was doing a great deal, certainly, but not enough.

"Be bold!" he cried to it. "A thousand reforms must be achieved. Let us achieve them!"

Coming to the scene of the great man's arrival, he omitted neither the "martial bearing of our militia," nor "our sprightly village lasses," nor the bald-headed ancients who contributed their patriarchal presence — some of them the "survivors of our immortal legions," who "felt their hearts beat once more in time to the manly roll of the drums." He mentioned himself among the foremost of the judges, and even reminded his readers in a footnote that M. Homais, pharmacist, had sent a treatise on cider to the Agricultural Society. When he got to the prize-giving, he painted the delight of the winners in dithyrambic strokes. Brother embraced brother, the father his son, the husband his wife. Many a one displayed his modest medal with pride, and doubtless, when he returned home to his good wife, hung it up, with tears in his eyes, on the wall of his humble cottage.

"At six o'clock a banquet, held in Monsieur Liégeard's meadow, assembled the leading personages of the Show. The utmost cordiality reigned throughout. Divers toasts were drunk, Monsieur Lieuvain proposing 'The King,' Monsieur Tuvache 'The Prefect,' Monsieur Homais 'Industry and The Arts, those twin sisters,' and Monsieur Leplichey 'Progress.' At night the sky was suddenly illumined by a brilliant firework display. 'Twas a veritable kaleidoscope, an operatic scena. For an instant our little town imagined itself transplanted into the midst of an Arabian Night's dream.

"Be it said that no untoward event came to upset our happy family gathering."

And he added:

"Only the absence of the clergy was remarked. No doubt the churches have their own idea of progress. . . . As you will, reverend apostles of Loyola!"

Emma and Léon *

While studying for his law degree, Monsieur Léon had been a not infrequent visitor at the *Thatched Cottage,* where he made quite a hit with the *grisettes,* who thought he looked "distinguished." He was the most presentable of the students, he wore his hair neither too short nor too long, he did not squander his term's allowance on the first of the month, and he kept on good terms with his tutors. And he had always abstained from excesses, as much from pusillanimity as from fastidiousness.

* From Part Three, chapter 1. Rodolphe has left Emma, who becomes ill and nearly dies. To encourage her recovery, Charles proposes a trip to hear the opera in Rouen, and there she meets Léon again.

Many a time when he stayed indoors reading, or when he sat under the lime-trees in the Luxembourg of an evening, his law-book would drop from his hands, and thoughts of Emma would return to him. But little by little his feeling for her lost its force and was overlaid by a mass of other appetites, though never quite extinguished by them, for Léon had not entirely abandoned hope, and the future dangled a vague promise before him, like a golden fruit hanging from some fantastic tree.

Now, seeing her again after a gap of three years, his passion re-awakened. This time, he thought, he must be bold, and try to win her. His shyness had, in fact, been rubbed off by contact with his gay companions, and he came back to the provinces full of contempt for whosoever had not trodden the asphalt of the boulevards in patent-leather shoes. In the presence of a Parisian lady in lace, or in the salon of some scholastic celebrity, some honoured personage with a carriage-and-four, the humble clerk would doubtless have trembled like a child. But here on the quayside at Rouen, talking to this country practitioner's wife, he felt at his ease, secure in the foreknowledge that he would shine. Assurance depends on one's surroundings. Words that go well enough in the top attic are useless in the drawing-room; the wealthy woman seems to have all her bank-notes about her to defend her virtue, like so much armour-plate inside the lining of her bodice.

After taking leave of Monsieur and Madame Bovary the night before, Léon had followed them at a distance along the street. When he saw them go in at the Red Cross, he had about-turned and spent the rest of the night thinking out a plan.

Consequently, at about five o'clock next day, he walked into the lobby of the hotel, with a tight feeling in his throat, a white face, and that coward's courage that nothing can stop.

"The gentleman isn't in," a servant told him.

That augured well. He went up.

Far from being disconcerted by his arrival, Emma apologised for having forgotten to tell him where they were staying.

"Oh, I guessed!" said Léon.

"How?"

He pretended he had been guided to her by instinct. She started smiling, and he hastened to retrieve that asininity by saying that he had spent the morning calling at every hotel in the place in search of her.

"So you decided to stay."

"Yes, though I ought not to," she said, "for there's no sense in acquiring tastes you can't indulge, when there are a hundred and one things that have a claim on you. . . ."

"Oh yes, I can imagine."

"I doubt if you can. You're not a woman."

Ah, but men had their trials too. . . . The conversation got under

way with sundry philosophical reflections. Emma dwelt on the poverty
of all earthly affection and the perpetual isolation that enshrouds the
human heart.

Whether he wished to sound impressive, or whether his mood were
naïvely following the lead of her melancholy, the young man declared
that he had been prodigiously bored all the time he was a student. Legal
procedure got on his nerves, other professions had attracted him, his
mother never stopped nagging at him in every letter she wrote. . . .
So they went into ever greater detail on the subject of their sorrows,
each growing somewhat excited as they went further in confidence. At
times they stopped short of expressing all they had in mind — yet felt
for phrases to convey their meaning none the less. She did not confess
her love for another man; he did not say he had forgotten her.

Perhaps he could no longer recall those suppers after the dance with
the girls in fancy dress. Presumably she had no recollection of those
assignations of old, those mornings when she used to run through the
long grass to her lover's [6] mansion. The noises of the town scarcely
reached them here; the room seemed small, as though to emphasize their
intimacy. Emma, wearing a dimity dressing-gown, leant back against
the aged armchair. The yellow wallpaper behind her gave her a sort of
gold background, and her bare head was reflected in the mirror, with
the white line of the parting in the middle and the tips of her ears
peeping out from under the plaits of her hair.

"But forgive me, I must be boring you with all my troubles," she said.

"No, never, never!"

"If you only knew," she said, and she lifted her beautiful eyes to the
ceiling as a tear formed, "if you only knew the dreams I've dreamed."

"I, too! I've suffered! I often used to go out and wander along by
the river, trying to deaden my thoughts in the noise of the crowd, yet
still unable to banish the obsession that pursued me. There's a picture-
shop along the Boulevard with an Italian print in the window, of one
of the Muses. She's draped in a tunic, looking at the moon, and she's
got forget-me-nots in her flowing hair. Something was for ever drawing
me towards that shop. I've stood there for hours on end." In a trembling voice he added: "She was something like you."

Madame Bovary turned away to hide the smile she felt rising irresistibly to her lips.

"Many a time I wrote to you, and then tore up the letter," he went on.
She made no answer.

"I fancied sometimes that chance would bring you to me. I thought
I saw you at street-corners, I went chasing after a cab whenever I
caught sight of a shawl or a veil like yours fluttering at the window."

She seemed determined to let him talk on without interruption. Folding her arms and lowering her head, she gazed down at the rosettes on
her slippers, and now and then gently moved her toes inside the satin.

At last she sighed. "What can be more distressing than to drag out

6. That is, Rodolphe.

a futile existence like mine? If only our sorrows could be of use to someone, we might find some consolation in the thought of our sacrifice."

He proceeded to pay tribute to virtue, duty, and silent immolation. *He* had an unbelievable, unsatisfied longing to dedicate himself.

"I should very much like to be a Sister of Mercy," she said.

"Alas," he replied, "there are no such sacred missions for men, nor any vocation at all, as far as I can see, unless perhaps that of a doctor. . . ."

With a little shrug of her shoulders, Emma broke in to tell him how dreadfully ill she had been, how near she had come to dying. A pity she hadn't died: she would now be suffering no more. . . . Immediately Léon yearned for the "peace of the tomb." One night he had actually made his will, asking that he should be buried in the beautiful rug with the velvet stripes which she had given him. . . . For this was how they would have liked it all to be: they were both constructing an ideal of themselves and adapting their past lives to it. Speech acts invariably as an enlarger of sentiments.

However, this tale about the rug made her ask, "Why?"

"Why?" He hesitated. "Because — I loved you!"

And while he congratulated himself on having taken the leap, he watched her face out of the corner of his eye.

It was like the sky when the wind blows the clouds away. The dark mass of sombre thoughts seemed to lift from her blue eyes, her whole face was radiant.

He waited, and at last she said, "I always suspected it."

And then they recounted all the little events of those far-off days whose joys and sorrows they had just summed up in a single word. He spoke of the bower of clematis, the dresses she used to wear, the furniture in her room, everything in the house.

"And our poor cactuses, what of them?"

"The frost killed them this winter."

"Ah, you don't know how I used to think about them. I saw them in my mind's eye, with the sun beating down on the blinds of a summer morning, and your bare arms moving among the plants."

"Poor Léon!" said she, holding out her hand to him.

Léon promptly pressed it to his lips. Then, when he had taken a deep breath —

"You had a sort of mysterious, captivating power over me in those days. There was one time, for instance, when I came to call — but I don't suppose you remember?"

"Yes, I do. Go on."

"You were downstairs in the hall, at the foot of the stairs, just going out — yes, you were wearing a hat with little blue flowers on it! Without waiting to be asked, I went with you, I couldn't help it. Yet every moment I grew more and more conscious of my silliness. I went along at your heels, not quite daring to walk beside you, yet unable to leave you. When you turned into a shop, I stood fast in the street and watched through the window as you took off your gloves and counted out the money. Then you went and rang at Madame Tuvache's. Someone let you in, and I stood there like an idiot staring at the big door closing behind you."

Listening to him, Madame Bovary was surprised to discover how old she was. All those glimpses of the past returning made her life seem larger; gave her, as it were, vast tracts of feeling over which she might rove. From time to time, with eyes half-closed, she murmured, "Yes, that's right. That's right."

They heard eight o'clock strike from the various clocks in the Beauvoisine quarter, which is full of boarding-schools, churches, and big derelict mansions. They had stopped talking, but as they looked at one another they felt a humming in their heads, as though some vibrant message had passed between their gazing eyes. They had joined hands; and past and future, memory and dream, all mingled together in the sweetness of their ecstasy. The shadows deepened along the walls; only the four crudely coloured prints that hung there, showing scenes from *La Tour de Nesle*, with inscriptions underneath in French and Spanish, still gleamed faintly in the twilight. Through the sash-window a patch of dark sky was visible between gabled roofs.

She rose to light a pair of candles on the chest of drawers, then came and sat down again.

"Well?" said Léon.

"Well?" she replied.

He was wondering how to resume after this interruption, when she said, "How is it no one has ever expressed such sentiments to me before?"

The clerk declared that idealistic natures were not easily understood. *He* had fallen in love with her at first sight. It made him frantic to think of the happiness they might have had, if it had only been granted them to meet earlier in life and be joined together in an indissoluble union.

"I have thought of that sometimes," she said.

"What a dream!" murmured Léon. And delicately toying with the blue border of her long white girdle, he added, "Why shouldn't we begin again now?"

"No, my friend," she replied. "I am too old, you're too young. Forget me. Other women will love you . . . you will love them."

"Not as I love you!" he cried.

"What a child you are! Come, we must be sensible. I ask it of you."

She pointed out all the reasons why love was impossible between them. They should remain just good friends, as they had been before.

Was she in earnest when she said that? Emma could hardly have known herself — preoccupied as she was with the temptation to which she was exposed and the necessity of withstanding it. Gazing at the young man with pity in her eyes, she gently repelled the shy caresses that his trembling hands essayed.

"I'm sorry!" he said, drawing back.

And Emma felt vaguely alarmed at this timidity, more dangerous for her than Rodolphe boldly advancing upon her with open arms. No man had ever seemed to her so handsome; there was an exquisite candour in his bearing. He lowered his long, fine, curving lashes. His smooth cheek flushed — with desire for her, she thought. Emma felt an almost ungovernable yearning to lay her lips upon it.

She bent forward and pretended to look at the clock. "Goodness, how late it is! How we chatter!"

He took the hint and reached for his hat.

"I've forgotten all about the opera, too. And poor Charles left me here especially for it! I was going with Monsieur and Madame Lormeaux from the Rue Grand-Pont."

And it had been her last chance. She was leaving next day.

"Leaving?" exclaimed Léon.

"Yes."

"But I must see you again," he said. "There's something I want to tell you. . . ."

"What is it?"

"Something — important. Something very serious. No, no, you can't, you mustn't go. If you only knew. . . . Listen. . . . You haven't understood me, then? You haven't guessed?"

"But you've talked very well!"

"You're laughing at me. Please! For pity's sake let me see you once more — just once!"

"Well . . . ," she said and paused; then, as a thought struck her, "No, not here!"

"Anywhere you like."

"Will you . . ." She seemed to ponder. Then, tersely: "Eleven tomorrow, in the Cathedral."

"I shall be there," he cried, and seized her hands; she pulled them away.

And as they were both standing up now, he behind her, Emma with lowered head, he bent over and kissed her, very deliberately, on the nape of the neck.

"Oh, you're crazy, you're crazy!" she cried, giving vibrant little laughs as the kisses rained down.

Leaning his head over her shoulder, he seemed to be seeking her eyes' consent. They fell upon him full of a frigid majesty.

Léon stepped back, to go. He halted at the door and whispered in a trembling voice, "Till tomorrow!"

She nodded in reply and vanished into the next room.

That night Emma wrote the clerk a long rambling letter withdrawing from the appointment: it was all a thing of the past, for their own good they ought not to meet again. But when the letter was sealed, Emma realised that she didn't know Léon's address. She was in a quandary.

"I'll give it him myself," she said. "He'll come."

Next day, with his window flung open and a song on his lips, Léon sat on his balcony polishing away at his pumps. He put on white trousers, smart socks and a green coat, drenched his handkerchief in every kind of scent he possessed, and after having his hair curled, uncurled it again to give it a greater natural elegance.

"Too soon yet!" he thought as he glanced at the hairdresser's cuckoo-clock, which pointed to nine.

He flicked through an old fashion-magazine, went out, smoked a cigar, wandered along three streets, then decided it was time to set off in the direction of Notre Dame.

It was a fine summer morning. Silverware glittered in the jewellers' shops; the light sloping down on the Cathedral set little points of brilliance dancing on the grey stones. A flock of birds wheeled in the blue sky, round the trefoiled bell-turrets. The square resounded with cries. It was fragrant with the flowers that bordered its pavement — roses, jasmine, pinks, narcissi, tuberoses, alternating irregularly with moist green plants, catmint and chickweed. The fountain gurgled in the centre, and under broad umbrellas, among pyramids of melons, bare-headed flower-women were wrapping bunches of violets in twists of paper.

The young man asked for a bunch. It was the first time he had ever bought flowers for a woman, and as he sniffed their scent his bosom swelled with pride, as though the homage intended for her came home again to him.

However, he was afraid of being observed. He walked resolutely into the Cathedral.

On the threshold, in the centre of the left-hand porch, under the *Marianne Dancing,* stood the beadle, his plumed hat on his head, rapier at his calf and cane in hand, more majestic than a cardinal and as highly polished as a sacred pyx.

He came forward to greet Léon, with that smile of wheedling benignity that churchmen use when they address children.

"A stranger hereabouts, I expect, sir. You wish to see over the Cathedral?"

"No," said Léon. And first he walked round the aisles. Then he went out and looked across the square. No sign of Emma. He turned back and walked up into the choir. The nave was mirrored in the brimming fonts, with the beginnings of the arches and part of the windows. The reflection of the stained glass broke at the edge of the marble and continued on the flagstones beyond like a chequered carpet. Broad daylight shone in through the three open doors and stretched down the whole length of the Cathedral in three enormous rays. Now and again a sacristan crossed at the far end, making the oblique genuflexion of piety in a hurry. The crystal chandeliers hung motionless. In the choir a silver lamp was burning. From the side-chapels and darker corners of the church came occasionally a sound like the exhaling of a sigh, and a clanking noise, as a grating was shut, that echoed on and on beneath the vaulted roof.

Léon walked gravely round the walls. Never had life seemed so good to him. Presently she would come, charming and animated, glancing round at the eyes that followed her; in flounced dress and dainty shoes, with her gold eye-glass and all manner of adornments new to his experience; and in all, the ineffable charm of virtue surrendering. The Cathedral was like a gigantic boudoir prepared for her. The arches leaned down into the shadows to catch her confession of love, the windows shone resplendent to light her face, and the censers would burn that she might appear as an angel in an aromatic cloud.

But still she did not come. He sat down on a chair, his eyes lighted on a blue window depicting fishermen with baskets. He looked at it long and attentively, counting the fishes' scales and the button-holes in the jerkins, while his thoughts strayed in quest of Emma.

The beadle kept his distance, inwardly furious with this individual who presumed to admire the Cathedral by himself. It seemed to him a monstrous way to behave — a kind of stealing what was his — sacrilege, almost.

There was a rustle of silk over the stone slabs, the brim of a hat, a black cape — she had come! Léon rose and hastened to meet her.

Emma was white-faced, walking quickly.

"Read this!" she said, holding out a sheet of paper — "No, don't!" — and she snatched her hand back again. Then she went into the Lady Chapel, where she knelt down against a chair and began to pray.

The young man felt annoyed at this sudden piety. But then he found a certain charm in seeing her, at their place of tryst, thus wrapped in her devotions, like an Andalusian marquesa. Then he grew impatient, for she seemed to be going on for ever.

Emma was praying, or trying to pray, in the hope that Heaven would suddenly fill her with resolution. To elicit the divine aid she feasted her eyes on the splendours of the tabernacle, breathed in the scent of the white rocket-flowers blooming in the big vases, and listened to the stillness of the Cathedral — which only emphasized the tumult in her heart.

She rose, and they were about to leave, when the beadle came hurrying up to them.

"A stranger hereabouts, I expect, ma'am! You wish to see over the Cathedral?"

"No!" said the clerk.

"Why not?" said she — her tottering virtue clinging for support to the Virgin, the sculptures, the tombs, whatever offered.

To do the thing properly, the beadle took them right back to the entrance on the square, where he pointed with his cane to a large circle of black paving-stones with no inscription or carving.

"Here," he proclaimed majestically, "you see the outer casing of the lovely bell of Amboise. It weighed eighteen tons. There was not its like in all Europe. The workman who cast it died of joy. . . ."

"Come on," said Léon.

The old fellow started off again. Returned to the Lady Chapel, he spread out his arms in a comprehensive gesture of demonstration, prouder than a country smallholder showing off his wall-fruit.

"Beneath this plain stone lies Pierre de Brézé, Lord of Varenne and Brissac, Grand Marshal of Poitou and Governor of Normandy, killed at the Battle of Montlhéry on the 16th July, 1465."

Léon bit his lip, fuming.

"While on the right, this nobleman encased in iron, on a prancing steed, is his grandson Louis de Brézé, Lord of Breval and Montchauvet, Count of Maulevrier and Baron of Mauny, King's Chamberlain, Knight of the Order, and likewise Governor of Normandy, who died on the 23rd July, 1531, a Sunday, as the inscription tells. This figure underneath, about to descend into the tomb, shows you once more the self-same man. It would surely be impossible to find a more perfect representation of death!"

Madame Bovary held up her eye-glass. Léon stood still and watched her, no longer attempting the least word or gesture, utterly discouraged by this double defence of volubility and indifference. The interminable guide ran on: "This woman on her knees beside him, weeping, is his wife Diane de Poitiers, Countess of Brézé and Duchess of Valentinois, born 1499, died 1566. And on the left, with the child in her arms, is the Blessed Virgin. Now turn this way. Here we have the Amboise tombs. Both were Cardinals and Archbishops of Rouen. That one was a Minister under King Louis XII. He did much for the Cathedral. In his will he left thirty thousand gold crowns to the poor."

Talking all the time, he pushed them straight on into a chapel which was cluttered up with hand-rails, one or two of which he moved aside to reveal a sort of block that might once have been a crudely carved statue.

"Once upon a time," he said with a long groan, "it adorned the tomb of Richard Cœur-de-Lion, King of England and Duke of Normandy. It was reduced to its present state, sir, by the Calvinists. They buried it, for spite, in the ground beneath the episcopal throne. Look, here is the doorway leading to the Bishop's residence! We pass on now to the Dragon Windows. . . ."

Léon quickly pulled a silver coin from his pocket, and took Emma by the arm. The beadle was left standing in amazement, unable to comprehend such premature munificence, when there were still so many things for the strangers to see. He shouted after him, "The spire, sir, the spire!"

"No, thanks," said Léon.

"You shouldn't miss it, sir. It is four hundred and forty feet high, only nine less than the Great Pyramid of Egypt. It is all of cast iron, it . . ."

Léon fled, for it seemed to him that his love, which for close on two hours had been immobilised like the stones around him in the church, was now about to vanish like smoke through that kind of truncated funnel, oblong cage or fretwork chimney, that perches so grotesquely on top of the Cathedral like an essay in the extravagant by some whimsical tinker.

"Where are we going?" said Emma.

He strode on without answering; and Madame Bovary was actually dipping her finger in the holy-water font at the door, when they heard a heavy, panting breath behind them, punctuated by the tap-tap of a stick. Léon turned round.

"Sir!"

"What is it?"

There stood the beadle, a score or so of stout paper-bound volumes stuffed under his arm or balanced against his belly. They were works "treating of the Cathedral."

"Idiot!" growled Léon, and he darted outside.

A street urchin was playing on the pavement.

"Go and get me a cab!"

The youngster shot off down the Rue des Quatre Vents, and they were left for a minute face to face, in some embarrassment.

"Oh, Léon! Really — I don't know — whether I ought . . . ," she simpered affectedly. Then she looked serious. "You know it's not the thing!"

"Why not?" retorted the clerk. "It's done in Paris!"

And that word, with its unassailable logic, decided her.

The cab hadn't arrived yet, though; Léon was afraid she might retreat inside the Cathedral again. At last it came in sight.

"At any rate you ought to go out through the North Door!" cried the beadle, who had halted in the porch, "and see the *Resurrection,* the *Last Judgment,* the *Paradise, King David,* and the *Damned in the Flames of Hell!*"

"Where to, sir?" said the cabby.

"Where you like!" said Léon, pushing Emma into the carriage; and the lumbering machine set off.

It went down the Rue Grand-Pont, across the Place des Arts, along the Quai Napoléon, over the Pont Neuf, and pulled up sharply before the statue of Pierre Corneille.

"Keep on!" came a voice from inside.

The cab started off again, and gathering speed down the hill beyond the Carrefour La Fayette, drove into the station yard at full gallop.

"No! Straight on!" cried the voice again.

It passed out through the iron gates, and presently striking the Drive, trotted gently along between the tall elms. The cabby mopped his brow, stuck his leather hat between his legs and turned off beyond the side-avenues towards the green by the waterside.

All along the river, on the pebble-paved towing-path, went the fiacre, past the islands and a good way towards Oyssel.

Then suddenly it switched off through Quatre Mares, Sotteville, the

Grande Chaussée, the Rue d'Elbeuf, and halted for the third time out-side the Botanical Gardens.

"Go on, will you!" cried the voice yet more furiously.

Immediately it moved off again, past St Sever, the Quai des Curan-diers, the Quai aux Meules, back over the bridge, across the Drill Square and behind the workhouse gardens, where old men in black jackets are to be seen strolling in the sunshine along the ivy-mantled terrace. It drove along the Boulevard Bouvreuil, down the Boulevard Cauchoise, and all the way up Mont Riboudet as far as the Côte de Deville.

There it turned and came back again, then went roaming at random, without aim or course. It was seen at St Pol and Lescure, at Mont Gargan, at the Rouge Mare and in the Place du Gaillardbois; in the Rue Maladrerie, the Rue Dinanderie, outside St Romain, St Vivien, St Maclou and St Nicaise; at the Customs House, at the Old Tower, the "Three Pipes," the Monumental Cemetery. Every now and then the driver, perched up on his box, would cast despairing glances at the public houses. He couldn't conceive what mania for locomotion pos-sessed these individuals that they should want to drive on for ever. Once or twice he did slow up, and angry exclamations immediately broke out behind him; whereupon he whipped up his sweating hacks still harder, jolting the cab recklessly, banging into things right and left and not caring, demoralised, almost weeping with thirst, fatigue and despondency.

And by the harbour, in the midst of the wagons and barrels, in the streets, at every corner, the citizens opened their eyes wide in amaze-ment at the spectacle, so extraordinary in a provincial town, of a car-riage with drawn blinds, continually reappearing, sealed tighter than a tomb and being buffeted about like a ship at sea.

Once, in the middle of the day, when they were right out in the country and the sun was beating down at its fiercest on the old silver-plated carriage-lamps, an ungloved hand stole out beneath the little yellow canvas blinds and tossed away some scraps of paper, which were carried off on the wind and landed like white butterflies in a field of red clover in full bloom.

At about six o'clock the cab drew up in a side-street in the Beau-voisine quarter, and a woman got out; she walked away with her veil lowered, and without a backward glance.

The Death of Emma Bovary *

She bore it bravely next day when Maître Hareng the bailiff arrived, with two witnesses, to draw up a list of goods to be distrained.

They started with Bovary's consulting-room. His phrenological head they ruled out as being "professional equipment." But in the kitchen they counted the plates and the pots, the chairs and the candlesticks,

---

* From Part Three, chapters 7 and 8. The affair with Léon, after a brief period of pleasure, deteriorates, and then Emma's financial extravagances begin to bring disaster.

and in the bedroom all the knickknacks in the cabinet. They examined her linen, her clothes, her dressing-room; her whole existence was spread out like a corpse at a post-mortem, for the three men to pry into its inmost secrets.

Maître Hareng was buttoned up in a thin black coat, and wore a white cravat and tightly fastened boot-straps. "If you'll allow me, Madame, if you'll allow me," he would say from time to time — with frequent exclamations of "Charming!" or "Very pretty!" — after which he would resume his writing, dipping his pen into the ink-horn which he carried in his left hand.

When they had been over the rest of the house, they went up to the attic.

There was a desk up there in which she kept Rodolphe's letters. It had to be opened.

"Ah! Your correspondence," Maître Hareng smiled discreetly. "I must make sure the box contains nothing else, however. Allow me."

He tilted the papers gently as though he would shake out the gold pieces. That made her furious, to see that thick hand, the fingers red and soft like slugs, resting on the pages she had held to her beating heart.

At last they went. Félicité came back indoors — she had been put on guard to keep Bovary away — and they hurriedly installed the bailiff's man at the top of the house, where he promised to remain.

During the evening Charles seemed preoccupied. Emma watched him in an agony, reading accusation in every line of his face. Then, as her eyes travelled over the fireplace with its ornamental Chinese screens, over the big curtains, the armchairs, all the things that had softened the bitterness of her life, she was smitten with remorse, or rather with an immense regret which, far from extinguishing her passion, served only to awaken it. Charles sat with his feet on the fender, placidly poking the fire.

Once the bailiff's man, bored no doubt in his hiding-place, made a slight noise.

"Is that someone upstairs?" said Charles.

"No," she answered, "it's only an open window rattling in the wind."

The following day, a Sunday, she set off for Rouen, to call on all the bankers whose names she knew. They were out of town, or away on a journey. She refused to give in. Those she did manage to see she asked for money, declaring that she *must* have it and would pay it back. Some of them laughed in her face; all of them refused.

At two o'clock she hurried to Léon's and knocked at his door. No answer. Eventually he appeared.

"What brings you here?"

"Do you mind?"

"No, but . . ." and he admitted that the landlord didn't like them to have "women" there.

"I've got to talk to you," she said.

He reached for his key, but she stopped him. "No, let's go to our place."

They went to their room at the Hotel de Boulogne. As soon as they got inside, she drained a large glass of water. She was very pale.

She said to him:

"Léon, you've got to do something for me."

She gripped his hands tight and gave him a shake.

"Listen. I need three hundred pounds."

"You're crazy."

"Not yet. . . ."

She told him about the bailiffs and the predicament she was in. Charles knew nothing of it. Her mother-in-law hated her. Her father couldn't help. But he, Léon, he must set about finding this sum that she must have.

"And how do you expect . . . ?"

"Oh, don't be so helpless!" she cried.

Stupidly he said: "It can't be as bad as you make out. A hundred or so would probably keep the fellow quiet."

All the more reason for trying to do something! Surely it wasn't impossible to find a hundred pounds? And Léon could stand surety instead of her.

"Go on, go and try! You must! Oh, hurry, hurry! I will love you so!"

He went away. At the end of an hour he returned looking solemn. "I've been to three people," he said. "Nothing doing."

They sat facing one another on either side of the fireplace, motionless, silent. Emma shrugged her shoulders, tapped her foot on the floor.

"I'd soon get it if I were in your place," he heard her murmur.

"Where from?"

"Your office!" And she gave him a look.

In her blazing eyes was a diabolical recklessness; their lids narrowed with sensual invitation. The young man felt himself succumbing to the mute will-power of this woman who was urging him to a crime. He took fright, and to forestall anything more explicit, clapped his hand to his forehead with an exclamation:

"Morel is coming back tonight! I shouldn't think he'd refuse me." (Morel was a friend of his, the son of a wealthy business man.) "I can bring it you tomorrow."

Emma didn't appear to welcome this idea as cordially as he had hoped. Did she guess he was lying? He reddened and went on: "Don't wait, though, darling, if I'm not here by three o'clock. Now, I'm afraid I must be off. Good-bye!"

He grasped her hand, but it was quite lifeless in his. Emma had no energy left to feel anything.

The clock struck four. Yielding mechanically to force of habit, she rose to return to Yonville.

The weather was fine. It was one of those sharp, bright March days when the sun shines in a perfectly clear sky. The folk of Rouen were strolling contentedly in their Sunday clothes. She reached the Cathedral. Vespers were just over, and the people were pouring out through the three doors like a river beneath the arches of a bridge; in the middle, firmer than a rock, stood the beadle.

She remembered the day when she had gone in there, tense and expectant, with that great vault rising high above her, yet overtopped by her love. . . . She walked on, weeping beneath her veil, dazed, unsteady, almost fainting.

"Look out!" came a cry as a carriage gate swung open.

She stopped to let a tilbury emerge, with a black horse prancing in the shafts and a gentleman in sable furs driving. Who was it? Where had she seen . . . The carriage sprang forward and was gone.

Why, it was he! The Viscount! She turned round. The street was empty. She felt so overwhelmed with misery that she leaned against a wall to prevent herself falling.

Then she thought she must have been mistaken. She could be sure of nothing now. She felt lost, forsaken by everything within and around her, whirling through a bottomless chaos; and it was almost with joy that she arrived at the Red Cross to find the good Homais watching a crate of chemist's supplies being loaded on to the *Hirondelle,* and with a silk handkerchief in his hand in which he was carrying six *cheminots* for his wife.

Madame Homais was very fond of these small, heavy loaves, shaped like a turban, which are eaten with salt butter during Lent: a last survival of Gothic fare, perhaps going back to the time of the Crusades, with which the sturdy Normans used once to gorge themselves, fancying that they saw in the yellow torchlight on the table, between the jugs of mead and the huge joints of pork, Saracens' heads to devour. The chemist's wife crunched them up in the same heroic manner despite her dreadful teeth, and Homais never failed to bring some back from his trips into Rouen, always buying them at the big shop in the Rue Massacre.

"Delighted to see you!" he greeted Emma, and offered his hand to help her up into the coach.

He hung the *cheminots* on the netting of the rack and sat with bare head and folded arms, in a pensive Napoleonic attitude. But when the blind man came in sight as usual at the foot of the hill, he broke out:

"I can't understand the authorities tolerating such scandals nowadays. The poor wretches ought to be shut up and forced to work. Upon my word, progress goes at a snail's pace! We wallow in utter barbarism."

The blind man proffered his hat. It swung to and fro outside the carriage window, like a piece of upholstery hanging loose.

"That," said the chemist, "is a scrofulous complaint." And though he knew the poor devil well enough, he pretended he had never seen him before, muttered the words "cornea," "corneal opacity," "sclerotic," "facies," then asked him paternally: "Have you had that terrible affliction long, my friend? Instead of getting drunk at the pub, you'd do better to go on a diet."

He advised him to take good wine, good beer, and good roast meat.

The blind man went on singing his song; he seemed half-witted. At last Monsieur Homais opened his purse.

"Here you are, here's a penny: give me back a halfpenny. And don't forget my advice; it'll do you good."

Hivert ventured openly to doubt its efficacy, but the chemist guaranteed to cure the man himself, with an antiphlogiston ointment of his own preparation, and he gave him his address. "Monsieur Homais, Market-place. Anyone'll tell you."

"Now then," said Hivert, "after all that, you can do your act."

The blind man crouched down on his haunches, threw back his head, rolled his dark green eyes and stuck out his tongue, rubbed his stomach with both hands and uttered a sort of dull howl, like a famished dog. Disgusted, Emma tossed him a half-crown piece over her shoulder. It was the sum of her wealth; it seemed glorious to fling it away like that.

The carriage was moving off again when Homais suddenly leaned out of the window and called after him: "No starch, no milk food! Wear wool next the skin and expose the diseased parts to the smoke of juniper berries!"

The familiar sights rolling by gradually distracted Emma from her present miseries. An intolerable weariness overcame her, and she arrived home in a dispirited stupor, almost asleep.

"What will be, will be," she said to herself.

And you never knew, something quite unexpected might happen at any moment. Lheureux might even die.

At nine o'clock the next morning she was awakened by voices in the square. A mob of people was gathered round the market to read a large notice pasted up on one of the pillars. She saw Justin climb up and tear at it; as he did so, the hand of the village policeman descended on his shoulder. Homais came out of his shop; old Mother Lefrançois could be seen in the middle of the crowd, apparently delivering a harangue.

"Madame! Madame!" cried Félicité, running in. "It's a scandal!" And in great agitation the poor girl handed her a sheet of yellow paper she had just torn off the door. Emma read at a glance that all her furniture was for sale.

They gazed at one another in silence. Servant and mistress had no secrets from one another now.

"If I were you, Madame," Félicité sighed at last, "I'd go to Monsieur Guillaumin."

"You would?" said she. Which meant: "Has your Théodore's master ever spoken of me, then?"

"Yes, you go. It's the best thing you can do."

She dressed, put on her black frock and her bonnet with the jet beads, and to avoid being seen (for there were still a number of people in the market-place) she turned away from the village and went along the path by the water.

She reached the lawyer's gate quite out of breath. The sky was heavy, with a little snow falling.

In answer to her ring Théodore appeared at the top of the steps in his red waistcoat; he came and let her in almost familiarly, as he might have let in an acquaintance, and showed her into the dining-room.

A large porcelain stove was humming in a recess, the remainder of which was filled up with a cactus. In black wooden frames against oak-grained wallpaper hung Steuben's *Esmeralda* and Schopin's *Potiphar*. The table ready laid, the two silver dish-warmers, the crystal door-knobs, the parquet floor and the furniture, all shone with a meticulous, English cleanness. The windows were decorated at each corner with little square panes of coloured glass.

"This is the sort of dining-room," thought Emma, "that I ought to have."

The notary entered, clasping his palm-leaf dressing-gown against his body with his left arm, while with his other hand he quickly raised and replaced the maroon velvet cap that he wore tilted pretentiously to the right side of his head, over the ends of three strands of fair hair which were gathered up at the back and twisted round his bald skull.

Having offered her a chair, he sat down to breakfast with much apology for his incivility.

"Monsieur," said she, "I want to ask you . . ."

"What, Madame? I am listening."

She proceeded to explain her position.

Maître Guillaumin was aware of it, for he had a secret connection with the draper, from whom he used to obtain capital for mortgages.

He knew even better than she the long story of the notes — trifling at first, endorsed by various signatures, made payable at long intervals and continually renewed, until the day when the dealer had gathered up all his claims and deputed his friend Vinçart to institute the necessary proceedings in his own name — for Lheureux did not wish to be considered a shark among his fellow-townsmen.

She punctuated her account with recriminations against Lheureux, and from time to time the lawyer grunted noncommittally in response.

Eating his cutlet and drinking his tea, he kept his chin thrust down into his sky-blue cravat, which was fastened by a pair of diamond tie-pins linked with a little gold chain; and he smiled a peculiar, sugary, ambiguous smile.

He noticed that her feet were damp.

"Come and dry them by the stove. . . . Higher up . . . against the porcelain."

She was afraid of dirtying it.

"Pretty things never do any harm," the lawyer remarked with gallantry.

She set to work upon his feelings, became moved herself, started telling him of her household troubles, her difficulties, her needs. Yes, he could understand — a smart woman like her! Without ceasing to eat, he turned right round to face her, so that his knee brushed against her boot, the sole of which curled up as it steamed against the stove.

But when she asked him for a hundred and twenty pounds, he pursed his lips and declared that he was extremely sorry not to have had the management of her property earlier; for there were any number of ways, even for a lady, of turning one's money to account. She could have invested in the Grumesnil peat-bogs or the building sites at Le Havre and got big returns with practically no risk at all. He worked her into a devouring rage at the thought of the fabulous profits she would have been certain to make.

"Why didn't you come to me?" he asked.

"I don't really know," she said.

"I wonder. Were you frightened of me? Well, it's my loss, for we hardly know each other! Though I'm most interested in you: I hope you don't doubt that?"

He put out his hand and took hers, covered it with a greedy kiss, then held it on his knee, daintily toying with her fingers while he whispered softly in her ear.

His toneless voice babbled on like a running brook. Through his shiny spectacles she saw a glint in his eye. His hands slid up Emma's sleeve and stroked her arm. She felt a panting breath on her cheek. The man revolted her.

She sprang to her feet.

"I am waiting, sir!" she said.

"What, what . . ." stammered the lawyer, turning suddenly white.

"The money . . ."

"But . . ." Then, yielding to the uprush of an overpowering desire: "All right — yes!"

He dragged himself on his knees towards her, careless of his dressing-gown. "For pity's sake stay! I love you!"

He seized her round the waist.

A wave of crimson flooded Madame Bovary's face. She drew back, terrible to see.

"You take a despicable advantage of my distress, Monsieur! I am to be pitied . . . I am not to be bought!"

And she was gone.

The lawyer was left dumbfounded, his eyes fixed on his beautiful embroidered slippers. They were a love gift; eventually the sight of them consoled him. He reflected also that such an adventure might have taken him too far.

"What a wretch! What a blackguard! . . . What wickedness!" she said to herself as she fled on nervous feet beneath the aspens at the side of the road. Disappointment at failure reinforced indignation at the outrage to her modesty. It seemed that Providence was bent on persecuting her. The thought gave a fillip to her pride. Never had she felt so high an esteem for herself or so great a contempt for everybody else. She was in a fighting fury. She would have liked to hit men, to spit in their faces, to trample on them. She strode rapidly forward, pale, quivering, mad with rage, scanning the empty horizon with tear-filled eyes, gloating, almost, over the hatred that choked her.

The sight of her house paralysed her. She couldn't go on. Yet she must. Where else was there?

Félicité was waiting at the door.

"Well?"

"No," said Emma.

For a quarter of an hour they considered together the various people in Yonville who might be willing to help her. But each name that Félicité suggested was met with: "No! No, I'm sure they wouldn't!"

"And the doctor'll be in directly!"

"I know. . . . Leave me to myself."

She had tried everything. There was nothing else she could do. When Charles arrived she would have to say to him, "Keep out! The carpet on which you are treading belongs to us no longer. There's not a chair or a pin or a wisp of straw in your house, that's yours. And it is I, poor man, I who have ruined you!"

There would be a great sob, many tears, and in the end, recovered from the shock, he would forgive . . .

"Yes," she muttered, gritting her teeth, "he'll forgive me — he, whom I'd never forgive for having known me though he had a million to offer me! No, never, never!"

She felt furious at the idea of Bovary's being superior to herself. And whether she confessed or not, soon, very soon — tomorrow! — he'd know of the calamity just the same. She must await that horrible scene and bear the burden of his magnanimity.

She had an impulse to go back to Lheureux. But what was the use? To write to her father — it was too late. And she was perhaps beginning to regret that she hadn't yielded to that man, when she heard the sound of a horse trotting up the lane. It was Charles. He was opening the gate, his face whiter than the plaster on the wall. Running down the staircase, she dashed out across the square; and the mayor's wife, who was talking to Lestiboudois in front of the church, saw her go in at the tax-collector's.

This lady ran off to tell Madame Caron; together they climbed up to her attic, and under cover of some linen that was hanging out to air, took up a position commanding the interior of Binet's house.

He was alone in his garret, engaged in making a wood copy of one of those indescribable ivory carvings which are composed of crescents and spheres fitted one inside the other, the whole erect as an obelisk, and completely useless. And he was just starting on the last piece, the final touch! In the light and shade of his workshop the yellow sawdust flew off his machine like a shower of sparks from the hooves of a galloping horse. The wheels went whirring round. Binet was smiling, chin down, nostrils dilated — absorbed in one of those utter joys, belonging doubt-less only to mediocre tasks, which entertain the mind with simple dif-ficulties and satisfy it in a fulfilment where all aspiration ends.

"There she is!" said Madame Tuvache.

But they could hear scarcely anything that she said for the noise of the lathe.

At last the two ladies thought they caught the word "pounds."

"She's asking for time to pay her taxes," whispered Madame Tuvache.

"Looks like it!" the other agreed.

They watched her moving about the room, examining the serviette-rings on the walls, the candlesticks and bannister-knobs, while Binet sat complacently stroking his beard.

"Do you think she's gone to order something from him?" said the mayor's wife.

"He never sells anything!" her neighbour answered.

The tax-collector appeared to be listening, a blank stare of incompre-hension on his face. She went on in a tender, supplicating manner. She drew closer to him. Her breast heaved. They had stopped talking.

"Is she making up to him?" exclaimed Madame Tuvache.

Binet had gone red to the roots of his hair. She took his hands in hers. "Well, of all the . . .!"

And it must indeed have been a scandalous proposition that she was putting to him, for the tax-collector — albeit a man of mettle, who had fought at Bautzen and Lutzen, taken part in the French campaign and even been recommended for a decoration — suddenly sprang back as if he had seen a snake.

"Madame!" he cried. "How can you think of such a thing!"

"Women like that ought to be whipped!" said Madame Tuvache.

"Where's she gone?" said Madame Caron.

For she had vanished as they were speaking. When they saw her hurry along the High Street and then turn right as though making for the cemetery, they plunged into a whirl of conjecture.

"Mother Rollet," she said as she entered the nurse's house, "I can't breathe! Unlace me!"

She dropped on the bed, sobbing. Madame Rollet covered her with a petticoat, and stood beside her. But as she made no remark, the good woman moved away and set to work at her spinning-wheel.

"Stop!" muttered Emma, thinking she could hear Binet's lathe.

"What's troubling her?" the nurse wondered. "Why has she come here?"

She had fled there at the urging of a kind of panic that drove her from her own house.

Lying on her back, motionless, her eyes staring, she could not see things clearly though she strained with imbecile persistency to fix her attention upon them. She gazed at the plaster flaking off the wall, at the two sticks smouldering end to end on the fire, at a large spider crawling along a crack in the beam above her head. At last she collected her thoughts. She remembered . . . one day with Léon . . . (how long ago!) . . . the river glittering in the sun . . . the scent of the clematis . . . Swept head-long down the seething torrent of her memories, she soon returned to the recollection of the previous day.

"What time is it?" she asked.

Mother Rollet went outside, held up the fingers of her right hand in the direction where the sky was brightest, and came slowly in again.

"Three o'clock nearly."

"Ah, thank you, thank you!"

For he would come. Of course he would! He would have found some money. Perhaps he'd go to her house, though, never imagining that she'd be here. She told the nurse to run and fetch him.

"Hurry!"

"Yes, dear lady, I'm going, I'm going!"

She was surprised now that she hadn't thought of him at first. He had given his word yesterday; he wouldn't go back on it. She already saw herself laying the three bank-notes on Lheureux's desk. Then she'd have to think up some tale to explain matters to Bovary. What should it be?

The nurse was a long time coming back. But as there was no clock in the cottage, Emma thought that perhaps it seemed longer than it was. She started pacing slowly round the garden. Then she went out along the path by the hedge, and hurried back hoping the woman might have come home a different way. At last, tired of waiting, assailed by suspicions that she tried to thrust from her, knowing no longer whether she had been there an age or a minute, she sat down in a corner, shut her eyes and stopped her ears. The gate creaked. She started to her feet. Before she could say anything, Mother Rollet told her, "There's nobody come!"

"What?"

"Nobody! And your husband's crying. He keeps calling for you. They're looking for you."

Emma made no answer. She was panting and rolling her eyes, and the peasant-woman, scared at the look on her face, shrank back instinctively, thinking she had gone mad. All at once Emma clapped her hands to her forehead and gave a cry: like a flash of lightning on a dark night, the thought of Rodolphe had come to her. He was so kind, so considerate, so generous! And if he should hesitate to do her this service she could soon make him, for a single glance would suffice to remind him of their lost love. So she set off for La Huchette, unaware that she was hastening to expose herself to what a little while before had so enraged her, never for a moment suspecting prostitution.

"What shall I say? How shall I begin?" she asked herself as she went. And as she drew nearer she recognised the shrubs and trees, the furze on the hill-side and, down in the hollow, the château. She was back among the sensations of her first love, and her poor constricted heart swelled again with the tenderness of it. A warm breeze fanned her face. The snow was melting: it fell drop by drop from the young shoots on to the grass.

She went in at the same little park-gate and came to the courtyard with the double border of bushy lime-trees. Their long branches rustled as they swayed to and fro. The dogs in the kennels all barked, but no one appeared at their clamour.

Emma climbed the straight wide staircase with the wooden bannisters that led to the dusty stone corridor from which several rooms opened off in a row as in an hotel or a monastery. His was at the far end, the last one on the left. With her hand on the latch her strength suddenly deserted her. She felt afraid he wouldn't be there; she almost wished he were not; yet he was her one hope, her last chance. She waited a minute composing herself, then, re-tempering her courage in the awareness of her present need, she entered.

He was sitting in front of the fire with both feet on the fender, smoking a pipe.

"Lord! It's you!" he said, getting up hastily.

"Yes, it's me. . . . Rodolphe, I want some advice. . . ." But try as she might, she couldn't get another word out.

"You haven't changed. You're charming as ever!"

"Sad charms, my friend," she answered bitterly, "since you disdained them."

He launched into an explanation of his conduct, offering vague excuses for want of a more plausible story.

She let herself succumb to his words, more still to the sound of his voice and the sight of him — to the point of pretending to believe him (or perhaps she really did believe him) when he said that his motive for breaking with her was a secret on which depended the honour, even the life, of a third person.

"I've suffered, all the same," she said, looking at him unhappily.

"Life is like that!" he answered philosophically.

"Has it, at any rate, been kind to you since we parted?"

"Oh, neither kind nor unkind."

"It might have been better if we'd stayed together."

"Yes. Perhaps!"

"Do you think so?" she said, going up to him.

She sighed. "Oh, Rodolphe, if you only knew! . . . I loved you so!"

And then she took his hand, and for a while they sat with fingers intertwined — as on that first day at the Show. His pride struggled against his feeling; but she nestled against him and said: "How did you expect me to live without you? Do you think it's easy to part with happiness? I was desperate. I thought I should die. I'll tell you everything. . . . And you, you kept away from me!"

He had, indeed, carefully avoided her for the last three years, with that innate cowardice that characterises the stronger sex.

Emma went on, with pretty little movements of her head, coaxing him like an amorous kitten: "You've got other women: own up! Oh, I understand. I forgive them. You'll have fascinated them as you fascinated me. You are a man! You've everything to make a woman love you. . . . But we'll start again, won't we? We'll love each other? Look, I'm laughing, I'm happy! . . . Talk to me!"

And she was lovely to see, with a tear trembling in her eye like a raindrop in a blue petal.

He took her on his knees and stroked her smooth hair with the back of his hand; on those plaited coils a last ray of sunshine gleamed like a golden arrow in the fading light. She bent her head, and at last he kissed her very gently on the eyelids, just brushing them with his lips.

"You've been crying!" he said. "Why?"

She burst out sobbing. Rodolphe thought it was her passion finding its release. She said nothing; he took her silence for a final reserve of modesty, and exclaimed: "Oh, forgive me! You are the only one I care for. I have been foolish and wicked! I love you and I shall always love you! . . . What is it? Tell me!" And he went down on his knees.

"Very well. . . . I'm ruined, Rodolphe! You've got to lend me a hundred and twenty pounds!"

"But . . . but . . ." said he, gradually rising to his feet, his face assuming a grave expression.

"You know," she went on hurriedly, "my husband had put all his money into the hands of a lawyer? He disappeared. We had to borrow. The patients didn't pay. And my father-in-law's estate isn't yet wound up. We shall have that some time. But to-day, unless we can get a hundred and twenty pounds, the bailiffs will be arriving — now — this very instant. . . . And so, relying on your friendship, I came to you!"

"So that's it!" thought Rodolphe, going suddenly quite pale. After a pause, he said calmly: "I haven't got it, my dear lady."

He was not lying. If he had had it he would doubtless have given it to her, distasteful though it usually is to perform such noble deeds: a request for money being of all the icy blasts that blow upon love the coldest and most uprooting.

She kept her gaze on him for some minutes. "You haven't got it. . . . You haven't got it," she repeated. "I might have spared myself this last humiliation. You never loved me! You're no better than the rest!"

She was giving herself away, losing her head.

Rodolphe interrupted to say he happened to be "a bit short" himself.

"Oh, I'm sorry for you," said Emma. "I *am* sorry for you."

She let her gaze rest on a damascened rifle that glittered in a rack on the wall.

"When people are poor, they don't put silver on the butts of their guns! Or buy a clock inlaid with tortoise-shell!" she added, pointing to his Buhl timepiece, "or silver-plated whistles for their whips" (she touched them) "or trinkets for their watches! Oh, he wants for nothing! A liqueur-stand in his bedroom, even. You love yourself too much:

you live well, you've got a country-house, farms and woods, you ride to hounds, you go up to Paris. . . . Why, these alone," she cried, picking up his cuff-links from the mantelpiece, "the smallest of these fripperies can be turned into money! . . . No, keep them, I don't want them!"

And she flung the links away from her. Their gold chain snapped as they struck against the wall.

"And I, I'd have given you everything, sold everything I had, worked with my hands, begged in the streets, just for a smile, for a glance, just to hear you say 'Thank you.' And you sit there quite calmly in your easy-chair, as if you hadn't made me suffer enough already! Do you know I could have been happy if I'd never known you? Why did you have to do it? Was it for a wager? No, you loved me, you told me so. Just now, even . . . Oh, you'd have done better to send me away at once. My hands are still burning from your kisses. And here's the place on the carpet where you knelt at my feet and vowed me an eternity of love. And I believed you. For two years you led me on through the sweetest and most magnificent of dreams. Ha! Our plans for going away — do you remember? Oh, that letter, that letter, it tore my heart in two! And now when I come back to him, him with his money, his happiness, his freedom, to beg help that any casual stranger might give — entreating him, bringing back to him all my love — he turns me away because it'd cost him a hundred and twenty pounds!"

"I haven't got it," Rodolphe answered with that perfect calm which is the defence of a resigned anger.

She went. The walls were quivering, the ceiling pressing down upon her. She made her way back up the long drive, stumbling among the heaps of dead leaves that were scattering in the wind. At last she reached the ditch, the gate; in her haste to get it open she tore her nails on the latch. A hundred yards farther on, breathless, tottering, she halted, turned and looked back once more at the impassive mansion, the park, the gardens, the three courtyards, all the windows of the façade.

She stood in a daze, conscious of herself only through the throbbing of her arteries, which she fancied she could hear going forth like a deafening music and filling the countryside around. The ground seemed to give beneath her like water, the furrows looked like vast brown waves breaking into foam. All the thoughts and memories in her mind came rushing out together like a thousand fireworks going off at once. She saw her father: Lheureux's office: the room at Rouen: a different landscape. Madness was laying hold on her. Terrified, she managed to pull herself together, though in some bewilderment; for the thing that had brought her to this frightful condition — her need of money — she could not recall. Only in her love did she suffer; through the thought of that she felt her soul escape from her as a wounded man in his last agony feels life flow out through his bleeding gashes.

Night was falling. Some rooks flew overhead.

All at once it seemed as if the air were bursting with little globes of fire, like bullets, flattening out as they exploded. Round and round they went and finally melted in the snow amid the branches of the trees. In the centre of each the face of Rodolphe appeared. They multiplied, clustered together, bored into her. Then everything vanished, and she saw the lights of the houses glimmering through the mist far away.

And once again the deep hopelessness of her plight came back to her. Her lungs heaved as though they would burst. Then, in a transport of heroism which made her almost gay, she ran down the hill and across the cow-plank, hurried along the path, up the lane, through the market-place, and arrived in front of the chemist's shop.

It was empty. She was about to go in; but the bell would ring and someone might come. She slipped through the side gate holding her breath, and felt her way along the wall to the kitchen door. Inside, a candle was burning on the range. Justin, in his shirt-sleeves, was taking in a dish.

"They're at dinner. Wait."

He returned. She tapped on the window. He came out.

"The key! The key for upstairs, where the . . ."

"What?" He stared at her, astonished at the pallor of her face, which stood out white in the darkness. She looked so extraordinarily beautiful, possessed of a ghostly majesty. Without understanding what she wanted, he had a presentiment of something terrible.

She went on quickly in a low voice, a voice that was sweet and melting: "I want it! Give it me!"

Through the thin wall came the clatter of knives and forks from the dining-room. She said she wanted to kill some rats that were keeping her awake.

"I'll have to tell the master."

"No! Stop! . . . It's not worth bothering," she added more casually, "I'll tell him directly. Now, show me a light!"

She went down the passage off which the laboratory opened. Hanging on the wall was a key labelled *Capharnaum*.

"Justin!" shouted the chemist, who was growing impatient.

"Upstairs!" she whispered. And he followed her.

The key turned in the lock. She went straight over to the third shelf, so well did her memory guide her. She seized the blue jar, tugged at the cork, plunged her hand inside, and drew it out full of white powder which she proceeded to cram into her mouth.

"Stop!" he cried, hurling himself upon her.

"Be quiet! They'll come!"

He was desperate; he wanted to shout out.

"Don't say anything. All the blame will be put on your master!"

And she went away, suddenly at peace, serene as in the consciousness of duty done.

When Charles got home, overwrought at the news of the distraint, Emma had just gone. He called for her, wept, fainted away, but she did not return. Where could she be? He sent Félicité to the Homais', to Monsieur Tuvache's, to Lheureux's, to the Golden Lion, everywhere; and in the intervals of his anguish he saw his reputation lost, his money gone, Berthe's future wrecked. Through what cause? No word to tell him! He waited till six o'clock, then could stand it no longer. Fancying that she must have set off for Rouen, he walked a mile and a half along the highroad, met nobody, waited a while, turned back home again.

She had come in.

"What happened? What was it? Tell me!"

She sat down at her desk and wrote a letter, which she slowly sealed, adding the date and time.

"Read it tomorrow," she said in a solemn voice. "Till then, please don't ask me a single question. . . . No, not one!"

"But . . ."

"No, leave me alone!"

She lay down full length on the bed.

An acrid taste in her mouth awoke her. She saw Charles and closed her eyes again.

She watched with curiosity for any sign of pain. No, nothing yet. She heard the clock ticking, the fire crackling, Charles breathing as he stood beside her.

"There's not much in dying," she thought. "I shall go to sleep, and it will all be over."

She gulped down some water, and turned to the wall.

That dreadful inky taste was still there.

"I'm thirsty . . . I'm so thirsty!" she whispered.

"What can it be?" said Charles, handing her the glass.

"It's nothing . . . Open the window . . . I feel choked!"

And she vomited so suddenly that she barely had time to grab her handkerchief from under the pillow.

"Take it out! Throw it away!" she said quickly.

He started questioning her. She didn't answer. She kept quite still, afraid that the least agitation might make her sick. She began to feel an icy coldness mounting from her feet towards her heart.

"That's it, it's beginning!" she mumbled.

"What did you say?"

She rolled her head with a gentle, anguished movement, trying to open her jaws all the while as though she had a heavy weight on her tongue. At eight o'clock the vomiting began again.

Charles noticed a sort of white sediment clinging to the bottom of the basin.

"That's queer! That's funny!" he kept saying.

"No, it's nothing," she said in a firm voice.

Very gently, almost caressingly, he passed his hand over her stomach. She gave a shriek. He started back in terror.

She began to groan, feebly at first. A violent shudder went through her shoulders, she turned whiter than the sheet she was clutching in her fingers. Her wavering pulse could hardly be felt at all now.

Drops of sweat stood on her blue-veined face, which looked as if it had been petrified by exposure to some metallic vapour. Her teeth chattered, her pupils were dilated, her eyes stared vaguely about her. To every question she responded with simply a shake of the head. Two or three times she smiled. Little by little her groans grew louder. A muffled scream broke from her. She pretended to be feeling better and said she would soon be getting up. But then she was seized with convulsions.

"Oh, God, it's ghastly!" she cried.

He went down on his knees beside her.

"Tell me what you've eaten! For God's sake answer!" And he looked at her with such tenderness in his eyes as she had never seen before.

"All right," she said in a faltering voice. "There . . . over there. . . ."

He sprang to the desk, broke the seal and read aloud, "No one is guilty . . ." He stopped, passed his hand over his eyes, read on.

"What . . . Help! Oh, help!" And he could only utter the one word, "Poisoned! Poisoned!"

Félicité ran to get Homais, who shouted the news across the square. Madame Lefrançois heard him at the Golden Lion, several people got out of bed to tell their neighbours, and the village was awake all night.

Aghast, mouthing, hardly able to stand, Charles stumbled round the room, bumping into the furniture, tearing at his hair. Never had the chemist thought to see so appalling a sight.

He returned to his own house to write to Monsieur Canivet and Dr. Larivière. He lost his head and made over a dozen rough drafts. Hippolyte set off for Neufchâtel, Justin spurred Bovary's horse so unmercifully that he had to leave it on the hill at Bois-Guillaume foundered and three parts dead.

Charles tried to turn over the pages of his medical dictionary; but he could see nothing, the lines danced.

"Keep calm!" said the chemist. "It's only a matter of administering some powerful antidote. What poison was it?"

Charles pointed to the letter. It was arsenic.

"Right!" said Homais. "We must analyse."

For he knew that in all cases of poisoning it was necessary to analyse. Charles, not understanding, answered, "Yes, yes, go on! Save her!"

He went over to her again, sank down on the carpet and knelt with his head against the edge of the bed, sobbing.

"Don't cry!" she said. "Soon I shall be troubling you no more."

"Why did you? What made you?"

"It had to be, my dear," she replied.

"Weren't you happy? Is it my fault? I did all I could . . ."

"Yes . . . that's true. . . . You are a good man." And she passed her hand over his hair slowly. The sweetness of that sensation overcharged his grief. He felt his whole being dissolve in despair at the thought that he must lose her, just when she was showing more love for him than ever before. And he didn't know, he couldn't think, what to do; he didn't dare do anything — the necessity of an immediate decision serving to paralyse him completely.

She had done, she was thinking, with all the treachery and the squalor and the numberless desires that had racked her. She hated no one now; a twilight confusion was descending on her mind, and of all the noises of the earth Emma could no longer hear any but the intermittent lamentation of that poor soul at her side, blurred and tender as the last echo of a symphony dying in the distance.

"Bring me Berthe!" she said, raising herself on her elbow.

"You're not feeling worse?" asked Charles.

"No, no!"

The little girl arrived in her nurse's arms, her bare feet sticking out from under her long nightdress — solemn-faced and scarcely out of her dreams. She stared with wondering eyes at the untidy room, blinked at the dazzling candles that were burning on the tables. They must have reminded her of New Year's Day or mid-Lent when, woken early like this by candlelight, she used to get into her mother's bed to be given her presents; for she at once asked: "Where is it, Mummy?"

No one spoke.

"I can't see my stocking!"

And while Félicité held her over the bed, she kept her eyes turned towards the fireplace.

"Has nurse taken it?" she asked.

At the word "nurse," which revived the memory of her lusts and her miseries, Madame Bovary turned her head aside as though another, stronger, poison were rising nauseously in her throat. Berthe remained perched on the bed.

"Oh, mummy, what big eyes you've got! How pale you are! You're sticky!"

Her mother looked at her.

"I'm frightened!" said the child, shrinking away.

Emma took her hand and tried to kiss it. She struggled.

"That'll do! Take her away!" cried Charles, who was sobbing in the corner.

Then for a moment the symptoms ceased. She seemed less agitated, and at every slightest word, at every quieter breath she drew, he took fresh hope. When Canivet at last walked in, Charles threw himself into his arms, weeping.

"It's you! Thank you, it is kind of you! But she's better now. Look — !"

His colleague by no means shared this opinion; and without — as he put it — beating about the bush, he prescribed an emetic to clear the stomach completely.

Not long afterwards she started vomiting blood. Her lips pressed tighter together, her limbs writhed, brown spots broke out over her body, her pulse slid between the fingers like a taut wire, like a harp-string about to snap.

She began to scream, horribly. She damned and cursed the poison, begged it to be quick, and with her stiffening arms pushed away every-thing that Charles, in a still worse agony than she, kept trying to make her drink. He stood with his handkerchief to his lips, croaking, crying, choked by the sobs that shook his frame. Félicité ran hither and thither about the room. Homais stood motionless, sighing deeply; Monsieur Canivet, though still preserving his swagger, had none the less begun to feel uneasy.

"Damn! . . . But she's purged now, and the minute you stop the cause . . ."

"You stop the effect," said Homais. "That's obvious."

"Save her!" cried Bovary.

Accordingly, paying no heed to the chemist, who ventured the fur-ther hypothesis that it "might be a salutary paroxysm," Canivet was preparing to give her an antidote, when they heard the crack of a whip outside; the window-panes rattled, and a stage-coach, whisked along by three horses, in full harness and up to their ears in mud, came hurtling round the corner of the market. It was Dr. Larivière.

The advent of a god could have caused no greater commotion. Bovary lifted up his hands. Canivet stopped short. Homais removed his skull-cap long before the great man entered.

He belonged to that great line of surgeons that sprang from Bichat, that now-vanished generation of philosopher-healers who cherished their art with a fanatical love and practised it with zeal and sagacity. When Dr. Larivière was angry, the whole hospital quaked. His pupils re-vered him to the point of trying to imitate him in everything as soon as they set up in practice themselves; consequently, every town for miles around had its replica of his long merino greatcoat and his loose black jacket, the cuffs of which hung down unbuttoned over his firm hands — beautiful hands, always ungloved, as though to be the readier to plunge to the relief of suffering. Disdaining all academic honours, titles and decorations, hospitable and generous, like a father to the poor, practising goodness without believing in it, he might almost have passed for a saint had not his mental acuity caused him to be feared as a demon. Sharper than a lancet, his eyes looked straight into your soul, piercing through all pretence and reticence to dissect the lie be-neath. So he went his way, in all the easy majesty that comes of the consciousness of great talent, wealth and forty years of hard work and irreproachable living.

He closed the door behind him and his brows contracted at sight of Emma's cadaverous face, as she lay there on her back, her mouth agape. While apparently listening to Canivet, he rubbed his nostril with his forefinger and said, "Good, good. . . ." But his shoulders lifted in a slow gesture. Bovary noticed it. They looked at one another. And that man who was so accustomed to the sight of grief, could not restrain a tear; it dropped down on his shirt-front. He tried to take Canivet aside into the next room; Charles followed them.

"She's very bad, isn't she? Could we try poulticing? I don't know . . . Oh, think of something! You have saved so many lives!"

Charles had pinioned the doctor with both arms and was fixing him with a gaze of terrified entreaty, half-swooning on his chest.

"Come, my poor boy. Be brave! . . . There's nothing I can do." And Dr. Larivière turned away.

"Are you going?"

"I'm coming back."

He went out as though to give orders to the coachman, and Canivet followed, being no less reluctant to have Emma die under his care.

The chemist joined them in the market-place. He was temperamentally incapable of tearing himself away from celebrities and he accordingly requested Dr. Larivière to do him the signal honour of taking luncheon at his house.

Orders were hastily sent to the Golden Lion for pigeons, to the butcher's for all the cutlets he had in his shop, to Tuvache's for cream and to Lestiboudois for eggs. The chemist took a hand in the preparations himself.

"You'll excuse us, sir," said Madame Homais, tugging at the strings of her bodice. "In our little village, you know, unless we're warned the day before . . ."

"The wine-glasses!!!" whispered Homais.

"If we lived in town, now, we'd always have stuffed trotters to fall back on. . . ."

"Quiet! . . . Will you take your seat, Doctor!"

After a few mouthfuls he thought fit to impart certain details of the tragedy.

"First, we had a parched feeling in the pharnyx, then horrible pains in the epigastrium, superpurgation, and coma."

"How did she poison herself?"

"I've no idea, Doctor. Neither do I know where she could have obtained that arsenious acid."

Justin, who had just come in with a pile of plates, started trembling violently.

"What's the matter with you?" said the chemist.

So addressed, the young man let his whole load go crashing to the floor.

"Fool!" yelled Homais. "Clumsy blockhead! Pitiable idiot!"

Suddenly regaining control of himself, he went on: "I decided to attempt an analysis, Doctor. First, I carefully introduced into a tube . . ."

"You'd have done better," said the surgeon, "to introduce your fingers into her throat!"

His colleague remained silent; he had just received, in private, a severe rebuke on the subject of his emetic, and in consequence, the worthy Canivet, who had been so arrogant and loquacious at the time of the club-foot operation, today sat very quiet, wearing a continuous smile of approval.

Homais expanded in his hostly pride, and the distressing thought of Bovary lent, by contrast, a certain spice to his pleasure. The presence of the doctor quite enraptured him; he showed off all his erudition, pouring out allusions to cantharides, the upas, the manchineel, the viper.

"I've even read of people becoming intoxicated — struck down, you might say — by black puddings that had been submitted to an excessively strong fumigation! At least, so we were told in an excellent report composed by one of our leading pharmacists — one of our masters, the illustrious Cadet de Gassicourt!"

Madame Homais reappeared, carrying one of those rickety contrivances that you heat with a spirit-lamp: for Homais insisted on making his coffee at table. What was more, he had previously roasted, ground and blended it himself.

"*Saccharum,* Doctor?" he said as he passed the sugar.

Then he had all his children brought downstairs to hear what the surgeon thought of their constitutions.

And then, when Monsieur Larivière was on the point of leaving, Madame Homais asked him to examine her husband. He was "thickening his blood" by going to sleep every evening after dinner.

"Oh, it's not his *blood* that's thick." And with a little smile at this unnoticed witticism, the doctor opened the door. The shop was thronged with people, and he had great difficulty in getting away from Monsieur Tuvache, who suspected inflammation in his wife's lungs because she was always spitting in the fire; then from Monsieur Binet, who sometimes had hunger-pangs, and from Madame Caron, who had pins and needles; from Lheureux with his vertigo, Lestiboudois with his rheumatism, and Madame Lefrançois with her heartburn. When the three horses finally trotted off, the general opinion was that he had been most unobliging.

Public attention was distracted, however, by the appearance of Monsieur Bournisien coming through the market with the holy oils.

Homais owed it to his principles to compare priests with crows attracted by the smell of the dead. The sight of an ecclesiastic was physically repugnant to him, for the cassock put him in mind of the shroud, and his abomination of the one was partly due to his dread of the other.

Nevertheless, not shrinking from what he called his "mission," he returned to Bovary's house, together with Canivet, whom Monsieur Larivière, before leaving, had strongly urged to remain. But for his wife's remonstrances, the chemist would have taken his two sons along with him as well, to accustom them to painful occasions and give them a lesson, an example, a solemn picture that would remain in their minds thereafter.

The bedroom, when they entered, was filled with a mournful solemnity. On the work-table, covered with a white cloth, were five or six little balls of cotton-wool in a silver dish and a large crucifix standing between a pair of lighted candles. Emma lay with her chin sunk on her breast, her eyelids unnaturally wide apart, and her poor hands trailing over the sheets in that hideous, gentle movement of the dying, who seem prematurely eager to wrap themselves in the winding-sheet. Pale as a statue, with eyes like burning coals, Charles, not weeping now, stood facing her at the foot of the bed, while the priest knelt down and mumbled under his breath.

Slowly she turned her face, and when her eyes lighted on the violet stole she seemed to be seized with a sudden joy. Doubtless she was finding again in the midst of a wondrous appeasement the lost ecstasy of her first flights of mysticism, and beginning to see visions of eternal blessedness.

The priest rose to take the crucifix. Reaching forward like one in thirst, she glued her lips to the body of the Man-God and laid upon it with all her failing strength the most mighty kiss of love she had ever given. The priest recited the *Misereatur* and the *Indulgentiam;* then he dipped his right thumb into the oil and began the unctions: first on the eyes, that had so coveted all earthly splendours; then on the nostrils, that had loved warm breezes and amorous perfumes; then on the mouth, that had opened for falsehood, had groaned with pride and cried out in lust; then on the hands, that had revelled in delicious contacts; lastly on the soles of the feet, that once had run so swiftly to the assuaging of her desires, and now would walk no more.

The *curé* wiped his fingers, threw the oily wads of cotton-wool on the fire and sat down once more beside the dying woman, to tell her that she must now unite her sufferings with those of Jesus Christ and cast herself on the Divine Mercy.

As he finished his exhortation, he tried to put into her hand a consecrated taper, symbolic of the celestial glories by which she was soon to be surrounded. Emma was too weak to close her fingers on it, and Monsieur Bournisien caught it as it fell to the floor.

However, she was less pale now and her face wore an expression of serenity, as though the sacrament had healed her.

The priest did not fail to remark on this. Indeed, he explained to Bovary that the Lord did sometimes prolong people's lives when He deemed it meet for their salvation; and Charles remembered another day when she had been near to death like this and had received the communion.

"There may still be hope," he thought.

And just then she looked all round her, slowly, as one waking from a dream. In a clear voice she asked for her mirror, and remained bowed over it for some time, until big tears began to trickle out of her eyes. Then she threw up her head with a sigh and fell back on the pillow.

At once her lungs began to heave rapidly, the whole of her tongue protruded from her mouth, her rolling eyes turned pale like the globes of two guttering lamps: she might have been dead already but for the frightful oscillation of her ribs, that shook with furious gusts as though her soul were leaping to get free. Félicité knelt before the crucifix; even the chemist bent his knees a little; Monsieur Canivet stared vaguely out into the square. Bournisien had started praying again, his face bowed over the edge of the bed, his long black cassock trailing across the floor behind him. Charles knelt opposite, his arms stretched out towards Emma. He had taken her hands and was pressing them in his, shuddering at every beat of her heart as at the reverberation of a falling ruin. As the death-rattle grew louder, the priest hastened his orisons; they mingled with Bovary's stifled sobs, and sometimes everything seemed to be drowned in the dull murmur of the Latin syllables, that sounded like the tolling of a knell.

Suddenly there was a clumping of sabots on the pavement outside, the scraping of a stick, and a voice came up, a hoarse voice singing:

> *"When the sun shines warm above,*
> *It turns a maiden's thoughts to love."*

Emma sat up like a corpse galvanised, her hair dishevelled, her eyes fixed, gaping.

> *"All across the furrows brown*
> *See Nanette go bending down,*
> *Gathering up with careful hand*
> *The golden harvest from the land."*

"The blind man!" she cried.

And Emma started laughing, a ghastly, frantic, desperate laugh, fancying she could see the hideous face of the beggar rising up like a nightmare amid the eternal darkness.

> *"The wind it blew so hard one day,*
> *Her little petticoat flew away!"*

A convulsion flung her down upon the mattress. They moved nearer. She was no more.

Charles Baudelaire (1821–1867)

LIFE: The disorder of his early years, arising from the violent passion of his relations with his mother and stepfather, established the pattern of his life and became the source of his poetry. Sent to the Far East to relieve sensibilities at home, he returned with his half-caste mistress Jeanne Duval and thereupon jumped into the political and literary revolutions of Paris. Like Flaubert, whom he admired, Baudelaire was harassed and prosecuted for the immorality of his work; he finally left Paris for Brussels and lived there for two years until, physically and mentally paralyzed, he returned to die, in great pain but reconciled at last with his mother.

WORKS: *The Flowers of Evil* (1857); *Artificial Paradises* (1860); *Little Poems in Prose* (1869).

THE FLOWERS OF EVIL

To the Reader *

Folly and error, avarice and vice,
Employ our souls and waste our bodies' force.
As mangy beggars incubate their lice,
We nourish our innocuous remorse.

Our sins are stubborn, craven our repentance.   5
For our weak vows we ask excessive prices.
Trusting our tears will wash away the sentence,
We sneak off where the muddy road entices.

Cradled in evil, that Thrice-Great Magician,
The Devil, rocks our souls, that can't resist;   10
And the rich metal of our own volition
Is vaporized by that sage alchemist.

The Devil pulls the strings by which we're worked:
By all revolting objects lured, we slink
Hellwards; each day down one more step we're jerked   15
Feeling no horror, through the shades that stink.

Just as a lustful pauper bites and kisses
The scarred and shrivelled breast of an old whore,
We steal, along the roadside, furtive blisses,
Squeezing them like stale oranges for more.   20

Packed tight, like hives of maggots, thickly seething,
Within our brains a host of demons surges.
Deep down into our lungs at every breathing,
Death flows, an unseen river, moaning dirges.

If rape or arson, poison, or the knife   25
Has wove no pleasing patterns in the stuff

* Translated by Roy Campbell.

Of this drab canvas we accept as life —
It is because we are not bold enough!

Amongst the jackals, leopards, mongrels, apes,
Snakes, scorpions, vultures, that with hellish din,   30
Squeal, roar, writhe, gambol, crawl, with monstrous shapes,
In each man's foul menagerie of sin —

There's one more damned than all. He never gambols,
Nor crawls, nor roars, but, from the rest withdrawn,
Gladly of this whole earth would make a shambles   35
And swallow up existence with a yawn . . .

Boredom! He smokes his hookah, while he dreams
Of gibbets, weeping tears he cannot smother.
You know this dainty monster, too, it seems —
Hypocrite reader! — You! — My twin! — My brother!   40

Elevation *

Above the valleys and the lakes: beyond
The woods, seas, clouds, and mountain-ranges: far
Above the sun, the aethers silver-swanned
With nebulae, and the remotest star,

My spirit! with agility you move   5
Like a strong swimmer with the seas to fight,
Through the blue vastness furrowing your groove
With an ineffable and male delight.

Far from these foetid marshes, be made pure
In the pure air of the superior sky,   10
And drink, like some most exquisite liqueur,
The fire that fills the lucid realms on high.

Beyond where cares and boredom hold dominion,
Which charge our fogged existence with their spleen,
Happy is he who with a stalwart pinion   15
Can seek those fields so shining and serene:

Whose thoughts, like larks, rise on the freshening breeze,
Who fans the morning with his tameless wings,
Skims over life, and understands with ease
The speech of flowers and other voiceless things.   20

* Translated by Roy Campbell.

Beauty *

I am as lovely as a dream in stone;
My breast on which each finds his death in turn
Inspires the poet with a love as lone
As everlasting clay, and as taciturn.

Swan-white of heart, a sphinx no mortal knows,   5
My throne is in the heaven's azure deep;
I hate all movement that disturbs my pose;
I smile not ever, neither do I weep.

Before my monumental attitudes,
Taken from the proudest plastic arts,   10
My poets pray in austere studious moods,

For I, to fold enchantment round their hearts,
Have pools of light where beauty flames and dies,
The placid mirrors of my luminous eyes.

Correspondences †

Nature is a temple whose living colonnades
Breathe forth a mystic speech in fitful sighs;
Man wanders among symbols in those glades
Where all things watch him with familiar eyes.

Like dwindling echoes gathered far away   5
Into a deep and thronging unison
Huge as the night or as the light of day,
All scents and sounds and colors meet as one.

Perfumes there are as sweet as the oboe's sound,
Green as the prairies, fresh as a child's caress,   10
— And there are others, rich, corrupt, profound

And of an infinite pervasiveness,
Like myrrh, or musk, or amber, that excite
The ecstasies of sense, the soul's delight.

Invitation to the Voyage †

My child, my sister, dream
How sweet all things would seem

* From Baudelaire, *Flowers of Evil*, Marthiel and Jackson Mathews, eds. Translated by F. P. Sturm. Copyright 1955 by New Directions. Reprinted by permission of New Directions Publishing Corporation.
† From *Things of This World*, © 1956, by Richard Wilbur. Reprinted by permission of Harcourt, Brace & World, Inc., and Richard Wilbur.

Were we in that kind land to live together,
   And there love slow and long,
   There love and die among   5
Those scenes that image you, that sumptuous weather.
   Drowned suns that glimmer there
   Through cloud-dishevelled air
Move me with such a mystery as appears
   Within those other skies   10
   Of your treacherous eyes
When I behold them shining through their tears.

There, there is nothing else but grace and measure,
Richness, quietness, and pleasure.

   Furniture that wears   15
   The lustre of the years
Softly would glow within our glowing chamber,
   Flowers of rarest bloom
   Proffering their perfume
Mixed with the vague fragrances of amber;   20
   Gold ceilings would there be,
   Mirrors deep as the sea,
The walls all in an Eastern splendor hung —
   Nothing but should address
   The soul's loneliness,   25
Speaking her sweet and secret native tongue.

There, there is nothing else but grace and measure,
Richness, quietness, and pleasure.

   See, sheltered from the swells
   There in the still canals   30
Those drowsy ships that dream of sailing forth;
   It is to satisfy
   Your least desire, they ply
Hither through all the waters of the earth.
   The sun at close of day   35
   Clothes the fields of hay,
Then the canals, at last the town entire
   In hyacinth and gold:
   Slowly the land is rolled
Sleepward under a sea of gentle fire.   40

There, there is nothing else but grace and measure,
Richness, quietness, and pleasure.

The Voyage *

To Maxime du Camp.

I

For children crazed with maps and prints and stamps —
The universe can sate their appetite.
How vast the world is by the light of lamps,
But in the eyes of memory how slight!

One morning we set sail, with brains on fire,   5
And hearts swelled up with rancorous emotion,
Balancing, to the rhythm of its lyre,
Our infinite upon the finite ocean.

Some wish to leave their venal native skies,
Some flee their birthplace, others change their ways,   10
Astrologers who've drowned in Beauty's eyes,
Tyrannic Circe with the scent that slays.

Not to be changed to beasts, they have their fling
With space, and splendour, and the burning sky,
The suns that bronze them and the frosts that sting   15
Efface the mark of kisses by and by.

But the true travellers are those who go
Only to get away: hearts like balloons
Unballasted, with their own fate aglow,
Who know not why they fly with the monsoons: 20

Those whose desires are in the shape of clouds,
Who dream, as raw recruits of shot and shell,
Of mighty raptures in strange, transient crowds
Of which no human soul the name can tell.

II

Horror! We imitate the top and bowl   25
In swerve and bias. Through our sleep it runs.
It's Curiosity that makes us roll,
As the fierce Angel whips the whirling suns.

Singular game! where the goal changes places;
The winning-post is nowhere, yet all round;   30
Where Man tires not of the mad hope he races
Thinking, some day, that respite will be found.

---

* Translated by Roy Campbell.

Our soul's like a three-master, where one hears
A voice that from the bridge would warn all hands.
Another from the foretop madly cheers   35
"Love, joy, and glory" . . . Hell! we're on the sands!

The watchmen think each isle that heaves in view
An Eldorado, shouting their belief;
Imagination riots in the crew
Who in the morning only find a reef.   40

The fool that dotes on far, chimeric lands —
Put him in irons, or feed him to the shark!
The drunken sailor's visionary lands
Can only leave the bitter truth more stark.

So some old vagabond, in mud who grovels,   45
Dreams, nose in air, of Edens sweet to roam;
Wherever smoky wicks illumine hovels
He sees another Capua or Rome.

III

Amazing travellers, what noble stories
We read in the deep oceans of your gaze!   50
Show us your memory's casket, and the glories
Streaming from gems made out of stars and rays!

We, too, would roam without a sail or steam,
And to combat the boredom of our jail,
Would stretch, like canvas on our souls, a dream,   55
Framed in horizons, of the seas you sail.

What have you seen?

IV

"We have seen stars and waves,
We have seen sands and shores and oceans too,
In spite of shocks and unexpected graves,   60
We have been bored, at times, the same as you.

The solar glories on the violet ocean
And those of spires that in the sunset rise,
Lit, in our hearts, a yearning, fierce emotion
To plunge into those ever-luring skies.   65

The richest cities and the scenes most proud
In nature, have no magic to enamour

Like those which hazard traces in the cloud
While wistful longing magnifies their glamour.

(Enjoyment adds more fuel for desire,   70
Old tree, to which all pleasure is manure;
As the bark hardens, so the boughs shoot higher,
And nearer to the sun would grow mature.

Tree, will you always flourish, more vivacious
Than cypress?) None the less, these views are yours: 75
We took some photographs for your voracious
Album, who only care for distant shores.

We have seen idols elephantine-snouted,
And thrones with living gems bestarred and pearled,
And palaces whose riches would have routed   80
The dreams of all the bankers in the world.

We have seen wonder-striking robes and dresses,
Women whose nails and teeth the betel stains
And jugglers whom the rearing snake caresses."

v

What then? What then?

VI

"O childish little brains,   85
Not to forget the greatest wonder there —
We've seen in every country, without searching,
From top to bottom of the fatal stair
Immortal sin ubiquitously lurching:

Woman, a vile slave, proud in her stupidity,   90
Self-worshipping, without the least disgust:
Man, greedy, lustful, ruthless in cupidity,
Slave to a slave, and sewer to her lust:

The torturer's delight, the martyr's sobs,
The feasts where blood perfumes the giddy rout: 95
Power sapping its own tyrants: servile mobs
In amorous obeisance to the knout:

Some similar religions to our own,
All climbing skywards: Sanctity who treasures,
As in his downy couch some dainty drone,   100
In horsehair, nails, and whips, his dearest pleasures.

Prating Humanity, with genius raving,
As mad today as ever from the first,
Cries in fierce agony, its Maker braving,
'O God, my Lord and likeness, be thou cursed!'   105

But those less dull, the lovers of Dementia,
Fleeing the herd which fate has safe impounded,
In opium seek for limitless adventure.
— That's all the record of the globe we rounded."

VII

It's bitter knowledge that one learns from travel.   110
The world so small and drab, from day to day,
The horror of our image will unravel,
A pool of dread in deserts of dismay.

Must we depart, or stay? Stay if you can.
Go if you must. One runs: another hides   115
To baffle Time, that fatal foe to man.
And there are runners, whom no rest betides,

Like the Apostles or the Wandering Jew,
Whom neither ship nor waggon can enable
To cheat the retiary. But not a few   120
Have killed him without stirring from their cradle.

But when he sets his foot upon our nape
We still can hope and cry "Leave all behind!"
As in old times to China we'd escape
With eyes turned seawards, hair that fans the wind,   125

We'll sail once more upon the sea of Shades
With heart like that of a young sailor beating.
I hear the rich, sad voices of the Trades
Who cry "This Way! all you who would be eating

The scented Lotus. Here it is they range   130
The piles of magic fruit. O hungry friend,
Come here and swoon away into the strange
Trance of an afternoon that has no end."

In the familiar tones we sense the spectre;
Our Pylades stretch arms across the seas.   135
"To salve your heart, now swim to your Electra,"
She cries, of whom we used to kiss the knees.

135. *Pylades:* A friend of Orestes, he was with him when he killed his mother Clytemnestra, and thereafter shared his tortured wanderings.
136. Electra: Orestes' sister, who eventually married Pylades.

VIII

O Death, old Captain, it is time. Weigh anchor!
To sail beyond the doldrums of our days.
Though black as pitch the sea and sky, we hanker   140
For space; you know our hearts are full of rays.

Pour us your poison to revive our soul!
It cheers the burning quest that we pursue,
Careless if Hell or Heaven be our goal,
Beyond the known world to seek out the New!   145

Fyodor Dostoevsky (1821–1881)

LIFE: The son of a doctor killed by one of his peasants, Dostoevsky
himself felt death and survived: he was arrested for revolutionary activities, sentenced to be shot, led to the place of execution, and then
reprieved. It was no doubt the central experience of his life. Everything after it — the ten years of imprisonment in Siberia, the extreme
poverty, compulsive gambling, anguished wandering over the face of
Europe, the chaos of his personal life, the terror of epilepsy — merely
fired the emotional and psychological vision which used the experience
to create the passionate fiction.

WORKS: *The Double* (1846); *Notes from Underground* (1864); *Crime
and Punishment* (1866); *The Idiot* (1869); *The Possessed* (1871–72);
The Brothers Karamazov (1880).

NOTES FROM UNDERGROUND *,†

Part I — Underground

I

I am a sick man. I am a spiteful man. I am an unattractive man.
I believe my liver is diseased. However, I know nothing at all about

Reprinted by permission of the publisher, The Vanguard Press, from *A Treasury of Russian Literature*, edited by Bernard Guilbert Guerney. Copyright 1943, by Vanguard Press, Inc. Translated by Constance Garnett, revised by Bernard Guerney.

* 1864. Our text contains the complete story.

† The author of the diary and the diary itself are, of course, imaginary. Nevertheless it is clear
that such persons as the writer of these notes not only may, but positively must, exist in our
society, when we consider the circumstances in the midst of which our society is formed. I have
tried to expose to the view of the public, more distinctly than is commonly done, one of the
characters of the recent past. He is one of the representatives of a generation still living. In this
fragment, entitled *Underground*, this person introduces himself and his views and, as it were, tries
to explain the causes owing to which he has made his appearance and was bound to make his
appearance in our midst. In the second fragment there are added the actual notes of this person
concerning certain events in his life. — *Author's Note.*

my disease and do not know for certain what ails me. I don't consult a doctor for it, and never have, though I have a respect for medicine and doctors. Besides, I am extremely superstitious, sufficiently so to respect medicine, at any rate (I am well-educated enough not to be superstitious, even though I am). No, I refuse to consult a doctor out of spite. That is something you probably will not understand. Well, I do. Of course, I can't explain whom precisely I am mortifying in this case by my spite: I am perfectly well aware that I cannot "get even" with the doctors by not consulting them; I know better than anyone that by all this I am only injuring myself and no one else. But still, if I don't consult a doctor it is out of spite. My liver is bad, well — let it get worse!

I have been going on like that for a long time — twenty years. Now I am forty. I used to be in the government service, but am no longer. I was a spiteful official. I was rude and took pleasure in being so. I did not take bribes, you see, so I was bound to find a recompense in that, at least. (A poor jest, but I will not cross it out. I wrote it thinking it would sound very witty; but now that I have perceived myself that I was merely trying to show off in a despicable way, I will purposely refrain from crossing it out!)

When petitioners would come to my desk for information, I would grind my teeth at them and feel intense enjoyment whenever I succeeded in making anybody unhappy. I almost always did succeed. For the most part they were all timid people — of course, since they were petitioners. But of the uppity ones there was one officer in particular I could not endure. He simply would not be humble, and kept clanking his sword in a disgusting way. I carried on a feud with him for eighteen months over that sword. At last I got the better of him. He left off clanking it. That happened in my youth, though.

But do you know, gentlemen, what was the chief point about my spite? Why, the whole point, the real sting of it lay in the fact that continually, even in the moment of the acutest spleen, I was inwardly conscious with shame that I was not only not a spiteful man but not even an embittered one, that I was simply scaring sparrows at random and amusing myself by it. I might foam at the mouth, but bring me a doll to play with, give me a cup of tea with sugar in it, and I could be appeased. I might even be genuinely touched, though probably I should grind my teeth at myself afterward and lie awake at night from shame for months after. That was my way.

I was lying when I said just now that I was a spiteful official. I was lying from spite. I was simply amusing myself with the petitioners and with the officer, and in reality I never could become spiteful. I was conscious every moment in myself of many, very many elements absolutely opposite to that. I felt them positively swarming in me, these opposed elements. I knew that they had been swarming in me all my life and craving some outlet from me, but let them out I would not. I would not let them, I purposely would not let them come out. They tormented me till I was ashamed; they drove me to convulsions and at last sickened me — how they sickened me! Now, aren't you imagining, gentlemen, that I am expressing remorse over something, that I am asking your forgiveness for something? I am sure you are. However, I assure you I don't care about that.

It was not only that I could not become spiteful; I did not know how to become anything: either spiteful or kind, either a rascal or an honest man, either a hero or an insect. Now I am living out my life in my corner, taunting myself with the spiteful and useless consolation that an intelligent man cannot seriously become anything and it is only the fool who becomes something. Yes, a man in the nineteenth century must and morally ought to be pre-eminently a characterless creature; a man of character, an active man is pre-eminently a limited creature. That is my conviction of forty years. I am forty years old now, and you know forty years is a whole lifetime; you know it is extreme old age. To live longer than forty years is bad manners, it's vulgar, immoral. Who lives beyond forty? Answer that, sincerely and honestly. I will tell you who: fools and good-for-nothings. I tell all old men that to their faces, all these venerable old men, all these silver-haired and reverend ancients! I tell the whole world that to its face! I have a right to say so, for I'll go on living to sixty myself. To seventy! To eighty! Hold on, let me catch my breath.

No doubt, gentlemen, you imagine that I wish to amuse you. You are mistaken in that, too. I am by no means such a mirthful person as you imagine, or may imagine; however, irritated by all this babble (and I feel that you are irritated), you think fit to ask me who am I; my answer is, I am a Collegiate Assessor. I went into Civil Service so as to have something to eat (that and nothing else), and when last year a distant relation left me six thousand rubles in his will I immediately retired from the Service and settled down in my hole. I used to live in this hole before, but now I have settled down in it. My room is a wretched, horrid one on the outskirts of the town. My servant is an old countrywoman, ill-natured from stupidity, and, moreover, there is always a nasty smell about her. I am told that the Petersburg climate is bad for me, and that with my small means it is very expensive to live there. I know all that better than all these sage and experienced counselors and preceptors. But I am remaining in Petersburg; I am not going away from Petersburg! I am not going away because — eh, it absolutely doesn't matter whether I am going away or not going away.

But what can a decent man speak of with most pleasure?

Answer: Of himself.

Well, then, I will talk about myself.

II

And now, gentlemen, whether you care to hear it or not, I want to tell you why I could not become even an insect. I tell you solemnly that I have tried to become an insect, many's the time. But I was not equal even to that. I swear, gentlemen, that to be too conscious is an illness — a real out-and-out illness. For man's everyday needs it would have been quite enough to have the ordinary human consciousness, that is, half or a quarter of the amount which falls to the lot of a cultivated man of our unhappy nineteenth century, especially one who has the fatal ill-luck to inhabit Petersburg, the most theoretical and intentional town on the whole terrestrial globe. (There are intentional and unintentional towns.) It would have been quite enough, for instance, to have the consciousness by which all so-called straightforward persons and men of action live. I'll bet you think I am writing all this from affectation, to be witty at the expense of men of action; and what is more, that from ill-bred affectation I am clanking a sword, like my officer. But, gentlemen, whoever can pride himself on his diseases and even swagger over them?

Although, after all, everyone does do just that; people do pride themselves on their diseases, and I, perhaps, more than anyone else. We will not dispute it; my contention was absurd. And yet I am firmly persuaded that a great deal of consciousness — every sort of consciousness, in fact — is a disease. I stick to that. But let's leave that, too, for a minute. Tell me this: why does it happen that at the very — yes, at the *very* — moments when I am most capable of feeling every refinement of all that is *good and beautiful* (as they used to say at one time), I would, as though on purpose, happen not only to feel but to do such ugly things that — well, in short, such actions as perhaps all men commit, but which, as though purposely, came at the very time when I was most conscious that they ought not to be committed. The more conscious I was of goodness and of all that was *good and beautiful,* the more deeply I sank into my mire and the more ready I was to sink in it altogether. But the chief point was that all this was not accidental in me, as it were, but apparently had to be so. It was as though it were my most normal condition, and not in the least disease or depravity, so that at last all desire in me to struggle against this depravity passed. It ended by my almost (perhaps actually) believing that this was perhaps my normal condition.

But at first, in the beginning, what agonies I endured in that struggle! I did not believe it was the same with other people, and all my life I hid this fact about myself as a secret. I was ashamed (even now, perhaps, I am ashamed); I got to the point of feeling a sort of secret, abnormal, despicable enjoyment in returning home to my hole on some disgustingly inclement Petersburg night, acutely conscious that that day I had committed a loathsome action again, that what was done could never be undone, and secretly, inwardly gnawing, gnawing at myself for it, rending and consuming myself till at last the bitterness turned into a sort of shameful accursed sweetness, and at last into positive real enjoyment! Yes, into enjoyment — into enjoyment! I insist upon that. I have spoken of this because I keep wanting to know for a fact whether other people feel such enjoyment? I will explain: the enjoyment was just from the too intense consciousness of one's own degradation; it was from feeling that you had reached the last barrier, that it was horrible, but that it could not be otherwise; that there was no escape for you; that you never could become a different man; that even if time and faith were still left you to change into something different you would most likely not wish to change; or if you did wish to, even then you would do nothing, because perhaps in reality there was nothing for you to change into.

And the worst of it, and the root of it all, was that it was all in accord with the normal fundamental laws of overacute consciousness, and with the inertia that was the direct result of those laws, and that consequently one was not only unable to change but could do absolutely nothing. Thus it would follow, as the result of acute consciousness, that one is not to blame in being a scoundrel; as though that were any consolation to the scoundrel once he has come to realize that he actually is a scoundrel. But enough! Eh, I've talked a lot of nonsense, yet what have I explained? How is such enjoyment to be explained? Yet explain it I will. I will get to the bottom of it! That is why I have taken up my pen. . . .

I, for instance, have a great deal of *amour propre*. I am as suspicious and prone to take offense as a hunchback or a dwarf. But, upon my word, I sometimes have had moments when, if I had happened to be slapped in the face, I should, perhaps, have been positively glad of it. I say, in earnest, that I should probably have been able to discover even in that a peculiar sort of enjoyment — the enjoyment, of course, of despair; but in despair there are the most intense enjoyments, especially when one is very acutely conscious of the hopelessness of one's position. And when one is slapped in the face — why, then the consciousness of being rubbed into a pulp would positively overwhelm one. The worst of it is, look at it which way you will, it still turns out that I was always most to blame in everything. And what is most humiliating of all, to blame for no fault of my own but, so to say, through the laws of nature. In the first place, I was to blame because I am cleverer than any of the people surrounding me. (I have always considered myself cleverer than any of the people surrounding me, and sometimes, would you believe it, have been positively ashamed of it. At any rate, I have all my life, as it were, turned my eyes away and never could look people straight in the face.) I was to blame, finally, because even if I had had magnanimity, I should only have had more suffering from the sense of its uselessness. I should certainly have never been able to do anything because of being magnanimous — either to forgive (for my assailant would perhaps have slapped me from the laws of nature, and one cannot forgive the laws of nature) or to forget (for even if the slap were owing to the laws of nature, it is insulting all the same). Finally, even if I had wanted to be anything but magnanimous, had desired on the contrary to avenge myself on my assailant, I could not have avenged myself on anyone for anything, because I should certainly never have made up my mind to do anything, even if I had been able to. Why shouldn't I have made up my mind? I want to say a few words about that in particular.

III

With people who know how to avenge themselves and to stand up for themselves in general, how is it done? Why, when they are possessed, let us suppose, by the feeling of revenge, then for the time being there is nothing else but that feeling left in their whole being. Such a gentleman simply dashes straight for his object like an infuriated bull with its horns down, and nothing but a wall will stop him. (By the way: facing the wall, such gentlemen — that is, the *straightforward* persons and men of action — are genüinely nonplused. For them a wall is not an evasion, as for us who think and consequently do nothing; it is not an excuse for turning aside, an excuse which we always are very glad of, though we scarcely believe in it ourselves, as a rule. No, they are nonplused in all sincerity. The wall has for them something tranquilizing, morally soothing, final — perhaps even something mysterious — but of this wall more later.)

Well, such a straightforward person I regard as the real normal man, as his tender Mother Nature wished to see him when she graciously brought him into being on the earth. I envy such a man till I am green in the face. He is stupid. I am not disputing that, but perhaps, for all we know, the normal man should be stupid. Perhaps it's all very beautiful, in fact. And I am the more persuaded of that suspicion, if one can call it so, by the fact that if you take, for instance, the antithesis of the normal man, that is, the man of acute consciousness, who has come, of course, not out of the lap of nature but out of a retort (this is almost mysticism, gentlemen, but I suspect that this, too, is so), this retort-made man is sometimes so nonplused in the presence of his antithesis that with all his exaggerated consciousness he genuinely thinks of himself as a mouse and not a man. It may be an acutely conscious mouse, yet it is a mouse, while the other is a man, and, therefore, *et cetera, et cetera*. And the worst of it is, he himself, his very own self, looks on himself as a mouse; no one asks him to do so; and that is an important point. Now let us look at this mouse in action. Let us suppose, for instance, that it feels insulted, too (and it almost always does feel insulted), and wants to revenge itself likewise. There may even be a greater accumulation of spite in it than in *l'homme de la nature et de la vérité*.[1] The base and nasty desire to vent that spite on its assailant rankles perhaps even more nastily in it than in *l'homme de la nature et de la vérité*. For through his innate stupidity the latter looks upon his revenge as justice, pure and simple; while in conse-

---

1. That is, the man of nature and of truth — as Rousseau described himself in the opening paragraph of his *Confessions*.

quence of its acute consciousness the mouse does not believe in the justice of it.

To come at last to the deed itself, to the very act of revenge. Apart from the one fundamental nastiness the luckless mouse succeeds in creating around it, so many other nastinesses in the form of doubts and questions add to the one question so many unsettled questions that there inevitably works up around it a sort of fatal ferment, a stinking mess, made up of its doubts, emotions, and of the contempt spat upon it by the *straightforward* men of action who stand solemnly about it as judges and arbitrators, laughing at it till their healthy sides ache. Of course, the only thing left for it is to dismiss all that with a wave of its paw and, with a smile of assumed contempt in which it does not even itself believe, creep ignominiously into its mousehole. There in its nasty, stinking, underground home our insulted, crushed and ridiculed mouse promptly becomes absorbed in cold, malignant, and, above all, everlasting spite. For forty years together it will remember its injury down to the smallest, most ignominious details, and every time will add, of itself, details still more ignominious, spitefully teasing and tormenting itself with its own imagination. It will itself be ashamed of its imaginings, but yet it will recall everything, it will go over and over every detail, it will invent unheard-of things against itself, pretending that those things might happen, and will forgive nothing. Perhaps it will take to avenging itself, too, but piecemeal, as it were, in trivial ways, from behind the stove, incognito, without believing either in its own right to vengeance or in the success of its revenge, knowing that from all its efforts at revenge it will suffer a hundred times more than he on whom it revenges itself, while the victim, I daresay, will not even know a thing about it. On its deathbed the mouse will recall everything all over again, with interest compounded through all the years, and —

But it is just in that cold, abominable half-despair, half-belief, in that conscious burying of oneself alive for grief in the underworld for forty years, in that acutely recognized and yet partly doubtful hopelessness of one's position, in that hell of unsatisfied, introverted desires, in that fever of oscillations, of resolutions determined for ever and repented of again a minute later — that the savor of that strange enjoyment of which I have spoken lies. It is so subtle, so difficult of analysis, that persons who are a little limited, or even simply persons of strong nerves, will not understand a single atom of it. "Possibly," you will add on your own account with a grin, "people who have never received a slap in the face will not understand it either," and in that way you will politely hint to me that I, too, perhaps, have had the experience of a slap in the face in my life, and therefore speak as one who knows. I'll bet that's what you're thinking. But set your minds at rest, gentlemen, I have not received a slap in the face, though it is absolutely a matter of indifference to me what you may think about it. Possibly I even regret, myself, that I have given so few slaps in the face during my life. But enough — not another word on that subject of such extreme interest to you.

I will continue calmly concerning persons with strong nerves who do not understand a certain refinement of enjoyment. Though in certain circumstances these gentlemen bellow their loudest like bulls, though this, let us suppose, does them the greatest credit, yet, as I have said already, confronted with the impossible they subside at once. The impossible means the stone wall! What stone wall? Why, of course, the laws of nature, the deductions of natural science, mathematics. As soon as they prove to you, for instance, that you are descended from a monkey, there's no use scowling, accept it for a fact. When they prove to you that in reality one drop of your own suet must be dearer to you than a hundred thousand of your fellow creatures, and that this conclusion is the final solution of all the so-called virtues and duties and all such prejudices and fancies, why, you just have to accept it; there's no help for it, for two times two is a law of mathematics. Just try refuting it!

"Upon my word," they will shout at you, "it is no use protesting: it's a case of two times two making four! Nature does not ask your permission, she has nothing to do with your wishes, and whether you like her laws or dislike them, you're bound to accept her as she is, and consequently all her conclusions. A wall, you see, is a wall — " and so on and so on.

Merciful Heavens! But what do I care for the laws of nature and arithmetic, when, for some reason, I dislike those laws and the fact that two times two makes four? Of course I can't break through the wall by battering my head against it if I really haven't the strength to knock it down, but I'm not going to be reconciled to it simply because it is a stone wall and I haven't the strength.

As though such a stone wall really were a consolation and really did contain some word of conciliation, simply because it is as true as that two times two makes four. Oh, absurdity of absurdities! How much better it is to understand all, to recognize all — all the impossibilities and the stone wall; not to be reconciled to one of those impossibilities and stone walls if it disgusts you to be reconciled to it; by the way of the most inevitable, logical combinations to reach the most revolting conclusions on the everlasting theme: that you yourself are somehow to blame even for the stone wall, though again it is as clear as day you are not to blame in the least, and therefore grinding your teeth in silent impotence to sink into luxurious inertia, brooding on the fact that there's no one for you even to feel vindictive against, that you have not, and perhaps never will have, an object for your spite, that it is a sleight of hand, a bit of jugglery, a cardsharper's trick, that it is simply a mess, no knowing what and no knowing who. But in spite of all these uncertainties and juggleries, there is still an ache in you, and the more you do not know, the worse the ache.

IV

"Ha, ha, ha! You'll be finding enjoyment in toothache next," you cry with a laugh.

"Well? There is enjoyment even in toothache," I answer. I had a toothache for a whole month and I know there is. In that case, of course, people aren't silently spiteful but moan; the moans, however, are not candid but malevolent. And it is in their malevolence that the whole point lies. The enjoyment of the sufferer finds expression in those moans; if he did not feel enjoyment in them he would not moan. It is a good example, gentlemen, and I will develop it. Those moans express in the first place all the aimlessness of your pain, which is so humiliating to your consciousness; the whole legal system of nature on which you spit disdainfully, of course, but from which you suffer all the same while nature doesn't. They express the consciousness that you have no enemy to punish, but that you do have pain; the consciousness that in spite of all possible autosuggestionists you are in complete slavery to your teeth; that if someone wishes it, your teeth will leave off aching, and if he does not, they will go on aching another three months; and that, finally, if you are still contumacious and still protest, all that is left you for your own gratification is to beat yourself, or beat your wall with your fists as hard as you can — that, and absolutely nothing more. Well, these mortal insults, these jeers on the part of someone unknown, end at last in an enjoyment which sometimes reaches the highest degree of voluptuousness.

I ask you, gentlemen, listen sometimes to the moans of an educated man of the nineteenth century suffering from toothache on the second or third day of the attack, when he is beginning to moan not as he moaned on the first day — that is, not simply because he has toothache, not just as any coarse peasant, but as a man affected by progress and European civilization, a man who is "divorced from the soil and the national elements," as they express it nowadays. His moans become nasty, disgustingly malevolent, and go on for whole days and nights. And of course he himself knows that he isn't doing himself the least good with his moans; he knows better than anyone that he is only lacerating and harassing himself and others for nothing; he knows that even the audience before whom he is making his efforts, and his whole family, listen to him with loathing, without the least belief in him, and inwardly understand that he might moan differently, more simply, without trills and grace notes, and that he is only amusing himself like that from ill-humor, from malevolency. Well, it is in all these recognitions and disgraces that the voluptuous pleasure lies. As though he would say: "I am worrying you, I am lacerating your hearts, I am keeping everyone in the house awake. Well, stay awake; then you, too, will feel every moment that I have toothache. I am not a hero to you now, as I tried to seem before, but simply a nasty person, an impostor. Well, so be it, then! I am very glad that you see through me. It is nasty for you to hear my despicable moans; well, let it be nasty; there, I'll let you have a nastier quaver in just a moment!" You do not understand even now, gentlemen? No, it seems our development and our consciousness must go further to understand all the intricacies of this pleasure. You laugh? Delighted! My jests, gentlemen, are of course in bad taste, abrupt, involved, lacking in self-confidence. But of course that is because I do not respect myself. Can a man of perception respect himself at all?

V

Come, can a man who attempts to find enjoyment in the very feeling of his own degradation possibly have a spark of respect for himself? I am not saying this now from any mawkish kind of remorse. And, indeed, I could never endure saying: "Forgive me, Papa, I won't do it again" — not because I am incapable of saying that; on the contrary, perhaps just because I have been too capable of it, and how, at that! As though on purpose, I used to get into trouble in cases when I was not to blame in any way. That was the nastiest part of it. At the same time I was genuinely touched and penitent; I used to shed tears and, of course, deceived myself, though I was not acting in the least and there was a sick feeling in my heart at the time. For that, one could not blame even the laws of nature, though the laws of nature have continually all my life offended me more than anything else. It is loathsome to remember it all, but it was loathsome even then. Of course, a minute or so later I would realize wrathfully that it was all a lie, a revolting lie, a stilted lie — I mean all this penitence, this emotion, these vows of reform. You will ask why I upset myself with such antics: the answer is because it was very dull to sit with one's hands folded, and so I began cutting capers. That's it, really. Observe yourselves more carefully, gentlemen, then you will understand that it's so. I invented adventures for myself and made up a life, so as at least to live in some way. How many times it has happened to me — well, for instance, to take offense simply on purpose, for nothing; and you know yourself, of course, that you're offended at nothing, that you're putting on an act, and yet you bring yourself at last to the point of being really offended. All my life have I had an impulse to play such pranks, so that in the end I could not control that impulse in myself.

Another time — twice, in fact — I tried hard to fall in love. I suffered, too, gentlemen, I assure you. In the depth of my heart there was no faith in my suffering, only a faint stir of mockery, yet suffer I did, and that in the real, orthodox way; I was jealous, beside myself — and it was all from ennui, gentlemen, all from ennui; inertia overcame me. You know the direct, legitimate fruit of consciousness is inertia, that is, conscious sitting-with-your-hands-folded. I have referred to this already. I repeat, I repeat with emphasis: all *straightforward* persons and men of action are active just because they are stupid and limited. How explain that? I will tell you: in consequence of their limitation they take immediate and secondary causes for primary ones, and in that way persuade themselves more quickly and easily than other people that they have found an infallible basis for their activity, and their minds are at ease and that, you know, is the chief thing. To begin to act, you know, you must first have your mind completely at ease and no trace of doubt left in it. Why, how am I, for example, to set my mind at rest? Where are the primary causes on which I am to build? Where are my bases? Where am I to get them from? I exercise myself in reflection, and consequently with me every primary cause at once draws after itself another still more primary, and so on to infinity. That is just the essence of every sort of consciousness and reflection. It must be a case of the laws of nature again. What is the result of it in the end? Why, the same unvarying one.

Remember I spoke just now of vengeance. (I am sure you did not take it in.) I said that a man avenges himself because he sees justice in it. Therefore he has found a primary cause — that is, justice. And so he is at rest all around, and consequently he carries out his revenge calmly and successfully, being persuaded that he is doing a just and honest thing. But I see no justice in it, I find no sort of virtue in it, either, and consequently if I attempt to avenge myself, it is only out of spite. Spite, of course, might overcome everything, all my doubts and so might serve quite successfully in place of a primary cause, precisely because it is not a cause. But what is to be done if I have not even spite (I began with that just now, you know)? In consequence again of those accursed laws of consciousness, anger in me is subject to chemical disintegration. You look into it, the object flies off into air, your reasons evaporate, the criminal is not to be found, the wrong becomes not a wrong but a phantom, something like the toothache, for which no one is to blame, and consequently there is only the same outlet left again — that is, to pound the wall as hard as you can. So you give it up with a wave of the hand because you have not found a fundamental cause. And you try letting yourself be carried away by your feelings, blindly, without reflection, without a primary cause, repelling consciousness at least for a time; you hate or love, just so as not to sit with your hands folded. The day after tomorrow, at the latest, you will begin despising yourself for having knowingly deceived yourself. Result: a soap bubble and inertia. Oh, gentlemen, do you know, perhaps I consider myself an intelligent man only because all my life I have been able neither to begin nor to finish anything. Granted I am a babbler, a harmless, vexatious babbler, like all of us. But what is to be done if the direct and sole vocation of every intelligent man is babbling — that is, the intentional pouring of water through a sieve?

VI

Oh, if I had done nothing simply from laziness! Heavens, how I should have respected myself then! I should have respected myself because I should at least have been capable of being lazy; there would at least have been one positive quality, as it were, in me, in which I could have believed myself. Question: What is he? Answer: A sluggard. How very pleasant it would have been to hear that of oneself! It would mean that I was positively defined, it would mean that there was something to say about me. "Sluggard" — why, it is a calling and vocation, it is a career.

Do not jest — it is so. I should then be a member of the best club, by right, and should find my occupation in continually respecting myself. I knew a gentleman who prided himself all his life on being a connoisseur of Lafitte. He considered this as his positive virtue and never doubted himself. He died not simply with a tranquil but with a triumphant conscience, and he was quite right, too. Then I should have chosen a career for myself, I should have been a sluggard and a glutton, not a simple one, but, for instance, one with sympathies for everything good and beautiful. How do you like that? I have long had visions of it. That *good and beautiful* weighs heavily on my mind at forty. But that is at forty; then — oh, then it would have been different! I should have found for myself a form of activity in keeping with it — to be precise, drinking to the health of everything *good and beautiful*. I should have snatched at every opportunity to drop a tear into my glass and then to drain it to all that is *good and beautiful*. I should then have turned everything into the good and the beautiful; in the nastiest, unquestionable trash, I should have sought out the *good and the beautiful*. I should have exuded tears as a wet sponge exudes water. An artist, for instance, paints a picture worthy of Ge.[2] At once I drink to the health of the artist who painted the picture worthy of Ge, because I love all that is *good and beautiful*. An author has written *As You Like It*:[3] at once I drink to the health of *As You Like It* because I love all that is *good and beautiful*.

I should claim respect for doing so. I should persecute anyone who would not show me respect. I should live at ease, I should die with dignity, why, it's charming, utterly charming! And what a good round belly I'd grow, what a triple chin I'd fit myself out with, what a ruby nose I'd color for myself, so that everyone would say, looking at me: "Here is an asset! Here is something real and solid!"

And, say what you like, it is very agreeable to hear such remarks about oneself in this negative age.

VII

But these are all golden dreams. Oh, tell me, who was it first announced, who was it first proclaimed, that man only does nasty things because he does not know his own interests; and that if he were enlightened, if his eyes were opened to his real normal interests, man would at once cease to do nasty things, would at once become good and noble because, being enlightened and understanding his real advantage, he would see his own advantage in the good and nothing else, and we all know that not one man can, consciously, act against his own interests, consequently, so to say, through necessity, he would begin doing good? Oh, the babe! Oh, the pure, innocent child! Why, in the first place, when in all these thousands of years has there been a time when man has acted

2. N. N. Ge, a contemporary Russian painter whose work Dostoevsky had criticized.
3. Not the play by Shakespeare, but an article by M. E. Saltykov-Shchedrin on ways of improving man. The narrator is, of course, being bitterly ironic.

only from his own interest? What is to be done with the millions of facts that bear witness that men, *consciously*, that is, fully understanding their real interests, have left them in the background and have rushed headlong on another path, to meet peril and danger, compelled to this course by nobody and by nothing, but, as it were, simply disliking the beaten track, and have obstinately, willfully, beaten another difficult, absurd path, seeking it almost in the darkness? So, I suppose, this obstinacy and perversity were pleasanter to them than any advantage. Advantage! What is advantage? And will you take it upon yourself to define with perfect accuracy of what the advantage of man consists? And what if it so happens that a man's advantage, *sometimes*, not only may, but even must, consist in his desiring in certain cases what is harmful to himself and not advantageous? And if so, if there can be such a case, the whole principle falls into dust. What do you think — are there such cases? You laugh; laugh away, gentlemen, but only answer me: have man's advantages been reckoned up with perfect certainty? Are there not some which not only have not been included but cannot possibly be included under any classification?

You see, you gentlemen have, to the best of my knowledge, taken your whole register of human advantages from the averages of statistical figures and politico-economical formulas. Your advantages are prosperity, wealth, freedom, peace — and so on, and so on. So that the man who should, for instance, go openly and knowingly in opposition to all that list would, to your thinking, and indeed mine, too, of course, be an obscurantist or an absolute madman: wouldn't he? But, you know, this is what is surprising: why does it so happen that all these statisticians, sages and lovers of humanity, when they reckon up human advantages, invariably leave out one? They don't even take it into their reckoning in the form in which it should be taken, yet the whole reckoning depends upon that. It would be no great matter, they would simply have to take it, this advantage, and add it to the list. But the trouble is that this strange advantage does not fall under any classification and is out of place in any list. I have a friend, for instance — Eh, gentleman, but of course he is your friend, too; and indeed there is no one — no one! — to whom he is not a friend! When he prepares for any undertaking this gentleman immediately explains to you, elegantly and clearly, exactly how he must act in accordance with the laws of reason and truth. What is more, he will talk to you with animation and passion of the true normal interests of man; with irony he will upbraid the shortsighted fools who do not understand their own interests, nor the true significance of virtue; and, within a quarter of an hour, without any sudden outside provocation, but simply through something inside him which is stronger than all his interests, he will go off on quite a different tack — that is, act in direct opposition to what he has just been saying about himself, in opposition to the laws of reason, in opposition to his own advantage, in fact, in opposition to everything. I warn you that my friend is a compound personality, and therefore it is difficult to blame him as an individual.

The fact is, gentlemen, there apparently must really exist something that is dearer to almost every man than his greatest advantages, or (not to be illogical) there is a most advantageous advantage (the very one omitted, of which we spoke just now) which is more important and more advantageous than all other advantages, for the sake of which a man if necessary is ready to act in opposition to all laws; that is, in opposition to reason, honor, peace, prosperity — in fact, in opposition to all those excellent and useful things if only he can attain that fundamental, most advantageous advantage which is dearer to him than all.

"Yes, but it's an advantage all the same," you will retort. But excuse me, I'll make the point clear, and it isn't a case of playing upon words, either. What matters is that this advantage is remarkable from the very fact that it breaks down all our classifications and continually shatters every system constructed by lovers of mankind for the benefit of mankind. In fact, it upsets everything. But before mentioning this advantage to you, I want to compromise myself personally, and therefore I boldly declare that all these fine systems — all these theories for explaining to mankind its real normal interests, so that inevitably striving to pursue these interests men may at once become good and noble — are, in my opinion, so far, mere logical exercises! Yes, logical exercises. Why, to maintain this theory of the regeneration of mankind by means of the pursuit of its own advantage is to my mind almost the same thing as — as to affirm, for instance, following Buckle,[4] that through civilization mankind becomes softer, and consequently less bloodthirsty and less fitted for warfare. Logically it does seem to follow from his arguments. But man has such a predilection for systems and abstract deductions that he is ready to distort the truth intentionally, he is ready to deny the evidence of his senses only to justify his logic.

I take this example because it is the most glaring instance of it. Only look about you: blood is being spilt in streams, and in the merriest way, as though it were champagne. Take the whole of the nineteenth century in which Buckle lived. Take Napoleon — the Great, and also the present one. Take North America — the eternal Union. Take the farce of Schleswig-Holstein.[5] And what is it that civilization softens in us? The only gain of civilization for mankind is the greater capacity for variety of sensations — and absolutely nothing more. And through the development of this many-sidedness man may come to finding enjoyment in bloodshed. In fact, this has already happened to him. Have you noticed that it is the most civilized gentlemen who have been the subtlest slaughterers, to whom the Attilas and Stenka Razins[6] could not hold a candle? And if they are not so conspicuous as the Attilas and Stenka Razins, it is simply because they are so often met with, are so ordinary and have become so familiar to us. In any case, civilization has made mankind, if not more bloodthirsty, at least more vilely, more loathsomely bloodthirsty.

4. Henry Thomas Buckle (1821–62), whose two volume *History of Civilization in England* asserted the progressive intellectual evolution of man.
5. For this disputed territory Austria and Germany invaded Denmark. (Ibsen exiled himself from Norway in disgust over its failure to aid Denmark.)
6. A seventeenth-century Cossack rebel as bloodthirsty and savage as Attila, the fifth-century Hun.

In the old days man saw justice in bloodshed, and with his conscience at peace exterminated people as he saw fit. Now we do think bloodshed abominable and yet we engage in this abomination, and with more energy than ever. Which is worse? Decide that for yourselves. They say that Cleopatra (excuse an instance from Roman history) was fond of sticking gold pins into her slave-girls' breasts and derived gratification from their screams and writhings. You will say that that was in the comparatively barbarous times; that these are barbarous times, too, because also, comparatively speaking, pins are stuck in even now; that though man has now learned to see more clearly than in barbarous ages, he is still far from having learned to act as reason and science would dictate. But yet you are fully convinced that he will be sure to learn when he gets rid of certain old bad habits, and when common sense and science have completely re-educated human nature and turned it in a normal direction. You are confident that then man will cease from *intentional* error and, so to say, will be compelled not to want to set his will against his normal interests. That is not all; then, you say, science itself will teach man (though to my mind it's a superfluous luxury) that he never has really had any caprice or will of his own, and that he himself is something in the nature of a piano-key or the stop of an organ, and that there are, besides, things called the laws of nature; so that everything he does is not done by his willing it, but is done by itself, by the laws of nature. Consequently we have only to discover these laws of nature, and man will no longer have to answer for his actions and life will become exceedingly easy for him. All human actions will then, of course, be tabulated according to these laws, mathematically, like tables of logarithms up to 108,000, and entered in an index; or, better still, there would be published certain edifying works in the nature of encyclopedic lexicons, in which everything will be so clearly calculated and explained that there will be no more incidents or adventures in the world.

Then — it is you who are saying all this — new economic relations will be established, all ready-made and worked out with mathematical exactitude, so that every possible question will vanish in the twinkling of an eye, simply because every possible answer to it will be provided. Then will the Palace of Crystal [7] be built. Then . . . in fact, those will be halcyon days. Of course, there is no guaranteeing (this is my comment) that it will not be, for instance, frightfully dull then (for what will one have to do when everything will be calculated and tabulated?), but on the other hand everything will be extraordinarily rational. Of course boredom may lead you to anything. It is boredom that sets one to sticking golden pins into people, but all that would not matter. What is bad (this is my comment again) is that, I dare say, people will be thankful for the gold pins then. Man is stupid, you know, phenomenally stupid; or rather he is not at all stupid, but he is so ungrateful that you could not find his like in all creation.

---

7. It had already been built, of course, in London and was much admired. Like so many of the other allusions, this one too is scornful.

I, for instance, would not be in the least surprised if all of a sudden, *à propos* of nothing, in the midst of general prosperity, a gentleman with an ignoble, or rather with a reactionary and ironical, countenance were to arise and, putting his arms akimbo, say to us all: "I say, gentlemen, hadn't we better kick over the whole show and scatter rationalism to the winds, simply to send these logarithms to the devil, and to enable us to live once more at our own sweet foolish will?"

That, again, would not matter; but what is annoying is that he would be sure to find followers — such is the nature of man. And all that for the most foolish reason, which, one would think, was hardly worth mentioning: that is, that man everywhere and at all times, whoever he may be, has preferred to act as he chose and not in the least as his reason and advantage dictated. And one may choose what is contrary to one's own interests, and sometimes one *positively ought* (that is my idea). One's own free, unfettered choice, one's own caprice, however wild it may be, one's own fancy worked up at times to frenzy — is that very *most advantageous advantage* which we have overlooked, which comes under no classification and against which all systems and theories are continually being shattered to atoms. And how do these wiseacres know that man wants a normal, a virtuous choice? What has made them conceive that man must want a rationally advantageous choice? What man wants is simply *independent* choice, whatever that independence may cost and wherever it may lead. And a choice, of course, whose nature only the devil knows.

VIII

"Ha! ha! ha! But you know there is no such thing as choice in reality, say what you like," you will interpose with a chuckle. "Science has succeeded in so far analyzing man that we know already that choice and what is called freedom of will is nothing else than — "

Hold on, gentlemen, I meant to begin with that myself. I confess I was rather frightened. I was just going to say that the devil only knows what choice depends on, and that perhaps that was a very good thing, but I remembered the teachings of science — and pulled myself up short. And here you have begun upon it. Indeed, if a formula for all our desires and caprices is really discovered some day — that is, an explanation of what they depend upon, by which laws they arise, how they develop, what they are aiming at in this case and that, and so on, that is, a real mathematical formula — then, most likely, man will at once cease to feel desire; indeed, he will be certain to cease feeling desire. For who would want to choose by rule? Besides, he will at once be transformed from a human being into an organ-stop or something of the sort; for what is a man without desires, without free will and without choice, if not a stop in an organ? What do you think? Let us reckon the chances — can such a thing happen or not?

"H'm!" you decide. "Our choice is usually mistaken from a false view of our advantage. We sometimes choose absolute nonsense because in our foolishness we see in that nonsense the easiest means for attaining a supposed advantage. But when all that is explained and worked out on paper (which is perfectly possible, for it is contemptible and senseless to suppose that some laws of nature man will never understand), then certainly so-called desires will no longer exist. For if a desire should come into conflict with reason we shall then reason and not desire, because it will be impossible, retaining our reason, to be *senseless* in our desires, and in that way knowingly act against reason and desire to injure ourselves. And as all choice and reasoning can be really calculated — because there will some day be discovered the laws of our so-called free will — so, joking apart, there may one day be something like a table constructed of them, so that we really shall choose in accordance with it. If, for instance, some day they calculate and prove to me that I thumbed my nose at someone because I could not help thumbing my nose at him and that I had to do it in that particular way, what *freedom* is left me, especially if I am a learned man and have taken my degree somewhere? Then I should be able to calculate my whole life for thirty years beforehand. In short, if this could be arranged there would be nothing left for us to do; anyway, that would have to be our understanding. And, in fact, we ought unwearyingly to repeat to ourselves that at such and such a time and in such and such circumstances nature does not ask our leave; that we have got to take her as she is and not fashion her to suit our fancy, and if we really aspire to formulas and tables of rules, and — well, even to the chemical retort — there's no help for it, we must accept the retort, too, or else it will be accepted without our consent."

Yes, but here I come to a stop! Gentlemen, you must excuse me for being overphilosophical; it's the result of forty years underground! Allow me to indulge my fancy. You see, gentlemen, reason is an excellent thing, there's no disputing that, but reason is nothing but reason and satisfies only the rational side of man's nature, while will is a manifestation of the whole life, that is, of the whole human life including reason and all the impulses. And although our life, in this manifestation of it, is often worthless, yet it is life and not simply extracting square roots. Here I, for instance, quite naturally want to live, in order to satisfy all my capacities for life, and not simply my capacity for reasoning, that is, not simply one-twentieth of my capacity for life. What does reason know? Reason only knows what it has succeeded in learning (some things, perhaps, it will never learn; this is a poor comfort, but why not say so frankly?), and human nature acts as a whole, with everything that is in it, consciously or unconsciously, and, even if it goes wrong, it still lives on. I suspect, gentlemen, that you're looking at me with compassion; you tell me again that an enlightened and developed man, such, in short, as the future man will be, cannot consciously desire anything disadvantageous to himself, that this can be proved mathematically. I thoroughly agree it can — by mathematicians.

But I repeat for the hundredth time, there is one case, one only, when man may consciously, purposely, desire what is injurious to himself, what is stupid, very stupid — simply in order to have the right to desire for himself even what is very stupid and not to be bound by an obligation to desire only what is sensible.

Of course, this very stupid thing, this caprice of ours, may be in reality, gentlemen, more advantageous for us than anything else on earth, especially in certain cases. And in particular it may be more advantageous than any advantage even when it does us obvious harm and contradicts the soundest conclusions of our reason concerning our advantage — for it preserves for us, at any rate, what is most precious and most important — that is, our personality, our individuality. Some, you see, maintain that this really is the most precious thing for mankind; choice, of course, if it chooses, can be in agreement with reason; and especially if the choice be not abused but kept within bounds. It is profitable and sometimes even praiseworthy. But very often, and even most often, choice is utterly and stubbornly opposed to reason . . . and . . . and . . . do you know that that, too, is profitable, sometimes even praiseworthy?

Gentlemen, let us suppose that man is not stupid. (Indeed, one cannot refuse to suppose that, if only from the one consideration, that, if man is stupid, then who is wise?) But if he is not stupid, he is monstrously ungrateful! Phenomenally ungrateful. In fact, I believe that the best definition of man is the ungrateful biped. But that is not all, that is not his worst defect; his worst defect is his perpetual moral obliquity, perpetual — from the days of the Flood to the Schleswig-Holstein period. Moral obliquity and consequently lack of good sense; for it has long been accepted that lack of good sense is due to no other cause than moral obliquity. Put it to the test and cast your eyes upon the history of mankind. What will you see? Is it a grand spectacle? Grand, if you like. Take the Colossus of Rhodes,[8] for instance, that's worth something. With good reason Mr. Anaevski testifies of it that some say that it is the work of man's hands, while others maintain that it has been created by nature herself. Is history motley with many colors? Maybe it is, at that: if you take the dress uniforms, military and civilian, of all peoples in all ages — that alone is worth something, and if you take the undress uniforms you'll never get to the end of the thing; no historian would be equal to the job. Is it monotonous? Maybe it's monotonous, too: it's all fighting and fighting; they are fighting now, they fought first and they fought last — you will admit that it's almost too monotonous.

In short, one may say anything about the history of the world — anything that might enter the most disordered imagination. The only thing you can't say is that it's rational. The very word sticks in your throat. And, indeed, this is the odd thing that is continually happening:

8. A gigantic statue on the island of Rhodes; it was one of the Seven Wonders of the Ancient World.

there are continually turning up in life moral and rational persons, sages and lovers of humanity, who make it their object to live all their lives as morally and rationally as possible, to be, so to speak, a light to their neighbors simply in order to show them that it is possible to live morally and rationally in this world. And yet we all know that those very people sooner or later have been false to themselves, playing some queer trick, often a most unseemly one. Now I ask you: what can be expected of man since he is a being endowed with such strange qualities? Shower upon him every earthly blessing, drown him in a sea of happiness, so that nothing but bubbles of bliss can be seen on the surface; give him economic prosperity, such that he should have nothing else to do but sleep, live on cakes and ale and busy himself with the continuation of his species, and even then out of sheer ingratitude, sheer spite, man would play you some nasty trick. He would even risk his cakes and ale and would deliberately desire the most fatal rubbish, the most uneconomical absurdity, simply to introduce into all this positive good sense his fatal fantastic element. It is just his fantastic dreams, his vulgar folly, that he will desire to retain, simply in order to prove to himself — as though that were so necessary — that men still are men and not the keys of a piano, which the laws of nature threaten to control so completely that soon one will not be able to desire anything but by the calendar. And that is not all: even if man really were nothing but a piano-key, even if this were proved to him by natural science and mathematics, even then he would not become reasonable, but would purposely do something perverse out of simple ingratitude, simply to gain his point. And if he does not find means he will contrive destruction and chaos, will contrive sufferings of all sorts, only to gain his point! He will launch a curse upon the world, and as only man can curse (it is his privilege, the primary distinction between him and other animals), maybe by his curse alone he will attain his object — that is, convince himself that he is a man and not a piano-key! If you say that all this, too, can be calculated and tabulated — chaos and darkness and curses, so that the mere possibility of calculating it all beforehand would stop it all, and reason would reassert itself — then man would purposely go mad in order to be rid of reason and gain his point! I believe in it, I answer for it, for the whole work of man really seems to consist in nothing but proving to himself every minute that he is a man and not a piano-key! It may be at the cost of his skin, it may be by cannibalism! And this being so, can one help being tempted to rejoice that it has not yet come off, and that desire still depends on something we don't know?

You will scream at me (that is, if you condescend to do so) that no one is touching my free will, that all they are concerned with is that my will should of itself, of its own free will, coincide with my own normal interests, with the laws of nature and arithmetic.

Good Heavens, gentlemen, what sort of free will is left when we come to tabulation and arithmetic, when it will all be a case of two times two making four? Two times two makes four without my will. As if free will meant that!

IX

Gentlemen, I am joking, and I know myself that my jokes are not brilliant, but you know one can't take everything as a joke. I am, perhaps, jesting against the grain. Gentlemen, I am tormented by questions; answer them for me. You, for instance, want to cure men of their old habits and reform their will in accordance with science and good sense. But how do you know, not only that it is possible, but also that it is *desirable,* to reform man in that way? And what leads you to the conclusion that man's inclinations *need* reforming? In short, how do you know that such a reformation will be a benefit to man? And to go to the root of the matter — why are you so positively convinced that not to act against his real normal interests as guaranteed by the conclusions of reason and arithmetic is certainly always advantageous for man, and must always be a law for mankind? So far, you know, this is only your supposition. It may be the law of logic, but not the law of humanity. You think, gentlemen, perhaps that I am mad? Allow me to defend myself. I agree that man is pre-eminently a creative animal, predestined to strive consciously for an object and to engage in engineering — that is, incessantly and eternally to make new roads, *wherever they may lead.* But the reason why he wants sometimes to go off at a tangent may be precisely because he is *predestined* to make the road, and perhaps, too, that however stupid the straightforward practical man may be, the thought sometimes will occur to him that the road almost always does lead *somewhere,* and that the destination it leads to is less important than the process of making it, and that the chief thing is to save the well-conducted child from despising engineering, and so giving way to fatal idleness, which, as we all know, is the mother of all the vices.

Man likes to make roads and to create, that's a fact beyond dispute. But why has he such a passionate love for destruction and chaos also? Tell me that! But on that point I want to say a couple of words myself. May it not be that he loves chaos and destruction (there can be no disputing that he does sometimes love them) because he is instinctively afraid of attaining his object and completing the edifice he is constructing? Who knows, perhaps he only loves that edifice from a distance, and is by no means in love with it at close quarters; perhaps he only loves building it and does not want to live in it, but will leave it, when completed, for the use of *les animaux domestiques* — such as the ants, the sheep, and so on. Now the ants have quite a different taste. They have a marvelous edifice of that pattern which endures forever — the ant heap.

With the ant heap the respectable race of ants began and with the ant heap it will probably end, which does the greatest credit to the

perseverance and good sense of ants. But man is a frivolous and ludicrous creature, and perhaps, like a chess player, loves the process of
the game, not the end of it. And who knows (there is no saying this
with certainty), perhaps the only goal on earth to which mankind is
striving lies in this incessant process of attaining (in other words, in
life itself), and not in the thing to be attained, which must always be
expressed as a formula, as positive as that two times two makes four,
and such positiveness is not life, gentlemen, but is the beginning of
death. Anyway, man has always been afraid of this mathematical certainty, and I am afraid of it now. Granted man does nothing but seek
that mathematical certainty, he traverses oceans, he sacrifices his life
in the quest; but I assure you, he dreads to succeed, really to find it.
He feels that when he has found it there will be nothing for him to
look for. When workmen have finished their work they do at least
receive their pay, they go to the tavern, then they are taken to the police
station — and there is occupation for a week. But where can man go?
Anyway, one can observe a certain awkwardness about him when he
has attained such objects. He loves the process of attaining, but does
not quite like to have attained, and that, of course, is very absurd.
In fact, man is a comical creature; there seems to be a kind of jest in
it all. But yet mathematical certainty is, after all, something insufferable. Two times two making four seems to me simply a piece of insolence. Two times two making four is a pert coxcomb who stands with
arms akimbo barring your path and spitting. I admit that two times
two making four is an excellent thing, but if we are to give everything
its due, two times two making five is sometimes a very charming thing,
too.

And why are you so firmly, so triumphantly convinced that only the
normal and the positive — in other words, only what is conducive to
welfare — is for the advantage of man? Is not reason in error as regards
advantage? Does not man, perhaps, love something besides well-being?
Perhaps he is just as fond of suffering? Perhaps suffering is just as
great a benefit to him as well-being? Man is sometimes extraordinarily,
passionately in love with suffering, and that's a fact. There is no need
to appeal to universal history to prove that; only ask yourself, if you are
a man and have lived at all. As far as my personal opinion is concerned,
to care only for well-being seems to me positively ill-bred. Whether it's
good or bad, it is sometimes very pleasant, too, to smash things. I hold
no brief for suffering nor for well-being either. I am standing for . . .
my caprice, and for its being guaranteed to me when necessary. Suffering
would be out of place in musical comedies, for instance; I know that. In
the Palace of Crystal it is unthinkable; suffering means doubt, negation,
and what would be the good of a *palace of crystal* if there could be any
doubt about it? And yet I think man will never renounce real suffering,
that is, destruction and chaos. Why, suffering is the sole origin of consciousness. Though I did lay it down at the beginning that consciousness
is the greatest misfortune for man, yet I know man prizes it and would

not give it up for any satisfaction. Consciousness, for instance, is infinitely superior to two times two making four. Once you have mathematical certainty there is nothing left to do or to understand. There will be nothing left but to bottle up your five senses and plunge into contemplation. While if you stick to consciousness, even though the same result is attained, you can at least flog yourself at times, and that will, at any rate, liven you up. Reactionary as it is, corporal punishment is better than nothing.

X

You believe in a *palace of crystal* that can never be destroyed — a palace at which one will not be able to put out one's tongue or thumb one's nose on the sly. And perhaps that is just why I am afraid of this edifice, that it is of crystal, and can never be destroyed, and that one can't put one's tongue out at it even on the sly.

You see, if it were not a palace, but a henhouse, I might creep into it to avoid getting wet, and yet I would not call the henhouse a palace out of gratitude to it for keeping me dry. You laugh and say that in such circumstances a henhouse is as good as a mansion. Yes, I answer, if one had to live simply to keep out of the rain.

But what is to be done if I have taken it into my head that that is not the only object in life, and that if one must live one had better live in a mansion? That is my choice, my desire. You will only eradicate it when you have changed my preference. Well, do change it, allure me with something else, give me another ideal. But meanwhile I will not take a henhouse for a mansion. The *palace of crystal* may be an idle dream, it may be that it is inconsistent with the laws of nature and that I have invented it only through my own stupidity, through the old-fashioned irrational habits of my generation. But what does it matter to me that it is inconsistent? That makes no difference, since it exists in my desires, or rather exists as long as my desires exist. Perhaps you are laughing again? Laugh away; I will put up with any mockery rather than pretend that I am sated when I am hungry. I know, anyway, that I will not be put off with a compromise, with a recurring zero, simply because it is consistent with the laws of nature and actually exists. I will not accept as the crown of my desires a block of slum tenements on a lease of a thousand years, and perhaps with a signboard of a dentist hanging out. Destroy my desires, eradicate my ideals, show me something better, and I will follow you. You will say, perhaps, that it is not worth your trouble; but in that case I can give you the same answer. We are discussing things seriously; but if you won't deign to give me your attention, I'll drop your acquaintance. I can retreat into my underground hole.

But while I am alive and have desires I would rather my hand were withered off than bring one brick to such a building! Don't remind me that I have just rejected the *palace of crystal* for the sole reason that one cannot put out one's tongue at it. I did not say that because I am so fond of putting my tongue out. Perhaps the thing I resented was that of all your edifices there has not been one at which one could not put out one's tongue. On the contrary, I would let my tongue be cut off out of gratitude if things could be so arranged that I should lose all desire to put it out. It's not my fault that things cannot be so arranged, and that one must be satisfied with model flats. Then why am I made with such desires? Can I have been constructed simply in order to come to the conclusion that all my construction is a cheat? Can this be my whole purpose? I do not believe it.

But do you know what? I'm convinced that we underground folk ought to be kept in check. Though we may sit forty years underground without speaking, when we do come out into the light of day and break out we talk and talk *and* talk . . .

XI

The long and the short of it is, gentlemen, that it's better to do nothing! Better conscious inertia! And so hurrah for the underground! Though I have said that I envy the normal man to the last drop of my bile, yet I should not care to be in his place such as he is now (though I shall not cease envying him). No, no; anyway, the underground life is more advantageous. There, at any rate, one can. . . . Oh, but even now I'm lying! I'm lying because I know myself that it is not the underground that is better, but something different, quite different, for which I am thirsting, but which I cannot find. Damn the underground!

I will tell you another thing that would be better, and that is, if I myself believed in anything of what I have just written. I swear to you, gentlemen, there is not one thing, not one word of what I have written that I really believe. That is, I believe it, perhaps, but at the same time I feel and suspect that I am lying like a politician.

"Then why have you written all this?" you will say to me.

"I ought to put you underground for forty years without anything to do and then come to you in your cellar, to find out what stage you have reached! How can a man be left with nothing to do for forty years?"

"Isn't that shameful, isn't that humiliating?" you will say, perhaps, wagging your heads contemptuously. "You thirst for life and try to settle the problems of life by a logical tangle. And how persistent, how insolent are your sallies, and at the same time what a fright you are in! You spout nonsense and are pleased with it; you say impudent things and are in continual alarm and apologizing for them. You declare that you are afraid of nothing and at the same time try to ingratiate yourself in our good opinion. You declare that you are gnashing your teeth and at the same time you try to be witty so as to amuse us. You know that your witticisms are not witty, but you are evidently well satisfied with their literary value. You may, perhaps, have really suffered, but you have no respect for your own suffering. You may have sincerity, but you have no modesty; out of the pettiest vanity you expose your sincerity to publicity and ignominy. You doubtless mean to say something but hide your last word through fear, because you haven't the resolution to utter it and have only a cowardly impudence. You boast of consciousness, but you are not sure of your ground, for though your mind works, yet your heart is darkened and corrupt, and you cannot have a full, genuine consciousness without a pure heart. And how intrusive you are, how you insist and grimace! Lies, lies, lies!"

Of course I have myself made up all the things you say. That, too, is of the underground. I have been for forty years listening to you through a crack under the floor. I have invented them myself, there was nothing else I could invent. It is no wonder that I have learned it all by heart and it has taken a literary form.

But can you really be so credulous as to think that I will print all this and give it to you to read, too? And another problem: Why do I call you "gentlemen," why do I address you as though you really were my readers? Such confessions as I intend to make are never printed nor given to other people to read. Anyway, I am not strong-minded enough for that, and I don't see why I should be. But, you see, a fancy has struck me and I want to realize it at all costs. Let me explain.

Every man has reminiscences which he would not tell to everyone, but only to his friends. He has other matters in his mind which he would not reveal even to his friends, but only to himself, and that in secret. But there are other things which a man is afraid to tell even to himself, and every decent man has a number of such things stored away in his mind. The more decent he is, the greater the number of such things in his mind. Anyway, I have only lately determined to remember some of my early adventures. Till now I have always avoided them, even with a certain uneasiness. Now, when I am not only recalling them, but have actually decided to write an account of them, I want to try the experiment whether one can, even with oneself, be perfectly open and not take fright at the whole truth. I will observe, in parentheses, that Heine says that a true autobiography is almost an impossibility, and that man is bound to lie about himself. He considers that Rousseau certainly told lies about himself in his *Confessions*, and even intentionally lied, out of vanity. I am convinced that Heine is right; I quite understand how sometimes one may, out of sheer vanity, attribute regular crimes to oneself, and indeed I can very well conceive that kind of vanity. But Heine judged of people who made their confessions to the public. I write only for myself, and I wish to declare once and for all that if I write as though I were addressing readers, that is simply because it is easier for me to write in that form. It is a form, an empty form — I'll never have readers. I have made this plain already.

I don't wish to be hampered by any restrictions in the compilation of my notes. I shall not attempt any system or method. I will jot things down as I remember them.

But here, perhaps, someone will catch at the word and ask me: "If you really don't reckon on readers, why do you make such compacts with yourself — and on paper, too — as that you won't attempt any system or method, that you'll jot things down as you remember them, and so on, and so on? Why the explanations? Why the apologies?"

"There, now!" I answer.

There is a whole psychology in all this, though. Perhaps it is simply that I am a coward. And perhaps that I purposely imagine an audience before me in order that I may be more dignified while I write. There are perhaps thousands of reasons. Again, what precisely is my object in writing? If it is not for the benefit of the public why should I not simply recall these incidents in my own mind without putting them on paper?

Quite so; but yet it is more imposing on paper. There's something more impressive about it; I'll be better able to criticize myself and improve my style. Besides, I may obtain actual relief from writing. Today, for instance, I'm particularly oppressed by one memory of a distant past. It came back vividly to my mind a few days ago, and has remained haunting me like an annoying tune that one cannot get rid of. And yet get rid of it I must, somehow. I have hundreds of such reminiscences; but at times some one of them stands out from a hundred others and oppresses me. For some reason I believe that if I wrote it down I'd get rid of it. Why not try?

Besides, I'm bored, and I never have anything to do. Writing will be a sort of work. They say work makes man kindhearted and honest. Well, here is a chance for me, anyway.

Snow is falling today, yellow and dingy. It fell yesterday, too, as well as a few days ago. I fancy it is the wet snow that has reminded me of that incident which I cannot shake off now. And so let it be a story *à propos* of the falling snow.

Part II — *À propos of the Wet Snow*

From out dark error's subjugation
My words of passionate exhortation
　　Had wrenched thy fainting spirit free;
And writhing prone in thine affliction
Thou didst recall with malediction
　　The vice that had encompassed thee:
And then, thy slumbering conscience fretting
　　From recollection's torturing flame,
Thou didst reveal the hideous setting
　　Of thy life's current ere I came;
And suddenly I saw thee sicken,
　　And weeping, hide thine anguished face,
Revolted, maddened, horror-stricken,
　　At memories of foul disgrace.

　　　　　　　　　　NECRASSOV [9]

9. A nineteenth-century lyric poet who dealt realistically with social wrongs.

I

At that time I was only twenty-four. My life was even then gloomy, ill-regulated, and as solitary as that of a savage. I made friends with no one and positively avoided speech, burying myself more and more in my hole. At work in the office I never looked at anyone, and I was perfectly well aware that my companions looked upon me not only as a queer fellow, but even — I always fancied this — with a sort of loathing. I sometimes wondered why it was that nobody else fancied that he was looked upon with aversion. One of the clerks had a most repulsive, pock-marked face, which looked positively villainous. I believe I should not have dared to look at anyone with such an unsightly countenance. Another had such a very dirty old uniform that there was an unpleasant odor in his proximity. Yet neither of these gentlemen showed in any way the slightest self-consciousness, either about his clothes or his countenance or his character. Neither of them ever imagined that he was looked at with disgust; if they had imagined it they would not have minded — so long as their superiors did not look at them in that way.

It is clear to me now that, owing to my unbounded vanity and to the high standard I set for myself, I often looked at myself with furious discontent, which verged on loathing, and so I inwardly attributed the same feeling to everyone. I hated my face, for instance: I thought it disgusting, and even suspected that there was something base in my expression, and so every day when I turned up at the office I tried to behave as independently as possible and to assume a lofty expression, so that I might not be suspected of being abject. "My face may be ugly," I thought, "but let it be lofty, expressive, and, above all, *extremely* intelligent." But I was positively and painfully certain that it was impossible for my countenance ever to express those qualities. And what was worst of all, I thought it actually stupid-looking, and I would have been quite satisfied if I could have looked intelligent. In fact, I would even have put up with looking base if, at the same time, my face could have been thought strikingly intelligent.

Of course, I hated my fellow clerks one and all, and I despised them all, yet at the same time I was, as it were, afraid of them. In fact, it happened at times that I thought more highly of them than of myself. It somehow happened quite suddenly that I alternated between despising them and thinking them superior to myself. A cultivated and decent man cannot be vain without setting a fearfully high standard for himself, and without despising and almost hating himself at certain moments. But whether I despised them or thought them superior, I dropped my eyes almost every time I met anyone. I even made experiments whether I could face so-and-so's looking at me, and I was always the first to drop my eyes. This worried me to distraction. I had a sickly dread, too, of being ridiculous, and so had a slavish passion for the conventional in everything external. I loved to fall into the common rut and had a wholehearted terror of any kind of eccentricity in myself. But how could I live up to it? I was morbidly sensitive, as a man of our age should be. They were all stupid and as like one another as so many sheep. Perhaps I was the only one in the office who fancied that I was a coward and a slave, and I fancied it just because I was more highly developed. But it was not only that I fancied it, it really was so. I *was* a coward and a slave. I say this without the slightest embarrassment. Every decent man of our age must be a coward and a slave. That is his normal condition. Of that I am firmly convinced. He is made and constructed to that very end. And not only at the present time, owing to certain casual circumstances, but always, at all times, a decent man is bound to be a coward and a slave. It is the law of nature for all decent people all over the earth. If any one of them happens to be valiant about something, he need not be comforted nor carried away by that; he would show the white feather just the same before something else. That's how it invariably and inevitably ends. Only donkeys and mules are valiant, and then only till they are up against the wall. It's not worth while to pay attention to them, for they really don't count.

Another circumstance, too, worried me in those days: that there was no one like me and that I was not like anyone else. "I am unique, but they are like all," I thought — and pondered.

From which it's evident that I was still a youngster.

Sometimes the very opposite would happen. It was loathsome sometimes to go to the office; things reached such a point that I often came home ill. But all at once, *à propos* of nothing, there would come a phase of skepticism and indifference (everything happened in phases to me), and I myself would laugh at my intolerance and fastidiousness, I would reproach myself with being *romantic*. At one time I was unwilling to speak to anyone, while at other times I would not merely talk with people but go to the extent of contemplating friendship with them. All my fastidiousness would suddenly, without rhyme or reason, vanish. Who knows, perhaps I never had really had it, and it had simply been affected and gotten out of books. I haven't decided that question even up to now. Once I actually made friends with them, visited their homes, played cards, drank vodka, talked of promotions. But here let me make a digression.

We Russians, speaking generally, have never had those foolish transcendental *romantics* (German, and still more, French) on whom nothing produces any effect; if there were an earthquake, if all France perished at the barricades, the French *romantics* would still be the same, they would not even have the decency to affect a change, but would still go on singing their transcendental songs to the hour of their death, because they are fools. We, in Russia, have no fools; that's something everybody knows well. That's what distinguishes our land from others. Consequently these transcendental natures are not found amongst us in their pure form. The idea that they are so found is due to our *realistic* journalists and critics of the day, always on the lookout for

Kostanzhoglos [10] and Uncle Peter Ivanichs [11] and foolishly accepting them as our ideal; they have slandered our *romantics*, taking them for the same transcendental sort as in Germany or France. On the contrary, the characteristics of our *romantics* are absolutely and directly opposed to the transcendental European type, and no European standard can be applied to them. (Allow me to make use of this word *romantic* — an old-fashioned and much-respected word which has done good service and is familiar to all.) The characteristics of our *romantic* are to understand everything, *to see everything and to see it often incomparably more clearly than our most realistic minds see it;* to refuse to accept anyone or anything, but at the same time not to despise anything; to give way, to yield, from policy; never to lose sight of a useful practical object (such as rent-free quarters at the government expense, pensions, decorations), to keep an eye on that object through all the enthusiasms and volumes of lyrical poems, and at the same time to preserve *the good and the beautiful* inviolate within them to the hour of their death, and to preserve themselves also, incidentally, like some precious jewel wrapped in cotton wool, if only for the benefit of *the good and the beautiful.* Our *romantic* is a man of great breadth and the greatest rogue of all our rogues, I assure you. I can assure you of that from experience, indeed. Of course, that is, if he is intelligent. But what am I saying? The *romantic* is always intelligent, and I only meant to observe that although we have had foolish romantics they don't count, and they were foolish only because in the flower of their youth they degenerated into Germans and, to preserve their precious jewel more comfortably, settled somewhere out there — by preference in Weimar or the Black Forest.

I, for instance, genuinely despised my official work and did not openly abuse it simply because I was in it myself and got a salary out of it. Anyway, take note, I did not openly abuse it. Our *romantic* would rather go out of his mind — a thing, however, which very rarely happens — than take to open abuse, unless he had some other career in view; and he is never kicked out. At most, they would take him to the lunatic asylum as "the King of Spain" if he should go very mad.[12] But it is only the slim, fair-haired lads who go out of their minds in Russia. Innumerable *romantics* attain later in life to considerable rank in the Service. Their many-sidedness is remarkable! And what a faculty they have for the most contradictory sensations! I was comforted by this thought even in those days, and I am of the same opinion now. That is why there are so many *broad natures* among us who never lose their ideal even in the depths of degradation; and though they never stir a finger for their ideal, though they are arrant thieves and knaves, yet they tearfully cherish their first ideal and are extraordinarily honest at heart. Yes, it is only among us that the most incorrigible

10. The good landlord in Part II of Gogol's *Dead Souls.*
11. The hero's wise teacher in Goncharov's *The Same Old Story.*
12. An allusion to Gogol's "The Diary of a Madman."

rogue can be absolutely and loftily honest at heart without in the least ceasing to be a rogue. I repeat, our *romantics,* frequently, become such accomplished rascals (I use the term *rascals* affectionately), suddenly display such a sense of reality and practical knowledge, that their bewildered superiors and the public generally can only ejaculate in amazement.

Their many-sidedness is really amazing, and goodness knows what it may develop into later on, and what the future has in store for us. It is not a poor material! I do not say this from any foolish or boastful patriotism. But I feel sure that you are again imagining that I am joking. Or perhaps it's just the contrary, and you are convinced that I really think so. Anyway, gentlemen, I shall welcome both views as an honor and a special favor. And do forgive my digression.

I did not, of course, maintain friendly relations with my comrades and soon was at loggerheads with them, and in my youth and inexperience I even gave up bowing to them, as though I had cut off all relations. That, however, only happened to me once. As a rule, I was always alone.

In the first place I spent most of my time at home, reading. I tried to stifle all that was continually seething within me by means of external impressions. And the only external means I had was reading. Reading, of course, was a great help — stirring me, giving me pleasure and pain. Yet at times it bored me fearfully. One longed for movement in spite of everything, and I plunged all at once into dark, underground, loathsome vice of the pettiest kind. My wretched passions were acute, smarting, from my continual, sickly irritability. I had hysterical impulses, accompanied by tears and convulsions. I had no resource except reading — that is, there was nothing in my surroundings which I could respect and which attracted me. I was overwhelmed with depression, too; I had an hysterical craving for incongruity and for contrast, and so I took to vice. I have not said all this to justify myself.. . . . But, no — I'm lying. I did want to justify myself. I made that little observation for my own benefit, gentlemen. I don't want to lie. I vowed to myself I wouldn't.

And so, furtively, timidly, in solitude, at night, I indulged in filthy vice, with a feeling of shame which never deserted me, even at the most loathsome moments, and which at such moments nearly made me curse. Already even then I had my underground world in my soul. I was fearfully afraid of being seen, of being met, of being recognized. I visited various obscure haunts.

One night as I was passing a tavern I saw through a lighted window some gentlemen fighting with billiard cues, and saw one of them thrown out of a window. At other times I should have felt very much disgusted, but I was in such a mood at the time that I actually envied the gentleman thrown out of a window — and I envied him so much that I even went into the tavern and into the billiard room. "Perhaps," I thought, "I'll have a fight, too, and they'll throw me out of a window."

I wasn't drunk — but what is one to do? Depression will drive a man to such a pitch of hysteria! But nothing happened. It seemed that I was not even up to being thrown out of a window, and I went away without having had my fight.

An officer put me in my place from the first moment.

I was standing by the billiard table and in my ignorance blocking up the way, and he wanted to pass; he took me by the shoulders and without a word — without a warning or explanation — thrust me from where I was standing to another spot and passed by as though he had not noticed me. I could have forgiven blows, but I could not forgive his having thrust me aside without noticing me.

The devil knows what I would have given for a real, regular quarrel — a more decent, a more *literary* one, so to speak. I had been treated like a fly. This officer was over six feet, while I was a spindly little fellow. But the quarrel was in my hands. I had only to protest and I certainly would have been thrown out of a window. But I changed my mind and preferred to beat a resentful retreat.

From the tavern I went straight home, confused and troubled, and the next night I went out again with the same lewd intentions, still more furtively, abjectly and miserably than before, as it were, with tears in my eyes — but still I did go out again. Don't imagine, though, it was cowardice which made me slink away from the officer: I never have been a coward at heart, though I have always been a coward in action. Don't be in a hurry to laugh — I assure you I can explain it all.

Oh, if only that officer had been one of the sort who would consent to fight a duel! But no, he was one of those gentlemen (alas, long extinct!) who preferred fighting with cues or, like Gogol's Lieutenant Pirogov,[13] appealing to the police. They did not fight duels and would have thought a duel with a civilian like me an utterly unseemly procedure in any case — and they looked upon the duel altogether as something impossible, something freethinking and French. But they were quite ready to bully, especially when they were over six feet.

I did not slink away through cowardice, but through an unbounded vanity. I was afraid not of his six-foot height, nor of getting a sound thrashing and being thrown out of a window; I should have had physical courage enough, I assure you; but I hadn't the moral courage. What I was afraid of was that everyone present, from the insolent marker down to the lowest little stinking, pimply clerk in a greasy collar, would jeer at me and fail to understand when I began to protest and to address them in literary language. For of the point of honor — not of honor, but of the point of honor (*point d'honneur*) — one cannot speak among us except in literary language. You can't allude to the *point of honor* in ordinary language. I was fully convinced (the sense of reality, in spite of all my romanticism!) that they would all simply split their sides with laughter, and that the officer would not simply beat me (that is, without insulting me), but would

13. In his story "The Nevski Prospect."

certainly give me his knee in the back, kick me round the billiard table, and only then, perhaps, have pity and drop me out of a window.

Of course, for me this trivial incident could not end in that. I often met that officer afterward in the street and noticed him very carefully. I'm not quite sure whether he recognized me; I imagine not. I judge from certain signs. But I — I stared at him with spite and hatred, and so it went on — for several years! My resentment grew even deeper with the years. At first I began making stealthy inquiries about this officer. It was difficult for me to do so, for I knew no one. But one day I heard someone shout his last name in the street as I was following him at a distance, as though I were tied to him — and so I learned his last name. Another time I followed him to his flat, and for a small silver coin learned from the janitor where he lived, on which floor, whether he lived alone or with others, and so on — in fact, everything one could learn from a janitor. One morning, though I had never tried my hand with the pen, it suddenly occurred to me to write a satire on this officer in the form of a novel which would unmask his villainy. I wrote the novel with relish. I did unmask his villainy, I even exaggerated it; at first I so altered his last name that it could easily be recognized, but on second thoughts I changed it and sent the story to *Notes of the Fatherland*. But at that time such attacks were not the fashion and my story was not printed. Which was a great vexation to me.

Sometimes I was positively choked with resentment. At last I determined to challenge my enemy to a duel. I composed a splendid, charming letter to him, imploring him to apologize to me and hinting rather plainly at a duel in case of refusal. The letter was so composed that if the officer had had the least understanding of the good and the beautiful he would certainly have flung himself on my neck and have offered me his friendship. And how fine that would have been! How we should have got on together! "He could have shielded me with his higher rank, while I could have improved his mind with my culture, and, well . . . my ideas; and all sorts of things might have happened." Just imagine, this was two years after his insult to me, and my challenge would have been a ridiculous anachronism, in spite of all the ingenuity of my letter in disguising and explaining away the anachronism. But, thank God (to this day I thank the Almighty with tears in my eyes), I did not send the letter to him. Cold shivers run down my back when I think of what might have happened if I had sent it.

And all at once I revenged myself in the simplest way, by a stroke of genius! A brilliant thought suddenly dawned upon me. Sometimes on holidays I used to stroll along the sunny side of the Nevski Prospect about four o'clock in the afternoon. Though it was hardly a stroll so much as a series of innumerable miseries, humiliations and resentments; but no doubt that was just what I wanted. I used to squirm along in a most unseemly fashion, like an eel, continually moving aside to make way for generals, for officers of the guards and hussars, or for ladies. At such moments there used to be a convulsive twinge at my heart, and I used to feel hot all down my back at the mere thought of the wretchedness of my attire, of the wretchedness and abjectness of my little scurrying figure. This was a regular martyrdom; a continual, intolerable humiliation at the thought, which passed into an incessant and direct sensation, that I was a mere fly in the eyes of all this world, a nasty, disgusting fly — more intelligent, more highly developed, more refined in feeling than any of them, of course — but a fly that was continually making way for everyone, insulted and injured by everyone. Why I inflicted this torture upon myself, why I went to the Nevski Prospect, I don't know. I felt simply drawn there at every possible opportunity.

Already then I began to experience a rush of the enjoyment of which I spoke in the first chapter. After my affair with the officer I felt even more drawn there than before: it was on the Nevski Prospect that I met him most frequently; there I could admire him. He, too, went there chiefly on holidays. He, too, turned out of his path for generals and persons of high rank, and he, too, squirmed in and out among them like an eel; but people like me, or even those better dressed, yet like me, he simply walked over; he made straight for them as though there was nothing but empty space before him, and never, under any circumstances, turned aside. I gloated over my resentment, watching him and — always made way for him resentfully. It exasperated me that even in the street I could not be on an even footing with him.

"Why must you invariably be the first to move aside?" I kept asking myself in hysterical rage, waking up sometimes at three o'clock in the morning. "Why you and not he? There's no regulation about it; there's no written law. Let there be equality about making way, as there usually is when refined people meet: he moves halfway and you move halfway; you pass with mutual respect."

But that never happened, and I always moved aside, while he didn't as much as notice my making way for him. And lo and behold, a bright idea dawned upon me! "What," I thought, "if I meet him and don't move to one side? What if I don't move aside on purpose, even if I bump against him? How would that do?" This audacious idea took such a hold on me that it gave me no peace. I was dreaming of it continually, horribly, and I purposely went more frequently to the Nevski Prospect in order to picture more vividly how I should do it when I did do it. I was delighted. This intention seemed to me more and more practical and feasible.

"Of course I won't really jostle him," I thought, already more good-natured in my joy. "I simply won't turn aside, will run up against him, not very violently, but merely shouldering him — just as much as decency permits. I'll jostle against him just as much as he jostles against me." At last I made up my mind completely. But my preparations took a great deal of time. To begin with, when I carried out my plan I'd have to look rather more decent, and so I had to think of my getup.

"In case of emergency, if, for instance, there were any sort of public scandal (and the public there is of the most *recherché*: the Countess walks there; Prince D— walks there; all the literary world is there), I must be well dressed; that inspires respect and of itself puts us on an equal footing in the eyes of society."

With this object I asked for some of my salary in advance and bought at Churkin's a pair of black gloves and a decent hat. Black gloves seemed to me both more dignified and *bon ton* than the lemon-colored ones which I had contemplated at first. "The color is too gaudy; it looks as though one were trying to be conspicuous," and I did not take the lemon-colored ones. I had got ready long beforehand a good shirt, with white bone studs; my overcoat was the only thing that held me back. The coat in itself was a very good one, it kept me warm; but it was quilted and it had a raccoon collar, which was the height of vulgarity. I had to change the collar at any sacrifice, and get one of beaver, like an officer's. For this purpose I began visiting the Drapers' Row and after several attempts I decided upon some cheap German beaver. Though German beaver soon grows stagey and looks wretched, yet at first it looks exceedingly well, and I only needed it for one occasion. I asked the price; even so, it was too expensive. After thinking it over thoroughly I decided to sell my raccoon collar; the rest of the sum (a considerable one for me) I decided to borrow from Anton Antonich Syetochkin, my immediate superior, an unassuming person, though grave and judicious. He never lent money to anyone, but I had, on entering the service, been specially recommended to him by an important personage who had got me my job. I was horribly worried. To borrow from Anton Antonich seemed to me monstrous and shameful. I did not sleep for two or three nights. Indeed, I did not sleep well at that time, I was in a fever; I had a vague sinking at my heart or else a sudden throbbing, throbbing, throbbing! Anton Antonich was surprised at first, then he frowned, then he reflected, and after all lent me the money, receiving from me a written authorization to take from my salary a fortnight later the sum that he had lent me.

In this way everything was at last ready. The handsome beaver replaced the mean-looking raccoon, and I began by degrees to get ready for action. It would never have done to act offhand, at random; the plan had to be carried out skillfully, by degrees. But I must confess that after many efforts I began to despair: we simply could not run into each other. I made every preparation, I was quite determined — it seemed as though we should run into one another directly — and before I knew what I was doing I had stepped aside for him again and he had passed without noticing me. I even prayed as I approached him that God would grant me determination. One time I had made up my mind thoroughly, but it ended in my stumbling and falling at his feet because at the very last instant when I was only six inches from him my courage failed me. He very calmly stepped over me, while I flew to one side like a ball. That night I was ill again, feverish and delirious.

And suddenly it ended most happily. The night before I had made up my mind not to carry out my fatal plan and to abandon it all, and with that object I went to the Nevski Prospect for the last time, just to see how I would abandon it all. Suddenly, three paces from my enemy, I unexpectedly made up my mind — I closed my eyes, and we ran full tilt, shoulder to shoulder, against one another! I did not budge an inch and passed him on a perfectly equal footing! He did not even look round and pretended not to notice it; but he was only pretending, I am convinced of that. I am convinced of that to this day! Of course, I got the worst of it — he was stronger, but that was not the point. The point was that I had attained my object; I had kept up my dignity, I had not yielded a step and had put myself publicly on an equal social footing with him. I returned home feeling that I was fully avenged for everything. I was delighted. I was triumphant and sang Italian arias. Of course, I will not describe to you what happened to me three days later; if you have read my first chapter you can guess that for yourself. The officer was afterwards transferred; I have not seen him now for fourteen years. What is the dear fellow doing now? Whom is he trampling now?

II

But the period of my dissipation would end, and I always felt very sick afterward. It was followed by remorse — I tried to drive it away: I felt too sick. By degrees, however, I grew used to that, too. I grew used to everything, or rather I voluntarily resigned myself to enduring it. But I had a means of escape that reconciled everything — that was to find refuge in *the good and the beautiful* — in dreams, of course. I was a terrible dreamer, I would dream for three months on end, tucked away in my corner, and you may believe me that at those moments I had no resemblance to the gentleman who, in his chickenhearted perturbation, had put a collar of German beaver on his overcoat. I suddenly became a hero. I would not have admitted my six-foot lieutenant even if he had called on me. I could not even picture him before me then. What were my dreams and how could I satisfy myself with them? It is hard to say now, but at the time I was satisfied with them. Though, indeed, even now, I am to some extent satisfied with them.

Dreams were particularly sweet and vivid after a spell of dissipation; they came with remorse and with tears, with curses and transports. There were moments of such positive intoxication, of such happiness, that there was not the faintest trace of irony within me, on my honor. I had faith, hope, love. I believed blindly at such times that by some miracle, by some external circumstance, all this would suddenly open out, expand; that suddenly a vista of suitable activity — beneficent, good, and, above all, *ready-made* (what sort of activity I had no idea, but the great thing was that it should be all ready for me) — would rise up before me — and I should come out into the light of day, well-nigh riding a white horse and crowned with laurel. Anything but the foremost place I could not conceive for myself, and for that very reason, in reality, I quite contentedly occupied the lowest. Either to be a hero or to grovel in the mud — there was nothing between. That was my ruin, for when I was in the mud I comforted myself with the thought that at other times I was a hero, and the hero was a cloak for the mud; for an ordinary man it was shameful to defile himself, but a hero was too lofty to be utterly defiled, and so he might defile himself. It is worth noting that these attacks of *the good and the beautiful* visited me even during the period of dissipation and just at the times when I was touching bottom. They came in separate spurts, as though reminding me of themselves, but did not banish the dissipation by their appearance. On the contrary, they seemed to add a zest to it by contrast, and were only sufficiently present to serve as an appetizing sauce. That sauce was made up of contradictions and sufferings, of agonizing inward analysis, and all these pangs and pinpricks gave a certain piquancy, even a significance, to my dissipation — in fact, completely answered the purpose of an appetizing sauce. There was a certain depth of meaning in it. And I could hardly have resigned myself to the simple, vulgar, direct debauchery of a clerk and have endured all the filthiness of it. What could have allured me about it then and have drawn me at night into the street? No, I had a lofty way of getting out of it all.

And what loving-kindness, O Lord, what loving-kindness I felt at times in those dreams of mine, in those flights into *the good and the beautiful.* Though it was fantastic love, though it was never applied to anything human in reality, yet there was so much of this love that one did not feel afterward even the impulse to apply it in reality — that would have been superfluous. Everything, however, passed satisfactorily by a lazy and fascinating transition into the sphere of art, that is, into the beautiful forms of life, lying ready, largely stolen from the poets and novelists and adapted to all sorts of needs and uses. I, for instance, was triumphant over everyone; everyone, of course, was in dust and ashes, and was forced spontaneously to recognize my superiority, and I forgave them all. I was a poet and a grand gentleman; I fell in love; I came in for countless millions and immediately devoted them to humanity, and at the same time I confessed before all the people my shameful deeds, which, of course, were not merely shameful but had in them much that was *good and beautiful,* something in the style of Manfred.[14] Everyone would kiss me and weep (what idiots they would be if they didn't), while I'd go barefoot and hungry preaching new ideas and fighting a victorious Austerlitz [15] against the obscurantists. Then the band would play a march, an amnesty would be declared, the Pope would agree to retire from Rome to Brazil; then there would be a ball for the whole of Italy at the Villa Borghese on the shores of the Lake of Como (the Lake of Como being for that purpose transferred

14. The great Byronic hero.
15. Where Napoleon defeated the Russians.

to the neighborhood of Rome); then would come a scene in the bushes, and so on, and so on — as though you didn't know all about it!

You will say that it is vulgar and contemptible to drag all this out before everybody after all the tears and transports which I have myself confessed. But why is it contemptible? Can you imagine that I am ashamed of it all, and that it was stupider than anything in your life, gentlemen? And I can assure you that some of these fancies were by no means badly composed. It did not all happen on the shores of Lake Como. And yet you are right — it really is vulgar and contemptible. And most contemptible of all is the fact that I am now attempting to justify myself to you. And even more contemptible than that is my making this remark now. But that's enough, or there will be no end to it: each step will be more contemptible than the last. . . .

I could never stand more than three months of dreaming at a time without feeling an irresistible desire to plunge into society. To plunge into society meant to visit my superior at the office, Anton Antonich Syetochkin. He was the only permanent acquaintance I ever had in my life, and I wonder at the fact myself now. But I only went to see him when that phase came over me and when my dreams had reached such a point of bliss that it became essential at once to embrace my fellows and all mankind; and for that purpose I needed, at least, one human being, actually existing. I had to call on Anton Antonich, however, on Tuesday — his at-home day, so I always had to time my passionate desire to embrace humanity so that it might fall on a Tuesday.

This Anton Antonich lived on the fourth floor in a house in Five Corners, in four low-pitched rooms, each smaller than the next, of a particularly frugal and sere appearance. He had two daughters, and the daughters had an aunt, who used to pour out the tea. Of the daughters one was thirteen and the other fourteen; they both had snub noses, and I was awfully shy in their presence because they were always whispering and giggling together. The master of the house usually sat in his study on a leather couch in front of the table with some gray-headed gentleman, usually a colleague from our office or some other department. I never saw more than two or three visitors there, always the same. They talked about the excise duties, about matters in the Senate, about salaries, about promotions, about His Excellency, and the best means of pleasing him, and so on. I had the patience to sit like a fool beside these people for four hours at a stretch, listening to them without knowing what to say to them or venturing to say a word. I became stupefied, several times I felt myself perspiring, I was overcome by a sort of paralysis; but this was pleasant and good for me. On returning home I deferred for a time my desire to embrace all mankind.

I had, however, one other acquaintance of a sort, Simonov, who was an old schoolfellow. In fact, I had a number of schoolfellows in Petersburg, but I did not associate with them and had even given up nodding to them in the street. I believe I had asked to be transferred into the department I was in simply to avoid their company and to cut off all connection with my hateful childhood. Curses on that school and all those terrible years of penal servitude! In short, I parted from my schoolfellows as soon as I got out into the world. There were two or three left to whom I did nod in the street. One of them was Simonov, who had been in no way distinguished at school, and was of a quiet and equable disposition; but I discovered in him a certain independence of character and even honesty. I don't even suppose that he was particularly stupid. I had at one time spent some rather soulful moments with him, but these had not lasted long and had somehow been suddenly clouded over. He was evidently uncomfortable at these recollections and was, I imagine, always afraid that I might take up the same tone again. I suspected that he had an aversion for me, but still I went on going to see him, not being quite certain of it.

And so on one occasion, unable to endure my solitude and knowing that since it was Thursday Anton Antonich's door would be closed, I thought of Simonov. Climbing up to his fourth-floor flat, I was thinking that the man disliked me and that it was a mistake to go and see him. But as it always happened that such reflections impelled me, as though purposely, to put myself into a false position, I went in. It was almost a year since I had last seen Simonov.

III

I found two of my old schoolfellows with him. They seemed to be discussing an important matter. All of them took scarcely any notice of my entrance, which was strange, for I had not met them for years. Evidently they looked upon me as something on the level of a common housefly. I had not been treated like that even at school, though they had all hated me. I knew, of course, that they must despise me now for my lack of success in the Service, and for my having let myself sink so low, going about badly dressed, and so on — which seemed to them a sign of my incapacity and insignificance. But I had not expected such contempt. Simonov was positively surprised at my turning up. Even in the old days he had always seemed surprised at my coming. All this disconcerted me. I sat down, feeling rather miserable, and began listening to what they were saying.

They were engaged in warm and earnest conversation about a farewell dinner which they wanted to arrange for the next day to a comrade of theirs called Zvercov, an officer in the army, who was going away to a distant province. This Zvercov, too, had been at school all the time I was there. I had begun to hate him, particularly in the upper grades. In the lower grades he had simply been a pretty, playful boy whom everybody liked. I had hated him, however, even in the lower grades, just because he was a pretty and playful boy. He was always poor at his lessons and got worse and worse as he went on; however, he left with a good certificate, since he had influential people interested in him. During his last year at school he came in for an estate of two hundred serfs, and as almost all of us were poor he took to swaggering among us. He was vulgar in the extreme, but at the same time he was a good-natured fellow, even in his swaggering. In spite of superficial, fantastic and sham notions of honor and dignity, all but very few of us positively groveled before Zvercov, and the more he swaggered the more they groveled. And it was not from any interested motive that they groveled, but simply because he had been favored by the gifts of nature. Moreover, it was, as it were, an accepted idea among us that Zvercov was a specialist in tact and the social graces. This last fact particularly infuriated me. I hated the abrupt self-confident tone of his voice, his admiration of his own witticisms, which were often frightfully stupid, though he was bold in his language; I hated his handsome but stupid face (for which I would, however, have gladly exchanged my intelligent one), and the free-and-easy military manners in fashion in the forties.

I hated the way in which he used to talk of his future conquests of women (he did not venture to begin his attacks upon women until he had the epaulettes of an officer, and was looking forward to them with impatience), and boasted of the duels he would constantly be fighting. I remember how I, invariably so taciturn, suddenly fastened upon Zvercov, when one day while talking at a leisure moment with his schoolfellows of his future relations with the fair sex, and growing as sportive as a puppy in the sun, he all at once declared that he would not leave a single village girl on his estate unnoticed, that that was his *droit de seigneur,* and that if the peasants dared to protest he would have them all flogged and double the tax on them, the bearded rascals. Our servile rabble applauded, but I attacked him, not from compassion for the girls and their fathers, but simply because they were applauding such an insect. I got the better of him on that occasion, but though Zvercov was stupid he was also lively and impudent, and so laughed it off, and in such a way that my victory was not really complete: the laugh was on his side. He got the better of me on several occasions afterward, but without malice, jestingly, casually. I remained angrily and contemptuously silent and would not answer him.

When we left school he made advances to me; I did not rebuff them, for I was flattered, but we soon parted, and quite naturally. Afterward I heard of his barrack-room success as a lieutenant, and of the fast life he was leading. Then there came other rumors — of his successes in the Service. By then he had taken to cutting me in the street, and I suspected that he was afraid of compromising himself by greeting a personage as insignificant as myself. I saw him once at a theater, in the third tier of boxes. By then he was wearing shoulder straps. He was twisting and turning, ingratiating himself with the daughters of an ancient general. In three years he had become considerably shopworn, though he was still rather handsome and adroit. One could see that by the time he was thirty he would be corpulent.

So it was to this Zvercov that my schoolfellows were going to give a dinner on his departure. They had kept up with him for those three years, though privately they did not consider themselves on an equal footing with him, I am convinced of that.

Of Simonov's two visitors, one was Ferfichkin, a Russianized German — a little fellow with the face of a monkey, a blockhead who was always deriding everyone, a very bitter enemy of mine from our days in the lower grades — a vulgar, impudent, swaggering fellow, who affected a most sensitive feeling of personal honor, though, of course, he was a wretched little coward at heart. He was one of those worshipers of Zvercov who made up to the latter from interested motives, and often borrowed money from him. Simonov's other visitor, Trudolyubov, was a person in no way remarkable — a tall young fellow, in the army, with a cold face, fairly honest, though he worshiped success of every sort, and was capable only of thinking about promotion. He was some sort of distant relation of Zvercov's, and this, foolish as it seems, gave him a certain importance among us. He always thought me of no consequence whatever; his behavior to me, though not quite courteous, was tolerable.

"Well, with seven rubles each," said Trudolyubov, "which is twenty-one rubles for the three of us, we ought to be able to get a good dinner. Zvercov, of course, won't pay."

"Of course not, since we're inviting him," Simonov decided.

"Can you imagine," Ferfichkin interrupted hotly and conceitedly, like some insolent flunky boasting of his master's, the general's, decorations, "can you imagine that Zvercov will let us pay alone? He'll accept from delicacy, but he'll order half a dozen bottles of champagne."

"Do we want half a dozen for the four of us?" observed Trudolyubov, taking notice only of the half dozen.

"It's settled then — the three of us, with Zvercov for the fourth, twenty-one rubles, at the Hôtel de Paris, at five o'clock tomorrow," Simonov, who had been asked to make the arrangements, concluded finally.

"How do you figure twenty-one rubles?" I asked in some agitation, with a show of being offended. "If you count me it won't be twenty-one but twenty-eight rubles."

It seemed to me that to invite myself so suddenly and unexpectedly would be positively graceful, and that they would all be conquered at once and would look upon me with respect.

"Do you want to join, too?" Simonov observed, with no appearance of pleasure, seeming to avoid looking at me. He knew me through and through.

It infuriated me that he knew me so thoroughly.

"Why not? I'm an old schoolfellow of his, too, I believe, and I must own I feel hurt at your having left me out," I said, boiling over again.

"And where were we to find you?" Ferfichkin put in rudely.

"You never were on good terms with Zvercov," Trudolyubov added, frowning.

But I had already grabbed at the idea and would not give it up.

"It seems to me that no one has a right to form an opinion upon that," I retorted in a shaky voice, as though something tremendous had happened. "Perhaps that is just my reason for wishing it now, that I have not always been on good terms with him."

"Oh, there's no making you out — with all these refinements," Trudolyubov jeered.

"We'll put your name down," Simonov decided, addressing me. "Tomorrow at five o'clock, at the Hôtel de Paris."

"What about the money?" Ferfichkin began in an undertone, indicating me to Simonov, but he broke off, for even Simonov was embarrassed.

"That will do," said Trudolyubov, getting up. "If he wants to come so much, let him."

"But it's a private affair, among friends," Ferfichkin said crossly as he, too, picked up his hat. "It's not an official gathering."

They went away. Ferfichkin did not greet me in any way as he went out, Trudolyubov barely nodded. Simonov, with whom I was left tête-à-tête, was in a state of vexation and perplexity, and looked at me queerly. He did not sit down nor did he ask me to.

"H'm . . . yes . . . tomorrow, then. Will you pay your share now? I'm merely asking to make sure," he muttered in embarrassment.

I flushed crimson, and as I did so I remembered that I had owed Simonov fifteen rubles for ages — which I had, indeed, never forgotten, though I had not paid it.

"You will understand, Simonov, that I could have no idea of this when I came here. I'm very much embarrassed that I have forgotten — "

"All right, all right, that doesn't matter. You can pay tomorrow after the dinner. I simply wanted to know. Please don't — "

He broke off and began pacing the room, still more vexed. As he walked he began to stamp with his heels.

"Am I keeping you?" I asked after two minutes of silence.

"Oh!" he said, starting, "for — to be truthful — yes. I have to go and see someone — not far from here," he added in an apologetic voice, somewhat abashed.

"My goodness, why didn't you say so?" I cried, seizing my cap, with an astonishing free-and-easy air, which was the last thing I should have expected of myself.

"It's close by — not two steps away," Simonov repeated, accompanying me to the front door with a fussy air which did not suit him at all. "So five o'clock, punctually, tomorrow," he called down the stairs after me. He was very glad to get rid of me. I was furious.

"What possessed me — what possessed me to force myself upon them?" I wondered, grinding my teeth as I strode along the street, "for a scoundrel, a swine like that Zvercov! Of course, I'd better not go; of course, I must just snap my fingers at them. I'm not bound in any way. I'll send Simonov a note by tomorrow's mail — "

But what made me furious was that I knew for certain that I should go, that I should make a point of going; and the more tactless, the more unseemly my going would be, the more certainly I would go.

And there was a positive obstacle to my going: I had no money. All I had was nine rubles. I had to give seven of that to my servant, Apollon, for his monthly wages. That was all I paid him — he had to keep himself.

Not to pay him was impossible, considering his character. But I will talk about that fellow, about that plague of mine, another time.

However, I knew I would go and wouldn't pay him his wages.

That night I had the most hideous dreams. No wonder; all the evening I had been oppressed by memories of my miserable days at school, and I couldn't shake them off. I had been sent to the school by distant relations, upon whom I was dependent and of whom I have heard nothing since; they had sent me there a forlorn, silent boy, already crushed by their reproaches, already troubled by doubt, and looking with savage distrust at everyone. My schoolfellows met me with spiteful and merciless gibes because I was unlike any of them. But I could not endure their taunts; I could not give in to them with the ignoble readiness with which they gave in to one another. I hated them from the first, and shut myself away from everyone in timid, wounded, and disproportionate pride. Their coarseness revolted me. They laughed cynically at my face, at my clumsy figure; and yet what stupid faces they had themselves! In our school the boys' faces seemed in a special way to degenerate and grow stupider. How many fine-looking boys came to us! In a few years they became repulsive. Even at sixteen I wondered at them morosely; even then I was struck by the pettiness of their thoughts, the stupidity of their pursuits, their games, their conversations. They had no understanding of things that were so essential, they took no interest in matters that were so striking, so impressive, that I could not help considering them inferior to myself.

It was not wounded vanity that drove me to this, and for God's sake do not thrust upon me your hackneyed remarks, repeated *ad nauseam,* that "I was only a dreamer," while they even then had an understanding of life. They understood nothing, they had no idea of real life, and I swear that that was what made me most indignant about them. On the contrary, the most obvious, striking reality they accepted with fantastic stupidity and even at that time were accustomed to respect success. Everything that was just, but oppressed and looked down upon, they laughed at heartlessly and shamefully. They took rank for intelligence; even at sixteen they were already talking about a snug berth. Of course, a great deal of it was due to their stupidity, to the bad examples with which they had always been surrounded in their childhood and boyhood. They were monstrously depraved. Of course, a great deal of that, too, was superficial and an assumption of cynicism; of course, there were glimpses of youth and freshness even in their depravity; but even that freshness was not attractive, and showed itself in a certain rakishness.

I hated them horribly, though perhaps I was worse than any of them. They repaid me in the same way, and did not conceal their aversion for me. But by then I did not desire their affection: on the contrary, I continually longed for their humiliation. To escape from their derision I purposely began to make all the progress I could with my studies and forced my way to the very top. This impressed them. Moreover, they all began by degrees to grasp that I had already read books none of them could read, and understood things (not forming part of our school curriculum) of which they had not even heard. They took a savage and sarcastic view of it, but were morally impressed, especially as the teachers began to notice me on those grounds. The mockery ceased, but the hostility remained, and cold and strained relations became permanent between us. In the end I could not put up with it; with years a craving for society, for friends, developed in me. I attempted to get on friendly terms with some of my schoolfellows, but somehow or other my intimacy with them was always strained and soon ended of itself.

Once, indeed, I did have a friend. But I was already a tyrant at heart; I wanted to exercise unbounded sway over him; I tried to instill in him a contempt for his surroundings; I required of him a disdainful and complete break with those surroundings. I frightened him with my passionate affection; I reduced him to tears, to hysterics. He was a simple and devoted soul; but when he devoted himself to me entirely I began to hate him immediately and repulsed him — as though all I needed him for was to win a victory over him, to subjugate him and nothing else. But I could not subjugate all of them; my friend was not at all like them either; he was, in fact, a rare exception. The first thing I did on leaving school was to give up the special job for which I had been destined, so as to break all ties, to curse my past and shake its dust from off my feet. And goodness knows why, after all that, I should go trudging off to Simonov's!

Early next morning I roused myself and jumped out of bed with excitement, as though it were all about to happen at once. But I believed that some radical change in my life was coming, and would come inevitably on that day. Owing to its rarity, perhaps, any external event, however trivial, always made me feel as though some radical change in my life were at hand. I went to the office, however, as usual, but sneaked away home two hours earlier to get ready. The great thing, I thought, was not to be the first to arrive, or they would think me overjoyed at coming. But there were thousands of such great points to consider, and they all agitated and overwhelmed me. I polished my boots a second time with my own hands; nothing in the world would have induced Apollon to clean them twice a day, as he considered that it was more than his duties required of him. I stole the brushes to clean them from the passage, being careful he should not detect it, for fear of his contempt. Then I minutely examined my clothes and thought that everything looked old, worn, and threadbare. I had let myself get too slovenly. My uniform, perhaps, was tidy, but I could hardly go out to dinner in it. The worst of it was that there was a big yellow stain on the knees of my trousers. I had a foreboding that that stain would deprive me of nine-tenths of my personal dignity. I knew, too, that it was very bad to think so. "But this is no time for thinking: now I am in for the real thing," I thought, and my heart sank.

I knew, too, perfectly well even then, that I was monstrously exaggerating the facts. But how could I help it? I could not control myself and was already shaking with fever. With despair I pictured to myself how coldly and disdainfully that scoundrel Zvercov would meet me; with what dull-witted, invincible contempt that blockhead Trudolyubov would look at me; with what impudent rudeness that insect Ferfichkin would snigger at me in order to curry favor with Zvercov; how completely Simonov would take it all in, and how he would despise me for the abjectedness of my vanity and lack of spirit — and worst of all, how paltry, *unliterary,* commonplace it would all be. Of course, the best thing would be not to go at all. But that was most impossible of all: if I feel impelled to do anything, I seem to be pitchforked into it. I should have jeered at myself ever afterward: "So you fell down, you fell down, you fell down when it came to the *real thing!*" On the contrary, I passionately longed to show all that "rabble" that I was by no means such a spiritless creature as I seemed to myself.

What is more, even in the acutest paroxysm of this cowardly fever, I dreamed of getting the upper hand, of dominating them, carrying them away, making them like me — if only for my "elevation of thought and unmistakable wit." They would abandon Zvercov, he would sit to one side, silent and ashamed, while I would crush him. Then, perhaps, we'd be reconciled and drink to our everlasting friendship; but what was most bitter and most humiliating for me was that I knew even then, knew fully and for certain that I really needed nothing of all this, that I did not really want to crush, to subdue, to attract them, and that I didn't really care a straw for the result, even if I did achieve it. Oh, how I prayed for the day to pass quickly! In unutterable anguish I went to the window, opened the ventilator, and looked out into the troubled darkness of the thickly falling wet snow.

At last my wretched little clock hissed out five. I seized my hat and, trying not to look at Apollon, who had been all day expecting his month's wages, but in his foolishness was unwilling to be the first to speak about it, I slipped out between him and the door and, jumping into a high-class sleigh on which I spent my last half ruble, I drove up in grand style to the Hôtel de Paris.

IV

I had been certain the day before that I should be the first to arrive. But it was not a question of being the first to arrive. Not only were they not there, but I had difficulty in finding our room. The table had not been laid even. What did it mean? After a good many questions I elicited from the waiters that the dinner had been ordered not for five but for six o'clock. This was confirmed at the bar as well. I felt really ashamed to go on questioning them. It was only twenty-five minutes past five. If they had changed the dinner hour they ought at least to have let me know — that's what the mail is for — and not put me in an absurd position in my own eyes and . . . and even before the waiters. I sat down; the servant began laying the table; I felt even more humiliated when he was present. Toward six o'clock they brought in candles, though there were lamps burning in the room. It had not occurred to the waiter, however, to bring them in at once when I arrived. In the next room two gloomy, angry-looking persons were eating their dinners in silence at two different tables. There was a great deal of noise, even shouting, in a room further away; one could hear the laughter of a crowd of people and nasty little shrieks in French: there were ladies at the dinner. It was sickening, in fact. I rarely passed more unpleasant moments, so much so that when they did arrive all together punctually at six I was overjoyed to see them, as though they were my deliverers, and even forgot that I really ought to show resentment.

Zvercov walked in at the head of them; evidently he was the leading spirit. He and all of them were laughing; but, seeing me, Zvercov drew himself up a little and walked up to me deliberately with a slight, rather jaunty bend from the waist. He shook hands with me in a friendly, but not overfriendly, fashion, with a sort of circumspect courtesy like that of a general, as though in giving me his hand he were warding off something. I had imagined, on the contrary, that on coming in he would at once break into his habitual thin, shrill laugh and fall to making his insipid jokes and witticisms. I had been preparing for them ever since the previous day, but I had not expected such condescension, such high-official courtesy. So, then, he felt himself ineffably superior to me in every respect! If he only meant to insult me by that high-official tone it would not matter, I thought — I could pay him back for it one way or another. But what if, in reality, without the least desire to be offensive, that muttonhead had a notion in earnest that he was superior to me and could only look at me in a patronizing way? The very supposition made me gasp.

"I was surprised to hear of your desire to join us," he began, lisping and drawling, which was something new. "You and I seem to have seen nothing of each other. You fight shy of us. You shouldn't. We're not such dreadful people as you think. Well, anyway, I am glad to renew our acquaintance."

And he turned carelessly to put down his hat on the window.

"Have you been waiting long?" Trudolyubov inquired.

"I arrived at five o'clock as you told me yesterday," I answered loudly, with an irritability that threatened an explosion.

"Didn't you let him know that we had changed the hour?" said Trudolyubov to Simonov.

"No, I didn't. I forgot," the latter replied, with no sign of regret, and, without even apologizing to me, he went off to order the hors d'oeuvres.

"So you've been here a whole hour? Oh, you poor fellow!" Zvercov cried out ironically, for to his notion this was bound to be extremely funny. That rascal Ferfichkin chimed in with his nasty little snigger, like a puppy yapping. My position struck him, too, as exquisitely ludicrous and embarrassing.

"It isn't funny at all!" I cried to Ferfichkin, more and more irritated. "It wasn't my fault, but that of others. They neglected to let me know. It was . . . it was . . . it was simply absurd!"

"It's not only absurd, but something else as well," muttered Trudolyubov, naïvely taking my part. "You're too mild about it. It was simply rudeness — unintentional, of course. And how could Simonov — h'm!"

"If a trick like that had been played on me," observed Ferfichkin, "I'd — "

"But you should have ordered something for yourself," Zvercov interrupted, "or simply asked for dinner without waiting for us."

"You'll admit that I might have done that without your permission," I rapped out. "If I waited, it was because — "

"Let us sit down, gentlemen," called out Simonov, coming in. "Everything is ready; I can answer for the champagne; it is capitally iced. You see, I didn't know your address; where was I to look for you?" He suddenly turned to me, but again he seemed to avoid looking at me. Evidently he had something against me. It must have been what had happened yesterday.

All sat down; I did the same. It was a round table. Trudolyubov was on my left, Simonov on my right. Zvercov was sitting opposite, Ferfichkin next to him, between him and Trudolyubov.

"Tell me, are you . . . in a government office?" Zvercov went on being attentive to me. Seeing that I was embarrassed, he seriously thought that he ought to be friendly to me, and, so to speak, cheer me up.

"Does he want me to throw a bottle at his head?" I thought, in a rage. In my novel surroundings I was unnaturally ready to be irritated.

"In the N—— office," I answered jerkily, with my eyes on my plate.

"And ha-ave you a goo-ood berth? I say, what ma-a-de you leave your original job?"

"What ma-a-de me was that I wanted to leave my original job," I drawled more than he, hardly able to control myself. Ferfichkin went off into a guffaw. Simonov looked at me sarcastically. Trudolyubov left off eating and began looking at me with curiosity.

Zvercov winced, but he tried not to notice anything.

"And the remuneration?"

"What remuneration?"

"I mean, your sa-a-lary?"

"Why are you cross-examining me?" However, I told him at once what my salary was. I turned horribly red.

"It's not very handsome," Zvercov observed majestically.

"Yes, you can't afford to dine at cafés on that," Ferfichkin added insolently.

"To my thinking it's very poor," Trudolyubov observed gravely.

"And how thin you have grown! How you have changed!" added Zvercov, with a shade of venom in his voice, scanning me and my attire with a sort of insolent compassion.

"Oh, spare his blushes," cried Ferfichkin, sniggering.

"My dear Sir, allow me to tell you I am not blushing," I broke out at last: "Do you hear? I am dining here, at this café, at my own expense, not at other people's — note that, Mr. Ferfichkin."

"Wha-at? Isn't everyone here dining at his own expense? You seem to be — " Ferfichkin turned on me, becoming as red as a lobster and looking me in the face with fury.

"We won't go into tha-at," I mimicked in answer, feeling I had gone too far. "And I imagine it would be better to talk of something more intelligent."

"You intend to show off your intelligence, I suppose?"

"Don't upset yourself; that would be quite out of place here."

"Why are you jabbering away like that, my good Sir, eh? Have you gone out of your wits in your office?"

"Enough, gentlemen, enough!" Zvercov cried authoritatively.

"How stupid all this is!" muttered Simonov.

"It really is stupid. We've met here, a party of friends, for a farewell dinner to a comrade, and you carry on a fight," said Trudolyubov, rudely addressing himself to me alone. "You invited yourself to join us, so don't disturb the general harmony."

"Enough, enough!" cried Zvercov. "Quit it, gentlemen, it's out of place. Better let me tell you how I nearly got married the day before yesterday — "

And then followed a burlesque narrative of how this gentleman had almost been married two days before. There was not a word about the marriage, however, but the story was adorned with generals, colonels, and gentlemen-in-waiting, while Zvercov almost took the lead among them. It was greeted with approving laughter; Ferfichkin positively squealed.

No one paid any attention to me, and I sat crushed and humiliated.

"Good Heavens, these are not the people for me!" I thought. "And what a fool I have made of myself before them! I let Ferfichkin go too far, though. The brutes imagine they are doing me an honor in letting me sit down with them. They don't understand that it's an honor to them and not to me! I've grown thinner! My clothes! Oh, damn my trousers! Zvercov noticed the yellow stain on the knee as soon as he came in. But what's the use! I must get up at once, this very minute, take my hat and simply go without a word — with contempt! And tomorrow I can send a challenge. The scoundrels! As though I cared about the seven rubles. They may think . . . Damn it! I don't care about the seven rubles. I'll go this minute!"

Of course I remained. I drank sherry and Lafitte by the glassful in my discomfiture. Being unaccustomed to it, I was quickly affected. My annoyance increased as the wine went to my head. I longed, all of a sudden, to insult them all in a most flagrant manner and then go away. To seize the moment and show what I could do, so that they would say: "He's clever, though he's absurd," and . . . and . . . in fact, damn them all!

I scanned them all insolently with my drowsy eyes. But they seemed to have forgotten me altogether. They were noisy, vociferous, cheerful. Zvercov was talking all the time. I began listening. Zvercov was talking of some exuberant lady whom he had at last led on to declaring her love (of course he was lying like a trooper), and how he had been helped in this affair by an intimate friend of his, a Prince Nicky, an officer in the hussars, who had three thousand serfs.

"And yet this Nicky, who has three thousand serfs, hasn't put in an appearance here tonight to see you off," I cut in suddenly.

For a minute everyone was silent. "You are drunk already." Trudolyubov deigned to notice me at last, glancing contemptuously in my direction. Zvercov, without a word, examined me as though I were an insect. I dropped my eyes. Simonov made haste to fill up the goblets with champagne.

Trudolyubov raised his goblet, as did everyone else but me.

"Your health and good luck on the journey!" he said to Zvercov. "To old times, to our future, hurrah!"

They all tossed off their goblets and crowded around Zvercov to kiss him. I didn't stir; my full goblet stood untouched before me.

"Why, aren't you going to drink the toast?" roared Trudolyubov, losing patience and turning menacingly to me.

"I want to make a speech separately, on my own account — and then I'll drink to it, Mr. Trudolyubov."

"Spiteful brute!" muttered Simonov.

I drew myself up in my chair and feverishly seized my goblet, prepared for something extraordinary, though I did not know myself precisely what I was going to say.

"*Silence!*" cried Ferfichkin. "Now for a display of wit!"

Zvercov waited very gravely, knowing what was coming.

"Lieutenant Zvercov, Sir," I began, "let me tell you that I hate phrases, phrasemongers, and men who wear corsets — that's the first point, and there's a second one to follow it."

There was a general stir.

"The second point is: I hate loose talk and loose talkers. Especially loose talkers! The third point: I love justice, truth, and honesty." I went on almost mechanically, for I was beginning to shiver with horror myself and had no idea how I had come to be talking like this. "I love thought, Monsieur Zvercov; I love true comradeship, on an equal foot-ing and not — h'm! I love — but, however, why not? I'll drink your health, too, Monsieur Zvercov. Seduce the Circassian girls, shoot the enemies of the fatherland, and — and — here's to your health, Mon-sieur Zvercov!"

Zvercov got up from his seat, bowed to me, and said:

"I'm very much obliged to you." He was frightfully offended and had turned pale.

"Damn the fellow!" roared Trudolyubov, bringing his fist down on the table.

"Well, he ought to get a punch in the nose for that," squealed Ferfichkin.

"We ought to turn him out," muttered Simonov.

"Not a word, gentlemen, not a move!" cried Zvercov gravely, check-ing the general indignation. "I thank you all, but I am able to show him myself how much value I attach to his words."

"Mr. Ferfichkin, you will give me satisfaction tomorrow for your words just now!" I said aloud, turning with dignity to Ferfichkin.

"A duel, you mean? Certainly," he answered. But probably I was so ridiculous as I challenged him, and it was so out of keeping with my appearance, that everyone, including Ferfichkin, was prostrate with laughter.

"Yes, let him alone, of course! He's quite drunk," Trudolyubov said with disgust.

"I'll never forgive myself for letting him join us," Simonov muttered again.

"Now is the time to throw a bottle at their heads," I thought to myself. I picked up the bottle — and filled my glass.

"No, I'd better sit on to the end," I went on thinking; "you would be pleased, my friends, if I went away. Nothing will induce me to go. I'll go on sitting here and drinking to the end, on purpose, just to show that I don't think you of the slightest consequence. I'll go on sitting and drinking, because this is a tavern and I paid my entrance money. I'll sit here and drink, for I look upon you as so many pawns, so many inanimate pawns. I'll sit here and drink — and sing if I want to. Yes, sing, for I have the right to — to sing. H'm!"

But I did not sing. I simply tried not to look at any of them. I assumed various attitudes, ever so unconcerned, and waited with im-patience for them to speak *first*. But alas, they did not address me! And oh, how I wished at that moment to be reconciled to them! It struck eight, and nine, at last. They moved from the table to the sofa. Zvercov stretched himself on a lounge and put one foot on a round table. Wine was brought there. He did, as a fact, order three bottles on his own account. I, of course, was not invited to join them. They all sat round him on the sofa. They listened to him, almost with reverence. It was evident that they were fond of him.

"What for? What for?" I wondered. From time to time they were moved to drunken enthusiasm and kissed one another. They talked of the Caucasus, of the nature of true passion, of snug berths in the Service, of the income of an hussar called Podharzhevski, whom none of them knew personally, and rejoiced at the hugeness of it, at the extraordinary grace and beauty of a Princess D——, whom none of them had ever seen; then it came to Shakespeare's being immortal.

I smiled contemptuously and walked up and down the other side of the room, opposite the sofa, from the table to the stove and back again. I tried my very utmost to show them that I could do without them, and yet I purposely made a noise with my shoes, thumping my heels. But it was all in vain. They paid no attention. I had the patience to walk up and down in front of them from eight o'clock till eleven, in the same place, from the table to the stove and back again. "I walk up and down to please myself, and no one can prevent me." The waiter who came into the room stopped, from time to time, to look at me. I was somewhat giddy from turning round so often; at moments it seemed to me that I was in delirium. During those three hours I was three times soaked with sweat and dry again.

At times, with an intense, acute pang, I was stabbed to the heart by the thought that ten years, twenty years, forty years would pass, and that even in forty years I would remember with loathing and humiliation those filthiest, most ludicrous, and most awful moments of my life. No one could have gone out of his way to degrade himself more shamelessly, and I fully realized it, fully, and yet I went on pacing up and down from the table to the stove. "Oh, if you only knew what thoughts and feelings I am capable of, how cultured I am!" I thought at moments, mentally addressing the sofa on which my enemies were sitting. But my enemies behaved as though I were not in the room. Once — only once — they turned toward me, just when Zvercov was talking about Shakespeare, and I suddenly gave a contemptuous laugh. I laughed in such an affected and disgusting way that they all at once broke off their conversation and silently and gravely for two minutes watched me walking up and down from the table to the stove, *taking no notice of them.* But nothing came of it: they said nothing, and two minutes later they ceased to notice me again. It struck eleven.

"Friends," cried Zvercov, getting up from the sofa, "let us all go *there* now!"

"Of course, of course," the others assented. I turned sharply to Zvercov. I was so harassed, so exhausted, that I would have cut my throat to put an end to it. I was in a fever; my hair, soaked with perspiration, stuck to my forehead and temples.

"Zvercov, I beg your pardon," I said abruptly and resolutely. "Ferfichkin, yours, too, and everyone's, everyone's: I have insulted you all!"

"Aha! A duel is not in your line, old man," Ferfichkin got out venomously through clenched teeth.

It sent a sharp pang to my heart.

"No, it's not the duel I'm afraid of, Ferfichkin! I'm ready to fight you tomorrow, after we're reconciled. I insist upon it, in fact, and you cannot refuse. I want to show you that I am not afraid of a duel. You'll fire first and I'll fire into the air."

"He's comforting himself," said Simonov.

"He's simply raving," said Trudolyubov.

"Look, let us pass. Why are you barring our way? What do you want?" Zvercov answered disdainfully.

They were all flushed; their eyes were bright; they had been drinking heavily.

"I ask for your friendship, Zvercov; I insulted you, but — "

"Insulted? *You* insulted *me*? Understand, Sir, that you never, under any circumstances, could possibly insult *me*."

"And that's enough for you. Out of the way!" concluded Trudolyubov.

"Olympia is mine, friends, that's agreed!" cried Zvercov.

"We won't dispute your right, we won't dispute your right," the others answered, laughing.

I stood there as though they had spat upon me. The party went noisily out of the room. Trudolyubov struck up some stupid song. Simonov remained behind for a moment to tip the waiters. I suddenly went up to him.

"Simonov, give me six rubles!" I said with desperate resolution.

He looked at me in extreme amazement, with vacant eyes. He, too, was drunk.

"You don't mean you're coming with us?"

"Yes."

"I've no money," he snapped out, and with a scornful laugh he went toward the door.

I clutched at his overcoat. It was a nightmare.

"Simonov, I saw you had money. Why do you refuse me? Am I a scoundrel? Beware of refusing me: if you knew, if you but knew why I'm asking! My whole future, my whole plans depend upon it!"

Simonov pulled out the money and almost flung it at me.

"Take it, if you have no sense of shame!" he uttered pitilessly, and ran to overtake the others.

I was left alone for a moment. Disorder, the remains of dinner, a broken wineglass on the floor, spilt wine, cigarette ends, fumes of drink and delirium in my brain, an agonizing misery in my heart and finally the waiter, who had seen and heard all and was looking inquisitively into my face.

"I'm going there!" I cried. "Either they'll all go down on their knees to beg for my friendship or I'll give Zvercov a slap in the face!"

V

"So this is it, this is it at last — contact with real life," I muttered as I ran headlong down the stairs. "This is very different from the

Pope's leaving Rome and going to Brazil, very different from the ball on Lake Como!"

"You're a scoundrel," a thought flashed through my mind, "if you laugh at this now."

"No matter!" I cried, answering myself. "Now everything is lost!"

There was no trace to be seen of them, but that made no difference — I knew where they had gone.

At the steps stood a solitary nighthawk of a sleigh driver in a rough peasant coat, powdered over with the still-falling snow, wet and seemingly warm. It felt hot and steamy. The little shaggy piebald horse was also covered with snow and wheezing — I remember that very well. I made a rush for the ramshackle sleigh, but as soon as I raised my foot to get into it, the recollection of how Simonov had just given me six rubles seemed to double me up and I tumbled into the sledge like a sack.

"No, I must do a great deal to make up for all this!" I cried. "But I will make up for it or perish on the spot this very night. Get going!" I told the driver.

We set off. My head was all in a whirl.

"They won't go down on their knees to beg for my friendship. That's a mirage, a cheap mirage, revolting, romantic, and fantastical — that's another ball on Lake Como. And so I'm bound to slap Zvercov's face! It's my duty to. And so it's settled; I'm rushing to give him a slap in the face. Hurry up!"

The driver tugged at the reins.

"Soon as I go in I'll let him have it. Should I say a few words by way of preface before giving him a slap in the face? No. I'll simply go in and let him have it. They will all be sitting in the drawing room, and be with Olympia on the sofa. That damned Olympia! She laughed at my looks on one occasion and turned me down. I'll pull Olympia's hair, pull Zvercov's ears! No, better one ear, and drag him by it round the room. Maybe they'll all begin beating me and will kick me out. That's most likely, indeed. No matter! Anyway, I'll first slap him; the initiative will be mine; and by the laws of honor that's everything: he'll be branded and unable to wipe off the slap by any blows, by nothing short of a duel. He'll be forced to fight. And let them beat me now. Let them, the ungrateful wretches! Trudolyubov will beat me hardest, he's so strong; Ferfichkin will be sure to edge in and tug at my hair. But no matter, no matter! That's what I'm going for. The blockheads will be forced at last to see the tragedy of it all! When they drag me to the door I'll call out to them that in reality they're not worth my little finger. Hurry, driver, hurry!" I cried. He started and flicked his whip, so savagely had I shouted.

"We'll fight at daybreak, that's settled. I've done with my job. Ferfichkin made fun of it just now. But where can I get pistols? Nonsense! I'll get my salary in advance and buy them. And powder and bullets? That's the second's business. And how can it all be done by daybreak? And where am I to get a second? I have no friends. Non-

sense!" I cried, working myself up more and more. "It's of no consequence! The first person I meet in the street is bound to be my second,
just as he would be bound to pull a drowning man out of water. The
most peculiar things may happen. Even if I were to ask the director
himself to be my second tomorrow, he'd be bound to consent, if only
from a feeling of chivalry, and to keep the secret! Anton Antonich — "

The fact is that at that very minute the disgusting absurdity of my
plan and the other side of the question was clearer and more vivid to
my imagination than it could be to anyone else on earth. But —

"Hurry, driver! Hurry, you! Hurry!"

"Yes, Sir!" said the son of toil, and grunted.

Cold shivers suddenly ran down my back. Wouldn't it be better
to . . . go straight home? My God, my God! Why did I invite myself
to this dinner yesterday? But no, it's impossible. And my pacing up
and down for three hours from the table to the stove? No, they, *they*
and no one else must pay for that promenade of mine! They must wipe
out that dishonor! Drive on!

And what if they give me into custody? They won't dare! They'll be
afraid of the scandal. And what if Zvercov is so contemptuous that he
refuses to fight a duel? He's sure to; but in that case I'll show them!
I'll turn up at the posting station when he is setting off tomorrow, I'll
catch him by the leg, I'll pull off his coat when he gets into the carriage. I'll sink my teeth into his hand, I'll bite him. "See what lengths
you can drive a desperate man to!" He may hit me on the head and
they may belabor me from behind. I'll shout to the assembled multitude: "Look at this puppy who's driving off to captivate the Circassian
girls after letting me spit in his face!"

Of course, after that everything will be over! The office will have
vanished off the face of the earth. I shall be arrested, I shall be tried,
I shall be dismissed from the Service, thrown in prison, sent to Siberia.
Never mind! In fifteen years when they let me out of prison I'll trudge
off to him, a beggar, in rags. I shall find him in some provincial town.
He'll be married and happy. He'll have a grown-up daughter. . . .
I'll say to him: "Look, monster, at my hollow cheeks and my rags! I've
lost everything — my career, my happiness, art, science, *the woman I
loved*, and all through you. Here are pistols. I have come to discharge
my pistol in the air and — and — I forgive you. Then I'll fire into the
air and he'll hear nothing more of me. . . ."

I was actually on the point of tears, though I knew perfectly well
at that moment that all this was out of Pushkin's *Sylvio* and Lermon-
tov's *Masquerade*. And all at once I felt horribly ashamed, so ashamed
that I stopped the horse, got out of the sleigh, and stood still in the
snow in the middle of the street. The driver gazed at me with a gasping
wonder.

What was I to do? I could not go on there — it was evidently stupid,
and I could not leave things as they were, because that would seem as
though . . . Heavens, how could I leave things just so? And after such

insults! "No!" I cried, throwing myself into the sleigh again. "It is ordained! It is fate! Drive on, drive on!"

And in my impatience I hit the back of the driver's neck.

"What are you up to? What are you hitting me for?" the peasant shouted, but he whipped up his nag so that it began kicking.

The snow was falling in big wet flakes; I opened my coat in spite of that. I forgot everything else, for I had finally decided on slapping Zvercov's face, and felt with horror that the thing was going to happen *now, at once,* and that *no force could stop it.* The deserted street lamps gleamed sullenly in the snowy darkness like torches at a funeral. The snow drifted under my greatcoat, under my coat, under my cravat, and melted there. I did not wrap myself up — all was lost, anyway.

At last we arrived. I jumped out, almost unconscious, ran up the steps, and began knocking and kicking at the door. I felt fearfully weak, particularly in my legs and knees. The door was opened quickly as though they knew I was coming. As a fact, Simonov had warned them that perhaps another gentleman would arrive, and this was a place in which one had to give notice and to observe certain precautions. It was one of those *millinery emporia* which the police had closed down some time ago. By day it really was a shop; but at night, if one had an introduction, one might visit it for other purposes.

I walked rapidly through the dark shop into the familiar drawing room, where there was only one candle burning, and stood still in amazement: there was no one there. "Where are they?" I asked somebody. But by now, of course, they had separated. Before me was standing a person with a stupid smile, the *madam* herself, who had seen me before. A minute later a door opened and another person came in.

Taking no notice of anything, I strode about the room and, I believe, I talked to myself. I felt as though I had been saved from death and was conscious of this, joyfully, all over: I should have given that slap, I should certainly, certainly have given it! But now they were not here and . . . everything had vanished and changed! I looked around. I could not realize my condition yet. I looked mechanically at the girl who had come in, and had a glimpse of a fresh, young, rather pale face, with straight, dark eyebrows, and with grave, as it were wondering, eyes that attracted me at once; I should have hated her if she had been smiling. I began looking at her more intently and with something like an effort. I had not fully collected my thoughts. There was something simple and good-natured in her face, yet somehow strangely grave. I am sure that this stood in her way here, and no one of those fools had noticed her. She could not, however, have been called a beauty, though she was tall, strong-looking, and well built. She was very simply dressed. Something loathsome stirred within me. I went straight up to her.

I chanced to look into the glass. My harassed face struck me as revolting in the extreme, pale, wrought-up, abject, with disheveled hair.

"No matter, I'm glad of it," I thought: "I'm glad I'll seem repulsive to her; I like that."

VI

Somewhere behind a screen a clock began wheezing, as though oppressed by something, as though someone were strangling it. After an unnaturally prolonged wheezing there followed a shrill, nasty, and, as it were, unexpectedly rapid, chime — as though someone were suddenly leaping forward. It struck two. I woke up, though I hadn't really been asleep but lying half conscious.

It was almost completely dark in the narrow, cramped, low-ceiled room, cumbered up with an enormous wardrobe and piles of cardboard boxes and all sorts of frippery and litter. The candle end that had been burning on the table was going out and gave a faint flicker from time to time. In a few minutes there would be complete darkness.

I was not long in coming to myself; everything came back to my mind at once, without an effort, as though it had been in ambush to pounce out on me again. And, indeed, even while I was unconscious a point seemed continually to remain in my memory unforgotten, and round it my dreams moved drearily. But, strange to say, everything that had happened to me in that day seemed to me now, on waking, to be in the far, faraway past, as though I had long, long since lived all that down.

My head was full of fumes. Something seemed to be hovering over me, rousing me, exciting me, and making me restless. Misery and spite seemed surging up in me again and seeking an outlet. Suddenly I saw beside me two wide-open eyes scrutinizing me curiously and persistently. The look in those eyes was coldly detached, sullen, utterly remote, as it were; it weighed upon me.

A grim idea came into my brain and passed all over my body, as a horrible sensation, such as one feels when one goes into a damp and moldy cellar. There was something unnatural in those two eyes, beginning to look at me only now. I recalled, too, that during those two hours I had not said a single word to this creature, and had, in fact, considered it utterly superfluous; in fact, the silence had for some reason gratified me. Now I suddenly realized vividly the hideous idea — revolting as a spider — of vice, which, without love, grossly and shamelessly begins with that in which true love finds its consummation. For a long time we gazed at each other like that, but she did not drop her eyes before mine and her expression did not change, so that at last I felt uncomfortable.

"What is your name?" I asked abruptly, to put an end to it.

"Liza," she answered almost in a whisper, but somehow far from graciously, and she turned her eyes away.

I was silent.

"What weather! The snow is disgusting!" I said, almost to myself, putting my arm under my head despondently and gazing at the ceiling.

She made no answer. This was horrible.

"Have you always lived in Petersburg?" I asked a minute later, almost angrily, turning my head slightly toward her.

"No."

"Where do you come from?"

"From Riga," she answered reluctantly.

"Are you a German?"

"No, Russian."

"Have you been here long?"

"Where?"

"In this house?"

"A fortnight."

She spoke more and more jerkily. The candle went out; I could no longer distinguish her face.

"Have you a father and mother?"

"Yes . . . no. Yes, I have."

"Where are they?"

"There — in Riga."

"Who are they?"

"Oh, nobody in particular."

"Nobody? Why, what do they do?"

"They're tradespeople."

"Have you always lived with them?"

"Yes."

"How old are you?"

"Twenty."

"Why did you leave them?"

"Oh, for no special reason."

That answer meant "Let me alone; I feel sick, sad."

We were silent.

God knows why I did not go away. I felt myself more and more sick and dreary. The images of the previous day began of themselves, apart from my will, flitting through my memory in confusion. I suddenly recalled something I had seen that morning when, full of anxious thoughts, I was hurrying to the office.

"I saw them carrying a coffin out yesterday and they nearly dropped it," I suddenly said aloud, not that I desired to open the conversation, but by accident, as it were.

"A coffin?"

"Yes, in the Hay Market; they were bringing it up out of a cellar."

"From a cellar?"

"Not from a cellar, but from a basement. Oh, you know — from somewhere underground — from a sporting house. It was all so filthy there. Eggshells, rubbish, stink. It was loathsome."

Silence.

"A nasty day to be buried," I began, simply to avoid being silent.

"Nasty — in what way?"

"The snow, the wet." (I yawned.)

"It makes no difference," she said suddenly, after a brief silence.

"No, it's horrid." (I yawned again.) "The gravediggers must have sworn at getting wet from the snow. And there must have been water in the grave."

"Why should there be water in the grave?" she asked with a sort of curiosity, but speaking even more harshly and abruptly than before.

I suddenly began to feel provoked.

"Why, there must have been water at the bottom a foot deep. You can't dig a dry grave in Volkovo Cemetery."

"Why?"

"Why? Because the place is quaggy. It's a regular marsh. So they bury them in water. I've seen it myself — many times."

(I had never seen it once; as a matter of fact, I'd never been in Volkovo and had only heard stories of it.)

"Do you mean to say, you don't mind how you die?"

"But why should I die?" she answered, as though defending herself.

"Why, some day you'll die, and you'll die just the same as that dead woman. She was a — girl — like you. She died of consumption."

"A tart would have died in a hospital . . ." (She knows all about it already: she said *tart*, not *girl*.)

"She was in debt to her madam," I retorted, more and more provoked by the discussion; "and went on earning money for her up to the end, though she had consumption. The sleigh drivers standing about were talking about her to some soldiers and telling them so. No doubt they knew her. They were laughing. They were going to meet in a pothouse to drink to her memory."

A great deal of this was my own invention. Silence followed, profound silence. She did not stir.

"And is it better to die in a hospital?"

"Isn't it just the same? Besides, why should I die?" she added irritably.

"If not now, a little later."

"Why a little later?"

"Why, indeed? Now you're young, not bad-looking, fresh, you fetch a high price. But after another year of this life you'll be very different — you'll pop off."

"In a year?"

"Anyway, in a year you'll be worth less," I continued maliciously. "You'll go from here to something lower, to some other house; a year later — to a third, lower and lower, and in seven years you will come to a basement around the Hay Market. That is, if you're lucky. But it would be much worse if you got some disease, tuberculosis, say. All you have to do is catch a chill or something. It's not easy to get over an illness in your way of life. If you catch anything you may not get rid of it. And so you'll die."

"Oh, well, then I'll die," she answered quite vindictively, and she made a quick movement.

"Still, one feels sorry."

"Sorry for whom? Or what?"

"Sorry for life."

Silence.

"Were you ever engaged? Eh?"

"What's it to you?"

"Oh, I'm not cross-examining you. It's nothing to me. Why are you so cross? Of course you may have had your own troubles. What's it to me? It's simply that I felt sorry."

"Sorry for whom?"

"Sorry for you."

"No need," she whispered hardly audibly, and again made a faint movement.

That incensed me at once. What! I was so gentle with her, but she —

"Why, do you think that you're on the right path?"

"I don't think anything."

"That's just what's wrong. You don't think. Come to your senses while there's still time. There still *is* time. You are still young, not bad-looking; you might love, be married, be happy — "

"Not all married women are happy," she snapped in the rude, abrupt tone she had used at first.

"Not all, of course, but anyway it's much better than the life here. Infinitely better. Besides, with love one can live even without happiness. Even in sorrow life is sweet; life is sweet however one lives. But here — what is there except . . . filth? Phew!"

I turned away with disgust; I was no longer reasoning coldly. I myself began to feel what I was saying and warmed to the subject. I was already longing to expound the cherished ideas I had brooded over in my cubbyhole. Something suddenly flared up in me. An object had appeared before me.

"Never mind my being here, I'm no example for you. I am, perhaps, worse than you are. I was drunk when I came here, though," I nevertheless hastened to say in self-defense. "Besides, a man is no example for a woman. It's a different thing. I may degrade and defile myself, but I'm not anybody's slave. I come and go, and that's the end of it. I shake it off and I'm a different man. But you are a slave from the start. Yes, a slave! You give up everything, your whole freedom. If you want to break your chains afterward, you won't be able to: you'll get more and more tangled. It's an accursed bondage. I know it. I won't speak of anything else, maybe you won't understand, but tell me: no doubt you're in debt to your madam? There, you see," I added, though she made no answer, but only listened in silence, entirely absorbed, "that's bondage for you! You'll never buy your freedom.

They'll see to that. It's like selling your soul to the Devil. And besides, perhaps I, too, am just as unlucky — how do you know — and wallow in the mud on purpose, out of misery? You know, men take to drink from grief; well, maybe I'm here from grief. Come, tell me, what is there good here? Here you and I . . . came together . . . just now and didn't say a single word to each other all the time, and it was only afterward you began staring at me like a wild creature, and I at you. Is that love? Is that how one human being should meet another? It's hideous, that's what it is!"

"Yes!" she assented sharply and quickly.

I was positively astounded by the promptitude of this "Yes." So the same thought may have been straying through her mind when she was staring at me just before. So she, too, was capable of certain thoughts? "Damn it all, this was interesting, this was a point of likeness!" I thought, almost rubbing my hands. And indeed it's easy to turn a young soul like that!

It was the exercise of my power that attracted me most.

She turned her head nearer to me, and it seemed to me in the darkness that she propped herself on her arm. Perhaps she was scrutinizing me. How I regretted that I could not see her eyes. I heard her deep breathing.

"Why have you come here?" I asked her, with a note of authority already in my voice.

"Oh, I don't know."

"But how fine it would be to be living in your father's house! It's warm, and no one bothers you; you have a home of your own."

"But what if it's worse than this?"

"I must take the right tone," flashed through my mind. "I may not get far with sentimentality." But it was only a momentary thought. I swear she really did interest me. Besides, I was exhausted and moody. And cunning so easily goes hand-in-hand with feeling.

"Who denies it!" I hastened to answer. "Anything may happen. I am convinced that someone has wronged you, and that you are more sinned against than sinning. Of course, I know nothing of your story, but it's not likely a girl like you has come here of her own inclination. . . ."

"A girl like me?" she whispered, hardly audibly; but I heard it.

Damn it all, I was flattering her. That was horrid. But perhaps it was a good thing. . . . She was silent.

"Look, Liza, I'll tell you about myself. If I had had a home from childhood, I shouldn't be what I am now. I often think that. However bad it may be at home, anyway they are your father and mother, and not enemies, strangers. Once a year, at least, they'll show their love of you. Anyhow, you know you are at home. I grew up without a home, and perhaps that's why I've turned so — unfeeling."

I waited again. "Perhaps she doesn't understand," I thought, "and, indeed, it's absurd, this moralizing."

"If I were a father and had a daughter, I believe I'd really love my daughter more than my sons," I began indirectly, as though talking of something else, to distract her attention. I must confess I blushed.

"Why so?" she asked.

Ah! so she was listening!

"I don't know, Liza. I knew a father who was a stern, austere man, but used to go down on his knees to his daughter, used to kiss her hands, her feet, he couldn't make enough of her, really. When she danced at parties he used to stand for five hours at a stretch, gazing at her. He was mad over her: I understand that! She'd fall asleep tired at night, and he'd wake to kiss her in her sleep and make the sign of the cross over her. He would go about in a dirty old coat, he was stingy to everyone else, but would spend his last penny for her, giving her expensive presents, and it was his greatest delight when she was pleased with what he gave her. Fathers always love their daughters more than the mothers do. Some girls live happily at home! And I believe I'd never let my daughters marry."

"What next?" she asked with a faint smile.

"I'd be jealous, I really should. To think that she should kiss anyone else! That she should love a stranger more than her father! It's painful to imagine it. Of course, that's all nonsense; of course, every father would be reasonable at last. But I believe before I should let her marry I'd worry myself to death; I'd find fault with all her suitors. But I'd end by letting her marry whomever she herself loved. The one whom the daughter loves always seems the worst to the father, you know. That's always so. So many family troubles come from that."

"Some are glad to sell their daughters rather than to marry them off honorably."

Ah, so that was it!

"Such a thing, Liza, happens in those accursed families in which there is neither love nor God," I retorted warmly, "and where there is no love, there is no sense either. There are such families, it's true, but I am not speaking of them. You must have seen wickedness in your own family, if you talk like that. Truly, you must have been unlucky. H'm! That sort of thing mostly comes about through poverty."

"And is it any better with the gentry? Even among the poor, honest people live happily."

"H'm . . . yes. Perhaps. Another thing, Liza, man is fond of reckoning up his troubles, but does not count his joys. If he counted them up as he ought, he'd see that every lot has enough happiness provided for it. And what if all goes well with the family, if the blessing of God is upon it, if the husband is a good one, loves you, cherishes you, never leaves you! There's happiness in such a family! Even sometimes there is happiness in the midst of sorrow; and indeed sorrow is everywhere. If you marry *you will find out for yourself*. But think of the first years of married life with one you love: what happiness, what happiness there sometimes is in it! And indeed it's the usual thing. In those early days even quarrels with one's husband end happily. Some women get up quarrels with their husbands just because they love them. Indeed, I knew a woman like that: she seemed to say that because she loved him she'd torment him and make him feel it. You know that you may torment a man on purpose through love. Women are particularly given to that, thinking to themselves 'I will love him so, I will make so much of him afterward, that it's no sin to torment him a little now.' And all in the house rejoice at the sight of you, and you are happy and gay and peaceful and honored. Then there are some women who are jealous. I knew one such woman; she couldn't restrain herself, but would jump up at night and run off on the sly to find out where he was, if he went off anywhere, whether he was with some other woman. That's a pity. And the woman knows herself it's wrong, and her heart fails her and she suffers, but she loves — it's all through love. And how sweet it is to make up after quarrels, to own herself in the wrong or to forgive him! And they are both suddenly so happy — as though they had met anew, been married over again, as though their love had begun afresh. And no one, no one should know what passes between husband and wife if they love one another. And whatever quarrels there may be between them, they ought not to call in even their own mothers to judge between them and tell tales of one another. They are their own judges. Love is a holy mystery and ought to be hidden from all other eyes, whatever happens. That makes it holier and better. They respect one another more, and much is built on respect. And if once there has been love, if they have been married for love, why should love pass away? Surely one can keep it! It is rare that one can't keep it. And if the husband is kind and straightforward, why should not love last? The first phase of married love will pass, it's true, but then there will come a love that is better still. Then there will be the union of souls, they will have everything in common, there'll be no secrets between them. And once they have children, the most difficult times will seem to them happy, so long as there is love and courage. Even toil will be a joy; you may deny yourself bread for your children and even that will be a joy. They'll love you for it afterward, so you are putting something away for your future. As the children grow up you feel that you're an example, a support for them; that even after you die, your children will always keep your thoughts and feelings, because they have received them from you; they will take on your semblance and likeness. So you see this is a great duty. How can it fail to draw the father and mother nearer? People say it's a trial to have children. Who says that? It is heavenly happiness! Are you fond of little children, Liza? I'm awfully fond of them. You know — a little rosy baby boy at your bosom, and what husband's heart isn't touched, seeing his wife nursing his child! A plump little rosy baby, sprawling and snuggling, chubby little hands and feet, clean tiny little nails, so tiny that it makes one laugh to look at them; eyes that look as if they understand everything. And while it sucks it clutches at your bosom with its little hand and plays. When its father comes up, the child tears itself away from the bosom, flings itself back, looks at its father, laughs, as though it were fearfully funny, and falls to sucking again. Or it will bite its mother's breast when its little teeth are coming, while it looks sideways at her, with its little eyes as though to say, 'Look, I'm biting!' Isn't it happiness when the three are together, husband, wife, and child? One can forgive a great deal for the sake of such moments. Yes, Liza, one must first learn to live oneself before one blames others!"

"It's by pictures, pictures like that one must get at you," I thought to myself, though I did speak with real feeling, and all at once I flushed crimson. "What if she were suddenly to burst out laughing, what should I do then?" That idea drove me to fury. Toward the end of my speech I really was excited, and now my vanity was somehow wounded. The silence continued. I almost nudged her.

"Why are you — " she began and stopped. But I understood: there was a quiver of something different in her voice, not abrupt, harsh, and unyielding as before, but something soft and shamefaced, so shamefaced that I suddenly felt ashamed and guilty.

"What?" I asked with tender curiosity.

"Why, you — "

"What?"

"Why, you — talk like a book, somehow," she said, and again there was a note of irony in her voice.

That remark sent a pang through my heart. It wasn't what I had been expecting.

I did not understand that she was hiding her feelings under irony, that this is usually the last refuge of modest and chaste-souled people when the privacy of their soul is coarsely and unfeelingly invaded, and that their pride makes them refuse to surrender till the last moment and shrink from giving expression to their feelings before you. I ought to have guessed the truth from the timidity with which she had repeatedly approached her sarcasm, only bringing herself to utter it at last with an effort. But I did not guess, and an evil feeling took possession of me.

"Wait a bit!" I thought.

VII

"Oh, hush, Liza! How can you talk about talking like a book, when it makes even me, an outsider, feel sick? Though I don't look at it as an outsider, for, indeed, it touches me to the heart. Is it possible — is it possible that you do not feel sick at being here yourself? Evidently habit does wonders! God knows what habit can do with anyone. Can you seriously think that you'll never grow old, that you'll never lose your looks, and that they'll keep you here for ever and ever? I say nothing of the loathsomeness of the life here. Though let me tell you this about it — about your present life, I mean; here though you are young now, attractive, nice, with soul and feeling, yet you know as soon as I came to myself just now I felt at once sick at being here with you! One can only come here when one is drunk. But if you were anywhere else, living as good people live, I would perhaps be more than attracted by you, fall in love with you, be glad of a look from you, let alone a word; I'd hang about your door, go down on my knees to you, look upon you as my betrothed and think it an honor. I would not dare to have an impure thought about you. But here, you see, I know that I have only to whistle and you have to come with me whether you like it or not. I don't consult your wishes, but you mine. The lowest laborer hires himself as a workman but he doesn't make a slave of himself altogether, besides, he knows that he will be free again presently. But when are you free? Only think what you're giving up here! What are you enslaving? Your soul, together with your body; you're selling your soul, which you have no right to dispose of! You give your love to be outraged by every drunkard! Love! But that's everything, you know, it's a priceless diamond, it's a maiden's treasure; love — why, a man would be ready to give his soul, to face death to gain that love. But how much is your love worth now? You are sold, all of you, body and soul, and there's no need to strive for love when one can have everything without love. And you know there's no greater insult to a girl than that, do you understand? To be sure, I've heard that they comfort you poor fools, they let you have lovers of your own here. But you know that's simply a farce, that's simply a sham, it's just mockery, and you're taken in by it! Why, do you suppose he really loves you, that lover of yours? I don't believe it. How can he love you when he knows you may be called away from him, any minute? He would be a low fellow if he did! Will he have a grain of respect for you? What have you in common with him? He laughs at you and robs you — that's all his love amounts to! You are lucky if he doesn't beat you. Very likely he does beat you, too. Ask him if you have got one, whether he'll marry you. He'll laugh in your face, if he doesn't spit in it or give you a blow — though maybe he isn't worth a damn himself. And for what have you ruined your life, if you come to think of it? For the coffee they give you to drink and the plentiful meals? But with what object are they fattening you? An honest girl couldn't swallow the food, for she'd know what she was being fed for. You're in debt here, and, of course, you'll always be in debt, and you will go on being in debt to the very end, till the visitors here begin to scorn you. And that'll happen soon enough. Don't rely upon your youth — all that flies by express here, you know. You'll be kicked out. And not simply kicked out; long before that the madam will begin nagging at you, scolding you, abusing you, as though you had not sacrificed your health for her, had not thrown away your youth and your soul for her benefit, but as though you had ruined her, beggared her, robbed her. And don't expect anyone to take your part: the others, your companions, will attack you, too, to win her favor, for all are in slavery here, and here they have lost all conscience and pity long ago. They have become utterly vile, and nothing on earth is viler, more loathsome, and more insulting than their abuse. And you're laying down everything here, unconditionally, youth and health and beauty and hope, and at twenty-two you will look like a woman of five-and-thirty, and you'll be lucky if you're not diseased; pray to God to save you from that! No doubt you are thinking now that you have a fine time and no work to do! Yet there is no work harder or more dreadful in the world or ever has been. One would think that the heart alone would be worn out with tears. And you won't dare to say a word, not half a word, when they drive you away from here; you'll go away as though you were to blame. You'll change to another house, then to a third, then somewhere else, till you come down at last to the Hay Market. There you'll be beaten at every turn; that's good manners there, the visitors don't know how to be friendly without beating you. You don't believe that it's so hateful there? Go and look for yourself some time, you can see with your own eyes. Once, one New Year's Day, I saw a woman at a door. They had turned her out as a joke, to give her a taste of the frost because she had been crying so much, and they shut the door behind her. At nine o'clock in the morning she was already quite drunk, disheveled, half naked, covered with bruises, her face was powdered but she had a black eye, blood was trickling from her nose and her teeth; some cabman had just given her a drubbing. She was sitting on the stone steps, a salt fish of some sort in her hand; she was crying, wailing something about her luck and slapping the fish on the steps, and cabmen and drunken soldiers were crowding in the doorway taunting her. You don't believe that you'll ever get to be like that? I'd be sorry to believe it, too, but how do you know — maybe ten years, eight years ago, that very woman with the salt fish came here fresh as a cherub, innocent, pure, knowing no evil, blushing at every word. Perhaps she was like you, proud, ready to take offense, not like the others; perhaps she looked like a queen, and knew what happiness was in store for the man who should love her and whom she should love. Do you see how it ended? And what if at that very moment when she was pounding her salted fish on the filthy steps, drunken and disheveled — what if at that very moment she recalled the early days of her purity in her father's house, when she used to go to school and the neighbor's son watched for her on the way, declaring that he'd love her as long as he lived, that he'd devote his life to her, and when they vowed to love one another for ever and be married as soon as they were grown up! No, Liza, it would be happy for you if you were to die soon of tuberculosis in some corner, in some cellar like that woman just now. In the hospital, do you say? You'll be lucky if they take you, but what if you are still of use to the madam here? Tuberculosis is a queer disease; it's not like fever. The patient goes on hoping till the last minute and says he's all right. He deludes himself. And that just suits your madam. Never doubt it, that's how it is. You've sold your soul, and what is more, you owe money, so you daren't say a word. But when you're dying, everyone will abandon you, everyone will turn away from you, for then there will be nothing to get from you. What's more, they will reproach you for cumbering the place, for being so long over dying. However you beg you won't get a drink of water without abuse: 'Whenever are you going off, you nasty hussy, you won't let us sleep with your moaning, you make the gentlemen sick.' That's true, I've heard such things said myself. They will thrust you dying into the filthiest corner in the cellar — in the damp and the darkness; what will your thoughts be, lying there alone? When you die, strange hands will lay you out, with grumbling and impatience; no one will bless you, no one will sigh for you, all they want is to get rid of you as soon as possible; they'll buy a coffin, drag you to the grave as they did that poor woman today, and celebrate your memory at some pothouse. There'll be sleet, filth, melting snow in the grave — no need to put themselves out for you. 'Let her down, Vanuha. It's just like her luck — even here she's upside down, the hussy. Tauten the rope, you scalawag.' 'It's all right as it is.' 'All right, is it? Why, she's on her side! She was a fellow creature, after all! But, never mind, throw the earth on her.' And they won't care to waste much time quarreling over you. They'll throw on the wet blue clay as quick as they can and go off to the pothouse — and there all memory of you on earth will end; other women have children to go to their graves, fathers, husbands. But for you there'll be never a tear, nor a sigh, nor any remembrance; no one in the whole world will ever come to you, your name will vanish from off the face of the earth — as though you'd never existed, never been born at all! Nothing but filth and mud, however you knock at your coffin lid at night, when the dead arise, however you cry: 'Let me out, kind people, to live in the light of day! My life was no life at all; my life was thrown away like a dishclout; it was drunk away in the pothouse at the Hay Market; let me out, kind people, to live in the world again!' "

And I worked myself up to such a pitch that I began to have a lump in my throat myself, and . . . and all at once I stopped, sat up in dismay, and, bending over apprehensively, began to listen with a beating heart. I had reason to be worried.

I had felt for some time that I was turning her soul inside out and rending her heart, and — and the more I was convinced of it, the more eagerly I desired to gain my object as quickly and as effectually as possible. It was the exercise of my skill that carried me away; yet it was more than mere sport.

I knew I was speaking stiffly, artificially, even bookishly; in fact, I could not speak except "like a book." But that did not trouble me: I knew, I felt that I should be understood and that this very bookishness might be a help. But now, having attained my effect, I was suddenly panic-stricken. Never before had I witnessed such despair! She was lying on her face, thrusting her face into the pillow and clutching at it with both hands. Her heart was being rent. Her youthful body was shuddering all over as though in convulsions. Suppressed sobs rent her bosom and suddenly burst out in weeping and wailing, whereupon she buried her face deeper in the pillow: she did not want anyone here, not a living soul, to know of her anguish and her tears. She bit the pillow, bit her hand till it bled (I saw that afterward), or, plunging her fingers into her disheveled hair, seemed rigid with the effort of restraint, holding her breath and clenching her teeth. I started to say something, begging her to calm herself, but felt that I did not dare; and all at once, in a sort of cold shiver, almost in terror, began fumbling in the dark, trying hurriedly to get dressed and then go. It was dark: though I tried my best I could not finish dressing quickly. Suddenly I felt a box of matches and a candlestick with a whole candle in it. As soon as the room was lighted up, Liza sprang up, sat up in bed, and with a contorted face, with a half-insane smile, looked at me almost senselessly. I sat down beside her and took her hands; she came to herself, made an impulsive movement toward me, would have caught hold of me, but did not dare, and slowly bowed her head before me.

"Liza, my dear, I was wrong — forgive me, my dear," I began, but she squeezed my hand in her fingers so tightly that I felt I was saying the wrong thing and stopped.

"This is my address, Liza. Come to me."

"I'll come," she answered resolutely, her head still bowed.

"But now I am going, good-by — till we meet again."

I got up. She, too, stood up and suddenly flushed all over, gave a shudder, snatched up a shawl that was lying on a chair, and muffled herself in it to her chin. As she did this she gave another sickly smile, blushed and looked at me strangely. I felt wretched; I was in haste to get away — to disappear.

"Wait a minute," she said suddenly in the passage just at the doorway, stopping me with her hand on my overcoat. She put down the candle in hot haste and ran off; evidently she had thought of something or wanted to show me something. As she ran away she flushed, her eyes shone, and there was a smile on her lips — what was the meaning of it? Against my will I waited; she came back a minute later with an expression that seemed to ask forgiveness for something. In fact, it was not the same face, not the same look as the evening before — sullen, mistrustful, and obstinate. Her eyes now were imploring, soft, and at the same time trustful, caressing, timid. The expression with which children look at people they are very fond of, of whom they are asking a favor. Her eyes were a light hazel, they were lovely eyes, full of life, and capable of expressing love as well as sullen hatred.

Making no explanation, as though I, as a sort of higher being, must understand everything without explanations, she held out a piece of paper to me. Her whole face was positively beaming at that instant with naïve, almost childish triumph. I unfolded it. It was a letter to her from a medical student or someone of that sort — a very highflown and flowery, but extremely respectable, love letter. I don't recall the words now, but I remember well that through the highflown phrases there was apparent a genuine feeling, which could not be feigned. When I had finished reading it I met her glowing, questioning, and childishly impatient eyes fixed upon me. She fixed her eyes upon my face and waited impatiently for what I should say. In a few words, hurriedly, but with a sort of joy and pride, she explained to me that she had been to a dance somewhere in a private house, a family of "very nice people, *who knew nothing,* absolutely nothing, for she had only come here so lately, and it was only through chance she'd gotten in here . . . and she hadn't made up her mind to stay and was certainly going away as soon as she'd paid her debt. . . ." And the student had been at that party and had danced with her all evening. He had talked to her, and it turned out that he'd known her in the old days at Riga when he was a child, they had played together, but a very long time ago — and he knew her parents, but *about this* he knew nothing, nothing whatever, and had no suspicion! And the day after the dance (three days ago) he had sent her that letter through the friend with whom she had gone to the party . . . and . . . well, that was all.

She dropped her shining eyes with a sort of bashfulness as she finished.

The poor girl was keeping that student's letter as a precious treasure, and had run to fetch it, her only treasure, because she did not want me to go away without knowing that she, too, was honestly and genuinely loved; that she, too, was addressed respectfully. No doubt that letter was destined to lie in her box and lead to nothing. But none the less I am certain that she would keep it all her life as a precious treasure, as her pride and justification, and now at such a minute she had thought of that letter and brought it with naïve pride to raise herself in my eyes that I might see; that I, too, might think well of her. I said nothing, pressed her hand, and went out. I very much longed to get away. I walked all the way home, in spite of the fact that the snow was still falling in heavy melting flakes. I was exhausted, shattered, in bewilderment. But behind the bewilderment the truth was already glinting. The loathsome truth.

VIII

It was some time, however, before I consented to recognize that truth. Waking up in the morning after some hours of heavy, leaden sleep, and immediately realizing all that had happened on the previous day, I was positively amazed at my last night's *sentimentality* with Liza, at all those "outcries of horror and pity." "To think of having such an attack of womanish hysteria, pah!" I concluded. And what did I thrust my address upon her for? What if she comes? Let her come, though; it doesn't matter. But *obviously,* that was not now the chief and the most important matter: I had to make haste and at all costs save my reputation in the eyes of Zvercov and Simonov as quickly as possible; that was the chief business. And I was so taken up that morning that I actually forgot all about Liza.

First of all I had at once to repay what I had borrowed the day before from Simonov. I resolved on a desperate measure: to borrow fifteen rubles at once from Anton Antonich. As luck would have it, he was in the best of moods that morning and gave me the sum right away, without waiting to be asked twice. I was so delighted at this that, as I signed the I O U with a swaggering air, I told him casually that the night before "I'd been hitting it up with some friends at the Hôtel de Paris; we were giving a farewell party to a comrade, in fact, I might say a friend of my childhood, and you know — a desperate rake, fearfully spoilt — of course, he belongs to a good family, and has considerable means, a brilliant career; he's witty, charming, a regular Don Juan, you understand; we drank an extra half-dozen and — "

And it went off all right; all this was uttered very casually, unconstrainedly, and complacently.

On reaching home I promptly wrote to Simonov.

To this hour I am lost in admiration when I recall the truly gentlemanly, good-humored, candid tone of my letter. With tact and good breeding and, above all, entirely without superfluous words, I blamed myself for all that had happened. I defended myself, "if I really may be allowed to defend myself," by alleging that being utterly unaccustomed to wine, I had been intoxicated with the first glass, which I said I had drunk before they arrived, while waiting for them at the Hôtel de Paris between five and six o'clock. I begged Simonov's pardon in particular. I asked him to convey my explanations to all the others, especially to Zvercov, whom "I seemed to remember insulting as though in a dream." I added that I would have called upon all of them myself, but my head ached, and besides I could not face them. I was particularly pleased with a certain lightness, almost nonchalance (strictly within the bounds of politness, however), which was apparent in my style, and better than any possible arguments gave them at once to understand that I took rather an independent view of "all that unpleasantness last night," that I was by no means so utterly crushed as you, my friends, probably imagine, but on the contrary looked upon it as a gentleman serenely respecting himself should. "On a young hero's past no censure is cast!"

"There is actually an aristocratic playfulness about it!" I thought admiringly as I read over the letter. And it's all because I am an intellectual and cultured man! Another man in my place would not have known how to extricate himself, but here I have gotten out of it and am again as jolly as ever, and all because I am "a cultured and educated man of our day." And, indeed, perhaps everything was due to the wine yesterday. H'm! No, it wasn't the wine. I hadn't drunk anything at all between five and six when I was waiting for them. I had lied to Simonov; I had lied shamelessly; and indeed I wasn't ashamed now. Hang it all, though, the great thing was that I was rid of the mess.

I put six rubles in the letter, sealed it up, and asked Apollon to take it to Simonov. When he learned that there was money in the letter, Apollon became more respectful and agreed to take it. Toward evening I went out for a walk. My head was still aching and dizzy after yesterday. But as evening came on and the twilight deepened, my impressions and, following them, my thoughts grew more and more different and confused. Something was not dead within me, in the depths of my heart and conscience it would not die, and it evinced itself in acute depression. For the most part I jostled my way through the most crowded business streets, along Meshchanski Street, along Sadovyi Street, and in Yusupov Garden. I always liked particularly sauntering along these streets in the dusk, just when there were crowds of working people of all sorts going home from their daily work, with faces looking cross from worry. What I liked was just that cheap bustle, that bald prose. On this occasion the jostling of the streets irritated me more than ever. I could not make out what was wrong with me, I could not find the clue, something seemed rising up in my soul continually, painfully, and refusing to be appeased. I returned home completely upset. It was just as though some crime were lying on my conscience.

The thought that Liza was coming worried me continually. It seemed queer to me that of all my recollections of yesterday this, seemingly, tormented me especially, quite by itself, as it were. Everything else I had quite succeeded in forgetting by evening; I dismissed it all and was still perfectly satisfied with my letter to Simonov. But on this point I was not satisfied at all. It was as though I were worried only by Liza. "What if she comes?" I thought incessantly. "Well, it doesn't matter, let her come! H'm, it's horrid that she should see how I live, for instance. Yesterday I seemed such a hero to her, while now — h'm! It's horrid, though, that I have let myself go so; my room looks like a beggar's. And I brought myself to go out to dinner in such a suit! And my leatheroid sofa with the stuffing sticking out, and my dressing gown which won't cover me, it's so tattered. And she'll see all this — and Apollon, too. That beast is certain to insult her. He'll fasten upon her in order to be rude to me. And, of course, I'll be panic-stricken as usual; I'll begin bowing and scraping before her and pulling my dressing gown about me; I'll begin smiling, telling lies. Oh, the loathsomeness of it all! And it isn't the loathsomeness that matters most! There's something more important, more loathsome, viler! Yes, viler! And to put on that dishonest lying mask again!"

When I reached that thought I fired up all at once.

"Why dishonest? How dishonest? I was speaking sincerely last night. I remember there was real feeling in me, too. What I wanted was to excite an honorable feeling in her. . . . Her crying was a good thing; it'll have a good effect."

Yet I could not feel at ease. All that evening, even when I had come back home, even after nine o'clock, when I calculated that Liza could not possibly come, she still haunted me, and what was worse she came back to my mind always in the same attitude. One moment out of all that had happened last night stood vividly before my imagination: the moment when I struck a match and saw her pale, distorted face, with its look of torture. And what a pitiful, what an unnatural, what a distorted smile she had at that moment! But I did not know then that fifteen years later I should still see Liza in my imagination, always with the pitiful, distorted, incongruous smile which was on her face at that moment.

Next day I was ready again to look upon it all as nonsense, due to overexcited nerves, and, above all, as *exaggerated*. I was always conscious of that weak point of mine, and sometimes very much afraid of it. "I exaggerate everything; that's where I go wrong," I repeated to myself every hour. But, however, "Liza will very likely come all the same" was the refrain with which all my reflections ended. I was so uneasy that I sometimes flew into a fury: "She'll come, she's certain to come!" I cried, dashing about the room, "if not today then tomorrow; she'll find me out! The damnable romanticism of these pure hearts! Oh, the vileness — oh, the silliness — oh, the stupidity of these "wretched sentimental.souls"! Why, how could one fail to understand? How could one?

But at this point I stopped short, and in great confusion, at that.

And how few, how few words, I thought, in passing, were needed; how little of the idyllic (and affectedly, bookishly, artificially idyllic too) had sufficed to turn a whole human life at once according to my will. That's virginity, to be sure! Freshness of soil!

At times a thought occurred to me, to go to her to "tell her all," and beg her not to come to me. But this thought stirred up such wrath in me that I believed I would have crushed that "damned" Liza if she had chanced to be near me at the time. I would have insulted her, have spat at her, have turned her out, have struck her!

One day passed, however, then another and another; she did not come and I began to grow calmer. I felt particularly bold and cheerful after nine o'clock. I even sometimes began dreaming and rather sweetly: I, for instance, became Liza's salvation, simply through her coming to me and my talking to her. I developed her, educated her. Finally, I noticed that she loved me, loved me passionately. I pretended not to understand (I don't know, however, why I pretended — just for effect, perhaps). At last all in confusion, transfigured, trembling and sobbing, she flung herself at my feet and said that I was her savior, and that she loved me better than anything in the world. I was amazed, but — "Liza," I said, "can you imagine that I have not noticed your love? I saw it all, I divined it, but I did not dare to approach you first, because I had an influence over you and was afraid that you would force yourself, from gratitude, to respond to my love, would try to rouse in your heart a feeling which was perhaps absent, and I did not wish that — because it would be tyranny. It would be indelicate [in short, I launched off at that point into Continental, inexplicably lofty subtleties à la George Sand],[16] but now, now you are mine, you are my creation, you are pure, you are good, you are my noble wife.

16. The nineteenth-century French woman novelist and feminist.

> 'And into my house, calm and fearless,
> As its full mistress walk thou in.' "

Then we began living together, went abroad, and so on and so on. In fact, in the end it seemed vulgar to my own self, and I began putting out my tongue at myself.

Besides, they won't let the hussy out, I thought. They don't let them go out very readily, especially in the evening (for some reason I fancied she would come in the evening, and at seven o'clock precisely). Though she did say she was not altogether a slave there yet, and had certain rights, so — h'm! Damn it all, she will come, she's sure to come!

It was a good thing, in fact, that Apollon distracted my attention at that time by his rudeness. He drove me beyond all patience! He was the bane of my life, the curse laid upon me by Providence. We had been squabbling continually for years, and I hated him. My God, how I hated him! I believe I had never hated anyone in my life as I hated him, especially at certain moments. He was an elderly, dignified man, who worked part of his time as a tailor. But for some unknown reason he despised me beyond all measure, and looked down upon me insufferably. Though, for that matter, he looked down upon everyone. Simply to glance at that flaxen, smoothly brushed head, at the tuft of hair he combed up on his forehead and oiled with sunflower oil, at that dignified mouth, compressed into the shape of the letter B, made one feel one was confronting a man who never had any doubts of himself. He was a pedant, to the utmost degree, the greatest pedant I had met on this earth, and with that had a vanity befitting only Alexander of Macedonia. He was in love with every button on his coat, every nail on his fingers — absolutely in love with them, and he looked it! In his behavior to me he was a perfect tyrant, he spoke very little to me, and if he chanced to glance at me he gave me a firm, majestically self-confident and invariably sarcastic look that sometimes drove me to fury. He did his work with the air of doing me the greatest favor — though he did scarcely anything for me, and did not, indeed, consider himself bound to do anything. There could be no doubt that he looked upon me as the greatest fool on earth, and that he did not "get rid" of me was simply so he could get wages from me every month. He consented to do nothing for me for seven rubles a month. Many sins should be forgiven me for what I suffered from him.

My hatred reached such a point that sometimes his very step almost threw me into convulsions. What I loathed particularly was his lisp. His tongue must have been a little too long or something of that sort, for he continually lisped, and seemed to be very proud of it, imagining that it greatly added to his dignity. He spoke in a slow, measured tone, with his hands behind his back and his eyes fixed on the ground. He maddened me particularly when he read aloud the Psalms to himself behind his partition. Many a battle I waged over that reading! But he was awfully fond of reading aloud in the evenings, in a slow, even, singsong voice, as though over the dead. Interestingly enough, that's just how he wound up his career: he hired himself out to read the Psalms over the dead, and at the same time killed rats and made shoe-blacking. But at that time I could not get rid of him; it was as though he were chemically combined with my existence. Besides, nothing would have induced him to consent to leaving me. I could not live in furnished lodgings: my lodging was my private solitude, my shell, my cave, in which I concealed myself from all mankind, and Apollon seemed to me, for some reason, an integral part of that flat, and for seven years I could not turn him away.

To be two or three days behind with his wages, for instance, was impossible. He would have made such a fuss that I wouldn't have known where to hide my head. But I was so exasperated with everyone during those days that I made up my mind for some reason and with some object to *punish* Apollon and not to pay him for a fortnight the wages that were due him. I had for a long time — for the last two years — been intending to do this, simply in order to teach him not to give himself airs before me, and to show him that if I liked I could withhold his wages. I proposed to say nothing to him about it, and was indeed purposely silent, in order to score off his pride and force him to be the first to speak of his wages. Then I would take the seven rubles out of a drawer, show him I had the money put aside on purpose, but that I wouldn't, I wouldn't, I simply wouldn't pay him his wages; I wouldn't, just because that was "my wish," because "I was master, and it was for me to decide," because he had been disrespectful, because he had been rude; but if he were to ask respectfully I might be softened and give it to him, otherwise he might wait another fortnight, another three weeks, a whole month.

But angry as I was, he nevertheless got the better of me. I could not hold out for four days. He began as he always did in such cases, for there had been such cases already, there had been attempts (and it may be observed I knew all this beforehand, I knew his nasty tactics by heart). He would begin by fixing upon me an exceedingly severe stare, keeping it up for several minutes at a time, particularly on meeting me or seeing me out of the house. If I held out and pretended not to notice these stares he would, still in silence, proceed to further tortures. All at once, à propos of nothing, he would glide softly into my room, when I was pacing up and down or reading, stand at the door, one hand behind his back and one foot back of the other, and fix upon me a stare more than severe, utterly contemptuous. If I suddenly asked him what he wanted he would make me no answer but continue staring at me persistently for some seconds, then, with a peculiar compression of his lips and a most significant air, deliberately turn around and deliberately go back to his room. Two hours later he would come out again, and again present himself before me in the same way. Sometimes I was so infuriated I did not even ask him what he wanted but simply raised my head sharply and imperiously and began staring back at him. We stared at one another for two minutes; at last he turned with deliberation and dignity and went back again for two hours.

If I were still not brought to reason by all this but persisted in my revolt, he would suddenly begin sighing while he looked at me, long, deep sighs as though measuring by them the depths of my moral degradation, and, of course, it ended at last by his triumphing completely: I raged and shouted, but still was forced to do what he wanted.

This time the usual staring maneuvers had scarcely begun when I lost my temper and flew at him in a fury. I was irritated beyond endurance, and not only on his account.

"Wait!" I cried in a frenzy as he was slowly and silently turning, with one hand behind his back, to go to his room. "Wait! Come back, come back, I tell you!" and I must have screamed so unnaturally that he turned around and even looked at me with some wonder. However, he persisted in saying nothing, and that infuriated me.

"How dare you come and look at me like that without being sent for? Answer me!"

After looking at me calmly for half a minute, he began turning round again.

"Wait!" I roared, running up to him. "Don't stir! There. Answer, now — what did you come to look at?"

"If you have any order to give me it's my duty to carry it out," he answered after another silent pause, with a slow, measured lisp, raising his eyebrows and calmly twisting his head from side to side, all this with exasperating composure.

"That's not what I'm asking you about, you torturer!" I shouted, turning crimson with anger. "I'll tell you myself why you came here. You see, I don't give you your wages, but you are so proud you don't want to bow down and ask for them, and so you come to punish me with your stupid stares, to worry me, and you have no sus-pi-cion how stupid it is — stupid, stupid, stupid, stupid!"

He would have turned around again without a word, but I seized him.

"Listen," I shouted to him, "here's the money, do you see, here it is [I took it out of the table drawer], here are the seven rubles, in full, but you're not going to get them. You — are — not — going — to — get — them until you come respectfully with bowed head and beg my pardon. You hear?"

"That cannot be," he answered with the most preternatural self-confidence.

"It shall be so," I said. "I give you my word of honor it shall be!"

"And there's nothing for me to beg your pardon for," he went on, as though he had not noticed my exclamations at all. "And, besides, you called me a 'torturer,' for which I can summon you to the police station at any time, for an insulting action."

"Go, summon me," I roared. "Go at once, this very minute, this very second! You are a torturer all the same! A torturer!"

But he merely looked at me, then turned, and, regardless of my loud calls to him, walked to his room with an even step and without looking around.

"If it had not been for Liza nothing of this would have happened," I decided inwardly. Then, after waiting a minute, I went myself behind his screen with a dignified and solemn air, though my heart was beating slowly and violently.

"Apollon," I said quietly and emphatically, though I was breathless, "go at once without a minute's delay and fetch the police officer."

He had meanwhile settled himself at his table, put on his spectacles, and picked up some garment he was mending. But, hearing my order, he burst into a guffaw.

"At once, go this minute! Go on or else you can't imagine what will happen."

"You are certainly out of your mind," he observed without even raising his head, lisping as deliberately as ever and threading his needle. "Whoever heard of a man sending for the police against himself? And as for being frightened — you are upsetting yourself about nothing, for nothing will come of it."

"Go!" I shrieked, shaking him by the shoulder. I felt I would strike him in a minute.

But I did not notice the door from the passage softly and slowly open at that instant and a figure come in, stop short, and begin staring at us in perplexity. I glanced, nearly swooned with shame, and rushed back to my room. There, clutching at my hair with both hands, I leaned my head against the wall and stood thus motionless.

Two minutes later I heard Apollon's deliberate footsteps.

"There's some woman asking for you," he said, looking at me with peculiar severity. Then he stood aside and let in Liza. He would not go away, but stared at us sarcastically.

"Go away, go away," I commanded in desperation. At that moment my clock began whirring and wheezing and struck seven.

IX

And into my house, calm and fearless,
As its full mistress walk thou in.

I stood before her crushed, crestfallen, revoltingly confused, and I believe I smiled as I did my utmost to wrap myself in the folds of my ragged quilted dressing gown — exactly as, in a fit of depression, I had imagined the scene not long before. After standing over us for a couple of minutes Apollon went away, but that did not put me any more at ease. What made it worse was that she, too, was overwhelmed with confusion — more so, in fact, than I might have expected. Overwhelmed at the sight of me, of course.

"Sit down," I said mechanically, moving a chair up to the table, and I sat down on the sofa. She obediently seated herself at once and gazed at me open-eyed, evidently expecting something from me at once.

This naïveté of expectation drove me to fury, but I restrained myself.

She ought to have tried not to notice, as though everything had been as usual, while instead of that, she. . . . And I dimly felt that I should make her pay dearly for *all this*.

"You have found me in a strange position, Liza," I began, stammering and knowing that this was the wrong way to begin. "No, no, don't imagine anything," I cried, seeing that she had suddenly flushed. "I am not ashamed of my poverty. On the contrary, I regard my poverty with pride. I am poor but honorable. One can be poor and honorable," I mumbled. "However . . . Would you like tea?"

"No" — she was about to refuse.

"Wait a minute."

I leaped up and ran to Apollon. I had to get out of the room somehow.

"Apollon," I whispered in feverish haste, flinging down before him the seven rubles which had remained all the time in my clenched fist, "here are your wages. See, I give them to you; but for that you must come to my rescue: bring me tea and a dozen zwieback from the restaurant. If you won't go, you'll make me a miserable man! You don't know who this woman is. This is — everything! You may be imagining something — but you don't know what that woman is!"

Apollon, who had already sat down to his work and put on his spectacles again, at first glanced askance at the money without speaking or putting down his needle; then, without paying the slightest attention to me or making any answer, he went on busying himself with his needle, which he had not yet threaded. I waited before him for three minutes with my arms crossed à la Napoleon. My temples were dank with sweat. I was pale, I felt. But, thank God, he must have been moved to pity, looking at me. Having threaded his needle he deliberately got up from his seat, deliberately moved back his chair, deliberately took off his spectacles, deliberately counted the money, and, finally asking me over his shoulder: "Shall I get enough for two?", deliberately walked out of the room. As I was going back to Liza the thought occurred to me: Shouldn't I run away just as I was in my dressing gown, no matter where, and then let come what might?

I sat down again. She looked at me uneasily. For some minutes we were silent.

"I will kill him," I shouted suddenly, striking the table with my fist so that the ink spurted out of the inkstand.

"What are you saying!" she cried, starting.

"I will kill him! Kill him!" I shrieked, suddenly striking the table in absolute frenzy and at the same time fully understanding how stupid it was to be so frenzied. "You don't know, Liza, what a torturer he is to me. He is my torturer. He went just now to fetch something; he — "

And suddenly I burst into tears. It was an hysterical attack. How ashamed I felt in the midst of my sobs! But still I could not restrain them.

She was frightened.

"What's the matter? What's wrong?" she cried, fussing about me.

"Water, give me water! Over there!" I muttered faintly, though I was inwardly conscious that I could have got on very well without water and without muttering faintly. But I was what is called *putting on an act*, to save appearances, though the attack was a genuine one.

She gave me water, looking at me in bewilderment. At that moment Apollon brought in the tea. It suddenly seemed to me that this commonplace, prosaic tea was horribly undignified and paltry after all that had happened, and I blushed crimson. Liza looked at Apollon with positive alarm. He went out without a glance at either of us.

"Liza, do you despise me?" I asked, looking at her fixedly, trembling with impatience to know what she was thinking.

She was confused and did not know what to answer.

"Drink your tea," I said to her angrily. I was angry with myself, but, of course, it was she who would have to pay for it. A horrible spite against her suddenly surged up in my heart; I believe I could have killed her. To revenge myself on her I swore inwardly not to say a word to her all the time. "She is the cause of it all," I thought.

Our silence lasted for five minutes. The tea stood on the table; we did not touch it. I had got to the point of purposely refraining from breaking the silence in order to embarrass her further; it was awkward for her to begin. Several times she glanced at me with mournful perplexity. I was obstinately silent. I was, of course, myself the chief sufferer, because I was fully conscious of the disgusting meanness of my spiteful stupidity, and yet at the same time I could not restrain myself.

"I want to — get away from there altogether," she began, to break the silence in some way, but, poor girl, that was just what she ought not to have spoken about at such a stupid moment to a man as stupid as I was. My heart positively ached with pity for her tactless and unnecessary straightforwardness. But something hideous at once stifled all compassion in me; it even provoked me to greater venom. I did not care what happened. Another five minutes passed.

"Perhaps I am in your way," she began with timidity, hardly audibly, and was getting up.

But as soon as I saw this first impulse of wounded dignity I positively trembled with spite, and at once burst out:

"Why have you come to me? Tell me that, please?" I began, gasping for breath and disregarding all logical connection in my words. I longed to have it all out at once, at one sweep; I did not even trouble how to begin. "Why have you come? Answer me, answer me!" I cried, hardly knowing what I was doing. "I'll tell you, my good girl, why you have come. You've come because I talked sentimental bosh to you that time. So now you are soft as butter and longing for fine sentiments again. But you may as well know that I was laughing at you then. And I'm laughing at you now. Why are you shuddering? Yes, I was laughing at you! I had been insulted just before, at dinner, by the

fellows who came that evening before me. I came to you, meaning to
thrash one of them, an officer. But I didn't succeed, I didn't find him;
I had to avenge the insult on someone to get even; you turned up,
I vented my spleen on you and laughed at you. I had been humiliated,
so I wanted to humiliate; I had been treated like a rag, so I wanted
to show my power. That's what it was, and you imagined I had come
there on purpose to save you. Yes? You imagined that? You imagined
that?"

I knew that she would perhaps be muddled and not take it all in
exactly, but I knew, too, that she would grasp the gist of it, very well
indeed. And so, in fact, she did. She turned white as linen, tried to
say something, and her lips worked painfully; but she sank on a chair
as though she had been felled by an ax. And all the time afterward
she listened to me with her lips parted and her eyes wide open, shuddering in awful terror. The cynicism, the cynicism of my words overwhelmed her.

"Save you!" I went on, jumping up from my chair and dashing up
and down the room before her. "Save you from what? But perhaps I
myself am worse than you. Why didn't you throw it in my teeth when
I was giving you that sermon: 'But what did you yourself come here
for? Was it to read me a sermon?' Power, power was what I wanted
then, sport was what I wanted; I wanted to wring out your tears, your
humiliation, your hysteria — that was what I wanted then! Of course,
I couldn't keep it up then, because I'm a foolishly wretched creature,
I was frightened, and, the devil knows why, foolishly gave you my
address. Afterward, before I got home, I was cursing and swearing at
you because of that address; I hated you already because of the lies
I had told you. Because I only like playing with words, only dreaming.
But, do you know, what I really want is that you should all go to hell.
That's what I want. I want peace; yes, I'd sell the whole world for a
copper, straight off, if only I'd be left in peace. Is the world to go to
pot or am I to go without my tea? I say that the world may go to pot
for all I care, so long as I always get my tea. Did you know that or
not? Well, anyway, I know that I'm a blackguard, a scoundrel, an
egoist, a sluggard. Here I've been shuddering for the last three days
at the thought of your coming. And do you know what has worried me
particularly for these three days? That I posed as such a hero to you,
and now you would see me in a wretched, torn dressing gown, beggarly,
loathsome. I told you just now that I was not ashamed of my poverty;
well, you may as well know that I am ashamed of it. I am ashamed of
it more than of anything, more afraid of it than of being found out if
I were a thief, because I am as touchy as though I had been flayed,
and the very air blowing on me hurts. Surely by now you must realize
that I shall never forgive you for having found me in this wretched
dressing gown, just as I was flying at Apollon like a spiteful cur. The
savior, the former hero, was flying like a mangy, unkempt sheep dog
at his flunky, and the flunky was jeering at him! And I shall never

forgive you for the tears I could not help shedding before you just now, like some silly woman put to shame! And for what I am confessing to you now I'll never forgive *you* either! Yes — you must answer for it all because you turned up like this, because I am a blackguard, because I am the nastiest, stupidest, absurdest, and most envious of all the worms on earth, who are not a bit better than I am, but, the devil knows why, are never embarrassed, while I shall always be insulted by every louse. That is my doom! And what is it to me that you don't understand a word of this? And what do I care, what do I care about you, and whether you go to ruin there or not? Do you understand? How I'll hate you now after saying this, for having been here and listening. Why, it's not once in a lifetime a man speaks out like this, and then it is in hysterics! What more do you want? Why do you still stand confronting me, after all this? Why are you upsetting me? Why don't you go?"

But at this point a strange thing happened. I was so accustomed to thinking and imagining everything from books, and to picturing everything in the world to myself just as I had made it up in my dreams beforehand, that I could not all at once take in this strange circumstance. What happened was this: Liza, insulted and crushed by me, understood a great deal more than I imagined. She understood from all this what a woman understands first of all, if she feels genuine love, that is, that I was myself unhappy.

The frightened and wounded expression on her face was followed first by a look of sorrowful perplexity. When I began calling myself a scoundrel and a blackguard and my tears flowed (the tirade was accompanied throughout by tears), her whole face worked convulsively. She was on the point of getting up and stopping me; when I finished she took no notice of my shouting: "Why are you here, why don't you go away?" but realized only that it must have been very bitter for me to say all this. Besides, she was so crushed, poor girl; she considered herself infinitely beneath me; how could she feel anger or resentment? She suddenly leaped up from her chair with an irresistible impulse and held out her hands, yearning toward me, though still timid and not daring to move forward. At this point there was a revulsion in my heart, too. Then she suddenly rushed to me, threw her arms around me, and burst into tears. I, too, could not restrain myself and sobbed as I never had before.

"They won't let me — I can't be good!" I managed to articulate; then I went to the sofa, fell on it face downward, and sobbed on it for a quarter of an hour in genuine hysterics. She came close to me, put her arms around me, and stayed thus, motionless. But the trouble was that the hysterics could not go on forever, and (I am writing the loathsome truth) lying face down on the sofa with my face thrust into my nasty leatheroid cushion, I began by degrees to be aware of a faraway, involuntary but irresistible feeling that it would be awkward now for me to raise my head and look Liza straight in the face. Why was I ashamed? I don't know, but I was ashamed. The thought, too, came into my overwrought brain that our parts now were completely reversed, that she was now the heroine, while I was just such a crushed and humiliated creature as she had been before me that night — four days before. And all this came into my mind during the minutes I was lying on my face on the sofa.

My God! Surely I was not envious of her then.

I don't know, to this day I cannot decide, and at the time, of course, I was still less able than now to understand, what I was feeling. I cannot get on without domineering and tyrannizing over someone, but . . . there is no explaining anything by reasoning and so it is useless to reason.

I mastered myself, however, and raised my head; I had to do so sooner or later. And I am convinced to this day that it was just because I was ashamed to look at her that another feeling was suddenly kindled and flamed up in my heart — a feeling of mastery and possession. My eyes gleamed with passion and I gripped her hands tightly. How I hated her and how I was drawn to her at that minute! The one feeling intensified the other. It was almost like an act of vengeance. At first there was a look of amazement, even of terror on her face, but only for one instant. She warmly and rapturously embraced me.

X

A quarter of an hour later I was rushing up and down the room in frenzied impatience; from minute to minute I went up to the screen and peeped through the crack at Liza. She was sitting on the ground with her head leaning against the bed, and must have been crying. But she did not go away, and that irritated me. This time she understood it all. I had insulted her finally, but . . . there's no need to describe it. She realized that my outburst of passion had been simply revenge, a fresh humiliation, and that to my earlier, almost causeless hatred was added now a *personal hatred,* born of envy. Though I do not maintain positively that she understood all this distinctly; but she certainly did fully understand that I was a despicable man, and, what was worse, incapable of loving her.

I know I shall be told that this is incredible — but it is incredible to be as spiteful and stupid as I was; it may be added that it was strange I should not love her, or, at any rate, appreciate her love. Why is it strange? In the first place, by then I was incapable of love, for I repeat, with me loving meant tyrannizing and showing my moral superiority. I have never in my life been able to imagine any other sort of love, and have nowadays come to the point of sometimes thinking that love really consists in the right — freely given by the beloved — to tyrannize over her.

Even in my underground dreams I did not imagine love except as a struggle. I began it always with hatred and ended it with moral subjugation, and afterward I never knew what to do with the subjugated object. And what is there to wonder at in that, since I had succeeded in so corrupting myself, since I was so out of touch with "real life," as to have actually thought of reproaching her and putting her to shame for having come to me to hear "fine sentiments"; and did not even guess that she had come, not to hear fine sentiments but to love me, because to a woman all reformation, all salvation from any sort of ruin, and all moral renewal, is contained in love and can only show itself in that form.

I did not hate her so much, however, when I was dashing about the room and peeping through the crack in the screen. I was only insufferably oppressed by her being here. I wanted her to disappear. I wanted "peace," to be left alone in my underground world. Real life oppressed me with its novelty so much that I could hardly breathe.

But several minutes passed and she still remained, without stirring, as though she were unconscious. I had the shamelessness to tap softly on the screen as though to remind her. She started, sprang up, and flew to seek her kerchief, her hat, her coat, as though making her escape from me. Two minutes later she came from behind the screen and, with heavy eyes, looked at me. I gave a spiteful grin, which was forced, however, to *keep up appearances,* and turned away from her eyes.

"Good-by," she said, going toward the door.

I ran up to her, seized her hand, opened it, thrust something in it, and closed it again. Then I turned at once and dashed away in haste to the other corner of the room to avoid seeing her, at any rate.

I did mean a moment ago to tell a lie — to write that I did this accidentally, not knowing through foolishness, through having lost my head, what I was doing. But I don't want to lie, and so I'll say right out that I opened her hand and put the money in it from spite. It came into my head to do this while I was dashing up and down the room and she was sitting behind the screen. But this I can say for certain: though I did that cruel thing purposely, it was not an impulse from the heart, but came from my evil brain. This cruelty was so affected, so purposely made up, so completely a product of the brain, of books, that I could not even keep it up a minute — first I dashed away to avoid seeing Liza, and then in shame and despair rushed after her. I opened the door in the passage and began listening.

"Liza! Liza!" I cried on the stairs, but in a low voice, not boldly.

There was no answer, but I fancied I heard her footsteps, lower down on the stairs.

"Liza!" I cried more loudly.

No answer. But at that minute I heard the unwieldy outer glass door open heavily with a creak and slam violently, the sound echoing up the stairs.

She had gone. I went back to my room hesitatingly. I felt horribly oppressed.

I stood still at the table, beside the chair on which she had sat, and looked aimlessly before me. A minute passed, suddenly I started; straight before me on the table I saw — in short, I saw a crumpled blue five-ruble note, the one I had thrust into her hand a minute before. It was the same note; it could be no other, there was no other in the flat. So she had managed to fling it from her hand on the table at the moment when I had dashed into the corner furthest from her.

Well! I might have expected that she would do that. Might I have expected it? No, I was such an egoist, I was so lacking in respect for my fellow creatures that I could not even imagine she would do so. I could not endure it. A minute later I flew like a madman to dress, flinging on what I could at random and ran headlong after her. She could not have got two hundred paces away when I ran out into the street.

It was a still night, and the snow was coming down thick and falling almost perpendicularly, covering the pavement and the empty street as though with a pillow. There was no one in the street; not a sound was to be heard. The street lamps gave a disconsolate and ineffectual glimmer. I ran two hundred paces to the street intersection and stopped short.

Where had she gone? And why was I running after her?

Why? To fall down before her, to sob with remorse, to kiss her feet, to entreat her forgiveness! I longed for that, my whole breast was being rent to pieces, and never, never shall I recall that moment with indifference. "But — what for?" I thought. Should I not begin to hate her, perhaps, even tomorrow, just because I had kissed her feet today? Should I give her happiness? Had I not recognized that day, for the hundredth time, what I was worth? Should I not torture her?

I stood in the snow, gazing into the troubled darkness, and pondered this.

"And will it not be better," I mused fantastically afterward at home, stifling the living pang of my heart with fantastic dreams — "will it not be better that she should keep the resentment of the insult forever? Resentment — why, it is purification; it is a most stinging and painful consciousness! Tomorrow I should have defiled her soul and have exhausted her heart, while now the feeling of insult will never die in her heart, and however loathsome the filth awaiting her, the feeling of insult will elevate and purify her through hatred. H'm! Perhaps, too, by forgiveness. . . . Will all that make things easier for her, though?"

And, indeed, I will ask an idle question here on my own account: Which is better — cheap happiness or exalted sufferings? Well, which *is* better?

So I dreamed as I sat at home that evening, almost dead with the pain in my soul. Never had I endured such suffering and remorse, yet could there have been the faintest doubt when I ran out from my lodging that I should turn back halfway?

I never met Liza again and I have heard nothing of her. I will add, too, that I remained for a long time afterward pleased with the phrase about the benefit from resentment and hatred in spite of the fact that I almost fell ill from misery.

Even now, so many years later, all this is somehow a very evil memory. I have many evil memories now, but — hadn't I better end my "Notes" here? I believe I made a mistake in beginning to write them; anyway, I have felt ashamed all the time I've been writing this story. So it's hardly literature as much as a corrective punishment. Why, to tell long stories, showing how I have spoiled my life through morally rotting in my cubbyhole, through lack of fitting environment, through divorce from real life and rankling spite in my underground world, would certainly not be interesting; a novel needs a hero, and all the traits for an antihero are *expressly* gathered together here, and (what matters most) it all produces an unpleasant impression, for we are all divorced from life, we are all cripples, every one of us, more or less.

We are so divorced from it that we feel at once a sort of loathing for real life, and so cannot bear to be reminded of it. Why, we have come almost to look upon real life as an effort, almost as hard work, and we are all privately agreed that it is better in books. And why do we fuss and fume sometimes? Why are we perverse, asking for something else, without ourselves knowing what? It would be the worse for us if our petulant prayers were answered. Come, try, give any one of us, for instance, a little more independence, untie our hands, widen the spheres of our activity, relax the control and we — yes, I assure you — we'd be begging to be under control again at once. I know that you will very likely be angry with me for that, and will begin shouting and stamping. Speak for yourself, you will say, and for your miseries in your underground holes, and don't dare to say "all of us." Excuse me, gentlemen, I'm not justifying myself with that "all of us."

As for what concerns me in particular, I have in my life only carried to an extreme what you have not dared to carry halfway, and what's more, you have taken your cowardice for good sense, and have found comfort in deceiving yourselves. So that perhaps, after all, there is more life in me than in you. Look into it more carefully! Why, we don't even know what living means now, what it is, and what it is called. Leave us alone without books and we'll be lost and in confusion at once. We'll not know what to join to, what to cling to, what to love and what to hate, what to respect and what to despise. We are oppressed at being men — men with real individual flesh and blood, we are ashamed of it, we think it a disgrace and try to contrive to be some sort of impossible generalized man. We are stillborn, and for generations past have been begotten not by living fathers, and that suits us more and more. We are developing a taste for it. Soon we shall contrive to be born from an idea somehow. But enough; I don't want to write more from *underground*.

[The notes of this paradoxalist do not end here, however. He could not refrain from going on with them, but it seems to us that we may stop here.]

Arthur Rimbaud (1854–1891)

LIFE: At the age of nineteen, disappointed by the reception of his first book, *A Season in Hell,* he burned his manuscripts and gave up the writing of poetry. His career thereafter was as melodramatic as his relationship with the poet Paul Verlaine, who shot Rimbaud when he threatened to break off their friendship. Verlaine went to prison for two years; Rimbaud wandered through Europe, the Middle East, and Africa, gun-running, perhaps slave-trading; an infection brought him back to Marseilles, where his leg was amputated and where, after a brief return to his home in Charleville, near the Belgian border, he finally died.

WORKS: *A Season in Hell* (1873); *The Illuminations* (begun in 1872, first published in 1886); the first accurate edition of his complete poems appeared in 1895.

THE DRUNKEN BOAT *

As I came down the impassible Rivers,
I felt no more the bargemen's guiding hands,
Targets for yelling red-skins they were nailed
Naked to painted poles.

What did I care for any crews,   5
Carriers of English cotton or of Flemish grain!
Bargemen and all that hubbub left behind,
The waters let me go my own free way.

In the furious lashings of the tides,
Emptier than children's minds, I through that winter   10
Ran! And great peninsulas unmoored
Never knew more triumphant uproar than I knew.

The tempest blessed my wakings on the sea.
Light as a cork I danced upon the waves,

* Written in 1871.

Eternal rollers of the deep sunk dead,   15
Nor missed at night the lanterns' idiot eyes!

Sweeter than sour apples to a child,
Green waters seeped through all my seams,
Washing the stains of vomit and blue wine,
And swept away my anchor and my helm.   20

And since then I've been bathing in the Poem
Of star-infused and milky Sea,
Devouring the azure greens, where, flotsam pale,
A brooding corpse at times drifts by;

Where, dyeing suddenly the blue,   25
Rhythms delirious and slow in the blaze of day,
Stronger than alcohol, vaster than your lyres,
Ferment the bitter reds of love!

I know the lightning-opened skies, waterspouts,
Eddies and surfs; I know the night,   30
And dawn arisen like a colony of doves,
And sometimes I have seen what men have thought they saw!

I've seen the low sun, fearful with mystic signs,
Lighting with far flung violet arms,
Like actors in an ancient tragedy,   35
The fluted waters shivering far away.

I've dreamed green nights of dazzling snows,
Slow kisses on the eyelids of the sea,
The terrible flow of unforgettable saps,
And singing phosphors waking yellow and blue.   40

Months through I've followed the assaulting tides
Like maddened cattle leaping up the reefs,
Nor ever thought the Marys' luminous feet
Could curb the muzzle of the panting Deep.

I've touched, you know, fantastic Floridas   45
Mingling the eyes of panthers, human-skinned, with flowers!
And rainbows stretched like endless reins
To glaucous flocks beneath the seas.

I've seen fermenting marshes like enormous nets
Where in the reeds a whole Leviathan decays!   50

50. *Leviathan:* see Job 41:1.

Crashings of waters in the midst of calms!
Horizons toward far chasms cataracting!

Glaciers and silver suns, fiery skies and pearly seas,
Hideous wrecks at the bottom of brown gulfs
Where giant serpents vermin ridden   55
Drop with black perfumes from the twisted trees!

I would show children those dorados,
And golden singing fishes in blue seas.
Foam flowers have blest my aimless wanderings,
Ineffable winds have given me wings.   60

Tired of poles and zones, sometimes the martyred sea,
Rolling me gently on her sobbing breast,
Lifted her shadow flowers with yellow cups toward me
And I stayed there like a woman on her knees.

Island, I sailed, and on my gunnels tossed   65
Quarrels and droppings of the pale-eyed birds,
While floating slowly past my fragile bands,
Backward the drowned went dreaming by.

But I, lost boat in the cove's trailing tresses,
Tossed by the tempest into birdless space,   70
Whose water-drunken carcass never would have salvaged
Old Monitor or Galleon of the Hanseatic League;

Who, ridden by violent mists, steaming and free,
Pierced the sky reddening like a wall,
Covered with lichens of the sun and azure's phlem,   75
Preserves that all good poets love,

Who, spotted with electric crescents ran,
Mad plank with escort of black hypocamps,
While Augusts with their hammer blows tore down
The sea-blue, spiral-flaming skies;   80

Who trembling felt Behemoth's rut
And Maelstroms groaning fifty leagues away,
Eternal scudder through the quiescent blue,
I long for Europe's parapets!

I've seen sidereal archipelagos! Islands   85
Whose delirious skies open for wanderers:

81. *Behemoth:* see Job 40:15.

"Is it in such bottomless nights you sleep, exiled,
O countless golden birds, O Force to come?"

True I have wept too much! Dawns are heartbreaking;
Cruel all moons and bitter the suns.   90
Drunk with love's acrid torpors,
O let my keel burst! Let me go to the sea!

If I desire any European water, it's the black pond
And cold, where toward perfumed evening
A sad child on his knees sets sail   95
A boat as frail as a May butterfly.

I can no longer, bathed in your languors, O waves,
Obliterate the cotton carriers' wake,
Nor cross the pride of pennants and of flags,
Nor swim past prison hulks' hateful eyes!   100

Stéphane Mallarmé (1842–1898)

LIFE: The obscurities of his poetry are only matched by the mysteries of his life — or what seems a quiet mystery when juxtaposed to the melodramatic lives of the French poets who were his contemporaries. He first became known through his translation of Poe's "The Raven"; he taught English at various schools in Paris and the provinces; he gathered about him a small group of disciples, with whom he revolutionized French poetry and for whom he remained the master.

WORKS: *Poems* (1887); *Album of Verse and Prose* (1887); *Divagations* (1897).

THE AFTERNOON OF A FAUN *

Eclogue

THE FAUN

I would perpetuate these nymphs.

So clear,
their light carnation, that it drifts on the air
drowsy with tufted slumbers.

From *French Symbolist Poetry*, translated by C. F. MacIntyre. Reprinted by permission of the publisher, the University of California Press.

* First published in 1876.

So I loved a dream?
My doubt, a mass of ancient night, concludes
in many a subtle branch, which, since the real woods   5
remain, proves, alas! what I offered to myself
as triumph was the ideal lack of roses.
Let's think it over . . .

if those girls whom you explain
be but an itching in your fabulous brain!
Faun, the illusion escapes from the blue eyes   10
and cold of the more chaste, like a weeping spring:
but the other one, all sighs, you say, contrasts
like a day-breeze warm upon your fleece!
But no! through the immobile and heavy swoon
stifling with heat the cool morning if it resists,   15
murmurs no water but that poured from my flute
on the grove sprinkled with harmonies; the only wind
prompt to exhale from the twin-pipes before
it can disperse the sound in an arid rain,
is, on the horizon unstirred by a wrinkle,   20
the visible and serene artificial breath
of inspiration, which regains the sky.
O Sicilian borders of a peaceful marsh
which like unto the sun my vanity plunders,
tacit under the flowers of sparks, RELATE   25
"How I was cutting here the hollow reeds
tamed by my talent; when, on the glaucous gold
of distant verdures dedicating their vines
to the fountains, undulated an animal whiteness,
reposing: and to the slow prelude whence the pipes   30
are born, this flight of swans, no! of Naiades
goes scampering off or dives . . ."

Inert, all things
burn in the tawny hour, not noticing
by what are together fled this too much hymen
desired by who seeks for *la:* then I'll awaken   35
to the primal fervor, erect and alone,
under the antique flood of light, O lilies!
and the one among you all for artlessness.

Besides this sweet nothing by their lips made known,
the kiss, that reveals, though hushed, some faithless ones,   40
my breast, virgin of proof, vouches a bite,
mysterious, from some illustrious tooth;
but enough! as confidant such arcanum chose
the great twin-reeds one plays beneath the azure:
which, diverting to themselves the cheeks' excitement,   45

dream, in a long solo, that we may amuse
the beauties hereabout by false confusions
between them even and our credulous song;
and to make as high as love can modulate
vanish from the banal dream of backs   50
or pure flanks pursued in my closed eyes,
a sonorous and vain, monotonous line.

Try then, instrument of flights, O evil
Syrinx, to flower again by the lakes where you wait!
Proud of my noise, I am going to talk at length   55
of the goddesses; and by idolatrous paintings
to lift again the cinctures from their shadows:
so, when I have sucked the bright juice of the grapes,
to banish a regret by my pretense discarded,
laughing, I raise to the summer sky the empty   60
hulls and, puffing into these luminous skins,
craving drunkenness, I gaze through them till evening.

O nymphs, we swell with divers MEMORIES.
"Piercing the reeds, my eyes speared each immortal
neck, that drowns its burning in the water   65
with a cry of rage flung to the forest sky;
and the splendid bath of tresses disappeared
in shimmerings and shiverings, O jewels!
I rush up; when, at my feet, entwine (bruised
by the languor drunk from this harm of being two)   70
girls sleeping in each other's perilous arms;
I seize them, not untangling them, and run
to this clump, hated by the frivolous shade,
of roses exhausting all their scent in the sun,
where our frolic should be like a squandered day."   75
I adore you, anger of virgins, O fierce delight
of the sacred naked burden that slips to flee
the fiery drinking of my lips, like the crack
of lightning! the secret terror of the flesh:
from the feet of the heartless one to the heart of the timid   80
abandoned at the same time by an innocence, humid
with foolish tears or less melancholy vapors.
"My crime is, gay at vanquishing their traitress
fears, to have parted the disheveled tangle
of kisses that the gods kept so well mingled;   85
for I was just going to hide a glowing laugh
in the happy creases of one (even while I kept
with only a finger — so that her plume's candor
should be stained by the frenzy of her sister

54. *Syrinx:* a chaste nymph who fled from Pan's insistent passion. She begged for help from the
gods and was changed into a reed; Pan unwittingly cut her down to make one of his pipes.

who burned — the little one, naïve, not blushing a bit:) 90
when from my arms, relaxed by the vague death,
this prey, forever ungrateful, frees itself,
not pitying the sob that still bedrunkened me."
Too bad! but others will lead me toward happiness,
knotting the horns on my brow with many a tress; 95
you know, my passion, how, crimson and already ripe,
every pomegranate bursts and murmurs with bees;
and our blood, burning for who is going to receive it,
flows for all the eternal swarm of desire.
At the hour when this wood is stained with gold and ashes 100
a feast exults among extinguished leaves:
Etna! it is on you visited by Venus
upon your lava setting her candid feet
when thunders a sad slumber or the flame expires.
I embrace the queen!

Sure punishment . . .

No, but the spirit 105
empty of words now and the body numbed
unto noon's haughty silence at last succumb:
enough! on the thirsty sand, forgetful of
the outrage, I must sleep, and as I love
open my mouth to the powerful star of wine! 110

Sweet pair, farewell. I shall see the shades you became.

Leo Tolstoy (1828–1910)

LIFE: The celebrated religious conversion (in 1879) which seemed to
mark a revolutionary change in his attitude toward the purpose and
function of life and art, including his own, had its roots in the existence
lived until that moment: the restless search for a career, for an experience of value, for a way of transforming his country. The novels he
wrote (as well as the attempts to educate the peasants) can be read as
foreshadowings of the later compulsion to reform the world; and there
is even a logical, though tragic, inevitability to his death: after a quarrel
with his wife about the chaos which his new vision had produced in the
life of his family, he left her, to die in a stationmaster's house, miles
from his home, an old man, Lear without even the dead Cordelia to ease
his going.

WORKS: *War and Peace* (1862–69); *Anna Karenina* (1875–77); *The
Death of Iván Ilých* (1886); *The Kreutzer Sonata* (1889); *What Is
Art?* (1897); *Resurrection* (1900).

THE DEATH OF IVÁN ILÝCH *

I

During an interval in the Melvínski trial in the large building of the Law Courts the members and public prosecutor met in Iván Egórovich Shébek's private room, where the conversation turned on the celebrated Krasóvski case. Fëdor Vasílievich warmly maintained that it was not subject to their jurisdiction, Iván Egórovich maintained the contrary, while Peter Ivánovich, not having entered into the discussion at the start, took no part in it but looked through the *Gazette* which had just been handed in.

"Gentlemen," he said, "Iván Ilých has died!"

"You don't say so!"

"Here, read it yourself," replied Peter Ivánovich, handing Fëdor Vasílievich the paper still damp from the press. Surrounded by a black border were the words: "Praskóvya Fëdorovna Goloviná, with profound sorrow, informs relatives and friends of the demise of her beloved husband Iván Ilých Golovín, Member of the Court of Justice, which occurred on February the 4th of this year 1882. The funeral will take place on Friday at one o'clock in the afternoon."

Iván Ilých had been a colleague of the gentlemen present and was liked by them all. He had been ill for some weeks with an illness said to be incurable. His post had been kept open for him, but there had been conjectures that in case of his death Alexéev might receive his appointment, and that either Vínnikov or Shtábel would succeed Alexéev. So on receiving the news of Iván Ilých's death the first thought of each of the gentlemen in that private room was of the changes and promotions it might occasion among themselves or their acquaintances.

"I shall be sure to get Shtábel's place or Vínnikov's," thought Fëdor Vasílievich. "I was promised that long ago, and the promotion means an extra eight hundred rubles a year for me besides the allowance."

"Now I must apply for my brother-in-law's transfer from Kalúga," thought Peter Ivánovich. "My wife will be very glad, and then she won't be able to say that I never do anything for her relations."

"I thought he would never leave his bed again," said Peter Ivánovich aloud. "It's very sad."

"But what really was the matter with him?"

"The doctors couldn't say — at least they could, but each of them said something different. When last I saw him I thought he was getting better."

"And I haven't been to see him since the holidays. I always meant to go."

Reprinted from *The Death of Iván Ilých*, translated by Aylmer Maude, and published by the Oxford University Press.

* 1886.

"Had he any property?"

"I think his wife had a little — but something quite trifling."

"We shall have to go to see her, but they live so terribly far away."

"Far away from you, you mean. Everything's far away from your place."

"You see, he never can forgive my living on the other side of the river," said Peter Ivánovich, smiling at Shébek. Then, still talking of the distances between different parts of the city, they returned to the Court.

Besides considerations as to the possible transfers and promotions likely to result from Iván Ilých's death, the mere fact of the death of a near acquaintance aroused, as usual, in all who heard of it the complacent feeling that, "it is he who is dead and not I."

Each one thought or felt, "Well, he's dead but I'm alive!" But the more intimate of Iván Ilých's acquaintances, his so-called friends, could not help thinking also that they would now have to fulfil the very tiresome demands of propriety by attending the funeral service and paying a visit of condolence to the widow.

Fëdor Vasílievich and Peter Ivánovich had been his nearest acquaintances. Peter Ivánovich had studied law with Iván Ilých and had considered himself to be under obligations to him.

Having told his wife at dinner-time of Iván Ilých's death, and of his conjecture that it might be possible to get her brother transferred to their circuit, Peter Ivánovich sacrificed his usual nap, put on his evening clothes, and drove to Iván Ilých's house.

At the entrance stood a carriage and two cabs. Leaning against the wall in the hall downstairs near the cloak-stand was a coffin-lid covered with cloth of gold, ornamented with gold cord and tassels, that had been polished up with metal powder. Two ladies in black were taking off their fur cloaks. Peter Ivánovich recognized one of them as Iván Ilých's sister, but the other was a stranger to him. His colleague Schwartz was just coming downstairs, but on seeing Peter Ivánovich enter he stopped and winked at him, as if to say: "Iván Ilých has made a mess of things — not like you and me."

Schwartz's face with his Piccadilly whiskers, and his slim figure in evening dress, had as usual an air of elegant solemnity which contrasted with the playfulness of his character and had a special piquancy here, or so it seemed to Peter Ivánovich.

Peter Ivánovich allowed the ladies to precede him and slowly followed them upstairs. Schwartz did not come down but remained where he was, and Peter Ivánovich understood that he wanted to arrange where they should play bridge that evening. The ladies went upstairs to the widow's room, and Schwartz with seriously compressed lips but a playful look in his eyes, indicated by a twist of his eyebrows the room to the right where the body lay.

Peter Ivánovich, like everyone else on such occasions, entered feeling uncertain what he would have to do. All he knew was that at such times it is always safe to cross oneself. But he was not quite sure whether one should make obeisances while doing so. He therefore adopted a middle course. On entering the room he began crossing himself and made a slight movement resembling a bow. At the same time, as far as the motion of his head and arm allowed, he surveyed the room. Two young men — apparently nephews, one of whom was a high-school pupil — were leaving the room, crossing themselves as they did so. An old woman was standing motionless, and a lady with strangely arched eyebrows was saying something to her in a whisper. A vigorous, resolute Church Reader, in a frock-coat, was reading something in a loud voice with an expression that precluded any contradiction. The butler's assistant, Gerásim, stepping lightly in front of Peter Ivánovich, was strewing something on the floor. Noticing this, Peter Ivánovich was immediately aware of a faint odour of a decomposing body.

The last time he had called on Iván Ilých, Peter Ivánovich had seen Gerásim in the study. Iván Ilých had been particularly fond of him and he was performing the duty of a sick nurse.

Peter Ivánovich continued to make the sign of the cross slightly inclining his head in an intermediate direction between the coffin, the Reader, and the icons on the table in a corner of the room. Afterwards, when it seemed to him that this movement of his arm in crossing himself had gone on too long, he stopped and began to look at the corpse.

The dead man lay, as dead men always lie, in a specially heavy way, his rigid limbs sunk in the soft cushions of the coffin, with the head forever bowed on the pillow. His yellow waxen brow with bald patches over his sunken temples was thrust up in the way peculiar to the dead, the protruding nose seeming to press on the upper lip. He was much changed and had grown even thinner since Peter Ivánovich had last seen him, but, as is always the case with the dead, his face was handsomer and above all more dignified than when he was alive. The expression on the face said that what was necessary had been accomplished, and accomplished rightly. Besides this there was in that expression a reproach and a warning to the living. This warning seemed to Peter Ivánovich out of place, or at least not applicable to him. He felt a certain discomfort and so he hurriedly crossed himself once more and turned and went out of the door — too hurriedly and too regardless of propriety, as he himself was aware.

Schwartz was waiting for him in the adjoining room with legs spread wide apart and both hands toying with his top-hat behind his back. The mere sight of that playful, well-groomed, and elegant figure refreshed Peter Ivánovich. He felt that Schwartz was above all these happenings and would not surrender to any depressing influences. His very look said that this incident of a church service for Iván Ilých could not be a sufficient reason for infringing the order of the session — in other words, that it would certainly not prevent his unwrapping a new pack of cards and shuffling them that evening while a footman placed four fresh candles on the table: in fact, there was no reason for supposing that this incident would hinder their spending the evening agreeably. Indeed he said this in a whisper as Peter Ivánovich passed him, proposing that they should meet for a game at Fëdor Vasílievich's. But apparently Peter Ivánovich was not destined to play bridge that evening. Praskóvya Fëdorovna (a short, fat woman who despite all efforts to the contrary had continued to broaden steadily from her shoulders downwards and who had the same extraordinarily arched eyebrows as the lady who had been standing by the coffin), dressed all in black, her head covered with lace, came out of her own room with some other ladies, conducted them to the room where the dead body lay, and said: "The service will begin immediately. Please go in."

Schwartz, making an indefinite bow, stood still, evidently neither accepting nor declining this invitation. Praskóvya Fëdorovna recognizing Peter Ivánovich, sighed, went close up to him, took his hand, and said: "I know you were a true friend to Iván Ilých . . ." and looked at him awaiting some suitable response. And Peter Ivánovich knew that, just as it had been the right thing to cross himself in that room, so what he had to do here was to press her hand, sigh, and say, "Believe me. . . ." So he did all this and as he did it felt that the desired result had been achieved: that both he and she were touched.

"Come with me. I want to speak to you before it begins," said the widow. "Give me your arm."

Peter Ivánovich gave her his arm and they went to the inner rooms, passing Schwartz who winked at Peter Ivánovich compassionately.

"That does for our bridge! Don't object if we find another player. Perhaps you can cut in when you do escape," said his playful look.

Peter Ivánovich sighed still more deeply and despondently, and Praskóvya Fëdorovna pressed his arm gratefully. When they reached the drawing-room, upholstered in pink cretonne and lighted by a dim lamp, they sat down at the table — she on a sofa and Peter Ivánovich on a low pouffe, the springs of which yielded spasmodically under his weight. Praskóvya Fëdorovna had been on the point of warning him to take another seat, but felt that such a warning was out of keeping with her present condition and so changed her mind. As he sat down on the pouffe Peter Ivánovich recalled how Iván Ilých had arranged this room and had consulted him regarding this pink cretonne with green leaves. The whole room was full of furniture and knick-knacks, and on her way to the sofa the lace of the widow's black shawl caught on the carved edge of the table. Peter Ivánovich rose to detach it, and the springs of the pouffe, relieved of his weight, rose also and gave him a push. The widow began detaching her shawl herself, and Peter Ivánovich again sat down, suppressing the rebellious springs of the pouffe under him. But the widow had not quite freed herself and Peter Ivánovich got up again, and again the pouffe rebelled and even creaked. When this was all over she took out a clean cambric handkerchief and began to weep. The episode with the shawl and the struggle with the pouffe had cooled Peter Ivánovich's emotions and he sat there with a sullen look on his face. This awkward situation was interrupted by Sokolóv, Iván Ilých's butler, who came to report that the plot in the cemetery that Praskóvya Fëdorovna had chosen would cost two hundred rubles. She stopped weeping and, looking at Peter Ivánovich with the air of a victim, remarked in French that it was very hard for her. Peter Ivánovich made a silent gesture signifying his full conviction that it must indeed be so.

"Please smoke," she said in a magnanimous yet crushed voice, and turned to discuss with Sokolóv the price of the plot for the grave.

Peter Ivánovich while lighting his cigarette heard her inquiring very circumstantially into the price of different plots in the cemetery and finally decide which she would take. When that was done she gave instructions about engaging the choir. Sokolóv then left the room.

"I look after everything myself," she told Peter Ivánovich, shifting the albums that lay on the table; and noticing that the table was endangered by his cigarette-ash, she immediately passed him an ashtray, saying as she did so: "I consider it an affectation to say that my grief prevents my attending to practical affairs. On the contrary, if anything can — I won't say console me, but — distract me, it is seeing to everything concerning him." She again took out her handkerchief as if preparing to cry, but suddenly, as if mastering her feeling, she shook herself and began to speak calmly. "But there is something I want to talk to you about."

Peter Ivánovich bowed, keeping control of the springs of the pouffe, which immediately began quivering under him.

"He suffered terribly the last few days."

"Did he?" said Peter Ivánovich.

"Oh, terribly! He screamed unceasingly, not for minutes but for hours. For the last three days he screamed incessantly. It was unendurable. I cannot understand how I bore it; you could hear him three rooms off. Oh, what I have suffered!"

"Is it possible that he was conscious all that time?" asked Peter Ivánovich.

"Yes," she whispered. "To the last moment. He took leave of us a quarter of an hour before he died, and asked us to take Volódya away."

The thought of the sufferings of this man he had known so intimately, first as a merry little boy, then as a school-mate, and later as a grown-up colleague, suddenly struck Peter Ivánovich with horror, despite an unpleasant consciousness of his own and this woman's dissimulation. He again saw that brow, and that nose pressing down on the lip, and felt afraid for himself.

"Three days of frightful suffering and then death! Why, that might suddenly, at any time, happen to me," he thought, and for a moment felt terrified. But — he did not himself know how — the customary reflection at once occurred to him that this had happened to Iván Ilých and not to him, and that it should not and could not happen to him, and that to think that it could would be yielding to depression which he ought not to do, as Schwartz's expression plainly showed. After which reflection Peter Ivánovich felt reassured, and began to ask with interest about the details of Iván Ilých's death, as though death was an accident natural to Iván Ilých but certainly not to himself.

After many details of the really dreadful physical sufferings Iván Ilých had endured (which details he learnt only from the effect those sufferings had produced on Praskóvya Fëdorovna's nerves) the widow apparently found it necessary to get to business.

"Oh, Peter Ivánovich, how hard it is! How terribly, terribly hard!" and she again began to weep.

Peter Ivánovich sighed and waited for her to finish blowing her nose. When she had done so he said, "Believe me . . . ," and she again began talking and brought out what was evidently her chief concern with him — namely, to question him as to how she could obtain a grant of money from the government on the occasion of her husband's death. She made it appear that she was asking Peter Ivánovich's advice about her pension, but he soon saw that she already knew about that to the minutest detail, more even than he did himself. She knew how much could be got out of the government in consequence of her husband's death, but wanted to find out whether she could not possibly extract something more. Peter Ivánovich tried to think of some means of doing so, but after reflecting for a while and, out of propriety, condemning the government for its niggardliness, he said he thought that nothing more could be got. Then she sighed and evidently began to devise means of getting rid of her visitor. Noticing this, he put out his cigarette, rose, pressed her hand, and went out into the anteroom.

In the dining-room where the clock stood that Iván Ilých had liked so much and had bought at an antique shop, Peter Ivánovich met a priest and a few acquaintances who had come to attend the service, and he recognized Iván Ilých's daughter, a handsome young woman. She was in black and her slim figure appeared slimmer than ever. She had a gloomy, determined, almost angry expression, and bowed to Peter Ivánovich as though he were in some way to blame. Behind her, with the same offended look, stood a wealthy young man, an examining magistrate, whom Peter Ivánovich also knew and who was her fiancé, as he had heard. He bowed mournfully to them and was about to pass into the death-chamber, when from under the stairs appeared the figure of Iván Ilých's schoolboy son, who was extremely like his father. He seemed a little Iván Ilých, such as Peter Ivánovich remembered when they studied law together. His tear-stained eyes had in them the look that is seen in the eyes of boys of thirteen or fourteen who are not pure-minded. When he saw Peter Ivánovich he scowled morosely and shame-facedly. Peter Ivánovich nodded to him and entered the death-chamber. The service began: candles, groans, incense, tears, and sobs. Peter Ivánovich stood looking gloomily down at his feet. He did not look once at the dead man, did not yield to any depressing influence, and was one of the first to leave the room. There was no one in the anteroom, but Gerásim darted out of the dead man's room, rummaged with his strong hands among the fur coats to find Peter Ivánovich's and helped him on with it.

"Well, friend Gerásim," said Peter Ivánovich, so as to say something. "It's a sad affair, isn't it?"

"It's God's will. We shall all come to it some day," said Gerásim, displaying his teeth — the even, white teeth of a healthy peasant — and, like a man in the thick of urgent work, he briskly opened the front door, called the coachman, helped Peter Ivánovich into the sledge, and sprang back to the porch as if in readiness for what he had to do next.

Peter Ivánovich found the fresh air particularly pleasant after the smell of incense, the dead body, and carbolic acid.

"Where to, sir?" asked the coachman.

"It's not too late even now. . . . I'll call round on Fëdor Vasílievich."

He accordingly drove there and found them just finishing the first rubber, so that it was quite convenient for him to cut in.

II

Iván Ilých's life had been most simple and most ordinary and therefore most terrible.

He had been a member of the Court of Justice, and died at the age of forty-five. His father had been an official who after serving in various ministries and departments in Petersburg had made the sort of career which brings men to positions from which by reason of their long service they cannot be dismissed, though they are obviously unfit to hold any responsible position, and for whom therefore posts are specially created, which though fictitious carry salaries of from six to ten thousand rubles that are not fictitious, and in receipt of which they live on to a great age.

Such was the Privy Councillor and superfluous member of various superfluous institutions, Ilyá Epímovich Golovín.

He had three sons, of whom Iván Ilých was the second. The eldest son was following in his father's footsteps only in another department, and was already approaching that stage in the service at which a similar sinecure would be reached. The third son was a failure. He had ruined his prospects in a number of positions and was now serving in the railway department. His father and brothers, and still more their wives, not merely disliked meeting him, but avoided remembering his existence unless compelled to do so. His sister had married Baron Greff, a Petersburg official of her father's type. Iván Ilých was *le phénix de la famille* [1] as people said. He was neither as cold and formal as his elder brother nor as wild as the younger, but was a happy mean between them — an intelligent, polished, lively and agreeable man. He had studied with his younger brother at the School of Law, but the latter had failed to complete the course and was expelled when he was in the fifth class. Iván Ilých finished the course well. Even when he was at the School of Law

1. The phoenix of the family, that is, the unusual one.

he was just what he remained for the rest of his life: a capable, cheerful, good-natured, and sociable man, though strict in the fulfilment of what he considered to be his duty: and he considered his duty to be what was so considered by those in authority. Neither as a boy nor as a man was he a toady, but from early youth was by nature attracted to people of high station as a fly is drawn to the light, assimilating their ways and views of life and establishing friendly relations with them. All the enthusiasms of childhood and youth passed without leaving much trace on him; he succumbed to sensuality, to vanity, and latterly among the highest classes to liberalism, but always within limits which his instinct unfailingly indicated to him as correct.

At school he had done things which had formerly seemed to him very horrid and made him feel disgusted with himself when he did them; but when later on he saw that such actions were done by people of good position and that they did not regard them as wrong, he was able not exactly to regard them as right, but to forget about them entirely or not be at all troubled at remembering them.

Having graduated from the School of Law and qualified for the tenth rank of the civil service, and having received money from his father for his equipment, Iván Ilých ordered himself clothes at Scharmer's, the fashionable tailor, hung a medallion inscribed *respice finen* [2] on his watch-chain, took leave of his professor and the prince who was patron of the school, had a farewell dinner with his comrades at Donon's first-class restaurant, and with his new and fashionable portmanteau, linen, clothes, shaving and other toilet appliances, and a travelling rug, all purchased at the best shops, he set off for one of the provinces where, through his father's influence, he had been attached to the Governor as an official for special service.

In the province Iván Ilých soon arranged as easy and agreeable a position for himself as he had had at the School of Law. He performed his official tasks, made his career, and at the same time amused himself pleasantly and decorously. Occasionally he paid official visits to country districts, where he behaved with dignity both to his superiors and inferiors, and performed the duties entrusted to him, which related chiefly to the sectarians, with an exactness and incorruptible honesty of which he could not but feel proud.

In official matters, despite his youth and taste for frivolous gaiety, he was exceedingly reserved, punctilious, and even severe; but in society he was often amusing and witty, and always good-natured, correct in his manner, and *bon enfant*, as the governor and his wife — with whom he was like one of the family — used to say of him.

In the provinces he had an affair with a lady who made advances to the elegant young lawyer, and there was also a milliner; and there were carousals with aides-de-camp who visited the district, and after-supper visits to a certain outlying street of doubtful reputation; and there was too some obsequiousness to his chief and even to his chief's wife, but all

2. Look to the end.

this was done with such a tone of good breeding that no hard names could be applied to it. It all came under the heading of the French saying: *"Il faut que jeunesse se passe."* [3] It was all done with clean hands, in clean linen, with French phrases, and above all among people of the best society and consequently with the approval of people of rank.

So Iván Ilých served for five years and then came a change in his official life. The new and reformed judicial institutions were introduced, and new men were needed. Iván Ilých became such a new man. He was offered the post of Examining Magistrate, and he accepted it though the post was in another province and obliged him to give up the connexions he had formed and to make new ones. His friends met to give him a send-off; they had a group-photograph taken and presented him with a silver cigarette-case, and he set off to his new post.

As examining magistrate Iván Ilých was just as *comme il faut* and decorous a man, inspiring general respect and capable of separating his official duties from his private life, as he had been when acting as an official on special service. His duties now as examining magistrate were far more interesting and attractive than before. In his former position it had been pleasant to wear an undress uniform made by Scharmer, and to pass through the crowd of petitioners and officials who were timorously awaiting an audience with the governor, and who envied him as with free and easy gait he went straight into his chief's private room to have a cup of tea and a cigarette with him. But not many people had then been directly dependent on him — only police officials and the sectarians when he went on special missions — and he liked to treat them politely, almost as comrades, as if he were letting them feel that he who had the power to crush them was treating them in this simple, friendly way. There were then but few such people. But now, as an examining magistrate, Iván Ilých felt that everyone without exception, even the most important and self-satisfied, was in his power, and that he need only write a few words on a sheet of paper with a certain heading, and this or that important, self-satisfied person would be brought before him in the role of an accused person or a witness, and if he did not choose to allow him to sit down, would have to stand before him and answer his questions. Iván Ilých never abused his power; he tried on the contrary to soften its expression, but the consciousness of it and of the possibility of softening its effect, supplied the chief interest and attraction of his office. In his work itself, especially in his examinations, he very soon acquired a method of eliminating all considerations irrelevant to the legal aspect of the case, and reducing even the most complicated case to a form in which it would be presented on paper only in its externals, completely excluding his personal opinion of the matter, while above all observing every prescribed formality. The work was new and Iván Ilých was one of the first men to apply the new Code of 1864. [4]

3. "Youth must have its fling" [translator's note].
4. The emancipation of the serfs in 1861 was followed by a thorough all-round reform of judicial proceedings [translator's note].

On taking up the post of examining magistrate in a new town, he made new acquaintances and connexions, placed himself on a new footing, and assumed a somewhat different tone. He took up an attitude of rather dignified aloofness towards the provincial authorities, but picked out the best circle of legal gentlemen and wealthy gentry living in the town and assumed a tone of slight dissatisfaction with the government, of moderate liberalism, and of enlightened citizenship. At the same time, without at all altering the elegance of his toilet, he ceased shaving his chin and allowed his beard to grow as it pleased.

Iván Ilých settled down very pleasantly in this new town. The society there, which inclined towards opposition to the Governor, was friendly, his salary was larger, and he began to play *vint* [a form of bridge], which he found added not a little to the pleasure of life, for he had a capacity for cards, played good-humouredly, and calculated rapidly and astutely, so that he usually won.

After living there for two years he met his future wife, Praskóvya Fëdorovna Míkhel, who was the most attractive, clever, and brilliant girl of the set in which he moved, and among other amusements and relaxations from his labours as examining magistrate, Iván Ilých established light and playful relations with her.

While he had been an official on special service he had been accustomed to dance, but now as an examining magistrate it was exceptional for him to do so. If he danced now, he did it as if to show that though he served under the reformed order of things, and had reached the fifth official rank, yet when it came to dancing he could do it better than most people. So at the end of an evening he sometimes danced with Praskóvya Fëdorovna, and it was chiefly during these dances that he captivated her. She fell in love with him. Iván Ilých had at first no definite intention of marrying, but when the girl fell in love with him he said to himself: "Really, why shouldn't I marry?"

Praskóvya Fëdorovna came of a good family, was not bad looking, and had some little property. Iván Ilých might have aspired to a more brilliant match, but even this was good. He had his salary, and she, he hoped, would have an equal income. She was well connected, and was a sweet, pretty, and thoroughly correct young woman. To say that Iván Ilých married because he fell in love with Praskóvya Fëdorovna and found that she sympathized with his views of life would be as incorrect as to say that he married because his social circle approved of the match. He was swayed by both these considerations: the marriage gave him personal satisfaction, and at the same time it was considered the right thing by the most highly placed of his associates.

So Iván Ilých got married.

The preparations for marriage and the beginning of married life, with its conjugal caresses, the new furniture, new crockery, and new linen, were very pleasant until his wife became pregnant — so that Iván Ilých had begun to think that marriage would not impair the easy, agreeable, gay and always decorous character of his life, approved of by society and regarded by himself as natural, but would even improve it. But from the first months of his wife's pregnancy, something new, unpleasant, depressing, and unseemly, and from which there was no way of escape, unexpectedly showed itself.

His wife, without any reason — *de gaieté de cœur* as Iván Ilých expressed it to himself — began to disturb the pleasure and propriety of their life. She began to be jealous without any cause, expected him to devote his whole attention to her, found fault with everything, and made coarse and ill-mannered scenes.

At first Iván Ilých hoped to escape from the unpleasantness of this state of affairs by the same easy and decorous relation to life that had served him heretofore: he tried to ignore his wife's disagreeable moods, continued to live in his usual easy and pleasant way, invited friends to his house for a game of cards, and also tried going out to his club or spending his evenings with friends. But one day his wife began upbraiding him so vigorously, using such coarse words, and continued to abuse him every time he did not fulfil her demands, so resolutely and with such evident determination not to give way till he submitted — that is, till he stayed at home and was bored just as she was — that he became alarmed. He now realized that matrimony — at any rate with Praskóvya Fëdorovna — was not always conducive to the pleasures and amenities of life but on the contrary often infringed both comfort and propriety, and that he must therefore entrench himself against such infringement. And Iván Ilých began to seek for means of doing so. His official duties were the one thing that imposed upon Praskóvya Fëdorovna, and by means of his official work and the duties attached to it he began struggling with his wife to secure his own independence.

With the birth of their child, the attempts to feed it and the various failures in doing so, and with the real and imaginary illnesses of mother and child, in which Iván Ilých's sympathy was demanded but about which he understood nothing, the need of securing for himself an existence outside his family life became still more imperative.

As his wife grew more irritable and exacting and Iván Ilých transferred the centre of gravity of his life more and more to his official work, so did he grow to like his work better and became more ambitious than before.

Very soon, within a year of his wedding, Iván Ilých had realized that marriage, though it may add some comforts to life, is in fact a very intricate and difficult affair towards which in order to perform one's duty, that is, to lead a decorous life approved of by society, one must adopt a definite attitude just as towards one's official duties.

And Iván Ilých evolved such an attitude towards married life. He only required of it those conveniences — dinner at home, housewife, and bed — which it could give him, and above all that propriety of external forms required by public opinion. For the rest he looked for light-hearted pleasure and propriety, and was very thankful when he found them, but if he met with antagonism and querulousness he at once retired into his separate fenced-off world of official duties, where he found satisfaction.

Iván Ilých was esteemed a good official, and after three years was made Assistant Public Prosecutor. His new duties, their importance, the possibility of indicting and imprisoning anyone he chose, the publicity his speeches received, and the success he had in all these things, made his work still more attractive.

More children came. His wife became more and more querulous and ill-tempered, but the attitude Iván Ilých had adopted towards his home life rendered him almost impervious to her grumbling.

After seven years' service in that town he was transferred to another province as Public Prosecutor. They moved, but were short of money and his wife did not like the place they moved to. Though the salary was higher the cost of living was greater, besides which two of their children died and family life became still more unpleasant for him.

Praskóvya Fëdorovna blamed her husband for every inconvenience they encountered in their new home. Most of the conversations between husband and wife, especially as to the children's education, led to topics which recalled former disputes, and those disputes were apt to flare up again at any moment. There remained only those rare periods of amorousness which still came to them at times but did not last long. These were islets at which they anchored for a while and then again set out upon that ocean of veiled hostility which showed itself in their aloofness from one another. This aloofness might have grieved Iván Ilých had he considered that it ought not to exist, but he now regarded the position as normal, and even made it the goal at which he aimed in family life. His aim was to free himself more and more from those unpleasantnesses and to give them a semblance of harmlessness and propriety. He attained this by spending less and less time with his family, and when obliged to be at home he tried to safeguard his position by the presence of outsiders. The chief thing however was that he had his official duties. The whole interest of his life now centred in the official world and that interest absorbed him. The consciousness of his power, being able to ruin anybody he wished to ruin, the importance, even the external dignity of his entry into court, or meetings with his subordinates, his success with superiors and inferiors, and above all his masterly handling of cases, of which he was conscious — all this gave him pleasure and filled his life, together with chats with his colleagues, dinners, and bridge. So that on the whole Iván Ilých's life continued to flow as he considered it should do — pleasantly and properly.

So things continued for another seven years. His eldest daughter was already sixteen, another child had died, and only one son was left, a schoolboy and a subject of dissension. Iván Ilých wanted to put him in the School of Law, but to spite him Praskóvya Fëdorovna entered him at the High School. The daughter had been educated at home and had turned out well: the boy did not learn badly either.

III

So Iván Ilých lived for seventeen years after his marriage. He was already a Public Prosecutor of long standing, and had declined several proposed transfers while awaiting a more desirable post, when an unanticipated and unpleasant occurrence quite upset the peaceful course of his life. He was expecting to be offered the post of presiding judge in a University town, but Happe somehow came to the front and obtained the appointment instead. Iván Ilých became irritable, reproached Happe, and quarrelled both with him and with his immediate superiors — who became colder to him and again passed him over when other appointments were made.

This was in 1880, the hardest year of Iván Ilých's life. It was then that it became evident on the one hand that his salary was insufficient for them to live on, and on the other that he had been forgotten, and not only this, but that what was for him the greatest and most cruel injustice appeared to others a quite ordinary occurrence. Even his father did not consider it his duty to help him. Iván Ilých felt himself abandoned by everyone, and that they regarded his position with a salary of 3,500 rubles [about £350] as quite normal and even fortunate. He alone knew that with the consciousness of the injustices done him, with his wife's incessant nagging, and with the debts he had contracted by living beyond his means, his position was far from normal.

In order to save money that summer he obtained leave of absence and went with his wife to live in the country at her brother's place.

In the country, without his work, he experienced *ennui* for the first time in his life, and not only *ennui* but intolerable depression, and he decided that it was impossible to go on living like that, and that it was necessary to take energetic measures.

Having passed a sleepless night pacing up and down the veranda, he decided to go to Petersburg and bestir himself, in order to punish those who had failed to appreciate him and to get transferred to another ministry.

Next day, despite many protests from his wife and her brother, he started for Petersburg with the sole object of obtaining a post with a salary of five thousand rubles a year. He was no longer bent on any particular department, or tendency, or kind of activity. All he now wanted was an appointment to another post with a salary of five thousand rubles, either in the administration, in the banks, with the railways, in one of the Empress Márya's Institutions,[5] or even in the customs — but it had to carry with it a salary of five thousand rubles and be in a ministry other than that in which they had failed to appreciate him.

And this quest of Iván Ilých's was crowned with remarkable and unexpected success. At Kursk an acquaintance of his, F. I. Ilyín, got into the first-class carriage, sat down beside Iván Ilých, and told him

5. Empress Márya, wife of Alexander III, gave her name and energy to the charitable "department of the institution."

of a telegram just received by the Governor of Kursk announcing that a change was about to take place in the ministry: Peter Ivánovich was to be superseded by Iván Semënovich.

The proposed change, apart from its significance for Russia, had a special significance for Iván Ilých, because by bringing forward a new man, Peter Petróvich, and consequently his friend Zachár Ivánovich, it was highly favourable for Iván Ilých, since Zachár Ivánovich was a friend and colleague of his.

In Moscow this news was confirmed, and on reaching Petersburg Iván Ilých found Zachár Ivánovich and received a definite promise of an appointment in his former department of Justice.

A week later he telegraphed to his wife: "Zachár in Miller's place. I shall receive appointment on presentation of report."

Thanks to this change of personnel, Iván Ilých had unexpectedly obtained an appointment in his former ministry which placed him two stages above his former colleagues besides giving him five thousand rubles salary and three thousand five hundred rubles for expenses conrnected with his removal. All his ill humor towards his former enemies and the whole department vanished, and Iván Ilých was completely happy.

He returned to the country more cheerful and contented than he had been for a long time. Praskóvya Fëdorovna also cheered up and a truce was arranged between them. Iván Ilých told of how he had been his enemies fêted by everybody in Petersburg, how all those who had been his enemies were put to shame and now fawned on him, how envious they were of his appointment, and how much everybody in Petersburg had liked him.

Praskóvya Fëdorovna listened to all this and appeared to believe it. She did not contradict anything, but only made plans for their life in the town to which they were going. Iván Ilých saw with delight that these plans were his plans, that he and his wife agreed, and that, after a stumble, his life was regaining its due and natural character of pleasant lightheartedness and decorum.

Iván Ilých had come back for a short time only, for he had to take up his new duties on the 10th of September. Moreover, he needed time to settle into the new place, to move all his belongings from the province, and to buy and order many additional things: in a word, to make such arrangements as he had resolved on, which were almost exactly what Praskóvya Fëdorovna too had decided on.

Now that everything had happened so fortunately, and that he and his wife were at one in their aims and moreover saw so little of one another, they got on together better than they had done since the first years of marriage. Iván Ilých had thought of taking his family away with him at once, but the insistence of his wife's brother and her sister-in-law, who had suddenly become particularly amiable and friendly to him and his family, induced him to depart alone.

So he departed, and the cheerful state of mind induced by his success and by the harmony between his wife and himself, the one intensifying the other, did not leave him. He found a delightful house, just the thing both he and his wife had dreamt of. Spacious, lofty reception rooms in the old style, a convenient and dignified study, rooms for his wife and daughter, a study for his son — it might have been specially built for them. Iván Ilých himself superintended the arrangements, chose the wall-papers, supplemented the furniture (preferably with antiques which he considered particularly *comme il faut*), and supervised the upholstering. Everything progressed and progressed and approached the ideal he had set himself: even when things were only half completed they exceeded his expectations. He saw what a refined and elegant character, free from vulgarity, it would all have when it was ready. On falling asleep he pictured to himself how the reception-room would look. Looking at the yet unfinished drawing-room he could see the fireplace, the screen, the what-not, the little chairs dotted here and there, the dishes and plates on the walls, and the bronzes, as they would be when everything was in place. He was pleased by the thought of how his wife and daughter, who shared his taste in this matter, would be impressed by it. They were certainly not expecting as much. He had been particularly successful in finding, and buying cheaply, antiques which gave a particularly aristocratic character to the whole place. But in his letters he intentionally understated everything in order to be able to surprise them. All this so absorbed him that his new duties — though he liked his official work — interested him less than he had expected. Sometimes he even had moments of absent-mindedness during the Court Sessions, and would consider whether he should have straight or curved cornices for his curtains. He was so interested in it all that he often did things himself, rearranging the furniture, or rehanging the curtains. Once when mounting a step-ladder to show the upholsterer, who did not understand, how he wanted the hangings draped, he made a false step and slipped, but being a strong and agile man he clung on and only knocked his side against the knob of the window frame. The bruised place was painful but the pain soon passed, and he felt particularly bright and well just then. He wrote: "I feel fifteen years younger." He thought he would have everything ready by September, but it dragged on till mid-October. But the result was charming not only in his eyes but to everyone who saw it.

In reality it was just what is usually seen in the houses of people of moderate means who want to appear rich, and therefore succeed only in resembling others like themselves: there were damasks, dark wood, plants, rugs, and dull and polished bronzes — all the things people of a certain class have in order to resemble other people of that class. His house was so like the others that it would never have been noticed, but to him it all seemed to be quite exceptional. He was very happy when he met his family at the station and brought them to the newly furnished house all lit up, where a footman in a white tie opened the door into the hall decorated with plants, and when they went on into the drawing-room and the study uttering exclamations of delight. He conducted them everywhere, drank in their praises eagerly, and beamed with pleasure. At tea that evening, when Praskóvya Fëdorovna among other things asked him about his fall, he laughed, and showed them how he had gone flying and had frightened the upholsterer.

"It's a good thing I'm a bit of an athlete. Another man might have been killed, but I merely knocked myself, just here; it hurts when it's touched, but it's passing off already — it's only a bruise."

So they began living in their new home — in which, as always happens, when they got thoroughly settled in they found they were just one room short — and with the increased income, which as always was just a little (some five hundred rubles) too little, but it was all very nice.

Things went particularly well at first, before everything was finally arranged and while something had still to be done: this thing bought, that thing ordered, another thing moved, and something else adjusted. Though there were some disputes between husband and wife, they were both so well satisfied and had so much to do that it all passed off without any serious quarrels. When nothing was left to arrange it became rather dull and something seemed to be lacking, but they were then making acquaintances, forming habits, and life was growing fuller.

Iván Ilých spent his mornings at the law court and came home to dinner, and at first he was generally in a good humour, though he occasionally became irritable just on account of his house. (Every spot on the tablecloth or the upholstery, and every broken window-blind string, irritated him. He had devoted so much trouble to arranging it all that every disturbance of it distressed him.) But on the whole his life ran its course as he believed life should do: easily, pleasantly, and decorously.

He got up at nine, drank his coffee, read the paper, and then put on his undress uniform and went to the law courts. There the harness in which he worked had already been stretched to fit him and he donned it without a hitch: petitioners, inquiries at the chancery, the chancery itself, and the sittings public and administrative. In all this the thing was to exclude everything fresh and vital, which always disturbs the regular course of official business, and to admit only official relations with people, and then only on official grounds. A man would come, for instance, wanting some information. Iván Ilých, as one in whose sphere the matter did not lie, would have nothing to do with him: but if the man had some business with him in his official capacity, something that could be expressed on officially stamped paper, he would do everything, positively everything he could within the limits of such relations, and in doing so would maintain the semblance of friendly human relations, that is, would observe the courtesies of life. As soon as the official relations ended, so did everything else. Iván Ilých possessed this capacity to separate his real life from the official side of affairs and not mix the two, in the highest degree, and by long practice and natural aptitude had brought it to such a pitch that sometimes, in the manner of a virtuoso, he would even allow himself to let the human and official relations mingle. He let himself do this just because he felt that he could at any time he chose resume the strictly official attitude again and drop the human relation. And he did it all easily, pleasantly, correctly, and even artistically. In the intervals between the sessions he smoked, drank tea, chatted a little about politics, a little about general topics, a little about cards, but most of all about official appointments. Tired, but with the feelings of a virtuoso — one of the first violins who has played his part in an orchestra with precision — he would return home to find that his wife and daughter had been out paying calls, or had a visitor, and that his son had been to school, had done his homework with his tutor, and was duly learning what is taught at High Schools. Everything was as it should be. After dinner, if they had no visitors, Iván Ilých sometimes read a book that was being much discussed at the time, and in the evening settled down to work, that is, read official papers, compared the depositions of witnesses, and noted paragraphs of the Code applying to them. This was neither dull nor amusing. It was dull when he might have been playing bridge, but if no bridge was available it was at any rate better than doing nothing or sitting with his wife. Iván Ilých's chief pleasure was giving little dinners to which he invited men and women of good social position, and just as his drawing-room resembled all other drawing-rooms so did his enjoyable little parties resemble all other such parties.

Once they even gave a dance. Iván Ilých enjoyed it and everything went off well, except that it led to a violent quarrel with his wife about the cakes and sweets. Praskóvya Fëdorovna had made her own plans, but Iván Ilých insisted on getting everything from an expensive confectioner and ordered too many cakes, and the quarrel occurred because some of those cakes were left over and the confectioner's bill came to forty-five rubles. It was a great and disagreeable quarrel. Praskóvya Fëdorovna called him "a fool and an imbecile," and he clutched at his head and made angry allusions to divorce.

But the dance itself had been enjoyable. The best people were there, and Iván Ilých had danced with Princess Trúfonova, a sister of the distinguished founder of the Society "Bear my Burden."

The pleasures connected with his work were pleasures of ambition; his social pleasures were those of vanity; but Iván Ilých's greatest pleasure was playing bridge. He acknowledged that whatever disagreeable incident happened in his life, the pleasure that beamed like a ray of light above everything else was to sit down to bridge with good players, not noisy partners, and of course to four-handed bridge (with five players it was annoying to have to stand out, though one pretended not to mind), to play a clever and serious game (when the cards allowed it) and then to have supper and drink a glass of wine. After a game of bridge, especially if he had won a little (to win a large sum was unpleasant), Iván Ilých went to bed in specially good humour.

So they lived. They formed a circle of acquaintances among the best people and were visited by people of importance and by young folk. In their views as to their acquaintances, husband, wife and daughter were entirely agreed, and tacitly and unanimously kept at arm's length and shook off the various shabby friends and relations who, with much show of affection, gushed into the drawing-room with its Japanese plates on the walls. Soon these shabby friends ceased to obtrude themselves and only the best people remained in the Golovíns' set.

Young men made up to Lisa, and Petríschhev, an examining magistrate and Dmítri Ivánovich Petríschhev's son and sole heir, began to be so attentive to her that Iván Ilých had already spoken to Praskóvya Fëdorovna about it, and considered whether they should not arrange a party for them, or get up some private theatricals.

So they lived, and all went well, without change, and life flowed pleasantly.

IV

They were all in good health. It could not be called ill health if Iván Ilých sometimes said that he had a queer taste in his mouth and felt some discomfort in his left side.

But this discomfort increased and, though not exactly painful, grew into a sense of pressure in his side accompanied by ill humour. And his irritability became worse and worse and began to mar the agreeable, easy, and correct life that had established itself in the Golovín family. Quarrels between husband and wife became more and more frequent, and soon the ease and amenity disappeared and even the decorum was barely maintained. Scenes again became frequent, and very few of those islets remained on which husband and wife could meet without an explosion. Praskóvya Fëdorovna now had good reason to say that her husband's temper was trying. With characteristic exaggeration she said he had always had a dreadful temper, and that it had needed all her good nature to put up with it for twenty years. It was true that now the quarrels were started by him. His bursts of temper always came just before dinner, often just as he began to eat his soup. Sometimes he noticed that a plate or dish was chipped, or the food was not right, or his son put his elbow on the table, or his daughter's hair was not done as he liked it, and for all this he blamed Praskóvya Fëdorovna. At first she retorted and said disagreeable things to him, but once or twice he fell into such a rage at the beginning of dinner that she realized it was due to some physical derangement brought on by taking food, and so she restrained herself and did not answer, but only hurried to get the dinner over. She regarded this self-restraint as highly praiseworthy. Having come to the conclusion that her husband had a dreadful temper and made her life miserable, she began to feel sorry for herself, and the more she pitied herself the more she hated her husband. She began to wish he would die; yet she did not want him to die because then his salary would cease. And this irritated her against him still more. She considered herself dreadfully unhappy just because not even his death could save her, and though she concealed her exasperation, that hidden exasperation of hers increased his irritation also.

After one scene in which Iván Ilých had been particularly unfair and after which he had said in explanation that he certainly was irritable but that it was due to his not being well, she said that if he was ill it should be attended to, and insisted on his going to see a celebrated doctor.

He went. Everything took place as he had expected and as it always does. There was the usual waiting and the important air assumed by the doctor, with which he was so familiar (resembling that which he himself assumed in court), and the sounding and listening, and the questions which called for answers that were foregone conclusions and were evidently unnecessary, and the look of importance which implied that "if only you put yourself in our hands we will arrange everything — we know indubitably how it has to be done, always in the same way for everybody alike." It was all just as it was in the law courts. The doctor put on just the same air towards him as he himself put on towards an accused person.

The doctor said that so-and-so indicated that there was so-and-so inside the patient, but if the investigation of so-and-so did not confirm this, then he must assume that and that. If he assumed that and that, then . . . and so on. To Iván Ilých only one question was important: was his case serious or not? But the doctor ignored that inappropriate question. From his point of view it was not the one under consideration, the real question was to decide between a floating kidney, chronic catarrh, or appendicitis. It was not a question of Iván Ilých's life or death, but one between a floating kidney and appendicitis. And that question the doctor solved brilliantly, as it seemed to Iván Ilých, in favour of the appendix, with the reservation that should an examination of the urine give fresh indications the matter would be reconsidered. All this was just what Iván Ilých had himself brilliantly accomplished a thousand times in dealing with men on trial. The doctor summed up just as brilliantly, looking over his spectacles triumphantly and even gaily at the accused. From the doctor's summing up Iván Ilých concluded that things were bad, but that for the doctor, and perhaps for everybody else, it was a matter of indifference, though for him it was bad. And this conclusion struck him painfully, arousing in him a great feeling of pity for himself and of bitterness towards the doctor's indifference to a matter of such importance.

He said nothing of this, but rose, placed the doctor's fee on the table, and remarked with a sigh: "We sick people probably often put inappropriate questions. But tell me, in general, is this complaint dangerous, or not? . . ."

The doctor looked at him sternly over his spectacles with one eye, as if to say: "Prisoner, if you will not keep to the questions put to you, I shall be obliged to have you removed from the court."

"I have already told you what I consider necessary and proper. The analysis may show something more." And the doctor bowed.

Iván Ilých went out slowly, seated himself disconsolately in his sledge, and drove home. All the way home he was going over what the doctor had said, trying to translate those complicated, obscure, scientific phrases into plain language and find in them an answer to the question: "Is my condition bad? Is it very bad? Or is there as yet nothing much wrong?" And it seemed to him that the meaning of what the doctor had said was that it was very bad. Everything in the streets seemed depressing. The cabmen, the houses, the passers-by, and the shops, were dismal. His ache, this dull gnawing ache that never ceased for a moment, seemed to have acquired a new and more serious significance from the doctor's dubious remarks. Iván Ilých now watched it with a new and oppressive feeling.

He reached home and began to tell his wife about it. She listened, but in the middle of his account his daughter came in with her hat on, ready to go out with her mother. She sat down reluctantly to listen to this tedious story, but could not stand it long, and her mother too did not hear him to the end.

"Well, I am very glad," she said. "Mind now to take your medicine regularly. Give me the prescripion and I'll send Gerásim to the chemist's." And she went to get ready to go out.

While she was in the room Iván Ilých had hardly taken time to breathe, but he sighed deeply when she left it.

"Well," he thought, "perhaps it isn't so bad after all."

He began taking his medicine and following the doctor's directions, which had been altered after the examination of the urine. But then it happened that there was a contradiction between the indications drawn from the examination of the urine and the symptoms that showed themselves. It turned out that what was happening differed from what the doctor had told him, and that he had either forgotten, or blundered, or hidden something from him. He could not, however, be blamed for that, and Iván Ilých still obeyed his orders implicitly and at first derived some comfort from doing so.

From the time of his visit to the doctor, Iván Ilých's chief occupation was the exact fulfilment of the doctor's instructions regarding hygiene and the taking of medicine, and the observation of his pain and his excretions. His chief interests came to be people's ailments and people's health. When sickness, deaths, or recoveries, were mentioned in his presence, especially when the illness resembled his own, he listened with agitation which he tried to hide, asked questions, and applied what he heard to his own case.

The pain did not grow less, but Iván Ilých made efforts to force himself to think that he was better. And he could do this so long as nothing agitated him. But as soon as he had any unpleasantness with his wife, any lack of success in his official work, or held bad cards at bridge, he was at once acutely sensible of his disease. He had formerly borne such mischances, hoping soon to adjust what was wrong, to master it and attain success, or make a grand slam. But now every mischance upset him and plunged him into despair. He would say to himself: "There now, just as I was beginning to get better and the medicine had begun to take effect, comes this accursed misfortune, or unpleasantness . . ." And he was furious with the mishap, or with the people who were causing the unpleasantness and killing him, for he felt that this fury was killing him but could not restrain it. One would have thought that it should have been clear to him that this exasperation with circumstances and people aggravated his illness, and that he ought therefore to ignore unpleasant occurrences. But he drew the very opposite conclusion: he said that he needed peace, and he watched for everything that might disturb it and became irritable at the slightest infringement of it. His condition was rendered worse by the fact that he read medical books and consulted doctors. The progress of his disease was so gradual that he could deceive himself when comparing one day with another — the difference was so slight. But when he consulted the doctors it seemed to him that he was getting worse, and even very rapidly. Yet despite this he was continually consulting them.

That month he went to see another celebrity, who told him almost the same as the first had done but put his questions rather differently, and the interview with this celebrity only increased Iván Ilých's doubts and fears. A friend of a friend of his, a very good doctor, diagnosed his illness again quite differently from the others, and though he predicted recovery, his questions and suppositions bewildered Iván Ilých still more and increased his doubts. A homoeopathist diagnosed the disease in yet another way, and prescribed medicine which Iván Ilých took secretly for a week. But after a week, not feeling any improvement and having lost confidence both in the former doctor's treatment and in this one's, he became still more despondent. One day a lady acquaintance mentioned a cure effected by a wonder-working icon. Iván Ilých caught himself listening attentively and beginning to believe that it had occurred. This incident alarmed him. "Has my mind really weakened to such an extent?" he asked himself. "Nonsense! It's all rubbish. I mustn't give way to nervous fears but having chosen a doctor must keep strictly to his treatment. That is what I will do. Now it's all settled. I won't think about it, but will follow the treatment seriously till summer, and then we shall see. From now there must be no more of this wavering!" This was easy to say but impossible to carry out. The pain in his side oppressed him and seemed to grow worse and more incessant, while the taste in his mouth grew stranger and stranger. It seemed to him that his breath had a disgusting smell, and he was conscious of a loss of appetite and strength. There was no deceiving himself: something terrible, new, and more important than anything before in his life, was taking place within him of which he alone was aware. Those about him did not understand or would not understand it, but thought everything in the world was going on as usual. That tormented Iván Ilých more than anything. He saw that his household, especially his wife and daughter who were in a perfect whirl of visiting, did not understand anything of it and were annoyed that he was so depressed and so exacting, as if he were to blame for it. Though they tried to disguise it he saw that he was an obstacle in their path, and that his wife had adopted a definite line in regard to his illness and kept to it regardless of anything he said or did. Her attitude was this: "You know," she would say to her friends, "Iván Ilých can't do as other people do, and keep to the treatment prescribed for him. One day he'll take his drops and keep strictly to his diet and go to bed in good time, but the next day unless I watch him he'll suddenly forget his medicine, eat sturgeon — which is forbidden — and sit up playing cards till one o'clock in the morning."

"Oh, come, when was that?" Iván Ilých would ask in vexation. "Only once at Peter Ivánovich's."

"And yesterday with Shébek."

"Well, even if I hadn't stayed up, this pain would have kept me awake."

"Be that as it may you'll never get well like that, but will always make us wretched."

Praskóvya Fëdorovna's attitude to Iván Ilých's illness, as she expressed it both to others and to him, was that it was his own fault and was another of the annoyances he caused her. Iván Ilých felt that this opinion escaped her involuntarily — but that did not make it easier for him.

At the law courts too, Iván Ilých noticed, or thought he noticed, a strange attitude towards himself. It sometimes seemed to him that people were watching him inquisitively as a man whose place might soon be vacant. Then again, his friends would suddenly begin to chaff him in a friendly way about his low spirits, as if the awful, horrible, and unheard-of thing that was going on within him, incessantly gnawing at him and irresistibly drawing him away, was a very agreeable subject for jests. Schwartz in particular irritated him by his jocularity, vivacity, and *savoir-faire*, which reminded him of what he himself had been ten years ago.

Friends came to make up a set and they sat down to cards. They dealt, bending the new cards to soften them, and he sorted the diamonds in his hand and found he had seven. His partner said "No trumps" and supported him with two diamonds. What more could be wished for? It ought to be jolly and lively. They would make a grand slam. But suddenly Iván Ilých was conscious of that gnawing pain, that taste in his mouth, and it seemed ridiculous that in such circumstances he should be pleased to make a grand slam.

He looked at his partner Mikháil Mikháylovich, who rapped the table with his strong hand and instead of snatching up the tricks pushed the cards courteously and indulgently towards Iván Ilých that he might have the pleasure of gathering them up without the trouble of stretching out his hand for them. "Does he think I am too weak to stretch out my arm?" thought Iván Ilých, and forgetting what he was doing he over-trumped his partner, missing the grand slam by three tricks. And what was most awful of all was that he saw how upset Mikháil Mikháylovich was about it but did not himself care. And it was dreadful to realize why he did not care.

They all saw that he was suffering, and said: "We can stop if you are tired. Take a rest." Lie down? No, he was not at all tired, and he finished the rubber. All were gloomy and silent. Iván Ilých felt that he had diffused this gloom over them and could not dispel it. They had supper and went away, and Iván Ilých was left alone with the consciousness that his life was poisoned and was poisoning the lives of others, and that this poison did not weaken but penetrated more and more deeply into his whole being.

With this consciousness, and with physical pain besides the terror, he must go to bed, often to lie awake the greater part of the night. Next morning he had to get up again, dress, go to the law courts, speak, and write; or if he did not go out, spend at home those twenty-four hours a day each of which was a torture. And he had to live thus all alone on the brink of an abyss, with no one who understood or pitied him.

V

So one month passed and then another. Just before the New Year his brother-in-law came to town and stayed at their house. Iván Ilých was at the law courts and Praskóvya Fëdorovna had gone shopping. When Iván Ilých came home and entered his study he found his brother-in-law there — a healthy, florid man — unpacking his portmanteau himself. He raised his head on hearing Iván Ilých's footsteps and looked up at him for a moment without a word. That stare told Iván Ilých everything. His brother-in-law opened his mouth to utter an exclamation of surprise but checked himself, and that action confirmed it all.

"I have changed, eh?"

"Yes, there is a change."

And after that, try as he would to get his brother-in-law to return to the subject of his looks, the latter would say nothing about it. Praskóvya Fëdorovna came home and her brother went out to her. Iván Ilých locked the door and began to examine himself in the glass, first full face, then in profile. He took up a portrait of himself taken with his wife, and compared it with what he saw in the glass. The change in him was immense. Then he bared his arms to the elbow, looked at them, drew the sleeves down again, sat down on an ottoman, and grew blacker than night.

"No, no, this won't do!" he said to himself, and jumped up, went to the table, took up some law papers and began to read them, but could not continue. He unlocked the door and went into the reception-room. The door leading to the drawing-room was shut. He approached it on tiptoe and listened.

"No, you are exaggerating!" Praskóvya Fëdorovna was saying.

"Exaggerating! Don't you see it? Why, he's a dead man! Look at his eyes — there's no light in them. But what is it that is wrong with him?"

"No one knows. Nikoláevich [that was another doctor] said something, but I don't know what. And Leshchetítsky [this was the celebrated specialist] said quite the contrary . . ."

Iván Ilých walked away, went to his own room, lay down, and began musing: "The kidney, a floating kidney." He recalled all the doctors had told him of how it detached itself and swayed about. And by an effort of imagination he tried to catch that kidney and arrest it and support it. So little was needed for this, it seemed to him. "No, I'll go to see Peter Ivánovich again." [That was the friend whose friend was a doctor.] He rang, ordered the carriage, and got ready to go.

"Where are you going, Jean?" asked his wife, with a specially sad and exceptionally kind look.

This exceptionally kind look irritated him. He looked morosely at her.

"I must go to see Peter Ivánovich."

He went to see Peter Ivánovich, and together they went to see his friend, the doctor. He was in, and Iván Ilých had a long talk with him.

Reviewing the anatomical and physiological details of what in the doctor's opinion was going on inside him, he understood it all.

There was something, a small thing, in the vermiform appendix. It might all come right. Only stimulate the energy of one organ and check the activity of another, then absorption would take place and everything would come right. He got home rather late for dinner, ate his dinner, and conversed cheerfully, but could not for a long time bring himself to go back to work in his room. At last, however, he went to his study and did what was necessary, but the consciousness that he had put something aside — an important, intimate matter which he would revert to when his work was done — never left him. When he had finished his work he remembered that this intimate matter was the thought of his vermiform appendix. But he did not give himself up to it, and went to the drawing-room for tea. There were callers there, including the examining magistrate who was a desirable match for his daughter, and they were conversing, playing the piano, and singing. Iván Ilých, as Praskóvya Fëdorovna remarked, spent that evening more cheerfully than usual, but he never for a moment forgot that he had postponed the important matter of the appendix. At eleven o'clock he said good-night and went to his bedroom. Since his illness he had slept alone in a small room next to his study. He undressed and took up a novel by Zola,[6] but instead of reading it he fell into thought, and in his imagination that desired improvement in the vermiform appendix occurred. There was the absorption and evacuation and the reestablishment of normal activity. "Yes, that's it!" he said to himself. "One need only assist nature, that's all." He remembered his medicine, rose, took it, and lay down on his back watching for the beneficent action of the medicine and for it to lessen the pain. "I need only take it regularly and avoid all injurious influences. I am already feeling better, much better." He began touching his side: it was not painful to the touch. "There, I really don't feel it. It's much better already." He put out the light and turned on his side . . . "The appendix is getting better, absorption is occurring." Suddenly he felt the old, familiar, dull, gnawing pain, stubborn and serious. There was the same familiar loathsome taste in his mouth. His heart sank and he felt dazed. "My God! My God!" he muttered. "Again, again! And it will never cease." And suddenly the matter presented itself in a quite different aspect. "Vermiform appendix! Kidney!" he said to himself. "It's not a question of appendix or kidney, but of life and . . . death. Yes, life was there and now it is going, going and I cannot stop it. Yes. Why deceive myself? Isn't it obvious to everyone but me that I'm dying, and that it's only a question of weeks, days . . . it may happen this moment. There was light and now there is darkness. I was here and now I'm going there! Where?" A chill came over him, his breathing ceased, and he felt only the throbbing of his heart.

"When I am not, what will there be? There will be nothing. Then where shall I be when I am no more? Can this be dying? No, I don't want to!" He jumped up and tried to light the candle, felt for it with trembling hands, dropped candle and candlestick on the floor, and fell back on his pillow.

"What's the use? It makes no difference," he said to himself, staring with wide-open eyes into the darkness. "Death. Yes, death. And none of them know or wish to know it, and they have no pity for me. Now they are playing." (He heard through the door the distant sound of a song and its accompaniment.) "It's all the same to them, but they will die too! Fools! I first, and they later, but it will be the same for them. And now they are merry . . . the beasts!"

Anger choked him and he was agonizingly, unbearably miserable. "It is impossible that all men have been doomed to suffer this awful horror!" He raised himself.

"Something must be wrong. I must calm myself — must think it all over from the beginning." And he again began thinking. "Yes, the beginning of my illness: I knocked my side, but I was still quite well that day and the next. It hurt a little, then rather more. I saw the doctors, then followed despondency and anguish, more doctors, and I

6. After his conversion, Tolstoy had nothing but bitter scorn for the famous French naturalistic writer.

drew nearer to the abyss. My strength grew less and I kept coming nearer and nearer, and now I have wasted away and there is no light in my eyes. I think of the appendix — but this is death! I think of mending the appendix, and all the while here is death! Can it really be death?" Again terror seized him and he gasped for breath. He leant down and began feeling for the matches, pressing with his elbow on the stand beside the bed. It was in his way and hurt him, he grew furious with it, pressed on it still harder, and upset it. Breathless and in despair he fell on his back, expecting death to come immediately.

Meanwhile the visitors were leaving. Praskóvya Fëdorovna was seeing them off. She heard something fall and came in.

"What has happened?"

"Nothing. I knocked it over accidentally."

She went out and returned with a candle. He lay there panting heavily, like a man who has run a thousand yards, and stared upwards at her with a fixed look.

"What is it, Jean?"

"No . . . o . . . thing. I upset it." ("Why speak of it? She won't understand," he thought.)

And in truth she did not understand. She picked up the stand, lit his candle, and hurried away to see another visitor off. When she came back he still lay on his back, looking upwards.

"What is it? Do you feel worse?"

"Yes."

She shook her head and sat down.

"Do you know, Jean, I think we must ask Leshchetítsky to come and see you here."

This meant calling in the famous specialist, regardless of expense. He smiled malignantly and said "No." She remained a little longer and then went up to him and kissed his forehead.

While she was kissing him he hated her from the bottom of his soul and with difficulty refrained from pushing her away.

"Good-night. Please God you'll sleep."

"Yes."

VI

Iván Ilých saw that he was dying, and he was in continual despair. In the depth of his heart he knew he was dying, but not only was he not accustomed to the thought, he simply did not and could not grasp it.

The syllogism he had learnt from Kiezewetter's Logic: "Caius is a man, men are mortal, therefore Caius is mortal," had always seemed to him correct as applied to Caius, but certainly not as applied to himself. That Caius — man in the abstract — was mortal, was perfectly correct, but he was not Caius, not an abstract man, but a creature quite separate from all others. He had been little Ványa, with a mamma and a papa, with Mítya and Volódya, with the toys, a coachman and a nurse, afterwards with Kátenka and with all the joys, griefs, and delights of childhood, boyhood, and youth. What did Caius know of the smell of that striped leather ball Ványa had been so fond of? Had Caius kissed his mother's hand like that, and did the silk of her dress rustle so for Caius? Had he rioted like that at school when the pastry was bad? Had Caius been in love like that? Could Caius preside at a session as he did? "Caius really was mortal, and it was right for him to die; but for me, little Ványa, Iván Ilých, with all my thoughts and emotions, it's altogether a different matter. It cannot be that I ought to die. That would be too terrible."

Such was his feeling.

"If I had to die like Caius I should have known it was so. An inner voice would have told me so, but there was nothing of the sort in me and I and all my friends felt that our case was quite different from that of Caius. And now here it is!" he said to himself. "It can't be. It's impossible! But here it is. How is this? How is one to understand it?"

He could not understand it, and tried to drive this false, incorrect, morbid thought away and to replace it by other proper and healthy thoughts. But that thought, and not the thought only but the reality itself, seemed to come and confront him.

And to replace that thought he called up a succession of others, hoping to find in them some support. He tried to get back into the former current of thoughts that had once screened the thought of death from him. But strange to say, all that had formerly shut off, hidden, and destroyed, his consciousness of death, no longer had that effect. Iván Ilých now spent most of his time in attempting to reestablish that old current. He would say to himself: "I will take up my duties again — after all I used to live by them." And banishing all doubts he would go to the law courts, enter into conversation with his colleagues, and sit carelessly as was his wont, scanning the crowd with a thoughtful look and leaning both his emaciated arms on the arms of his oak chair; bending over as usual to a colleague and drawing his papers nearer he would interchange whispers with him, and then suddenly raising his eyes and sitting erect would pronounce certain words and open the proceedings. But suddenly in the midst of those proceedings the pain in his side, regardless of the stage the proceedings had reached, would begin its own gnawing work. Iván Ilých would turn his attention to it and try to drive the thought of it away, but without success. It would come and stand before him and look at him, and he would be petrified and the light would die out of his eyes, and he would again begin asking himself whether It alone was true. And his colleagues and subordinates would see with surprise and distress that he, the brilliant and subtle judge, was becoming confused and making mistakes. He would shake himself, try to pull himself together, manage somehow to bring the sitting to a close, and return home with the sorrowful consciousness that his judicial labours could not as formerly hide from him what he wanted them to hide, and could not deliver him from *It*. And what was worst of all was that *It* drew his attention to itself not in order to make him take some action but only that he should look at *It*, look it straight in the face: look at it and without doing anything, suffer inexpressibly.

And to save himself from this condition Iván Ilých looked for consolations — new screens — and new screens were found and for a while seemed to save him, but then they immediately fell to pieces or rather became transparent, as if *It* penetrated them and nothing could veil *It*.

In these latter days he would go into the drawing-room he had arranged — that drawing-room where he had fallen and for the sake of which (how bitterly ridiculous it seemed) he had sacrificed his life — for he knew that his illness originated with that knock. He would enter and see that something had scratched the polished table. He would look for the cause of this and find that it was the bronze ornamentation of an album, that had got bent. He would take up the expensive album which he had lovingly arranged, and feel vexed with his daughter and her friends for their untidiness — for the album was torn here and there and some of the photographs turned upside down. He would put it carefully in order and bend the ornamentation back into position. Then it would occur to him to place all those things in another corner of the room, near the plants. He would call the footman, but his daughter or wife would come to help him. They would not agree, and his wife would contradict him, and he would dispute and grow angry. But that was all right, for then he did not think about *It*. *It* was invisible.

But then, when he was moving something himself, his wife would say: "Let the servants do it. You will hurt yourself again." And suddenly *It* would flash through the screen and he would see it. It was just a flash, and he hoped it would disappear, but he would involuntarily pay attention to his side. "It sits there as before, gnawing just the same!" And he could no longer forget *It*, but could distinctly see it looking at him from behind the flowers. "What is it all for?"

"It really is so I lost my life over that curtain as I might have done when storming a fort. Is that possible? How terrible and how stupid. It can't be true! It can't, but it is."

He would go to his study, lie down, and again be alone with *It*: face to face with *It*. And nothing could be done with *It* except to look at it and shudder.

VII

How it happened it is impossible to say because it came about step by step, unnoticed, but in the third month of Iván Ilých's illness, his wife, his daughter, his son, his acquaintances, the doctors, the servants, and above all he himself, were aware that the whole interest he had for other people was whether he would soon vacate his place, and at last release the living from the discomfort caused by his presence and be himself released from his sufferings.

He slept less and less. He was given opium and hypodermic injections of morphine, but this did not relieve him. The dull depression he experienced in a somnolent condition at first gave him a little relief, but only as something new, afterwards it became as distressing as the pain itself or even more so.

Special foods were prepared for him by the doctors' orders, but all those foods became increasingly distasteful and disgusting to him.

For his excretions also special arrangements had to be made, and this was a torment to him every time — a torment from the uncleanliness, the unseemliness, and the smell, and from knowing that another person had to take part in it.

But just through this most unpleasant matter, Iván Ilých obtained comfort. Gerásim, the butler's young assistant, always came in to carry the things out. Gerásim was a clean, fresh peasant lad, grown stout on town food and always cheerful and bright. At first the sight of him, in his clean Russian peasant costume, engaged on that disgusting task embarrassed Iván Ilých.

Once when he got up from the commode too weak to draw up his trousers, he dropped into a soft armchair and looked with horror at his bare, enfeebled thighs with the muscles so sharply marked on them.

Gerásim with a firm light tread, his heavy boots emitting a pleasant smell of tar and fresh winter air, came in wearing a clean Hessian apron, the sleeves of his print shirt tucked up over his strong bare young arms; and refraining from looking at his sick master out of consideration for his feelings, and restraining the joy of life that beamed from his face, went up to the commode.

"Gerásim!" said Iván Ilých in a weak voice.

Gerásim started, evidently afraid he might have committed some blunder, and with a rapid movement turned his fresh, kind, simple young face which just showed the first downy signs of a beard.

"Yes, sir?"

"That must be very unpleasant for you. You must forgive me. I am helpless."

"Oh, why, sir," and Gerásim's eyes beamed and he showed his glistening white teeth, "what's a little trouble? It's a case of illness with you, sir."

And his deft strong hands did their accustomed task, and he went out of the room stepping lightly. Five minutes later he as lightly returned.

Iván Ilých was still sitting in the same position in the armchair.

"Gerásim," he said when the latter had replaced the freshly washed utensil. "Please come here and help me." Gerásim went up to him. "Lift me up. It is hard for me to get up, and I have sent Dmítri away."

Gerásim went up to him, grasped his master with his strong arms deftly but gently, in the same way that he stepped — lifted him, supported him with one hand, and with the other drew up his trousers and would have set him down again, but Iván Ilých asked to be led to the sofa. Gerásim, without an effort and without apparent pressure, led him, almost lifting him, to the sofa and placed him on it.

"Thank you. How easily and well you do it all!"

Gerásim smiled again and turned to leave the room. But Iván Ilých felt his presence such a comfort that he did not want to let him go.

"One thing more, please move up that chair. No, the other one — under my feet. It is easier for me when my feet are raised."

Gerásim brought the chair, set it down gently in place, and raised Iván Ilých's legs on to it. It seemed to Iván Ilých that he felt better while Gerásim was holding up his legs.

"It's better when my legs are higher," he said. "Place that cushion under them."

Gerásim did so. He again lifted the legs and placed them, and again Iván Ilých felt better while Gerásim held his legs. When he set them down Iván Ilých fancied he felt worse.

"Gerásim," he said. "Are you busy now?"

"Not at all, sir," said Gerásim, who had learnt from the townsfolk how to speak to gentlefolk.

"What have you still to do?"

"What have I to do? I've done everything except chopping the logs for to-morrow."

"Then hold my legs up a bit higher, can you?"

"Of course I can. Why not?" And Gerásim raised his master's legs higher and Iván Ilých thought that in that position he did not feel any pain at all.

"And how about the logs?"

"Don't trouble about that, sir. There's plenty of time."

Iván Ilých told Gerásim to sit down and hold his legs, and began to talk to him. And strange to say it seemed to him that he felt better while Gerásim held his legs up.

After that Iván Ilých would sometimes call Gerásim and get him to hold his legs on his shoulders, and he liked talking to him. Gerásim did it all easily, willingly, simply, and with a good nature that touched Iván Ilých. Health, strength, and vitality in other people were offensive to him, but Gerásim's strength and vitality did not mortify but soothed him.

What tormented Iván Ilých most was the deception, the lie, which for some reason they all accepted, that he was not dying but was simply ill, and that he only need keep quiet and undergo a treatment and then something very good would result. He however knew that do what they would nothing would come of it, only still more agonizing suffering and death. This deception tortured him — their not wishing to admit what they all knew and what he knew, but wanting to lie to him con-

cerning his terrible condition, and wishing and forcing him to partici-
pate in that lie. Those lies — lies enacted over him on the eve of his
death and destined to degrade this awful, solemn act to the level of
their visitings, their curtains, their sturgeon for dinner — were a terrible agony for Iván Ilých. And strangely enough, many times when
they were going through their antics over him he had been within a
hairbreadth of calling out to them: "Stop lying! You know and I know
that I am dying. Then at least stop lying about it!" But he had never
had the spirit to do it. The awful, terrible act of his dying was, he
could see, reduced by those about him to the level of a casual, unpleasant, and almost indecorous incident (as if someone entered a
drawing-room diffusing an unpleasant odour) and this was done by
that very decorum which he had served all his life long. He saw that
no one felt for him, because no one even wished to grasp his position.
Only Gerásim recognized it and pitied him. And so Iván Ilých felt at
ease only with him. He felt comforted when Gerásim supported his
legs (sometimes all night long) and refused to go to bed, saying:
"Don't you worry, Iván Ilých. I'll get sleep enough later on," or when
he suddenly became familiar and exclaimed: "If you weren't sick it
would be another matter, but as it is, why should I grudge a little
trouble?" Gerásim alone did not lie; everything showed that he alone
understood the facts of the case and did not consider it necessary to
disguise them, but simply felt sorry for his emaciated and enfeebled
master. Once when Iván Ilých was sending him away he even said
straight out: "We shall all of us die, so why should I grudge a little
trouble?" — expressing the fact that he did not think his work burdensome, because he was doing it for a dying man and hoped someone
would do the same for him when his time came.

Apart from this lying, or because of it, what most tormented Iván
Ilých was that no one pitied him as he wished to be pitied. At certain
moments after prolonged suffering he wished most of all (though he
would have been ashamed to confess it) for someone to pity him as
a sick child is pitied. He longed to be petted and comforted. He knew
he was an important functionary, that he had a beard turning grey,
and that therefore what he longed for was impossible, but still he
longed for it. And in Gerásim's attitude towards him there was something akin to what he wished for, and so that attitude comforted him.
Iván Ilých wanted to weep, wanted to be petted and cried over, and
then his colleague Shébek would come, and instead of weeping and
being petted, Iván Ilých would assume a serious, severe, and profound
air, and by force of habit would express his opinion on a decision of
the Court of Cassation [7] and would stubbornly insist on that view. This
falsity around him and within him did more than anything else to
poison his last days.

7. That is, a court of appeal.

VIII

It was morning. He knew it was morning because Gerásim had gone, and Peter the footman had come and put out the candles, drawn back one of the curtains, and begun quietly to tidy up. Whether it was morning or evening, Friday or Sunday, made no difference, it was all just the same: the gnawing, unmitigated, agonizing pain, never ceasing for an instant, the consciousness of life inexorably waning but not yet extinguished, that approach of that ever dreaded and hateful Death which was the only reality, and always the same falsity. What were days, weeks, hours, in such a case?

"Will you have some tea, sir?"

"He wants things to be regular, and wishes the gentlefolk to drink tea in the morning," thought Iván Ilých, and only said "No."

"Wouldn't you like to move onto the sofa, sir?"

"He wants to tidy up the room, and I'm in the way. I am uncleanliness and disorder," he thought, and said only:

"No, leave me alone."

The man went on bustling about. Iván Ilých stretched out his hand. Peter came up, ready to help.

"What is it, sir?"

"My watch."

Peter took the watch which was close at hand and gave it to his master.

"Half-past eight. Are they up?"

"No sir, except Vladímir Ivánich" (the son) "who has gone to school. Praskóvya Fëdorovna ordered me to wake her if you asked for her. Shall I do so?"

"No, there's no need to." "Perhaps I'd better have some tea," he thought, and added aloud: "Yes, bring me some tea."

Peter went to the door but Iván Ilých dreaded being left alone. "How can I keep him here? Oh yes, my medicine." "Peter, give me my medicine." "Why not? Perhaps it may still do me some good." He took a spoonful and swallowed it. "No, it won't help. It's all tomfoolery, all deception," he decided as soon as he became aware of the familiar, sickly, hopeless taste. "No, I can't believe in it any longer. But the pain, why this pain? If it would only cease just for a moment!" And he moaned. Peter turned towards him. "It's all right. Go and fetch me some tea."

Peter went out. Left alone Iván Ilých groaned not so much with pain, terrible though that was, as from mental anguish. Always and for ever the same, always these endless days and nights. If only it would come quicker! If only *what* would come quicker? Death, darkness? . . . No, no! Anything rather than death!

When Peter returned with the tea on a tray, Iván Ilých stared at him for a time in perplexity, not realizing who and what he was. Peter was disconcerted by that look and his embarrassment brought Iván Ilých to himself.

"Oh, tea! All right, put it down. Only help me to wash and put on a clean shirt."

And Iván Ilých began to wash. With pauses for rest, he washed his hands and then his face, cleaned his teeth, brushed his hair, and looked in the glass. He was terrified by what he saw, especially by the limp way in which his hair clung to his pallid forehead.

While his shirt was being changed he knew that he would be still more frightened at the sight of his body, so he avoided looking at it. Finally he was ready. He drew on a dressing-gown, wrapped himself in a plaid, and sat down in the armchair to take his tea. For a moment he felt refreshed, but as soon as he began to drink the tea he was again aware of the same taste, and the pain also returned. He finished it with an effort, and then lay down stretching out his legs, and dismissed Peter.

Always the same. Now a spark of hope flashes up, then a sea of despair rages, and always pain; always pain, always despair, and always the same. When alone he had a dreadful and distressing desire to call someone, but he knew beforehand that with others present it would be still worse. "Another dose of morphine — to lose consciousness. I will tell him, the doctor, that he must think of something else. It's impossible, impossible, to go on like this."

An hour and another pass like that. But now there is a ring at the door bell. Perhaps it's the doctor? It is. He comes in fresh, hearty, plump, and cheerful, with that look on his face that seems to say: "There now, you're in a panic about something, but we'll arrange it all for you directly!" The doctor knows this expression is out of place here, but he has put it on once for all and can't take it off — like a man who has put on a frock-coat in the morning to pay a round of calls.

The doctor rubs his hands vigorously and reassuringly.

"Brr! How cold it is! There's such a sharp frost; just let me warm myself!" he says, as if it were only a matter of waiting till he was warm, and then he would put everything right.

"Well now, how are you?"

Iván Ilých feels that the doctor would like to say: "Well, how are our affairs?" but that even he feels that this would not do, and says instead: "What sort of a night have you had?"

Iván Ilých looks at him as much as to say: "Are you really never ashamed of lying?" But the doctor does not wish to understand this question, and Iván Ilých says: "Just as terrible as ever. The pain never leaves me and never subsides. If only something . . ."

"Yes, you sick people are always like that. . . . There, now I think I am warm enough. Even Praskóvya Fëdorovna, who is so particular, could find no fault with my temperature. Well, now I can say good-morning," and the doctor presses his patient's hand.

Then, dropping his former playfulness, he begins with a most serious face to examine the patient, feeling his pulse and taking his temperature, and then begins the sounding and auscultation.

Iván Ilých knows quite well and definitely that all this is nonsense and pure deception, but when the doctor, getting down on his knee, leans over him, putting his ear first higher then lower, and performs various gymnastic movements over him with a significant expression on his face, Iván Ilých submits to it all as he used to submit to the speeches of the lawyers, though he knew very well that they were all lying and why they were lying.

The doctor, kneeling on the sofa, is still sounding him when Praskóvya Fëdorovna's silk dress rustles at the door and she is heard scolding Peter for not having let her know of the doctor's arrival.

She comes in, kisses her husband, and at once proceeds to prove that she has been up a long time already, and only owing to a misunderstanding failed to be there when the doctor arrived.

Iván Ilých looks at her, scans her all over, sets against her the whiteness and plumpness and cleanness of her hands and neck, the gloss of her hair, and the sparkle of her vivacious eyes. He hates her with his whole soul. And the thrill of hatred he feels for her makes him suffer from her touch.

Her attitude towards him and his disease is still the same. Just as the doctor had adopted a certain relation to his patient which he could not abandon, so had she formed one towards him — that he was not doing something he ought to do and was himself to blame, and that she reproached him lovingly for this — and she could not now change that attitude.

"You see he doesn't listen to me and doesn't take his medicine at the proper time. And above all he lies in a position that is no doubt bad for him — with his legs up."

She described how he made Gerásim hold his legs up.

The doctor smiled with a contemptuous affability that said: "What's to be done? These sick people do have foolish fancies of that kind, but we must forgive them."

When the examination was over the doctor looked at his watch, and then Praskóvya Fëdorovna announced to Iván Ilých that it was of course as he pleased, but she had sent to-day for a celebrated specialist who would examine him and have a consultation with Michael Danílovich (their regular doctor).

"Please don't raise any objections. I am doing this for my own sake," she said ironically, letting it be felt that she was doing it all for his sake and only said this to leave him no right to refuse. He remained silent, knitting his brows. He felt that he was so surrounded and involved in a mesh of falsity that it was hard to unravel anything.

Everything she did for him was entirely for her own sake, and she told him she was doing for herself what she actually was doing for

1732 🏵 LEO TOLSTOY

herself, as if that was so incredible that he must understand the opposite.

At half-past eleven the celebrated specialist arrived. Again the sounding began and the significant conversations in his presence and in another room, about the kidneys and the appendix, and the questions and answers, with such an air of importance that again, instead of the real question of life and death which now alone confronted him, the question arose of the kidney and appendix which were not behaving as they ought to and would now be attacked by Michael Danílovich and the specialist and forced to amend their ways.

The celebrated specialist took leave of him with a serious though not hopeless look, and in reply to the timid question Iván Ilých, with eyes glistening with fear and hope, put to him as to whether there was a chance of recovery, said that he could not vouch for it but there was a possibility. The look of hope with which Iván Ilých watched the doctor out was so pathetic that Praskóvya Fëdorovna, seeing it, even wept as she left the room to hand the doctor his fee.

The gleam of hope kindled by the doctor's encouragement did not last long. The same room, the same pictures, curtains, wall-paper, medicine bottles, were all there, and the same aching suffering body, and Iván Ilých began to moan. They gave him a subcutaneous injection and he sank into oblivion.

It was twilight when he came to. They brought him his dinner and he swallowed some beef tea with difficulty, and then everything was the same again and night was coming on.

After dinner, at seven o'clock, Praskóvya Fëdorovna came into the room in evening dress, her full bosom pushed up by her corset, and with traces of powder on her face. She had reminded him in the morning that they were going to the theatre. Sarah Bernhardt [8] was visiting the town and they had a box, which he had insisted on their taking. Now he had forgotten about it and her toilet offended him, but he concealed his vexation when he remembered that he had himself insisted on their securing a box and going because it would be an instructive and aesthetic pleasure for the children.

Praskóvya Fëdorovna came in, self-satisfied but yet with a rather guilty air. She sat down and asked how he was but, as he saw, only for the sake of asking and not in order to learn about it, knowing that there was nothing to learn — and then went on to what she really wanted to say: that she would not on any account have gone but that the box had been taken and Helen and their daughter were going, as well as Petríshchev (the examining magistrate, their daughter's fiancé) and that it was out of the question to let them go alone; but that she would have much preferred to sit with him for a while; and he must be sure to follow the doctor's orders while she was away.

"Oh, and Fëdor Petróvich" (the fiancé) "would like to come in. May he? And Lisa?"

8. The famous French actress.

"All right."

Their daughter came in in full evening dress, her fresh young flesh exposed (making a show of that very flesh which in his own case caused so much suffering), strong, healthy, evidently in love, and impatient with illness, suffering, and death, because they interfered with her happiness.

Fëdor Petróvich came in too, in evening dress, his hair curled *à la Capoul*, a tight stiff collar round his long sinewy neck, an enormous white shirt-front and narrow black trousers tightly stretched over his strong thighs. He had one white glove tightly drawn on, and was holding his opera hat in his hand.

Following him the schoolboy crept in unnoticed, in a new uniform, poor little fellow, and wearing gloves. Terribly dark shadows showed under his eyes, the meaning of which Iván Ilých knew well.

His son had always seemed pathetic to him, and now it was dreadful to see the boy's frightened look of pity. It seemed to Iván Ilých that Vásya was the only one besides Gerásim who understood and pitied him.

They all sat down and again asked how he was. A silence followed. Lisa asked her mother about the opera-glasses, and there was an altercation between mother and daughter as to who had taken them and where they had been put. This occasioned some unpleasantness.

Fëdor Petróvich inquired of Iván Ilých whether he had ever seen Sarah Bernhardt. Iván Ilých did not at first catch the question, but then replied: "No, have you seen her before?"

"Yes, in *Adrienne Lecouvreur*." [9]

Praskóvya Fëdorovna mentioned some roles in which Sarah Bernhardt was particularly good. Her daughter disagreed. Conversation sprang up as to the elegance and realism of her acting — the sort of conversation that is always repeated and is always the same.

In the midst of the conversation Fëdor Petróvich glanced at Iván Ilých and became silent. The others also looked at him and grew silent. Iván Ilých was staring with glittering eyes straight before him, evidently indignant with them. This had to be rectified, but it was impossible to do so. The silence had to be broken, but for a time no one dared to break it and they all became afraid that the conventional deception would suddenly become obvious and the truth become plain to all. Lisa was the first to pluck up courage and break that silence, but by trying to hide what everybody was feeling, she betrayed it.

"Well, if we are going it's time to start," she said, looking at her watch, a present from her father, and with a faint and significant smile at Fëdor Petróvich relating to something known only to them. She got up with a rustle of her dress.

They all rose, said good-night, and went away.

When they had gone it seemed to Iván Ilých that he felt better; the

9. Written in collaboration by the French dramatists Legouvé and Scribe, whom Tolstoy also scorned.

falsity had gone with them. But the pain remained — that same pain and that same fear that made everything monotonously alike, nothing harder and nothing easier. Everything was worse.

Again minute followed minute and hour followed hour. Everything remained the same and there was no cessation. And the inevitable end of it all became more and more terrible.

"Yes, send Gerásim here," he replied to a question Peter asked.

IX

His wife returned late at night. She came in on tiptoe, but he heard her, opened his eyes, and made haste to close them again. She wished to send Gerásim away and to sit with him herself, but he opened his eyes and said: "No, go away."

"Are you in great pain?"

"Always the same."

"Take some opium."

He agreed and took some. She went away.

Till about three in the morning he was in a state of stupefied misery. It seemed to him that he and his pain were being thrust into a narrow, deep black sack, but though they were pushed further and further in they could not be pushed to the bottom. And this, terrible enough in itself, was accompanied by suffering. He was frightened yet wanted to fall through the sack, he struggled but yet co-operated. And suddenly he broke through, fell, and regained consciousness. Gerásim was sitting at the foot of the bed dozing quietly and patiently, while he himself lay with his emaciated stockinged legs resting on Gerásim's shoulders; the same shaded candle was there and the same unceasing pain.

"Go away, Gerásim," he whispered.

"It's all right, sir. I'll stay a while."

"No. Go away."

He removed his legs from Gerásim's shoulders, turned sideways onto his arm, and felt sorry for himself. He only waited till Gerásim had gone into the next room and then restrained himself no longer but wept like a child. He wept on account of his helplessness, his terrible loneliness, the cruelty of man, the cruelty of God, and the absence of God.

"Why hast Thou done all this? Why hast Thou brought me here? Why, why dost Thou torment me so terribly?"

He did not expect an answer and yet wept because there was no answer and could be none. The pain again grew more acute, but he did not stir and did not call. He said to himself: "Go on! Strike me! But what is it for? What have I done to Thee? What is it for?"

Then he grew quiet and not only ceased weeping but even held his breath and became all attention. It was as though he were listening not to an audible voice but to the voice of his soul, to the current of thoughts arising within him.

"What is it you want?" was the first clear conception capable of expression in words, that he heard.

"What do you want? What do you want?" he repeated to himself. "What do I want? To live and not to suffer," he answered.

And again he listened with such concentrated attention that even his pain did not distract him.

"To live? How?" asked his inner voice.

"Why, to live as I used to — well and pleasantly."

"As you lived before, well and pleasantly?" the voice repeated.

And in imagination he began to recall the best moments of his pleasant life. But strange to say none of these best moments of his pleasant life now seemed at all what they had then seemed — none of them except the first recollections of childhood. There, in childhood, there had been something really pleasant with which it would be possible to live if it could return. But the child who had experienced that happiness existed no longer, it was like a reminiscence of somebody else.

As soon as the period began which had produced the present Iván Ilých, all that had then seemed joys now melted before his sight and turned into something trivial and often nasty.

And the further he departed from childhood and the nearer he came to the present the more worthless and doubtful were the joys. This began with the School of Law. A little that was really good was still found there — there was light-heartedness, friendship, and hope. But in the upper classes there had already been fewer of such good moments. Then during the first years of his official career, when he was in the service of the Governor, some pleasant moments again occurred: they were the memories of love for a woman. Then all became confused and there was still less of what was good; later on again there was still less that was good, and the further he went the less there was. His marriage, a mere accident, then the disenchantment that followed it, his wife's bad breath and the sensuality and hypocrisy: then that deadly official life and those preoccupations about money, a year of it, and two, and ten, and twenty, and always the same thing. And the longer it lasted the more deadly it became. "It is as if I had been going downhill while I imagined I was going up. And that is really what it was. I was going up in public opinion, but to the same extent life was ebbing away from me. And now it is all done and there is only death."

"Then what does it mean? Why? It can't be that life is so senseless and horrible. But if it really has been so horrible and senseless, why must I die and die in agony? There is something wrong!"

"Maybe I did not live as I ought to have done," it suddenly occurred to him. "But how could that be, when I did everything properly?" he replied, and immediately dismissed from his mind this, the sole solution of all the riddles of life and death, as something quite impossible.

"Then what do you want now? To live? Live how? Live as you lived in the law courts when the usher proclaimed 'The judge is coming!'

The judge is coming, the judge!" he repeated to himself. "Here he is, the judge. But I am not guilty!" he exclaimed angrily. "What is it for?" And he ceased crying, but turning his face to the wall continued to ponder on the same question: Why, and for what purpose, is there all this horror? But however much he pondered he found no answer. And whenever the thought occurred to him, as it often did, that it all resulted from his not having lived as he ought to have done, he at once recalled the correctness of his whole life and dismissed so strange an idea.

X

Another fortnight passed. Iván Ilých now no longer left his sofa. He would not lie in bed but lay on the sofa, facing the wall nearly all the time. He suffered ever the same unceasing agonies and in his loneliness pondered always on the same insoluble question: "What is this? Can it be that it is Death?" And the inner voice answered: "Yes, it is Death."

"Why these sufferings?" And the voice answered, "For no reason — they just are so." Beyond and besides this there was nothing.

From the very beginning of his illness, ever since he had first been to see the doctor, Iván Ilých's life had been divided between two contrary and alternating moods: now it was despair and the expectation of this uncomprehended and terrible death, and now hope and an intently interested observation of the functioning of his organs. Now before his eyes there was only a kidney or an intestine that temporarily evaded its duty, and now only that incomprehensible and dreadful death from which it was impossible to escape.

These two states of mind had alternated from the very beginning of his illness, but the further it progressed the more doubtful and fantastic became the conception of the kidney, and the more real the sense of impending death.

He had but to call to mind what he had been three months before and what he was now, to call to mind with what regularity he had been going downhill, for every possibility of hope to be shattered.

Latterly during that loneliness in which he found himself as he lay facing the back of the sofa, a loneliness in the midst of a populous town and surrounded by numerous acquaintances and relations but that yet could not have been more complete anywhere — either at the bottom of the sea or under the earth — during that terrible loneliness Iván Ilých had lived only in memories of the past. Pictures of his past rose before him one after another. They always began with what was nearest in time and then went back to what was most remote — to his childhood — and rested there. If he thought of the stewed prunes that had been offered him that day, his mind went back to the raw shrivelled French plums of his childhood, their peculiar flavour and the flow of saliva when he sucked their stones, and along with the memory of that taste came a whole series of memories of those days: his nurse, his brother, and their toys. "No, I mustn't think of that. . . . It is too painful," Iván Ilých said to himself, and brought himself back to the present — to the button on the back of the sofa and the creases in its morocco. "Morocco is expensive, but it does not wear well: there had been a quarrel about it. It was a different kind of quarrel and a different kind of morocco that time when we tore father's portfolio and were punished, and mamma brought us some tarts. . . ." And again his thoughts dwelt on his childhood, and again it was painful and he tried to banish them and fix his mind on something else.

Then again together with that chain of memories another series passed through his mind — of how his illness had progressed and grown worse. There also the further back he looked the more life there had been. There had been more of what was good in life and more of life itself. The two merged together. "Just as the pain went on getting worse and worse so my life grew worse and worse," he thought. "There is one bright spot there at the back, at the beginning of life, and afterwards all becomes blacker and blacker and proceeds more and more rapidly — in inverse ratio to the square of the distance from death," thought Iván Ilých. And the example of a stone falling downwards with increasing velocity entered his mind. Life, a series of increasing sufferings, flies further and further towards its end — the most terrible suffering. "I am flying. . . ." He shuddered, shifted himself, and tried to resist, but was already aware that resistance was impossible, and again with eyes weary of gazing but unable to cease seeing what was before them, he stared at the back of the sofa and waited — awaiting that dreadful fall and shock and destruction.

"Resistance is impossible!" he said to himself. "If I could only understand what it is all for! But that too is impossible. An explanation would be possible if it could be said that I have not lived as I ought to. But it is impossible to say that," and he remembered all the legality, correctitude, and propriety of his life. "That at any rate can certainly not be admitted," he thought, and his lips smiled ironically as if some-one could see that smile and be taken in by it. "There is no explanation! Agony, death. . . . What for?"

XI

Another two weeks went by in this way and during that fortnight an event occurred that Iván Ilých and his wife had desired. Petrísh-chev formally proposed. It happened in the evening. The next day Praskóvya Fëdorovna came into her husband's room considering how best to inform him of it, but that very night there had been a fresh change for the worse in his condition. She found him still lying on the sofa but in a different position. He lay on his back, groaning and star-ing fixedly straight in front of him.

She began to remind him of his medicines, but he turned his eyes towards her with such a look that she did not finish what she was saying; so great an animosity, to her in particular, did that look express.

"For Christ's sake let me die in peace!" he said.

She would have gone away, but just then their daughter came in and went up to say good morning. He looked at her as he had done at his wife, and in reply to her inquiry about his health said dryly that he would soon free them all of himself. They were both silent and after sitting with him for a while went away.

"Is it our fault?" Lisa said to her mother. "It's as if we were to blame! I am sorry for papa, but why should we be tortured?"

The doctor came at his usual time. Iván Ilých answered "Yes" and "No," never taking his angry eyes from him, and at last said: "You know you can do nothing for me, so leave me alone."

"We can ease your sufferings."

"You can't even do that. Let me be."

The doctor went into the drawing-room and told Praskóvya Fëdorovna that the case was very serious and that the only resource left was opium to allay her husband's sufferings, which must be terrible.

It was true, as the doctor said, that Iván Ilých's physical sufferings were terrible, but worse than the physical sufferings were his mental sufferings which were his chief torture.

His mental sufferings were due to the fact that that night, as he looked at Gerásim's sleepy, good-natured face with its prominent cheekbones, the question suddenly occurred to him: "What if my whole life has really been wrong?"

It occurred to him that what had appeared perfectly impossible before, namely that he had not spent his life as he should have done, might after all be true. It occurred to him that his scarcely perceptible attempts to struggle against what was considered good by the most highly placed people, those scarcely noticeable impulses which he had immediately suppressed, might have been the real thing, and all the rest false. And his professional duties and the whole arrangement of his life and of his family, and all his social and official interests, might all have been false. He tried to defend all those things to himself and suddenly felt the weakness of what he was defending. There was nothing to defend.

"But if that is so," he said to himself, "and I am leaving this life with the consciousness that I have lost all that was given me and it is impossible to rectify it — what then?"

He lay on his back and began to pass his life in review in quite a new way. In the morning when he saw first his footman, then his wife, then his daughter, and then the doctor, their every word and movement confirmed to him the awful truth that had been revealed to him during the night. In them he saw himself — all that for which he had lived — and saw clearly that it was not real at all, but a terrible and huge deception which had hidden both life and death. This consciousness intensified his physical suffering tenfold. He groaned and tossed about, and pulled at his clothing which choked and stifled him. And he hated them on that account.

He was given a large dose of opium and became unconscious, but at noon his sufferings began again. He drove everybody away and tossed from side to side.

His wife came to him and said:

"Jean, my dear, do this for me. It can't do any harm and often helps. Healthy people often do it."

He opened his eyes wide.

"What? Take communion? Why? It's unnecessary! However. . . ."

She began to cry.

"Yes, do, my dear. I'll send for our priest. He is such a nice man."

"All right. Very well," he muttered.

When the priest came and heard his confession, Iván Ilých was softened and seemed to feel a relief from his doubts and consequently from his sufferings, and for a moment there came a ray of hope. He again began to think of the vermiform appendix and the possibility of correcting it. He received the sacrament with tears in his eyes.

When they laid him down again afterwards he felt a moment's ease, and the hope that he might live awoke in him again. He began to think of the operation that had been suggested to him. "To live! I want to live!" he said to himself.

His wife came in to congratulate him after his communion, and when uttering the usual conventional words she added:

"You feel better, don't you?"

Without looking at her he said "Yes."

Her dress, her figure, the expression of her face, the tone of her voice, all revealed the same thing. "This is wrong, it is not as it should be. All you have lived for and still live for is falsehood and deception, hiding life and death from you." And as soon as he admitted that thought, his hatred and his agonizing physical suffering again sprang up, and with that suffering a consciousness of the unavoidable, approaching end. And to this was added a new sensation of grinding shooting pain and a feeling of suffocation.

The expression of his face when he uttered that "yes" was dreadful. Having uttered it, he looked her straight in the eyes, turned on his face with a rapidity extraordinary in his weak state and shouted:

"Go away! Go away and leave me alone!"

XII

From that moment the screaming began that continued for three days, and was so terrible that one could not hear it through two closed doors without horror. At the moment he answered his wife he realized that he was lost, that there was no return, that the end had come, the very end, and his doubts were still unsolved and remained doubts.

"Oh! Oh! Oh!" he cried in various intonations. He had begun by screaming "I won't!" and continued screaming on the letter "o."

For three whole days, during which time did not exist for him, he struggled in that black sack into which he was being thrust by an invisible, resistless force. He struggled as a man condemned to death struggles in the hands of the executioner, knowing that he cannot save himself. And every moment he felt that despite all his efforts he was drawing nearer and nearer to what terrified him. He felt that his agony was due to his being thrust into that black hole and still more to his not being able to get right into it. He was hindered from getting into it by his conviction that his life had been a good one. That very justification of his life held him fast and prevented his moving forward, and it caused him most torment of all.

Suddenly some force struck him in the chest and side, making it still harder to breathe, and he fell through the hole and there at the bottom was a light. What had happened to him was like the sensation one sometimes experiences in a railway carriage when one thinks one is going backwards while one is really going forwards and suddenly becomes aware of the real direction.

"Yes, it was all not the right thing," he said to himself, "but that's no matter. It can be done. But what *is* the right thing?" he asked himself, and suddenly grew quiet.

This occurred at the end of the third day, two hours before his death. Just then his schoolboy son had crept softly in and gone up to the bedside. The dying man was still screaming desperately and waving his arms. His hand fell on the boy's head, and the boy caught it, pressed it to his lips, and began to cry.

At that very moment Iván Ilých fell through and caught sight of the light, and it was revealed to him that though his life had not been what it should have been, this could still be rectified. He asked himself, "What *is* the right thing?" and grew still, listening. Then he felt that someone was kissing his hand. He opened his eyes, looked at his son, and felt sorry for him. His wife came up to him and he glanced at her. She was gazing at him open-mouthed, with undried tears on her nose and cheek and a despairing look on her face. He felt sorry for her too.

"Yes, I am making them wretched," he thought. "They are sorry, but it will be better for them when I die." He wished to say this but had not the strength to utter it. "Besides, why speak? I must act," he thought. With a look at his wife he indicated his son and said: "Take him away . . . sorry for him . . . sorry for you too. . . ." He tried to add, "forgive me," but said "forego" and waved his hand, knowing that He whose understanding mattered would understand.

And suddenly it grew clear to him that what had been oppressing him and would not leave him was all dropping away at once from two sides, from ten sides, and from all sides. He was sorry for them, he must act so as not to hurt them: release them and free himself from these sufferings. "How good and how simple!" he thought. "And the pain?" he asked himself. "What has become of it? Where are you, pain?"

He turned his attention to it.

"Yes, here it is. Well, what of it? Let the pain be."

"And death . . . where is it?"

He sought his former accustomed fear of death and did not find it. "Where is it? What death?" There was no fear because there was no death.

In place of death there was light.

"So that's what it is!" he suddenly exclaimed aloud. "What joy!"

To him all this happened in a single instant, and the meaning of that instant did not change. For those present his agony continued for another two hours. Something rattled in his throat, his emaciated body twitched, then the gasping and rattle became less and less frequent.

"It is finished!" said someone near him.

He heard these words and repeated them in his soul.

"Death is finished," he said to himself. "It is no more!"

He drew in a breath, stopped in the midst of a sigh, stretched out, and died.

Henrik Ibsen (1828–1906)

LIFE: Born in Skien, Norway, he was apprenticed, after his father went bankrupt, to a pharmacist in the small town of Grimstad, where he lived in isolation for six years, alienated from his family and the world. This early separation outlined the pattern of his life. After a brief career as the Artistic Director of a theater in Oslo, he quit Norway in 1864, in disgust over its policy toward Denmark in the war with Germany, and began his wanderings through Europe. He lived in Rome, Dresden, and Munich, and did not return permanently to his native country until 1891. He never fully recovered from the stroke he suffered in 1900: yet another exile to round off his life.

WORKS: *Peer Gynt* (1867); *A Doll's House* (1879); *Ghosts* (1881); *An Enemy of the People* (1882); *The Wild Duck* (1884); *Rosmersholm* (1886); *Hedda Gabler* (1890); *The Master Builder* (1892); *Little Eyolf* (1894); *When We Dead Awaken* (1899).

HEDDA GABLER *

CHARACTERS

GEORGE TESMAN, *research graduate, in cultural history*

HEDDA, *his wife*

MISS JULIANA TESMAN, *his aunt*

From *Hedda Gabler and Three Other Plays* by Henrik Ibsen, translated by Michael Meyer. Copyright © 1961 by Michael Meyer. Reprinted by permission of Doubleday & Company, Inc.

* Written in 1890.

MRS. ELVSTED
JUDGE BRACK
EILERT LOEVBORG
BERTHA, *a maid*

The action takes place in TESMAN'S *villa in the fashionable quarter of town.*

ACT I

A large drawing room, handsomely and tastefully furnished; decorated in dark colours. In the rear wall is a broad open doorway, with curtains drawn back to either side. It leads to a smaller room, decorated in the same style as the drawing room. In the right-hand wall of the drawing room, a folding door leads out to the hall. The opposite wall, on the left, contains french windows, also with curtains drawn back on either side. Through the glass we can see part of a verandah, and trees in autumn colours. Downstage stands an oval table, covered by a cloth and surrounded by chairs. Downstage right, against the wall, is a broad stove tiled with dark porcelain; in front of it stand a high-backed armchair, a cushioned footrest, and two footstools. Upstage right, in an alcove, is a corner sofa, with a small, round table. Downstage left, a little away from the wall, is another sofa. Upstage of the french windows, a piano. On either side of the open doorway in the rear wall stand what-nots holding ornaments of terra cotta and majolica. Against the rear wall of the smaller room can be seen a sofa, a table, and a couple of chairs. Above this sofa hangs the portrait of a handsome old man in general's uniform. Above the table a lamp hangs from the ceiling, with a shade of opalescent, milky glass. All round the drawing room bunches of flowers stand in vases and glasses. More bunches lie on the tables. The floors of both rooms are covered with thick carpets. Morning light. The sun shines in through the french windows.

MISS JULIANA TESMAN, *wearing a hat and carrying a parasol, enters from the hall, followed by* BERTHA, *who is carrying a bunch of flowers wrapped in paper.* MISS TESMAN *is about sixty-five, of pleasant and kindly appearance. She is neatly but simply dressed in grey outdoor clothes.* BERTHA, *the maid, is rather simple and rustic-looking. She is getting on in years.*

MISS TESMAN *stops just inside the door, listens, and says in a hushed voice.* No, bless my soul! They're not up yet.

BERTHA, *also in hushed tones.* What did I tell you, miss? The boat didn't get in till midnight. And when they did turn up — Jesus, miss, you should have seen all the things Madam made me unpack before she'd go to bed!

MISS TESMAN. Ah, well. Let them have a good lie in. But let's have some nice fresh air waiting for them when they do come down.

Goes to the french windows and throws them wide open.

BERTHA, *bewildered at the table, the bunch of flowers in her hand.* I'm blessed if there's a square inch left to put anything. I'll have to let it lie here, miss.

Puts it on the piano.

MISS TESMAN. Well, Bertha dear, so now you have a new mistress. Heaven knows it nearly broke my heart to have to part with you.

BERTHA *snivels.* What about me, Miss Juju? How do you suppose I felt? After all the happy years I've spent with you and Miss Rena?

MISS TESMAN. We must accept it bravely, Bertha. It was the only way. George needs you to take care of him. He could never manage without you. You've looked after him ever since he was a tiny boy.

BERTHA. Oh, but, Miss Juju, I can't help thinking about Miss Rena, lying there all helpless, poor dear. And that new girl! She'll never learn the proper way to handle an invalid.

MISS TESMAN. Oh, I'll manage to train her. I'll do most of the work myself, you know. You needn't worry about my poor sister, Bertha dear.

BERTHA. But Miss Juju, there's another thing. I'm frightened Madam may not find me suitable.

MISS TESMAN. Oh, nonsense, Bertha. There may be one or two little things to begin with —

BERTHA. She's a real lady. Wants everything just so.

MISS TESMAN. But of course she does! General Gabler's daughter! Think of what she was accustomed to when the General was alive. You remember how we used to see her out riding with her father? In that long black skirt? With the feather in her hat?

BERTHA. Oh, yes, miss. As if I could forget! But, Lord! I never dreamed I'd live to see a match between her and Master Georgie.

MISS TESMAN. Neither did I. By the way, Bertha, from now on you must stop calling him Master Georgie. You must say: Dr. Tesman.

BERTHA. Yes, Madam said something about that too. Last night — the moment they'd set foot inside the door. Is it true, then, miss?

MISS TESMAN. Indeed it is. Just imagine, Bertha, some foreigners have made him a doctor. It happened while they were away. I had no idea till he told me when they got off the boat.

BERTHA. Well, I suppose there's no limit to what he won't become. He's that clever. I never thought he'd go in for hospital work, though.

MISS TESMAN. No, he's not that kind of doctor.

Nods impressively.

In any case, you may soon have to address him by an even grander title.

BERTHA. You don't say! What might that be, miss?

MISS TESMAN *smiles.* Ah! If you only knew!

Moved.

Dear God, if only poor dear Joachim could rise out of his grave and see what his little son has grown into!

Looks round.

But Bertha, why have you done this? Taken the chintz covers off all the furniture!

BERTHA. Madam said I was to. Can't stand chintz covers on chairs, she said.

MISS TESMAN. But surely they're not going to use this room as a parlour?

BERTHA. So I gathered, miss. From what Madam said. He didn't say anything. The Doctor.

GEORGE TESMAN *comes into the rear room, from the right, humming, with an open, empty travelling bag in his hand. He is about thirty-three, of medium height and youthful appearance, rather plump, with an open, round, contented face, and fair hair and beard. He wears spectacles, and is dressed in comfortable, indoor clothes.*

MISS TESMAN. Good morning! Good morning, George!

TESMAN, *in open doorway.* Auntie Juju! Dear Auntie Juju!

Comes forward and shakes her hand.

You've come all the way out here! And so early! What?

MISS TESMAN. Well, I had to make sure you'd settled in comfortably.

TESMAN. But you can't have had a proper night's sleep.

MISS TESMAN. Oh, never mind that.

TESMAN. We were so sorry we couldn't give you a lift. But you saw how it was — Hedda had so much luggage — and she insisted on having it all with her.

MISS TESMAN. Yes, I've never seen so much luggage.

BERTHA, *to* TESMAN. Shall I go and ask Madam if there's anything I can lend her a hand with?

TESMAN. Er — thank you, Bertha; no, you needn't bother. She says if she wants you for anything she'll ring.

BERTHA, *over to right.* Oh. Very good.

TESMAN. Oh, Bertha — take this bag, will you?

BERTHA *takes it.* I'll put it in the attic.

Goes out into the hall.

TESMAN. Just fancy, Auntie Juju, I filled that whole bag with notes for my book. You know, it's really incredible what I've managed to find rooting through those archives. By Jove! Wonderful old things no one even knew existed —

MISS TESMAN. I'm sure you didn't waste a single moment of your honeymoon, George dear.

TESMAN. No, I think I can truthfully claim that. But, Auntie Juju, do take your hat off. Here. Let me untie it for you. What?

MISS TESMAN, *as he does so.* Oh dear, oh dear! It's just as if you were still living at home with us.

TESMAN *turns the hat in his hand and looks at it.* I say! What a splendid new hat!

MISS TESMAN. I bought it for Hedda's sake.

TESMAN. For Hedda's sake? What?

MISS TESMAN. So that Hedda needn't be ashamed of me, in case we ever go for a walk together.

TESMAN *pats her cheek.* You still think of everything, don't you, Auntie Juju?

Puts the hat down on a chair by the table.

Come on, let's sit down here on the sofa. And have a little chat while we wait for Hedda.

They sit. She puts her parasol in the corner of the sofa.

MISS TESMAN *clasps both his hands and looks at him.* Oh, George, it's so wonderful to have you back, and be able to see you with my own eyes again! Poor dear Joachim's own son!

TESMAN. What about me! It's wonderful for me to see you again, Auntie Juju. You've been a mother to me. And a father, too.

MISS TESMAN. You'll always keep a soft spot in your heart for your old aunties, won't you, George dear?

TESMAN. I suppose Auntie Rena's no better? What?

MISS TESMAN. Alas, no. I'm afraid she'll never get better, poor dear. She's lying there just as she has for all these years. Please God I may be allowed to keep her for a little longer. If I lost her I don't know what I'd do. Especially now I haven't you to look after.

TESMAN *pats her on the back.* There, there, there!

MISS TESMAN, *with a sudden change of mood.* Oh but George, fancy you being a married man! And to think it's you who've won Hedda Gabler! The beautiful Hedda Gabler! Fancy! She was always so surrounded by admirers.

TESMAN *hums a little and smiles contentedly.* Yes, I suppose there are quite a few people in this town who wouldn't mind being in my shoes. What?

MISS TESMAN. And what a honeymoon! Five months! Nearly six.

TESMAN. Well, I've done a lot of work, you know. All those archives to go through. And I've had to read lots of books.

MISS TESMAN. Yes, dear, of course.

Lowers her voice confidentially.

But tell me, George — haven't you any — any extra little piece of news to give me?

TESMAN. You mean, arising out of the honeymoon?

MISS TESMAN. Yes.

TESMAN. No, I don't think there's anything I didn't tell you in my letters. My doctorate, of course — but I told you about that last night, didn't I?

MISS TESMAN. Yes, yes, I didn't mean that kind of thing. I was just wondering — are you — are you expecting — ?

TESMAN. Expecting what?

MISS TESMAN. Oh, come on, George, I'm your old aunt!

TESMAN. Well actually — yes, I am expecting something.

MISS TESMAN. I knew it!

TESMAN. You'll be happy to hear that before very long I expect to become a professor.

MISS TESMAN. Professor?

TESMAN. I think I may say that the matter has been decided. But, Auntie Juju, you know about this.

MISS TESMAN *gives a little laugh*. Yes, of course. I'd forgotten.

Changes her tone.

But we were talking about your honeymoon. It must have cost a dreadful amount of money, George?

TESMAN. Oh well, you know, that big research grant I got helped a good deal.

MISS TESMAN. But how on earth did you manage to make it do for two?

TESMAN. Well, to tell the truth it was a bit tricky. What?

MISS TESMAN. Especially when one's travelling with a lady. A little bird tells me that makes things very much more expensive.

TESMAN. Well, yes, of course it does make things a little more expensive. But Hedda has to do things in style, Auntie Juju. I mean, she has to. Anything less grand wouldn't have suited her.

MISS TESMAN. No, no, I suppose not. A honeymoon abroad seems to be the vogue nowadays. But tell me, have you had time to look round the house?

TESMAN. You bet. I've been up since the crack of dawn.

MISS TESMAN. Well, what do you think of it?

TESMAN. Splendid. Absolutely splendid. I'm only wondering what we're going to do with those two empty rooms between that little one and Hedda's bedroom.

MISS TESMAN *laughs slyly*. Ah, George dear, I'm sure you'll manage to find some use for them — in time.

TESMAN. Yes, of course, Auntie Juju, how stupid of me. You're thinking of my books. What?

MISS TESMAN. Yes, yes, dear boy. I was thinking of your books.

TESMAN. You know, I'm so happy for Hedda's sake that we've managed to get this house. Before we became engaged she often used to say this was the only house in town she felt she could really bear to live in. It used to belong to Mrs. Falk — you know, the Prime Minister's widow.

MISS TESMAN. Fancy that! And what a stroke of luck it happened to come into the market. Just as you'd left on your honeymoon.

TESMAN. Yes, Auntie Juju, we've certainly had all the luck with us. What?

MISS TESMAN. But, George dear, the expense! It's going to make a dreadful hole in your pocket, all this.

TESMAN, *a little downcast*. Yes, I — I suppose it will, won't it?

MISS TESMAN. Oh, George, really!

TESMAN. How much do you think it'll cost? Roughly, I mean? What?

MISS TESMAN. I can't possibly say till I see the bills.

TESMAN. Well, luckily Judge Brack's managed to get it on very favourable terms. He wrote and told Hedda so.

MISS TESMAN. Don't you worry, George dear. Anyway I've stood security for all the furniture and carpets.

TESMAN. Security? But dear, sweet Auntie Juju, how could you possibly stand security?

MISS TESMAN. I've arranged a mortgage on our annuity.

TESMAN *jumps up.* What? On your annuity? And — Auntie Rena's?

MISS TESMAN. Yes. Well, I couldn't think of any other way.

TESMAN *stands in front of her.* Auntie Juju, have you gone completely out of your mind? That annuity's all you and Auntie Rena have.

MISS TESMAN. All right, there's no need to get so excited about it. It's a pure formality, you know. Judge Brack told me so. He was so kind as to arrange it all for me. A pure formality; those were his very words.

TESMAN. I dare say. All the same —

MISS TESMAN. Anyway, you'll have a salary of your own now. And, good heavens, even if we did have to fork out a little — tighten our belts for a week or two — why, we'd be happy to do so for your sake.

TESMAN. Oh, Auntie Juju! Will you never stop sacrificing yourself for me?

MISS TESMAN *gets up and puts her hands on his shoulders.* What else have I to live for but to smooth your road a little, my dear boy? You've never had any mother or father to turn to. And now at last we've achieved our goal. I won't deny we've had our little difficulties now and then. But now, thank the good Lord, George dear, all your worries are past.

TESMAN. Yes, it's wonderful really how everything's gone just right for me.

MISS TESMAN. Yes! And the enemies who tried to bar your way have been struck down. They have been made to bite the dust. The man who was your most dangerous rival has had the mightiest fall. And now he's lying there in the pit he dug for himself, poor misguided creature.

TESMAN. Have you heard any news of Eilert? Since I went away?

MISS TESMAN. Only that he's said to have published a new book.

TESMAN. What! Eilert Loevborg? You mean — just recently? What?

MISS TESMAN. So they say. I don't imagine it can be of any value, do you? When your new book comes out, that'll be another story. What's it going to be about?

TESMAN. The domestic industries of Brabant in the Middle Ages.

MISS TESMAN. Oh, George! The things you know about!

TESMAN. Mind you, it may be some time before I actually get down to writing it. I've made these very extensive notes, and I've got to file and index them first.

MISS TESMAN. Ah, yes! Making notes; filing and indexing; you've always been wonderful at that. Poor dear Joachim was just the same.

TESMAN. I'm looking forward so much to getting down to that. Especially now I've a home of my own to work in.

MISS TESMAN. And above all, now that you have the girl you set your heart on, George dear.

TESMAN *embraces her.* Oh, yes, Auntie Juju, yes! Hedda's the loveliest thing of all!

Looks towards the doorway.

I think I hear her coming. What?

HEDDA *enters the rear room from the left, and comes into the drawing room. She is a woman of twenty-nine. Distinguished, aristocratic face and figure. Her complexion is pale and opalescent. Her eyes are steel-grey, with an expression of cold, calm serenity. Her hair is of a handsome auburn colour, but is not especially abundant. She is dressed in an elegant, somewhat loose-fitting morning gown.*

MISS TESMAN *goes to greet her.* Good morning, Hedda dear! Good morning!

HEDDA *holds out her hand.* Good morning, dear Miss Tesman. What an early hour to call. So kind of you.

MISS TESMAN *seems somewhat embarrassed.* And has the young bride slept well in her new home?

HEDDA. Oh — thank you, yes. Passably well.

TESMAN *laughs.* Passably. I say, Hedda, that's good! When I jumped out of bed, you were sleeping like a top.

HEDDA. Yes. Fortunately. One has to accustom oneself to anything new, Miss Tesman. It takes time.

Looks left.

Oh, that maid's left the french windows open. This room's flooded with sun.

MISS TESMAN *goes towards the windows.* Oh — let me close them.

HEDDA. No, no, don't do that. Tesman dear, draw the curtains. This light's blinding me.

TESMAN, *at the windows.* Yes, yes, dear. There, Hedda, now you've got shade and fresh air.

HEDDA. This room needs fresh air. All these flowers — But my dear Miss Tesman, won't you take a seat?

MISS TESMAN. No, really not, thank you. I just wanted to make sure you have everything you need. I must see about getting back home. My poor dear sister will be waiting for me.

TESMAN. Be sure to give her my love, won't you? Tell her I'll run over and see her later today.

MISS TESMAN. Oh yes, I'll tell her that. Oh, George —

Fumbles in the pocket of her skirt.

I almost forgot. I've brought something for you.

TESMAN. What's that, Auntie Juju? What?

MISS TESMAN *pulls out a flat package wrapped in newspaper and gives it to him.* Open and see, dear boy.

TESMAN *opens the package.* Good heavens! Auntie Juju, you've kept them! Hedda, this is really very touching. What?

HEDDA, *by the what-nots, on the right.* What is it, Tesman?

TESMAN. My old shoes! My slippers, Hedda!

HEDDA. Oh, them. I remember you kept talking about them on our honeymoon.

TESMAN. Yes, I missed them dreadfully.

Goes over to her.

Here, Hedda, take a look.

HEDDA *goes away towards the stove.* Thanks, I won't bother.

TESMAN *follows her.* Fancy, Hedda, Auntie Rena's embroidered them for me. Despite her being so ill. Oh, you can't imagine what memories they have for me.

HEDDA, *by the table.* Not for me.

MISS TESMAN. No, Hedda's right there, George.

TESMAN. Yes, but I thought since she's one of the family now —

HEDDA *interrupts.* Tesman, we really can't go on keeping this maid.

MISS TESMAN. Not keep Bertha?

TESMAN. What makes you say that, dear? What?

HEDDA *points.* Look at that! She's left her old hat lying on the chair.

TESMAN, *appalled, drops his slippers on the floor.* But, Hedda — !

HEDDA. Suppose someone came in and saw it?

TESMAN. But Hedda — that's Auntie Juju's hat.

HEDDA. Oh?

MISS TESMAN *picks up the hat.* Indeed it's mine. And it doesn't happen to be old, Hedda dear.

HEDDA. I didn't look at it very closely, Miss Tesman.

MISS TESMAN, *tying on the hat.* As a matter of fact, it's the first time I've worn it. As the good Lord is my witness.

TESMAN. It's very pretty, too. Really smart.

MISS TESMAN. Oh, I'm afraid it's nothing much really.

Looks round.

My parasol? Ah, here it is.

Takes it.

This is mine, too.

Murmurs.

Not Bertha's.

TESMAN. A new hat and a new parasol! I say, Hedda, fancy that!

HEDDA. Very pretty and charming.

TESMAN. Yes, isn't it? What? But Auntie Juju, take a good look at Hedda before you go. Isn't she pretty and charming?

MISS TESMAN. Dear boy, there's nothing new in that. Hedda's been a beauty ever since the day she was born.

Nods and goes right.

TESMAN *follows her.* Yes, but have you noticed how strong and healthy she's looking? And how she's filled out since we went away?

MISS TESMAN *stops and turns.* Filled out?

HEDDA *walks across the room.* Oh, can't we forget it?

TESMAN. Yes, Auntie Juju — you can't see it so clearly with that dress on. But I've good reason to know —

HEDDA, *by the french windows, impatiently.* You haven't good reason to know anything.

TESMAN. It must have been the mountain air up there in the Tyrol —

HEDDA, *curtly, interrupts him.* I'm exactly the same as when I went away.

TESMAN. You keep on saying so. But you're not. I'm right, aren't I, Auntie Juju?

MISS TESMAN *has folded her hands and is gazing at her.* She's beautiful — beautiful. Hedda is beautiful.

Goes over to HEDDA, *takes her head between her hands, draws it down and kisses her hair.*

God bless and keep you, Hedda Tesman. For George's sake.

HEDDA *frees herself politely.* Oh — let me go, please.

MISS TESMAN, *quietly, emotionally.* I shall come and see you both every day.

TESMAN. Yes, Auntie Juju, please do. What?

MISS TESMAN. Good-bye! Good-bye!

She goes out into the hall. TESMAN *follows her. The door remains open,* TESMAN *is heard sending his love to* AUNT RENA *and thanking* MISS TESMAN *for his slippers. Meanwhile* HEDDA *walks up and down the room raising her arms and clenching her fists as though in desperation. Then she throws aside the curtains from the french windows and stands there, looking out. A few moments later,* TESMAN *returns and closes the door behind him.*

TESMAN *picks up his slippers from the floor.* What are you looking at, Hedda?

HEDDA, *calm and controlled again.* Only the leaves. They're so golden. And withered.

TESMAN *wraps up the slippers and lays them on the table.* Well, we're in September now.

HEDDA, *restless again.* Yes. We're already into September.

TESMAN. Auntie Juju was behaving rather oddly, I thought, didn't you? Almost as though she was in church or something. I wonder what came over her. Any idea?

HEDDA. I hardly know her. Does she often act like that?

TESMAN. Not to the extent she did today.

HEDDA *goes away from the french windows.* Do you think she was hurt by what I said about the hat?

TESMAN. Oh, I don't think so. A little at first, perhaps —

HEDDA. But what a thing to do, throw her hat down in someone's drawing room. People don't do such things.

TESMAN. I'm sure Auntie Juju doesn't do it very often.

HEDDA. Oh well, I'll make it up with her.

TESMAN. Oh Hedda, would you?

HEDDA. When you see them this afternoon invite her to come out here this evening.

TESMAN. You bet I will! I say, there's another thing which would please her enormously.

HEDDA. Oh?

TESMAN. If you could bring yourself to call her Auntie Juju. For my sake, Hedda? What?

HEDDA. Oh no, really, Tesman, you mustn't ask me to do that. I've told you so once before. I'll try to call her Aunt Juliana. That's as far as I'll go.

TESMAN, *after a moment.* I say, Hedda, is anything wrong? What?

HEDDA. I'm just looking at my old piano. It doesn't really go with all this.

TESMAN. As soon as I start getting my salary we'll see about changing it.

HEDDA. No, no, don't let's change it. I don't want to part with it. We can move it into that little room and get another one to put in here.

TESMAN, *a little downcast.* Yes, we — might do that.

HEDDA *picks up the bunch of flowers from the piano.* These flowers weren't here when we arrived last night.

TESMAN. I expect Auntie Juju brought them.

HEDDA. Here's a card.

Takes it out and reads.

"Will come back later today." Guess who it's from?

TESMAN. No idea. Who? What?

HEDDA. It says: "Mrs. Elvsted."

TESMAN. No, really? Mrs. Elvsted! She used to be Miss Rysing, didn't she?

HEDDA. Yes. She was the one with that irritating hair she was always showing off. I hear she used to be an old flame of yours.

TESMAN *laughs.* That didn't last long. Anyway, that was before I got to know you, Hedda. By Jove, fancy her being in town!

HEDDA. Strange she could call. I only knew her at school.

TESMAN. Yes, I haven't seen her for — oh, heaven knows how long. I don't know how she manages to stick it out up there in the north. What?

HEDDA *thinks for a moment, then says suddenly.* Tell me, Tesman, doesn't he live somewhere up in those parts? You know — Eilert Loevborg?

TESMAN. Yes, that's right. So he does.

BERTHA *enters from the hall.*

BERTHA. She's here again, madam. The lady who came and left the flowers.

Points.

The ones you're holding.

HEDDA. Oh, is she? Well, show her in.

BERTHA *opens the door for* MRS. ELVSTED *and goes out.* MRS. ELVSTED

*is a delicately built woman with gentle, attractive features. Her eyes
are light blue, large, and somewhat prominent, with a frightened,
questioning expression. Her hair is extremely fair, almost flaxen, and
is exceptionally wavy and abundant. She is two or three years younger
than* HEDDA. *She is wearing a dark visiting dress, in good taste but not
quite in the latest fashion.*

HEDDA *goes cordially to greet her.* Dear Mrs. Elvsted, good morning.
How delightful to see you again after all this time.

MRS. ELVSTED, *nervously, trying to control herself.* Yes, it's many years
since we met.

TESMAN. And since *we* met. What?

HEDDA. Thank you for your lovely flowers.

MRS. ELVSTED. Oh, please — I wanted to come yesterday afternoon. But
they told me you were away —

TESMAN. You've only just arrived in town, then? What?

MRS. ELVSTED. I got here yesterday, around midday. Oh, I became almost
desperate when I heard you weren't here.

HEDDA. Desperate? Why?

TESMAN. My dear Mrs. Rysing — Elvsted —

HEDDA. There's nothing wrong, I hope?

MRS. ELVSTED. Yes, there is. And I don't know anyone else here whom I
can turn to.

HEDDA *puts the flowers down on the table.* Come and sit with me on the
sofa —

MRS. ELVSTED. Oh, I feel too restless to sit down.

HEDDA. You must. Come along, now.

She pulls MRS. ELVSTED *down on to the sofa and sits beside her.*

TESMAN. Well? Tell us, Mrs. — er —

HEDDA. Has something happened at home?

MRS. ELVSTED. Yes — that is, yes and no. Oh, I do hope you won't misunderstand me —

HEDDA. Then you'd better tell us the whole story, Mrs. Elvsted.

TESMAN. That's why you've come. What?

MRS. ELVSTED. Yes — yes, it is. Well, then — in case you don't already
know — Eilert Loevborg is in town.

HEDDA. Loevborg here?

TESMAN. Eilert back in town? By Jove, Hedda, did you hear that?

HEDDA. Yes, of course I heard.

MRS. ELVSTED. He's been here a week. A whole week! In this city. Alone.
With all those dreadful people —

HEDDA. But my dear Mrs. Elvsted, what concern is he of yours?

MRS. ELVSTED *gives her a frightened look and says quickly.* He's been
tutoring the children.

HEDDA. Your children?

MRS. ELVSTED. My husband's. I have none.

HEDDA. Oh, you mean your stepchildren.

MRS. ELVSTED. Yes.

TESMAN, *gropingly.* But was he sufficiently — I don't know how to put it — sufficiently regular in his habits to be suited to such a post? What?

MRS. ELVSTED. For the past two to three years he has been living irreproachably.

TESMAN. You don't say! By Jove, Hedda, hear that?

HEDDA. I hear.

MRS. ELVSTED. Quite irreproachably, I assure you. In every respect. All the same — in this big city — with money in his pockets — I'm so dreadfully frightened something may happen to him.

TESMAN. But why didn't he stay up there with you and your husband?

MRS. ELVSTED. Once his book had come out, he became restless.

TESMAN. Oh, yes — Auntie Juju said he'd brought out a new book.

MRS. ELVSTED. Yes, a big new book about the history of civilisation. A kind of general survey. It came out a fortnight ago. Everyone's been buying it and reading it — it's created a tremendous stir —

TESMAN. Has it really? It must be something he's dug up, then.

MRS. ELVSTED. You mean from the old days?

TESMAN. Yes.

MRS. ELVSTED. No, he's written it all since he came to live with us.

TESMAN. Well, that's splendid news, Hedda. Fancy that!

MRS. ELVSTED. Oh, yes! If only he can go on like this!

HEDDA. Have you met him since you came here?

MRS. ELVSTED. No, not yet. I had such dreadful difficulty finding his address. But this morning I managed to track him down at last.

HEDDA *looks searchingly at her.* I must say I find it a little strange that your husband — him —

MRS. ELVSTED *starts nervously.* My husband! What do you mean?

HEDDA. That he should send you all the way here on an errand of this kind. I'm surprised he didn't come himself to keep an eye on his friend.

MRS. ELVSTED. Oh, no, no — my husband hasn't the time. Besides, I — er — wanted to do some shopping here.

HEDDA, *with a slight smile.* Ah. Well, that's different.

MRS. ELVSTED *gets up quickly, restlessly.* Please, Mr. Tesman, I beg you — be kind to Eilert Loevborg if he comes here. I'm sure he will. I mean, you used to be such good friends in the old days. And you're both studying the same subject, as far as I can understand. You're in the same field, aren't you?

TESMAN. Well, we used to be, anyway.

MRS. ELVSTED. Yes — so I beg you earnestly, do please, please, keep an eye on him. Oh, Mr. Tesman, do promise me you will.

TESMAN. I shall be only too happy to do so, Mrs. Rysing.

HEDDA. Elvsted.

TESMAN. I'll do everything for Eilert that lies in my power. You can rely on that.

MRS. ELVSTED. Oh, how good and kind you are!

Presses his hands.

Thank you, thank you, thank you.

Frightened.

My husband's so fond of him, you see.

HEDDA *gets up.* You'd better send him a note, Tesman. He may not come to you of his own accord.

TESMAN. Yes, that'd probably be the best plan, Hedda. What?

HEDDA. The sooner the better. Why not do it now?

MRS. ELVSTED, *pleadingly.* Oh yes, if only you would!

TESMAN. I'll do it this very moment. Do you have his address, Mrs. — er — Elvsted?

MRS. ELVSTED. Yes.

Takes a small piece of paper from her pocket and gives it to him.

TESMAN. Good, good. Right, well I'll go inside and —

Looks round.

Where are my slippers? Oh yes, here.

Picks up the package and is about to go.

HEDDA. Try to sound friendly. Make it a nice long letter.

TESMAN. Right, I will.

MRS. ELVSTED. Please don't say anything about my having seen you.

TESMAN. Good heavens no, of course not. What?

Goes out through the rear room to the right.

HEDDA *goes over to* MRS. ELVSTED, *smiles, and says softly.* Well! Now we've killed two birds with one stone.

MRS. ELVSTED. What do you mean?

HEDDA. Didn't you realise I wanted to get him out of the room?

MRS. ELVSTED. So that he could write the letter?

HEDDA. And so that I could talk to you alone.

MRS. ELVSTED, *confused.* About this?

HEDDA. Yes, about this.

MRS. ELVSTED, *in alarm.* But there's nothing more to tell, Mrs. Tesman. Really there isn't.

HEDDA. Oh, yes there is. There's a lot more. I can see that. Come along, let's sit down and have a little chat.

She pushes MRS. ELVSTED *down into the armchair by the stove and seats herself on one of the footstools.*

MRS. ELVSTED *looks anxiously at her watch.* Really, Mrs. Tesman, I think I ought to be going now.

HEDDA. There's no hurry. Well? How are things at home?

MRS. ELVSTED. I'd rather not speak about that.

HEDDA. But my dear, you can tell me. Good heavens, we were at school together.

MRS. ELVSTED. Yes, but you were a year senior to me. Oh, I used to be terribly frightened of you in those days.

HEDDA. Frightened of me?

MRS. ELVSTED. Yes, terribly frightened. Whenever you met me on the staircase you used to pull my hair.

HEDDA. No, did I?

MRS. ELVSTED. Yes. And once you said you'd burn it all off.

HEDDA. Oh, that was only in fun.

MRS. ELVSTED. Yes, but I was so silly in those days. And then afterwards — I mean, we've drifted so far apart. Our backgrounds were so different.

HEDDA. Well, now we must try to drift together again. Now listen. When we were at school we used to call each other by our Christian names —

MRS. ELVSTED. No, I'm sure you're mistaken.

HEDDA. I'm sure I'm not. I remember it quite clearly. Let's tell each other our secrets, as we used to in the old days.

Moves closer on her footstool.

There, now.

Kisses her on the cheek.

You must call me Hedda.

MRS. ELVSTED *squeezes her hands and pats them.* Oh, you're so kind. I'm not used to people being so nice to me.

HEDDA. Now, now, now. And I shall call you Tora, the way I used to.

MRS. ELVSTED. My name is Thea.

HEDDA. Yes, of course. Of course. I meant Thea.

Looks at her sympathetically.

So you're not used to kindness, Thea? In your own home?

MRS. ELVSTED. Oh, if only I had a home! But I haven't. I've never had one.

HEDDA *looks at her for a moment.* I thought that was it.

MRS. ELVSTED *stares blankly and helplessly.* Yes — yes — yes.

HEDDA. I can't remember exactly now, but didn't you first go to Mr. Elvsted as a housekeeper?

MRS. ELVSTED. Governess, actually. But his wife — at the time, I mean — she was an invalid, and had to spend most of her time in bed. So I had to look after the house too.

HEDDA. But in the end, you became mistress of the house.

MRS. ELVSTED, *sadly.* Yes, I did.

HEDDA. Let me see. Roughly how long ago was that?

MRS. ELVSTED. When I got married, you mean?

HEDDA. Yes.

MRS. ELVSTED. About five years.

HEDDA. Yes; it must be about that.

MRS. ELVSTED. Oh, those five years! Especially the last two or three. Oh, Mrs. Tesman, if you only knew — !

HEDDA *slaps her hand gently.* Mrs. Tesman? Oh, Thea!

MRS. ELVSTED. I'm sorry, I'll try to remember. Yes — if you had any idea —

HEDDA, *casually.* Eilert Loevborg's been up there too, for about three years, hasn't he?

MRS. ELVSTED *looks at her uncertainly.* Eilert Loevborg? Yes, he has.

HEDDA. Did you know him before? When you were here?

MRS. ELVSTED. No, not really. That is — I knew him by name, of course.

HEDDA. But up there, he used to visit you?

MRS. ELVSTED. Yes, he used to come and see us every day. To give the children lessons. I found I couldn't do that as well as manage the house.

HEDDA. I'm sure you couldn't. And your husband — ? I suppose being a magistrate he has to be away from home a good deal?

MRS. ELVSTED. Yes. You see, Mrs. — you see, Hedda, he has to cover the whole district.

HEDDA *leans against the arm of* MRS. ELVSTED'S *chair.* Poor, pretty little Thea! Now you must tell me the whole story. From beginning to end.

MRS. ELVSTED. Well — what do you want to know?

HEDDA. What kind of a man is your husband, Thea? I mean, as a person. Is he kind to you?

MRS. ELVSTED, *evasively.* I'm sure he does his best to be.

HEDDA. I only wonder if he isn't too old for you. There's more than twenty years between you, isn't there?

MRS. ELVSTED, *irritably.* Yes, there's that too. Oh, there are so many things. We're different in every way. We've nothing in common. Nothing whatever.

HEDDA. But he loves you, surely? In his own way?

MRS. ELVSTED. Oh, I don't know. I think he just finds me useful. And then I don't cost much to keep. I'm cheap.

HEDDA. Now you're being stupid.

MRS. ELVSTED *shakes her head.* It can't be any different. With him. He doesn't love anyone except himself. And perhaps the children — a little.

HEDDA. He must be fond of Eilert Loevborg, Thea.

MRS. ELVSTED *looks at her.* Eilert Loevborg? What makes you think that?

HEDDA. Well, if he sends you all the way down here to look for him—
    Smiles almost imperceptibly.
Besides, you said so yourself to Tesman.

MRS. ELVSTED, *with a nervous twitch.* Did I? Oh yes, I suppose I did.
    Impulsively, but keeping her voice low.
Well, I might as well tell you the whole story. It's bound to come out sooner or later.

HEDDA. But my dear Thea — ?

MRS. ELVSTED. My husband had no idea I was coming here.

HEDDA. What? Your husband didn't know?

MRS. ELVSTED. No, of course not. As a matter of fact, he wasn't even there. He was away at the assizes. Oh, I couldn't stand it any longer, Hedda! I just couldn't. I'd be so dreadfully lonely up there now.

HEDDA. Go on.

MRS. ELVSTED. So I packed a few things. Secretly. And went.

HEDDA. Without telling anyone?

MRS. ELVSTED. Yes. I caught the train and came straight here.

HEDDA. But my dear Thea! How brave of you!

MRS. ELVSTED *gets up and walks across the room.* Well, what else could I do?

HEDDA. But what do you suppose your husband will say when you get back?

MRS. ELVSTED, *by the table, looks at her.* Back there? To him?

HEDDA. Yes. Surely — ?

MRS. ELVSTED. I shall never go back to him.

HEDDA *gets up and goes closer.* You mean you've left your home for good?

MRS. ELVSTED. Yes. I didn't see what else I could do.

HEDDA. But to do it so openly!

MRS. ELVSTED. Oh, it's no use trying to keep a thing like that secret.

HEDDA. But what do you suppose people will say?

MRS. ELVSTED. They can say what they like.

Sits sadly, wearily on the sofa.

I had to do it.

HEDDA, *after a short silence.* What do you intend to do now? How are you going to live?

MRS. ELVSTED. I don't know. I only know that I must live wherever Eilert Loevborg is. If I am to go on living.

HEDDA *moves a chair from the table, sits on it near* MRS. ELVSTED *and strokes her hands.* Tell me, Thea, how did this — friendship between you and Eilert Loevborg begin?

MRS. ELVSTED. Oh, it came about gradually. I developed a kind of — power over him.

HEDDA. Oh?

MRS. ELVSTED. He gave up his old habits. Not because I asked him to. I'd never have dared to do that. I suppose he just noticed I didn't like that kind of thing. So he gave it up.

HEDDA *hides a smile.* So you've made a new man of him. Clever little Thea!

MRS. ELVSTED. Yes — anyway, he says I have. And he's made a — sort of — real person of me. Taught me to think — and to understand all kinds of things.

HEDDA. Did he give you lessons too?

MRS. ELVSTED. Not exactly lessons. But he talked to me. About — oh, you've no idea — so many things! And then he let me work with him. Oh, it was wonderful. I was so happy to be allowed to help him.

HEDDA. Did he allow you to help him!

MRS. ELVSTED. Yes. Whenever he wrote anything we always — did it together.

HEDDA. Like good pals?

MRS. ELVSTED, *eagerly.* Pals! Yes — why, Hedda, that's exactly the word he used! Oh, I ought to feel so happy. But I can't. I don't know if it will last.

HEDDA. You don't seem very sure of him.

MRS. ELVSTED, *sadly.* Something stands between Eilert Loevborg and me. The shadow of another woman.

HEDDA. Who can that be?

MRS. ELVSTED. I don't know. Someone he used to be friendly with in — in the old days. Someone he's never been able to forget.

HEDDA. What has he told you about her?

MRS. ELVSTED. Oh, he only mentioned her once, casually.

HEDDA. Well! What did he say?

MRS. ELVSTED. He said when he left her she tried to shoot him with a pistol.

HEDDA, *cold, controlled.* What nonsense. People don't do such things. The kind of people we know.

MRS. ELVSTED. No. I think it must have been that red-haired singer he used to —

HEDDA. Ah yes, very probably.

MRS. ELVSTED. I remember they used to say she always carried a loaded pistol.

HEDDA. Well then, it must be her.

MRS. ELVSTED. But Hedda, I hear she's come back, and is living here. Oh, I'm so desperate — !

HEDDA *glances towards the rear room.* Ssh! Tesman's coming.

Gets up and whispers.

Thea, we mustn't breathe a word about this to anyone.

MRS. ELVSTED *jumps up.* Oh, no, no! Please don't!

GEORGE TESMAN *appears from the right in the rear room with a letter in his hand, and comes into the drawing room.*

TESMAN. Well, here's my little epistle all signed and sealed.

HEDDA. Good. I think Mrs. Elvsted wants to go now. Wait a moment — I'll see you as far as the garden gate.

TESMAN. Er — Hedda, do you think Bertha could deal with this?

HEDDA *takes the letter.* I'll give her instructions.

BERTHA *enters from the hall.*

BERTHA. Judge Brack is here and asks if he may pay his respects to Madam and the Doctor.

HEDDA. Yes, ask him to be so good as to come in. And — wait a moment — drop this letter in the post box.

BERTHA *takes the letter.* Very good, madam.

She opens the door for JUDGE BRACK, *and goes out.* JUDGE BRACK *is forty-five; rather short, but well-built, and elastic in his movements. He has a roundish face with an aristocratic profile. His hair, cut short, is still almost black, and is carefully barbered. Eyes lively and humorous. Thick eyebrows. His moustache is also thick, and is trimmed square at the ends. He is wearing outdoor clothes which are elegant but a little too youthful for him. He has a monocle in one eye; now and then he lets it drop.*

BRACK, *hat in hand, bows.* May one presume to call so early?

HEDDA. One may presume.

TESMAN *shakes his hand.* You're welcome here any time. Judge Brack — Mrs. Rysing.

HEDDA *sighs.*

BRACK *bows.* Ah — charmed —

HEDDA *looks at him and laughs.* What fun to be able to see you by daylight for once, Judge.

BRACK. Do I look — different?

HEDDA. Yes. A little younger, I think.

BRACK. Obliged.

TESMAN. Well, what do you think of Hedda? What? Doesn't she look well? Hasn't she filled out — ?

HEDDA. Oh, do stop it. You ought to be thanking Judge Brack for all the inconvenience he's put himself to —

BRACK. Nonsense, it was a pleasure —

HEDDA. You're a loyal friend. But my other friend is pining to get away. Au revoir, Judge. I won't be a minute.

Mutual salutations. MRS. ELVSTED *and* HEDDA *go out through the hall.*

BRACK. Well, is your wife satisfied with everything?

TESMAN. Yes, we can't thank you enough. That is — we may have to shift one or two things around, she tells me. And we're short of one or two little items we'll have to purchase.

BRACK. Oh? Really?

TESMAN. But you mustn't worry your head about that. Hedda says she'll get what's needed. I say, why don't we sit down? What?

BRACK. Thanks, just for a moment.

Sits at the table.

There's something I'd like to talk to you about, my dear Tesman.

TESMAN. Oh? Ah yes, of course.

Sits.

After the feast comes the reckoning. What?

BRACK. Oh, never mind about the financial side — there's no hurry about that. Though I could wish we'd arranged things a little less palatially.

TESMAN. Good heavens, that'd never have done. Think of Hedda, my dear chap. You know her. I couldn't possibly ask her to live like a suburban housewife.

BRACK. No, no — that's just the problem.

TESMAN. Anyway, it can't be long now before my nomination comes through.

BRACK. Well, you know, these things often take time.

TESMAN. Have you heard any more news? What?

BRACK. Nothing definite.

Changing the subject.

Oh, by the way, I have one piece of news for you.

TESMAN. What?

BRACK. Your old friend Eilert Loevborg is back in town.

TESMAN. I know that already.

BRACK. Oh? How did you hear that?

TESMAN. She told me. That lady who went out with Hedda.

BRACK. I see. What was her name? I didn't catch it.

TESMAN. Mrs. Elvsted.

BRACK. Oh, the magistrate's wife. Yes, Loevborg's been living up near them, hasn't he?

TESMAN. I'm delighted to hear he's become a decent human being again.

BRACK. Yes, so they say.

TESMAN. I gather he's published a new book, too. What?

BRACK. Indeed he has.

TESMAN. I hear it's created rather a stir.

BRACK. Quite an unusual stir.

TESMAN. I say, isn't that splendid news! He's such a gifted chap — and I was afraid he'd gone to the dogs for good.

BRACK. Most people thought he had.

TESMAN. But I can't think what he'll do now. How on earth will he manage to make ends meet? What?

As he speaks his last words, HEDDA *enters from the hall.*

HEDDA, *to* BRACK, *laughs slightly scornfully.* Tesman is always worrying about making ends meet.

TESMAN. We were talking about poor Eilert Loevborg, Hedda dear.

HEDDA *gives him a quick look.* Oh, were you?

Sits in the armchair by the stove and asks casually.

Is he in trouble?

TESMAN. Well, he must have run through his inheritance long ago by now. And he can't write a new book every year. What? So I'm wondering what's going to become of him.

BRACK. I may be able to enlighten you there.

TESMAN. Oh?

BRACK. You mustn't forget he has relatives who wield a good deal of influence.

TESMAN. Relatives? Oh, they've quite washed their hands of him, I'm afraid.

BRACK. They used to regard him as the hope of the family.

TESMAN. Used to, yes. But he's put an end to that.

HEDDA. Who knows?

With a little smile.

I hear the Elvsteds have made a new man of him.

BRACK. And then this book he's just published —

TESMAN. Well, let's hope they find something for him. I've just written him a note. Oh, by the way, Hedda, I asked him to come over and see us this evening.

BRACK. But my dear chap, you're coming to me this evening. My bachelor party. You promised me last night when I met you at the boat.

HEDDA. Had you forgotten, Tesman?

TESMAN. Good heavens, yes, I'd quite forgotten.

BRACK. Anyway, you can be quite sure he won't turn up here.

TESMAN. Why do you think that? What?

BRACK, *a little unwillingly, gets up and rests his hands on the back of his chair.* My dear Tesman — and you, too, Mrs. Tesman — there's something I feel you ought to know.

TESMAN. Concerning Eilert?

BRACK. Concerning him and you.

TESMAN. Well, my dear Judge, tell us, please!

BRACK. You must be prepared for your nomination not to come through quite as quickly as you hope and expect.

TESMAN *jumps up uneasily.* Is anything wrong? What?

BRACK. There's a possibility that the appointment may be decided by competition —

TESMAN. Competition! By Jove, Hedda, fancy that!

HEDDA *leans further back in her chair.* Ah! How interesting!

TESMAN. But who else — ? I say, you don't mean — ?

BRACK. Exactly. By competition with Eilert Loevborg.

TESMAN *clasps his hands in alarm.* No, no, but this is inconceivable! It's absolutely impossible! What?

BRACK. Hm. We may find it'll happen, all the same.

TESMAN. No, but — Judge Brack, they couldn't be so inconsiderate towards me!

Waves his arms.

I mean, by Jove, I — I'm a married man! It was on the strength of this that Hedda and I *got* married! We ran up some pretty hefty debts. And borrowed money from Auntie Juju! I mean, good heavens, they practically promised me the appointment. What?

BRACK. Well, well, I'm sure you'll get it. But you'll have to go through a competition.

HEDDA, *motionless in her armchair.* How exciting, Tesman. It'll be a kind of duel, by Jove.

TESMAN. My dear Hedda, how can you take it so lightly?

HEDDA, *as before.* I'm not. I can't wait to see who's going to win.

BRACK. In any case, Mrs. Tesman, it's best you should know how things stand. I mean before you commit yourself to these little items I hear you're threatening to purchase.

HEDDA. I can't allow this to alter my plans.

BRACK. Indeed? Well, that's your business. Good-bye.

To TESMAN.

I'll come and collect you on the way home from my afternoon walk.

TESMAN. Oh, yes, yes. I'm sorry, I'm all upside down just now.

HEDDA, *lying in her chair, holds out her hand.* Good-bye, Judge. See you this afternoon.

BRACK. Thank you. Good-bye, good-bye.

TESMAN *sees him to the door.* Good-bye, my dear Judge. You will excuse me, won't you?

JUDGE BRACK *goes out through the hall.*

TESMAN, *pacing up and down.* Oh, Hedda! One oughtn't to go plunging off on wild adventures. What?

HEDDA *looks at him and smiles.* Like you're doing?

TESMAN. Yes. I mean, there's no denying it, it was a pretty big adventure to go off and get married and set up house merely on expectation.

HEDDA. Perhaps you're right.

TESMAN. Well, anyway, we have our home, Hedda. By Jove, yes. The home we dreamed of. And set our hearts on. What?

HEDDA *gets us slowly, wearily.* You agreed that we should enter society. And keep open house. That was the bargain.

TESMAN. Yes. Good heavens, I was looking forward to it all so much. To seeing you play hostess to a select circle! By Jove! What? Ah, well, for the time being we shall have to make do with each other's company, Hedda. Perhaps have Auntie Juju in now and then. Oh dear, this wasn't at all what you had in mind —

HEDDA. I won't be able to have a liveried footman. For a start.

TESMAN. Oh no, we couldn't possibly afford a footman.

HEDDA. And that thoroughbred horse you promised me —

TESMAN, *fearfully.* Thoroughbred horse!

HEDDA. I mustn't even think of that now.

TESMAN. Heaven forbid!

HEDDA *walks across the room.* Ah, well. I still have one thing left to amuse myself with.

TESMAN, *joyfully.* Thank goodness for that. What's that, Hedda? What?

HEDDA, *in the open doorway, looks at him with concealed scorn.* My pistols, George darling.

TESMAN, *alarmed.* Pistols!

HEDDA, *her eyes cold.* General Gabler's pistols.

She goes into the rear room and disappears.

TESMAN *runs to the doorway and calls after her.* For heaven's sake, Hedda dear, don't touch those things. They're dangerous. Hedda — please — for my sake! What?

ACT II

The same as in Act One, except that the piano has been removed and an elegant little writing table, with a bookcase, stands in its place. By the sofa on the left a smaller table has been placed. Most of the flowers have been removed. MRS. ELVSTED'S *bouquet stands on the larger table, downstage. It is afternoon.*

HEDDA, *dressed to receive callers, is alone in the room. She is standing by the open french windows, loading a revolver. The pair to it is lying in an open pistol case on the writing table.*

HEDDA *looks down into the garden and calls.* Good afternoon, Judge.

BRACK, *in the distance, below.* Afternoon, Mrs. Tesman.

HEDDA *raises the pistol and takes aim.* I'm going to shoot you, Judge Brack.

BRACK *shouts from below.* No, no, no! Don't aim that thing at me!

HEDDA. This'll teach you to enter houses by the back door. *Fires.*

BRACK, *below.* Have you gone completely out of your mind?

HEDDA. Oh dear! Did I hit you?

BRACK, *still outside.* Stop playing these silly tricks.

HEDDA. All right, Judge. Come along in.

JUDGE BRACK, *dressed for a bachelor party, enters through the french windows. He has a light overcoat on his arm.*

BRACK. For God's sake! Haven't you stopped fooling around with those things yet? What are you trying to hit?

HEDDA. Oh, I was just shooting at the sky.

BRACK *takes the pistol gently from her hand.* By your leave, ma'am.

Looks at it.

Ah, yes — I know this old friend well.

Looks around.

Where's the case? Oh, yes.

Puts the pistol in the case and closes it.

That's enough of that little game for today.

HEDDA. Well, what on earth *am* I to do?

BRACK. You haven't had any visitors?

HEDDA *closes the french windows.* Not one. I suppose the best people are all still in the country.

BRACK. Your husband isn't home yet?

HEDDA *locks the pistol away in a drawer of the writing table.* No. The moment he'd finished eating he ran off to his aunties. He wasn't expecting you so early.

BRACK. Ah, why didn't I think of that? How stupid of me.

HEDDA *turns her head and looks at him.* Why stupid?

BRACK. I'd have come a little sooner.

HEDDA *walks across the room.* There'd have been no one to receive you. I've been in my room since lunch, dressing.

BRACK. You haven't a tiny crack in the door through which we might have negotiated?

HEDDA. You forgot to arrange one.

BRACK. Another stupidity.

HEDDA. Well, we'll have to sit down here. And wait. Tesman won't be back for some time.

BRACK. Sad. Well, I'll be patient.

HEDDA *sits on the corner of the sofa.* BRACK *puts his coat over the back of the nearest chair and seats himself, keeping his hat in his hand. Short pause. They look at each other.*

HEDDA. Well?

BRACK, *in the same tone of voice.* Well?

HEDDA. I asked first.

BRACK *leans forward slightly.* Yes, well, now we can enjoy a nice, cosy little chat — Mrs. Hedda.

HEDDA *leans further back in her chair.* It seems such ages since we had a talk. I don't count last night or this morning.

BRACK. You mean: *à deux?*

HEDDA. Mm — yes. That's roughly what I meant.

BRACK. I've been longing so much for you to come home.

HEDDA. So have I.

BRACK. You? Really, Mrs. Hedda? And I thought you were having such a wonderful honeymoon.

HEDDA. Oh, yes. Wonderful!

BRACK. But your husband wrote such ecstatic letters.

HEDDA. He! Oh, yes! He thinks life has nothing better to offer than rooting around in libraries and copying old pieces of parchment, or whatever it is he does.

BRACK, *a little maliciously.* Well, that *is* his life. Most of it, anyway.

HEDDA. Yes, I know. Well, it's all right for him. But for me! Oh no, my dear Judge. I've been bored to death.

BRACK, *sympathetically.* Do you mean that? Seriously?

HEDDA. Yes. Can you imagine? Six whole months without ever meeting a single person who was one of us, and to whom I could talk about the kind of things we talk about.

BRACK. Yes, I can understand. I'd miss that, too.

HEDDA. That wasn't the worst, though.

BRACK. What was?

HEDDA. Having to spend every minute of one's life with — with the same person.

BRACK *nods.* Yes. What a thought! Morning; noon; and —

HEDDA, *coldly.* As I said: every minute of one's life.

BRACK. I stand corrected. But dear Tesman is such a clever fellow, I should have thought one ought to be able —

HEDDA. Tesman is only interested in one thing, my dear Judge. His special subject.

BRACK. True.

HEDDA. And people who are only interested in one thing don't make the most amusing company. Not for long, anyway.

BRACK. Not even when they happen to be the person one loves?

HEDDA. Oh, don't use that sickly, stupid word.

BRACK *starts.* But, Mrs. Hedda — !

HEDDA, *half laughing, half annoyed.* You just try it, Judge. Listening to the history of civilisation morning, noon and —

BRACK *corrects her.* Every minute of one's life.

HEDDA. All right. Oh, and those domestic industries of Brabant in the Middle Ages! That really is beyond the limit.

BRACK *looks at her searchingly.* But, tell me — if you feel like this why on earth did you — ? Ha —

HEDDA. Why on earth did I marry George Tesman?

BRACK. If you like to put it that way.

HEDDA. Do you think it so very strange?

BRACK. Yes — and no, Mrs. Hedda.

HEDDA. I'd danced myself tired, Judge. I felt my time was up —
    Gives a slight shudder.
No, I mustn't say that. Or even think it.

BRACK. You've no rational cause to think it.

HEDDA. Oh — cause, cause —

Looks searchingly at him.

After all, George Tesman — well, I mean, he's a very respectable man.

BRACK. Very respectable, sound as a rock. No denying that.

HEDDA. And there's nothing exactly ridiculous about him. Is there?

BRACK. Ridiculous? N-no, I wouldn't say that.

HEDDA. Mm. He's very clever at collecting material and all that, isn't he? I mean, he may go quite far in time.

BRACK *looks at her a little uncertainly.* I thought you believed, like everyone else, that he would become a very prominent man.

HEDDA *looks tired.* Yes, I did. And when he came and begged me on his bended knees to be allowed to love and to cherish me, I didn't see why I shouldn't let him.

BRACK. No, well — if one looks at it like that —

HEDDA. It was more than my other admirers were prepared to do, Judge dear.

BRACK *laughs.* Well, I can't answer for the others. As far as I myself am concerned, you know I've always had a considerable respect for the institution of marriage. As an institution.

HEDDA, *lightly.* Oh, I've never entertained any hopes of you.

BRACK. All I want is to have a circle of friends whom I can trust, whom I can help with advice or — or by any other means, and into whose houses I may come and go as a — trusted friend.

HEDDA. Of the husband?

BRACK *bows.* Preferably, to be frank, of the wife. And of the husband too, of course. Yes, you know, this kind of — triangle is a delightful arrangement for all parties concerned.

HEDDA. Yes, I often longed for a third person while I was away. Oh, those hours we spent alone in railway compartments —

BRACK. Fortunately your honeymoon is now over.

HEDDA *shakes her head.* There's a long, long way still to go. I've only reached a stop on the line.

BRACK. Why not jump out and stretch your legs a little, Mrs. Hedda?

HEDDA. I'm not the jumping sort.

BRACK. Aren't you?

HEDDA. No. There's always someone around who —

BRACK *laughs.* Who looks at one's legs?

HEDDA. Yes. Exactly.

BRACK. Well, but surely —

HEDDA, *with a gesture of rejection.* I don't like it. I'd rather stay where I am. Sitting in the compartment. *À deux.*

BRACK. But suppose a third person were to step into the compartment?

HEDDA. That would be different.

BRACK. A trusted friend — someone who understood —

HEDDA. And was lively and amusing —

BRACK. And interested in — more subjects than one —

HEDDA *sighs audibly.* Yes, that'd be a relief.

BRACK *hears the front door open and shut.* The triangle is completed.

HEDDA, *half under breath.* And the train goes on.

GEORGE TESMAN, *in grey walking dress with a soft felt hat, enters from the hall. He has a number of paper-covered books under his arm and in his pockets.*

TESMAN *goes over to the table by the corner sofa.* Phew! It's too hot to be lugging all this around.

Puts the books down.

I'm positively sweating, Hedda. Why, hullo, hullo! You here already, Judge? What? Bertha didn't tell me.

BRACK *gets up.* I came in through the garden.

HEDDA. What are all those books you've got there?

TESMAN *stands glancing through them.* Oh, some new publications dealing with my special subject. I had to buy them.

HEDDA. Your special subject?

BRACK. His special subject, Mrs. Tesman.

BRACK *and* HEDDA *exchange a smile.*

HEDDA. Haven't you collected enough material on your special subject?

TESMAN. My dear Hedda, one can never have too much. One must keep abreast of what other people are writing.

HEDDA. Yes. Of course.

TESMAN, *rooting among the books.* Look — I bought a copy of Eilert Loevborg's new book, too.

Holds it out to her.

Perhaps you'd like to have a look at it, Hedda? What?

HEDDA. No, thank you. Er — yes, perhaps I will, later.

TESMAN. I glanced through it on my way home.

BRACK. What's your opinion — as a specialist on the subject?

TESMAN. I'm amazed how sound and balanced it is. He never used to write like that.

Gathers his books together.

Well, I must get down to these at once. I can hardly wait to cut the pages. Oh, I've got to change, too.

To BRACK.

We don't have to be off just yet, do we? What?

BRACK. Heavens, no. We've plenty of time yet.

TESMAN. Good, I needn't hurry, then.

Goes with his books, but stops and turns in the doorway.

Oh, by the way, Hedda, Auntie Juju won't be coming to see you this evening.

HEDDA. Won't she? Oh — the hat, I suppose.

TESMAN. Good heavens, no. How could you think such a thing of Auntie Juju? Fancy — ! No, Auntie Rena's very ill.

HEDDA. She always is.

TESMAN. Yes, but today she's been taken really bad.

HEDDA. Oh, then it's quite understandable that the other one should want to stay with her. Well, I shall have to swallow my disappointment.

TESMAN. You can't imagine how happy Auntie Juju was in spite of everything. At your looking so well after the honeymoon!

HEDDA, *half beneath her breath, as she rises.* Oh, these everlasting aunts!

TESMAN. What?

HEDDA *goes over to the french windows.* Nothing.

TESMAN. Oh. All right.

Goes into the rear room and out of sight.

BRACK. What was that about the hat?

HEDDA. Oh, something that happened with Miss Tesman this morning. She'd put her hat down on a chair.

Looks at him and smiles.

And I pretended to think it was the servant's.

BRACK *shakes his head.* But my dear Mrs. Hedda, how could you do such a thing? To that poor old lady?

HEDDA, *nervously, walking across the room.* Sometimes a mood like that hits me. And I can't stop myself.

Throws herself down in the armchair by the stove.

Oh, I don't know how to explain it.

BRACK, *behind her chair.* You're not really happy. That's the answer.

HEDDA *stares ahead of her.* Why on earth should I be happy? Can you give me a reason?

BRACK. Yes. For one thing you've got the home you always wanted.

HEDDA *looks at him.* You really believe that story?

BRACK. You mean it isn't true?

HEDDA. Oh, yes, it's partly true.

BRACK. Well?

HEDDA. It's true I got Tesman to see me home from parties last summer —

BRACK. It was a pity my home lay in another direction.

HEDDA. Yes. Your interests lay in another direction, too.

BRACK *laughs.* That's naughty of you, Mrs. Hedda. But to return to you and Tesman —

HEDDA. Well, we walked past this house one evening. And poor Tesman was fidgeting in his boots trying to find something to talk about. I felt sorry for the great scholar —

BRACK *smiles incredulously.* Did you? Hm.

HEDDA. Yes, honestly I did. Well, to help him out of his misery, I happened to say quite frivolously how much I'd love to live in this house.

BRACK. Was that all?

HEDDA. That evening, yes.

BRACK. But — afterwards?

HEDDA. Yes. My little frivolity had its consequences, my dear Judge.

BRACK. Our little frivolities do. Much too often, unfortunately.

HEDDA. Thank you. Well, it was our mutual admiration for the late Prime Minister's house that brought George Tesman and me together on common ground. So we got engaged, and we got married, and we went on our honeymoon, and — Ah well, Judge, I've — made my bed and I must lie in it, I was about to say.

BRACK. How utterly fantastic! And you didn't really care in the least about the house?

HEDDA. God knows I didn't.

BRACK. Yes, but now that we've furnished it so beautifully for you?

HEDDA. Ugh — all the rooms smell of lavender and dried roses. But perhaps Auntie Juju brought that in.

BRACK *laughs.* More likely the Prime Minister's widow, rest her soul.

HEDDA. Yes, it's got the odour of death about it. It reminds me of the flowers one has worn at a ball — the morning after.

> *Clasps her hands behind her neck, leans back in the chair and looks up at him.*

Oh, my dear Judge, you've no idea how hideously bored I'm going to be out here.

BRACK. Couldn't you find some kind of occupation, Mrs. Hedda? Like your husband?

HEDDA. Occupation? That'd interest me?

BRACK. Well — preferably.

HEDDA. God knows what. I've often thought —

> *Breaks off.*

No, that wouldn't work either.

BRACK. Who knows? Tell me about it.

HEDDA. I was thinking — if I could persuade Tesman to go into politics, for example.

BRACK *laughs.* Tesman! No, honestly, I don't think he's quite cut out to be a politician.

HEDDA. Perhaps not. But if I could persuade him to have a go at it?

BRACK. What satisfaction would that give you? If he turned out to be no good? Why do you want to make him do that?

HEDDA. Because I'm bored.

> *After a moment.*

You feel there's absolutely no possibility of Tesman becoming Prime Minister, then?

BRACK. Well, you know, Mrs. Hedda, for one thing he'd have to be pretty well off before he could become that.

HEDDA *gets up impatiently.* There you are!

> *Walks across the room.*

It's this wretched poverty that makes life so hateful. And ludicrous. Well, it is!

BRACK. I don't think that's the real cause.

HEDDA. What is, then?

BRACK. Nothing really exciting has ever happened to you.

HEDDA. Nothing serious, you mean?

BRACK. Call it that if you like. But now perhaps it may.

HEDDA *tosses her head.* Oh, you're thinking of this competition for that wretched professorship? That's Tesman's affair. I'm not going to waste my time worrying about that.

BRACK. Very well, let's forget about that then. But suppose you were to find yourself faced with what people call — to use the conventional phrase — the most solemn of human responsibilities?

Smiles.

A new responsibility, little Mrs. Hedda.

HEDDA, *angrily.* Be quiet! Nothing like that's going to happen.

BRACK, *warily.* We'll talk about it again in a year's time. If not earlier.

HEDDA, *curtly.* I've no leanings in that direction, Judge. I don't want any — responsibilities.

BRACK. But surely you must feel some inclination to make use of that — natural talent which every woman —

HEDDA, *over by the french windows.* Oh, be quiet, I say! I often think there's only one thing for which I have any natural talent.

BRACK *goes closer.* And what is that, if I may be so bold as to ask?

HEDDA *stands looking out.* For boring myself to death. Now you know.

Turns, looks toward the rear room and laughs.

Talking of boring, here comes the Professor.

BRACK, *quietly, warningly.* Now, now, now, Mrs. Hedda!

GEORGE TESMAN, *in evening dress, with gloves and hat in his hand, enters through the rear room from the right.*

TESMAN. Hedda, hasn't any message come from Eilert? What?

HEDDA. No.

TESMAN. Ah, then we'll have him here presently. You wait and see.

BRACK. You really think he'll come?

TESMAN. Yes, I'm almost sure he will. What you were saying about him this morning is just gossip.

BRACK. Oh?

TESMAN. Yes. Auntie Juju said she didn't believe he'd ever dare to stand in my way again. Fancy that!

BRACK. Then everything in the garden's lovely.

TESMAN *puts his hat, with his gloves in it, on a chair, right.* Yes, but you really must let me wait for him as long as possible.

BRACK. We've plenty of time. No one'll be turning up at my place before seven or half past.

TESMAN. Ah, then we can keep Hedda company a little longer. And see if he turns up. What?

HEDDA *picks up* BRACK'S *coat and hat and carries them over to the corner sofa.* And if the worst comes to the worst, Mr. Loevborg can sit here and talk to me.

BRACK, *offering to take his things from her.* No, please. What do you mean by "if the worst comes to the worst"?

HEDDA. If he doesn't want to go with you and Tesman.

TESMAN *looks doubtfully at her.* I say, Hedda, do you think it'll be all right for him to stay here with you? What? Remember Auntie Juju isn't coming.

HEDDA. Yes, but Mrs. Elvsted is. The three of us can have a cup of tea together.

TESMAN. Ah, that'll be all right then.

BRACK *smiles.* It's probably the safest solution as far as he's concerned.

HEDDA. Why?

BRACK. My dear Mrs. Tesman, you always say of my little bachelor parties that they should be attended only by men of the strongest principles.

HEDDA. But Mr. Loevborg is a man of principle now. You know what they say about a reformed sinner —

BERTHA *enters from the hall.*

BERTHA. Madam, there's a gentleman here who wants to see you —

HEDDA. Ask him to come in.

TESMAN, *quietly.* I'm sure it's him. By Jove. Fancy that!

EILERT LOEVBORG *enters from the hall. He is slim and lean, of the same age as* TESMAN, *but looks older and somewhat haggard. His hair and beard are of a blackish-brown; his face is long and pale, but with a couple of reddish patches on his cheekbones. He is dressed in an elegant and fairly new black suit, and carries black gloves and a top hat in his hand. He stops just inside the door and bows abruptly. He seems somewhat embarrassed.*

TESMAN *goes over and shakes his hand.* My dear Eilert! How grand to see you again after all these years!

EILERT LOEVBORG *speaks softly.* It was good of you to write, George.

Goes nearer to HEDDA.

May I shake hands with you, too, Mrs. Tesman?

HEDDA *accepts his hand.* Delighted to see you, Mr. Loevborg.

With a gesture.

I don't know if you two gentlemen —

LOEVBORG *bows slightly.* Judge Brack, I believe.

BRACK, *also with a slight bow.* Correct. We — met some years ago —

TESMAN *puts his hands on* LOEVBORG'S *shoulders.* Now you're to treat this house just as though it were your own home, Eilert. Isn't that right, Hedda? I hear you've decided to settle here again? What?

LOEVBORG. Yes, I have.

TESMAN. Quite understandable. Oh, by the bye — I've just bought your new book. Though to tell the truth I haven't found time to read it yet.

LOEVBORG. You needn't bother.

TESMAN. Oh? Why?

LOEVBORG. There's nothing much in it.

TESMAN. By Jove, fancy hearing that from you!

BRACK. But everyone's praising it.

LOEVBORG. That was exactly what I wanted to happen. So I only wrote what I knew everyone would agree with.

BRACK. Very sensible.

TESMAN. Yes, but my dear Eilert —

LOEVBORG. I want to try to re-establish myself. To begin again — from the beginning.

TESMAN, *a little embarrassed.* Yes, I — er — suppose you do. What?

LOEVBORG *smiles, puts down his hat and takes a package wrapped in paper from his coat pocket.* But when this gets published — George Tesman — read it. This is my real book. The one in which I have spoken with my own voice.

TESMAN. Oh, really? What's it about?

LOEVBORG. It's the sequel.

TESMAN. Sequel? To what?

LOEVBORG. To the other book.

TESMAN. The one that's just come out?

LOEVBORG. Yes.

TESMAN. But my dear Eilert, that covers the subject right up to the present day.

LOEVBORG. It does. But this is about the future.

TESMAN. The future! But, I say, we don't know anything about that.

LOEVBORG. No. But there are one or two things that need to be said about it.

Opens the package.

Here, have a look.

TESMAN. Surely that's not your handwriting?

LOEVBORG. I dictated it.

Turns the pages.

It's in two parts. The first deals with the forces that will shape our civilisation.

Turns further on towards the end.

And the second indicates the direction in which that civilisation may develop.

TESMAN. Amazing! I'd never think of writing about anything like that.

HEDDA, *by the french windows, drumming on the pane.* No. You wouldn't.

LOEVBORG *puts the pages back into their cover and lays the package on the table.* I brought it because I thought I might possibly read you a few pages this evening.

TESMAN. I say, what a kind idea! Oh, but this evening — ?

Glances at BRACK.

I'm not quite sure whether —

LOEVBORG. Well, some other time, then. There's no hurry.

BRACK. The truth is, Mr. Loevborg, I'm giving a little dinner this evening. In Tesman's honour, you know.

LOEVBORG *looks round for his hat.* Oh — then I mustn't —

BRACK. No, wait a minute. Won't you do me the honour of joining us?

LOEVBORG, *curtly, with decision.* No I can't. Thank you so much.

BRACK. Oh, nonsense. Do — please. There'll only be a few of us. And I can promise you we shall have some good sport, as Mrs. Hed— as Mrs. Tesman puts it.

LOEVBORG. I've no doubt. Nevertheless —

BRACK. You could bring your manuscript along and read it to Tesman at my place. I could lend you a room.

TESMAN. By Jove, Eilert, that's an idea. What?

HEDDA *interposes*. But Tesman, Mr. Loevborg doesn't want to go. I'm sure Mr. Loevborg would much rather sit here and have supper with me.

LOEVBORG *looks at her*. With you, Mrs. Tesman?

HEDDA. And Mrs. Elvsted.

LOEVBORG. Oh.

Casually.

I ran into her this afternoon.

HEDDA. Did you? Well, she's coming here this evening. So you really must stay, Mr. Loevborg. Otherwise she'll have no one to see her home.

LOEVBORG. That's true. Well — thank you, Mrs. Tesman, I'll stay then.

HEDDA. I'll just tell the servant.

> *She goes to the door which leads into the hall, and rings.* BERTHA *enters.* HEDDA *talks softly to her and points towards the rear room.* BERTHA *nods and goes out.*

TESMAN, *to* LOEVBORG, *as* HEDDA *does this.* I say, Eilert. This new subject of yours — the — er — future — is that the one you're going to lecture about?

LOEVBORG. Yes.

TESMAN. They told me down at the bookshop that you're going to hold a series of lectures here during the autumn.

LOEVBORG. Yes, I am. I — hope you don't mind, Tesman.

TESMAN. Good heavens, no! But — ?

LOEVBORG. I can quite understand it might queer your pitch a little.

TESMAN, *dejectedly.* Oh well, I can't expect you to put them off for my sake.

LOEVBORG. I'll wait till your appointment's been announced.

TESMAN. You'll wait! But — but — aren't you going to compete with me for the post? What?

LOEVBORG. No. I only want to defeat you in the eyes of the world.

TESMAN. Good heavens! Then Auntie Juju was right after all! Oh, I knew it, I knew it! Hear that, Hedda? Fancy! Eilert *doesn't* want to stand in our way.

HEDDA, *curtly.* Our? Leave me out of it, please.

> *She goes towards the rear room, where* BERTHA *is setting a tray with decanters and glasses on the table.* HEDDA *nods approval, and comes back into the drawing room.* BERTHA *goes out.*

TESMAN, *while this is happening.* Judge Brack, what do you think about all this? What?

BRACK. Oh, I think honour and victory can be very splendid things —

TESMAN. Of course they can. Still —

HEDDA *looks at* TESMAN *with a cold smile.* You look as if you'd been hit by a thunderbolt.

TESMAN. Yes, I feel rather like it.

BRACK. There was a black cloud looming up, Mrs. Tesman. But it seems to have passed over.

HEDDA *points towards the rear room*. Well, gentlemen, won't you go in and take a glass of cold punch?

BRACK *glances at his watch*. A stirrup cup? Yes, why not?

TESMAN. An admirable suggestion, Hedda. Admirable! Oh, I feel so relieved!

HEDDA. Won't you have one, too, Mr. Loevborg?

LOEVBORG. No, thank you. I'd rather not.

BRACK. Great heavens, man, cold punch isn't poison. Take my word for it.

LOEVBORG. Not for everyone, perhaps.

HEDDA. I'll keep Mr. Loevborg company while you drink.

TESMAN. Yes, Hedda dear, would you?

He and BRACK *go into the rear room, sit down, drink punch, smoke cigarettes and talk cheerfully during the following scene.* EILERT LOEVBORG *remains standing by the stove.* HEDDA *goes to the writing table.*

HEDDA, *raising her voice slightly*. I've some photographs I'd like to show you, if you'd care to see them. Tesman and I visited the Tyrol on our way home.

She comes back with an album, places it on the table by the sofa and sits in the upstage corner of the sofa. EILERT LOEVBORG *comes towards her, stops and looks at her. Then he takes a chair and sits down on her left, with his back towards the rear room.*

HEDDA *opens the album*. You see these mountains, Mr. Loevborg? That's the Ortler group. Tesman has written the name underneath. You see: "The Ortler Group near Meran."

LOEVBORG *has not taken his eyes from her; says softly, slowly*. Hedda — Gabler!

HEDDA *gives him a quick glance*. Ssh!

LOEVBORG *repeats softly*. Hedda Gabler!

HEDDA *looks at the album*. Yes, that used to be my name. When we first knew each other.

LOEVBORG. And from now on — for the rest of my life — I must teach myself never to say: Hedda Gabler.

HEDDA, *still turning the pages*. Yes, you must. You'd better start getting into practice. The sooner the better.

LOEVBORG, *bitterly*. Hedda Gabler married? And to George Tesman?

HEDDA. Yes. Well — that's life.

LOEVBORG. Oh, Hedda, Hedda! How could you throw yourself away like that?

HEDDA *looks sharply at him*. Stop it.

LOEVBORG. What do you mean?

TESMAN comes in and goes towards the sofa.

HEDDA *hears him coming and says casually*. And this, Mr. Loevborg, is the view from the Ampezzo valley. Look at those mountains.

Glances affectionately up at TESMAN.

What did you say those curious mountains were called, dear?

TESMAN. Let me have a look. Oh, those are the Dolomites.

HEDDA. Of course. Those are the Dolomites, Mr. Loevborg.

TESMAN. Hedda, I just wanted to ask you, can't we bring some punch in here? A glass for you, anyway. What?

HEDDA. Thank you, yes. And a biscuit or two, perhaps.

TESMAN. You wouldn't like a cigarette?

HEDDA. No.

TESMAN. Right.

He goes into the rear room and over to the right. BRACK *is sitting there, glancing occasionally at* HEDDA *and* LOEVBORG.

LOEVBORG, *softly, as before.* Answer me, Hedda. How could you do it?

HEDDA, *apparently absorbed in the album.* If you go on calling me Hedda I won't talk to you any more.

LOEVBORG. Mayn't I even when we're alone?

HEDDA. No. You can think it. But you mustn't say it.

LOEVBORG. Oh, I see. Because you love George Tesman.

HEDDA *glances at him and smiles.* Love? Don't be funny.

LOEVBORG. You don't love him?

HEDDA. I don't intend to be unfaithful to him. That's not what I want.

LOEVBORG. Hedda — just tell me one thing —

HEDDA. Ssh!

TESMAN *enters from the rear room, carrying a tray.*

TESMAN. Here we are! Here come the goodies!

Puts the tray down on the table.

HEDDA. Why didn't you ask the servant to bring it in?

TESMAN *fills the glasses.* I like waiting on you, Hedda.

HEDDA. But you've filled both glasses. Mr. Loevborg doesn't want to drink.

TESMAN. Yes, but Mrs. Elvsted'll be here soon.

HEDDA. Oh yes, that's true. Mrs. Elvsted —

TESMAN. Had you forgotten her? What?

HEDDA. We're so absorbed with these photographs.

Shows him one.

You remember this little village?

TESMAN. Oh, that one down by the Brenner Pass. We spent a night there —

HEDDA. Yes, and met all those amusing people.

TESMAN. Oh yes, it was there, wasn't it? By Jove, if only we could have had you with us, Eilert! Ah, well.

Goes back into the other room and sits down with BRACK.

LOEVBORG. Tell me one thing, Hedda.

HEDDA. Yes?

LOEVBORG. Didn't you love me either? Not — just a little?

HEDDA. Well now, I wonder? No, I think we were just good pals — Really good pals who could tell each other anything.

Smiles.

You certainly poured your heart out to me.

LOEVBORG. You begged me to.

HEDDA. Looking back on it, there was something beautiful and fascinating — and brave — about the way we told each other everything. That secret friendship no one else knew about.

LOEVBORG. Yes, Hedda, yes! Do you remember? How I used to come up to your father's house in the afternoon — and the General sat by the window and read his newspapers — with his back towards us —

HEDDA. And we sat on the sofa in the corner —

LOEVBORG. Always reading the same illustrated magazine —

HEDDA. We hadn't any photograph album.

LOEVBORG. Yes, Hedda. I regarded you as a kind of confessor. Told you things about myself which no one else knew about — then. Those days and nights of drinking and — Oh, Hedda, what power did you have to make me confess such things?

HEDDA. Power? You think I had some power over you?

LOEVBORG. Yes — I don't know how else to explain it. And all those — oblique questions you asked me —

HEDDA. You knew what they meant.

LOEVBORG. But that you could sit there and ask me such questions! So unashamedly —

HEDDA. I thought you said they were oblique.

LOEVBORG. Yes, but you asked them so unashamedly. That you could question me about — about that kind of thing!

HEDDA. You answered willingly enough.

LOEVBORG. Yes — that's what I can't understand — looking back on it. But tell me, Hedda — what you felt for me — wasn't that — love? When you asked me those questions and made me confess my sins to you, wasn't it because you wanted to wash me clean?

HEDDA. No, not exactly.

LOEVBORG. Why did you do it, then?

HEDDA. Do you find it so incredible that a young girl, given the chance to do so without anyone knowing, should want to be allowed a glimpse into a forbidden world of whose existence she is supposed to be ignorant?

LOEVBORG. So that was it?

HEDDA. One reason. One reason — I think.

LOEVBORG. You didn't love me, then. You just wanted — knowledge. But if that was so, why did you break it off?

HEDDA. That was your fault.

LOEVBORG. It was you who put an end to it.

HEDDA. Yes, when I realised that our friendship was threatening to develop into something — something else. Shame on you, Eilert Loevborg! How could you abuse the trust of your dearest friend?

LOEVBORG *clenches his fists.* Oh, why didn't you do it? Why didn't you shoot me dead? As you threatened to?

HEDDA. I was afraid. Of the scandal.

LOEVBORG. Yes, Hedda. You're a coward at heart.

HEDDA. A dreadful coward.

Changes her tone.

Luckily for you. Well, now you've found consolation with the Elvsteds.

LOEVBORG. I know what Thea's been telling you.

HEDDA. I dare say you told her about us.

LOEVBORG. Not a word. She's too silly to understand that kind of thing.

HEDDA. Silly?

LOEVBORG. She's silly about that kind of thing.

HEDDA. And I am a coward.

Leans closer to him, without looking him in the eyes, and says quietly. But let me tell you something. Something you don't know.

LOEVBORG, *tensely.* Yes?

HEDDA. My failure to shoot you wasn't my worst act of cowardice that evening.

LOEVBORG *looks at her for a moment, realises her meaning and whispers passionately.* Oh, Hedda! Hedda Gabler! Now I see what was behind those questions. Yes! It wasn't knowledge you wanted! It was life!

HEDDA *flashes a look at him and says quietly.* Take care! Don't you delude yourself!

It has begun to grow dark. BERTHA, *from outside, opens the door leading into the hall.*

HEDDA *closes the album with a snap and cries, smiling.* Ah, at last! Come in, Thea dear!

MRS. ELVSTED *enters from the hall, in evening dress. The door is closed behind her.*

HEDDA, *on the sofa, stretches out her arms towards her.* Thea darling, I thought you were never coming!

MRS. ELVSTED *makes a slight bow to the gentlemen in the rear room as she passes the open doorway, and they to her. Then she goes to the table and holds out her hand to* HEDDA. EILERT LOEVBORG *has risen from his chair. He and* MRS. ELVSTED *nod silently to each other.*

MRS. ELVSTED. Perhaps I ought to go in and say a few words to your husband?

HEDDA. Oh, there's no need. They're happy by themselves. They'll be going soon.

MRS. ELVSTED. Going?

HEDDA. Yes, they're off on a spree this evening.

MRS. ELVSTED, *quickly, to* LOEVBORG. You're not going with them?

LOEVBORG. No.

HEDDA. Mr. Loevborg is staying here with us.

MRS. ELVSTED *takes a chair and is about to sit down beside him.* Oh, how nice it is to be here!

HEDDA. No, Thea darling, not there. Come over here and sit beside me. I want to be in the middle.

MRS. ELVSTED. Yes, just as you wish.

She goes round the table and sits on the sofa, on HEDDA'S *right.* LOEV-
BORG *sits down again in his chair.*

LOEVBORG, *after a short pause, to* HEDDA. Isn't she lovely to look at?

HEDDA *strokes her hair gently.* Only to look at?

LOEVBORG. Yes. We're just good pals. We trust each other implicitly.
We can talk to each other quite unashamedly.

HEDDA. No need to be oblique?

MRS. ELVSTED *nestles close to* HEDDA *and says quietly.* Oh, Hedda, I'm so
happy. Imagine — he says I've inspired him!

HEDDA *looks at her with a smile.* Dear Thea! Does he really?

LOEVBORG. She has the courage of her convictions, Mrs. Tesman.

MRS. ELVSTED. I? Courage?

LOEVBORG. Absolute courage. Where friendship is concerned.

HEDDA. Yes. Courage. Yes. If only one had that —

LOEVBORG. Yes?

HEDDA. One might be able to live. In spite of everything.

Changes her tone suddenly.

Well, Thea darling, now you're going to drink a nice glass of cold punch.

MRS. ELVSTED. No, thank you. I never drink anything like that.

HEDDA. Oh. You, Mr. Loevborg?

LOEVBORG. Thank you, I don't either.

MRS. ELVSTED. No, he doesn't, either.

HEDDA *looks into his eyes.* But if I want you to?

LOEVBORG. That doesn't make any difference.

HEDDA *laughs.* Have I no power over you at all? Poor me!

LOEVBORG. Not where this is concerned.

HEDDA. Seriously, I think you should. For your own sake.

MRS. ELVSTED. Hedda!

LOEVBORG. Why?

HEDDA. Or perhaps I should say for other people's sake.

LOEVBORG. What do you mean?

HEDDA. People might think you didn't feel absolutely and unashamedly
sure of yourself. In your heart of hearts.

MRS. ELVSTED, *quietly.* Oh, Hedda, no!

LOEVBORG. People can think what they like. For the present.

MRS. ELVSTED, *happily.* Yes, that's true.

HEDDA. I saw it so clearly in Judge Brack a few minutes ago.

LOEVBORG. Oh. What did you see?

HEDDA. He smiled so scornfully when he saw you were afraid to go in
there and drink with them.

LOEVBORG. Afraid! I wanted to stay here and talk to you.

MRS. ELVSTED. That was only natural, Hedda.

HEDDA. But the Judge wasn't to know that. I saw him wink at Tesman
when you showed you didn't dare to join their wretched little party.

LOEVBORG. Didn't dare! Are you saying I didn't dare?

HEDDA. I'm not saying so. But that was what Judge Brack thought.

LOEVBORG. Well, let him.

HEDDA. You're not going, then?

LOEVBORG. I'm staying here with you and Thea.

MRS. ELVSTED. Yes, Hedda, of course he is.

HEDDA *smiles, and nods approvingly to* LOEVBORG. Firm as a rock! A man of principle! That's how a man should be!

Turns to MRS. ELVSTED *and strokes her cheek.*

Didn't I tell you so this morning when you came here in such a panic —

LOEVBORG *starts.* Panic?

MRS. ELVSTED, *frightened.* Hedda! But — Hedda!

HEDDA. Well, now you can see for yourself. There's no earthly need for you to get scared to death just because —

Stops.

Well! Let's all three cheer up and enjoy ourselves.

LOEVBORG. Mrs. Tesman, would you mind explaining to me what this is all about?

MRS. ELVSTED. Oh, my God, my God, Hedda, what are you saying? What are you doing?

HEDDA. Keep calm. That horrid Judge has his eye on you.

LOEVBORG. Scared to death, were you? For my sake?

MRS. ELVSTED, *quietly, trembling.* Oh, Hedda! You've made me so unhappy!

LOEVBORG *looks coldly at her for a moment. His face is distorted.* So that was how much you trusted me.

MRS. ELVSTED. Eilert dear, please listen to me —

LOEVBORG *takes one of the glasses of punch, raises it and says quietly, hoarsely.* Skoal, Thea!

Empties the glass, puts it down and picks up one of the others.

MRS. ELVSTED, *quietly.* Hedda, Hedda! Why did you want this to happen?

HEDDA. *I* — want it? Are you mad?

LOEVBORG. Skoal to you too, Mrs. Tesman. Thanks for telling me the truth. Here's to the truth!

Empties his glass and refills it.

HEDDA *puts her hand on his arm.* Steady. That's enough for now. Don't forget the party.

MRS. ELVSTED. No, no, no!

HEDDA. Ssh! They're looking at you.

LOEVBORG *puts down his glass.* Thea, tell me the truth —

MRS. ELVSTED. Yes!

LOEVBORG. Did your husband know you were following me?

MRS. ELVSTED. Oh, Hedda!

LOEVBORG. Did you and he have an agreement that you should come here and keep an eye on me? Perhaps he gave you the idea? After all, he's a magistrate. I suppose he needed me back in his office. Or did he miss my companionship at the card table?

MRS. ELVSTED, *quietly, sobbing.* Eilert, Eilert!

LOEVBORG *seizes a glass and is about to fill it.* Let's drink to him, too.

HEDDA. No more now. Remember you're going to read your book to Tesman.

LOEVBORG, *calm again, puts down his glass.* That was silly of me, Thea. To take it like that, I mean. Don't be angry with me, my dear. You'll see — yes, and they'll see, too — that though I fell, I — I have raised myself up again. With your help, Thea.

MRS. ELVSTED, *happily.* Oh, thank God!

> BRACK *has meanwhile glanced at his watch. He and* TESMAN *get up and come into the drawing room.*

BRACK *takes his hat and overcoat.* Well, Mrs. Tesman, it's time for us to go.

HEDDA. Yes, I suppose it must be.

LOEVBORG *gets up.* Time for me too, Judge.

MRS. ELVSTED, *quietly, pleadingly.* Eilert, please don't!

HEDDA *pinches her arm.* They can hear you.

MRS. ELVSTED *gives a little cry.* Oh!

LOEVBORG *to* BRACK. You were kind enough to ask me to join you.

BRACK. Are you coming?

LOEVBORG. If I may.

BRACK. Delighted.

LOEVBORG *puts the paper package in his pocket and says to* TESMAN. I'd like to show you one or two things before I send it off to the printer.

TESMAN. I say, that'll be fun. Fancy — ! Oh, but Hedda, how'll Mrs. Elvsted get home? What?

HEDDA. Oh, we'll manage somehow.

LOEVBORG *glances over towards the ladies.* Mrs. Elvsted? I shall come back and collect her, naturally.

> *Goes closer.*

About ten o'clock, Mrs. Tesman? Will that suit you?

HEDDA. Yes. That'll suit me admirably.

TESMAN. Good, that's settled. But you mustn't expect me back so early, Hedda.

HEDDA. Stay as long as you c— as long as you like, dear.

MRS. ELVSTED, *trying to hide her anxiety.* Well then, Mr. Loevborg, I'll wait here till you come.

LOEVBORG, *his hat in his hand.* Pray do, Mrs. Elvsted.

BRACK. Well, gentlemen, now the party begins. I trust that, in the words of a certain fair lady, we shall enjoy good sport.

HEDDA. What a pity the fair lady can't be there, invisible.

BRACK. Why invisible?

HEDDA. So as to be able to hear some of your uncensored witticisms, your honour.

BRACK *laughs.* Oh, I shouldn't advise the fair lady to do that.

TESMAN *laughs too.* I say, Hedda, that's good. By Jove! Fancy that!

BRACK. Well, good night, ladies, good night!

LOEVBORG *bows farewell.* About ten o'clock, then.

> BRACK, LOEVBORG *and* TESMAN *go out through the hall. As they do so,*

BERTHA *enters from the rear room with a lighted lamp. She puts it on the drawing-room table, then goes out the way she came.*

MRS. ELVSTED *has got up and is walking uneasily to and fro.* Oh Hedda, Hedda! How is all this going to end?

HEDDA. At ten o'clock, then. He'll be here. I can see him. With a crown of vine-leaves in his hair. Burning and unashamed!

MRS. ELVSTED. Oh, I do hope so!

HEDDA. Can't you see? Then he'll be himself again! He'll be a free man for the rest of his days!

MRS. ELVSTED. Please God you're right.

HEDDA. That's how he'll come!

Gets up and goes closer.

You can doubt him as much as you like. I believe in him! Now we'll see which of us —

MRS. ELVSTED. You're after something, Hedda.

HEDDA. Yes, I am. For once in my life I want to have the power to shape a man's destiny.

MRS. ELVSTED. Haven't you that power already?

HEDDA. No, I haven't. I've never had it.

MRS. ELVSTED. What about your husband?

HEDDA. Him! Oh, if you could only understand how poor I am. And you're allowed to be so rich, so rich!

Clasps her passionately.

I think I'll burn your hair off after all!

MRS. ELVSTED. Let me go! Let me go! You frighten me, Hedda!

BERTHA, *in the open doorway.* I've laid tea in the dining room, madam.

HEDDA. Good, we're coming.

MRS. ELVSTED. No, no, no! I'd rather go home alone! Now — at once!

HEDDA. Rubbish! First you're going to have some tea, you little idiot. And then — at ten o'clock — Eilert Loevborg will come. With a crown of vine-leaves in his hair!

She drags MRS. ELVSTED *almost forcibly towards the open doorway.*

ACT III

The same. The curtains are drawn across the open doorway, and also across the french windows. The lamp, half turned down, with a shade over it, is burning on the table. In the stove, the door of which is open, a fire has been burning, but it is now almost out.

MRS. ELVSTED, *wrapped in a large shawl and with her feet resting on a footstool, is sitting near the stove, huddled in the armchair.* HEDDA *is lying asleep on the sofa, fully dressed, with a blanket over her.*

MRS. ELVSTED, *after a pause, suddenly sits up in her chair and listens tensely. Then she sinks wearily back again and sighs.* Not back yet! Oh, God! Oh, God! Not back yet!

BERTHA *tiptoes cautiously in from the hall. She has a letter in her hand.*

MRS. ELVSTED *turns and whispers.* What is it? Has someone come?

BERTHA, *quietly.* Yes, a servant's just called with this letter.

MRS. ELVSTED, *quickly, holding out her hand.* A letter! Give it to me!

BERTHA. But it's for the Doctor, madam.

MRS. ELVSTED. Oh. I see.

BERTHA. Miss Tesman's maid brought it. I'll leave it here on the table.

MRS. ELVSTED. Yes, do.

BERTHA *puts down the letter.* I'd better put the lamp out. It's starting to smoke.

MRS. ELVSTED. Yes, put it out. It'll soon be daylight.

BERTHA *puts out the lamp.* It's daylight already, madam.

MRS. ELVSTED. Yes. Broad day. And not home yet.

BERTHA. Oh dear, I was afraid this would happen.

MRS. ELVSTED. Were you?

BERTHA. Yes. When I heard that a certain gentleman had returned to town, and saw him go off with them. I've heard all about him.

MRS. ELVSTED. Don't talk so loud. You'll wake your mistress.

BERTHA *looks at the sofa and sighs.* Yes. Let her go on sleeping, poor dear. Shall I put some more wood on the fire?

MRS. ELVSTED. Thank you, don't bother on my account.

BERTHA. Very good.

Goes quietly out through the hall.

HEDDA *wakes as the door closes and looks up.* What's that?

MRS. ELVSTED. It was only the maid.

HEDDA *looks round.* What am I doing here? Oh, now I remember.

Sits up on the sofa, stretches herself and rubs her eyes.

What time is it, Thea?

MRS. ELVSTED. It's gone seven.

HEDDA. When did Tesman get back?

ELVSTED. He's not back yet.

HEDDA. Not home yet?

MRS. ELVSTED *gets up.* No one's come.

HEDDA. And we sat up waiting for them till four o'clock.

MRS. ELVSTED. God! How I waited for him!

HEDDA *yawns and says with her hand in front of her mouth.* Oh, dear. We might have saved ourselves the trouble.

MRS. ELVSTED. Did you manage to sleep?

HEDDA. Oh, yes. Quite well, I think. Didn't you get any?

MRS. ELVSTED. Not a wink. I couldn't, Hedda. I just couldn't.

HEDDA *gets up and comes over to her.* Now, now, now. There's nothing to worry about. I know what's happened.

MRS. ELVSTED. What? Please tell me.

HEDDA. Well, obviously the party went on very late —

MRS. ELVSTED. Oh dear, I suppose it must have. But —

HEDDA. And Tesman didn't want to come home and wake us all up in the middle of the night.

Laughs.

Probably wasn't too keen to show his face either, after a spree like that.

MRS. ELVSTED. But where could he have gone?

HEDDA. I should think he's probably slept at his aunts'. They keep his old room for him.

MRS. ELVSTED. No, he can't be with them. A letter came for him just now from Miss Tesman. It's over there.

HEDDA. Oh?

Looks at the envelope.

Yes, it's Auntie Juju's handwriting. Well, he must still be at Judge Brack's, then. And Eilert Loevborg is sitting there, reading to him. With a crown of vine-leaves in his hair.

MRS. ELVSTED. Hedda, you're only saying that. You don't believe it.

HEDDA. Thea, you really are a little fool.

MRS. ELVSTED. Perhaps I am.

HEDDA. You look tired to death.

MRS. ELVSTED. Yes. I am tired to death.

HEDDA. Go to my room and lie down for a little. Do as I say, now; don't argue.

MRS. ELVSTED. No, no. I couldn't possibly sleep.

HEDDA. Of course you can.

MRS. ELVSTED. But your husband'll be home soon. And I must know at once —

HEDDA. I'll tell you when he comes.

MRS. ELVSTED. Promise me, Hedda?

HEDDA. Yes, don't worry. Go and get some sleep.

MRS. ELVSTED. Thank you. All right, I'll try.

She goes out through the rear room. HEDDA *goes to the french windows and draws the curtains. Broad daylight floods into the room. She goes to the writing table, takes a small hand mirror from it and arranges her hair. Then she goes to the door leading into the hall and presses the bell. After a few moments,* BERTHA *enters.*

BERTHA. Did you want anything, madam?

HEDDA. Yes, put some more wood on the fire. I'm freezing.

BERTHA. Bless you, I'll soon have this room warmed up.

She rakes the embers together and puts a fresh piece of wood on them. Suddenly she stops and listens.

There's someone at the front door, madam.

HEDDA. Well, go and open it. I'll see to the fire.

BERTHA. It'll burn up in a moment.

She goes out through the hall. HEDDA *kneels on the footstool and puts more wood in the stove. After a few seconds,* GEORGE TESMAN *enters from the hall. He looks tired, and rather worried. He tiptoes towards the open doorway and is about to slip through the curtains.*

HEDDA, *at the stove, without looking up.* Good morning.

TESMAN *turns.* Hedda!

Comes nearer.

Good heavens, are you up already? What?

HEDDA. Yes, I got up very early this morning.

TESMAN. I was sure you'd still be sleeping. Fancy that!

HEDDA. Don't talk so loud. Mrs. Elvsted's asleep in my room.

TESMAN. Mrs. Elvsted? Has she stayed the night here?

HEDDA. Yes. No one came to escort her home.

TESMAN. Oh. No, I suppose not.

HEDDA *closes the door of the stove and gets up.* Well. Was it fun?

TESMAN. Have you been anxious about me? What?

HEDDA. Not in the least. I asked if you'd had fun.

TESMAN. Oh yes, rather! Well, I thought, for once in a while — The first part was the best; when Eilert read his book to me. We arrived over an hour too early — what about that, eh? By Jove! Brack had a lot of things to see to, so Eilert read to me.

HEDDA *sits at the right-hand side of the table.* Well? Tell me about it.

TESMAN *sits on a footstool by the stove.* Honestly, Hedda, you've no idea what a book that's going to be. It's really one of the most remarkable things that's ever been written. By Jove!

HEDDA. Oh, never mind about the book —

TESMAN. I'm going to make a confession to you, Hedda. When he'd finished reading a sort of beastly feeling came over me.

HEDDA. Beastly feeling?

TESMAN. I found myself envying Eilert for being able to write like that. Imagine that, Hedda!

HEDDA. Yes. I can imagine.

TESMAN. What a tragedy that with all those gifts he should be so incorrigible.

HEDDA. You mean he's less afraid of life than most men?

TESMAN. Good heavens, no. He just doesn't know the meaning of the word moderation.

HEDDA. What happened afterwards?

TESMAN. Well, looking back on it I suppose you might almost call it an orgy, Hedda.

HEDDA. Had he vine-leaves in his hair?

TESMAN. Vine-leaves? No, I didn't see any of them. He made a long rambling oration in honour of the woman who'd inspired him to write this book. Yes, those were the words he used.

HEDDA. Did he name her?

TESMAN. No. But I suppose it must be Mrs. Elvsted. You wait and see!

HEDDA. Where did you leave him?

TESMAN. On the way home. We left in a bunch — the last of us, that is — and Brack came with us to get a little fresh air. Well, then, you see, we agreed we ought to see Eilert home. He'd had a drop too much.

HEDDA. You don't say?

TESMAN. But now comes the funny part, Hedda. Or I should really say the tragic part. Oh, I'm almost ashamed to tell you. For Eilert's sake, I mean —

HEDDA. Why, what happened?

TESMAN. Well, you see, as we were walking towards town I happened to drop behind for a minute. Only for a minute — er — you understand —

HEDDA. Yes, yes — ?

TESMAN. Well then, when I ran on to catch them up, what do you think I found by the roadside. What?

HEDDA. How on earth should I know?

TESMAN. You mustn't tell anyone, Hedda. What? Promise me that — for Eilert's sake.

Takes a package wrapped in paper from his coat pocket.
Just fancy! I found this.

HEDDA. Isn't this the one he brought here yesterday?

TESMAN. Yes! The whole of that precious, irreplaceable manuscript! And he went and lost it! Didn't even notice! What about that? By Jove! Tragic.

HEDDA. But why didn't you give it back to him?

TESMAN. I didn't dare to, in the state he was in.

HEDDA. Didn't you tell any of the others?

TESMAN. Good heavens, no. I didn't want to do that. For Eilert's sake, you understand.

HEDDA. Then no one else knows you have his manuscript?

TESMAN. No. And no one must be allowed to know.

HEDDA. Didn't it come up in the conversation later?

TESMAN. I didn't get a chance to talk to him any more. As soon as we got into the outskirts of town, he and one or two of the others gave us the slip. Disappeared, by Jove!

HEDDA. Oh? I suppose they took him home.

TESMAN. Yes, I imagine that was the idea. Brack left us, too.

HEDDA. And what have you been up to since then?

TESMAN. Well, I and one or two of the others — awfully jolly chaps, they were — went back to where one of them lived, and had a cup of morning coffee. Morning-after coffee — what? Ah, well. I'll just lie down for a bit and give Eilert time to sleep it off, poor chap, then I'll run over and give this back to him.

HEDDA *holds out her hand for the package.* No, don't do that. Not just yet. Let me read it first.

TESMAN. Oh no, really, Hedda dear, honestly, I daren't do that.

HEDDA. Daren't?

TESMAN. No — imagine how desperate he'll be when he wakes up and finds his manuscript's missing. He hasn't any copy, you see. He told me so himself.

HEDDA. Can't a thing like that be rewritten?

TESMAN. Oh no, not possibly, I shouldn't think. I mean, the inspiration, you know —

HEDDA. Oh, yes. I'd forgotten that.

Casually.
By the way, there's a letter for you.

TESMAN. Is there? Fancy that!

HEDDA *holds it out to him.* It came early this morning.

TESMAN. I say, it's from Auntie Juju! What on earth can it be?

Puts the package on the other footstool, opens the letter, reads it and jumps up.

Oh, Hedda! She says poor Auntie Rena's dying.

HEDDA. Well, we've been expecting that.

TESMAN. She says if I want to see her I must go quickly. I'll run over at once.

HEDDA *hides a smile.* Run?

TESMAN. Hedda dear, I suppose you wouldn't like to come with me? What about that, eh?

HEDDA *gets up and says wearily and with repulsion.* No, no, don't ask me to do anything like that. I can't bear illness or death. I loathe anything ugly.

TESMAN. Yes, yes. Of course.

In a dither.

My hat? My overcoat? Oh yes, in the hall. I do hope I won't get there too late, Hedda? What?

HEDDA. You'll be all right if you run.

BERTHA *enters from the hall.*

BERTHA. Judge Brack's outside and wants to know if he can come in.

TESMAN. At this hour? No, I can't possibly receive him now.

HEDDA. I can.

To BERTHA.

Ask his honour to come in.

BERTHA *goes.*

HEDDA *whispers quickly.* The manuscript, Tesman.

She snatches it from the footstool.

TESMAN. Yes, give it to me.

HEDDA. No, I'll look after it for now.

She goes over to the writing table and puts it in the bookcase. TESMAN *stands dithering, unable to get his gloves on.* JUDGE BRACK *enters from the hall.*

HEDDA *nods to him.* Well, you're an early bird.

BRACK. Yes, aren't I?

To TESMAN.

Are you up and about, too?

TESMAN. Yes, I've got to go and see my aunts. Poor Auntie Rena's dying.

BRACK. Oh dear, is she? Then you mustn't let me detain you. At so tragic a —

TESMAN. Yes, I really must run. Good-bye! Good-bye!

Runs out through the hall.

HEDDA *goes nearer.* You seem to have had excellent sport last night — Judge.

BRACK. Indeed yes, Mrs. Hedda. I haven't even had time to take my clothes off.

HEDDA. *You* haven't either?

BRACK. As you see. What's Tesman told you about last night's escapades?

HEDDA. Oh, only some boring story about having gone and drunk coffee somewhere.

BRACK. Yes, I've heard about that coffee party. Eilert Loevborg wasn't with them, I gather?

HEDDA. No, they took him home first.

BRACK. Did Tesman go with him?

HEDDA. No, one or two of the others, he said.

BRACK *smiles*. George Tesman is a credulous man, Mrs. Hedda.

HEDDA. God knows. But — has something happened?

BRACK. Well, yes, I'm afraid it has.

HEDDA. I see. Sit down and tell me.

She sits on the left of the table, BRACK *at the long side of it, near her.*

HEDDA. Well?

BRACK. I had a special reason for keeping track of my guests last night. Or perhaps I should say some of my guests.

HEDDA. Including Eilert Loevborg?

BRACK. I must confess — yes.

HEDDA. You're beginning to make me curious.

BRACK. Do you know where he and some of my other guests spent the latter half of last night, Mrs. Hedda?

HEDDA. Tell me. If it won't shock me.

BRACK. Oh, I don't think it'll shock you. They found themselves participating in an exceedingly animated *soirée*.

HEDDA. Of a sporting character?

BRACK. Of a highly sporting character.

HEDDA. Tell me more.

BRACK. Loevborg had received an invitation in advance — as had the others. I knew all about that. But he had refused. As you know, he's become a new man.

HEDDA. Up at the Elvsteds', yes. But he went?

BRACK. Well, you see, Mrs. Hedda, last night at my house, unhappily, the spirit moved him.

HEDDA. Yes, I hear he became inspired.

BRACK. Somewhat violently inspired. And as a result, I suppose, his thoughts strayed. We men, alas, don't always stick to our principles as firmly as we should.

HEDDA. I'm sure you're an exception, Judge Brack. But go on about Loevborg.

BRACK. Well, to cut a long story short, he ended up in the establishment of a certain Mademoiselle Danielle.

HEDDA. Mademoiselle Danielle?

BRACK. She was holding the *soirée*. For a selected circle of friends and admirers.

HEDDA. Has she got red hair?

BRACK. She has.

HEDDA. A singer of some kind?

BRACK. Yes — among other accomplishments. She's also a celebrated huntress — of men, Mrs. Hedda. I'm sure you've heard about her. Eilert Loevborg used to be one of her most ardent patrons. In his salad days.

HEDDA. And how did all this end?

BRACK. Not entirely amicably, from all accounts. Mademoiselle Danielle began by receiving him with the utmost tenderness and ended by resorting to her fists.

HEDDA. Against Loevborg?

BRACK. Yes. He accused her, or her friends, of having robbed him. He claimed his pocketbook had been stolen. Among other things. In short, he seems to have made a bloodthirsty scene.

HEDDA. And what did this lead to?

BRACK. It led to a general free-for-all, in which both sexes participated. Fortunately, in the end the police arrived.

HEDDA. The police too?

BRACK. Yes. I'm afraid it may turn out to be rather an expensive joke for Master Eilert. Crazy fool!

HEDDA. Oh?

BRACK. Apparently he put up a very violent resistance. Hit one of the constables on the ear and tore his uniform. He had to accompany them to the police station.

HEDDA. Where did you learn all this?

BRACK. From the police.

HEDDA, *to herself*. So that's what happened. He didn't have a crown of vine-leaves in his hair.

BRACK. Vine-leaves, Mrs. Hedda?

HEDDA, *in her normal voice again*. But, tell me, Judge, why do you take such a close interest in Eilert Loevborg?

BRACK. For one thing it'll hardly be a matter of complete indifference to me if it's revealed in court that he came there straight from my house.

HEDDA. Will it come to court?

BRACK. Of course. Well, I don't regard that as particularly serious. Still, I thought it my duty, as a friend of the family, to give you and your husband a full account of his nocturnal adventures.

HEDDA. Why?

BRACK. Because I've a shrewd suspicion that he's hoping to use you as a kind of screen.

HEDDA. What makes you think that?

BRACK. Oh, for heaven's sake, Mrs. Hedda, we're not blind. You wait and see. This Mrs. Elvsted won't be going back to her husband just yet.

HEDDA. Well, if there were anything between those two there are plenty of other places where they could meet.

BRACK. Not in anyone's home. From now on every respectable house will once again be closed to Eilert Loevborg.

HEDDA. And mine should be too, you mean?

BRACK. Yes. I confess I should find it more than irksome if this gentleman were to be granted unrestricted access to this house. If he were superfluously to intrude into —

HEDDA. The triangle?

BRACK. Precisely. For me it would be like losing a home.

HEDDA *looks at him and smiles.* I see. You want to be the cock of the walk.

BRACK *nods slowly and lowers his voice.* Yes, that is my aim. And I shall fight for it with — every weapon at my disposal.

HEDDA, *as her smile fades.* You're a dangerous man, aren't you? When you really want something.

BRACK. You think so?

HEDDA. Yes, I'm beginning to think so. I'm deeply thankful you haven't any kind of hold over me.

BRACK *laughs equivocally.* Well, well, Mrs. Hedda — perhaps you're right. If I had, who knows what I might not think up?

HEDDA. Come, Judge Brack. That sounds almost like a threat.

BRACK *gets up.* Heaven forbid! In the creation of a triangle — and its continuance — the question of compulsion should never arise.

HEDDA. Exactly what I was thinking.

BRACK. Well, I've said what I came to say. I must be getting back. Good-bye, Mrs. Hedda.

Goes towards the french windows.

HEDDA *gets up.* Are you going out through the garden?

BRACK. Yes, its shorter.

HEDDA. Yes. And it's the back door, isn't it?

BRACK. I've nothing against back doors. They can be quite intriguing — sometimes.

HEDDA. When people fire pistols out of them, for example?

BRACK, *in the doorway, laughs.* Oh, people don't shoot tame cocks.

HEDDA *laughs too.* I suppose not. When they've only got one.

They nod good-bye, laughing. He goes. She closes the french windows behind him, and stands for a moment, looking out pensively. Then she walks across the room and glances through the curtains in the open doorway. Goes to the writing table, takes LOEVBORG'S *package from the bookcase and is about to leaf through the pages when* BERTHA *is heard remonstrating loudly in the hall.* HEDDA *turns and listens. She hastily puts the package back in the drawer, locks it and puts the key on the inkstand.* EILERT LOEVBORG, *with his overcoat on and his hat in his hand, throws the door open. He looks somewhat confused and excited.*

LOEVBORG *shouts as he enters.* I must come in, I tell you! Let me pass!

He closes the door, turns, sees HEDDA, *controls himself immediately and bows.*

HEDDA, *at the writing table.* Well, Mr. Loevborg, this is rather a late hour to be collecting Thea.

LOEVBORG. And an early hour to call on you. Please forgive me.

HEDDA. How do you know she's still here?

LOEVBORG. They told me at her lodgings that she has been out all night.

HEDDA *goes to the table.* Did you notice anything about their behaviour when they told you?

LOEVBORG *looks at her, puzzled.* Notice anything?

HEDDA. Did they sound as if they thought it — strange?

LOEVBORG *suddenly understands.* Oh, I see what you mean. I'm dragging her down with me. No, as a matter of fact I didn't notice anything. I suppose Tesman isn't up yet?

HEDDA. No, I don't think so.

LOEVBORG. When did he get home?

HEDDA. Very late.

LOEVBORG. Did he tell you anything?

HEDDA. Yes. I gather you had a merry party at Judge Brack's last night.

LOEVBORG. He didn't tell you anything else?

HEDDA. I don't think so. I was so terribly sleepy —

MRS. ELVSTED *comes through the curtains in the open doorway.*

MRS. ELVSTED *runs towards him.* Oh, Eilert! At last!

LOEVBORG. Yes — at last. And too late.

MRS. ELVSTED. What is too late?

LOEVBORG. Everything — now. I'm finished, Thea.

MRS. ELVSTED. Oh, no, no! Don't say that!

LOEVBORG. You'll say it yourself, when you've heard what I —

MRS. ELVSTED. I don't want to hear anything!

HEDDA. Perhaps you'd rather speak to her alone? I'd better go.

LOEVBORG. No, stay.

MRS. ELVSTED. But I don't want to hear anything, I tell you!

LOEVBORG. It's not about last night.

MRS. ELVSTED. Then what — ?

LOEVBORG. I want to tell you that from now on we must stop seeing each other.

MRS. ELVSTED. Stop seeing each other!

HEDDA, *involuntarily.* I knew it!

LOEVBORG. I have no further use for you, Thea.

MRS. ELVSTED. You can stand there and say that! No further use for me! Surely I can go on helping you? We'll go on working together, won't we?

LOEVBORG. I don't intend to do any more work from now on.

MRS. ELVSTED, *desperately.* Then what use have I for my life?

LOEVBORG. You must try to live as if you had never known me.

MRS. ELVSTED. But I can't!

LOEVBORG. Try to, Thea. Go back home —

MRS. ELVSTED. Never! I want to be wherever you are! I won't let myself be driven away like this! I want to stay here — and be with you when the book comes out.

HEDDA *whispers.* Ah, yes! The book!

LOEVBORG *looks at her.* Our book; Thea's and mine. It belongs to both of us.

MRS. ELVSTED. Oh, yes! I feel that, too! And I've a right to be with you when it comes into the world. I want to see people respect and honour you again. And the joy! The joy! I want to share it with you!

LOEVBORG. Thea — our book will never come into the world.

HEDDA. Ah!

MRS. ELVSTED. Not — ?

LOEVBORG. It cannot. Ever.

MRS. ELVSTED. Eilert — what have you done with the manuscript? Where is it?

LOEVBORG. Oh Thea, please don't ask me that!

MRS. ELVSTED. Yes, yes — I must know. I've a right to know. Now!

LOEVBORG. The manuscript. I've torn it up.

MRS. ELVSTED *screams.* No, no!

HEDDA, *involuntarily.* But that's not — !

LOEVBORG *looks at her.* Not true, you think?

HEDDA *controls herself.* Why — yes, of course it is, if you say so. It just sounded so incredible —

LOEVBORG. It's true, nevertheless.

MRS. ELVSTED. Oh, my God, my God, Hedda — he's destroyed his own book!

LOEVBORG. I have destroyed my life. Why not my life's work, too?

MRS. ELVSTED. And you — did this last night?

LOEVBORG. Yes, Thea. I tore it into a thousand pieces. And scattered them out across the fjord. It's good, clean, salt water. Let it carry them away; let them drift in the current and the wind. And in a little while, they will sink. Deeper and deeper. As I shall, Thea.

MRS. ELVSTED. Do you know, Eilert — this book — all my life I shall feel as though you'd killed a little child?

LOEVBORG. You're right. It is like killing a child.

MRS. ELVSTED. But how could you? It was my child, too!

HEDDA, *almost inaudibly.* Oh — the child — !

MRS. ELVSTED *breathes heavily.* It's all over, then. Well — I'll go now, Hedda.

HEDDA. You're not leaving town?

MRS. ELVSTED. I don't know what I'm going to do. I can't see anything except — darkness.

She goes out through the hall.

HEDDA *waits a moment.* Aren't you going to escort her home, Mr. Loevborg?

LOEVBORG. I? Through the streets? Do you want me to let people see her with me?

HEDDA. Of course I don't know what else may have happened last night. But is it so utterly beyond redress?

LOEVBORG. It isn't just last night. It'll go on happening. I know it. But the curse of it is, I don't want to live that kind of life. I don't want to start all that again. She's broken my courage. I can't spit in the eyes of the world any longer.

HEDDA, *as though to herself.* That pretty little fool's been trying to shape a man's destiny.

Looks at him.

But how could you be so heartless towards her?

LOEVBORG. Don't call me heartless!

HEDDA. To go and destroy the one thing that's made her life worth living? You don't call that heartless?

LOEVBORG. Do you want to know the truth, Hedda?

HEDDA. The truth?

LOEVBORG. Promise me first — give me your word — that you'll never let Thea know about this.

HEDDA. I give you my word.

LOEVBORG. Good. Well; what I told her just now was a lie.

HEDDA. About the manuscript?

LOEVBORG. Yes. I didn't tear it up. Or throw it in the fjord.

HEDDA. You didn't? But where is it, then?

LOEVBORG. I destroyed it, all the same. I destroyed it, Hedda!

HEDDA. I don't understand.

LOEVBORG. Thea said that what I had done was like killing a child.

HEDDA. Yes. That's what she said.

LOEVBORG. But to kill a child isn't the worst thing a father can do to it.

HEDDA. What could be worse than that?

LOEVBORG. Hedda — suppose a man came home one morning, after a night of debauchery, and said to the mother of his child: "Look here. I've been wandering round all night. I've been to — such-and-such a place and such-and-such a place. And I had our child with me. I took him to — these places. And I've lost him. Just — lost him. God knows where he is or whose hands he's fallen into."

HEDDA. I see. But when all's said and done, this was only a book —

LOEVBORG. Thea's heart and soul were in that book. It was her whole life.

HEDDA. Yes. I understand.

LOEVBORG. Well, then you must also understand that she and I cannot possibly ever see each other again.

HEDDA. Where will you go?

LOEVBORG. Nowhere. I just want to put an end to it all. As soon as possible.

HEDDA *takes a step towards him.* Eilert Loevborg, listen to me. Do it — beautifully!

LOEVBORG. Beautifully?

Smiles.

With a crown of vine-leaves in my hair? The way you used to dream of me — in the old days?

HEDDA. No. I don't believe in that crown any longer. But — do it beautifully, all the same. Just this once. Good-bye. You must go now. And don't come back.

LOEVBORG. Adieu, madam. Give my love to George Tesman.

Turns to go.

HEDDA. Wait. I want to give you a souvenir to take with you.

She goes over to the writing table, opens the drawer and the pistol-case, and comes back to LOEVBORG *with one of the pistols.*

LOEVBORG *looks at her.* This? Is this the souvenir?

HEDDA *nods slowly.* You recognise it? You looked down its barrel once.

LOEVBORG. You should have used it then.

HEDDA. Here! Use it now!

LOEVBORG *puts the pistol in his breast pocket.* Thank you.

HEDDA. Do it beautifully, Eilert Loevborg. Only promise me that!

LOEVBORG. Good-bye, Hedda Gabler.

He goes out through the hall. HEDDA *stands by the door for a moment, listening. Then she goes over to the writing table, takes out the package containing the manuscript, glances inside it, pulls some of the pages half out and looks at them. Then she takes it to the arm-chair by the stove and sits down with the package in her lap. After a moment, she opens the door of the stove; then she opens the packet.*

HEDDA *throws one of the pages into the stove and whispers to herself.*

I'm burning your child, Thea! You with your beautiful wavy hair!

She throws a few more pages into the stove.

The child Eilert Loevborg gave you.

Throws the rest of the manuscript in.

I'm burning it! I'm burning your child!

ACT IV

The same. It is evening. The drawing room is in darkness. The small room is illuminated by the hanging lamp over the table. The curtains are drawn across the french windows. HEDDA, *dressed in black, is walking up and down in the darkened room. Then she goes into the small room and crosses to the left. A few chords are heard from the piano. She comes back into the drawing room.*

BERTHA *comes through the small room from the right with a lighted lamp, which she places on the table in front of the corner sofa in the drawing room. Her eyes are red with crying, and she has black ribbons on her cap. She goes quietly out, right.* HEDDA *goes over to the french windows, draws the curtains slightly to one side and looks out into the darkness.*

A few moments later, MISS TESMAN *enters from the hall. She is dressed in mourning, with a black hat and veil.* HEDDA *goes to meet her and holds out her hand.*

MISS TESMAN. Well, Hedda, here I am in the weeds of sorrow. My poor sister has ended her struggles at last.

HEDDA. I've already heard. Tesman sent me a card.

MISS TESMAN. Yes, he promised me he would. But I thought, no, I must go and break the news of death to Hedda myself — here, in the house of life.

HEDDA. It's very kind of you.

MISS TESMAN. Ah, Rena shouldn't have chosen a time like this to pass away. This is no moment for Hedda's house to be a place of mourning.

HEDDA, *changing the subject.* She died peacefully, Miss Tesman?

MISS TESMAN. Oh, it was quite beautiful! The end came so calmly. And she was so happy at being able to see George once again. And say good-bye to him. Hasn't he come home yet?

HEDDA. No. He wrote that I mustn't expect him too soon. But please sit down.

MISS TESMAN. No, thank you, Hedda dear — bless you. I'd like to. But I've so little time. I must dress her and lay her out as well as I can. She shall go to her grave looking really beautiful.

HEDDA. Can't I help with anything?

MISS TESMAN. Why, you mustn't think of such a thing! Hedda Tesman mustn't let her hands be soiled by contact with death. Or her thoughts. Not at this time.

HEDDA. One can't always control one's thoughts.

MISS TESMAN *continues.* Ah, well, that's life. Now we must start to sew poor Rena's shroud. There'll be sewing to be done in this house too before long, I shouldn't wonder. But not for a shroud, praise God.

GEORGE TESMAN *enters from the hall.*

HEDDA. You've come at last! Thank heavens!

TESMAN. Are you here, Auntie Juju? With Hedda? Fancy that!

MISS TESMAN. I was just on the point of leaving, dear boy. Well, have you done everything you promised me?

TESMAN. No, I'm afraid I forgot half of it. I'll have to run over again tomorrow. My head's in a complete whirl today. I can't collect my thoughts.

MISS TESMAN. But George dear, you mustn't take it like this.

TESMAN. Oh? Well — er — how should I?

MISS TESMAN. You must be happy in your grief. Happy for what's happened. As I am.

TESMAN. Oh, yes, yes. You're thinking of Aunt Rena.

HEDDA. It'll be lonely for you now, Miss Tesman.

MISS TESMAN. For the first few days, yes. But it won't last long. I hope. Poor dear Rena's little room isn't going to stay empty.

TESMAN. Oh? Whom are you going to move in there? What?

MISS TESMAN. Oh, there's always some poor invalid who needs care and attention.

HEDDA. Do you really want another cross like that to bear?

MISS TESMAN. Cross! God forgive you, child. It's been no cross for me.

HEDDA. But now — if a complete stranger comes to live with you — ?

MISS TESMAN. Oh, one soon makes friends with invalids. And I need so much to have someone to live for. Like you, my dear. Well, I expect there'll soon be work in this house too for an old aunt, praise God!

HEDDA. Oh — please!

TESMAN. By Jove, yes! What a splendid time the three of us could have together if —

HEDDA. If?

TESMAN, *uneasily*. Oh, never mind. It'll all work out. Let's hope so — what?

MISS TESMAN. Yes, yes. Well, I'm sure you two would like to be alone. *Smiles.*

Perhaps Hedda may have something to tell you, George. Good-bye. I must go home to Rena.

Turns to the door.

Dear God, how strange! Now Rena is with me and with poor dear Joachim.

TESMAN. Fancy that. Yes, Auntie Juju! What?

MISS TESMAN *goes out through the hall.*

HEDDA *follows* TESMAN *coldly and searchingly with her eyes.* I really believe this death distresses you more than it does her.

TESMAN. Oh, it isn't just Auntie Rena. It's Eilert I'm so worried about.

HEDDA, *quickly.* Is there any news of him?

TESMAN. I ran over to see him this afternoon. I wanted to tell him his manuscript was in safe hands.

HEDDA. Oh? You didn't find him?

TESMAN. No. He wasn't at home. But later I met Mrs. Elvsted and she told me he'd been here early this morning.

HEDDA. Yes, just after you'd left.

TESMAN. It seems he said he'd torn the manuscript up. What?

HEDDA. Yes, he claimed to have done so.

TESMAN. You told him we had it, of course?

HEDDA. No.

Quickly.

Did you tell Mrs. Elvsted?

TESMAN. No, I didn't like to. But you ought to have told him. Think if he should go home and do something desperate! Give me the manuscript, Hedda. I'll run over to him with it right away. Where did you put it?

HEDDA, *cold and motionless, leaning against the armchair.* I haven't got it any longer.

TESMAN. Haven't got it? What on earth do you mean?

HEDDA. I've burned it.

TESMAN *starts, terrified.* Burned it! Burned Eilert's manuscript!

HEDDA. Don't shout. The servant will hear you.

TESMAN. Burned it! But in heaven's name — ! Oh, no, no, no! This is impossible!

HEDDA. Well, it's true.

TESMAN. But Hedda, do you realise what you've done? That's appropriating lost property! It's against the law! By Jove! You ask Judge Brack and see if I'm not right.

HEDDA. You'd be well advised not to talk about it to Judge Brack or anyone else.

TESMAN. But how could you go and do such a dreadful thing? What on earth put the idea into your head? What came over you? Answer me! What?

HEDDA *represses an almost imperceptible smile.* I did it for your sake, George.

TESMAN. For my sake?

HEDDA. When you came home this morning and described how he'd read his book to you —

TESMAN. Yes, yes?

HEDDA. You admitted you were jealous of him.

TESMAN. But, good heavens, I didn't mean it literally!

HEDDA. No matter. I couldn't bear the thought that anyone else should push you into the background.

TESMAN, *torn between doubt and joy.* Hedda — is this true? But — but — but I never realised you loved me like that! Fancy —

HEDDA. Well, I suppose you'd better know. I'm going to have —

Breaks off and says violently.

No, no — you'd better ask your Auntie Juju. She'll tell you.

TESMAN. Hedda! I think I understand what you mean.

Clasps his hands.

Good heavens, can it really be true! What?

HEDDA. Don't shout. The servant will hear you.

TESMAN, *laughing with joy.* The servant! I say, that's good! The servant! Why, that's Bertha! I'll run out and tell her at once!

HEDDA *clenches her hands in despair.* Oh, it's destroying me, all this — it's destroying me!

TESMAN. I say, Hedda, what's up? What?

HEDDA, *cold, controlled.* Oh, it's all so — absurd — George.

TESMAN. Absurd? That I'm so happy? But surely — ? Ah, well — perhaps I won't say anything to Bertha.

HEDDA. No, do. She might as well know too.

TESMAN. No, no, I won't tell her yet. But Auntie Juju — I must let her know! And you — you called me George! For the first time! Fancy that! Oh, it'll make Auntie Juju so happy, all this! So very happy!

HEDDA. Will she be happy when she hears I've burned Eilert Loevborg's manuscript — for your sake?

TESMAN. No, I'd forgotten about that. Of course no one must be allowed to know about the manuscript. But that you're burning with love for me, Hedda, I must certainly let Auntie Juju know that. I say,

I wonder if young wives often feel like that towards their husbands?
What?

HEDDA. You might ask Auntie Juju about that too.

TESMAN. I will, as soon as I get the chance.

Looks uneasy and thoughtful again.

But I say, you know, that manuscript. Dreadful business. Poor Eilert!

MRS. ELVSTED, *dressed as on her first visit, with hat and overcoat, enters from the hall.*

MRS. ELVSTED *greets them hastily and tremulously.* Oh, Hedda dear, do please forgive me for coming here again.

HEDDA. Why, Thea, what's happened?

TESMAN. Is it anything to do with Eilert Loevborg? What?

MRS. ELVSTED. Yes — I'm so dreadfully afraid he may have met with an accident.

HEDDA *grips her arm.* You think so?

TESMAN. But, good heavens, Mrs. Elvsted, what makes you think that?

MRS. ELVSTED. I heard them talking about him at the boarding-house, as I went in. Oh, there are the most terrible rumours being spread about him in town today.

TESMAN. Fancy. Yes, I heard about them too. But I can testify that he went straight home to bed. Fancy that!

HEDDA. Well — what did they say in the boarding-house?

MRS. ELVSTED. Oh, I couldn't find out anything. Either they didn't know, or else — They stopped talking when they saw me. And I didn't dare to ask.

TESMAN *fidgets uneasily.* We must hope — we must hope you misheard them, Mrs. Elvsted.

MRS. ELVSTED. No, no, I'm sure it was he they were talking about. I heard them say something about a hospital —

TESMAN. Hospital!

HEDDA. Oh no, surely that's impossible!

MRS. ELVSTED. Oh, I became so afraid. So I went up to his rooms and asked to see him.

HEDDA. Do you think that was wise, Thea?

MRS. ELVSTED. Well, what else could I do? I couldn't bear the uncertainty any longer.

TESMAN. But *you* didn't manage to find him either? What?

MRS. ELVSTED. No. And they had no idea where he was. They said he hadn't been home since yesterday afternoon.

TESMAN. Since yesterday? Fancy that!

MRS. ELVSTED. I'm sure he must have met with an accident.

TESMAN. Hedda, I wonder if I ought to go into town and make one or two enquiries?

HEDDA. No, no, don't you get mixed up in this.

JUDGE BRACK *enters from the hall, hat in hand.* BERTHA, *who has opened the door for him, closes it. He looks serious and greets them silently.*

TESMAN. Hullo, my dear Judge. Fancy seeing you!

BRACK. I had to come and talk to you.

TESMAN. I can see Auntie Juju's told you the news.

BRACK. Yes, I've heard about that too.

TESMAN. Tragic, isn't it?

BRACK. Well, my dear chap, that depends how you look at it.

TESMAN *looks uncertainly at him.* Has something else happened?

BRACK. Yes.

HEDDA. Another tragedy?

BRACK. That also depends on how you look at it, Mrs. Tesman.

MRS. ELVSTED. Oh, it's something to do with Eilert Loevborg!

BRACK *looks at her for a moment.* How did you guess? Perhaps you've heard already — ?

MRS. ELVSTED, *confused.* No, no, not at all — I —

TESMAN. For heaven's sake, tell us!

BRACK *shrugs his shoulders.* Well, I'm afraid they've taken him to the hospital. He's dying.

MRS. ELVSTED *screams.* Oh God, God!

TESMAN. The hospital! Dying!

HEDDA, *involuntarily.* So quickly!

MRS. ELVSTED, *weeping.* Oh, Hedda! And we parted enemies!

HEDDA *whispers.* Thea — Thea!

MRS. ELVSTED, *ignoring her.* I must see him! I must see him before he dies!

BRACK. It's no use, Mrs. Elvsted. No one's allowed to see him now.

MRS. ELVSTED. But what's happened to him? You must tell me!

TESMAN. He hasn't tried to do anything to himself? What?

HEDDA. Yes, he has. I'm sure of it.

TESMAN. Hedda, how can you — ?

BRACK, *who has not taken his eyes from her.* I'm afraid you've guessed correctly, Mrs. Tesman.

MRS. ELVSTED. How dreadful!

TESMAN. Attempted suicide! Fancy that!

HEDDA. Shot himself!

BRACK. Right again, Mrs. Tesman.

MRS. ELVSTED *tries to compose herself.* When did this happen, Judge Brack?

BRACK. This afternoon. Between three and four.

TESMAN. But, good heavens — where? What?

BRACK, *a little hesitantly.* Where? Why, my dear chap, in his rooms of course.

MRS. ELVSTED. No, that's impossible. I was there soon after six.

BRACK. Well, it must have been somewhere else, then. I don't know exactly. I only know that they found him. He'd shot himself — through the breast.

MRS. ELVSTED. Oh, how horrible! That he should end like that!

HEDDA, *to* BRACK. Through the breast, you said?

BRACK. That is what I said.

HEDDA. Not through the head?

BRACK. Through the breast, Mrs. Tesman.

HEDDA. The breast. Yes; yes. That's good, too.

BRACK. Why, Mrs. Tesman?

HEDDA. Oh — no, I didn't mean anything.

TESMAN. And the wound's dangerous, you say? What?

BRACK. Mortal. He's probably already dead.

MRS. ELVSTED. Yes, yes — I feel it! It's all over. All over. Oh Hedda — !

TESMAN. But, tell me, how did you manage to learn all this?

BRACK, *curtly.* From the police. I spoke to one of them.

HEDDA, *loudly, clearly.* At last! Oh, thank God!

TESMAN, *appalled.* For God's sake, Hedda, what are you saying?

HEDDA. I am saying there's beauty in what he has done.

BRACK. Hm — Mrs. Tesman —

TESMAN. Beauty! Oh, but I say!

MRS. ELVSTED. Hedda, how can you talk of beauty in connection with a thing like this?

HEDDA. Eilert Loevborg has settled his account with life. He's had the courage to do what — what he had to do.

MRS. ELVSTED. No, that's not why it happened. He did it because he was mad.

TESMAN. He did it because he was desperate.

HEDDA. You're wrong! I know!

MRS. ELVSTED. He must have been mad. The same as when he tore up the manuscript.

BRACK *starts.* Manuscript? Did he tear it up?

MRS. ELVSTED. Yes. Last night.

TESMAN *whispers.* Oh, Hedda, we shall never be able to escape from this.

BRACK. Hm. Strange.

TESMAN *wanders round the room.* To think of Eilert dying like that. And not leaving behind him the thing that would have made his name endure.

MRS. ELVSTED. If only it could be pieced together again!

TESMAN. Yes, fancy! If only it could! I'd give anything —

MRS. ELVSTED. Perhaps it can, Mr. Tesman.

TESMAN. What do you mean?

MRS. ELVSTED *searches in the pocket of her dress.* Look! I kept the notes he dictated it from.

HEDDA *takes a step nearer.* Ah!

TESMAN. You kept them, Mrs. Elvsted! What?

MRS. ELVSTED. Yes, here they are. I brought them with me when I left home. They've been in my pocket ever since.

TESMAN. Let me have a look.

MRS. ELVSTED *hands him a wad of small sheets of paper.* They're in a terrible muddle. All mixed up.

TESMAN. I say, just fancy if we can sort them out! Perhaps if we work on them together — ?

MRS. ELVSTED. Oh, yes! Let's try, anyway!

TESMAN. We'll manage it. We must! I shall dedicate my life to this.

HEDDA. *You*, George? Your life?

TESMAN. Yes — well, all the time I can spare. My book'll have to wait. Hedda, you do understand? What? I owe it to Eilert's memory.

HEDDA. Perhaps.

TESMAN. Well, my dear Mrs. Elvsted, you and I'll have to pool our brains. No use crying over spilt milk, what? We must try to approach this matter calmly.

MRS. ELVSTED. Yes, yes, Mr. Tesman. I'll do my best.

TESMAN. Well, come over here and let's start looking at these notes right away. Where shall we sit? Here? No, the other room. You'll excuse us, won't you, Judge? Come along with me, Mrs. Elvsted.

MRS. ELVSTED. Oh, God! If only we can manage to do it!

TESMAN *and* MRS. ELVSTED *go into the rear room. He takes off his hat and overcoat. They sit at the table beneath the hanging lamp and absorb themselves in the notes.* HEDDA *walks across to the stove and sits in the armchair. After a moment,* BRACK *goes over to her.*

HEDDA, *half aloud.* Oh, Judge! This act of Eilert Loevborg's — doesn't it give one a sense of release!

BRACK. Release, Mrs. Hedda? Well, it's a release for him, of course —

HEDDA. Oh, I don't mean him — I mean me! The release of knowing that someone can do something really brave! Something beautiful!

BRACK *smiles.* Hm — my dear Mrs. Hedda —

HEDDA. Oh, I know what you're going to say. You're a bourgeois at heart too, just like — ah, well!

BRACK *looks at her.* Eilert Loevborg has meant more to you than you're willing to admit to yourself. Or am I wrong?

HEDDA. I'm not answering questions like that from you. I only know that Eilert Loevborg has had the courage to live according to his own principles. And now, at last, he's done something big! Something beautiful! To have the courage and the will to rise from the feast of life so early!

BRACK. It distresses me deeply, Mrs. Hedda, but I'm afraid I must rob you of that charming illusion.

HEDDA. Illusion?

BRACK. You wouldn't have been allowed to keep it for long, anyway.

HEDDA. What do you mean?

BRACK. He didn't shoot himself on purpose.

HEDDA. Not on purpose?

BRACK. No. It didn't happen quite the way I told you.

HEDDA. Have you been hiding something? What is it?

BRACK. In order to spare poor Mrs. Elvsted's feelings, I permitted myself one or two small — equivocations.

HEDDA. What?

BRACK. To begin with, he is already dead.

HEDDA. He died at the hospital?

BRACK. Yes. Without regaining consciousness.

HEDDA. What else haven't you told us?

BRACK. The incident didn't take place at his lodgings.

HEDDA. Well, that's utterly unimportant.

BRACK. Not utterly. The fact is, you see, that Eilert Loevborg was found shot in Mademoiselle Danielle's boudoir.

HEDDA *almost jumps up, but instead sinks back in her chair.* That's impossible. He can't have been there today.

BRACK. He was there this afternoon. He went to ask for something he claimed they'd taken from him. Talked some crazy nonsense about a child which had got lost —

HEDDA. Oh! So that was the reason!

BRACK. I thought at first he might have been referring to his manuscript. But I hear he destroyed that himself. So he must have meant his pocketbook — I suppose.

HEDDA. Yes, I suppose so. So they found him there?

BRACK. Yes; there. With a discharged pistol in his breast pocket. The shot had wounded him mortally.

HEDDA. Yes. In the breast.

BRACK. No. In the — hm — stomach. The — lower part —

HEDDA *looks at him with an expression of repulsion.* That too! Oh, why does everything I touch become mean and ludicrous? It's like a curse!

BRACK. There's something else, Mrs. Hedda. It's rather disagreeable, too.

HEDDA. What?

BRACK. The pistol he had on him —

HEDDA. Yes? What about it?

BRACK. He must have stolen it.

HEDDA *jumps up.* Stolen it! That isn't true! He didn't!

BRACK. It's the only explanation. He must have stolen it. Ssh!

TESMAN *and* MRS. ELVSTED *have got up from the table in the rear room and come into the drawing room.*

TESMAN, *his hands full of papers.* Hedda, I can't see properly under that lamp. Think!

HEDDA. I am thinking.

TESMAN. Do you think we could possibly use your writing table for a little? What?

HEDDA. Yes, of course.

Quickly.

No, wait! Let me tidy it up first.

TESMAN. Oh, don't you trouble about that. There's plenty of room.

HEDDA. No, no, let me tidy it up first, I say. I'll take this in and put them on the piano. Here.

She pulls an object, covered with sheets of music, out from under the bookcase, puts some more sheets on top and carries it all into the rear room and away to the left. TESMAN *puts his papers on the writing table and moves the lamp over from the corner table. He and* MRS. ELVSTED *sit down and begin working again.* HEDDA *comes back.*

HEDDA, *behind* MRS. ELVSTED'S *chair, ruffles her hair gently.* Well, my pretty Thea! And how is work progressing on Eilert Loevborg's memorial?

MRS. ELVSTED *looks up at her, dejectedly.* Oh, it's going to be terribly difficult to get these into any order.

TESMAN. We've got to do it. We must! After all, putting other people's papers into order is rather my specialty, what?

HEDDA *goes over to the stove and sits on one of the footstools.* BRACK *stands over her, leaning against the armchair.*

HEDDA *whispers.* What was that you were saying about the pistol?

BRACK, *softly.* I said he must have stolen it.

HEDDA. Why do you think that?

BRACK. Because any other explanation is unthinkable, Mrs. Hedda, or ought to be.

HEDDA. I see.

BRACK *looks at her for a moment.* Eilert Loevborg was here this morning. Wasn't he?

HEDDA. Yes.

BRACK. Were you alone with him?

HEDDA. For a few moments.

BRACK. You didn't leave the room while he was here?

HEDDA. No.

BRACK. Think again. Are you sure you didn't go out for a moment?

HEDDA. Oh — yes, I might have gone into the hall. Just for a few seconds.

BRACK. And where was your pistol-case during this time?

HEDDA. I'd locked it in that —

BRACK. Er — Mrs. Hedda?

HEDDA. It was lying over there on my writing table.

BRACK. Have you looked to see if both the pistols are still there?

HEDDA. No.

BRACK. You needn't bother. I saw the pistol Loevborg had when they found him. I recognised it at once. From yesterday. And other occasions.

HEDDA. Have you got it?

BRACK. No. The police have it.

HEDDA. What will the police do with this pistol?

BRACK. Try to trace the owner.

HEDDA. Do you think they'll succeed?

BRACK *leans down and whispers.* No, Hedda Gabler. Not as long as I hold my tongue.

HEDDA *looks nervously at him.* And if you don't?

BRACK *shrugs his shoulders.* You could always say he'd stolen it.

HEDDA. I'd rather die!

BRACK *smiles.* People say that. They never do it.

HEDDA, *not replying.* And suppose the pistol wasn't stolen? And they trace the owner? What then?

BRACK. There'll be a scandal, Hedda.

HEDDA. A scandal!

BRACK. Yes, a scandal. The thing you're so frightened of. You'll have to appear in court. Together with Mademoiselle Danielle. She'll have to explain how it all happened. Was it an accident, or was it — homicide? Was he about to take the pistol from his pocket to threaten her? And did it go off? Or did she snatch the pistol from his hand, shoot him and then put it back in his pocket? She might quite easily have done it. She's a resourceful lady, is Mademoiselle Danielle.

HEDDA. But I had nothing to do with this repulsive business.

BRACK. No. But you'll have to answer one question. Why did you give Eilert Loevborg this pistol? And what conclusions will people draw when it is proved you did give it to him?

HEDDA *bows her head.* That's true. I hadn't thought of that.

BRACK. Well, luckily there's no danger as long as I hold my tongue.

HEDDA *looks up at him.* In other words, I'm in your power, Judge. From now on, you've got your hold over me.

BRACK *whispers, more slowly.* Hedda, my dearest — believe me — I will not abuse my position.

HEDDA. Nevertheless, I'm in your power. Dependent on your will, and your demands. Not free. Still not free!

Rises passionately.

No. I couldn't bear that. No.

BRACK *looks half-derisively at her.* Most people resign themselves to the inevitable, sooner or later.

HEDDA *returns his gaze.* Possibly they do.

She goes across to the writing table.

HEDDA *represses an involuntary smile and says in* TESMAN'S *voice.* Well, George. Think you'll be able to manage? What?

TESMAN. Heaven knows, dear. This is going to take months and months.

HEDDA, *in the same tone as before.* Fancy that, by Jove!

Runs her hands gently through MRS. ELVSTED'S *hair.*

Doesn't it feel strange, Thea? Here you are working away with Tesman just the way you used to work with Eilert Loevborg.

MRS. ELVSTED. Oh — if only I can inspire your husband too!

HEDDA. Oh, it'll come. In time.

TESMAN. Yes — do you know, Hedda, I really think I'm beginning to feel a bit — well — that way. But you go back and talk to Judge Brack.

HEDDA. Can't I be of use to you two in any way?

TESMAN. No, none at all.

Turns his head.

You'll have to keep Hedda company from now on, Judge, and see she doesn't get bored. If you don't mind.

BRACK *glances at* HEDDA. It'll be a pleasure.

HEDDA. Thank you. But I'm tired this evening. I think I'll lie down on the sofa in there for a little while.

TESMAN. Yes, dear — do. What?

HEDDA goes into the rear room and draws the curtains behind her. Short pause. Suddenly she begins to play a frenzied dance melody on the piano.

MRS. ELVSTED *starts up from her chair.* Oh, what's that?

TESMAN *runs to the doorway.* Hedda dear, please! Don't play dance music tonight! Think of Auntie Rena. And Eilert.

HEDDA *puts her head out through the curtains.* And Auntie Juju. And all the rest of them. From now on I'll be quiet.

Closes the curtains behind her.

TESMAN, *at the writing table.* It distresses her to watch us doing this. I say, Mrs. Elvsted, I've an idea. Why don't you move in with Auntie Juju? I'll run over each evening, and we can sit and work there. What?

MRS. ELVSTED. Yes, that might be the best plan.

HEDDA, *from the rear room.* I can hear what you're saying, Tesman. But how shall I spend the evenings out here?

TESMAN, *looking through his papers.* Oh, I'm sure Judge Brack'll be kind enough to come over and keep you company. You won't mind my not being here, Judge?

BRACK, *in the armchair, calls gaily.* I'll be delighted, Mrs. Tesman. I'll be here every evening. We'll have great fun together, you and I.

HEDDA, *loud and clear.* Yes, that'll suit you, won't it, Judge? The only cock on the dunghill — !

A shot is heard from the rear room. TESMAN, MRS. ELVSTED *and* JUDGE BRACK *start from their chairs.*

TESMAN. Oh, she's playing with those pistols again.

He pulls the curtains aside and runs in. MRS. ELVSTED *follows him.* HEDDA *is lying dead on the sofa. Confusion and shouting.* BERTHA *enters in alarm from the right.*

TESMAN *screams to* BRACK. She's shot herself! Shot herself in the head! By Jove! Fancy that!

BRACK *half paralysed in the armchair.* But, good God! People don't do such things!

Anton Chekhov (1860–1904)

LIFE: He was the son of a shopkeeper and the grandson of a serf; poverty shadowed his early years, tuberculosis his maturity. He became a doctor but it was as a writer that he supported his family: beginning with short humorous sketches for magazines and newspapers, he slowly developed the craft which made the details of his stories sound tones of multiple resonance. His success in the theatre was much slower but no less permanent, and when he died he was the master of his second craft.

WORKS: There are many volumes of short stories; among the plays
are *The Sea Gull* (1896), *The Three Sisters* (1901), and *The Cherry
Orchard* (1904).

GOOSEBERRIES *

The whole sky had been overcast with rain-clouds from early morning; it was a still day, not hot, but heavy, as it is in gray dull weather
when the clouds have been hanging over the country for a long while,
when one expects rain and it does not come. Ivan Ivanovich, the veterinary surgeon, and Burkin, the high school teacher, were already tired
from walking, and the fields seemed to them endless. Far ahead of them
they could just see the windmills of the village of Mironositskoe; on
the right stretched a row of hillocks which disappeared in the distance
behind the village, and they both knew that this was the bank of the
river, that there were meadows, green willows, homesteads there, and
that if one stood on one of the hillocks one could see from it the same
vast plain, telegraph-wires, and a train which in the distance looked
like a crawling caterpillar, and that in clear weather one could even
see the town. Now, in still weather, when all nature seemed mild and
dreamy, Ivan Ivanovich and Burkin were filled with love of the countryside, and both thought how great, how beautiful a land it was.

"Last time we were in Prokofy's barn," said Burkin, "you were about
to tell me a story."

"Yes; I meant to tell you about my brother."

Ivan Ivanovich heaved a deep sigh and lighted a pipe to begin to tell
his story, but just at that moment the rain began. And five minutes
later heavy rain came down, covering the sky, and it was hard to tell
when it would be over. Ivan Ivanovich and Burkin stopped in hesitation; the dogs, already drenched, stood with their tails between their
legs gazing at them feelingly.

"We must take shelter somewhere," said Burkin. "Let us go to
Alehin's; it's close by."

"Come along."

They turned aside and walked through mown fields, sometimes going
straight forward, sometimes turning to the right, till they came out on
the road. Soon they saw poplars, a garden, then the red roofs of barns;
there was a gleam of the river, and the view opened onto a broad expanse of water with a windmill and a white bathhouse: this was Sofino,
where Alehin lived.

The watermill was at work, drowning the sound of the rain; the dam

Reprinted with permission of The Macmillan Company from *The Wife and Other Stories* by Anton
Chekhov. Translated by Constance Garnett. Copyright 1918 by The Macmillan Company, renewed 1946
by Constance Garnett.

* 1898.

was shaking. Here wet horses with drooping heads were standing near their carts, and men were walking about covered with sacks. It was damp, muddy, and desolate; the water looked cold and malignant. Ivan Ivanovich and Burkin were already conscious of a feeling of wetness, messiness, and discomfort all over; their feet were heavy with mud, and when, crossing the dam, they went up to the barns, they were silent, as though they were angry with one another.

In one of the barns there was the sound of a winnowing machine, the door was open, and clouds of dust were coming from it. In the doorway was standing Alehin himself, a man of forty, tall and stout, with long hair, more like a professor or an artist than a landowner. He had on a white shirt that badly needed washing, a rope for a belt, drawers instead of trousers, and his boots, too, were plastered up with mud and straw. His eyes and nose were black with dust. He recognized Ivan Ivanovich and Burkin, and was apparently much delighted to see them.

"Go into the house, gentlemen," he said, smiling; "I'll come directly, this minute."

It was a big two-storied house. Alehin lived in the lower story, with arched ceilings and little windows, where the bailiffs had once lived; here everything was plain, and there was a smell of rye bread, cheap vodka, and harness. He went upstairs into the best rooms only on rare occasions, when visitors came. Ivan Ivanovich and Burkin were met in the house by a maidservant, a young woman so beautiful that they both stood still and looked at one another.

"You can't imagine how delighted I am to see you, my friends," said Alehin, going into the hall with them. "It is a surprise! Pelageya," he said, addressing the girl, "give our visitors something to change into. And, by the way, I will change too. Only I must first go and wash, for I almost think I have not washed since spring. Wouldn't you like to come into the bathhouse? And meanwhile they will get things ready here."

Beautiful Pelageya, looking so refined and soft, brought them towels and soap, and Alehin went to the bathhouse with his guests.

"It's a long time since I had a wash," he said, undressing. "I have got a nice bathhouse, as you see — my father built it — but I somehow never have time to wash."

He sat down on the steps and soaped his long hair and his neck, and the water round him turned brown.

"Yes, I must say," said Ivan Ivanovich meaningly, looking at his head.

"It's a long time since I washed . . ." said Alehin with embarrassment, giving himself a second soaping, and the water near him turned dark blue, like ink.

Ivan Ivanovich went outside, plunged into the water with a loud splash, and swam in the rain, flinging his arms out wide. He stirred the water into waves which set the white lilies bobbing up and down; he swam to the very middle of the millpond and dived, and came up a minute later in another place, and swam on, and kept on diving, trying to touch bottom.

"Oh, my goodness!" he repeated continually, enjoying himself thoroughly. "Oh, my goodness!" He swam to the mill, talked to the peasants there, then returned and lay on his back in the middle of the pond, turning his face to the rain. Burkin and Alehin were dressed and ready to go, but he still went on swimming and diving. "Oh, my goodness! . . ." he said. "Oh, Lord, have mercy on me! . . ."

"That's enough!" Burkin shouted to him.

They went back to the house. And only when the lamp was lighted in the big drawing-room upstairs, and Burkin and Ivan Ivanovich, attired in silk dressing-gowns and warm slippers, were sitting in armchairs; and Alehin, washed and combed, in a new coat, was walking about the drawing-room, evidently enjoying the feeling of warmth, cleanliness, dry clothes, and light shoes; and when lovely Pelageya, stepping noiselessly on the carpet and smiling softly, handed tea and jam on a tray — only then Ivan Ivanovich began on his story, and it seemed as though not only Burkin and Alehin were listening, but also the ladies, young and old, and the officers who looked down upon them sternly and calmly from their gold frames.

"There are two of us brothers," he began — "I, Ivan Ivanovich, and my brother, Nikolay Ivanovich, two years younger. I went in for a learned profession and became a veterinary surgeon, while Nikolay sat in a government office from the time he was nineteen. Our father, Chimsha-Himalaisky, was the son of a private, but he himself rose to be an officer and left us a little estate and the rank of nobility. After his death the little estate went in debts and legal expenses; but, anyway, we had spent our childhood running wild in the country. Like peasant children, we passed our days and nights in the fields and the woods, looked after horses, stripped the bark off the trees, fished and so on. . . . And, you know, whoever has once in his life caught perch or has seen the migrating of the thrushes in autumn, watched how they float in flocks over the village on bright, cool days, he will never be a real townsman, and will have a yearning for freedom to the day of his death. My brother was miserable in the government office. Years passed by, and he went on sitting in the same place, went on writing the same papers and thinking of one and the same thing — how to get into the country. And this yearning by degrees passed into a definite desire, into a dream of buying himself a little farm somewhere on the banks of a river or a lake.

"He was a gentle, good-natured fellow, and I was fond of him, but I never sympathized with this desire to shut himself up for the rest of his life in a little farm of his own. It's the correct thing to say that a man needs no more than six feet of earth. But six feet is what a corpse needs, not a man. And they say, too, now, that if our intellectual classes are attracted to the land and yearn for a farm, it's a good thing. But these farms are just the same as six feet of earth. To retreat from town, from the struggle, from the bustle of life, to retreat and bury oneself in one's farm — it's not life, it's egoism, laziness, it's monasticism of a sort, but monasticism without good works. A man does not need six feet of earth or a farm, but the whole globe, all nature, where he can have room to display all the qualities and peculiarities of his free spirit.

"My brother Nikolay, sitting in his government office, dreamed of how he would eat his own cabbages, which would fill the whole yard with such a savory smell, take his meals on the green grass, sleep in the sun, sit for whole hours on the seat by the gate gazing at the fields and the forest. Gardening books and the agricultural hints in calendars were his delight, his favorite spiritual sustenance; he enjoyed reading newspapers, too, but the only things he read in them were the advertisements of so many acres of arable land and a grass meadow with farmhouses and buildings, a river, a garden, a mill and millponds, for sale. And his imagination pictured the garden-paths, flowers and fruit, starling cotes, the carp in the pond, and all that sort of thing, you know. These imaginary pictures were of different kinds according to the advertisements which he came across, but for some reason in every one of them he always had to have gooseberries. He could not imagine a homestead, he could not picture an idyllic nook, without gooseberries.

" 'Country life has its conveniences,' he would sometimes say. 'You sit on the veranda and you drink tea, while your ducks swim on the pond, there is a delicious smell everywhere, and . . . and the gooseberries are growing.'

"He used to draw a map of his property, and in every map there were the same things — (a) house for the family, (b) servants' quarters, (c) kitchen-garden, (d) gooseberry-bushes. He lived parsimoniously, was frugal in food and drink, his clothes were beyond description; he looked like a beggar, but kept on saving and putting money in the bank. He grew fearfully avaricious. I did not like to look at him, and I used to give him something and send him presents for Christmas and Easter, but he used to save that too. Once a man is absorbed by an idea there is no doing anything with him.

"Years passed: he was transferred to another province. He was over forty, and he was still reading the advertisements in the papers and saving up. Then I heard he was married. Still with the same object of buying a farm and having gooseberries, he married an elderly and ugly widow without a trace of feeling for her, simply because she had filthy lucre. He went on living frugally after marrying her, and kept her short of food, while he put her money in the bank in his name.

"Her first husband had been a postmaster, and with him she was accustomed to pies and homemade wines, while with her second husband she did not get enough black bread; she began to pine away with this sort of life, and three years later she gave up her soul to God. And I need hardly say that my brother never for one moment imagined that he was responsible for her death. Money, like vodka, makes a man queer.

In our town there was a merchant who, before he died, ordered a plate-ful of honey and ate up all his money and lottery tickets with the honey, so that no one might get the benefit of it. While I was inspecting cattle at a railway-station a cattle-dealer fell under an engine and had his leg cut off. We carried him into the waiting-room, the blood was flowing — it was a horrible thing — and he kept asking them to look for his leg and was very much worried about it; there were twenty roubles in the boot on the leg that had been cut off, and he was afraid they would be lost."

"That's a story from a different opera," said Burkin.

"After his wife's death," Ivan Ivanovich went on, after thinking for half a minute, "my brother began looking out for an estate for himself. Of course, you may look about for five years and yet end by making a mistake, and buying something quite different from what you have dreamed of. My brother Nikolay bought through an agent a mortgaged estate of three hundred and thirty acres, with a house for the family, with servants' quarters, with a park, but with no orchard, no goose-berry-bushes, and no duck-pond; there was a river, but the water in it was the color of coffee, because on one side of the estate there was a brickyard and on the other a factory for burning bones. But Nikolay Ivanovich did not grieve much; he ordered twenty gooseberry-bushes, planted them, and began living as a country gentleman.

"Last year I went to pay him a visit. I thought I would go and see what it was like. In his letters my brother called his estate 'Chumbaro-klov Waste, alias Himalaiskoe.' I reached 'alias Himalaiskoe' in the afternoon. It was hot. Everywhere there were ditches, fences, hedges, fir-trees planted in rows, and there was no knowing how to get to the yard, where to put one's horse. I went up to the house, and was met by a fat red dog that looked like a pig. It wanted to bark, but was too lazy. The cook, a fat, barefooted woman, came out of the kitchen, and she, too, looked like a pig, and said that her master was resting. I went in to see my brother. He was sitting up in bed with a quilt over his legs; he had grown older, fatter, wrinkled; his cheeks, his nose, and his mouth all stuck out — he looked as though he might begin grunting into the quilt at any moment.

"We embraced each other, and shed tears of joy and of sadness at the thought that we had once been young and now were both gray-headed and near the grave. He dressed, and led me out to show me the estate.

" 'Well, how are you getting on here?' I asked.

" 'Oh, all right, thank God; I am getting on very well.'

"He was no more a poor timid clerk, but a real landowner, a gentle-man. He was already accustomed to it, had grown used to it, and liked it. He ate a great deal, went to the bathhouse, was growing stout, was already at law with the village commune and both factories, and was very much offended when the peasants did not call him 'your Honor.' And he concerned himself with the salvation of his soul in a substantial, gentlemanly manner, and performed deeds of charity, not simply, but with an air of consequence. And what deeds of charity! He treated the peasants for every sort of disease with soda and castor oil, and on his name-day had a thanksgiving service in the middle of the village, and then treated the peasants to a gallon of vodka — he thought that was the thing to do. Oh, those horrible gallons of vodka! One day the fat landowner hauls the peasants up before the district captain for trespass, and next day, in honor of a holiday, treats them to a gallon of vodka, and they drink and shout 'Hurrah!' and when they are drunk bow down to his feet. A change of life for the better and being well fed and idle develop in a Russian the most insolent self-conceit. Nikolay Ivanovich, who at one time in the government office was afraid to have any views of his own, now could say nothing that was not gospel truth, and uttered such truths in the tone of a prime minister. 'Education is essential, but for the peasants it is premature.' 'Corporal punishment is harmful as a rule, but in some cases it is necessary and there is nothing to take its place.'

" 'I know the peasants and understand how to treat them,' he would say. 'The peasants like me. I need only to hold up my little finger and the peasants will do anything I like.'

"And all this, observe, was uttered with a wise, benevolent smile. He repeated twenty times over 'We noblemen,' 'I as a noble'; obviously he did not remember that our grandfather was a peasant, and our father a soldier. Even our surname Chimsha-Himalaisky, in reality so incongruous, seemed to him now melodious, distinguished, and very agreeable.

"But the point just now is not he, but myself. I want to tell you about the change that took place in me during the brief hours I spent at his country place. In the evening, when we were drinking tea, the cook put on the table a plateful of gooseberries. They were not bought, but his own gooseberries, gathered for the first time since the bushes were planted. Nikolay Ivanovich laughed and looked for a minute in silence at the gooseberries, with tears in his eyes; he could not speak for excitement. Then he put one gooseberry in his mouth, looked at me with the triumph of a child who has at last received his favorite toy, and said:

" 'How delicious!'

"And he ate them greedily, continually repeating, 'Ah, how delicious! Do taste them!'

"They were sour and unripe, but, as Pushkin says:

> *Dearer to us the falsehood that exalts*
> *Than hosts of baser truths.*

"I saw a happy man whose cherished dream was so obviously fulfilled, who had attained his object in life, who had gained what he wanted, who was satisfied with his fate and himself. There is always, for some reason, an element of sadness mingled with my thoughts of human happiness, and, on this occasion, at the sight of a happy man I was overcome by an oppressive feeling that was close upon despair. It was particularly oppressive at night. A bed was made up for me in the room next to my brother's bedroom, and I could hear that he was awake, and that he kept getting up and going to the plate of gooseberries and taking one. I reflected how many satisfied, happy people there really are! What an overwhelming force it is! You look at life: the insolence and idleness of the strong, the ignorance and brutishness of the weak, incredible poverty all about us, overcrowding, degeneration, drunkenness, hypocrisy, lying . . . Yet all is calm and stillness in the houses and in the streets; of the fifty thousand living in a town, there is not one who would cry out, who would give vent to his indignation aloud. We see the people going to market for provisions, eating by day, sleeping by night, talking their silly nonsense, getting married, growing old, serenely escorting their dead to the cemetery; but we do not see and we do not hear those who suffer, and what is terrible in life goes on somewhere behind the scenes. . . . Everything is quiet and peaceful, and nothing protests but mute statistics: so many people gone out of their minds, so many gallons of vodka drunk, so many children dead from malnutrition. . . . And this order of things is evidently necessary; evidently the happy man only feels at ease because the unhappy bear their burden in silence, and without that silence happiness would be impossible. It's a case of general hypnotism. There ought to be behind the door of every happy, contented man someone standing with a hammer continually reminding him with a tap that there are unhappy people; that however happy he may be, life will show him her jaws sooner or later, trouble will come for him — disease, poverty, losses, and no one will see or hear, just as now he neither sees nor hears others. But there is no man with a hammer; the happy man lives at his ease, the trivial daily cares faintly agitate him like the wind in the aspen-tree — and all goes well.

"That night I realized that I, too, was happy and contented," Ivan Ivanovich went on, getting up. "I, too, at dinner and at the hunt liked to lay down the law on life and religion, and the way to manage the peasantry. I, too, used to say that science was light, that culture was essential, but for the simple people reading and writing was enough for the time. Freedom is a blessing, I used to say; we can no more do without it than without air, but we must wait a little. Yes, I used to talk like that, and now I ask, 'For what reason are we to wait?'" asked Ivan Ivanovich, looking angrily at Burkin. "Why wait, I ask you? What grounds have we for waiting? I shall be told, it can't be done all at once; every idea takes shape in life gradually, in its due time. But who is it says that? Where is the proof that it's right? You will fall back upon the natural order of things, the uniformity of phenomena; but is there order and uniformity in the fact that I, a living, thinking man, stand over a chasm and wait for it to close of itself, or to fill up with mud at the very time when perhaps I might leap over it or build a bridge across it? And again, wait for the sake of what? Wait till there's no strength to live? And meanwhile one must live, and one wants to live!

"I went away from my brother's early in the morning, and ever since then it has been unbearable for me to be among people. I am oppressed by peace and quiet; I am afraid to look at the windows, for there is no spectacle more painful to me now than the sight of a happy family sitting round the table drinking tea. I am old and am not fit for the struggle; I am not even capable of hatred; I can only grieve inwardly, feel irritated and vexed; but at night my head is hot from the rush of ideas, and I cannot sleep. . . . Ah, if I were young!"

Ivan Ivanovich walked backwards and forwards in excitement, and repeated: "If I were young!"

He suddenly went up to Alehin and began pressing first one of his hands and then the other.

"Pavel Konstantinovich," he said in an imploring voice, "don't be calm and contented, don't let yourself be put to sleep! While you are young, strong, confident, be not weary in well-doing! There is no happiness, and there ought not to be; but if there is a meaning and an object in life, that meaning and object is not our happiness, but something greater and more rational. Do good!"

And all this Ivan Ivanovich said with a pitiful, imploring smile, as though he were asking him a personal favor.

Then all three sat in armchairs at different ends of the drawing-room and were silent. Ivan Ivanovich's story had not satisfied either Burkin or Alehin. When the generals and ladies gazed down from their gilt frames, looking in the dusk as though they were alive, it was dreary to listen to the story of the poor clerk who ate gooseberries. They felt inclined for some reason to talk about elegant people, about women. And their sitting in the drawing-room where everything — the chandeliers in their covers, the armchairs, and the carpet under their feet — reminded them that those very people who were now looking down from their frames had once moved about, sat, drunk tea in this room, and the fact that lovely Pelageya was moving noiselessly about was better than any story.

Alehin was fearfully sleepy; he had got up early, before three o'clock in the morning, to look after his work, and now his eyes were closing; but he was afraid his visitors might tell some interesting story after he had gone, and he lingered on. He did not go into the question whether what Ivan Ivanovich had just said was right and true. His visitors did not talk of groats, nor of hay, nor of tar, but of something that had no direct bearing on his life, and he was glad and wanted them to go on.

"It's bedtime, though," said Burkin, getting up. "Allow me to wish you good night."

Alehin said good night and went downstairs to his own domain, while the visitors remained upstairs. They were both taken for the night to a big room where there stood two old wooden beds decorated with carvings, and in the corner was an ivory crucifix. The big cool beds, which had been made by the lovely Pelageya, smelt agreeably of clean linen.

Ivan Ivanovich undressed in silence and got into bed.

"Lord forgive us sinners!" he said, and put his head under the quilt.

His pipe lying on the table smelt strongly of stale tobacco, and Burkin could not sleep for a long while, and kept wondering where the oppressive smell came from.

The rain was pattering on the windowpanes all night.

The Modern World: Twentieth Century

The difficulties which adhere to the naming or defining of earlier cultural periods seem trivial when the historian is confronted with his own time, or the recent past. Does he allude to the two world wars and speak of an apocalyptic age? Does he use the literature which issues from existentialist anxiety to speak of an age of estrangement, or alienation? After living through three decades of the twentieth century, Freud wrote a book called *Civilization and Its Discontents,* in which he describes the unbearable demands made on the individual in the name of progress, and the neurosis which inevitably results from the repression of those instincts society believes inimical to its survival. The language Freud uses is uniquely his own, but the conflict he isolates is as old as the recorded history of the Western world: it no doubt first arose when men came together for their mutual protection and were thus forced to sacrifice some individual desire to the security of the larger group. In *The Interpretation of Dreams,* Freud characterizes the longing for an unfettered past by a metaphor taken from an area of human activity he considered an "illusion":

> When we look back at this unashamed period of childhood it seems to us a Paradise; and Paradise itself is no more than a group phantasy of the childhood of the individual. That is why mankind were naked in Paradise and were without shame in one another's presence; till a moment arrived when shame and anxiety awoke, expulsion followed, and sexual life and the tasks of cultural activity began. But we can regain this Paradise every night in our dreams.

We cannot, of course, return to Paradise in our conscious lives, but much of the literature in this anthology records the symbolic journey. It is, therefore, appropriate that the Modern World begin with Freud's interpretation of the significance of that journey, and of the needs which drive men to attempt it. Such a journey can become no more than a romantic escape into the past, or into the solipsistic universe of the human imagination.

1813

The problem for the artist, no matter how realistically objective his technique, has always been to translate the distortions of his personal vision into a recognizable truth about the nature of man. Even the most idiosyncratic wanderings of a Rimbaud demand that we hear something of ourselves in the resonances of his introversion. Freud himself, in the opinion of his biographer Ernest Jones, had a wildly speculative imagination which he had to restrain with some effort. He also felt that the science he was creating was not new: poets grasped intuitively and had recorded what he learned empirically as he listened to and analyzed the confessions of his patients. The Modern World, then, is characterized in part by the way in which science began to catch up with the apparently improbable speculations of writers, like Dostoevsky, who detested science and all it implied about the inadequacies of the emotional life and the power of reason. Freud, of course, wished to create both a theory of the mind and a therapeutic technique; he believed that, in spite of the ability of the unconscious to control our waking and sleeping lives, man would learn to impose a semblance of order on his experience, if only by acknowledging the reality and significance of those forces the existence of which the poets had been proclaiming for thousands of years. The irony is that even though writers who came after Freud used his "discoveries" to recreate the modern world, they would not let go of the illusions he wished to cure them of; it has been argued that without the neurotic tensions which spring from their conflicts with external reality they would cease to be artists.

Freud's influence on his time does not necessarily reflect a close reading of his work: his ideas were popularized, his jargon came into common usage, but very often knowledge of his theories was second hand, by way of his critics or magazines. It can be an enlightening experience, then, to enter into the actual presence of the world he created, and to observe its creator moving through material the resistance to which he anticipates by his tactful, cautious exposition of ideas that are conventionally distasteful (see, for example, his discussion of the child's wish for the death of others on page 1829). It is also revealing of the quality of Freud's mind that he attempts to persuade his readers of the validity of his theory of the Oedipus complex by exploring in detail the original literary model. His willingness to use works of art as evidence suggests one of the reasons so many artists find his ideas congenial; but analogy as a rhetorical device became, for Freud, an integral part of his system — so much so that at times he appears to believe that analogy is a sufficient substitute for scientific demonstration or proof. Perhaps such a belief is merely another manifestation of that duality in his nature Jones speaks of: the impulse to uncontrollable speculation coexisting with the necessary restraints imposed by reasonable, empirical discourse.

The same duality seems to be present in the work of Freud's most famous disciple. Jung's break with his master resulted, in part at least, from his unwillingness to believe that the individual's sexual life was central to the development of his personality. Like Freud, Jung felt the necessity of demonstrating his theories by a rigorous examination and use of substantive data; like Freud, he also felt the pressures of a wide-ranging, at times unmanageable predisposition to assert as demonstrable, unchanging truth what could be believed but not proved; and his concept of the "collective unconscious" is one that Freud himself, while denying that Jung originated it, used when, later in his life, he took up the origins of monotheism. Unlike Freud, however, Jung was willing to use the revelations and intuitions of religion to establish the validity of his hypotheses; and his application of the created world of artists was even more extensive than Freud's, so that his language, too, has come to be part of the vocabulary of literary criticism.

The life and work of André Gide can be read as an emblem of the psychological tensions which characterize the modern world and of the consequent ambiguities which are part of the artist's search for a form to dramatize them. Gide was concerned with the achievement and uses of freedom; he sought release from the restrictions of his harsh Protestant background, but realized the dangers of sacrificing all the value to be derived from a life lived according to predetermined, persistent ideas of good and evil. Michel, the narrator of his novel *The Immoralist*, attempts to discover the unlimited possibilities of human experience by allowing those unconscious forces which are assumed to be evil to become part of his conscious life. He wishes to break with a past that denies him his freedom; his ambiguous failure illustrates the difficulty of maintaining the freedom which is achieved with so much pain — of discovering the means whereby the commitment to the sensual experience of the present can be carried into the future. Alissa in *Strait is the Gate* is faced with a similar opportunity, but she chooses renunciation, a denial of those instincts and emotions and desires which demand expression in the creation of a self. Her choice is no less heroic than Michel's and her success no less ambiguous. Like Dostoevsky, Gide seems to be saying that sometimes it is necessary to contrive one's destruction in order to demonstrate that one is free — a cruel paradox that defines man's essentially tragic fate. The purity of Alissa's motives and of her life, reflecting her will to achieve a goodness purged of all weakness, becomes so intense and excessive that her submission isolates and then undermines her humanity — the very quality that had prevented her from appearing to be merely perverse. Yet even that impression is qualified by the self-doubts which dominate some of her entries:

> I can neither pray nor sleep. I went out again into the dark garden. I was afraid — in my room — everywhere in the house — I was afraid. My anguish brought me once more to the door behind which I had left him. I opened it with a mad hope that he might have come back. I called. I groped in the darkness. I have come in again to write to him. I cannot accept my grief.

She is poised on the thin edge which marks off pleasure and pain; her soul is suspended between the demands of self-sacrifice and the instinct of self-gratification.

Forty-three years elapsed between the publication of the first chapters of *Felix Krull* and the novel, which Mann left unfinished at his death; during those years the German writer established his reputation as an artist concerned with the serious, ambiguous role of the individual in a world apparently committed to preventing him from discovering his true self. *Death in Venice,* the short novel Mann wrote when he put aside *Felix Krull,* reveals the Germanic intensity and somberness of his exploration of man's psychological nature. The hero von Aschenbach has devoted his life to the composition of books which, in their classical severity, deny the forces, subterranean, uncontrollable, that demand expression and are repressed at great cost to the stability of the soul. Mann associates these forces with the demonic spirits that were so congenial to writers like Baudelaire and Balzac: von Aschenbach, too, takes a journey into the hell of his own psyche and there discovers the price he must pay for his new consciousness. In *Death In Venice,* as in *The Immoralist,* demons are those of homosexual desire, which liberate a force that tragically destroys the newly created self. The adventures of Felix Krull are comic variations on the theme which Mann explored with such passionate seriousness throughout his creative life. Felix, a hero out of the great tradition of the picaresque novel, is a rogue — a young man living by his wits, and outwitting a society whose main function is to punish the individual for denying its power over him. Felix is motivated in part by the same greed for possessions and personal gratification which characterizes those who accept the values of society. What distinguishes him is his unwillingness to mask or repress his desires with references to duty or love or charity. Felix stands outside the group, observing, learning, taking himself seriously, and when it suits his needs, playing the social and moral games which are necessary for survival. When he discovers his natural talent for taking advantage of the empty rules by which men live, he is able to triumph over his adversaries. The scene in which he enacts an epileptic seizure to evade the draft depends for its comic effect on the seriousness with which Felix plays the game and the pompous self-confidence with which the doctor makes his judgments; but the conclusion Felix draws from the experience transforms it into a significant comment on the nature of his self-discovery:

> . . . if I lived *like* a soldier, it would have been a silly misapprehension to believe that I should therefore live *as* a soldier; yes, if it is permissible to describe and define intellectually an emotional treasure as noble as freedom, then it may be said that to live like a soldier but not as a soldier, figuratively but not literally, to be allowed in short to live symbolically, spells true freedom.

Like Gide, Mann establishes freedom as a certain, absolute value, but the rogue, like so many other modern heroes, must pay for his freedom. Felix is forced to enter into the very society he is defying — in effect, he is ensuring its survival by acknowledging that it does, after all, have the power to punish him. The identity of the confidence man, no less than the people he is deceiving, depends on his ability to convince them that he is something he is not, so that although Felix stands for the outlaw which exists in everyone — that part of us concerned only with self-gratification — he must lose his identity, his sense of himself as a person, his freedom, when society discovers what he is not. At that moment Felix Krull ceases to exist.

Dostoevsky's "underground man" was so paralyzed by his self-consciousness that he "could not become even an insect." Kafka begins *The Metamorphosis* with a man so acutely aware of his inadequacies that he is, indeed, transformed into "some monstrous kind of vermin." The idea of a physical change is as old as myths and fairy tales: in Ovid's *Metamorphoses* the changes often occur as a punishment for a misdeed or as a means of escape from danger. In his own eyes and the eyes of others already a "bug," Gregor Samsa becomes one in fact; his change is an escape from the unbearable burden of being judged inadequate. But that withdrawal dramatizes the even more powerful fear — the dread — of becoming what, in man's worst nightmares, he suspects is his true nature. The nightmare is intensified by the quiet tone of the narrative: Gregor's initial reactions to his self-discovery are absurdly natural, and normal. Kafka's strategic economy is artfully deployed: as he describes realistically what it is like to be a bug, he is revealing the kind of man Gregor was. There are two conflicts in the story: the first is an external one, between Gregor and his family, which reaches its climax when his father hurls the apples at him. The second conflict is internal, between Gregor's determination not to accept what he is and his masochistic submission to it. His descent into the filth of his identity and his family's joyful celebration of their freedom after his death complete the nightmare, which for many readers has never been more powerfully realized than in Kafka's symbolic drama. The transformation of Gregor Samsa has become an image of modern man.

The pessimistic sense that life always frustrates man's expectations, that it finally defeats him, dominates the "underground man"; it assumes the limitations of man's power to redeem himself, to become something different from what he fears he will always be. Gregor Samsa feels that despair. Chekhov's short story "Gooseberries" gently, sadly, ironically exposes the barrier between man's idealistic longings and the harsh reality he is continually forced to experience. Nevertheless, he holds onto his illusions, unwilling to face himself without the comfort of believing that there are further, as yet unexplored, possibilities for happiness. Pirandello, in his long story "Such Is Life," examines the same predisposition to deceive oneself about the nature of human experience. Signora Leuca has denied those instincts which she has been taught are base, punishing herself with guilt, expiating her guilt by performing acts of charitable love she does not feel. She knows her life is built on self-deception, but such is its power that when she allows her husband to return, she convinces herself that she is once again doing it for reasons that have nothing to do with her buried emotions. Existence is a continual struggle between illusion and reality, between what one believes and what one knows, between the impulse to deny and the need to affirm those instincts and emotions which an imposed morality has condemned.

In a slightly different form, Babel's short story "My First Goose" dramatizes a similar conflict. The young Jewish intellectual must pay with blood for his commitment to the violent world of the Cossacks. He does not have any illusions about the meaning of such an involvement, but he is not quite prepared for the terrible intensity of its effect on him:

> I dreamed: and in my dreams saw women. But my heart, stained with bloodshed, grated and brimmed over.

The world of men in action — the world of passion and death — brutalizes the man of reason; but without it, the self is incomplete.

The perception of an irreconcilable duality in man's nature exacerbated the consciousness of the "underground man." It becomes the strategy of Brecht's *The Good Woman of Setzuan*. The German playwright's "epic theater" was an attempt to create a new kind of drama, in which the assumption that the audience must identify with the characters on the stage and the illusion that they were "real" people were discarded, to be replaced by an action which continually reminded the spectator that it was only a performance, not an actual experience. Brecht strived to achieve a detachment which would allow the audience to speculate on the meaning of the play and come to the necessary conclusions about the relationship of man to his social and moral world. The conclusion that he apparently wished his audience to reach is that man is torn by the duality of his nature. The prostitute Shen Te is the only good person in Setzuan and so she is rewarded by the gods with enough money to succeed in the world, but she is too gentle and loving to survive. Like the narrator in Babel's story, she must learn the techniques of those who never lose: she becomes her calculating cousin Shui Ta, who represents the power of unencumbered, unsentimental reason. Brecht seems to be suggesting that these two warring principles — love and cruelty, reason and emotion — can never be reconciled. In spite of the "pious hope" of the epilogue, he is as pessimistic as Chekhov and Pirandello about the possibility of changing a world in which a good woman cannot defend herself against the harsh, necessitous demands of an impersonal reality.

The despair which links so many contemporary writers persists. Whatever form it takes, it seems to deny imperatively that man can transcend it in order to re-create the world which is its source. Yet two ways are offered, tentatively, by the poets Rilke and Lorca and by Camus: the first is the way of the artist, who symbolically orders the universal chaos and violence and thus cheats the world bent on destroying him by robbing death of its objective reality. It is a way which depends on a belief in the power of art to arrest time, if only for the moment; it is a way which demands that we accept on faith the permanence of the imagination, and emotions.

> Show him how happy a thing can be, how guileless and ours;
> how even the moaning of grief purely determines on form,
> serves as a thing, or dies into a thing, — to escape
> to a bliss beyond the fiddle. These things that live on departure
> understand when you praise them: fleeting, they look for
> rescue through something in us, the most fleeting of all.
> Want us to change them entirely, within our invisible hearts,
> into — oh, endlessly — into ourselves! Whosoever we are.
>
> (Rilke, "The Ninth Elegy")

> Nobody knows you. No. But I sing of you.
> For posterity I sing of your profile and grace.
>
> (Lorca, *Lament*)

Camus' way is harder; it accepts man's fate, which is to die, and does not speak of immortality; it asserts the primacy of human consciousness, which means the experience of pain. It does not give the absurdity of suffering form, or beauty; rather, it celebrates ritualistically a succession of single moments, which may end now. It requires a commitment, no more reasonable than Rilke's, but perhaps more accessible.

> I leave Sisyphus at the foot of the mountain! One always finds one's burden again. But Sisyphus teaches the higher fidelity that negates the gods and raises rocks. He too concludes that all is well. This universe henceforth without a master seems to him neither sterile nor futile. Each atom of that stone, each mineral flake of that night-filled mountain, in itself forms a world. The struggle itself toward the heights is enough to fill a man's heart. One must imagine Sisyphus happy.

Sigmund Freud (1856–1939)

LIFE: In his personal life he was very much of the nineteenth century: monogamous, patriarchal, conservative in his tastes, habits, and behavior; but the life of his mind helped to make and enrage modern man. The painful triumph of his self-analysis, which resulted in *The Interpretation of Dreams*, steeled him against the scorn and distaste with which his work was received. A refugee from the Nazis, he died in London of the cancer he had suffered for sixteen years.

WORKS: *The Interpretation of Dreams* (1900); *Three Essays on the Theory of Sexuality* (1905); *Totem and Taboo* (1912–13); *Civilization and Its Discontents* (1930).

TYPICAL DREAMS *

Embarrassing Dreams of Being Naked

Dreams of being naked or insufficiently dressed in the presence of strangers sometimes occur with the additional feature of there being a complete absence of any such feeling as shame on the dreamer's part. We are only concerned here, however, with those dreams of being naked in which one *does* feel shame and embarrassment and tries to escape or hide, and is then overcome by a strange inhibition which prevents one from moving and makes one feel incapable of altering one's distressing situation. It is only with this accompaniment that the dream is typical; without it, the gist of its subject-matter may be included in every variety of context or may be ornamented with individual trimmings. Its essence lies in a distressing feeling in the nature of shame and in the fact that one wishes to hide one's nakedness, as a rule by locomotion, but finds one is unable to do so. I believe the great majority of my readers will have found themselves in this situation in dreams.

The nature of the undress involved is customarily far from clear. The dreamer may say "I was in my chemise," but this is rarely a dis-

From *The Interpretation of Dreams*, by Sigmund Freud, translated and edited by James Strachey, Basic Books, Inc., Publishers, New York, 1955.

* From *The Interpretation of Dreams*, chapter V. Although the book was dated 1900, it was actually published in 1899.

tinct picture. The kind of undress is usually so vague that the description is expressed as an alternative: "I was in my chemise or petticoat." As a rule the defect in the dreamer's toilet is not so grave as to appear to justify the shame to which it gives rise. In the case of a man who has worn the Emperor's uniform, nakedness is often replaced by some breach of the dress regulations: "I was walking in the street without my sabre and saw some officers coming up," or "I was without my necktie," or "I was wearing civilian check trousers," and so on.

The people in whose presence one feels ashamed are almost always strangers, with their features left indeterminate. In the typical dream it never happens that the clothing which causes one so much embarrassment is objected to or so much as noticed by the onlookers. On the contrary, they adopt indifferent or (as I observed in one particularly clear dream) solemn and stiff expressions of face. This is a suggestive point.

The embarrassment of the dreamer and the indifference of the onlookers offer us, when taken together, a contradiction of the kind that is so common in dreams. It would after all be more in keeping with the dreamer's feelings if strangers looked at him in astonishment and derision or with indignation. But this objectionable feature of the situation has, I believe, been got rid of by wish-fulfilment, whereas some force has led to the retention of the other features; and the two portions of the dream are consequently out of harmony with each other. We possess an interesting piece of evidence that the dream in the form in which it appears — partly distorted by wish-fulfilment — has not been rightly understood. For it has become the basis of a fairy tale which is familiar to us all in Hans Andersen's version, *The Emperor's New Clothes,* and which has quite recently been put into verse by Ludwig Fulda [1] in his *Der Talisman.* Hans Andersen's fairy tale tells us how two impostors weave the Emperor a costly garment which, they say, will be visible only to persons of virtue and loyalty. The Emperor walks out in this invisible garment, and all the spectators, intimidated by the fabric's power to act as a touchstone, pretend not to notice the Emperor's nakedness. . . .

The impostor is the dream and the Emperor is the dreamer himself; the moralizing purpose of the dream reveals an obscure knowledge of the fact that the latent dream-content is concerned with forbidden wishes that have fallen victim to represssion. For the context in which dreams of this sort appear during my analyses of neurotics leaves no doubt that they are based upon memories from earliest childhood. It is only in our childhood that we are seen in inadequate clothing both by members of our family and by strangers — nurses, maid-servants, and visitors; and it is only then that we feel no shame at our nakedness. We can observe how undressing has an almost intoxicating effect on many children even in their later years, instead of making them feel ashamed. They laugh and jump about and slap themselves, while their

1. German playwright, 1862–1939.

mother, or whoever else may be there, reproves them and says: "Ugh! Shocking! You mustn't ever do that!" Children frequently manifest a desire to exhibit. One can scarcely pass through a country village in our part of the world without meeting some child of two or three who lifts up his little shirt in front of one — in one's honour, perhaps. One of my patients has a conscious memory of a scene in his eighth year, when at bed-time he wanted to dance into the next room where his little sister slept, dressed in his night-shirt, but was prevented by his nurse. In the early history of neurotics an important part is played by exposure to children of the opposite sex; in paranoia delusions of being observed while dressing and undressing are to be traced back to experiences of this kind; while among persons who have remained at the stage of perversion there is one class in which this infantile impulse has reached the pitch of a symptom — the class of "exhibitionists."

When we look back at this unashamed period of childhood it seems to us to be a Paradise; and Paradise itself is no more than a group phantasy of the childhood of the individual. That is why mankind were naked in Paradise and were without shame in one another's presence; till a moment arrived when shame and anxiety awoke, expulsion followed, and sexual life and the tasks of cultural activity began. But we can regain this Paradise every night in our dreams. I have already expressed a suspicion that impressions of earliest childhood (that is, from the prehistoric epoch [2] until about the end of the third year of life) strive to achieve reproduction, from their very nature and irrespectively perhaps of their actual content, and that their repetition constitutes the fulfilment of a wish. Thus dreams of being naked are dreams of exhibiting.

The core of a dream of exhibiting lies in the figure of the dreamer himself (not as he was as a child but as he appears at the present time) and his inadequate clothing (which emerges indistinctly, whether owing to superimposed layers of innumerable later memories of being in undress or as a result of the censorship). Added to these are the figures of the people in whose presence the dreamer feels ashamed. I know of no instance in which the actual spectators of the infantile scene of exhibiting have appeared in the dream; a dream is scarcely ever a simple memory. Curiously enough, the people upon whom our sexual interest was directed in childhood are omitted in all the reproductions which occur in dreams, in hysteria and in obsessional neurosis. It is only in paranoia that these spectators reappear and, though they remain invisible, their presence is inferred with fanatical conviction. What takes their place in dreams — "a lot of strangers" who take no notice of the spectacle that is offered — is nothing more nor less than the wishful contrary of the single familiar individual before whom the dreamer exposed himself. Incidentally, "a lot of strangers" frequently appear in dreams in many other connections, and they always stand as the wishful contrary of "secrecy." It is to be noticed that even in

2. The period before the child has a conscious memory.

paranoia, where the original state of things is restored, this reversal into a contrary is observed. The subject feels that he is no longer alone, he has no doubt that he is being observed, but the observers are "a lot of strangers" whose identity is left curiously vague.

In addition to this, repression plays a part in dreams of exhibiting; for the distress felt in such dreams is a reaction on the part of the second system against the content of the scene of exhibiting having found expression in spite of the ban upon it. If the distress was to be avoided, the scene should never have been revived.

We shall return later to the feeling of being inhibited. It serves admirably in dreams to represent a conflict in the will or a negative. The unconscious purpose requires the exhibiting to proceed; the censorship demands that it shall be stopped.

There can be no doubt that the connections between our typical dreams and fairy tales and the material of other kinds of creative writing are neither few nor accidental. It sometimes happens that the sharp eye of a creative writer has an analytic realization of the process of transformation of which he is habitually no more than the tool. If so, he may follow the process in a reverse direction and so trace back the imaginative writing to a dream. One of my friends has drawn my attention to the following passage in Gottfried Keller's *Der grüne Heinrich*:[3] "I hope, my dear Lee, that you may never learn from your own personal experience the peculiar and *piquant* truth of the plight of Odysseus when he appeared, naked and covered with mud, before the eyes of Nausicaä and her maidens![4] Shall I tell you how that can happen? Let us look into our example. If you are wandering about in a foreign land, far from your home and from all that you hold dear, if you have seen and heard many things, have known sorrow and care, and are wretched and forlorn, then without fail you will dream one night that you are coming near to your home; you will see it gleaming and shining in the fairest colours, and the sweetest, dearest and most beloved forms will move towards you. Then suddenly you will become aware that you are in rags, naked and dusty. You will be seized with a nameless shame and dread, you will seek to find covering and to hide yourself, and you will awake bathed in sweat. This, so long as men breathe, is the dream of the unhappy wanderer; and Homer has evoked the picture of his plight from the deepest and eternal nature of man."

The deepest and eternal nature of man, upon whose evocation in his hearers the poet is accustomed to rely, lies in those impulses of the mind which have their roots in a childhood that has since become prehistoric. Suppressed and forbidden wishes from childhood break through in the dream behind the exile's unobjectionable wishes which are capable of entering consciousness; and that is why the dream which finds concrete expression in the legend of Nausicaä ends as a rule as an anxiety-dream.

---

3. Gottfried Keller (1819–90) was a Swiss poet, novelist, and short story writer.
4. In Book VI of Homer's *Odyssey*.

My own dream [5] of running upstairs and of soon afterwards finding myself glued to the steps was equally a dream of exhibiting, since it bears the essential marks of being one. It should be possible, therefore, to trace it back to experiences during my childhood, and if these could be discovered they should enable us to judge how far the maid-servant's behavior to me — her accusing me of dirtying the carpet [6] — helped to give her her place in my dream. I can, as it happens, provide the necessary particulars. In a psycho-analysis one learns to interpret propinquity in time as representing connection in subject-matter. Two thoughts which occur in immediate sequence without any apparent connection are in fact part of a single unity which has to be discovered; in just the same way, if I write an *"a"* and a *"b"* in succession, they have to be pronounced as a single syllable *"ab."* The same is true of dreams. The staircase dream to which I have referred was one of a series of dreams; and I understood the interpretation of the other members of the series. Since this particular dream was surrounded by the others it must have dealt with the same subject. Now these other dreams were based on a recollection of a nurse in whose charge I had been from some date during my earliest infancy till I was two and a half. I even retain an obscure conscious memory of her. According to what I was told not long ago by my mother, she was old and ugly, but very sharp and efficient. From what I can infer from my own dreams her treatment of me was not always excessive in its amiability and her words could be harsh if I failed to reach the required standard of cleanliness. And thus the maid-servant, since she had undertaken the job of carrying on his educational work, acquired the right to be treated in my dream as a reincarnation of the prehistoric old nurse. It is reasonable to suppose that the child loved the old woman who taught him these lessons, in spite of her rough treatment of him.

Dreams of the Death of Persons of Whom the Dreamer Is Fond

Another group of dreams which may be described as typical are those containing the death of some loved relative — for instance, of a parent, of a brother or sister, or of a child. Two classes of such dreams must at once be distinguished: those in which the dreamer is unaffected by grief, so that on awakening he is astonished at his lack of feeling, and those in which the dreamer feels deeply pained by the death and may even weep bitterly in his sleep.

We need not consider the dreams of the first of these classes, for they have no claim to be regarded as "typical." If we analyse them, we find that they have some meaning other than their apparent one, and that

5. Freud records it in Chapter V of *The Interpretation of Dreams:* "I was very incompletely dressed and was going upstairs from a flat on the ground floor to a higher storey. I was going up three steps at a time and was delighted at my agility. Suddenly I saw a maid-servant coming down the stairs — coming towards me, that is. I felt ashamed and tried to hurry, and at this point the feeling of being inhibited set in: I was glued to the steps and unable to budge from the spot."

6. In his analysis of the dream Freud remembers that a maid had criticized him for not wiping the dirt from his boots when he climbed the stairs to visit a patient.

they are intended to conceal some other wish. Such was the dream of the aunt who saw her sister's only son lying in his coffin. It did not mean that she wished her little nephew dead; as we have seen, it merely concealed a wish to see a particular person of whom she was fond and whom she had not met for a long time — a person whom she had once before met after a similarly long interval beside the coffin of another nephew. This wish, which was the true content of the dream, gave no occasion for grief, and no grief, therefore, was felt in the dream. . . .

Very different are the dreams of the other class — those in which the dreamer imagines the death of a loved relative and is at the same time painfully affected. The meaning of such dreams, as their content indicates, is a wish that the person in question may die. And since I must expect that the feelings of all of my readers and any others who have experienced similar dreams will rebel against my assertion, I must try to base my evidence for it on the broadest possible foundation.

I have already discussed a dream which taught us that the wishes which are represented in dreams as fulfilled are not always present-day wishes. They may also be wishes of the past which have been abandoned, overlaid and repressed, and to which we have to attribute some sort of continued existence only because of their re-emergence in a dream. They are not dead in our sense of the word but only like the shades in the *Odyssey*, which awoke to some sort of life as soon as they had tasted blood. . . .[7]

If anyone dreams, with every sign of pain, that his father or mother or brother or sister has died, I should never use the dream as evidence that he wishes for that person's death *at the present time*. The theory of dreams does not require as much as that; it is satisfied with the inference that this death has been wished for at some time or other during the dreamer's childhood. I fear, however, that this reservation will not appease the objectors; they will deny the possibility of their *ever* having had such a thought with just as much energy as they insist that they harbour no such wishes now. I must therefore reconstruct a portion of the vanished mental life of children on the basis of the evidence of the present.

Let us first consider the relation of children to their brothers and sisters. I do not know why we presuppose that that relation must be a loving one; for instances of hostility between adult brothers and sisters force themselves upon everyone's experience and we can often establish the fact that the disunity originated in childhood or has always existed. But it is further true that a great many adults, who are on affectionate terms with their brothers and sisters and are ready to stand by them to-day, passed their childhood on almost unbroken terms of enmity with them. The elder child ill-treats the younger, maligns him and robs him of his toys; while the younger is consumed with impotent rage against the elder, envies and fears him, or meets his oppressor with the first

7. In Book XI of the *Odyssey*.

stirrings of a love of liberty and a sense of justice. Their parents complain that the children do not get on with one another, but cannot discover why. It is easy to see that the character of even a good child is not what we should wish to find it in an adult. Children are completely egoistic; they feel their needs intensely and strive ruthlessly to satisfy them — especially as against the rivals, other children, and first and foremost as against their brothers and sisters. But we do not on that account call a child "bad," we call him "naughty"; he is no more answerable for his evil deeds in our judgement than in the eyes of the law. And it is right that this should be so; for we may expect that, before the end of the period which we count as childhood, altruistic impulses and morality will awaken in the little egoist. . . . It is true, no doubt, that morality does not set in simultaneously all along the line and that the length of non-moral childhood varies in different individuals. If this morality fails to develop, we like to talk of "degeneracy," though what in fact faces us is an inhibition in development. After the primary character has already been overlaid by later development, it can still be laid bare again, at all events in part, in cases of hysterical illness. There is a really striking resemblance between what is known as the hysterical character and that of a naughty child. Obsessional neurosis, on the contrary, corresponds to a super-morality imposed as a reinforcing weight upon fresh stirrings of the primary character.

Many people, therefore, who love their brothers and sisters and would feel bereaved if they were to die, harbour evil wishes against them in their unconscious, dating from earlier times; and these are capable of being realized in dreams.

It is of quite particular interest, however, to observe the behaviour of small children up to the age of two or three or a little older towards their younger brothers and sisters. Here, for instance, was a child who had so far been the only one; and now he was told that the stork had brought a new baby. He looked the new arrival up and down and then declared decisively: "The stork can take him away again!" I am quite seriously of the opinion that a child can form a just estimate of the set-back he has to expect at the hands of the little stranger. A lady of my acquaintance, who is on very good terms to-day with a sister four years her junior, tells me that she greeted the news of her first arrival with this qualification: "But all the same I shan't give her my red cap!" Even if a child only comes to realize the situation later on, his hostility will date from that moment. I know of a case in which a little girl of less than three tried to strangle an infant in its cradle because she felt that its continued presence boded her no good. Children at that time of life are capable of jealousy of any degree of intensity and obviousness. Again, if it should happen that the baby sister does in fact disappear after a short while, the elder child will find the whole affection of the household once more concentrated upon himself. If after that the stork should bring yet another baby, it seems only logical that the little favourite should nourish a wish that his new competitor may meet with the same fate as the earlier one, so that he himself may be as happy as he was originally and during the interval. Normally, of course, this attitude of a child towards a younger brother or sister is a simple function of the difference between their ages. Where the gap in time is sufficiently long, an elder girl will already begin to feel the stirring of her maternal instincts towards the helpless newborn baby.

Hostile feelings towards brothers and sisters must be far more frequent in childhood than the unseeing eye of the adult observer can perceive.

In the case of my own children, who followed each other in rapid succession, I neglected the opportunity of carrying out observations of this kind; but I am now making up for this neglect by observing a small nephew, whose autocratic rule was upset, after lasting for fifteen months, by the appearance of a female rival. I am told, it is true, that the young man behaves in the most chivalrous manner to his little sister, that he kisses her hand and strokes her; but I have been able to convince myself that even before the end of his second year he made use of his powers of speech for the purpose of criticizing someone whom he could not fail to regard as superfluous. Whenever the conversation touched upon her he used to intervene in it and exclaim petulantly: "Too 'ickle! too 'ickle!" During the last few months the baby's growth has made enough progress to place her beyond this particular ground for contempt, and the little boy has found a different basis for his assertion that she does not deserve so much attention: at every suitable opportunity he draws attention to the fact that she has no teeth. We all of us recollect how the eldest girl of another of my sisters, who was then a child of six, spent half-an-hour in insisting upon each of her aunts in succession agreeing with her: "Lucie can't understand that yet, can she?" she kept asking. Lucie was her rival — two and a half years her junior.

In none of my women patients, to take an example, have I failed to come upon this dream of the death of a brother or sister, which tallies with an increase in hostility. I have only found a single exception; and it was easy to interpret this as a confirmation of the rule. On one occasion during an analytic session I was explaining this subject to a lady, since in view of her symptom its discussion seemed to me relevant. To my astonishment she replied that she had never had such a dream. Another dream, however, occurred to her, which ostensibly had no connection with the topic — a dream which she had first dreamt when she was four years old and at that time the youngest of the family, and which she had dreamt repeatedly since: *A whole crowd of children — all her brothers, sisters and cousins of both sexes — were romping in a field. Suddenly they all grew wings, flew away and disappeared.* She had no idea what this dream meant; but it is not hard to recognize that in its original form it had been a dream of the death of all her brothers and sisters, and had been only slightly influenced by the censorship. I may venture to suggest the following analysis. On the occasion of the death of one of this crowd of children (in this instance the children of two brothers had been brought up together as a single family) the dreamer, not yet four years old at the time, must have asked some wise grown-up person what became of children when they were dead. The reply must have been: "They grow wings and turn into little angels." In the dream which followed upon this piece of information all the dreamer's brothers and sisters had wings like angels and — which is the main point — flew away. Our little baby-killer was left alone, strange to say: the only survivor of the whole crowd! We can hardly be wrong in supposing that the fact of the children romping in a *field* before flying away points to butterflies. It is as though the child was led by the same chain of thought as the peoples of antiquity to picture the soul as having a butterfly's wings.

At this point someone will perhaps interrupt: "Granted that children have hostile impulses towards their brothers and sisters, how can a child's mind reach such a pitch of depravity as to wish for the *death* of his rivals or of playmates stronger than himself, as though the death penalty were the only punishment for every crime?" Anyone who talks like this has failed to bear in mind that a child's idea of being "dead" has nothing much in common with ours apart from the word. Children know nothing of the horrors of corruption, of freezing in the ice-cold grave, of the terrors of eternal nothingness — ideas which grown-up people find it so hard to tolerate, as is proved by all the myths of a future life. The fear of death has no meaning to a child; hence it is that he will play with the dreadful word and use it as a threat against a playmate: "If you do that again, you'll die, like Franz!" Meanwhile the poor mother gives a shudder and remembers, perhaps, that the greater half of the human race fail to survive their childhood years. It was actually possible for a child, who was over eight years old at the time, coming home from a visit to the Natural History Museum, to say to his mother: "I'm so fond of you, Mummy: when you die I'll have you stuffed and I'll keep you in this room, so that I can see you *all* the time." So little resemblance is there between a child's idea of being dead and our own!

To children, who, moreover, are spared the sight of the scenes of suffering which precede death, being "dead" means approximately the same as being "gone" — not troubling the survivors any longer. A child makes no distinction as to how this absence is brought about: whether it is due to a journey, to a dismissal, to an estrangement, or to death. If, during a child's prehistoric epoch, his nurse has been dismissed, and if soon afterwards his mother has died, the two events are superimposed on each other in a single series in his memory as revealed in analysis. When people are absent, children do not miss them with any great intensity; many mothers have learnt this to their sorrow when, after being away from home for some weeks on a summer holiday, they are met on their return by the news that the children have not once asked after their mummy. If their mother does actually make the journey to that "undiscover'd country, from whose bourn no traveller returns," [8] children seem at first to have forgotten her, and it is only later on that they begin to call their dead mother to mind.

Thus if a child has reasons for wishing the absence of another, there is nothing to restrain him from giving his wish the form of the other child being dead. And the psychical reaction to dreams containing death-wishes proves that, in spite of the different content of these wishes in the case of children, they are nevertheless in some way or other the same as wishes expressed in the same terms by adults.

If, then, a child's death-wishes against his brothers and sisters are explained by the childish egoism which makes him regard them as his rivals, how are we to explain his death-wishes against his parents, who surround him with love and fulfil his needs and whose preservation that same egoism should lead him to desire?

A solution of this difficulty is afforded by the observation that dreams of the death of parents apply with preponderant frequency to the parent who is of the same sex as the dreamer: that men, that is, dream mostly of their father's death and women of their mother's. I cannot pretend that this is universally so, but the preponderance in the direction I have indicated is so evident that it requires to be explained by a factor of general importance. It is as though — to put it bluntly — a sexual preference were making itself felt at an early age: as though boys regarded their fathers and girls their mothers as their rivals in love; whose elimination could not fail to be to their advantage.

Before this idea is rejected as a monstrous one, it is as well in this case, too, to consider the real relations obtaining — this time between parents and children. We must distinguish between what the cultural standards of filial piety demand of this relation and what everyday observation shows it in fact to be. More than one occasion for hostility lies concealed in the relation between parents and children — a relation which affords the most ample opportunities for wishes to arise which cannot pass the censorship.

Let us consider first the relation between father and son. The sanctity which we attribute to the rules laid down in the Decalogue [9] has, I think, blunted our powers of perceiving the real facts. We seem scarcely to venture to observe that the majority of mankind disobey the Fifth Commandment.[10] Alike in the lowest and in the highest strata of human society filial piety is wont to give way to other interests. The obscure information which is brought to us by mythology and legend from the primaeval ages of human society gives an unpleasing picture of the father's despotic power and of the ruthlessness with which he made use of it. Kronos devoured his children, just as the wild boar devours

---

8. From Hamlet's famous soliloquy in Act III, scene 1.
9. The Ten Commandments.
10. Honor thy father and thy mother.

the sow's litter;[11] while Zeus emasculated his father[12] and made himself ruler in his place. The more unrestricted was the rule of the father in the ancient family, the more must the son, as his destined successor, have found himself in the position of an enemy, and the more impatient must he have been to become ruler himself through his father's death. Even in our middle-class families fathers are as a rule inclined to refuse their sons independence and the means necessary to secure it and thus to foster the growth of the germ of hostility which is inherent in their relation. A physician will often be in a position to notice how a son's grief at the loss of his father cannot suppress his satisfaction at having at length won his freedom. In our society to-day fathers are apt to cling desperately to what is left of a now sadly antiquated *potestas partis familias;*[13] and an author who, like Ibsen, brings the immemorial struggle between fathers and sons into prominence in his writings may be certain of producing his effect.

Occasions for conflict between a daughter and her mother arises when the daughter begins to grow up and long for sexual liberty, but finds herself under her mother's tutelage; while the mother, on the other hand, is warned by her daughter's growth that the time has come when she herself must abandon her claims to sexual satisfaction.

All of this is patent to the eyes of everyone. But it does not help us in our endeavour to explain dreams of a parent's death in people whose piety towards their parents has long been unimpeachably established. Previous discussions, moreover, will have prepared us to learn that the death-wish against parents dates back to earliest childhood.

This supposition is confirmed with a certainty beyond all doubt in the case of psychoneurotics when they are subjected to analysis. We learn from them that a child's sexual wishes — if in their embryonic stage they deserve to be so described — awaken very early, and that a girl's first affection is for her father and a boy's first childish desires are for his mother. Accordingly, the father becomes a disturbing rival to the boy and the mother to the girl; and I have already shown in the case of brothers and sisters how easily such feelings can lead to a death-wish. The parents too give evidence as a rule of sexual partiality: a natural predilection usually sees to it that a man tends to spoil his little daughters, while his wife takes her sons' part; though both of them, where their judgement is not disturbed by the magic of sex, keep a strict eye upon their children's education. The child is very well aware of this partiality and turns against that one of his parents who is opposed to showing it. Being loved by an adult does not merely bring a child the satisfaction of a special need; it also means that he will get what he wants in every other respect as well. Thus he will be following his own sexual instinct and at the same time giving fresh strength to

11. Kronos ate his children to prevent the fulfillment of the prophecy that one of his sons would kill him. Zeus was saved from this fate by his mother.
12. It was Kronos who castrated *his* father, Uranus.
13. Paternal authority.

the inclination shown by his parents if his choice between them falls in with theirs.

The signs of these infantile preferences are for the most part over-looked; yet some of them are to be observed even after the first years of childhood. An eight-year-old girl of my acquaintance, if her mother is called away from the table, makes use of the occasion to proclaim herself her successor: "I'm going to be Mummy now. Do you want some more greens, Karl? Well, help yourself, then!" and so on. A particularly gifted and lively girl of four, in whom this piece of child psychology is especially transparent, declared quite openly: "Mummy can go away now. Then Daddy must marry me and I'll be his wife." Such a wish occurring in a child is not in the least inconsistent with her being tenderly attached to her mother. If a little boy is allowed to sleep beside his mother when his father is away from home, but has to go back to the nursery and to someone of whom he is far less fond as soon as his father returns, he may easily begin to form a wish that his father should *always* be away, so that he himself could keep his place beside his dear, lovely Mummy. One obvious way of attaining this wish would be if his father were dead; for the child has learnt one thing by experience — namely that "dead" people, such as Grandaddy, are always away and never come back.

Though observations of this kind on small children fit in perfectly with the interpretation I have proposed, they do not carry such complete conviction as is forced upon the physician by psycho-analyses of adult neurotics. In the latter case dreams of the sort we are considering are introduced into the analysis in such a context that it is impossible to avoid interpreting them as *wishful* dreams

One day one of my women patients was in a distressed and tearful mood. "I don't want ever to see my relations again," she said, "they must think me horrible." She then went on, with almost no transition, to say that she remembered a dream, though of course she had no idea what it meant. When she was four years old she had a dream that *a lynx or fox was walking on the roof; then something had fallen down or she had fallen down; and then her mother was carried out of the house dead* — and she wept bitterly. I told her that this dream must mean that when she was a child she had wished she could see her mother dead, and that it must be on account of the dream that she felt her relations must think her horrible. I had scarcely said this when she produced some material which threw light on the dream. "Lynx-eye" was a term of abuse that had been thrown at her by a street-urchin when she was a very small child. When she was three years old, a tile off the roof had fallen on her mother's head and made it bleed violently.

I once had an opportunity of making a detailed study of a young woman who passed through a variety of psychical conditions. Her illness began with a state of confusional excitement during which she displayed a quite special aversion to her mother, hitting and abusing her whenever she came near her bed, while at the same period she was docile and affectionate towards a sister who was many years her senior. This was followed by a state in which she was lucid but somewhat apathetic and suffered from badly disturbed sleep. It was during this phase that I began treating her and analysing her dreams. An immense number of these dreams were concerned, with a greater or less degree of disguise, with the death of her mother: at one time she would be attending an old woman's funeral, at another she and her sister would be sitting at table dressed in mourning. There could be no question as to the meaning of these dreams. As her condition improved still further, hysterical phobias developed. The most tormenting of these was a fear that something might have happened to her mother. She was obliged to hurry home, wherever she might be, to convince herself that her mother was still alive. This case, taken in conjunction with what I had learnt from other sources, was highly instructive: it exhibited, translated as it were into different languages, the various ways in which the psychical apparatus reacted to one and the same exciting idea. In the confusional state, in which, as I believe, the second psychical agency was overwhelmed by the normally suppressed first one, her unconscious hostility to her mother found a powerful *motor* expression. When the calmer condition set in, when the rebellion was suppressed and the domination of the censorship re-established, the only region left open in which her hostility could realize the wish for her mother's death was that of dreaming. When a normal state was still more firmly established, it led to the production of her exaggerated worry about her mother as a hysterical counter-reaction and defensive phenomenon. In view of this it is no longer hard to understand why hysterical girls are so often attached to their mothers with such exaggerated affection.

On another occasion I had an opportunity of obtaining a deep insight into the unconscious mind of a young man whose life was made almost impossible by an obsessional neurosis. He was unable to go out into the street because he was tortured by the fear that he would kill everyone he met. He spent his days in preparing his alibi in case he might be charged with one of the murders committed in the town. It is unnecessary to add that he was a man of equally high morals and education. The analysis (which, incidentally, led to his recovery) showed that the basis of this distressing obsession was an impulse to murder his somewhat over-severe father. This impulse, to his astonishment, had been consciously expressed when he was seven years old, but it had, of course, originated much earlier in his childhood. After his father's painful illness and death, the patient's obsessional self-reproaches appeared — he was in his thirty-first year at the time — taking the shape of a phobia transferred on to strangers. A person, he felt, who was capable of wanting to push his own father over a precipice from the top of a mountain was not to be trusted to respect the lives of those less closely related to him; he was quite right to shut himself up in his room.

In my experience, which is already extensive, the chief part in the mental lives of all children who later become psychoneurotics is played by their parents. Being in love with the one parent and hating the other are among the essential constituents of the stock of psychical impulses which is formed at that time and which is of such importance in determining the symptoms of the later neurosis. It is not my belief, however, that psychoneurotics differ sharply in this respect from other human beings who remain normal — that they are able, that is, to create something absolutely new and peculiar to themselves. It is far more probable — and this is confirmed by occasional observations on normal children — that they are only distinguished by exhibiting on a magnified scale feelings of love and hatred to their parents which occur less obviously and less intensely in the minds of most children.

This discovery is confirmed by a legend that has come down to us from classical antiquity: a legend whose profound and universal power to move can only be understood if the hypothesis I have put forward in regard to the psychology of children has an equally universal validity. What I have in mind is the legend of King Oedipus and Sophocles' drama which bears his name.

Oedipus, son of Laïus, King of Thebes, and of Jocasta, was exposed as an infant because an oracle had warned Laïus that the still unborn child would be his father's murderer. The child was rescued, and grew up as a prince in an alien court, until, in doubts as to his origin, he too questioned the oracle and was warned to avoid his home since he was destined to murder his father and take his mother in marriage. On the road leading away from what he believed was his home, he met King Laïus and slew him in a sudden quarrel. He came next to Thebes and solved the riddle set him by the Sphinx who barred his way. Out of gratitude the Thebans made him their king and gave his Jocasta's hand in marriage. He reigned long in peace and honour, and she who, unknown to him, was his mother bore him two sons and two daughters. Then at last a plague broke out and the Thebans made enquiry once more of the oracle. It is at this point that Sophocles' tragedy opens. The messengers bring back the reply that the plague will cease when the murderer of Laïus has been driven from the land.

> But he, where is he? Where shall now be read
> The fading record of this ancient guilt? [14]

The action of the play consists in nothing other than the process of revealing, with cunning delays and ever-mounting excitement — a process that can be likened to the work of a psychoanalysis — that Oedipus himself is the murderer of Laïus, but further that he is the son of the

14. From the translation by Lewis Campbell. See lines 112–113 of the play in this anthology.

murdered man and of Jocasta. Appalled at the abomination which he has unwittingly perpetrated, Oedipus blinds himself and forsakes his home. The oracle has been fulfilled.

Oedipus Rex is what is known as a tragedy of destiny. Its tragic effect is said to lie in the contrast between the supreme will of the gods and the vain attempts of mankind to escape the evil that threatens them. The lesson which, it is said, the deeply moved spectator should learn from the tragedy is submission to the divine will and realization of his own impotence. Modern dramatists have accordingly tried to achieve a similar tragic effect by weaving the same contrast into a plot invented by themselves. But the spectators have looked on unmoved while a curse or an oracle was fulfilled in spite of all the efforts of some innocent man: later tragedies of destiny have failed in their effect.

If *Oedipus Rex* moves a modern audience no less than it did the contemporary Greek one, the explanation can only be that its effect does not lie in the contrast between destiny and human will, but is to be looked for in the particular nature of the material on which that contrast is exemplified. There must be something which makes a voice within us ready to recognize the compelling force of destiny in the *Oedipus,* while we can dismiss as merely arbitrary such dispositions as are laid down in *Die Ahnfrau* [15] or other modern tragedies of destiny. And a factor of this kind is in fact involved in the story of King Oedipus. His destiny moves us only because it might have been ours — because the oracle laid the same curse upon us before our birth as upon him. It is the fate of all of us, perhaps, to direct our first sexual impulse towards our mother and our first hatred and our first murderous wish against our father. Our dreams convince us that that is so. King Oedipus, who slew his father Laïus and married his mother Jocasta, merely shows us the fulfilment of our own childhood wishes. But, more fortunate than he, we have meanwhile succeeded, in so far as we have not become psychoneurotics, in detaching our sexual impulses from our mothers and in forgetting our jealousy of our fathers. Here is one in whom these primaeval wishes of our childhood have been fulfilled, and we shrink back from him with the whole force of the repression by which those wishes have since that time been held down within us. While the poet, as he unravels the past, brings to light the guilt of Oedipus, he is at the same time compelling us to recognize our own inner minds, in which those same impulses, though suppressed, are still to be found. The contrast with which the closing Chorus leaves us confronted —

> . . . Fix on Oedipus your eyes,
> Who resolved the dark enigma, noblest champion and most wise.
> Like a star his envied fortune mounted beaming far and wide:
> Now he sinks in seas of anguish, whelmed beneath a raging tide . . . [16]

15. By Frans Grillparzer (1791–1872), the Austrian dramatic poet.
16. See lines 1467–1471 of the play in this anthology.

— strikes as a warning at ourselves and our pride, at us who since our childhood have grown so wise and so mighty in our own eyes. Like Oedipus, we live in ignorance of these wishes, repugnant to morality, which have been forced upon us by Nature, and after their revelation we may all of us well seek to close our eyes to the scenes of our childhood.

There is an unmistakable indication in the text of Sophocles' tragedy itself that the legend of Oedipus sprang from some primaeval dream-material which had as its content the distressing disturbance of a child's relation to his parents owing to the first stirrings of sexuality. At a point when Oedipus, though he is not yet enlightened, has begun to feel troubled by his recollection of the oracle, Jocasta consoles him by referring to a dream which many people dream, though, as she thinks, it has no meaning:

> Many a man ere now in dreams hath lain
> With her who bare him. He hath least annoy
> Who with such omens troubleth not his mind.[17]

To-day, just as then, many men dream of having sexual relations with their mothers, and speak of the fact with indignation and astonishment. It is clearly the key to the tragedy and the complement to the dream of the dreamer's father being dead. The story of Oedipus is the reaction of the imagination to these two typical dreams. And just as these dreams, when dreamt by adults, are accompanied by feelings of repulsion, so too the legend must include horror and self-punishment. Its further modification originates once again in a misconceived secondary revision of the material, which has sought to exploit it for theological purposes. The attempt to harmonize divine omnipotence with human responsibility must naturally fail in connection with this subject-matter just as with any other.

Another of the great creations of tragic poetry, Shakespeare's *Hamlet*, has its roots in the same soil as *Oedipus Rex*. But the changed treatment of the same material reveals the whole difference in the mental life of these two widely separated epochs of civilization: the secular advance of repression in the emotional life of mankind. In the *Oedipus* the child's wishful phantasy that underlies it is brought into the open and realized as it would be in a dream. In *Hamlet* it remains repressed; and — just as in the case of a neurosis — we only learn of its existence from its inhibiting consequences. Strangely enough, the overwhelming effect produced by the more modern tragedy has turned out to be compatible with the fact that people have remained completely in the dark as to the hero's character. The play is built up on Hamlet's hesitations over fulfilling the task of revenge that is assigned to him; but its text offers no reasons or motives for these hesitations

17. See lines 982–84 of the play in this anthology.

and an immense variety of attempts at intepreting them have failed to produce a result. According to the view which was originated by Goethe [18] and is still the prevailing one to-day, Hamlet represents the type of man whose power of direct action is paralysed by an excessive development of his intellect. (He is "sicklied o'er with the pale cast of thought.") According to another view, the dramatist has tried to portray a pathologically irresolute character which might be classed as neurasthenic. The plot of the drama shows us, however, that Hamlet is far from being represented as a person incapable of taking any action. We see him doing so on two occasions: first in a sudden outburst of temper, when he runs his sword through the eavesdropper behind the arras, and secondly in a premeditated and even crafty fashion, when, with all the callousness of a Renaissance prince, he sends the two courtiers to the death that had been planned for himself. What is it, then, that inhibits him in fulfilling the task set him by his father's ghost? The answer, once again, is that it is the peculiar nature of the task. Hamlet is able to do anything — except take vengeance on the man who did away with his father and took that father's place with his mother, the man who shows him the repressed wishes of his own childhood realized. Thus the loathing which should drive him on to revenge is replaced in him by self-reproaches, by scruples of conscience, which remind him that he himself is literally no better than the sinner whom he is to punish. Here I have translated into conscious terms what was bound to remain unconscious in Hamlet's mind; and if anyone is inclined to call him a hysteric, I can only accept the fact as one that is implied by my interpretation. The distaste for sexuality expressed by Hamlet in his conversation with Ophelia fits in very well with this: the same distaste which was destined to take possession of the poet's mind more and more during the years that followed, and which reached its extreme expression in *Timon of Athens*. For it can of course only be the poet's own mind which confronts us in Hamlet. I observe in a book on Shakespeare by Georg Brandes (1896) a statement that *Hamlet* was written immediately after the death of Shakespeare's father (in 1601), that is, under the immediate impact of his bereavement and, as we may well assume, while his childhood feelings about his father had been freshly revived. It is known, too, that Shakespeare's own son who died at an early age bore the name of "Hamnet," which is identical with "Hamlet." Just as *Hamlet* deals with the relation of a son to his parents, so *Macbeth* (written at approximately the same period) is concerned with the subject of childlessness. But just as all neurotic symptoms, and, for that matter, dreams, are capable of being "over-interpreted" and indeed need to be, if they are to be fully understood, so all genuinely creative writings are the product of more than a single motive and more than a single impulse in the poet's mind, and are open to more than a single interpretation. In what I have written I have only attempted to interpret the deepest layer of impulses in the mind of the creative writer.

18. In *Wilhelm Meister's Apprenticeship*, Book IV, chapter 13.

Carl Gustav Jung (1875–1961)

LIFE: Born in Switzerland, he began his career as a psychiatrist after receiving (like Freud) a degree in medicine; when he met Freud in 1907, he accepted the role of disciple, just as the older man saw in Jung his successor; but like so many converts to the new "science," the son rebelled against the father: Jung refused to accept the irreducible importance which Freud assigned to the influence of sexuality in human behavior, and the two men broke off their personal and professional relationship. Even as the controversy surrounding Jung's later career — he was the editor of a journal (in the 1930's) which seemed to promulgate racist doctrines — begins to abate, his own disciples explore the significance and vitality of his psychology.

WORKS: In addition to the many papers and books dealing with the development of his theories, he wrote a study of flying saucers (1958) and an autobiography, *Memories, Dreams, Reflections* (begun when he was eighty-three).

THE PERSONAL AND THE COLLECTIVE UNCONSCIOUS *

In Freud's view, as most people know, the contents of the unconscious are limited to infantile tendencies which are repressed because of their incompatible character. Repression is a process that begins in early childhood under the moral influence of the environment and lasts throughout life. Through analysis the repressions are removed and the repressed wishes made conscious.

According to this theory, the unconscious contains only those parts of the personality which could just as well be conscious and are in fact suppressed only through upbringing. Although from one point of view the infantile tendencies of the unconscious are the most conspicuous, it would nonetheless be incorrect to define or evaluate the unconscious entirely in these terms. The unconscious has still another side to it: it includes not only repressed contents, but also all psychic material that lies below the threshold of consciousness. It is impossible to explain the subliminal nature of all this material on the principle of repression; otherwise, through the removal of repressions, a man would acquire a phenomenal memory which would thenceforth forget nothing.

Collected Works of C. G. Jung, Volume 7: Two Essays on Analytical Psychology, "The Personal and the Collective Unconscious," translated by R. F. C. Hull. Bollingen Series XX.7. 2nd edition copyright 1953 by Bollingen Foundation, New York. Distributed by Princeton University Press.

* From *Two Essays on Analytical Psychology* by C. G. Jung, Volume 7 of the Collected Works, Bollingen Series XX, Pantheon. The translation is by R. F. C. Hull.

We therefore emphatically say that in addition to the repressed material the unconscious contains all those psychic components that have fallen below the threshold, including subliminal sense-perceptions. Moreover we know, from abundant experience as well as for theoretical reasons, that the unconscious also contains components that have *not yet* reached the threshold of consciousness. These are the seeds of future conscious contents. Equally we have reason to suppose that the unconscious is never at rest in the sense of being inactive, but is continually engaged in grouping and regrouping its contents. Only in pathological cases can this activity be regarded as completely autonomous; normally it is co-ordinated with the conscious mind in a compensatory relationship.

It is to be assumed that all these contents are personal in so far as they are acquired during the individual's life. Since this life is limited, the number of acquired contents in the unconscious must also be limited. This being so, it might be thought possible to empty the unconscious either by analysis or by making a complete inventory of unconscious contents, on the ground that the unconscious cannot produce anything more than is already known and accepted in the conscious mind. We should also have to infer, as already indicated, that if one could stop the descent of conscious contents into the unconscious by doing away with repression, unconscious productivity would be paralysed. This is possible only to a very limited extent, as we know from experience. We urge our patients to hold fast to repressed contents that have been reassociated with consciousness, and to assimilate them into their plan of life. But this procedure, as we may daily convince ourselves, makes no impression on the unconscious, since it calmly continues to produce dreams and fantasies which, according to Freud's original theory, must arise from personal repressions. If in such cases we pursue our observations systematically and without prejudice, we shall find material which, although similar in form to the previous personal contents, yet seems to contain allusions that go far beyond the personal sphere. . . .

There are present in every individual, besides his personal memories, the great "primordial" images, as Jacob Burckhardt once aptly called them, the inherited powers of human imagination as it was from time immemorial. The fact of this inheritance explains the truly amazing phenomenon that certain motifs from myths and legends repeat themselves the world over in identical forms. It also explains why it is that our mental patients can reproduce exactly the same images and associations that are known to us from the old texts. I give some examples of this in my book *Symbols of Transformation*. In so doing I do not by any means assert the inheritance of ideas, but only of the possibility of such ideas, which is something very different.

In this further stage of treatment, then, when fantasies are produced which no longer rest on personal memories, we have to do with the manifestations of a deeper layer of the unconscious where the primordial images common to humanity lie sleeping. I have called these images or motifs "archetypes," also "dominants" of the unconscious. For a further elucidation of the idea I must refer the reader to the relevant literature.

This discovery means another step forward in our understanding: the recognition, that is, of two layers in the unconscious. We have to distinguish between a personal unconscious and an impersonal or transpersonal unconscious. We speak of the latter also as the collective unconscious, because it is detached from anything personal and is entirely universal, and because its contents can be found everywhere, which is naturally not the case with the personal contents. The personal unconscious contains lost memories, painful ideas that are repressed (i.e., forgotten on purpose), subliminal perceptions, by which are meant sense-perceptions that were not strong enough to reach consciousness, and finally, contents that are not yet ripe for consciousness. It corresponds to the figure of the shadow so frequently met with in dreams.

The primordial images are the most ancient and the most universal "thought-forms" of humanity. They are as much feelings as thoughts; indeed, they lead their own independent life rather in the manner of part-souls, as can easily be seen in those philosophical or Gnostic systems which rely on awareness of the unconscious as the source of knowledge. The idea of angels, archangels, "principalities and powers" in St. Paul, the archons of the Gnostics, the heavenly hierarchy of Dionysius the Areopagite,[1] all come from the perception of the relative autonomy of the archetypes. . . .

The greatest and best thoughts of man shape themselves upon these primordial images as upon a blueprint. I have often been asked where the archetypes or primordial images come from. It seems to me that their origin can only be explained by assuming them to be deposits of the constantly repeated experiences of humanity. One of the commonest and at the same time most impressive experiences is the apparent movement of the sun every day. We certainly cannot discover anything of the kind in the unconscious, so far as the known physical process is concerned. What we do find, on the other hand, is the myth of the sun-hero in all its countless modifications. It is this myth, and not the physical process, that forms the sun archetype. The same can be said of the phases of the moon. The archetype is a kind of readiness to produce over and over again the same or similar mythical ideas. Hence it seems as though what is impressed upon the unconscious were exclusively the subjective fantasy-ideas aroused by the physical process. Therefore we may take it that archetypes are recurrent impressions

1. Gnosticism was a . . . philosophical-religious movement which, in pre-Christian times, fused elements of Babylonian astral mythology, cabalistic Judaism, Persian Zoroastrianism, and Greek philosophy; at its first contact with Christianity, Gnosticism absorbed the doctrine of Christ as the Redeemer; it came down through the Middle Ages in the beliefs and mystical symbolism of alchemy. . . . Dionysius the Areopagite was a first-century Athenian converted by the apostle Paul; in the Middle Ages certain writings of the late fifth or early sixth century were erroneously attributed to him; as author of these, he is now known as the "pseudo-Dionysius." These treatises, on such subjects as "The Celestial Hierarchies" and "The Divine Names," brought to medieval scholasticism — particularly through Thomas Aquinas — the concepts of neo-Platonism and the theology of angels. . . .

made by subjective reactions. Naturally this assumption only pushes the problem further back without solving it. There is nothing to prevent us from assuming that certain archetypes exist even in animals, that they are grounded in the peculiarities of the living organism itself and are therefore direct expressions of life whose nature cannot be further explained. Not only are the archetypes, apparently, impressions of ever-repeated typical experiences, but, at the same time, they behave empirically like agents that tend towards the repetition of these same experiences. For when an archetype appears in a dream, in a fantasy, or in life, it always brings with it a certain influence or power by virtue of which it either exercises a numinous [2] or a fascinating effect, or impels to action.

"No mortal mind can plumb the depths of nature" — nor even the depths of the unconscious. We do know, however, that the unconscious never rests. It seems to be always at work, for even when asleep we dream. There are many people who declare that they never dream, but the probability is that they simply do not remember their dreams. It is significant that people who talk in their sleep mostly have no recollection either of the dream which started them talking, or even of the fact that they dreamed at all. Not a day passes but we make some slip of the tongue, or something slips our memory which at other times we know perfectly well, or we are seized by a mood whose cause we cannot trace, etc. These things are all symptoms of some consistent unconscious activity which becomes directly visible at night in dreams, but only occasionally breaks through the inhibitions imposed by our daytime consciousness.

So far as our present experience goes, we can lay it down that the unconscious processes stand in a compensatory relation to the conscious mind. I expressly use the word "compensatory" and not the word "opposed," because conscious and unconscious are not necessarily in opposition to one another, but complement one another to form a totality, which is the *self*. According to this definition the self is a quantity that is superordinate to the conscious ego. It embraces not only the conscious but also the unconscious psyche, and is therefore, so to speak, a personality which we *also* are. It is easy enough to think of ourselves as possessing part-souls. Thus we can, for instance, see ourselves as a persona without too much difficulty.[3] But it transcends our powers of imagination to form a clear picture of what we are as a self, for in this operation the part would have to comprehend the whole. There is little hope of our ever being able to reach even approximate consciousness of the self, since however much we may make conscious there will always exist an indeterminate and indeterminable amount of unconscious material which belongs to the totality of the self. Hence the self will always remain a superordinate quantity.

---

2. Having "numen," a divine force or significance.
3. . . . In Jung's psychology, a "persona" is the character we adopt in public, the appearance we present to other people, the personality we have formed to deal with all our public behavior.

The unconscious processes that compensate the conscious ego contain all those elements that are necessary for the self-regulation of the psyche as a whole. On the personal level, these are the not consciously recognized personal motives which appear in dreams, or the meanings of daily situations which we have overlooked, or conclusions we have failed to draw, or affects we have not permitted, or criticisms we have spared ourselves. But the more we become conscious of ourselves through self-knowledge, and act accordingly, the more the layer of the personal unconscious that is superimposed on the collective unconscious will be diminished. In this way there arises a consciousness which is no longer imprisoned in the petty, oversensitive, personal world of the ego, but participates freely in the wider world of objective interests. This widened consciousness is no longer that touchy, egotistical bundle of personal wishes, fears, hopes, and ambitions which always has to be compensated or corrected by unconscious counter-tendencies; instead, it is a function of relationship to the world of objects, bringing the individual into absolute, binding, and indissoluble communion with the world at large. The complications arising at this stage are no longer egotistic wish-conflict, but difficulties that concern others as much as oneself. At this stage it is fundamentally a question of collective problems, which have activated the collective unconscious because they require collective rather than personal compensation. We can now see that the unconscious produces contents which are valid not only for the person concerned, but for others as well, in fact for a great many people and possibly for all.

The Elgonyi, natives of the Elgon forests, of central Africa, explained to me that there are two kinds of dreams: the ordinary dream of the little man, and the "big vision" that only the great man has, e.g., the medicine-man or chief. Little dreams are of no account, but if a man has a "big dream" he summons the whole tribe in order to tell it to everybody.

How is a man to know whether his dream is a "big" or a "little" one? He knows it by an instinctive feeling of significance. He feels so overwhelmed by the impression it makes that he would never think of keeping the dream to himself. He *has* to tell it, on the psychologically correct assumption that it is of general significance. Even with us the collective dream has a feeling of importance about it that impels communication. It springs from a conflict of relationship and must therefore be built into our conscious relations, because it compensates these and not just some inner personal quirk.

The processes of the collective unconscious are concerned not only with the more or less personal relations of an individual to his family or to a wider social group, but with his relations to society and to the human community in general. The more general and impersonal the condition that releases the unconscious reaction, the more significant, bizarre, and overwhelming will be the compensatory manifestation. It impels not just private communication, but drives people to revelations and confessions, and even to a dramatic representation of their fantasies.

I will explain by an example how the unconscious manages to compensate relationships. A somewhat arrogant gentleman once came to me for treatment. He ran a business in partnership with his younger brother. Relations between the two brothers were very strained, and this was one of the essential causes of my patient's neurosis. From the information he gave me, the real reason for the tension was not altogether clear. He had all kinds of criticisms to make of his brother, whose gifts he certainly did not show in a very favourable light. The brother frequently came into his dreams, always in the role of a Bismarck, Napoleon, or Julius Caesar. His house looked like the Vatican or Yildiz Kiosk. My patient's unconscious evidently had the need to exalt the rank of the younger brother. From this I concluded that he was setting himself too high and his brother too low. The further course of analysis entirely justified this inference.

Another patient, a young woman who clung to her mother in an extremely sentimental way, always had very sinister dreams about her. She appeared in the dreams as a witch, as a ghost, as a pursuing demon. The mother had spoilt her beyond all reason and had so blinded her by tenderness that the daughter had no conscious idea of her mother's harmful influence. Hence the compensatory criticism exercised by the unconscious.

I myself once happened to put too low a value on a patient, both intellectually and morally. In a dream I saw a castle perched on a high cliff, and on the topmost tower was a balcony, and there sat my patient. I did not hesitate to tell her this dream at once, naturally with the best results.

We all know how apt we are to make fools of ourselves in front of the very people we have unjustly underrated. Naturally the case can also be reversed, as once happened to a friend of mine. While still a callow student he had written to Virchow, the pathologist, craving an audience with "His Excellency." When, quaking with fear, he presented himself and tried to give his name, he blurted out, "My name is Virchow." Whereupon His Excellency, smiling mischievously, said, "Ah! So your name is Virchow too?" The feeling of his own nullity was evidently too much for the unconscious of my friend, and in consequence it instantly prompted him to present himself as equal to Virchow in grandeur.

In these more personal relations there is of course no need for any very collective compensations. On the other hand, the figures employed by the unconscious in our first case are of a definitely collective nature: they are universally recognized heroes. Here there are two possible interpretations: either my patient's younger brother is a man of acknowledged and far-reaching collective importance, or my patient is over-estimating his own importance not merely in relation to his brother but in relation to everybody else as well. For the first assumption there was no support at all, while for the second there was the evidence of one's own eyes. Since the man's extreme arrogance affected not only himself, but a far wider social group, the compensation availed itself of a collective image.

The same is true of the second case. The "witch" is a collective image; hence we must conclude that the blind dependence of the young woman applied as much to the wider social group as it did to her mother personally. This was indeed the case, in so far as she was still living in an exclusively infantile world, where the world was identical with her parents. These examples deal with relations within the personal orbit. There are, however, impersonal relations which occasionally need unconscious compensation. In such cases collective images appear with a more or less mythological character. Moral, philosophical, and religious problems are, on account of their universal validity, the most likely to call for mythological compensation. . . .

The universal problem of evil and sin is another aspect to our impersonal relations to the world. Almost more than any other, therefore, this problem produces collective compensations. One of my patients, aged sixteen, had as the initial symptom of a severe compulsion neurosis the following dream: *He is walking along an unfamiliar street. It is dark, and he hears steps coming behind him. With a feeling of fear he quickens his pace. The footsteps come nearer, and his fear increases. He begins to run. But the footsteps seem to be overtaking him. Finally he turns round, and there he sees the devil. In deathly terror he leaps into the air and hangs there suspended.* This dream was repeated twice, a sign of its special urgency.

It is a notorious fact that the compulsion neuroses, by reason of their meticulousness and ceremonial punctilio, not only have the surface appearance of a moral problem but are indeed brim-full of inhuman beastliness and ruthless evil, against whose integration the otherwise very delicately organized personality puts up a desperate struggle. This explains why so many things have to be performed in ceremonially "correct" style, as though to counteract the evil hovering in the background. After this dream the neurosis started, and its essential feature was that the patient had, as he put it, to keep himself in a "provisional" or "uncontaminated" state of purity. For this purpose he either severed or made "invalid" all contact with the world and with everything that reminded him of the transitoriness of human existence, by means of lunatic formalities, scrupulous cleansing ceremonies, and the anxious observance of innumerable rules and regulations of an unbelievable complexity. Even before the patient had any suspicion of the hellish existence that lay before him, the dream showed him that if he wanted to come down to earth again there would have to be a pact with evil.

Elsewhere I have described a dream that illustrates the compensation of a religious problem in a young theological student. He was involved in all sorts of difficulties of belief, a not uncommon occurrence in the man of today. In his dream he was the pupil of the "white magician," who, however, was dressed in black. After having instructed him up to a certain point, the white magician told him that they now needed the "black magician." The black magician appeared, but clad in a white robe. He declared that he had found the keys of paradise, but needed the wisdom of the white magician in order to understand how to use them. This dream obviously contains the problem of opposites which, as we know, has found in Taoist philosophy a solution very different from the views prevailing in the West.[4] The figures employed by the dream are impersonal collective images corresponding to the nature of the impersonal religious problem. . . .

We should certainly not conclude from these compensations that, as the conscious mind becomes more deeply engrossed in universal problems, the unconscious will bring forth correspondingly far-reaching compensations. There is what one might call a legitimate and an illegitimate interest in impersonal problems. Excursions of this kind are legitimate only when they arise from the deepest and truest needs of the individual; illegitimate when they are either mere intellectual curiosity or a flight from unpleasant reality. In the latter case the unconscious produces all too human and purely personal compensations, whose manifest aim is to bring the conscious mind back to ordinary reality. People who go illegitimately mooning after the infinite often have absurdly banal dreams which endeavour to damp down their ebullience. Thus, from the nature of the compensation, we can at once draw conclusions as to the seriousness and rightness of the conscious strivings.

There are certainly not a few people who are afraid to admit that the unconscious could ever have "big" ideas. They will object, "But do you really believe that the unconscious is capable of offering anything like a constructive criticism of our Western mentality?" Of course, if we take the problem intellectually and impute rational intentions to the unconscious, the thing becomes absurd. But it would never do to foist our conscious psychology upon the unconscious. Its mentality is an instinctive one; it has no differentiated functions, and it does not "think" as we understand "thinking." It simply creates an image that answers to the conscious situation. This image contains as much thought as feeling, and is anything rather than a product of rationalistic reflection. Such an image would be better described as an artistic vision. We tend to forget that a problem like the one which underlies the dream last mentioned cannot, even to the conscious mind of the dreamer, be an intellectual problem, but is profoundly emotional. For a moral man the ethical problem is a passionate question which has its roots in the deepest instinctual processes as well as in his most idealistic aspirations. The problem for him is devastatingly real. It is not surprising, therefore, that the answer likewise springs from the depths of his nature. The fact that everyone thinks his psychology is the measure of all

4. Taoism is the traditional philosophy and religion of China, founded, according to legend, by Lao-tse (or Lao-tzu) in the sixth century B.C. While the opposites of "good" and "evil" are pitted against each other in Christianity, in Taoism both are integral to the whole of nature and experience.

things, and, if he also happens to be a fool, will inevitably think that such a problem is beneath his notice, should not trouble the psychologist in the least, for he has to take things objectively, as he finds them, without twisting them to fit his subjective suppositions. The richer and more capacious natures may legitimately be gripped by an impersonal problem, and to the extent that this is so, their unconscious can answer in the same style. And just as the conscious mind can put the question, "Why is there this frightful conflict between good and evil?," so the unconscious can reply, "Look closer! Each needs the other. The best, just because it is the best, holds the seed of evil, and there is nothing so bad but good can come of it."

It might then dawn on the dreamer that the apparently insoluble conflict is, perhaps, a prejudice, a frame of mind conditioned by time and place. The seemingly complex dream-image might easily reveal itself as plain, instinctive common sense, as the tiny germ of a rational idea, which a maturer mind could just as well have thought consciously. At all events Chinese philosophy thought of it ages ago. The singularly apt, plastic configuration of thought is the prerogative of that primitive, natural spirit which is alive in all of us and is only obscured by a one-sided conscious development. If we consider the unconscious compensations from this angle, we might justifiably be accused of judging the unconscious too much from the conscious standpoint. And indeed, in pursuing these reflections, I have always started from the view that the unconscious simply reacts to the conscious contents, albeit in a very significant way, but that it lacks initiative. It is, however, far from my intention to give the impression that the unconscious is merely reactive in all cases. On the contrary, there is a host of experiences which seem to prove that the unconscious is not only spontaneous but can actually take the lead. There are innumerable cases of people who lingered on in a pettifogging unconsciousness, only to become neurotic in the end. Thanks to the neurosis contrived by the unconscious, they are shaken out of their apathy, and this in spite of their own laziness and often desperate resistance.

Yet it would, in my view, be wrong to suppose that in such cases the unconscious is working to a deliberate and concerted plan and is striving to realize certain definite ends. I have found nothing to support this assumption. The driving force, so far as it is possible for us to grasp it, seems to be in essence only an urge towards self-realization. If it were a matter of some general teleological plan, then all individuals who enjoy a surplus of unconsciousness would necessarily be driven towards higher consciousness by an irresistible urge. That is plainly not the case. There are vast masses of the population who, despite their notorious unconsciousness, never get anywhere near a neurosis. The few who are smitten by such a fate are really persons of the "higher" type who, for one reason or another, have remained too long on a primitive level. Their nature does not in the long run tolerate persistence in what is for them an unnatural torpor. As a result of their narrow conscious outlook and their cramped existence they save energy; bit by bit it accumulates in the unconscious and finally explodes in the form of a more or less acute neurosis. This simple mechanism does not necessarily conceal a "plan." A perfectly understandable urge towards self-realization would provide a quite satisfactory explanation. We could also speak of a retarded maturation of the personality.

Since it is highly probable that we are still a long way from the summit of absolute consciousness, presumably everyone is capable of wider consciousness, and we may assume accordingly that the unconscious processes are constantly supplying us with contents which, if consciously recognized, would extend the range of consciousness. Looked at in this way, the unconscious appears as a field of experience of unlimited extent. If it were merely reactive to the conscious mind, we might aptly call it a psychic mirror-world. In that case, the real source of all contents and activities would lie in the conscious mind, and there would be absolutely nothing in the unconscious except the distorted reflections of conscious contents. The creative process would be shut up in the conscious mind, and anything new would be nothing but conscious invention or cleverness. The empirical facts give the lie to this. Every creative man knows that spontaneity is the very essence of creative thought. Because the unconscious is not just a reactive mirror-reflection, but an independent, productive activity, its realm of experience is a self-contained world, having its own reality, of which we can only say that it affects us as we affect it — precisely what we say about our experience of the outer world. And just as material objects are the constituent elements of this world, so psychic factors constitute the objects of that other world.

The idea of psychic objectivity is by no means a new discovery. It is in fact one of the earliest and most universal achievements of humanity: it is nothing less than the conviction as to the concrete existence of a spirit-world. The spirit-world was certainly never an invention in the sense that fire-boring was an invention; it was far rather the experience, the conscious acceptance of a reality in no way inferior to that of the material world. I doubt whether primitives exist anywhere who are not acquainted with magical influence or a magical substance. ("Magical" is simply another word for "psychic.") It would also appear that practically all primitives are aware of the existence of spirits. "Spirit" is a psychic fact. Just as we distinguish our own bodiliness from bodies that are strange to us, so primitives — if they have any notion of "souls" at all — distinguish between their own souls and the spirits, which are felt as strange and as "not belonging." They are objects of outward perception, whereas their own soul (or one of several souls where a plurality is assumed), though believed to be essentially akin to the spirits, is not usually an object of so-called sensible perception. After death the soul (or one of the plurality of souls) becomes a spirit which survives the dead man, and often it shows a marked deterioration of character that partly contradicts the notion of personal immortality. The Bataks, of Sumatra, go so far as to assert that the people who were good in this life turn into malign and dangerous spirits. Nearly everything that the primitives say about the tricks which the spirits play on the living, and the general picture they give of the *revenants*,[5] corresponds down to the last detail with the phenomena established by spiritualistic experience. And just as the communications from the "Beyond" can be seen to be the activities of broken-off bits of the psyche, so these primitive spirits are manifestations of unconscious complexes. The importance that modern psychology attaches to the "parental complex" is a direct continuation of primitive man's experience of the dangerous power of the ancestral spirits. Even the error of judgment which leads him unthinkingly to assume that the spirits are realities of the external world is carried on in our assumption (which is only partially correct) that the real parents are responsible for the parental complex. In the old trauma theory of Freudian psychoanalysis, and in other quarters as well, this assumption even passed for a scientific explanation. (It was in order to avoid this confusion that I advocated the term "parental imago." [6])

The simple soul is of course quite unaware of the fact that his nearest relations, who exercise immediate influence over him, create in him an image which is only partly a replica of themselves, while its other part is compounded of elements derived from himself. The imago is built up of parental influences plus the specific reactions of the child; it is therefore an image that reflects the object with very considerable qualifications. Naturally, the simple soul believes that his parents are as he sees them. The image is unconsciously projected, and when the parents die, the projected image goes on working as though it were a spirit existing on its own. The primitive then speaks of parental spirits who return by night (*revenants*), while the modern man calls it a father or mother complex.

The more limited a man's field of consciousness is, the more numerous the psychic contents (imagos) which meet him as quasi-external apparitions, either in the form of spirits, or as magical potencies projected upon living people (magicians, witches, etc.). At a rather higher stage of development, where the idea of the soul already exists, not all the imagos continue to be projected (where this happens, even trees and stones talk), but one or the other complex has come near enough to consciousness to be felt as no longer strange, but as somehow "belonging." Nevertheless, the feeling that it "belongs" is not at first sufficiently strong for the complex to be sensed as a subjective content of consciousness. It remains in a sort of no man's land between con-

5. From the French verb *revenir*, to come back: the spirits of the dead who come back to the realm of the living.

6. In its derivation from the Latin, "imago" means simply "image," copy, or reflection; but as used in modern psychology, an "imago" . . . is not the same thing as an exact image or reflection of something external, . . . but is a conception built up by the unconscious mind, a conception which may not have any exact resemblance to, for instance, the actual parent.

scious and unconscious, in the half-shadow, in part belonging or akin
to the conscious subject, in part an autonomous being, and meeting
consciousness as such. At all events it is not necessarily obedient to
subjective intentions, it may even be of a higher order, more often than
not a source of inspiration or warning, or of "supernatural" information. Psychologically such a content could be explained as a partly
autonomous complex that is not yet fully integrated. The archaic souls,
the *ba* and *ka* of the Egyptians, are complexes of this kind. At a still
higher level, and particularly among the civilized peoples of the West,
this complex is invariably of the feminine gender . . . a fact for which
deeper and cogent reasons are not lacking.

André Gide (1869–1951)

LIFE: Like Rousseau before him, he exposed his life in his work, as
autobiography, fiction, dialogue. Born into a French protestant family,
he moved from the intense, puritanical piety of his upbringing to the
complete freedom of self-realization — a revolution in behavior brought
about by his famous trip to North Africa in 1893. Thereafter the ruthless honesty, which was the product of his struggle to record the self-
doubts, appealed to a whole generation of writers who used his example
to reveal their own truths.

WORKS: *The Immoralist* (1902); *Return of the Prodigal* (1907);
Strait is the Gate (1909); *The Counterfeiters* (1925); *If It Die* (1926).

ALISSA'S JOURNAL *

Aigues-Vives.

Left Le Havre [1] the day before yesterday; yesterday arrived at
Nîmes; my first journey! With no housekeeping to do and no cooking
to look after, and consequently with a slight feeling of idleness, today,
the 23rd May, 188–, my twenty-fifth birthday, I begin this journal —
without much pleasure, a little for the sake of company; for, perhaps
for the first time in my life, I feel lonely — in a different, a foreign
land almost, one with which I have not yet made acquaintance. It has,
no doubt the same things to say to me as Normandy — the same that
I listen to untiringly at Fongueusemare — for God is nowhere different
from Himself — but this southern land speaks a language I have not
yet learned, and to which I listen wondering.

* From *Strait is the Gate* (1909) by Andre Gide, trans. Dorthy Bussy. Copyright 1924 and renewed
1951 by Alfred A. Knopf, Inc. Reprinted by permission.
1. Alissa has left her home at Fongueusemare, in the vicinity of Le Havre, to be with her
sister Juliette during the final weeks of her pregnancy.

24th May.

Juliette is dozing on a sofa near me — in the open gallery that is the chief charm of the house, built as it is after the Italian fashion. The gallery opens on to the graveled courtyard that is a continuation of the garden. Without leaving her sofa, Juliette can see the lawn sloping down to the piece of water, where a tribe of parti-colored ducks disport themselves and two swans sail. A stream which, they say, never runs dry in the heat of any summer, feeds it and then flows through the garden, which merges into a grove of ever-increasing wildness, more and more shut in by the bed of a dried torrent on the one side and the vineyards on the other, and finally strangled altogether between them.

Édouard Teissières[2] yesterday showed my father the garden, the farm, the cellars, and the vineyards, while I stayed behind with Juliette — so that this morning, while it was still very early, I was able to make my first voyage of discovery in the park, by myself. A great many plants and strange trees, whose names, however, I should have liked to know. I pick a twig of each of them so as to be told what they are at lunch. In some of them I recognize the evergreen oaks that Jerome[3] admired in the gardens of the Villa Borghese or Doria-Pamphili — so distantly related to our northern tree, of such a different character! Almost at the farthest end of the park there is a narrow, mysterious glade that they shelter, bending over a carpet of grass so soft to the feet that it seems an invitation to the choir of nymphs. I wonder — I am almost scared that my feeling for nature, which at Fongueusemare is so profoundly Christian, should here become, in spite of myself, half pagan. And yet the kind of awe which oppressed me more and more was religious too. I whispered the words: *"hic nemus."*[4] The air was crystalline; there was a strange silence. I was thinking of Orpheus,[5] of Armida,[6] when all at once there rose a solitary bird's song, so near me, so pathetic, so pure, that it seemed suddenly as though all nature had been awaiting it. My heart beat violently; I stayed for a moment leaning against a tree, and then came in before anyone was up.

26th May.

Still no letter from Jerome. If he had written to me at Le Havre, his letter would have been forwarded. . . . I can confide my anxiety to no one but this book; for the last three days I have not been distracted from it for an instant, either by our excursion yesterday to Les Baux, or by reading, or by prayer. Today I can write of nothing else; the curious melancholy from which I have been suffering ever since I arrived at Aigues-Vives has, perhaps, no other cause — and yet I feel it at such a depth within me that it seems to me now as if it had been

2. Juliette's husband.
3. Alissa's cousin, whose passionate love for her she has renounced. Jerome is the narrator of the novel; shortly after Alissa's death he receives, and then records, her journal.
4. "This grove." Nemus was also the name of the sacred grove of Diana at Aricia.
5. For the story of this legendary singer see Ovid's *Metamorphoses* in this anthology.
6. The beautiful sorceress in the romantic epic *Jerusalem Delivered* (1575) by the Italian poet Torquato Tasso (1544–95).

there for a long time past, and as if the joy on which I prided myself did no more than cover it over.

27th May.

Why should I lie to myself? It is by an effort of mind that I rejoice in Juliette's happiness. That happiness which I longed for so much, to the extent of offering my own in sacrifice to it, is painful to me, now that I see that she has obtained it without trouble, and that it is so different from what she and I imagined. How complicated it all is! Yes . . . I see well enough that a horrible revival of egoism in me is offended at her having found her happiness elsewhere than in my sacrifice — at her not having needed my sacrifice in order to be happy.

And now I ask myself, as I feel what uneasiness Jerome's silence causes me: Was that sacrifice really consummated in my heart? I am, as it were, humiliated, to feel that God no longer exacts it. Can it be that I was not equal to it?

28th May.

How dangerous this analysis of my sadness is! I am already growing attached to this book. Is my personal vanity, which I thought I had mastered, reasserting its rights here? No; may my soul never use this journal as a flattering mirror before which to attire itself! It is not out of idleness that I write, as I thought at first, but out of sadness. Sadness is a *state of sin,* which had ceased to be mine, which I hate, from whose *complications* I wish to free my soul. This book must help me to find my happiness in myself once more.

Sadness is a complication. I never used to analyze my happiness.

At Fongueusemare I was alone, too, still more alone — why did I not feel it? And when Jerome wrote to me from Italy, I was willing that he should see without me, that he should live without me; I followed him in thought, and out of his joy I made my own. And now, in spite of myself, I want him; without him, every new thing I see is irksome to me.

10th June.

Long interruption of this journal, which I had scarcely begun; birth of little Lise; long hours of watching beside Juliette; I take no pleasure in writing anything here that I can write to Jerome. I should like to keep myself from the intolerable fault which is common to so many women — that of writing too much. Let me consider this notebook as a means of perfection.

There followed several pages of notes made in the course of her reading, extracts, etc. Then, dated from Fongueusemare once more:

16th July.

Juliette is happy; she says so, seems so; I have no right, no reason to doubt it.[7] Whence comes this feeling of dissatisfaction, of discomfort,

7. It was Juliette's unconfessed love for Jerome which initially caused Alissa to renounce him.

which I have now when I am with her? Perhaps from feeling that such happiness is so practical, so easily obtained, so perfectly "to measure" that it seems to cramp the soul and stifle it. . . .

And I ask myself now whether it is really happiness that I desire so much as the progress toward happiness. Oh, Lord! preserve me from a happiness to which I might too easily attain! Teach me to put off my happiness, to place it as far away from me as Thou art.

Several pages here had been torn out; they referred, no doubt, to our painful meeting at Le Havre. The journal did not begin again till the following year; the pages were not dated, but had certainly been written at the time of my stay at Fongueusemare.

Sometimes as I listen to him talking, I seem to be watching myself think. He explains me and discovers me to myself. Should I exist without him? I *am* only when I am with him. . . .

Sometimes I hesitate as to whether what I feel for him is really what people call love — the picture that is generally drawn of love is so different from that which I should like to draw. I should like nothing to be said about it, and to love him without knowing that I love him. I should like, above all, to love him without his knowing it.

I no longer get any joy out of that part of life which has to be lived without him. My virtue is all only to please him — and yet, when I am with him, I feel my virtue weakening.

I used to like learning the piano, for it seemed to me that I was able to make some progress in it every day. That too, perhaps, is the secret of the pleasure I take in reading a book in a foreign language; not, indeed, that I prefer any other language whatever to our own, or that the writers I admire in it appear to me in any way inferior to those of other countries — but the slight difficulty that lies in the pursuit of their meaning and feeling, the unconscious pride of overcoming this difficulty, and of overcoming it more and more successfully, adds to my intellectual pleasure a certain spiritual contentment, which it seems to me I cannot do without.

However blessed it might be, I cannot desire a state without progress. I imagine Heavenly joy not as a confounding of the spirit with God, but as an infinite, a perpetual drawing near to Him . . . and if I were not afraid of playing upon words I should say that I did not care for any joy that was not *progressive*.

This morning we were sitting on the bench in the avenue; we were not talking and did not feel any need to talk. . . . Suddenly he asked me if I believed in a future life.

"Oh! Jerome!" I cried at once, "it is more than hope I have; it is certainty."

And it seemed to me, on a sudden, that my whole faith had, as it were, been poured into that exclamation.

"I should like to know," he added. He stopped a few moments; then: "Would you act differently without your faith?"

"How can I tell?" I answered; and I added: "And you, my dear, you yourself, and in spite of yourself, can no longer act otherwise than as if you were inspired by the liveliest faith. And I should not love you if you were different."

No, Jerome, no, it is not after a future recompense that our virtue is striving; it is not for recompense that our love is seeking. A generous soul is hurt by the idea of being rewarded for its efforts; nor does it consider virtue an adornment; no, virtue is the form of its beauty.

Papa is not so well again; nothing serious, I hope, but he has been obliged to go back to his milk diet for the last three days.

Yesterday evening, Jerome had just gone up to his room; Papa, who was sitting up with me for a little, left me alone for a few minutes. I was sitting on the sofa, or rather — a thing I hardly ever do — I was lying down, I don't know why. The lampshade was shading my eyes and the upper part of my body from the light; I was mechanically looking at my feet, which showed a little below my dress in the light thrown upon them by the lamp. When Papa came back, he stood for a few moments at the door, staring at me oddly, half smiling, half sad. I got up with a vague feeling of shyness; then he called me: "Come and sit beside me," said he; and, though it was already late, he began speaking to me about my mother,[8] which he had never done since their separation. He told me how he had married her, how much he had loved her, and how much she had at first been to him.

"Papa," I said to him at last, "do, please, say why are you telling me this this evening — what makes you tell me this just this particular evening?"

"Because, just now, when I came into the drawing-room and saw you lying on the sofa, I thought for a moment it was your mother."

The reason I asked this so insistently was because that very evening, Jerome had been reading over my shoulder, standing leaning over me. I could not see him, but I felt his breath and, as it were, the warmth and pulsation of his body. I pretended to go on reading, but my mind had stopped working; I could not even distinguish the lines; so strange a perturbation took possession of me that I was obliged to get up from my chair quickly while I still could; I managed to leave the room for a few minutes, luckily without his noticing anything. But a little later, when I was alone in the drawing-room and lay down on the sofa, where

8. Who had run away, presumably with another man.

Papa thought I looked like my mother, at that very moment I was thinking of her.

I slept very badly last night; I was disturbed, oppressed, miserable, haunted by the recollection of the past, which came over me like a wave of remorse.

Lord, teach me the horror of all that has any appearance of evil.

Poor Jerome! If he only knew that sometimes he would have but a single sign to make, and that sometimes I wait for him to make it. . . .

When I was a child, even then it was because of him that I wanted to be beautiful. It seems to me now that I have never striven after perfection, except for him. And that this perfection can only be attained without him is of all Thy teachings, my God! the one that is most disconcerting to my soul.

How happy must that soul be for whom virtue is one with love! Sometimes I doubt whether there is any other virtue than love . . . to love as much as possible and continually more and more. . . . But at other times, alas! virtue appears to me to be nothing but resistance to love. What! shall I dare to call virtue that which is the most natural inclination of my heart? Oh, tempting sophism! Specious allurement! Cunning mirage of happiness!

This morning I read in La Bruyère: [9] "In the course of this life one sometimes meets with pleasures so dear, promises so tender, which are yet forbidden us, that it is natural to desire at least that they might be permitted: charms so great can be surpassed only when virtue teaches us to renounce them."

Why did I invent here that there was anything forbidden? Can it be that I am secretly attracted by a charm more powerful and a sweetness greater still than that of love? Oh! that it were possible to carry our two souls forward together, by force of love, beyond love!

Alas! I understand now only too well: between God and him there is no other obstacle but myself. If perhaps, as he says, his love for me at first inclined him to God, now that very love hinders him; he lingers with me, prefers me, and I am become the idol that keeps him back from making further progress in virtue. One of us two must needs attain to it; and as I despair of overcoming the love in my coward heart, grant me, my God, vouchsafe me strength to teach him to love me no longer, so that at the cost of my merits I may bring Thee his, which are so infinitely preferable . . . and if today my soul sobs with grief at losing him, do I not lose him to find him again hereafter in Thee?

Tell me, oh, my God! what soul ever deserved Thee more? Was he not born for something better than to love me? And should I love him

---

9. Jean de la Bruyère (1645–96), French satirist, whose only book (published in 1688) is called *The Characters*, a collection of sketches of social types, moral observations, and epigrams.

so much if he were to stop short at myself? How much all that might become heroic dwindles in the midst of happiness!

Sunday.

"God having provided some better thing for us."

Monday, 3rd May.

To think that happiness is here, close by, offering itself, and that one only has to put out one's hand to grasp it. . . .

This morning, as I was talking to him, I consummated the sacrifice.

Monday evening.

He leaves tomorrow . . .

Dear Jerome, I still love you with infinite tenderness; but never more shall I be able to tell you so. The constraint that I lay upon my eyes, upon my lips, upon my soul, is so hard that to leave you is a relief and a bitter satisfaction.

I strive to act according to reason, but at the moment of action the reasons that made me act escape me, or appear foolish; I no longer believe in them.

The reasons that make me fly from him? I no longer believe in them. . . . And yet I fly from him, sadly and without understanding why I fly.

Lord! that we might advance toward Thee, Jerome and I together, each beside the other, each helping the other; that we might walk along the way of life like two pilgrims, of whom one says at times to the other: "Lean on me, brother, if you are weary," and to whom the other replies: "It is enough to feel you near me. . . ." But no! The way Thou teachest, Lord, is a strait way — so strait that two cannot walk in it abreast.

5th July.

More than six weeks have gone by without my opening this book. Last month, as I was rereading some of its pages, I became aware of a foolish, wicked anxiety to write well . . . which I owe to *him.* . . .

As though in this book, which I began only so as to help myself to do without *him,* I was continuing to write to *him.*

I have torn up all the pages that seemed to me to be *well written.* (I know what I mean by this.) I ought to have torn up all those in which there was any question of him. I ought to have torn them all up. I could not.

And already, because I tore up those few pages, I had a little feeling of pride . . . a pride that I should laugh at if my heart were not so sick.

It really seemed as though I had done something meritorious, and as though what I had destroyed had been of some importance!

6th July.

I have been obliged to banish from my bookshelves. . . .

I fly from him in one book only to find him in another. I hear his voice reading me even those pages which I discover without him. I care only for what interests him, and my mind has taken the form of his to such an extent that I can distinguish one from the other no better than I did at the time when I took pleasure in feeling they were one.

Sometimes I force myself to write badly in order to escape from the rhythm of his phrases; but even to struggle against him is still to be concerned with him. I have made a resolution to read nothing but the Bible (perhaps the *Imitation*) [10] and to write nothing more in this book, except every evening the chief text of my reading.

There followed a kind of diary, in which the date of each day, starting with July 1st, was accompanied by a text. I transcribe only those which are accompanied by some commentary.

20th July.

"Sell all that thou hast and give it to the poor."

I understand that I ought to give to the poor this heart of mine, which belongs only to Jerome. And by so doing should I not teach him at the same time to do likewise? . . . Lord, grant me this courage.

24th July.

I have stopped reading the *Interior Consolation.* The old-fashioned language greatly charmed me, but it was distracting, and the almost pagan joy it gives me is far removed from the edification that I set myself to get from it.

I have taken up the *Imitation* again, and not even in the Latin text, which I was vain of understanding. I am glad that the translation in which I read it should not even be signed. It is true that it is Protestant, but "adapted to the use of all Christian communities," says the title.

"Oh, if thou wert sensible, how much peace thou wouldest procure for thyself and joy for others, by rightly ordering thyself, methinks thou wouldest be more solicitous for thy spiritual progress!"

10th August.

If I were to cry to Thee, my God, with the impulsive faith of a child and with the heavenly tongues of angels. . . .

All this comes to me, I know, not from Jerome, but from Thee.

Why, then, between Thee and me, dost Thou everywhere set his image?

14th August.

Only two months more in which to complete my work. . . . Oh, Lord, grant me Thy help!

10. *Imitation of Christ,* the famous book (originally written in Latin) whose author was probably Thomas à Kempis (1380–1471), the German mystic and ascetic.

20th August.

I feel — I feel by my *unhappiness* that the sacrifice is not consummated in my heart. My God, grant that henceforth I owe to none but Thee the joy that he alone used to give me.

28th August.

How mediocre, and miserable is the virtue to which I attain! Do I then exact too much from myself? . . . To suffer no more.

What cowardice makes me continually implore God for His strength? My prayers now are nothing but complainings.

29th August.

"Consider the lilies of the field. . . ."

This simple saying plunged me this morning into a sadness from which nothing could distract me. I went out into the country and these words, which I kept continually repeating to myself, filled my heart and eyes with tears. I contemplated the vast and empty plain where the laborer was toiling, bent over his plough. . . . "The lilies of the field. . . ." But, Lord, where are they . . . ?

16th September, 10 o'clock at night.

I have seen him again. He is here under this roof. I see the light from his window shining on the grass. He is still up as I write these lines, and perhaps he is thinking of me. He has not changed. He says so, and I feel it. Shall I be able to show myself to him as I have resolved to be, so that his love may disown me?

24th September.

Oh, torturing conversation in which I succeeded in feigning indifference — coldness, when my heart was fainting within me! Up till then I had contented myself with avoiding him. This morning I was able to believe that God would give me strength to be victorious and that to slink forever out of the combat was to prove myself a coward. Did I triumph? Does Jerome love me a little less? Alas! I both hope and fear it together. I have never loved him more.

And if it is Thy Will, Lord, that to save him from me I must compass my own perdition, so be it.

"Enter into my heart and into my soul in order to bear in them my sufferings and to continue to endure in me what remains to Thee to suffer of Thy Passion."

We spoke of Pascal. . . . What did I say? What shameful, foolish words? I suffered even as I uttered them, but tonight I repent them as a blasphemy. I turned again to the heavy volume of the *Pensées,* which opened of itself at this passage in the letters to Mademoiselle de

Roannez: [11] "We do not feel our bonds as long as we follow willingly him who leads; but as soon as we begin to resist and to draw away, then indeed we suffer."

These words affected me so personally that I did not have strength to go on reading; but opening the book in another place I came across an admirable passage which I did not know and which I have just copied out.

The first volume of the Journal came to an end here. No doubt the next had been destroyed, for in the papers that Alissa left behind, the Journal did not begin again till three years later — still at Fongueuse-mare — in September — a short time, that is to say, before our last meeting.

The last volume begins with the sentences that follow.

17th September.

My God, Thou knowest I have need of him to love Thee.

20th September.

My God, give him to me so that I may give Thee my heart.

My God, let me see him only once more.

My God, I engage to give Thee my heart. Grant me what my love beseeches. I will give what remains to me of life to Thee alone.

My God, forgive me this despicable prayer, but I cannot keep his name from my lips nor forget the anguish of my heart.

My God, I cry to Thee. Do not forsake me in my distress.

21st September.

"Whatever ye shall ask the Father in my name . . ."

Lord, in Thy name, I dare not.

But though I no longer formulate my prayer, wilt Thou be the less aware of the delirious longing of my heart?

27th September.

Ever since the morning a great calm. Spent nearly the whole night in meditation, in prayer. Suddenly I was conscious of a kind of luminous peace like the imagination I had as a child of the Holy Ghost; it seemed to wrap me round, to descend into me. I went to bed at once, fearing that my joy was due only to nervous exaltation. I went to sleep fairly quickly without this felicity leaving me. It is still here this morning in all its completeness. I have the certainty now that he will come.

30th September.

Jerome, my friend! you whom I still call brother, but whom I love infinitely more than a brother. . . . How many times I have cried your

11. Charlotte de Roannez is said to have been the object of Pascal's passionate love. It is somewhat more probable that for a few years before his conversion in 1654 he lived a rather dissolute life in the company of, among others, Charlotte's brother, the duc de Roannez.

name in the beech copse. Every evening toward dusk I go out by the little gate of the kitchen-garden and walk down the avenue where it is already dark. If you were suddenly to answer me, if you were to appear there from behind the stony bank around which I so eagerly seek you, or if I were to see you in the distance, seated on the bench waiting for me, my heart would not leap . . . no! I am astonished at not seeing you.

1st October.

Nothing yet. The sun has set in a sky of incomparable purity. I am waiting. I know that soon I shall be sitting with him on this very bench. I hear his voice already. I like it so much when he says my name. He will be here! I shall put my hand in his hand. I shall let my head lean on his shoulder. I shall breathe beside him. Yesterday I brought out some of his letters with me to reread, but I did not look at them — I was too much taken up with the thought of him. I took with me, too, the amethyst cross he used to like, and which one summer I used to wear every evening as long as I did not want him to go. I should like to give him this cross. For a long time past I have had a dream — that he was married and I godmother to his first daughter, a little Alissa, to whom I gave this ornament. . . . Why have I never dared tell him?

2nd October.

My soul today is as light and joyful as a bird would be that had made its nest in the sky. For today he will come. I feel it! I know it! I should like to proclaim it aloud to the world. I feel I must write it here. I cannot hide my joy any longer. Even Robert,[12] who is usually so inattentive and indifferent to what concerns me, noticed it. His questions embarrassed me, and I did not know what to answer. How shall I be able to wait till this evening? . . .

Some kind of strange transparent bandage over my eyes seems to show me his image everywhere — his image magnified — and all love's rays are concentrated on a single burning spot in my heart.

Oh! how this waiting tires me!

Lord, unclose for me one moment the wide gateways of gladness.

3rd October.

All is over. Alas! he has slipped out of my arms like a shadow. He was here! He was here! I feel him still. I call him. My hands, my lips seek him in vain in the night. . . .

I can neither pray nor sleep. I went out again into the dark garden. I was afraid — in my room — everywhere in the house — I was afraid. My anguish brought me once more to the door behind which I had left him. I opened it with a mad hope that he might have come back. I called. I groped in the darkness. I have come in again to write to him. I cannot accept my grief.

12. Alissa's brother.

What has happened? What did I say to him? What did I do? Why do I always want to exaggerate my virtue to him? What can be the worth of a virtue that my whole heart denies? I was secretly false to the words God set upon my lips. In spite of all that my heart was bursting with, I could bring nothing out. Jerome! Jerome, my unhappy friend, in whose presence my heart bleeds and in whose absence I perish, believe nothing of all I said to you just now, but only the words spoken by my love.

Tore up my letter, then wrote again. . . . Here is the dawn, gray, wet with tears, as sad as my thoughts. I hear the first sounds of the farm and everything that was sleeping reawakens to life. . . . "Arise, now. The hour is at hand. . . ."
My letter shall not go.

5th October.
Oh, jealous God, who hast despoiled me, take Thou possession of my heart. All warmth henceforth has forsaken it; nothing will touch it more. Help me to triumph over the melancholy remnant of myself. This house, this garden encourage my love intolerably. I must fly to some place where I shall see none but Thee.

Thou wilt help me to bestow upon Thy poor what fortune I possessed; let me leave Fongueusemare, which I cannot dispose of easily, to Robert. I have made my will, it is true, but I am ignorant of the necessary formalities, and yesterday I could not talk to the lawyer properly, as I was afraid he might suspect the decision I had taken and warn Juliette and Robert. I will finish this business in Paris.

10th October.
Arrived here so tired that I was obliged to stay in bed the first two days. The doctor, who was sent for against my will, speaks of an operation that he considers necessary. What is the use of objecting? But I easily made him believe that I was frightened at the idea of an operation and preferred waiting till I had "regained my strength a little."
I have managed to conceal my name and address. I have deposited enough money with the management of the house for them to make no difficulty about taking me in and keeping me for as long as God shall continue to think it necessary.
I like this room. The walls need no other decoration than their perfect cleanliness. I was quite astonished to feel almost joyful. The reason is that I expect nothing more from life — that I must be content now with God, and His love is sweet only if it fills to completion whatever space there is within us. . . .

The only book I have brought with me is the Bible; but today there sounded in me louder than any words I find there, this wild and passionate sob of Pascal's: "Whatever is not God cannot satisfy my longings."

Oh! too human joy, that my imprudent heart desired. . . . Was it to wring this cry from me, Lord, that Thou hast thus bereft me?

12th October.

Thy Kingdom come! May it come in me; so that Thou alone mayest reign over me and reign over the whole of me. I will no longer grudge Thee my heart.

Though I am as tired as if I were very old, my soul keeps a strange childishness. I am still the little girl, who could not go to sleep before everything in her room was tidy and the clothes she had taken off were neatly folded beside her bed. . . . That is how I should like to get ready to die.

13th October.

Reread my journal before destroying it. "It is unworthy of noble natures to spread round them the disturbance they feel." It is, I think, Clotilde de Vaux [13] who says this so finely.

Just as I was going to throw this journal into the fire, I felt a kind of warning that held me back. It seemed to me that it no longer belonged to me, that I had no right to deprive Jerome of it, that I had never written it except for him. My anxieties, my doubts, seem to me now so foolish that I can no longer attach any importance to them or believe that they will disturb Jerome. My God, grant that he may at times catch in these lines the unskilled accent of a heart passionately desirous of urging him to those heights of virtue which I myself despaired of reaching.

"My God, lead me to the rock that is higher than I."

15th October.

"Joy, joy, joy, tears of joy. . . ."

Above human joy and beyond all suffering, yes, I foresee that radiant joy. The "rock that is higher than I" bears, I know, the name of happiness . . . I understand that my whole life has been vain, except in so far as it culminates in happiness. . . . Ah! Lord, but Thy promise to the pure and renouncing soul was this: "Blessed *from henceforth*" said Thy holy word, "Blessed are they which die in the Lord from henceforth." Must I wait until I die? This is the point where my faith wavers. Lord! I cry unto Thee with all my strength. I am in the night! I am waiting for the dawn. I cry unto Thee with a crying that wastes me to death. Come and slake the thirst of my heart. It is now, at once, that I thirst for happiness. . . . Or ought I to persuade myself that I have it? And as the pipe of the impatient bird before daybreak calls

13. Intimate friend of Auguste Comte (1798–1857), the French philosopher.

rather than heralds the light, ought I to sing, without waiting for the night to dwindle?

16th October.
Jerome, I wish I could teach you perfect joy.

This morning I was shattered by a fit of sickness. And afterwards I felt so weak that for a moment I hoped I was going to die. But no; first a great calm fell upon my whole being; then a pang of anguish pierced me, a shudder of my flesh and soul; it was like the sudden and disenchanting *illumination* of my life. It seemed to me that I saw for the first time the walls of my room in their atrocious bareness. I was seized with fear. Even now I am writing to reassure myself, to calm myself. Oh Lord! may I reach the end without blasphemy!

I was able to get up again. I went down on my knees like a child. . . .

I should like to die now, quickly, before again realizing that I am alone.

Marcel Proust (1871–1922)

LIFE: After the death of his mother in 1905, when he was thirty-four, Proust, already suffering from asthma, withdrew into his cork-lined room and there composed his long meditation on the world he had chosen to leave — and from that stationary journey he recovered the self which had once touched the world.

WORKS: *Remembrance of Things Past* (in French *À la Recherche du temps perdu,* 1913–27) ; *Jean Santeuil* (1952).

REMEMBRANCE OF THINGS PAST

Overture *

For a long time I used to go to bed early. Sometimes, when I had put out my candle, my eyes would close so quickly that I had not even time to say "I'm going to sleep." And half an hour later the thought that it was time to go to sleep would awaken me; I would try to put away the book which, I imagined, was still in my hands, and to blow out the light; I had been thinking all the time while I was asleep, of what I had just been reading, but my thoughts had run into a channel

* From the beginning of the first volume, called *Swann's Way* (1913). Translated by C. K. Scott Moncrieff.

of their own, until I myself seemed actually to have become the subject of my book: a church, a quartet, the rivalry between François I and Charles V.[1] This impression would persist for some moments after I was awake; it did not disturb my mind, but it lay like scales upon my eyes and prevented them from registering the fact that the candle was no longer burning. Then it would begin to seem unintelligible, as the thoughts of a former existence must be to a reincarnate spirit; the subject of my book would separate itself from me, leaving me free to choose whether I would form part of it or no; and at the same time my sight would return and I would be astonished to find myself in a state of darkness, pleasant and restful enough for the eyes, and even more, perhaps, for my mind, to which it appeared incomprehensible, without a cause, a matter dark indeed.

I would ask myself what o'clock it could be; I could hear the whistling of trains, which, now nearer and now farther off, punctuating the distance like the note of a bird in a forest, shewed me in perspective the deserted countryside through which a traveller would be hurrying towards the nearest station: the path that he followed being fixed for ever in his memory by the general excitement due to being in a strange place, to doing unusual things, to the last words of conversation, to farewells exchanged beneath an unfamiliar lamp which echoed still in his ears amid the silence of the night; and to the delightful prospect of being once again at home.

I would lay my cheeks gently against the comfortable cheeks of my pillow, as plump and blooming as the cheeks of babyhood. Or I would strike a match to look at my watch. Nearly midnight. The hour when an invalid, who has been obliged to start on a journey and to sleep in a strange hotel, awakens in a moment of illness and sees with glad relief a streak of daylight shewing under his bedroom door. Oh, joy of joys! it is morning. The servants will be about in a minute: he can ring, and some one will come to look after him. The thought of being made comfortable gives him strength to endure his pain. He is certain he heard footsteps: they come nearer, and then die away. The ray of light beneath his door is extinguished. It is midnight; some one has turned out the gas; the last servant has gone to bed, and he must lie all night in agony with no one to bring him any help.

I would fall asleep, and often I would be awake again for short snatches only, just long enough to hear the regular creaking of the wainscot, or to open my eyes to settle the shifting kaleidoscope of the darkness, to savour, in an instantaneous flash of perception, the sleep which lay heavy upon the furniture, the room, the whole surroundings of which I formed but an insignificant part and whose unconsciousness I should very soon return to share. Or, perhaps, while I was asleep I had returned without the least effort to an earlier stage in my life, now for ever outgrown; and had come under the thrall of one of my childish terrors, such as that old terror of my great-uncle's pulling my

1. Their rivalry dominated the history of Europe in the first half of the sixteenth century.

curls, which was effectually dispelled on the day — the dawn of a new era to me — on which they were finally cropped from my head. I had forgotten that event during my sleep; I remembered it again immediately I had succeeded in making myself wake up to escape my great-uncle's fingers; still, as a measure of precaution, I would bury the whole of my head in the pillow before returning to the world of dreams.

Sometimes, too, just as Eve was created from a rib of Adam, so a woman would come into existence while I was sleeping, conceived from some strain in the position of my limbs. Formed by the appetite that I was on the point of gratifying, she it was, I imagined, who offered me that gratification. My body, conscious that its own warmth was permeating hers, would strive to become one with her, and I would awake. The rest of humanity seemed very remote in comparison with this woman whose company I had left but a moment ago: my cheek was still warm with her kiss, my body bent beneath the weight of hers. If, as would sometimes happen, she had the appearance of some woman whom I had known in waking hours, I would abandon myself altogether to the sole quest of her, like people who set out on a journey to see with their own eyes some city that they have always longed to visit, and imagine that they can taste in reality what has charmed their fancy. And then, gradually, the memory of her would dissolve and vanish, until I had forgotten the maiden of my dream.

When a man is asleep, he has in a circle round him the chain of the hours, the sequence of the years, the order of the heavenly host. Instinctively, when he awakes, he looks to these, and in an instant reads off his own position on the earth's surface and the amount of time that has elapsed during his slumbers; but this ordered procession is apt to grow confused, and to break its ranks. Suppose that, towards morning, after a night of insomnia, sleep descends upon him while he is reading, in quite a different position from that in which he normally goes to sleep, he has only to lift his arm to arrest the sun and turn it back in its course, and, at the moment of waking, he will have no idea of the time, but will conclude that he has just gone to bed. Or suppose that he gets drowsy in some even more abnormal position; sitting in an armchair, say, after dinner: then the world will fall topsy-turvy from its orbit, the magic chair will carry him at full speed through time and space, and when he opens his eyes again he will imagine that he went to sleep months earlier and in some far distant country. But for me it was enough if, in my own bed, my sleep was so heavy as completely to relax my consciousness; for then I lost all sense of the place in which I had gone to sleep, and when I awoke at midnight, not knowing where I was, I could not be sure at first who I was; I had only the most rudimentary sense of existence, such as may lurk and flicker in the depths of an animal's consciousness; I was more destitute of human qualities than the cave-dweller; but then the memory, not yet of the place in which I was, but of various other places where I had lived, and might now very possibly be, would come like a rope let down from heaven to draw me up out of the abyss of not-being, from which I could never have escaped by myself: in a flash I would traverse and surmount centuries of civilisation, and out of a half-visualised succession of oil-lamps, followed by shirts with turned-down collars, would put together by degrees the component parts of my ego.

Perhaps the immobility of the things that surround us is forced upon them by our conviction that they are themselves, and not anything else, and by the immobility of our conceptions of them. For it always happened that when I awoke like this, and my mind struggled in an unsuccessful attempt to discover where I was, everything would be moving round me through the darkness: things, places, years. My body, still too heavy with sleep to move, would make an effort to construe the form which its tiredness took as an orientation of its various members, so as to induce from that where the wall lay and the furniture stood, to piece together and to give a name to the house in which it must be living. Its memory, the composite memory of its ribs, knees, and shoulder-blades, offered it a whole series of rooms in which it had at one time or another slept; while the unseen walls kept changing, adapting themselves to the shape of each successive room that it remembered, whirling madly through the darkness. And even before my brain, lingering in consideration of when things had happened and of what they had looked like, had collected sufficient impressions to enable it to identify the room, it, my body would recall from each room in succession what the bed was like, where the doors were, how daylight came in at the windows, whether there was a passage outside, what I had had in my mind when I went to sleep, and had found there when I awoke. The stiffened side underneath my body would, for instance, in trying to fix its position, imagine itself to be lying, face to the wall, in a big bed with a canopy; and at once I would say to myself, "Why, I must have gone to sleep after all, and Mamma never came to say good night!" for I was in the country with my grandfather, who died years ago; and my body, the side upon which I was lying, loyally preserving from the past an impression which my mind should never have forgotten, brought back before my eyes the glimmering flame of the night-light in its bowl of Bohemian glass, shaped like an urn and hung by chains from the ceiling, and the chimney-piece of Sienna marble in my bedroom at Combray, in my great-aunt's house, in those far distant days which, at the moment of waking, seemed present without being clearly defined, but would become plainer in a little while when I was properly awake.

Then would come up the memory of a fresh position; the wall slid away in another direction; I was in my room in Mme. de Saint-Loup's house in the country; good heavens, it must be ten o'clock, they will have finished dinner! I must have overslept myself, in the little nap which I always take when I come in from my walk with Mme. de Saint-Loup, before dressing for the evening. For many years have now elapsed since the Combray days, when, coming in from the longest and latest walks, I would still be in time to see the reflection of the sunset glowing in the panes of my bedroom window. It is a very different kind of existence at Tansonville now with Mme. de Saint-Loup, and a different kind of pleasure that I now derive from taking walks only in the evenings, from visiting by moonlight the roads on which I used to play, as a child, in the sunshine; while the bedroom, in which I shall presently fall asleep instead of dressing for dinner, from afar off I can see it, as we return from our walk, with its lamp shining through the window, a solitary beacon in the night.

These shifting and confused gusts of memory never lasted for more than a few seconds; it often happened that, in my spell of uncertainty as to where I was, I did not distinguish the successive theories of which that uncertainty was composed any more than, when we watch a horse running, we isolate the successive positions of its body as they appear upon a bioscope. But I had seen first one and then another of the rooms in which I had slept during my life, and in the end I would revisit them all in the long course of my waking dream: rooms in winter, where on going to bed I would at once bury my head in a nest, built up out of the most diverse materials, the corner of my pillow, the top of my blankets, a piece of a shawl, the edge of my bed, and a copy of an evening paper, all of which things I would contrive, with the infinite patience of birds building their nests, to cement into one whole; rooms where, in a keen frost, I would feel the satisfaction of being shut in from the outer world (like the sea-swallow which builds at the end of a dark tunnel and is kept warm by the surrounding earth), and where, the fire keeping in all night, I would sleep wrapped up, as it were, in a great cloak of snug and savoury air, shot with the glow of the logs which would break out again in flame: in a sort of alcove without walls, a cave of warmth dug out of the heart of the room itself, a zone of heat whose boundaries were constantly shifting and altering in temperature as gusts of air ran across them to strike freshly upon my face, from the corners of the room, or from parts near the window or far from the fireplace which had therefore remained cold — or rooms in summer, where I would delight to feel myself a part of the warm evening, where the moonlight striking upon the half-opened shutters would throw down to the foot of my bed its enchanted ladder; where I would fall asleep, as it might be in the open air, like a titmouse which the breeze keeps poised in the focus of a sunbeam — or sometimes the Louis XVI room, so cheerful that I could never feel really unhappy, even on my first night in it: that room where the slender columns which lightly supported its ceiling would part, ever so gracefully, to indicate where the bed was and to keep it separate; sometimes again that little room with the high ceiling, hollowed in the form of a pyramid out of two separate storeys, and partly walled with mahogany, in which from the first moment my mind was drugged by the unfamiliar scent of flowering grasses, convinced of the hostility of the violet curtains and of the insolent indifference of a clock that chattered on at the top of its voice as though I were not there; while a strange and pitiless mirror with square feet, which stood across one corner of the room, cleared for itself a site I had not looked to find tenanted in the quiet surroundings of my normal field of vision: that room in which my mind, forcing itself for hours on end to leave its moorings, to elongate itself upwards so as to take on the exact shape of the room, and to reach to the summit of that monstrous funnel, had passed so many anxious nights while my body lay stretched out in bed, my eyes staring upwards, my ears straining, my nostrils sniffing uneasily, and my heart beating; until custom had changed the colour of the curtains, made the clock keep quiet, brought an expression of pity to the cruel, slanting face of the glass, disguised or even completely dispelled the scent of flowering grasses, and distinctly reduced the apparent loftiness of the ceiling. Custom! that skilful but unhurrying manager who begins by torturing the mind for weeks on end with her provisional arrangements; whom the mind, for all that, is fortunate in discovering, for without the help of custom it would never contrive, by its own efforts, to make any room seem habitable.

Certainly I was now well awake; my body had turned about for the last time and the good angel of certainty had made all the surrounding objects stand still, had set me down under my bedclothes, in my bed-room, and had fixed, approximately in their right places in the uncertain light, my chest of drawers, my writing-table, my fireplace, the window overlooking the street, and both the doors. But it was no good my knowing that I was not in any of those houses of which, in the stupid moment of waking, if I had not caught sight exactly, I could still believe in their possible presence; for memory was now set in motion; as a rule I did not attempt to go to sleep again at once, but used to spend the greater part of the night recalling our life in the old days at Combray with my great-aunt, at Balbec, Paris, Doncières, Venice, and the rest; remembering again all the places and people that I had known, what I had actually seen of them, and what others had told me.

At Combray, as every afternoon ended, long before the time when I should have to go up to bed, and to lie there, unsleeping, far from my mother and grandmother, my bedroom became the fixed point on which my melancholy and anxious thoughts were centred. Some one had had the happy idea of giving me, to distract me on evenings when I seemed abnormally wretched, a magic lantern, which used to be set on top of my lamp while we waited for dinner-time to come: in the manner of the master-builders and glass-painters of gothic days it substituted for the opaqueness of my walls an impalpable iridescence, supernatural phenomena of many colours, in which legends were depicted, as on a shifting and transitory window. But my sorrows were only increased, because this change of lighting destroyed, as nothing else could have done, the customary impression I had formed of my room, thanks to which the room itself, but for the torture of having to go to bed in it, had become quite endurable. For now I no longer recognised it, and I became uneasy, as though I were in a room in some hotel or furnished lodging, in a place where I had just arrived, by train, for the first time.

Riding at a jerky trot, Golo, his mind filled with an infamous design, issued from the little three-cornered forest which dyed dark-green the slope of a convenient hill, and advanced by leaps and bounds towards the castle of poor Geneviève de Brabant. This castle was cut off short by a curved line which was in fact the circumference of one of the transparent ovals in the slides which were pushed into position through a slot in the lantern. It was only the wing of a castle, and in front of it stretched a moor on which Geneviève stood, lost in contemplation, wearing a blue girdle. The castle and the moor were yellow, but I could tell their colour without waiting to see them, for before the slides made their appearance the old-gold sonorous name of Brabant had given me an unmistakable clue. Golo stopped for a moment and listened sadly to the little speech read aloud by my great-aunt, which he seemed perfectly to understand, for he modified his attitude with a docility not devoid of a degree of majesty, so as to conform to the indications given in the text; then he rode away at the same jerky trot. And nothing could arrest his slow progress. If the lantern were moved I could still distinguish Golo's horse advancing across the window-curtains, swelling out with their curves and diving into their folds. The body of Golo himself, being of the same supernatural substance as his steed's, overcame all material obstacles — everything that seemed to bar his way — by taking each as it might be a skeleton and embodying it in himself: the door-handle, for instance, over which, adapting itself at once, would float invincibly his red cloak or his pale face, never losing its nobility or its melancholy, never shewing any sign of trouble at such a transubstantiation.

And, indeed, I found plenty of charm in these bright projections, which seemed to have come straight out of a Merovingian past, and to shed around me the reflections of such ancient history. But I cannot express the discomfort I felt at such an intrusion of mystery and beauty into a room which I had succeeded in filling with my own personality until I thought no more of the room than of myself. The anaesthetic effect of custom being destroyed, I would begin to think and to feel very melancholy things. The door-handle of my room, which was different to me from all the other door-handles in the world, inasmuch as it seemed to open of its own accord and without my having to turn it, so unconscious had its manipulation become; lo and behold, it was now an astral body for Golo. And as soon as the dinner-bell rang I would run down to the dining-room, where the big hanging lamp, ignorant of Golo and Bluebeard but well acquainted with my family and the dish of stewed beef, shed the same light as on every other evening; and I would fall into the arms of my mother, whom the misfortunes of Geneviève de Brabant had made all the dearer to me, just as the crimes of Golo had driven me to a more than ordinarily scrupulous examination of my own conscience.

But after dinner, alas, I was soon obliged to leave Mamma, who stayed talking with the others, in the garden if it was fine, or in the little parlour where everyone took shelter when it was wet. Everyone except my grandmother, who held that "It is a pity to shut oneself indoors in the country," and used to carry on endless discussions with my father on the very wettest days, because he would send me up to my room with a book instead of letting me stay out of doors. "That is not the way to make him strong and active," she would say sadly, "especially this little man, who needs all the strength and character that he can get." My father would shrug his shoulders and study the barometer, for he took an interest in meteorology, while my mother, keeping very quiet so as not to disturb him, looked at him with tender respect, but not too hard, not wishing to penetrate the mysteries of his superior mind. But my grandmother, in all weathers, even when the rain was coming down in torrents and Françoise had rushed indoors with the precious wicker armchairs, so that they should not get soaked, you would see my grandmother pacing the deserted garden, lashed by the storm, pushing back her grey hair in disorder so that her brows might be more free to imbibe the life-giving draughts of wind and rain. She would say, "At last one can breathe!" and would run up and down the soaking paths — too straight and symmetrical for her liking, owing to the want of any feeling for nature in the new gardener, whom my father had been asking all morning if the weather were going to improve — with her keen, jerky little step regulated by the various effects wrought upon her soul by the intoxication of the storm, the force of hygiene, the stupidity of my education and of symmetry in gardens, rather than by any anxiety (for that was quite unknown to her) to save her plum-coloured skirt from the spots of mud under which it would gradually disappear to a depth which always provided her maid with a fresh problem and filled her with fresh despair.

When these walks of my grandmother's took place after dinner there was one thing which never failed to bring her back to the house: that was if (at one of those points when the revolutions of her course brought her, moth-like, in sight of the lamp in the little parlour where the liqueurs were set out on the card-table) my great-aunt called out to her: "Bathilde! Come in and stop your husband from drinking brandy!" For, simply to tease her (she had brought so foreign a type of mind into my father's family that everyone made a joke of it), my great-aunt used to make my grandfather, who was forbidden liqueurs, take just a few drops. My poor grandmother would come in and beg and implore her husband not to taste the brandy; and he would become annoyed and swallow his few drops all the same, and she would go out again sad and discouraged, but still smiling, for she was so humble and so sweet that her gentleness towards others, and her continual subordination of herself and of her own troubles, appeared on her face blended in a smile which, unlike those seen on the majority of human faces, had no trace in it of irony, save for herself, while for all of us kisses seemed to spring from her eyes, which could not look upon those she loved without yearning to bestow upon them passionate caresses. The torments inflicted on her by my great-aunt, the sight of my grandmother's vain entreaties, of her in her weakness conquered before she began, but still making the futile endeavour to wean my grandfather from his liqueur-glass — all these were things of the sort to which, in later years, one can grow so well accustomed as to smile at them, to take the tormentor's side with a happy determination which deludes one into the belief that it is not, really, tormenting; but in those days they filled me with such horror that I longed to strike my great-aunt. And yet, as soon as I heard her "Bathilde! Come in and stop your husband from drinking brandy!" in my cowardice I became at once a man, and did what all we grown men do when face to face with suffering and injustice; I preferred not to see them; I ran up to the top of the house to cry by myself in a little room beside the schoolroom and beneath the roof, which smelt of orrisroot, and was scented also by a wild currant-bush which had climbed up between the stones of the outer wall and thrust a flowering branch in through the half-opened window. Intended for a more special and a baser use, this room, from which, in the day-time, I could see as far as the keep of Roussainville-le-Pin, was for a long time my place of refuge, doubtless because it was the only room whose door I was allowed to lock, whenever my occupation was such as required an inviolable solitude; reading or dreaming, secret tears or paroxysms of desire. Alas! I little knew that my own lack of will-power, my delicate health, and the consequent uncertainty as to my future weighed far more heavily on my grandmother's mind than any little breach of the rules by her husband, during those endless perambulations, afternoon and evening, in which we used to see passing up and down, obliquely raised towards the heavens, her handsome face with its brown and wrinkled cheeks, which with age had acquired almost the purple hue of tilled fields in autumn, covered, if she were walking abroad, by a half-lifted veil, while upon them either the cold or some sad reflection invariably left the drying traces of an involuntary tear.

My sole consolation when I went upstairs for the night was that Mamma would come in and kiss me after I was in bed. But this good night lasted for so short a time: she went down again so soon that the moment in which I heard her climb the stairs, and then caught the sound of her garden dress of blue muslin, from which hung little tassels of plaited straw, rustling along the double-doored corridor, was for me a moment of the keenest sorrow. So much did I love that good night that I reached the stage of hoping that it would come as late as possible, so as to prolong the time of respite during which Mamma would not yet have appeared. Sometimes when, after kissing me, she opened the door to go, I longed to call her back, to say to her "Kiss me just once again," but I knew that then she would at once look displeased, for the concession which she made to my wretchedness and agitation in coming up to me with this kiss of peace always annoyed my father, who thought such ceremonies absurd, and she would have liked to try to induce me to outgrow the need, the custom of having her there at all, which was a very different thing from letting the custom grow up of my asking her for an additional kiss when she was already crossing the threshold. And to see her look displeased destroyed all the sense of tranquillity she had brought me a moment before, when she bent her loving face down over my bed, and held it out to me like a Host, for an act of Communion in which my lips might drink deeply the sense of her real presence, and with it the power to sleep. But those evenings on which Mamma stayed so short a time in my room were sweet indeed compared to those on which we had guests to dinner, and therefore she did not come at all. Our 'guests' were practically limited to M. Swann, who, apart from a few passing strangers, was almost the only person who ever came to the house at Combray, sometimes to a neighbourly dinner (but less frequently since his unfortunate marriage, as my family did not care to receive his wife) and sometimes after dinner, uninvited. On those evenings when, as we sat in front of the house beneath the big chestnut-tree and round the iron table, we heard, from the far end of the garden, not the large and noisy rattle which heralded and deafened as he approached with its ferruginous, interminable, frozen sound any member of the household who had put it out of action by coming in 'without ringing,' but the double peal — timid, oval, gilded — of the visitors' bell, everyone would at once exclaim "A visitor! Who in the world can it be?" but they knew quite well that it could only be M. Swann. My great-aunt, speaking in a loud voice, to set an example, in a tone which she endeavoured to make sound natural, would tell the others not to whisper so; that nothing could be more unpleasant for a stranger coming in, who would be led to think that people were saying things about him which he was not meant to hear; and then my grandmother would be sent out as a scout, always happy to find an excuse for an additional turn in the garden, which she would utilise to remove surreptitiously, as she passed, the stakes of a rosetree or two, so as to make the roses look a little more natural, as a mother might run her hand through her boy's hair, after the barber had smoothed it down, to make it stick out properly round his head.

And there we would all stay, hanging on the words which would fall from my grandmother's lips when she brought us back her report of the enemy, as though there had been some uncertainty among a vast number of possible invaders, and then, soon after, my grandfather would say: "I can hear Swann's voice." And, indeed, one could tell him only by his voice, for it was difficult to make out his face with its arched nose and green eyes, under a high forehead fringed with hair, almost red hair, dressed in the Bressant style, because in the garden we used as little light as possible, so as not to attract mosquitoes: and I would slip away as though not going for anything in particular, to tell them to bring out the syrups; for my grandmother made a great point, thinking it 'nicer,' of their not being allowed to seem anything out of the ordinary, which we kept for visitors only. Although a far younger man, M. Swann was very much attached to my grandfather, who had been an intimate friend, in his time, of Swann's father, an excellent but an eccentric man in whom the least little thing would, it seemed, often check the flow of his spirits and divert the current of his thoughts. Several times in the course of a year I would hear my grandfather tell at table the story, which never varied, of the behaviour of M. Swann the elder upon the death of his wife, by whose bedside he had watched day and night. My grandfather, who had not seen him for a long time, hastened to join him at the Swanns' family property on the outskirts of Combray, and managed to entice him for a moment, weeping profusely, out of the death-chamber, so that he should not be present when the body was laid in its coffin. They took a turn or two in the park, where there was a little sunshine. Suddenly M. Swann seized my grandfather by the arm and cried, "Oh, my dear old friend, how fortunate we are to be walking here together on such a charming day! Don't you see how pretty they are, all these trees — my hawthorns, and my new pond, on which you have never congratulated me? You look as glum as a night-cap. Don't you feel this little breeze? Ah! whatever you may say, it's good to be alive all the same, my dear Amédée!" And then, abruptly, the memory of his dead wife returned to him, and probably thinking it too complicated to inquire into how, at such a time, he could have allowed himself to be carried away by an impulse of happiness, he confined himself to a gesture which he habituálly employed whenever any perplexing question came into his mind: that is, he passed his hand across his forehead, dried his eyes, and wiped his glasses. And he could never be consoled for the loss of his wife, but used to say to my grandfather, during the two years for which he survived her, "It's a funny thing, now; I very often think of my poor wife, but I cannot think of her very much at any one time." "Often, but a little at a time, like poor old Swann," became one of my grandfather's favourite phrases, which he would apply to all kinds of things. And I should have assumed that this father of Swann's had been a monster if my grandfather, whom I regarded as a better judge than myself, and whose word was my law and often led me in the long run to pardon offences which I should have been inclined to condemn, had not gone on to exclaim, "But, after all, he had a heart of gold."

For many years, albeit — and especially before his marriage — M. Swann the younger came often to see them at Combray, my great-aunt and grandparents never suspected that he had entirely ceased to live in the kind of society which his family had frequented, or that, under the sort of incognito which the name of Swann gave him among us, they were harbouring — with the complete innocence of a family of honest innkeepers who have in their midst some distinguished high-wayman and never know it — one of the smartest members of the Jockey Club, a particular friend of the Comte de Paris and of the Prince of Wales, and one of the men most sought after in the aristocratic world of the Faubourg Saint-Germain.

Our utter ignorance of the brilliant part which Swann was playing in the world of fashion was, of course, due in part to his own reserve and discretion, but also to the fact that middle-class people in those days took what was almost a Hindu view of society, which they held to consist of sharply defined castes, so that everyone at his birth found himself called to that station in life which his parents already occupied, and nothing, except the chance of a brilliant career or of a 'good' marriage, could extract you from that station or admit you to a superior caste. M. Swann, the father, had been a stockbroker; and so 'young Swann' found himself immured for life in a caste where one's fortune, as in a list of taxpayers, varied between such and such limits of income. We knew the people with whom his father had associated, and so we knew his own associates, the people with whom he was 'in a position to mix.' If he knew other people besides, those were youthful acquaintances on whom the old friends of the family, like my relatives, shut their eyes all the more good-naturedly that Swann himself, after he was left an orphan, still came most faithfully to see us; but we would have been ready to wager that the people outside our acquaintance whom Swann knew were of the sort to whom he would not have dared to raise his hat, had he met them while he was walking with ourselves. Had there been such a thing as a determination to apply to Swann a social coefficient peculiar to himself, as distinct from all the other sons of other stockbrokers in his father's position, his coefficient would have been rather lower than theirs, because, leading a very simple life, and having always had a craze for 'antiques' and pictures, he now lived and piled up his collections in an old house which my grandmother longed to visit, but which stood on the Quai d'Orléans, a neighbourhood in which my great-aunt thought it most degrading to be quartered. "Are you really a connoisseur, now?" she would say to him; "I ask for your own sake, as you are likely to have 'fakes' palmed off on you by the dealers," for she did not, in fact, endow him with any critical faculty, and had no great opinion of the intelligence of a man who, in conversation, would avoid serious topics and shewed a very dull preciseness, not only when he gave us kitchen recipes, going into the most minute details, but even when my grandmother's sisters were talking to him about art. When challenged by them to give an opinion, or to express his admiration for some picture, he would remain almost impolitely silent, and would then make amends by furnishing (if he could) some fact or other about the gallery in which the picture was hung, or the date at which it had been painted. But as a rule he would content himself with trying to amuse us by telling us the story of his latest adventure — and he would have a fresh story for us on every occasion — with some one whom we ourselves knew, such as the Combray chemist, or our cook, or our coachman. These stories certainly used to make my great-aunt laugh, but she could never tell whether that was on account of the absurd parts which Swann invariably made himself play in the adventures, or of the wit that he shewed in telling us of them. "It is easy to see that you are a regular 'character,' M. Swann!"

As she was the only member of our family who could be described as a trifle 'common,' she would always take care to remark to strangers, when Swann was mentioned, that he could easily, if he had wished to, have lived in the Boulevard Haussmann or the Avenue de l'Opéra, and that he was the son of old M. Swann who must have left four or five million francs, but that it was a fad of his. A fad which, moreover, she thought was bound to amuse other people so much that in Paris, when M. Swann called on New Year's Day bringing her a little packet of *marrons glacés,* she never failed, if there were strangers in the room, to say to him: "Well, M. Swann, and do you still live next door to the Bonded Vaults, so as to be sure of not missing your train when you go to Lyons?" and she would peep out of the corner of her eye, over her glasses, at the other visitors.

But if anyone had suggested to my aunt that this Swann, who, in his capacity as the son of old M. Swann, was 'fully qualified' to be received by any of the 'upper middle class,' the most respected barristers and solicitors of Paris (though he was perhaps a trifle inclined to let this hereditary privilege go into abeyance), had another almost secret existence of a wholly different kind: that when he left our house in Paris, saying that he must go home to bed, he would no sooner have turned the corner than he would stop, retrace his steps, and be off to some drawing-room on whose like no stockbroker or associate of stockbrokers had ever set eyes — that would have seemed to my aunt as extraordinary as, to a woman of wider reading, the thought of being herself on terms of intimacy with Aristaeus,[2] of knowing that he would, when he had finished his conversation with her, plunge deep into the realms of Thetis, into an empire veiled from mortal eyes, in which Virgil depicts him as being received with open arms; or — to be content with an image more likely to have occurred to her, for she had seen it painted on the plates we used for biscuits at Combray — as the thought of having had to dinner Ali Baba, who, as soon as he found himself alone and unobserved, would make his way into the cave, resplendent with its unsuspected treasures.

One day when he had come to see us after dinner in Paris, and had begged pardon for being in evening clothes, Françoise, when he had gone, told us that she had got it from his coachman that he had been dining "with a princess." "A pretty sort of princess," drawled my aunt, "I know them," and she shrugged her shoulders without raising her eyes from her knitting, serenely ironical.

Altogether, my aunt used to treat him with scant ceremony. Since she was of the opinion that he ought to feel flattered by our invitations, she thought it only right and proper that he should never come to see us in summer without a basket of peaches or raspberries from his

2. The story of his descent into the "realms of Thetis" is told in Virgil's *Georgics.*

garden, and that from each of his visits to Italy he should bring back some photographs of old masters for me.

It seemed quite natural, therefore, to send to him whenever we wanted a recipe for some special sauce or for a pineapple salad for one of our big dinner-parties, to which he himself would not be invited, not seeming of sufficient importance to be served up to new friends who might be in our house for the first time. If the conversation turned upon the Princess of the House of France, "Gentlemen you and I will never know, will we, and don't want to, do we?" my great-aunt would say tartly to Swann, who had, perhaps, a letter from Twickenham in his pocket; she would make him play accompaniments and turn over music on evenings when my grandmother's sister sang; manipulating this creature, so rare and refined at other times and in other places, with the rough simplicity of a child who will play with some curio from the cabinet no more carefully than if it were a penny toy. Certainly the Swann who was a familiar figure in all the clubs of those days differed hugely from the Swann created in my great-aunt's mind when, of an evening, in our little garden at Combray, after the two shy peals had sounded from the gate, she would vitalise, by injecting into it everything she had ever heard about the Swann family, the vague and unrecognisable shape which began to appear, with my grandmother in its wake, against a background of shadows, and could at last be identified by the sound of its voice. But then, even in the most insignificant details of our daily life, none of us can be said to constitute a material whole, which is identical for everyone, and need only be turned up like a page in an account-book or the record of a will; our social personality is created by the thoughts of other people. Even the simple act which we describe as "seeing some one we know" is, to some extent, an intellectual process. We pack the physical outline of the creature we see with all the ideas we have already formed about him, and in the complete picture of him which we compose in our minds those ideas have certainly the principal place. In the end they come to fill out so completely the curve of his cheeks, to follow so exactly the line of his nose, they blend so harmoniously in the sound of his voice that these seem to be no more than a transparent envelope, so that each time we see the face or hear the voice it is our own ideas of him which we recognise and to which we listen. And so, no doubt, from the Swann they had built up for their own purposes my family had left out, in their ignorance, a whole crowd of the details of his daily life in the world of fashion, details by means of which other people, when they met him, saw all the Graces enthroned in his face and stopping at the line of his arched nose as at a natural frontier; but they contrived also to put into a face from which its distinction had been evicted, a face vacant and roomy as an untenanted house, to plant in the depths of its unvalued eyes a lingering sense, uncertain but not unpleasing, half-memory and half-oblivion, of idle hours spent together after our weekly dinners, round the card-table or in the garden, during our companionable country life. Our friend's bodily frame had been so well lined with this sense, and with various earlier memories of his family, that their own special Swann had become to my people a complete and living creature; so that even now I have the feeling of leaving some one I know for another quite different person when, going back in memory, I pass from the Swann whom I knew later and more intimately to this early Swann — this early Swann in whom I can distinguish the charming mistakes of my childhood, and who, incidentally, is less like his successor than he is like the other people I knew at that time, as though one's life were a series of galleries in which all the portraits of any one period had a marked family likeness, the same (so to speak) tonality — this early Swann abounding in leisure, fragrant with the scent of the great chestnut-tree, of baskets of raspberries and of a sprig of tarragon. . . .

But the only one of us in whom the prospect of Swann's arrival gave rise to an unhappy foreboding was myself. And that was because on the evenings when there were visitors, or just M. Swann in the house, Mamma did not come up to my room. I did not, at that time, have dinner with the family: I came out to the garden after dinner, and at nine I said good night and went to bed. But on these evenings I used to dine earlier than the others, and to come in afterwards and sit at table until eight o'clock, when it was understood that I must go upstairs; that frail and precious kiss which Mamma used always to leave upon my lips when I was in bed and just going to sleep I had to take with me from the dining-room to my own, and to keep inviolate all the time that it took me to undress, without letting its sweet charm be broken, without letting its volatile essence diffuse itself and evaporate; and just on those very evenings when I must needs take most pains to receive it with due formality, I had to snatch it, to seize it instantly and in public, without even having the time or being properly free to apply to what I was doing the punctiliousness which madmen use who compel themselves to exclude all other thoughts from their minds while they are shutting a door, so that when the sickness of uncertainty sweeps over them again they can triumphantly face and overcome it with the recollection of the precise moment in which the door was shut. . . .

I never took my eyes off my mother. I knew that when they were at table I should not be permitted to stay there for the whole of dinnertime, and that Mamma, for fear of annoying my father, would not allow me to give her in public the series of kisses that she would have had in my room. And so I promised myself that in the dining-room as they began to eat and drink and as I felt the hour approach, I would put beforehand into this kiss, which was bound to be so brief and stealthy in execution, everything that my own efforts could put into it: would look out very carefully first the exact spot on her cheek where I would imprint it, and would so prepare my thoughts that I might be able, thanks to these mental preliminaries, to consecrate the whole of the minute Mamma would allow me to the sensation of her cheek against my lips, as a painter who can have his subject for short sittings only prepares his palette, and from what he remembers and from rough notes does in advance everything which he possibly can do in the sitter's absence. But tonight, before the dinner-bell had sounded, my grandfather said with unconscious cruelty: "The little man looks tired; he'ld better go up to bed. Besides, we are dining late tonight."

And my father, who was less scrupulous than my grandmother or mother in observing the letter of a treaty, went on: "Yes; run along; to bed with you."

I would have kissed Mamma then and there, but at that moment the dinner-bell rang.

"No, no, leave your mother alone. You've said good night quite enough. These exhibitions are absurd. Go on upstairs."

And so I must set forth without viaticum; must climb each step of the staircase 'against my heart,' as the saying is, climbing in opposition to my heart's desire, which was to return to my mother, since she had not, by her kiss, given my heart leave to accompany me forth. That hateful staircase, up which I always passed with such dismay, gave out a smell of varnish which had to some extent absorbed, made definite and fixed the special quality of sorrow that I felt each evening, and made it perhaps even more cruel to my sensibility because, when it assumed this olfactory guise, my intellect was powerless to resist it. When we have gone to sleep with a maddening toothache and are conscious of it only as a little girl whom we attempt, time after time, to pull out of the water, or as a line of Molière which we repeat incessantly to ourselves, it is a great relief to wake up, so that our intelligence can disentangle the idea of toothache from any artificial semblance of heroism or rhythmic cadence. It was the precise converse of this relief which I felt when my anguish at having to go up to my room invaded my consciousness in a manner infinitely more rapid, instantaneous almost, a manner at once insidious and brutal as I breathed in — a far more poisonous thing than any moral penetration — the peculiar smell of the varnish upon that staircase.

Once in my room I had to stop every loophole, to close the shutters, to dig my own grave as I turned down the bedclothes, to wrap myself in the shroud of my nightshirt. But before burying myself in the iron bed which had been placed there because, on summer nights, I was too hot among the rep curtains of the four-poster, I was stirred to revolt, and attempted the desperate stratagem of a condemned prisoner. I wrote to my mother begging her to come upstairs for an important reason which I could not put in writing. My fear was that Françoise, my aunt's cook who used to be put in charge of me when I was at Combray, might refuse to take my note. I had a suspicion that, in her eyes, to carry a message to my mother when there was a stranger in the room would appear flatly inconceivable, just as it would be for the door-keeper of a theatre to hand a letter to an actor upon the stage.

For things which might or might not be done she possessed a code at once imperious, abundant, subtle, and uncompromising on points themselves imperceptible or irrelevant, which gave it a resemblance to those ancient laws which combine such cruel ordinances as the massacre of infants at the breast with prohibitions, of exaggerated refinement, against "seething the kid in his mother's milk," or "eating of the sinew which is upon the hollow of the thigh." This code, if one could judge it by the sudden obstinacy which she would put into her refusal to carry out certain of our instructions, seemed to have foreseen such social complications and refinements of fashion as nothing in Françoise's surroundings or in her career as a servant in a village household could have put into her head; and we were obliged to assume that there was latent in her some past existence in the ancient history of France, noble and little understood, just as there is in those manufacturing towns where old mansions still testify to their former courtly days. . . .

In this particular instance, the article of her code which made it highly improbable that — barring an outbreak of fire — Françoise would go down and disturb Mamma when M. Swann was there for so unimportant a person as myself was one embodying the respect she shewed not only for the family (as for the dead, for the clergy, or for royalty), but also for the stranger within our gates; a respect which I should perhaps have found touching in a book, but which never failed to irritate me on her lips, because of the solemn and gentle tones in which she would utter it, and which irritated me more than usual this evening when the sacred character in which she invested the dinner-party might have the effect of making her decline to disturb its ceremonial. But to give myself one chance of success I lied without hesitation, telling her that it was not in the least myself who had wanted to write to Mamma, but Mamma who, on saying good night to me, had begged me not to forget to send her an answer about something she had asked me to find, and that she would certainly be very angry if this note were not taken to her. I think that Françoise disbelieved me, for, like those primitive men whose senses were so much keener than our own, she could immediately detect, by signs imperceptible by the rest of us, the truth or falsehood of anything that we might wish to conceal from her. She studied the envelope for five minutes as though an examination of the paper itself and the look of my handwriting could enlighten her as to the nature of the contents, or tell her to which article of her code she ought to refer the matter. Then she went out with an air of resignation which seemed to imply: "What a dreadful thing for parents to have a child like this!"

A moment later she returned to say that they were still at the ice stage and that it was impossible for the butler to deliver the note at once, in front of everybody; but that when the finger-bowls were put round he would find a way of slipping it into Mamma's hand. At once my anxiety subsided; it was now no longer (as it had been a moment ago) until tomorrow that I had lost my mother, for my little line was going — to annoy her, no doubt, and doubly so because this contrivance would make me ridiculous in Swann's eyes — but was going all the same to admit me, invisibly and by stealth, into the same room as herself, was going to whisper from me into her ear; for that forbidden and unfriendly dining-room, where but a moment ago the ice itself — with burned nuts in it — and the finger-bowls seemed to me to be concealing pleasures that were mischievous and of a mortal sadness because Mamma was tasting of them and I was far away, had opened its doors to me and, like a ripe fruit which bursts through its skin, was going to pour out into my intoxicated heart the gushing sweetness of Mamma's attention while she was reading what I had written. Now I was no longer separated from her; the barriers were down; an exquisite thread was binding us. Besides, that was not all, for surely Mamma would come.

As for the agony through which I had just passed, I imagined that Swann would have laughed heartily at it if he had read my letter and had guessed its purpose; whereas, on the contrary, as I was to learn in due course, a similar anguish had been the bane of his life for many years, and no one perhaps could have understood my feelings at that moment so well as himself; to him, that anguish which lies in knowing that the creature one adores is in some place of enjoyment where one-self is not and cannot follow — to him that anguish came through Love, to which it is in a sense predestined, by which it must be equipped and adapted; but when, as had befallen me, such an anguish possesses one's soul before Love has yet entered into one's life, then it must drift, awaiting Love's coming, vague and free, without precise attachment, at the disposal of one sentiment today, of another tomorrow, of filial piety or affection for a comrade. And the joy with which I first bound myself apprentice, when Françoise returned to tell me that my letter would be delivered, Swann, too, had known well that false joy which a friend can give us, or some relative of the woman we love, when on his arrival at our house or theatre where she is to be found, for some ball or party or 'first-night' at which he is to meet her, he sees us wandering outside, desperately awaiting some opportunity of communi-cating with her. He recognises us, greets us familiarly, and asks what we are doing there. And when we invent a story of having some urgent message to give to his relative or friend, he assures us that nothing could be more simple, takes us in at the door, and promises to send her down to us in five minutes. How much we love him — as at that moment I loved Françoise — the good-natured intermediary who by a single word has made supportable, human, almost propitious the incon-ceivable, infernal scene of gaiety in the thick of which we had been imagining swarms of enemies, perverse and seductive, beguiling away from us, even making laugh at us, the woman whom we love. If we are to judge of them by him, this relative who has accosted us and who is himself an initiate in those cruel mysteries, then the other guests cannot be so very demoniacal. Those inaccessible and torturing hours into which she had gone to taste of unknown pleasures — behold, a breach in the wall, and we are through it. Behold, one of the moments whose series will go to make up their sum, a moment as genuine as the rest, if not actually more important to ourself because our mistress is more intensely a part of it; we picture it to ourselves, we possess it, we intervene upon it, almost we have created it: namely, the moment in which he goes to tell her that we are waiting there below. And very probably the other moments of the party will not be essentially different, will contain nothing else so exquisite or so well able to make us suffer, since this kind friend has assured us that "Of course, she will be delighted to come down! It will be far more amusing for her to talk to you than to be bored up there." Alas! Swann had learned by experience that the good intentions of a third party are powerless to control a woman who is annoyed to find herself pursued even into a ball-room by a man whom she does not love. Too often, the kind friend comes down again alone.

My mother did not appear, but with no attempt to safeguard my self-respect (which depended upon her keeping up the fiction that she had asked me to let her know the result of my search for something or other) made Françoise tell me, in so many words "There is no answer" — words I have so often, since then, heard the hall-porters in 'mansions' and the flunkeys in gambling-clubs and the like, repeat to some poor girl, who replies in bewilderment: "What! he's said nothing? It's not possible. You did give him my letter, didn't you? Very well, I shall wait a little longer." And just as she invariably protests that she does not need the extra gas which the porter offers to light for her, and sits on there, hearing nothing further, except an occasional remark on the weather which the porter exchanges with a messenger whom he will send off suddenly, when he notices the time, to put some customer's wine on the ice; so, having declined Françoise's offer to make me some tea or to stay beside me, I let her go off again to the servants' hall, and lay down and shut my eyes, and tried not to hear the voices of my family who were drinking their coffee in the garden.

But after a few seconds I realised that, by writing that line to Mamma, by approaching — at the risk of making her angry — so near to her that I felt I could reach out and grasp the moment in which I should see her again, I had cut myself off from the possibility of going to sleep until I actually had seen her, and my heart began to beat more and more painfully as I increased my agitation by ordering myself to keep calm and to acquiesce in my ill fortune. Then, suddenly, my anxiety subsided, a feeling of intense happiness coursed through me, as when a strong medicine begins to take effect and one's pain vanishes: I had found a resolution to abandon all attempts to go to sleep without seeing Mamma, and had decided to kiss her at all costs, even with the certainty of being in disgrace with her for long afterwards, when she herself came up to bed. The tranquillity which followed my anguish made me extremely alert, no less than my sense of expectation, my thirst for and my fear of danger.

Noiselessly I opened the window and sat down on the foot of my bed;

hardly daring to move in case they should hear me from below. Things outside seemed also fixed in mute expectation, so as not to disturb the moonlight which, duplicating each of them and throwing it back by the extension, forwards, of a shadow denser and more concrete than its substance, had made the whole landscape seem at once thinner and longer, like a map which, after being folded up, is spread out upon the ground. What had to move — a leaf of the chestnut-tree, for instance — moved. But its minute shuddering, complete, finished to the least detail and with utmost delicacy of gesture, made no discord with the rest of the scene, and yet was not merged in it, remaining clearly outlined. Exposed upon this surface of silence, which absorbed nothing from them, the most distant sounds, those which must have come from gardens at the far end of the town, could be distinguished with such exact 'finish' that the impression they gave of coming from a distance seemed due only to their 'pianissimo' execution, like those movements on muted strings so well performed by the orchestra of the Conservatoire that, although one does not lose a single note, one thinks all the same that they are being played somewhere outside, a long way from the concert hall, so that all the old subscribers, and my grandmother's sisters too, when Swann had given them his seats, used to strain their ears as if they had caught the distant approach of an army on the march, which had not yet rounded the corner of the Rue de Trévise.

I was well aware that I had placed myself in a position than which none could be counted upon to involve me in graver consequences at my parents' hands; consequences far graver, indeed, than a stranger would have imagined, and such as (he would have thought) could follow only some really shameful fault. But in the system of education which they had given me faults were not classified in the same order as in that of other children, and I had been taught to place at the head of the list (doubtless because there was no other class of faults from which I needed to be more carefully protected) those in which I can now distinguish the common feature that one succumbs to them by yielding to a nervous impulse. But such words as these last had never been uttered in my hearing; no one had yet accounted for my temptations in a way which might have led me to believe that there was some excuse for my giving in to them, or that I was actually incapable of holding out against them. Yet I could easily recognise this class of transgressions by the anguish of mind which preceded, as well as by the rigour of the punishment which followed them; and I knew that what I had just done was in the same category as certain other sins for which I had been severely chastised, though infinitely more serious than they. When I went out to meet my mother as she herself came up to bed, and when she saw that I had remained up so as to say good night to her again in the passage, I should not be allowed to stay in the house a day longer, I should be packed off to school next morning; so much was certain. Very good: had I been obliged, the next moment, to hurl myself out of the window, I should still have preferred such a fate. For what I wanted now was Mamma, and to say good night to her. I had gone too far along the road which led to the realisation of this desire to be able to retrace my steps.

I could hear my parents' footsteps as they went with Swann; and, when the rattle of the gate assured me that he had really gone, I crept to the window. Mamma was asking my father if he had thought the lobster good, and whether M. Swann had had some more of the coffee-and-pistachio ice. "I thought it rather so-so," she was saying; "next time we shall have to try another flavour."

"I can't tell you," said my great-aunt, "what a change I find in Swann. He is quite antiquated!" She had grown so accustomed to seeing Swann always in the same stage of adolescence that it was a shock to her to find him suddenly less young than the age she still attributed to him. And the others too were beginning to remark in Swann that abnormal, excessive, scandalous senescence, meet only in a celibate, in one of that class for whom it seems that the great day which knows no morrow must be longer than for other men, since for such a one it is void of promise, and from its dawn the moments steadily accumulate without any subsequent partition among his offspring.

"I fancy he has a lot of trouble with that wretched wife of his, who 'lives' with a certain Monsieur de Charlus, as all Combray knows. It's the talk of the town."

My mother observed that, in spite of this, he had looked much less unhappy of late. "And he doesn't nearly so often do that trick of his, so like his father, of wiping his eyes and passing his hand across his forehead. I think myself that in his heart of hearts he doesn't love his wife any more."

"Why, of course he doesn't," answered my grandfather. "He wrote me a letter about it, ages ago, to which I took care to pay no attention, but it left no doubt as to his feelings, let alone his love for his wife. Hullo! you two; you never thanked him for the Asti!" he went on, turning to his sisters-in-law.

"What! we never thanked him? I think, between you and me, that I put it to him quite neatly," replied my aunt Flora.

"Yes, you managed it very well; I admired you for it," said my aunt Céline.

"But you did it very prettily, too."

"Yes: I liked my expression about 'nice neighbours.'"

"What! Do you call that thanking him?" shouted my grandfather. "I heard that all right, but devil take me if I guessed it was meant for Swann. You may be quite sure he never noticed it."

"Come, come; Swann is not a fool. I am positive he appreciated the compliment. You didn't expect me to tell him the number of bottles, or to guess what he paid for them."

My father and mother were left alone and sat down for a moment; then my father said: "Well, shall we go up to bed?"

"As you wish, dear, though I don't feel in the least like sleeping.

I don't know why; it can't be the coffee-ice — it wasn't strong enough to keep me awake like this. But I see a light in the servants' hall: poor Françoise has been sitting up for me, so I will get her to unhook me while you go and undress."

My mother opened the latticed door which led from the hall to the staircase. Presently I heard her coming upstairs to close her window. I went quietly into the passage; my heart was beating so violently that I could hardly move, but at least it was throbbing no longer with anxiety, but with terror and with joy. I saw in the well of the stair a light coming upwards, from Mamma's candle. Then I saw Mamma herself: I threw myself upon her. For an instant she looked at me in astonishment, not realising what could have happened. Then her face assumed an expression of anger. She said not a single word to me; and, for that matter, I used to go for days on end without being spoken to, for far less offences than this. A single word from Mamma would have been an admission that further intercourse with me was within the bounds of possibility, and that might perhaps have appeared to me more terrible still, as indicating that, with such a punishment as was in store for me, mere silence, and even anger, were relatively puerile.

A word from her then would have implied the false calm in which one converses with a servant to whom one has just decided to give notice; the kiss one bestows on a son who is being packed off to enlist, which would have been denied him if it had merely been a matter of being angry with him for a few days. But she heard my father coming from the dressing-room, where he had gone to take off his clothes, and, to avoid the 'scene' which he would make if he saw me, she said, in a voice half-stifled by her anger: "Run away at once. Don't let your father see you standing there like a crazy jane!"

But I begged her again to "Come and say good night to me!" terrified as I saw the light from my father's candle already creeping up the wall, but also making use of his approach as a means of blackmail, in the hope that my mother, not wishing him to find me there, as find me he must if she continued to hold out, would give in to me, and say: "Go back to your room. I will come."

Too late: my father was upon us. Instinctively I murmured, though no one heard me, "I am done for!"

I was not, however. My father used constantly to refuse to let me do things which were quite clearly allowed by the more liberal charters granted me by my mother and grandmother, because he paid no heed to 'Principles,' and because in his sight there were no such things as 'Rights of man.' For some quite irrelevant reason, or for no reason at all, he would at the last moment prevent me from taking some particular walk, one so regular and so consecrated to my use that to deprive me of it was a clear breach of faith; or again, as he had done this evening, long before the appointed hour he would snap out: "Run along up to bed now; no excuses!" But then again, simply because he was devoid of principles (in my grandmother's sense), so he could not, properly speaking, he called inexorable. He looked at me for a moment with an air of annoyance and surprise, and then when Mamma had told him, not without some embarrassment, what had happened, said to her: "Go along with him, then; you said just now that you didn't feel like sleep, so stay in his room for a little. I don't need anything."

"But, dear," my mother answered timidly, "whether or not I feel like sleep is not the point; we must not make the child accustomed . . ."

"There's no question of making him accustomed," said my father, with a shrug of the shoulders; "you can see quite well that the child is unhappy. After all, we aren't goalers. You'll end by making him ill, and a lot of good that will do. There are two beds in his room; tell Françoise to make up the big one for you, and stay beside him for the rest of the night. I'm off to bed, anyhow; I'm not nervous like you. Good night."

It was impossible for me to thank my father; what he called my sentimentality would have exasperated him. I stood there, not daring to move; he was still confronting us, an immense figure in his white nightshirt, crowned with the pink and violet scarf of Indian cashmere in which, since he had begun to suffer from neuralgia, he used to tie up his head, standing like Abraham in the engraving after Benozzo Gozzoli [3] which M. Swann had given me, telling Sarah that she must tear herself away from Isaac. Many years have passed since that night. The wall of the staircase, up which I had watched the light of his candle gradually climb, was long ago demolished. And in myself, too, many things have perished which, I imagined, would last for ever, and new structures have arisen, giving birth to new sorrows and new joys which in those days I could not have foreseen, just as now the old are difficult of comprehension. It is a long time, too, since my father has been able to tell Mamma to "Go with the child." Never again will such hours be possible for me. But of late I have been increasingly able to catch, if I listen attentively, the sound of the sobs which I had the strength to control in my father's presence, and which broke out only when I found myself alone with Mamma. Actually, their echo has never ceased: it is only because life is now growing more and more quiet round about me that I hear them afresh, like those convent bells which are so effectively drowned during the day by the noises of the streets that one would suppose them to have been stopped for ever, until they sound out again through the silent evening air.

Mamma spent that night in my room: when I had just committed a sin so deadly that I was waiting to be banished from the household, my parents gave me a far greater concession than I should ever have won as the reward of a good action. Even at the moment when it manifested itself in this crowning mercy, my father's conduct towards me was still somewhat arbitrary, and regardless of my deserts, as was characteristic of him and due to the fact that his actions were generally dictated by chance expediencies rather than based on any formal plan.

3. A fifteenth-century Italian painter.

And perhaps even what I called his strictness, when he sent me off to bed, deserved that title less, really, than my mother's or grandmother's attitude, for his nature, which in some respects differed more than theirs from my own, had probably prevented him from guessing, until then, how wretched I was every evening, a thing which my mother and grandmother knew well; but they loved me enough to be unwilling to spare me that suffering, which they hoped to teach me to overcome, so as to reduce my nervous sensibility and to strengthen my will. As for my father, whose affection for me was of another kind, I doubt if he would have shewn so much courage, for as soon as he had grasped the fact that I was unhappy he had said to my mother: "Go and comfort him."

Mamma stayed all night in my room, and it seemed that she did not wish to mar by recrimination those hours, so different from anything that I had had a right to expect; for when Françoise (who guessed that something extraordinary must have happened when she saw Mamma sitting by my side, holding my hand and letting me cry unchecked) said to her: "But, Madame, what is little Master crying for?" she replied: "Why, Françoise, he doesn't know himself: it is his nerves. Make up the big bed for me quickly and then go off to your own." And thus for the first time my unhappiness was regarded no longer as a fault for which I must be punished, but as an involuntary evil which had been officially recognised, a nervous condition for which I was in no way responsible: I had the consolation that I need no longer mingle apprehensive scruples with the bitterness of my tears; I could weep henceforward without sin. I felt no small degree of pride, either, in Françoise's presence at this return to humane conditions which, not an hour after Mamma had refused to come up to my room and had sent the snubbing message that I was to go to sleep, raised me to the dignity of a grown-up person, brought me of a sudden to a sort of puberty of sorrow, to emancipation from tears. I ought then to have been happy; I was not. It struck me that my mother had just made a first concession which must have been painful to her, that it was a first step down from the ideal she had formed for me, and that for the first time she, with all her courage, had to confess herself beaten. It struck me that if I had just scored a victory it was over her; that I had succeeded, as sickness or sorrow or age might have succeeded, in relaxing her will, in altering her judgment; that this evening opened a new era, must remain a black date in the calendar. And if I had dared now, I should have said to Mamma: "No, I don't want you; you mustn't sleep here." But I was conscious of the practical wisdom, of what would be called nowadays the realism, with which she tempered the ardent idealism of my grandmother's nature, and I knew that now the mischief was done she would prefer to let me enjoy the soothing pleasure of her company, and not to disturb my father again. Certainly my mother's beautiful features seemed to shine again with youth that evening, as she sat gently holding my hands and trying to check my tears; but, just for that reason, it seemed to me that this should not have happened; her anger would have been less difficult to endure than this new kindness which my childhood had not known; I felt that I had with an impious and secret finger traced a first wrinkle upon her soul and made the first white hair shew upon her head. This thought redoubled my sobs, and then I saw that Mamma, who had never allowed herself to go to any length of tenderness with me, was suddenly overcome by my tears and had to struggle to keep back her own. Then, as she saw that I had noticed this, she said to me, with a smile: "Why, my little buttercup, my little canary-boy, he's going to make Mamma as silly as himself if this goes on. Look, since you can't sleep, and Mamma can't either, we mustn't go on in this stupid way; we must do something; I'll get one of your books." But I had none there. "Would you like me to get out the books now that your grandmother is going to give you for your birthday? Just think it over first, and don't be disappointed if there is nothing new for you then." . . .

Mamma sat down by my bed; she had chosen *François le Champi*, whose reddish cover and incomprehensible title gave it a distinct personality in my eyes and a mysterious attraction. I had not then any real novels. I had heard it said that George Sand [4] was a typical novelist. That prepared me in advance to imagine that *François le Champi* contained something inexpressibly delicious. The course of the narrative, where it tended to arouse curiosity or melt to pity, certain modes of expression which disturb or sadden the reader, and which, with a little experience, he may recognise as 'common form' in novels, seemed to me then distinctive — for to me a new book was not one of a number of similar objects, but was like an individual man, unmatched, and with no cause of existence beyond himself — an intoxicating whiff of the peculiar essence of *François le Champi*. Beneath the everyday incidents, the commonplace thoughts and hackneyed words, I could hear, or overhear, an intonation, a rhythmic utterance fine and strange. The 'action' began: to me it seemed all the more obscure because in those days, when I read to myself, I used often, while I turned the pages, to dream of something quite different. And to the gaps which this habit made in my knowledge of the story more were added by the fact that when it was Mamma who was reading to me aloud she left all the love-scenes out. And so all the odd changes which take place in the relations between the miller's wife and the boy, changes which only the birth and growth of love can explain, seemed to me plunged and steeped in a mystery, the key to which (as I could readily believe) lay in that strange and pleasant-sounding name of *Champi*, which draped the boy who bore it, I knew not why, in its own bright colour, purpurate and charming. If my mother was not a faithful reader, she was, none the less, admirable when reading a work in which she found the note of true feeling by the respectful simplicity of her interpretation and by the sound of her sweet and gentle voice. It was the same in her

4. The pseudonym of Amandine Aurore Lucie Dupin, the nineteenth-century woman novelist and eccentrically aggressive feminist.

daily life, when it was not works of art but men and women whom she was moved to pity or admire: it was touching to observe with what deference she would banish from her voice, her gestures, from her whole conversation, now the note of joy which might have distressed some mother who had long ago lost a child, now the recollection of an event or anniversary which might have reminded some old gentleman of the burden of his years, now the household topic which might have bored some young man of letters. And so, when she read aloud the prose of George Sand, prose which is everywhere redolent of that generosity and moral distinction which Mamma had learned from my grandmother to place above all other qualities in life, and which I was not to teach her until much later to refrain from placing, in the same way, above all other qualities in literature; taking pains to banish from her voice any weakness or affectation which might have blocked its channel for that powerful stream of language, she supplied all the natural tenderness, all the lavish sweetness which they demanded to phrases which seemed to have been composed for her voice, and which were all, so to speak, within her compass. She came to them with the tone that they required, with the cordial accent which existed before they were, which dictated them, but which is not to be found in the words themselves, and by these means she smoothed away, as she read on, any harshness there might be or discordance in the tenses of verbs, endowing the imperfect and the preterite with all the sweetness which there is in generosity, all the melancholy which there is in love; guided the sentence that was drawing to an end towards that which was waiting to begin, now hastening, now slackening the pace of the syllables so as to bring them, despite their difference of quantity, into a uniform rhythm, and breathed into this quite ordinary prose a kind of life, continuous and full of feeling.

My agony was soothed; I let myself be borne upon the current of this gentle night on which I had my mother by my side. I knew that such a night could not be repeated; that the strongest desire I had in the world, namely, to keep my mother in my room through the sad hours of darkness, ran too much counter to general requirements and to the wishes of others for such a concession as had been granted me this evening to be anything but a rare and casual exception. Tomorrow night I should again be the victim of anguish and Mamma would not stay by my side. But when these storms of anguish grew calm I could no longer realise their existence; besides, tomorrow evening was still a long way off; I reminded myself that I should still have time to think about things, albeit that remission of time could bring me no access of power, albeit the coming event was in no way dependent upon the exercise of my will, and seemed not quite inevitable only because it was still separated from me by this short interval.

And so it was that, for a long time afterwards, when I lay awake at night and revived old memories of Combray. I saw no more of it than this sort of luminous panel, sharply defined against a vague and shadowy background, like the panels which a Bengal fire or some electric sign will illuminate and dissect from the front of a building the other parts of which remain plunged in darkness: broad enough at its base, the little parlour, the dining-room, the alluring shadows of the path along which would come M. Swann, the unconscious author of my sufferings, the hall through which I would journey to the first step of that staircase, so hard to climb, which constituted, all by itself, the tapering 'elevation' of an irregular pyramid; and, at the summit, my bedroom, with the little passage through whose glazed door Mamma would enter; in a word, seen always at the same evening hour, isolated from all its possible surroundings, detached and solitary against its shadowy background, the bare minimum of scenery necessary (like the setting one sees printed at the head of an old play, for its performance in the provinces) to the drama of my undressing, as though all Combray had consisted of but two floors joined by a slender staircase, and as though there had been no time there but seven o'clock at night. I must own that I could have assured any questioner that Combray did include other scenes and did exist at other hours than these. But since the facts which I should then have recalled would have been prompted only by an exercise of the will, by my intellectual memory, and since the pictures which that kind of memory shews us of the past preserve nothing of the past itself, I should never have had any wish to ponder over this residue of Combray. To me it was in reality all dead.

Permanently dead? Very possibly.

There is a large element of hazard in these matters, and a second hazard, that of our own death, often prevents us from awaiting for any length of time the favours of the first.

I feel that there is much to be said for the Celtic belief that the souls of those whom we have lost are held captive in some inferior being, in an animal, in a plant, in some inanimate object, and so effectively lost to us until the day (which to many never comes) when we happen to pass by the tree or to obtain possession of the object which forms their prison. Then they start and tremble, they call us by our name, and as soon as we have recognised their voice the spell is broken. We have delivered them: they have overcome death and return to share our life.

And so it is with our own past. It is a labour in vain to attempt to recapture it: all the efforts of our intellect must prove futile. The past is hidden somewhere outside the realm, beyond the reach of intellect, in some material object (in the sensation which that material object will give us) which we do not suspect. And as for that object, it depends on chance whether we come upon it or not before we ourselves must die.

Many years had elapsed during which nothing of Combray, save what was comprised in the theatre and the drama of my going to bed there, had any existence for me, when one day in winter, as I came home, my mother, seeing that I was cold, offered me some tea, a thing I did not ordinarily take. I declined at first, and then, for no particular reason, changed my mind. She sent out for one of those short, plump little cakes called 'petites madeleines,' which look as though they had been moulded in the fluted scallop of a pilgrim's shell. And soon, mechanically, weary after a dull day with the prospect of a depressing morrow, I raised to my lips a spoonful of the tea in which I had soaked a morsel of the cake. No sooner had the warm liquid, and the crumbs with it, touched my palate than a shudder ran through my whole body, and I stopped, intent upon the extraordinary changes that were taking place. An exquisite pleasure had invaded my senses, but individual, detached, with no suggestion of its origin. And at once the vicissitudes of life had become indifferent to me, its disasters innocuous, its brevity illusory — this new sensation having had on me the effect which love has of filling me with a precious essence; or rather this essence was not in me, it was myself. I had ceased now to feel mediocre, accidental, mortal. Whence could it have come to me, this all-powerful joy? I was conscious that it was connected with the taste of tea and cake, but that it infinitely transcended those savours, could not, indeed, be of the same nature as theirs. Whence did it come? What did it signify? How could I seize upon and define it?

I drink a second mouthful, in which I find nothing more than in the first, a third, which gives me rather less than the second. It is time to stop; the potion is losing its magic. It is plain that the object of my quest, the truth, lies not in the cup but in myself. The tea has called up in me, but does not itself understand, and can only repeat indefinitely, with a gradual loss of strength, the same testimony; which I, too, cannot interpret, though I hope at least to be able to call upon the tea for it again and to find it there presently, intact and at my disposal, for my final enlightenment. I put down my cup and examine my own mind. It is for it to discover the truth. But how? What an abyss of uncertainty whenever the mind feels that some part of it has strayed beyond its own borders; when it, the seeker, is at once the dark region through which it must go seeking, where all its equipment will avail it nothing. Seek? More than that: create. It is face to face with something which does not so far exist, to which it alone can give reality and substance, which it alone can bring into the light of day.

And I begin again to ask myself what it could have been, this unremembered state which brought with it no logical proof of its existence, but only the sense that it was a happy, that it was a real state in whose presence other states of consciousness melted and vanished. I decide to attempt to make it reappear. I retrace my thoughts to the moment at which I drank the first spoonful of tea. I find again the same state, illumined by no fresh light. I compel my mind to make one further effort, to follow and recapture once again the fleeting sensation. And that nothing may interrupt it in its course I shut out every obstacle, every extraneous idea, I stop my ears and inhibit all attention to the sounds which come from the next room. And then, feeling that my mind is growing fatigued without having any success to report, I compel it for a change to enjoy that distraction which I have just denied it, to think of other things, to rest and refresh itself before the supreme attempt. And then for the second time I clear an empty space in front of it. I place in position before my mind's eye the still recent taste of that first mouthful, and I feel something start within me, something that leaves its resting-place and attempts to rise, something that has been embedded like an anchor at a great depth; I do not know yet what it is, but I can feel it mounting slowly; I can measure the resistance, I can hear the echo of great spaces traversed.

Undoubtedly what is thus palpitating in the depths of my being must be the image, the visual memory which, being linked to that taste, has tried to follow it into my conscious mind. But its struggles are too far off, too much confused; scarcely can I perceive the colourless reflection in which are blended the uncapturable whirling medley of radiant hues, and I cannot distinguish its form, cannot invite it, as the one possible interpreter, to translate to me the evidence of its contemporary, its inseparable paramour, the taste of cake soaked in tea; cannot ask it to inform me what special circumstance is in question, of what period in my past life.

Will it ultimately reach the clear surface of my consciousness, this memory, this old, dead moment which the magnetism of an identical moment has travelled so far to importune, to disturb, to raise up out of the very depths of my being? I cannot tell. Now that I feel nothing, it has stopped, has perhaps gone down again into its darkness, from which who can say whether it will ever rise? Ten times over I must essay the task, must lean down over the abyss. And each time the natural laziness which deters us from every difficult enterprise, every work of importance, has urged me to leave the thing alone, to drink my tea and to think merely of the worries of today and of my hopes for tomorrow, which let themselves be pondered over without effort or distress of mind.

And suddenly the memory returns. The taste was that of the little crumb of madeleine which on Sunday mornings at Combray (because on those mornings I did not go out before church-time), when I went to say good day to her in her bedroom, my aunt Léonie used to give me, dipping it first in her own cup of real or of lime-flower tea. The sight of the little madeleine had recalled nothing to my mind before I tasted it; perhaps because I had so often seen such things in the interval, without tasting them, on the trays in pastry-cooks' windows, that their image had dissociated itself from those Combray days to take its place among others more recent; perhaps because of those memories, so long abandoned and put out of mind, nothing now survived, everything was scattered; the forms of things, including that of the little scallop-shell of pastry, so richly sensual under its severe, religious folds, were either obliterated or had been so long dormant as to have lost the power of expansion which would have allowed them to resume their place in my consciousness. But when from a long-distant past nothing subsists, after the people are dead, after the things are broken and scattered, still, alone, more fragile, but with more vitality, more unsubstantial, more persistent, more faithful, the smell and taste of things remain poised a long time, like souls, ready to remind us, waiting and hoping for their moment, amid the ruins of all the rest; and bear unfaltering, in the tiny and almost impalpable drop of their essence, the vast structure of recollection.

And once I had recognised the taste of the crumb of madeleine soaked in her decoction of lime-flowers which my aunt used to give me (although I did not yet know and must long postpone the discovery of why this memory made me so happy) immediately the old grey house upon the street, where her room was, rose up like the scenery of a theatre to attach itself to the little pavilion, opening on to the garden, which had been built out behind it for my parents (the isolated panel which until that moment had been all that I could see); and with the house the town, from morning to night and in all weathers, the Square where I was sent before luncheon, the streets along which I used to run errands, the country roads we took when it was fine. And just as the Japanese amuse themselves by filling a porcelain bowl with water and steeping in it little crumbs of paper which until then are without character or form, but, the moment they become wet, stretch themselves and bend, take on colour and distinctive shape, become flowers or houses or people, permanent and recognisable, so in that moment all the flowers in our garden and in M. Swann's park, and the water-lilies on the Vivonne and the good folk of the village and their little dwellings and the parish church and the whole of Combray and of its surroundings, taking their proper shapes and growing solid, sprang into being, town and gardens alike, from my cup of tea.

Georges Poulet

The first volume of *Studies in Human Time*, from which the following excerpt was taken, established Georges Poulet's reputation as a philosophical critic of literature.

PROUST

I

And when I awoke in the middle of the night, not knowing where I was, I did not even know at first who I was; I had only in its

From *Studies in Human Time* by Georges Poulet. Reprinted by permission of The Johns Hopkins Press.

primal simplicity a sense of existing, such as may flicker in the depths of an animal's consciousness; I was more destitute than the cave-dweller.[1]

At the beginning of the Proustian novel there is, then, an instant which is not preceded by any other . . . But if this instant is of a "primal simplicity," that is because it is about to become the starting point of the immense development that follows it; but it is oriented not toward this "becoming" but toward the nothingness which precedes it. Here, this first moment is neither a moment of fullness nor of birth. It is pregnant neither with its future possibilities nor with its present realities. And if it reveals a fundamental emptiness, that is not because it needs anything from "ahead" but because it lacks something from "behind": something which *is no longer;* not something which *is not yet.* One might call it the first moment of a being that has lost everything, that has lost itself, because it is dead: "We have slept too long, we no longer exist. Our waking is barely felt, mechanically and without consciousness. . . ."[2]

The sleeper awakes from sleep more naked than a cave man. His nakedness is the nakedness of a lack of knowledge. If he is reduced to the state in which he is, that is because he does not know who he is. And he does not know who he is because he does not know who he has been. He knows *no longer.* He is a being who has lost his being because memory and the past have been lost:

Then from those profound slumbers we awake in a dawn, not knowing who we are, being nobody, newly born, ready for anything, our brain being emptied of that past which was previously our life. And perhaps it is more wonderful still when our landing at the waking-point is abrupt and the thoughts of our sleep, hidden by a cloak of oblivion, have no time to return to us progressively, before sleep ceases. Then, from the black tempest through which we seem to have passed (but we do not even say *we*) we emerge, prostrate, without a thought, a "we" that is without content. What hammer-blow has the being or the thing that is lying there received to make it unconscious of anything . . . ?[3]

He who surges now into existence seems less a being than one emptied of his being. He is a being *in vacuo,* in emptiness; a being "without consciousness," since consciousness can only be consciousness of something. He is "without content," "more lifeless than a jelly-fish," returned to "the most elementary kingdoms of nature"; a being that cannot be described otherwise than by calling it "the being or the thing that is there."

But how is this thing which is there, in a moment "outside of time and all measures," how is it going to be able to leave this moment which

1. *Remembrance of Things Past* (2 vols.; New York: Random House, 1927–32) I, 5.
2. *Ibid.,* II, 464.
3. *Ibid.,* p. 271.

isolates it before and behind? How shall it repair its monstrous ignorance of time, place, and its own person? Doubtless, to the animal feeling of its own existence there corresponds the feeling of the existence
of a world in which it seems confusedly immersed. Awakened, and at
the very instant when it awakes, this sleeper discovers himself and discovers at the same time that he *is there* — there, that is to say somewhere: at a certain time; in a place; among things. But suppose he
awakens in the middle of the night, in darkness: in what room is he?
in what place? in what time? Certain images of places and times come
and go, excluding each other and superimposing themselves upon him:

> Perhaps the immobility of the things that surround us is forced
> upon them by our conviction that they are themselves, and not any-
> thing else, and by the immobility of our conceptions of them. For
> it always happened that when I awoke like this, and my mind strug-
> gled in an unsuccessful attempt to discover where I was, everything
> would be moving round me through the darkness: things, places,
> years.[4]

Vertigo of images. The world, as the awakened sleeper discovers it,
is indeed a world of things, but of interchangeable things, in which
nothing is attached to one particular point of space or duration; a
world of things doubtful rather than certain; possible rather than
necessary; a world similar to the legendary images of Golo and of
Geneviève de Brabant which the play of the magic lantern substituted
for the walls of the room of the child Proust, to make "a stained glass
window, flickering and momentary."

The being that is uncertain of himself wants to lean upon the stability of things. But what stability can be offered by things which are
"even more unreal than the projections of the magic lantern"? Unreal
as the forms he has just encountered in the world of sleep:

> . . . deep slumber in which are opened to us a return to childhood,
> the recapture of past years, of lost feelings, the disincarnation, the
> transmigration of the soul, the evoking of the dead, the illusions of
> madness, retrogression towards the most elementary of the natural
> kingdoms (for we say that we often see animals in our dreams, but
> we forget almost always that we are ourself then an animal deprived
> of that reasoning power which projects upon things the light of cer-
> tainty; we present on the contrary to the spectacle of life only a
> *dubious vision, destroyed afresh every moment by oblivion*, the for-
> mer reality fading before that which follows it as one projection of
> a magic lantern fades before the next as we change the slide).[5]

The awakened sleeper, Proust, is never entirely able to detach himself from this first figuration of the world. One would say that, if
Goethe taught himself to represent the universe as a theater of mario-

4. *Ibid.*, I, 5.
5. *Ibid.*, p. 617.

nettes, Proust learned to represent existence as the "flickering and momentary" play of the light of a magic lantern. The Proustian world is always to be an intermittent world. A world in which things project themselves before the eyes in instantaneous images which in turn are replaced by other images belonging to other moments and other places; a world in which the apparition of any one image does not necessarily entail the apparition of the one following; where one may find oneself going backward as well as forward; where "the magic chair may carry us at all speed in time and space"; a world of "doubtful visions," whose lacunae the mind will have to fill up by its conjectures, whose vacillations it will have to remedy by its beliefs. The Proustian world is a world anachronistic in itself, without a home, wandering in duration as well as in extent, a world to which the mind must precisely assign a certain place in duration and space, by imposing its own certitude upon it, by realizing oneself in the face of it.

But in order to impose our certainties upon the world, we must first find them in ourselves. Now what certainties can a consciousness without content find in itself? What can it offer, denuded of all, beggar that it is? The human being on the threshold of awakening, the child at the onset of the night, finds itself face to face with "doubtful visions destroyed every minute," and confronted by things of which it is impossible to know "whether they are themselves and not others." Thus the child Proust, in the room that the projection of the magic lantern metamorphosized: "The mere change of lighting destroyed the customary impression I had formed of my room, thanks to which the room itself, but for the torture of having to go to bed in it, had become quite endurable. For now I no longer recognized it, and I became uneasy, as though I were in a room in some hotel or "chalet," in a place where I had just arrived for the first time. . . ." [6] It is a place one no longer recognizes, which therefore can be any other place, a place which has become doubtful, strange, anonymous; a place disconnected from its occupant, because nothing in it responds to the demand of his thought. Then, in the consciousness of the hostile refusal of things to put themselves in touch with the mind, the child Proust takes account of the depth of his solitude, and the anguish begins:

Having no world, no room, no body now that was not menaced by the enemies thronging round, invaded to the very bones by fever, I was alone, I wanted to die.[7]

For the anguish of solitude is not only that of being detached from things and beings: it is being detached from fixity, from the permanence one would like to have beings and things possess and give us by return; it is to feel oneself betrayed, without any help from them, to the indeterminate power of thought, which ceaselessly imposes upon us metamorphoses, which perpetually changes us into another "self," and which every instant makes of us, and for us, a stranger.

6. *Ibid.*, p. 8.
7. *Ibid.*, p. 506.

Thence proceed those contractions and rebellions of the threatened parts of our whole selves "which we must recognize to be a secret, partial, tangible and true aspect of our resistance to death, of the long resistance, desperate and daily renewed, to a fragmentary and reiterated death such as interpolates itself through the whole course of our life . . ." [8] successive deaths, more imminent, more reiterated, more total in proportion as a thought without content finds in itself no resource for establishing fixity and consistence.

The human being, for Proust, therefore, is a being who tries to find justification for his existence. Not knowing who he is, either he is like someone striken with amnesia who goes from door to door asking people to tell him his name, or he feels himself to be what things indifferently become in him: a bundle of anonymous images that obliterate themselves and reform, like the iridescent spray from fountains of water. He is nothing or anything by turns, anything which is still nothing. Now this being who is nothing finds himself thrown into a moment lost in the midst of others, that is to say, a moment which resembles nothing and rests on nothing. And since this instant is inevitably going to be annihilated by another, he sees in this instant his own death, and he does not know whether he will be born again, or into what sort of being he will be reborn. . . . For to be dead, for Proust, is not simply to be no more; it is to be *another being*. Such is a man who after an illness is shocked to see that his hair has turned white.

And when I realized that I felt no joy at the thought of her being alive, that I no longer loved her, I ought to have been more astounded than a person who, looking at his reflexion in the glass, after months of travel, or of sickness discovers that he has white hair and a different face, that of a middle aged or an old man. This appalls us because its message is: "the man that I was, the fair young man, no longer exists, I am another person." And yet, was not the impression that I now felt, the proof of as profound a change, as total a death of my former self and of the no less complete substitution of a new self for that former self, as is proved by the sight of a wrinkled face capped with a snowy poll instead of the face of long ago? [9]

What is death but to be different from oneself? The fear of death is not so much the fear of no longer feeling and no longer being conscious; it is the fear of no longer feeling that which one feels, and of no longer being conscious of that of which one is conscious. Yet such a death seems an ineluctable reality, not only at the end of total existence, but at the end of each of these tiny closed existences, of these "drops of time" which are each one of the moments of our life:

. . . truly a death of ourselves, a death followed, it is true, by resurrection, but in a different ego, the life, the love of which are beyond the reach of those elements of the existing ego that are doomed to die.[10]

8. *Ibid.*, p. 510.
9. *Ibid.*, II, 833.

10. *Ibid.*, I, 510.

Condemned, then, to a fragmentary and successive death, not knowing whether he will come to life again or in whom he will come to life, the human being such as Proust depicts is haunted by the anguish of this substitution of self for self which for him is death. Against this anguish he has only one recourse: to give himself the assurance of this survival; to believe that, beyond all this, one will be able to find *oneself again*. But it is impossible for this faith to assure him as to the future, since one cannot find there anything imaginable; since this future is the present of the monstrously inconceivable being into which death will have changed us. From this side, *from the side of the death to come,* the grave is insuperable. The future is closed by death; confronting the closed future, we are in anguish.

Free-floating anguish, indeterminate, "at the service one day of one feeling, the next day of another." But whether it presents itself under the form of the indefinable dejection into which the spectacle of a strange room throws us, or under the form of the anxiety of the child who waits in vain for the kiss of his mother before going to sleep, fundamentally this anguish is of a being who, finding himself in an existence which nothing, it seems, can justify, incapable of discovering for himself a reason for being, incapable at the same time of finding anything which guarantees the continuation of his being, experiences simultaneously horror of a future which changes him, contempt for a present which seems powerless to establish him, and the exclusive need of saving himself, come what may, from his cruel contingency by discovering in the past the basis of this being that he is, and yet that *he no longer is.*

For if it is impossible beforehand to burst open the precincts of death, is it not possible to do so, one might say, behindhand? If we are always *on this side* of our death to come, are we not always *on that side* of a death *already come,* a death beyond which lies our past life? Is there not then an act by which one might be able to rediscover himself and the basis of his existence?

This question is answered in the strange beginning of Proust's novel, where, with hardly an initial moment admitted, the thought gets underway and begins to march, but in reverse. A journey backwards, as if at the very moment the being discovers his existence, he experiences as well the need of sustaining rather than fulfilling it, of giving himself reasons for being rather than reasons for acting.

Proust's novel is the history of a search: that is to say a series of efforts to *find again* something that one has lost. It is the novel of an existence in search of its essence.

One is no longer a person. How then, seeking for one's mind, one's personality, as one seeks for a thing that is lost, does one recover one's own self rather than any other? . . . What is it that guides us, when there has been an actual interruption . . . ? There has indeed been death, as when the heart has ceased to beat and a rhythmical friction of the tongue revives us. . . . The resurrection at our awakening — after that healing attack of mental alienation which is sleep — must after all be similar to what occurs when we recapture a name, a line, a refrain that we had forgotten. And perhaps the resurrection of the soul after death is to be conceived as a phenomenon of memory.[11]

II

In Proustian thought memory plays the same supernatural role as grace in Christian thought. It is this inexplicable phenomenon that comes to apply itself to a fallen nature, irremediably separated from its origins, not to restore it integrally and at once to its first condition, but to give it the efficacy to find the highway of its salvation. Remembrance is a "succour from on high" which comes to the being in order "to draw him from the nothingness out of which, by himself, he would not have been able to emerge." Also it appears continually in the work of Proust under a form at once human and superhuman. It is at one and the same time an unforeseeable, "involuntary" thing that is added to the being, and the very act of this being, the most personal act because constitutive of the person. And, as there are some graces which fall on rich soil, and others on barren ground, some graces to which one responds and others which one ignores, so it is with memories. There are numerous examples in the work of Proust of these mysterious solicitations which a spirit distraught by its own ends fails to heed. More numerous still are those in which a debased memory finds itself reduced to being only a vassal of the intelligence or a sort of habit: grace corrupted, which then loses its efficacy and becomes a "frozen memory," a "memory of facts." . . . A memory no longer supernatural, a fallen memory by the will of which it is vain to hope to "re-establish ourselves in that state we were in," for we can do nothing by our own strength and our own will, and all depends from the first on supernatural chance.

But if it all depends from the first on this miraculous contingency, if it is this originally which is the first cause, it is not a unique cause; it calls for our collaboration; it exacts the maximum effort from us. The Proustian memory has often been identified with the affective memory of the psychologists. And — psychologically speaking — it is that without doubt: that is to say, a revival in us of a forgotten state of mind. Furthermore the very term *involuntary,* by which Proust qualifies it, seems to confirm this identification, since for the psychologist the affective memory is in the final analysis spontaneous and unforeseeable, the simple raising of old emotions up into the mind; a raising up in which the mind assists less as an actor than as a patient. But for Proust profound remembrance is not only that, something involuntarily undergone, but at its point of arrival in us something which is or which ought to be the point of departure for our spiritual action. It is an

11. *Ibid.,* p. 776.

invitation, an appeal, which is addressed to all our being, and to which all our being ought to respond. It opens to us a road through the depths, but it is up to us to advance on that road. Paradise lost is returned to us if we wish it, but only if we wish it.

It is for that reason that there are in the Proustian novel so many examples of abortive memories and portions of the past ultimately lost. For that reason also there are many more memories which, brought to light, leave only, after the spectacle of their brief resurrection, the regret for a "paradise lost," lost for the second time. Just as for the Scholastics there was an infinity of degrees in the "perfection" of grace, so for Proust there is an infinity of degrees in the "perfection" of memory. But in his case each of these degrees is like that of one descending scale, and sometimes the being seems stopped at one level, sometimes a little lower, when what he seeks is away below. But most of the time "we lack the strength to penetrate to the very depths where truth lies, the real universe, our authentic impression." . . .

From this point of view the most famous of all the passages of Proust, the episode of the madeleine, ought not at all to seem to us to have exhausted the meaning of the novel. It contains it without doubt, but it does not reveal it. Or rather, if it reveals something of it, it is precisely that the whole mystery lies beyond the psychological explanation of it: "I still did not know and must long postpone the discovery of *why* the memory made me happy."

The real significance of the episode of the madeleine resides entirely in precisely this: that it gives us a moment of happiness. To the unhappy instant with which the book began there now succeeds a happy instant, as if the grace of memory consisted in exchanging the one for the other. In the moment of awakening one sees the hero discover a nocturnal world, anguished, in which he knows neither who he is nor whether things are as they seem; in the moment of remembrance we watch him find himself in diurnal life, in the broad daylight of a Sunday morning of his childhood, surrounded by customary things, in a familiar time and place: "Everything that took *form and solidity* had sprung, town and gardens, from my cup of tea."

Form and solidity. If it is true then that remembrance is an exchange, it is also true that the moment exchanged has no longer the tragic inconsistency of what it replaces. It is a moment in which things have a form, in which they are solid, in which one knows what they are as well as one knows who one is. And it is such a moment because it represents this daily face of the life of childhood, this *face of the sun,* in which things in full light offer their form and solidity to a being who addresses toward them his desire and his faith. Deep remembrance is only the return of a deep impression. Now if it appears to us so beautiful, if its return makes us so happy, that is because it expresses between the being who feels and the object felt a spontaneous accord in which the desire of the one meets with the solidity of the other; as if the external world were now precisely what we would desire it to be:

For a desire seems to us more beautiful, we repose on it with more confidence, when we know that outside ourselves there is a reality which conforms to it, even if, for us, it is not to be realized.[12]

If reality conforms to it, then and only then, we can *believe in it* and not simply feel it. Thus the deep impressions are not merely impressions we are content to submit to, even in a repetitive fashion, but experiences in which we add something to what they bring us, namely the adherence of our *complete being,* that is to say, our love. Such a desire is experienced by Marcel for the milk-seller who passes along the length of the train:

> She passed down the line of windows, offering coffee and milk to a few awakened passengers. Reddened with the glow of morning, her face was rosier than the sky. I felt in her presence that desire to live which is reborn in us whenever we become conscious anew of beauty and happiness. . . . Alien to the models of beauty which my fancy was wont to sketch when I was by myself, this strapping girl gave me at once the sensation of a certain happiness (the sole form, always individual, in which we may learn the sensation of happiness), of a happiness that would be realized by my staying by her side. . . . I was giving the milk-girl the benefit of what was really my own entire being, ready to taste the keenest joys. . . .[13]

> When we are young, at the age I had reached at the period of my walks along the Méséglise way, our desires, our faith bestow on a woman's clothing an individual personality, an irreducible essence.[14]

Desire and belief: terms almost interchangeable which express the two aspects of the same activity, an activity of all one's being. For just as the perfection of memory demands the conjunction of a given object and an effort of the mind, so that which is discovered deeper than memory, the primitive impression, contains for us a given object and a movement on our part to seize it. A movement which, insofar as it issues from the being, is called *desire,* and which insofar as it applies itself to and rests in the object is called *faith.*

In the depths of being, then, what comes to light is a moment of the past which is exactly the inverse of the present moment of awakening: a moment when, instead of being separated from things, and of not being sure whether they are themselves or other things, one is sure they are different from all others; and that because one now has the power to bind oneself to them, to confer upon them an individual particularity, an irreducible essence:

> Moreover — just as in moments of musing contemplation of nature, the normal actions of the mind being suspended, and our abstract ideas of things set on one side, we believe with profound faith in the originality, in the individual existence of the place in

12. *Ibid.,* p. 539.
13. *Ibid.,* p. 498.
14. *Ibid.,* p. 994.

which we may happen to be — the passing figure which my desire evoked seemed to be not any one example of the general type of "woman," but a necessary and natural product of the soil. For at that time everything which was not myself, the earth and the creatures upon it, seemed to me more precious, more important, endowed with a more real existence than they appear to full-grown men. And between the earth and its creatures I made no distinction.[15]

If the primitive impression, then, is worthy of *faith,* that is because it involves a *moment* and a *place;* and not, as with the being of awakening, a moment which can be any moment, a place that can be any place; but a moment so well defined in time and space that it cannot be confounded with any other, and of so great an authenticity that we cannot doubt it. Extreme depth where truth lies, little universe having its own particular time and place in which our *authentic impression* rediscovers itself in its lost reality, thanks to memory:

> What I had long lost, the feeling which makes us not merely regard a thing as a spectacle, but believe in it as in a creature without parallel. . . .[16]

What was lost and what is found is not just time, but a fragment of time to which clings a fragment of space; and in the interior of this small universe, the self, the individual is indivisibly bound by its faith and its desire to this moment of time and to this point in space. From a feeling of existence detached from times and places, the being finds himself brought back by deep remembrance to a first feeling, truly original, constituent of himself and of the world, the act of faith by which the sentient being adheres instantaneously, locally, to sensible reality.

In bringing us back thus, across the past, to a primitive impression, Proust reminds us of Condillac:[17] "The only means of acquiring knowledge," Condillac says, "is to go back to the origin of our ideas, to follow the generation of them, and to compare them . . ." But if Proust goes back to the origin, it is not by analysis and a taking of things apart, but by a synthetic intuition — remembrance — because it is not for him a question of arriving at a simple entity, but at a primitive complex which analysis would irremediably lose.

It is rather to Rousseau that he must be compared. For the one, as for the other, at bottom, at the origin, there is a natural identity between the feeling self and the thing felt. But with Rousseau identity is posed simply as such; with Proust, on the contrary, it appears as proposed rather than given; it must be achieved in a movement of the self toward the object and culminate in belief:

15. *Ibid.,* p. 146.
16. *Ibid.,* p. 50.
17. Étienne Bonnot de Mably de Condillac (1715–80), French philosopher, founder of Sensationalism.

For this is the point to which we must always return, to these beliefs with which most of the time we are quite unconsciously filled, but which for all that are of more importance to our happiness than is the average person whom we see, for it is through them that we see him, it is they that impart his transitory grandeur to the person seen.[18]

Only a transitory grandeur, to be sure, as happens with all correspondences between him who regards and that which is regarded; but an imperishable grandeur as well, because the object thus transfigured by belief, detached by the very fact of the general motion of things and the flux of duration, leaves upon the mind of him who *believed in it* an indelible image. The image *will be found again*. In the midst of a magic-lantern world, a vacillating unreal world made of "doubtful visions" in which one cannot believe, the awakened sleeper, if he remembers, will find once more in the depths of his memory, in his first impressions, this *passing grandeur* which an act of childlike faith has fixed in him forever.

18. *Remembrance of Things Past*, I, 708.

Thomas Mann (1875–1955)

LIFE: Like Goethe before him, he was the contemporary master of German literature and the symbolic center of German culture; but he left his country when the Nazis came to power and eventually became an American citizen. His fiction records the persistent conflict between the needs of the artist and the repressive demands of society and civilization.

WORKS: *Buddenbrooks* (1900); *Death in Venice* (1913); *The Magic Mountain* (1924); *Joseph and His Brothers* (1933); *Doctor Faustus* (1947); *The Holy Sinner* (1951); *Confessions of Felix Krull, Confidence Man* (1954).

FELIX KRULL *

I shall pass quickly over the first confused days following our arrival in Frankfurt,[1] for it pains me to recall the distressing role we were obliged to play in that rich and resplendent centre of commerce, and I should be afraid of earning the reader's displeasure by a circumstantial account of our situation. I say nothing of the dingy hostelry

* From *Confessions of Felix Krull, Confidence Man*, chapters IV and V.
1. Where the young Felix has come after the bankruptcy and suicide of his father.

or rooming-house, unworthy of the name of hotel which it arrogated to itself, where, for reasons of economy, my mother and I spent several nights, my sister Olympia having parted company with us at the junction in Wiesbaden in order to seek her fortune in Cologne with Meerschaum, the agent. For my own part, I spent those nights on a sofa teeming with vermin that both stung and bit. I say nothing of our painful wanderings through that great, cold-hearted city, so unfriendly to poverty, in search of an abode we could afford, until, in a mean section, we finally came on one that had just been vacated and that corresponded fairly well to my mother's idea of a starting-place. It consisted of four small, sunless rooms and an even smaller kitchen, and was situated on the ground floor of a rear building, with a view of ugly courtyards. As, however, it cost only forty marks a month, and as it ill became us to be fastidious, we rented it on the spot and moved in the same day.

Whatever is new holds infinite charm for the young, and although this gloomy domicile could not be compared even faintly with our cheerful villa at home, I nevertheless felt cheered by the unfamiliar surroundings and satisfied to the point of boisterousness. With rough and ready helpfulness I joined my mother in the necessary preliminaries, moving furniture, unpacking cups and plates from protective woodshavings, stocking shelves and cupboards with pots and pans; I also undertook to negotiate with our landlord, a repulsively fat man with vulgar manners, about the necessary alterations in our quarters. Fatbelly, however, obstinately refused to pay for them, and in the end my mother had to dip into her own pocketbook so that the rooms we hoped to rent would not look completely dilapidated. This came hard, for the costs of moving and settling in had been high, and if our paying guests did not put in an appearance, our establishment would be threatened with bankruptcy before it was properly started.

On the very evening, as we were standing in the kitchen eating our supper of fried eggs, we decided, for reasons of pious and happy memory,[2] to call our establishment "Pension Loreley," and we immediately communicated this decision to my godfather, Schimmelpreester,[3] on a postcard we jointly composed; next day I hurried to the office of Frankfurt's leading newspaper with an advertisement couched in modest yet enticing terms and designed, by the use of bold-face type to impress that poetic name on the public consciousness. Because of the expense, we were unable for several days to put up a sign on the house facing the street that would attract the attention of passers-by to our establishment. How describe our jubilation when, on the sixth or seventh day after our arrival, the mail from home brought a package of mysterious shape with my godfather Schimmelpreester's name on it? It contained a metal sign, one end of which was bent at a right angle and pierced by four holes. It bore, painted by the artist's own hand, that female figure clothed only in jewelry which had adorned our bottle

2. His father had produced a bad champagne called *Loreley extra cuvée.*
3. Whose name meant, in Felix's words, "high priest of mould."

labels, with the inscription: "Pension Loreley" emblazoned in gold letters beneath it. When this had been fastened to the corner of the house facing the street in such a way that the fairy of the rock pointed with outstretched, ring-bedecked hand across the courtyard to our establishment, it produced the most beautiful effect.

As it turned out, we did get customers: first of all in the person of a young technician or mechanical engineer, a solemn, quiet, even morose man, clearly discontented with his lot, who nevertheless paid punctually and led a discreet and orderly life. He had been with us barely a week when two other guests arrived together: members of the theatrical profession — a comic bass, unemployed because of having lost his voice completely, heavy and jolly in appearance but in a furious temper as a result of his misfortune and determined to restore his organ through persistent and futile exercises which sounded as though someone were drowning inside a hogshead and shouting for help: and with him his female supplement, a red-haired chorus girl with long, rose-coloured fingernails, who wore a dirty dressing-gown — a pathetic, frail creature who seemed to have chest trouble, but whom the singer, either on account of her shortcomings or simply to give vent to his general bitterness, beat frequently and severely with his braces, without, however, making her at all dubious about him or his affection for her.

These two, then, occupied a room together, the machinist another; the third served as a dining-room, where we all consumed the meals my mother skilfully concocted out of very little. As I did not wish to share a room with my mother, for obvious reasons of propriety, I slept on a kitchen bench with bedding spread over it, and washed myself at the kitchen sink, mindful that this state of affairs could not last and that, in one way or another, my road would soon have a turning.

The Pension Loreley began to flourish; the guests, as I have indicated, drove us into a corner, and my mother could properly look forward to an enlargement of the enterprise and the acquisition of a maid. In any case, the business was on its feet, my assistance was no longer required, and, left to myself, I saw that until I departed for Paris [4] or was compelled to put on a uniform, there would be a prolonged period of leisurely waiting of the sort that is so welcome to a high-minded youth — indeed, so necessary for his inner development. Education is not won in dull toil and labour; rather it is the fruit of freedom and apparent idleness; one does not achieve it by exertion, one breathes it in; some secret machinery is at work to that end; a hidden industry of the senses and the spirit, consonant with an appearance of complete vagabondage, is hourly active to promote it, and you could go so far as to say that one who is chosen learns even in his sleep. For one must after all be of educable stuff in order to be educated. No one grasps what he has not possessed from birth, and you can never

4. Where his godfather had arranged for him to become a hotel waiter.

yearn for what is alien. He who is made of common clay will never acquire education; he who does acquire it was never crude. And here once again it is very hard to draw a just and clear distinction between personal desert and what are called favourable circumstances; if, on the one hand, beneficent fortune had placed me in a big city at the right moment and granted me time in abundance, on the other hand it must be said that I was entirely deprived of the means which alone throw open the many places of entertainment and education such a city contains. And in my studies I had, as it were, to be content with pressing my face against the magnificent gates of a pleasure garden.

At this time I devoted myself to sleep almost to excess, usually sleeping until lunchtime, often until much later, eating a warmed-over meal in the kitchen or even a cold one, and afterward lighting a cigarette, a gift from our machinist (who knew how greedy I was for this pleasure and how unable I was to provide it for myself out of my own funds). I did not leave the Pension Loreley until late in the afternoon, four or five o'clock. At that hour the fashionable life of the city reached its height, rich ladies rode out in their carriages to pay calls or go shopping, the coffee houses were filling, and the store windows began to come magnificently alight. Then it was that I betook myself to the centre of town, embarking on a journey of pleasure and entertainment through the populous streets of the famous city, from which I would not return to my mother's house until the grey of dawn, though usually with much profit.

Now observe this youth in ragged clothes, alone, friendless, and lost in the crowd, wandering through this bright and alien world. He has no money with which to take any real part in the joys of civilization. He sees them proclaimed and touted on the placards stuck on advertising pillars, so excitingly that they would arouse curiosity and desire in even the dullest (whereas he is especially impressionable) — and he must content himself with reading their names and being aware of their existence. He sees the portals of the theatres festively open and dares not join the crowd that goes streaming in; he stands dazzled in the unearthly light that spills across the sidewalk from music halls and vaudeville houses, in front of which, perhaps, some gigantic Negro, his countenance and purple costume blanched by the white brilliance, towers fabulously in tricorn hat, waving his staff — and he cannot accept the flashing-toothed invitation and the enticements of the spiel. But his senses are lively, his mind attentive and alert; he sees, he enjoys, he assimilates; and if at first the rush of noise and faces confuses this son of a sleepy country town, bewilders him, frightens him indeed, nevertheless he possesses mother wit and strength of mind enough slowly to become master of his inner turmoil and turn it to good purpose for his education, his enthusiastic researches.

And what a happy institution the shop window is! How lucky that stores, bazaars, salons, that market places and emporia of luxury do not stingily hide their treasures indoors, but shower them forth in glittering profusion, in inexhaustible variety, spreading them out like a splendid offering behind shining plate glass. Brighter than day on a winter's afternoon is the illumination of these displays; rows of little gas flames at the bottoms of the windows keep the panes from frosting over. And there stood I, protected from the cold only by a woollen scarf wrapped around my neck (for my overcoat, inherited from my poor father, had long since gone to the pawnshop for a paltry sum), devouring with my eyes these wares, these precious and splendid wares, and paying no attention to the cold and damp that worked their way up from my feet to my thighs.

Whole suites were arranged in the windows of the furniture stores: drawing-rooms of stately luxury, bed-chambers that acquainted one with every intimate refinement of cultivated life; inviting little dining-rooms, where the damask-covered, flower-bedecked tables, surrounded by comfortable chairs, shimmered enchantingly with silver, fine porcelain, and fragile glassware; princely salons in formal style with candelabra, fireplaces, and brocaded armchairs; and I never tired of observing how firmly and splendidly the legs of that noble furniture rested on the colourful, softly glowing Persian carpets. Farther on, the windows of a haberdasher and a fashion shop drew my attention. Here I saw the wardrobes of the rich and great, from satin dressing-gowns and silk-lined smoking-jackets to the evening severity of the tail-coat, from the alabaster collar in the latest, most favoured style to the delicate spat and the mirror-bright patent-leather shoe, from the pin-striped or dotted shirt with French cuffs to the costly fur jacket; here their hand luggage was displayed before me, those knapsacks of luxury, of pliant calfskin or expensive alligator, which looks as though it were made out of little squares; and I learned to know the appurtenances of a high and discriminating way of life, the bottles, the hairbrushes, the dressing-cases, the boxes with plates and cutlery and collapsible alcohol stoves of finest nickel; fancy waistcoats, magnificent ties, sybaritic underclothes, morocco slippers, silk-lined hats, deerskin gloves, and socks of gauzy silk were strewn in seductive display; the youth could fix in his memory the wardrobe requirements of a man of fashion down to the last, sturdy, convenient button. But perhaps I needed only to slip across the street, carefully and adroitly dodging between carriages and honking buses, to arrive at the windows of an art gallery. There I saw the treasures of the decorative industry, such objects of a high and cultivated visual lust as oil paintings by the hands of masters, gleaming porcelain figures of animals of various sorts, beautifully shaped earthenware vessels, small bronze statues, and dearly would I have liked to pick up and fondle those poised and noble bodies.

But what sort of splendour was it a few steps farther on that held me rooted to the spot in amazement? It was the window display of a big jeweller and goldsmith — and here nothing but a fragile pane of glass divided the covetousness of a freezing boy from all the treasures of fairyland. Here, more than anywhere else, my first dazzled enchantment was combined with the eagerest desire to learn. Pearl necklaces, palely shimmering on lace runners, arranged one above another, big as cherries in the middle and decreasing symmetrically toward the sides, ending in diamond clasps, and worth whole fortunes; diamond jewelry bedded on satin, sharply glittering with all the colours of the rainbow and worthy to adorn the neck, the bosom, the head of queens; smooth golden cigarette cases and cane heads, seductively displayed on glass shelves; and everywhere, carelessly strewn, polished precious stones of magnificent colour: blood-red rubies; grass-green, glossy emeralds; transparent blue sapphires that held a star-shaped light; amethysts whose precious violet shade is said to be due to organic content; mother-of-pearl opals whose colour changed as I shifted my position; single topazes; fanciful arrangements of gems in all the shadings of the spectrum — all this was not only a joy to the senses, I studied it, I immersed myself completely in it, I tried to decipher the few price tags that were visible, I compared, I weighed by eye, for the first time I became aware of my love for the precious stones of the earth, those essentially quite worthless crystals whose elements through a playful whim of Nature have combined to form these precious structures. It was at this time that I laid the groundwork for my later reliable connoisseurship in this magical domain.

Shall I speak too of the flower shops out of whose doors, when they were opened, gushed the moist, warm perfumes of paradise, and behind whose windows I saw those sumptuous flower baskets, adorned with gigantic silk bows, that one sends to women as evidence of one's attention? Or of the stationery stores whose displays taught me what sort of notepaper a cavalier uses for his correspondence, and how the initials of one's name are engraved on it with crest and coat of arms? Or the windows of the perfumers and hairdressers, where in glittering, elegant rows shone the many different scents and essences that come from France, and the delicate instruments used for the manicure and the care of the face were displayed in richly lined cases? The gift of seeing had been granted me and it was my be-all and end-all at this time — an instructive gift, to be sure, when material things, the enticing, educational aspects of the world, are its object. But how much more profoundly does the gift of perception engage one's feelings! Perception, that visual feasting on the human spectacle as it unfolds in the fashionable districts of a great city — whither I went by preference — how very different from the attraction of inanimate objects must be the pull it exerts on the longings and curiosity of a passionately ambitious youth!

O scenes of the beautiful world! Never have you presented yourselves to more appreciative eyes. Heaven knows why one in particular among the nostalgic pictures I stored up at that time has sunk so deeply into me and clings so persistently in my memory that despite its unimportance, its insignificance indeed, it fills me with delight even today. I shall not resist the temptation to record it here, though I know very well that a story-teller — and it is as a story-teller that I present myself in these pages — ought not to encumber the reader with incidents of which "nothing comes," to put the matter bluntly, since they in no way advance what is called "the action." But perhaps it is in some measure permissible, in the description of one's own life, to follow not the laws of art but the dictates of one's heart.

Once more, it was nothing, it was only charming. The stage was above my head — an open balcony of the *bel étage* of the great Hotel Zum Frankfurter Hof. Onto it stepped one afternoon — it was so simple that I apologize — two young people, as young as myself, obviously a brother and sister, possibly twins — they looked very much alike — a young man and a young woman moving out together into the wintry weather. They did so out of pure high spirits, hatless, without protection of any kind. Slightly foreign in appearance, dark-haired, they might have been Spanish, Portuguese, South American, Argentinian, Brazilian — I am simply guessing — but perhaps, on the other hand, they were Jews — I could not swear they were not and I would not on that account be shaken in my enthusiasm, for gently reared children of that race can be most attractive. Both were pretty as pictures — the youth not a whit less than the girl. In evening dress, both of them, the youth with a pearl in his shirt front, the girl wearing one diamond clip in her rich, dark, attractively dressed hair and another at her breast, where the flesh-coloured silk of her princess gown met the transparent lace of the yoke and sleeves.

I trembled for the safety of their attire, for a few damp snowflakes were falling and some of them came to rest on their wavy black hair. But they carried on their childish family prank for only two minutes at most, only long enough to point out to each other, as they leaned laughing over the railing, some incident in the street. Then they pretended to shiver with cold, knocked one or two snowflakes from their clothes, and withdrew into their room, where the light was at once turned on. They were gone, the enchanting phantasmagoria of an instant, vanished never to be seen again. But for a long time I continued to lean against the lamppost, staring up at their balcony, while I tried in imagination to force my way into their existence; and not on that night only but on many following nights, when I lay down on my kitchen bench exhausted from wandering and watching, my dreams were of them.

Dreams of love, dreams of delight and a longing for union — I cannot name them otherwise, though they concerned not a single image but a double creature, a pair fleetingly but profoundly glimpsed, a brother and sister — a representative of my own sex and of the other, the fair one. But the beauty here lay in the duality, in the charming doubleness, and if it seems more than doubtful that the appearance of the youth alone on the balcony would have inflamed me in the slightest, apart perhaps from the pearl in his shirt, I am almost equally sure that the image of the girl alone, without her fraternal complement, would never have lapped my spirit in such sweet dreams. Dreams of love, dreams that I loved precisely because — I firmly believe — they were of primal indivisibility and indeterminateness, double; which really means that only then is there a significant whole blessedly embracing what is beguilingly human in both sexes.

Dreamer and idler! I hear the reader addressing me. Where are your adventures? Do you propose to entertain me throughout your whole book with such fine-spun quiddities, the so-called experiences of your covetous idleness? No doubt, until the policeman drove you away, you pressed your forehead and nose against the big glass panes and peered into the interior of elegant restaurants through the openings in the cream-coloured curtains — stood in the mixed, spicy odours that drifted up from the kitchen through cellar gratings and saw Frankfurt's high society, served by attentive waiters, dining at little tables on which stood shaded candles and candelabra and crystal vases with rare flowers? So I did — and I am astounded at how accurately the reader is able to report the visual joys I purloined from the beau monde, just exactly as though he had had his own nose pressed against that pane. So far as "idleness" is concerned, he will very soon see the inaccuracy of any such description and will, like a gentleman, withdraw it and apologize. Let it be said right now, however, that, divorcing myself from the spectator's role, I sought and found a personal relationship with that world to which I was drawn by nature. I would, to wit, linger around the entrances of the theatres at closing-time and, like an active and obliging lad, make myself useful to the exalted public that streamed chattering out of the lobbies, stimulated by the delights of art. I would do this by hailing droshkies and summoning waiting carriages. I would rush out in front of a droshky to stop it in front of the marquee for my patron, or I would run some distance up the street to catch one and then drive back, sitting beside the coachman. Swinging down like a lackey, I would open the door for the people who were waiting with a bow so perfect as to startle them. To summon the private coupés and coaches, I would inquire in flattering fashion the names of their fortunate owners and I took no small delight in shouting those names and titles down the street in a clear, strong voice — Privy Councillor Streisand! Consul General Ackerbloom! Lieutenant-Colonel von Stralenheim or Adelebsen! And then the horses would drive up. Many names were quite difficult and their owners hesitated to tell them to me, doubtful of my ability to pronounce them. A dignified married couple, for example, with an obviously unmarried daughter, was named Crequis de Mont-en-fleur, and what pleased surprise all three showed at the correctness and elegance with which that name rang out when they finally entrusted it to me, that name compounded, as it were, of sneezes and giggles terminating in a nasal but flowery poesy! It came to the ears of their fairly far-off and aged family coachman like the clarion morning call of chanticleer, so that there was no delay in bringing up the old-fashioned but well-washed carriage and the plump, dun-coloured pair.

Many a welcome coin, often enough a silver one, was slipped into my hand for these services tendered to Society. But more precious to my heart, a dearer, more reassuring reward was mine as well — an intercepted look of astonishment, of attentive kindliness on the part of the world, a glance that measured me with pleased surprise, a smile that dwelt on my person with amazement and curiosity; and so carefully did I treasure up these secret triumphs that I could today report them more easily than almost anything else, however significant and profound.

What a wonderful phenomenon it is, carefully considered, when the human eye, that jewel of organic structures, concentrates its moist brilliance on another human creature! This precious jelly, made up of just such ordinary elements as the rest of creation, affirming, like a precious stone, that the elements count for nothing, but their imaginative and happy combination counts for everything — this bit of slime embedded in a bony hole, destined some day to moulder lifeless in the grave, to dissolve back into watery refuse, is able, so long as the spark of life remains alert there, to throw such beautiful, airy bridges across all the chasms of strangeness that lie between man and man!

Of delicate and subtle matters one should speak delicately and subtly, and so a supplementary observation will be cautiously inserted here. Only at the two opposite poles of human contact, where there are no words or at least no more words, in the glance and in the embrace, is happiness really to be found, for there alone are unconditional freedom, secrecy, and profound ruthlessness. Everything by way of human contact and exchange that lies between is lukewarm and insipid; it is determined, conditioned, and limited by manners and social convention. Here the word is master — that cool, prosaic device, that first begetter of tame, mediocre morality, so essentially alien to the hot, inarticulate realm of nature that one might say every word exists in and for itself and is therefore no better than claptrap. I say this, I, who am engaged in the labour of describing my life and am exerting every conceivable effort to give it a belletristic form. And yet verbal communication is not my element; my truest interest does not lie there. It lies rather in the extreme, silent regions of human intercourse — that one, first of all, where strangeness and social rootlessness still maintain a free, primordial condition and glances meet and marry irresponsibly in dreamlike wantonness; but then, too, the other in which the greatest possible closeness, intimacy, and commingling re-establish completely that wordless primordial condition.

But I am conscious of a look of concern on the reader's face lest as a result of all these tokens of kindliness I may have forgotten, frivolously and completely, the matter of my military obligations, and so I hasten to assure him that this was by no means the case; I had instead kept my eye fixed constantly and uneasily on that fatal question. It is true that after I had reached a decision about handling this unpleasant problem, my uneasiness turned, to a certain extent, into the kind of happy nervousness we feel when we are about to test our abilities in a great, indeed excessive, enterprise and — here I must curb my pen and, out of calculation, resist in some measure the temptation to blurt out everything in advance. For since my intention has steadily strengthened to give this little composition to the press, if I ever get to the end of it, and thus present it to the public, I should be much in the wrong if I did not obey those general rules and maxims professional writers use to maintain interest and tension, against which I should be sinning grossly if I yielded to my inclination to blurt out the best at once and, so to speak, burn up all my powder in advance.

Let just this much be said: I went to work with great thoroughness, with scientific precision, in fact, and took good care not to underestimate the difficulties in my path, for plunging ahead was never my way of undertaking a serious enterprise; instead I have always felt that precisely those actions of extreme daring which are most incredible to the common crowd require the coolest consideration and the most delicate foresight, if their result is not to be defeat, shame, and ridicule — and I have not fared badly. Not content with informing myself exactly as to the methods and practices of the recruiting-office and the nature of the regulations on which it acted (which I accomplished partly through conversations with our machinist boarder who had seen military service, and partly with the help of a general reference work in several volumes which another boarder, hopeful of improving himself, had installed in his room), once my plan was sketched in general outline I saved up one and a half marks from my tips for fetching carriages to buy a publication I had discovered in a bookstore window, a publication of clinical character, in the reading of which I immersed myself with both enthusiasm and profit.

Just as a ship requires ballast, so talent requires knowledge, but it is equally certain that we can really assimilate, indeed have a real right to, only just so much knowledge as our talent demands and hungrily draws to itself in each urgent, individual instance, in order to acquire the requisite substance and solidity. I devoured with the greatest joy the instructive content of that little book, and translated what I had acquired into certain practical exercises carried out by candlelight in front of a mirror in the nightly privacy of my kitchen, exercises that would have looked foolish to a secret observer but with which I was pursuing a clear and reasoned goal. Not a word more about it here! The reader will be compensated shortly for this momentary deprivation.

Before the end of January, in compliance with official regulations, I had reported in writing to the military authorities, enclosing my birth certificate, which was in perfect order, as well as the necessary certificate of good behaviour from the Police Bureau, the reticent and negative form of which (to wit, that concerning my way of life nothing reprehensible was known to the authorities) made me childishly angry and uncomfortable. At the beginning of March, just as twittering birds and sweet breezes were charmingly heralding the advent of spring, I was obliged by statute to present myself at the recruiting-center for an initial interview and, summoned to Wiesbaden, I travelled thither by train, fourth class, in a fairly relaxed state of mind, for I knew that the die could hardly be cast that day and that almost everyone comes up before the final authority, which is known as the Superior Draft Commission on the Fitness and Recruitment of Youth. My expectations proved correct. The episode was brief, hurried, unimportant, and my memories of it have faded. I was measured up and down, tapped and questioned, and received no information in return. Dismissed and, for the time being, free, as though on the end of a long tether, I went for a walk in the splendid parks that adorn the spa, amused myself by training my eye in the fine stores in the casino colonnade, and returned to Frankfurt the same day.

But when two more months had passed (half of May was over and a premature midsummer heat hung over the district), the day arrived when my respite ended, the long tether I spoke of figuratively was hauled in, and I had to present myself for recruitment. My heart beat hard when I found myself seated once more on the narrow bench of a fourth-class compartment in the Wiesbaden train, surrounded by characters of the lower sort, and borne on wings of steam toward the moment of decision. The prevailing closeness lulled my travelling-companions into a nodding doze, but could not be allowed to enervate me; awake and alert I sat there, automatically on guard against leaning back, while I tried to picture the circumstances in which I should have to prove myself, and which, to judge by experience, would turn out to be quite different from any I could prefigure. If my feelings were apprehensive as well as happy, it was not because I had any serious doubts about the outcome. That was quite definite in my mind. I was completely determined to go all the way, yes, even if it proved necessary to put all the latent powers of body and soul into the game (in my opinion, it is silly to undertake any great enterprise without being prepared to do this), and I did not for an instant doubt that I was bound to succeed. What made me apprehensive was simply my being uncertain how much of myself I should have to give, what sort of sacrifice in enthusiasm and energy I should have to make to gain my ends — in other words, a sort of tenderness toward myself which had been part of my character from of old and could quite easily have turned into softness and cowardice had not more manly qualities evened the balance and held it steady.

I can still see before my eyes the low, large room, with wooden beams, into which I was roughly herded by the guard and which I found, on entering, filled with a great crowd of young men. Located on the second floor of a dilapidated and abandoned barracks on the outer edge of the city, this cheerless room offered through four bare windows a view of suburban fields disfigured by all sorts of refuse, tin cans, rubbish, and waste. Seated behind an ordinary kitchen table, papers and writing-materials spread out before him, a harsh-voiced sergeant called out names. Those summoned had to pass through a doorless entry into a passage where they stripped to a state of nature and then entered an adjoining room, the real scene of the examination. The behaviour of the man in charge was brutal and deliberately frightening. Frequently he thrust out his fists and legs, yawning like an animal, or made merry, as he ran through the roster, over the impressive degrees of those who appeared before him, headed for that decisive corridor. "Doctor of philosophy!" he shouted, laughing derisively as though he meant to say: "We'll beat it out of you, my young friend!" All this aroused fear and revulsion in my heart.

The business of conscription was in full swing, but it advanced slowly, and as it proceeded in alphabetical order, those whose names began with letters well along in the alphabet had to resign themselves to a long wait. An oppressive silence hung over the assembly, which consisted of young men from the most varied walks of life. You saw helpless country bumpkins and unruly young representatives of the urban proletariat; semi-refined shop employees and simple sons of toil; there was even a member of the theatrical profession, who aroused much covert merriment by his plump, dark appearance; hollow-eyed youths of uncertain profession, without collars and with cracked patent-leather shoes; mothers' darlings just out of Latin school, and gentlemen of more advanced years with pointed beards, pallid faces, and the cultivated deportment of scholars, pacing through the room, restless and painfully intent, conscious of their undignified position. Three or four of the potential recruits whose names would soon be called stood barefooted near the door, stripped to their undershirts, their clothes over their arms, hat and shoes in their hands. Others were sitting on the narrow benches that ran around the room or, perched on one thigh on the window-sills, were making friends and exchanging subdued comments on one another's physical peculiarities and the vicissitudes of conscription. Once in a while, no one knew how, rumours circulated from the room where the board was sitting that the number of those already accepted for service was very large and so the chances of escaping, for those who had not yet been examined, were improving, rumours no one was in a position to verify. Here and there in the crowd jokes and coarse comments broke out about the men already called up, who had to stand about almost entirely naked, and they were laughed at with increasing openness until the biting voice of the uniformed man at the table restored a respectful silence.

I for my part remained aloof as always, took no part in the idle chatter or the coarse jokes, and replied in chilly and evasive fashion when I was spoken to. Standing at an open window (for the human smell in the room had become distressing), I glanced from the desolate landscape outside to the mixed gathering in the room, and let the hours run by. I should have liked to get a glimpse of the neighbouring room where the commission sat, so as to form an impression of the examining doctor; but this was impossible and I kept emphasizing to myself that nothing depended on that particular individual and that my fate rested not in his hands but in mine alone. Boredom weighed heavily on the spirits of those around me. I, however, did not suffer from it, first because I have always been patient by nature, can endure long periods unoccupied, and love the free time those addicted to mindless activity either squander or obliterate; moreover, I was in no hurry to engage in the daring and difficult feat that awaited me, but was instead grateful for the prolonged leisure in which to collect, accustom, and prepare myself.

Noon was already approaching when names beginning with the letter *K* came to my ears. But, as though fate were bent on teasing me, there were a great many, and the list of Kammachers, Kellermanns, and Kilians, as well as Knolls and Krolls, seemed to have no end, so that when my name was finally pronounced by the man at the table, I set about the prescribed toilet rather unnerved and weary. I can declare, however, that my weariness not only failed to detract from my resolution but actually strengthened it.

For that particular day I had put on one of those starched white shirts my godfather had given me at parting, which until now I had conscientiously saved; I had realized in advance that here one's linen would be of special importance and so I now stood at the entrance to the passage, between two fellows in checked, faded cotton shirts, conscious that I could afford to be seen. To the best of my knowledge, no word of ridicule was directed at me from the room, and even the sergeant at the table looked at me with the sort of respect that underlings, used to being subordinate, never deny to elegance of manner and attire. I was quick to notice how curiously he compared the information on his list with my appearance; indeed, he was so engrossed in this study that for a moment he neglected to call my name again at the appropriate time, and I had to ask him whether I was to step inside. He said yes. I crossed the threshold on bare soles and, alone in the passage, placed my clothes on the bench beside those of my predecessor, put my shoes underneath, and took off my starched shirt as well; I folded it neatly and added it to the rest of my outfit. Then I waited alertly for further instructions.

My feeling of tension was painful, my heart hammered irregularly, and I incline to believe that the blood left my face. But with this agitation there was mixed another, happier feeling, to describe which there are no words readily available. Somewhere or other — perhaps in an aphorism or *aperçu* that I came on while reading in prison or glancing through the daily paper — this notion has come to my attention: that nakedness, the condition in which Nature brought us forth, is levelling and that no sort of injustice or order of precedence can obtain between naked creatures. This statement, which immediately aroused my anger and resistance, may seem flatteringly self-evident to the crowd, but it is not true in the least, and one might almost say by way of correction that the true and actual order of precedence is established only in that original state, and that nakedness can only be called just in so far as it proclaims the naturally unjust constitution of the human race, unjust in that it is aristocratic. I had perceived this long ago, when my godfather Schimmelpreester's artistry had conjured up my likeness on canvas in its higher significance, and on all those other occasions, as in public baths, where men are freed of their accidental trappings and step forth in and for themselves. So, too, from that moment on, I was filled with joy and lively pride that I was to present myself before a high commission not in the misleading garb of a beggar but in my own free form.

The end of the passage adjoining the committee room was open, and although a wooden partition blocked my view of the examination scene, I was able to follow its course very accurately by ear. I heard the words of command with which the staff doctor directed the recruit to bend this way and that, to show himself from all sides, heard the short questions and the answers, rambling accounts of an inflammation of the lung, which obviously failed of their transparent purpose, for they were presently cut short by a declaration of unconditional fitness for service. This verdict was repeated by other voices, further instructions followed, the order to withdraw was given, pattering steps approached, and presently the conscript joined me: a poor specimen, I saw, with a brown streak around his neck, plump shoulders, yellow spots on his upper arms, coarse knees, and big, red feet. In the narrow space I was careful to avoid contact with him. At that moment my name was called in a sharp nasal voice and simultaneously the assisting noncom appeared in front of the cabinet and motioned to me; I stepped out from behind the partition, turned to the left, and strode with dignified but modest bearing to the place where the doctor and the commission awaited me.

At such moments one is blind, and it was only in blurred outline that the scene penetrated to my at once excited and bemused consciousness: obliquely to my right a longish table cut off one corner of the room, and at this the gentlemen sat in a row, some bending forward, some leaning back, some in uniform, some in civilian clothes. To the left of the table stood the doctor, he too very shadowy in my eyes, especially since he had the window at his back. I, however, inwardly repelled by so many importunate glances turned on me, bemused by the dreamlike sensation of being in a highly vulnerable and defenceless position, seemed to myself to be alone, cut off from every relationship, nameless, ageless, floating free and pure in empty space, a sensation I have preserved in memory as not only not disagreeable but actually precious. The fibres of my body might continue to quiver, my pulse go on beating wildly and irregularly; nevertheless, from then on, my spirit, if not sober, was yet completely calm, and what I said and did in the sequel happened as though without my co-operation and in the most natural fashion — indeed, to my own momentary amazement. Here exactly lies the value of long advance preparation and conscientious immersion in what is to come: at the critical moment something somnambulistic occurs, halfway between action and accident, doing and being dealt with, which scarcely requires our attention, all the less so because the demands actuality makes on us are usually lighter than we expected, and we find ourselves, so to speak, in the situation of a man who goes into battle armed to the teeth only to discover that the adroit use of a single weapon is all he needs for victory. To protect himself the more readily in minor contingencies the prudent man practises what is most difficult, and he is happy if he needs only the most delicate and subtle weapons in order to triumph, for he is naturally averse to anything gross and crude and accommodates himself to their use only in cases of necessity.

"That's a one-year man," I heard a deep, benevolent voice say from the commission table, as though in explanation, but immediately thereafter I was disgusted to hear another, that sharp and nasal voice, declare by way of correction that I was only a recruit.

"Step up," said the staff doctor. His voice was a rather weak tremolo. I obeyed with alacrity and, standing close in front of him, I made this statement with an absurd but not unpleasant assurance.

"I am entirely fit for service."

"That's not for you to judge," he broke in angrily, thrusting his head forward and shaking it violently. "Answer what I ask you and refrain from such remarks!"

"Certainly, Surgeon General," I said softly, although I knew very well that he was nothing but a senior staff doctor, and I looked at him with startled eyes. I could now make him out a little better. He was lean of build, and his uniform blouse hung on him in loose folds. His sleeves, their facings reaching almost to the elbows, were so long that half of each hand was covered and only the thin fingers stuck out. A full beard, sparse and narrow, of a neutral dark shade like the wiry hair on his head, lengthened his face, and this effect was the more pronounced because of his hollow cheeks and his habit of letting his lower jaw sag with his mouth half open. A pince-nez in a silver frame that was bent out of shape sat in front of his narrowed, reddened eyelids in such a way that one lens rested awkwardly against the lid while the other stood far out.

This was the external appearance of my partner. He smiled woodenly at my manner of address and glanced out of the corner of his eye at the table where the commission sat.

"Lift your arms. State your position in civil life," he said, and at the same time, like a tailor, put a green tape measure with white figures on it around my chest.

"It is my intention," I replied, "to devote myself to hotel service."

"Hotel service? So, it is your intention. When do you intend to do this?"

"I and mine have reached an understanding that I am to begin this career after I have finished my military service."

"Hm. I did not ask about your people. Who are your people?"

"Professor Schimmelpreester, my godfather, and my mother, the widow of a champagne-manufacturer."

"So, so, the widow of a champagne-manufacturer. And what are you doing at present? Are you nervous? Why are your shoulders jerking and twitching that way?"

I had in fact begun, since I had been standing there, half unconsciously and entirely spontaneously, an oddly contrived twisting of the shoulders, an action by no means obtrusive but recurring frequently, which had somehow seemed appropriate. I replied thoughtfully:

"No. It has never for an instant crossed my mind that I might be nervous."

"Then stop that jerking!"

"Yes, Surgeon General," I said shamefacedly, and yet at the same instant I jerked again, a fact he appeared to overlook.

"I am not the Surgeon General," he bleated at me sharply, and shook his outstretched head so violently that the pince-nez threatened to drop off and he was forced to push it back in place with all five fingers of his right hand, an action that could do nothing to remedy the root of the trouble, the fact that it was bent.

"Then I beg your pardon," I replied very softly and penitently.

"Just answer my question!"

Confused, without comprehension, I looked around me, glanced, too, as though in entreaty at the row of commissioners, in whose deportment I thought I had detected a certain sympathy and interest. Finally I sighed without speaking.

"I have asked about your present occupation."

"I assist my mother," I replied with restrained enthusiasm, "in the operation of a quite large boarding-house or rooming-house in Frankfurt am Main."

"My compliments," he said ironically. "Cough!" he then commanded immediately, for he had placed a black stethoscope against my chest and was bending over to listen to my heart.

I had to cough again and again while he poked about on my body with his instrument. Thereupon he exchanged the stethoscope for a little hammer that he picked up from a nearby table, and he began to tap.

"Have you had any serious illnesses?" he asked.

I replied: "No, colonel! Never serious ones! To the best of my knowledge I am entirely healthy and have always been so, if I may pass over certain insignificant fluctuations in my health, and I feel myself qualified in the highest degree for any form of military service."

"Silence!" he said, suddenly interrupting his auscultation and glancing angrily up into my face from his stooping position. "Leave the question of your military fitness to me and don't make so many irrelevant observations! You continually talk irrelevancies!" he repeated as though distracted, and, interrupting his examination, he straightened up and stepped back from me a little, "Your manner of speech is lacking in restraint. That struck me some time ago. What is your position anyway? What schools have you attended?"

"I went through six grades at high school," I replied softly, feigning distress at having alienated and offended him.

"And why not the seventh?"

I let my head hang and threw him an upward glance that may well have spoken for me and struck the recipient to the heart. "Why do you torment me?" I asked with this look. "Why do you force me to speak? Don't you hear, don't you feel, don't you see that I am a refined and remarkable youth who, beneath an agreeable and conventional exterior, hides deep wounds that life has cruelly inflicted on him? Is it delicate of you to force me to reveal my shame before so many respectable gentlemen?" Thus my glance; and, discriminating reader, it was by no means a lie, even though its piteous plaint at this particular instant was the product of calculation and design. For lies and hypocrisy refer properly to a sensation that is illegitimately produced because its outward expression corresponds to no true and deep experience, a state of affairs that can only result in pathetic, bungling apishness. Should we not, however, be able to command the timely and useful manifestation of our own precious experiences? Briefly, sadly, and reproachfully my glance spoke of early acquaintance with the injustices and misfortunes of life. Then I sighed deeply.

"Answer," said the senior staff doctor in a milder tone.

Struggling with myself, I replied hesitantly: "I was passed over at school and did not complete the course because of a recurrent indisposition that on several occasions confined me to my bed and frequently prevented me from attending class. Also, the teachers thought it their duty to reproach me with lack of attention and diligence, which depressed me very much and disheartened me, since I was not aware of any failure or carelessness in this respect. And yet it so happened that at times a good deal escaped me, I did not hear it or absorb it, whether a classroom exercise was in question or the prescribed homework, whose completion I neglected because I knew nothing about it, not because I entertained other and unsuitable thoughts but because it was exactly as though I had not been present, had not been there in the classroom when the assignments were given out, and this led to reprimands and severe disciplinary measures on the part of the authorities, and on my own part to great — "

Here I could no longer find words, grew confused, fell silent, with my shoulders twitching strangely.

"Stop!" he said. "Do you have trouble hearing? Step farther back there! Repeat what I say." And now with laughable distortion of his thin lips and sparse beard, he began to whisper cautiously: "Nineteen, twenty-seven," and other figures, which I took pains to say after him promptly and exactly; for like all my faculties my hearing was not simply normal but of a special acuity and fineness, and I saw no reason to hide this fact. And so I understood and repeated compound numbers that he only breathed out, and my unusual talent seemed to fascinate him, for he pressed on with the experiment further and further, sending me into the remotest corner of the room in order to hide rather than communicate numbers of four figures at a distance of six or seven yards, and then with pursed mouth he directed significant glances at the commissioners' table when I, half-guessing, understood and repeated what he believed he had barely let slip across his lips.

"Well," he said finally with pretended indifference, "you hear very well. Step up here again and tell us precisely how this indisposition that occasionally kept you from school manifested itself."

Obediently I approached.

"Our family doctor," I replied, "Health Councillor Düsing, used to explain it as a kind of migraine."

"So, you had a family doctor. Health Councillor, was he? And he explained it as migraine! Well, how did it show itself, this migraine? Describe an attack for us. Did you have headaches?"

"Headaches, too!" I replied in surprise, looking at him with respect. "A kind of roaring in both ears and especially a great feeling of distress and fear or rather a timorousness of the whole body, which finally turns into a spasm of choking so violent that it almost hurls me out of bed."

"Spasms of choking?" he said. "Any other spasms?"

"No, certainly no others," I assured him with great earnestness.

"But roaring in the ears."

"A roaring in the ears did certainly often accompany it."

"And when did the attacks occur? Possibly when there had been preceding excitement of some sort? Some specific cause?"

"If I am right," I replied hesitantly and with a questioning glance, "during my school days they often ensued upon just such an incident — that is, a difficulty of the sort I told — "

"When you failed to hear certain things just as though you had not been there?"

"Yes, Surgeon-in-Chief."

"Hm," he said. "And now just think back and tell us carefully whether you noticed any signs that regularly preceded and heralded this condition when it seemed to you that you weren't present. Don't be hesitant. Overcome your natural embarrassment and tell us frankly whether you noticed anything of the sort at such times."

I looked at him, looked him resolutely in the eye for a considerable time, while I nodded my head, heavily, slowly, and as it were in bitter reflection.

"Yes, I often feel strange; strange, alas, was and is very often my state of mind," I finally said softly and reflectively. "Often it seems as though I have suddenly come close to an oven or a fire, so hot do my limbs feel, first my legs, then the upper parts, and this is accompanied by a kind of tickling or prickling that astonishes me, all the more so because at the same time I have before my eyes a play of colour that is really beautiful but that nevertheless terrifies me; and if I may come back to the prickling for a moment, one might describe it as ants running over one."

"Hm. And after this you fail to hear certain things?"

"Yes, that is so, superintendent, sir! There is a great deal I don't understand about my nature, and even at home it has caused me embarrassment, for at times I know I have involuntarily dropped my spoon at the table and stained the tablecloth with soup, and afterward my mother scolds me because I, a full-grown man, behave so boorishly in the presence of our guests — theatrical artists and scholars they are, for the most part."

"So, you drop your spoon? And only notice it a bit later? Tell me, did you ever tell your family doctor, this Health Councillor or whatever that civilian title is, about these little irregularities?"

Softly and dejectedly I replied that I had not.

"And why not?" the other persisted.

"Because I was ashamed," I replied falteringly, "and did not want to tell anyone; it seemed to me that I must keep it secret. And then, too, I hoped secretly that in time it would go away. And I would never have thought I could have enough confidence in anyone to confess to him what very strange experiences I sometimes have."

"Hm," he said, twitching his sparse beard derisively, "because you probably thought they would simply explain it all as migraine. Didn't you say," he went on, "that your father was a distiller?"

"Yes — that is, he owned a sparkling-wine establishment on the Rhine," I said, politely confirming his words and at the same time correcting them.

"Right, a sparkling-wine establishment! And so your father was probably a distinguished connoisseur of wine, was he not?"

"He was indeed, superintendent, sir!" I said happily, while a wave of amusement visibly swept the commission table. "Yes, he was indeed."

"And no hypocrite about himself either, rather a man who loved a good drop, was he not, and, as the saying goes, a mighty drinker before the Lord?"

"My father," I replied evasively, as though withdrawing my levity, "was love of life itself. That much I can agree to."

"So, so, love of life. And what did he die of?"

I was silent. I glanced at him, then bowed my head. And in an altered voice I replied:

"May I most humbly request the battalion surgeon to be so kind as not to insist on an answer?"

"You are not permitted to refuse any information whatsoever!" he replied in a shrill bleat. "What I ask you is asked with deliberation, and your answers are important. In your own interest I warn you to tell us truthfully the manner of your father's death."

"He received a church funeral," I said with heaving breast, and my excitement was too great for me to report things in their proper order.

"I can bring you papers to prove that he was buried from a church, and inquiries will show that a number of officers and Professor Schimmelpreester walked behind the coffin. Spiritual Counsellor Chateau himself said in his funeral oration," I went on with increasing vehemence, "that the gun went off accidentally as my father was examining it, and if his hand shook and he was not completely master of himself, that was because we had been visited by a great calamity."

I said "great calamity" and made use of other extravagant and figurative expressions. "Ruin had knocked at our door with her bony knuckle," I said, beside myself, knocking in the air with my own bent index finger by way of illustration, "for my father had fallen into the toils of evil men, blood-suckers, who cut his throat, and everything was sold and squandered — the glass — harp," I stammered foolishly, and felt myself change colour, for now something altogether astounding was about to happen to me, "the æolian — wheel — " and at that instant this is what occurred.

My face became contorted — but that tells very little. In my opinion, it was contorted in an entirely new and terrifying fashion, such as no human passion could produce, but only a satanic influence and impulse. My features were literally thrust apart in all directions, upward and downward, right and left, only to be violently contracted toward the centre immediately thereafter; a horrible, one-sided grin tore at my left, then at my right cheek, compressing each eye in turn with frightful force while the other became so enormously enlarged that I had the distinct and frightful feeling that the eyeball must pop out — and it could have done so for all of me — let it happen! Whether or not it popped out was hardly the important question, and in any case this was not the moment for tender solicitude about my eye. If, however, so unnatural a play of expression might well have aroused in those present that extreme distaste which we call horror, it was nevertheless only the introduction and prelude to a real witches' Sabbath of face-making, a whole battle of grimaces, fought out during the following seconds on my youthful countenance. To recount in detail the distortions of my features, to describe completely the horrible positions in which mouth, nose, brows, and cheeks — in short, all the muscles of my face — were involved, changing constantly, moreover, so that not a single one of these facial deformities repeated itself — such a description would be far too great an undertaking. Let just this much be said, that the emotional experiences which might correspond to these physiognomical phenomena, the sensations of mindless cheerfulness, blank astonishment, wild lust, inhuman torment, and tooth-grinding rage, simply could not be of this world, but must rather belong to an infernal region where our earthly passions, magnified to monstrous proportions, would find themselves horribly reproduced. But is it not true that those emotions whose expressions we assume really do reproduce themselves in premonitory and shadowy fashion in our souls? Meanwhile, the rest of my body was not still, though I remained standing in one spot. My head lolled and several times it twisted almost entirely around just as if Old Nick were in the act of breaking my neck; my shoulders and arms seemed on the point of being wrenched out of their sockets, my hips were bowed, my knees turned inward, my belly was hollowed, while my ribs seemed to burst the skin over them; my teeth were clamped together; not a single finger but was fantastically bent into a claw. And so, as though stretched on a hellish engine of torture, I remained for perhaps two thirds of a minute.

I was not conscious during this most difficult and consequently lengthy period, at least I was not aware of my surroundings and audience, for to keep them in mind was rendered wholly impossible by the rigours of my condition. Rough shouts reached my ears as though from a great distance without my being able to understand them. Coming to myself on a chair, which the army doctor had hurriedly pushed under me, I choked violently on some stale, warmish tap water which this scholar in uniform had been at pains to pour down my throat. Several of the gentlemen of the commission had sprung up and were bending forward over the green table with expressions of consternation, indignation, and even disgust. Others revealed more sympathetically their amazement at the impressions they had received. I saw one who was holding both fists against his ears; probably through some kind of contagion he had twisted his own face into a grimace; another had two fingers of his right hand pressed against his lips and was blinking his eyelids with extraordinary rapidity. As far as I myself was concerned, I had no sooner looked about me with a restored but naturally shocked expression than I hastened to put an end to a scene that could only appear unseemly to me. I rose from my chair quickly and bewilderedly and took up a military posture beside it, which, to be sure, ill suited my naked human state.

The doctor had stepped back, with the glass still in his hand.

"Have you come to your senses?" he asked with a mixture of anger and sympathy.

"At your service, sir," I replied in a zealous tone.

"And do you retain any recollection of what you have just gone through?"

"I humbly beg your pardon," I replied. "For a moment I was a little distraught."

Short, rather harsh laughter answered me from the commission table. There was repeated murmuring of the word "distraught."

"You certainly didn't seem to be paying very close attention," the doctor said dryly. "Did you come here in a state of excitement? Were you especially anxious about the decision on your fitness for service?"

"I must admit," I replied, "that it would have been a great disappointment to be turned down, and I hardly know how I could have broken such news to my mother. In earlier days she was used to having many members of the officers' corps in her home, and she regards the Army with the greatest admiration. For this reason it is especially important to her for me to be taken into the service, and she not only looks forward to conspicuous advantages in respect of my education but also, and particularly, to a desirable strengthening of my health, which occasionally leaves something to be desired."

He seemed to regard my words with contempt and as worthy of no further consideration.

"Rejected," he said, putting down the glass on the little table where lay the instruments of his profession, the measuring-tape, stethoscope, and little hammer. "The barracks are not a health resort," he snapped at me over his shoulder, turning to the gentlemen at the commission table.

"This individual called up for service," he explained in a thin bleat, "suffers from epileptoid attacks, the so-called equivalents, which are sufficient to negate absolutely his fitness for service. My examination shows that there is obviously a hereditary taint from his alcoholic father, who, after his business failure, ended his life by suicide. The appearance of the so-called aura was unmistakable in the patient's obviously embarrassed descriptions. Furthermore, the feeling of severe distress which, as we heard, at times confined him to bed and which my colleague in civil life" (here a wooden derision appeared once more on his thin lips) "attempted to diagnose as so-called migraine, is to be scientifically designated as a depressed condition following a precedent attack. Especially significant for the nature of the illness is the secrecy the patient observed in regard to his symptoms; for though he is obviously of a communicative character, he kept them secret from everyone, as we heard. It is worth noting that even today there persists in the consciousness of many epileptics something of that mystical, religious attitude which the ancient world adopted toward this nervous disorder. This individual came here in a tense and excited emotional state. Indeed, his exalted way of speaking made me suspicious. Furthermore there were indications of a nervous disorder in the extremely irregular though organically sound beat of his heart and the habitual twitching of the shoulders, which he appeared unable to control. As an especially fascinating symptom I should like to draw your attention to the really astounding hyperacuity of hearing which the patient manifested upon further examination. I have no hesitation in connecting this supernormal sensory sharpness with the rather severe attack we have witnessed, which had perhaps been latent for hours and was instantly precipitated by the excitement I induced in the patient through my unwelcome questions. I recommend to you" — he concluded his clear and learned survey and turned condescendingly to me — "that you put yourself in the hands of a competent doctor. You are rejected."

"Rejected," repeated the sharp, nasal voice that I knew.

Aghast I stood there, not moving from the spot.

"You are exempt from service and may go." These words were spoken, not without some traces of sympathy and kindliness, by that bass voice whose possessor had discriminatingly taken me for a one-year service-man.

Then I rose on tiptoe and said with beseechingly raised brows: "Would it not be possible to try? Is it not conceivable that a soldier's life would improve my health?"

Some of the gentlemen at the commission table laughed so that their shoulders shook, but the doctor remained harsh and truculent.

"I repeat," he said, rudely throwing the words at my feet, "that the barracks are not a health resort. Dismissed!" he bleated.

"Dismissed!" repeated the sharp, nasal voice, and a new name was called. "Latte" it was, if I remember correctly, for it was now the turn of the letter L, and a tramp with shaggy chest appeared on the scene. I, however, bowed and withdrew to the passage. While I put on my clothes the assisting noncom kept me company.

Happy of course and yet serious in mood; wearied by experiences so extreme as hardly to lie within the human range, experiences to which I had yielded myself, acting and being acted upon; still preoccupied in particular by the significant comments the army doctor had made about the esteem formerly attached to the mysterious sickness from which he believed I was suffering, I paid hardly any attention to the intimate chatter of the underling, with his inadequate stripes, watered hair, and waxed moustaches; it was only later that I remembered his simple words.

"Too bad," he said, looking at me, "too bad about you, Krull, or whatever your name is! You're a promising fellow, you might have amounted to something in the Army. One can see right away whether a man is going to get anywhere with us. Too bad about you; you have what it takes, that's certain, you would certainly have made a first-rate soldier. Who knows if you mightn't have made sergeant major if you'd only given in!"

It was only afterward, as I have said, that this confidential speech reached my consciousness. While hurrying wheels bore me homeward, I thought to myself that the fellow might well have been right; yes, when I pictured how admirably, how naturally and convincingly a uniform would have become me, what a satisfying effect my figure would have made in it, I almost regretted that I had had to dismiss on principle this way of attaining a form of existence that would so well become me and a world where a sense for the natural hierarchy is obviously so highly developed.

More mature consideration, however, compelled me to realize that my entering that world would have been a gross mistake and error. I had not, after all, been born under the sign of Mars — at least not in the specific and actual sense! For although martial severity, self-discipline, and danger have been the conspicuous characteristics of my strange life, its primary prerequisite and basis has been freedom, a necessity completely irreconcilable with any kind of commitment to a grossly factual situation. Accordingly, if I lived *like* a soldier, it would have been a silly misapprehension to believe that I should therefore live *as* a soldier; yes, if it is permissible to describe and define intellectually an emotional treasure as noble as freedom, then it may be said that to live like a soldier but not as a soldier, figuratively but not literally, to be allowed in short to live symbolically, spells true freedom.

Franz Kafka (1883–1924)

LIFE: Born into a Jewish family in Prague, he was the eldest of six children, the only surviving son, and the putative heir of his strong-willed father's middle-class interests. The conflict between his desire to please and his need to reject intensified the acute awareness of his own limitations as he tried to make his way in a world that respected his father's accomplishments; but it was not until he fell in love that he was able to confront and accept his own nature. He never married, but he finally left Prague in 1923 for Berlin, where even as he was dying painfully of tuberculosis he lived the happiest months of his life with the brilliant actress Dora Dymant.

WORKS: Most of Kafka's major work was published posthumously: *The Trial* (1925); *The Castle* (1926); *Amerika* (1927).

THE METAMORPHOSIS *

I

As Gregor Samsa awoke one morning from a troubled dream, he found himself changed in his bed to some monstrous kind of vermin.

He lay on his back, which was as hard as armor plate, and, raising his head a little, he could see the arch of his great, brown belly, divided by bowed corrugations. The bedcover was slipping helplessly off the summit of the curve, and Gregor's legs, pitiably thin compared with their former size, fluttered helplessly before his eyes.

"What has happened?" he thought. It was no dream. His room, a real man's room — though rather small — lay quiet within its four familiar walls. Over the table, where a collection of cloth samples was scattered — Samsa was a commercial traveler — hung the picture that he had recently cut from an illustrated paper and had put in a pretty gilded frame. This picture showed a lady sitting very upright, wearing a small fur hat and a fur boa; she offered to the gaze a heavy muff into which her arm was thrust up to the elbow.

* 1916. Translator unknown.

Gregor looked toward the window; rain could be heard falling on the panes; the foggy weather made him sad. "How would it be if I go to sleep again for awhile and forget all this stupidity?" he thought; but it was absolutely impossible, for he was used to sleeping on the right side and in his present plight he could not get into that position. However hard he tried to throw himself violently on his side, he always turned over on his back with a little swinging movement. He tried a hundred times, closing his eyes so that he should not see the trembling of his legs, and he did not give up until he felt in his side a slight but deep pain, never before experienced.

"God!" he thought, "What a job I've chosen. Traveling day in, day out. A much more worrying occupation than working in the office! And apart from business itself, this plague of traveling: the anxieties of changing trains, the irregular, inferior meals, the ever changing faces, never to be seen again, people with whom one has no chance to be friendly. To hell with it all!" He felt a little itch above his stomach and wriggled nearer to the bedpost, dragging himself slowly on his back so that he might more easily raise his head; and he saw, just where he was itching, a few little white points, whose purpose he could not guess at; he tried to scratch the place with one of his feet but he had to draw it back quickly, for the contact made him shudder coldly.

He turned to his former position. He said to himself: "Nothing is more degrading than always to have to rise so early. A man must have his sleep. Other travelers can live like harem women. When I return to the hotel in the morning to enter my orders, I find these gentlemen still at breakfast. I'd like to see what my boss would say if I tried it; I should be sacked immediately. Who knows if that wouldn't be a good thing, after all! If I didn't hold back because of my parents, I would have given notice long ago; I would have gone to the boss and I wouldn't have minced matters. He would have fallen from his desk. That's a funny thing; to sit on a desk so as to speak to one's employees from such a height, especially when one is hard of hearing and people must come close! Still, all hope is not lost; once I have got together the money my parents owe him — that will be in about five or six years — I shall certainly do it. Then I'll take the big step! Meanwhile, I must get up, for my train goes at five."

He looked at the alarm clock which was ticking on the chest. "My God!" he thought; it was half-past six; quarter to seven was not far off. Hadn't the alarm gone? From the bed it could be seen that the little hand was set at four, right enough; the alarm had sounded. But had he been able to sleep calmly through that furniture-shattering din? Calmly, no; his sleep had not been calm; but he had slept only the sounder for that. What should he do now?

The next train went at seven; to catch it he must hurry madly, and his collection of samples was not packed; besides, he himself did not feel at all rested nor inclined to move. And even if he did catch the train, his employer's anger was inevitable, since the firm's errand boy

would have been waiting at the five o'clock train and would have noti-
fied the firm of his lapse. He was just a toady to his boss, a stupid and
servile boy. Supposing Gregor pretended to be ill? But that would be
very tiresome, and suspicious, too, for during the four years he had
been with the firm he had never had the slightest illness. The manager
would come with the Health Insurance doctor; he would reproach his
parents for their son's idleness and would cut short any objections by
giving the doctor's arguments that no people are sick, only idle. And
would he be so far wrong, in such a case? Gregor felt in very good
fettle, apart from his unnecessary need for more sleep after such a
long night; he even had an unusually keen appetite.

Just as he was quickly turning these thoughts over in his mind without being able to decide to leave the bed — while the alarm clock struck
a quarter to seven — he heard a cautious knock on his door, close by
his bed's head.

"Gregor," someone called — it was his mother — "it is a quarter to
seven. Didn't you want to catch the train?"

What a soft voice! Gregor trembled as he heard his own voice reply.
It was unmistakably his former voice, but with it could be heard, as if
from below, a painful whining, which only allowed the words their real
shape for a moment, immediately to confuse their sound so that one
wondered if one had really heard aright. Gregor would have liked to
answer fully and to give an explanation but, in these circumstances, he
contented himself by saying, "Yes, yes, thank you, mother. I am just
getting up." No doubt the door prevented her from judging the change
in Gregor's voice, for the explanation reassured his mother, who went
away, shuffling in her slippers. But because of this little dialogue the
other members of the family had become aware that, contrary to custom,
Gregor was still in the house, and his father started to knock on one
of the side doors, softly, but with his fists.

"Gregor, Gregor," he cried, "what is the matter?" And, after a
moment, in a warning tone, "Gregor! Gregor!"

At the other side door, the young man's sister softly called, "Gregor,
aren't you well? Do you need anything?"

"I am getting ready," said Gregor, answering both sides and forcing
himself to pronounce carefully and to separate each word with a long
pause, to keep a natural voice.

His father went back to breakfast, but the sister still whispered,
"Gregor, open the door, I beg you." But Gregor had no intention of
answering this request; on the contrary, he complimented himself on
having learned the habit of always locking his door, as if in a hotel.

He would get up quietly, without being bothered by anyone; he
would dress, and, above all, he would have breakfast; then would come
the time to reflect, for he felt it was not in bed that a reasonable solution could be found. He recalled how often an unusual position adopted
in bed had resulted in slight pains which proved imaginary as soon as
he arose, and Gregor was curious to see his present hallucination grad-

ually dissolve. As for the change in his voice, his private opinion was that it was the prelude to some serious quinsy, the occupational malady of travelers.

He had no difficulty in turning back the coverlet; he needed only to blow himself up a little, and it fell of its own accord. But beyond that he was impeded by his tremendous girth. To get up, he needed arms and hands; but he had only numerous little legs, in perpetual vibration, over which he had no control. Before he could bend one leg, he first had to stretch it out; and when at last he had performed the desired movement, all the other legs worked uncontrollably, in intensely painful agitation. "I must not stay uselessly in bed," said Gregor to himself.

To get his body out of bed, he first tried moving the hind part. But unfortunately this hind part, which he had not yet seen, and of which he could form no very precise idea, went so slowly it proved to be very difficult to move; he summoned all his strength to throw himself forward but, ill-calculating his course, he hurled himself violently against one of the bedposts, and the searing pain he felt showed that the lower part of his body was without doubt the most sensitive.

He then tried to start with the fore part of his body and cautiously turned his head toward the side of the bed. In this he succeeded quite easily, and the rest of his body, despite its weight and size, followed the direction of his head. But when his head left the bed and was hanging in mid-air, he was afraid to continue any further; if he were to fall in this position, it would be a miracle if he did not crack his head; and this was no moment to lose his senses — better to stay in bed.

But when, panting after his efforts, he again found himself stretched out just as before, when he saw his little legs struggling more wildly than ever, despairing of finding any means of bringing peace and order into this chaotic procedure, he once again realized that he absolutely could not stay in bed and that it was perfectly reasonable to sacrifice everything to the slightest chance of getting out. At the same time he did not forget that cool and wise reflection would be far better than desperate resolutions. Ordinarily, at such moments he turned his eyes to the window to gain encouragement and hope. But this day the fog prevented him from seeing the other side of the street; the window gave him neither confidence nor strength. "Seven o'clock already," he said as he listened once more to the sound of the alarm clock. "Seven o'clock already, and the fog has got no thinner!" He lay back again for a moment, breathing weakly, as though, in the complete silence, he could calmly await the return to his normal self.

Then he said, "Before a quarter past it is absolutely essential for me to be up. In any case, someone will be sent from the office to ask for me before then, for the place opens at seven." And he began to rock on his back in order to get his whole body out of bed in one movement. In this manner he would be able to protect his head by raising it sharply as he fell. His back seemed to be hard; nothing would be risked by falling on it to the floor; his only fear was that the noise of his fall, which must surely resound through the whole house, might arouse terror, or, at the very least, uneasiness. However, that would have to be risked.

When Gregor had half his body out of bed — the new method seemed more like a game than a task, for he had only to swing himself on his back — he began to think how easily he could have got up if only he had had a little assistance. Two strong people — he thought of his father and the servant girl — would have been quite enough; they would have needed only to pass their arms under his round back, raise it from the bed, quickly lean forward with their burden, and then wait carefully till he had completed the operation of settling himself on the ground, where he hoped his feet would at last find a way of working together. But even if the doors had not been closed, would it have been wise for him to call for help? At this idea, despite his misery, he could not repress a smile.

Now he had progressed so far that, by sharply accentuating his swinging movement, he felt he was nearly losing his balance; he would have to take a serious decision, for in five minutes it would be a quarter to eight — but suddenly there was a knock at the front door.

"Someone from the office," he said to himself, and he felt his blood run cold, while his little legs quickened their saraband. For a moment all was quiet.

"They're not going to the door," thought Gregor, in an access of absurd hope. But of course the maid, with a firm tread, went to the door and opened it. Gregor needed to hear only the caller's first words of greeting to know immediately who it was — the manager himself. Why was Gregor, particularly, condemned to work for a firm where the worst was suspected at the slightest inadvertence of the employees? Were the employees, without exception, all scoundrels? Was there among their number not one devoted, faithful servant, who, if it did so happen that by chance he missed a few hours work one morning, might have found himself so numbed with remorse that he just could not leave his bed? Would it not have been enough to send some apprentice to put things right — if, in any case, it was necessary to make inquiries at all — instead of the manager himself having to come, in order to let the whole innocent family know that the clearing-up of so suspicious an affair could only be entrusted to a person of his importance? These thoughts so irritated Gregor that he swung himself out of bed with all his might. This made a loud thud, but not the terrible crash that he had feared. The carpet somewhat softened the blow, and Gregor's back was more elastic than he had thought, and so his act was not accompanied by any din. Only his head had been slightly hurt. Gregor had not raised it enough, and it had been knocked in the fall. He turned over a little to rub it on the carpet, in pain and anger.

"Something fell in there just then," cried the manager, in the room on the left. Gregor tried to imagine his employer's face if such a mishap had occurred to him; for such a thing was possible, he had to admit. But, as if in brutal reply, the manager began pacing up and down in the next room, making his patent-leather boots creak.

And in the other room on the right, Gregor's sister whispered to warn her brother, "Gregor, the manager is here."

"I know," said Gregor to himself, but he dared not raise his voice enough for his sister to hear.

"Gregor," said his father in the room on the left, "the manager has come to find out why you didn't catch the early train. We don't know what to say. He wants to speak to you personally. So please open the door. I'm sure he will be kind enough to excuse the untidiness of your room."

"Good morning, good morning, Mr. Samsa," interrupted the manager, cordial and brisk.

"He is not well," said his mother to the manager, while his father went on shouting through the door. "Believe me, he is not well, sir. How else could Gregor have missed the train? The boy thinks of nothing but his work! It makes me upset to see how he never goes out after supper; do you know he's just spent a whole week here and been at home every evening! He sits down with us at the table and stays there, quietly reading the paper or studying his timetables. His greatest indulgence is to do a little fretwork. Just lately he made a small picture frame. It was finished in two or three evenings, and you'd be surprised how pretty it is; it is hanging up in his room. As soon as Gregor opens his door, you will be able to see it. I am so glad you came, sir, because without you we would never have got Gregor to open his door, he is so obstinate; and surely he must be ill, even though he denied it this morning."

"I am just coming," said Gregor slowly and carefully, but he continued to lie still, so as not to miss a word of the conversation.

"I can offer no other suggestion," declared the manager. "Let us only hope it is nothing serious. However, we businessmen must often — fortunately or not, as you will — get on with our jobs and ignore our little indispositions."

"Well, can the manager come in now?" asked his father impatiently, rapping on the door again.

"No," said Gregor. In the room on the left there was a painful silence; in that on the right the sister began to sob.

Why did she not go to the others? Possibly she had only just got out of bed and was not yet dressed. And why did she weep? Because he did not get up to let the manager in, because he risked losing his position, and because the boss would once more worry his parents about their old debts? These were misplaced troubles! Gregor was still there and had not the slightest intention of letting his family down. At this very moment he was stretched out on the carpet, and nobody seeing him in this state could seriously have demanded that he should let the manager enter his room. But it was not on account of this slight impoliteness — for which in normal times he could easily have made his excuses later — that Gregor would be dismissed. And he thought it would be more reasonable, just now, to leave him alone rather than to upset him with tears and speeches. But it was just this uncertainty which was making the others uneasy and which excused their behavior.

"Herr Samsa," now cried the manager, raising his voice, "what is the matter? You barricade yourself in your room, you don't answer yes or no, you needlessly upset your parents, and you neglect your professional duties in an unheard-of manner. I am speaking in the name of your employer and of your parents, and I beg you seriously to give us a satisfactory explanation immediately. I am astonished, astonished! I took you for a quiet, reasonable young man, and here you suddenly give yourself airs, behaving in an absolutely fantastic manner! The head of the firm, speaking to me this morning in your absence, suggested an explanation which I rejected; he mentioned the samples which were entrusted to you a while ago. I gave him my word of honor that this had nothing to do with the affair, but now that I have been witness to your obstinacy, I can assure you, Herr Samsa, that it deprives me of any wish to defend you. Your job is by no means safe! I had intended to tell you this in private but, since you oblige me to waste my time here for nothing, I see no reason for keeping quiet before your parents. I'd have you know that lately your work has been far from satisfactory; we realize, of course, that the time of the year is not propitious for big business, but you must understand, Herr Samsa, that a period with no business at all should not and can not be tolerated!"

Gregor was beside himself; in his anxiety he forgot everything else. "But, sir," he cried, "I will open the door immediately. I will open it. I felt a little ill; a slight giddiness prevented me from getting up. I am still in bed. But I feel better already. I am just getting up. Only a moment's patience. I am not quite so well as I thought. But I am all right, really. How can it be that illness should take one so quickly? Only yesterday I felt quite well, my parents can tell you; and then last evening I had a slight symptom. They must have noticed it. Why didn't I let them know at the office! But then, one always thinks one will be able to get rid of an illness without staying at home. Please, sir, spare my parents. The complaints you made just now are really without foundation. No one has even suggested them before. Perhaps you have not seen the last orders I sent in. I will leave on the eight o'clock train; these few moments of rest have done me a great deal of good. Please don't stay, sir, I shall be at the office immediately; and please inform the director of what has happened and put in a good word for me."

And while Gregor hastily cried these words, scarcely realizing what he said, he had, with an ease due to his previous exertions, approached the chest of drawers, against which he now tried to raise himself. He wanted to open the door; he wanted to be seen and to speak with the manager. He was curious to know what impression he would make on these people who were so imperiously demanding his presence. If he frightened them, that would be reassuring, for he would stop being cross-questioned and be left in peace. If they took everything quietly then he, too, need not be alarmed. And if he hurried he might still catch the eight o'clock train. The chest was polished, and Gregor slipped on it several times but, by a supreme effort, he managed to get upright. He paid no attention to the pains in his stomach, though they were hurting him. He let himself drop forward onto the top of a near-by chair and clung there with his little legs. Then, finding himself master of his body, he stayed very quiet in order to listen to what the manager had to say.

"Did you understand a word of what he said?" the manager asked the parents. "Is he trying to make fools of us?"

"Good heavens," cried the mother, already in tears. "Perhaps he is seriously ill, and here we are torturing him all this while! Grete! Grete!" she called.

"Mother!" cried the daughter from the other side. They were separated by Gregor's room.

"Fetch a doctor immediately. Gregor is ill. A doctor, quickly! Did you hear him speak?"

"It was an animal's voice," said the manager; after the cries of the women, his voice seemed curiously gentle.

"Anna, Anna!" shouted the father through the hall into the kitchen, clapping his hands. "Get a locksmith, quick!" And already the two young girls — how could his sister have dressed so soon? — ran along the corridor with rustling skirts and opened the front door. No one heard the door close; no doubt it had been left open, as is the custom in houses to which a great misfortune has come.

However, Gregor had become calmer. Doubtless they had not understood his words, though they had seemed clear enough to him, clearer, indeed, than the first time; perhaps his ears were becoming more accustomed to the sounds. But at least they were obliged to realize that his case was not normal, and they were ready, now, to help him. The assurance and resourcefulness with which the first steps had been taken comforted him considerably. He felt himself integrated into human society once again, and, without differentiating between them, he hoped for great and surprising things from the locksmith and the doctor. To clear his throat for the decisive conversation which he would have to hold soon, he coughed a little, but as quietly as possible, for he feared that even his cough might not sound human. Meanwhile, in the next room, it had become quiet. Perhaps his parents were sitting at table in a secret conference with the manager; perhaps everyone was leaning against the door, listening.

Gregor made his way slowly toward it with the chair; then he abandoned the chair and flung himself at the door, holding himself erect against the woodwork — for the bottoms of his feet secreted a sticky substance — and he rested a moment from his efforts. After this, he tried to turn the key in the lock with his mouth. Unfortunately, it seemed he had no proper teeth. How could he take hold of the key?

In compensation, instead of teeth he possessed a pair of very strong mandibles and succeeded in seizing the key in the lock, regardless of the pain this caused him; a brownish liquid flowed out of his mouth, spread over the lock, and dropped to the floor.

"Listen!" said the manager in the next room. "He is just turning the key."

This was valuable encouragement for Gregor; he would have liked his father, his mother, everybody, to start calling to him, "Courage, Gregor, go on, push hard!" And, with the idea that everyone was following his efforts with passionate attention, he clutched the key with all the power of his jaws until he was nearly unconscious. Following the progress of the turning key, he twisted himself around the lock, hanging on by his mouth, and, clinging to the key, pressed it down again, whenever it slipped, with all the weight of his body. The clear click of the lock as it snapped back awoke Gregor from his momentary coma.

"I have dispensed with the locksmith," he thought, and sighed and leaned his head against the handle to open one panel of the double doors completely.

This method, the only possible one, prevented the others from seeing him for some time, even with the door open. Still erect, he had to grope his way round the door with great caution in order not to spoil his entry by falling flat on his back; so he was concentrating toward this end, with all his attention absorbed by the maneuver, when he heard the manager utter a sonorous, "Oh!" such as the roaring of the wind produces, and saw him — he was just by the door — press his hand over his open mouth and slowly stagger back as if some invisible and intensely powerful force were driving him from the spot. His mother — who, despite the presence of the manager, was standing by with her hair in curlers, still disordered by sleep — began to look at the father, clasping her hands; then she made two steps toward Gregor and fell backward into the family circle in the midst of a confusion of skirts which spread around her, while her face, falling on her breast, was concealed from sight. The father clenched his fists with a menacing air, as if to beat Gregor back into his room; then he looked around the dining room in perplexity, covered his eyes with his hand, and wept with great sobs which shook his powerful chest.

Gregor did not enter the room; he stood against the closed half of the double doors, allowing only a part of his body to be seen, while, above, he turned his head to one side to see what would happen. Meanwhile, it had grown much lighter; on either side of the street a part of the long, dark building opposite could clearly be seen — it was a hospital, with regular windows startlingly pitting its façade; it was still raining, but in great separate drops which fell to the ground, one by one. The breakfast crockery was spread all over the table, for breakfast was the most important meal of the day for Gregor's father; he would prolong it for hours while he read various newspapers. On the wall hung a photograph of Gregor in lieutenant's uniform, taken while he was in military service; he was smiling; his hand lay on the hilt of his sword. By his expression, he seemed happy to be alive; by his gesture, he appeared to command respect for his rank. The living-room door was ajar, and, as the front door was also open, the balcony and the first steps of the stairway could just be seen.

"Now," said Gregor, and he realized that he was the only one to have kept calm, "now I will get dressed, collect my samples, and go. Will you, will you let me go? Surely you can now see, sir, that I am not obstinate, that I do mean to work; commercial traveling is tiresome, I admit, but without it I cannot live. Where are you going, sir? To the office? Yes? Will you give them a faithful account of what has happened? After all, anyone might find for a moment that they were incapable of resuming their work, but that's just a good opportunity to review the work they have been doing, and to bear in mind that, once the obstacle is removed, they will be able to return with twice the heart. I owe so much to the director, as you know very well. I have my parents and my sister to consider. I am in an awkward position, but I shall return to work. Only, please do not make things more difficult for me; they are hard enough as it is. Take my part at the office. I know only too well they don't like travelers. They think we earn our money too easily, that we lead too grand a life. I realize that the present situation doesn't encourage the removal of this prejudice; but you, sir, the manager, can judge the circumstances better than the rest of the staff, better than the director himself — though this is between ourselves — for in his executive capacity he is often easily misled by an employee's prejudice. You know quite well that the traveler, who is hardly ever in the office the whole year round, is often the victim of scandal, of a chance, undeserved complaint against which he is powerless to defend himself, for he does not even know that he is being accused; he only learns of it as he returns, exhausted, at the end of his trip, when the sad consequences of an affair, whose circumstances he can no longer recall, painfully confront him. Please, sir, don't leave me without a word to show that you think all this at least a little reasonable."

But, at Gregor's first words, the manager had turned away and only glanced back, with snarling lips, over his trembling shoulder. During Gregor's speech, he had not stood still for a moment; instead, he had retreated furtively, step by step, toward the door — always keeping Gregor in sight — as if some secret law forbade him to leave the room. He had already reached the hall and, as he took the very last step out of the living room, one would have thought the floor was burning his shoes, so sharply did he spring. Then he stretched his hand toward the balustrade, as if some unearthly deliverance awaited him at the foot of the stairs.

Gregor realized that, if he were to keep his job, on no account must the manager be allowed to leave in this condition. Unfortunately, his parents did not realize the position very clearly; they had for so long held the idea that Gregor was settled in the firm for life and were so taken up with their present troubles that they had little thought for such a contingency. But Gregor had more foresight. The manager must be stopped, calmed, convinced, and finally won over. The future of Gregor and of his family depended on it! If only his sister were there! She had understood, she had actually begun to weep while Gregor still lay quietly on his back. And the manager, who liked women, would have listened to her; he would have let himself be guided by her; she would have closed the door and would have proved to him, in the hall, how unreasonable his terror was. But she was not there; Gregor himself must manage this affair. And without even considering whether he would ever be able to return to work, nor whether his speech had been understood, he let go of the doorpost to glide through the opening and overtake the manager (who was clutching the balustrade with both hands in a ridiculous manner), vainly sought for a foothold, and, uttering a cry, he fell, with his frail little legs crumpled beneath him.

Suddenly, for the first time that whole morning, he experienced a feeling of physical well-being; his feet were on firm ground; he noticed with joy that his legs obeyed him wonderfully and were even eager to carry him wherever he might wish. But while, under the nervous influence of his need for haste, he hesitated on the spot, not far from his mother, he saw her suddenly jump, fainting though she seemed to be, and throw her arms about with outspread fingers, crying, "Help, for God's sake, help!" She turned her head, the better to see Gregor; then, in flagrant contradiction, she began to retreat madly, having forgotten that behind her stood the table, still laden with breakfast things. She staggered against it and sat down suddenly, like one distraught, regardless of the fact that, at her elbow, the overturned coffeepot was making a pool of coffee on the carpet.

"Mother, mother," whispered Gregor, looking up at her. The manager had quite gone out of his mind. Seeing the coffee spilling, Gregor could not prevent himself from snapping his jaws several times in the air, as if he were eating. Thereupon his mother again began to shriek and quickly jumped up from the table and fell into the arms of the father, who had rushed up behind her. But Gregor had no time to bother about them. The manager was already on the stairs; with his chin on the balustrade, he was looking back for the last time.

Gregor summoned all his courage to try to bring him back; the manager must have suspected something of the sort, for he leaped several steps at a single bound and disappeared with a cry of "Huh!" which resounded in the hollow of the stair well. This flight had the unfortunate effect of causing Gregor's father — who till now had remained master of himself — to lose his head completely; instead of running after the manager, or at least not interfering with Gregor in his pursuit, he seized in his right hand the manager's walking stick, which had been left behind on a chair with his overcoat and hat, took up in his left a newspaper from the table, and began stamping his feet and brandishing the newspaper and the cane to drive Gregor back into his room. Gregor's prayers were unavailing, were not even understood; he had turned to his father a supplicating head, but, meek though he showed himself, his father merely stamped all the louder. In the dining room, despite the cold, the mother had opened the window wide and was leaning out as far as possible, pressing her face in her hands. A great rush of air swept the space between the room and the stairway; the curtains billowed, the papers rustled, and a few sheets flew over the carpet. But the father pursued Gregor pitilessly, whistling and whooping like a savage, and Gregor, who was not used to walking backward, progressed but slowly.

Had he been able to turn around, he could have reached his room quickly, but he feared to make his father impatient by the slowness of his turning and feared also that at any moment he might receive a mortal blow on his head or on his back from this menacing stick. Soon Gregor had no choice; for he realized with terror that when he was going backward he was not master of his direction and, still fearfully watching the attitude of his father out of the corner of his eye, he began his turning movement as quickly as possible, which was really only very slowly. Perhaps his father realized his good intention for, instead of hindering this move, he guided him from a little distance away, helping Gregor with the tip of the stick. If only he had left off that insupportable whistling! Gregor was completely losing his head. He had nearly completed his turn when, bewildered by the din, he mistook his direction and began to go back to his former position. When at last, to his great joy, he found himself facing the half-opened double doors, he discovered that his body was too big to pass through without hurt. Naturally, it never occurred to his father, in his present state, to open the other half of the double doors in order to allow Gregor to pass. He was dominated by the one fixed idea that Gregor should be made to return to his room as quickly as possible. He would never have entertained the long-winded performance which Gregor would have needed to rear up and pass inside. Gregor heard him storming behind him, no doubt to urge him through as though there were no obstacle in his path; the hubbub no longer sounded like the voice of one single father. Now was no time to play, and Gregor — come what may — hurled himself into the doorway. There he lay, jammed in a slanting position, his body raised up on one side and his flank crushed by the door jamb, whose white paint was now covered with horrible brown stains. He was caught fast and could not free himself unaided; on one side his little legs fluttered in the air, on the other they were painfully pressed under his body; then his father gave him a tremendous blow from behind with the stick. Despite the pain, this was almost a relief; he was lifted bodily into the middle of the room and fell, bleeding thickly. The door was slammed by a thrust of the stick, and then, at last, all was still.

II

It was dusk when Gregor awoke from his heavy, deathlike sleep. Even had he not been disturbed, he would doubtless soon have awakened, for he felt he had had his fill of rest and sleep; however, he seemed to have been awakened by the cautious, furtive noise of a key turning in the lock of the hall door. The reflection of the electric tramway lay dimly here and there about the ceiling and on the upper parts of the furniture, but below, where Gregor was, it was dark. Slowly he dragged himself toward the door to ascertain what had happened and fumbled around clumsily with his feelers, whose use he was at last learning to appreciate. His left side seemed to him to be one long, irritating scar, and he limped about on his double set of legs. One of his legs had been seriously injured during the morning's events — it was a miracle that only one should be hurt — and it dragged lifelessly behind.

When he reached the door, he realized what had attracted him: the smell of food. For there was a bowl of sweetened milk in which floated little pieces of bread. He could have laughed with delight, his appetite had grown so since morning; he thrust his head up to the eyes in the milk. But he drew it back quickly; his painful left side gave him some difficulty, for he could only eat by convulsing his whole body and snorting; also, he could not bear the smell of milk, which once had been his favorite drink and which his sister had no doubt prepared for this special reason. He turned from the bowl in disgust and dragged himself to the middle of the room.

The gas was lit in the dining room; he could see it through the cracks of the door. Now was the time when, ordinarily, his father would read aloud to his family from the evening paper, but this time Gregor heard nothing. Perhaps this traditional reading, which his sister always retailed to him in her conversation and in her letters, had not lapsed entirely from the customs of the household. But everywhere was still, and yet surely someone was in the room.

"What a quiet life my family has led," thought Gregor, staring before him in the darkness, and he felt very proud, for it was to him that his parents and his sister owed so placid a life in so nice a flat. What would happen now, if this peace, this satisfaction, this well-being should end in terror and disaster? In order to dissipate such gloomy thoughts, Gregor began to take a little exercise and crawled back and forth over the floor.

Once during the evening he saw the door on the left open slightly, and once it was the door on the right; someone had wished to enter but had found the task too risky. Gregor resolved to stop by the dining-room door and to entice the hesitant visitor as best he might or at least to see who it was; but the door never opened again, and Gregor waited in vain. That morning, when the door had been locked, everyone had tried to invade his room; but now that they had succeeded in opening it no one came to see him; they had even locked his doors on the outside.

Not till late was the light extinguished, and Gregor could guess that his parents and his sister had been waiting till then, for he heard them all go off on tiptoe. Now no one would come to him till the morning, and so he would have the necessary time to reflect on the ordering of his new life; but his great room, in which he was obliged to remain flat on his stomach on the floor, frightened him in a way that he could not understand — for he had lived in it for the past five years — and, with a half-involuntary action of which he was a little ashamed, he hastily slid under the couch; he soon found that here his back was a little crushed and he could not raise his head; he only regretted that his body was too large to go entirely under the couch.

He spent the whole night there, sometimes in a half-sleep from which the pangs of hunger would wake him with a start, sometimes ruminating on his misfortune and his vague hopes, always concluding that his duty was to remain docile and to try to make things bearable for his family, whatever unpleasantness the situation might impose upon them.

Early in the morning he had a chance to test the strength of his new resolutions; it was still almost dark; his sister, already half dressed, opened the hall door and looked in curiously. She did not see Gregor at once but when she perceived him under the sofa — "Heavens, he must be somewhere; he can't have flown away!" — she was overcome by an unmanageable terror and rushed off, slamming the door. Then, repenting her gesture, she opened it again and entered on tiptoe, as if it were the room of a stranger or one seriously ill. Gregor stretched his head out from the side of the sofa and watched her. Would she notice that he had left the milk, and not from lack of appetite? Would she bring him something which suited his taste better? If she did not do so of her own accord, he would rather have died of hunger than draw her attention to these things, despite his overwhelming desire to rush out of his hiding place, to throw himself at his sister's feet, and to beg for something to eat. But suddenly the sister saw the full bowl in astonishment. A little milk had been spilled around it; using a piece of paper, she took up the bowl without touching it and carried it off to the kitchen. Gregor waited anxiously to see what she would bring him in its place and racked his brains to guess. But he had never realized to what lengths his sister's kindness would go. In order to discover her brother's likes, she brought a whole choice of eatables spread on an old newspaper. There were half-rotted stumps of vegetables, the bones of yesterday's dinner covered with a thick white sauce, a few currants and raisins, some almonds, some cheese that Gregor, a few days before, had declared uneatable, a stale loaf, a piece of salted bread and butter, and another without salt. Besides this she brought back the bowl which had become so important to Gregor. This time it was filled with water, and, guessing that her brother would not like to eat before her, she very kindly retired, closing and locking the door to show him that he might eat in peace. Now that his meal was ready, Gregor felt all his legs trembling. His wounds seemed cured, for he felt not the slightest hindrance, and he was astonished to remember that when he had been human and had cut his finger slightly only a few months ago, it had pained him for several days after.

"Have I become less sensitive?" he wondered; but already he had begun sucking at the cheese, which had suddenly and imperiously attracted him above all the other food. Gluttonously he swallowed in turn the cheese, the vegetables, and the sauce, his eyes moist with satisfaction; as to the fresh things, he wanted none of them; their smell repelled him, and, in order to eat, he separated them from the others.

When he had finished and was idly making up his mind to return to his place, his sister slowly began to turn the key in the lock to give him the signal for retreat. He was very frightened, though he was half asleep, and hurried to reach the sofa. It needed great determination to remain beneath it during the time, however short, that his sister was in the room; his heavy meal had so swollen his body that he could scarcely breathe in his retreat. Between two fits of suffocation he saw, with his eyes filled with tears, that his sister, intending no harm, was sweeping up the remains of his meal with the very things that he had not touched, as if he needed them no more; she put the refuse into a bucket, which she covered with a wooden lid and hastily carried away. Hardly had she turned the handle before Gregor struggled out from his hiding place to expand his body to its proper size.

So he was fed each day; in the morning, before his parents and the maid were awake, and in the afternoon, when lunch was over and while his parents were taking their nap and the maid had been provided with some task or other by his sister. Certainly they did not wish Gregor to die of hunger but perhaps they preferred to know nothing about his meals except by hearsay — they could not have borne to see him — perhaps, also, in order to diminish their disgust, his sister was taking pains to spare them the slightest trouble. He must realize that they, too, had their share of misfortune.

Gregor never learned what excuses they had made to rid themselves of the doctor and the locksmith, for, as no one attempted to understand him, no one, not even his sister, imagined that he could understand them. He had to be content, when she came into his room, to listen to her invoking the saints between her sighs. It was only much later, when Grete had become somewhat accustomed to the new situation — to which she never really became reconciled — that Gregor would occasionally overhear an expression which showed some kindness or allowed him to guess at such a meaning. When he had eaten all the food off the newspaper she would say, "He liked what I brought today"; at other times, when he had no appetite — and lately this had become more frequent — she would say, almost sadly, "Now he has left it all."

But even if he could learn no news directly, Gregor overheard a good deal of what was said in the dining room; as soon as he heard anyone speak, he would hurry to the most propitious door and press his whole body close against it. At first, especially, there was little conversation which did not bear more or less directly on his predicament. For two whole days, the mealtimes were given over to deliberating on the new attitude which must be maintained toward Gregor; even between meals they spoke mostly on the same theme, for now at least two members of the household always remained at home, each one fearing to remain alone and, particularly, to leave Gregor unwatched.

It was not very clear how much the maid knew of what had happened, but, on the very first day, she had fallen on her knees and begged his mother to let her go; and a quarter of an hour later she had left the house in tearful gratitude, as if her release were the greatest evidence of the kindness she had met with in the house; and of her own accord she took a long and boring oath never to reveal the secret to anyone. Now his sister and his mother had to look after the cooking; this entailed little trouble, for the appetite of the Samsa family had gone. Occasionally Gregor would hear one member of the family vainly exhorting another to eat. The reply was always the same: "Thank you, I have had enough," or some such phrase. Perhaps, also, they did not drink. Often his sister would ask her father if he would like some beer; she would cheerfully offer to fetch it, or, faced with her father's silence, she would say, to remove any scruples on his part, that the landlady could go for it, but her father would always reply with a loud, "No!" and nothing more would be said.

In the course of the very first day, the father had clearly explained their precise financial situation to his wife and daughter. From time to time he would get up from the table and hunt for some paper or account book in his Wertheim safe, which he had saved from the crash when his business had failed five years before. He could be heard opening the complicated locks of the safe and closing it again after he had taken out what he sought. Ever since he became a prisoner, nothing had given Gregor such pleasure as these financial explanations. He had always imagined that his father had been unable to save a penny from the ruins of his business; in any case, his father had never said anything to undeceive him, and Gregor had never questioned him upon the matter; he had done all he could to help his family to forget as quickly as possible the disaster which had plunged them into such despair.

He had set to work with splendid ardor; in less than no time, from being a junior clerk he had been promoted to the position of traveler, with all the benefits of such a post; and his successes were suddenly transformed into hard cash which could be spread on the table before the surprised and delighted eyes of his family. Those were happy times —they had never since recovered such a sense of delight, though Gregor now earned enough to feed the whole Samsa family. Everyone had grown accustomed to it, his family as much as himself; they took the money gratefully, he gave it willingly, but the act was accompanied by no remarkable effusiveness. Only his sister had remained particularly affectionate toward Gregor, and it was his secret plan to have her enter the conservatory next year regardless of the considerable cost of such an enterprise, which he would try to meet in some way; for, unlike him, Grete was very fond of music and wished to take up the study of the violin. This matter of the conservatory recurred often in the brief conversations between Gregor and his sister, whenever Gregor had a few days to spend with his family; they hardly ever spoke of it except as a dream impossible to realize; his parents did not much like the innocent allusions to the subject, but Gregor thought very seriously of it and had promised himself that he would solemnly announce his plan next Christmas Eve.

It was ideas of this kind, ideas completely unsuited to his present situation, which now passed constantly through Gregor's mind while he held himself pressed erect against the door, listening. He would get so tired that he could no longer hear anything; then he would let himself go and allow his head to fall against the door; but he would draw it back immediately, for the slightest noise was noticed in the dining room and would be followed by an interval of silence.

"What can he be doing now?" his father would say after a moment's pause, turning, no doubt, toward the door; the interrupted conversation would only gradually be resumed.

His father was often obliged to repeat his explanations in order to recall forgotten details or to make them understood by his wife, who did not always grasp them the first time. Gregor thus learned, by what the father said, that, despite all their misfortunes, his parents had been able to save a certain amount from their former property — little enough, it is true, but it had been augmented, to some extent, by interest. Also, they had not spent all the money that Gregor, keeping only a few shillings for himself, had handed over to his family each week, enabling them to gather together a little capital. Behind his door, Gregor nodded his head in approval; he was so happy at this unexpected foresight and thrift. Doubtless, with these savings his father could have more rapidly paid off the debt he had contracted to Gregor's employer, which would have brought nearer the date of Gregor's release; but under the circumstances it was much better that his father had acted as he had.

Unfortunately this money was not quite sufficient to enable the family to live on its interest; it would last a year, perhaps two, but no more. It was a sum which must not be touched, which must be kept for a case of urgent necessity. As for money on which to live, that would have to be earned. Now, despite his good health, the father was nevertheless an old man who had ceased to work five years before and who could not be expected to entertain any foolish hopes of getting employment; during these five years of retirement — his first holiday in a life entirely devoted to work and unsuccess — he had become very fat and moved with great difficulty. And the old mother would not be able to earn much, suffering as she did from asthma, for even now it was an effort for her to get about the house; she passed a good deal of her time each day lying on the sofa, panting and wheezing under the open window. And was the breadwinner to be the sister, who was still but a child, seventeen years old, so suited to the life she had led till then, nicely dressed, getting plenty of sleep, helping in the house, taking part in a few harmless little entertainments, and playing her violin? Whenever the conversation fell on this topic, Gregor left the door and lay on the leather sofa, whose coolness was so soothing to his body, burning as it was with anxiety and shame.

Often he lay all night, sleepless, and hearing no sound for hours on end save the creak of the leather as he turned. Or, uncomplainingly, he would push his armchair toward the window, crawl up on it, and, propped on the seat, he would lean against the window, not so much to enjoy the view as to recall the sense of release he once used to feel whenever he looked across the pavements; for now he was daily becoming more shortsighted, he could not even make out the hospital opposite, which he had cursed when he was human because he could see it all too clearly; and had he not known so well that he was living in Charlottenstrasse, a quiet but entirely urban street, he might have thought his window gave out on a desert, where the gray of the sky and the gray of the earth merged indistinguishably together. His attentive sister had only to see the armchair by the window twice to understand; from then on, each time she tidied the room she would push the armchair to the window, and would always leave its lower half open.

If only Gregor had been able to speak to his sister, to thank her for all she was doing for him, he could have borne her services easier; but as it was, they pained and embarrassed him. Grete naturally tried to hide any appearance of blame or trouble regarding the situation, and as time went on she played her part even better, but she could not prevent her brother from realizing his predicament more and more clearly. Each time she entered his room, it was terrible for Gregor. Hardly had she entered, when, despite the pains she always took to spare the others the sight of its interior, she would not even take time to shut the door but would run to the window, open it hastily with a single push, as if to escape imminent suffocation, and would stand there for a minute, however cold it might be, breathing deeply. Twice a day she terrified Gregor with this rush and clatter; he shrank trembling under the couch the whole time; he knew his sister would have spared him this had she been able to stand being in the room with him with the window shut.

One day — it must have been a month after Gregor's change, and his sister had no grounds for astonishment at his appearance — she came a little earlier than usual and found him looking out of the window, motionless and in such a position as to inspire terror. If she had not liked to enter, that would not have surprised Gregor, for his position prevented her from opening the window. But not only would she not enter; she sprang back, slammed the door, and locked it; a stranger might have thought that Gregor was lying in wait for his sister, to attack her. Naturally he hid himself under the couch immediately, but he had to wait till midday for Grete's return, and, when she did come, she appeared unusually troubled. He realized that his appearance was still disgusting to the poor girl, that it would always be so, and that she must fiercely resist her own impulse to flee the moment she caught sight of the tiniest part of Gregor's body protruding from under the sofa. To spare her this sight, he took a sheet on his back, dragged it to the sofa — a task which occupied some hours — and spread it in such a way that his sister could see nothing under the sofa, even if she stooped. Had she found this precaution unnecessary, she would have taken the sheet away, for she guessed that Gregor did not so completely shut himself away for pleasure; but she left the sheet where it lay, and Gregor, prudently parting the curtain with his head to see what impression this new arrangement had made upon his sister, thought he detected a look of gratitude in her face.

During the first fortnight his parents had not been able to bring themselves to enter his room, and he often heard them praising the zeal of his sister, whom they had regarded, so far, as a useless young girl and of whom they had often complained. But now, both his father and mother would wait quite frequently outside Gregor's door while his sister was tidying the room, and scarcely had she come out again before they would make her tell them in detail exactly how she had found the room, what Gregor had eaten, and, in detail, what he was doing at that moment; they would ask her, too, if there were the slightest signs of improvement. His mother seemed impatient to see Gregor, but the father and sister restrained her with argument to which she listened very attentively and with which she wholly agreed. Later, however, they had to use force, and when his mother began to cry, "Let me go to Gregor! My poor boy! Don't you understand that I must see him!" Gregor thought that perhaps it would be as well if his mother did come in, not every day, of course, but perhaps once a week; she would understand things better than his sister, who was but a child, for all her courage, and had perhaps taken on such a difficult task out of childish lightheartedness.

Gregor's wish to see his mother was soon realized. Gregor avoided showing himself at the window during the day, out of consideration to his parents; but his restricted walks around the floor did not fully compensate him for this self-denial, nor could he bear to lie still for long, even during the night; he took no more pleasure in eating, and it soon became his habit to distract himself by walking — around the room, back and forth along the walls, and across the ceiling, on which he would hang; it was quite a different matter from walking across the floor. His breathing became freer, a light, swinging motion went through his body, and he felt so elated that now and then, to his own surprise, he would let himself go and fall to the floor. But by now, knowing better how to manage his body, he succeeded in rendering these falls harmless. His sister soon noticed his new pastime, for he left sticky marks here and there in his track, and Grete took it into her head to help him in his walks by removing all the furniture likely to be a hindrance, particularly the chest and the desk. Unfortunately, she was not strong enough to manage this on her own and dared not ask the help of her father; as for the maid, she certainly would have refused, for if this sixteen-year-old child had worked bravely since the former cook had left, it was on condition that she could stay continually barricaded in the kitchen, whose doors she would only open on special demand. So there was nothing else for it; Grete would have to enlist the mother's help one day when the father was away.

The mother gladly consented, but her exclamations of joy were hushed before Gregor's door. The sister first made sure that everything was in order in the room; then she allowed the mother to enter. In his great haste, Gregor had pulled the sheet down further than usual, and the many folds in which it fell gave the scene the air of a still life. This time he refrained from peeping under the sheet to spy on his mother but he was delighted to have her near.

"You may come in; he is not in sight," said his sister; and, taking her mother by the hand, she led her into the room. Then Gregor heard the two frail women struggling to remove the heavy old chest; the sister undertook the hardest part of the task, despite the warnings of her mother, who feared she might do herself some harm. It took a long time. They had been struggling with the chest for four hours when the mother declared that it might be best to leave it where it was, that it was too heavy for them, that they would not finish moving it before the father returned, and that, with the chest in the middle of the room, Gregor would be considerably impeded in his movements, and, finally, who knew whether he might not be displeased by the removal of his furniture?

The mother thought he would be; the sight of the bare walls struck cold at her heart; might Gregor not feel the same, having long grown so accustomed to the furniture, and would he not feel forsaken in his empty room? "Isn't it a fact," said the mother in a low voice — she had spoken in whispers ever since she entered the room, so that Gregor whose hiding place she had not yet discovered, might not overhear, not so much what she was saying — for she was persuaded that he could not understand — but the very sound of her voice. "Isn't it a fact that when we remove the furniture, we seem to imply that we are giving up all hope of seeing him cured and are wickedly leaving him to his fate? I think it would be better to keep the room just as it was before, so that Gregor will find nothing changed when he comes back to us and will be able the more easily to forget what has happened meanwhile."

Hearing his mother's words, Gregor realized how these two monotonous months, in the course of which nobody had addressed a word to him, must have affected his mind; he could not otherwise explain his desire for an empty room. Did he really wish to allow this warm, comfortable room with its genial furniture to be transformed into a cavern in which, in rapid and complete forgetfulness of his human past, he might exercise his right to crawl all over the walls? It seemed he was already so near to forgetting; and it had required nothing less than his mother's voice, which he had not heard for so long, to rouse him. Nothing should be removed, everything must stay as it is, he could not bear to forego the good influence of his furniture, and, if it prevented him from indulging his crazy impulses, then so much the better.

Unfortunately, his sister was not of this opinion; she had become accustomed to assume authority over her parents where Gregor was concerned — this was not without cause — and now the mother's remarks were enough to make her decide to remove not only the desk and the chest — which till now had been their only aim — but all the other furniture as well, except the indispensable sofa. This was not the result of mere childish bravado, nor the outcome of that new feeling of self-confidence which she had just acquired so unexpectedly and painfully. No, she really believed that Gregor had need of plenty of room for exercise and that, as far as she could see, he never used the furniture. Perhaps, also, the romantic character of girls of her age was partly responsible for her decision, a sentiment which strove to satisfy itself on every possible occasion and which now drove her to dramatize her brother's situation to such an extent so that she could devote herself to Gregor even more passionately than hitherto; for in a room over whose bare walls Gregor reigned alone, no one but Grete dare enter and stay.

She did not allow herself to be turned from her resolve by her mother, made irresolute by the oppressive atmosphere of the room, and who did not hesitate now to remove the chest as best she could. Gregor could bear to see the chest removed, at a pinch, but the desk must stay. And hardly had the women left the room, panting as they pushed the chest, than Gregor put out his head to examine the possibilities of making a prudent and tactful appearance. But unfortunately it was his mother who returned first, while Grete, in the side room, her arms around the chest, was rocking it from side to side without being able to settle it in position. The mother was not used to the sight of Gregor; it might give her a serious shock. Terrified, he hastened to retreat to the other end of the sofa, but he could not prevent the sheet from fluttering slightly, which immediately attracted his mother's attention. She stopped short, stood stockstill for a moment, then hurried back to Grete.

Gregor assured himself that nothing extraordinary was happening — they were merely removing a few pieces of furniture — but the coming and going of the women, their little cries, the scraping of the furniture over the floor, seemed to combine in such an excruciating din that, however much he withdrew his head, contracted his legs, and pressed himself to the ground, he had to admit that he could not bear this torture much longer. They were emptying his room, taking away from him all that he loved; they had already removed the chest in which he kept his saw and his fretwork outfit; now they were shifting his desk, which had stood so solid and fast to the floor all the time it was in use, that desk on which he had written his lessons while he was at the commercial school, at the secondary school, even at the preparatory school. However, he could no longer keep pace with their intentions, for so absent minded had he become he had almost forgotten their existence, now that fatigue had quietened them and the clatter of their weary feet could no longer be heard.

So he came out — the women were only leaning against the desk in the next room, recovering their breath — and he found himself so bewildered that he changed his direction four times; he really could not decide what he should first salvage — when suddenly he caught sight of the picture of the woman in furs which assumed tremendous importance on the bare wall; he hastily climbed up and pressed himself against the glass, which stuck to his burning belly and refreshed him delightfully. This picture, at least, which Gregor entirely covered, should not be snatched away from him by anyone. He turned his head toward the dining-room door to observe the women as they returned.

They had had but a short rest and were already coming back; Grete's arm was round her mother's waist, supporting her.

"Well, what shall we take now?" said Grete, and she looked around. Her eyes met those of Gregor on the wall. If she succeeded in keeping her presence of mind, it was only for her mother's sake, toward whom she leaned her head to prevent her from seeing anything and said, a little too quickly and with a trembling voice, "Come, wouldn't it be better to go back to the living room for a minute?" The girl's intention was clear to Gregor: she wished to put her mother in a safe place and then to drive him from the wall. Well, let her try! He lay over his picture, and he would not let it go. He would rather leap into his sister's face.

But Grete had merely disquieted her mother; now she turned, saw the gigantic brown stain spread over the wallpaper and, before she realized that it was Gregor she was seeing, she cried, "O God! O God!" in a screaming, raucous voice, fell on the sofa with outspread arms in a gesture of complete renunciation, and gave no further sign of life. "You, Gregor!" cried the sister, raising her fist and piercing Gregor with a look. It was the first word she had addressed to him directly ever since his metamorphosis. Then she ran to get some smelling salts from the dining room to rouse her mother from her swoon. Gregor decided to help — there was still time to save the picture — alas, he found he had stuck fast to the glass and had to make a violent effort to detach himself; then he hurried into the dining room as if able to give his sister some good advice, but he was obliged to content himself with remaining passively behind her while she rummaged among the bottles, and he frightened her so terribly when she turned around that a bottle fell and broke on the floor, a splinter wounded Gregor in the face, and a corrosive medicine flowed round his feet; then Grete hastily grabbed up all the bottles she could carry and rushed in to her mother, slamming the door behind her with her foot. Now Gregor was shut out from his mother, who perhaps was nearly dead through his fault; he dared not open the door lest he drive away his sister, who must stay by his mother; so there was nothing to do but wait, and, gnawed by remorse and distress, he began to wander over the walls, the furniture, and the ceilings so rapidly that everything began to spin around him, till in despair he fell heavily on to the middle of the huge table.

A moment passed; Gregor lay stretched there; around all was still; perhaps that was a good sign. But suddenly he heard a knock. The maid was naturally barricaded in her kitchen; Grete herself must go to the door. His father had returned.

"What has happened?" were his first words; no doubt Grete's expression had explained everything.

The girl replied in a stifled voice — probably she leaned her face against her father's breast — "Mother fainted, but she is better now. Gregor has got out."

"I was waiting for that," said the father, "I told you all along, but you women will never listen."

Gregor realized by these words that his father had misunderstood Grete's brief explanation and imagined that his son had broken loose in some reprehensible way. There was no time to explain. Gregor had to find some way of pacifying his father, so he quickly crawled to the door of his room and pressed himself against it for his father to see, as he came in, how he had every intention of returning to his own room immediately and that it was not at all necessary to drive him back with violence; one had only to open the door and he would quickly withdraw.

But his father was in no mood to notice these fine points. As he entered he cried, "Ah!" in a tone at once of joy and anger; Gregor turned his head away from the door and lifted it toward his father. He was astonished. He had never imagined his father as he stood before him now; it is true that for some time now he had neglected to keep himself acquainted with the events of the house, preferring to devote himself to his new mode of existence, and he had therefore been unaware of a certain change of character in his family. And yet — and yet, was that really his father? Was it really the same man who once had lain wearily in bed when Gregor had been leaving on his journeys, who met him, on his return, in his nightshirt, seated in an armchair out of which he could not even lift himself, throwing his arms high to show how pleased he was? Was this that same old man who, on the rare walks which the family would take together, two or three Sundays a year and on special holidays, would hobble between Gregor and his mother, while they walked slower and slower for him, as he, covered with an old coat, carefully set his stick before him and prudently worked his way forward; and yet, despite their slowness, he would be obliged to stop, whenever he wished to say anything, and call his escort back to him? How upstanding he had become since then!

Now he was wearing a blue uniform with gold buttons, without a single crease, just as you see the employees of banking houses wearing; above the big, stiff collar his double chin spread its powerful folds; under his bristly eyebrows the watchful expression of his black eyes glittered young and purposefully; his white hair, ordinarily untidy, had been carefully brushed till it shone. He threw on to the sofa his cap, ornamented with the gilded monogram of some bank, making it describe the arc of a circle across the room, and, with his hands in his trouser pockets, the long flaps of his coat turned back, he walked toward Gregor with a menacing air. He himself did not know what he was going to do; however, he raised his feet very high, and Gregor, astonished at the enormous size of the soles of his boots, took care to remain still, for he knew that, from the first day of his metamorphosis, his father had held the view that the greatest severity was the only attitude to take up toward Gregor. Then he began to beat a retreat before his father's approach, halting when the other stopped and beginning again at his father's slightest move. In this way they walked several times round the room without any decisive result; it did not even take on the appearance of a pursuit, so slow was their pace.

Gregor was provisionally keeping to the floor; he feared that if his father saw him climbing about the walls or rushing across the ceiling, he might take this maneuver for some refinement of bad behavior. However, he had to admit that he could not go on much longer in this way; in the little time his father needed to take a step, Gregor had to make a whole series of gymnastic movements and, as he had never had good lungs, he now began to pant and wheeze; he tried to recover his breath quickly in order to gather all his strength for a supreme effort, scarcely daring to open his eyes, so stupefied that he could think of no other way to safety than by pursuing his present course; he had already forgotten that the walls were at his disposal, and the carefully carved furniture, all covered with festoons of plush and lace as it was. Suddenly something flew sharply by him, fell to the ground, and rolled away. It was an apple, carelessly thrown; a second one flew by. Paralyzed with terror, Gregor stayed still. It was useless to continue his course, now that his father had decided to bombard him. He had emptied the bowls of fruit on the sideboard, filled his pockets, and now threw apple after apple, without waiting to take aim.

These little red apples rolled about the floor as if electrified, knocking against each other. One lightly-thrown apple struck Gregor's back and fell off without doing any harm, but the next one literally pierced his flesh. He tried to drag himself a little further away, as if a change of position could relieve the shattering agony he suddenly felt, but he seemed to be nailed fast to the spot and stretched his body helplessly, not knowing what to do. With his last, hopeless glance, he saw his door opened suddenly, and, in front of his sister, who was shouting at the top of her voice, his mother came running in, in her petticoat, for his sister had partly undressed her that she might breathe easier in her swoon. And his mother, who ran to the father, losing her skirts one by one, stumbled forward, thrust herself against her husband, embraced him, pressed him to her, and, with her hands clasped at the back of his neck — already Gregor could see no more — begged him to spare Gregor's life.

III

The apple which no one dared draw from Gregor's back remained embedded in his flesh as a palpable memory, and the grave wound which he now had borne for a month seemed to have reminded his father that Gregor, despite his sad and terrible change, remained none the less a member of the family and must not be treated as an enemy; on the contrary, duty demanded that disgust should be overcome and Gregor be given all possible help.

His wound had made him lose, irremediably, no doubt, much of his agility; now, merely to cross his room required a long, long time, as if he were an aged invalid; his walks across the walls could no longer be considered. But this aggravation of his state was largely compensated for, in his opinion, by the fact that now, every evening, the dining-room door was left open; for two hours he would wait for this. Lying in the darkness of his room, invisible to the diners, he could observe the whole family gathered round the table in the lamplight, and he could, by common consent, listen to all they had to say — it was much better than before.

It must be admitted that they no longer held those lively conversations of which, in former times, he had always thought with such sadness as he crept into his damp bed in some little hotel room. Most of the time, now, they discussed nothing in particular after dinner. The father would soon settle himself to doze in his armchair; the mother and daughter would bid each other be silent; the mother, leaning forward in the light, would sew at some fine needlework for a lingerie shop, and the sister, who had obtained a job as a shop assistant, would study shorthand or French in the hope of improving her position. Now and then the father would wake up and, as if he did not know that he had been asleep, would say to his wife, "How late you are sewing tonight!" and would fall off to sleep again, while the mother and sister would exchange a tired smile.

By some capricious obstinacy, the father always refused to take off his uniform, even at home; his dressing gown hung unused in the wardrobe, and he slept in his armchair in full livery, as if to keep himself always ready to carry out some order; even in his own home he seemed to await his superior's voice. Moreover, the uniform had not been new when it was issued to him, and now each day it became more shabby, despite the care which the two women devoted to it; and Gregor often spent the evening staring dully at this coat, so spotted and stained, whose polished buttons always shone so brightly, and in which the old man slept, uncomfortably but peacefully.

As soon as the clock struck ten, the mother, in a low voice, tried to rouse her husband and to encourage him to go to bed, as it was impossible to get proper sleep in such a position, and he must sleep normally before returning to work at six the next morning. But, with the obstinacy which had characterized him ever since he had obtained his position at the bank, he would stay at the table although he regularly dropped off to sleep, and thus it would become more and more difficult to induce him to change his armchair for the bed. The mother and sister might insist with their little warnings; he stayed there just the same, slowly nodding his head, his eyes shut tight, and would not get up. The mother might shake him by the wrist, might whisper endearments in his ear; the daughter might abandon her work to assist her mother, but all in vain. The old man would merely sink deeper in his chair. At last the two women would have to take him under the arms to make him open his eyes; then he would look at each in turn and say, "What a life! Is this the hard-earned rest of my old days?" and, leaning on the two women, he would rise painfully, as if he were a tremendous weight, and would allow himself to be led to the door by his wife and daughter; then he would wave them off and continue alone, while the mother and sister, the one quickly throwing down her pen, the other her needle, would run after him to help.

Who in the overworked and overtired family had time to attend to Gregor, except for his most pressing needs? The household budget was ever more and more reduced; at last the maid was dismissed. In her place, a gigantic charwoman with bony features and white hair, which stood up all around her head, came, morning and evening, to do the harder work. The rest was done by the mother, over and above her interminable mending and darning. It even happened that they were obliged to sell various family trinkets which formerly had been worn proudly by the mother and sister at ceremonies and festivals, as Gregor discovered one evening when he heard them discussing the price they hoped to get. But their most persistent complaints were about this flat, which was so much larger than they needed and which had now become too expensive for the family purse; they could not leave, they said, for they could not imagine how Gregor could be moved. Alas, Gregor understood that it was not really he who was the chief obstacle to this removal, for he might easily have been transported in a large wooden box pierced with a few air holes. No, what particularly prevented the family from changing their residence was their own despair, the idea that they had been stricken by such a misfortune as had never before occurred in the family or within the circle of their acquaintances.

Of all the deprivations which the world imposes on poor people, not one had been spared them; the father took his day-time meals with the lesser employees of the bank, the mother was killing herself mending the linen of strangers, the sister ran here and there behind her counter at the customers' bidding; but the family had energy for nothing further. It seemed to poor Gregor that his wound reopened whenever his mother and sister, returning from putting the father to bed, would leave their work in disorder and bring their chairs nearer to each other, till they were sitting almost cheek to cheek; then the mother would say, pointing to Gregor's room, "Close the door, Grete," and he would once more be left in darkness, while, outside, the two women mingled their tears or, worse, sat at the table staring with dry eyes.

These days and nights brought Gregor no sleep. From time to time he thought of taking the family affairs in hand, as he once used, the very next time the door was opened; at the end of a long perspective of time he dimly saw in his mind his employer and the manager, the clerks and apprentices, the porter with his narrow ideas, two or three acquaintances from other offices, a provincial barmaid — a fleeting but dear memory — and a cashier in a hat shop, whom he had pursued earnestly but too slowly; they passed through his mind in confusion, mingled with unknown and unforgotten faces; but none of them could bring help to him or his family; nothing was to be gained from them. He was pleased to be able to dismiss them from his mind but now he no longer cared what happened to his family; on the contrary, he only felt enraged because they neglected to tidy his room and, though nothing imaginable could excite his appetite, he began making involved plans for a raid on the larder, with a view to taking such food as he had a right to, even if he was not hungry. Nowadays his sister no longer tried to guess what might please him; she made a hasty appearance twice a day, in the morning and in the afternoon, before going to her shop, and pushed a few scraps of food into the room with her foot; in the evening, without even bothering to see whether he had touched his meal or whether he had left it entirely — and this was usually the case — she would sweep up the remains with a whisk of the broom.

As for tidying up the room, which Grete now did in the evenings, it could not have been done in a more hasty manner. Great patches of dirt streaked the wall, little heaps of dust and ordure lay here and there about the floor. At first Gregor would place himself in the filthiest places whenever his sister appeared, so that this might seem a reproach to her. But he could have stayed there for weeks, and still Grete would not have altered her conduct; she saw the dirt as well as he but she had finally decided to take no further trouble. This did not prevent her from taking even more jealous care than ever to insure that no other member of the family should presume on her right to the tidying of the room.

Once the mother undertook to give Gregor's room a great cleaning which required several buckets of water, and this deluge deeply upset poor Gregor, crouched under his sofa in bitter immobility — but the mother's punishment soon came. Hardly had the sister, coming home in the evening, noticed the difference in Gregor's room, than, feeling deeply offended, she ran crying and screaming into the dining room, despite the appeal of her mother, who raised her hands in supplication; the father, who was quietly seated at table, leaped up, astonished but powerless to pacify her. Then he, too, became agitated; shouting, he began to attack the mother, on the one hand, for not leaving the care and cleaning of Gregor's room to the girl and, on the other hand, he forbade his daughter ever again to dare to clean it; the mother tried to draw the old man, quivering with anger as he was, into the bedroom; the daughter, shaken with sobs, was banging on the table with her little fists, while Gregor loudly hissed with rage to think that no one had the decency or consideration to close the door and thus spare him the sight of all this trouble and uproar.

But even if the sister, tired out by her work in the shop, could not bother to look after Gregor as carefully as hitherto, she could still have arranged that he should not be neglected without necessarily calling on the aid of her mother, for there was always the charwoman. This old woman, whose bony frame had helped her out of worse trouble during her long life, could not really be said to feel any disgust with Gregor. Though she was not inquisitive, she had opened his door one day and had stood with her hands folded over her stomach, astonished at the sight of Gregor, who began to trot here and there in his alarm, though she had no thought of chasing him. From that day, morning and evening, the old woman never lost an opportunity of opening the door a little to peer into the room.

At first she would call Gregor to make him come out, crying in a familiar tone, "Come on, you old cockroach!" or, "Hey, look at the old cockroach!" To such invitations Gregor would not respond; instead he remained motionless beneath his sofa as if the door had not been opened. If they had only ordered the charwoman to clean his room out each day instead of allowing her to go on teasing and upsetting him! Early one morning, when heavy rain — perhaps a sign of approaching spring — beat on the roofs, Gregor was so annoyed by the old woman as she began to bait him again that he suddenly turned on her, in a somewhat cumbersome and uncertain manner, it must be admitted, but with every intention of attacking her. She was not at all frightened of him; there was a chair by the door; she took it up and brandished it, opening wide her mouth with the obvious intention of not closing it until she had brought the chair down with a crash on Gregor's back. "Ah, is that all?" she asked, seeing him return to his former position, and she quietly put the chair back in its place.

Nowadays Gregor hardly ate at all. When, by some chance, he passed by his scraps, he would amuse himself by taking a piece of food in his mouth and keeping it there for hours, usually spitting it out in the end. At first he had thought that his loss of appetite was due to the misery into which the state of his room had plunged him; no doubt this was a mistake, for he had soon become reconciled to the squalor of his surroundings. His family had got into the habit of piling into his room whatever could not be accommodated elsewhere, and this meant a great deal, now that one of the rooms had been let to three lodgers. They were very earnest and serious men; all three had thick beards — as Gregor saw one day when he was peering through a crack in the door — and they were fanatically tidy; they insisted on order, not only in their own room, but also, now that they were living here, thronghont the whole household, and especially in the kitchen.

They had brought with them all that they needed, and this rendered superfluous a great many things about the house which could neither be sold nor thrown away, and which were now all stacked in Gregor's room, as were the ash bucket and the rubbish bin. Everything that seemed for the moment useless would be dumped in Gregor's room by the charwoman, who was always in a breathless hurry to get through her work; he would just have time to see a hand brandishing some unwanted utensil, and then the door would slam again. Perhaps the old woman intended to return and find the objects she so carelessly relegated here when she needed them and had time to search; or perhaps she meant to throw them all away some day, but in actual fact they stayed in the room, on the very spot where they had first fallen, so that Gregor was obliged to pick his way among the rubbish to make a place for himself — a game for which his taste began to grow, in spite of the appalling misery and fatigue which followed these peregrinations, leaving him paralyzed for hours. As the lodgers sometimes dined at home in the living room, the door of this room would be shut on certain evenings; however, Gregor no longer attached any importance to this; for some while, now, he had ceased to profit by those evenings when the family would open the door and he would remain shrinking in the darkest corner of his room, where the family could not see him.

One day the woman forgot to close the dining-room door, and it was still ajar when the lodgers came in and lit the gas. They sat down at table in the places that previously had been occupied by the father, the mother, and Gregor; each unfolded his napkin and took up his knife and fork. Soon the mother appeared in the doorway with a plate of meat; the sister followed her, carrying a dish of potatoes. When their meal had been set before them, the lodgers leaned over to examine it, and the one who was seated in the middle and who appeared to have some authority over the others, cut a piece of meat as it lay on the dish to ascertain whether it was tender or whether he should send it back to the kitchen. He seemed satisfied, however, and the two women, who had been anxiously watching, gave each other a smile of relief.

The family itself lived in the kitchen. However, the father, before going into the kitchen, always came into the dining room and bowed once with his cap in his hand, then made his way around the table. The boarders rose together and murmured something in their beards. Once they were alone, they began to eat in silence. It seemed curious to Gregor that he could hear the gnashing of their teeth above all the clatter of cutlery; it was as if they wanted to prove to him that one must have real teeth in order to eat properly, and that the best mandibles in the world were but an unsatisfactory substitute. "I am hungry," thought Gregor sadly, "but not for these things. How these lodgers can eat! And in the meantime I might die, for all they care."

He could not remember hearing his sister play since the arrival of the lodgers; but this evening the sound of the violin came from the kitchen. The lodgers had just finished their meal; the middle one had brought a newspaper and had given a page to each of the others; now they all three read, leaning back in their chairs and smoking. The sound of the violin attracted their attention, and they rose and walked on tiptoe toward the hall door, where they halted and remained very close together.

Apparently they had been heard in the kitchen, for the father cried, "Does the violin upset you gentlemen? We'll stop it immediately."

"On the contrary," said the man in the middle. "Would Fräulein Samsa not like to come in and play to us here in the dining room, where it is much nicer and more comfortable?"

"Oh, thank you," said the father, as if he were the violinist.

The gentlemen walked back across the room and waited. Soon the father came in with the music stand, the mother with the sheets of music, and the sister with the violin. The sister calmly prepared to play; her parents, who had never before let their rooms, were exaggeratedly polite to the boarders and were afraid to seem presumptuous by sitting in their own chairs; the father leaned against the door, his right hand thrust between two buttons of his livery coat; but one of the gentlemen offered the mother a chair, in which she finally sat, not daring to move from her corner throughout the performance.

The girl now began to play, while her father and mother, from either side, watched the movement of her hands. Attracted by the music, Gregor had crawled forward a little and had thrust his head into the room. He was no longer astonished that nowadays he had entirely lost that consideration for others, that anxiety to cause no trouble that once had been his pride. Yet never had he more reason to remain hidden, for now, because of the dirt that lay about his room, flying up at the slightest movement, he was always covered with dust and fluff, with ends of cotton and hairs, and with morsels of stale food, which stuck to his back or to his feet and which he trailed after him wherever he went; his apathy had grown too great for him to bother any more about cleaning himself several times a day by lying on his back and rubbing himself on the carpet, as once he used to do. And this filthy state did not prevent him from crawling over the spotless floor without a moment's shame.

So far, no one had noticed him. The family was too absorbed by the music of the violin, and the lodgers, who had first stood with their hands in their pockets, very close to the music stand — which disturbed the sister a great deal as she was obliged to see their image dancing amid the notes — had at last retired toward the window, where they stood speaking together half aloud, with lowered heads, under the anxious gaze of the father, who was watching attentively. It had become only too evident that they had been deceived in their hopes of hearing some beautiful violin piece, or at least some amusing little tune; it seemed that what the girl was playing bored them and that now they only tolerated her out of politeness. By the way in which they puffed the smoke of their cigars, by the energy with which they blew it toward the ceiling through the mouth or the nose, one could guess how fidgety they were becoming. And the sister was playing so nicely. Her face leaning to one side, her glance followed the score carefully and sadly. Gregor crawled forward a little more and put his head as near as possible to the floor to meet her gaze. Could it be that he was only an animal, when music moved him so? It seemed to him to open a way toward that unknown nourishment he so longed for. He resolved to creep up to his sister and to pull at her dress, to make her understand that she must come with him, for no one here would appreciate her music as much as he. He would never let her out of his room — at least, while he lived — for once, his horrible shape would serve him some useful purpose; he would be at all doors at once, repulsing intruders with his raucous breath; but his sister would not be forced to stay there; she must live with him of her own accord; she would sit by him on the sofa, hearing what he had to say; then he would tell her in confidence that he had firmly intended to send her to the Conservatory and had planned to let everyone know last Christmas — was Christmas really past? — without listening to any objections, had his misfortune not overtaken him too soon. His sister, moved by this explanation, would surely burst into tears, and Gregor, climbing up on her shoulder, would kiss her neck; this would be all the easier, for she had worn neither collar nor ribbon ever since she had been working in the shop.

"Herr Samsa," cried the middle lodger, and he pointed at Gregor, who slowly came into the room. The violin was suddenly silenced, the middle lodger turned to his friends, grinning and shaking his head, then once more he stared at Gregor. The father seemed to consider it more urgent to reassure the lodgers than to drive his son from the room, though the lodgers did not seem to be at all upset by the spectacle; in fact, Gregor seemed to amuse them more highly than did the violin. The father hurried forward and, with outstretched arms, tried to drive them into their room, hiding Gregor from them with his body. Now they began to be really upset, but it is not known whether this was on account of the father's action or because they had been living with such a monstrous neighbor as Gregor without being made aware of it. They demanded explanations, waving their arms in the air; and, fidgeting nervously with their beards, they retreated toward their own door. Meanwhile the sister had recovered from the distress that the sudden interruption of her music had caused her; after remaining a moment completely at a loss, with the violin and the bow hanging from her helpless hands, following the score with her eyes as if she were still playing, she suddenly came back to life, laid the violin in her mother's lap — the mother sat suffocating in her chair, her lungs working violently — and rushed into the next room, toward which the lodgers were rapidly retreating before Herr Samsa's onslaught. One could see how quickly, under Grete's practised hand, pillows and covers were set in order on the beds. The lodgers had not yet reached the room when their beds were already prepared, and Grete had slipped out. The father seemed so possessed by his strange fury that he had quite forgotten the respect due to lodgers.

He drove them to the door of the room, where the middle lodger suddenly came to a stop, stamping thunderously on the floor. "I wish to inform you," said this man, raising his hand and looking around for the two women, "that in view of the disgusting circumstances which govern this family and this house" — and here he spat quickly on the carpet — "I hereby immediately give up my room. Naturally, you will not get a penny for the time I have been living here; on the contrary, I am considering whether I should not claim compensation from you, damages which should easily be awarded in any court of law; it is a matter about which I shall inquire, believe me." He was silent and stared into space, as if awaiting something. Accordingly, his two friends also spoke up: "We, too, give our notice." Thereupon the gentleman in the middle seized the door handle, and they went inside. The door closed with a crash.

The father stumbled toward his chair, put his trembling hands upon the arms, and let himself drop into it; he looked exactly as if he were settling himself for his customary evening nap, but the way his head drooped heavily from side to side showed that he was thinking of something other than sleep. All this time Gregor had stayed still on the spot where he had surprised the lodgers. He felt completely paralyzed with bewilderment at the checking of his plans — perhaps, also, with weakness due to his prolonged fasting. He feared that the whole household would fall upon him immediately; he foresaw the precise moment when this catastrophe would happen, and now he waited. Even the violin did not frighten him as it fell with a clatter from the trembling fingers of his mother, who until now had held it in her lap.

"My dear parents," said his sister, who beat with her hand on the table by way of introduction. "Things cannot go on like this. Even if you do not realize it, I can see it quite clearly. I will not mention my brother's name when I speak of this monster here; I merely want to say: we must find some means of getting rid of it. We have done all that is humanly possible to care for it, to put up with it; I believe that nobody could reproach us in the least."

"She's a thousand times right," said the father. But the mother who had not yet recovered her breath, coughed helplessly behind her hand, her eyes haggard.

The sister hurried toward her mother and held her forehead. Grete's words seemed to have made up the father's mind, for now he sat up in his armchair and fidgeted with his cap among the dishes on the table, from which the lodgers' meal had not yet been cleared; from time to time he stared at Gregor.

"We must find a way of getting rid of it," repeated the sister, now speaking only to her father, for her mother, shaken by her coughing, could hear nothing. "It will bring you both to the grave. I can see it coming. When people have to work all day, as we must, we cannot bear this eternal torture each time we come home at night. I can stand it no longer." And she wept so bitterly that her tears fell on her mother's face, who wiped them off with a mechanical movement of her hand.

"But what can we do, child?" said the father in a pitiful voice. It was surprising to see how well he understood his daughter.

The sister merely shrugged her shoulders as a sign of the perplexity which, during her tears, had replaced her former assurance.

"If he could only understand us," said the father in a half-questioning tone, but the sister, through her tears, made a violent gesture with her hand as a sign that this was not to be thought of.

"If only he could understand us," repeated the father — and he shut his eyes as he spoke, as if to show that he agreed with the sister that such a thing was quite impossible. "If only he could understand us, perhaps there would be some way of coming to an agreement. But as it is . . ."

"It must go!" cried the sister. "That's the only way out. You must get the idea out of your head that this is Gregor. We have believed that for too long, and that is the cause of all our unhappiness. How could it be Gregor? If it were really he, he would long ago have realized that he could not live with human beings and would have gone off on his own accord. I haven't a brother any longer, but we can go on living and can honor his memory. In his place we have this monster that pursues us and drives away our lodgers; perhaps it wants the whole flat to itself, to drive us out into the streets. Look, father, look!" she suddenly screamed, "it's beginning again!" And in an access of terror, which Gregor could not understand, she let go her mother so suddenly that she bounced in the seat of the armchair; it seemed as if the sister would rather sacrifice her mother than stay near Gregor; she hastily took refuge behind her father, who was very upset by her behavior and now stood up, spreading his arms to protect her.

But Gregor had no thought of frightening anyone, least of all his sister. He had merely started to turn around in order to go back to his room; but it must be realized that this looked very alarming, for his weakness obliged him to assist his difficult turning movement with his head, which he raised and lowered many times, clutching at the carpet with his mandibles. At last he ceased and stared at the family. It seemed they realized his good intentions. They were watching him in mute sadness. The mother lay in her armchair, her outstretched legs pressed tightly together, her eyes nearly closed with fatigue; the father and sister were sitting side by side, and the girl's arm was round her father's neck.

"Now, perhaps, they will let me turn," thought Gregor, and he once more set about his task. He could not repress a sigh of weariness; he was obliged to rest from time to time. However, no one hurried him; they left him entirely alone. When he had completed his turn, he immediately beat a retreat, crawling straight ahead. He was astonished at the distance which separated him from his room; he did not realize that this was due merely to his weak state and that a little before he could have covered the distance without noticing it. His family did not disturb him by a single cry, a single exclamation; but this he did not even notice, so necessary was it to concentrate all his will on getting back to his room. It was only when he had at long last reached his door that he thought of turning his head, not completely, because his neck had become very stiff, but sufficiently to reassure himself that nothing had changed behind him; only his sister was now standing up. His last look was toward his mother, who, by this time, was fast asleep.

Hardly was he in his room before the door was slammed, locked, and double bolted. So sudden was the crash that Gregor's legs gave way. It was his sister who had rushed to the door. She had stood up so as to be ready immediately and at the right moment had run forward so lightly that he had not heard her come; as she turned the key in the lock, she cried to her parents, "At last!"

"What now?" asked Gregor, looking around himself in the darkness. He soon discovered that he could not move. This did not surprise him in the least; it seemed to him much more remarkable that such frail legs had hitherto been able to bear his weight. Now he experienced a feeling of relative comfort. True, his whole body ached, but it seemed that these aches became less and less until finally they disappeared. Even the rotted apple embedded in his back hardly hurt him now; no more did the inflammation of the surrounding parts, covered with fine dust, cause him any further discomfort. He thought of his family in tender solicitude. He realized that he must go, and his opinion on this point was even more firm, if possible, than that of his sister. He lay in this state of peaceful and empty meditation till the clock struck the third morning hour. He saw the landscape grow lighter through the window; then, against his will, his head fell forward and his last feeble breath streamed from his nostrils.

When the charwoman arrived early in the morning — and though she had often been forbidden to do so, she always slammed the door so loudly in her vigor and haste that once she was in the house it was impossible to get any sleep — she did not at first notice anything unusual as she paid her customary morning visit to Gregor. She imagined that he was deliberately lying motionless in order to play the role of an "injured party," as she herself would say — she deemed him capable of such refinements; as she had a long broom in her hand, she tried to tickle him from the doorway. Meeting with little success, she grew angry; she gave him one or two hard pushes, and it was only when his body moved unresistingly before her thrusts that she became curious. She quickly realized what had happened, opened her eyes wide, and whistled in astonishment, but she did not stay in the room; she ran to the bedroom, opened the door, and loudly shouted into the darkness, "Come and look! He's stone dead! He's lying there, absolutely dead as a doornail!"

Herr and Frau Samsa sat up in their bed and tried to calm each other; the old woman had frightened them so much and they did not realize the sense of her message immediately. But now they hastily scrambled out of bed, Herr Samsa on one side, his wife on the other; Herr Samsa put the coverlet over his shoulders, Frau Samsa ran out, clad only in her nightdress; and it was thus that they rushed into Gregor's room. Meanwhile, the dining-room door was opened — Grete had been sleeping there since the arrival of the lodgers — she was fully dressed, as if she had not slept all night, and the pallor of her face seemed to bear witness to her sleeplessness.

"Dead?" said Frau Samsa, staring at the charwoman with a questioning look, though she could see as much for herself without further examination.

"I should say so," said the charwoman, and she pushed Gregor to one side with her broom, to support her statement. Frau Samsa made a movement as if to hold back the broom, but she did not complete her gesture.

"Well," said Herr Samsa, "we can thank God for that!" He crossed himself and signed the three women to do likewise.

Grete, whose eyes had never left the corpse, said, "Look how thin he was! It was such a long time since he had eaten anything. His meals used to come out of the room just as they were taken in." And, indeed, Gregor's body was quite flat and dry; this could be seen more easily now that he was no longer supported on his legs and there was nothing to deceive one's sight.

"Come with us a moment, Grete!" said Frau Samsa with a sad smile, and Grete followed her parents into their bedroom, not without turning often to gaze at the corpse. The charwoman closed the door and opened the French windows. Despite the early hour, the fresh morning air had a certain warmth. It was already the end of March.

The three lodgers came out of their room and gazed around in astonishment for their breakfast; they had been forgotten. "Where is our breakfast?" the middle lodger petulantly demanded of the old woman. But she merely laid her finger to her mouth and signed them, with a mute and urgent gesture, to follow her into Gregor's room. So they entered and stood around Gregor's corpse, with their hands in the pockets of their rather shabby coats, in the middle of the room already bright with sunlight.

Then the bedroom door opened and Herr Samsa appeared in his uniform with his wife on one arm, his daughter on the other. All seemed to have been weeping, and from time to time Grete pressed her face against her father's arm.

"Leave my house immediately!" said Herr Samsa, and he pointed to the door, while the women still clung to his arms.

Somewhat disconcerted, the middle lodger said with a timid smile, "Whatever do you mean?"

The two others clasped their hands behind their backs and kept on rubbing their palms together, as if they were expecting some great dispute which could only end in triumph for them.

"I mean exactly what I say!" answered Herr Samsa and, in line with the two women, he marched straight at the lodger. The latter, however, stood quietly in his place, his eyes fixed on the floor, as if reconsidering what he should do.

"Well, then, we will go," he said at last, raising his eyes to Herr Samsa as if searching, in a sudden access of humility, for some slight approval of his resolution.

Herr Samsa merely nodded several times, opening his eyes very wide. Thereupon the lodger walked away with big strides and soon reached the anteroom; his two friends, who for some while had ceased wringing their hands, now bounded after him, as if afraid Herr Samsa might reach the door before them and separate them from their leader. Once they had gained the hall, they took down their hats from the pegs, grabbed their sticks from the umbrella stand, bowed silently, and left the flat.

With a suspicion which, it appears, was quite unjustified, Herr Samsa ran out onto the landing after them with the women and leaned over the balustrade to watch the three men as they slowly, but steadily, descended the interminable stairway, disappearing once as they reached a certain point on each floor, and then, after a few seconds, coming into view again. As they went farther down the staircase, so the Samsa family's interest diminished, and when they had been met and passed by a butcher's boy who came proudly up the stairs with his basket on his head, Herr Samsa and the women quickly left the landing and went indoors again with an air of relief.

They decided to spend the whole day resting; perhaps they might take a walk in the country; they had earned a respite and needed it urgently. And so they sat down to the table to write three letters of excuse: Herr Samsa to the manager of the Bank, Frau Samsa to her employer, and Grete to the head of her department at the shop. The charwoman came in while they were writing and announced that her work was done and that she was going. The three writers at first merely nodded their heads, without raising their eyes, but, as the old woman did not leave, they eventually laid down their pens and looked crossly at her.

"Well?" asked Herr Samsa. The charwoman was standing in the

doorway, smiling as if she had some very good news to tell them but which she would not impart till she had been begged to. The little ostrich feather which stood upright on her hat and which had always annoyed Herr Samsa so much ever since the old woman had entered their service, now waved lightly in all directions.

"Well, what is it?" asked Frau Samsa, toward whom the old woman had always shown so much more respect than to the others.

"Well . . ." she replied, and she laughed so much she could hardly speak for some while. "Well, you needn't worry about getting rid of that thing in there, I have fixed it already."

Frau Samsa and Grete leaned over the table as if to resume their letter-writing; Herr Samsa, noticing that the woman was about to launch forth into a detailed explanation, cut her short with a peremptory gesture of his outstretched hand. Then, prevented from speaking, she suddenly remembered that she was in a great hurry and, crying, "Goodbye, everyone," in a peevish tone, she half turned and was gone in a flash, savagely slamming the door behind her.

"This evening we must sack her," declared Herr Samsa; but neither his wife nor his daughter answered; the old woman had not been able to disturb their newly won tranquillity. They arose, went to the window, and stood there, with their arms around each other; Herr Samsa, turning toward them in his armchair, stared at them for a moment in silence. Then he cried, "Come, come, it's all past history now; you can start paying a little attention to me." The women immediately hurried to him, kissed him, and sat down to finish their letters.

Then they all left the apartment together, a thing they had been unable to do for many months past, and they boarded a tram which would take them some way into the country. There were no other passengers in the compartment, which was warm and bright in the sun. Casually leaning back in their seats, they began to discuss their future. On careful reflection, they decided that things were not nearly so bad as they might have been, for — and this was a point they had not hitherto realized — they had all three found really interesting occupations which looked even more promising in the future. They decided to effect what really should be the greatest improvement as soon as possible. That was to move from the flat they occupied at present. They would take a smaller, cheaper flat, but one more practical, and especially in a better neighborhood than the present one, which Gregor had chosen. Hearing their daughter speak in more and more lively tones, Herr and Frau Samsa noticed almost together that, during this affair, Grete had blossomed into a fine strapping girl, despite the make-up which made her cheeks look pale. They became calmer; almost unconsciously they exchanged glances; it occurred to both of them that it would soon be time for her to find a husband. And it seemed to them that their daughter's gestures were a confirmation of these new dreams of theirs, an encouragement for their good intentions, when, at the end of the journey, the girl rose before them and stretched her young body.

Paul Valéry (1871–1945)

LIFE: Born of a Corsican father and an Italian mother in the city of Sète on the Mediterranean, he came to Paris in 1892; there Gide introduced him to Mallarmé, who became his poetic master and friend; but for twenty years after the composition of his early poems Valéry published nothing: instead, he studied mathematics, architecture, and psychology. That silence, however, was followed by "La jeune parque," published in 1917; in 1922 appeared *Charmes*, containing "Le Cimetière marin"; and so began his public career: first as a member of the Académie Française; later as a lecturer at the Sorbonne, where he occupied a chair of poetry created for him; and finally as one of the most influential voices in French poetry and criticism of the twentieth century.

WORKS: *Album des vers anciens: 1890–1900* (1920); *Charmes* (1922); and various philosophical and esthetic studies, including five volumes of critical essays, *Variété* (1924–44).

THE GRAVEYARD BY THE SEA *

This quiet roof, where dove-sails saunter by,
Between the pines, the tombs, throbs visibly.
Impartial noon patterns the sea in flame —
That sea forever starting and re-starting.
When thought has had its hour, oh how rewarding   5
Are the long vistas of celestial calm!

What grace of light, what pure toil goes to form
The manifold diamond of the elusive foam!
What peace I feel begotten at that source!
When sunlight rests upon a profound sea,   10
Time's air is sparkling, dream is certainty —
Pure artifice both of an eternal Cause.

Sure treasure, simple shrine to intelligence,
Palpable calm, visible reticence,
Proud-lidded water, Eye wherein there wells   15
Under a film of fire such depth of sleep —
O silence! . . . Mansion in my soul, you slope
Of gold, roof of a myriad golden tiles.

* Published in 1922.

Temple of time, within a brief sigh bounded,
To this rare height inured I climb, surrounded
By the horizons of a sea-girt eye.   20
And, like my supreme offering to the gods,
That peaceful coruscation only breeds
A loftier indifference on the sky.

Even as a fruit's absorbed in the enjoying,
Even as within the mouth its body dying   25
Changes into delight through dissolution,
So to my melted soul the heavens declare
All bounds transfigured into a boundless air,
And I breathe now my future's emanation.   30

Beautiful heaven, true heaven, look how I change!
After such arrogance, after so much strange
Idleness — strange, yet full of potency —
I am all open to these shining spaces;
Over the homes of the dead my shadow passes,
Ghosting along — a ghost subduing me.   35

My soul laid bare to your midsummer fire,
O just, impartial light whom I admire,
Whose arms are merciless, you have I stayed
And give back, pure, to your original place.
Look at yourself . . . But to give light implies   40
No less a somber moiety of shade.

Oh, for myself alone, mine, deep within
At the heart's quick, the poem's fount, between
The void and its pure issue, I beseech
The intimations of my secret power.   45
O bitter, dark, and echoing reservoir
Speaking of depths always beyond my reach.

But know you — feigning prisoner of the boughs,
Gulf which eats up their slender prison-bars,
Secret which dazzles though mine eyes are closed —   50
What body drags me to its lingering end,
What mind draws *it* to this bone-peopled ground?
A star broods there on all that I have lost.

Closed, hallowed, full of insubstantial fire,
Morsel of earth to heaven's light given o'er —   55
This plot, ruled by its flambeaux, pleases me —
A place all gold, stone, and dark wood, where shudders

57. *flambeaux:* flaming torches.

So much marble above so many shadows:
And on my tombs, asleep, the faithful sea. 60

Keep off the idolaters, bright watch-dog, while —
A solitary with the shepherd's smile —
I pasture long my sheep, my mysteries,
My snow-white flock of undisturbéd graves!
Drive far away from here the careful doves, 65
The vain daydreams, the angels' questioning eyes!

Now present here, the future takes its time.
The brittle insect scrapes at the dry loam;
All is burnt up, used up, drawn up in air
To some ineffably rarefied solution . . . 70
Life is enlarged, drunk with annihilation,
And bitterness is sweet, and the spirit clear.

The dead lie easy, hidden in earth where they
Are warmed and have their mysteries burnt away.
Motionless noon, noon aloft in the blue 75
Broods on itself — a self-sufficient theme.
O rounded dome and perfect diadem,
I am what's changing secretly in you.

I am the only medium for your fears.
My penitence, my doubts, my baulked desires — 80
These are the flaw within your diamond pride . . .
But in their heavy night, cumbered with marble,
Under the roots of trees a shadow people
Has slowly now come over to your side.

To an impervious nothingness they're thinned, 85
For the red clay has swallowed the white kind;
Into the flowers that gift of life has passed.
Where are the dead? — their homely turns of speech,
The personal grace, the soul informing each?
Grubs thread their way where tears were once composed. 90

The bird-sharp cries of girls whom love is teasing,
The eyes, the teeth, the eyelids moistly closing,
The pretty breast that gambles with the flame,
The crimson blood shining when lips are yielded,
The last gift, and the fingers that would shield it — 95
All go to earth, go back into the game.

And you, great soul, is there yet hope in you
To find some dream without the lying hue

That gold or wave offers to fleshly eyes?
Will you be singing still when you're thin air?
All perishes. A thing of flesh and pore   100
Am I. Divine impatience also dies.

Lean immortality, all crêpe and gold,
Laurelled consoler frightening to behold,
Death is a womb, a mother's breast, you feign —   105
The fine illusion, oh the pious trick!
Who does not know them, and is not made sick —
That empty skull, that everlasting grin?

Ancestors deep down there, O derelict heads
Whom such a weight of spaded earth o'erspreads,
Who *are* the earth, in whom our steps are lost,   110
The real flesh-eater, worm unanswerable
Is not for you that sleep under the table:
Life is his meat, and I am still his host.

"Love," shall we call him? "Hatred of self," maybe?   115
His secret tooth is so intimate with me
That any name would suit him well enough,
Enough that he can see, will, daydream, touch —
My flesh delights him, even upon my couch
I live but as a morsel of his life.   120

Zeno, Zeno, cruel philosopher Zeno,
Have you then pierced me with your feathered arrow
That hums and flies, yet does not fly! The sounding
Shaft gives me life, the arrow kills. Oh, sun! —
Oh, what a tortoise-shadow to outrun   125
My soul, Achilles' giant stride left standing!

No, no! Arise! The future years unfold.
Shatter, O body, meditation's mould!
And, O my breast, drink in the wind's reviving!
A freshness, exhalation of the sea,   130
Restores my soul . . . Salt-breathing potency!
Let's run at the waves and be hurled back to living!

Yes, mighty sea with such wild frenzies gifted
(The panther skin and the rent chlamys), sifted
All over with sun-images that glisten,   135
Creature supreme, drunk on your own blue flesh,

121. *Zeno*: born about 490 B.C., Zeno of Elea invented, according to Aristotle, dialectic. The most famous of his surviving arguments deal with motion: Achilles can never beat the tortoise in a race because, when he reaches its starting-point, the tortoise is already a little farther along; an arrow in flight is at every given moment at rest because it is always opposite a piece of ground equal in length to itself.

Who in a tumult like the deepest hush
Bite at your sequin-glittering tail — yes, listen!

The wind is rising! . . . We must try to live!
The huge air opens and shuts my book: the wave   140
Dares to explode out of the rocks in reeking
Spray. Fly away, my sun-bewildered pages!
Break, waves! Break up with your rejoicing surges
This quiet roof where sails like doves were pecking.

CONCERNING *LE CIMETIÈRE MARIN* *

I do not know whether it is still the fashion to elaborate poems at length, to keep them between being and nonbeing, suspended for years in the presence of desire; to nourish doubts, scruples, and regrets — so that a work perpetually resumed and recast gradually takes on the secret importance of an exercise in self-reform.

This way of producing little was not uncommon among poets and some prose writers forty years ago. For them, time did not count; in that, they were rather like gods. Neither the Idol of Beauty nor the superstition of Literary Eternity had yet been destroyed; and belief in Posterity was not entirely abolished. There existed a kind of *Ethic of Form* that led to infinite labor. Those who devoted themselves to it well knew that the greater the labor, the fewer the people who understand and appreciate it; they toiled for very little — and, as it were, holily. . . .

Thus one moves away from the "natural" or ingenuous conditions of literature and comes little by little to confuse the composition of a work of the mind, which is a *finished* thing, with the very life of the mind — which is a power of transformation always in action. One ends by working for work's sake. In the eyes of these lovers of anxiety and perfection, a work is never *complete* — a word which to them is meaningless — but *abandoned;* and this abandonment, which delivers the work to the flames or to the public (whether it be the result of weariness or the necessity of delivering), is for them a kind of *accident* comparable to the interruption of a thought annulled by fatigue, an importunate person, or some sensation.

I had contracted this sickness, this perverse taste for endless revision, and this indulgence in the reversible state of works at the critical age when the intellectual man is formed and fixed. I rediscovered them in their full force when, toward the age of fifty, circumstances led me to

The Collected Works of Paul Valéry, Volume 7: The Art of Poetry, translated by Denise Folliot. Bollingen Series XLV. 7. Copyright 1958 by Bollingen Foundation, New York. Distributed by Princeton University Press. Pages 140–152: "Concerning *Le Cimetière Marin.*"

* First published in the *Nouvelle Revue française,* March 1, 1933. ("Le Cimetière marin": "The Graveyard by the Sea.")

start composing once more, I have therefore lived a good deal with my poems. For nearly ten years they were for me an undertaking of indeterminate duration — an exercise rather than an act, a search rather than a deliverance, a maneuver of myself by myself rather than a preparation intended for the public. It seems to me that they have taught me several things.

However, I do not advise the adoption of this system: I am not qualified to give anyone the slightest advice, and besides I doubt whether it would suit the young men of an urgent, confused time with no outlook. We are in a fog bank. . . .

If I have mentioned this long intimacy between a work and a "self," it is merely in order to give some idea of the strange sensation I experienced one morning at the Sorbonne on hearing M. Gustave Cohen develop *ex cathedra* an explication of *Le Cimetière marin.*

What I have published has never lacked commentaries, and I cannot complain of the least silence about my few writings. I am used to being elucidated, dissected, impoverished, enriched, exalted, and cast down — to the point of no longer knowing myself *what* I am or *who* is in question: but reading what has been written about you is as nothing to the peculiar sensation of hearing yourself commented on at the University in front of the blackboard, just like a dead author.

In my day the living did not exist for the professorial chair; but I do not find it entirely a bad thing that this should no longer be so.

The teaching of literature takes from it what the teaching of History might take from the analysis of the present — that is, the suspicion or the awareness of the *forces* that engender acts and forms. The past is only the *place* of forms without force; it is for us to provide it with life and necessity and to credit it with our passions and values.

I felt as though I were my own *shadow.* . . . I felt like a shadow taken captive, and yet I sometimes identified myself with one of the students who listened, made notes, and from time to time looked smilingly at the shadow whose poem their teacher was reading and commenting on stanza by stanza. . . .

I confess that *as a student* I discovered in myself little reverence for the poet — isolated, exposed, and embarrassed on his bench. My presence was oddly divided among several ways of being there.

Among the variety of sensations and reflections that made up this hour at the Sorbonne, the dominant one was indeed the sensation of the contrast between the memory of my toil, which was revived, and the finished figure, the determinate, fixed work to which M. Gustave Cohen applied his exegesis and analysis. This made me aware how our *being* is in opposition to our *seeming.* On the one hand was my poem, studied as an accomplished fact, revealing to expert examination its composition, intentions, modes of action, its place in the system of literary history, its affiliations, and its author's probable state of mind. . . . On the other hand was the memory of my attempts, my gropings, inner decipherings, those imperious verbal illuminations which suddenly impose a particular combination of words — as though a certain group possessed some kind of intrinsic power. . . . I nearly said: some kind of *will* to live, quite the opposite of the "freedom" or chaos of the mind, a will that can sometimes force the mind to deviate from its plan and the poem to become quite other than what it was going to be and something one did not dream it could be.

(One can see by this that the notion of an *Author* is not simple: it is so only *in the eyes of a third person.*)

As I listened to M. Cohen reading the stanzas of my text and giving to each its finished meaning and its right place in the development, I was divided between satisfaction at seeing how the aims and expressions of a poem reputedly very obscure were here perfectly understood and set forth and the odd, almost painful feeling to which I have just referred. I shall try to explain this briefly so as to complete the commentary of a particular poem considered as a *fact,* by a glance at the circumstances that accompanied the generation of that poem, or of what it was when it was within me in a state of desire and seeking.

Incidentally, I intrude only to introduce, by means (or by the digression) of a special case, a few remarks on the relationship between a poet and his poem.

It must first be said that the *Cimetière marin, as it stands,* is *for me* the result of the *intersection* of an inner labor and a fortuitous event. One afternoon in the year 1920, our much regretted friend Jacques Rivière,[1] coming to call on me, found me at one "stage" of my *Cimetière marin,* thinking of revising, suppressing, substituting, altering here and there. . . .

He did not rest until he was allowed to read it and, having read it, until he could snatch it away. Nothing is more decisive than the mind of an editor of a review.

Thus it was *by accident* that the form of this work was fixed. It was none of my doing. Moreover, in general I cannot go back over anything I have written without thinking that I should now make something quite different of it, if some outside intervention or some circumstance had not broken the enchantment of never finishing with it. I enjoy work only as work: beginnings bore me, and I suspect everything that comes at the first attempt of being capable of improvement. Spontaneity, even when excellent or seductive, has never seemed to me sufficiently *mine.* I do not say that "I am right," but that that is how I am. . . . The notion of Myself is no simpler than that of Author: a further degree of consciousness opposes a new *Self* to a new *Other.*

1. (1886–1925), critic, novelist, and editor of the *Nouvelle Revue française.*

Literature, then, interests me *profoundly* only to the extent to which it urges the mind to certain transformations — those in which the stimulating properties of language play the chief part. I can, indeed, take a liking for a book, read and reread it with delight; but it never possesses me wholly unless I find in it traces of a thought *whose power is equal to that of language itself*. The force to bend the common word to unexpected ends without violating the "time-honored forms," the capture and subjection of things that are difficult to say, and above all the simultaneous management of syntax, harmony, and ideas (which is the problem of the purest poetry) are in my eyes the supreme objects of our art.

This way of feeling is perhaps shocking. It makes of "creation" a means. It leads to excesses. Further, it tends to corrupt the innocent pleasure of *believing,* which engenders the innocent pleasure of producing and puts up with any kind of reading.

If the author knows himself rather too well, if the reader is active, what becomes of pleasure, what becomes of literature?

This glimpse of the difficulties that may arise between the "consciousness of self" and the habit of writing will no doubt explain certain *biases* with which I have sometimes been reproached. I have, for instance, been blamed for having published several, perhaps even contradictory, texts of the same poem. This reproach is barely intelligible to me, as might be expected after what I have just explained. On the contrary, I should be tempted (if I followed my inclinations) to engage poets to produce, like musicians, a diversity of variants or solutions of the same subject. Nothing would seem to me more consistent with the idea I like to hold of a poet and of poetry.

To my mind the poet is known by his idols and his liberties, which are not those of the majority. Poetry is distinguished from prose by having neither all the same restraints nor all the same licenses. The essence of prose is to perish — that is, to be "understood" — that is, to be dissolved, destroyed without return, entirely replaced by the image or the impulse that it conveys according to the convention of language. For prose always implies the universe of experiences and acts, a universe in which — or *thanks to which* — our perceptions and our acts or emotions have finally to correspond or answer each other in a single way — *uniformly*. The practical universe is reduced to a collection of *aims*. An aim being reached, the word expires. That universe excludes ambiguity, eliminates it; it demands that one should proceed by the shortest way, and it stifles as soon as possible the harmonics of each event that occurs in the mind.

But poetry requires or suggests a very different "Universe": a universe of reciprocal relations analogous to the universe of sounds within which musical thought is born and moves. In this poetic universe, resonance triumphs over causality, and "form," far from dissolving into its effects, is as it were *recalled* by them. The Idea claims its voice.

(The result is an *extreme* difference between the moments of constructing prose and the moments of creating poetry.)

In the same way, in the art of the Dance, the state of the dancer (or that of the lover of ballet) being the object of that art, the movements and displacements of the bodies have no limit in *space* — no visible aim, no *thing* which, being reached, annuls them; and it never occurs to anyone to impose on choreographic actions the law of *non-poetic* but *useful* acts, which is: to be accomplished *with the greatest possible economy of effort* and *in the shortest possible way.*

This comparison may give the impression that neither simplicity nor clarity is an absolute in poetry, where it is perfectly *reasonable* — and even necessary — to maintain oneself in a condition as remote as possible from that of prose, at the cost of losing (without too many regrets) as many readers as one must.

Voltaire said most felicitously that "Poetry is made up of nothing but beautiful details." I am saying no more than precisely that. The poetic universe of which I was speaking arises from the number, or rather from the density, of images, figures, consonances, dissonances, from the linking of turns of speech and rhythms — the essential being constantly to avoid anything that would lead back to prose, either by making it regretted or by following the *idea* exclusively. . . .

In short, the more a poem conforms to Poetry, the less it can be thought in prose without perishing. To summarize a poem or put it into prose is quite simply to misunderstand the essence of an art. Poetic necessity is inseparable from material form, and the thoughts uttered or suggested by the text of a poem are by no means the unique and chief objects of its discourse — but *means* which combine *equally* with the sounds, cadences, meter, and ornaments to produce and sustain a particular tension or exaltation, to engender within us a *world,* or *mode of existence,* of complete harmony.

If I am questioned; if anyone wonders (as happens sometimes quite peremptorily) what I "wanted to say" in a certain poem, I reply that I did not *want to say* but *wanted to make,* and that it was the intention of *making* which *wanted* what I *said.* . . .

As for the *Cimetière marin,* this intention was at first no more than a rhythmic figure, empty, or filled with meaningless syllables, which obsessed me for some time. I noticed that this figure was decasyllabic, and I pondered on that model, which is very little used in modern French poetry; it struck me as poor and monotonous. It was of little worth compared with the alexandrine, which three or four generations of great artists had prodigiously elaborated. The demon of generalization prompted me to try raising this *Ten* to the power of *Twelve*. It suggested a certain stanza of six lines, and the idea of a *composition* founded on the number of these stanzas and strengthened by a diversity of tones and functions to be assigned to them. Between the stanzas, contrasts or correspondences would be set up. This last condition soon required the potential poem to be a monologue of "self," in which the simplest and most enduring themes of my affective and intellectual life, as they had imposed themselves upon my adolescence, associated with the sea and the light of a particular spot on the Mediterranean coast, were called up, woven together, opposed. . . . All this led to the theme of death and suggested the theme of pure thought. (The chosen line of ten syllables bears some relation to the Dantesque line.)

My line had to be solid and strongly rhythmical. I knew I was tending toward a monologue as personal, but also as universal, as I could make it. The type of line chosen, and the form adopted for the stanzas, set me conditions that favored certain "movements," permitted certain changes of tone, called up a certain style. . . . The *Cimetière marin* was *conceived*. A rather long period of gestation ensued.

Whenever I think of the art of writing (in verse or in prose), the same "ideal" presents itself to my mind. The myth of "creation" lures us into wanting to make something from nothing. So I imagine that I discover my work little by little, beginning with pure conditions of form, more and more considered, defined to the point where they propose, or almost impose, a *subject* — or at least kinds of subject.

Note that precise conditions of form are nothing but the expression of the knowledge and consciousness we have of the *means* at hand, their capabilities, their limitations, and their defects. This is why I sometimes define the *writer* by a relationship between a particular "mind" and Language. . . .

But I know the illusory character of my "Ideal." The nature of language hardly lends itself to sustained combinations; moreover, the formation and habits of the modern reader, to whom his accustomed pabulum of incoherence and immediate effects renders imperceptible all concern for structure, hardly encourage one to wander so far from him. . . .

Yet the sole thought of constructions of this kind remains for me the most *poetic* of ideas: the idea of composition.

I pause on this word. . . . It would lead me into all kinds of diffuseness. Nothing in poets has more amazed me, or caused me more regret, than the little study they have given to composition. In the most famous lyrics I find almost nothing but developments that are purely linear, or . . . delirious — that is, which proceed bit by bit with no more sustained organization than is shown by a flame following a trail of powder. (I am not speaking of poems dominated by a story, where the chronology of events intervenes: these are mixed works — operas, not sonatas or symphonies.)

But my astonishment lasts only until I remember my own experiences and the almost discouraging difficulties I have met in my attempts to *compose* in the lyric order. The fact is that detail is here essential at each moment, and the cleverest and most beautiful scheme must come to terms with the uncertainty of discoveries. In the lyric universe each moment must consummate an indefinable alliance between the perceptible and the significant. The result is that, in some way, composition is continuous and can hardly withdraw into another time than that of execution. There is not one time for the "content" and another for the "form"; and composition in this *genre* is not only opposed to disorder or disproportion but also to *decomposition*. If the meaning and the sound (or the content and the form) can easily be dissociated, the poem *decomposes*.

Important result: the "ideas" that figure in a poetic work do not play the same part, are not at all *currency of the same kind,* as the ideas in prose.

I said that the *Cimetière marin* first came into my head in the shape of a composition in stanzas of six lines of ten syllables. This decision enabled me fairly easily to distribute through my work the perceptible, affective, and abstract content it needed so as to suggest a meditation by a particular *self,* translated into the poetic universe.

The necessity of producing contrasts, and of maintaining a kind of balance between the different moments of this *self,* led me (for example) to introduce at one point a certain touch of philosophy. The lines in which the famous arguments of Zeno of Elea appear (though here animated, confused, carried away in a burst of dialectic, like a whole rigging by a sudden gust of wind) have the role of offsetting by a metaphysical tonality the sensual and "too human" part of the preceding stanzas; also, they define more precisely *the person who is speaking,* a lover of abstractions; finally, they oppose to what in him was speculative and far too searching, the actual reflex power whose jerk breaks and dispels a state of somber fixity which is, as it were, complementary to the prevailing splendor — at the same time upsetting a mass of judgments on all human, inhuman, and superhuman things. I have corrupted those few images from Zeno to express the rebellion against the length and painfulness of a meditation that makes too cruelly felt the gap between *being* and *knowing* that is developed by the consciousness of consciousness. Naïvely, the *soul* wishes to exhaust the Eleatic's infinity.

But I meant no more than to borrow a little of the *color* of philosophy.

The various foregoing remarks may give some idea of an author's reflections when he is faced by a commentary on his work. He sees in the work what it should have been and what it could have been, rather than what it is. What, then, is more interesting to him than the result of a scrupulous examination and the impression of another's eye? It is not within myself that the real unity of my work is found. I wrote a "score" — but I can hear it performed only by the soul and mind of others.

This is why M. Cohen's work (leaving aside the far too amiable things in it about me) is particularly precious to me. He has sought my aims with remarkable care and method and has applied to a contemporary text the same learning and the same precision that he is in the habit of showing in his scholarly studies in literary history. He has with equal skill retraced the poem's architecture and called attention to its detail — noticing, for example, those recurrent terms which reveal the tendencies and characteristic repetitions of a mind. (Certain words above all others sound within us, like overtones of our deepest nature. . . .) Finally, I am very grateful to him for having so lucidly explained me to the young people who are his students.

As for the interpretation of the *letter,* I have already made myself clear elsewhere on this point; but it can never be too much insisted upon: *there is no true meaning to a text* — no author's authority. Whatever he may have *wanted to say,* he has written what he has written. Once published, a text is like an apparatus that anyone may use as he will and according to his ability: it is not certain that the one who constructed it can use it better than another. Besides, if he knows well what he meant to do, this knowledge always disturbs his perception of what he has done.

Rainer Maria Rilke (1875–1926)

LIFE: After five years in the academies which were to have been the prelude to a military career, he managed to get to Prague and Munich, where he began his study of the humanities. Thereafter the Austrian poet set out on those travels which took him to Russia, where he met and came under the influence of Tolstoy; to Paris, where he was employed as secretary to the great French sculptor Rodin; and to the homes and castles of European nobility, where he wrote the poetry which attempted to impose his intensely personal vision of order on the chaos of reality.

WORKS: *The Book of Hours* (1905); *New Poems,* 2 volumes (1907–08); *The Notebooks of Malte Laurids Brigge* (1910); *Duino Elegies* (1923); *Sonnets to Orpheus* (1923).

DUINO ELEGIES

The Third Elegy *

One thing to sing the beloved, another, alas!
that hidden guilty river-god of the blood.
He whom she knows from afar, her lover, what does he know
of that Lord of Pleasure, who often, out of his lonely heart,
before she had soothed him, often as though she did not exist,
streaming from, oh, what unknowable depths, would uplift
his god-head, uprousing the night to infinite uproar?
Oh, the Neptune within our blood, oh, his terrible trident!
Oh, the gloomy blast of his breast from the twisted shell!
Hark, how the night grows fluted and hollowed. You stars,   10
is it not from you that the lover's delight in the loved one's
face arises? Does not his intimate insight
into her purest face come from the purest star?

It was not you, alas! It was not his mother
that bent his brows into such an expectant arch.
Not to meet yours, girl feeling him, not to meet yours
did his lips begin to assume that more fruitful curve.
Do you really suppose your gentle approach could have so
convulsed him, you, that wander like morning-breezes?
You terrified his heart, indeed; but more ancient terrors   20
rushed into him in that instant of shattering contact.
Call him . . . you can't quite call him away from those sombre com-
      panions.
Truly, he tries to, he does escape them; disburdenedly settles
into your intimate heart, receives and begins himself there.
Did he ever begin himself, though?
Mother, you made him small, it was you that began him;
he was new to you, you arched over those new eyes
the friendly world, averting the one that was strange.
Where, oh where, are the years when you simply displaced
for him, with your slender figure, the surging abyss?   30
You hid so much from him then; made the nightly-suspected room
harmless, and out of your heart full of refuge
mingled more human space with that of his nights.
Not in the darkness, no, but within your far nearer presence

Reprinted from *Duino Elegies* by Rainer Maria Rilke. Translation, Introduction, and Commentary by J. B. Leishman and Stephen Spender. Copyright 1939 by W. W. Norton & Company, Inc. Copyright Renewed © 1967 by Stephen Spender and J. B. Leishman.

* Rilke began writing the *Elegies* at the home of his friend, Princess Marie von Thurn und Taxis-Hohenlohe, at Schloss Duino, near Trieste, during the winter of 1911–12, but did not finish them until ten years later.

you placed the light, and it shone as though out of friendship.
Nowhere a creak you could not explain with a smile,
as though you had long known *when* the floor would behave itself
    thus . . .
And he listened to you and was soothed. So much it availed,
gently, your coming; his tall cloaked destiny stepped
behind the chest of drawers, and his restless future,   40
that easily got out of place, conformed to the folds of the curtain.

And he himself as he lay there in such relief,
mingling, under his drowsy eyelids, the sweetness
of your light shaping with foretaste of coming sleep,
seemed to be under protection . . . Within, though: who could avert,
divert, the floods of origin flowing within him?
Alas! there *was* no caution within that sleeper; sleeping,
yes, but dreaming, yes, but feverish: what he embarked on!
He, so new, so timorous, how he got tangled
in ever-encroaching roots of inner event,   50
twisted to primitive patterns, to throttling growths, to bestial
preying forms! How he gave himself up to it! Loved.
Loved his interior world, his interior jungle,
that primal forest within, on whose mute overthrownness,
green-lit, his heart stood. Loved. Left it, continued
into his own roots and out into violent beginning
where his tiny birth was already outlived. Descended,
lovingly, into the older blood, the ravines
where Frightfulness lurked, still gorged with his fathers. And every
terror knew him, and winked, and quite understood.   60
Yes, Horror smiled at him . . . Seldom
did you, Mother, smile so tenderly. How could he help
loving what smiled at him? Long before you
he loved it, for, even while you bore him,
it was there, dissolved in the water that lightens the seed.

Look, we don't love like flowers, with only a single
season behind us; immemorial sap
mounts in our arms when we love. Oh, maid,
this: that we've loved, *within* us, not one, still to come, but all
the innumerable fermentation; not just a single child,   70
but the fathers, resting like mountain-ruins
within our depths; — but the dry river-bed
of former mothers; — yes, and the whole of that
soundless landscape under its cloudy or
cloudless destiny: — *this* got the start of you, maid.

And you yourself, how can you tell, — you have conjured up
prehistoric time in your lover. What feelings

whelmed up from beings gone by! What women
hated you in him! What sinister men
you roused in his youthful veins! Dead children
were trying to reach you . . . Oh gently, gently
show him daily a loving, confident task done, — guide him
close to the garden, give him those counter-
balancing nights . . . . . .
Withhold him . . . . . .

80

The Ninth Elegy

Why, when this span of life might be fleeted away
as laurel, a little darker than all
the surrounding green, with tiny waves on the border
of every leaf (like the smile of a wind) : — oh, why
have to be human, and, shunning Destiny,
long for Destiny? . . .
Not because happiness really
exists, that premature profit of imminent loss.
Not out of curiosity, not just to practise the heart,
that could still be there in laurel. . . . .
But because being here amounts to so much, because all
this Here and Now, so fleeting, seems to require us and strangely
concerns us. Us the most fleeting of all. Just once,
everything, only for once. Once and no more. And we, too,
once. And never again. But this
having been once, though only once,
having been once on earth — can it ever be cancelled?

10

And so we keep pressing on and trying to perform it,
trying to contain it within our simple hands,
in the more and more crowded gaze, in the speechless heart.
Trying to become it. To give it to whom? We'd rather
hold on to it all for ever. . . . Alas, but the other relation, —
what can be taken across? Not the art of seeing, learnt here
so slowly, and nothing that's happened here. Nothing at all.
Sufferings, then. Above all, the hardness of life,
the long experience of love; in fact,
purely untellable things. But later,
under the stars, what then? the more deeply untellable stars?
For the wanderer doesn't bring from the mountain slope
a handful of earth to the valley, untellable earth, but only
some word he has won, a pure word, the yellow and blue
gentian. Are we, perhaps, here just for saying: House,
Bridge, Fountain, Gate, Jug, Olive tree, Window, —
possibly: Pillar, Tower? . . . . but for saying, remember,
oh, for such saying as never the things themselves

20

30

hoped so intensely to be. Is not the secret purpose
of this sly earth, in urging a pair of lovers,
just to make everything leap with ecstasy in them?
Threshold: how much it can mean
to two lovers, that they should be wearing their own
worn threshold a little, they too, after the many before,
before the many to come, ... as a matter of course! 40

Here is the time for the Tellable, *here* is its home.
Speak and proclaim. More than ever
the things we can live with are falling away, and their place
being oustingly taken up by an imageless act.
Act under crusts, that will readily split as soon
as the doing within outgrows them and takes a new outline.
Between the hammers lives on
our heart, as between the teeth
the tongue, which, nevertheless, 50
remains the bestower of praise.

Praise the world to the Angel, not the untellable: you
can't impress him with the splendour you've felt; in the cosmos
where he more feelingly feels you're only a tyro. So show him
some simple thing, remoulded by age after age,
till it lives in our hands and eyes as a part of ourselves.
Tell him *things*. He'll stand more astonished; as you did
beside the roper in Rome or the potter in Egypt.
Show him how happy a thing can be, how guileless and ours;
how even the moaning of grief purely determines on form, 60
serves as a thing, or dies into a thing, — to escape
to a bliss beyond the fiddle. These things that live on departure
understand when you praise them: fleeting, they look for
rescue through something in us, the most fleeting of all.
Want us to change them entirely, within our invisible hearts,
into — oh, endlessly — into ourselves! Whosoever we are.

Earth, isn't this what you want: an invisible
re-arising in us? Is it not your dream
to be one day invisible? Earth! invisible!
What is your urgent command, if not transformation? 70
Earth, you darling, I will! Oh, believe me, you need
your Springs no longer to win me: a single one,
just one, is already more than my blood can endure.
I've now been unspeakably yours for ages and ages.
You were always right, and your holiest inspiration's
Death, that friendly Death.
Look, I am living. On what? Neither childhood nor future
are growing less. . . . . Supernumerous existence
wells up in my heart. 80

Isaac Babel (1894–?)

LIFE: Born in Odessa, where, as in the rest of Russia, the official anti-semitism of Nicholas II made mere survival a triumph, he left his family and went first to Kiev, then to St. Petersburg, to begin his life as artist and intellectual. In 1916 he met the writer Maxim Gorky, who published two of his stories and then advised him to stop writing and go "among the people." Babel served in the Tsar's army during World War I, but joined and fought in the Revolution, which he apparently saw as yet another test of his ability to survive and endure. By the early thirties he had become a popular and esteemed Soviet writer, but after 1932 he no longer published any new stories, and the ambiguous address he delivered to the first Writers' Congress seems to have foreshadowed his disappearance during the great purges, which reached their climax in the trials of 1937. It is probable that he died in a concentration camp in 1939 or 1940.

WORKS: *Odessa Tales* (1924); *Red Cavalry* (1926).

MY FIRST GOOSE *

Savitsky, Commander of the VI Division, rose when he saw me, and I wondered at the beauty of his giant's body. He rose, the purple of his riding breeches and the crimson of his little tilted cap and the decorations stuck on his chest cleaving the hut as a standard cleaves the sky. A smell of scent and the sickly sweet freshness of soap emanated from him. His long legs were like girls sheathed to the neck in shining riding boots.

He smiled at me, struck his riding whip on the table, and drew toward him an order that the Chief of Staff had just finished dictating. It was an order for Ivan Chesnokov to advance on Chugunov-Dobryvodka with the regiment entrusted to him, to make contact with the enemy and destroy the same.

"For which destruction," the Commander began to write, smearing the whole sheet, "I make this same Chesnokov entirely responsible, up to and including the supreme penalty, and will if necessary strike him down on the spot; which you, Chesnokov, who have been working with me at the front for some months now, cannot doubt."

The Commander signed the order with a flourish, tossed it to his orderlies and turned upon me gray eyes that danced with merriment.

I handed him a paper with my appointment to the Staff of the Division.

* From *Red Cavalry* (1926).

"Put it down in the Order of the Day," said the Commander. "Put him down for every satisfaction save the front one. Can you read and write?"

"Yes, I can read and write," I replied, envying the flower and iron of that youthfulness. "I graduated in law from St. Petersburg University."

"Oh, are you one of those grinds?" he laughed. "Specs on your nose, too! What a nasty little object! They've sent you along without making any enquiries; and this is a hot place for specs. Think you'll get on with us?"

"I'll get on all right," I answered, and went off to the village with the quartermaster to find a billet for the night.

The quartermaster carried my trunk on his shoulder. Before us stretched the village street. The dying sun, round and yellow as a pumpkin, was giving up its roseate ghost to the skies.

We went up to a hut painted over with garlands. The quartermaster stopped, and said suddenly, with a guilty smile:

"Nuisance with specs. Can't do anything to stop it, either. Not a life for the brainy type here. But you go and mess up a lady, and a good lady too, and you'll have the boys patting you on the back."

He hesitated, my little trunk on his shoulder; then he came quite close to me, only to dart away again despairingly and run to the nearest yard. Cossacks were sitting there, shaving one another.

"Here, you soldiers," said the quartermaster, setting my little trunk down on the ground. "Comrade Savitsky's orders are that you're to take this chap in your billets, so no nonsense about it, because the chap's been through a lot in the learning line."

The quartermaster, purple in the face, left us without looking back. I raised my hand to my cap and saluted the Cossacks. A lad with long straight flaxen hair and the handsome face of the Ryazan Cossacks went over to my little trunk and tossed it out at the gate. Then he turned his back on me and with remarkable skill emitted a series of shameful noises.

"To your guns — number double-zero!" an older Cossack shouted at him, and burst out laughing. "Running fire!"

His guileless art exhausted, the lad made off. Then, crawling over the ground, I began to gather together the manuscripts and tattered garments that had fallen out of the trunk. I gathered them up and carried them to the other end of the yard. Near the hut, on a brick stove, stood a cauldron in which pork was cooking. The steam that rose from it was like the far-off smoke of home in the village, and it mingled hunger with desperate loneliness in my head. Then I covered my little broken trunk with hay, turning it into a pillow, and lay down on the ground to read in *Pravda* Lenin's speech at the Second Congress of the Comintern. The sun fell upon me from behind the toothed hillocks, the Cossacks trod on my feet, the lad made fun of me untiringly, the beloved lines came toward me along a thorny path and could not reach me. Then I put aside the paper and went out to the landlady, who was spinning on the porch.

"Landlady," I said, "I've got to eat."

The old woman raised to me the diffused whites of her purblind eyes and lowered them again.

"Comrade," she said, after a pause, "what with all this going on, I want to go and hang myself."

"Christ!" I muttered, and pushed the old woman in the chest with my fist. "You don't suppose I'm going to go into explanations with you, do you?"

And turning around I saw somebody's sword lying within reach. A severe-looking goose was waddling about the yard, inoffensively preening its feathers. I overtook it and pressed it to the ground. Its head cracked beneath my boot, cracked and emptied itself. The white neck lay stretched out in the dung, the wings twitched.

"Christ!" I said, digging into the goose with my sword. "Go and cook it for me, landlady."

Her blind eyes and glasses glistening, the old woman picked up the slaughtered bird, wrapped it in her apron, and started to bear it off toward the kitchen.

"Comrade," she said to me, after a while, "I want to go and hang myself." And she closed the door behind her.

The Cossacks in the yard were already sitting around their cauldron. They sat motionless, stiff as heathen priests at a sacrifice, and had not looked at the goose.

"The lad's all right," one of them said, winking and scooping up the cabbage soup with his spoon.

The Cossacks commenced their supper with all the elegance and restraint of peasants who respect one another. And I wiped the sword with sand, went out at the gate, and came in again, depressed. Already the moon hung above the yard like a cheap earring.

"Hey, you," suddenly said Surovkov, an older Cossack. "Sit down and feed with us till your goose is done."

He produced a spare spoon from his boot and handed it to me. We supped up the cabbage soup they had made, and ate the pork.

"What's in the newspaper?" asked the flaxen-haired lad, making room for me.

"Lenin writes in the paper," I said, pulling out *Pravda*. "Lenin writes that there's a shortage of everything."

And loudly, like a triumphant man hard of hearing, I read Lenin's speech out to the Cossacks.

Evening wrapped about me the quickening moisture of its twilight sheets; evening laid a mother's hand upon my burning forehead. I read on and rejoiced, spying out exultingly the secret curve of Lenin's straight line.

"Truth tickles everyone's nostrils," said Surovkov, when I had come to the end. "The question is, how's it to be pulled from the heap. But he goes and strikes at it straight off like a hen pecking at a grain!"

This remark about Lenin was made by Surovkov, platoon commander of the Staff Squadron; after which we lay down to sleep in the hayloft. We slept, all six of us, beneath a wooden roof that let in the stars, warming one another, our legs intermingled. I dreamed: and in my dreams saw women. But my heart, stained with bloodshed, grated and brimmed over.

Federico García Lorca (1899–1936)

LIFE: In spite of his early successes as poet and dramatist, he left Spain in 1929 to live first in New York and then Cuba, where for a few months he was happy. When he returned to his homeland, he directed the traveling university-theatre *La Barraca*, saw more of his plays produced, went to Argentina to teach and direct; and then came home again, to be executed during the Spanish Civil War by Falangists occupying Granada.

WORKS: *Libro de Poemas* (1921); *Gypsy Ballads* (1928); *Mariana Pineda* (1928); *Poet in New York* (1929–30); *Blood Wedding* (1933); *The House of Bernarda Alba* (1945).

THE KING OF HARLEM

With a spoon
he scooped out the eyes of crocodiles
and spanked the monkeys on their bottoms.
With a spoon.

Fire of all times slept in the flints
and the beetles drunk with anis
forgot the moss of the villages.

That old man covered with mushrooms
went to the place where the Negroes were weeping
while the spoon of the King crackled
and the tanks of putrid water arrived.

Roses escaped along the edge of the final curves of the air,
and in the heaps of saffron

From *Selected Poems of Federico García Lorca*. Translated by Stephen Spender and J. L. Gili. Copyright 1955 by New Directions. Reprinted by permission of New Directions Publishing Corporation.

the boys were mauling small squirrels
with a flush of stained frenzy.

It is necessary to cross the bridges
and to reach the black murmur,
so that the perfume of lungs strikes our temples
with its suit of warm pineapple.

Necessary to murder the blonde seller of brandy,
and all the friends of the apple and sand,
necessary to bang with closed fists
the small Jewesses that tremble full of bubbles,
so that the King of Harlem sings with his multitude,
so that the crocodiles sleep in long rows
under the asbestos of the moon,
so that nobody doubts the infinite beauty of funnels,
graters, feather-dusters, and saucepans in kitchens.

Ah Harlem! Ah Harlem! Ah Harlem!
There is no anxiety comparable to your oppressed scarlets,
to your blood shaken within your dark eclipse,
to your garnet violence deaf and dumb in the penumbra,
to your great King, a prisoner with a commissionaire's uniform.

The night had a fissure
and still ivory salamanders.
The American girls carried babies and coins in their bellies
and the boys fainted stretched on the cross of lassitude.

They are.
They are those who take silver whisky near the volcanoes
and devour bits of heart through the frozen mountains of the bear.

That night the King of Harlem with a very hard spoon
scooped out the eyes of crocodiles
and spanked the monkeys on their bottoms.
With a spoon.
The Negroes cried abased
among umbrellas and golden suns,
the mulattoes were stretching gum, anxious to reach the white torso,
and the wind blurred mirrors
and burst open the veins of the dancers.

Negroes, Negroes, Negroes, Negroes.
The blood has no doors in your night face upwards.
There is no blushing. Furious blood under the skins,

alive in the thorn of the dagger and in the breast of landscapes,
under the pincers and the broom of the celestial Moon of Cancer.

Blood that searches through thousand ways deaths covered in flour and
        ashes of nards,
still skies, slanting, where the colonies of planets
rumble along beaches with abandoned objects.

Blood that looks slowly through the tail of the eye
made of squeezed esparto and subterranean nectars.
Blood that oxidizes the unaware trade wind in a footprint
and dissolves the butterflies in the windowpanes.

This is the blood that comes, that will come
through roofs and terraces, by every way,
to burn the chlorophyll of blonde women,
to groan at the foot of beds facing insomnia of basins
and to crash against a dawn of tobacco and subdued yellow.

One has to flee,
to flee from the shores and lock oneself up in the top storeys
because the marrow of the woods will penetrate through the crevices,
to leave in your flesh a slight print of eclipse
and a false sadness of faded glove and chemical rose.

Through the most wise silence
when the waiters and cooks and those that clean with their tongues
the wounds of millionaires
look for the King through the streets and in angles of saltpeter.

An oblique South Wind of wood in the black mud
spits at the broken boats and pierces nails in its shoulders;
a South Wind that carries
fangs, sunflowers, alphabets
and a voltaic battery with suffocated wasps.

Oblivion was expressed by three drops of ink on the monocle,
love, by a single face, invisible on the surface of stone.
Marrows and corollas were composing on the clouds
a desert of stems without a single rose.

From the left, from the right, from the South, and from the North,
there rises the wall impassive
to the mole and the needle of water.
Do not seek, Negroes, for the cleft
to find the infinite mask.
Seek for the great Sun of the center

made into a buzzing cluster.
The Sun that slides through the woods
certain of not meeting a nymph,
the Sun that destroys numbers and has never crossed a dream,
the tattooed Sun that goes down the river
and bellows followed by alligators.

Negroes, Negroes, Negroes, Negroes.

Never snake, nor goat, nor mule
grew pale at death.

The wood-cutter does not know when
the clamorous trees which he fells expire.
Wait under the vegetable shadow of your King
until the hemlock, thistles and stinging nettles disturb the furthermost
     terraces.

Then, Negroes, then, then,
you will be able to kiss with frenzy the wheels of bicycles,
to put pairs of microscopes in the caves of the squirrels
and dance at last, without fear, while the spiked flowers
assassinate our Moses almost in the reeds of Heaven!

Ah, masqueraded Harlem!
Ah, Harlem, threatened by a mob wearing clothes without heads!
Your rumour reaches me,
your rumour reaches me, crossing tree trunks and lifts,
across the grey plates
where your cars float covered with teeth,
across the dead horses and the minute crimes,
across your great despairing King,
whose beard reaches the sea.

LAMENT FOR IGNACIO SANCHEZ MEJIAS *

1. *Cogida* † *and Death*

At five in the afternoon.
It was exactly five in the afternoon.
A boy brought the white sheet
at five in the afternoon.
A frail of lime ready prepared   5

* 1935.
† Goring.

at five in the afternoon.
The rest was death, and death alone
at five in the afternoon.

The wind carried away the cottonwool
at five in the afternoon.   10
And the oxide scattered crystal and nickel
at five in the afternoon.
Now the dove and the leopard wrestle
at five in the afternoon.
And a thigh with a desolate horn   15
at five in the afternoon.
The bass-string struck up
at five in the afternoon.
Arsenic bells and smoke
at five in the afternoon.   20
Groups of silence in the corners
at five in the afternoon.
And the bull alone with a high heart!
At five in the afternoon.
When the sweat of snow was coming   25
at five in the afternoon,
when the bull ring was covered in iodine
at five in the afternoon.
death laid eggs in the wound
at five in the afternoon.   30
At five in the afternoon.
Exactly at five o'clock in the afternoon.

A coffin on wheels is his bed
at five in the afternoon.
Bones and flutes resound in his ears   35
at five in the afternoon.
Now the bull was bellowing through his forehead
at five in the afternoon.
The room was iridescent with agony
at five in the afternoon.   40
In the distance the gangrene now comes
at five in the afternoon.
Horn of the lily through green groins
at five in the afternoon.
The wounds were burning like suns   45
at five in the afternoon,
and the crowd was breaking the windows
at five in the afternoon.
At five in the afternoon.
Ah, that fatal five in the afternoon!   50

It was five by all the clocks!
It was five in the shade of the afternoon!

2. *The Spilled Blood*

I will not see it!

Tell the moon to come   55
for I do not want to see the blood
of Ignacio on the sand.

I will not see it!

The moon wide open.
Horse of still clouds,   60
and the grey bull ring of dreams
with willows in the barreras.

I will not see it!

Let my memory kindle!
Warn the jasmines   65
of such minute whiteness!

I will not see it!

The cow of the ancient world
passed her sad tongue
over a snout of blood   70
spilled on the sand,
and the bulls of Guisando,
partly death and partly stone,
bellowed like two centuries
sated with treading the earth.   75
No.
I do not want to see it!
I will not see it!

Ignacio goes up the tiers
with all his death on his shoulders.
He sought for the dawn   80
but the dawn was no more.
He seeks for his confident profile
and the dream bewilders him.
He sought for his beautiful body
and encountered his opened blood.   85
I will not see it!
I do not want to hear it spurt

each time with less strength:
that spurt that illuminates
the tiers of seats, and spills   90
over the corduroy and the leather
of a thirsty multitude.
Who shouts that I should come near!
Do not ask me to see it!

His eyes did not close   95
when he saw the horns near,
but the terrible mothers
lifted their heads.
And across the ranches,
an air of secret voices rose,   100
shouting to celestial bulls,
herdsmen of pale mist.
There was no prince in Seville
who could compare with him,
nor sword like his sword   105
nor heart so true.
Like a river of lions
was his marvellous strength,
and like a marble torso
his firm drawn moderation.   110
The air of Andalusian Rome
gilded his head
where his smile was a spikenard
of wit and intelligence.
What a great torero in the ring!   115
What a good peasant in the sierra!
How gentle with the sheaves!
How hard with the spurs!
How tender with the dew!
How dazzling in the fiesta!   120
How tremendous with the final
banderillas of darkness!

But now he sleeps without end.
Now the moss and the grass
open with sure fingers   125
the flower of his skull.
And now his blood comes out singing;
singing along marshes and meadows,
sliding on frozen horns,
faltering soulless in the mist,   130
stumbling over a thousand hoofs
like a long, dark, sad tongue,

to form a pool of agony
close to the starry Guadalquivir.
Oh, white wall of Spain! 135
Oh, black bull of sorrow!
Oh, hard blood of Ignacio!
Oh, nightingale of his veins!
No.
I will not see it! 140
No chalice can contain it,
no swallows can drink it,
no frost of light can cool it,
nor song nor deluge of white lilies,
no glass can cover it with silver. 145
No.
I will not see it!

3. *The Laid Out Body*

Stone is a forehead where dreams grieve
without curving waters and frozen cypresses.
Stone is a shoulder on which to bear Time 150
with trees formed of tears and ribbons and planets.

I have seen grey showers move towards the waves
raising their tender riddled arms,
to avoid being caught by the lying stone
which loosens their limbs without soaking the blood. 155

For stone gathers seed and clouds,
skeleton larks and wolves of penumbra:
but yields not sounds nor crystals nor fire,
only bull rings and bull rings and more bull rings without walls.

Now, Ignacio the well born lies on the stone. 160
All is finished. What is happening? Contemplate his face:
death has covered him with pale sulphur
and has placed on him the head of a dark minotaur.

All is finished. The rain penetrates his mouth.
The air, as if mad, leaves his sunken chest, 165
and Love, soaked through with tears of snow,
warms itself on the peak of the herd.

What are they saying? A stenching silence settles down.
We are here with a body laid out which fades away,
with a pure shape which had nightingales 170
and we see it being filled with depthless holes.

Who creases the shroud? What he says is not true!
Nobody sings here, nobody weeps in the corner,
nobody pricks the spurs, nor terrifies the serpent.
Here I want nothing else but the round eyes 175
to see this body without a chance of rest.

Here I want to see those men of hard voice.
Those that break horses and dominate rivers;
those men of sonorous skeleton who sing
with a mouth full of sun and flint. 180

Here I want to see them. Before the stone.
Before this body with broken reins.
I want to know from them the way out
for this captain strapped down by death.

I want them to show me a lament like a river 185
which will have sweet mists and deep shores,
to take the body of Ignacio where it loses itself
without hearing the double panting of the bulls.

Loses itself in the round bull ring of the moon
which feigns in its youth a sad quiet bull: 190
loses itself in the night without song of fishes
and in the white thicket of frozen smoke.

I don't want them to cover his face with handkerchiefs
that he may get used to the death he carries.
Go, Ignacio; feel not the hot bellowing. 195
Sleep, fly, rest: even the sea dies!

4. *Absent Soul*

The bull does not know you, nor the fig tree,
nor the horses, nor the ants in your own house.
The child and the afternoon do not know you
because you have died for ever. 200

The back of the stone does not know you,
nor the black satin in which you crumble.
Your silent memory does not know you
because you have died for ever.

The autumn will come with small white snails,
misty grapes and with clustered hills, 205
but no one will look into your eyes
because you have died for ever.

Because you have died for ever,   210
like all the dead of the Earth,
like all the dead who are forgotten
in a heap of lifeless dogs.

Nobody knows you. No. But I sing of you.
For posterity I sing of your profile and grace.
Of the signal maturity of your understanding.   215
Of your appetite for death and the taste of its mouth.
Of the sadness of your once valiant gaiety.

It will be a long time, if ever, before there is born
an Andalusian so true, so rich in adventure.
I sing of his elegance with words that groan,   220
and I remember a sad breeze through the olive trees.

Luigi Pirandello (1867–1936)

LIFE: The son of a wealthy Sicilian mine-owner, he studied at Rome
and Bonn, taught literature, and wrote the plays which anticipated the
contemporary "theater of the absurd." The tragedy of his personal life
— his wife was committed to an asylum sixteen years after their marriage — seems to have been the source for that exploration of the nature
of reality and illusion which is the subject of both his fiction and his
drama. He received the Nobel Prize for literature in 1934.

WORKS: In addition to the fiction — novels and short stories, most of
which were written before World War I — he composed more than fifty
plays, among them: *Right You Are If You Think You Are* (1917);
Six Characters in Search of an Author (1920); *Henry IV* (1922).

SUCH IS LIFE *

Reflective silence, floors smelling of wax, spick-and-span muslin curtains at the windows: Signora Leuca's house had been like that for the
past eleven years. But now a strange suspense hung over those rooms.
Was it possible that Signora Leuca had agreed after a separation of
eleven years to let her husband return to live with her?
The measured ticking of the big clock in the dining room was dis-

From Pirandello, *Short Stories*. Copyright © 1959, by Gli Eredi di Luigi Pirandello. Reprinted by permission of Simon and Schuster, Inc.

* First published in 1920. Translated by Lily Duplaix.

turbing as it echoed through those voiceless rooms — as if time itself could continue to flow as evenly and serenely as before.

Yesterday, in the little sitting room with the highly sensitive floor, the small silver and crystal objects had tinkled. It was almost as if the teardrops of the gilded candelabra over the mantelpiece and the little liquor glasses on the tea table were shuddering with fear and indignation after Lawyer Arico's visit — "the old cricket," Signora Leuca called him to her friends.

"Ah, life . . . life . . ." he kept repeating after his long harangue, hunching his shoulders, half closing his large eyes in his sallow face, and painfully stretching his thin neck.

All those crystal and silver objects hung there in suspense, waiting for Signora Leuca to protest at least by a shake of her head. But no, she stood tall and erect, fresh and pink-and-white as ever, her spectacles high on her aquiline nose, as she faced the little man who twisted all over at one more leave-taking and went on repeating in the doorway: "Life . . . Ah! Life. . . ."

Was life really like that — a burning shame too great to confess, an agony to be suffered by hunching one's shoulders and squinting one's eyes, or a hard, bitter pill to be swallowed by stretching the neck? Was it not life, after all, that Signora Leuca had spent here in this spotless, demure house for eleven years, receiving occasional visits from her good friends, the ladies of the Charity Society, the learned priest of Sant' Agnese or the organist, Signor Ildebrando? Had she not enjoyed a life of unending peace, spotless order, and silence marked only by the slow, even ticking of the big clock indolently striking the hours and half-hours inside its glass case?

Signorina Trecke, an old maid, ran like a frightened dove to the parish house of Sant' Agnese to sound the alarm.

"Signora Leuca . . . Signora Leuca and her husband . . ." she panted.

Her anxiety turned to amazement, her amazement dissolved into a vague smile before the unruffled nod with which the priest received her news, which he already knew.

Long-legged, short-waisted and stooped, Signorina Trecke was still blond at sixty-six. She was half Russian, half German, yet perhaps more Russian than German. She had been converted to Catholicism by her brother-in-law, God rest his soul, and was most zealous. Her eyes in her pale, flabby face were as blue as when she was eighteen, like two clear lakes obstinately reflecting the smiling, innocent skies of her youth, though who knows how many storm clouds had since passed to darken them. But Signorina Trecke went on feigning ignorance. She did not wish the gall of dismal experience to eat away at the fixity of her new faith, so she appeared completely naïve, to the great annoyance of her friends.

Melting into that empty smile of hers, she asked uneasily if Signor

Marco Leuca really deserved to be forgiven, something she had never questioned because — perhaps it was slander, since His Reverence approved a reconciliation — but didn't Signora Leuca's husband have three children, three little girls with a . . . how do you say it ? . . . by another woman? And what now? Would he abandon them to become reconciled with his wife? No? Then what? The wife here, another woman there, with three — how do you say it ? — three *natural* daughters?

"Nothing of the kind!" the priest tried to reassure her, his usual serenity tinged with a mildly protective air.

Though there were catacombs under Sant' Agnese and even a gloomy, solemn, subterranean church, the parish house stood in the open, surrounded by soft, leafy green amid plenty of air and sunlight. One could see in the priest's limpid eyes and hear in his warm voice the good effects of this environment not only on the body but the soul!

"My dear Signorina Trecke, it is not a question of two households or of abandonment either; it is not even a question of an out-and-out reconciliation. We will have, God willing, a simple, friendly relationship, a few brief visits from time to time, and that is all . . . to bring a little comfort."

"To him?" asked Signorina Trecke.

"Of course to *him!*" the priest said. "To relieve the burden of his guilt, a kind word to soothe his gnawing remorse. He asks nothing more and, for that matter, our excellent Signora Leuca could not grant anything less. Now, don't worry!"

The priest placed his words like beautiful little porcelain vases on the table before him, there, there and there — each one graced with an artificial flower with green tissue paper twisted around the wire stem, charmingly effective at no cost whatsoever. But the organist, that good Signor Ildebrando who also acted as secretary, should have been told not to approve every word the priest said with honeyed smiles and little nods. It virtually turned Signorina Trecke's stomach.

Signor Ildebrando had never been able to forgive his long-dead parents for imposing such a sonorous name on him, most unsuitable for his slender, frail body as well as his temperament. He disliked ruddy, aggressive, noisy men who cocked an eye, hanging one thumb in the armhole of their vests like the great *I am!* His nature was tepid, mediocre, colorless, and whenever possible he hung back, clinging to the shadows. He thought that Signorina Trecke, drab as she was, should do the same, instead of putting herself forward in the thick of things, meddling where she was not directly concerned.

"Well, in that case," she was now saying to the priest, "I could invite him to my house for supper, couldn't I ?"

"Of course not!" said the priest, taken aback. "What have you to do with it, Signorina Trecke?"

"Well, if he is to be pitied — my niece says she knows him," she haggled, widening her mouth in a bland smile.

"You will do well, my dear signorina," the priest replied severely, "to keep closer watch over your niece."

"I? But how can I, Father? I really don't understand these things, as I've just proved to you . . . absolutely nothing," she said, opening her arms wide and bowing to take her leave, with a stupid smile still on her face and her childlike eyes clouded because of the hopeless ignorance with which she was afflicted.

Three days later Signor Marco Leuca, accompanied by Arico, the lawyer, paid his first visit.

Disheveled, shabby, blushing for shame, he looked bewildered in that impeccable house so delicately furnished, so jealously chaste. Trembling all over like a wounded animal, he could not utter a word. Then, in desperation, he dropped mutely to his knees before her. Signora Leuca was distressed and frightened by his appearance, aged and shockingly coarsened after eleven years, and she backed away in panic before his helpless gesture although her first impulse had been to help him up.

"Oh, no. God! No!" she moaned.

Then when he almost came to blows with the lawyer who turned on him angrily, loudly commanding him to be calm and not to make a scene, she wanted to run out of the room. He made a furious lunge to shove Arico aside, determined to present himself before her in all his abjection and despair. Hanging his head, he was mortified that his theatrical gesture had misfired; he had fervently hoped she would place her hand tenderly on his hair, not as a caress, but in forgiveness.

How in heaven's name could Signora Leuca have done that? He might have known it was impossible. Pity, patience, even compassion she had, not only for him but for all poor wretches with the same insatiable penchant for vice.

Ah! Life . . .

It was violently marked on his loose face with the telltale sag of the lower lip and the dark pouches around his sad, troubled eyes. But, as the lawyer said, he could at last perhaps enjoy the peace and sweetness of a home — now that his hair was gray and hers completely white . . .

"The sweetness of a home, did you say, Lawyer Arico?"

Signora Leuca knew very well that her house no longer had sweetness, only great calm. She did not say it depressed her, only that she was accustomed to it. She read, busied herself working for the poor, took up collections with the other ladies of the Charity Society, went to church or to the dressmaker — for she liked to dress well — and, when necessary, made calls on Arico, the lawyer, who was in charge of her affairs. All in all, she never had an idle moment. She was content this way, since God had not blessed her life with more intimate joys. At times, in the silence between one stitch and the next on the little shirt she was knitting for a poor child of the neighborhood, or between one line and the next of the book she was reading, she would suddenly sink into a timeless mood where thought seemed vain and comfortless.

She would stare, then, at a familiar object in the room as if seeing it for the first time and as if it had no significance for her. She regretted the things she had never known and suffered that her own heart should have deceived her into supposing she could have been happy by marrying a man who — well, a man. Now Signora Leuca did not even despise him any more.

Yes, life.

It was not as her young girl's heart had dreamed. It was even wrong perhaps for her to speak of her revulsion for that physical contact which sullied one. Although difficult, it was also to be pitied since the price of pleasure had later to be paid in bitter tears.

It was in answer to the priest's exclamation, "In God's name, whoever said compassion was easy?" that she had let herself be persuaded to receive her husband briefly from time to time.

Her charity work, she knew, was really another way of passing the time. True, she did more than she really was able to do and exhausted herself going up and down stairs, or working late into the night for the poor. She threw off this fatigue by sheer will power. A good part of her income went to the needy, and she deprived herself of many things which, for her, were not entirely superfluous. But she could not say that she had ever made a real sacrifice, such as overcoming the recoil of her flesh at the thought of an insufferable contact, or risking the harmony of her neat, orderly life. She was afraid she could never do it.

The same impulses sprang up in her as in everyone else, but where others surrendered blindly she was wary. Her natural instincts were too guarded, her life too hushed, rarefied to a point where ordinary things no longer had substance. She would suddenly notice new, strange aspects of them which disturbed her, as if for the fraction of a second she could penetrate a hidden reality different from that commonly attributed to them. At such times, she feared she was losing her mind.

It should have annoyed her, therefore, that others thought her life so undisturbed and considered her the picture of serenity. Instead it pleased her. She wanted to believe it, convinced that she rejected every longing as soon as it arose within her because of her instinctive aversion for a soiled life. To be sure, she worked at her charities in the midst of sordidness, but she could not have mingled freely with the poor had she not felt herself immune. The only sacrifice she could make, after all, was to expose and eventually to conquer her own squeamishness. It was little enough. She did even more in subduing her own body, her own flesh and all that takes place in intimacy — even involuntarily — and which one never dares confess.

Meanwhile Signorina Trecke, with her usual air of feckless innocence, brought her niece to call and to hear the latest news. Other friends, Signora Marzorati, her daughter, and Signora Mielli, were already there. Urged to talk, Signora Leuca tried to say as little as possible about her husband's first visit.

Signorina Trecke exclaimed, "Ah, so he did come!"

Annoyed, her niece snapped back, "Why pretend not to know it, when you do?"

"I knew? I knew only that he was coming, not that he had come."

Her niece shrugged and turned away to talk to young Signorina Marzorati. The girl's mother bridled, not at all pleased to see her daughter talking with Signorina Trecke's niece, who was a scandal, not only because of her manner of dress, but because of all the gossip that raged around her.

Only Signora Leuca understood that it was not entirely the niece's fault but was partly due to what went on every day between her aunt and herself. They were engaged in a dangerous conflict, the aunt refusing to see any harm in the younger woman's behavior, and the niece doing her utmost to shock her aunt out of her hypocritical pretense. There was no telling where this might lead. What was to be done when Signorina Trecke, who saw harm in the most harmless things, refused to recognize evil when it was flung in her face?

Here, for example, she had expected Signora Leuca to be distraught after her ordeal and instead found her calmly discussing her husband's visit as if nothing out of the ordinary had happened.

"But really nothing did happen," Signora Leuca said, smiling. "He stayed for about fifteen minutes with Lawyer Arico."

"Ah! I'm glad it was with the lawyer!" sighed Signorina Trecke. "I was so afraid he would come alone."

"But why were you afraid?" asked Signora Leuca.

"My niece told me he was so fiery. Nella teaches in the school where he brings the oldest child every morning — goodness, even though they're not legitimate, I suppose they should be called his daughters, shouldn't they? Although they don't bear his name! Nella, what did you say their name was?" she asked.

"Smacca!" replied her niece sharply.

"Probably their mother's name," observed Signora Mielli, who always seemed to have dropped from the clouds when she did happen to say a few words.

"Yes, probably," Signorina Trecke went on. "Imagine! Right in front of my niece, he gave his daughter a — a slap one morning, and so hard it knocked the poor child down. Her cheek was quite scratched by his fingernail. When he saw how he had hurt her, my niece says he started to cry. Oh, I suppose he did some crying here too!"

As the other two ladies turned, expecting a reply, Signora Leuca felt obliged to say yes, that he had cried.

Although the niece was deep in conversation with Signorina Marzorati, she followed every word the women were saying and now she flashed out at her aunt, "No harm done! Her husband's tears never hurt Signora Leuca at all. I'm telling you this so you won't pretend to be shocked!"

Signora Leuca could not help noting the contemptuous tone of the girl's voice but she did not quite understand the reason for it, unless the niece meant to offend her aunt by ridiculing her attitude. A look of chilled amazement passed between her other two friends, Signora Mielli and Signora Marzorati. She herself smiled sadly, trying to enlist their sympathy for poor Signorina Trecke, who, as usual, chose to find nothing amiss.

"He must have changed a lot," Nella Trecke confided in Signorina Marzorati's ear, "but I'll wager Signora Leuca's husband was *something* in his day!"

Signora Marzorati was obviously more and more upset by her daughter's interest in whatever it was that that terrible girl was saying to her. The daughter wore glasses and had bulging breasts; her alarming naïveté was sometimes stormed by secret thoughts which made her blush crimson, because she feared she would no longer be taken for the overgrown child everyone considered her.

All this was clear to Signora Leuca but it gave her no satisfaction that her eyes could see through things so plainly, completely aware that she was not deceived. Then there was Signora Mielli with that air of never knowing what she was doing or saying, as though in a dream, so that in a pinch she might always exclaim, "Really? Did I do this? Did I say that?"

When her five friends finally left, Signora Leuca felt tired and depressed. She looked at the empty, displaced chairs in the sitting room whose disorder seemed to ask what had been the reason for this visit and whether or not it had been really necessary. Yes, it seemed so, for one must look into others' lives, to see what was going on in them, what others thought and what they had to say. This curiosity satisfied a desire in human beings to see beyond themselves, to vary the monotony of every day. It was a diversion from the irritations and difficulties of life. It helped pass the time. A misfortune? A scandal? And they would all run to see and hear about it. Who? Why? No, really? Impossible! When nothing happened, there was boredom and the agony of watching daylight slowly fade and die, as Signora Leuca was now doing through the windowpane.

The priest and the lawyer arranged that Marco Leuca would never come alone to visit his wife, that his visits would always be short and that they would not exceed two a month. However, a few days after the first visit he returned, alone this time and with the pitiful look of an unwanted dog expecting a kick.

Signora Leuca was annoyed, but concealed her agitation as she led him into the little dining room. He buried his face in his big hands and started to sob as soon as he sat down, but without dramatics this time. She looked at him and realized that it would take no more than an understanding word from her to dry his tears.

And then?

No. No. It was already too much that he had returned so soon and

alone. Were she to encourage him with kind words, it would be tantamount to accepting his visits every day and asking for who knows
what else, then farewell to the conditions of their agreement. No. He
would have to stop crying of his own accord and find enough courage
to say why he had come, giving a specific reason if he had one.

Dear God! After two hours of torture, Signora Leuca sat there
stunned, trembling in every fiber of her body. He had come, he said,
to confess. In vain she had reiterated that it was unnecessary, that she
already knew everything, that Lawyer Arico had told her all. He had
still wanted to confess.

He found the courage ruthlessly to expose his life, and seemed to
enjoy debasing himself more and more, that she might trample on him
and that her foot might be sullied in the mire with him.

Signora Leuca was stupefied by certain unheard-of obscenities. The
outrage of it all held her gaze fixed on his clear portrayal of every
loathsome detail. Her cheeks burned. She was conscious of the queasi-
ness with which she held a hundred-lire note between her fingers, which
he quickly snatched out of her furtive hand as if to hide it from himself also.

Although she had given him the money to rid herself of him, afterward she wondered whether this had been the real motive of his visit.
Perhaps not. In all conscience, she had to admit that he had not asked
for it, at least not directly. He had said, to move her, no doubt, that
he had turned over to Lawyer Arico for his children the small sum remaining from his inheritance and had instructed him to pay that
woman only the interest for household expenses. She was so stingy, he
said, that she did not give him a cent to buy a cigar or even a cup of
coffee if he felt like standing at a café bar. How could he possibly have
asked his wife for anything after that confession, accusing himself of
a weak character, a prey to all temptations, dumping all the blame on
that woman's back? He had beseeched her, with hands joined as if in
prayer, to help him overcome his weakness if only by letting him see
her.

After that, it was evil of her to have given him money just to get
rid of him. She had played on the very weakness he had implored her
to combat. Signora Leuca's humiliation only increased as she thought
that perhaps he had felt no compunction whatsoever in accepting the
money.

She turned to the window to look out at the bright green of the
vacant lots for sale across the way. A row of cypress trees and a few
pines were the sole survivors of the princely old villa which had fallen
into decay and disappeared. The azure sky on that clear day filled the
silent house with light.

"Dear Lord," Signora Leuca cried, covering her face with her hands.
"The evil we do . . . the evil that is done unto us!"

Her face still hidden, she recalled the candid look of an old English
minister that summer in Ari at a boardinghouse which stood on top of

the hill like a castle. How green! How sunny! And that swarm of young girls flocking around her every time she stopped to admire the broad valley!

"Marzietta di Lama . . ."

That was her name . . . the girl with the piercing eyes . . . the one with the rippling laugh as she raised her arm to show the Signora a little scratch on her nose. If only she could have been a mother, how much it would have meant . . . but even that joy had been denied her.

Glancing at her hands, she saw her wedding ring and felt an impulse to throw it out the window. A symbol of her married state, it now reflected all the ignominy of that man's confession, she thought, as she twisted her hands in her lap.

Still, if she had been governed by her flesh, fascinated and led astray by insatiable desires, she too would probably have fallen headlong.

As she glanced about the dining room, the furniture seemed to draw back as if waiting for her to return to the quiet of her orderly life. But in her turmoil she hardly noticed; the disturbing violence of that man's body had entered here to challenge the stability of all she had sought to build around and within herself — her conscience, her whole house.

But who had advised and influenced her, and how far was her charity supposed to go, sinking into contact with such hidden shame? Everyone's shame, perhaps more so for those who did not show it because they managed to hide it from themselves than for that poor fiend who wore it blazoned across his face.

Was this, then, her punishment? Punishment for what? Did they suppose that she was to blame for not knowing how to hold him when he left the house eleven years ago to wind up in such degradation?

It was not true: she had never denied him anything which, as her husband, he had the right to expect — and not only out of duty. No. She had always tried to be honest with herself, however painful the truth might be, so that now she was forced to consider how her body had consented, knowing full well that duty would be no excuse to ease her conscience when it later awoke with disgust after all love and respect for the man had gone.

No, she had not sent him away; he left her when she no longer satisfied him.

Having succeeded in freeing herself of all desire, Signora Leuca wanted indignantly to ask those who advised her to show this "difficult proof of a charitable spirit" if that were not a bit too simple. If, on the contrary, it were not more mandatory to pity those who had struggled to resist passion? She wanted the proud satisfaction of being pitied, but in quite a different way. She wanted pity, not admiration! After all, she was not made of marble and was tired of insipid admiration. What did they think, that her deliverance had cost her nothing?

For the first time, the shining order of her house annoyed her. She was bored with it all and, jumping to her feet, she shook her head and cried, "Hypocrisy!"

Marco Leuca walked away from his wife's house reeling with satisfaction. It seemed to him, as he swelled out his chest to breathe, that the road opened before him, making a way between the houses and the trees. By God, he was free! And to prove it he had only to thrust one hand into his pants pocket and crumple that note between his fingers. He was free of all those tiresome restrictions laid down by the priest and the lawyer who boosted him up the stairs of redemption to his wife's house.

She had placed a barrier between them when she had slipped him that hundred-lire note [1] — she stood on one side, he on the other, and there would be no more passing over. On his side he could befoul himself as much as he pleased. What a relief! What joy! And let her not dare presume, with her grand manner, that he no longer needed charity.

A hundred lire! Drink! Drink yourself drunk!

He laughed and glanced around, a mad gleam in his eyes.

How well he had played his part! In return — one hundred lire! Almost a lira for every tear. He had enjoyed seeing her blench at certain descriptions; her eyes were troubled but gaping wide behind those glasses set on the bridge of her nose. When one hits on a way to reveal certain secret things, although they may be shocking, they also magnetize. Revulsion itself, shrinking like meat over a fire, with alarmed "whys," thirsts for more detail — but always from a distance, not close enough to touch! Here, come here and risk one little touch — it will not hurt. It will entice you . . .

He let out a loud guffaw and people turned to stare at him. Nice, those girls over there by the fountain of Sant' Agnese! Cute! If only he could stroke them, under the pretense of taking a drink of water. But no, he wanted wine — and in a first-class place, like a gentleman! Besides, those girls lacked zest. It was the others, with flanks like mares and caverns which so completely seized one with pleasure, from whom it was impossible to break away.[2]

She said that whether they cried or not, the children's hair had to be combed; or else with all the dust and filth . . .

Or else, what?

1. "When this story was written, around 1920, one hundred lire were equivalent to about $12.50" [Translator's note].

2. "The revision begun by the author in the autumn of 1936 comes to an end here, although he intended to continue the development of this, his favorite work. In fact, among his papers, notes were found outlining three new chapters:

(I) *Coming out after the visit and the confession with one hundred lire to spend for a spree. Degradation, wine, women, the bodies of women with flanks like mares. It was no good any more.*

(II) *This woman: She ran away once and then came back. Doubts about the last child. The mediocrity of Sandrina and Lauretta. Elodina, the musician's orphan . . . a delicate stem, a rare flower.*

(III) *Nella Trecke at home, seduction before our eyes*" [Translator's note].

Lice! That's what. Then every morning there would be more tears getting rid of them with a fine-tooth comb — if that would suffice! Sometimes it was necessary to take a razor and shave off all the hair . . . then wouldn't they look pretty, the three of them, with shaved heads!

Oh, God! Why did she have to pull their hair so hard? Plaited that tightly, it curled against their necks like little pigs' tails, the ends tied off with string. It hardly looked as if they had any hair, soaked with oil as it was and parted clear down the back, just two pigtails, and yet Sandrina's hair was very thick.

Walking past the Villa Borghese, he glanced back at the tight little braids on her shoulders and felt tempted to stop and undo them. They took the short cut through the park to save time, also because he wanted to prepare his daughter for the visit they were about to make. It was a long way from Via Flaminia to Sant' Agnese where his wife lived, and he wondered if it was not too far for the child to walk.

Poor Sandrina! It wasn't only her hair. With that dress on, that hat and those wretched little drawers showing below her petticoat, she seemed to feel ungraceful and walked along like a little old woman. But lately, whenever he had complained at home about the way the children were dressed or tried to loosen their braids, *she* had threatened, "Beware, or I'll kiss them!"

For a few months now she had had a swelling on her lip which had grown until it was as round and hard as a pea and almost black.

It could not amount to much because, even when she pressed it, it did not hurt her. They advised her to see a doctor but she said that was nothing compared to other things: headaches, constant fatigue, and always a little fever toward evening. She did not need a doctor to tell her what was wrong — it was the terrible life she had to lead.

However, she stopped kissing the children. But she kissed him at night all right, laughing wildly and holding his head between her hands so that he could not move. She planted those kisses on his mouth . . . there . . . there . . . and there because, just in case what the neighbors said was true, she wanted him to catch it in the same place. It was a wicked joke, but a joke nevertheless because she knew what they said was not true.

He didn't believe it either, or rather it seemed unlikely anyone could die from a little lump which was not even painful. Also he dared not believe it, because it would be such a wonderful stroke of luck. So he laughed resentfully under those kisses she intended as poisonous stings. But one day he stopped before a mirror in a shop window to examine his lips carefully, passing a finger slowly across them and stretching the skin to make sure there was no crack. He, too, now refrained from kissing the children or, at most, he kissed the hair of the smallest one whose adorable little ways and sayings were hard to resist.

The other two, Sandrina and Lauretta, always had a dazed look on their faces as if in constant fear of something. The violent quarrels they witnessed almost every day had left them terrified. But when their father and mother locked themselves in their room it was even worse. Screams came through the door, crying, slaps, blows, kicks, running and falling and the noise of flying objects crashing to bits.

There had been a fight last night and he was now wearing a handkerchief wound around his right hand to hide a long scratch — if it was not a bite. There was another long scratch on his neck.

"Are you, tired, Sandrina?"

"No, Papa."

"Would you like to sit over there on that bench to rest a little while?"

"No, Papa."

"Well, we'll take the streetcar on Via Veneto. Tell me . . . would you like to go to a beautiful house?"

Sandrina looked up from under her hat with an uncertain smile. She had already noticed that he spoke in a different tone of voice. It pleased her though she did not know what to make of it. She nodded her head.

"To see a lady . . . whom I know," he went on. "But you . . ."

He stopped, not knowing how to put it. Sandrina quietly grew very attentive, waiting for him to go on, but as he said nothing more, she risked a question.

"What is her name?"

"She's . . . your aunt," he told her. "But be careful not to mention this at home to your mamma, and not to Lauretta or Rosina either. Nobody at all, understand?"

He stopped to look at her. Sandrina glanced up at him but quickly lowered her eyes.

"You understand?" he repeated roughly, leaning down to look squarely in her eyes.

Sandrina hurriedly nodded her head several times.

"To no one!"

"No one."

"Do you know why I don't want you to tell?" he asked, walking on. "Because your mamma . . . and this . . . this aunt have quarreled. If she ever found out I'd taken you there . . . well, you saw what happened yesterday? It would be even worse! Do you understand?"

"Yes, Papa."

"Don't say a word to anyone . . . or there will be trouble."

After all these instructions and threats, Sandrina stole a look at her father's gloomy face and no longer felt any pleasure at going to the aunt's beautiful house. She understood that her father was not going there to please her, after all, but because he wanted to go even at the risk of another fight if his visit were found out — certainly not through her . . . but suppose her mother asked her where they had gone? Frightened, Sandrina immediately turned to her father.

"Papa . . ."

"What is it?"

"What shall I tell Mama?"

He jerked her hand violently and pulled her arm.

"Nothing . . . nothing, I said. You mustn't say anything at all!"

"I know, but if she asks me where we've been . . ." Sandrina pointed out, more dismayed than ever.

He regretted his roughness and leaned down to caress her.

"Sweet, my little sweet," he murmured. "I didn't understand . . . of course I'll tell you. I'll tell you just what to say if she asks where you've been. Now, perk up! Show me one of your pretty smiles. Quick, a little smile like the one you had when I took you to the puppet show."

His tenderness was more for himself than for the child. It made him feel he was being *good*. His heart swelled with joy as he caught the approving smile of a lady who happened to be passing as he bent solicitously over his daughter. He wanted Sandrina to give him a better reward, but although she tried obediently to smile, her cold, sad little face seemed to plead with him to accept it: the smile was the best she could do.

Sandrina was hardly ten but she knew she would have to protect herself first from her father, then from her mother and sisters as well. Her face was pale and too thin to be pretty; the perky little nose did not match her eyes, which were grim and serious and, when fixed attentively or glancing slyly to either side, did not have a sweet expression.

He sensed his daughter's secret hostility and straightened up resentfully, thinking that he was a fool to expect anything from the children of such a mother.

For quite a while, Signor Leuca had been thinking that it would be a good thing if his wife were to agree to raise his three children. Should their mother die — although he did not believe it likely — or should he take off one day, his rich wife could help these children as she did so many others. If it was not right to bring children into the world and then cast them off, at least he would have taken a step to insure their future. So this time Signora Leuca's husband came to visit her with a little girl.

He was afraid his wife would see through his scheme, as she had before when she suspected his visits of another motive than the need for moral comfort. Also he was not quite sure if, in her eyes, it would not seem brazen to bring this living proof of infidelity into her house.

He came in very doubtfully but brightened when he noticed her delight at sight of the child. He opened his arms wide and quietly let out a huge sigh of relief, smiling tremulously.

Signora Leuca welcomed the little girl tenderly, and Sandrina looked up at her with wide, bewildered eyes.

"Ah, look who is here! What is your name? Sandrina? That's a lovely name. You're the oldest, aren't you? And do you go to school? Oh, already in the fourth grade! Would you like to take off your little hat? We will put it here. Come, sit down beside me."

"Perhaps she doesn't know who I am?" she asked, turning to her husband who stood there tearfully looking on.

"My aunt," Sandrina supplied promptly.

"Yes, darling, your aunt," Signora Leuca agreed; surprised and touched by this answer, she leaned down to kiss the little girl's hand.

Many little children called her "aunt," affectionately prompted by their mothers to show their gratitude. But she felt especially pleased that he had suggested it, even though certainly for a different reason.

Very well, since she was her aunt, this little niece was to have a special treat: chocolate, cookies, and bread-and-butter spread with jam. Seating the child on a cushion at the table, nice and high like a grown-up, she tied a little napkin around her neck.

"Ummm, it's good like this," Signora Leuca said as she prepared a slice of bread, first with butter, then with jam. "Now a spoonful of jam all by itself, to put in your mouth! Would you like that? Yes, I think you would."

Sandrina looked at her and smiled happily as though it were all too good to be true.

When she smiled, that ugly little dress and the way her hair was skinned back distressed Signora Leuca. Poor little thing! As soon as she had finished eating, they went into the bedroom to undo those miserable braids and make one large loose plait, tied halfway down with a satin bow. She then arranged Sandrina's hair becomingly over her forehead to soften her thin face, now pink with pleasure. How her eyes shone! Sandrina looked so entirely different that, seeing her own image in the mirror surrounded by the reflection of all the beautiful things in the bedroom, she did not know herself.

Signora Leuca was mystified by her husband's worried frown when she brought the child back, her face glowing and looking so changed.

Possibly this transformation in his daughter gave him the same feeling she herself had had while she combed the little girl's hair, but she did not want him to mistake her affection for regret that this little girl was not her own. Why, she had even forgotten he was waiting there in the next room while she was busy fussing over the child!

When they left, Signora Leuca went to the window to watch that lovely tassel of hair hanging down her back. After waiting for a while and not seeing them come out the door, she tiptoed to the head of the stairs, curious to see what was keeping them. Then she understood why he had been so dismayed. Her mind at ease, she could not help smiling.

There he was sitting on the steps below, intently trying to do up those two horrible little pigtails again. He had slipped the handkerchief off his hand and from above Signora Leuca saw the long scratch, and an even worse one on his neck.

She was sorry that she had so thoughtlessly put him in this predicament and, remembering the two pieces of dirty string lying on her dressing table, she realized he could never tie off the ends without them, or manage to pull the hair tightly enough with his clumsy hands. If that horrid woman who scratched him like that was not to know about this visit, the child must go home with the same pieces of string. Quickly she ran back to her room and then hurried down the stairs.

"Wait, wait!" she called out. "Let me do it. I'm sorry. I didn't think. You're perfectly right."

As he got up, very embarrassed, she quickly took his place and plaited the braids. Then she bent over Sandrina to kiss her. He slyly took her hand and, before she could snatch it back, she felt the revolting contact of his lips upon it.

A long time afterward, in her little dining room, Signora Leuca sat, still rubbing her hand.

Three weeks, a month went by and her husband did not return. Signora Leuca had expected him to come with the other two children as he had said he would. Maybe that woman had found out about the last visit and had made a scene, or perhaps after his promise he was ashamed to come alone. She supposed he was ill, or possibly one of the children was sick or even the woman herself. Maybe he was still embarrassed because she had discovered him on the stairs . . . and she smiled over that. Or had he perhaps noticed her disgust when she had pulled her hand away?

Signora Leuca supposed so many things. Her friends of the Charity Society, stopping in to see her at that time, observed in a roundabout way that she supposed too much: if it was painful to receive her husband occasionally for short visits, then she should be happy that of himself he had spaced them out. To tell the truth, they said, those visits had grown rather frequent and were not, it would seem, any too brief either.

Finally she agreed that she did suppose too much but that she was still curious to know why he had not returned. It never occurred to her to question the reason for her concern. She said that she wanted to know if something had happened to him — not that it made any difference to her if he no longer came to see her.

Finally it no longer mattered. Everything seemed remote, even the closest things; as soon as she was conscious of them for an instant, they vanished. Curiosity was a thing of the past. She accepted, even welcomed, suffering, but it never touched her deeply. She seemed now to be immune to all the unhappiness life had to offer.

Then one day, instead of her husband, Lawyer Arico and the old priest came to see her. There could be no more doubt: something had happened. But what?

It was difficult to say whether the news was good or bad. The woman was dead . . . that woman.

"Dead?"

She had died suddenly of pneumonia. But the doctor who treated her said she had a cancer on her mouth and would not have lived very long in any case.

At this, Signora Leuca became suspicious. She asked the lawyer and the priest if they had known about the woman's condition when they suggested her husband's visits. Both protested — the priest before God, and the lawyer on his word of honor.

"And did he?" Signora Leuca questioned.

"Did he what?"

"Did he know it?"

"Ah, that, yes," the little lawyer had to confess, twisting on his chair. "He said that . . . he had vaguely . . . vaguely suspected it, he said."

Seeing Signora Leuca frown, the old priest asked, "Do you suppose he foresaw her death? I don't think so."

"Oh, Father," Signora Leuca burst out, "for pity's sake, don't misunderstand me. If you only knew how humiliated I feel! Believe me, my charity does not depend on the washing of a dirty child's face. I'm afraid you do not think very highly of me, Father."

"Not at all! Not at all!" the old priest protested, smiling and blushing a little.

"I'm sorry, but it is true," Signora Leuca insisted.

Seeing how deeply upset she was, the priest grew serious.

"Let us take care not to sin out of spiritual pride, my dear signora."

"I?"

"Yes, you. One sins through pride in many ways. If, for example, you disparage the object of your charity by a suspicion of this kind and so make your act more commendable before God, or rather before your own conscience, your charity changes and becomes something different."

"My own conscience?"

"Yes, Signora."

"Away from God."

"Yes, Signora. I am warning you: for some time now I have noticed this tendency of yours and I am sorry to have to say it. I mean this searching for reasons . . . this suspicious questioning of every motive. You must guard against it."

Signora Leuca bowed her head sadly and covered her face with her hands, regretting her outburst.

"Yes, it's true," she murmured. "I am like that."

Then Lawyer Arico, always impatient of discussions that did not come straight to the point, ventured to say, "So now, Signora . . ."

"No, wait, Signor Arico," she looked up and quickly cut him off. "It is bad, very bad, what you reproach me of, Father, and I thank you. But believe me, it is not out of pride. Quite the contrary . . ."

"To disparage the object of one's charity?"

"No, myself, myself, Father! I would be more prone to disparage myself if I have had a wicked thought. In that case, I think he would be helped by someone worse off than he — if it is true that he had no ulterior motive. Perhaps I don't express myself clearly. I mean that, even though he became reconciled with me knowing this woman might die, I would still have done all I could for his children and for him.

Wait! Wait! Let me finish. Because it seems more natural to me that way, more humane, even more merciful, without any appearance of . . . of exaltation or false grandeur . . . because, well, we are like that . . . and if he is not, then all the better. That is all I wanted to say."

"Well, now . . ." the lawyer quickly put in, seeing that the priest was satisfied with this explanation, smiling and nodding his approval.

But he had no luck with the blessed woman — very noble and all that, but a nuisance for a man with a lot of work to do. There she was, turning around again.

"No, please wait, Lawyer Arico."

What more could she have to say? Now she wanted to strip herself of all merit for her charity. Ah, dear God! Whatever had made that priest talk of spiritual pride? Just listen to that! She said it would not be charity but a real pleasure for her to take three children into her home, educate them and look after them like a mother. Fine! Now, that was that. If it was a pleasure for her . . . That was more than they had ever hoped to achieve by this visit. There was nothing left to do but thank her and go.

But that was not all . . . no, indeed! It could not be that simple! Now she wanted to know what price they thought she would have to pay for the joy of being a mother to those three little ones.

Lawyer Arico stared at the priest and felt annoyed when he appeared to understand the hidden meaning of that question — he even appeared to be confronted by a case of conscience which had never occurred to him: Yes, with those three little ones there was also the question of the husband . . . If he were to come back again to live under the same roof with her . . .

"Oh, so that's it!" exclaimed Arico, scratching his neck with one finger. "Never mind, Signora, I'll speak to him myself. His Reverence will speak to him too. He certainly can't expect the impossible."

"And then?" she asked curtly.

"Then what?"

"Signor Arico, you can speak to him as much as you like, but you will never change him. We know him, dear God, and we must accept him as he is. He will promise, he will swear to both of you, and then . . . then the moment will come when he will forget his promises. Well, given the inevitable outcome . . . I say this for *me,* mind you, not for him!"

"How do you mean . . . for you?"

"For my responsibility in this, Signor Arico. I must foresee what is bound to happen, knowing as I do the man I am taking back! You will see. He will leave the children and go off, blaming me again and saying that I opened the door with my own hands to throw him back into his former life."

"But, not at all, Signora . . ."

"Don't be so quick to deny it. Wait and see if it does not turn out just as I have said."

"Well, in that case it'll be just too bad for him! You're already doing

too much taking in those children. If he wants to behave like a —
forgive me, it almost slipped out — that's his responsibility, not yours
by a long shot."

But Signora Leuca was not looking at the indignant little lawyer but
at the silent priest. She knew from his silence that he no longer thought
her conscience had strayed away from God. It meant that she must look
to Him for inspiration — that the final issue was up to life, life as it is
and always shall be.

Farewell, reflective silence, spotless order, calm.

Signora Leuca's house was turned inside out to allow for more guests
than it could hold: four must be accommodated by pulling all the rooms
apart and putting them together again — eliminating the little sitting
room and the dressing room, piling up furniture, and carrying pieces
off to the basement to make space for three little beds and other new
furnishings yet to be bought.

Signora Leuca would give up her own room to the three little girls
and she would sleep in what had been the sitting room, relinquishing
her wardrobe with its three-way mirror because it would not fit. Her
husband would have to make do with the dressing room, large enough
but rather dark.

She did not regret her comforts or all the beloved objects which now
had to be discarded. She was gay in the midst of these scrambled rooms
— so lonely before in their undisturbed order and now seemingly full
of life because of their very confusion.

The new arrangement of the rooms, more practical than beautiful,
nevertheless gave her pleasure. It represented another way of life to
her. With old things in new places and new things arriving little by
little, all her former uncertainty disappeared.

Meanwhile she saw herself going about these unfamiliar rooms, meeting her responsibilities and problems as they arose.

She wanted everything to be new for the children's room and spent
whole mornings shopping: three little iron beds, enameled white — if
there had been only one to buy she would have preferred to have it in
wood, but three wooden beds were out of the question now that she had
to economize. Everything must be white: chests of drawers, chairs, the
little wardrobe with its mirror and the writing tables with shelves to
one side. Perhaps it was not practical to have white desks, with the risk
of spilled ink, but she wanted to teach them to take care of their things,
and when they did their homework, she would supervise — not to protect the desks but to see to it that the girls worked well. Beside each
bed was a little pink rug, and the curtains at the windows were pink,
as well as the coverlets on the beds. The whole room was pink and white.

That nasty old cricket, Arico, said she spent too much and that it
would have been a saving to bring the beds, chairs and tables from the
other house for their use. She would not hear of it. She wanted nothing

from there, not so much as a nail. But what if she were the only one to feel this aversion? What if he and the little ones wanted something familiar to keep? Without more ado, she decided to visit the house on Via Flaminia.

"What!" cried Arico. "After you've gone and spent all that money?"

The neighbors in the house, friends and acquaintances of the dead woman, all leaned out of their windows or ran to stand in the old, dilapidated doorway to see her step down from the carriage — tall, erect and elegantly dressed, a veil over her face. And what comments there were as soon as she walked into the vestibule and turned to the right, up the steps leading to a kind of terrace where two French doors opened out.

"Did you see her white hair?"

"Yes, but she looks young. What age would you say . . . forty?"

"A real lady . . ."

"And all for that old brute in there!"

"Still, it looks as if she's come to take him back!"

"Yes, he's probably good for something after all."

"Say what you like, for me a woman with glasses . . ."

Whether it was because the day was overcast, or because she had just come from outside, at first Signora Leuca could not make out a thing. Then, as she began to discern the poverty and filth around her, her heart ached that he had been reduced to living in such a place. A rank odor of stale flowers and medicines still lingered about the room.

"Where is he?"

Sandrina came in her petticoat to open the door. Her thin arms were bare, her hair uncombed. She was surprised by this unexpected visit of her beautiful aunt with the rich shining house, and said that her father was lying down and that the dressmaker had come.

"Ah, good!" Signora Leuca smiled and lifted her veil to kiss the little girl. "The dressmaker, did you say? We'll go in. Are you glad to see your aunt, dear? My poor child. Now that I am here . . . perhaps it would be best if I spoke to the dressmaker. Has she taken your measurements?"

"Everything is finished."

"What! Already?"

Holding the child's hand, Signora Leuca started toward the back room — and there he was, disheveled, his shirt open on his hairy chest, hurriedly pulling on an old black coat.

"You — here! Come in. The dressmaker . . . for . . . for their mourning clothes . . ."

His voice betrayed his distress and he seemed to be hurrying her, either in an effort to hide his emotion or because he was ashamed of his dirty surroundings.

But before looking at the mourning clothes, she wanted to get acquainted with the other two children. Oh, just look at that little one, what a love! Her chubby legs were bare under her little skirt and her arms were raised to lift the rumpled mass of jet-black curls at her neck. What eyes! Wasn't she a little headstrong, Signora Leuca wondered?

"Rosetta? Is that her name? What a darling!"

"No, Rosina," corrected Sandrina.

Rosina? Rosetta would be better suited to her roundness. But neither Rosina nor Rosetta really, with that black hair and those black eyes — dear God, how penetrating they were — and that bud of a mouth, a fiery bud, and a little nose that was hardly a nose at all . . .

Was she five or not quite? Certainly one of those black dresses could not be meant for her. She should have a white one with a black satin sash. But later on she would attend to all that . . .

"And this is Lauretta?"

Try as she might to sound affectionate, her voice was cold. It seemed as if she had already met this child in Sandrina — the same afflicted look, the same set, serious eyes in a long, pale face, — the same miserably straight hair.

It was clear at a glance that the two older sisters had nothing in common with this little one, born a few years later. Lauretta was already over eight, fourteen months younger than Sandrina.

Signora Leuca checked a suspicion which rose in her mind, knowing about her husband's jealous fights with that woman. But now she was dead, and it was obvious the littlest one . . .

To conceal her doubt, she quickly turned to the dressmaker and exchanged a few words about the horrid dresses; then she told her husband the purpose of her visit. He agreed with her that nothing need be taken from the house. He would sell whatever he could and distribute the rest among the neighbors. He only wanted to take his clothes and whatever the children could still wear.

Signora Leuca had turned toward the bureau to look at the children's clothes when she spied her husband's gesture to restrain her and immediately saw the reason for it. On top of the dresser stood a photograph in a cheap copper frame. She realized it must be of that woman and pretended not to notice it. She told him there was no hurry about the girls' clothes; whatever they could not use should be given to the needy.

Then she asked Sandrina if she would like to go with her. Sandrina clapped her hands with delight, and Lauretta wanted to go too. Why not the little one, then? They could all go with her this evening because their room was ready.

But the baby refused to budge. She would not be separated from her father. Without her father she would not leave, and he had to stay on a few more days to liquidate his sorry past.

That evening Signora Leuca returned home with two little girls dressed in black.

"This is your room. Do you like it?"

Sandrina and Lauretta were spellbound.

"You will sleep here," she told Sandrina, "and Lauretta there. Rosina will sleep in the smaller bed between you."

Then she showed them the little desks where they would do their homework, assigning a desk to each one.

"Both desks are exactly alike," she pointed out, "each one has a little shelf."

She explained that they would attend another school, close by in Via Novara, and that she hoped they would study well, behave nicely and be neat. As for their clothing, for the moment they would keep the things they had until new frocks could be bought, pretty dresses to go walking in and others to wear at home with protective pinafores.

Meanwhile she bathed them, combed their hair and showed them through the house — where their father would sleep, where she would sleep. Finally she seated them at the table with her for supper.

There were so many things the little girls needed to be taught, but for this evening it was best to allow them to do everything their own way. They were in a trance. They didn't know how to take up a glass or hold the small-scale knives and forks bought especially for them, but they would learn in time. And she too must learn not to spoil them by overindulgence.

She kept them with her after supper, talking, although she was careful not to let her curiosity about many things lead her into questioning them. However, nothing would induce Lauretta to speak; she sat watching her sister Sandrina who was at ease, having been there before.

When Signora Leuca put them in bed, she discovered that they had not been taught to make the sign of the cross before going to sleep. She explained this to them as best she could and persuaded them to repeat a short prayer after her. Then, for the first time, she heard the sound of Lauretta's voice.

A little later, listening at their door to find out if they were asleep, she heard a terrible fight going on. They sounded like cats, pulling each other's hair, kicking and clawing. What was she to do? Open the door? Surprise them? If they kept their voices so low it must be because they had misgivings and did not want her to hear them. Then Lauretta tiptoed back to bed and there was silence, except for Sandrina's sobs half muffled under the covers.

That night Signora Leuca stayed awake a long time. She wondered what these children had for her that the others she had helped before did not have — all those children she could no longer afford to comfort. She had never before spent so much money for charitable work nor gone to so much trouble, and never once had she dreamed of taking one of the others into her home.

Was it because they were her husband's children? And for that matter, who knew if they really were, even one of them? No, that was not it. She had taken them in to fill the emptiness of her life, in spite of all the worry and difficulty this would mean for her . . . and certainly not only because of the children themselves.

So this was what it amounted to: She was the object of her own charity, to the detriment of those poor unfortunates whom she would no longer have time to care for and think about. It hardly seemed right. Even though it was impossible to do as much for them as for the two sleeping in there, already in a sense her own, she would feel conscience-stricken if she did nothing at all — at least for some of them: that little sick girl in Via Reggio, and — oh God! — the little orphan, Elodina, in Via Alessandria! She could not abandon them to their wretched fate when everything here was pink and white — beds, rugs, coverlets, and when she considered the pleasure she found in just thinking of things she wanted to buy for them — dainty underclothes, pretty shoes — and all the pains she would take to have them becomingly dressed. No! No! It was too unfair. And why, after all? Who were these children, really?

Tomorrow would she feel gratified to be praised for her generosity because she was taking in her husband's three children by another woman? And by a woman like that one? No. The very thought that such praise was inevitable made her regret what she had done. Were these children to be rewarded for their mother's shame and their father's guilt, "generously" forgiven by her? She had nothing to forgive, having suffered no more from her husband's actions than she suffered from so many other wrongs — for instance, the wrong she herself was now doing by excluding so many poor children because these three were more vital to her.

Ah! She would atone for her wrongdoing!

Suddenly she was aware of the slow, distinct ticking of the clock across the same gaping silence as before. It must be very late. Hovering and forlorn, she saw all her thoughts, her deeds, every feature of her life, more painfully than ever before.

And there, peering through the shadows in the luster of its cheap copper frame, sat the picture of the dead woman on the dresser. What was he doing alone at this hour in that horrible house? And why did she imagine him standing in front of the dresser with the child, looking intently at that photograph?

Her fault lay in having climbed all the way to the top of a high mountain — not for the vainglory of climbing. What glory was there in that? Or should she consider it a punishment . . . or fate . . . rather than a fault?

She well knew the chill, the silence of the summit, from which everything appears small and distant, blurred by a mist of solitary sorrow which perhaps does not exist below, at close range, but which here, aloof and apart, forms a cloud between the viewer and day-to-day reality.

Three days later her husband arrived, the little one clinging around his neck like a wild, scared kitten. Exasperated by this untamed child and the weight of the two heavy suitcases he carried, one in each hand, he was indifferent to the happy, affectionate greetings of Lauretta and Sandrina and blind to their completely new appearance.

The two little girls, who were expecting their father to admire their good behavior, their rosy cleanliness, their well-combed hair, their new black pinafores with white lace collars and cuffs, their dainty stockings and shoes, were disappointed and hurt.

It was a miracle that he did not curse, strangled as he was by Rosina's plump arms viciously gripping him tighter and tighter. Finally, unable to make her let go, he wrenched her off violently and threw her into a chair.

"There, be quiet or I'll let you have it!"

At this the frantic child rolled over on the floor, screaming and kicking, hiding her face in her arms, her hands clutching her hair. Infuriated, he turned his back and strode to the window.

"I can't stand any more!" he cried, facing his wife. "For sixteen days I have been shackled like this!"

As the baby crawled after him, howling like a wild thing, he added, "There! You see! You see!"

And just as Rosina was about to grab his leg, he lifted it up. Sandrina and Lauretta began to laugh.

"Oh, don't laugh!" Signora Leuca admonished them. "Shame on you, when your little sister is crying like that! Go, bring the toys we bought yesterday."

"Toys! Do you hear?" said her father, picking up the child.

The little one was somewhat mollified in his arms, although still convulsed with sobs. But as soon as Sandrina and Lauretta came back with the toys and she heard the tinkle of tiny cymbals struck by a mechanical clown, she buried her face in her father's neck, not to see or hear.

Signora Leuca had the impression that this clinging child was a bedevilment of the dead woman, tethering him to all she had represented for him in life: misery, vulgarity and bondage.

She realized the impossibility of taming the little creature, who was as dark as if impregnated with the vice from which she had sprung, and whose blood, she sensed, was a savage mixture. Signora Leuca did not even attempt to take her from her father or persuade her to play with her sisters. She knew it was useless and might even make things worse.

She showed her husband to his room as if apologizing because it was not better, but immediately realized that this was the wrong attitude. In fact his reply, synchronizing with her thoughts, affected her strangely.

"Not at all! What are you trying to say?"

He frowned when he saw the single bed, having slept in a double bed until now, and asked, pointing to the child, "What about this nuisance?"

"She has her own bed in the girls' room," Signora Leuca told him. "Come, I'll show you."

He stood in the doorway admiring the lovely pink-and-white room with its three little beds. He was pleased and touched but ill at ease because he found it difficult to tell her that, since the death of that woman, the baby had taken her mother's place at night and might now refuse to sleep alone.

"Well, we shall see this evening," Signora Leuca replied. "If we manage to put her to bed in here, you might stay with her until she goes to sleep. Otherwise, we can move her little bed into your room and she can sleep there."

As she spoke, she saw that Sandrina and Lauretta would be only too happy to have this lovely room all to themselves. They had quickly adopted an air of well-brought-up little girls since they had come into her house, but their little sister clearly did not want to change. Their father was not too welcome either in the older girls' room in this lovely house where they were so happy, enjoying a new life with their "aunt."

In truth, their gloomy, unkempt father did not look as if he would ever adjust to these surroundings but must always feel a stranger, not daring to look about him, not knowing what to say, confused, embarrassed, repeating hoarsely, "It's too much, too much!"

He now asked permission to go to his room to unpack his bags, as though he were afraid someone might do it for him.

"Auntie, why are we in mourning for Mama, when Papa isn't?"

Signora Leuca, who had not noticed the color of her husband's clothes, stared at the child and did not know how to reply; not that it was so difficult to think up an answer but she suddenly realized that he was not wearing black out of regard for her, unwilling to parade his mourning for another woman before her eyes.

It saddened and upset her. How he must have wept for that woman! The horrible things he had confessed were still vivid in her mind and she knew that, although he might have hated her for enslaving him, he probably would give much to have her back, now that she was gone, and who knew how deep and lasting his grief would be. Unless . . .

Signora Leuca broke off this supposition which had troubled her for many days. She was more than ever convinced that her prediction would come to pass, if not today or tomorrow, then as soon as his first embarrassment had passed and he regained his old self-confidence.

Her agitation mounted as she began to notice ways of his, familiar gestures and expressions which should, on the contrary, have reassured her. His humility and the patience and the affection he had for the children were all but unbelievable . . . so many things which aroused her sympathy for him in his position — sympathy more real than she had been prepared, out of duty, to show him.

She was impressed at dinner, as they were discussing the little lawyer, to see him lift one eyebrow and contract the other in an intelligent frown — an all-but-forgotten trait of his which had always pleased her. His natural good manners at table impressed her also. He was self-conscious only when she looked at him; then he would glance aside. His air of quiet good breeding came as a surprise to the two older girls who stared as if they did not recognize him. However, Signora Leuca, to her delight, saw him fall into the spontaneous, charming manner she had known long ago.

Wine! What torture! She had to wrench her eyes from the bottle every time, though it remained almost untouched. Her eyes betrayed her and it was useless to try to hide the fact that she knew about his habit of getting drunk every night. It must be hard on him now to drink hardly anything, yet he did not show it. Tonight was the first time in many years that they had sat together at table. Who knew if tomorrow, at lunch or at dinner, he would still be able to control himself?

After dinner, a tender, paternal smile moved his discolored lips under the graying mustache as he silently called her attention to the sleeping child in his lap. He asked quietly if it would not be better to undress her there before putting her to bed in the room where the other children were sleeping

As she leaned over the child, her shoulder brushed his chest and she felt his breath on her hair. She touched him several times as she undressed the little one on his lap, but her apprehension disturbed her more than the actual contact. She was anxious lest her hands betray her nervousness.

Finally, when the child had been carefully put to bed and they both had tiptoed from the room, the dangerous moment was at hand, the moment when they were alone together in the intimacy of the house.

Yet, nothing happened. The door of the children's room was hardly closed before he sighed with relief and smilingly told her that he would now have peace until morning because Rosina never waked during the night. Then humbly and quietly he wished her good night and went to his room.

Signora Leuca lay in her bed turning many things over in her mind. She was especially irritated with herself because of her apprehension, the more unjustified when confronted by his withdrawn attitude. He dared not look at her and certainly never dreamed of drawing closer than she would allow, for the moment.

What was it she feared then? She had locked the door behind her as soon as she entered her own room. This precaution now made her angry. She was tempted to jump out of bed and unlock the door.

The priest noticed it, he said, after the last meeting of the Charity Society in the parish house. Her friends, Signora Mielli and Signora Marzorati, had of course noticed it; and so had good Signorina Trecke, impossible as it might seem.

Signora Leuca's zeal had cooled: she had not attended the meetings of the Charity Society for two months now. Not only that but she had skipped Mass for several weeks. And she treated her friends with indifference as if she suspected them of being partly responsible for the state in which she now found herself — with those three children in the house and that man who, for all the respect he showed her, must weigh like a stone around her neck.

There could be no question that the three children gave her a lot of work, but if this was so — and no doubt it was, since they had not even known how to make the sign of the cross when they first came to her — then all the more reason to attend Mass regularly every Sunday. Her attitude was incomprehensible, especially at the very time of the Novena in preparation for the Feast of the Immaculate Conception of the Blessed Virgin Mary.

Signora Mielli remarked that their friend, always so careful about her appearance, had begun to neglect herself. Her hair was badly combed, if at all, as if she no longer looked at herself in the mirror. Of course, she had *four* children to care for, not three, and all the worry of the house, but she could still have found time to groom herself properly had she wanted to. Evidently, with the serene, unruffled life she had led before, she did not know what a struggle it was to bring up children. But merit lay in conquering difficulties, not in going slack under their weight.

Too bad she had had to part with the devoted servant who had been with her so many years. But it was only natural. She should have taken in someone to help, for one person alone could not possibly do all the work now with three children and a man in the house.

"She hired another maid, yes, she certainly did!" said Signorina Trecke. "But she had to discharge her on the spot, because it seems that her husband . . . well, I don't know . . ."

"What? Her husband!" exclaimed Signora Marzorati making a wry face.

Signorina Trecke opened her mouth in one of her usual smiles. She didn't quite understand what it was Signora Leuca had discovered, but her niece had laughed her head off when she heard it.

"She laughed like a fool. I can't think why."

"Of course," mused Signora Mielli with a faraway look in her eyes, "Now surely, that man . . ."

"Dear God!" cried Signora Marzorati. "If Signora Leuca . . . of course she's right, poor woman. In her place as a wife, I'd rather put up with . . . I don't know what! I mean, you understand, Signora Mielli . . . well, *out*side the house, at least!"

When the two ladies had exchanged a few words, heavy with innuendoes, Signorina Trecke remarked angelically that Signor Leuca did go outside the house — every evening, as a matter of fact.

"I happen to know this," she said, "because he comes to my house." Surprised, Signora Marzorati scowled at her.

"To *your* house! What for?"

"To see my niece," replied Signorina Trecke.

There could be no harm in Signor Leuca's visits now that he was reconciled with Signora Leuca and the priest himself had favored this reconciliation.

"What reconciliation?" Signora Marzorati exploded. "Do you know, at least, what your niece and Signor Leuca talk about when they are together?"

Signorina Trecke lowered her aging eyelids with roguish cunning over her cloudless blue eyes.

"They talk about the Republic of Ecuador," she said.

"About the Republic of Ecuador!" gasped Signora Mielli, not so far off for once.

"Yes," explained Signorina Trecke. "Because an expedition of big industrialists has left for the Republic of Ecuador. Everything is still to be done there: bridges, roads, railroads, electricity, schools . . . My niece knows a member of the expedition. She says that soon an even larger group will go: workmen, farmers, engineers, even lawyers and teachers. She says that she will go too — my niece, that is — to this Republic of Ecuador! That's all they talk about."

Signorina Trecke looked so stupid as she told them this news that Signora Marzorati and Signora Nielli were annoyed and, restraining their curiosity, changed the subject, turning away to discuss other things between themselves.

It was all over.

Signora Leuca, contrary to all her expectations, was hurt not so much by what had actually happened as by what she suffered within. It was because the harm she had foreseen, feared and awaited had failed to materialize that she now endured this torment.

She was certain, despite the scorn she felt for her own flesh, that she would not have yielded if her husband had seized her one of those nights in the silence of the house, but would have pushed him away. She would have been deaf to the promptings of her conscience which made her realize that if she rejected him she only gave him a fresh excuse to fall back once more into that horrible life. She had to admit that she would never have relented even though later her remorse would not be denied.

Yes, but it was equally certain that, if this had happened, her suffering would have been less cruel than what she now endured because it had not occurred.

For little by little her horror of his body, aroused by all those indelible images with which his confession had seeded her mind, had become a horror of her own flesh. Every evening when she closed her door — without locking it — she looked at her body in the mirror and wondered if it was really so undesirable that it did not even merit a sidelong glance from a man like that, who had found pleasure until recently in such a vulgar woman.

She was still beautiful and she knew it, thanks to the glances of men who turned to look at her in the street when she least expected it. Her hair, turned white as snow before the age of thirty, brought out the youthful freshness of her skin, and gave an ambiguous grace, like an innocent lie, to her smile every time she said, "Now, I am old . . ."

Her smooth throat rising like an unblemished column from her shapely bosom, her . . . God! How frightful this intimate analysis of her whole body was in its vain attempt to reassure herself that she was still beautiful, still desirable! Her former assurance was, after all, the reason why she had so clearly forecast for the lawyer and the priest what demands her husband was sure to make on her, in consequence of which she would have been obliged to put him out of the house.

She had lost interest in her appearance as she became progressively convinced of her husband's indifference — although he continued to show her every polite consideration. Refusing to admit the reason to herself, she pretended she had no time to dress her hair properly, what with the two older girls to look after and get off early to school.

And when, by accident, she had found that awful woman's picture in his dresser drawer, how greedily her eyes had devoured it! What a disappointment it was, after having imagined that she was so beautiful! Provocative, yes, but in fact quite ugly with a mad look in her eyes, and she was common. But it was only natural that he would have been attracted to that type of woman.

However, Nella, the vivacious niece of Signorina Trecke, certainly was not common in appearance and she clearly pleased and attracted him. Sandrina had been in her class two years ago when she first began to teach near the Porta del Popolo. What a coincidence that she should find her former pupil at the school in Via Novara where she was now teaching! She had walked home with her after class, Sandrina's father holding one hand and she the other. But now that it was all over, Signora Leuca did not want to complain even about the Trecke girl's betrayal. She had always felt an instinctive aversion for her and had recognized her as an enemy.

Considering his past reputation there should have been little need to seduce him, yet that is what Nella Trecke did under Signora Leuca's eyes, using her pupil as an excuse to come to the house nearly every day. She felt, no doubt, that a lady like Signora Leuca would not deign to notice, or would at most feel a little more scorn for that wretched man she had taken in — along with his daughters — out of charity.

Signora Leuca had accepted the challenge at first and closed her eyes to the young girl's smiles and blandishments, not wanting to admit the obscure, hidden jealousy they awakened in her. However, when she could bear it no longer, she had forbidden the girl to come to the house. But, afraid of betraying her own distress, she had not warned Nella's stupid aunt or the old priest, and thus had abetted their scheme.

Then the scandal broke.

The priest and the ladies of the Charity Society blamed Signorina Trecke for having given the pair the opportunity to meet every evening at her house and plan their flight together to the Republic of Ecuador.

Signorina Trecke wept inconsolably not so much over the disgrace that her niece had brought on her as over the fact that she was still quite unable to see the evil she had fostered and which had now brought down so many reproaches on her head — all well deserved, of course. Unfortunately, no healthy suspicions were ever to cloud her childlike eyes, which would now be red from crying because her ungrateful niece had left her.

To crown it all, even Signora Leuca found herself accused of doing things by halves, always, of course, because of that over-niceness which had so often hindered her from giving free rein to her charitable instincts, especially in the difficult task she had attempted this time.

Heavens! Having taken her husband back into her house, why could she not have accepted the role of a wife in every sense? One has crosses to bear, but virtue lies in resignation.

Signora Leuca let them talk; she even let them think it was her fault. The wound was too deep: let their words fall into it like so many drops of acid. She did not mind — the more it stung, the better.

She smilingly received Lawyer Arico's compliments — which he saw fit to present to her privately — on having freed herself of that lecherous brute, an offensive encumbrance in her house, no matter what the priest said about it. She herself had only objected to *his* return, the lawyer recalled, but hadn't she said that the children would be a pleasure? Well, now he was gone, and what's more she had not had to drive him out; and she had the children.

"What could be better?" he concluded.

In fact, what could be better?

Was she to confide to Lawyer Arico that suddenly, as soon as she had heard of her husband's flight, the pleasure of having the children in the house had vanished as if by magic and a heavy burden of responsibility had settled on her shoulders, making the children seem strangers to her?

Signora Leuca did not even want to admit this to herself. She showered more attention and more affection on the three abandoned orphans than ever — but Signora Leuca felt a change come over her feelings for the little one, that savage little creature. She knew why only too well, but would not name the reason.

"Do you love me?"

"Ess!"

Kneeling in her lap, Rosina would stretch her little clawlike hands up to her neck, wrinkle her tiny nose, and purse that rosebud of a mouth.

"Oh! Not like that! My goodness! You look ugly that way!"

"*You* ugly!"

Signora Leuca had won her over to the extent that she now allowed herself to be picked up and cared for — but at the price of scratches, kicks and even spittings in the face!

The other two stood by, watching a little enviously. They thought it unfair for their aunt to take such trouble with Rosina in front of them — Rosina, who was downright naughty while they were always good as gold.

Only once had Sandrina, evidently speaking for Lauretta too, asked her, "Where is Papa?"

They must have understood something vaguely either from gossip at school or from the priest's words when he had come, very upset, to announce the elopement; or perhaps the copious tears Signorina Trecke had shed the following day, when she begged forgiveness for her niece, had told them more clearly than words.

"Papa has gone away but he will come back," Signora Leuca answered calmly, and they were satisfied.

But would he come back? Signora Leuca was certain that he never would. In any case, even if he did turn up one day or another, what could it now matter to her?

It was all over.

Her spirit sadly on guard under its mask of candid serenity, Signora Leuca was inwardly torn by a distress no one suspected; she was left with the three children to care for and bring up, but what was more, she bore an ever-present torment, not for herself alone, who was perhaps better off than many others, but for all things, all earthly creatures as she saw them in the infinite anguish of her love and pity, in that constant painful awareness — assuaged only by fleeting peaceful moments which brought relief and consolation — of the futility of living like this . . .

Bertolt Brecht (1898–1956)

LIFE: A Marxist who embarrassed the East Germans and aroused the suspicions of the Americans, Brecht lived in Germany until 1933; he fled Nazism to settle, after eight years of wandering through Europe and Asia, in California; when the war was over, he returned to Europe and at the invitation of the government of East Germany created the Berliner Ensemble, the company which made his name and work known to the world. The gradually increasing frequency with which his plays are now performed suggests that the influence and practice of his ideas about the theater will last longer than the years of oblivion.

WORKS: Among his plays are: *Baal; Man Is Man; The Threepenny Opera; The Private Life of the Master Race; Puntilla; Mother Courage; The Caucasian Chalk Circle; The Good Woman of Setzuan; Galileo.*

THE GOOD WOMAN OF SETZUAN *

Characters

WONG, *a water seller*

THREE GODS

SHEN TE, *a prostitute, later a shopkeeper*

MRS. SHIN, *former owner of Shen Te's shop*

A FAMILY OF EIGHT (*husband, wife, brother, sister-in-law, grandfather, nephew, niece, boy*)

AN UNEMPLOYED MAN

A CARPENTER

MRS. MI TZU, *Shen Te's landlady*

YANG SUN, *an unemployed pilot, later a factory manager*

AN OLD WHORE

A POLICEMAN

AN OLD MAN

AN OLD WOMAN, *his wife*

MR. SHU FU, *a barber*

MRS. YANG, *mother of Yang Sun*

GENTLEMEN, VOICES, CHILDREN (*three*), *etc.*

PROLOGUE

At the gates of the half-Westernized city of Setzuan. Evening. WONG *the water seller introduces himself to the audience.*

WONG: I sell water here in the city of Setzuan. It isn't easy. When water is scarce, I have long distances to go in search of it, and when it is plentiful, I have no income. But in our part of the world there is nothing unusual about poverty. Many people think only the gods can save the situation. And I hear from a cattle merchant — who travels a lot — that some of the highest gods are on their way here at this very moment. Informed sources have it that heaven is quite disturbed at all the complaining. I've been coming out here to the city gates for three days now to bid these gods welcome. I want to be the first to greet them. What about those fellows over there? No, no, they *work*. And that one there has ink on his fingers, he's no god, he must be a clerk from the cement factory. *Those* two are another story. They look as though they'd like to beat you. But gods don't need to beat you, do they?

© 1947, 1948, 1956, 1961 by Eric Bentley. Epilogue © Copyright 1965 by Eric Bentley. Originally published in the volume *Parables for the Theatre: Two Plays by Bertolt Brecht* by the University of Minnesota Press, Minneapolis. Reprinted by permission.

* Written at the end of the nineteen-thirties.

THREE GODS *appear.*

What about those three? Old-fashioned clothes — dust on their feet — they *must* be gods! (*He throws himself at their feet.*) Do with me what you will, illustrious ones!

FIRST GOD (*with an ear trumpet*): Ah! (*He is pleased.*) So we were expected?

WONG (*giving them water*): Oh, yes. And I *knew* you'd come.

FIRST GOD: We need somewhere to stay the night. You know of a place?

WONG: The whole town is at your service, illustrious ones! What sort of a place would you like?

The GODS *eye each other.*

FIRST GOD: Just try the first house you come to, my son.

WONG: That would be Mr. Fo's place.

FIRST GOD: Mr. Fo.

WONG: One moment! (*He knocks at the first house.*)

VOICE FROM MR. FO'S: No!

WONG *returns a little nervously.*

WONG: It's too bad. Mr. Fo isn't in. And his servants don't dare do a thing without his consent. He'll have a fit when he finds out who they turned away, won't he?

FIRST GOD (*smiling*): He will, won't he?

WONG: One moment! The next house is Mr. Cheng's. Won't he be thrilled!

FIRST GOD: Mr. Cheng.

WONG *knocks.*

VOICE FROM MR. CHENG'S: Keep your gods. We have our own troubles!

WONG (*back with the* GODS): Mr. Cheng is very sorry, but he has a houseful of relations. I think some of them are a bad lot, and naturally, he wouldn't like you to see them.

THIRD GOD: Are we so terrible?

WONG: Well, only with bad people, of course. Everyone knows the province of Kwan is always having floods.

SECOND GOD: Really? How's that?

WONG: Why, because they're so irreligious.

SECOND GOD: Rubbish. It's because they neglected the dam.

FIRST GOD (*to* SECOND): Sh! (*To* WONG:) You're still in hopes, aren't you, my son?

WONG: Certainly. All Setzuan is competing for the honor! What happened up to now is pure coincidence. I'll be back. (*He walks away, but then stands undecided.*)

SECOND GOD: What did I tell you?

THIRD GOD: It *could* be pure coincidence.

SECOND GOD: The same coincidence in Shun, Kwan, and Setzuan? People just aren't religious any more, let's face the fact. Our mission has failed!

FIRST GOD: Oh come, we might run into a good person any minute.

THIRD GOD: How did the resolution read? (*Unrolling a scroll and reading from it:*) "The world can stay as it is if enough people are found (*at the word "found" he unrolls it a little more*) living lives worthy of human beings." Good people, that is. Well, what about this water seller himself? *He's* good, or I'm very much mistaken.

SECOND GOD: You're very much mistaken. When he gave us a drink, I had the impression there was something odd about the cup. Well, look! (*He shows the cup to the* FIRST GOD.)

FIRST GOD: A false bottom!

SECOND GOD: The man is a swindler.

FIRST GOD: Very well, count *him* out. That's one man among millions. And as a matter of fact, we only need one on *our* side. These atheists are saying, "The world must be changed because no one can *be* good and *stay* good." No one, eh? I say: let us find one — just one — and we have those fellows where we want them!

THIRD GOD (*to* WONG): Water seller, is it so hard to find a place to stay?

WONG: Nothing could be easier. It's just me. I don't go about it right.

THIRD GOD: Really?

He returns to the others. A GENTLEMAN *passes by.*

WONG: Oh dear, they're catching on. (*He accosts the* GENTLEMAN.) Excuse the intrusion, dear sir, but three gods have just turned up. Three of the very highest. They need a place for the night. Seize this rare opportunity — to have real gods as your guests!

GENTLEMAN (*laughing*): A new way of finding free rooms for a gang of crooks. (*Exit* GENTLEMAN.)

WONG (*shouting at him*): Godless rascal! Have you no religion, gentleman of Setzuan? (*Pause.*) Patience, illustrious ones! (*Pause.*) There's only one person left. Shen Te, the prostitute. She *can't* say no. (*Calls up to a window:*) Shen Te!

SHEN TE *opens the shutters and looks out.*

WONG: Shen Te, it's Wong. *They're* here, and nobody wants them. Will you take them?

SHEN TE: Oh, no, Wong, I'm expecting a gentleman.

WONG: Can't you forget about him for tonight?

SHEN TE: The rent has to be paid by tomorrow or I'll be out on the street.

WONG: This is no time for calculation, Shen Te.

SHEN TE: Stomachs rumble even on the Emperor's birthday, Wong.

WONG: Setzuan is one big dung hill!

SHEN TE: Oh, very well! I'll hide till my gentleman has come and gone. Then I'll take them. (*She disappears.*)

WONG: They mustn't see her gentleman or they'll know what she is.

FIRST GOD (*who hasn't heard any of this*): I think it's hopeless.

They approach WONG.

WONG (*jumping, as he finds them behind him*): A room has been found, illustrious ones! (*He wipes sweat off his brow.*)

SECOND GOD: Oh, good.

THIRD GOD: Let's see it.

WONG (*nervously*): Just a minute. It has to be tidied up a bit.

THIRD GOD: Then we'll sit down here and wait.

WONG (*still more nervous*): No, no! (*Holding himself back.*) Too much traffic, you know.

THIRD GOD (*with a smile*): Of course, if you *want* us to move.

They retire a little. They sit on a doorstep. WONG *sits on the ground.*

WONG (*after a deep breath*): You'll be staying with a single girl — the finest human being in Setzuan!

THIRD GOD: That's nice.

WONG (*to the audience*): They gave me such a look when I picked up my cup just now.

THIRD GOD: You're worn out, Wong.

WONG: A little, maybe.

FIRST GOD: Do people here have a hard time of it?

WONG: The good ones do.

FIRST GOD: What about yourself?

WONG: You mean I'm not good. That's true. And I don't have an easy time either!

During this dialogue, a GENTLEMAN *has turned up in front of Shen Te's house, and has whistled several times. Each time* WONG *has given a start.*

THIRD GOD (*to* WONG, *softly*): Psst! I think he's gone now.

WONG (*confused and surprised*): Ye-e-es.

The GENTLEMAN *has left now, and* SHEN TE *has come down to the street.*

SHEN TE (*softly*): Wong!

Getting no answer, she goes off down the street. WONG *arrives just too late, forgetting his carrying pole.*

WONG (*softly*): Shen Te! Shen Te! (*To himself:*) So she's gone off to earn the rent. Oh dear, I can't go to the gods *again* with no room to offer them. Having failed in the service of the gods, I shall run to my den in the sewer pipe down by the river and hide from their sight!

He rushes off. SHEN TE *returns, looking for him, but finding the* GODS. *She stops in confusion.*

SHEN TE: You are the illustrious ones? My name is Shen Te. It would please me very much if my simple room could be of use to you.

THIRD GOD: Where is the water seller, Miss . . . Shen Te?

SHEN TE: I missed him, somehow.

FIRST GOD: Oh, he probably thought you weren't coming, and was afraid of telling us.

THIRD GOD (*picking up the carrying pole*): We'll leave this with you. He'll be needing it.

Led by SHEN TE, *they go into the house. It grows dark, then light. Dawn. Again escorted by* SHEN TE, *who leads them through the half-light with a little lamp, the* GODS *take their leave.*

FIRST GOD: Thank you, thank you, dear Shen Te, for your elegant hospitality! We shall not forget! And give our thanks to the water seller — he showed us a good human being.

SHEN TE: Oh, *I'm* not good. Let me tell you something: when Wong asked me to put you up, I hesitated.

FIRST GOD: It's all right to hesitate if you then go ahead! And in giving us that room you did much more than you knew. You proved that good people still exist, a point that has been disputed of late — even in heaven. Farewell!

SECOND GOD: Farewell!

THIRD GOD: Farewell!

SHEN TE: Stop, illustrious ones! I'm not sure you're right. I'd like to be good, it's true, but there's the rent to pay. And that's not all: I sell myself for a living. Even so I can't make ends meet, there's too much competition. I'd like to honor my father and mother and speak nothing but the truth and not covet my neighbor's house. I should love to stay with one man. But how? How is it done? Even breaking a few of your commandments, I can hardly manage.

FIRST GOD (*clearing his throat*): These thoughts are but, um, the misgivings of an unusually good woman!

THIRD GOD: Good-bye, Shen Te! Give our regards to the water seller!

SECOND GOD: And above all: be good! Farewell!

FIRST GOD: Farewell!

THIRD GOD: Farewell!

They start to wave good-bye.

SHEN TE: But everything is so expensive, I don't feel sure I can do it!

SECOND GOD: That's not in our sphere. We never meddle with economics.

THIRD GOD: One moment. (*They stop.*) Isn't it true she might do better if she had more money?

SECOND GOD: Come, come! How could we ever account for it Up Above?

FIRST GOD: Oh, there are ways. (*They put their heads together and confer in dumb show. To* SHEN TE, *with embarrassment:*) As you say you can't pay your rent, well, um, we're not paupers, so of course we *insist* on paying for our room. (*Awkwardly thrusting money into her hand.*) There! (*Quickly.*) But don't tell anyone! The incident is open to misinterpretation.

SECOND GOD: It certainly is!

FIRST GOD (*defensively*): But there's no law against it! It was never decreed that a god mustn't pay hotel bills!

The GODS *leave.*

1

A small tobacco shop. The shop is not as yet completely furnished and hasn't started doing business.

SHEN TE (*to the audience*): It's three days now since the gods left. When they said they wanted to pay for the room, I looked down at my hand, and there was more than a thousand silver dollars! I bought a tobacco shop with the money, and moved in yesterday. I don't own the building, of course, but I can pay the rent, and I hope to do a lot of good here. Beginning with Mrs. Shin, who's just coming across the square with her pot. She had the shop before me, and yesterday she dropped in to ask for rice for her children. (*Enter* MRS. SHIN. *Both women bow.*) How do you do, Mrs. Shin.

MRS. SHIN: How do you do, Miss Shen Te. You like your new home?

SHEN TE: Indeed, yes. Did your children have a good night?

MRS. SHIN: In that hovel? The youngest is coughing already.

SHEN TE: Oh, dear!

MRS. SHIN: You're going to learn a thing or two in these slums.

SHEN TE: Slums? That's not what you said when you sold me the shop!

MRS. SHIN: Now don't start nagging! Robbing me and my innocent children of their home and then calling it a slum! That's the limit! (*She weeps.*)

SHEN TE (*tactfully*): I'll get your rice.

MRS. SHIN: And a little cash while you're at it.

SHEN TE: I'm afraid I haven't sold anything yet.

MRS. SHIN (*screeching*): I've got to have it. Strip the clothes from my back and then cut my throat, will you? I know what I'll do: I'll dump my children on your doorstep! (*She snatches the pot out of* SHEN TE'S *hands.*)

SHEN TE: Please don't be angry. You'll spill the rice.

Enter an elderly HUSBAND *and* WIFE *with their shabbily dressed* NEPHEW.

WIFE: Shen Te, dear! You've come into money, they tell me. And we haven't a roof over our heads! A tobacco shop. We had one too. But it's gone. Could we spend the night here, do you think?

NEPHEW (*appraising the shop*): Not bad!

WIFE: He's our nephew. We're inseparable!

MRS. SHIN: And who are these . . . ladies and gentlemen?

SHEN TE: They put me up when I first came in from the country. (*To the audience:*) Of course, when my small purse was empty, they put me out on the street, and they may be afraid I'll do the same to them. (*To the newcomers, kindly:*) Come in, and welcome, though I've only one little room for you — it's behind the shop.

HUSBAND: That'll do. Don't worry.

WIFE (*bringing* SHEN TE *some tea*): We'll stay over here, so we won't be in your way. Did you make it a tobacco shop in memory of your first real home? We can certainly give you a hint or two! That's one reason we came.

MRS. SHIN (*to* SHEN TE): Very nice! As long as you have a few customers too!

HUSBAND: Sh! A customer!

Enter an UNEMPLOYED MAN, *in rags.*

UNEMPLOYED MAN: Excuse me. I'm unemployed.

MRS. SHIN *laughs.*

SHEN TE: Can I help you?

UNEMPLOYED MAN: Have you any damaged cigarettes? I thought there might be some damage when you're unpacking.

WIFE: What nerve, begging for tobacco! (*Rhetorically.*) Why don't they ask for bread?

UNEMPLOYED MAN: Bread is expensive. One cigarette butt and I'll be a new man.

SHEN TE (*giving him cigarettes*): That's very important — to be a new man. You'll be my first customer and bring me luck.

The UNEMPLOYED MAN *quickly lights a cigarette, inhales, and goes off, coughing.*

WIFE: Was that right, Shen Te, dear?

MRS. SHIN: If this is the opening of a shop, you can hold the closing at the end of the week.

HUSBAND: I bet he had money on him.

SHEN TE: Oh, no, he said he hadn't!

NEPHEW: How d'you know he wasn't lying?

SHEN TE (*angrily*): How do you know he was?

WIFE (*wagging her head*): You're too good, Shen Te, dear. If you're going to keep this shop, you'll have to learn to say no.

HUSBAND: Tell them the place isn't yours to dispose of. Belongs to . . . some relative who insists on all accounts being strictly in order . . .

MRS. SHIN: That's right! What do you think you are — a philanthropist?

SHEN TE (*laughing*): Very well, suppose I ask you for my rice back, Mrs. Shin?

WIFE (*combatively, at* MRS. SHIN): So that's *her* rice?

Enter the CARPENTER, *a small man.*

MRS. SHIN (*who, at the sight of him, starts to hurry away*): See you tomorrow, Miss Shen Te! (*Exit* MRS. SHIN.)

CARPENTER: Mrs. Shin, it's you I want!

WIFE (*to* SHEN TE): Has she some claim on you?

SHEN TE: She's hungry. That's a claim.

CARPENTER: Are you the new tenant? And filling up the shelves already? Well, they're not yours till they're paid for, ma'am. I'm the carpenter, so I should know.

SHEN TE: I took the shop "furnishings included."

CARPENTER: You're in league with that Mrs. Shin, of course. All right. I demand my hundred silver dollars.

SHEN TE: I'm afraid I haven't got a hundred silver dollars.

CARPENTER: Then you'll find it. Or I'll have you arrested.

WIFE (*whispering to* SHEN TE): That relative: make it a cousin.

SHEN TE: Can't it wait till next month?

CARPENTER: No!

SHEN TE: Be a little patient, Mr. Carpenter, I can't settle all claims at once.

CARPENTER: Who's patient with me? (*He grabs a shelf from the wall.*) Pay up — or I take the shelves back!

WIFE: Shen Te! Dear! Why don't you let your . . . cousin settle this affair? (*To* CARPENTER:) Put your claim in writing. Shen Te's cousin will see you get paid.

CARPENTER (*derisively*): Cousin, eh?

HUSBAND: Cousin, yes.

CARPENTER: I know these cousins!

NEPHEW: Don't be silly. He's a personal friend of mine.

HUSBAND: What a man! Sharp as a razor!

CARPENTER: All right. I'll put my claim in writing. (*Puts shelf on floor, sits on it, writes out bill.*)

WIFE (*to* SHEN TE): He'd tear the dress off your back to get his shelves. Never recognize a claim. That's my motto.

SHEN TE: He's done a job, and wants something in return. It's shameful that I can't give it to him. What will the gods say?

HUSBAND: You did your bit when you took *us* in.

Enter the BROTHER, *limping, and the* SISTER-IN-LAW, *pregnant.*

BROTHER (*to* HUSBAND *and* WIFE): So this is where you're hiding out! There's family feeling for you! Leaving us on the corner!

WIFE (*embarrassed, to* SHEN TE): It's my brother and his wife. (*To them:*) Now stop grumbling, and sit quietly in that corner. (*To* SHEN TE:) It can't be helped. She's in her fifth month.

SHEN TE: Oh yes. Welcome!

WIFE (*to the couple*): Say thank you. (*They mutter something.*) The cups are there. (*To* SHEN TE:) Lucky you bought this shop when you did!

SHEN TE (*laughing and bringing tea*): Lucky indeed!

Enter MRS. MI TZU, *the landlady.*

MRS. MI TZU: Miss Shen Te? I am Mrs. Mi Tzu, your landlady. I hope our relationship will be a happy one. I like to think I give my tenants modern, personalized service. Here is your lease. (*To the others, as* SHEN TE *reads the lease:*) There's nothing like the opening of a little shop, is there? A moment of true beauty! (*She is looking around.*) Not very much on the shelves, of course. But everything in the gods' good time! Where are your references, Miss Shen Te?

SHEN TE: Do I *have* to have references?

MRS. MI TZU: After all, I haven't a notion who you are!

HUSBAND: Oh, *we'd* be glad to vouch for Miss Shen Te! We'd go through fire for her!

MRS. MI TZU: And who may *you* be?

HUSBAND (*stammering*): Ma Fu, tobacco dealer.

MRS. MI TZU: Where is your shop, Mr. . . . Ma Fu?

HUSBAND: Well, um, I haven't got a shop — I've just sold it.

MRS. MI TZU: I see. (*To* SHEN TE:) Is there no one else that knows you?

WIFE (*whispering to* SHEN TE): Your cousin! Your cousin!

MRS. MI TZU: This is a respectable house, Miss Shen Te. I never sign a lease without certain assurances.

SHEN TE (*slowly, her eyes downcast*): I have . . . a cousin.

MRS. MI TZU: On the square? Let's go over and see him. What does he do?

SHEN TE (*as before*): He lives . . . in another city.

WIFE (*prompting*): Didn't you say he was in Shung?

SHEN TE: That's right. Shung.

HUSBAND (*prompting*): I had his name on the tip of my tongue. Mr. . . .

SHEN TE (*with an effort*): Mr. . . . Shui . . . Ta.

HUSBAND: That's it! Tall, skinny fellow!

SHEN TE: Shui Ta!

NEPHEW (*to* CARPENTER): *You* were in touch with him, weren't you? About the shelves?

CARPENTER (*surlily*): Give him this bill. (*He hands it over.*) I'll be back in the morning. (*Exit* CARPENTER.)

NEPHEW (*calling after him, but with his eyes on* MRS. MI TZU): Don't worry! Mr. Shui Ta pays on the nail!

MRS. MI TZU (*looking closely at* SHEN TE): I'll be happy to make his acquaintance, Miss Shen Te. (*Exit* MRS. MI TZU.)

Pause.

WIFE: By tomorrow morning she'll know more about you than you do yourself.

SISTER-IN-LAW (*to* NEPHEW): This thing isn't built to last.

Enter GRANDFATHER.

WIFE: It's Grandfather! (*To* SHEN TE:) Such a good old soul!

The BOY *enters.*

BOY (*over his shoulder*): Here they are!

WIFE: And the boy, how he's grown! But he always could eat enough for ten.

Enter the NIECE.

WIFE (*to* SHEN TE): Our little niece from the country. There are more of us now than in your time. The less we had, the more there were of us; the more there were of us, the less we had. Give me the key. We must protect ourselves from unwanted guests. (*She takes the key and locks the door.*) Just make yourself at home. I'll light the little lamp.

NEPHEW (*a big joke*): I hope her cousin doesn't drop in tonight! The strict Mr. Shui Ta!

SISTER-IN-LAW *laughs.*

BROTHER (*reaching for a cigarette*): One cigarette more or less . . .

HUSBAND: One cigarette more or less.

They pile into the cigarettes. The BROTHER *hands a jug of wine round.*

NEPHEW: Mr. Shui Ta'll pay for it!

GRANDFATHER (*gravely, to* SHEN TE): How do you do?

SHEN TE, *a little taken aback by the belatedness of the greeting, bows. She has the carpenter's bill in one hand, the landlady's lease in the other.*

WIFE: How about a bit of a song? To keep Shen Te's spirits up?

NEPHEW: Good idea. Grandfather: you start!

SONG OF THE SMOKE

GRANDFATHER:
I used to think (before old age beset me)
  That brains could fill the pantry of the poor.
But where did all my cerebration get me?
  I'm just as hungry as I was before.
    So what's the use?
      See the smoke float free
    Into ever colder coldness!
      It's the same with me.

HUSBAND:
The straight and narrow path leads to disaster
  And so the crooked path I tried to tread.
That got me to disaster even faster.
  (They say we shall be happy when we're dead.)

So what's the use?
    See the smoke float free
Into ever colder coldness!
    It's the same with me.

NIECE:
You older people, full of expectation,
    At any moment now you'll walk the plank!
The future's for the younger generation!
    Yes, even if that future is a blank.
        So what's the use?
            See the smoke float free
        Into ever colder coldness!
            It's the same with me.

NEPHEW (*to the* BROTHER): Where'd you get that wine?

SISTER-IN-LAW (*answering for the* BROTHER): He pawned the sack of tobacco.

HUSBAND (*stepping in*): What? That tobacco was all we had to fall back on! You pig!

BROTHER: *You'd* call a man a pig because your wife was frigid! Did you refuse to drink it?

They fight. The shelves fall over.

SHEN TE (*imploringly*): Oh don't! Don't break everything! Take it, take it, take it all, but don't destroy a gift from the gods!

WIFE (*disparagingly*): This shop isn't big enough. I should never have mentioned it to Uncle and the others. When *they* arrive, it's going to be disgustingly overcrowded.

SISTER-IN-LAW: And did you hear our gracious hostess? She cools off quick!

Voices outside. Knocking at the door.

UNCLE'S VOICE: Open the door!

WIFE: Uncle! Is that you, Uncle?

UNCLE'S VOICE: Certainly, it's me. Auntie says to tell you she'll have the children here in ten minutes.

WIFE (*to* SHEN TE): I'll have to let him in.

SHEN TE (*who scarcely hears her*):
The little lifeboat is swiftly sent down
Too many men too greedily
Hold on to it as they drown.

1a

Wong's den in a sewer pipe.

WONG (*crouching there*): All quiet! It's four days now since I left the city. The gods passed this way on the second day. I heard their steps on the bridge over there. They must be a long way off by this time, so I'm safe. (*Breathing a sigh of relief, he curls up and goes to sleep. In his dream the pipe becomes transparent, and the* GODS *appear. Raising an arm, as if in self-defense:*) I know, I know, illustrious ones! I found no one to give you a room — not in all Setzuan! There, it's out. Please continue on your way!

FIRST GOD (*mildly*): But you did find someone. Someone who took us in for the night, watched over us in our sleep, and in the early morning lighted us down to the street with a lamp.

WONG: It was . . . Shen Te that took you in?

THIRD GOD: Who else?

WONG: And I ran away! "She isn't coming," I thought, "she just can't afford it."

GODS (*singing*):
O you feeble, well-intentioned, and yet feeble chap
Where there's need the fellow thinks there is
    no goodness!
When there's danger he thinks courage starts to
    ebb away!
Some people only see the seamy side!
What hasty judgment! What premature desperation!

WONG: I'm *very* ashamed, illustrious ones.

FIRST GOD: Do us a favor, water seller. Go back to Setzuan. Find Shen Te, and give us a report on her. We hear that she's come into a little money. Show interest in her goodness — for no one can be good for long if goodness is not in demand. Meanwhile we shall continue the search, and find other good people. After which, the idle chatter about the impossibility of goodness will stop!

The GODS *vanish.*

2

A knocking.

WIFE: Shen Te! Someone at the door. Where is she anyway?

NEPHEW: She must be getting the breakfast. Mr. Shui Ta will pay for it.

The WIFE *laughs and shuffles to the door. Enter* MR. SHUI TA *and the* CARPENTER.

WIFE: Who is it?

SHUI TA: I am Miss Shen Te's cousin.

WIFE: What?

SHUI TA: My name is Shui Ta.

WIFE: Her cousin?

NEPHEW: Her cousin?

NIECE: But that was a joke. She hasn't got a cousin.

HUSBAND: So early in the morning?

BROTHER: What's all the noise?

SISTER-IN-LAW: This fellow says he's her cousin.

BROTHER: Tell him to prove it.

NEPHEW: Right. If you're Shen Te's cousin, prove it by getting the breakfast.

SHUI TA (*whose regime begins as he puts out the lamp to save oil; loudly, to all present, asleep or awake*): Would you all please get dressed! Customers will be coming! I wish to open my shop!

HUSBAND: *Your* shop? Doesn't it belong to our good friend Shen Te?

SHUI TA *shakes his head.*

SISTER-IN-LAW: So we've been cheated. Where *is* the little liar?

SHUI TA: Miss Shen Te has been delayed. She wishes me to tell you there will be nothing she can do — now I am here.

WIFE (*bowled over*): I thought she was good!

NEPHEW: Do you have to believe *him?*

HUSBAND: I don't.

NEPHEW: Then do something.

HUSBAND: Certainly! I'll send out a search party at once. You, you, you, and you, go out and look for Shen Te. (*As the* GRANDFATHER *rises and makes for the door.*) Not you, Grandfather, you and I will hold the fort.

SHUI TA: You won't find Miss Shen Te. She has suspended her hospitable activity for an unlimited period. There are too many of you. She asked me to say: this is a tobacco shop, not a gold mine.

HUSBAND: Shen Te never said a thing like that. Boy, food! There's a bakery on the corner. Stuff your shirt full when they're not looking!

SISTER-IN-LAW: Don't overlook the raspberry tarts.

HUSBAND: And don't let the policeman see you.

The BOY *leaves.*

SHUI TA: Don't you depend on this shop now? Then why give it a bad name by stealing from the bakery?

NEPHEW: Don't listen to him. Let's find Shen Te. She'll give him a piece of her mind.

SISTER-IN-LAW: Don't forget to leave us some breakfast.

BROTHER, SISTER-IN-LAW, *and* NEPHEW *leave.*

SHUI TA (*to the* CARPENTER): You see, Mr. Carpenter, nothing has changed since the poet, eleven hundred years ago, penned these lines:

A governor was asked what was needed
To save the freezing people in the city.
He replied:
"A blanket ten thousand feet long
to cover the city and all its suburbs."

He starts to tidy up the shop.

CARPENTER: Your cousin owes me money. I've got witnesses. For the shelves.

SHUI TA: Yes, I have your bill. (*He takes it out of his pocket.*) Isn't a hundred silver dollars rather a lot?

CARPENTER: No deductions! I have a wife and children.

SHUI TA: How many children?

CARPENTER: Three.

SHUI TA: I'll make you an offer. Twenty silver dollars.

The HUSBAND *laughs.*

CARPENTER: You're crazy. Those shelves are real walnut.

SHUI TA: Very well. Take them away.

CARPENTER: What?

SHUI TA: They cost too much. Please take them away.

WIFE: Not bad! (*And she, too, is laughing.*)

CARPENTER (*a little bewildered*): Call Shen Te, someone! (*To* SHUI TA:) She's *good!*

SHUI TA: Certainly. She's ruined.

CARPENTER (*provoked into taking some of the shelves*): All right, you can keep your tobacco on the floor.

SHUI TA (*to the* HUSBAND): Help him with the shelves.

HUSBAND (*grins and carries one shelf over to the door where the* CARPENTER *now is*): Good-bye, shelves!

CARPENTER (*to the* HUSBAND): You dog! You want my family to starve?

SHUI TA: I repeat my offer. I have no desire to keep my tobacco on the floor. Twenty silver dollars.

CARPENTER (*with desperate aggressiveness*): One hundred!

SHUI TA *shows indifference, looks through the window. The* HUSBAND *picks up several shelves.*

CARPENTER (*to* HUSBAND): You needn't smash them against the door-post, you idiot! (*To* SHUI TA:) These shelves were made to measure. They're no use anywhere else!

SHUI TA: Precisely.

The WIFE *squeals with pleasure.*

CARPENTER (*giving up, sullenly*): Take the shelves. Pay what you want to pay.

SHUI TA (*smoothly*): Twenty silver dollars.

He places two large coins on the table. The CARPENTER *picks them up.*

HUSBAND (*brings the shelves back in*): And quite enough too!

CARPENTER (*slinking off*): Quite enough to get drunk on.

HUSBAND (*happily*): Well, we got rid of *him!*

WIFE (*weeping with fun, gives a rendition of the dialogue just spoken*): "Real walnut," says he. "Very well, take them away," says his lordship. "I have three children," says he. "Twenty silver dollars," says his lordship. "They're no use anywhere else," says he. "Pre-cisely," said his lordship! (*She dissolves into shrieks of merriment.*)

SHUI TA: And now: go!

HUSBAND: What's that?

SHUI TA: You're thieves, parasites. I'm giving you this chance. Go!

HUSBAND (*summoning all his ancestral dignity*): That sort deserves no answer. Besides, one should never shout on an empty stomach.

WIFE: Where's that boy?

SHUI TA: Exactly. The boy. I want no stolen goods in this shop. (*Very loudly.*) I strongly advise you to leave! (*But they remain seated, noses in the air. Quietly.*) As you wish. (SHUI TA *goes to the door. A* POLICEMAN *appears.* SHUI TA *bows.*) I am addressing the officer in charge of this precinct?

POLICEMAN: That's right, Mr., um, what was the name, sir?

SHUI TA: Mr. Shui Ta.

POLICEMAN: Yes, of course, sir.

They exchange a smile.

SHUI TA: Nice weather we're having.

POLICEMAN: A little on the warm side, sir.

SHUI TA: Oh, a little on the warm side.

HUSBAND (*whispering to the* WIFE): If he keeps it up till the boy's back, we're done for. (*Tries to signal* SHUI TA.)

SHUI TA (*ignoring the signal*): Weather, of course, is one thing indoors, another out on the dusty street!

POLICEMAN: Oh, quite another, sir!

WIFE (*to the* HUSBAND): It's all right as long as he's standing in the doorway — the boy will see him.

SHUI TA: Step inside for a moment! It's quite cool indoors. My cousin and I have just opened the place. And we attach the greatest importance to being on good terms with the, um, authorities.

POLICEMAN (*entering*): Thank you, Mr. Shui Ta. It *is* cool!

HUSBAND (*whispering to the* WIFE): And now the boy *won't* see him.

SHUI TA (*showing* HUSBAND *and* WIFE *to the* POLICEMAN): Visitors, I think my cousin knows them. They were just leaving.

HUSBAND (*defeated*): Ye-e-es, we were . . . just leaving.

SHUI TA: I'll tell my cousin you couldn't wait.

Noise from the street. Shouts of "Stop, Thief!"

POLICEMAN: What's that?

The BOY *is in the doorway with cakes and buns and rolls spilling out of his shirt. The* WIFE *signals desperately to him to leave. He gets the idea.*

POLICEMAN: No, you don't! (*He grabs the* BOY *by the collar.*) Where's all this from?

BOY (*vaguely pointing*): Down the street.

POLICEMAN (*grimly*): So that's it. (*Prepares to arrest the* BOY.)

WIFE (*stepping in*): And *we* knew nothing about it. (*To the* BOY:) Nasty little thief!

POLICEMAN (*dryly*): Can you clarify the situation, Mr. Shui Ta?

SHUI TA *is silent.*

POLICEMAN (*who understands silence*): Aha. You're all coming with me — to the station.

SHUI TA: I can hardly say how sorry I am that my establishment . . .

WIFE: Oh, he saw the boy leave not ten minutes ago!

SHUI TA: And to conceal the theft asked a policeman in?

POLICEMAN: Don't listen to her, Mr. Shui Ta, I'll be happy to relieve you of their presence one and all! (*To all three:*) Out! (*He drives them before him.*)

GRANDFATHER (*leaving last, gravely*): Good morning!

POLICEMAN: Good morning!

SHUI TA, *left alone, continues to tidy up.* MRS. MI TZU *breezes in.*

MRS. MI TZU: You're her cousin, are you? Then have the goodness to explain what all this means — police dragging people from a respectable house! By what right does your Miss Shen Te turn my property into a house of assignation? — Well, as you see, I know all!

SHUI TA: Yes. My cousin has the worst possible reputation: that of being poor.

MRS. MI TZU: No sentimental rubbish, Mr. Shui Ta. Your cousin was a common . . .

SHUI TA: Pauper. Let's use the uglier word.

MRS. MI TZU: I'm speaking of her conduct, not her earnings. But there must have *been* earnings, or how did she buy all this? Several elderly gentlemen took care of it, I suppose. I repeat: this is a respectable house! I have tenants who prefer not to live under the same roof with such a person.

SHUI TA (*quietly*): How much do you want?

MRS. MI TZU (*he is ahead of her now*): I beg your pardon.

SHUI TA: To reassure yourself. To reassure your tenants. How much will it cost?

MRS. MI TZU: You're a cool customer.

SHUI TA (*picking up the lease*): The rent is high. (*He reads on.*) I assume it's payable by the month?

MRS. MI TZU: Not in her case.

SHUI TA (*looking up*): What?

MRS. MI TZU: Six months' rent payable in advance. Two hundred silver dollars.

SHUI TA: Six . . . ! Sheer usury! And where am I to find it?

MRS. MI TZU: You should have thought of that before.

SHUI TA: Have you no heart, Mrs. Mi Tzu? It's true Shen Te acted foolishly, being kind to all those people, but she'll improve with time. I'll see to it she does. She'll work her fingers to the bone to pay her rent and all the time be as quiet as a mouse, as humble as a fly.

MRS. MI TZU: Her social background . . .

SHUI TA: Out of the depths! She came out of the depths! And before she'll go back there, she'll work, sacrifice, shrink from nothing. . . . Such a tenant is worth her weight in gold, Mrs. Mi Tzu.

MRS. MI TZU: It's silver we were talking about, Mr. Shui Ta. Two hundred silver dollars or . . .

Enter the POLICEMAN.

POLICEMAN: Am I intruding, Mr. Shui Ta?

MRS. MI TZU: This tobacco shop is well known to the police, I see.

POLICEMAN: Mr. Shui Ta has done us a service, Mrs. Mi Tzu. I am here to present our official felicitations!

MRS. MI TZU: That means less than nothing to me, sir. Mr. Shui Ta, all I can say is: I hope your cousin will find my terms acceptable. Good day, gentlemen. (*Exit.*)

SHUI TA: Good day, ma'am.

Pause.

POLICEMAN: Mrs. Mi Tzu a bit of a stumbling block, sir?

SHUI TA: She wants six months' rent in advance.

POLICEMAN: And you haven't got it, eh? (SHUI TA *is silent.*) But surely you can get it, sir? A man like you?

SHUI TA: What about a woman like Shen Te?

POLICEMAN: You're not staying, sir?

SHUI TA: No, and I won't be back. Do you smoke?

POLICEMAN (*taking two cigars, and placing them both in his pocket*): Thank you, sir — I see your point. Miss Te — let's mince no words — Miss Shen Te lived by selling herself. "What else could she have done?" you ask. "How else was she to pay the rent?" True. But the fact remains, Mr. Shui Ta, it is not respectable. Why not? A very deep question. But, in the first place, love — love isn't bought and sold like cigars, Mr. Shui Ta. In the second place, it isn't respectable to go waltzing off with someone that's paying his way, so to speak — it must be for love! Thirdly and lastly, as the proverb has it: not for a handful of rice but for love! (*Pause. He is thinking hard.*) "Well," you may say, "and what good is all this wisdom if the milk's already spilt?" Miss Shen Te is what she is. Is *where* she is. We have to face the fact that if she doesn't get hold of six months' rent pronto, she'll be back on the streets. The question then as I see it — everything in this world is a matter of opinion — the question as I see it is: *how* is she to get hold of this rent? How? Mr. Shui Ta: I don't know. (*Pause.*) I take that back, sir. It's just come to me. A husband. We must find her a husband!

Enter a little OLD WOMAN.

OLD WOMAN: A good cheap cigar for my husband, we'll have been married forty years tomorrow and we're having a little celebration.

SHUI TA: Forty years? And you still want to celebrate?

OLD WOMAN: As much as we can afford to. We have the carpet shop across the square. We'll be good neighbors, I hope?

SHUI TA: I hope so too.

POLICEMAN (*who keeps making discoveries*): Mr. Shui Ta, you know what we need? We need capital. And how do we acquire capital? We get married.

SHUI TA (*to* OLD WOMAN): I'm afraid I've been pestering this gentleman with my personal worries.

POLICEMAN (*lyrically*): We can't pay six months' rent, so what do we do? We marry money.

SHUI TA: That might not be easy.

POLICEMAN: Oh, I don't know. She's a good match. Has a nice, growing business. (*To the* OLD WOMAN:) What do you think?

OLD WOMAN (*undecided*): Well —

POLICEMAN: Should she put an ad in the paper?

OLD WOMAN (*not eager to commit herself*): Well, if she agrees —

POLICEMAN: I'll write it for her. *You* lend us a hand, and *we* write an ad for you! (*He chuckles away to himself, takes out his notebook, wets the stump of a pencil between his lips, and writes away.*)

SHUI TA (*slowly*): Not a bad idea.

POLICEMAN: "What . . . *respectable* . . . man . . . with small capital . . . widower . . . not excluded . . . desires . . . marriage . . . into flourishing . . . tobacco shop?" And now let's add: "Am . . . pretty . . . " No! . . . "Prepossessing appearance."

SHUI TA: If you don't think that's an exaggeration?

OLD WOMAN: Oh, not a bit. I've seen her.

The POLICEMAN *tears the page out of his notebook, and hands it over to* SHUI TA.

SHUI TA (*with horror in his voice*): How much luck we need to keep our heads above water! How many ideas! How many friends! (*To the* POLICEMAN:) Thank you, sir, I think I see my way clear.

3

Evening in the municipal park. Noise of a plane overhead. YANG SUN, *a young man in rags, is following the plane with his eyes: one can tell that the machine is describing a curve above the park.* YANG SUN *then takes a rope out of his pocket, looking anxiously about him as he does so. He moves toward a large willow. Enter two prostitutes, one the* OLD WHORE, *the other the* NIECE *whom we have already met.*

NIECE: Hello. Coming with me?

YANG SUN (*taken aback*): If you'd like to buy me a dinner.

OLD WHORE: Buy you a dinner! (*To the* NIECE:) Oh, we know him — it's the unemployed pilot. Waste no time on him!

NIECE: But he's the only man left in the park. And it's going to rain.

OLD WHORE: Oh, how do you know?

And they pass by. YANG SUN *again looks about him, again takes his rope, and this time throws it round a branch of the willow tree. Again*

*he is interrupted. It is the two prostitutes returning — and in such a
hurry they don't notice him.*

NIECE: It's going to pour!

Enter SHEN TE.

OLD WHORE: There's that *gorgon* Shen Te! That *drove* your family out
into the cold!

NIECE: It wasn't her. It was that cousin of hers. She offered to pay for
the cakes. I've nothing against her.

OLD WHORE: I have, though. (*So that* SHEN TE *can hear.*) Now where
could the little lady be off to? She may be rich now but that won't stop
her snatching our young men, will it?

SHEN TE: I'm going to the tearoom by the pond.

NIECE: Is it true what they say? You're marrying a widower — with
three children?

SHEN TE: Yes. I'm just going to see him.

YANG SUN (*his patience at breaking point*): Move on there! This is a
park, not a whorehouse!

OLD WHORE: Shut your mouth!

But the two prostitutes leave.

YANG SUN: Even in the farthest corner of the park, even when it's raining, you can't get rid of them! (*He spits.*)

SHEN TE (*overhearing this*): And what right have you to scold them?
(*But at this point she sees the rope.*) Oh!

YANG SUN: Well, what are you staring at?

SHEN TE: That rope. What is it for?

YANG SUN: Think! Think! I haven't a penny. Even if I had, I wouldn't
spend it on you. I'd buy a drink of water.

The rain starts.

SHEN TE (*still looking at the rope*): What is the rope for? You mustn't!

YANG SUN: What's it to you? Clear out!

SHEN TE (*irrelevantly*): It's raining.

YANG SUN: Well, don't try to come under this tree.

SHEN TE: Oh, no. (*She stays in the rain.*)

YANG SUN: Now go away. (*Pause.*) For one thing, I don't like your looks, you're bowlegged.

SHEN TE (*indignantly*): That's not true!

YANG SUN: Well, don't show 'em to me. Look, it's raining. You better come under this tree.

Slowly, she takes shelter under the tree.

SHEN TE: Why did you want to do it?

YANG SUN: You really want to know? (*Pause.*) To get rid of you! (*Pause.*) You know what a flyer is?

SHEN TE: Oh yes, I've met a lot of pilots. At the tearoom.

YANG SUN: You call *them* flyers? Think they know what a machine is? Just 'cause they have leather helmets. They gave the airfield director a bribe, that's the way *those* fellows got up in the air! Try one of them out sometime. "Go up to two thousand feet," tell them, "then let it fall, then pick it up again with a flick of the wrist at the last moment." Know what he'll say to that? "It's not in my contract." Then again, there's the landing problem. It's like landing on your own backside. It's no different, planes are human. Those fools don't understand. (*Pause.*) And I'm the biggest fool for reading the book on flying in the Peking school and skipping the page where it says: "We've got enough flyers and we don't need you." I'm a mail pilot with no mail. You understand that?

SHEN TE (*shyly*): Yes. I do.

YANG SUN: No, you don't. You'd never understand that.

SHEN TE: When we were little we had a crane with a broken wing. He made friends with us and was very good-natured about our jokes. He would strut along behind us and call out to stop us going too fast for him. But every spring and autumn when the cranes flew over the villages in great swarms, he got quite restless. (*Pause.*) I understand that. (*She bursts out crying.*)

YANG SUN: Don't!

SHEN TE (*quieting down*): No.

YANG SUN: It's bad for the complexion.

SHEN TE (*sniffing*): I've stopped.

She dries her tears on her big sleeve. Leaning against the tree, but not looking at her, he reaches for her face.

YANG SUN: You can't even wipe your own face. (*He is wiping it for her with his handkerchief. Pause.*)

SHEN TE (*still sobbing*) : I don't know *anything!*

YANG SUN : You interrupted me! What for?

SHEN TE : It's such a rainy day. You only wanted to do . . . *that* because it's such a rainy day. (*To the audience:*)

In our country
The evenings should never be somber
High bridges over rivers
The gray hour between night and morning
And the long, long winter:
Such things are dangerous
For, with all the misery,
A very little is enough
And men throw away an unbearable life.

Pause.

YANG SUN : Talk about yourself for a change.

SHEN TE : What about me? I have a shop.

YANG SUN (*incredulous*) : You have a shop, have you? Never thought of walking the streets?

SHEN TE : I did walk the streets. Now I have a shop.

YANG SUN (*ironically*) : A gift of the gods, I suppose!

SHEN TE : How did you know?

YANG SUN (*even more ironical*) : One fine evening the gods turned up saying: here's some money!

SHEN TE (*quickly*) : One fine morning.

YANG SUN (*fed up*) : This isn't much of an entertainment.

Pause.

SHEN TE : I can play the zither a little. (*Pause.*) And I can mimic men. (*Pause.*) I got the shop, so the first thing I did was to give my zither away. I can be as stupid as a fish now, I said to myself, and it won't matter.

I'm rich now, I said
I walk alone, I sleep alone
For a whole year, I said
I'll have nothing to do with a man.

YANG SUN : And now you're marrying one! The one at the tearoom by the pond?

SHEN TE *is silent.*

YANG SUN : What do you know about love?

SHEN TE : Everything.

YANG SUN : Nothing. (*Pause.*) Or d'you just mean you enjoyed it?

SHEN TE : No.

YANG SUN (*again without turning to look at her, he strokes her cheek with his hand*) : You like that?

SHEN TE : Yes.

YANG SUN (*breaking off*) : You're easily satisfied, I must say. (*Pause.*) What a town!

SHEN TE : You have no friends?

YANG SUN (*defensively*) : Yes, I have! (*Change of tone.*) But they don't want to hear I'm still unemployed. "What?" they ask. "Is there still water in the sea?" You have friends?

SHEN TE (*hesitating*) : Just a . . . cousin.

YANG SUN : Watch him carefully.

SHEN TE : He only came once. Then he went away. He won't be back. (YANG SUN *is looking away.*) But to be without hope, they say, is to be without goodness!

Pause.

YANG SUN : Go on talking. A voice is a voice.

SHEN TE : Once, when I was a little girl, I fell, with a load of brushwood. An old man picked me up. He gave me a penny too. Isn't it funny how people who don't have very much like to give some of it away? They must like to show what they can do, and how could they show it better than by being kind? Being wicked is just like being clumsy. When we sing a song, or build a machine, or plant some rice, we're being kind. You're kind.

YANG SUN : You make it sound easy.

SHEN TE : Oh, no. (*Little pause.*) Oh! A drop of rain!

YANG SUN : Where'd you feel it?

SHEN TE : Between the eyes.

YANG SUN : Near the right eye? Or the left?

SHEN TE : Near the left eye.

YANG SUN : Oh, good. (*He is getting sleepy.*) So you're through with men, eh?

SHEN TE (*with a smile*): But I'm not bowlegged.

YANG SUN: Perhaps not.

SHEN TE: Definitely not.

Pause.

YANG SUN (*leaning wearily against the willow*): I haven't had a drop to drink all day, I haven't eaten anything for *two* days. I couldn't love you if I tried.

Pause.

SHEN TE: I like it in the rain.

Enter WONG *the water seller, singing.*

THE SONG OF THE WATER SELLER IN THE RAIN

"Buy my water," I am yelling
And my fury restraining
For no water I'm selling
'Cause it's raining, 'cause it's raining!
  I keep yelling: "Buy my water!"
  But no one's buying
  Athirst and dying
  And drinking and paying!
  Buy water!
  Buy water, you dogs!

Nice to dream of lovely weather!
Think of all the consternation
Were there no precipitation
Half a dozen years together!
  Can't you hear them shrieking: "Water!"
  Pretending they adore me?
  They all would go down on their knees before me!
  Down on your knees!
  Go down on your knees, you dogs!

What are lawns and hedges thinking?
What are fields and forests saying?
"At the clouds' breast we are drinking!
And we've no idea who's paying!"
  I keep yelling: "Buy my water!"
  But no one's buying
  Athirst and dying
  And drinking and paying!
  Buy water!
  Buy water, you dogs!

The rain has stopped now. SHEN TE *sees* WONG *and runs toward him.*

SHEN TE: Wong! You're back! Your carrying pole's at the shop.

WONG: Oh, thank you, Shen Te. And how is life treating *you?*

SHEN TE: I've just met a brave and clever man. And I want to buy him a cup of your water.

WONG (*bitterly*): Throw back your head and open your mouth and you'll have all the water you need —

SHEN TE (*tenderly*):
I want *your* water, Wong
The water that has tired you so
The water that you carried all this way
The water that is hard to sell because
  it's been raining.

I need it for the young man over there — he's a flyer!

A flyer is a bold man:
Braving the storms
In company with the clouds
He crosses the heavens
And brings to friends in faraway lands
The friendly mail!

She pays WONG, *and runs over to* YANG SUN *with the cup. But* YANG SUN *is fast asleep.*

SHEN TE (*calling to* WONG, *with a laugh*): He's fallen asleep! Despair and rain and I have worn him out!

3a

Wong's den. The sewer pipe is transparent, and the GODS *again appear to* WONG *in a dream.*

WONG (*radiant*): I've seen her, illustrious ones! And she hasn't changed!

FIRST GOD: That's good to hear.

WONG: She loves someone.

FIRST GOD: Let's hope the experience gives her the strength to stay good!

WONG: It does. She's doing good deeds all the time.

FIRST GOD: Ah? What sort? What sort of good deeds, Wong?

WONG: Well, she has a kind word for everybody.

FIRST GOD (*eagerly*): And then?

WONG: Hardly anyone leaves her shop without tobacco in his pocket — even if he can't pay for it.

FIRST GOD: Not bad at all. Next?

WONG: She's putting up a family of eight.

FIRST GOD (*gleefully, to the* SECOND GOD): Eight! (*To* WONG:) And that's not all, of course!

WONG: She bought a cup of water from me even though it was raining.

FIRST GOD: Yes, yes, yes, all these smaller good deeds!

WONG: Even they run into money. A little tobacco shop doesn't make so much.

FIRST GOD (*sententiously*): A prudent gardener works miracles on the smallest plot.

WONG: She hands out rice every morning. That eats up half her earnings.

FIRST GOD (*a little disappointed*): Well, as a beginning . . .

WONG: They call her the Angel of the Slums — whatever the carpenter may say!

FIRST GOD: What's this? A carpenter speaks ill of her?

WONG: Oh, he only says her shelves weren't paid for in full.

SECOND GOD (*who has a bad cold and can't pronounce his n's and m's*): What's this? Not paying a carpenter? Why was that?

WONG: I suppose she didn't have the money.

SECOND GOD (*severely*): One pays what one owes, that's in our book of rules! First the letter of the law, then the spirit.

WONG: But it wasn't Shen Te, illustrious ones, it was her cousin. She called *him* in to help.

SECOND GOD: Then her cousin must never darken her threshold again!

WONG: Very well, illustrious ones! · But in fairness to Shen Te, let me say that her cousin is a businessman.

FIRST GOD: Perhaps we should inquire what is customary. I find business quite unintelligible. But everybody's doing it. Business! Did the Seven Good Kings do business? Did Kung the Just sell fish?

SECOND GOD: In any case, such a thing must not occur again!

The GODS *start to leave.*

THIRD GOD: Forgive us for taking this tone with you, Wong, we haven't been getting enough sleep. The rich recommend us to the poor, and the poor tell us they haven't enough room.

SECOND GOD: Feeble, feeble, the best of them!

FIRST GOD: No great deeds! No heroic daring!

THIRD GOD: On such a *small* scale!

SECOND GOD: Sincere, yes, but what is actually *achieved?*

One can no longer hear them.

WONG (*calling after them*): I've thought of something, illustrious ones: Perhaps you shouldn't ask — too — much — all — at — once!

4

The square in front of Shen Te's tobacco shop. Besides Shen Te's place, two other shops are seen: the carpet shop and a barber's. Morning. Outside Shen Te's the GRANDFATHER, the SISTER-IN-LAW, the UNEMPLOYED MAN, and MRS. SHIN stand waiting.

SISTER-IN-LAW: She's been out all night again.

MRS. SHIN: No sooner did we get rid of that crazy cousin of hers than Shen Te herself starts carrying on! Maybe she does give us an ounce of rice now and then, but can you depend on her? Can you depend on her?

Loud voices from the barber's.

VOICE OF SHU FU: What are you doing in my shop? Get out — at once!

VOICE OF WONG: But sir. They all let me sell . . .

WONG *comes staggering out of the barber's shop pursued by* MR. SHU FU, *the barber, a fat man carrying a heavy curling iron.*

SHU FU: Get out, I said! Pestering my customers with your slimy old water! Get out! Take your cup!

He holds out the cup. WONG *reaches out for it.* MR. SHU FU *strikes his hand with the curling iron, which is hot.* WONG *howls.*

SHU FU: You had it coming, my man!

Puffing, he returns to his shop. The UNEMPLOYED MAN *picks up the cup and gives it to* WONG.

UNEMPLOYED MAN: You can report that to the police.

WONG: My hand! It's smashed up!

UNEMPLOYED MAN: Any bones broken?

WONG: I can't move my fingers.

UNEMPLOYED MAN: Sit down. I'll put some water on it.

WONG *sits*.

MRS. SHIN: The water won't cost you anything.

SISTER-IN-LAW: You might have got a bandage from Miss Shen Te till she took to staying out all night. It's a scandal.

MRS. SHIN (*despondently*): If you ask me, she's forgotten we ever existed!

Enter SHEN TE *down the street, with a dish of rice.*

SHEN TE (*to the audience*): How wonderful to see Setzuan in the early morning! I always used to stay in bed with my dirty blanket over my head afraid to wake up. This morning I saw the newspapers being delivered by little boys, the streets being washed by strong men, and fresh vegetables coming in from the country on ox carts. It's a long walk from where Yang Sun lives, but I feel lighter at every step. They say you walk on air when you're in love, but it's even better walking on the rough earth, on the hard cement. In the early morning, the old city looks like a great heap of rubbish! Nice, though, with all its little lights. And the sky, so pink, so transparent, before the dust comes and muddies it! What a lot you miss if you never see your city rising from its slumbers like an honest old craftsman pumping his lungs full of air and reaching for his tools, as the poet says! (*Cheerfully, to her waiting guests:*) Good morning, everyone, here's your rice! (*Distributing the rice, she comes upon* WONG.) Good morning, Wong, I'm quite light-headed today. On my way over, I looked at myself in all the shop windows. I'd love to be beautiful.

She slips into the carpet shop. MR. SHU FU *has just emerged from his shop.*

SHU FU (*to the audience*): It surprises me how beautiful Miss Shen Te is looking today! I never gave her a passing thought before. But now I've been gazing upon her comely form for exactly three minutes! I begin to suspect I am in love with her. She is overpoweringly attractive! (*Crossly, to* WONG:) Be off with you, rascal!

He returns to his shop. SHEN TE *comes back out of the carpet shop with the* OLD MAN, *its proprietor, and his wife — whom we have already met — the* OLD WOMAN. SHEN TE *is wearing a shawl. The* OLD MAN *is holding up a looking glass for her.*

OLD WOMAN: Isn't it lovely? We'll give you a reduction because there's a little hole in it.

SHEN TE (*looking at another shawl on the* OLD WOMAN'S *arm*): The other one's nice too.

OLD WOMAN (*smiling*) : Too bad there's no hole in that!

SHEN TE : That's right. My shop doesn't make very much.

OLD WOMAN : And your good deeds eat it all up! Be more careful, my dear. . . .

SHEN TE (*trying on the shawl with the hole*) : Just now, I'm light-headed! Does the color suit me?

OLD WOMAN : You'd better ask a man.

SHEN TE (*to the* OLD MAN) : Does the color suit me?

OLD MAN : You'd better ask your young friend.

SHEN TE : I'd like to have your opinion.

OLD MAN : It suits you very well. But wear it this way: the dull side out.

SHEN TE *pays up*.

OLD WOMAN : If you decide you don't like it, you can exchange it. (*She pulls* SHEN TE *to one side.*) Has he got money?

SHEN TE (*with a laugh*) : Yang Sun? Oh, no.

OLD WOMAN : Then how're you going to pay your rent?

SHEN TE : I'd forgotten about that.

OLD WOMAN : And next Monday is the first of the month! Miss Shen Te, I've got something to say to you. After we (*indicating her husband*) got to know you, we had our doubts about that marriage ad. We thought it would be better if you'd let *us* help you. Out of our savings. We reckon we could lend you two hundred silver dollars. We don't need anything in writing — you could pledge us your tobacco stock.

SHEN TE : You're prepared to lend money to a person like me?

OLD WOMAN : It's folks like you that need it. We'd think twice about lending anything to your cousin.

OLD MAN (*coming up*) : All settled, my dear?

SHEN TE : I wish the gods could have heard what your wife was just saying, Mr. Ma. They're looking for good people who're happy — and helping me makes you happy because you know it was love that got me into difficulties!

The OLD COUPLE *smile knowingly at each other.*

OLD MAN : And here's the money, Miss Shen Te.

He hands her an envelope. SHEN TE *takes it. She bows. They bow back. They return to their shop.*

SHEN TE (*holding up her envelope*): Look, Wong, here's six months' rent! Don't you believe in miracles now? And how do you like my new shawl?

WONG: For the young fellow I saw you with in the park?

SHEN TE *nods*.

MRS. SHIN: Never mind all that. It's time you took a look at his hand!

SHEN TE: Have you hurt your hand?

MRS. SHIN: That barber smashed it with his hot curling iron. Right in front of our eyes.

SHEN TE (*shocked at herself*): And I never noticed! We must get you to a doctor this minute or who knows what will happen?

UNEMPLOYED MAN: It's not a doctor he should see, it's a judge. He can ask for compensation. The barber's filthy rich.

WONG: You think I have a chance?

MRS. SHIN (*with relish*): If it's really good and smashed. But is it?

WONG: I think so. It's very swollen. Could I get a pension?

MRS. SHIN: You'd need a witness.

WONG: Well, you all saw it. You could all testify.

He looks round. The UNEMPLOYED MAN, *the* GRANDFATHER, *and the* SISTER-IN-LAW *are all sitting against the wall of the shop eating rice. Their concentration on eating is complete.*

SHEN TE (*to* MRS. SHIN): You saw it yourself.

MRS. SHIN: I want nothing to do with the police. It's against my principles.

SHEN TE (*to* SISTER-IN-LAW): What about you?

SISTER-IN-LAW: Me? I wasn't looking.

SHEN TE (*to the* GRANDFATHER, *coaxingly*): Grandfather, *you'll* testify, won't you?

SISTER-IN-LAW: And a lot of good that will do. He's simple-minded.

SHEN TE (*to the* UNEMPLOYED MAN): You seem to be the only witness left.

UNEMPLOYED MAN: My testimony would only hurt him. I've been picked up twice for begging.

SHEN TE: Your brother is assaulted, and you shut your eyes?
He is hit, cries out in pain, and you are silent?

The beast prowls, chooses and seizes his victim, and you say:
"Because we showed no displeasure, he has spared us."
If no one present will be a witness, I will. I'll say *I* saw it.

MRS. SHIN (*solemnly*) : The name for that is perjury.

WONG: I don't know if I can accept that. Though maybe I'll have to.
(*Looking at his hand.*) Is it swollen enough, do you think? The swelling's not going down?

UNEMPLOYED MAN: No, no. The swelling's holding up well.

WONG: Yes. It's *more* swollen if anything. Maybe my wrist is broken after all. I'd better see a judge at once.

Holding his hand very carefully, and fixing his eyes on it, he runs off.
MRS. SHIN *goes quickly into the barber's shop.*

UNEMPLOYED MAN (*seeing her*) : She is getting on the right side of Mr. Shu Fu.

SISTER-IN-LAW: You and I can't change the world, Shen Te.

SHEN TE: Go away! Go away all of you!

The UNEMPLOYED MAN, *the* SISTER-IN-LAW, *and the* GRANDFATHER *stalk off, eating and sulking.*

To the audience:

They've stopped answering
They stay put
They do as they're told
They don't care
Nothing can make them look up
But the smell of food.

Enter MRS. YANG, *Yang Sun's mother, out of breath.*

MRS. YANG: Miss Shen Te. My son has told me everything. I am Mrs. Yang, Sun's mother. Just think. He's got an offer. Of a job as a pilot. A letter has just come. From the director of the airfield in Peking!

SHEN TE: So he can fly again? Isn't that wonderful!

MRS. YANG (*less breathlessly all the time*) : They won't give him the job for nothing. They want five hundred silver dollars.

SHEN TE: We can't let money stand in his way, Mrs. Yang!

MRS. YANG: If only you could help him out!

SHEN TE: I have the shop. I can try! (*She embraces* MRS. YANG.) I happen to have two hundred with me now. Take it. (*She gives her the old couple's money.*) It was a loan but they said I could repay it with my tobacco stock.

MRS. YANG: And they were calling Sun the Dead Pilot of Setzuan! A friend in need!

SHEN TE: We must find another three hundred.

MRS. YANG: How?

SHEN TE: Let me think. (*Slowly.*) I know someone who can help. I didn't want to call on his services again, he's hard and cunning. But a flyer must fly. And I'll make this the last time.

Distant sound of a plane.

MRS. YANG: If the man you mentioned can do it. . . . Oh, look, there's the morning mail plane, heading for Peking!

SHEN TE: The pilot can see us, let's wave!

They wave. The noise of the engine is louder.

MRS. YANG: You know that pilot up there?

SHEN TE: Wave, Mrs. Yang! I know the pilot who will be up there. He gave up hope. But he'll do it now. One man to raise himself above the misery, above us all. (*To the audience:*)

Yang Sun, my lover:
Braving the storms
In company with the clouds
Crossing the heavens
And bringing to friends in faraway lands
The friendly mail!

4a

In front of the inner curtain. Enter SHEN TE, *carrying Shui Ta's mask. She sings.*

THE SONG OF DEFENSELESSNESS

In our country
A useful man needs luck
Only if he finds strong backers
Can he prove himself useful.
The good can't defend themselves and
Even the gods are defenseless.

Oh, why don't the gods have their own ammunition
And launch against badness their own expedition
Enthroning the good and preventing sedition
And bringing the world to a peaceful condition?

Oh, why don't the gods do the buying and selling
Injustice forbidding, starvation dispelling
Give bread to each city and joy to each dwelling?
Oh, why don't the gods do the buying and selling?

She puts on SHUI TA's *mask and sings in his voice.*

You can only help one of your luckless brothers
By trampling down a dozen others.

Why is it the gods do not feel indignation
And come down in fury to end exploitation
Defeat all defeat and forbid desperation
Refusing to tolerate such toleration?

Why is it?

5

Shen Te's tobacco shop. Behind the counter, MR. SHUI TA, *reading the paper.* MRS. SHIN *is cleaning up. She talks and he takes no notice.*

MRS. SHIN: And when certain rumors get about, what *happens* to a little place like this? It goes to pot. *I* know. So, if you want my advice, Mr. Shui Ta, find out just what has been going on between Miss Shen Te and that Yang Sun from Yellow Street. And remember: a certain interest in Miss Shen Te has been expressed by the barber next door, a man with twelve houses and only one wife, who, for that matter, is likely to drop off at any time. A certain interest has been expressed. He was even inquiring about her means and, if *that* doesn't prove a man is getting serious, what would? (*Still getting no response, she leaves with her bucket.*)

YANG SUN'S VOICE: Is that Miss Shen Te's tobacco shop?

MRS. SHIN'S VOICE: Yes, it is, but it's Mr. Shui Ta who's here today.

SHUI TA *runs to the mirror with the short, light steps of* SHEN TE, *and is just about to start primping, when he realizes his mistake, and turns away, with a short laugh. Enter* YANG SUN. MRS. SHIN *enters behind him and slips into the back room to eavesdrop.*

YANG SUN: I am Yang Sun. (SHUI TA *bows.*) Is Shen Te in?

SHUI TA: No.

YANG SUN: I guess you know our relationship? (*He is inspecting the stock.*) Quite a place! And I thought she was just talking big. I'll be flying again, all right. (*He takes a cigar, solicits and receives a light from* SHUI TA.) You think we can squeeze the other three hundred out of the tobacco stock?

SHUI TA: May I ask if it is your intention to sell at once?

YANG SUN: It was decent of her to come out with the two hundred but they aren't much use with the other three hundred still missing.

SHUI TA: Shen Te was overhasty promising so much. She might have to sell the shop itself to raise it. Haste, they say, is the wind that blows the house down.

YANG SUN: Oh, she isn't a girl to keep a man waiting. For one thing or the other, if you take my meaning.

SHUI TA: I take your meaning.

YANG SUN (*leering*): Uh, huh.

SHUI TA: Would you explain what the five hundred silver dollars are for?

YANG SUN: Want to sound me out? Very well. The director of the Peking airfield is a friend of mine from flying school. I give him five hundred: he gets me the job.

SHUI TA: The price is high.

YANG SUN: Not as these things go. He'll have to fire one of the present pilots — for negligence. Only the man he has in mind isn't negligent. Not easy, you understand. You needn't mention that part of it to Shen Te.

SHUI TA (*looking intently at* YANG SUN): Mr. Yang Sun, you are asking my cousin to give up her possessions, leave her friends, and place her entire fate in your hands. I presume you intend to marry her?

YANG SUN: I'd be prepared to.

Slight pause.

SHUI TA: Those two hundred silver dollars would pay the rent here for six months. If you were Shen Te wouldn't you be tempted to continue in business?

YANG SUN: What? Can you imagine Yang Sun the flyer behind a counter? (*In an oily voice.*) "A strong cigar or a mild one, worthy sir?" Not in this century!

SHUI TA: My cousin wishes to follow the promptings of her heart, and, from her own point of view, she may even have what is called the right to love. Accordingly, she has commissioned me to help you to this post. There is nothing here that I am not empowered to turn immediately into cash. Mrs. Mi Tzu, the landlady, will advise me about the sale.

Enter MRS. MI TZU.

MRS. MI TZU: Good morning, Mr. Shui Ta, you wish to see me about the rent? As you know it falls due the day after tomorrow.

SHUI TA: Circumstances have changed, Mrs. Mi Tzu: my cousin is getting married. Her future husband here, Mr. Yang Sun, will be taking her to Peking. I am interested in selling the tobacco stock.

MRS. MI TZU: How much are you asking, Mr. Shui Ta?

YANG SUN: Three hundred sil —

SHUI TA: Five hundred silver dollars.

MRS. MI TZU: How much did she pay for it, Mr. Shui Ta?

SHUI TA: A thousand. And very little has been sold.

MRS. MI TZU: She was robbed. But I'll make you a special offer if you'll promise to be out by the day after tomorrow. Three hundred silver dollars.

YANG SUN (*shrugging*): Take it, man, take it.

SHUI TA: It is not enough.

YANG SUN: Why not? Why not? Certainly, it's enough.

SHUI TA: Five hundred silver dollars.

YANG SUN: But why? We only need three!

SHUI TA (*to* MRS. MI TZU): Excuse me. (*Takes* YANG SUN *on one side.*) The tobacco stock is pledged to the old couple who gave my cousin the two hundred.

YANG SUN: Is it in writing?

SHUI TA: No.

YANG SUN (*to* MRS. MI TZU): Three hundred will do.

MRS. MI TZU: Of course, I need an assurance that Miss Shen Te is not in debt.

YANG SUN: Mr. Shui Ta?

SHUI TA: She is not in debt.

YANG SUN: When can you let us have the money?

MRS. MI TZU: The day after tomorrow. And remember: I'm doing this because I have a soft spot in my heart for young lovers! (*Exit.*)

YANG SUN (*calling after her*): Boxes, jars and sacks — three hundred for the lot and the pain's over! (*To* SHUI TA:) Where else can we raise money by the day after tomorrow?

SHUI TA: Nowhere. Haven't you enough for the trip and the first few weeks?

YANG SUN: Oh, certainly.

SHUI TA: How much, exactly.

YANG SUN: Oh, I'll dig it up, even if I have to steal it.

SHUI TA: I see.

YANG SUN: Well, don't fall off the roof. I'll get to Peking somehow.

SHUI TA: Two people can't travel for nothing.

YANG SUN (*not giving* SHUI TA *a chance to answer*): I'm leaving *her* behind. No millstones round *my* neck!

SHUI TA: Oh.

YANG SUN: Don't look at me like that!

SHUI TA: How precisely is my cousin to live?

YANG SUN: Oh, you'll think of something.

SHUI TA: A small request, Mr. Yang Sun. Leave the two hundred silver dollars here until you can show me two tickets for Peking.

YANG SUN: You learn to mind your own business, Mr. Shui Ta.

SHUI TA: I'm afraid Miss Shen Te may not wish to sell the shop when she discovers that . . .

YANG SUN: You don't know women. She'll want to. Even then.

SHUI TA (*a slight outburst*): She is a human being, sir! And not devoid of common sense!

YANG SUN: Shen Te is a woman: she *is* devoid of common sense. I only have to lay my hand on her shoulder, and church bells ring.

SHUI TA (*with difficulty*): Mr. Yang Sun!

YANG SUN: Mr. Shui Whatever-it-is!

SHUI TA: My cousin is devoted to you . . . because . . .

YANG SUN: Because I have my hands on her breasts. Give me a cigar. (*He takes one for himself, stuffs a few more in his pocket, then changes his mind and takes the whole box.*) Tell her I'll marry her, then bring me the three hundred. Or let her bring it. One or the other. (*Exit.*)

MRS. SHIN (*sticking her head out of the back room*): Well, he has your cousin under his thumb, and doesn't care if all Yellow Street knows it!

SHUI TA (*crying out*): I've lost my shop! And he doesn't love me! (*He runs berserk through the room, repeating these lines incoherently. Then stops suddenly, and addresses* MRS. SHIN.) Mrs. Shin, you grew up in the gutter, like me. Are we lacking in hardness? I doubt it. If you steal a penny from me, I'll take you by the throat till you spit it out! You'd do the same to me. The times are bad, this city is hell, but we're like ants, we keep coming, up and up the walls, however smooth! Till bad luck comes. Being in love, for instance. One weakness is enough, and love is the deadliest.

MRS. SHIN (*emerging from the back room*): You should have a little talk with Mr. Shu Fu, the barber. He's a real gentleman and just the thing for your cousin. (*She runs off.*)

SHUI TA:
A caress becomes a stranglehold
A sigh of love turns to a cry of fear
Why are there vultures circling in the air?
A girl is going to meet her lover.

SHUI TA *sits down and* MR. SHU FU *enters with* MRS. SHIN.

SHUI TA: Mr. Shu Fu?

SHU FU: Mr. Shui Ta.

They both bow.

SHUI TA: I am told that you have expressed a certain interest in my cousin Shen Te. Let me set aside all propriety and confess: she is at this moment in grave danger.

SHU FU: Oh, dear!

SHUI TA: She has lost her shop, Mr. Shu Fu.

SHU FU: The charm of Miss Shen Te, Mr. Shui Ta, derives from the goodness, not of her shop, but of her heart. Men call her the Angel of the Slums.

SHUI TA: Yet her goodness has cost her two hundred silver dollars in a single day: we must put a stop to it.

SHU FU: Permit me to differ, Mr. Shui Ta. Let us, rather, open wide the gates to such goodness! Every morning, with pleasure tinged by affection, I watch her charitable ministrations. For they are hungry, and she giveth them to eat! Four of them, to be precise. Why only four? I ask. Why not four hundred? I hear she has been seeking shelter for the homeless. What about my humble cabins behind the cattle run? They are at her disposal. And so forth. And so on. Mr. Shui Ta, do you think Miss Shen Te could be persuaded to listen to certain ideas of mine? Ideas like these?

SHUI TA: Mr. Shu Fu, she would be honored.

Enter WONG *and the* POLICEMAN. MR. SHU FU *turns abruptly away and studies the shelves.*

WONG: Is Miss Shen Te here?

SHUI TA: No.

WONG: I am Wong the water seller. You are Mr. Shui Ta?

SHUI TA: I am.

WONG: I am a friend of Shen Te's.

SHUI TA: An intimate friend, I hear.

WONG (*to the* POLICEMAN): You see? (*To* SHUI TA:) It's because of my hand.

POLICEMAN: He hurt his hand, sir, that's a fact.

SHUI TA (*quickly*): You need a sling, I see. (*He takes a shawl from the back room, and throws it to* WONG.)

WONG: But that's her new shawl!

SHUI TA: She has no more use for it.

WONG: But she bought it to please someone!

SHUI TA: It happens to be no longer necessary.

WONG (*making the sling*): She is my only witness.

POLICEMAN: Mr. Shui Ta, your cousin is supposed to have seen the barber hit the water seller with a curling iron.

SHUI TA: I'm afraid my cousin was not present at the time.

WONG: But she was, sir! Just ask her! Isn't she in?

SHUI TA (*gravely*): Mr. Wong, my cousin has her own troubles. You wouldn't wish her to add to them by committing perjury?

WONG: But it was she that told me to go to the judge!

SHUI TA: Was the judge supposed to heal your hand?

MR. SHU FU *turns quickly around.* SHUI TA *bows to* SHU FU, *and vice versa.*

WONG (*taking the sling off, and putting it back*): I see how it is.

POLICEMAN: Well, I'll be on my way. (*To* WONG:) And you be careful. If Mr. Shu Fu wasn't a man who tempers justice with mercy, as the saying is, you'd be in jail for libel. Be off with you!

Exit WONG, *followed by* POLICEMAN.

SHUI TA: Profound apologies, Mr. Shu Fu.

SHU FU: Not at all, Mr. Shui Ta. (*Pointing to the shawl.*) The episode is over?

SHUI TA: It may take her time to recover. There are some fresh wounds.

SHU FU: We shall be discreet. Delicate. A short vacation could be arranged. . . .

SHUI TA: First, of course, you and she would have to talk things over.

SHU FU: At a small supper in a small, but high-class restaurant.

SHUI TA: I'll go and find her. (*Exit into back room.*)

MRS. SHIN (*sticking her head in again*): Time for congratulations, Mr. Shu Fu?

SHU FU: Ah, Mrs. Shin! Please inform Miss Shen Te's guests they may take shelter in the cabins behind the cattle run!

MRS. SHIN *nods, grinning.*

SHU FU (*to the audience*): Well? What do you think of me, ladies and gentlemen? What could a man do more? Could he be less selfish? More farsighted? A small supper in a small but . . . Does that bring rather vulgar and clumsy thoughts into your mind? Ts, ts, ts. Nothing of the sort will occur. She won't even be touched. Not even accidentally while passing the salt. An exchange of ideas only. Over the flowers on the table — white chrysanthemums, by the way (*he writes down a note of this*) — yes, over the white chrysanthemums, two young souls will . . . shall I say "find each other"? We shall NOT exploit the misfortune of others. Understanding? Yes. An offer of assistance? Certainly. But quietly. Almost inaudibly. Perhaps with a single glance. A glance that could also — also mean more.

MRS. SHIN (*coming forward*): Everything under control, Mr. Shu Fu?

SHU FU: Oh, Mrs. Shin, what do you know about this worthless rascal Yang Sun?

MRS. SHIN: Why, he's the most worthless rascal . . .

SHU FU: Is he really? You're sure? (*As she opens her mouth.*) From now on, he doesn't exist! Can't be found anywhere!

Enter YANG SUN.

YANG SUN: What's been going on here?

MRS. SHIN: Shall I call Mr. Shui Ta, Mr. Shu Fu? He wouldn't want strangers in here!

SHU FU: Mr. Shui Ta is in conference with Miss Shen Te. Not to be disturbed.

YANG SUN: Shen Te here? I didn't see her come in. What kind of conference?

SHU FU (*not letting him enter the back room*): Patience, dear sir! And if by chance I have an inkling who you are, pray take note that Miss Shen Te and I are about to announce our engagement.

YANG SUN: What?

MRS. SHIN: You didn't expect that, did you?

YANG SUN *is trying to push past the barber into the back room when* SHEN TE *comes out.*

SHU FU: My dear Shen Te, ten thousand apologies! Perhaps you . . .

YANG SUN: What is it, Shen Te? Have you gone crazy?

SHEN TE (*breathless*): My cousin and Mr. Shu Fu have come to an understanding. They wish me to hear Mr. Shu Fu's plans for helping the poor.

YANG SUN: Your cousin wants to part us.

SHEN TE: Yes.

YANG SUN: And you've agreed to it?

SHEN TE: Yes.

YANG SUN: They told you I was bad. (SHEN TE *is silent.*) And suppose I am. Does that make me need you less? I'm low, Shen Te, I have no money, I don't do the right thing but at least I put up a fight! (*He is near her now, and speaks in an undertone.*) Have you no eyes? Look at him. Have you forgotten already?

SHEN TE: No.

YANG SUN: How it was raining?

SHEN TE: No.

YANG SUN: How you cut me down from the willow tree? Bought me water? Promised me money to fly with?

SHEN TE (*shakily*): Yang Sun, what do you want?

YANG SUN: I want you to come with me.

SHEN TE (*in a small voice*): Forgive me, Mr. Shu Fu, I want to go with Mr. Yang Sun.

YANG SUN: We're lovers you know. Give me the key to the shop. (SHEN TE *takes the key from around her neck.* YANG SUN *puts it on the counter. To* MRS. SHIN:) Leave it under the mat when you're through. Let's go, Shen Te.

SHU FU: But this is rape! Mr. Shui Ta!!

YANG SUN (*to* SHEN TE): Tell him not to shout.

SHEN TE: Please don't shout for my cousin, Mr. Shu Fu. He doesn't agree with me, I know, but he's wrong. (*To the audience:*)

I want to go with the man I love
I don't want to count the cost
I don't want to consider if it's wise
I don't want to know if he loves me
I want to go with the man I love.

YANG SUN: That's the spirit.

And the couple leave.

5a

In front of the inner curtain. SHEN TE *in her wedding clothes, on the way to her wedding.*

SHEN TE: Something terrible has happened. As I left the shop with Yang Sun, I found the old carpet dealer's wife waiting on the street, trembling all over. She told me her husband had taken to his bed sick with all the worry and excitement over the two hundred silver dollars they lent me. She said it would be best if I gave it back now. Of course, I had to say I would. She said she couldn't quite trust my cousin Shui Ta or even my fiancé Yang Sun. There were ears in her eyes. With my emotions in an uproar, I threw myself into Yang Sun's arms, I couldn't resist him. The things he'd said to Shui Ta had taught Shen Te nothing. Sinking into his arms, I said to myself:

To let no one perish, not even oneself
To fill everyone with happiness, even oneself
Is so good

How could I have forgotten those two old people? Yang Sun swept me away like a small hurricane. But he's not a bad man, and he loves me. He'd rather work in the cement factory than owe his flying to a crime. Though, of course, flying *is* a great passion with Sun. Now, on the way to my wedding, I waver between fear and joy.

6

The "private dining room" on the upper floor of a cheap restaurant in a poor section of town. With SHEN TE: *the* GRANDFATHER, *the* SISTER-

IN-LAW, *the* NIECE, MRS. SHIN, *the* UNEMPLOYED MAN. *In a corner, alone, a* PRIEST. *A* WAITER *pouring wine. Downstage,* YANG SUN *talking to his* MOTHER. *He wears a dinner jacket.*

YANG SUN: Bad news, Mamma. She came right out and told me she can't sell the shop for me. Some idiot is bringing a claim because he lent her the two hundred she gave you.

MRS. YANG: What did you say? Of course, you can't marry her now.

YANG SUN: It's no use saying anything to *her.* I've sent for her cousin, Mr. Shui Ta. He said there was nothing in writing.

MRS. YANG: Good idea. I'll go and look for him. Keep an eye on things.

Exit MRS. YANG. SHEN TE *has been pouring wine.*

SHEN TE (*to the audience, pitcher in hand*): I wasn't mistaken in him. He's bearing up well. Though it must have been an awful blow — giving up flying. I do love him so. (*Calling across the room to him:*) Sun, you haven't drunk a toast with the bride!

YANG SUN: What do we drink to?

SHEN TE: Why, to the future!

YANG SUN: When the bridegroom's dinner jacket won't be a hired one!

SHEN TE: But when the bride's dress will still get rained on sometimes!

YANG SUN: To everything we ever wished for!

SHEN TE: May all our dreams come true!

They drink.

YANG SUN (*with loud conviviality*): And now, friends, before the wedding gets under way, I have to ask the bride a few questions. I've no idea what kind of wife she'll make, and it worries me. (*Wheeling on* SHEN TE.) For example. Can you make five cups of tea with three tea leaves?

SHEN TE: No.

YANG SUN: So I won't be getting very much tea. Can you sleep on a straw mattress the size of that book? (*He points to the large volume the* PRIEST *is reading.*)

SHEN TE: The two of us?

YANG SUN: The one of you.

SHEN TE: In that case, no.

YANG SUN: What a wife! I'm shocked!

While the audience is laughing, his MOTHER *returns. With a shrug of her shoulders, she tells* YANG SUN *the expected guest hasn't arrived. The* PRIEST *shuts the book with a bang, and makes for the door.*

MRS. YANG: Where are *you* off to? It's only a matter of minutes.

PRIEST (*watch in hand*): Time goes on, Mrs. Yang, and I've another wedding to attend to. Also a funeral.

MRS. YANG (*irately*): D'you think we planned it this way? I was hoping to manage with one pitcher of wine, and we've run through two already. (*Points to empty pitcher. Loudly.*) My dear Shen Te, I don't know where your cousin can be keeping himself!

SHEN TE: My cousin?!

MRS. YANG: Certainly. I'm old-fashioned enough to think such a close relative should attend the wedding.

SHEN TE: Oh, Sun, is it the three hundred silver dollars?

YANG SUN (*not looking her in the eye*): Are you deaf? Mother says she's old-fashioned. And I say I'm considerate. We'll wait another fifteen minutes.

HUSBAND: Another fifteen minutes.

MRS. YANG (*addressing the company*): Now you all know, don't you, that my son is getting a job as a mail pilot?

SISTER-IN-LAW: In Peking, too, isn't it?

MRS. YANG: In Peking, too! The two of us are moving to Peking!

SHEN TE: Sun, tell your mother Peking is out of the question now.

YANG SUN: Your cousin'll tell her. If he agrees. I don't agree.

SHEN TE (*amazed, and dismayed*): Sun!

YANG SUN: I hate this godforsaken Setzuan. What people! Know what they look like when I half close my eyes? Horses! Whinnying, fretting, stamping, screwing their necks up! (*Loudly.*) And what is it the thunder says? They are su-per-flu-ous! (*He hammers out the syllables.*) They've run their last race! They can go trample themselves to death! (*Pause.*) I've got to get out of here.

SHEN TE: But I've promised the money to the old couple.

YANG SUN: And since you always do the wrong thing, it's lucky your cousin's coming. Have another drink.

SHEN TE (*quietly*): My cousin can't be coming.

YANG SUN: How d'you mean?

SHEN TE: My cousin can't be where I am.

YANG SUN: Quite a conundrum!

SHEN TE (*desperately*): Sun, I'm the one that loves you. Not my cousin. He was thinking of the job in Peking when he promised you the old couple's money —

YANG SUN: Right. And that's why he's bringing the three hundred silver dollars. Here — to my wedding.

SHEN TE: He is not bringing the three hundred silver dollars.

YANG SUN: Huh? What makes you think that?

SHEN TE (*looking into his eyes*): He says you only bought one ticket to Peking.

Short pause.

YANG SUN: That was yesterday. (*He pulls two tickets part way out of his inside pocket, making her look under his coat.*) Two tickets. I don't want Mother to know. She'll get left behind. I sold her furniture to buy these tickets, so you see . . .

SHEN TE: But what's to become of the old couple?

YANG SUN: What's to become of me? Have another drink. Or do you believe in moderation? If I drink, I fly again. And if you drink, you may learn to understand me.

SHEN TE: You want to fly. But I can't help you.

YANG SUN: "Here's a plane, my darling — but it's only got one wing!"

The WAITER *enters.*

WAITER: Mrs. Yang!

MRS. YANG: Yes?

WAITER: Another pitcher of wine, ma'am?

MRS. YANG: We have enough, thanks. Drinking makes me sweat.

WAITER: Would you mind paying, ma'am?

MRS. YANG (*to everyone*): Just be patient a few moments longer, everyone, Mr. Shui Ta is on his way over! (*To the* WAITER:) Don't be a spoilsport.

WAITER: I can't let you leave till you've paid your bill, ma'am.

MRS. YANG: But they know me here!

WAITER: That's just it.

PRIEST (*ponderously getting up*): I humbly take my leave. (*And he does.*)

MRS. YANG (*to the others, desperately*): Stay where you are, everybody! The priest says he'll be back in two minutes!

YANG SUN: It's no good, Mamma. Ladies and gentlemen, Mr. Shui Ta still hasn't arrived and the priest has gone home. We won't detain you any longer.

They are leaving now.

GRANDFATHER (*in the doorway, having forgotten to put his glass down*): To the bride! (*He drinks, puts down the glass, and follows the others.*)

Pause.

SHEN TE: Shall I go too?

YANG SUN: You? Aren't you the bride? Isn't this your wedding? (*He drags her across the room, tearing her wedding dress.*) If we can wait, you can wait. Mother calls me her falcon. She wants to see me in the clouds. But I think it may be St. Nevercome's Day before she'll go to the door and see my plane thunder by. (*Pause. He pretends the guests are still present.*) Why such a lull in the conversation, ladies and gentlemen? Don't you like it here? The ceremony is only slightly postponed — because an important guest is expected at any moment. Also because the bride doesn't know what love is. While we're waiting, the bridegroom will sing a little song. (*He does so.*)

THE SONG OF ST. NEVERCOME'S DAY

On a certain day, as is generally known,
  One and all will be shouting: Hooray, hooray!
For the beggar maid's son has a solid-gold throne
  And the day is St. Nevercome's Day
On St. Nevercome's, Nevercome's, Nevercome's Day
  He'll sit on his solid-gold throne

Oh, hooray, hooray! That day goodness will pay!
  That day badness will cost you your head!
And merit and money will smile and be funny
  While exchanging salt and bread
On St. Nevercome's, Nevercome's, Nevercome's Day
  While exchanging salt and bread

And the grass, oh, the grass will look down at the sky
  And the pebbles will roll up the stream
And all men will be good without batting an eye
  They will make of our earth a dream
On St. Nevercome's, Nevercome's, Nevercome's Day
  They will make of our earth a dream

And as for me, that's the day I shall be
  A flyer and one of the best
Unemployed man, you will have work to do
  Washerwoman, you'll get your rest
On St. Nevercome's, Nevercome's, Nevercome's Day
  Washerwoman, you'll get your rest

MRS. YANG: It looks like he's not coming.

The three of them sit looking at the door.

6a

Wong's den. The sewer pipe is again transparent and again the GODS appear to WONG in a dream.

WONG: I'm so glad you've come, illustrious ones. It's Shen Te. She's in great trouble from following the rule about loving thy neighbor. Perhaps she's *too* good for this world!

FIRST GOD: Nonsense! You are eaten up by lice and doubts!

WONG: Forgive me, illustrious one, I only meant you might deign to intervene.

FIRST GOD: Out of the question! My colleague here intervened in some squabble or other only yesterday. (*He points to the* THIRD GOD *who has a black eye.*) The results are before us!

WONG: She had to call on her cousin again. But not even he could help. I'm afraid the shop is done for.

THIRD GOD (*a little concerned*): Perhaps we should help after all?

FIRST GOD: The gods help those that help themselves.

WONG: What if we *can't* help ourselves, illustrious ones?

Slight pause.

SECOND GOD: Try, anyway! Suffering ennobles!

FIRST GOD: Our faith in Shen Te is unshaken!

THIRD GOD: We certainly haven't found any *other* good people. You can see where we spend our nights from the straw on our clothes.

WONG: You might help her find her way by —

FIRST GOD: The good man finds his own way here below!

SECOND GOD: The good woman too.

FIRST GOD: The heavier the burden, the greater her strength!

THIRD GOD: We're only onlookers, you know.

FIRST GOD: And everything will be all right in the end, O ye of little faith!

They are gradually disappearing through these last lines.

7

The yard behind Shen Te's shop. A few articles of furniture on a cart. SHEN TE *and* MRS. SHIN *are taking the washing off the line.*

MRS. SHIN: If you ask me, you should fight tooth and nail to keep the shop.

SHEN TE: How can I? I have to sell the tobacco to pay back the two hundred silver dollars today.

MRS. SHIN: No husband, no tobacco, no house and home! What are you going to live on?

SHEN TE: I can work. I can sort tobacco.

MRS. SHIN: Hey, look, Mr. Shui Ta's trousers! He must have left here stark naked!

SHEN TE: Oh, he may have another pair, Mrs. Shin.

MRS. SHIN: But if he's gone for good as you say, why has he left his pants behind?

SHEN TE: Maybe he's thrown them away.

MRS. SHIN: Can I take them?

SHEN TE: Oh, no.

Enter MR. SHU FU, *running.*

SHU FU: Not a word! Total silence! I know all. You have sacrificed your own love and happiness so as not to hurt a dear old couple who had put their trust in you! Not in vain does this district — for all its malevolent tongues — call you the Angel of the Slums! That young man couldn't rise to your level, so you left him. And now, when I see you closing up the little shop, that veritable haven of rest for the multitude, well, I cannot, I cannot let it pass. Morning after morning I have stood watching in the doorway not unmoved — while you graciously handed out rice to the wretched. Is that never to happen again? Is the good woman of Setzuan to disappear? If only you would allow *me* to assist you! Now don't say anything! No assurances, no exclamations of gratitude! (*He has taken out his checkbook.*) Here! A blank check. (*He places it on the cart.*) Just my signature. Fill it out as you wish. Any sum in the world. I herewith retire from the scene, quietly, unobtrusively, making no claims, on tiptoe, full of veneration, absolutely selflessly . . . (*He has gone.*)

MRS. SHIN: Well! You're saved. There's always some idiot of a man. . . . Now hurry! Put down a thousand silver dollars and let me fly to the bank before he comes to his senses.

SHEN TE: I can pay you for the washing without any check.

MRS. SHIN: What? You're not going to cash it just because you might have to marry him? Are you crazy? Men like him *want* to be led by the nose! Are you still thinking of that flyer? All Yellow Street knows how he treated you!

SHEN TE: When I heard his cunning laugh, I was afraid
But when I saw the holes in his shoes, I loved him dearly.

MRS. SHIN: Defending that good-for-nothing after all that's happened!

SHEN TE (*staggering as she holds some of the washing*): Oh!

MRS. SHIN (*taking the washing from her, dryly*): So you feel dizzy when you stretch and bend? There couldn't be a little visitor on the way? If that's it, you can forget Mr. Shu Fu's blank check: it wasn't meant for a christening present!

She goes to the back with a basket. SHEN TE'*s eyes follow* MRS. SHIN *for a moment. Then she looks down at her own body, feels her stomach, and a great joy comes into her eyes.*

SHEN TE: O joy! A new human being is on the way. The world awaits him. In the cities the people say: he's got to be reckoned with, this new human being! (*She imagines a little boy to be present, and introduces him to the audience.*) This is my son, the well-known flyer!

Say: Welcome
To the conqueror of unknown mountains and unreachable regions
Who brings us our mail across the impassable deserts!

She leads him up and down by the hand.

Take a look at the world, my son. That's a tree. Tree, yes. Say: "Hello, tree!" And bow. Like this. (*She bows.*) Now you know each other. And, look, here comes the water seller. He's a friend, give him your hand. A cup of fresh water for my little son, please. Yes, it *is* a warm day. (*Handing the cup.*) Oh dear, a policeman, we'll have to make a circle round *him.* Perhaps we can pick a few cherries over there in the rich Mr. Pung's garden. But we mustn't be seen. You want cherries? Just like children with fathers. No, no, you can't go straight at them like that. Don't pull. We must learn to be reasonable. Well, have it your own way. (*She has let him make for the cherries.*) Can you reach? Where to put them? Your mouth is the best place. (*She tries one herself.*) Mmm, they're good. But the policeman, we must run! (*They run.*) Yes, back to the street. Calm now, so no one will notice us. (*Walking the street with her child, she sings.*)

🌼 BERTOLT BRECHT

Once a plum — 'twas in Japan —
Made a conquest of a man
But the man's turn soon did come
For he gobbled up the plum

Enter WONG, *with a* CHILD *by the hand. He coughs.*

SHEN TE: Wong!

WONG: It's about the carpenter, Shen Te. He's lost his shop, and he's been drinking. His children are on the streets. This is one. Can you help?

SHEN TE (*to the* CHILD): Come here, little man. (*Takes him down to the footlights. To the audience:*)

You there! A man is asking you for shelter!
A man of tomorrow says: what about today?
His friend the conqueror, whom you know,
Is his advocate!

(*To* WONG:) He can live in Mr. Shu Fu's cabins. I may have to go there myself. I'm going to have a baby. That's a secret — don't tell Yang Sun — we'd only be in his way. Can you find the carpenter for me?

WONG: I knew you'd think of something. (*To the* CHILD:) Good-bye, son, I'm going for your father.

SHEN TE: What about your hand, Wong? I wanted to help, but my cousin . . .

WONG: Oh, I can get along with one hand, don't worry. (*He shows how he can handle his pole with his left hand alone.*)

SHEN TE: But your right hand! Look, take this cart, sell everything that's on it, and go to the doctor with the money . . .

WONG: She's still good. But first I'll bring the carpenter. I'll pick up the cart when I get back. (*Exit* WONG.)

SHEN TE (*to the* CHILD): Sit down over here, son, till your father comes.

The CHILD *sits cross-legged on the ground. Enter the* HUSBAND *and* WIFE, *each dragging a large, full sack.*

WIFE (*furtively*): You're alone, Shen Ten, dear?

SHEN TE *nods. The* WIFE *beckons to the* NEPHEW *off-stage. He comes on with another sack.*

WIFE: Your cousin's away? (SHEN TE *nods.*) He's not coming back?

SHEN TE: No. I'm giving up the shop.

WIFE: That's why we're here. We want to know if we can leave these things in your new home. Will you do us this favor?

SHEN TE: Why, yes, I'd be glad to.

HUSBAND (*cryptically*): And if anyone asks about them, say they're yours.

SHEN TE: Would anyone ask?

WIFE (*with a glance back at her husband*): Oh, someone might. The police, for instance. They don't seem to like us. Where can we put it?

SHEN TE: Well, I'd rather not get in any more trouble . . .

WIFE: Listen to her! The good woman of Setzuan!

SHEN TE *is silent.*

HUSBAND: There's enough tobacco in those sacks to give us a new start in life. We could have our own tobacco factory!

SHEN TE (*slowly*): You'll have to put them in the back room.

The sacks are taken off-stage, while the CHILD *is alone. Shyly glancing about him, he goes to the garbage can, starts playing with the contents, and eating some of the scraps. The others return.*

WIFE: We're counting on you, Shen Te!

SHEN TE: Yes. (*She sees the* CHILD *and is shocked.*)

HUSBAND: We'll see you in Mr. Shu Fu's cabins.

NEPHEW: The day after tomorrow.

SHEN TE: Yes. Now, go. Go! I'm not feeling well.

Exeunt all three, virtually pushed off.

He is eating the refuse in the garbage can!
Only look at his little gray mouth!

Pause. Music.

As this is the world *my* son will enter
I will study to defend him.
To be good to you, my son,
I shall be a tigress to all others
If I have to.
And I shall have to.

She starts to go.

One more time, then. I hope really the last.

Exit SHEN TE, *taking Shui Ta's trousers.* MRS. SHIN *enters and watches her with marked interest. Enter the* SISTER-IN-LAW *and the* GRAND-FATHER.

SISTER-IN-LAW: So it's true, the shop has closed down. And the furniture's in the back yard. It's the end of the road!

MRS. SHIN (*pompously*): The fruit of high living, selfishness, and sensuality! Down the primrose path to Mr. Shu Fu's cabins — with you!

SISTER-IN-LAW: Cabins? Rat holes! He gave them to us because his soap supplies only went moldy there!

Enter the UNEMPLOYED MAN.

UNEMPLOYED MAN: Shen Te is moving?

SISTER-IN-LAW: Yes. She was sneaking away.

MRS. SHIN: She's ashamed of herself, and no wonder!

UNEMPLOYED MAN: Tell her to call Mr. Shui Ta or she's done for this time!

SISTER-IN-LAW: Tell her to call Mr. Shui Ta or *we're* done for this time.

Enter WONG *and* CARPENTER, *the latter with a* CHILD *on each hand.*

CARPENTER: So we'll have a roof over our heads for a change!

MRS. SHIN: Roof? Whose roof?

CARPENTER: Mr. Shu Fu's cabins. And we have little Feng to thank for it. (FENG, *we find, is the name of the* CHILD *already there; his* FATHER *now takes him. To the other two:*) Bow to your little brother, you two!

The CARPENTER *and the two new arrivals bow to* FENG. *Enter* SHUI TA.

UNEMPLOYED MAN: Sst! Mr. Shui Ta!

Pause.

SHUI TA: And what is this crowd here for, may I ask?

WONG: How do you do, Mr. Shui Ta. This is the carpenter, Miss Shen Te promised him space in Mr. Shu Fu's cabins.

SHUI TA: That will not be possible.

CARPENTER: We can't go there after all?

SHUI TA: All the space is needed for other purposes.

SISTER-IN-LAW: You mean we have to get out? But we've got nowhere to go.

SHUI TA: Miss Shen Te finds it possible to provide employment. If the proposition interests you, you may stay in the cabins.

SISTER-IN-LAW (*with distaste*): You mean *work?* Work for Miss Shen Te?

SHUI TA: Making tobacco, yes. There are three bales here already. Would you like to get them?

SISTER-IN-LAW (*trying to bluster*): We have our own tobacco! We were in the tobacco business before you were born!

SHUI TA (*to the* CARPENTER *and the* UNEMPLOYED MAN): You *don't* have your own tobacco. What about you?

The CARPENTER *and the* UNEMPLOYED MAN *get the point, and go for the sacks. Enter* MRS. MI TZU.

MRS. MI TZU: Mr. Shui Ta? I've brought you your three hundred silver dollars.

SHUI TA: I'll sign your lease instead. I've decided not to sell.

MRS. MI TZU: What? You don't need the money for that flyer?

SHUI TA: No.

MRS. MI TZU: And you can pay six months' rent?

SHUI TA (*takes the barber's blank check from the cart and fills it out*): Here is a check for ten thousand silver dollars. On Mr. Shu Fu's account. Look! (*He shows her the signature on the check.*) Your six months' rent will be in your hands by seven this evening. And now, if you'll excuse me.

MRS. MI TZU: So it's Mr. Shu Fu now. The flyer has been given his walking papers. These modern girls! In my day they'd have said she was flighty. That poor, deserted Mr. Yang Sun!

Exit MRS. MI TZU. *The* CARPENTER *and the* UNEMPLOYED MAN *drag the three sacks back on the stage.*

CARPENTER (*to* SHUI TA): I don't know why I'm doing this for you.

SHUI TA: Perhaps your children want to eat, Mr. Carpenter.

SISTER-IN-LAW (*catching sight of the sacks*): Was my brother-in-law here?

MRS. SHIN: Yes, he was.

SISTER-IN-LAW: I thought as much. I know those sacks! That's our tobacco!

SHUI TA: Really? I thought it came from my back room! Shall we consult the police on the point?

SISTER-IN-LAW (*defeated*): No.

SHUI TA: Perhaps you will show me the way to Mr. Shu Fu's cabins?

Taking FENG *by the hand,* SHUI TA *goes off, followed by the* CARPENTER *and his two older children, the* SISTER-IN-LAW, *the* GRANDFATHER, *and the* UNEMPLOYED MAN. *Each of the last three drags a sack. Enter* OLD MAN *and* OLD WOMAN.

MRS. SHIN: A pair of pants — missing from the clothesline one minute — and next minute on the honorable backside of Mr. Shui Ta.

OLD WOMAN: We thought Miss Shen Te was here.

MRS. SHIN (*preoccupied*): Well, she's not.

OLD MAN: There was something she was going to give us.

WONG: She was going to help me too. (*Looking at his hand.*) It'll be too late soon. But she'll be back. This cousin has never stayed long.

MRS. SHIN (*approaching a conclusion*): No, he hasn't, has he?

7a

The Sewer Pipe: WONG *asleep. In his dream, he tells the* GODS *his fears. The* GODS *seem tired from all their travels. They stop for a moment and look over their shoulders at the water seller.*

WONG: Illustrious ones. I've been having a bad dream. Our beloved Shen Te was in great distress in the rushes down by the river — the spot where the bodies of suicides are washed up. She kept staggering and holding her head down as if she was carrying something and it was dragging her down into the mud. When I called out to her, she said she had to take your Book of Rules to the other side, and not get it wet, or the ink would all come off. You had talked to her about the virtues, you know, the time she gave you shelter in Setzuan.

THIRD GOD: Well, but what do you suggest, my dear Wong?

WONG: Maybe a little relaxation of the rules, Benevolent One, in view of the bad times.

THIRD GOD: As for instance?

WONG: Well, um, good will, for instance, might do instead of love?

THIRD GOD: I'm afraid that would create new problems.

WONG: Or, instead of justice, good sportsmanship?

THIRD GOD: That would only mean more work.

WONG: Instead of honor, outward propriety?

THIRD GOD: Still more work! No, no! The rules will have to stand, my dear Wong!

Wearily shaking their heads, all three journey on.

8

Shui Ta's tobacco factory in Shu Fu's cabins. Huddled together behind bars, several families, mostly women and children. Among these people the SISTER-IN-LAW, *the* GRANDFATHER, *the* CARPENTER, *and his* THREE CHILDREN. *Enter* MRS. YANG *followed by* YANG SUN.

MRS. YANG (*to the audience*): There's something I just *have* to tell you: strength and wisdom are wonderful things. The strong and wise Mr. Shui Ta has transformed my son from a dissipated good-for-nothing into a model citizen. As you may have heard, Mr. Shui Ta opened a small tobacco factory near the cattle runs. It flourished. Three months ago — I shall never forget it — I asked for an appointment, and Mr. Shui Ta agreed to see us — me and my son. I can see him now as he came through the door to meet us. . . .

Enter SHUI TA *from a door.*

SHUI TA: What can I do for you, Mrs. Yang?

MRS. YANG: This morning the police came to the house. We find you've brought an action for breach of promise of marriage. In the name of Shen Te. You also claim that Sun came by two hundred silver dollars by improper means.

SHUI TA: That is correct.

MRS. YANG: Mr. Shui Ta, the money's all gone. When the Peking job didn't materialize, he ran through it all in three days. I know he's a good-for-nothing. He sold my furniture. He was moving to Peking without me. Miss Shen Te thought highly of him at one time.

SHUI TA: What do *you* say, Mr. Yang Sun?

YANG SUN: The money's gone.

SHUI TA (*to* MRS. YANG): Mrs. Yang, in consideration of my cousin's incomprehensible weakness for your son, I am prepared to give him another chance. He can have a job — here. The two hundred silver dollars will be taken out of his wages.

YANG SUN: So it's the factory or jail?

SHUI TA: Take your choice.

YANG SUN: May I speak with Shen Te?

SHUI TA: You may not.

Pause.

YANG SUN (*sullenly*): Show me where to go.

MRS. YANG: Mr. Shui Ta, you are kindness itself: the gods will reward you! (*To* YANG SUN:) And honest work will make a man of you, my boy. (YANG SUN *follows* SHUI TA *into the factory.* MRS. YANG *comes down again to the footlights.*) Actually, honest work didn't agree with him — at first. And he got no opportunity to distinguish himself till — in the third week — when the wages were being paid . . .

SHUI TA *has a bag of money. Standing next to his foreman — the former* UNEMPLOYED MAN — *he counts out the wages. It is* YANG SUN's *turn.*

UNEMPLOYED MAN (*reading*): Carpenter, six silver dollars. Yang Sun, six silver dollars.

YANG SUN (*quietly*): Excuse me, sir. I don't think it can be more than five. May I see? (*He takes the foreman's list.*) It says six working days. But that's a mistake, sir. I took a day off for court business. And I won't take what I haven't earned, however miserable the pay is!

UNEMPLOYED MAN: Yang Sun. Five silver dollars. (*To* SHUI TA:) A rare case, Mr. Shui Ta!

SHUI TA: How is it the book says six when it should say five?

UNEMPLOYED MAN: I must've made a mistake, Mr. Shui Ta. (*With a look at* YANG SUN.) It won't happen again.

SHUI TA (*taking* YANG SUN *aside*): You don't hold back, do you? You give your all to the firm. You're even honest. Do the foreman's mistakes always favor the workers?

YANG SUN: He does have . . . friends.

SHUI TA: Thank you. May I offer you any little recompense?

YANG SUN: Give me a trial period of one week, and I'll prove my intelligence is worth more to you than my strength.

MRS. YANG (*still down at the footlights*): Fighting words, fighting words! That evening, I said to Sun: "If you're a flyer, then fly, my falcon! Rise in the world!" And he got to be foreman. Yes, in Mr. Shui Ta's tobacco factory, he worked real miracles.

We see YANG SUN *with his legs apart standing behind the workers who are handing along a basket of raw tobacco above their heads.*

YANG SUN: Faster! Faster! You, there, d'you think you can just stand around, now you're not foreman any more? It'll be your job to lead us in song. Sing!

UNEMPLOYED MAN *starts singing. The others join in the refrain.*

SONG OF THE EIGHTH ELEPHANT

Chang had seven elephants — all much the same —
    But then there was Little Brother
The seven, they were wild, Little Brother, he was tame
    And to guard them Chang chose Little Brother
      Run faster!
      Mr. Chang has a forest park
      Which must be cleared before tonight
      And already it's growing dark!

When the seven elephants cleared that forest park
    Mr. Chang rode high on Little Brother
While the seven toiled and moiled till dark
    On his big behind sat Little Brother
      Dig faster!
      Mr. Chang has a forest park
      Which must be cleared before tonight
      And already it's growing dark!

And the seven elephants worked many an hour
    Till none of them could work another
Old Chang, he looked sour, on the seven he did glower
    But gave a pound of rice to Little Brother
      What was that?
      Mr. Chang has a forest park
      Which must be cleared before tonight
      And already it's growing dark!

And the seven elephants hadn't any tusks
    The one that had the tusks was Little Brother
Seven are no match for one, if the one has a gun!
    How old Chang did laugh at Little Brother!
      Keep on digging!
      Mr. Chang has a forest park
      Which must be cleared before tonight
      And already it's growing dark!

Smoking a cigar, SHUI TA *strolls by.* YANG SUN, *laughing, has joined in the refrain of the third stanza and speeded up the tempo of the last stanza by clapping his hands.*

MRS. YANG: And that's why I say: strength and wisdom are wonderful things. It took the strong and wise Mr. Shui Ta to bring out the best in Yang Sun. A real superior man is like a bell. If you ring it, it rings, and if you don't, it don't, as the saying is.

9

Shen Te's shop, now an office with club chairs and fine carpets. It is raining. SHUI TA, *now fat, is just dismissing the* OLD MAN *and* OLD WOMAN. MRS. SHIN, *in obviously new clothes, looks on, smirking.*

SHUI TA: No! I can NOT tell you when we expect her back.

OLD WOMAN: The two hundred silver dollars came today. In an envelope. There was no letter, but it must be from Shen Te. We want to write and thank her. May we have her address?

SHUI TA: I'm afraid I haven't got it.

OLD MAN (*pulling* OLD WOMAN'*s sleeve*): Let's be going.

OLD WOMAN: She's got to come back some time!

They move off, uncertainly, worried. SHUI TA *bows.*

MRS. SHIN: They lost the carpet shop because they couldn't pay their taxes. The money arrived too late.

SHUI TA: They could have come to me.

MRS. SHIN: People don't like coming to you.

SHUI TA (*sits suddenly, one hand to his head*): I'm dizzy.

MRS. SHIN: After all, you *are* in your seventh month. But old Mrs. Shin will be there in your hour of trial! (*She cackles feebly.*)

SHUI TA (*in a stifled voice*): Can I count on that?

MRS. SHIN: We all have our price, and mine won't be too high for the great Mr. Shui Ta! (*She opens* SHUI TA'*s collar.*)

SHUI TA: It's for the child's sake. All of this.

MRS. SHIN: "All for the child," of course.

SHUI TA: I'm so fat. People must notice.

MRS. SHIN: Oh no, they think it's 'cause you're rich.

SHUI TA (*more feelingly*): What will happen to the child?

MRS. SHIN: You ask that nine times a day. Why, it'll have the best that money can buy!

SHUI TA: He must never see Shui Ta.

MRS. SHIN: Oh, no. Always Shen Te.

SHUI TA: What about the neighbors? There are rumors, aren't there?

MRS. SHIN: As long as Mr. Shu Fu doesn't find out, there's nothing to worry about. Drink this.

Enter YANG SUN *in a smart business suit, and carrying a businessman's briefcase.* SHUI TA *is more or less in* MRS. SHIN'*s arms.*

YANG SUN (*surprised*): I guess I'm in the way.

SHUI TA (*ignoring this, rises with an effort*): Till tomorrow, Mrs. Shin.

MRS. SHIN *leaves with a smile, putting her new gloves on.*

YANG SUN: Gloves now! She couldn't be fleecing you? And since when did *you* have a private life? (*Taking a paper from the briefcase.*) You haven't been at your desk lately, and things are getting out of hand. The police want to close us down. They say that at the most they can only permit twice the lawful number of workers.

SHUI TA (*evasively*): The cabins are quite good enough.

YANG SUN: For the workers maybe, not for the tobacco. They're too damp. We must take over some of Mrs. Mi Tzu's buildings.

SHUI TA: Her price is double what I can pay.

YANG SUN: Not unconditionally. If she has me to stroke her knees she'll come down.

SHUI TA: I'll never agree to that.

YANG SUN: What's wrong? Is it the rain? You get so irritable whenever it rains.

SHUI TA: Never! I will never . . .

YANG SUN: Mrs. Mi Tzu'll be here in five minutes. *You* fix it. And Shu Fu will be with her. . . . What's all that noise?

During the above dialogue, WONG *is heard off-stage, calling:* "The good Shen Te, where is she? Which of you has seen Shen Te, good people? Where is Shen Te?" *A knock. Enter* WONG.

WONG: Mr. Shui Ta, I've come to ask when Miss Shen Te will be back, it's six months now. . . . There are rumors. People say something's happened to her.

SHUI TA: I'm busy. Come back next week.

WONG (*excited*): In the morning there was always rice on her doorstep — for the needy. It's been there again lately!

SHUI TA: And what do people conclude from this?

WONG: That Shen Te is still in Setzuan! She's been . . . (*He breaks off.*)

SHUI TA: She's been what? Mr. Wong, if you're Shen Te's friend, talk a little less about her, that's my advice to you.

WONG: I don't want your advice! Before she disappeared, Miss Shen Te told me something very important — she's pregnant!

YANG SUN: What? What was that?

SHUI TA (*quickly*): The man is lying.

WONG: A good woman isn't so easily forgotten, Mr. Shui Ta.

He leaves. SHUI TA *goes quickly into the back room.*

YANG SUN (*to the audience*): Shen Te pregnant? So that's why. Her cousin sent her away, so I wouldn't get wind of it. I have a son, a Yang appears on the scene, and what happens? Mother and child vanish into thin air! That scoundrel, that unspeakable . . . (*The sound of sobbing is heard from the back room.*) What was that? Someone sobbing? Who was it? Mr. Shui Ta the Tobacco King doesn't weep his heart out. And where does the rice come from that's on the doorstep in the morning? (SHUI TA *returns. He goes to the door and looks out into the rain.*) Where is she?

SHUI TA: Sh! It's nine o'clock. But the rain's so heavy, you can't hear a thing.

YANG SUN: What do you want to hear?

SHUI TA: The mail plane.

YANG SUN: What?!

SHUI TA: I've been told *you* wanted to fly at one time. Is that all forgotten?

YANG SUN: Flying mail is night work. I prefer the daytime. And the firm is very dear to me — after all it belongs to my ex-fiancée, even if she's not around. And she's not, is she?

SHUI TA: What do you mean by that?

YANG SUN: Oh, well, let's say I haven't altogether — lost interest.

SHUI TA: My cousin might like to know that.

YANG SUN: I might not be indifferent — if I found she was being kept under lock and key.

SHUI TA: By whom?

YANG SUN: By you.

SHUI TA: What could you do about it?

YANG SUN: I could submit for discussion — my position in the firm.

SHUI TA: You are now my manager. In return for a more . . . appropriate position, you might agree to drop the inquiry into your ex-fiancée's whereabouts?

YANG SUN: I might.

SHUI TA: What position *would* be more appropriate?

YANG SUN: The one at the top.

SHUI TA: My own? (*Silence.*) And if I preferred to throw you out on your neck?

YANG SUN: I'd come back on my feet. With suitable escort.

SHUI TA: The police?

YANG SUN: The police.

SHUI TA: And when the police found no one?

YANG SUN: I might ask them not to overlook the back room. (*Ending the pretense.*) In short, Mr. Shui Ta, my interest in this young woman has not been officially terminated. I should like to see more of her. (*Into* SHUI TA's *face:*) Besides, she's pregnant and needs a friend. (*He moves to the door.*) I shall talk about it with the water seller.

Exit. SHUI TA *is rigid for a moment, then he quickly goes into the back room. He returns with Shen Te's belongings: underwear, etc. He takes a long look at the shawl of the previous scene. He then wraps the things in a bundle, which, upon hearing a noise, he hides under the table. Enter* MRS. MI TZU *and* MR. SHU FU. *They put away their umbrellas and galoshes.*

MRS. MI TZU: I thought your manager was here, Mr. Shui Ta. He combines charm with business in a way that can only be to the advantage of all of us.

SHU FU: You sent for us, Mr. Shui Ta?

SHUI TA: The factory is in trouble.

SHU FU: It always is.

SHUI TA: The police are threatening to close us down unless I can show that the extension of our facilities is imminent.

SHU FU: Shui Ta, I'm sick and tired of your constantly expanding projects. I place cabins at your cousin's disposal; you make a factory of them. I hand your cousin a check; you present it. Your cousin disappears; you find the cabins too small and start talking of yet more —

SHUI TA: Mr. Shu Fu, I'm authorized to inform you that Miss Shen Te's return is now imminent.

SHU FU: Imminent? It's becoming his favorite word.

MRS. MI TZU: Yes, what does it mean?

SHUI TA: Mrs. Mi Tzu, I can pay you exactly half what you asked for your buildings. Are you ready to inform the police that I am taking them over?

MRS. MI TZU: Certainly, if I can take over your manager.

SHU FU: What?

MRS. MI TZU: He's so efficient.

SHUI TA: I'm afraid I need Mr. Yang Sun.

MRS. MI TZU: So do I.

SHUI TA: He will call on you tomorrow.

SHU FU: So much the better. With Shen Te likely to turn up at any moment, the presence of that young man is hardly in good taste.

SHUI TA: So we have reached a settlement. In what was once the good Shen Te's little shop we are laying the foundations for the great Mr. Shui Ta's twelve magnificent super tobacco markets. You will bear in mind that though they call me the Tobacco King of Setzuan, it is my cousin's interests that have been served . . .

VOICES (*off*): The police, the police! Going to the tobacco shop! Something must have happened!

Enter YANG SUN, WONG *and the* POLICEMAN.

POLICEMAN: Quiet there, quiet, quiet! (*They quiet down.*) I'm sorry, Mr. Shui Ta, but there's a report that you've been depriving Miss Shen Te of her freedom. Not that I believe all I hear, but the whole city's in an uproar.

SHUI TA: That's a lie.

POLICEMAN: Mr. Yang Sun has testified that he heard someone sobbing in the back room.

SHU FU: Mrs. Mi Tzu and myself will testify that no one here has been sobbing.

MRS. MI TZU: We have been quietly smoking our cigars.

POLICEMAN: Mr. Shui Ta, I'm afraid I shall have to take a look at that room. (*He does so. The room is empty.*) No one there, of course, sir.

YANG SUN: But I heard sobbing. What's that? (*He finds the clothes.*)

WONG: Those are Shen Te's things. (*To crowd:*) Shen Te's clothes are here!

VOICES (*off, in sequence*):
— Shen Te's clothes!
— They've been found under the table!
— Body of murdered girl still missing!
— Tobacco King suspected!

POLICEMAN: Mr. Shui Ta, unless you can tell us where the girl is, I'll have to ask you to come along.

SHUI TA: I do not know.

POLICEMAN: I can't say how sorry I am, Mr. Shui Ta. (*He shows him the door.*)

SHUI TA: Everything will be cleared up in no time. There are still judges in Setzuan.

YANG SUN: I heard sobbing!

9a

Wong's den. For the last time, the GODS appear to the water seller in his dream. They have changed and show signs of a long journey, extreme fatigue, and plenty of mishaps. The FIRST no longer has a hat; the THIRD has lost a leg; all three are barefoot.

WONG: Illustrious ones, at last you're here. Shen Te's been gone for months and today her cousin's been arrested. They think he murdered her to get the shop. But I had a dream and in this dream Shen Te said her cousin was keeping her prisoner. You must find her for us, illustrious ones!

FIRST GOD: We've found very few good people anywhere, and even they didn't keep it up. Shen Te is still the only one that stayed good.

SECOND GOD: If she *has* stayed good.

WONG: Certainly she has. But she's vanished.

FIRST GOD: That's the last straw. All is lost!

SECOND GOD: A little moderation, dear colleague!

FIRST GOD (*plaintively*): What's the good of moderation now? If she can't be found, we'll have to resign! The world is a terrible place! Nothing but misery, vulgarity, and waste! Even the countryside isn't what it used to be. The trees are getting their heads chopped off by telephone wires, and there's such a noise from all the gunfire, and I can't stand those heavy clouds of smoke, and —

THIRD GOD: The place is absolutely unlivable! Good intentions bring people to the brink of the abyss, and good deeds push them over the edge. I'm afraid our book of rules is destined for the scrap heap —

SECOND GOD: It's people! They're a worthless lot!

THIRD GOD: The world is too cold!

SECOND GOD: It's people! They're too weak!

FIRST GOD: Dignity, dear colleagues, dignity! Never despair! As for this world, didn't we agree that we only have to find one human being who can stand the place? Well, we found her. True, we lost her again. We must find her again, that's all! And at once!

They disappear.

10

Courtroom. Groups: SHU FU *and* MRS. MI TZU; YANG SUN *and* MRS. YANG; WONG, *the* CARPENTER, *the* GRANDFATHER, *the* NIECE, *the* OLD MAN, *the* OLD WOMAN; MRS. SHIN, *the* POLICEMAN; *the* UNEMPLOYED MAN, *the* SISTER-IN-LAW.

OLD MAN: So much power isn't good for one man.

UNEMPLOYED MAN: And he's going to open twelve super tobacco markets!

WIFE: One of the judges is a friend of Mr. Shu Fu's.

SISTER-IN-LAW: Another one accepted a present from Mr. Shui Ta only last night. A great fat goose.

OLD WOMAN (*to* WONG): And Shen Te is nowhere to be found.

WONG: Only the gods will ever know the truth.

POLICEMAN: Order in the court! My lords the judges!

Enter the THREE GODS *in judges' robes. We overhear their conversation as they pass along the footlights to their bench.*

THIRD GOD: We'll never get away with it, our certificates were so badly forged.

SECOND GOD: My predecessor's "sudden indigestion" will certainly cause comment.

FIRST GOD: But he *had* just eaten a whole goose.

UNEMPLOYED MAN: Look at that! *New* judges.

WONG: New judges. And what good ones!

The THIRD GOD *hears this, and turns to smile at* WONG. *The* GODS *sit. The* FIRST GOD *beats on the bench with his gavel. The* POLICEMAN *brings in* SHUI TA *who walks with lordly steps. He is whistled at.*

POLICEMAN (*to* SHUI TA): Be prepared for a surprise. The judges have been changed.

SHUI TA *turns quickly round, looks at them, and staggers.*

NIECE: What's the matter now?

WIFE: The great Tobacco King nearly fainted.

HUSBAND: Yes, as soon as he saw the new judges.

WONG: Does *he* know who they are?

SHUI TA *picks himself up, and the proceedings open.*

FIRST GOD: Defendant Shui Ta, you are accused of doing away with your cousin Shen Te in order to take possession of her business. Do you plead guilty or not guilty?

SHUI TA: Not guilty, my lord.

FIRST GOD (*thumbing through the documents of the case*): The first witness is the policeman. I shall ask him to tell us something of the respective reputations of Miss Shen Te and Mr. Shui Ta.

POLICEMAN: Miss Shen Te was a young lady who aimed to please, my lord. She liked to live and let live, as the saying goes. Mr. Shui Ta, on the other hand, is a man of principle. Though the generosity of Miss Shen Te forced him at times to abandon half measures, unlike the girl he was always on the side of the law, my lord. One time, he even unmasked a gang of thieves to whom his too trustful cousin had given shelter. The evidence, in short, my lord, proves that Mr. Shui Ta was *incapable* of the crime of which he stands accused!

FIRST GOD: I see. And are there others who could testify along, shall we say, the same lines?

SHU FU *rises.*

POLICEMAN (*whispering to* GODS): Mr. Shu Fu — a very important person.

FIRST GOD (*inviting him to speak*): Mr. Shu Fu!

SHU FU: Mr. Shui Ta is a businessman, my lord. Need I say more?

FIRST GOD: Yes.

SHU FU: Very well, I will. He is Vice President of the Council of Commerce and is about to be elected a Justice of the Peace. (*He returns to his seat.*)

MRS. MI TZU *rises.*

WONG: Elected! *He* gave him the job!

With a gesture the FIRST GOD *asks who* MRS. MI TZU *is.*

POLICEMAN: Another very important person. Mrs. Mi Tzu.

MRS. MI TZU: My lord, as Chairman of the Committee on Social Work, I wish to call attention to just a couple of eloquent facts: Mr. Shui Ta not only has erected a model factory with model housing in our city, he is a regular contributor to our home for the disabled. (*She returns to her seat.*)

POLICEMAN (*whispering*): And she's a great friend of the judge that ate the goose!

FIRST GOD (*to the* POLICEMAN): Oh, thank you. What next? (*To the Court, genially:*) Oh, yes. We should find out if any of the evidence is less favorable to the defendant.

WONG, *the* CARPENTER, *the* OLD MAN, *the* OLD WOMAN, *the* UNEMPLOYED MAN, *the* SISTER-IN-LAW, *and the* NIECE *come forward.*

POLICEMAN (*whispering*): Just the riffraff, my lord.

FIRST GOD (*addressing the "riffraff"*): Well, um, riffraff — do you know anything of the defendant, Mr. Shui Ta?

WONG: Too much, my lord.

UNEMPLOYED MAN: What don't we know, my lord.

CARPENTER: He ruined us.

SISTER-IN-LAW: He's a cheat.

NIECE: Liar.

WIFE: Thief.

BOY: Blackmailer.

BROTHER: Murderer.

FIRST GOD: Thank you. We should now let the defendant state his point of view.

SHUI TA: I only came on the scene when Shen Te was in danger of losing what I had understood was a gift from the gods. Because I did the filthy jobs which someone had to do, they hate me. My activities were restricted to the minimum, my lord.

SISTER-IN-LAW: He had us arrested!

SHUI TA: Certainly. You stole from the bakery!

SISTER-IN-LAW: Such concern for the bakery! You didn't want the shop for yourself, I suppose!

SHUI TA: I didn't want the shop overrun with parasites.

SISTER-IN-LAW: We had nowhere else to go.

SHUI TA: There were too many of you.

WONG: What about this old couple: Were *they* parasites?

OLD MAN: We lost our shop because of you!

OLD WOMAN: And we gave your cousin money!

SHUI TA: My cousin's fiancé was a flyer. The money had to go to *him*.

WONG: Did you care whether he flew or not? Did you care whether she married him or not? You wanted her to marry someone else! (*He points at* SHU FU.)

SHUI TA: The flyer unexpectedly turned out to be a scoundrel.

YANG SUN (*jumping up*): Which was the reason you made him your manager?

SHUI TA: Later on he improved.

WONG: And when he improved, you sold him to her? (*He points out* MRS. MI TZU.)

SHUI TA: She wouldn't let me have her premises unless she had him to stroke her knees!

MRS. MI TZU: What? The man's a pathological liar. (*To him:*) Don't mention my property to me as long as you live! Murderer! (*She rustles off, in high dudgeon.*)

YANG SUN (*pushing in*): My lord, I wish to speak for the defendant.

SISTER-IN-LAW: Naturally. He's your employer.

UNEMPLOYED MAN: And the worst slave driver in the country.

MRS. YANG: That's a lie! My lord, Mr. Shui Ta is a great man. He . . .

YANG SUN: He's this and he's that, but he is not a murderer, my lord. Just fifteen minutes before his arrest I heard Shen Te's voice in his own back room.

FIRST GOD: Oh? Tell us more!

YANG SUN: I heard sobbing, my lord!

FIRST GOD: But lots of women sob, we've been finding.

YANG SUN: Could I fail to recognize her voice?

SHU FU: No, you made her sob so often yourself, young man!

YANG SUN: Yes. But I also made her happy. Till he (*pointing at* SHUI TA) decided to sell her to you!

SHUI TA: Because you didn't love her.

WONG: Oh, no: it was for the money, my lord!

SHUI TA: And what was the money for, my lord? For the poor! And for Shen Te so she could go on being good!

WONG: For the poor? That he sent to his sweatshops? And why didn't you let Shen Te be good when you signed the big check?

SHUI TA: For the child's sake, my lord.

CARPENTER: What about *my* children? What did he do about them?

SHUI TA *is silent.*

WONG: The shop was to be a fountain of goodness. That was the gods' idea. You came and spoiled it!

SHUI TA: If I hadn't, it would have run dry!

MRS. SHIN: There's a lot in that, my lord.

WONG: What have you done with the good Shen Te, bad man? She *was* good, my lords, she was, I swear it! (*He raises his hand in an oath.*)

THIRD GOD: What's happened to your hand, water seller?

WONG (*pointing to* SHUI TA): It's all his fault, my lord, *she* was going to send me to a doctor — (*To* SHUI TA:) You were her worst enemy!

SHUI TA: I was her only friend!

WONG: Where is she then? Tell us where your good friend is!

The excitement of this exchange has run through the whole crowd.

ALL: Yes, where is she? Where is Shen Te? (*Etc.*)

SHUI TA: Shen Te . . . had to go.

WONG: Where? Where to?

SHUI TA: I cannot tell you! I cannot tell you!

ALL: Why? Why did she have to go away? (*Etc.*)

WONG (*into the din with the first words, but talking on beyond the others*): Why not, why not? Why did she have to go away?

SHUI TA (*shouting*): Because you'd all have torn her to shreds, that's why! My lords, I have a request. Clear the court! When only the judges remain, I will make a confession.

ALL (*except* WONG, *who is silent, struck by the new turn of events*): So he's guilty? He's confessing! (*Etc.*)

FIRST GOD (*using the gavel*): Clear the court!

POLICEMAN: Clear the court!

WONG: Mr. Shui Ta has met his match this time.

MRS. SHIN (*with a gesture toward the judges*): You're in for a little surprise.

The court is cleared. Silence.

SHUI TA: Illustrious ones!

The GODS *look at each other, not quite believing their ears.*

SHUI TA: Yes, I recognize you!

SECOND GOD (*taking matters in hand, sternly*): What have you done with our good woman of Setzuan?

SHUI TA: I have a terrible confession to make: I am she! (*He takes off his mask, and tears away his clothes.* SHEN TE *stands there.*)

SECOND GOD: Shen Te!

SHEN TE: Shen Te, yes. Shui Ta *and* Shen Te. Both.

Your injunction
To be good and yet to live
Was a thunderbolt:
It has torn me in two
I can't tell how it was
But to be good to others
And myself at the same time
I could not do it
Your world is not an easy one, illustrious ones!
When we extend our hand to a beggar, he tears it off for us
When we help the lost, we are lost ourselves
And so
Since not to eat is to die
Who can long refuse to be bad?
As I lay prostrate beneath the weight of good intentions
Ruin stared me in the face
It was when I was unjust that I ate good meat
And hobnobbed with the mighty
Why?
Why are bad deeds rewarded?
Good ones punished?
I enjoyed giving
I truly wished to be the Angel of the Slums
But washed by a foster mother in the water of the gutter
I developed a sharp eye
The time came when pity was a thorn in my side
And, later, when kind words turned to ashes in my mouth
And anger took over

I became a wolf
Find me guilty, then, illustrious ones,
But know:
All that I have done I did
To help my neighbor
To love my lover
And to keep my little one from want
For your great, godly deeds, I was too poor, too small.

Pause.

FIRST GOD (*shocked*): Don't go on making yourself miserable, Shen Te!
We're overjoyed to have found you!

SHEN TE: I'm telling you I'm the bad man who committed all those
crimes!

FIRST GOD (*using — or failing to use — his ear trumpet*): The good
woman who did all those good deeds?

SHEN TE: Yes, but the bad man too!

FIRST GOD (*as if something had dawned*): Unfortunate coincidences!
Heartless neighbors!

THIRD GOD (*shouting in his ear*): But how is she to continue?

FIRST GOD: Continue? Well, she's a strong, healthy girl . . .

SECOND GOD: You didn't hear what she said!

FIRST GOD: I heard every word! She is confused, that's all. (*He begins
to bluster.*) And what about this book of rules — we can't renounce
our rules, can we? (*More quietly.*) Should the world be changed? How?
By whom? The world should *not* be changed! (*At a sign from him,
the lights turn pink, and music plays.*) [1]
And now the hour of parting is at hand.
Dost thou behold, Shen Te, yon fleecy cloud?
It is our chariot. At a sign from me
'Twill come and take us back from whence we came
Above the azure vault and silver stars. . . .

SHEN TE: No! Don't go, illustrious ones!

FIRST GOD: Our cloud has landed now in yonder field
From which it will transport us back to heaven.
Farewell, Shen Te, let not thy courage fail thee. . . .

Exeunt GODS.

SHEN TE: What about the old couple? They've lost their shop! What
about the water seller and his hand? And I've got to defend myself

---

1. The rest of this scene has been adapted for the many American theatres that do not have
"fly-space" to lower things from ropes.

against the barber, because I don't love him! And against Sun, because I do love him! How? How?

SHEN TE's *eyes follow the* GODS *as they are imagined to step into a cloud which rises and moves forward over the orchestra and up beyond the balcony.*

FIRST GOD (*from on high*): We have faith in you, Shen Te!

SHEN TE: There'll be a child. And he'll have to be fed. I can't stay here. Where shall I go?

FIRST GOD: Continue to be good, good woman of Setzuan!

SHEN TE: I need my bad cousin!

FIRST GOD: But not very often!

SHEN TE: Once a week at least!

FIRST GOD: Once a month will be quite enough!

SHEN TE (*shrieking*): No, no! Help!

But the cloud continues to recede as the GODS *sing.*

VALEDICTORY HYMN

What rapture, oh, it is to know
    A good thing when you see it
And having seen a good thing, oh,
    What rapture 'tis to flee it

Be good, sweet maid of Setzuan
    Let Shui Ta be clever
Departing, we forget the man
    Remember your endeavor

Because through all the length of days
    Her goodness faileth never
    Sing hallelujah! Make Shen Te's
    Good name live on forever!

SHEN TE: Help!

EPILOGUE

You're thinking, aren't you, that this is no right
Conclusion to the play you've seen tonight? [2]
After a tale, exotic, fabulous,
A nasty ending was slipped up on us.
We feel deflated too. We too are nettled
To see the curtain down and nothing settled.

2. *At afternoon performances:*
    We quite agree, our play this afternoon
    Collapsed upon us like a pricked balloon.

How could a better ending be arranged?
Could one change people? Can the world be changed?
Would new gods do the trick? Will atheism?
Moral rearmament? Materialism?
It is for you to find a way, my friends,
To help good men arrive at happy ends.
You write the happy ending to the play!
There must, there must, there's got to be a way! [3]

3. When I first received the German manuscript of *Good Woman* from Brecht in 1945 it had no Epilogue. He wrote it a little later, influenced by misunderstandings of the ending in the press on the occasion of the Viennese première of the play. I believe that the Epilogue has sometimes been spoken by the actress playing Shen Te, but the actor playing Wong might be a shrewder choice, since the audience has already accepted him as a kind of chorus. On the other hand, it is not *Wong* who should deliver the Epilogue: whichever actor delivers it should drop the character he has been playing. — E. B.

Albert Camus (1913–1960)

LIFE: He was an Algerian farm-laborer's son who studied philosophy, became a journalist, and wrote plays before he moved to Paris in 1940; there, during the German occupation, he joined the underground movement, writing for the newspaper *Combat,* and published those books — novels, existential meditations — which made him as influential as Sartre, his great antagonist. He received the Nobel Prize for literature in 1957 and three years later was killed in an automobile accident.

WORKS: *The Stranger* (1942); *The Myth of Sisyphus* (1942); *The Plague* (1948); *The Rebel* (1954); *The Fall* (1957); *Exile and the Kingdom* (1958); *Caligula and Other Plays* (1958).

THE MYTH OF SISYPHUS *

An Absurd Reasoning

ABSURDITY AND SUICIDE

There is but one truly serious philosophical problem, and that is suicide. Judging whether life is or is not worth living amounts to answering the fundamental question of philosophy. All the rest — whether or not the world has three dimensions, whether the mind has nine or twelve categories — comes afterwards. These are games; one must first answer. And if it is true, as Nietzsche claims, that a philosopher, to deserve our respect, must preach by example, you can appreciate the importance of

From *The Myth of Sisyphus,* by Albert Camus and translated by Justin O'Brien. © Copyright 1955 by Alfred A. Knopf, Inc. Reprinted by permission.

* 1942.

that reply, for it will precede the definitive act. These are facts the heart can feel; yet they call for careful study before they become clear to the intellect.

If I ask myself how to judge that this question is more urgent than that, I reply that one judges by the actions it entails. I have never seen anyone die for the ontological argument. Galileo, who held a scientific truth of great importance, abjured it with the greatest ease as soon as it endangered his life. In a certain sense, he did right.[1] That truth was not worth the stake. Whether the earth or the sun revolves around the other is a matter of profound indifference. To tell the truth, it is a futile question. On the other hand, I see many people die because they judge that life is not worth living. I see others paradoxically getting killed for the ideas or illusions that give them a reason for living (what is called a reason for living is also an excellent reason for dying). I therefore conclude that the meaning of life is the most urgent of questions. How to answer it? On all essential problems (I mean thereby those that run the risk of leading to death or those that intensify the passion of living) there are probably but two methods of thought: the method of La Palisse [2] and the method of Don Quixote. Solely the balance between evidence and lyricism can allow us to achieve simultaneously emotion and lucidity. In a subject at once so humble and so heavy with emotion, the learned and classical dialectic must yield, one can see, to a more modest attitude of mind deriving at one and the same time from common sense and understanding.

Suicide has never been dealt with except as a social phenomenon. On the contrary, we are concerned here, at the outset, with the relationship between individual thought and suicide. An act like this is prepared within the silence of the heart, as is a great work of art. The man bimself is ignorant of it. One evening he pulls the trigger or jumps. Of an apartment-building manager who had killed himself I was told that he had lost his daughter five years before, that he had changed greatly since, and that that experience had "undermined" him. A more exact word cannot be imagined. Beginning to think is beginning to be undermined. Society has but little connection with such beginnings. The worm is in man's heart. That is where it must be sought. One must follow and understand this fatal game that leads from lucidity in the face of existence to flight from light.

There are many causes for a suicide, and generally the most obvious ones were not the most powerful. Rarely is suicide committed (yet the hypothesis is not excluded) through reflection. What sets off the crisis is almost always unverifiable. Newspapers often speak of "personal sorrows" or of "incurable illness." These explanations are plausible. But one would have to know whether a friend of the desperate man had not

1. From the point of view of the relative value of truth. On the other hand, from the point of view of virile behavior, this scholar's fragility may well make us smile [author's note].

2. A distinguished soldier (c. 1470–1525), ridiculed for his simplicity in a song by Bernard de la Monnoye (1641–1728). A phrase from the song — "Verité de Monsieur de la Palisse" — came to mean "self-evident truth."

that very day addressed him indifferently. He is the guilty one. For that is enough to precipitate all the rancors and all the boredom still in suspension.[3]

But if it is hard to fix the precise instant, the subtle step when the mind opted for death, it is easier to deduce from the act itself the consequences it implies. In a sense, and as in melodrama, killing yourself amounts to confessing. It is confessing that life is too much for you or that you do not understand it. Let's not go too far in such analogies, however, but rather return to everyday words. It is merely confessing that that "is not worth the trouble." Living, naturally, is never easy. You continue making the gestures commanded by existence for many reasons, the first of which is habit. Dying voluntarily implies that you have recognized, even instinctively, the ridiculous character of that habit, the absence of any profound reason for living, the insane character of that daily agitation, and the uselessness of suffering.

What, then, is that incalculable feeling that deprives the mind of the sleep necessary to life? A world that can be explained even with bad reasons is a familiar world. But, on the other hand, in a universe suddenly divested of illusions and lights, man feels an alien, a stranger. His exile is without remedy since he is deprived of the memory of a lost home or the hope of a promised land. This divorce between man and his life, the actor and his setting, is properly the feeling of absurdity. All healthy men having thought of their own suicide, it can be seen, without further explanation, that there is a direct connection between this feeling and the longing for death.

The subject of this essay is precisely this relationship between the absurd and suicide, the exact degree to which suicide is a solution to the absurd. The principle can be established that for a man who does not cheat, what he believes to be true must determine his action. Belief in the absurdity of existence must then dictate his conduct. It is legitimate to wonder, clearly and without false pathos, whether a conclusion of this importance reqires forsaking as rapidly as possible an incomprehensible condition. I am speaking, of course, of men inclined to be in harmony with themselves. . . .

In the face of such contradictions and obscurities must we conclude that there is no relationship between the opinion one has about life and the act one commits to leave it? Let us not exaggerate in this direction. In a man's attachment to life there is something stronger than all the ills in the world. The body's judgment is as good as the mind's, and the body shrinks from annihilation. We get into the habit of living before acquiring the habit of thinking. In that race which daily hastens us toward death, the body maintains its irreparable lead. In short, the essence of that contradiction lies in what I shall call the act of eluding because it is both less and more than diversion in the Pascalian sense.

---

3. Let us not miss this opportunity to point out the relative character of this essay. Suicide may indeed be related to much more honorable considerations — for example, the political suicides of protest, as they were called, during the Chinese revolution [author's note].

Eluding is the invariable game. The typical act of eluding, the fatal evasion that constitutes the third theme of this essay, is hope. Hope of another life one must "deserve" or trickery of those who live not for life itself but for some great idea that will transcend it, refine it, give it a meaning, and betray it.

Thus everything contributes to spreading confusion. Hitherto, and it has not been wasted effort, people have played on words and pretended to believe that refusing to grant a meaning to life necessarily leads to declaring that it is not worth living. In truth, there is no necessary common measure between these two judgments. One merely has to refuse to be misled by the confusions, divorces, and inconsistencies previously pointed out. One must brush everything aside and go straight to the real problem. One kills oneself because life is not worth living, that is certainly a truth — yet an unfruitful one because it is a truism. But does that insult to existence, that flat denial in which it is plunged come from the fact that it has no meaning? Does its absurdity require one to escape it through hope or suicide — this is what must be clarified, hunted down, and elucidated while brushing aside all the rest. Does the Absurd dictate death? This problem must be given priority over others, outside all methods of thought and all exercises of the disinterested mind. Shades of meaning, contradictions, the psychology that an "objective" mind can always introduce into all problems have no place in this pursuit and this passion. It calls simply for an unjust — in other words, logical — thought. That is not easy. It is always easy to be logical. It is almost impossible to be logical to the bitter end. Men who die by their own hand consequently follow to its conclusion their emotional inclination. Reflection on suicide gives me an opportunity to raise the only problem to interest me: is there a logic to the point of death? I cannot know unless I pursue, without reckless passion, in the sole light of evidence, the reasoning of which I am here suggesting the source. This is what I call an absurd reasoning. Many have begun it. I do not yet know whether or not they kept to it. . . .

ABSURD WALLS

Like great works, deep feelings always mean more than they are conscious of saying. The regularity of an impulse or a repulsion in a soul is encountered again in habits of doing or thinking, is reproduced in consequences of which the soul itself knows nothing. Great feelings take with them their own universe, splendid or abject. They light up with their passion an exclusive world in which they recognize their climate. There is a universe of jealousy, of ambition, of selfishness, or of generosity. A universe — in other words, a metaphysic and an attitude of mind. What is true of already specialized feelings will be even more so of emotions basically as indeterminate, simultaneously as vague and as "definite," as remote and as "present" as those furnished us by beauty or aroused by absurdity.

At any streetcorner the feeling of absurdity can strike any man in the face. As it is, in its distressing nudity, in its light without effulgence, it is elusive. But that very difficulty deserves reflection. It is probably true that a man remains forever unknown to us and that there is in him something irreducible that escapes us. But *practically* I know men and recognize them by their behavior, by the totality of their deeds, by the consequences caused in life by their presence. Likewise, all those irrational feelings which offer no purchase to analysis. I can define them *practically,* appreciate them *practically,* by gathering together the sum of their consequences in the domain of the intelligence, by seizing and noting all their aspects, by outlining their universe. It is certain that apparently, though I have seen the same actor a hundred times, I shall not for that reason know him any better personally. Yet if I add up the heroes he has personified and if I say that I know him a little better at the hundredth character counted off, this will be felt to contain an element of truth. For this apparent paradox is also an apologue. There is a moral to it. It teaches that a man defines himself by his make-believe as well as by his sincere impulses. There is thus a lower key of feelings, inaccessible in the heart but partially disclosed by the acts they imply and the attitudes of mind they assume. It is clear that in this way I am defining a method. But it is also evident that that method is one of analysis and not of knowledge. For methods imply metaphysics; unconsciously they disclose conclusions that they often claim not to know yet. Similarly, the last pages of a book are already contained in the first pages. Such a link is inevitable. The method defined here acknowledges the feeling that all true knowledge is impossible. Solely appearances can be enumerated and the climate make itself felt.

Perhaps we shall be able to overtake that elusive feeling of absurdity in the different but closely related worlds of intelligence, of the art of living, or of art itself. The climate of absurdity is in the beginning. The end is the absurd universe and that attitude of mind which lights the world with its true colors to bring out the privileged and implacable visage which that attitude has discerned in it.

All great deeds and all great thoughts have a ridiculous beginning. Great works are often born on a streetcorner or in a restaurant's revolving door. So it is with absurdity. The absurd world more than others derives its nobility from that abject birth. In certain situations, replying "nothing" when asked what one is thinking about may be pretense in a man. Those who are loved are well aware of this. But if that reply is sincere, if it symbolizes that odd state of soul in which the void becomes eloquent, in which the chain of daily gestures is broken, in which the heart vainly seeks the link that will connect it again, then it is as it were the first sign of absurdity.

It happens that the stage sets collapse. Rising, streetcar, four hours in the office or the factory, meal, streetcar, four hours of work, meal, sleep, and Monday Tuesday Wednesday Thursday Friday and Saturday according to the same rhythm — this path is easily followed most of the time. But one day the "why" arises and everything begins in that weariness tinged with amazement. "Begins" — this is important. Weariness comes at the end of the acts of a mechanical life, but at the same time it inaugurates the impulse of consciousness. It awakens consciousness and provokes what follows. What follows is the gradual return into the chain or it is the definitive awakening. At the end of the awakening comes, in time, the consequence: suicide or recovery. In itself weariness has something sickening about it. Here, I must conclude that it is good. For everything begins with consciousness and nothing is worth anything except through it. . . .

Likewise and during every day of an unillustrious life, time carries us. But a moment always comes when we have to carry it. We live on the future: "tomorrow," "later on," "when you have made your way," "you will understand when you are old enough." Such irrelevancies are wonderful, for, after all, it's a matter of dying. Yet a day comes when a man notices or says that he is thirty. Thus he asserts his youth. But simultaneously he situates himself in relation to time. He takes his place in it. He admits that he stands at a certain point on a curve that he acknowledges having to travel to its end. He belongs to time, and by the horror that seizes him, he recognizes his worst enemy. Tomorrow, he was longing for tomorrow, whereas everything in him ought to reject it. That revolt of the flesh is the absurd.[4]

A step lower and strangeness creeps in: perceiving that the world is "dense," sensing to what a degree a stone is foreign and irreducible to us, with what intensity nature or a landscape can negate us. At the heart of all beauty lies something inhuman, and these hills, the softness of the sky, the outline of these trees at this very minute lose the illusory meaning with which we had clothed them, henceforth more remote than a lost paradise. The primitive hostility of the world rises up to face us across millennia. For a second we cease to understand it because for centuries we have understood in it solely the images and designs that we had attributed to it beforehand, because henceforth we lack the power to make use of that artifice. The world evades us because it becomes itself again. That stage scenery masked by habit becomes again what it is. It withdraws at a distance from us. Just as there are days when under the familiar face of a woman, we see as a stranger her we had loved months or years ago, perhaps we shall come even to desire what suddenly leaves us so alone. But the time has not yet come. Just one thing: that denseness and that strangeness of the world is the absurd.

Men, too, secrete the inhuman. At certain moments of lucidity, the mechanical aspect of their gestures, their meaningless pantomime makes silly everything that surrounds them. A man is talking on the telephone behind a glass partition; you cannot hear him, but you see his incomprehensible dumb show: you wonder why he is alive. This discomfort in the

---

4. But not in the proper sense. This is not a definition, but rather an enumeration of the feelings that may admit of the absurd. Still, the enumeration finished, the absurd has nevertheless not been exhausted [author's note].

face of man's own inhumanity, this incalculable tumble before the image of what we are, this "nausea," as a writer of today calls it, is also the absurd. Likewise the stranger who at certain seconds comes to meet us in a mirror, the familiar and yet alarming brother we encounter in our own photographs is also the absurd.

I come at last to death and to the attitude we have toward it. On this point everything has been said and it is only proper to avoid pathos. Yet one will never be sufficiently surprised that everyone lives as if no one "knew." This is because in reality there is no experience of death. Properly speaking, nothing has been experienced but what has been lived and made conscious. Here, it is barely possible to speak of the experience of others' deaths. It is a substitute, an illusion, and it never quite convinces us. That melancholy convention cannot be persuasive. The horror comes in reality from the mathematical aspect of the event. If time frightens us, this is because it works out the problem and the solution comes afterward. All the pretty speeches about the soul will have their contrary convincingly proved, at least for a time. From this inert body on which a slap makes no mark the soul has disappeared. This elementary and definitive aspect of the adventure constitutes the absurd feeling. Under the fatal lighting of that destiny, its uselessness becomes evident. No code of ethics and no effort are justifiable *a priori* in the face of the cruel mathematics that command our condition.

Let me repeat: all this has been said over and over. I am limiting myself here to making a rapid classification and to pointing out these obvious themes. They run through all literatures and all philosophies. Everyday conversation feeds on them. There is no question of reinventing them. But it is essential to be sure of these facts in order to be able to question oneself subsequently on the primordial question. I am interested — let me repeat again — not so much in absurd discoveries as in their consequences. If one is assured of these facts, what is one to conclude, how far is one to go to elude nothing? Is one to die voluntarily or to hope in spite of everything? Beforehand, it is necessary to take the same rapid inventory on the plane of the intelligence.

The mind's first step is to distinguish what is true from what is false. However, as soon as thought reflects on itself, what it first discovers is a contradiction. Useless to strive to be convincing in this case. Over the centuries no one has furnished a clearer and more elegant demonstration of the business than Aristotle: "The often ridiculed consequence of these opinions is that they destroy themselves. For by asserting that all is true we assert the truth of the contrary assertion and consequently the falsity of our own thesis (for the contrary assertion does not admit that it can be true). And if one says that all is false, that assertion is itself false. If we declare that solely the assertion opposed to ours is false or else that solely ours is not false, we are nevertheless forced to admit an infinite number of true or false judgments. For the one who expresses a true assertion proclaims simultaneously that it is true, and so on *ad infinitum*."

This vicious circle is but the first of a series in which the mind that studies itself gets lost in a giddy whirling. The very simplicity of these paradoxes makes them irreducible. Whatever may be the plays on words and the acrobatics of logic, to understand is, above all, to unify. The mind's deepest desire, even in its most elaborate operations, parallels man's unconscious feeling in the face of his universe: it is an insistence upon familiarity, an appetite for clarity. Understanding the world for a man is reducing it to the human, stamping it with his seal. The cat's universe is not the universe of the anthill. The truism "All thought is anthropomorphic" has no other meaning. Likewise, the mind that aims to understand reality can consider itself satisfied only by reducing it to terms of thought. If man realized that the universe like him can love and suffer, he would be reconciled. If thought discovered in the shimmering mirrors of phenomena eternal relations capable of summing them up and summing themselves up in a single principle, then would be seen an intellectual joy of which the myth of the blessed would be but a ridiculous imitation. That nostalgia for unity, that appetite for the absolute illustrates the essential impulse of the human drama. But the fact of that nostalgia's existence does not imply that it is to be immediately satisfied. For if, bridging the gulf that separates desire from conquest, we assert with Parmenides the reality of the One (whatever it may be), we fall into the ridiculous contradiction of a mind that asserts total unity and proves by its very assertion its own difference and the diversity it claimed to resolve. This other vicious circle is enough to stifle our hopes.

These are again truisms. I shall again repeat that they are not interesting in themselves but in the consequences that can be deduced from them. I know another truism: it tells me that man is mortal. One can nevertheless count the minds that have deduced the extreme conclusions from it. It is essential to consider as a constant point of reference in this essay the regular hiatus between what we fancy we know and what we really know, practical assent and simulated ignorance which allows us to live with ideas which, if we truly put them to the test, ought to upset our whole life. Faced with this inextricable contradiction of the mind, we shall fully grasp the divorce separating us from our own creations. So long as the mind keeps silent in the motionless world of its hopes, everything is reflected and arranged in the unity of its nostalgia. But with its first move this world cracks and tumbles: an infinite number of shimmering fragments is offered to the understanding. We must despair of ever reconstructing the familiar, calm surface which would give us peace of heart. After so many centuries of inquiries, so many abdications among thinkers, we are well aware that this is true for all our knowledge. With the exception of professional rationalists, today people despair of true knowledge. If the only significant history of human thought were to be written, it would have to be the history of its successive regrets and its impotences.

Of whom and of what indeed can I say: "I know that!" This heart within me I can feel, and I judge that it exists. This world I can touch, and I likewise judge that it exists. There ends all my knowledge, and the rest is construction. For if I try to seize this self of which I feel sure, if I try to define and to summarize it, it is nothing but water slipping through my fingers. I can sketch one by one all the aspects it is able to assume, all those likewise that have been attributed to it, this upbringing, this origin, this ardor or these silences, this nobility or this vileness. But aspects cannot be added up. This very heart which is mine will forever remain indefinable to me. Between the certainty I have of my existence and the content I try to give to that assurance, the gap will never be filled. Forever I shall be a stranger to myself. In psychology as in logic, there are truths but no truth. Socrates' "Know thyself" has as much value as the "Be virtuous" of our confessionals. They reveal a nostalgia at the same time as an ignorance. They are sterile exercises on great subjects. They are legitimate only in precisely so far as they are approximate.

And here are trees and I know their gnarled surface, water and I feel its taste. These scents of grass and stars at night, certain evenings when the heart relaxes — how shall I negate this world whose power and strength I feel? Yet all the knowledge on earth will give me nothing to assure me that this world is mine. You describe it to me and you teach me to classify it. You enumerate its laws and in my thirst for knowledge I admit that they are true. You take apart its mechanism and my hope increases. At the final stage you teach me that this wondrous and multicolored universe can be reduced to the atom and that the atom itself can be reduced to the electron. All this is good and I wait for you to continue. But you tell me of an invisible planetary system in which electrons gravitate around a nucleus. You explain this world to me with an image. I realize then that you have been reduced to poetry: I shall never know. Have I the time to become indignant? You have already changed theories. So that science that was to teach me everything ends up in a hypothesis, that lucidity founders in metaphor, that uncertainty is resolved in a work of art. What need had I of so many efforts? The soft lines of these hills and the hand of evening on this troubled heart teach me much more. I have returned to my beginning. I realize that if through science I can seize phenomena and enumerate them, I cannot, for all that, apprehend the world. Were I to trace its entire relief with my finger, I should not know any more. And you give me the choice between a description that is sure but that teaches me nothing and hypotheses that claim to teach me but that are not sure. A stranger to myself and to the world, armed solely with a thought that negates itself as soon as it asserts, what is this condition in which I can have peace only by refusing to know and to live, in which the appetite for conquest bumps into walls that defy its assaults? To will is to stir up paradoxes. Everything is ordered in such a way as to bring into being that poisoned peace produced by thoughtlessness, lack of heart, or fatal renunciations.

Hence the intelligence, too, tells me in its way that this world is absurd. Its contrary, blind reason, may well claim that all is clear; I was waiting for proof and longing for it to be right. But despite so many pretentious centuries and over the heads of so many eloquent and persuasive men, I know that is false. On this plane, at least, there is no happiness if I cannot know. That universal reason, practical or ethical, that determinism, those categories that explain everything are enough to make a decent man laugh. They have nothing to do with the mind. They negate its profound truth, which is to be enchained. In this unintelligible and limited universe, man's fate henceforth assumes its meaning. A horde of irrationals has sprung up and surrounds him until his ultimate end. In his recovered and now studied lucidity, the feeling of the absurd becomes clear and definite. I said that the world is absurd, but I was too hasty. This world in itself is not reasonable, that is all that can be said. But what is absurd is the confrontation of this irrational and the wild longing for clarity whose call echoes in the human heart. The absurd depends as much on man as on the world. For the moment it is all that links them together. It binds them one to the other as only hatred can weld two creatures together. This is all I can discern clearly in this measureless universe where my adventure takes place. Let us pause here. If I hold to be true that absurdity that determines my relationship with life, if I become thoroughly imbued with that sentiment that seizes me in face of the world's scenes, with that lucidity imposed on me by the pursuit of a science, I must sacrifice everything to these certainties and I must see them squarely to be able to maintain them. Above all, I must adapt my behavior to them and pursue them in all their consequences. I am speaking here of decency. But I want to know beforehand if thought can live in those deserts.

I already know that thought has at least entered those deserts. There it found its bread. There it realized that it had previously been feeding on phantoms. It justified some of the most urgent themes of human reflection.

From the moment absurdity is recognized, it becomes a passion, the most harrowing of all. But whether or not one can live with one's passions, whether or not one can accept their law, which is to burn the heart they simultaneously exalt — that is the whole question. It is not, however, the one we shall ask just yet. It stands at the center of this experience. There will be time to come back to it. Let us recognize rather those themes and those impulses born of the desert. It will suffice to enumerate them. They, too, are known to all today. There have always been men to defend the rights of the irrational. The tradition of what may be called humiliated thought has never ceased to exist. The criticism of rationalism has been made so often that it seems unnecessary to begin again. Yet our epoch is marked by the rebirth of those paradoxical systems that strive to trip up the reason as if truly it had always forged ahead. But that is not so much a proof of the efficacy of the reason as of the intensity of its hopes. On the plane of history, such a constancy of two attitudes illustrates the essential passion of man torn between his urge toward unity and the clear vision he may have of the walls enclosing him. . . .

ABSURD FREEDOM

Now the main thing is done, I hold certain facts from which I cannot separate. What I know, what is certain, what I cannot deny, what I cannot reject — this is what counts. I can negate everything of that part of me that lives on vague nostalgias, except this desire for unity, this longing to solve, this need for clarity and cohesion. I can refute everything in this world surrounding me that offends or enraptures me, except this chaos, this sovereign chance and this divine equivalence which springs from anarchy. I don't know whether this world has a meaning that transcends it. But I know that I do not know that meaning and that it is impossible for me just now to know it. What can a meaning outside my condition mean to me? I can understand only in human terms. What I touch, what resists me — that is what I understand. And these two certainties — my appetite for the absolute and for unity and the impossibility of reducing this world to a rational and reasonable principle — I also know that I cannot reconcile them. What other truth can I admit without lying, without bringing in a hope I lack and which means nothing within the limits of my condition?

If I were a tree among trees, a cat among animals, this life would have a meaning, or rather this problem would not arise, for I should belong to this world. I should *be* this world to which I am now opposed by my whole consciousness and my whole insistence upon familiarity. This ridiculous reason is what sets me in opposition to all creation. I cannot cross it out with a stroke of the pen. What I believe to be true I must therefore preserve. What seems to me so obvious, even against me, I must support. And what constitutes the basis of that conflict, of that break between the world and my mind, but the awareness of it? If therefore I want to preserve it, I can through a constant awareness, ever revived, ever alert. This is what, for the moment, I must remember. At this moment the absurd, so obvious and yet so hard to win, returns to a man's life and finds its home there. At this moment, too, the mind can leave the arid, dried-up path of lucid effort. That path now emerges in daily life. It encounters the world of the anonymous impersonal pronoun "one," but henceforth man enters in with his revolt and his lucidity. He has forgotten how to hope. This hell of the present is his Kingdom at last. All problems recover their sharp edge. Abstract evidence retreats before the poetry of forms and colors. Spiritual conflicts become embodied and return to the abject and magnificent shelter of man's heart. None of them is settled. But all are transfigured. Is one going to die, escape by the leap, rebuild a mansion of ideas and forms to one's own scale? Is one, on the contrary, going to take up the heart-rending and marvelous wager of the absurd? Let's make a final effort in this regard and draw all our conclusions. The body, affection, creation, action, human nobility will then resume their places in this mad world. At last man will again find there the wine of the absurd and the bread of indifference on which he feeds his greatness.

Let us insist again on the method: it is a matter of persisting. At a certain point on his path the absurd man is tempted. History is not lacking in either religions or prophets, even without gods. He is asked to leap. All he can reply is that he doesn't fully understand, that it is not obvious. Indeed, he does not want to do anything but what he fully understands. He is assured that this is the sin of pride, but he does not understand the notion of sin; that perhaps hell is in store, but he has not enough imagination to visualize that strange future; that he is losing immortal life, but that seems to him an idle consideration. An attempt is made to get him to admit his guilt. He feels innocent. To tell the truth, that is all he feels — his irreparable innocence. This is what allows him everything. Hence, what he demands of himself is to live *solely* with what he knows, to accommodate himself to what is, and to bring in nothing that is not certain. He is told that nothing is. But this at least is a certainty. And it is with this that he is concerned: he wants to find out if it is possible to live *without appeal*.

Now I can broach the notion of suicide. It has already been felt what solution might be given. At this point the problem is reversed. It was previously a question of finding out whether or not life had to have a meaning to be lived. It now becomes clear, on the contrary, that it will be lived all the better if it has no meaning. Living an experience, a particular fate, is accepting it fully. Now, no one will live this fate, knowing it to be absurd, unless he does everything to keep before him that absurd brought to light by consciousness. Negating one of the terms of the opposition on which he lives amounts to escaping it. To abolish conscious revolt is to elude the problem. The theme of permanent revolution is thus carried into individual experience. Living is keeping the absurd alive. Keeping it alive is, above all, contemplating it. Unlike Eurydice, the absurd dies only when we turn away from it. One of the only coherent philosophical positions is thus revolt. It is a constant confrontation between man and his own obscurity. It is an insistence upon an impossible transparency. It challenges the world anew every second. Just as danger provided man the unique opportunity of seizing awareness, so metaphysical revolt extends awareness to the whole of experience. It is that constant presence of man in his own eyes. It is not aspiration, for it is devoid of hope. That revolt is the certainty of a crushing fate, without the resignation that ought to accompany it.

This is where it is seen to what a degree absurd experience is remote from suicide. It may be thought that suicide follows revolt — but wrongly. For it does not represent the logical outcome of revolt. It is just the contrary by the consent it presupposes. Suicide, like the leap, is acceptance at its extreme. Everything is over and man returns to his essential history. His future, his unique and dreadful future — he sees and rushes toward it. In its way, suicide settles the absurd. It engulfs the absurd in the same death. But I know that in order to keep alive, the absurd cannot be settled. It escapes suicide to the extent that it is simultaneously awareness and rejection of death. It is, at the extreme limit of the condemned man's last thought, that shoelace that despite everything he sees a few yards away, on the very brink of his dizzying fall. The contrary of suicide, in fact, is the man condemned to death.

That revolt gives life its value. Spread out over the whole length of a life, it restores its majesty to that life. To a man devoid of blinders, there is no finer sight than that of the intelligence at grips with a reality that transcends it. The sight of human pride is unequaled. No disparagement is of any use. That discipline that the mind imposes on itself, that will conjured up out of nothing, that face-to-face struggle have something exceptional about them. To impoverish that reality whose inhumanity constitutes man's majesty is tantamount to impoverishing him himself. I understand then why the doctrines that explain everything to me also debilitate me at the same time. They relieve me of the weight of my own life, and yet I must carry it alone. At this juncture, I cannot conceive that a skeptical metaphysics can be joined to an ethics of renunciation.

Consciousness and revolt, these rejections are the contrary of renunciation. Everything that is indomitable and passionate in a human heart quickens them, on the contrary, with its own life. It is essential to die unreconciled and not of one's own free will. Suicide is a repudiation. The absurd man can only drain everything to the bitter end, and deplete himself. The absurd is his extreme tension, which he maintains constantly by solitary effort, for he knows that in that consciousness and in that day-to-day revolt he gives proof of his only truth, which is defiance. This is a first consequence.

If I remain in that prearranged position which consists in drawing all the conclusions (and nothing else) involved in a newly discovered notion, I am faced with a second paradox. In order to remain faithful to that method, I have nothing to do with the problem of metaphysical liberty. Knowing whether or not man is free doesn't interest me. I can experience only my own freedom. As to it, I can have no general notions, but merely a few clear insights. The problem of "freedom as such" has no meaning. For it is linked in quite a different way with the problem of God. Knowing whether or not man is free involves knowing whether he can have a master. The absurdity peculiar to this problem comes from the fact that the very notion that makes the problem of freedom possible also takes away all its meaning. For in the presence of God there is less a problem of freedom than a problem of evil. You know the alternative: either we are not free and God the all-powerful is responsible for evil. Or we are free and responsible but God is not all-powerful. All the scholastic subtleties have neither added anything to nor subtracted anything from the acuteness of this paradox.

This is why I cannot get lost in the glorification or the mere definition of a notion which eludes me and loses its meaning as soon as it goes beyond the frame of reference of my individual experience. I cannot understand what kind of freedom would be given me by a higher being. I have lost the sense of hierarchy. The only conception of freedom I can have is that of the prisoner or the individual in the midst of the State. The only one I know is freedom of thought and action. Now if the absurd cancels all my chances of eternal freedom, it restores and magnifies, on the other hand, my freedom of action. That privation of hope and future means an increase in man's availability.

Before encountering the absurd, the everyday man lives with aims, a concern for the future or for justification (with regard to whom or what is not the question). He weighs his chances, he counts on "someday," his retirement or the labor of his sons. He still thinks that something in his life can be directed. In truth, he acts as if he were free, even if all the facts make a point of contradicting that liberty. But after the absurd, everything is upset. That idea that "I am," my way of acting as if everything has a meaning (even if, on occasion, I said that nothing has) — all that is given the lie in vertiginous fashion by the absurdity of a possible death. Thinking of the future, establishing aims for oneself, having preferences — all this presupposes a belief in freedom, even if one occasionally ascertains that one doesn't feel it. But at that moment I am well aware that that higher liberty, that freedom *to be,* which alone can serve as basis for a truth, does not exist. Death is there as the only reality. After death the chips are down. I am not even free, either, to perpetuate myself, but a slave, and, above all, a slave without hope of an eternal revolution, without recourse to contempt. And who without revolution and without contempt can remain a slave? What freedom can exist in the fullest sense without assurance of eternity?

But at the same time the absurd man realizes that hitherto he was bound to that postulate of freedom on the illusion of which he was living. In a certain sense, that hampered him. To the extent to which he imagined a purpose to his life, he adapted himself to the demands of a purpose to be achieved and became the slave of his liberty. Thus I could not act otherwise than as the father (or the engineer or the leader of a nation, or the post-office sub-clerk) that I am preparing to be. I think I can choose to be that rather than something else. I think so unconsciously, to be sure. But at the same time I strengthen my postulate with the beliefs of those around me, with the presumptions of my human environment (others are so sure of being free, and that cheerful mood is so contagious!). However far one may remain from any presumption, moral or social, one is partly influenced by them and even, for the best among them (there are good and bad presumptions), one adapts one's life to them. Thus the absurd man realizes that he was not really free. To speak clearly, to the extent to which I hope, to which I worry about a truth that might be individual to me, about a way of being or creating, to the extent to which I arrange my life and prove thereby that I accept its having a meaning, I create for myself barriers between which I confine my life. I do like so many bureaucrats of the mind and heart who only fill me with disgust and whose only vice, I now see clearly, is to take man's freedom seriously.

The absurd enlightens me on this point: there is no future. Henceforth this is the reason for my inner freedom. I shall use two comparisons here. Mystics, to begin with, find freedom in giving themselves. By losing themselves in their god, by accepting his rules, they become secretly free. In spontaneously accepted slavery they recover a deeper independence. But what does that freedom mean? It may be said, above all, that they *feel* free with regard to themselves, and not so much free as liberated. Likewise, completely turned toward death (taken here as the most obvious absurdity), the absurd man feels released from everything outside that passionate attention crystallizing in him. He enjoys a freedom with regard to common rules. It can be seen at this point that the initial themes of existential philosophy keep their entire value. The return to consciousness, the escape from everyday sleep represent the first steps of absurd freedom. But it is existential *preaching* that is alluded to, and with it that spiritual leap which basically escapes consciousness. In the same way (this is my second comparison) the slaves of antiquity did not belong to themselves. But they knew that freedom which consists in not feeling responsible.[5] Death, too, has patrician hands which, while crushing, also liberate.

Losing oneself in that bottomless certainty, feeling henceforth sufficiently remote from one's own life to increase it and take a broad view of it — this involves the principle of a liberation. Such new independence has a definite time limit, like any freedom of action. It does not write a check on eternity. But it takes the place of the illusions of *freedom,* which all stopped with death. The divine availability of the condemned man before whom the prison doors open in a certain early dawn, that unbelievable disinterestedness with regard to everything except for the pure flame of life — it is clear that death and the absurd are here the principles of the only reasonable freedom: that which a human heart can experience and live. This is a second consequence. The absurd man thus catches sight of a burning and frigid, transparent and limited universe in which nothing is possible but everything is given, and beyond which all is collapse and nothingness. He can then decide to accept such a universe and draw from it his strength, his refusal to hope, and the unyielding evidence of a life without consolation.

But what does life mean in such a universe? Nothing else for the moment but indifference to the future and a desire to use up everything that is given. Belief in the meaning of life always implies a scale of values, a choice, our preferences. Belief in the absurd, according to our definitions, teaches the contrary. But this is worth examining.

Knowing whether or not one can live *without appeal* is all that interests me. I do not want to get out of my depth. This aspect of life

---

5. I am concerned here with a factual comparison, not with an apology of humility. The absurd man is the contrary of the reconciled man [author's note].

being given me, can I adapt myself to it? Now, faced with this particular concern, belief in the absurd is tantamount to substituting the quantity of experiences for the quality. If I convince myself that this life has no other aspect than that of the absurd, if I feel that its whole equilibrium depends on that perpetual opposition between my conscious revolt and the darkness in which it struggles, if I admit that my freedom has no meaning except in relation to its limited fate, then I must say that what counts is not the best living but the most living. It is not up to me to wonder if this is vulgar or revolting, elegant or deplorable. Once and for all, value judgments are discarded here in favor of factual judgments. I have merely to draw the conclusions from what I can see and to risk nothing that is hypothetical. Supposing that living in this way were not honorable, then true propriety would command me to be dishonorable.

The most living; in the broadest sense, that rule means nothing. It calls for definition. It seems to begin with the fact that the notion of quantity has not been sufficiently explored. For it can account for a large share of human experience. A man's rule of conduct and his scale of values have no meaning except through the quantity and variety of experiences he has been in a position to accumulate. Now, the conditions of modern life impose on the majority of men the same quantity of experiences and consequently the same profound experience. To be sure, there must also be taken into consideration the individual's spontaneous contribution, the "given" element in him. But I cannot judge of that, and let me repeat that my rule here is to get along with the immediate evidence. I see, then, that the individual character of a common code of ethics lies not so much in the ideal importance of its basic principles as in the norm of an experience that it is possible to measure. To stretch a point somewhat, the Greeks had the code of their leisure just as we have the code of our eight-hour day. But already many men among the most tragic cause us to foresee that a longer experience changes this table of values. They make us imagine that adventurer of the everyday who through mere quantity of experiences would break all records (I am purposely using this sports expression) and would thus win his own code of ethics.[6] Yet let's avoid romanticism and just ask ourselves what such an attitude may mean to a man with his mind made up to take up his bet and to observe strictly what he takes to be the rules of the game.

Breaking all the records is first and foremost being faced with the world as often as possible. How can that be done without contradictions and without playing on words? For on the one hand the absurd teaches that all experiences are unimportant, and on the other it urges toward the greatest quantity of experiences. How, then, can one fail to do as so many of those men I was speaking of earlier — choose the form of life that brings us the most possible of that human matter, thereby

6. Quantity sometimes constitutes quality. If I can believe the latest restatements of scientific theory, all matter is constituted by centers of energy. Their greater or lesser quantity makes its specificity more or less remarkable. A billion ions and one ion differ not only in quantity but also in quality. It is easy to find an analogy in human experience [author's note].

introducing a scale of values that on the other hand one claims to reject?

But again it is the absurd and its contradictory life that teaches us. For the mistake is thinking that that quantity of experiences depends on the circumstances of our life when it depends solely on us. Here we have to be over-simple. To two men living the same number of years, the world always provides the same sum of experiences. It is up to us to be conscious of them. Being aware of one's life, one's revolt, one's freedom, and to the maximum, is living, and to the maximum. Where lucidity dominates, the scale of values becomes useless. Let's be even more simple. Let us say that the sole obstacle, the sole deficiency to be made good, is constituted by premature death. Thus it is that no depth, no emotion, no passion, and no sacrifice could render equal in the eyes of the absurd man (even if he wished it so) a conscious life of forty years and a lucidity spread over sixty years.[7] Madness and death are his irreparables. Man does not choose. The absurd and the extra life it involves *therefore do not depend on man's will*, but on its contrary, which is death.[8] Weighing words carefully, it is altogether a question of luck. One just has to be able to consent to this. There will never be any substitute for twenty years of life and experience.

By what is an odd inconsistency in such an alert race, the Greeks claimed that those who died young were beloved of the gods. And that is true only if you are willing to believe that entering the ridiculous world of the gods is forever losing the purest of joys, which is feeling, and feeling on this earth. The present and the succession of presents before a constantly conscious soul is the ideal of the absurd man. But the word "ideal" rings false in this connection. It is not even his vocation, but merely the third consequence of his reasoning. Having started from an anguished awareness of the inhuman, the meditation on the absurd returns at the end of its itinerary to the very heart of the passionate flames of human revolt.[9]

Thus I draw from the absurd three consequences, which are my revolt, my freedom, and my passion. By the mere activity of consciousness I transform into a rule of life what was an invitation to death — and I refuse suicide. I know, to be sure, the dull resonance that vibrates throughout these days. Yet I have but a word to say: that it is necessary. . . .

7. Same reflection on a notion as different as the idea of eternal nothingness. It neither adds anything to nor subtracts anything from reality. In psychological experience of nothingness, it is by the consideration of what will happen in two thousand years that our own nothingness truly takes on meaning. In one of its aspects, eternal nothingness is made up precisely of the sum of lives to come which will not be ours [author's note].

8. The will is only the agent here: it tends to maintain consciousness. It provides a discipline of life, and that is appreciable [author's note].

9. What matters is coherence. We start out here from acceptance of the world. But Oriental thought teaches that one can indulge in the same effort of logic by choosing *against* the world. That is just as legitimate and gives this essay its perspectives and its limits. But when the negation of the world is pursued just as rigorously, one often achieves (in certain Vedantic schools) similar results regarding, for instance, the indifference of works. In a book of great importance, *Le Choix*, Jean Grenier establishes in this way a veritable "philosophy of indifference" [author's note].

The gods had condemned Sisyphus to ceaselessly rolling a rock to the top of a mountain, whence the stone would fall back of its own weight. They had thought with some reason that there is no more dreadful punishment than futile and hopeless labor.

If one believes Homer, Sisyphus was the wisest and most prudent of mortals. According to another tradition, however, he was disposed to practice the profession of highwayman. I see no contradiction in this. Opinions differ as to the reasons why he became the futile laborer of the underworld. To begin with, he is accused of a certain levity in regard to the gods. He stole their secrets. Ægina, the daughter of Æsopus, was carried off by Jupiter. The father was shocked by that disappearance and complained to Sisyphus. He, who knew of the abduction, offered to tell about it on condition that Æsopus would give water to the citadel of Corinth. To the celestial thunderbolts he preferred the benediction of water. He was punished for this in the underworld. Homer tells us also that Sisyphus had put Death in chains. Pluto could not endure the sight of his deserted, silent empire. He dispatched the god of war, who liberated Death from the hands of her conqueror.

It is said also that Sisyphus, being near to death, rashly wanted to test his wife's love. He ordered her to cast his unburied body into the middle of the public square. Sisyphus woke up in the underworld. And there, annoyed by an obedience so contrary to human love, he obtained from Pluto permission to return to earth in order to chastise his wife. But when he had seen again the face of this world, enjoyed water and sun, warm stones and the sea, he no longer wanted to go back to the infernal darkness. Recalls, signs of anger, warnings were of no avail. Many years more he lived facing the curve of the gulf, the sparkling sea, and the smiles of earth. A decree of the gods was necessary. Mercury came and seized the impudent man by the collar and, snatching him from his joys, led him forcibly back to the underworld, where his rock was ready for him.

You have already grasped that Sisyphus is the absurd hero. He *is,* as much through his passions as through his torture. His scorn of the gods, his hatred of death, and his passion for life won him that unspeakable penalty in which the whole being is exerted toward accomplishing nothing. This is the price that must be paid for the passions of this earth. Nothing is told us about Sisyphus in the underworld. Myths are made for the imagination to breathe life into them. As for this myth, one sees merely the whole effort of a body straining to raise the huge stone, to roll it and push it up a slope a hundred times over; one sees the face screwed up, the cheek tight against the stone, the shoulder bracing the clay-covered mass, the foot wedging it, the fresh start with arms outstretched, the wholly human security of two earth-clotted hands. At the very end of his long effort measured by skyless space and time without depth, the purpose is achieved. Then Sisyphus watches the stone rush down in a few moments toward that lower world whence he will have to push it up again toward the summit. He goes back down to the plain.

It is during that return, that pause, that Sisyphus interests me. A face that toils so close to stones is already stone itself! I see that man going back down with a heavy yet measured step toward the torment of which he will never know the end. That hour like a breathing-space which returns as surely as his suffering, that is the hour of consciousness. At each of those moments when he leaves the heights and gradually sinks toward the lairs of the gods, he is superior to his fate. He is stronger than his rock.

If this myth is tragic, that is because its hero is conscious. Where would his torture be, indeed, if at every step the hope of succeeding upheld him? The workman of today works every day in his life at the same tasks, and this fate is no less absurd. But it is tragic only at the rare moments when it becomes conscious. Sisyphus, proletarian of the gods, powerless and rebellious, knows the whole extent of his wretched condition: it is what he thinks of during his descent. The lucidity that was to constitute his torture at the same time crowns his victory. There is no fate that cannot be surmounted by scorn.

If the descent is thus sometimes performed in sorrow, it can also take place in joy. This word is not too much. Again I fancy Sisyphus returning toward his rock, and the sorrow was in the beginning. When the images of earth cling too tightly to memory, when the call of happiness becomes too insistent, it happens that melancholy rises in man's heart: this is the rock's victory, this is the rock itself. The boundless grief is too heavy to bear. These are our nights of Gethsemane. But crushing truths perish from being acknowledged. Thus, Œdipus at the outset obeys fate without knowing it. But from the moment he knows, his tragedy begins. Yet at the same moment, blind and desperate, he realizes that the only bond linking him to the world is the cool hand of a girl. Then a tremendous remark rings out: "Despite so many ordeals, my advanced age and the nobility of my soul make me conclude that all is well." [10] Sophocles' Œdipus . . . thus gives the recipe for the absurd victory. Ancient wisdom confirms modern heroism.

One does not discover the absurd without being tempted to write a manual of happiness. "What! by such narrow ways — ?" There is but one world, however. Happiness and the absurd are two sons of the same earth. They are inseparable. It would be a mistake to say that happiness necessarily springs from the absurd discovery. It happens as well that the feeling of the absurd springs from happiness. "I conclude that all is well," says Œdipus, and that remark is sacred. It echoes in the wild and limited universe of man. It teaches that all is not, has not been, exhausted. It drives out of this world a god who had come into it with dissatisfaction and a preference for futile sufferings. It makes of fate a human matter, which must be settled among men.

All Sisyphus' silent joy is contained therein. His fate belongs to him.

10. In *Oedipus at Colonus*.

His rock is his thing. Likewise, the absurd man, when he contemplates his torment, silences all the idols. In the universe suddenly restored to its silence, the myriad wondering little voices of the earth rise up. Unconscious, secret calls, invitations from all the faces, they are the necessary reverse and price of victory. There is no sun without shadow, and it is essential to know the night. The absurd man says yes and his effort will henceforth be unceasing. If there is a personal fate, there is no higher destiny, or at least there is but one which he concludes is inevitable and despicable. For the rest, he knows himself to be the master of his days. At that subtle moment when man glances backward over his life, Sisyphus returning toward his rock, in that slight pivoting he contemplates that series of unrelated actions which becomes his fate, created by him, combined under his memory's eye and soon sealed by his death. Thus, convinced of the wholly human origin of all that is human, a blind man eager to see who knows that the night has no end, he is still on the go. The rock is still rolling.

I leave Sisyphus at the foot of the mountain! One always finds one's burden again. But Sisyphus teaches the higher fidelity that negates the gods and raises rocks. He too concludes that all is well. This universe henceforth without a master seems to him neither sterile nor futile. Each atom of that stone, each mineral flake of that night-filled mountain, in itself forms a world. The struggle itself toward the heights is enough to fill a man's heart. One must imagine Sisyphus happy.